ENCYCLOPEDIA OF
BODY LANGUAGE

WHAT EVERY MOVEMENT SAYS

ALAN ELANGOVAN

PARTRIDGE

Print information available on the last page.

To order additional copies of this book, contact
Toll Free +65 3165 7531 (Singapore)
Toll Free +60 3 3099 4412 (Malaysia)
orders.singapore@partridgepublishing.com

www.partridgepublishing.com/singapore

CONTENTS

ACKNOWLEDGEMENTS

Even though I have always longed to write a book on body language for decades, it eventually came to pass at this moment. It is better late than never. Without mincing words, there were numerous things that stood as stumbling blocks to the success of this work but I must appreciate those who made this possible. Most times, we don't know how life-changing and impactful our little acts of kindness towards people are. This project has made me realise how extraordinary they can be.

Let me start from my doorstep. I have come to understand the importance of family in one's life. No matter how successful one is, if one does not have a stable family, one's success is incomplete. The grace that flows on my relations has always spoken for me positively. My dearest sister, Anparasi, was a source of inspiration for this book. Her laudable ideas led to the birth of this book. The beauty of her intelligence resonated in all levels. Also, her beautiful daughter, Haley Magdalene King—my conversations with her were often laced with deep insights. And my ever-charming trio, outstanding and excellent daughters—Laavenya, Pavithiral and Senaiga—I have no precise words to describe the support, goodwill, and encouragements I enjoyed from them. When the whole world lost interest in me, they believed and stood by me. Their endless love for me was a catalyst for the success of this project.

Again, this book made me accept the fact that nobody is self-made. Countless experiences have culminated in the writing of this book. I am most grateful to my parents who brought me up in the right way; they ensured the environment was conducive enough for me to pursue my vision rather than be lost in the illusion of the world. My passion for understanding, reading people through their body movement started in my childhood.

Through intuition and curiosity, when I observed some deficiencies in people's behaviour and movement, I would approach them to ask relevant questions. Many of them were always taken aback that I was able to make a right guess of their thought through their physical actions. I also learnt through the experiences of those who were close to me—my family. Even at a very young age, a lot of people were surprised that I could spot inadequacies in their narratives. As you devour the pages of this book, you will come across recreations of many of those childhood experiences.

I eventually ventured in astrology and numerology. At this point, the behaviour of an average human being became crystal clear to me. Those things I was oblivious of during my childhood appeared clearer to me, and I kept learning for years. Even though some people may not agree with this dimension, I cannot wave it off due to the immeasurable contribution it made to who I am today.

At age ten, I had started reading books related to behavioural psychology. I was so much fascinated to the subject matter that I had little time to think of the essence of those books. Any voice of dissent could have talked me out of it because by then, it was passion without direction. I kept on reading books on psychology till I was nineteen. Unconsciously, I gave myself to practice, and they were working out well without my knowledge until my friend called my attention.

My days in the army were one of the most productive as I met with experienced colleagues on the field. They were ready to teach and correct and ultimately watch me grow in knowledge. I mastered the 'power of observation'. For this, I am most appreciative to my ITD commanding officer, LTC Arthur Lee Huai Siang. He taught me how I could look the enemy with intimidation. This worked for me beyond the army as I deployed its usage while serving in the Immigration and Checkpoints Authority (ICA).

As I was growing older, I became uncomfortable with things learnt through personal experience alone; I wanted more and as such, I began to read books of experts such as Joe Navarro (FBI Special Agent, Ret). Dr Paul Ekman, Allan Pease, Elizabeth Kuhnke, Jan Hargrave, Janine Driver, Amy Cuddy, and Julius Fast, among others. If you read between the lines, you will hear the silent voices of these pillars of intellectualism in the work. I have read some of them to the extent that I can reflect their style in my own writing.

At this point, let me sincerely acknowledge the countless opportunities offered to me by the Ex-Commissioners of Immigration, Mr Eric Tan and Mr Clarence Yeo. I never knew how invaluable the experiences they offered me were until later on in life. I was also fortunate to work under a dynamic supervisor since 1999. Mr Goh Choon Kin, Mr K. Kurusamy, Mr Phua Chew Hua, and Mr Poh Seng Hock gave me the exposure to profile criminals and tutoring. Before then, I had heard senior colleagues complain about this concept, but my knowledge on different aspects of the work gave me an edge. I was so versed in the field that I was eventually made a tutor on criminal profiling by the authorities of the ICA. I am grateful to them for offering me the platform to discover my potentials, nurture them for growth, and deploy them to use. There were equally other passionate people, yet they still found me worthy.

I commend the resilience, love, and optimistic spirit of Ganiish Subramanian, my childhood friend. For the past forty years, he had been my greatest fan. Any time I was stuck in a rough road, he was there to lift me up. When I felt inferior, he believed in me. When I thought I was empty, he pointed at the numerous potentials in me. Apart from the institutions earlier acknowledged, Ganiish was one of those who shook me out of my shell. May the cord of our friendship be stronger. Also, in the line of appreciation are S.P.Selvam and Leo Pichay, for being a source of encouragement and support to me for decades. I never took our partnership for granted.

It would have amounted to pure disaster for me to assume that my personal knowledge was enough to write a book of this volume. On this note, I want to appreciate all the scholars, essayists, opinion writers, and experts whose works were referenced in any part of the book. I want to thank them for permitting me to drink out of their wealth of knowledge. Joe Navarro, Christopher Philip, Farouk Radwan, David Strater, Hanan Parvez, Vanessa Van Edwards and Cherry Khedira deserve a special mention.

The contributions of the editors, publishing team, and figures of authority who provided holistic reviews of the book are so much appreciated. Without their mechanical and technical contributions, this book would have eternally remained a manuscript.

The Latin expression 'Qui docet discit', which is translated as 'He who teaches learns', is one of my most admired wise sayings. On this ground, I want to extend my appreciation to all participants in my numerous training sessions. I learnt so many things by teaching them, many of which were used in making this book what it is today. In fact, the resolve to find true solutions to many of the issues raised during our discussions propelled me to write the book.

Finally, I am grateful to you, the reader. Thank you for believing in me. Thank you for giving me the benefit of the doubt. Thank you for encouraging me to write more. Thank you for being responsive.

REVIEW
_____

This book presents in its entirety 23 body parts movement and their meanings—ways in which every human who are serious about their daily living can understand those they come across with in their business transactions. It gives an extensive account of the psychological feeling of people in each given situation. One of the differentiating features of this book is that it aptly fits into any given endeavour—health, law enforcement, family, education, and formal and corporate world, among others. The author's attention to detail and sense of responsibility to give examples across different fields make this book exceptional and give each reader a sense of belonging and importance.

The *Encyclopaedia of Body Language* eveals the secrets in our minds. It does not confer on us the ability to become soothsayers, but through it, we are able to understand the intents of others towards us or a proposal we have tabled before them. Most times, we are taken aback by people's weird and unwarranted behaviours not because they did not show the tendencies of those attributes but only because we were not attentive or were ignorant of the gestures. This book brings liberation to anyone who longs for a deep understanding of the motivation for people's behaviours in different circumstances.

The simplicity and expertise with which this book is written will keep you glued to it. The author reels out each body part and all the likely behaviours that are attached to it before linking such to the overall attitude of the person and other clusters. The relevant case studies that are further used in buttressing the points after each concept gives a pictorial view of what is discussed. Throughout the book, you feel the connection between each concept and the interplay of behaviours. This is an indication that humans are social beings, and there is no one who can survive in loneliness. If there are two sets of people who will be most appreciative of this book, it would be business professionals and law enforcement agents. The reason being that the relationship these people maintain is directly proportional to the utterances and bodily actions of their co-interlocutors.

_____

The book is masterfully structured to aptly code its message in a way that can be easily decoded by body language enthusiasts. For instance, while reading, you will understand that the hands are the most expressive parts of the body. As such, it was extensively explained throughout a chapter and conspicuously linked with other chapters throughout the discussion. However, I also opined that the lower parts of the body are the most reliable body language indicators. The reason being that both you and your subjects rarely pay attention to those parts of the body; we are conventionally focused on the face, which can be feigned and restructured to show what they want you to see. A fundamental lesson for every reader is how you can beam your searchlight in the lower parts of the body to decode the intents of the heart of an interlocutor.

Perhaps people rarely talk about colour in non-verbal communication because they see it as not relevant or not strong enough to reveal the minds of others to them, but this misconception is intellectually rebuffed in this book through a masterful discussion of the concept and how it can be interpreted around the globe.

CHAPTER 1

Introduction

The concept of human behaviour is what many of us cannot do without. In fact, our world is centrally built around the concept of psychology. I have been personally engulfed in decoding everything that has to do with human behaviour since childhood; how people acted and the circumstances that led them into portraying a particular attitude has always been an interest to me. Above all, I was curious to know *why* they acted in such manner. For the past five decades of my life, I have been in the business of keeping a close tab on the bodily movement of people.

I was always digging deep to understand the intent of people through their behaviour even when I had no inkling that I would end up as an immigration officer and master trainer of forces across nations. For the past thirty years, my observations as a child have taken a prominent place in my career as I go after criminals, engage terrorists in interviews, and arm people from all walks of life with the intellectual weaponry of reading body language. My keen interest on how people make use of their body and what propel them in doing so endowed me with the natural trajectory of understanding their subtle means of communication.

Although born and raised in Singapore, I have had the opportunity to travel to the different continents of the world. During my stay abroad, I always pay rapt attention to my surroundings, listen to the echoes of people's body, and understand what is in store for me each time. Unlike the natives, I never took anything for granted. Invariably, I am always focused on discovering the only thing that appears reasonable to me—*body language*. Through their look, countenance, softness or toughness of their eyes, use of hands, or facial expression, I understand what they are trying to say. Through this action, I could measure my limits and excesses—those who like me, those who care less about my existence, and probably where I can be hurt. Till date, there is simply no alternative for me to survive in a strange land other than observing people's body language.

Of course, there are usually noticeable differences in the body language of other countries compared with that of my native land, but I often rely on the universal aspect in decoding what they were trying to say. Without mincing words, my greatest source of discovering body language has been the home front. The reason being that apart from understanding the spoken words, I also have vast knowledge on the culture of the community. So there was no way I could be lost in a conversation, taking cognisance of my keen interest in body language observation.

Hence, I learnt about deception at a very early age. People are pathological liars, but their Achilles heel has always been their non-verbal aspect. It is always baffling to see people express their stance on a given issue verbally when their non-verbal is communicating the opposite. This is often worse in children who are unarguably bad liars. It is not rare to see a child nod in agreement to an accusation while they deny such verbally at the same time. As we grow older, we become the embodiment of lies and deception, but a well-trained person can still spot the traces of deception, no matter how perfect the lie seems to have been presented. Some of the common betrayalsare when the person seems to lack confidence in themselves, when they are not convinced about their assertions, and when they leave out important details in a narrative, do not properly arrange events, and add needless details. All these signals are expertly documented in this book in a practical manner.

As I become more mature in age, experience, and reasoning, I decided to make the non-verbals my utmost means of judgement. There is virtually anything I do without relying on non-verbal cues—in trainings, at work, at home, amidst friends, while conversing with my children—just *everything* about life! The opportunity I have had to have interacted and observed people from all walks of life has further helped me in understanding people across racial divides. As a way of formalising my experience and knowledge in the field, I have read many legends on the subject matter and attended schools, and I am still learning through unique encounters that cross my path on a daily basis. The power of non-verbal communication struck me the most the day I saw children with congenital disorders on the playground; it was unbelievably amazing.

As a security expert who has worked for decades both in the public and private sectors, my job has mainly revolved round speaking with people, interviewing suspects, and interacting with criminals to establish the true cause of an incident and the actual role they played in such. And as I passionate lover of my job, I am always ready for all the above-listed undertakings. I am one of the most respected in the Asian front when it comes to reading body language. In instances where people thought it was impossible to know what was going on, I give them the unexpected response. It is an open secret that my work requires an indescribable level of tenacity. Criminals will hardly tell you the truth, no matter how hard you try. They are very much aware of the consequences of their actions, and confessing to such makes it easy for them to be punished. So the herculean job is always on the interrogating officer to handle them professionally until they consciously come to the acceptance of their actions.

Reading through journals and other publications on body language and deceptions, I can authoritatively tell the kind of criminal or terrorist the author had words with. All these never came as an overnight thing; working passionately on the field in the past thirty years has taught me what no book can. In this encyclopaedia, I have tried to share all my experiences in addition to those of others who have been equally successful in dealing with body language. It is a reflection of my life, what science states, and how you can conquer deception.

How It Benefits All

This book is beneficial to humanity in many ways. The only way to lead a peaceful life is to build a crime-free world. This is not just the job of some group of people; it requires the involvement of *everyone*. This means you have a role to play. Whether you are in the law enforcement, banking sector, hospitality industry, education, private firms, business world, or even unemployed, we must join hands together to send crime out of our *society*. This is the sole message of this book. It teaches how to detect crime and make criminals confess through scientific reliance on non-verbal gestures. It is simple, practical, charming, engaging, and solution-driven.

How It Benefits the Law Enforcement Officers

All over the world, it is conventionally expected that law enforcement officers should keep the society safe from all kinds of crimes. Even though this is an unrealistic expectation placed on these professionals, all hands must be on deck to put an end to crime. Generally, law enforcement should play the leading role in this demanding task. Criminals are indescribably smart, and you cannot use yesterday's method to solve today's problems. Gone are those days when threats and other traditional methods produce results. Evil-minded people are smart in hiding their crimes and will tell you how you are violating their fundamental human rights when you threaten them.

The good news is that this book has come up with a masterful and result-oriented way to deal with criminals and terrorists; you can know the thoughts and culpability of subjects based on their body language. While a lot of them think that they can be verbally deceptive, little did they know that they will be betrayed by their body movements. The *Encyclopedia of Body Language* tells you how to win the war against illegalities without losing your peace. Here, you have the weapons against evildoers. It is practical and applicable to all situations.

How It Benefits the Private Security Firms/Bodyguards

Private security firms operate more as a business entity than as a law enforcement agency. This is because they want to outsmart their competitors in all ramifications. While the top management is coming up with different ideas to get this done, some employees may sabotage their efforts through laziness and connivance with others. Such individuals cannot be identified from the surface level; they are hypocritical in nature—they behave good in public and plan death or evil in private. To match up with the games of such entities, one needs to be versatile in reading non-verbal gestures.

Apart from internal sabotage, private security firms need the application of non-verbal cues in their jobs. When contracted to mount guard in a given location, through the body language of people, you can identify the wrong members of public from the right. This will prevent the guards from venting their anger on the wrong person. When confronted with terrorists, being able to read their body language will diffuse the attack before explosion. With this book, no one is permitted to claim ignorance of an unwanted scenario. Maintaining the security of a given territory goes beyond just putting on a stern face or high-level technology; you need to see the unseen and hear the unsaid.

How It Benefits the Human Lie Detectors

The human lie detector is one of the innovations that came in the world with the breakthrough of technology. However, as good as this instrument is, it is not self-sufficient—that is, it needs complementary efforts from other sources to live above board. From research, it has been discovered that human lie detector needs human knowledge to verify its results. This means humans have developed a tough skin against it; the machine can easily be manipulated. Con artists and other hardened criminals will confidently manipulate it, while innocent but fearful people are trapped in the offence that they know nothing of. Due to this fact, prisons all over the world are filled with innocent prisoners. We cannot continue like this; there is no essence caging the wrong persons while those who are supposed to be punished go about, mocking our ignorance.

In order to have this paradigm shift, we must deploy the machineries of non-verbal gestures in aiding the activities of human lie detectors—that is, after the machine have done its work, we should ask some relevant questions to confirm whether the result presented is right or wrong. Our ability to read people's non-verbal cues will give us the needed answers.

How It Benefits the Schools

Apart from the home, the school is another institution where a child is moulded for both personal and societal use. However, it has been discovered over time that no matter how skilled or gifted a teacher is, there are some students who will still prove difficult to control for him or her. At this point, there is a need for a display of higher skill, and that is simply deployment of the knowledge of body language. Radicalised students are criminals in waiting if their wings are not caught ahead of time. No matter how you manipulate them to reveal their mind, there would still be loads of unsaid stories. This is the point where you need to apply your knowledge of non-verbal cues to decode what is going on.

Students who are involved in gang activities are difficult to handle too, and it is necessary that decisive actions are taken to refine them into the system. This may be difficult if you are unaware of what their issues are exactly. However, beyond physical rascality and brutality, students with academic issues should also be given due attention. Such problematic students are usually shy, and you need the knowledge of reading body language as shared in this book, to understand them beyond their words.

How It Benefits the Parents

Parents, just like school administrators and teachers, are the builders of kids in the society. Young minds will always attempt to take to all forms of vices, but their parents and guardians must be on ground to guide and lead them aright. The act of parenting is a herculean and challenging one. That is why some end up disappointing the society through faulty rearing of their kids. This should be a source of concern to all and sundry as malreared kids are potential time bombs in the community. Parents must live up to responsibility by understanding the needs and thoughts of their children on virtually every issue of life.

From my personal experiences, I can affirm that not every parent wants to fail in giving their children the right upbringing, but they are overwhelmed by ignorance. In such instances, the children would have become wayward or defocused before it comes to the notice of their parents. This makes them reactionary rather than being proactive. The good news is that every parent can live above board through the understanding of non-verbal communication. Children are holistic in their use of body language, and you can rely on it to understand their intents. For instance, a child who is saying no and nodding simultaneously is telling lie. This book offers every parent the opportunity to understand their children better and build more cohesive relationships with them.

How It Benefits the Business Entrepreneurs

In the business world, you will meet people from different parts of the world. It is a transaction that is purely based on money and services. While some business entrepreneurs are value-driven, some are simply money-driven. Those in the latter category can go to any mile to play on the intelligence of their business partners. This is the point where you need to be alert of your relationships with those whom you transact business with.

Beyond scamming, being able to read body language helps you understand your clients better. Some of them may not fully express themselves, especially when they are shy to tell you how unsatisfactory your services are. If you are able to decode the unsaid, you will be able to ask the right questions to know how to serve them better.

Every single step and decision matters in business. This means you need to pay attention to your own non-verbal gestures too. This book helps you be composed and have a firm message at all times. It teaches you how to rightly behave, pass your message without controversies, and win people over to your side. This is a silent tool that helps you sell better.

How It Benefits the Corporate Companies

The corporate world is regarded as the home of ideas and intellectualism where people are expected to demonstrate an appreciable level of knowledge and integrity in all their undertakings. However, this appears to be mere wishful thinking as the sector has been bastardised by the despicable attitudes of some bad eggs. Since those who are passionate about the sanity of the institution cannot sit back and watch, there is need for them to take result-oriented actions. It is pertinent to note that curbing crime in such an environment is tantamount to being tossed between the devil and the deep blue sea. When you accuse people wrongly, that can backfire and affect in some other ways. Through informed reading of people's body gestures, you will be able to determine whether they are involved in an occurrence or not.

Through this, you can wage war against corruption among professionals. Your ability to identify criminals among other workers will give you an edge in all that you do; you will be respected and feared. This means none of them will dare you with those nauseating behaviour. Beyond scouting for troublemakers and criminals, you will notice it when any of the workers have issues. There are many of them with burdens, affecting their productivity. When you show them care even when they are yet to open their mouth, it helps in winning their heart. It is only through the help of right non-verbal interpretations that this can be done.

How It Benefits the Hotels and Hospitality Industry

The hospitality industry is one of the most important sectors in any given economy, and nations of the world consciously step up their spending in the sector in order to make it a cynosure of all eyes. Whenever a person or a group of persons is coming into a given location, their first point of contact is the hospitality industry. From the foregoing, two things are crystal clear—first, the hospitality industry is a multibillion-dollar one, and second, it is home to important people of the society. This makes it attractive to criminals and predators. The presence of law enforcement officers alone cannot guarantee the safety of the sector. This book highlights ways in which everyone in the industry can play their own roles to ensure its safety.

Through the understanding of people's body language, you will know when the wrong person is coming into the industry. People with ulterior motives would hide under the cover of sweet words, but their body language has always betrayed their lies. From the security check right into their rooms, the signs would be glaring for anyone who can see beyond the surface level. This book arms you with the right knowledge to make you swing into action when the situation calls for it.

How It Benefits the Airline Industry

Due to its convenience, a lot of people do prefer travelling through air rather than land. It easily connects different nations of the world. While we still celebrate the innovation of the Wright brothers and the subsequent modifications that had heralded the industry, some opportunists have taken advantage of that avenue to inflict pain on innocent people. Our world is more perverse than ever before. Since it is not ideal for airline administrators to begin to fill airplanes with security agents, it is high time that we think outside the box and find laudable and encompassing solutions we can hold on to. Without mincing words, the only tested and result-proven method is an apt understanding of non-verbal cues of everyone who has a business or another in the industry.

Workers in the industry will benefit numerously from this book as it teaches them all the gimmicks that people deploy to play on their intelligence. When pilots, check-in staff, and stewardesses, among others, live in the consciousness of unravelling the inner thoughts of people through their non-verbal cues, then all loopholes will be blocked and sanity will return to the industry. This is not rocket science; that is why the steps listed in this book were well tested and researched before publication.

How It Benefits the Finance and Banking Industry

Perhaps one of the most delicate sectors of the economy is banking and finance. The reason being that it is the powerhouse of all human activities—we all work for the sake of money. Since the natural part of humans will crave for rest before work, some undisciplined individuals will rather opt for illegal ways to meet their needs. This has exposed the sector to all kinds of attacks. Despite improvements in technology and modern security architecture, it appears that the war is still far from being won. This means something decisive has to be done, and that is where this subject matter fits in.

The *Encyclopedia of Body Language* arms you with an unseen weapon that will win the war for you with ease. Scammers and money launderers will always want to test their antics on everyone whom they cross paths with, but what is most important is how informed you are. This book exposes you to the eternal truths about an average criminal; it teaches you how to be proactive in your fight against financial crime. It is a liberation balm that gives you solution to all crime-related issues in the sector. After going through this book, you will be able to identify a suspected scammer even before they strike.

How It Benefits the Hospitals and Healthcare Industry

Some decades ago, not too many people will believe the projection that hospitals will become a target location for criminals. Not only is it happening now but it is also on a high note. As someone who does not believe in reactionary measures, I was able to carry out extensive research in that sector and capture practical and probable ways in which these attacks on hospitals can be curbed. With the potency of body language, you can curb numerous maladies in the healthcare industry. First, when it is well-deployed, medical practitioners can identify lawbreakers ahead of their action. This book teaches medical practitioners how they can rely on their instincts and other scientific models to point out people with criminal intents.

Further, a vast understanding of non-verbal gestures will help nurses and doctors in understanding their patients better. There are some illnesses that cannot be well explained by their victims; doctors need to depend on other means to have a clearer view of what the person is going through. Unfortunately, some staffers are also corrupt, both in the discharge of their duties and in relation to crime. When such problem arises, a firm reliance on body language will give you effortless victory.

How It Benefits the Sales Industry

Like every other sector that has been mentioned in this note, the sales industry is the core of existence; whether directly or indirectly, we all participate in buying and selling of either goods and services or ideas. The side you belong to each time (either as a buyer or seller), notwithstanding, requires that you are vast in your understanding of people's body language—that is, you need to decode your partner's body language with ease. This will indicate whether you are in the right business deal or not. If you are into insurance, property, or general sales, you must train your mind to understand the body language of your customers. No client is willing to part with their hard-earned money, no matter how strongly worded you are. So the question is, when and how do you know you have succeeded in convincing the client? This is where body language interpretation plays a vital role.

There is no need to be overly bothered on how to go about as everything has been covered in this book. You will know when someone is for you or against you and what you can do to win people's attention so that they can do your bidding.

How It Benefits the Junior Drama Artists

At the beginning of every career, people are bound to face challenges. It is generally believed that it is those challenges that mould them up. People who experience real growth are those who learn from their down moments to prepare a brighter future for themselves. However, not everyone can see things from the positive lens. Being in the drama sector is a great challenge; they are mimicking individuals and institutions in the society. It is expected to be perfectly done so that the intended message can be passed. This makes the job more demanding. For young artists to move up the ladder very quickly, they need an indisputable understanding of this concept.

Drama goes beyond just uttering words. In fact, it is more about movements that convey more meanings than the actual words that are uttered. When the movement contradicts the intended message, the people would be left confused. That is why some artists are not seen as the viewers' favourite. For junior drama artists to gain the admiration of people, they must understand the interpretation of non-verbal gestures as detailed in this book. The book details every important segment of the society and how body language is used by professionals in each sector. Since dramatists are required to know something about everything, this book provides them the opportunity.

How It Benefits the Sportsmen

Although the sporting world is seen as one that is predominantly meant for relaxation and entertainment, it should not be forgotten that it is tied to the livelihood and essence of living of some people. Those individuals are referred to as professional athletes. Athletics is not just about the demonstration of skills; it also involves the ability to understand your opponents—that is, an athlete who desires to do well must think about himself and his opponent. In sports, the only way you can know the thoughts and permutations of your opponent is to observe their body movements. Some vaguely refer to this as pattern of play, skill display, or carriage; but in the real sense, they are all making reference to the non-verbal communication of the person.

As a sports person, you need to think about the possible movement of an opponent in the twinkle of an eye and get ready so as not to be caught unawares. Without an iota of exaggeration, sports persons should be more concerned about understanding body language than every other group of people. To those who share the same belief with this, the *Encyclopedia of Body Language* has provided you with reliefs that will bolster your career and make you a rare breed.

How It Benefits the General Public

As I have earlier reiterated in the other parts of this introductory note, understanding body language should be the job of all, no matter what your professional calling is. In every human transaction, communication is expected to take place, and where there is communication, body language sits in the central point. Take for instance when a job applicant goes to an interview. They need the knowledge of non-verbal gestures to be better composed and to know if their responses meet the expectations of the interviewers or not. Relationship is the foundation of greatness as no man succeeds on their own. When you display the right body language cues at all times, you will attract the right persons and build solid relationships with them.

Further, the nuggets shared in this book will help you understand the thoughts of people concerning what you tell them; you can determine if they are receptive of your ideas or not. It is pertinent to state that this book does not make you a mind reader, but it helps you in making right guesses on situations each time. It sharpens your instincts and helps you have an informed thought on a matter. It puts you on the safe side in all your relationships.

All in all, this book is filled with liberating knowledge; it is evidence of well-researched, adequately written, and masterfully arranged book. It digs into the deepest part of the human heart and brings out a master key that unlocks hidden meanings in all human activities. We have longed for a solution like this for a while, but it seems we were not hungry enough to go for it. Non-verbal communication has been a part of humans since the creation of man, but we relegated it to the backwoods and believed more in consciously coined deceptions which have not been good for our development. The *Encyclopedia of Body Language* marks the birth of a revolution in human communication.

CHAPTER 2

The Head

The head is the powerhouse of the human body; it is an embodiment of the brain which controls all human activity. Hence, the head serves as the source of every human behaviour. Science has made us aware that the brain does not stop working. This means it controls both our conscious and subconscious actions. Being the seat of power, it is involved in all activities relating to the body. Digestion, regulation of the heart, breathing, and every other important bodily action start from the head. When a part of the brain is damaged, it affects the whole body's system. For instance, damage to the left side of the brain can cause stroke, affecting the hands and legs of the victims. In others, it brings about speech deficiency. That is why the head should be guarded with the highest degree of caution. Injuries inflicted on the head are life-threatening.

However, what is very important to us in this book is the exterior of the head. We reach a conclusion about the beauty or ugliness of a person by looking at their head. All the parts of the head—lips, hair, chin, nose, forehead, ears, eyes, and eyebrows—have their own specific message they pass across during a conversation; they communicate to people who can decipher non-verbal cues. In fact, you cannot look away from the head and rightly establish the state of emotion of a person. Hence, we are starting from the part of the body that matters most throughout our lifetime.

At different stages of our lives, we look to the head for pieces of information about a person. When we were still young, our parents look at our head to know how we feel, what is wrong with us, or if we are hurt or hungry. At this stage, we cannot verbally express ourselves, and they rely on the expressions on our face to know the next line of action. As we grow up, we focus on the head while communicating with our friends. Through the movement of their eyes, nose, and overall facial expression, we are able to establish what goes on in their mind. Also, we rely on the head to work seamlessly with our colleagues at the workplace. Deception is better detected through the expressions people wear each time. A colleague who frowns during a meeting where a new idea is tabled is surely not up for the suggestion. Although they may try to deny this verbally, but along the line, they will not give their best to the rightful implementation of such an idea. And ultimately, the head plays a huge role between spouses.

The saying 'The eyes are the window to the soul' explains the importance of a part of the head in having a good relationship with others. On a first date with a person, they may be shy in expressing their feelings verbally, so you need to read their facial expression to know how they feel. And it continues on that cycle till death calls. Hence, it is not out of place to start our discussion from the head.

A platform is dedicated to body language teachings. Study Body Language also discussed the concept of the head in a masterful way. According to the platform, 'The position of the head is one of the quickest giveaways to mood or attitude in body language.' This is because there's a direct correlation between how we feel and how we hold our head. The way we see the world around us is affected by the angle we look at it, no doubt (SBL 2009). This explains why different people looking at the same thing have varied opinion about such thing. Accumulation of past experiences also plays a key role in this. Ideally, those who are happy or elated about a situation keep their head very high; they portray confidence and readiness to engage the system. On the other hand, frustrated or depressed people bow their head; they lack the inner strength to hold their head high as they are not proud of the circumstance.

As we move on this segment, this information can help us discern, in one glance, many types of attitudes (SBL 2009):

- The general morale—happy versus sad, assured versus shaky.
- Who or what is the centre of attention of the person you observe?

- How involved and engaged is someone in a given scenario?
- Who's the superior and who's the subordinate in the social power struggle?

Without mincing words, the above-stated guidelines are not sacrosanct or truly holistic in determining the state of mind of a person—that is, it will be wrong of me to claim that someone is elated on the basis of the singular fact that they hold their head high. However, the fact remains that the head in reading body language is an essential barometer in determining the mental state of a person in the twinkle of an eye. That is, if you are given a moment to state the mood of a person, the head position should be your number 1 focus.

The head cannot take any shape without the neck. As important as the neck is, it is very vulnerable. It holds our head and supplies it with vital bloodstream through the carotid arteries. That's the reason we instinctively guard our neck when we feel vulnerable (physically or emotionally) or show it with pride when we feel secure or when trying to impress (SBL 2019). Generally, the higher the head is raised, the higher the emotional condition of the person—that is, they wholesomely feel stronger, more agile, and more energised. Further, when the head is oriented with the movement induced by the neck, it is an indication of where the interest of the person lies. This is synonymous to pointing with the fingers. When the head is kept in a balanced position, it becomes difficult for anyone to read meanings of its movement as it is just in its natural state. However, once you begin to tilt it, there are arrays of meanings that can be alluded to it, which would be considered in this segment.

2.1. Adorning the Head

Generic Interpretations of the Concept

This form of body language signal is used across cultures for various purposes. One of its predominant uses is the communication of leadership status. (This is witnessed among Native American chiefs that use feather headdresses.) It can mean to signal the profession of a person (the hard hat used by miners in various parts of the world), representation of social status (the infamous Yves Saint Laurent pillbox hat), or to connote people's hobbies or pastimes (helmet worn by those who ride bicycles or engage in mountaineering). Furthermore, head adornment is used in the religious circles—the Jewish yarmulke or the cardinal's cap. It may also mean a form of expressing an allegiance to a system, sports, or a given person—passionate sports club, union, or associations, among others. This form of body signal gives an insight about individuals in relation to the environment in which they are found.

It tells us about the thought pattern of individuals—where they belong to in the society, their preferences, religious affiliations, economic buoyancy, what they think of themselves each time, and allegiances among other issues. Adorning the head in a particular way explains if a person confines with the doctrines of a given society. Some intentionally adorn their head to register their grievances against the status quo of the individual communities. In its natural interpretation, adornment is worn with the purpose of beautifying the head and making a person look more attractive. If worn properly, it distinguishes the wearer from other people in an occasion. In a multicultural setting, it is not uncommon to see try to set themselves apart through the adornment of the head. The reason behind the adornment gives hint of how it will look like. Someone who does so to prove economic status will ensure that the item is rare and expensive for lower-class individuals to afford.

Scientific Explanations

There are different items usually used for adornment, such as facial hair, lip plates, braiding, headgear, clothing accessories, cosmetics, and jewellery. According to an article on the website of the University of Tennessee, US, 'Hats and headdresses can be full of meaning. They simultaneously announce our place in society and make statements about our individuality. A hat can identify which country a person comes from and to what cultural group he belongs. It may indicate how he makes his living or how he spends his free time. Hats can reveal people's religious affiliations and confirm their faith in God or their belief in animistic spirits. They may be worn to scare off enemies and demons or to attract a mate. The shape, design, and decoration of the headwear may also convey one's state of life as well as social position, power, and wealth.' The above quote emphasises what has been said in the opening paragraph.

These days, there is a profusion of shapes for hats and headdresses, and as such, these are used in artistic manner. This is in affirmation to the diversity of the world cultures. Head adornments may serve as reinforcement of attitudes, values shared by people, and bridge among cultures (UT 2019). People who adorn their heads should be careful of the message they intend to pass because the accuracy is lost most times. This is because a lot of people tend to overlook the non-verbal message that their hats, headdresses, facial tattoos, and other adornments are passing across. Wrong usage can turn people off and alienate potential benefactors from you. Depending on its usage, head adornment can signal the need to be unique, rebellious, or nonconformist; can contain an artistic form; or on the other hand, can signal the urge to fit into the higher or lower socio-economic standard. People choose their adornments based on the message they want to pass across to others (Chris 2014).

Practical Illustrations

Case Study I: Before interpreting a person's head adornment, you need to check for congruency between their non-verbal body language and general body carriage so as to determine if someone is real or fake about their adornment for some reasons. For instance, a person who uses expensive head adornment is expected to walk with confidence in public. This is a proof that they are really wealthy. However, if confidence is lacking in what they do, it is a hint that the adornments are only meant to serve as a cover-up for their fear or false socio-economic status.

Case Study II: In West Africa, when women use scarves, especially in the fourteenth century, it was used to connote spiritual protection. The typical head in most West African local communities is used to connote balance and character and, as such, should not just be made open to all. It is the most valued part of the body. Among the Yoruba of Nigeria, women do not want to leave their heads open, lest an unclean spirit touches it. Among the Indians, jewellery plays a huge role in their head adornment since the primitive age. It has been in use for the past 5,000 years. Indians have an indescribable love for gold. And to them, it is a way of acquiring wealth. When their women use jewellery, it is for the purpose of beautification and aesthetics. Popular among their head adornments is the *sarpech*, which evolved from Rajasthan. It developed in medieval India, and it was always worn as a princely turban. Using it for other purposes then would be tagged as fake.

Case Study III: Among the Japanese, hairstyle plays a major role—on both men and women. For the women, it is their crowning glory and a means of displaying their wealth. Some hairstyles can be found on the nobles, while some are signatures of royalty. In the traditional era, most women spend a fortune on their hair and make it look like a crown. However, when you see a woman in Japan wearing their hair in a bun or tied to the back, this is an indication that the person is an ordinary Japanese; they are not wealthy. So the hair is worn by these people for mere functionality and not style. For the geisha and maiko, their hair is seen as the most important aspect of their professional calling. These professionals change their hair according to the season. Their hair is used for the depiction of their functions, rank, and apprenticeship status.

Case Study IV: Women have also used this as a way out for their criminal activities. In different cases, I came across women who adorned their head with veil or burka for the purpose of concealing their identity. They did it as if it were part of their attire, but I discovered that such veils covered almost all their head such that it was difficult to establish their identity. A closer look later revealed that they were impostors; they wanted to use other people's identification to gain entrance into the country. The veil they adorned changed their appearance in a way that other officers and I were left confused whether they were the ones on the identity card or not. Our doubts were established when they were asked to take it off.

Case Study V: Another great experience that is worth sharing was one with some group of men who were doing covert recordings. They were undoubtedly criminals who wanted to understand the operations of the borders. They hid their cameras in their caps and took their time to converse with officers at the border. I became suspicious of their activities when they began to ask some sensitive questions. Of course, they were harmless, but my instinct told me that the way they carried their head and even how they wore their caps was not normal. At some point, I needed to order for a search, and they confessed after a few minutes into the process. I understood their criminal intent through their dressing and manner of communication.

2.2. Nodding

Generic Interpretations of the Concept

Head nodding is one of the most common body language cues in the world. People of all race and backgrounds make use of this sign, and in many instances, it connotes universal meaning, except in some few cases. In general terms, head nodding is used to signal agreement among interlocutors. In a discourse context, when a person nods their head, it means they are receptive of the point being discussed by their co-interlocutor. In other contexts, it means they are affirming what the person is saying; it is an indication that the person is saying the whole truth. In this context, people do not have reservations about what the other party is saying. However, I need to state that there are instances when head nodding does not mean agreement if it is accompanied with lip pursing. However, this explanation seems too straight to be real in this corruption-ridden world. In some instances, someone may be nodding their head and playing out other signs just to show that they are in tandem with what the other person is saying, but in reality, it is the opposite. They know that if they should disagree openly, something evil may end happening. This form of fake head nod comes in a very rapid, quick, and aggressive manner.

Scientific Explanations

Writing on Body Language Project, Chris Phillips (2013) affirms that 'the head nod is a familiar gesture that happens naturally to show agreement. The nod means that the listener is going along with what is being said, but it can also be used as a tool to actively stimulate conversations.' There seems to be something magical about the head nod as research shows that it has the ability to increase a speaker's speaking time in three to four places. This means that when you nod your head while a person is speaking, it encourages them to speak further. It makes the speaker admire us more. It has also been proven by research that 'head nodding breeds positive thoughts and is hardwired into the brain' (Chris 2013).

Head nod can be divided into two main categories—fast and slow nods. They have different interpretations. When the head nod is slow and lengthy, it is used to signal understanding and agreement. It is another means of saying 'I am in agreement with you. Take your time to explain yourself because I am listening.' If this small, slow nod is accompanied with a smile, it further encourages the speaker, and it builds a bond between the interlocutors. However, if the head nod is fast and rapid and, most importantly, if the listener is rubbing their face or touching their ear, it means they are impatient. The person is telling you to be fast with what you are saying because they want to leave or say their own. It is like saying 'Yes, I understand your point. Move to the next' (SBL 2019).

'Scientific experiments have shown that as the conscious mind invariably gets tired or distracted, the head nodding stops or changes direction' (Chris 2013). Hence, if the person you are speaking with does not look at you while nodding, it means that they are only nodding for a show because they are distracted already. Another interpretation is that they are still ruminating on a point you made earlier. The fact is that it is not easy to think deeply while you still maintain eye contact. In this situation, you need to excuse the person some few minutes to think through (SBL 2013).

In conclusion, if the head nod is not in congruent with what they say, one needs to be suspicious. A person saying 'Yes, I agree with you' but shaking their head from side to side is telling lies (Parvez 2019).

Practical Illustrations

Case Study I: As said earlier, the head nod is usually noticeable in personal conversations and public discourses, and the way it is used illustrates what it stands for. For instance, if you are speaking with one of your children at home and they shake their head and say 'Yes, daddy, it's true', they are telling lies. If it were actually true, they should nod their head in agreement. Body language is mostly released in the sincere form in children because it is unconsciously done. On the other hand, while speaking with your parents and they nod their head in a very fast pace and say 'Continue, I'm with you', this means they are not really listening. Maybe they are late for work, and they just want you to say whatever you have to say so that they can move out. They are not attentive to the content of your speech.

Case Study II: In an office setting, if you are in a board meeting and you are presenting a new idea to the members of the board and they are nodding slowly, it is an indication that they really love the proposal. This is even more effective if they add several nods when you are done with your speech. This is also very true if you are presenting the report of a feasibility study. If your experienced senior colleague is nodding slowly, it is an indication that you did a thorough job and that they agree with all the content of your presentation. The concept of head nod is really pronounced in a formal setting. In a public presentation, if the audience is nodding in a fast manner, it is an indication of two things. One, they are tired of your presentation and want you to leave the podium any time soon. Second, you have raised a point in your presentation that is prompting them to ask questions once you are done. So the head nod signals people who are impatient or tired.

Case Study III: Head nod is also used in a criminal situation. Non-verbal communication plays a huge role in every discourse context. If a terrorist comes to spy on your office and they are nodding their head to what you are saying, it is a means of encouraging you to say more. This means you are actually giving them the vital pieces of information they are on the lookout for. So they are unconsciously encouraging you through their head nod to say more. With this, they will get all the relevant information from you without your consent.

Case Study IV: A somewhat funny but an unforgettable experience was with a subject who doesn't understand English. I discovered that throughout the investigation, the suspect was nodding. His nod looked so real that I could not doubt the sincerity of his response. I thought to myself that it was a 'perfect' investigation as his nod was considered more as a self-indictment than an affirmation of my doubts. However, things became messier during cross-examination as it became clear that he doesn't understand English. With the language barrier noticed, I had to run the interview again with the help of a translator. So head nods should be confirmed to know what the person is really saying and if he understands you.

2.3.   Nodding the Head in Contradiction

Generic Interpretations of the Concept

This concept was briefly explained in the preceding subsection. Head nodding in contradiction is mostly witnessed in children. This is when the non-verbal message of a person differs from their verbal utterance. In simpler terms, it is when a person is saying yes with their mouth while their body is echoing no. This is not only exclusive to young children but also seen in teenagers, youths, and adults. It is a subconscious action that is used to reveal the innermost thought of an interlocutor. In this context of incongruence, one is always urged to embrace the non-verbal context. This is because before a person speaks, they would have thought about it. Hence, the truth can be wilfully subverted.

However, the non-verbal cue goes beyond human conscious control. People who nod their head in contradiction think they are trying to confuse their listeners, but in truth, it is a means of depicting themselves as a blatant liar. Since they are not conscious of this action at the point of displaying it, they do not know how weird such an action is. After thinking about it, they will most probably become ashamed of themselves or blame themselves on the head for not being composed enough to deceive their listener with lies.

Scientific Explanations

'If the nodding or shaking of the head is not congruent with what the person is saying, then you're well-advised to be suspicious. For example, during a conversation, if a person says "It sounds good" or "Okay, let's go for it" while shaking his head from side to side, then it's clear that he does not mean what he's saying' (Parvez 2019). He goes on to assert that when non-verbal cues are contradictory to their verbal counterpart, one should always go for the former because non-verbal messages cannot be easily subjected to manipulation and, as such, are mostly true.

Another platform dedicated to body language discourse, Changing Minds, states that when the head contradicts with spoken words, it is a means of sending a subtle message of disagreement. 'This can be done deliberately in order to confuse. It also may happen subconsciously when lying.' In most cases, the latter is usually the case. There is hardly anyone who wants to be deliberately misheard in communication; we want people to understand everything we say. Apart from the headshake, there are other accompanying gestures that buttress the point of contradiction in communication. For instance, if the person is nodding in contradiction and raises their eyebrow, it means they are actually interested in what is being discussed but they do not want to agree with the point raised.

At this point, let me clearly state the fact that not every nod means yes and, likewise, not every headshake stands for no. This 'universal' principle is only applicable in the Western world. There are some countries in the world where this is clearly different. Examples are Greece, Bulgaria, Albania, and Macedonia. In these countries, the concept of headshake and nodding is in reversed form. For instance, when in Bulgaria, when a person nods their head to mean no, the head must first go downward, and this is commonly accompanied with slight pouting. However, if the headshake stands for yes, apart from the head going left and right, it will also tilt to the side. This form of shaking is more tentative than what would be done for a *no* shake (Mind Corrosive 2014).

The situation is not different in India too. The usual head wag in India looks much like the shaking of the head and can be misinterpreted by a Westerner as saying no when, in actual fact, the person is acknowledging what is being said. This sign is also used by Indians to signal that what you are saying has been heard. So we need to take cognisance of these exceptions while interpreting a person.

Practical Illustrations

Case Study I: As established at different points in time, the head is a powerhouse of non-verbal communication, and the way it is moved communicates the deepest intent of a person. In an office setting, if a person nods their head and says 'I did not do it' when accused of something, it means they are telling lies. This is more so if they are rubbing their nose or pulling their collar. They are restless about that lie and have to fiddle with their own body. This is usually the case when you ask a colleague a question and they are caught unawares. So they lie with their mouth and say the truth with their head. As research has shown, what the body says is more truthful than what the mouth utters. However, if the person disagrees with you, they will say no and nod gently. This is a subtle disagreement meant not to hurt you emotionally.

Case Study II: This body language signal is most prevalent among little children. In a home setting, if a parent asks their child thus 'Did you break the cup?' and the child says no—as most of them will do—but nods, this is a contradictory behaviour, and it has sold out the child. At that moment, the child would be confused on what to do. The parent will surely know that the child did it, and the child would be taken as a liar. However, do not neglect the exceptions I earlier mentioned under the 'Scientific Explanation' section.

Case Study III: Another instance of this is witnessed during a criminal investigation (as an expert in the field, I have seen countless of this in my career). Hardened criminals are always prepared to answer every question with scripted responses. However, if they are caught unawares, they may nod to an accusative question and deny it with their mouth after maintaining composure. For instance, if you ask an accused 'Were you there when the fire incident broke out?' and they nod slowly to it and then say no, it is an indication that they are not sincere with their response. Maybe the fire incident led to the death of a person, so they understand that saying yes will make the investigator ask them what led to the fire outbreak and why they could not have curtailed it. Some of these possible questions that will indict them at the latter stage of the investigation would be avoided like a plague.

2.4.   Patting the Back of the Head

Generic Interpretations of the Concept

At one time or another, we have all found ourselves in this behaviour. It is generally among the circles of experts in the body language field that when the hand touches the head, it is meant to pacify and relieve stress. It is also the same thing when we use one of our hands to pat ourselves at the back of the head. It is normally done when we are mentally conflicted about a given issue. It is an indication that we are trying hard to think through, and in the midst of the intellectual storm, we are trying to pacify ourselves. In some advanced cases, a person may even use the hand to stroke down their head.

This is a soothing gesture due to the tactile sensation that accompanies it. When done consistently, it generates some warmth, which also makes the body return to its normal state. Apart from this gesture being a pacifying move, it is also very pronounced; everybody can easily notice that something is wrong with you. Once the hands are moved, it means the person is not trying to hide their feelings. However, instead of looking for succour elsewhere, they decide to take solace in themselves.

Scientific Explanations

In the Western part of the world, patting or stroking children or a person on the head is a sign of affection (Khan-Panni 2019). It means the person is deeply connected to you. If it is done by the person to themselves, it means they are affectionate to themselves. It is a means of showing self-love and arousing the emotion in oneself. If it is done to another person, it is a sign of our affection to them. Parents usually do this to their children to build their bond. It makes them grow closer and intimate. However, touching of another person's head should be avoided in the East. Easterners highly revere the head, and it is a shared sentiment that it is the abode of the soul. So touching the head is tantamount to playing with the soul of the person (Khan-Panni 2019).

It is crucial to emphasise the difference between patting the head and using your hand to hold the back of your head. While the former is a pacifying act, the latter is considered as a negative body language. When you rest your hands behind your head, it is said to mean superiority or big-headedness. Hence, it is a poor body language sign in a formal setting or in a not-too-friendly space, which will give others a bad impression about you. You may try doing this while in the midst of your close friends as they understand you better and will not try to misinterpret you (Chernoff 2019). Another related negative body attitude to this is trying to scratch the backside of the head or neck. It is a means of expressing doubt and uncertainty. In the African clime, it means forgetfulness and trying hard to remember something important. In most parts of the world, it does not connote something good. People tend not to believe whatever you say while you are scratching the back of your neck. In an interview setting, the panel will assume that you are not knowledgeable enough on the subject matter if you scratch the back of your neck. In short, you should try to avoid this sign like a plague while in public (Chernoff 2019).

Touching is a form of expression of power and intimacy. When it comes to patting, this is more pronounced. However, it has to be friendly and warm in order to communicate the intended message.

Practical Illustrations

Case Study I: This form of body language is witnessed in almost every sphere of life. For instance, it is normal that a person going to an interview will be a little bit nervous, no matter how intelligent they are. Nobody can vividly picture every question that can be asked in an interview. So before being called in by the panel, an applicant can pat themselves at the back. This is to pacify themselves and give a self-assurance that all will be well. It is to calm the person down, take out the stress of preparation, inject energy into them, show them love that no loved one is around to do, and ultimately, give them hope of a fruitful outcome. So this is acceptable at this point because nobody is watching them or making any decision based on their behaviour.

Case Study II: When a child pats themselves at the back of the head at school or while going through their assignment at home, they are trying to encourage themselves. Imagine working on a mathematics lesson, and things seem to be not working out well as earlier envisioned. So instead of chickening out, the self-pat is to reinvigorate and charge themselves. However, if a teacher or parent pats a child at the back, it is a means of developing intimacy with them. The teacher/parent is trying to bridge the gap and develop closeness. With this, the child will be naturally moved by the elderly person. They will be able to open up to them and discuss their challenges.

Case Study III: This signal is also noticed during an investigation session. While new criminals will scratch the back of their head and give themselves out easily, hardened ones will pat themselves at the back of the head so as to calm down. They are trying not to be nervous so as to be able to answer every question adequately. This means they are adopting a subtle means to take themselves out of pressure and face every question of the investigator. At this point, an experienced investigator knows that he or she has to intensify the questioning process and make it more intellectually demanding and dramatic just in a bid to unsettle the accused. I have used this method in different instances, and it produced the needed results. It is a means of taking charge of everything in the interview room; you are professionally closing their breath and making them face the reality of their offence.

Case Study IV: I have seen criminals pat the back of their head for various reasons during investigations. As someone who is vast in the interpretation of non-verbal cues, I take note of every movement and tailor my questions along that line. There was one who patted the back of his head after accidentally saying the truth. He tried changing the subject matter as a smart move to deceive me, but I resisted it. I had to ask further questions about what he said earlier, and he had no choice but to answer, even though he was reluctant. However, there were some other cases where the head pat was sincere—they couldn't recall a name or an event vividly, so they patted the back of their head as a metaphoric way of recalling such events.

2.5.   Scratching the Head

Generic Interpretation of the Concept

This is an embodiment of meanings; it has multiple interpretations and mostly universal ones. Except in the literal case of when people have dandruff or any other form of head infection, it is not normal to see a person scratch their head. Invariably, having established that a person scratching their head does not have any form of infection, then you are at liberty to attribute metaphorical meaning to their actions. However, I need to emphasise that meanings should be read in relation to the context of the event. Head scratching is a common attribute of those who are in doubt and are frustrated about an event. Maybe they have been trying hard to get something done, but all their efforts have been abortive. Frustration is bound to set in, and the best way they make this known is by scratching their head.

Also, people suffering to remember an event or a piece of information and are perplexed also scratch their head; they feel like perforating their head and dipping their hands into their brain so as to fetch out that piece of information. It is a means of saying that they are troubled for not being able to remember that particular thing. If the head scratching is very rapid, it is a signal of high level of stress and concern; it literally makes the person mad, so they are unable to scratch in a civil manner.

Finally, on this, the head scratching body language cue is a means of saying that one is confused on the next line of action. They are lost in between many options, and there seems to be no one to assure them of which action would be fruitful.

Scientific Explanations

According to Bob Whipple, it is very difficult to miss the meaning of the head scratching body language signal. We refer to it in our daily interactions, and it is becoming more of a conscious action. 'The link for scratching the head might originate in the inability of the brain to comprehend exactly what is happening at the moment. We may scratch our heads as a way to see more clearly the issue, much the same as we rake leaves so we can see the grass better' (Whipple 2019). In other words, this scholar says that head scratching is related to confusion.

Apart from that, it may be used to refer to uncertainty or doubt and even lying in some other instances. If someone starts to scratch his head while you are talking to him, check to see if the indication is that the person does not believe what you are saying. You would usually see another facial indication of doubt along with the head scratching (Whipple 2019).

Hanan Parvez also supports the view of Whipple that scratching the head is an emotional signifier of confusion. All over the world, the best place to notice this form of body language is in the examination hall. A student trying to solve a hard question will unconsciously scratch their head. When a teacher is trying to expatiate on a concept and some of the students are scratching their head, it is an indirect message that they did not understand. So a professional teacher will have to employ another means to explain the topic. It is not at all times that they make use of fingers; pencils, rulers, sharp objects, and pen, among others may be used (Parvez 2019).

If a person slaps or scratches their forehead, it is to indicate forgetfulness. It means the person is trying hard to remember something. Hence, this gesture is only witnessed when a person is going through some form of mental imbalance; they are really engaging their intellectual faculty.

Practical Illustrations

Case Study I: Permit me to state that there are infinite instances in the demonstrations of this signal—that is, it is seen in every aspect of life. In the home setting, if you ask your child a question and they scratch their head, it means they are confused. Maybe the question is not clear enough, and there is a misinterpretation of the whole scene. However, if the child hits their forehead, it means they have forgotten such a particular thing. Maybe they were sent by their teacher, but it escaped their mind to deliver the message to you. If the teacher eventually calls to tell you, then they will hit their forehead to indicate that they actually forgot. Another related illustration is witnessed in the exam hall. If a student hits their forehead, it means that they truly read on the topic being tested on but that they have forgotten what they read. If, however, they are scratching their head, it means they are really confused about the whole concept.

Case Study II: The situation is the same in an investigation context. Some criminals are smart and will try to play on the intelligence of an official. It takes expertise to successfully engage such kind of people. A criminal suspect who scratches his head continuously is subtly communicating their restlessness; they are not emotionally stable. It is an indication that everything is not well with the person. This feeling will intensify if you have incriminating evidence against the person because the criminal would be shocked that you have such evidence against them, and there is no way they would not be destabilised. They become hopeless on how best to defend themselves.

Case Study III: In an office setting, if you are addressing a colleague and the person is scratching their head, it is an indication of their disbelief in you; they think you are lying. You would usually see another facial indication of doubt along with the head scratching. For example, if the person furrows his brow while scratching his head, it may be a signal that you are damaging the trust this person had built up for you. Whatever the source of the emotion, the person making the gesture is usually not aware he is doing it unless someone points it out. We see the behaviour in others very quickly, but we are normally not conscious of when we do it ourselves (Whipple 2019). So we all must pay conscious attention to this sign as we go in our daily affairs. This is how to build rapport with people and gain their trust without fear.

2.6. Stroking the Head

Generic Interpretations of the Concept

In its literal interpretation, people stroke their head with their palms just to put their hair in place and make it look more fashionable. However, there are instances where this action carries more embedded meanings. The action serves as a soothing balm for people when they are stressed; they intend to create some warmth in the head, which will in turn circulate all over their body. This action is also carried out when people are confused about an issue. They have an array of options that look confusing, and they are careful about the choice they make in order not to make a costly mistake.

Another common occurrence of this body language signal is when a person is thinking hard on how to answer a given question. Head stroking is also seen when a woman is trying to pacify their child in some cultures that allow touch. Japanese culture does not really support this idea. Children usually become calm when pacified in this way. Another metaphoric explanation of this sign is conflict or uncertainty, most especially if it is done on the back of the head. It is a signal made by people in certain contexts to mean that they do not believe what you are saying. This feeling of disbelief is subtly expressed in order not to depress you.

Scientific Explanations

Head stroking is regarded as stroking of the chin or beard among many scholars in the field. When a person strokes their chin, it is an indication of how deep their thought is; they are buried in thought and lost to their physical world. This is an unintentional motion used when a person puts their entire intellectual faculty into action so as to birth a worthy thought. It means they are yet to reach a decision concerning a given issue (Your Dictionary 2019). In its own submission, Changing Minds (2019) opines that stroking the head usually signifies anxiety. So people give preferences to places they touch during their difficult times. 'This is a classic pattern that poker players look for in other players as signs of having good or bad hands' (Changing Minds 2019).

Further, people stroke their head while they are passing judgement on others. It means they are trying to evaluate their subject before passing on their judgement. This same process is also true for those striving to make a decision concerning a given issue (Changing Minds 20190). Describing the process in one sentence, Philips Chris notes that this body language sign is used for 'evaluation and thought process'. When a person is trying hard to develop a feasible solution, when they rub the chin or any other part of the head, it will activate the thinking and intellectual mindset to birth novel ideas. This may be seen in negotiations where people may be stroking their head to mean that they are yet to reach a final decision on the item. This means the buyer can still stick with the price proposed or bring it further down. Sellers should learn how to read this body language so as to take advantage of it at all times.

In the world at large, stroking the head or rubbing the chin can be used by people to wade off pressure from themselves. It is generally believed that those who rub their chin while asked a question are contemplating over the issue. Hence, the questioner will give the person more time to think through and present their argument. It is tantamount to the verbal postulation, 'I am thinking or assessing and I need to charge up my source of wisdom through head stroke' (Chris 2014).

Practical Illustrations

Case Study I: This body language signal is usually seen in our individual homes—in both parents and children. When you are stressed up after a hectic day, you tend to stroke your head. If you pay attention to your children, you will discover that they stroke their head after a busy day at school. This is an indication that they worked out themselves earlier in the day. Another instance at the home front is when a child is crying and the mother wants to calm them. Stroking the head of the child seems to possess some appeasing effect as it works like magic.

Case Study II: In a formal setting, if a colleague strokes their head, it is an indication of confusion. Most probably, they have many options to work with, and they have never been at that professional junction before. This will surely be intellectually demanding. An example is a person given two confusing locations for feasibility studies. At the end of the assignment, they have to conclude on one and make their recommendations. If the options are close to call, you may begin to see the portrayal of this body language signal in them. In the school setting, if you ask a student a question and they stroke their head, it means they are finding the poser hard to tackle. They will have to brood over it before they can utter any word.

Case Study III: For times without number, I have seen this body language clue while engaging criminal suspects. Those who are new in the business easily give themselves out due to the stern faces of the investigators. However, the hardened ones are always ready to challenge the authority of investigators. Their sessions are normally lengthy and engaging. If you pose a hard question about their involvement in an atrocity, if they are caught unawares, they will stroke their head first. This is an indication that they are trying to think through before saying something that will be later used against them, and they are usually defensive in their responses. This normally happens on the other side of the table too—when an investigator is looking at a suspect keenly so as to pass their judgement. This means the investigator is assessing their subject so as to pass an informed judgement over them. So this signal is seen in almost every realm of life. A terrorist stroking their head in public is trying to assess how good the location is for a potential attack.

2.7. Scratching the Head and Rubbing the Tummy (Simultaneous Actions)

Generic Interpretations of the Concept

This is what can be subtly called double action—both hands are engaged in different activities at the same time. This is an obvious action that can be seen by anyone within range. Apart from humans, this body signal is also prevalent among other primates. Physically, when a person engages in this action, it means all is not well; they have some troubling moments which may be caused by sickness or some unpalatable news. If it is none of the two cases, then we may begin to attribute meanings to it after setting our baseline. One of the probable interpretations of this action is wonder or doubt. The person does not believe in what they are told or something they are shown. If they are taken aback by an action, they will do the same thing.

In another dimension, it signals insecurity. A person who feels insecure will try their possible best to guard some parts of their body they consider as being volatile. In other instances, it may be an expression of confusion and, at the same time, self-appease. Scratching the head means they are confused, and they go ahead to assure and calm themselves down through the rubbing of the belly.

Scientific Explanations

Joe Navarro, the author of *What Every Body Is Saying* opines that the human brain requires some certain amount of hand-to-body touch whenever we come under stress. It is an act of pacifying. According to him, 'These *pacifiers* serve to soothe the individual when there is negative limbic arousal. Pacifiers are with us all day long, and they increase or are magnified when we are very stressed' (Navarro 2009). However, it is not only limited to threatening circumstances; if the brain perceives that some certain conditions are threatening, it would activate some actions involving the head and abdomen that are pacifying and protective.

Changing Minds (2019) is very straightforward about this by asserting that 'touching oneself is often a sign of uncertainty or discomfort. It is as if the person were reassuring themselves, using their own hands in place of the hands of a non-present parent or friend.' The main propeller of uncertainty is some form of insecurity or threatening situation in one's immediate environment. A person who touches their tummy may be suffering from an upset stomach and, as such, uncertain if they should be at the restroom or not.

Stress makes human muscles become tensed, and this may cause itching in the person. Hence, they may need to rub the affected body portions. Little did people know that lying is a very stressful event which is certainly stress-inducing.

Inasmuch as I would not like to generalise this point, it is worthy to note that a person that scratches their head and rubs their tummy simultaneously may be suffering from lie-induced stress. Again, do remember to set your baseline before passing judgement in any given circumstance (Changing Minds 2019).

Research shows that the tummy is an embodiment of many muscles that get activated when we are stressed. If a person is worrying excessively over an issue, they will be seen rubbing their belly. It is also a vulnerable part of the body. When a person considers himself insecure in a given circumstance, they will hold their belly because they understand that they are open to attack.

For different reasons, we hardly allow people to touch those two areas— belly and head. For the belly, it is due to insecurity and vulnerability, and for the head, this is culture-bound. For example, in parts of South East Asia, the head (particularly of others) is considered to contain the spirit and hence must not be touched (Changing Minds 2019).

Practical Illustrations

Case Study I: If a child is holding their belly and scratching their head at the same time, it calls for concern, even in adults. It may be physical discomfort, which must be catered for immediately. This may signal digestion problem due to overeating or other related issues. In a metaphorical sense, imagine telling your spouse a story of a fascinating event that occurred on your way back home from work but does not look plausible, your partner may express their disbelief in the narrative by scratching their head and rubbing their tummy at the same time. This is more so if you have a long-standing history of deception.

Case Study II: Apart from the home setting, this body language signal is also witnessed in an investigation setting. A criminal will scratch their head and subtly rub their belly when they feel insecure due to questions asked. They are feeling insecure because of their past actions. They have probably killed people in the past, and anything they consider antagonistic makes them feel insecure. It is tantamount to running away from one's shadow. In an ideal setting, no investigator will ever attack their subject. I have worked in the industry for more than thirty years, and this has never happened for once. In fact, we are always afraid of the hardened criminals pouncing on us when the session is getting tensed.

Case Study III: Career persons who look well will also see this body language behaviour in their offices. A colleague scratching their head and rubbing their belly simultaneously is surely confused about a given issue. The person may be given a difficult assignment which they have racked their brain on, all to no avail. So the head scratch is to register their frustration over the issue, and on the other hand, rubbing the belly is self-pacification. They consider this action as a necessary ingredient in being able to survive the tense environment. It is an indirect way of saying they need your help. At this point, if you approach them, they will easily open up on their travails.

Case Study IV: And finally, those who are telling lies portray this body language gesture too. Imagine your child who is just 'learning' to lie. It would be stressful for them at first because they are not used to it. Then gradually, they will begin to adjust. For the first few lies, this feeling of discomfort will be written over them. This means the person is not finding it comfortable undertaking such an assignment. The person is scratching the head and rubbing the tummy simultaneously as a way of displaying their internal feeling of discomfort.

2.8. Interlacing the Fingers to Support the Back of the Head

Generic Interpretations of the Concept

This is technically referred to as hooding in many quarters because it gives the person a cobra-like kind of posture; they become bigger than their real self. There are different meanings that can be attributed to this behaviour, and all of them happen to be positive interpretations. When a person appears bigger than they are, they command respect. People relate with them honourably. It is a territorial display that shows that the person is in charge. When you 'hood', it means you are in a relaxed position and nothing bothers you—at least there is a momentary display of superiority over every circumstance. People do not display this sign when they are not comfortable since it is a sign of comfort. When the fingers are interlaced at the back of the head, it is pacifying and soothing.

When the elbows are out, it is a projection of confidence. If a person is fearful, they will maintain a closed body posture; they will keep to themselves. Such people will shrink in their chair and feel like disappearing to their place of comfort. However, I need to state that you do not need to display this body language signal when you are in the presence of a superior. That will amount to challenging their position or being full of yourself.

Scientific Explanations

There are twenty-seven bones in the hands. The hand is a very expressive part of the body. With the hands, we can express ourselves and handle issues in our environment. Phillips Chris (2014) also called this form of body language gesture as interlocking fingers or entwined fingers. Before moving it to the back of the head, when the fingers are interlaced, they first produce some pacifying effects. Invariably, a person may have been fearful but employed the body cue to pacify themselves before moving it to the back of their head to demonstrate confidence.

Before moving further, there is a need to emphasise that mere interlaced fingers put on the table or any other body part is different from that which is used as a support of the head. In the case of the former, it represents frustrations, negative thoughts, self-restraint, and hostility, while the latter is used to portray calmness, confidence, authority, and respect (Chris 2014).

On his own part, Joe Navarro (2010) emphasises the importance of the hands in every discourse. According to him, if a person should hide their hands while talking, you will not gain anything from them because the hands are the most expressive part of the body. When people place their hands at the back of their head, it means they are comfortable, and that is why the blood flow is consistent. It is an indication of the fact that the person is not under stress. If the elbows are raised higher, it means the person is more confident and stronger. Space only disappears when we feel insecure (Navarro 2010).

Changing Minds (2019) gives another interpretation outside of the conventional ones. According to the platform, making use of the interlaced fingers to support the head hammers on the fragile nature of the head; it means it is delicate and we are protecting it. This is more pronounced when we close up the gap between the elbows. In some rare circumstances, it may be used in hiding something. There is a subconscious coverage of the ears when one supports one's head with interlaced fingers, so it may indicate a means of blocking one's ears from the opinion of others—that is, we do not want to hear what they have to say. It may also mean trying to protect that part of the body from shocking harm (Changing Minds 2019). The explanations are numerous, and you only need to pay attention to the context and then make your interpretations.

Practical Illustrations

Case Study I: This form of body language cue is mostly witnessed in the home or unofficial setting. In societies where male dominance is pronounced, such as in many parts of Asia, if a man uses their interlaced fingers to support the back of their head, it is a demonstration of their authority. They are implicitly trying to say, 'I am the head of this house.' It means they are bigger than every other person in the house, wife and children included, and they wish to exercise their dominance in that realm. In most cases, they will also stretch out their legs and expose their genitals. All these are open body language portraying confidence and lack of fear.

Case Study II: In the office, this form of body language can be seen mostly in superiors who want to make their status pronounced; they want to show every other person around that they are in charge of the affairs of the office. In the weird form, the person can stretch their legs on the table or another chair. This amounts to saying, 'I am in charge of every affair in this office. Do not contend my place with me.' If a junior worker should display this form of body language, it means they are challenging the authority of their superior, and this may not end well. From time immemorial, the formal setting has always been a place of competition where everyone struggles to establish their relevance and dominance. So one needs to be careful of the body language signs one displays.

Case Study III: The criminal world is not totally free of this sign too. Investigators may use their interlaced fingers to support the back of their head to tell the criminal suspect, 'Look, I'm in charge of everything and, as such, will dictate the tune of things in this room.' It is to create some form of fear in the criminal and make them drop their ego. However, I have seen some really weird instances whereby it is the criminal themselves that portray this sign. It is a means of intentionally challenging the authority of the investigators. In other words, they want to tell us that they are not afraid of us. They are saying, 'I have nothing to fear about you guys because I will appear triumphantly at the end of the exercise.' This is surely an abuse on the process of the investigation.

2.9. Suddenly Reaching for the Head

Generic Interpretations of the Concept

Without any reason, there is someone who will reach for their head in a stupefied form. It is an action that is employed to denote shock for an unexpected event. This is when a person suddenly places their two hands on their head very close to the ears, but not allowing them to touch the ears. While in this position, the elbows move towards frontal state. They can maintain this position for several seconds as they mentally try to make sense out of the shocking event that occurred. They are stupefied by the occurrence of the event, and they still do not want to believe that it has occurred.

The shock has made them place their hands on their head as a protective means. The head seems to be the most fragile part of the body, and that is why people try to protect it first during a dangerous situation. Pushing the elbows to the front is a means of guarding against a sudden attack from nowhere. Although this is a form of primitive action, but it is an indication of how shocking the event is. Inasmuch as they would not like to believe it, the reality stares them in the face. A person who sees their child falling into the drainage in broad daylight will display this action.

The event that prompts this action is not limited to outsiders alone; it can be as a result of one's own misdoing. When we take a step that backfires, we tend to display this action. I will expatiate on this under the 'Practical Illustrations' section.

Scientific Explanations

If we pretend not to have done it, one thing that is undeniable is that we cannot shy away from seeing this body language cue in horror scenes; it is the pose most people maintain when something hurtful befalls them. In the event of a disaster, if people do not put their hands on their mouth, they will hold their head with their two hands in a bewildered form. Gillian Mohney (2013) postulates that human reaction to disaster is universal—that is, we all maintain the same body language posture while reacting to something horrific. In fact, experts have also discovered that apart from disaster, 'There are universal gestures for victory, defeat, and stress that appear to transcend country and region' (Mohney 2013). This is because they all fall within the universal emotional response category. The emotion is an innate feeling connecting all humans from the world—that is, what makes us different from other creatures is how we react to events that happen in our community.

'Chris Ulrich, a senior instructor at the Body Language Institute in Washington D.C., said covering your mouth or putting your hands on your head is a response that helps make people feel safer and smaller from a perceived threat. Ulrich said by covering part of their face, they can feel hidden from the shocking event' (Mohney 2013). Another purpose alluded to this form of body cue is to serve as pacifying gesture. The hands are known for pacifying the body in times of need. So placing them on the head is a means of recovering from the shock. It is a soothing gesture that helps us at that very moment. The verbal translation of this is 'I will get through this troubling moment'. Touching the head is reassuring and typical of every human.

Changing Minds (2019) also submits that touching the head is a signal of anxiety; it means we are concerned about something. Poker players are always on the lookout of this sign in others to know if things are good or not. Hanan Parvez states that when hands are placed on the head, it is an indication of confusion.

Practical Illustrations

Case Study I: This sign is seen everywhere where disaster occurs. In the front pages of newspapers, we often come across witnesses of a disaster scene holding their heads. This is to show their regret over the incident. For instance, people who just arrived at a fatal accident scene will hold their head to register their shock and displeasure. Imagine leaving a location with someone, and they later end up having an accident that claimed their life. You would be surprised that such an event happened just a few moments after departing from each other. Unconsciously, you would cover your mouth with your hands or place them on your head in a stupefied form. This is an expression of shock that will easily communicate your message to anyone who sees you; they know something negative has happened to you.

Case Study II: Even at home, when someone is shocked, they will open their mouth and then place their hands on their head. If a child comes into the living room to meet their mother making love with their concubine, this action will take them aback and, as such, display this body language cue. A woman who leaves their food on the stove and it gets burnt will also be found in this category. In short, whenever there is a shocking event, we should always expect the display of this gesture. If you suddenly delete an important item on your computer system, this will be your first point of action. The frustration increases if you are unable to retrieve the file. If you should miss an all-important meeting which you had thought would not escape your mind, this is the sign you would display; such would be unbelievable to you while you glance at your watch over and over again.

Case Study III: In an investigation session, criminal suspects usually display this sign too. Some of them believe that nothing could reveal some of their deepest secrets. So if an investigator throws some of the facts at them, they will unconsciously open their mouth and put their hands on their head for such accusations. The secret they had thought was out of public view is now being painted to them. This scene can be very interesting for everyone in the room because we surely know that the job is half-done, and there is no way they (the criminal suspect) can intellectually defend such an action at that point. The shock will be evident on their face when they suddenly grab their head as if they want to confirm if their head is still there or not.

Case Study IV: Also, when criminals are busted and they can't do anything any more but confess, they may display this gesture. I have a handful of such cases where suspected criminals had to confess to me after some questioning sessions. They were ashamed of themselves, while some of them pretended to be. During the confessions, they spoke softly and suddenly placed their hand on their face, as if trying to hide from me. They also looked down simultaneously that I had no option than just to listen to their confession—it was almost impossible to pick any message from their face. I had to calm them so as to take their hands off their head so I can see their facial expressions.

2.10. Interlacing the Fingers on Top of the Head

Generic Interpretations of the Concept

This body language attitude stands out in all realms due to its physical portrayal. Let me state that it also connotes negativity. The interlaced fingers are placed on top of the head, and the elbows are well spread out. The original intent of this behaviour is to cover the head, but this has been betrayed by the spreading out of the elbows that makes other parts of the head exposed. It is a sign of being overwhelmed by an activity that is not too good. When people are lost in the midst of an unpalatable event, they display this body cue. It is also an indication that a person is striving with the reality of a devastating loss. Losing one's entire property to flooding will make one portray this body gesture.

When things do not turn out as planned, this is the body gesture which can be found on us. Inasmuch as I am careful about using the word *regret*, it most likely seems like one. It makes one think outside of the box in an undersigned manner. In a way, it is an expression of our frustration at a given event or circumstance. Nobody is happy when their plans do not turn out well, and the first reaction can always be weird because it is shocking and it caught us unawares. This unhappiness is seen by everyone who is within range.

Scientific Explanations

Talking of body language cues, the hands and the face are the two major parts of the body that play the most prominent roles; they are the most expressive part of the body. If they are now combined to pass a message, such a message becomes visible to the blind and audible to the deaf. Rehm et al. (2007) posit that being able to identify body language cues is dependent on our ability to interpret the contextual inclinations of the cues. Marc Chernoff (2019) speaks about some of the body language signs to avoid, and interlocked fingers placed on the head makes the list. It is an open expression of regret and disaster, which everyone can easily notice. In such case, they will begin to ask you what's wrong. Even the person who should not know anything about you will obviously do. In some communities that still practise communal living, you will become an object of pity as everyone struggles to sympathise with you. I am not trying to condemn this body gesture but to explain some of the possible outcomes of the attitude.

If the interlocked fingers are used to scratch the head through the thumbs, it is an indication of uncertainty and doubt (Chernoff 2019). This means the person has a collision of thoughts going on in their mind at the same time. After showing signs of their loss; they scratched to non-verbally communicate their ability to recover what they have lost. A person who loses their entire property to a hurricane may be uncertain of what they will do in order to retrieve such items.

'When someone has interlaced their fingers, the tightness with which they press their fingers together is related to how anxious they are feeling' (Unverbal 2013). Joe Navarro in his *What Every Body Is Saying* describes this act as a 'pacifying behaviour'. If they are feeling more insecure, they will further press their interlaced fingers on their head. This is an expression of extreme fear. Experts are of the opinion that although this body language gesture is an unconscious one, a person can decide to suppress it, especially in public, where you do not want to be seen as being weak.

Practical Illustrations

Case Study I: With the explanation I have given so far, by now, your mind should have been filled with pictorial images of all circumstances where this body language cue is normally displayed. Even if people try hard to suppress it in some situations, it is usually glaring in a devastating situation. For instance, a person whose two children were electrocuted before arriving home will display this sign. It is a sign of extreme pain and regret. Many ill thoughts will gush through their mind upon seeing their beloved children in that state. If they scratch their head, it means they cannot think through it. It signals someone who is trying to recover from a deep shock.

Case Study II: In an office setting, if a colleague is injured through your action or inaction, this becomes troubling. For instance, you carelessly dropped a file at the wrong place, and a colleague mistakenly pours water on the confidential file. This is a huge loss to the company, and you know that if an investigation is carried out, you will surely be indicted, which will have bad consequences at the end of the day. So when you display this sign, it is an expression of your regret and struggles. You will cast your mind back and how you could have avoided the situation if you were diligent enough. If this is done unconsciously, the person will understand that you did not just stress them for nothing.

Case Study III: When dealing with criminals and one of them displays this sign, it is a means of saying that their plans did not go as planned. It is a feeling of depression and frustration. A criminal who has planned to dodge police—perform the act and leave just before the arrival of law enforcement officers—will be heavily disappointed if by the time they are concluding their operation, law enforcement officials just show up. This means their plans did not pull through, and more painfully, they will most probably face the wrath of the law. So interlocking their fingers and placing their palms on top of their head is a means of surrendering to the unfortunate situation; they are regretting their action and are pained that they are trapped in the operation. For the officials, it is a thrilling experience because the criminals were caught red-handed.

Case Study IV: In the event of flooding, which you cannot obviously control, you will stand at a position for some few moments and watch in regret as the flood washes off your valued property. Since you are helpless in that circumstance, you will interlock your fingers and place them on your head, well-pressed together to pacify yourself and show that you are really threatened by the circumstance. When someone presses their interlocked fingers on their head in a pitiable condition, this means there is a negative event that changed their thought pattern.

2.11. Ventilating through Hat Lifting

Generic Interpretations of the Concept

Some people don't like wearing hats but others passionately like it. In some cultures, their dressing is not complete until they wear a hat to match it. Hence, the manner in which it is worn passes vital messages to people who can decode it. In this section, I will explore the act of removing the hat to ventilate oneself. If I may ask, what can prompt a person to subtly undress in public for the purpose of ventilating themselves? Obviously, there are many. I will expatiate some of them in this lesson, and you can always add more that come to mind; just be sure they are all correct.

A fundamental reason that can cause a person to lift their hat is when they feel hot; it may be sunny, and they need to take in some fresh air directly into their head. Apart from this physical and literal instance, if a person suddenly takes off their hat, there are metaphoric reasons alluded to it. During an intense argument, people take off their hat so as to be able to give them the opportunity to face the opposing side without any form of restraint. The hat may be covering a part of their face, and they actually want to have a full view of the other party. Further, they may lift their hat after a heated moment. After arguing intensely, they can take off their hat in order to feel the fresh breeze and rest well before engaging in some other activities.

A person receiving an undesirable news will take off their hat. They are grasping for breath and have become restless. So they will do anything that will give them the desired rest at that moment. In terms of safety, when a person becomes extremely angry—during a road-rage incident or a traffic accident—disrobing is the first point of action for a person who is ready to pounce on you. It is to show their readiness to fight.

Scientific Explanations

Some experts have opined that the use of ventilators indicates deception in both men and women. According to this school of thought, lifting a hat up or tilting it sideways means the person is telling lies. In the Western world, ventilators are primarily used when they are facing some issues that have to be dealt with immediately. Such issues are probably stress-inducing, and the ventilator (hat) will serve as a cooling tool for them. This does not symbolise the sign of lying at all times. It only means that they are stressed and need to cool down. For instance, if the person is receiving bad news, they will surely be stressed. Before regarding it as a sign of deception, you need to critically analyse the context before reaching a conclusion. There are arrays of reasons that can bring about ventilating—hot weather, malfunctioning air conditioner, or unfavourable, new climate, among others (Skills Converged 2019).

Body language expert Joe Navarro was point-blank in pointing out that ventilating is a sign of criminality. In a 2012 article, he said thus: 'About thirty-five years ago when I first got into law enforcement, I began to observe that suspects often ventilated themselves during interviews while the innocent did not.' According to him, he was able to maximise the opportunity created by this technique in asking questions that make suspects uncomfortable. Ventilating behaviours appear in real time without any form of delay.

Navarro lists fear, a sense of weakness, vulnerability, apprehension, and anxiety as some of the causes of ventilating behaviours. And more so, they all lead to psychological discomfort. Look at the way the person behaves before you attach a meaning to their behaviour. One who does not take off their hat completely is probably lying or hiding something (Navarro 2012).

Practical Illustrations

Case Study I: From the foregoing, I have pointed out that ventilating behaviours may be induced by stress or deceptive acts. In the case of stress, let's consider a young man who is a little bit behind schedule in getting to the airport. He will be stressed because he is afraid of missing his flight. If the person wears a hat, they will lift it up, use their hands to run through their hair, and demand endlessly for a cool breeze. In this circumstance, the person is not telling lies; the signs will disappear once the person catches up and is on board. In the same instance, a person who is not used to heat may display this behaviour when they come home from work and discover that their air conditioner is faulty. Perhaps, they returned home late that fateful day, and their wife might probably take the behaviour as a telltale sign of deception, but in the real sense, it is not. What is really behind it is the faulty item.

Case Study II: In your office, if a colleague receives a sack letter, you may see this behaviour on them. This is most probably if they have a pending offence that is worth being fired. Once the letter is given to them, they will lift up their hat. At that moment, there is an inexplicable stress level in them. Many thoughts are running in their mind. There is nobody who is willing to employ someone who was sacked due to an obvious reason because such action can still be repeated.

Case Study III: Just like Joe Navarro has revealed in his referenced piece, criminals do ventilate in the interview room, and this is always at the advantage of an experienced investigator. They do it in a subtle manner to pacify themselves and calm their nerves, but the kind of questions you ask is dependent on how hard you are able to nail them to the accusation without appearing bias. While asking the simple question 'Where were you last night?' once you have discovered this behaviour in the suspect, it can throw them off balance. They are already stressed and nervous, so the question is meant to completely uproot them from their comfort zone. With this, the coast is clear for you to make the session interesting and fruitful.

CHAPTER 3

The Hair

    The hair occupies the topmost part of the human body; it sits comfortably on the head. The hair embodies numerous messages in the non-verbal realm. Before switching to the non-verbal realm, let me quickly run through the physical form of the hair as it relates to all humans. We all desire healthy hair, and even this desire is registered in our subconscious mind. All over the world, when a person's hair is unkempt, dirty, smelly, uncared for, pulled out, or infection-ridden, it may be a signal of mental illness or poor health. People will avoid such a person like a plague. If they are in the corporate world, that alone can serve as the beginning to their downfall. I have travelled around the world and have not come across any culture that encourages people not to cater for their hair. It is what people firstly see when they set their eyes on you and, as such, must be made charming. There is no wonder why some spend a fortune on it. Inasmuch as I am not trying to encourage excessive hairdo, you must always appear simple, attractive, and classy. This fact is unarguable if you desire success without boundaries.

Hair is a symbol of attraction, enticement, conformity, and shock. I have explained some of these in the preceding paragraph. Imagine coming across an old classmate after some few decades and your hair is unkempt; they would think things have not been well with you since then or even think life has been more miserable to you. Chinese women are always a cynosure of all eyes because they do dedicate meaningful time to catering for their hair. The different styles with which they make their hair are always fascinating. They are every man's pride in any part of the world they meet themselves.

There are health benefits of keeping the hair in a proper manner. It provides thermal insulation from the sun and also guides against UV radiation. So growing straight hair is what everyone should be proud of. What many people are oblivious of is that hair communicates something about our professions. I know you will be thinking *how*, and I will try my best in establishing that fact in this segment before moving to the other aspects of our study, which is non-verbal communication. According to renowned anthropologist David Givens, hair serves as an 'unofficial résumé' that gives a hint of where a person ranks in the organisational ladder. This may sound weird, but if you take your time to observe this eternal truth, you will discover how it has been playing out in your firm in a subtle manner. At least, I have subconsciously given you an assignment that you will be occupied with for some time.

According to Cortney Cleveland (2012), 'Your appearance does not affect your ability to do a job, but it does impact your success. Keeping it cute can influence your salary as much as your work experience.' Cleveland has actually surmised all that I intend to say in the concept of hair as it concerns our individual career. According to a research outcome, those who are attractive earn an average of 4 per cent more than a person who does not look charming. That transcends to about $230,000 more than a not-too-good-looking worker over a lifetime. Is it not too huge a fund for you to miss just because of your look and not your ability? I know you will likely blame the system, but please do not apportion blame to a system that has been in place even before your own birth.

Hair surpasses the issue of fashion. It belongs to you but is seen by everyone. It is a demonstration of both public and private culture. Although the culture cannot be said to be a mainstream one, you need to pay attention to the kind of hair you carry to work. There was a time when people considered anything outside of straightened hair as the ideal and professional form of hairdo, but things have drastically changed. Most women are now companions of natural hairstyle, and that is a form of revolution among female professionals. In these days, what is considered as a professional hairstyle is one that is neat, out of the face, and clean. So the issue of texture has no place in deciding what hairstyle is professional or not. I understand that not every workplace has caught up with this reality, but they will soon do as things go on. However, never alter your look because you want to appear attractive. It is not acceptable anywhere in the world.

Whether in a conservative setting or not, being adventurous with your hair is what you should take as a personal business. According to Cleveland, 'Hair can serve as the ultimate declaration of individuality. It can set you apart, grab attention, and give a sense of your personal brand before you open your mouth.' In other words, your hair can serve as the only distinguishing factor. That is why I emphasised in the preceding paragraph that your hairstyle should not alter your look. At this point, may I ask, why will you refuse to harness the influence of the mane for your career gain?

There is no reason good enough for you to play with appearance; it personifies your identity and that of your workplace, and I am sure you want to be a good ambassador of your employer at all times. There is little wonder that most employers have dress codes for their workers so as to mirror what the organisation stands for at all times. Your weekend may not be a big deal, but you definitely need to conform from Monday to Friday. You just need to separate yourself from the crowd through your hairdo. In the same vein, people tend to follow both cultural norms and the trends in place. However, anyone who does not conform to this standard will stand out. This may either be positive or negative. In some instances, hair can be critical to romance and dating. I can go on and on, but let's stop here and explore the concept further as it relates to non-verbal communication.

3.1. Appearance of the Hair

Generic Interpretations of the Concept

I have dealt so much with this aspect of our discussion in the introductory aspect of our study and will, as such, run through it here with some scientific backups. The hair can be a source of respect or dishonour to you depending on how much attention you pay to it. It is the first point of contact when you meet with people, and that is what they make their first judgement on. If the hair is well-kempt, it is a symbol of attraction. Let me state at this point that what constitutes ugliness or beauty all begins and ends at the face. So once you can make the face look charming, people carry this perception about the whole of your body.

Hair appearance is an expression of one's culture. This is more pronounced among the conservatives who link everything to the roots. African women are known to be fond of natural hairdo. It is their pride, and since the continent is known to have favoured polygamous setting, they do different hairstyles so as to win the heart of their spouses. The situation is not all that different in China, where their women are so much concerned about the appearance of their hair, and by extension, South East Asia as a whole. A well-kempt hair, on a general note, shows that the person is a responsible member of the society. People are easily attracted to them and, as such, can win more business opportunities.

On the other hand, people with dirty, unkempt, and smelly hair are considered as vagabonds and criminals. In the case of a breakdown of law and order, they are the first suspects. Their hair appearance portrays them as nonconformists, and that is why every action that is against the society is attached to them. Many criminals—terrorists, kidnappers, and armed robbers, among others—usually look weird due to their hairdo. Many of them are usually from other countries or continents of the world, and that is why they look different and are easily suspected by an observant local.

Scientific Explanations

Changing Minds talks about the multipurpose use of the hair in non-verbal communication; this is to entrench its importance in every discourse context. No matter the length of their hair, it can be trimmed, cut, or shaped into various designs just to give the wearer a unique look. The kind of hairstyle we do each time contributes to our overall image and, thus, encodes some non-verbal cues. If the hairdo is conventional, it means the person is conservative and aligns with the societal standard. Those people are said to be upholding the basic social tenets. However, if the hair is well-styled, it is an indication to look charming and win the admiration of people around us. And finally, a hairstyle that does not conform to the pattern of the society depicts the person as being a social defiant. Such people normally face stiff opposition from the pillars of the society because they are perceived as threats to the culture of the local community (Changing Minds 2019).

We cannot properly discuss the body language of hair without giving a separate consideration to women and men. All over the world, men are known to be moderate in their social lifestyle. As such, the conventional ones normally keep their hair short and clean. If the hair is extremely short, it may connote aggression (Segev 2019). This is because the army usually keep their hair short so as to be able to combat enemies without any form of restraint. On the other hand, if a male's hair is long, it is a depiction of young dropouts. However, if the hair is unkempt, it indicates lack of care or low self-esteem (Changing Minds 2019).

On the other hand, women enjoy more liberty to wear different hairstyles for various reasons—to appear attractive to men, compete with other women, and look unique. Women's general mood can be uncovered through their hairstyle. Those who do long ones that partially cover their face may be suffering from low self-esteem. It may be a means of teasing a man by covering their beauty before unveiling it at the appointed time. On the other hand, those who keep it short may be displaying their superiority and to attract the attention of men through their natural look (Segev 2019).

Practical Illustrations

Case Study I: Concerning this aspect, you have an open cheque to make deductions about people's hairdo based on what we have perused so far. However, I will provide you with some examples that will further serve as a guide for you. While dating a lady, if the person likes doing long hair that partially covers their face when they are going for a date, it means they are trying to tease you about their beauty. They want you to try more and hallucinate over their beauty till they are probably taken to bed. You will see them smile in a charming manner and make sure that the aspect that is revealed is attractive enough that you will long to see other parts.

Case Study II: In your office, if a person uses their hairstyle to cover their face, it is an indication of low self-esteem. Probably, they are not good-looking compared with other colleagues or even sound intellectually. So they consider everyone as a threat to them. The hairstyle is to bolster their confidence so as to enable them to walk with their head held high. Another probable interpretation is that maybe they have offended someone and, as such, do not want the person to have a full view of their face. They are using their hairstyle to bury their head in shame. I needed to challenge a female colleague some years back, and I discovered that when she adjusted the hair on her face, she lost her voice and looked nervous before I smiled at her to ease her feelings.

Case Study III: If a woman leaves their hair short, they are probably the head of a department or an organisation and, as such, want to assert their authority. Women are fond of this; they always want to proclaim their high status. It may be a means of eyeing a man in the office. So they want the man to see how beautiful they are. I once asked one of my female friends why she used to leave her hair short, and she smiled at me, asking me how it would have been possible for men to have a glimpse of her beauty without her going having a low cut. She was intentional about her hairdo just to lure men to herself.

Case Study IV: As an experienced investigator, when we are interrogating a person whose hair is unkempt, it is an indication that they have something hidden and have a connection to evil; they cannot be taken as being totally blameless. Well, this is not to create a form of sentiment in your heart, but I just made the submission due to my experiences in the past. Let me back this up with an evergreen incident. I once investigated a man with an unkempt hair, and during the process, I discovered that he was into drugs. It was beginning to affect him psychologically, and he wasn't bothered about his looks again.

3.2.   Tossing the Hair

Generic Interpretations of the Concept

Let me start by asserting that this non-verbal clue is only found among women. So you can begin to imagine what it would be all about. When the head is tossed, it throws the hair backwards in a horizontal manner for the primary purpose of drawing the attention of others. It is to register the person's availability even when others do not care about their presence. That is why people consider this sign as being romantic. Those whose long hair covers their face will have to toss their hair backwards in order to make their face visible. The visibility of their face is the first step towards starting communication. It means 'I am available to discuss with you'.

Even if a woman is suffering from low self-esteem, there is a way in which they carry themselves to still be seen as an embodiment of value. One of such means is by not approaching men directly. They make use of subtle means to communicate their likeness to men. So in public space, if they see a man they are attracted to, instead of walking up to them to register their romantic attachment, they will make use of indirect means such as hair tossing. Even though the person may not be interested in the lady, but they have actually made their intent known. You will understand this better under the next segment.

Scientific Explanations

According to body language experts, when a lady is attracted to a man, she has the unconscious feeling to show more of her skin in a bid to attract the person. Hence, when a woman tosses her hair, it is a subtle way of showing her skin to someone she is attracted to. This form of body language has many variants, but, in every way, a woman makes use of one of her hands to move her hair to the side in order to make her neck and ear visible to her target. This sign of attraction is one of the most accurate body language cues that signal interest. Hence, if a lady tosses her hair while facing a man, it is a probable way of saying that she is into the man (Speeli 2019).

Before I move further, let me explain how you can be sure that it is truly a sign of attraction. In that case, you will discover that the hair toss happens for more than once—it is done consecutively for like three or more times. Then it must be done in the presence of a man or a woman (in the case of lesbians) whom they are attracted to. In fact, a woman can display this sign while they look away from their target; isn't that amazing? For instance, if a man is walking beside a lady, she can do the hair toss without looking at the passer-by. In such instance, the action will be done at the side where the man is (Speeli 2019). This can take place in a group, and it indicates that the lady is actually interested in one of the people present at the given place.

Farouk Radwan (2019) importantly notes that there are many factors to consider before arriving at the thought that this action signals attraction. First, merely touching the hair is different from tossing the hair—that is, a woman can merely touch the hair to fiddle with it without any form of attraction towards a man. It is simpler to explain this cue from a psychological point of view. Since the woman is attracted to another person, there is an unconscious feeling of revealing a part of their body to the man or woman—in this case, the ear and skin of the neck. What should be registered at the back of your mind is that this body clue is 100 per cent (Radwan 2019).

As I conclude, let me state that a woman can actually display this gesture for many other reasons. It may just signal intent to adjust the hair. And that is why it is crucial to see the signs more than once before reaching a conclusion.

Practical Illustrations

Case Study I: This signal can be noticed in different realms and at different places. This means you have to open your eyes wide and see. I know men will be more interested in this because it gives them the key to unlock the feelings of women towards them. Anyways, some practical illustrations will give you more understanding of what you should look out for. If you are in the club and a woman is looking at you consistently, this is their first registration of intent. If it now goes beyond that by flipping their hair consistently, this is a direct invitation. It means they cannot hide or suppress the urge they have for you. If they discover that you came with another woman, they will keep displaying this sign just to show you that they are better than the person you came with. This can be very herculean for a promiscuous man who does not want to offend their date yet want to take the golden opportunity at their disposal; you will see them looking restless and disturbed throughout the process.

Case Study II: This can also take place in the office too. Probably, a colleague has been eyeing you and has developed intense feelings for you. If they do not know how to tell you, they will always seize every opportunity that comes their way to sit beside you. By the moment they sit near you, they will begin to reveal some of their body part, especially the neck and beneath the ear, which is considered as being romantic to you so as to lure your heart to them. They will also look at you longingly, and when you exchange eye contact, you will observe their craving to have an emotional attachment with you.

Case Study III: In some weird instances, some female criminals also display this signal while in the interview room. If they know that there is nothing they can say to wash themselves off the case being investigated, then they will be willing to give in their body. The first form of advance is to toss their hair so that the official can see how beautiful they are and probably drop the case against them. The purpose of this gesture is to look attractive to the investigator and divert their attention from the main issue at hand. I have heard different instances where law enforcement officers fell for such antics.

3.3. Touching the Hair

Generic Interpretations of the Concept

We all touch our hair from time to time. However, the reasons obviously vary, and as such, we must find out why something happens before generalising the concept of hair touch. I need to state that this body language signal is seen more in women than in men. This sign is a form of invitation, just like the tossing of the hair. In some instances, it shows excess energy depicting that a person is not feeling too comfortable or they are anxious about something. You may be thinking all these interpretations do not relate at the surface level but they at the deeper level, there is deep connection. Context is the key when trying to interpret body language.

When people are under heat, they may touch their hair to feel the texture. Maybe they have an important function to embark on after leaving their present location, and they have a feeling that their hair has become rough. They would be forced to touch it in order to be certain of the state of things and see if they will rush to a nearby beauty house just to fix things up. This is usually the case with people who pay excessive attention to fashion, their outlook, and what people think of them each time.

In addition, hair touch with other aligning signals may be a subtle means of invitation. This means the person wants to talk to the person they are attracted to at that particular moment. They will display this signal over and over again until there is a reaction from their target. In some cases, they may be unfortunate enough not to get the much-needed reaction from the person. This will further weaken them and may even redirect their focus to any available person at the moment. All these are some of the many interpretations of the hair touch signal.

Scientific Explanations

The concept of hair is a topic widely explored by body language experts. And fortunately, many of them have consensus opinion about it. This means there are not too many arguments concerning this concept, and as such, our affirmations will not be contentious. Having said that, let's consider some scholarly submissions about the concept. According to Changing Minds (2019), 'Stroking the hair is a preening gesture, which can be deliberate checking that it is perfectly coiffed or an invitation to stroke also.' So this is very clear enough, and it is at the literal level of interpretation. People who do not want to see their hair go rough will check from time to time to be certain that they still look good.

The platform also affirms that 'playing with the hair is particularly flirtatious and invites the other person to do this for you'. This is a metaphoric interpretation of the concept. This is usually seen in places such as offices, nightclubs, hotels, or commercial vehicles, among others, where there are mixtures of men and women. When women want to flirt, they do it in a very weird way but maintain consistency until they draw the attention of their target. Playing with the hair can be romantic, so it is a form of invitation to the opposite sex: 'Won't you come and have a touch too?' or 'Aren't you moved by this sexy act?' If it is a man who understands non-verbal communication in the real form, they know that the door of a girl's heart has been opened to them and need not struggle before they snatch it away.

It is important to emphasise that this form of body language signal is a stand-alone sign. 'This means that its presence can indicate the presence of interest even if no other signs were there', says Farouk Radwan. This means that if a woman did this gesture in your presence many times, then she probably finds you attractive. However, in such a case, you need to make sure that the sign was sent for you and not for another person in the room. In fact, it can even happen from a far distance. Attraction can come from any direction, and you need to be smart enough to know if it is directed at you (Radwan 2019). This sign is done when the attraction is really at a high level. So they may not do the signal when the attraction is just building up.

Practical Illustrations

Case Study I: Before you begin to attach meanings to this signal in a person, first make sure you establish a baseline and then analyse the context critically. Here are simple illustrations of how it happens. In your home, if your spouse is touching their hair and stroking it in an unusual manner, it is an invitation to make love. Maybe your kids are around, and she does not want to make a direct request for sex in their presence, so this sign is a clarion call for you to go into the bedroom so that she can follow suit. This can be an interesting scene if the children are off to school or anywhere else; the action can start at the very place where the gesture was made.

Case Study II: A colleague may be stroking their hair in the office from time to time. If, in addition to this, they look at you and smile for no reason, it means they are into you. They are ready to make things work with you. This person will look for every avenue to be very close to you. If this non-verbal gesture becomes obvious, then it means the person is ready for nothing else but a romantic relationship.

Case Study III: Criminals may also use this sign as a form of distraction in a shopping mall. They will look for a very charming lady who will be an accomplice. The lady will make this flirtatious invitation to the guard or any other member of staff manning their targeted place so that the person can be carried away with their act while their partners in crime cart away with valuables. This can always prove to be a potent means of having a field day during a criminal operation. In interview rooms too, the situation is not different; they deploy all forms of cunning techniques to evade justice. Once they discover that there is a particular investigator trying to make things difficult for them, they will look for every non-verbal way to distract the investigator, and this flirtatious gesture has worked at different times.

3.4. Twisting the Hair

Generic Interpretations of the Concept

When we play with the hair, we are either stroking, twisting, or twirling it; and it is considered a pacifying attitude on a general note. This attitude is mostly found in women, and it can be an indication of many things when analysed in its very depth. Something unique about this body language gesture is that it can be a signal of both positive and negative attitude. For instance, if a person is playing with their hair while relaxing or reading, it means the person is in a good mood. However, if this cue is displayed while they are waiting for an interview or something tricky, it is an indication of stress.

Any time the palm of the hand directly faces the hair, it is surely a pacifying attitude (we will soon discuss the opposite, which is the *palm out*). The primary role of every pacifying behaviour is to soothe our psychological cravings when we are anxious or stressed. It helps us to wage war against the difficult moment when there is no support system from any other person. Pacifying acts change with time. In little children, what they mostly do is suck their thumbs, then bite their lip (or its counterpart, their nail), and then, to the topic under discussion, stroke their face. Hence, hair twisting is a body language gesture that is popular among adults. Lip biting or thumb sucking is very childish and irritating for an elderly person to do, especially in public. Interpreting this body gesture can be very simple and straightforward once you have established the baseline.

Scientific Explanations

Women communicate their emotions more with body language than with words. If you are always around them, you need to learn how to listen to their body than you do with their words because the body communicates their deepest intents. However, most men do not understand the subtle signs let out by women. Well, this encyclopaedia will bail out many ignorant men. If a lady keeps playing with her hair, it means she is into you. Robin Wood (2018) notes that 'when women try and act flirtatious with you, their hand automatically goes to their hair, and they start twirling it around or swiftly move them with fingers. It either means she is attracted to you or that she is in the mood to flirt around a little. Whatever it is, women playing with their hair while talking to you is a good sign.' According to the body language expert, this is the most obvious sign that a woman gives out if she is interested in a person.

While contributing to this subject matter, Wendy Rodewald (2013) asserts that when a person has amazing hair, there would be an urge to always touch it. He describes this gesture as a 'cue of innocence' because most ladies do not know how it resoundingly communicates their intents. This gesture is often employed to flirt. Rodewald also notes that since this sign makes us feel good, people also do it as a means of relaxation. Anyone who is a twirler will notice that they tend to display this gesture at similar times—twirl their hair when tired, while watching television or reading, and to some others, when they feel nervous about a thing.

Everything should be done with balance, or else, it would be tagged as being bad. This principle also applies to hair twirling. According to Health Research Funding (HRF), 'Some women take things up a notch with their hair twirling, and it actually turns into a bad habit called Trichotillomania. This is the extreme of hair twirling, where the hair is actually knotted around the finger and pulled out.' The platform notes that when a person sees you twirling your hair, they may interpret it as being childlike or see you as nervous or insecure. And it also complements the submissions of other scholars that it may be an indication of sexual interest. In the same vein, this gesture can be considered as being seductive when a woman is on a date.

Practical Illustrations

Case Study I: Hair twirling, as said earlier, is a means of self-expression usually found in women than in men. Depending on where it is displayed, the meanings vary. If a woman plays with their hair while at home after a long, tiring day at work, this is considered as a self-pacifying act. The act soothes them, and it gives them some psychological reinforcement at the moment. On the other hand, the woman may be doing it as a means of inviting their husband to a sexual scene. Probably, she discovers that the husband is ready to go out on a date with another woman. She will use this subconscious means to invite her spouse and keep him at home till he misses the other appointment. If she is the only person at home, she is most probably feeling the texture of her hair—she has amazing hair, and this plants the subconscious urge in her.

Case Study II: If a woman is playing with her hair while waiting to be invited into the interview room, this is an indication of fear. There is anxiety in her which she is subconsciously trying to suppress. This may be fear of questions she would be asked during the interview or the urge not to disappoint the panel. Whichever it is, hair twirling at that point is to provide a soothing relief for her. This is also similar to what is witnessed among many women during an investigation. When the session is getting tensed and the criminal suspect is on the verge of confessing, she would begin to touch her hair. This sign of self-pacification is a subtle sign of saying that all is not well at that very moment.

Case Study III: And finally, when a woman is on a date and she is stroking her hair, this is to draw the attention of her date to herself. She wants the guy to look at how beautiful she is and take his attention off any other person at the location. This is an effective way that women deploy to keep their men at dates. They know it may be wrong to accuse their man of looking at another lady, and he can easily deny such allegation. So when she uses this gesture, she is rest assured that he wouldn't have to look at any other place again.

3.5. Playing with Hair with the Palm Out

Generic Interpretations of the Concept

This is the direct opposite of the concept we just explored. While the former has to do with playing with hair with the palms closed, this deals with opening the palm out as your hands fiddle with your hair. This is a public display of comfort. It is a sign displayed by women which means that they are confident being around others; it is to show their contentment. When we expose the underside of our wrist, it means we are comfortable with the people around us; if we are insecure, we will keep close to ourselves. So this body gesture is a sign of being at ease with others.

The perfect place this body language gesture is normally seen is in dating contexts. Here, the woman is free with their date and very relaxed. They want to seize every given opportunity to communicate their love to the man. Here, she would play with her hair, leaving the palm out, and then engage in a conversation with their date. They have the assurance that the person cannot injure them. And in fact, they are craving for their touch at that given moment. It is also a gesture of openness; it means the woman is not hiding anything from her man.

Hence, this cue is clearly different from the palm-in one discussed above, which is primarily for self-soothing. This is one of the gestures women show when they are really into a man.

Scientific Explanations

Danielle Anne says that although body language as a concept reveals much about a person to you if you know how to read the signs, it does much more if you understand the power of touch. Something is universal about love. If you have ever liked someone, you want the person to know how you are feeling. This explains why some surmount the courage to walk up to their potential lovers just to confess their feelings. However, since it is practically impossible to read a person's mind, other methods have been put in place to understand the inner feelings of one another.

Since body language helps in the communication of behaviour and emotions, it cannot be discarded when it comes to understanding the intents of people. If a woman is playing with her hair with the palms out, this is a very rare exhibition of love, and it means she has gone too far to let you know that she is into you. What is required of a man at this point is to make her more comfortable—making her comfortable in the sense that the communication should be shifted to her topic of interest. Discuss something romantic, share your plans with her, let her know that you are ready for her, reveal your plans to her, and give her peace of mind concerning the relationship. At this point, the woman will know that you really care about her (Arangua 2018).

The problem is that most men do misinterpret this gesture with the pacifying signs. The fact that this gesture is rare should tell you that it connotes something different from what has been in vogue. Changing Minds (2019) notes that the most common reason people touch a part of their body is for self-affirmation. So in a way, this cue can mean that the woman is trying to say she is in charge of the man. As in a romantic context, if this gesture is repeated consistently, it is sending out a strong desire to the other person. This can be erotic if done with the highest level of stimulation. We cannot leave out such interpretations in some given contexts—bars, hotels, restaurants, or nightclubs, among others—where their primary purpose is to proclaim love in different guises. With this in mind, nothing can be hidden about the thought of a woman towards you any longer.

Practical Illustrations

Case Study I: This gesture can be seen in an office setting. It is mostly done by women in this sense to prove that they are in charge. Women are moved by positions and high status. They want to prove at all times that nothing can move them out of their high position and people should always bow to them. If a woman plays with her palms out, it means that she is not afraid of anyone around her; it means everybody in that location is beneath her—it is a show of authority and superiority. If anyone dare challenge their authority at this point, they will feel threatened and flare up.

Case Study II: At home, if a woman should display this signal, it means she is relaxed and feeling comfortable around her spouse—it is an expression of her trust in her partner. It means that 'being around you, there is nothing that can happen to me'. With this, they will sit very close to their spouse and discuss intimate issues. The manner and pace of the discussion will hint you that the woman has nothing to fear in that context.

Case Study III: However, this sign is mostly displayed during dates. This is the point where both the lady and the man are striving to outdo each other—they want to show that they are really into each other. It is at this stage that the love is described as incomparable. If the woman is playing with her hair with the palms out, it means she really loves the man and wants to have his attention by all means. She is subtly saying that the man should forget about every other thing and focus on her alone. This is the height of her love for him. If the man seems not to be getting the message, she will keep doing it until she wins his attention and then keeps it through a conversation or any other means.

Case Study IV: In some weird situations, I do see this in the interview room, and it is actually an affront on the part of the suspect. They are trying to tell the interviewer that they are relaxed and not moved about everything going on; it means they are not nervous. This is a subtle way of saying, 'You cannot implicate me on this matter.' To an official who understands the signal, it means they are trying to question his expertise—that is, the interviewee does not see the investigator as someone competent enough to nail them.

3.6.   Men Touching the Hair

Generic Interpretations of the Concept

Men are not known to be fascinated by their hair to the extent of touching it at all times. Hence, when you see them running their fingers through their hair, it means there is a reason for that. To some very few, they want to feel the texture of their hair and be sure that it is still coiffed. They are the fashion freaks. However, in the real sense, when a man runs his fingers through his hair, it is a symbol of being stressed. It is a soothing act that pacifies them at this point. Also, when a person is stressed, they will become restless and will crave for fresh air. So this body language gesture means they are ventilating their heads—they want to open the vascular surface of the scalp up for ventilation. They want the breeze to cool their head and calm them down so as to be able to think straight.

Another interpretation given to this gesture is to stimulate the nerves of the skin as the hair presses down. Apart from that, running the fingers through one's hair may signal doubt. Maybe the man wants to take a major step and is not certain of what would be its aftermath, so he may display this sign to show that he is on a crossroad. At this point, he is more than willing to relate his story to anybody who will give him a listening ear. Furthermore, the gesture is also seen in men when they are concerned about something. Life is not a bed of roses, and we all have our down moments. Hence, this gesture is related to when one is engulfed in thought about the reality of a given concept.

Scientific Explanations

Checking through what body language experts say concerning this, one really needs to be careful of the interpretation one alludes to this body language gesture. In short, you must know the context of the occurrence of the gesture before you pin it down to a possible meaning. When you see a man running his fingers through his hair, it may signal mere nervousness. Both men and women unconsciously play with their hair when they are nervous. It means something is troubling them, and they need a compliment from a loved one. Somebody must assure them that all would be well so as to make them leave the fear behind. Compliment is known to be a potent settler of nerves (Coleman 2019).

However, if the man displays this sign while having a conversation with a woman, it means they want to look good; he is placing emphasis on his appearance—he wants to appear charming, attractive, and sexy to the woman. This is done when a man wants to appear perfect before a woman (Coleman 2019). Parul Solanki (2018) corroborates this view. He likens this body gesture to how birds fluff up and smooth their feathers just to look good. He said this cue is similar to preening in birds. Hence, if a man leans towards a woman and runs his fingers through his hair, then he wants to look good to the woman so as to win her heart. So it simply means he is into her. In some other times, the man may try smoothening a lapel or stroking his tie all in the effort to look decent.

Sally Murphy (2011) urges women to appreciate this gesture by men because it is a sign that they (men) are not taking the person they love for granted; it is a symbol of respect for a man to try showing his best. Men are known to be rude and egoistic. So for them to drop their ego is a symbol of true love towards a woman.

Practical Illustrations

Case Study I: A man who sits behind his system and runs his fingers through his hair is most probably confused about an incident. Maybe he has been trying to get something done for a while and is proving abortive. At some point, he will become concerned, and the sign would be written all over him. Also, it may also be interpreted as doubt. Maybe, he has applied for a job, but upon checking through the job descriptions and comparing them with his curriculum vitae, he has written himself off. He does not have hope of being contacted.

Case Study II: A terrorist can display this sign too. For instance, if he has been stationed to bomb a high-density shopping mall but the mall's security is always beefed up, having got to the location, he may be confused on where to detonate the bomb so that it will claim many calamities. He may be ruminating on moving closer or standing aloof in order not to be detected. At this point, he would run his fingers through his hair—it is an indication of doubt. It is also an expression of confusion as he does not know the best action to take at that point in time that will guarantee the needed outcome.

Case Study III: When a man is on a date with a woman whom he is not sure if she is into him, he would do everything humanly possible to satisfy her, and it begins with his look. This means he is paying attention to his look and wants to make sure that nothing slacks in his bid to entrench himself in her heart. If you are on the bed with him, this means he wants to get closer to you. And invariably, it means he is demanding for sex. At least being on the bed in the first place is a sign of closeness. So if this sign is displayed, it is asking for the main deal.

Case Study IV: This body gesture is also witnessed in the interview room. If an applicant answers a question and runs his fingers through his hair, it means he is not certain of the appropriateness of the answer he provides. This is an implication of doubt. However, if it is a criminal suspect, it means he is really stressed by the questioning process—it is an indication of a fagged-out person. It is usually a herculean task for someone to tell many lies at a time. So the accumulation of this stress and the uncertainty of what becomes of his lot after the session makes him exhibit this gesture.

3.7. Women Ventilating the Hair

Generic Interpretations of the Concept

This is a very potent tool seen in women. Ventilating the hair can be very pacifying in the moment of stress and heat. The way in which women ventilate their hair is different from men. However, this does not mean that they pass different messages across. For women to ventilate, they lift up their hair at the back of their neck in a rapid manner. This action may be due to physical activities which brought about overheating and drastic change in temperature. However, if there is not any physical reason that can be alluded to it, it means there are other messages intended to be passed through it.

First on the list is stress. Different activities can bring about stress. Apart from physical functions, lying is a major stress inducer. It takes mental stress to conjoin and fabricate stories. If the person has to tell lies along a chain of events, they would be worn out easily, and this would be noticed in their behaviour. If this gesture is done repeatedly, it means that the person is really stressed. Another possible interpretation of this sign is that the person is upset. Women easily get irritated by events. If someone keeps doing what they hate, they will get infuriated, and ventilating their hair is a subconscious means of passing their message across. It may also mean that they are flustered.

Also, women do ventilate their hair when they are concerned about something. As I rightly noted in the preceding paragraph, ladies easily get irritated. In the same vein, when an issue is bothering them, you will easily know through their body gestures. Invariably, they are easily moved emotionally. When an issue comes up, instead of them relaxing and conducting a full analysis of the events bothering them, they feel like proffering a one-time solution to it, and that is why they normally become restless.

Scientific Explanations

Ex-FBI agent Joe Navarro simply tagged this body gesture as a 'cool' body language. This is in relation to the literal meaning of the gesture. The universally acknowledged body language expert submits that the first point of noticing this behaviour in a woman is when she is hot. However, he notes that people ventilate when they have something bothering them. When there are myriads of issues to battle with, you see women ventilating—it is done subconsciously. The ventilating behaviour is apt in recognising the feeling of a person because it appears in real time; there is no delay or thinking of how to act it out.

Leaving temperature out of the game, there are many other things that can cause the ventilating behaviour in a woman. Apprehension, doubt, fear, anxiety, sense of weakness, vulnerability, and insecurity are some of the things that can make a woman ventilate. Women are emotional-laden beings; they get truly excited or pained by the slightest occurrence. The ventilating behaviour is not particular to any given event; once a person feels psychologically distressed, they will ventilate. If there is not any psychological exigency attached, it is almost impossible for you to see a woman run her fingers through her hair multiple times in quick succession (Navarro 2012).

This signal is mostly overlooked, but scholars affirm that it is one of the truest indicators of stress, anxiety, and insecurity. It accurately shows that the woman has something bothering her (O'Callaghan 2018). Sankalan Baidya (2015) describes this body gesture as one of the 'most interesting pacifying acts'. In her interpretation, she supports the submissions of other scholars that it is always seen when a person is stressed, fearful, or apprehensive. She, however, notes that this sign is slightly different in pregnant women.

Practical Illustrations

Case Study I: This sign can be seen in various settings. There are some women who are not used to heat. If they meet themselves in an unfriendly area where the temperature is beyond what they can bear, they will use their hands to run through their hair. This would be unconsciously done, and it is a direct reaction to their present situation. If they were home, they could have undressed in no time, but being outside means enduring and showing this discomfort in a subtle way.

Case Study II: A woman who is not fully prepared for an interview may also display this sign. It means they are really bothered about what the outcome of the process would be. You can also see this when a woman is sitting in an exam. The ventilating behaviour in an examination hall means the questions are really tough for the person. It is an indication that the person is not getting it well and may perform below expectations. If a teacher or trainer is explaining a concept and their female student runs her fingers through her hair from the back of the head, it means they are confused about what the teacher is saying. The teacher needs to adopt another technique in explaining the topic and ensure that the countenance of the student has improved considerably well before moving to other aspects.

Case Study III: During a criminal investigation, if a woman shows this body gesture, it means they are really stressed. This may be a result of a lengthy duration or their own deceptive act since the interview started. However, this is usually a plus to any official who knows their onus; it tells you that they are not comfortable, and you should actually hit harder at that point. Lying can be the major cause of stress to them. To successfully deceive a person, you have to think in-depth, do word calculations, take cognisance of events, and then polish the outcome all in the twinkle of an eye. Hence, this can be very tasking. Thus, it wears people out easily.

Case Study IV: A female terrorist sent to bomb a given location would be stressed and become apprehensive if what she sees on ground is different from what they had planned. They would be confused whether to execute the plan or retreat. At that point, they are really between the devil and the deep blue sea. Then this body gesture can be seen playing itself out in the person.

3.8.   Flipping the Hair

Generic Interpretations of the Concept

Hair flipping is also known as hair touching. When we flip or touch the hair, it is a potent way of drawing the attention of another person, a potential mate in most cases. This means we want to get noticed and can go to any length to achieve our aim. I must state that this action is usually unconscious, and it is done when one's feeling has reached the extreme. There is no gainsaying that moving the hand to touch the hair is an adventurous action if the hair is attractive itself. There is a primitive reaction known as orientation reflex (OR) which alerts every human of any form of the movement within the body. It is widely believed that the OR is attuned to hand movement, and that explains the reason magicians have always counted on it.

Hand movement is always an obvious action that draws the attention of people. It becomes more prevalent if the hand goes to the direction of the head. Even people from far away can notice this sign and, for a moment, focus on the subject. If this action is maintained for some period (through playing with one's hair), everybody's attention would be focused on the person. Because the orientation reflex is a subconscious action, it can even be seen in coma patients. The eyes primarily track the movement of things and people. Unless the eyes are blind, they focus their attention towards a moving object.

Scientific Explanations

At this juncture, it is crucial to establish the fact that hair flipping, which is said to be an attention-seeking gesture, is not necessarily a show of love. Just because someone is calling your attention does not mean that he or she has a crush on you. This is the opinion of body language experts. More so, the subconscious behaviours for all forms of likeness are the same. Hence, a person saying they 'like' you is different from showing romantic interest. For instance, there is the likeness bond between friends and family, and there is the love bond between spouses. However, both bonds are expressed in the same manner in the realm of body language gestures. So before you take the hair flipping sign as a symbol of love, first make your enquiries (Pinkstone 2018).

Hair flipping as a symbol of attraction can be used by a person to build trust. This is seen in boardrooms where people want to be trusted and others to align with their opinion on a given issue. A scientist from the University of Dayton, Ohio, Dr Matthew Montoya, said, 'When we like someone, we act in ways to get them to trust us. From this perspective, we engage in these behaviours to increase the degree of overlap, interdependence, and commitment to an agreement.' So at this point, I can stand on the assertions of these authorities to dispel that the famed hair flipping is not necessarily a gesture of romantic attraction.

Hair flipping is totally an unconscious action—that is, the person will do it without even realising that they have done it. It is a gesture displayed by a woman who craves for attention. Although I have said that hair flipping does not necessarily translate to romantic interest, I need to also note that it is a stand-alone sign which indicates interest at every given point it is portrayed. This means that if a lady should display the sign before you in quick succession, it means she needs your attention for an undisclosed reason. Other signs of attraction include genuine smile, balanced eye contact, mimicry, and laughter, among others. I have listed all these out to correct the myopic notion that the signs of attraction are limited. Hence, if the person does not flip their hair, there are other signs which can still communicate attraction (Radwan 2019).

Let me conclude this section with these apt words from the Trust ambassador: 'One thing to observe when a person is fussing with his or her hair is what type of conversation is occurring or what the situation is. If the person typically does this in only one kind of conversation, like my male friend above, it is a habitual comfortable gesture that may not have a lot of meaning. However, if a person rarely does this then all of a sudden start combing her hair with her fingers, something of significance is going on. Look for other accompanying BL signals to find out what is happening.'

Practical Illustrations

Case Study I: If a woman is at home, sitting comfortably before the television set and flipping her hair, it is just a sign of relaxation. It means she is confident and comfortable with herself. However, if her spouse is within sight, this is targeted at getting his attention. Maybe after styling the hair, the spouse has overlooked it and did not compliment her new look. So the hair flip is to draw his attention to the hair. It may be another thing—to talk about something or to make him see a new development at home, among other things.

Case Study II: If she displays the sign at the office, it is a means of calling the attention of her colleagues. Probably, they are at a meeting, and it seems her idea is being suppressed. She would do everything within her means to gain the attention of the leader of the team. This non-verbal clue is an effective way of building trust, and then she can make her point thereafter. Apart from building trust, when she displays this gesture, it calls people's attention to her, and then she can say whatever is in her mind then.

Case Study III: A criminal who wants to steal can use her hair to distract you. In the same vein, a terrorist who is ready to attack can display this sign. With that, she can lure you to herself before detonating the bomb on her. The non-verbal gesture can be used for both good and evil. Terrorists do not leave any stone unturned in their bid to harm their target. They come under different guises, and once you fall into their trap, they become merciless about the way they would treat you. This is evident in their method of operation all over the world.

3.9. Pulling the Hair

Generic Interpretations of the Concept

Trichotillomania is the intentional and repetitive pulling of the hair. This habit is usually seen in teenagers and young children when they are stressed. However, this does not mean that adults are totally excluded from it. For men, they do pluck their hair from the corners of their eyebrows while it is far wide-ranging in women—they pluck their arm hair, eyelids, eyebrows, and head hair. It is a universal response to stress. Let me state that this is not peculiar to human beings alone as even birds are fond of pulling off their feathers when stressed.

When we pull off the hair like a nervous tic on a repetitive way, it serves as a pacifying behaviour. This behaviour is known for the stimulation of the nerves. However, this must be put under check because if nerve endings become severe, one will need to see the doctor. I have always emphasised balance at every point of this book because there is nothing that is good when it comes in excess. Even the mere act of pulling out one's hair requires dexterity and caution so that one would not have to wound oneself. This warning should be heeded by women who are known to have a wide-ranging option when it comes to this gesture.

Scientific Explanations

Forbes lists this form of body language gesture as part of the worst ten body language mistakes people make. As I have rightly said earlier, this sign is mostly seen among children and teenagers and, as such, considered childish. Come to think of it, how well does it portray an adult to be pulling off their hair in public? Under what guise will they hide? No matter the level of pacification one enjoys from this gesture, it does not portray one as being mature. There is no subtle manner in which this action can be carried out. Hence, people will always see you and focus their attention on you while you do this. I am not trying to say that you should suppress your innate feeling because of what people will think about you, but you must not allow this weird, irregular act to be a culture for you.

Áine Cain of the Business Insider describes this body gesture as part of the eleven horrible body language mistakes that are hard to quit. Conversation is not based on words alone. In saner climes, body language plays a huge role in understanding your co-interlocutors. This means that you cannot do away with non-verbal gestures and have a full understanding of what your co-interlocutor is saying.

At this point, I need to reiterate that there is difference between mere hair touching and hair pulling. While the former is a form of romantic gesture, the latter does not in any way relate to anything positive. A person who plays with their hair will do it in a slow and attention-grabbing manner, while a person intending to pull their hair do not care if anybody is looking at them or not. They are stressed and looking for ways to get rid of it. So hair pulling is said to be a pacifying act which many scholars have condemned in relation with the world culture (Changing Minds 2019).

Practical Illustrations

Case Study I: It is an open secret that there are different reasons for stress—the context and causes of stress vary in human beings. However, we can simply classify them as psychological and physical. Anybody who is stressed craves for some soothing relief, and if it does not come from any other source, they tend to pacify themselves. For instance, a child who has been worked out in school can display this sign during closing hour or even when a lecture is ongoing. Such a child will lose concentration and will focus on the subconscious action he or she is undertaking at the moment. For a male pupil, he would focus on only his eyebrow, while a female student has different options. If the teacher is professional enough, he or she will quickly notice this distractive behaviour. This body language gesture is related to a child who has pimples on her face and is trying to rub them off while another activity is ongoing.

Case Study II: We can also see this gesture in the office among our colleagues on a busy workday. A frustrated worker who has been struggling with a piece of assignment can become stressed if it seems there would be no headway soon. When this body gesture is consistently displayed, it may indicate depression too. If you notice that a co-worker is totally lost in this activity, it is time to approach them and enquire what is wrong so that you can be a source of relief to them. Although this body gesture is rare in adults, but it occurs during excessive stress.

Case Study III: Even in the home front, one's children can suddenly begin to pluck any of their hair. Maybe you have bombarded them with a lot of house chores, and they are weakened by the work rate. You will notice that the child, while plucking the hair, will lose focus on what they have been doing. It is a subtle message that they want to get themselves rid of every activity and cool their body.

Case Study IV: A criminal who has been struggling to get a heinous act done will also portray this sign. For instance, he or she has been sent to profile a place and then harm people at the location, but it has been very difficult for them to break the security rank and gain entrance for hours. All their strategies and planning have not been productive. No matter how resilient they prove to be, feelings of boredom will set in, and they will subconsciously begin to pluck their hair off. This can also happen to them while being investigated. Surely, every criminal knows that their action is bad and that it would lead them to jail or death. So when apprehended, they will conjoin all forms of lies to defend themselves. Lying is a stressful adventure, and one of the things they do to pacify themselves is to pluck their hair.

CHAPTER 4

The Forehead

Just like I have mentioned at different points in time in this book, the head is the first place a person focuses on when they come across you. This is not different even in less-contact cultures such as the Japanese. These cultures are not saying 'Don't look.' All that they profess is, 'Look, but don't tarry in that act.' When a person glances at your entire face, there is no way they will not see your forehead. Unknown to many people, the forehead is a body part with multiple body language cues for a person who is smart enough to decode. Also, you must know how to send out the right non-verbal signals with the use of your forehead. In this section, I will explain the concept of the forehead in its entirety so that you can always use it to your advantage.

From time immemorial, the forehead is seen as the engine room of information by people from all walks of life. For instance, even an infant who is less than a year old focuses on its mother's forehead for furrows. Seeing the furrows indicates that the mother is angry or frustrated with it—anything negative. The fact is that we cannot discountenance the message the small space between the hairline and bridge of the nose passes across. It is a potent tool in making us understand the feelings of people each time.

This part of the body has deep connection with the brain, and that is why it accurately reveals our emotional state concerning every given issue—that is, the brain sees the forehead as a ready avenue for the communication of human intents. Something unique about the forehead is that the feelings it depicts cannot be hidden. It is unlike the hands or feet where we can decide to suppress the feelings they display. That is why Paul Ekman refers to the face as the seat of true emotions. The microemotions displayed on the face come in the form of a flash and disappear almost immediately. This means that it is only the eagle-eyed beings who can decode those expressions. If anyone decides to consciously cover them up, this would be made glaring to people around. For instance, if you decide to cover the furrows on your forehead with your hands, people at the other side of the room will definitely see this and dig deeper to know what is actually going on.

In the spiritual realm, the forehead is said to connote divine love. People who share this sentiment are of the opinion that the furrow on the forehead is a mark of protection of God over his people. Those in the Christian faith have some scriptural references they use in supporting their claim. As you know, this book is not written with any religious colouration. However, I want to ensure to take cognisance of every view concerning the topic under consideration. That is why I decided to briefly mention that.

Now let's do a little bit of science before returning to our normal routine. 'In human anatomy, the forehead is an area of the head bounded by three features, two of the skull and one of the scalp. The top of the forehead is marked by the hairline, the edge of the area where hair on the scalp grows. The bottom of the forehead is marked by the supraorbital ridge, the bone feature of the skull above the eyes. The two sides of the forehead are marked by the temporal ridge, a bone feature that links the supraorbital ridge to the coronal suture line and beyond' (David and Mel 2001). This has given some simple analysis of the forehead and shed more light on it.

Talking of the structure of the forehead, its bone is the squamous part of the frontal bone. The overlying muscles are the occipitofrontalis, procerus, and corrugator supercilii muscles, all of which are under the control of the temporal branch of the facial nerve. The sensory nerves of the forehead connect to the ophthalmic branch of the trigeminal nerve and to the cervical plexus and lie within the subcutaneous fat. The motor nerves of the forehead connect to the facial nerve (Valencia et al. 2007).

The ophthalmic branch of the trigeminal nerve, the supraorbital nerve, divides at the orbital rim into two parts in the forehead. One part, the superficial division, runs over the surface of the occipitofrontalis muscle. This provides sensation for the skin of the forehead and for the front edge of the scalp. The other part, the deep division, runs into the occipitofrontalis muscle and provides frontoparietal sensation. Blood supply to the forehead is via the left and right superorbital, supertrochealar, and anterior branches of the superficial temporal artery (David and Mel 2001).

There are two functions that the forehead performs—used in expression and wrinkles. For the former, the forehead plays a crucial role in determining facial expression. According to Paul Ekman, there are seven basic emotions which can occur individually or in combination to form different expressions. The occipitofrontalis muscles can raise the eyebrows, either together or individually, forming expressions of surprise and quizzicality. The corrugator supercilii muscles can pull the eyebrows inward and down, forming a frown. The procerus muscles can pull down the centre portions of the eyebrows (Nigel et al. 2006).

Talking of the latter (wrinkles function), the movements of the muscles in the forehead produce characteristic wrinkles in the skin. The occipitofrontalis muscles produce the transverse wrinkles across the width of the forehead, and the corrugator supercilii muscles produce vertical wrinkles between the eyebrows above the nose. The procerus muscles cause the nose to wrinkle (Nigel et al. 2006).

In physiognomy and phrenology, the shape of the forehead was taken to symbolise intellect and intelligence. 'Animals, even the most intelligent of them,' wrote Samuel R. Wells in 1942, 'can hardly be said to have any forehead at all, and in natural total idiots it is very diminished'. Having laid this solid foundation, we can now discuss the various aspects of the forehead body language.

4.1. Expression of Tension

Generic Interpretations of the Concept

When some people are stressed, this is made manifest through the sudden tension of their forehead. This means that their underlying muscles have been stiffened and tensed beyond measure. Body language expert and foremost researcher on microexpressions Dr Paul Ekman makes it known that there are more than twenty unique muscle groups on the face which have the ability to create over four thousand different expressions. This is huge, but we cannot contend it because it is as a result of extensive research conducted on the field.

In particular, there are six muscles dedicated to the furrowing or tightening of the face when we are under stress.

One thing is obvious in every body language circumstance—one must establish the baseline of a person when they are in a calm environment before we can attach meanings to their body gestures. Something fantastic about the forehead tension is that it cannot necessarily be hidden from people; it is often noticeable when we are stressed. It is an apt indicator that all is not well. In simpler terms, when the forehead is tensed through furrowing, it means that something is wrong. It is a body language signal that accompanies negativity. You do not see it on people when they are happy or when things are going as planned. This sign of stress may indicate frustration or depression of not getting something done.

Scientific Explanations

According to Changing Minds (2019), 'The forehead has its place in body language communications, often as a part of a wider set of signals. It is near the eyes and can be looked at without sending other signals [for example looking the mouth can say "I want to kiss you"], which can make even small movements with it reliably observed and hence significant. Its main limitation is that it can only make a few movements.' The point I want to establish from this quotation is that signals from the forehead are reliable. So whether they are many or not is not the thrust of our discussion; what is important is what we make out of it each time.

For the forehead tension, scholars across the board are unanimous in their postulation that it is a sign of stress. Changing Minds makes it known that it is impossible to hide this gesture that is propelled by the inner muscles of the head. What can only be done is for the stressed individual to wear a hat and a long sunburn brim that will hide the head down. Most probably, this explains the reason gamblers are fond of this act; they do not want people to know how they feel.

In its own submission, Word of Mouth Experiment makes it known that the forehead tension is a signal of aggression. If the person were shy, their head would have been buried in a lowered form. The forehead tension means that the person is unable to manage their intense feelings; it means they are really agitated inward. If anyone should annoy them at this point, there is a likelihood that they will explode; all they need at this moment are calming words that will soothe their emotions and make them feel different.

The forehead tension is quite a strenuous activity, and the facial muscles may be put under undue risk. If this tension is sustained for a long period of time, it can lead to torturous headaches. The tension can lead to many other health maladies that space will not permit me to mention in this segment. What is most important is that people should learn how to put this signal under check immediately before they get agitated (WME 2019).

Practical Illustrations

Case Study I: Man A and Man B have been working on a particular project, and there is a given deadline for the project. On the day they were supposed to put some finishing touches to the project and submit it, Man A was nowhere to be found, and his phone is not connecting. Man B, having thought of his labour all these while, decided to surmount courage and finish up with the work. However, upon starting the work, he discovered that he had a limited knowledge on what is left—it is the area of expertise of Man A. After battling with the assignment for hours, he decided to leave it angrily and walk home. On his way home, he called Man A in his home, and to his utmost surprise, there he was, lying down and watching a TV show.

At this point, Man B becomes irritatingly annoyed at the excuse of Man A— that he was a little bit tired and did not know that his mobile phone had been set to flight mode. Man B was already stressed by the unsuccessful attempts to get the project done, and this is compounded by the lies of Man A that he was tired and his phone had technical issue. If you should focus on his head, you would notice the tension on his forehead.

Case Study II: Another instance where this body language gesture can be noticed is in the office. A situation whereby a senior colleague has been instructing a junior colleague to do related things at different times can be tiring. Since the junior colleague sees it as an abomination to question the authority of their boss, their body language will definitely bear this message. At this point, if the wrong person comes to their way, they will transfer the aggression to the ill-fated individual. The tension will be made glaring on their forehead.

Case Study III: Pardon me for always giving examples related to crime because it is my area of expertise. This gesture is also seen in a criminal who has gone into hiding and believes no one should find them out but is later apprehended by law enforcement agents. If the person is brought into the interview room, if you focus on their forehead, you would see tension written on them due to the stress they have gone through. Also, the brain would have been rehearsing how to deceive the officials to interrogate them. The accumulation of this in addition to physical exhaustion will make them wear out.

4.2. Furrowing the Forehead

Generic Interpretations of the Concept

When the forehead is furrowed as a means of responding to an event in real time, it means something is wrong somewhere. The issue may not be ascertained at that point in time, but it is a good indication for anyone dealing with them to tread carefully. Also, it is interpreted as a sign of insecurity. When a person is taken by fear, this sign is always seen on them. Maybe they are exposed to something that threatens their comfort zone or gets them out of their natural condition. The furrowing is like frowning at the unwarranted condition. The fortunate thing about this body gesture is that it appears immediately when one feels the stimulus. A person who has been barricaded by robbers at a certain location will furrow their forehead any time they get to that location—it is expressing their fear as if the robbers were still there.

This signal is also seen when a person is trying hard to concentrate on a given task or make sense out of a given concept. Hence, in this context, it is a mark of seriousness. This means the person has tried to have a grasp of the concept at a casual level, and it has been proven abortive. In general, this gesture is usually associated with anxiety, concern, doubt, or tension. Looking at the four emotional displays that I listed, they are all negative. This means that when a person is happy, they do not furrow their forehead. As I round off on this, let me alert you on this, most especially law enforcement officials and bank workers who deal with impostors at all times, you should know that Botox, which is used for cosmetic purposes by many people in obstructing the stress lines, can be used in masking the furrowed forehead. In other words, criminals can hide under this guise to package their true feelings.

Scientific Explanations

Body Language Project states on its site that this body signal is also known as wrinkled forehead, forehead furrow, or forehead creasing. So anywhere you see any of the aforementioned, they are referring to the same thing. Furrowed forehead is the act of frowning done by creasing the brow and forehead. Explaining this concept in a sentence, the platform notes that 'a furrowed forehead is a sign of negative thoughts'. Without mincing words, this actually explains it all, and it aligns with the assertion I made while giving the generic interpretation of the concept.

In order to make others see that all is not well with them, a person will furrow their forehead. This signal is, no doubt, effective in showing people's disapproval to an initiative or occurrence. This means that if you are not pleased with someone's attitude and you do not want to express it verbally, you can make use of this gesture. And since it is not a hidden one, the person would be forced to change their behaviour in order to suit you (Chris 2014).

It has been observed that furrowing the forehead works perfectly for both children and adults. In a way, it can be described as a signal that is used by people to coerce others into submission. According to Chris, 'The honest portrayal of disapproval through furrowed forehead works to influence others as people are strongly social and do not cope well with the anger of others.' So once they see that your forehead is furrowed, they understand that you are not pleased with their behaviour, and if they still have their conscience intact, they will do everything humanly possible to please you and get you out the angry mode. As I wrap up on this, when we show disapproval through non-verbal means, it makes us avoid heated verbal confrontations because the furrowed forehead is clear and glaring enough for every onlooker to see.

Practical Illustrations

Case Study I: While going out, if you tell your child to wash the dish, mop the house, iron your clothes, and prepare launch and by the time you are done listing all the chores they are expected to perform and you see them furrow their forehead, it is a means of telling you that the chores are too much for them. Some children are fearful and, as such, may not be able to express themselves through verbal means when they are displeased. If you fail to enquire the child to know what is wrong, you may return home to see the work undone or, at the very best, haphazardly done. If you want to punish the child, they may tell you that they have *told* you before you went out that they will not do everything.

Case Study II: As a teacher, if after explaining a topic you decide to test your students through a short exercise but you see their forehead furrowed, it means that you should explain better before testing them on that particular topic. In other words, the students are trying to say that they did not have a full grasp of the content you explained to them. If you should go ahead in testing them without re-explaining it, they will perform woefully.

Case Study III: A co-worker with a furrowed forehead is, no doubt, angry. Instead of facing you while talking, their head would be buried in the work they are doing. If this is how they have been behaving since they came to work that day, it means the problem is actually from home and not at work. However, if you should annoy them with the slightest mistake, there is a high possibility that they will redirect their aggression on you. Also, if a colleague is assigned multiple jobs at a time by a superior, they cannot verbally reject such due to the professional implications. However, they will furrow their forehead to communicate their disapproval to the person. If the superior does not rescind on their decision, the junior worker may end up not doing a satisfactory job. After all, the worker believes that they have communicated their intention to the superior, only that the superior decided not to heed to it.

Case Study IV: During investigations and when things become tough for criminal suspects, you will observe that they will begin to furrow their forehead; this is done unconsciously as they will do everything humanly possible to appear unmoved. When their forehead is furrowed, they are either sad, worried, bewildered, or concerned about something, concentrated on what you are saying because they are gripped with fear, anxious of the unknown, or even angry. In my sojourn in the field, I have seen all these cases at one point or another. When the forehead becomes furrowed, the suspect is almost losing their composure, and a few hard questions will give them out.

4.3. Botoxed Forehead

Generic Interpretations of the Concept

Knowledge is now increasing sporadically in our world, and people are taking advantage of it, both in the negative and positive sense of it. Excessive beauty is now the order of the day. In other words, the world of fashion is not left out in the new trends of the world. Reordering of our affairs seems to now be the culture of the world. Since looking good now seems to be the foundation of getting everything done in life, both men and women are devoting their fortunes in getting Botox injections. These injections are famous in erasing the stress lines on the foreheads. Everyone wants to look artificially happy and young. That is why they ironically stress themselves to incur Botox injections.

Without mincing words, this singular act has robbed us of many things; children, couples, and even the larger society are battling with the problem of unravelling the true feelings of people. Even a four-week-old child looks at the forehead of their parents to know how they feel. If this feeling has been artificially covered up, where then do we expect the child to get the information from? Imagine the psychological stress that the poor, innocent child would be subjected to. If a baby sees furrowed forehead on their parents, they know that it connotes something negative and, as such, will adjust their behaviour. Unfortunately, both adults and children have reported their inability to read their spouses, friends, colleagues, and parents who have made use of Botox for emotional enhancement as easily as they could before. This means that they now have to dig deeper, rely on other cues, and even make some verbal clarifications before they can understand the feelings of others.

Scientific Explanations

While commenting on this act that is fast becoming a culture among men and women, Jessie Cole, whose article is focused on women, took out time to explain how Botox was first taking away the facial expression of people. According to her, on a particular occasion where she visited her friend, the face that greeted her was not the familiar one, and as expected, she perused on the likely cause of the sudden change. According to her, one of the eyelids of her friend was sagged, and she then had a lopsided smile. Then her friend made it known that it was Botox. Read the response of Cole as captured in her article: 'It took me a while to fully process her answer. My startlingly confident, formidably intelligent, beautiful 31-year-old friend was getting Botox? And Botox had caused her eye to sag as though she'd had a stroke? Of course, I knew film stars and celebrities forked out in order to have this paralysing poison injected into their faces, but it wasn't something I'd anticipated someone I actually know would do.' What I need to bring out in this is that Botox is nothing but poisonous.

People who have shiny foreheads have definitely voted for Botox. Something common about Botoxed faces is that they maintain a strange vacancy on their faces—there is a glaring peculiar dullness. In simpler terms, one feels a kind of deadness around the face of a person who had Botox. Watching them closely, a lot of them look somehow angry and indifferent (Cole 2013). This body language expert really shares the feeling of many people about Botoxed faces thus: 'I've found myself feeling uneasy after spending time with these shiny-faced friends. The sense of connectedness we've always shared seems impeded by their impenetrable faces. In short, I miss their micro-expressions. I feel cut off from them and come away lonely and disturbed.'

Cole's stance is supported by a research from University of Wisconsin headed by Dr David Havas. He reports that 'blocking the expression of emotion changes how we understand and feel the emotion'. In short, a Botoxed face confuses everything (Vanessa 2019). Experts conclude that this problem is a two-way thing. While we find it difficult to read Botoxed faces, they also find it herculean to understand us.

Practical Illustrations

Case Study I: Mr A came home feeling dejected after being fired by his company by an offence that was mistakenly committed. He was hopeless about life, and nothing good had scaled through his mind after he received the letter. His official car has been taken from him and, as such, had to board a commercial transport home. His wife who had Botoxed her face was home preparing supper when he came in. Their only son who was watching a reality show was the first to notice the sad expression on the face of his father. He asked what was wrong, and the father patted him at the back, assuring him that all would be well; he felt the boy was too young to be bothered with an issue so huge at that.

When the wife came out from the kitchen, having heard the voice of Mr A, she hugged him and greeted him in the usual way; she could not read the expression of grief written on the face of her husband. At that point, Mr A was really expecting her to notice, ask, pacify him, and join him in a round table as they think of the way forward; but till midnight, it was surely a desire that never materialised. At dawn the next day, Mr A was so depressed by this occurrence that he committed suicide. There, the wife cried profusely when their eight-year-old son revealed that *something* was wrong with his dad the day before.

Case Study II: In another incident, a worker with a Botoxed face was really pained and frustrated because se had spent almost three hours looking for an item she had forgotten that she handed over to a colleague in the past. The colleague was seated right beside her, but he did not know that she was bothered about anything because the expression on her face was indifferent. After some few more hours of search, she decided to ask him, and he handed over the item to her in the twinkle of an eye. She felt like crying, but it was not the fault of the colleague after all.

Case Study III: Criminals do use a Botoxed face for the purpose of deception. People have argued that those who take to crime are lazy and running away from reality, and I have had reasons to tell them that, ironically, crime is more demanding than many legal jobs. Those who had Botox make it difficult for people to accurately read their expressions. With that, they will not have to be bothered about the probability of their co-interlocutors guessing what they are thinking through their facial expressions. If you try to read someone's facial expressions for a few times and hit the rocks, you will probably stop, and that is the exact intent of criminals, to frustrate you from digging deep into their ways.

4.4.   Stress Lines on the Forehead

Generic Interpretations of the Concept

By the mention of *stress lines*, almost everyone on the surface of the earth understands the point one is trying to make. In short, whether life is fair to you or not, stress lines are a common feature among humans. The only difference is that while some people have them at a very young age, in others, they only appear much more later in life. Stress lines are the deep grooves on our foreheads. Life is not a bed of roses; those of us who have sworn to toil and live through honest means struggle every day of our lives. As time goes by, the stress lines begin to appear on our forehead as a mark of our life experiences. They may be accompanied by furrows and other indentations.

When you see the stress lines on the forehead of a person, it is a reflection of a stressful or difficult life; the person has been etching it out with life. It means the life of the person can be summed up as struggle. Another possible interpretation is that the person has spent much time under the sun. A person who is always under the scorching sun will definitely have these marks more pronounced than others who tend to work under a cool atmosphere.

Scientific Explanations

Mentalizer Education describes this body language gesture as the 'most obvious expression that a person's forehead can show'. The reason being that when the forehead is wrinkled, people easily notice it. Stress lines are connected to the movement of the eyebrows in the upward position. Thus, we can reliably assert that this body gesture is meant to enhance facial expression cues. Mentalizer Education makes it known that this gesture is used in the depiction of negativity. It may be seen on a suffering person. Also, a person frowns their face if they do not get a desirable result where they had expected such. For instance, if a supervisor wrinkles his face, it means someone has done a bad job, and it means every other person has to sit tight because he can easily get annoyed at this point.

Another platform, Simply Body Language, refers to this signal as a scrunching body language. When the forehead is scrunched, it means the forehead muscles are forcefully pulled together in order for it to wrinkle at the centre. In the weirdest interpretation, it is usually described as a sign of madness. But in a subtle manner, it can be described as a signal of intense concentration. This sign can be seen in a person watching an interesting movie; they would be fully concentrated. If the person is talking, it means they are serious and concerned about what they are discussing; they crave for results, and something urgent should be done before situations get out of hand. However, since we cannot isolate non-verbal signals and have 100 per cent accuracy, I want to state that the interpretation of this gesture is still dependent on other factors (Simply Body Language 2019).

On his own part, Gregg Williams opines that when a person shows a wrinkled forehead—which is unnatural—it signals stress. Hence, if a person does not develop it, it means they are calm and easy-going; they have nothing to be bothered about. And finally, on this, I will discuss the postulation by Nick Morgan. He believes that for most people, our known attitude is expressed in the forehead. He affirms that this is most prevalent when one is above the age of thirty. He likens this behaviour to open body language. According to him, the deeper the wrinkles of a person are, the more open they are. Ideally, an open person does raise their eyebrows and wrinkle their forehead while they search for a response. Although people tend to fake almost everything, but I want you to be sure that this signal still remains one of the most reliable body language gestures.

Practical Illustrations

Case Study I: I have explored this concept under different interpretations and may not illustrate all in a practical form. However, let's consider the few that we can. A person who is always involved in hard work, such as working in the power room of a factory, will definitely show this body signal—it connotes their negative experiences over the years. Being under the sun coupled with the kind of work they do makes it appear on their face.

Case Study II: If you are dealing with a person in the interview room and they seem to be fully concentrated on you with their forehead wrinkled, this means that they are really stressed by the session. It does not necessarily mean the person is telling lies or so, they may not be used to such scenarios in times past. So coming under an intense intellectual conversation for the first time would be strange and baffling. In a way, they may be communicating the need to have a break so that they can have some rest and continue. If you should proceed with the process without heeding their request, they may begin to alter words that may be self-indicting because they are really tired.

Case Study III: When you are in the office and your supervisor is conducting a routine check and after going through the work of a colleague, you see him wrinkle his forehead, it means he is not satisfied with what he has just checked. You need to be prepared and make some final touches to yours because if they notice the same mistake in your work, they can explode at your inconsistency.

Case Study IV: At home, if you are speaking with your child while they are working on their homework and they wrinkle their forehead, it means they are fully concentrated on the academic exercise before them and not what you are saying. This is an indication that the work is somehow tedious for them, and they are trying to give it all the attention it deserves to get it done. At this point, nothing really bothers them like having a breakthrough concerning the work before them. The same thing applies to a wife focused on a TV show.

4.5. Sweating on the Forehead

Generic Interpretations of the Concept

Let me hit the nail on its head from the start of this topic. If you see a person sweating on their forehead, it is surely a sign of stress. Most probably, it is an indication of being highly stressed. However, let me pause a little bit and make some clarifications. Sweat is personal; how and what causes it in every individual is different. To some, climbing a few flights of stairs will make them sweat profusely, while to others, it is by sipping coffee. The reason for saying this is that you need to make sure you establish the baseline of a person before reaching a conclusion. So a person coming for an interview who just climbed a flight of stairs to your office may be sweating on the forehead. This does not translate to fear or pressure. This is also applied to a person offered with hot coffee in a boardroom.

From the foregoing, a baseline behaviour is defined as the 'normal behaviour of a person when they are relaxed or not under any pressure'. It is what we see in a person when they are not stressed or necessarily affected by the purgation of emotions propelled by any given incident. So having established the baseline, if there is nothing physical about it, it means the person is stressed.

Scientific Explanations

According to Changing Minds, 'We often sweat more from the forehead than other parts of the body, making it significant in sending moisture-related signals.' This is an indication that there is an array of reasons that can cause forehead sweating. When a person is hot, they can sweat on the forehead. This may be external temperature-induced caused by physical exercise or even the arousal of inner strength. The body language platform also notes that if the sweat is cold, it can be interpreted as a sign of extreme anxiety. For you to be sure, this is mostly accompanied by damp eyes (Changing Minds 2019).

Another body language expert, Christopher Philip, affirms that 'sweating is a universal signal of stress or of the body's attempt to regulate a high temperature'. This short expression aligns with both literal and metaphorical interpretations of the concept. So if you see a person sweating on the forehead, if it is not a sign of high temperature, it is an indication of being stressed. In short, sweating is not always taken to be a positive body gesture. Apart from a physical exercise situation, in the realm of business or formal gathering, sweating is a highly negative signal. For the sake of these reasons, you should consider controlling your sweat through the use of antiperspirants. If it, however, becomes extreme (involving medical situation), you need to go for treatment so that medical experts can eliminate such sweat from its roots (Chris 2014)

However, there is an exception to the interpretations we have given so far. Forehead sweating is generally considered a positive cue in dating scenarios. This is likened to the primitive animal condition. Photo shoots and infomercials are some of the events that can cause forehead sweating in emotional partners, which can in turn create arousal in both men and women. Sweating can also be as a result of heat generated through sex. It is a known fact that stress is energy-consuming. After a romp, both partners are usually left in a sweaty state (Chris 2014).

Mentalizer Education (2019) also aligns itself with this submission. It notes that after establishing the baseline and you see a person's forehead sweating, it means they are sexually aroused or excited about a given event. However, if you cannot pin any positive reason to this action, it is an indication that the person just got into an unimaginable trouble.

Practical Illustrations

Case Study I: If you are walking on the roadside and you see a person sweating, look at their dressing. If they are in shorts and vest, it means they are doing a physical exercise. However, if the person is formally addressed, walking on a fast pace, looking straight and somehow focused, it means they are troubled by something. Maybe he has missed an appointment or something ill has occurred where they are heading and their attention is needed immediately.

Case Study II: If you visit a couple at home and they are just coming out from the inner room, sweating and panting a little bit, this is an indication that you just stopped them from 'real action'. It means they were having sex when you came in. When you check the expression on their faces, you would most probably notice satisfaction (you should be able to read their facial expression if their face is not Botoxed).

Case Study III: If you see a colleague sweating through the forehead and you are certain that the air conditioning is working well, he or she may just be emotionally aroused. Maybe a good-looking client has just walked in who has charged their emotions. Also, it may indicate excitement. Imagine a co-worker who just complained to you some few hours ago that they were in dire need of money, and unexpectedly, the payment for the month was made before the scheduled payday. At first, they will not believe it, and their inner arousal will cause them to start sweating on the forehead.

Case Study IV: An applicant has been delayed outside for hours before being invited in, and when she got in, she met some stern faces focusing on her. This can be troubling for her. The feeling of boredom in her will suddenly change to pressure, and in no time, she would begin to sweat excessively. The various activities she has undergone have changed her body system, and the result is being displayed through sweating.

Case Study V: While interviewing a suspect and he begins to sweat on the forehead, it means he is trying to surrender himself to you. In other words, he is accepting the fact that he just landed in trouble. If you push further by asking questions related to the issue at hand, they will try hard to lie, and this is also a stress-inducing action. Hence, you will notice him sweating more.

4.6. Throbbing of the Temporal Vein

Generic Interpretations of the Concept

This is another body gesture that is related to the forehead when a person is under stress. However, this is a little bit unique because it is more an internal action rather than external. When you are under stress, your superficial temporal veins (those that are closest to the skin on your head and located beneath the eyes) may throb or pulse visibly. This accurately indicates autonomic arousal which may be propelled by anger, fear, concern, anxiety, or even excitement in some rare instances. This form of body language is a technique deployed by the brain to automatically switch to survival mode when threatened by an unusual occurrence. During this process, the human brain compels the lungs and heart to work on a faster pace in preparation for the physical activity that may accompany this action—that is, all the essential parts of the body are prepared to either fight or take flight.

When you are faced with an unusual action that threatens your peace, this part of the body, centrally controlled by the brain, is put into action. If you are met with stiff opposition in an unexpected place, having surveyed and weighed your options, you may decide to fight your way through or retreat. At this point, this body gesture would be seen on you. In simpler terms, this body gesture is an indication that you are not in your normal mode—either taken by a positive or negative action that is unusual.

Scientific Explanations

Scholars that contributed to this topic looked at it from the medical point of view. According to Harvard Medical School, when you feel throbbing pain on your temples, especially if the pain is felt at just the side, it is considered a sign of migraine. The temporal arteritis is caused by the inflammation of the large temporal arteritis located on either side of the head. Experts note that the pain in women is twice as that of men. People who usually witness this pain are of age fifty and above. People with this pain describe it as being severe, burning, and throbbing. Some aligning symptoms are fatigue, loss of weight, low-grade fever, tender scalp, or loss of appetite (HMS 2018).

At present, medical experts cannot explain what triggers this pain, but it is generally opined that it 'involves a misguided immune response in which antibodies attack the blood vessel walls'. This can affect smooth flow of blood. In many cases, the arteries become entirely blocked. If it affects the retina, the vision of the affected eye is threatened. If the artery serving the brain suffers impairment, one is likely to suffer from stroke. The soothing message here is that it can easily be treated if detected early.

Adrienne Santos (2018) lists stress as the first possible cause of feeling of pressure at the temples. If pressure in the temple is the only symptom you feel, there is a probability that the muscle in your neck, jaws, or face are tensed. However, in this study, our major focus is on the muscles of the face. This could be as a result of stress, fear, anxiety, poor posture, or even fatigue.

Changing Minds (2019) also shares the same sentiment while contributing to this topic. The platform notes that 'rubbing the temples either side can indicate stress as the person tries to massage away the actual or implicit headache'. This is where we dwell most as it provides a clear interpretation of the concept; it gives a psychological brief on body language. Note that this form of massaging is only possible when the headache is not severe—it is just developing. Having said all these, there is no gainsaying that this body gesture is more of biology than psychology, but being able to provide a balance is what makes the difference.

Practical Illustrations

Case Study I: Imagine you are just walking into your office on a Monday morning and something that resembles a corpse lies at the door of your office. There is no doubt that you would be taken aback. Hence, you may have to move back first and have a vivid look at what is happening.

Now let's make it gender specific. If it were a lady, she will run back, scream uncontrollably, and will never return until she has some escorts. For a courageous man, he would move back and then approach the lying object to see what it is. At this point, they will massage their temporal veins. For the lady, it is a sign of flight, while that of the man can be taken as fight (both are survival instincts activated by the brain).

Case Study II: At the home setting, your spouse picks up your phone while you were away, and a suspicious message dropped in, which aroused the curiosity in her. She decided to take a look at some of the contents on the phone. You thought you have a strong password that cannot be guessed by anyone, but there she is; she knows it. Upon opening the first app, what she saw is your conversation with some other woman on a dating platform. At this point, you returned to the living room. If her temporal veins throb visibly, this indicates excessive anger. She is angry at you and connotes that you are betraying her. At that point, she may feel like walking out, pouncing on you, or getting some other things done—she would be disorganised.

Case Study III: At the workplace, a colleague just went through an email that popped up and kept quiet. Maybe he was really happy and was conversing with you before the message came in, but immediately, he kept shut, and upon looking at his face, you saw the temporal veins throbbing in a very glaring way. This means the email he just read is serving as a source of concern to him. Probably, he has been transferred to another branch or given a demanding job. At this point, you can be empathetic enough to ask them what went wrong so as to take them out of the state of loneliness.

Case Study IV: When criminals do not find something as easy as earlier projected, they may also display this gesture. I can vividly recall the case of a human smuggler who was intercepted at the border. From the look of things, he had always had a field day until my colleagues and I were deployed to the location. His reactions to seeing new officers at the border showed someone who was bothered. I got to know this and invited him for questioning. Even before asking him any question at all, his temporal veins were throbbing in a visible manner that I had to calm him first. I knew he was a criminal before the interview, and not too long into the investigation, he confessed.

4.7. Massaging the Forehead

Generic Interpretations of the Concept

Forehead massaging is a literal action we all take when we have a mild headache; it is a pacifying act engineered to relieve us of our pain. However, there are many metaphorical actions emboldened in this body language gesture. First, we use our hands to massage or rub our forehead while processing information. It means we are really trying hard to digest the piece of information or recall something at that point in time. A person who is really moved by this action will hit their forehead spontaneously and frown a little bit. This indicates the sincerity of their forgetfulness and urge to recall the information at that point.

Second, this body gesture is noticed in a person when they have some concerns or worries. Sometimes, life decides to be unfair to us, and the way in which individuals handle such challenges are different. A worried person may decide not to disclose their challenges to anybody. So the act of rubbing their forehead is to assure themselves that they will get through the issue and return to their normal selves. Another possible interpretation of this gesture is anxiety. Fear is not necessarily being confronted by an unfortunate situation in the physical form; nurturing the thought can also birth this feeling in us. A person who had never made public presentation in their life but were told would be defending their last project before the company board would suddenly switch to this body gesture.

Forehead massage is a well-known body language cue for soothing apprehension and tension. It is not the absence of fear; it is being able to manage such emotional purgation. So when you see a person rubbing their forehead, it means something is wrong, but it is still within their control. Now we may consider what scholars say about it.

Scientific Explanations

As stated earlier, this is a well-known body language that is related to negative thoughts. Many platforms and scholars share their opinion about this gesture. Changing Minds notes that the forehead may be massaged with the intent of propping up the head; the thumb would be made to touch the side of the head. However, it goes beyond that. IYSS lists forehead massaging as part of the key discomfort signals. The platform believes that there are nerve endings in our face, and that is why some people will rub their forehead in a bid to comfort themselves. Other related behaviours are rubbing of the lips and eyes and playing with the hair. All these are means of self-pacification.

Christopher Philip (2014) gives a detailed explanation of the concept. According to him, massaging the forehead can propel to come up with unimaginable solutions. However, if this body gesture is not effective in birthing solution-driven thoughts, it is a means of showing others that we are working hard to get something done. When others see this gesture in us, they believe we are being mindful and trying to process a piece of information. Hence, they will give you the chance to think through and come up with something that is worth working with. According to Chris, the verbal translation of this gesture is this: 'I'm in distress, and I figure if I massage my head long enough, my brain will be able to come to some sort of conclusion or solution.' This body gesture has a similar meaning with rubbing the temples.

Study Body Language (SBL) notes that this gesture is a closed body language—it means you are not open to communication from anybody. You want to be left alone because you are trying to figure out something. The platform concludes that 'another common explanation is that it can be a contemplative state, thinking about new ideas or reflecting upon positive events'. This is in tandem with the submission of Chris.

Practical Illustrations

Case Study I: While in the interview room, you are engaging a suspect, and the session has been flowing in a very interesting manner. However, after asking the suspect a question, they decide to rub their hands on their forehead. This means they are trying to recall that particular information. What this suggests to the law enforcement official is that the suspect definitely knows something about what you have asked. If after thinking they now deny that they do know anything about it, they are lying. On the other hand, massaging their forehead means they are contemplating over an issue—*Should I say it or not?* They know that saying it may land them in trouble and that not saying it does not guarantee their freedom.

Case Study II: In the school setting, you are invigilating your pupils during exams, and moving nearer to a student, you saw him rubbing their forehead. This is an indication that he is trying to retrieve a piece of information. In order not to disrupt their chain of thought, you are expected to excuse yourself from the student. If you should utter a word at that point, it can destabilise the student and make him forget the entire concept he is ruminating on.

Case Study III: At home, if your child does not return home when he was supposed to and you try to call their school line but it is not connecting, at this point, you would be confused on the next step to take—should you wait further at home or trace him at school? Since the forehead massaging is an unconscious action, you would not know when you will start rubbing your forehead. This is an indication that you are worried. This is usually accompanied by a deep frowning. And then you will become restless for the meantime. Also, if a colleague is trying to narrate a story to you but you do not necessarily believe the content of the narrative, you may begin to subconsciously rub your forehead. If the other person understands how to decode body language, they will understand that this is an expression of doubt. It means you are not convinced on what the person is saying.

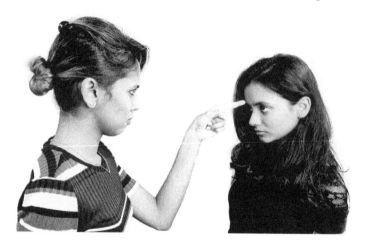

4.8.   Pointing at the Forehead

Generic Interpretations of the Concept

Without any reason, people will not point at the forehead. Of course, there are weird trends of fashion and show of style in the world these days, but we cannot discountenance the real meaning of this gesture. This gesture generally involves pointing a finger at the forehead or making use of the finger to make a screwing motion on the forehead. In most cultures, this is insulting. It is a means of directing your anger to the co-interlocutor or the observer. Since this is a negative body language gesture, it can be interpreted to mean all manners of things.

Some of the likely interpretations to the gesture are saying the observer is stupid, crazy, or ill-informed. It is a means of depicting the other person as being inferior to you intellectually—that is, you are telling them that you are more experienced and gifted than they are. This is usually done in a reaction to an unexpected event. Maybe you had expected the person to put up a good performance than they did, and in annoyance, you reacted to the disappointing outcome. However, it must be stated that this can also birth the same angry reaction from the observer. Nobody wants to be insulted, especially if done in public. Because they do not want to look stupid as you have proclaimed, they will ensure to pay you back in the same coin. If the situation is not stopped immediately, it can result into physical combat.

I need to state that this body gesture is culture-based—mostly seen in Austria, Germany, Switzerland, Africa, and even in the US. In these regions of the world, this body language cue is extremely offensive because of the negative meanings it carries. Hence, it should be avoided like a plague when you find yourself in any of the aforelisted regions before you have yourself to blame.

Scientific Explanations

When we point at a thing, this is an indication that we have interest in them. However, the interest can either be positive or negative. All the same, it is a means of drawing the person's attention to us. So pointing means that we are interested in hurling insults at the person. In groups or other formal gatherings, pointing at the forehead is considered abusive and can only be done by the superior. Even at that, others will consider the sign as being inappropriate and may even break protocol to engage the superior (Changing Minds 2019).

When you point with the twitch of the head to any direction, this is also a means of insult. However, if you should point at a person in this way and do not look at them, it means the insult is lashed out in a subtle manner. A person who makes use of this gesture is obviously informed of the consequences of their action. So in order not to put themselves in a glaring problem, they decide to look away and then demonstrate it. In this occasion, if a conflict should arise, the person can quickly defend himself that he was not focusing on the observer. This is mostly used if a subordinate wants to attack their superior using non-verbal means (Changing Minds 2019).

Pointing is considered as being rude and a threatening behaviour in many cultures of the world. Apart from the index finger, some people make use of the middle finger. It should be noted that the middle finger is considered as being more shocking and ruder. It is an invariable way of saying you do not give a dime about the thought of others. The pointing is done excessively when a person is indescribably angry. At this point, they are no longer under the influence of their conscious mind but the unconscious—that is why they are daring and can challenge any authority, something that could not have been done if they were normal (Changing Minds 2019).

Practical Illustrations

Case Study I: This gesture is usually noticeable when someone is angry or intentionally wants to get another person out of their nerves. It may be employed to pass a subtle message about your undiscerning spirit. For instance, if a terrorist should gain entrance to a location which they had thought was impossible, they will make use of this gesture to tell you how stupid you are as a security guard. Usually, while making this gesture, the terrorist will not look back in order not to be suspected; he would point at his forehead while he backs and keeps walking just as a way of mocking the laxity of the security system.

Case Study II: While in another country or region of the world where you do not really understand their culture, if you do something unexpected which they really frown at, they may point at their forehead to show how ill-informed you are. For instance, in Japan, it is believed that their culture does not favour looking at a person, especially a superior, in the face, an attitude that is highly encouraged in the Western world. If you are oblivious of this fact and keep staring at them, they will subtly insult you by pointing at their forehead. Others who are around may smile at your ignorance. Since you are lost in the labyrinth of cultural complexities, this may not really be meaningful to you—you would be wondering where you missed it until someone takes out time to explain everything to you.

Case Study III: Some rude students are found in the school setting too. Since they are intelligent, they think they can challenge the authority of their teachers at will. If the teacher should mistakenly write a wrong item on the board or miss a step while doing a calculation, they will openly call the attention of the teacher to it and even point at their forehead to mean that the teacher is stupid enough not to know that he or she has committed such a fatal error. If the student is not tamed on time, they will grow up with this rudeness and display it at any given opportunity.

Case Study IV: My encounter with prostitutes on different occasions has made this gesture an easy-to-remember one for me. Some of them will come into hotels and think they can do whatever pleases them. When you try to caution them, they will become angry, and at this point, it takes much efforts to stop them. As a way of getting back at me, they will begin to point at their forehead. Since I know what they are up to, I would be patient till everything calms down. In a few occasions, some of them would walk out of the hotel. Their intention is to create nuisance in the environment.

4.9.   Pressing the Hand on the Forehead

Generic Interpretations of the Concept

This gesture is a soothing one that is done when a person is stressed as a means of releasing tension from the head. The head houses the brain, and you believe it should first calm down before any other part of the body. This body language gesture is done by pressing the palm of the hand gently on the forehead for some moments while you feel the impulse. However, let me clarify that this cue is different from the slapping of the forehead gesture which is usually done as a means of self-punishment or showing that one is pained by a particular occurrence. Talking of this gesture (pressing the hand on the forehead), it is done as if you want to gently push the head backwards.

This is done by a person who is battling with doubt which they want to do away with. There are people who find it difficult to believe stories; this may be caused by their past experiences where people had betrayed their trust and taken them for granted. So any time they find themselves in that scenario, the subconscious mind quickly recalls the past events, and then they have to battle with acceptability or not. This induces stress and weakens their mental state. As a means of taking off the tension, they will place their hand on their forehead in a self-assuring manner. This moment is always solemn.

Also, the gesture is portrayed when a person is insecure. Insecurity can be caused by different reasons—psychological and physical. A person who is telling lies would be insecure because of the fear of being found out. Also, someone who is exposed to a physically challenging situation, such as armed robbery, bomb blast, or shooting spree, would be insecure. This is more so if they have never witnessed such a situation before. Immediately after the incident, they would be seen pacifying themselves. As with other touching non-verbal acts, this gesture is primarily designed to soothe the subject psychologically through the tactile pressure of the skin.

Scientific Explanations

In a way, this body gesture can be considered as cocooning—that is, body gesture that communicates our intent of not wanting to be bothered. When you place the palm of your hands on your forehead, you are communicating both literal and metaphorical messages. Literal in the sense that you want everyone to leave you to yourself; you want to be alone and pacify yourself until you are fully recovered. Covering the forehead will subtly block the eyes, and this means you are giving others around you 'the blinders up'. When people cannot have a full view of you, it would be difficult for them to initiate any form of conversation. On the metaphorical level, you are taking out tension. It is generally agreed among body language experts that when the hands touch any part of the body, they pacify those parts—there is a direct link of skin which generates some warmth that keeps the body alive (Chris 2014).

According to the view of Changing Minds, this sign is commonly used when a person is nervous; it is a gesture of anxiety. With the touch on the forehead, it is like refuelling and telling themselves that they can cross the bridge. In other words, it is like building their courage in order to do the unthinkable. It may also signal tiredness. The head is a little bit heavy, and when feeling weak, we use our hands to touch it. Pressing the palm to the forehead is to make sure that the head is relaxed. A person who has been on an intellectual assignment all day will touch their forehead so as to recuperate before finally taking their rest (Changing Minds 2019).

In some cases, people tend to do this after slapping their forehead. The slapping is a means of self-punishment for forgetting what they were not supposed to. However, after hitting themselves on the forehead, they will now pacify themselves by pressing their hand on the forehead. This is telling themselves that the forgetfulness was not entirely their fault and that they do not deserve to be punished (IndiaBIX 2019).

Practical Illustrations

Case Study I: Let me paint this scenario: your child was up early, took care of themselves, and then headed to school. It was on a Monday and, as such, the busiest day in school. As a prefect, he would be more engaged than many of his colleagues. Their mathematics teacher came in, explained a concept which seemed somehow difficult, but time was against the teacher. So he could not explain better before the end of the class. It is expected of the teacher to give a take-home assignment. Upon getting home, what your boy first did was to greet you, then he undressed and rushed to the study to battle with the assignment. He was there for some few hours before he had headway. Upon finishing up with that, he rushed out to help you with some chores before deciding to take some rest. Before falling back to bed, he pressed his palm on his forehead. This is not a sign of headache but self-pacification. He is trying to calm himself and then move on with life.

Case Study II: In the office, you saw a junior colleague bombarded with work by your superior, and for seven to eight hours, it seemed as if that colleague went dumb—no communication, no smile, no side talks. If at the end of shift you see them pressing their hand on their forehead, it means they are really tired and trying to recharge themselves before getting home. It is a way of rebuilding the body so that they can be physically strengthened. If not, they may not be able to drive home.

Case Study III: This scenario is commonly witnessed in the interview room too. A suspect who had thought that their fabricated stories would work against the officials would be forced to rearrange their fabricated stories if caught unawares. This is too much an intellectual rigour, which they can bear. If the process becomes more intense, they would feel like collapsing, and at this point, they would unconsciously place their hand on their forehead as a means of dousing tension. This tells you that they are feeling uncomfortable and looking for ways to stabilise themselves.

4.10. Looking in a Puzzled Manner

Generic Interpretations of the Concept

When the area between the eyes are pulled together, they normally lead to the furrowing of the eyebrows. In some instances, it may knit. During this process, the eyes may look away or squint. And some other times, the head is canted slightly to the side. What does this look signal? With the description given above, it surely connotes something negative. It is a feeling of being distressed. When the face of a person is puzzled, it means they are trying hard to figure out something mentally—that is, they have been given a piece of problem to solve which has been very demanding.

Although I referred to this as a connotation of negativity, but let me state that I only said that because of the physical state of the face when this gesture is being displayed. In the real sense, a puzzled look can only be seen on a person when they are intellectually engaged—that is, they are subjecting their cognitive ability into rigorous tests just to work their way around a given problem. The face is puzzled because of the high cognitive load which the head is battling with. It is either the person is recalling something or thinking arduously. In a way, we can say that the look on the face of the person signals confusion—that is, they are not sure of the thought they should align with in order to get a problem solved. So weighing different options is what makes them look confused.

Scientific Explanations

Most of the body language experts and platforms that commented on this body gesture agree that it is a feeling of confusion due to the intellectual assignment the person has currently embarked on. Christopher Philip (2014) describes this gesture as 'a face that is compressed or contorted by various muscles such as the one between the eyebrows. This muscle will force the eyebrows together creating a wrinkle. The eyes are squinted and the lips are compressed or pursed.' The above illustration paints a perfect picture of a face that is tense. Merely reading the face from afar, you would discover that it is either stressed or uneasy—that is, the person is bothered by something. Such face may indicate stress, discomfort, or worry.

A puzzled look is used to register dissatisfaction; this means the person is not content in a given situation. That is why managers and supervisors maintain this look when things do not go as planned. Also, it means that someone is emotionally and physically pained. Such people flex muscles in the face. Anyone who sees this reaction will enquire to know what is wrong. Another instance where a tense face is seen is when a person receives bad news. No right-thinking person will jump for joy when they receive ill news about something they hold dear. So the tense face is to unconsciously show that they are pained by the incident and, as such, the news is depressing. Hence, a puzzled look means you want to show others that you are not in your normal state or that something is disturbing you (Chris 2014).

Hope (2013) also buttresses the point made by Chris in his submission. He said for a person to know an expression of confusion, you need to focus on the forehead and nose. The forehead would be scrunched up, and in some cases, an eyebrow would be raised higher than the other. Even the lips are compressed as an aiding signal. This scholar traces the origin of human confusion to chimpanzees. He notes that 'confusion represents a lack of understanding, and the expression itself is created by one increasing their efforts to understand something. When a chimpanzee, especially a younger one, experiences a new sensation for the first time, a look of surprise or confusion appears that is very similar to the human one.' There is an innate desire in the two creatures to understand what goes around in their world; this is expressed at different levels though.

Practical Illustrations

Case Study I: The best place to see a puzzled look is at exams or job interviews. For instance, a student is asked to list, explain, and exemplify a concept. However, the concept looks very confusing, yet the ultimate rule in every examination setting is to do what you were told without asking any other person. At this point, many of the students will begin to rack their brain. If you should shift your attention to their facial expressions, you would see them squinting and looking puzzled. This means they are totally confused on the subject matter. Also, at the interview setting, if you ask a job applicant a question and instead of them looking at you directly and providing the answer, they are looking around, squinting their face, and looking tense. This means that they do not know the right answer. So they are trying to think hard and see if they will get an answer along that line to provide to the panellists. For that moment, you would see confusion written all over them.

Case Study II: Let me also duplicate the example given by Chris on his platform thus: 'As the details of the contract became clear, his face began to show signs of disagreement. When the split was offered at 40/60, his eyes squinted. When there was an additional royalty added, his lips compressed. The deal breaker came when he stated the he would be completely bought out of the company at the five-year mark. This caused his forehead to furrow in anger. His body language clearly signalled that he had had enough with the contract and he wouldn't sign it.'

Case Study III: Another instance where you can witness this body gesture is when a criminal is being investigated. The session is always tensed on a natural level. If you ask a suspect to tell you about their involvement in the crime under investigation, they will deny. Try asking them where they were on that particular day and time the event occurred. Listen to their defence and pay attention to their forehead as they answer the question. Since the question has made them uncomfortable, they will wear a tense face. This tells you that whatever answer you are fed with is fabricated just for the purpose of deceiving you.

4.11. Covering the Forehead with a Hat

Generic Interpretations of the Concept

My mantra is that nothing just happens out of the blue; before anything happens, the signs would have been made glaring enough to those observant enough to pick on. If a person should cover their forehead with a hat or a headgear, it means they are trying to run away from something. Sometimes, they make use of a hood or a visor. A major cause of this body language gesture is stress. When people have worked themselves out, they will cover their forehead with hat so that no one will know how they feel. At this point, I expected you to have known that stress-inducing activities are not just physical but also psychological. A criminal who went to spy on a mall and had to deceive people so as to get the needed information will surely be stressed, but because they have covered their forehead with a hat, it would be hard for anyone to know this and give them a challenge.

Although this sign is mostly seen in children and teenagers, adults also exhibit it. Watch law violators for this gesture. If any commercial driver is fined for overspeeding, they normal use their hat to cover their forehead as a means of expressing their shame. This is also a closed body language—that is, using a hat to cover their forehead will prevent people from talking with them. The hat is like a fence that blocks the wearer away from other people. Also, as social beings, we all subconsciously crave for open discussions where we are able to freely see the co-interlocutor in order to read the expressions on their face. If someone now intentionally covers their forehead just in a bid to prevent people from reading their non-verbal clues, it means they are blocking all forms of communication with people.

Scientific Explanations

When you cover the forehead with a hat, it is like lowering it because your head is buried. This is what most people do when they feel shameful of their act. If it is in public, they will keep the head tucked in until they leave that venue or till everyone departs. When you artificially cover the forehead, you will have to look at people you are dealing with under the eyebrow. When you cover the head, you are trying to guide it against an attack; it is a protective step. Just like any other closed body language, it means that trust is lacking in the conversation—the person covering their head does not trust you. They are afraid that you may do something evil to them, and that is why they are using their hat to guard one of the most delicate parts of the head (Chris 2013).

Primarily, this gesture comes like a childlike cue because kids are shorter than adults. Chris submits that 'as we age, we recall these gestures and go back to them when we wish to revive juvenile submissive feelings'. What I want to emphasise on is *submissive feelings*. After doing something bad, we cannot stand up to own our responsibilities, and hence, we become docile. We submit ourselves to the bidding of those around us so as to save ourselves from undue punishment. When you act like a child, it means you are submissive about your offences and ready to apologise if you have the opportunity. Threat is a recurring aspect in our lives, and that is why people are covering their forehead so as not to fall victim of undue situation. This gesture may also signal anger which is suppressed. If you do not want people to know that you are irritated by an event, you can cover your forehead with a hat (Chris 2013).

Linda (2019) also notes that this body gesture is reminiscence of negative feelings. She describes this body cue as both 'physical and psychological' threat. When you are in physical danger, you look for all means to protect your forehead;

when anything hits it, it is like hitting the brain. A person who maintains this gesture is invariably saying that they cannot defend themselves. Another possible interpretation to this body gesture is fatigue.

Practical Illustrations

Case Study I: She walks confidently into the shopping mall, performs some few security checks, goes around aimlessly in the mall, and pays attention to the alertness of the security guards. She picks some items and drops them immediately. She sees another face focusing on her. Here comes an opportunity for her to cart away with some valuables as it seems that the guard in this section is relaxed. Note that this is just a test run of the major operation. As she bends to pick the product, hide it, and dash for the main entrance, a pair of eyes is set on her—a fixed gaze for that matter. She is now between the devil and the deep blue sea—either she returns the product immediately and suffer some reproach or challenge the competence of the security guard and is later apprehended. The first option seems more plausible, and there she is, dropping the item gently with the guard's eyes still focused on her. What is now left is how she would surmount the courage to walk out of the mall. She uses her scarf to cover the forehead, and there she goes! This is a sign of embarrassment.

Case Study II: Another instance is a man who strolls to the house of his mistress on the other street, deceiving his spouse with some lies of having to exercise around the community. Upon getting to the mistress's place, there was the legal husband of the woman sitting and looking with a stern face. He wanted to hide under the pretext of a friend, but the woman knew that she would be asked endless questions when this 'friend' finally leaves. So she decided to deny knowing him at all. There was the husband who was physically ready to pounce but did not for the sake of the law. This embarrassed man had to run uncontrollably home, but the wife must not know that such a thing had happened. One of the most reliable means of understanding people is through their forehead language, but he had covered such with a hat because he did not want his wife to know.

Case Study III: Criminals do use this non-verbal gesture in different contexts to achieve their selfish purposes. While I was active in service, I saw this as a common display among those with expired permits. They are overstaying in the country, and they know their action is illegal. As such, they are common targets to law enforcement officers. Hence, while walking on the street, they will cover their forehead with a hat. This is to conceal their identity. Since you will have difficulty in identifying them, it means they may not be fished out any time soon. Also, covering their forehead will make it difficult for you to have a full view of their face to know how they look like.

CHAPTER 5

The Eyebrows

The eyebrows are an indispensable part of the human body, and they are also sacrosanct in understanding the innate thoughts of people. People erroneously think it is meant for beauty alone, but I can boldly say that it is one of the powerhouses of non-verbal expressions. Before I start relating it to body language, let me give a physical description and features of the eyebrows. They lie above the supraorbital arches of our eye sockets and serve different functions. Let's consider some of the functions in the succeeding paragraphs.

The major function of the eyebrows is to protect our eyes from sunlight, rain, and moisture. The way they are arched makes it possible for water to bypass the eyes. Our eyes are the most important part of the body, and as such, the eyebrows are serving as invaluable support system to their survival. Hence, the eyebrows keep the eyes free from invasion of particles from external sources (Squezze 2013). Since evolution, the human body has gone through changes with some unnecessary parts clipped off. If the eyebrows were not so important, they would have disappeared. The eyebrows are prominent for keeping our eyes free of moisture, which aids our visibility. It is an open secret that sweat is salty and, as such, not ideal for our eyes. It is the duty of the eyebrows to ensure that the sweat do not get into our eyes.

Research shows that genetics plays a huge role in how our individual eyebrows look like—that is, the shape, thickness, and colour of the eyebrows can be inherited. In a study carried out along this line in 2015, it was found that there is a strong link between an inherited eyebrow appearance and some given genes. For instance, there are four separate genes that may affect the eyebrow texture, one determines the shape, five other genes determine hair colour of our eyebrows, and finally, a gene determines if you will develop a monobrow or not (Cirino 2018).

In the same vein, we cannot discard the role of environmental factors in determining the development of eyebrows. Long duration of tweezing or waxing the eyebrows can change the shape permanently. Also, having injuries around the eyebrows can permanently alter their look and growth. Research also shows that the abnormalities with eyebrows can also be inherited. One is madarosis, which is the loss of eyebrows. This has been traced to some inherited disorders (Cirino 2018).

Eyebrows are also crucial in the identification of facial features. In a study led by neuroscientist Javid Sadr and colleagues at MIT, it was found that eyebrows help in the identification trait. And this explains one of the reasons why they have not disappeared from the human body. According to the scholars, a face without eyebrows is likened to a city without reference (Sadr 2003). The thrust of the study was to establish that eyebrows aid in facial recognition. The researchers invited about fifty volunteers to identify celebrities' faces. The photos of most of the celebrities were altered digitally—taking out the eyes or eyebrows in others. The result reveals that 60 per cent of the time, the volunteers could identify celebrities whose eyes have been altered, while on the other hand, only a paltry 46 per cent were able to recognise people whose eyebrows were altered. Hence, the study concludes that eyebrows are equally important as eyes in identifying people. For instance, if a person injects Botox on their face, alters the colour of the eyes, or even wears sunglasses, it would still be easy to identify the person. However, if the person should shave their eyebrows, it would be a herculean task to identify them with the naked eyes.

Sadr postulates that the key reason for eyebrows to be fundamental in facial recognition is that they themselves help in the expression of feelings and emotions. Thus, the eyebrows in addition to the lips may be the most expressive part of the body when it comes to body language gestures. Furthermore, the shape of our eyebrows reveals germane information about someone's gender, age, and other personal traits. For instance, women's eyebrows are a few millimetres longer than those of men. In the same vein, thick-set eyebrows in males are characteristic of alpha males, while thin, arched brows are common in stylish young females (Pincott 2011). The instances are just too numerous.

Cirino also emphasises the roles of eyebrows in non-verbal communication. According to him, 'Eyebrows are an important part of human expression and communication. They allow us to show our emotions. One raised eyebrow expresses scepticism or interest. Two raised eyebrows can express surprise' (Cirino 2018). Hence, if you want to understand the real emotions of people, you need to learn how to focus on their eyebrows while they talk. It is one of the few parts of the body that cannot be easily controlled, and that is why we refer to it as the seat of true emotions. They facilitate smooth communication among interlocutors—that is, if you are discussing with a person and you know how they feel even without them expressing themselves, you would know whether they are offended by what you are saying or not. So their feeling will hint you on whether to further discourse or change the topic. Desmond Morris (2008) aptly concludes that 'the primary function of the eyebrows is to signal changing mood of their owners'. This is precise and simple!

We have always relied on people's eyebrows to understand them right from our early age. That is why an infant would focus on the eyebrows of their mothers most times. In simpler terms, the eyebrows are very expressive of our individual feelings per time. As I gradually draw the curtain of this section to a close, it is pertinent to note that there is cultural dimension to the eyebrows too. During the Renaissance age, it was believed that shaving the eyebrows was a show of beauty, but there is divergent opinion on that during these contemporary times. More so, each region of the world believes they are culturally unique.

5.1. Flashing the Eyebrows

Generic Interpretations of the Concept

Anywhere you see this, it is a symbol of happiness; arching or flashing the eyebrows is a sign of the excitement of the person. When you receive happy news, your whole body system reacts, no matter how hard you try to keep it to yourself. However, this gesture is a microexpression—it is done in less than one-fifth of a second. This means that if you look away, you would not see this signal in a person. We refer to it as a gravity-defying attitude because it moves in an upward direction. As with other behaviours in this circle, it is a symbol of something positive. At the sight of seeing something pleasing, you flash your eyebrows. This means you are indescribably pleased by what you saw.

Even infants light up any time they see their mother flash up their eyebrows. Although they do not know the source of happiness of their parent, but they surely know through subconscious means that something pleasurable has happened to her. Also, when you are greeting a person and arch your eyebrows, it is a non-verbal means of saying that you are very happy to set your eyes on them. In most instances, they will mirror your behaviour.

There is no gainsaying that this gesture is great and can broker peace in some unexpected situations. Hence, I would not like you to view it as being insignificant in your dealings. In a way, when a person flashes their eyebrows, it is a means of showing empathy; they are telling you that they care about you and can go to any extent to make you happy. So this flash can be invaluably useful and powerful in every endeavour in our life. Imagine a seller flashing their eyebrows at a client. It communicates positivity to the client, and the client would stay with them even if there are some inconsistencies in their service delivery.

Scientific Explanations

According to recent research conducted on this subject matter, it reveals that this body language gesture is most effective when done with people who are already acquainted with each other and also potent among potential lovers. If you are in a crowded room and someone flashes their eyebrows at you, this is an expression of interest in you. In a way, they are trying to say you have met in times past—although this may birth some curiosity in you, but it is an avenue of creating familiarity by the person so that you can start a conversation (Chris 2013).

Although the eyebrow flash is said to be a general positive behaviour, if it is not done in a natural way, it becomes offensive—it can create hostility or anxiety in a person. Flashing your eyebrows at a person who is not in any way connected to you at a formal gathering can make them anxious; you would make them start wondering where they have met with you in times past. In a 1997 study by John Martin, it was discovered that 'the eyebrow flash was totally ineffective between strangers and sometimes even produced negative emotions. He found that people who were eye flashed keep more personal space between themselves and the flashers' (Chris 2013). The gesture is very positive among people who have met in times past. It serves as a means of rebirthing old memories and showing happiness in meeting the person again.

Research also shows that this gesture is better received between different sexes than within the same sex. That is why some experts consider it as a gesture of love. In fact, iVillage (2013) on Today.com listed it as the number one sign a man shows to register his love intent. When you see a person you are attracted to, your eyebrows rise and fall. If the person also likes you, their eyebrows would be raised. It is a microexpression that happens within one-fifth of a second, and it can be seen in every part of the world—it is a universal love gesture. This gesture makes our eyes look brighter and charming for the partner to see. However, it should not be deliberately done because this can be annoying, and the other person may not get the message that you are trying to pass (iVillage 2013).

Practical Illustrations

Case Study I: The eyebrow flash can happen at any given location. For instance, you attend the meeting of your thirty-year class reunion, and you are obviously looking different—you've dropped weight and you're looking smarter. From the other side of the room, you see an old crush, and you dash to their side to exchange pleasantries. Before getting to her, you give a few eyebrow flashes from a distance, and she returns it but quickly turns hers into a wrinkle. With the eyebrow flash, she has shown that she recognised you, but the wrinkle is an indication of confusion—she does not remember where exactly. This means she cannot recall past memories. Hence, you would see the grief muscles flexed between their eyes. This is a subtle gesture that you should not be too jovial with her because you may not like her response.

Case Study II: You are out on a date with your crush, and there was another good-looking man at the other side of the bar who has been keeping pace of your movements since you came in. He has been craving for your eyes to meet, but you are aware that your date is keeping tabs on your activities. Since you cannot stay glued to a direction for hours, you decided to flexibly look at the other side, and the man seated right there gave you an eyebrow flash. This is to tell you that he is interested in you. If you should return the flash immediately, you are giving them the assurance of your availability. Most times, this gesture occurs subconsciously, except for prostitutes that can display it consciously for the purpose of playing to the gallery.

Case Study III: At home, your spouse stays late at work due to some urgent demands and only managed to tell you that he would be coming home late. You are in the mood to play with him, have some intimae discussions, and share some romantic moment—your eyes would be focused on the door. If he eventually comes in and you raise your eyebrows, this is an indication that you are pleased to see him. This is also heart-warming as it would lighten up the mood of the husband.

Case Study IV: Criminal suspects who are into prostitution use this trick to tempt law enforcement officials. This is common to the beautiful ones among them. Since eye contact is an important factor in communication, suspects will take advantage of that to lure law enforcement agents out of the main issue. I remember the case of a lady who was showing all advances to me before going into the interview room, but I appeared to be ignorant of her antics. When we eventually started the investigation and she could not defend herself again, she would flash her eyebrows at me and accompany it with a charming smile. I was determined, and nothing could change my mind!

5.2. Greeting with Eyebrows

Generic Interpretations of the Concept

In this segment, I really want to focus on the social implication of the eyebrow flash. As noted earlier, if deployed appropriately, the eyebrow flash is a symbol of positivity. So I want to expatiate on how you can make the right use of it while trying to greet someone. When you see an old friend from afar or in public, you know that it is abnormal for you to start shouting because you would distract everyone or irritate many people, and ultimately, they will fix their gaze on you for a moment. And yet the person is very dear to you. So what is the way out? Flash your eyebrows at them! Hence, we flash the eyebrows at people we cannot have verbal conversations with at the very moment.

Another use of this gesture is to recognise the presence of a person. For instance, you are going through files and someone came into a meeting, so instead of being distracted, you will flash at them in order to make them know you are aware of their presence. In some instances, this flash is accompanied with a light smile. You should know that this is most appropriate in an informal setting where everything is casual.

If you greet a person with an eyebrow flash and they fail to mirror you, you would quickly notice this. This can be very depressing and frustrating, especially when it comes from people who you do not expect. This gesture is used to tell people that you hold them in high esteem and that despite all odds, you are still showing them some reverence. This gesture is simple but powerful. It is a means of brokering conversation. Also, this form of greeting is the best because of the cultural implications of others such as the handshake, which has different variants.

Scientific Explanations

German behavioural research scientist Eibl-Eibesfeldt has studied the concept of eyebrow flash used in social greeting for decades. One of his findings is that the eyebrow flash 'is a universally recognised long-distance social greeting'. However, there is the Japanese exception to this. In Japan, this gesture is interpreted as an overt sexual invitation. Hence, it is seen as being inappropriate. Apart from the Japanese, every other person sees this gesture as a means of greeting and brokering social relationship. This happens very briefly—within one-fifth of a second. This flash occurs about six to twelve feet away where verbal greetings cannot easily take place (Chris 2013).

Further, this form of greeting can be an expression of surprise. For instance, when you see a loved one in an unexpected location, you make this gesture to greet them. Hence, it can be interpreted verbally as this: 'Hey, I noticed you and am surprised but also fearful because I've been taken off guard.' In this sense, the eyebrow flash informs the person that you are not a threat. Another theory on this subject matter opines that this gesture draws attention to the face in order to make communication less ambiguous.

Another study submits that this body language gesture is rarely seen in people with strained relationship—those who are fighting. You can always try out this gesture with a person you recently had a misunderstanding with. If the person should flash at you, it means they have got over the issue. This gesture is likened to eye contact. When people are fighting, they try as much as possible not to exchange any eye contact under whatever guise. Probably, they do not want the greeting to lead to unwanted interactions. From the foregoing, we can carefully conclude that eyebrow flash is a non-verbal communication starter (Chris 2013).

Hanan Parvez (2019) notes that the eyebrow flash is a conscious action that we choose to elicit to anybody of our choice. It is mostly given out to people we are familiar with or know in times past.

Practical Illustrations

Case Study I: You can use the eyebrow flash to greet people in different occasions. In the office, you are just arriving, and your boss came a minute earlier—maybe he is at the door before he heard the sound of a car and turned back. Since both of you are a distance apart, it would be weird for you to shout and greet him. Instead, you can just flash the eyebrows at him. He may decide to return it with a smile. This means he is happy to see you. However, if it is greeted with a furrowed wrinkle, then you need to be careful. If not, you will ignite the anger in your boss.

Case Study II: Another instance where you can make use of this gesture at the office is when you have a strained relationship with a colleague—maybe you fought at the end of your shift the preceding day. So you want to know if they have got over the issue or not. Doing that verbally can be risky as they may explode and embarrass you! Instead, make use of the eyebrow flash. If the person should flash back, be sure you have been forgiven and can go ahead to apologise verbally. Then you can take things up from there. This is a good gimmick that will save you from unwanted embarrassments.

Case Study III: Surprisingly, I have seen some criminal suspects greet law enforcement officials with an eyebrow flash before the start of investigation. This means the person is confident about the process. There are two polar reasons that can birth this confidence—first, the person is a hardened criminal who knows his onus. He has been interrogated many times before, and he scaled through. As such, he sees this as one of those times. Secondly, it may be an indication that the person was ignorantly apprehended, and they are sure they would prove their innocence at the end of the day. So the person is greeting you because he thinks the whole scenario is not worth birthing unnecessary bitterness.

Case Study IV: Your child who is just coming back from school and never expected to meet you at home will put on a sigh of relief and flash their eyebrows at you once they are at the door as a means of telling you that they are pleased to see you home. Perhaps, you are an absentee parent who does not have time for them, but they internally yearn for it. If you return this flash, you would spur the happiness of the kid because they would subconsciously process this message.

5.3. Arching the Eyebrow in a Tense Situation

Generic Interpretations of the Concept

Not all surprises are pleasant; some can be rude and shocking. And to every action, there is an equal and opposite reaction. In other words, you cannot serve a person with hostility and expect them to be excited about it—they will reply to you in the same negative manner. Hence, eyebrow arching is done when a person is shocked with an occurrence or presented with an unpleasant surprise. When trying to read a person, you can look for other gestures that normally accompany this clue, such as compressed lips or tense face. In short, the overall facial expression of the person would be unwelcoming. This means the experience is really negative.

I know you may be wondering how the same face manages to show both positive and negative reactions. Well, the muscles of the face are the secret behind this. The tension in the muscle control is what differentiates this from the social concept of the eyebrow just discussed above. Another noticeable difference is that this tarries more on the face than the former. Hence, it is more glaring for others to see that something is really wrong with us. And as such, they can intervene in the situation if they care so much.

The muscles of the face ensure that we are able to communicate our innate feelings in an apt manner at all times.

Scientific Explanations

Microexpressions are an important part of understanding human emotions, and they mostly show through the face. You need to know that microexpressions 'are useful when they appear out of congruency with other gestures or language. It is when the facial expression is out of tune with what is being said. For example, telling a positive story while smiling and momentarily flashing a microexpression can mean that the person is lying.' I have taken my time to explain microexpressions because of their link to the gesture under discussion.

When the eyebrows arch to show surprise, they would be curved upwards, wrinkles would form in the forehead, and the eyes would widen to the extent that the whites in them would be very visible. If you focus on the jaws, you would notice that they would be slack and open. I am trying to give all these gestures so that you can pay attention to them while reading a person. Remember that body clues should be read in clusters.

Eyebrow arching is also used when expressing fear, and if you are not careful, you may confuse the facial expression with surprise because there are just a few differences between them. While displaying an expression of fear, the eyebrows rise and are pulled together in a way that they form a curve shape. However, the curve in this is lesser than the one seen in a surprised expression. Wrinkles also appear on the forehead but do not cover the entire forehead as witnessed in an expression of surprise (Chris 2013).

This form of body language gesture may also be used to signal confrontation, aggression, anxiety, or displeasure. When the eyebrows look tense, this is an indication that something bad is happening to the person. If the eyebrows are well-curved that they drop very low, this means that the person is insecure and weak. Weakness can be caused by different things. Workload, psychological activities, and mental depression, among others, are some of the possible causes of weakness in people. And also, when you are introduced to a threatening situation or when you find yourself in a place where you believe your atrocities may be easily found out, you would become insecure. When you see this clue on a person, it connotes defeat and invariably means that the person would not attack you. How do you expect a person in rude shock to fight you? That is why predators and bullies look for this sign in people to identify weak people to take as prey (Chris 2013).

Practical Illustrations

Case Study I: This is mostly seen in the courtrooms. Usually, criminals think that their disjointed lies are too intellectually woven enough to get them out of trouble. This is more so if the law enforcement official plays along with them. If they are eventually charged to court, they would erroneously assume that the proceedings would just be a walkover, after all, the prosecuting team does not have any incriminating evidence against them. However, after getting into the dock and the prosecutor begins to reel out facts about their participation in the crime, at that point, they would be shocked, and one of the clues you would see on their face is the arching of the eyebrows. This is an indication that they are unpleasantly surprised that you could gather such facts against them. In other words, they have given up already due to the magnanimity of facts presented before them.

Case Study II: This gesture is also seen in students after being handed their results for a semester. Many of them write extensively but out of point. So before the result is out, they would be grading themselves on how they had performed excellently. If the teacher now expertly marks and scores them below what they have imagined, they would be depressed and shocked. Their eyebrows would be curved and squinted to show their defeating surprise. At this time, they are depressed, and you will see their countenance being changed.

Case Study III: This gesture can also be witnessed at the workplace. We all love surprises spiced up with varieties. If you work with a company that has different branches across the country or the continent, you should obviously be prepared for transfer at any moment, and let's imagine you have been yearning for one and may have lobbied your way in. The letter eventually comes. You are eager to open the mail in order to know your next destination. After opening it, you discover that you are transferring to a branch whose workers are being overburdened with work. Surely, one of the signs that would be seen on your face is the eyebrows being arched. This is an expression of sadness and shock. This can be very depressing, and for the rest of that day, you may not be able to do anything productive.

5.4.   Arching the Eyebrow at the Chin through the Neck

Generic Interpretations of the Concept

When we arch our eyebrows, the mouth is always closed, chin from the neck. We do this when we hear something that is surprising. It is a doubtful look that we display as a form of reaction to an event that is unexpected. The mouth is closed because we do not want to scream. If we were not to close our mouth, we would scream uncontrollably at such occurrence. Weird occurrences do happen, but some can be extremely unbelievable. When we immediately hear anything like that, we would not be able to overlook such and, as such, will react appropriately.

This behaviour is also displayed in an embarrassing situation. This can be verbally translated as meaning 'I heard that, and I didn't like it.' Maybe what they did was disgusting, and we do not want the person to repeat that attitude. So it is an invariable way of warning the person before you show them your other side. This look is a puzzled form of reacting to an unwanted situation. For instance, when a student behaves in a rude manner, this is the look a teacher gives them as a way of warning before meting out appropriate punishment on them.

Scientific Explanations

This is a body language gesture of suspicion. It is an indication that we do not believe what the other person is saying. When you are discussing with a person and you see cocking their eyebrow, it means they are suspicious of what you are telling them. If you are truly lying, you need to just stop it because they have seen through your deceptive acts. If, however, you are being truthful, you need to do convince the person of the sincerity of your narrative. The verbal translation of this sign is, 'I'm suspicious of your motives so my eyes will show surprise by raising on one side and anger by lowering on the other.' That is, the chin arches towards the neck. This is a general disbelief that can still be corrected (Chris 2013).

This clue is both a representation of aggression and fear. A person may become fearful due to the type of information you are giving them, and this can in turn make them aggressive. Some people detest deception, even in the thinnest sense of it. So when they see the traces of it anywhere, their facial muscles would swing into action, and you would easily notice this sign in them. If you keep the storyline for a long time, they may become agitated and can even burst out verbally.

Also, due to the division of the high and low, when mixed, it is an indication of suspicion and scepticism. This means that there is an aspect of a story that looks very blurring and superficial to believe. This calls for reorientation or reweaving of the story or, in the very least, the need to change the focus of the discourse (Chris 2013). When you see this gesture, it is a call to normalcy, and that is why it has always been used by teachers to caution troublesome students. The gesture is also adopted in order to avoid embarrassment. For instance, if you flash at a person and the person fails to return it, it means there is no room for conversation. If you want to defy this subtle order and start any, you are surely heading for an unimaginable disgrace. The person can walk out of you or simply make you a laughing stock.

Practical Illustrations

Case Study I: Let me start my illustration from the school setting: a teacher has prepared her notes for the day, ready to influence the students and make the class interactive in order to make communication seamless. Upon entering the class, she knows that she is to spend just an hour and must cover the lesson. Hence, everything needs to go as pictured, or else, she should be ready to reply to queries from the management. Upon starting, the students are cooperative, and things have been going on well, until a student is called to make his own contribution to the concept—he has been noticed to be making side comments with some of his colleagues. Now when he has the floor, he starts to behave in a clownish manner and has set the whole class on fire due to his irritating statements. The teacher is gradually losing control of the class, and any member of the management team would show up at any given point for supervision. The teacher knows that she may not be able to caution all the students at once. So she targets the mastermind and sends her non-verbal message by arching her eyebrows and closing her mouth. This means she is trying to caution the troublesome student before unleashing the full wrath of the law on him. Fortunately, the student catches up with the signal.

Case Study II: This body gesture is also seen in the interview room. Most times, for the sake of fair hearing, the criminal suspects are given time to express themselves by saying everything they know about the issue being investigated on before law enforcement officials begin to ask questions. It is at the point of narrating the story that many of the suspects make some unbelievable fabrications. Even an infant would find some of their assertions difficult to believe all in the bid of washing themselves clean of the allegations levelled against them. During this process, it may become irresistible for the law enforcement official to keep things within themselves. So they may just show this body gesture instead of screaming. For a suspect who pays attention to body language, at this point, they will understand that their story is not making any sense to the man at the other side of the table.

Case Study III: This body signal can also be adopted in the home front. When children are just learning to lie, they do it in a very weird manner. They conjoin stories that do not match. Yet they would expect you to believe them hook, line, and sinker. However, with this cautionary sign, it means they should better be careful—that is, the child will get to know that their fabrications did not work out on you.

5.5. Asymmetry of the Eyebrows

Generic Interpretations of the Concept

This body language gesture is seen in people in order to register their uncertainty or doubt about a given topic. How do you notice this gesture? An eyebrow will arch higher while the other one will remain unmoved or, at the very best, move to a lower position than its original state. The asymmetry is meant to question what the other person is saying. In simpler terms, it means the person does not believe your words; they think you are being deceptive. This gesture makes you see the feeling of doubt on the face of the person. Jack Nicholson, a famous movie actor in the US, is famous for this gesture—both formally and informally.

What you are saying may not be entirely false, but the past experiences of the person can heighten their unbelief. For instance, the person has been a victim of falsehood for some period in the past. Their subconscious mind will quickly make them recall those ugly experiences, and they will be making their judgement based on those past incidents and not even the reality on what is on ground. That is why you may be pained that they are obviously making their decision based on what they think and not on the reality lying bare before them. So blame their circumstances and leave them out of the picture.

Scientific Explanations

Christopher Philip (2014) refers to this gesture as an eyebrow cock. This has to do with raising an eyebrow while the other is lowered or made to maintain its position. Hence, this creates a form of mixed eyebrow movement. There is a parallel movement of the two eyebrows—one goes higher, while the other goes lower. In a way, this obvious discrepancy between the two makes it very visible to observers. It is an indication that the person is in general disbelief about the comment you just passed or the action you just did. The verbal interpretation of this gesture can be so interesting. The eyebrow that goes up is communicating surprise. It means the person is disappointed in you for conveying such message; they had expected more from you. Maybe they have always revered your personality. On the other hand, the lowered eyebrow is used to communicate anger. It means they are angry at you for choosing to feed them with a deceptive story. The anger is birthed by the disappointment they have first encountered (Chris 2014).

There are clusters you can follow while reading this body gesture. For instance, if the head tilts to the side while displaying the eyebrow asymmetry, it means the person is sceptical about what you are telling them. However, if the person is communicating aggression with this cue, their eyes would squint and the lips would be compressed. With this, you would be able to know how to deal with people in different circumstances (Chris 2014).

Another body language platform, Study Body Language (SBL), notes that this gesture is used is sowing the seed of doubt into a person's heart. It states that 'if you pick the right moment with the right people, you can easily take advantage of it to undermine someone's authority'. However, if you consciously make it pronounced and extreme, it would be comical, and people will laugh at you instead of seeing it as a call to adjust.

The gesture can also be used for bonding between people. If you are three at a place and the other two are communicating through this means, they are subtly painting your stupidity to each other, and this would strengthen their bond. And finally, it may mean that someone is not impressed. This is usually done by superiors to their subordinates. They are invariably telling the other person to try harder to forge home their point (SBL 2019).

Practical Illustrations

Case Study I: At your workplace, you and your team were sent out to make some enquiries about the next big move of the company. So you wanted to know the feasibility of the initiative before implementing it. You really went to work and did some findings before preparing your report, and on an appointed date, you will be presenting the report to the management board for their evaluation. As the leader, you would be making the presentation on behalf of the team. You have prepared a PowerPoint presentation. After making the presentation for an hour, while some of the audience clapped and nodded at your effort, the CEO raises one of his eyebrows and lowers the other and then tilts his head to the side. This means he is sceptical about your findings—he does not believe it is worth working with. In other words, all the efforts you put into the project are not appreciated.

Case Study II: You and your friend decide to go out and have fun, and upon getting to the location, you meet with another person and, in an inexplicable way, you click with that person. In no time, discussion has started. And the person is the one dominating the discussion. If it gets to a point where you think most of what he is saying is not true and your friend shares the same sentiment with you, your friend can look at you, do the eyebrow asymmetry sign as a way of saying, 'Look, this guy doesn't really know what he's talking about, am I right?' With this, you build the bond with your friend, and if the stranger is not careful, you would soon send him packing.

Case Study III: This sign can also be used within the family. Let's illustrate with the story of a woman and her daughter. The daughter was accused of stealing a doughnut, which she denied. However, there was overwhelming evidence that point to the fact that the young lady was the brain behind the theft. Since the daughter was very vehement about her denial, her mother decided not to pester her further. The mom kept a close look at her, raised an eyebrow and lowered the other, and kept her lips closed. This is a non-verbal sign of suspicion towards the daughter.

Case Study IV: One of the Achilles heels of drug addicts is that they want to consume drugs at every given place. However, those who have been made to pay heavily for such display of illegalities are always cautious of the people around. There was a case of a drug addict in a public space. I guess he was longing for drugs and had some with him. I began to notice him when he became restless. I knew he was up to something, and I wasn't going to engage in any other thing until I see his end. At some point, he noticed me too, and he raised an eyebrow and lowered the other, frowned his face, and looked away. He was suspicious of my identity.

5.6.   Knitting the Eyebrows

Generic Interpretations of the Concept

The area just above the nose and between the eyes is referred to as glabella. When this area becomes furrowed or narrowed through the squinting of the eyebrows, it means all is not well. When a person is positive, they maintain an open body language and look cheerful and hospitable; there is eagerness to speak with other people written on their face. However, the furrowing of the glabella means the person is concerned about something, expressing their dislike over a given concept or trying to solve an issue. It is pertinent to state that this sign is universal—it connotes almost the same meaning all over the world. Looking at this gesture, doing it makes one look ugly and unattractive. So I would have been taken aback to see some cultures of the world using it to mean something positive.

Since it is a microexpression, it happens in the twinkle of an eye, and it takes only an eagle-eyed individual to see it happen. Expectedly, it is one of the truest ways of expressing emotions. Knitting the brow is done when one is told a disturbing story or when one is trying to figure out the sense in a story one is told. Anybody who is nearby will know a person is troubled even without anybody calling their attention to it. Narrowing the eyebrows is like trying to close the eyebrows to the event you are experiencing. It is tantamount to running away from something tragic.

Scientific Explanations

Eyebrows of grief, grief muscle flex, oblique eyebrows of grief, worry facial expression, and eyebrow scrunch are some of the names that Chris gave to this body gesture. Looking at all the synonyms listed above, there is none that hints on a positive idea. In order to identify this gesture in a person, you would notice that 'the eyebrows are raised simultaneously and drawn inward towards each other, producing both horizontal creases in the forehead and vertical creases between the eyebrows. In the oblique eyebrows of grief cue, the eyebrows are pulled upward more so than the other ends' (Chris 2014). In both cases, you would notice that there is forceful movement of the facial muscles. In short, knitting the eyebrows is a signal of physical pain or psychological grief.

To knit the eyebrows, you need to flex the muscles between the brows. This is most potent during your moment of anger, and you want to pass the message to the person who offended you. By looking at your face, they would have understood that you are flaring up. In other form, it can be used as a sign of disapproval. When people who reverence you see you being annoyed, they will quickly adjust their behaviour in order to calm your nerves. According to a research outcome, kids have the power to decode the facial expressions of adults. More so, facial expressions are very crucial to the children; they believe that how you carry your face every time is a true reflection of your internal feelings. In simpler terms, children hardly detect an angry voice like how they do to an angry face. Hence, we can boldly conclude that facial expression is more effective to kids and even to every other age group than verbal utterances (Chris 2014).

Westside Toastmasters (WSTM) notes that this body gesture makes a person look concerned and authoritative. According to the platform, when we lower the eyebrows, it is a means of showing dominance, aggression, or anger towards a thing or another person. When the eyebrows are open, it is a symbol of submissiveness. According to the outcome of a research by Keating and Keating, even other related creatures like monkeys and apes also make use of the same gestures for the same purpose. They also discovered that those who narrow their eyebrows are naturally perceived to be aggressive. Those seeking for one favour or another from people usually maintain the submissive facial expression because they do not want to be considered as being intolerant and aggressive.

Practical Illustrations

Case Study I: I will be starting with a criminal story this time around. A certain man was stopped at the border while trying to gain entrance into the country. The law enforcement official on duty demanded from him if he was carrying drugs or some other incriminating items. But he replied no. However, the official noticed that at the point of answering, the man's eyebrows immediately furrowed and narrowed at the glabella. As an expert in reading body language, the official was able to recognise the man's grief through his facial expression. So he was apprehended and detained. Then he was further questioned in order to establish the truth of the matter. The official was able to arrest him because the suspect's microexpression portrayed him as a liar.

Case Study II: Another example is seen at home. You send your child on an errand before going out to check on your sick friend in the next street and urge her to be fast with it so that everything would have been set for you to come and prepare supper when you are back. But after spending about two hours with the friend, you still came home to meet everything just as you left them. Instead of screaming at the girl, you should just flex your facial muscles and focus on the girl for some seconds before moving on with other activities. By this, you have successfully passed the message that you are annoyed by their uncouth action. You can also make use of this gesture on your spouse who comes home late without prior notice. You should even make this more pronounced if it is on a weekend when he was supposed to spend the substantial part of the day with you.

Case Study III: As a team leader at work or even a junior worker, you can appropriately deploy the use of this gesture. If you assign a duty to one of the workers and they fail to carry it out as expected, you can make use of this gesture to register your displeasure. Once the person discovers that your eyebrows are narrowed, it means you are unhappy with them. The person should also wear a remorseful look throughout the period until you find a solution to the problem they engineered.

CHAPTER 6

The Eyes

The importance of the eyes to every creature cannot be overemphasised. In fact, it is said in many quarters that it is the most important part of the body. Inasmuch as I would not want to buy into that opinion in order not to debase the other parts of the body, there is no gainsaying that the eyes are very crucial to us. It makes us avoid physical troubles and makes us see things clearly. The eyes are the gateway to everything around us. The eyes are the embodiment of non-verbal clues. Hence, that is why you would see that even infants scan at familiar faces, trying to read the expressions of their eyes. Also, it is the eyes that feed our brain with the new experiences they observe in the society. The human visual cortex, the largest part of the brain, is the part of the body dedicated to finding new and novel experiences.

The eyes depict how we feel every time. Some can intentionally feign their look with the purpose of intentionally sending away others from them or to make them prey of their ill intents. Before I discuss body language in details in relation to the eyes, let us consider some biological and psychological explanations to the concept.

Experts liken the structure of the eyes to a digital camera. In this, there are four basic connections reeled out by Liz Segre in her article posted on 'All About Vision'. First, the light of the eyes is basically catered for by the cornea. The cornea is the surface of the eyes which is clear, acting like the typical digital camera lens. Further, the iris of the eyes can be compared with the diaphragm of a digital camera. This controls the amount of light that reaches the back of the eyes. This is done by the automatic adjustment of the pupil's size—aperture (Segre 2019).

Thirdly, the crystalline lens of the eyes is positioned immediately behind the pupils and focuses more on the light that enters the body through the eyes. This process is known as accommodation. With the help of this lens, we are able to focus our attention on approaching and near objects. This process is the same thing with that of an autofocus camera lens that makes nearer images clear and sharp. And finally, the light focused by crystalline and cornea lens—which is limited by the pupils and iris—gets to the retina. The retina is the light-sensitive inner lining of the back of the eyes. It functions just like the electronic image sensor of a digital camera which converts optical images into electronic signals. The optic nerve is now laden with the duty of transferring the signals to the visual cortex. The cortex is the part of the brain dedicated to the control of the sense of sight—one of the five sense organs (Segre 2019).

Having given this practical insight about how the sight works, it is good that we run through the full anatomy of the eyes:

The eyelids. They are the thin folds of the skin covering and protecting the conjunctiva and cornea from physical and chemical injury.

The eyelashes. These are the stiff and short hair that covers our eyes from external irritants that can impede our clear vision. Dust and sweats are common examples (THE 2019).

Sclera. It is charged with the duty of protecting the inner structures of the eyes. It is the tough, opaque outer layer of the eyes which is popularly referred to as white of the eye.

Cornea. This is the five-layered membrane which is a subtle extension of the sclera. As said earlier, it protects the eyes from the light rays. However, its focusing power is not as flexible as that of a lens.

Conjunctiva. This is a transparent membrane covering the inner surface of the eyelids and sclera. It secretes a minute volume of tears and mucus that constantly keeps our eyes moist.

The tear gland. The basic function of this gland is to secrete tears that contain bacterial enzymes and salt which washes off external particles or irritants in the eye. It also lubricates the conjunctiva, which reduces friction between the eyelids and the eyeballs. With the tear gland active, the eyes cannot dry out (THE 2019).

The iris. This is a pigmented layer of the muscular tissue which provides the eye with its appearance—colour. It contains two sets of involuntary muscles—radial and circular. The muscles are charged with the control of the diameter of the pupils. Invariably, they also control the amount of light entering into the eyes.

The pupil. This is an opening located at the centre of the iris. It gives the light the opportunity to gain entrance into the eye (THE 2019).

Now we have captured all the biology explanations of the eyes in a very simple and straightforward manner. According to Alan Kozarsky (2017), 'The eyes are your body's most highly developed sensory organs. In fact, a far larger part of the brain is dedicated to vision than to hearing, taste, touch, or smell combined. We tend to take eyesight for granted; yet when vision problems develop, most of us will do everything in our power to restore our eyesight back to normal.' This aptly expresses the importance of the eyes and how trivial we handle them until something goes wrong with them. I cannot talk about the positive sides of the eyesight enough.

Now back to eyes in relation with body language! The eyes can be employed to communicate love, compassion, disdain, and fear. When a person brightens their welcoming eyes on us, it may be all we need for our day to be fulfilled. In the same vein, the position of the eyes can hint us that all is not well with a person—it can depict the person as being worried or concerned. When we adorn the eyes, we make it a source of attraction; however, if we keep them to ourselves, we want to intentionally avoid gazes.

6.1. Dilating the Pupils

Generic Interpretations of the Concept

Let me start by stating that pupil dilation is a subconscious action—we have no control over its activities. In other words, this is a very reliable means of determining the true emotion of a person. Since it cannot be feigned, it means once you see a person dilate their pupils, it's a true expression of their state of mind. What then does pupil dilation connote? It is an indication of comfort and happiness. When you come across a thing, concept, or person that you really like, your pupils will dilate to express this fact. Pupil dilation is one of the open behaviours of body language. When the pupil is dilated, it brightens the eyes, which in turn brightens the mind of the co-interlocutor. That explains why you notice this behaviour among lovers.

It has been discovered that location has an impact to play in determining this body language act. For instance, dimly lit bars or restaurants are considered a perfect meeting point for people because they provide a natural softness for the eyes and makes the pupils look larger than they are. This effect is processed by the brain as a receptive act, and that is why we feel relaxed, even among acquaintances. This psychological effect is felt in our body system through the eyes and makes us feel safe, even in public.

Scientific Explanations

A common assertion among scholars on this body language gesture is that it is seen when someone is asserted. The excitement, however, can be described in different phases—emotional, physical, or psychological, among others. Another consensus opinion among experts in the field is that this body language clue is subconscious—the sender hardly knows that he or she is sending out the signal. According to Study Body Language (SBL), the pupils dilate most when one is sexually aroused. This was made known in a study conducted on pupillometry—a work that focuses on how pupil size serves as a reflection of psychological condition. Both male and female reacted to the experiment in the same way— that is, their pupils were dilated when shown semi-naked photos. Apart from being aroused by the images of the opposite sex, that of babies and mothers also moved women (SBL 2019).

From the foregoing, we can assume that our pupils dilate when we are stimulated. The research also reports that it goes the other way around; people are moved by dilated pupils. There is little wonder that advertising agencies take advantage of this gesture by enlarging the pupils of models on the covers of magazines in order to tempt potential buyers (SBL 2019). In the same vein, Changing Minds (2019) notes that 'sexual desire is a common cause of pupil dilation and is sometimes called "doe eyes" or "bedroom eyes"'. This gesture is a reciprocal one—when an interlocutor's pupils dilate, we will mirror them, and when it constricts, ours contract too.

Another reason for pupil dilation is when rooms become darker—it opens to let in more light. This may probably be the reason bars, restaurants, clubs, and some other romantic locations make everything so dingy. Changing Minds submits that 'a fundamental cause of eye dilation is cognitive effort. When we are thinking more, our eyes dilate. This helps explain "doe eyes" as when we like other people, looking at them leads to significant thinking about how we may gain and sustain their attention.'

It has been reputed that those on the verge of making ill decisions will have their pupils more dilated. People with light irises are very easy to detect when their pupils dilate while those with dark irises look extremely charming. Another body language platform, Westside Toastmsters, opines that pupil dilation or contrition is a way of showing our mood. In general, when we are positive and happy, the pupils will dilate. The platform also reports that if the pupil is increased, it is an indication of a problem-solving activity. And it would dilate to maximum size when the person eventually arrives at a solution (WSTM 2019).

Practical Illustrations

Case Study I: Let me start from the office setting: A colleague has been sitting in an unusual position since they came to work that day and seem to be fixed on an activity. You have tried greeting them, and they respond passively. Of course, you know that he or she is busy, but what you don't know exactly is what's keeping them so engaged that they 'seem to be productive than the CEO'. To know whether they are trying to solve an issue or just worried about something, look at their pupils. Remember that the eyes are the window to the soul. If their eyes dilate, it means they are intellectually engaged on a piece. If by the end of the work their pupils dilate more with a general sigh of relief, this further confirms your doubt.

Case Study II: This sign can also be seen in a student. The teacher just finished teaching an interesting topic and decided to test the understanding of the students by giving them some few exercises. The teacher would know if the students were on the right path or not by paying attention to their pupils. Generally, a student who is solving the work a step after the other will put on a positive facial look. If they eventually arrive at the targeted solution, their pupils would be further dilated. This means that they have conquered the 'mountain', and as such, they are happy.

Case Study III: Popular instances can be found in the love world. You are on a date with a lady for the first time, and while sitting at the restaurant, having the usual chat, it seems their eyes are getting brighter, accompanied with smiles. This is an indication that they are relaxed and relieved being around you. In other interpretation, it means they are sexually stimulated—that is, they are ready for action. This is especially so when you are in a dark location. The first show of love can be seen through the eyes as the most active sense organ. Then other methods can now follow suit. Couples do the eye dilation a lot. When couples dilate their eyes to each other, it is a non-verbal way of confessing their love to each other. When you see such couples, you will most probably see them as happy couples.

Case Study IV: Criminals also dilate their pupils after an interview to express joy for overcoming investigative officers. A colleague was troubled after completing an investigation with a suspect, and the said suspect was smiling. When he told me, I suggested the suspect played on him, and after some few months, my doubts were established. Also, criminals dilate their pupils when a target is about to fall into their hands. They become happy for doing a *thorough job*, and as a way of self-commendation, their pupils become dilated. This may be accompanied with a smile. However, they are usually cautious of smiling because they don't want you to suspect of what they are up to. If someone is having a deal with you and you observe that they suddenly begin to dilate their pupils, with a suppressed smile, you need to consider the deal again before giving a final nod.

6.2. Constricting the Pupils

Generic Interpretations of the Concept

This is the polar opposite of the pupil dilation body language. Invariably, anything that concerns eye constriction is mainly negative. It is categorised under a closed body language whereby the eyes become small when it perceives something it does not like. This attitude is spurred when we have negative emotions towards someone or something. During the eye constriction process, the pupils will shrink suddenly, which hints that a negative event has occurred. This behaviour is easily detected in a light-coloured eye. It should be noted that this activity is primarily governed by the brain. In other words, it is a subconscious action, and it is immediate. This means that it cannot be easily feigned by anyone, and it is done as a reaction to an event that just transpired and not what has been done in times past.

The essence of the brain making the pupil to constrict at the occurrence of negative event is to ensure that we are focused on the distressed action. As the aperture becomes smaller, our vision becomes clearer. The message of the brain in this instance is that since a negative event is currently taking place, one should not lose focus of everything that transpires at the process in order not to make one a victim of an avoidable calamity. Hence, that is why our eyes squint in order to improve focus on that particular event as it unfolds.

From the foregoing, we can say that the ultimate reason for the constriction of the pupils is for our own safety and cannot be considered as a negative behaviour in this sense.

Scientific Explanations

There are handfuls of contributions from experts on this subject matter. In the submission of Changing Minds, when we constrict the pupils, it creates a greater depth of field in order to allow us more details. Animals mostly do this when they are determining the distance between them and their prey in order to know the aggressive approach to adopt in trapping the targeted prey down. However, it should also be noted that there is a literal interpretation for this behaviour. When the sun or lights are too bright, we constrict the pupils so as to reduce the rate of light entering into the eyes. The eyes do not need too much light in order to see clearly. Digital cameras also have apertures that control the rate of light getting into it (Changing Minds 2019).

Philips Christopher (2013) notes that our pupils constrict when we see an uninteresting or unpleasant stimulus. Watching a person being tortured, a war scene, or crippled beings, among other disgusting things, can lead to the constriction of the pupils. Changing Minds also supports this postulation. The platform submits that the pupils only constrict when we see something disgusting as a subtle way of saying 'I don't want to see you'. In another realm, this body language gesture may be an indication of overloaded brain—meaning the person has had more than enough to think about at a time. So the constriction is to shut every other thought or experience in their environment from getting into their brain.

This gesture can also imply uncertainty; the person is trying to think of something which they have actually arrived at a conclusion, but they are not certain of the correctness of their thought outcome. There is an unsubstantiated claim by Changing Minds that this body language gesture can be employed by liars who do not want others to detect their deception. There is no gainsaying that there are multiple interpretations for this gesture and, as such, must be considered in the clusters of clues or, at the very least, read the baseline of the subject before arriving at a conclusion.

Practical Illustrations

Case Study I: A popular scene in Continent DX had just been bombed by unidentified terrorists. And as expected, different media outfits across the world rushed to the venue to have a first-hand coverage of the event for their respective outfits. This would surely be the trending news for some time. Many people were trapped in the incidents—some sustained fatal injuries, some burnt beyond recognition, buildings destroyed, and properties worth millions of dollars washed down the drain. This was an ugly sight to behold. If you and others are watching the news report for this event, take time to focus on their pupils—you will discover that it is constricted. So also is yours. It is an invariable means of saying 'I don't want to see this'. Except for criminally minded people, it is usually difficult to watch a touching scene without being moved.

Case Study II: A mother who is catering for her sick daughter at the hospital will definitely not be happy. If she goes out to get something for the child and returns to see her in the same pitiable position, her pupils will constrict to show how concerned she is; it is an expression of her obvious sadness. This means she is worried and not excited that her daughter's situation is not getting better.

Case Study III: An employee can also constrict their pupils. Imagine someone who has been charged with the responsibility of conducting a feasibility study of the new branch his company intends to open in a targeted location. The same person is charged with the duty of drafting new policies for the firm on certain issues. Also, they are told to undertake a strategic study on the newly employed workers to understand their strengths and weaknesses. Yet they still have their day-to-day duties to accomplish, and the deadline for each assignment is close. This job is intellectually tasking, and while they sit to ruminate, you may just notice that they have constricted their pupils. This is an indication of safeguarding their thoughts from needless interruptions—that is, they are shutting themselves against their immediate environment for full concentration.

Case Study IV: You are visiting a special home for charity for the first time, and upon entering, you see all the special kids seated at some point and were playing. Some of them may be critically affected by various illnesses. Despite your love for them, you will still constrict your pupils because the sight is a little bit disgusting to you.

6.3. Relaxed Eyes

Generic Interpretations of the Concept

Relaxation is a symbol of comfort and peace. It means we are confident about something and not in any way perturbed about the future. For a moment, it may signal forgetting every negative issue and having the assurance that everything would be settled at the right time. When a person is at ease, you would discover that their facial muscles—those around the forehead, eyes, and cheeks— would be relaxed. However, the moment we become stressed due to an unpalatable experience, they become tense. We can aptly see this in babies whose facial muscles scrunch up before they begin to weep. The eye body language is the engine room for all body language interpretations. They are the windows to the soul. In other words, you need to always refer back to the eyes whenever you are reading any body language gesture for congruence.

Whenever the eye sockets, technically known as orbits, are relaxed, there is high tendency that nothing is out of hand. However, squinting or experiencing tension around the eyes means the person is probably stressed or trying to focus on something. From experience, it has been discovered that the muscles of the eyes react to stressors in a fast pace than other facial muscles. This means that the easiest means to understand the mental state of a person is to focus on the muscles of the eyes. From the foregoing, it is crystal clear that there is no way you can leave the eyes out in any body language interpretations. If you do not need them for the major gestures, you would rely on them as supporting evidence (clusters) for another gesture noticed in other parts of the body. That is why I usually say that the eyes are the mitochondria to the body.

Scientific Explanations

Let me start by submitting that relaxed eyes are seen as a sign of openness by scholars. When you are relaxed, it means you are comfortable and welcoming; you want to interact with people and vice versa. Body language expert Joe Navarro, in a 2009 article, notes that he focuses on the eyes to know if a person is relaxed and comfortable. In his own observation, he opines that we have the luxury to look away when we are most comfortable. I need to mention this as a means of dispelling the misconception in the field that when people do not maintain eye contact, they are deceptive and uncomfortable speaking with us. There is no research that backs up this argument. 'Looking away', as used here by Navarro, means having a relaxed look at the entire environment without being threatened. It is not good to focus one's gaze at a person or thing for a long time. It becomes threatening and distractive.

Changing Minds (2019) notes that when the muscles of the eyes are relaxed and there is slight defocusing, it means you are trying to take your person in what is known as doe eyes. This is an indication of sexual desire. If one is not relaxed, you cannot express sexual desire towards the opposite sex. A relaxed eye makes the eye shiny, dilated, and attractive for the purpose of hoodwinking a potential lover. In short, this body gesture is an expression of interest in others, not necessarily for emotional relationship.

As I bring this segment to a close, I need to state that there are cultural variants to this gesture, and you need to take cognisance of those while making your interpretations. Among the Japanese, Latin Americans, and African Americans, it is not deemed appropriate for one to focus on a person for a long time. Eye aversion, according to these cultures, is a way of showing respect to authorities. They look away so as to appear relaxed and respectful. Hence, Navarro (2019) concludes that 'eye contact is in fact a social/cultural phenomenon that is practised differently around the world'. Having this fact at the back of our mind at all times will help us while trying to pass our decision on the look of a person.

Practical Illustrations

Case Study I: Let's paint the scenario of a colleague who has been battling with some professional issues over the past one year. She actually committed an offence against the company due to her ignorance, and since ignorance is not an excuse before the law, the management of the firm had set up a disciplinary committee to investigate the matter. So for the past twelve calendar months, she had been frequenting the committee, answering questions. At some point, she had almost made up her mind that she would be shown the way out of the organisation. Hence, whenever you look at her, what you would see were concern, worry, lost hope, and trouble. Sometimes, you had had the course to approach her to assure her that whatever the outcome of the committee was, all would be well. However, on this particular occasion, you noticed that when she came out of the committee meeting, the muscles of her eyes were relaxed, looking fit, and attractive. This is an indication that she had been acquitted or the very least; the management had decided to pardon her. This means she is happy over the decision of the management.

Case Study II: Another instance is when your child goes for an important examination. If after returning home his face is relaxed and filled with the radiance of hope, this means that the examination was simple—he was able to answer most of the questions. Even without saying anything, you will also notice this happiness on his face.

Case Study III: This also plays out during a criminal interview. An open secret is that not every accused is actually guilty, and that is why professional investigators try to make the process as fair as possible in order not to implicate anybody in an undue manner. Just as Navarro has rightly noted, enforcement officials focus on the eyes of an interviewee for clues on questions and culpability. Someone who feel relaxed and communicate with you confidently without putting up disjointed stories may most probably be innocent. When you consider other body language cues, you would discover that they are open and ready to say everything they know concerning the issue at hand.

6.4. Narrowing the Eye Socket

Generic Interpretations of the Concept

When the eye sockets become narrow, it means we are trying to run away from or avoid something. As I have said at different points in time in this book, when you are comfortable, you maintain an open body language where anybody can approach you and discuss issues with you. However, the narrowing of the eye socket is used as a form of closed body gesture. The underlying muscles of the eye contract when we are faced with a stressful situation. When you see the orbits of the eyes of a person being narrowed, it means they are faced with a threatening situation. The gesture is used for the purgation of negative emotions. Hence, narrowing of the eye socket is a common gesture when a person is angry; physically, emotionally, and psychologically stressed; threatened; or feeling absurd.

This gesture is controlled by the brain and, as such, regarded as a subconscious action. When we are tensed or threatened, the brain makes the orbits smaller immediately as a way of responding to the apprehensive situation, doubt, or concern. To an observant person, this is a good indicator that something is amiss—that is, when the eye socket of a loved one narrows, you can always approach them to know what is wrong.

Scientific Explanations

Philips Chris (2014) opines that the narrowing of the eye sockets is 'due to physical and emotional pain'. The body language expert goes on to explain that if people do not want to hear what is being said or see what is displayed, they will narrow their eye sockets. This communicates a huge message to the people around them. However, the gesture only lasts for a fraction of a second. According to Chris, 'While people may not consciously perceive the signal, it will likely still register subconsciously. If the person for whom the cue is intended notices, they may revisit their proposal and add additional incentives to ease your negative judgement.' What I need to state concerning this point is that you should not force yourself to do it consciously because if it lasts for more than it should, it would look awkward and portray you as a fake. You still have to protect your integrity no matter what.

The verbal translation of eye socket narrowing is, 'What I'm seeing is causing me emotional or physical pain, and to prevent all that negativity from coming into my body, I'm going to squint and block to resist' (Chris 2013). In its own submission, Changing Minds (2019) notes that when the eye socket is narrowed, it is an indication of disbelief—that is, you are trying to evaluate what someone else said because you think it is not true. This is very similar to constriction of the pupils. And it also means uncertainty. Through this action, you are subtly telling your co-interlocutor that you cannot really see the point being emphasised in their story.

Expert Navarro says that his active years as a counterintelligence officer at the FBI taught him how to detect discomfort in people. According to him, when a person becomes suddenly troubled by an event or subject, he used to notice that their orbits also narrowed immediately. Hence, he opines authoritatively that 'squinting or the narrowing of the eye orbits indicates, very accurately, discomfort, stress, anger, or issues' (Navarro 2009). The behaviour is as old as man, and it aptly communicates our feelings to people in real time.

When you think of something and do not want to behold the shape of the internal image, you may narrow your eye socket involuntarily. In some instances, this gesture may mean tiredness. In conclusion, 'An eye blocking form of body language designed to prohibit distasteful images or even thoughts from being received at full view. Narrowing eyes indicates contempt, distaste and anger. A person will not only narrow their eye sockets from seeing objectionable sights but also negative thoughts or sounds' (Chris 2013).

Practical Illustrations

Case Study I: As said earlier, this is very similar to the pupil constriction gesture. This can be seen in a negotiation setting. You are negotiating a deal with a person and the talk has been going on well. However, when you got to the aspect of sealing the financial agreement, you discovered that when you first mentioned an amount, the other party put on a subtle smile. After bringing it a little bit lower, their eye socket immediately narrowed, and it seemed they lost their voice at that point. This is an indication that the person is not pleased with the amount offered and may not deliver the job as described if you insist on that offer.

Case Study II: Also, at the interview room, this can be used to know the capability of an applicant. You can try this out by reading the job requirements of a potential employee. To those who think they can adequately do them, they will nod and put on a sigh of relief, but if you read a portion and they squint, this is an indication that they are not pleased with that particular phase. Maybe they consider it as an aberration, or they are not intellectually capable for that role. The same technique is adopted by law enforcement officials across the world. While reading a statement of an event to a criminal suspect, officials would focus on their facial expressions. They would be unmoved when you read the point they think they can defend adequately. However, you read a section they never expected you would have known about, they would narrow their eye socket. This means that particular statement is incriminating, and they would not like to hear it. This gives you a hint of where to start your questioning from and how to make them confess.

Case Study III: At home, your spouse returns from work, and instead of him coming to you and giving you a hug as usual, he is reluctant, and it looks as if his eye sockets were narrowed. This is an indication he is stressed at work. This is the time to show him love and make him feel at home. If this is unusual, you need to create time to ask some relevant questions and show that you are really concerned.

6.5. Quivering under Eyes

Generic Interpretations of the Concept

This is another body language clue used to represent negative emotions. There are some tiny muscles lying immediately under the eyes; they can be located at the inferior underside of the *orbicularis oculi*. This means the muscles are just above the cheekbones and its surrounding tissues. The location of the muscles makes them very sensitive to stress. The location of the muscles is very delicate, and that is why they are central to understanding the mental state of a person. These muscles would quiver when you are frightened. It is as if every form of threat to the body is a threat to that part of the body. Remember that the eye is the part of the body that sees every incoming particle and takes note of the environment. It subconsciously closes if an object targets the eye. The same principle appeals to this soft area of the eyes.

When you see the muscles quivering, it also indicates concern. It means something is bothering the person. Anxiety is another probable cause of this gesture. Most times, anxiety is not caused by physical actions but also a product of our thoughts. When you picture a very frightening scene in your mind and see yourself in that scene, you will immediately feel this unconscious body gesture. It is serving as a warning to the eyes that something unpalatable is coming—it puts the protective mechanisms of the body at alert.

Scientific Explanations

While trying to draw the thin line between body language and microexpressions, Navarro (2011) speaks that this body gesture appears and disappears in the twinkle of an eye. According to him, this behaviour is difficult to observe due to its tininess. The body language expert also dispels the misconception that this body gesture is a sign of deception. Let me state that those gestures referred to as signals of deception are not necessarily one. It is difficult to use any body language gesture as a means of measuring *deceptive* statements. Instead, we should look at gestures in clusters. Navarro submits that twitching of the muscles beneath the eyes can be an indication of stress, anxiety, tension, concern, dislike, or psychological discomfort.

Linda Melone (2014) is another person who researched on this concept. She notes that this gesture—twitchy eyelid—is distractive to the person with the twitch. This is another subtle way of saying that this gesture is a negative sign, and it is sometimes noticed by other people. Some interpret this gesture as meaning dislike. This is true, but you should not take this personally against a person without finding out the reason behind their action. Dr Sandy T. Feldman, an eye surgeon and the medical director at ClearView Eye and Laser Medical Center in San Diego, notes that 'an eyelid twitch results from a spasm of the eyelids and may be indicative of stress or a medical condition'. From this point of view, we should regard this gesture less as a form of body language and see it more as an effect of caffeine, alcohol, or eye irritation. All these factors can lead to twitchy eyes. That is why I have always emphasised the place of baseline before reading the body language of others. In fact, if the eye twitches alongside the mouth, it is probably an indicator of neurological condition, and the person should see a doctor (Melone 2014).

So if you see this gesture in someone and you have established that it is not a medical disorder, then it is probably engineered by tension or stress. The irony of this behaviour is that if it becomes repetitive, it would be soothing to the body and would pacify the person. Hence, Navarro lists 'uncontrollable twitching of the eye' as a way of dealing with tension.

Practical Illustrations

Case Study I: When children are on the playground, they can display any form of behaviour. While some of them are being careful of causing harm on others, many of them are childish and reckless. At the point of playing, if there is a sharp object around (in rare cases though) and one of them tries to point the object at their mate, the other person, upon seeing such a threatening act from a close range, will develop some protective mechanisms against it. This includes immediate coming together of the eyelids to shut the eyes off the objects and then using their hands or arms to block the object. At this very point, the muscles of the eyes above the cheekbones would be filled with tension; the activity has actually charged their entire body system, and the message the gesture is communicating is that something is at risk.

Case Study II: Also, someone who just survived a crash on their way to work would display this gesture. Maybe a vehicle was about to ram into yours, but you were inexplicably delivered from it. By the time the vehicle was about to hit you, you would have lost consciousness—your body would develop resistance against the impending incident. Although the accident did not actually occur, but your mind had processed the fear due to a related incident you have witnessed in times past, which has been saved to your subconscious mind. So when this comes back to memories, it would be as if the event were taking place at that particular moment. And that is why the eyes would twitch during the incident.

Case Study III: An applicant who was coming for a job interview hoped that the terms and conditions of the job were not lucrative enough to lure many people to apply for it, but upon approaching the venue, when she saw that there was a mammoth of people waiting for the same purpose, she was greatly disappointed. The cause of the disappointment was that her expectations had been cut short. She would begin to think that her chances had become slim. She might be further threatened by the look and higher qualifications of others. With all these, she would be deeply concerned, and one of the ways of knowing this is to pay attention to the muscles of her eyes. If they quiver, this is an indication that the person is nervous, and it is to their own disadvantage.

Case Study IV: At the workplace, I have noticed this among illegal employees who were eventually nabbed. There was a time a company brought me in to help them with auditing their staff strength because it appeared that they were spending more than enough. Since I had no knowledge of accounting, I focused on observing the employees. I eventually fished some suspicious ones out and engaged them thoroughly. During my private chat with them, the first thing I established was to make them understand the implications of their actions. I looked into their eyes while making this assertion, and I saw the eyes of some of them quiver. This means they were not comfortable facing me and had some things to hide from me. It was a great hint for me to work with.

6.6.   Eye Blink Rate

Generic Interpretations of the Concept

There is no specific blink rate for an individual; we are all different, and the factors that influence the blink rate in individuals vary. Hence, we need to consider so many factors before giving meanings to the blink rate of a person. It is pertinent to state that there are many superstitious and unsubstantiated claims about this body language gesture, and I will try as much as possible to make things clear in this section. The amount of stress, the rate of arousal, and the environment are the major factors influencing the blinking rate. There is a widely shared belief that the typical blink rate is between sixteen to twenty times in a minute. This submission is also subjected to the rate of humidity and light present at the environment.

It has been observed that those who focus on the screen of their computer or other gadgets blink less. They may later end up complaining of dry eyes or other eye infections. Tears have been studied to have antibacterial features. So when a person blinks less, their eyes are normally dry, and there would not be moist to activate these antibacterial properties. On the other hand, those working at a dusty environment would blink more. Another thing you need to take cognisance of is that contact lenses increase blink rates in individuals.

And finally—this one seems metaphorical—being around a person who arouses our sexual interest increases our blink rate. This is why lovers blink more when they are with each other. It is a sign of arousal, which is subtly telling the lovers that they are into each other. From what I have said so far, it is obvious that I do not in any way connect this deception as more erroneously believed that those who lie blink more.

Scientific Explanations

Psychologist World (2019) states that the human eyes have been in existence for more than 540 million years. Apart from giving us sight, they are the embodiment of other messages. The platform submits that 'aside from our instinctive need to blink, our emotions and feelings towards the person we're talking to can cause us to subconsciously alter our blink rate'. So the truest expression of our emotion comes from the subconscious mind. Psychologist World also notes that when we blink for more than ten times in a minute while with an opposite sex or potential lover, this is an indication that we are attracted to the person. Hence, that is why some employ the gesture as a sign of flirting.

I like the description given to this gesture by Changing Minds. It states that 'blinking is a neat natural process whereby the eyelids wipe the eyes clean, much as a windscreen wiper on a car'. Note the use of the word *natural*, which means when you try to feign it, an observant fellow will know and cast you out. Changing Minds furthers that our blink rates tend to increase when we are intellectually engaged in complex thoughts or are stressed. In the same vein, it may be an indication of rapport. When we release positive body language gesture in a discussion, our co-interlocutors will subconsciously mirror us, and this makes the discourse interesting and unending.

However, looking beyond the random natural blinking, when a person blinks once, it is interpreted as a show of surprise. It means they are not convinced on what they see, and as such, they are trying to wipe off the tears in their eyes in order to have a clearer view. Also, a person paying rapt attention to your speech may likely blink once you are done with your presentation. In some instances, rapid blinking may be an indication of arrogance. This means the person sees himself or herself as being more important to the person standing at the other side of the table (Changing Minds 2019).

A research outcome reported in the article of Joe Navarro (2009) shows that nervousness or concern about an issue makes us increase our blink rate. Of course, this is often seen among liars, but seeing this gesture alone does not give you the licence to call anybody a liar. As said earlier, a person under stress can blink more rapidly.

Practical Illustrations

Case Study I: You are at the end-of-the-year dinner organised by your company as a way of unwinding the stressful year. And there is this particular lady who just got employed by the firm. It seems she is eyeing you, and you are also nursing interest in her. However, you have been careful so as not to be seen as a too-forward person. And more so, you have your professional reputation to safeguard. On the night of the dinner, both of you manage to sit on the same table, facing each other! Romantic conversation ensues in a subtle way, and in no time, you discover that her blink rate has tremendously increased without any noticeable external factor accounting for that. This is a pointer that you have a catch already! All you need to do is to come out straight and formalise things before events overrun the feeling.

Case Study II: If you are part of an interview panel mandated to select ten people out of about two hundred equally qualified applicants, you know that this is no doubt a tasking and daunting task. An interview is focused on impressions, and you definitely want to have the best hands to join your organisation. The kind of questions you would ask would be crafty. So during the process, if you see a person blinking rapidly, it is an indication that they are thinking hard—a stressful mental endeavour. You may decide to make them calm down or ask in a rapid succession so as to know how they would work under pressure.

Case Study III: You are sent out on a field trip by your organisation, and after presenting the report, the CEO blinks his eyes once. This is an indication of surprise. Maybe they are not expecting you to do such an in-depth assignment within the allotted time. So this is to show how they could not comprehend the depth of the report.

Case Study IV: Rapid blinking is a thing that is common to criminals too. I observed these numerous times during border patrol. A smuggler was apprehended unexpectedly. Since it was my culture to ask and establish the truth before acting, I called the suspected smuggler to the side and interrogated him. At first, he was articulate, but when the questions became 'hard', he calmed down and began to look pitiable. Upon asking how long he had been involved in the atrocity, he began to blink rapidly that this was obvious to everyone at the location. He knew the answer supplied would help in determining the extent of damage he had caused on the society.

6.7. Blinking Frequently

Generic Interpretations of the Concept

I have dealt with this concept briefly while explaining the concept of blinking in general. However, we will shed more light on it in this segment. When a person blinks rapidly, people tend to take it to mean a sign of deception. It is a known fact that lying is a stress-inducing activity, especially when one is on the hot seat, but every action related to this should not be ignorantly assumed to be an indicator of deception. You must get two to three other clues pointing to the direction of your thoughts before you can confirm it as being right. If an honest person is subjected to aggressive questioning, they would blink rapidly—does this mean they are deceptive? That is why some innocent people have been jailed and made to pay for the sin they know nothing about.

Blinking rapidly may be a sign of nervousness. A person who has attended about ten interviews within a month but nothing positive came out of it would definitely be filled with fear while going to the next one. Also, when a person is tense, there is no way we can take away rapid blinking from them. Stress from both physical and psychological activities has the tendency to make a person blink faster than usual. The list is countless, and the only way out of being trapped in the web of misconception is to find out the reason for a particular behaviour before passing judgement based on conventional beliefs.

Scientific Interpretations

According to Negotiation Ninja (2017), the eye's blink rate increases as stress increases. This is logical because blinking is primarily a protective mechanism. Hence, once the body is tired, it gives an appropriate response. The platform specifically warns that because someone is blinking on a fast rate does not make them a liar. It is just an increased probability that the person is lying and not a bare fact. In order to know whether they are lying or not, you would need to trick them into a situation whereby they would lie, and at that point, you would compare their blink rate to what you earlier noticed. If there is no difference, then you are right; if there is, then they are bothered about something. In addition, you need to keep tab on other body language gestures that your subject displays—intentional eye aversion, turning of heads, squirming in the chair, or even a slumping posture. All these are indicators of deceptions and not sure signs. By now, I need to be clear about the fact that you should not interpret any body language in isolation (Negotiation Ninja 2017).

In its submission on this subject matter, the first thing that Changing Minds notes is that the 'blink rate tends to increase when people are thinking more or are feeling stressed.' So there is a consensus among scholars that stress is the major propeller of frequent blinking. When a person blinks rapidly, it blocks the vision. Except for medical condition, if done by a superior to a subordinate, it may be considered as a subtle way of discarding the latter from their presence. It is a sign of arrogance in this sense. In another sense, this gesture flutters the eyelashes and, thus, makes them appealing for sexual invitation (Changing Minds 2019).

Tamsen Butler (2019) also says that rapid blinking among lovers or potential suitors is a sign of attraction. It means both parties are trying to get into each other. And also, when a particle drops into a person's eye and you are trying to get rid of it, you may start blinking in an unusual way as a means of recollecting the particles into the surface of the eyes and then pull it off.

Practical Illustrations

Case Study I: As a law enforcement officer, before starting an interview with a criminal suspect, you created a jovial atmosphere where they acted out themselves—you established their baseline when they are in a relaxed state. You took note of their facial expressions, use of hands, and other important body language gestures. Upon starting the interview, you discovered that their explanations to your questions were not convincing and did not even tally with the previous ones. You decided to hit the nail on its head by asking a question relating to the thrust of the matter, which really convicted the suspect of being the culprit. At this point, they began to squirm on their chair, maintained a closed posture, and blinked at a rapid pace—this signals discomfort. Ask a question that is off-topic to determine if they would lie or not; if they do, this is an indication that the frequent blinking is a signal of deception.

Case Study II: Another case of the use of the gesture is this: after a hectic week, you decided to go to the club on Friday to relax your muscles and catch some fun, and upon getting there, there was a lady who came on her own and was seated alone. You had previously sat on the table next to hers. And there was eye contact on three different occasions. You thought it was becoming too much, and as such, you tried looking away. The next time your eyes met, she was winking at you, and some sensational feelings were descending on you too. You took the courage as a man to move to the empty chair on her table, and after the first greeting from you, she replied coldly but was still feigning her focus on you. And when you started a general conversation, she began to speak up. At that point, there was no more 'shy' eye contact. You discovered that her blinking rate has increased, and unconsciously, you also began to blink at a rapid rate. This is a symbol of sexual attraction. Unlike its nervous counterpart, this frequent blinking will be accompanied with a smile and charming lip display just to lure the person into doing their bidding.

Case Study III: Your spouse sits at the study with some files, and for some moments, he keeps battling with a page of those files. He seems to have shut himself against the world. If this is accompanied by rapid blinking, it is an indication that he is thinking hard. At that moment, the best thing for you to do is to stay aloof—that is, do not go near him if you know you will just be a nuisance to him. Or better still, if you know you will be of great help, try helping him out of the difficulty.

6.8. Maintaining Eye Contact

Generic Interpretations of the Concept

This is also another body language gesture shrouded by unsubstantiated claims and superficial proclamations. Let me state right at the outset that this gesture is governed by individual preferences and cultural norms; it is just the personal principle of some people to either maintain or avoid eye contact in some certain circumstances. Also, some are culture-driven. Anyone who has ever interacted with Japanese, African Americans, Latin Americans, Africans, and other related cultures will understand the crucial role culture plays over the eye contact gesture.

In the above-mentioned cultures, if you dare look at a person beyond two seconds, it would be considered as a sign of rudeness; it means you are implicitly challenging the authority of the person, especially if the person is an older one or holding a position of authority. However, this is contrary to what is achieved in the Western world, where it is permissible to maintain eye contact with a person for about four seconds. Even within the Western world, this body gesture is further governed by the area one hails from. For instance, a person who is from New York City should not stare at a person for more than two seconds, or else, it would be tagged an affront.

In general, this body language gesture is determined by culture. While some see eye contact as a primary way of building rapport and making conversation flow, others see it as contesting the authority of figures of authority. Hence, some of these cultures teach their children to look down while addressing people who are older than them.

Scientific Explanations

Writing on eye contact in body language, Farouk Radwan (2019) captivatingly opens his essay thus: 'Maintaining proper eye contact during a conversation will give people the impression that you are interested in listening to them, that you are not shy and that you respect them.' The only problem we will have with this excerpt is that what exactly do we regard as 'proper eye contact'? Staring is different from maintaining eye contact. This is where most people miss it. *Staring* means keeping a fixed gaze on a person in a threatening manner, while *maintaining eye contact* is looking at a person for some time, looking around, and then returning the innocent gaze to the speaker.

Changing Minds (2019) says that eye contact is a powerful medium of communication between interlocutors. It may signal dominance, interest, or affection. When you look into the eyes of a person, it may signal acknowledgement of their presence and interest. If you were not interested in seeing them, you would have looked at the other side. Also, when you look at a person's eyes, it gives you a hint on where they focus their attention. Are they scanning through your body or focused on another thing entirely? If you were looking away when someone made a proclamation, and immediately you turned back to them, this means the person has succeeded in winning your attention.

The platform equally notes that prolonged eye contact is threatening; the ideal thing is to look away and look back again. If the eye contact breaks suddenly, it is an indication something has just been said which the listener is not pleased with. For instance, you called them out unexpectedly. However, this may also be spurred by internal discomfort. When a person looks at you, looks away, and then looks at you again almost immediately, it is a classic sign of flirtation.

If eye contact is prolonged, it carries different meanings, depending on the context where it is done. When a person is paying close attention to what we are saying, the eye contact will increase considerably. When someone likes us, he would fix his or her gaze on us. One that is common to women is to hold a man's gaze for about three seconds, look down for a second, and then look at the man they are attracted to again. However, it should be noted that prolonged eye contact is exhausting. Instead, you can focus on the person's nose (bridge of the nose). Sometimes, liars overcompensate this gesture just in a bid not to appear truthful (Changing Minds 2019).

Practical Illustrations

Case Study I: While communicating with your boss at work—he is seated on his chair, relaxed, and focused on you—you are looking away from time to time. After you are done with your speech, your superior still keeps his gaze on you while giving his responses to all that you have said. This form of eye contact from your boss is that of dominance; they are subtly proving their authority to you through non-verbal means.

Case Study II: In a criminal context, you are speaking with a person, and it seems that they are incongruent with their assertions. Something is odd about their speech, and it's superficial that even a kid would find it very difficult to believe without asking some curious questions. You have noticed some indicators of stress and tension in them. However, they are trying to conceal the telltale indicators, and one of the things they do is to look at you fixatedly. Since they have started their talk, they have never shifted their eyes to another direction. Now it feels threatening to you as it does not communicate any message. This means they are truly lying; he only wants to deceive you with the disconcerted look.

Case Study III: When a person meets you for the first time, it is expected that they will like to look at you again and again so as to recognise you in the future when you cross paths again. However, if you are far from the person, he would keep gazing at you, then after looking away, he would look back immediately. This is a show of interest. You will observe the curiosity on the face of the person. It means the person wants to have an emotional relationship with you. In such looks, distance is not a barrier.

Case Study IV: A colleague may try to appear authoritative to you by focusing on your eyes while speaking with you; instead of you looking at him, he is the one staring at you. Even though you are on the same pedestal at work, but he may be a domineering type who believes every other person should respect him. When there is no disconnection of eye contact when there is supposed to be ordinarily one, it means the person is up to something.

6.9. Avoiding Eye Contact

Generic Interpretations of the Concept

This body gesture is mostly a conscious action. When we feel like dodging a person or not having any form of relationship with them, we avoid having eye contact because this is seen as the foundation of every form of communication. Sometimes, we think it is not convenient to speak with a person. Hence, there is no reason to start what will not end well. People also hinder any communication with a person they consider to be repressive, obnoxious, or unlikeable. What is the point in discussing with a person you bear negative thoughts against? An employee who constantly has issues with their boss will avoid any form of eye contact with them.

This avoidance can be temporary or long term, depending on the context and the reason behind the decision. When someone does something unexpected or embarrassing, you can decide to avert eye contact. A student who does not want to answer questions will avert eye contact with their teacher so that their name does not come to the teacher's mind. Another reason for aversion of eye contact is proximity. In most parts of the world, when you are close to a person, you do not maintain eye contact, even if the person is known, because by that time, it would have turned to staring at the person. Consider being in an elevator with an acquaintance and other strangers. You would rather keep your discussions than start it there.

From the foregoing, it is crystal clear that eye avoidance is not a symbol of deception as many people have erroneously proclaimed. Of course, people tend to hide their face while lying so that one does not get to read their facial expressions, but we cannot assume that every form of avoidance of eye contact is orchestrated by this reason. Sometimes, it may be an indication of shame and embarrassment. If you feel inferior to a person, you would not like to maintain eye contact with them.

Scientific Interpretations

This is also known as eye avoidance, eye withdrawal, roving eyes, averting eyes, and gaze avoidance. It is the purposeful avoidance of making eye contact with another person. According to Chris, 'Avoiding eye contact signals that a person wants to avoid being called upon or that they want to create an air of superiority.' Avoiding eye contact is a powerful means of communication to anyone who understands how to use it. If you want to show your disdain for a person, you only need to ignore their presence. Also, when people averts eye contact, it makes them disappear—that is, people only have the tendency to be called upon when they have eye contact with their interlocutor. Students who do not know an answer to a question asked would ignore the teacher, while those who know it would passionately crave for the attention of the teacher (Chris 2014).

If you are trying to have eye contact with a person and the person is avoiding it by all means, this means they do not find you as the right person to communicate with. Generally, this body language gesture is used to signal discomfort or submission. A subordinate will usually avert eye contact as a way of honouring their boss/superior, while some do that because they are not comfortable looking at other people for long. This is more so if the person comes from one of the low-contact cultures.

There are two primary purposes this gesture is meant to serve. One is to avoid conflict. Conflict only arises when two people feel superior to each other. However, if one takes the bull by the horn, looks away, and focuses on other things, the other party would be forced to sheathe their sword. Another reason is for the purpose of power playing as explained in the preceding paragraph.

The signal may also mean that the person is trying to be defensive. If you do not want to accept the blame, you look away while someone is accusing you. It may also symbolise defeat. A defeated person would find it difficult to look at their opponent in the face. If you are nursing negative feelings and you do not want any other person to know about it, you can look away so that they will not have a hold of your face. This can also be used to allure and tease (Chris 2014).

Practical Illustrations

Case Study I: In the office, you have come to know your superior as a person who is dominant and wants to be respected so much. While speaking with him, you decided to look away. Your eye contact with him does not last before you fix your gaze on another thing. With this, your superior would not see you as a threat to his position of authority. With this, the boss will relate with you well because you have portrayed yourself as an embodiment of humility and support to their office.

Case Study II: You are having a minor disagreement with your colleague at work, and you are ready to slug it out with her because of some of her past 'offences' and how she has portrayed herself as being above others. However, as you are getting agitated, she just took her gaze off you. This is an indication that she is not ready to fight or even continue with the argument.

Case Study III: You are making a presentation, and you decide to make it interactive by calling people to talk and share their experiences on the concept being discussed. Some are afraid of public speaking, and by the moment you are making the decision to call people at random, they would feel like shrinking into their seat and disappear. What they do at the point of presentation is to bury their head and look away from you. This gesture is communicating defeat through the burying of the head. Another place where this is always seen is in the classroom. Students who do not wish to be called by their teachers will not be active about the whole lesson and will avoid eye contact with the teacher whenever the teacher is about to call on a student to answer a question.

Case Study IV: I once engaged some suspects who married for convenience. They claimed they were a couple and were not ready to say any other thing. I was troubled as my instinct kept telling me they were deceitful. Apart from the lack of flow that existed between couples, I also observed that they could not maintain eye contact for two seconds, and yet they were not looking at me. At some point, they had to look into each other's eyes, and the feeling of deceitfulness was well-written on their face. I had to separate them to ask questions that every couple should know about their spouse, and the answers were so contradictory that they later confessed their involvement in the sham marriage.

6.10. Superiority Gaze

Generic Interpretations of the Concept

People who hold positions of authority all over the world do subtly demand respect from their subordinates. This is universal. Hence, such high-status individuals engage in more eye contact than those in the lower rungs of the ladder. Whether an elderly person or an authoritative figure is speaking or listening to someone, they will focus on the person as a sign of showing their dominance. On the other hand, if you are a subordinate or less powerful to the person, you will only make more eye contact while listening to them and not when addressing them. This is more pronounced in Asia Pacific nations. Even in Japan, which is prominently known across the world to be a less-contact nation, this is obtained in the country.

Incidentally, people tend to respect and favour those who make direct eye contact with them especially if the person is a figure of authority. On the other hand, if we have the opportunity to speak with celebrities, movie stars, those holding prominent positions in society, and politicians, it make us feel favoured; it leaves a soothing and fulfilling impression on us. We think that they consider us being important and that they do not look down on us.

Scientific Illustrations

This is part of a dominant body language. The eyes serve as a powerful means of displaying superiority. Those who want to show superiority and dominance through the eye gesture will make prolonged eye contact. When a person holds his gaze, this is an indicator that he means what he says and nothing is going to make him change his stance on that particular issue. In other words, this gesture portrays the person as being strong-minded, dominant, unwilling, and potentially uncooperative. Sometimes, a person can show superiority by not looking at the person talking to them. This means the person is not worth their attention; the person addressing them is considered worthless (Skills Converged 2019).

Those who maintain this body gesture do not smile at all times. They do not want to be perceived as being weak. When a person does not smile always, he bars people from gaining unsolicited attention to their life (Skills Converged 2019).

Changing Minds also agrees to the fact that much dominance can be shown through the use of the face. The platform states that 'the eyes can be used to stare and hold the gaze for long period. They may also squint, preventing the other person seeing where you are looking. They may also look at anywhere but the other person, effectively saying that "you are not even worth looking at". Narrowing eyes shows suspicion or even dislike.' It can be seen that the platform is emphasising what Skills Converged opined.

When the gaze is prolonged without any form of blinking, this is like playing the long handshake which people use in showing dominance. When a male wants to show dominance through the eyes, he switches to the alpha face. Here, the person would lower his eyebrows, which gives them a stern look as if they were judging a person. Alternatively, the eyes can be narrowed, which will make the person appear as if they were evaluating their subject. While the person displays this gesture, he would close his mouth firmly and would not smile. When a person maintains a stern, prolonged eye contact, they quite understand that they are breaking the norm, but it is to show that they are powerful and can do anything against the rule.

The dominant eye gaze should not be viewed as being totally negative or challenging the status quo; we all need a dose of it at some point in life. Over the course of your life, you need to learn how to make use of the eyes to display interest, command respect, draw people's attention to yourself, create sensual feelings, and demonstrate superiority (WSTM).

Practical Illustrations

Case Study I: Let's assume you are working in a multinational company and heading one of its zonal offices in Country DT. On an annual basis, the organisation organises high-powered manpower training for all its executive officers across the world. Apart from the training, the programme also offers you the avenue to speak with other zonal coordinators about how they are getting along and the implementation of the company's goal. So on this particular occasion, there is a need for you to speak with the zonal head of Country DW branch. When you meet, he shakes your hands and holds on to it for a while. More so, he focuses his eyes on you throughout the period of discussion with little or no blink. The message he is trying to pass across with these body gestures is that he is superior to you. In other words, he is demanding respect from you.

Case Study II: You went out to buy a new car, and while negotiating with the dealer, he was friendly all throughout, trying to get a new client and making you feel at home. However, it got to a point where you offered an amount which they considered ridiculous but which you considered was not far from what he had initially pegged as the least price he could release the vehicle. If their rejection of your proposed amount is backed up by a prolonged eye contact, looking directly into your eyes, this is an indication of strong-mindedness—he was not going to budge from the price he had tabled before now. Invariably, he was unwilling to consider your proposal.

Case Study III: You had the opportunity to travel to Japan for a mini project which required you to interact with the locals. However, you discovered that every time you were to speak with those younger than you, they would not look straight into your eyes, but the baffling aspect was that you noticed that every time you were interacting with the elderly ones, reverse was the case—they would gaze at you for a prolonged time. Well, this is cultural, and the message is clear. They were not staring at you because you were a stranger but because it was always done as a mark of superiority or seniority.

Case Study IV: Con artists are fond of this look; since they have been committing crimes for years, they feel that there is no law enforcement officer who can match their level of knowledge. There was one who was apprehended by my colleague, and while he was being ushered into the interview room, he didn't look like a typical criminal—he wore a superior gaze that a friend had to ask me if my colleague did not arrest the wrong fellow. Interestingly, the interview with him lasted for hours before we could confirm his involvement in the said crime. Even after that, he was so sure of himself in court.

6.11. Seeking Eye Contact

Generic Interpretations of the Concept

At some point in life, we will desire and long to have a conversation with someone. However, breaking the barrier of starting the first conversation is usually herculean. It would be considered rude or inappropriate for you to just approach the person without any form of prior engagement. Hence, it becomes crucial and sacrosanct for one to understand the social ethics behind brokering relationship in every given context. One of the fundamental ways in which to seek attention is through the use of non-verbal clues. Although it is a cliché that 'the eyes are the window to the soul', but we cannot deny the fact that it is potent in every sense of its usage. Invariably, the eyes, if well socially deployed, can be an incredible means of brokering relationship with a person.

If you have an interest in starting a conversation with someone—be it formal, informal, or semi-formal—you can use the eyes to gain the attention of the person. When you look at the person longingly, scanning through their body until your eyes meet with theirs, then the person would see the urge in you. The eye contact at this point carries request to speak with the person; it is eye contact that shows that you are seeking their attention concerning something. Most times, the other party cannot resist it because it comes with passion and some form of pleading.

Scientific Explanations

Sarah Fader (2018) notes that 'it turns out that where and how we use our eyes is an extremely potent form of human communication. And you can use that to your advantage as you get to know someone and try to build lasting bonds with them.' However, the foundation of everything starts with our ability of being able to catch the person's attention through the eyes. Fader states the obvious that we all like being noticed, liked, and treated in an important way, be it to a group or an individual. In simpler terms, most people are after external validation. Eye contact is the primary way through which you can make others know this fact.

Humans are the only primates with white eyes. The function of the eyes is not only to see but also to make others see us. Making eye contact while communicating makes others remember whatever you say. When you strategically position your eyes, it makes it easy for people to notice you. When you win the attention of people through your facial look, they become more honest with you. This is a huge advantage to anyone seeking to build a bond with another person. Seeking eye contact is used as a foundation for making every relationship work. When you are successful in making another person have eye contact with you, they would be able to understand your emotions, and this will help the person understand how to relate with you. Lying with the eyes is not an easy exercise (Fader 2018).

There is need to emphasise that this body gesture should not be seen as a means of gaining the attention of an opposite gender alone; it is useful in all endeavours of life. Seeking the attention of others through eye contact is beneficial in relating with friends, relatives, colleagues, and even total strangers (Fader 2018).

This body gesture is a conscious glance. It is done when one is attracted to a person. So you want them to know that you are really attracted to them and want to converse with them. Once your gaze catches theirs, you may have to look away before returning your gaze to them so that it would not look as if you were staring at them. However, if the eyes of both of you meet and the person breaks theirs immediately, it means the person is indifferent to your presence, and they may not honour your non-verbal request (Fader 2018).

Another body language platform, Science of People, explains that when we want to seek the attention of a person, we raise our eyebrows in order to allow the face send a clear message to our target. If you pay attention to your subsequent actions, you would notice this. The platform submits that 'raising the eyebrows is a gesture of congeniality and an indication we want to get along and communicate better'. Hence, you should always note this fact at the back of your mind.

Practical Illustrations

Case Study I: You and your daughter went to a place, and she happened to be an introvert. You went a little bit late for the occasion, and being a very important one, things were done in an orderly manner. So both of you were not able to sit beside each other. Events began to unfold, and your daughter was not all that comfortable due to the kind of topic those seated beside her were discussing. You, on the other hand, were busy with some of your friends on your table. You were carried away that it escaped your mind to glance at your daughter to know if all was well with her. Your daughter had focused her gaze at your side, hoping that you would look at her so that you could read the discomfort written on her face. If you eventually looked at her side and there was a contact between the two of you, her eye gesture is referred to as seeking eye contact—that is, you would notice the longing desire to speak with you on her face.

Case Study II: In another instance, a man who saw a beautiful, charming lady from afar but who thought that approaching her directly would be absurd would seek a way to pass his message through non-verbal means. The man would tend to move closer to the lady and then look at her in a prolonged manner. The aim is to ensure they both have eye contact. If this eventually happens, the lady would see the hunger and thirst for the man to speak with her in his eyes. At this point, she could decide to open the door for conversation or not.

Case Study III: In the office setting, there are different ways in which this plays out. There was a reported case of a man who offended a female colleague. Since the female colleague was temperamental, he could not beg her in public.

The lady kept to herself all throughout, and she had been a sort of friend to the man. Not knowing what his fate would be if he should approach her, he looked longingly whenever the lady was passing by his desk. Of course, he was ignored for the first few instances, but at some point, she had to return the look, and that was the end of the conflict!

Case Study IV: Attention-seeking criminals do employ the use of this non-verbal cue. When criminals are about to appeal to the emotions of their targets before getting at them, they will devise a way that will facilitate their meeting. A criminal had traced his target to a restaurant, and it seemed the lady was not looking at his side. He changed his sitting position thrice, no success. However, when they eventually exchanged eye contact, he looked in a seeking manner that the lady had to inquire from him whether he needed something from her. The lady was gullible, and the criminal took advantage of her kind heart to exploit her till the case was reported to law enforcement agents.

6.12. Sentiments and Gaze

Generic Interpretations of the Concept

Let's explain this point from the stance of the love world so that you can have a practical insight of what we are to explicate under this section. One thing that seems to be common among humans is the language of love. This is why people from different continents marry each other without evil consequences. Taking the world of emotional relationship as a case study, it has been noticed that the first hint that makes us understand that couple's feeling for each other has changed is the way they look at each other. In other words, there is a particular way people who are truly in love look at each other. When anyone deviates from that conventional postulation, people around them will know that there are issues with the relationship.

Those who started their relationship on a friendship level and gradually moved it to a love affair will keep being friends even in their romantic relationship; there would be a look of increased interest from both parties. Lovers want to look at each other more, know how each partner is feeling, and then ensure that their partner is not looking away from them. From the foregoing, it is crystal clear that our gaze changes as a way of capturing our changing sentiments even before uttering verbal expressions towards that direction. This is very true in many endeavours in life. For instance, in the case of friends turned lovers given above, before they would open their mouth to confess their love for each other, it would have been done through the use of eyes. At that point, both partners would have known that they have feelings for each other. Hence, what would be left with the verbal aspect is the formalisation of everything. Again, this gesture can be used in expressing any feeling or emotions.

Scientific Explanations

Kendra Cherry (2019) explains that the eyes are referred to as the 'windows to the soul' due to the invaluable roles they perform in our lives. In every communication context, we take note of eye movement in a natural form; it is a part of every discourse process. Some of the things that we notice when watching people speak are if they are making direct eye contact with us or averting their gaze, if their pupils are dilated, and the rate of blinking.

A person who looks into your eye while you converse with them is subtly telling you that he or she is interested in you. Another sentiment shared here is that the person is paying close attention to what you are saying. So before opening their mouth to say 'I'm listening', their eye gaze has explained that through non-verbal means (Cherry 2019).

This can also be interpreted to mean something negative. A person who looks at you in a prolonged manner without budging even when there is a course for that is passing a message that they are a threat to you. Maybe you are trying to win over the heart of their date, and as such, he is looking at you in a stern manner, warning that if you keep on persisting for their date to be your friend, he can do any evil against you. It means they are not okay with your action and, as such, must desist from your behaviour or you face their wrath.

Gazing at one's eyes may also be employed to communicate discomfort or distraction or even conceal one's real feelings (Cherry 2019). Changing Minds also explains that eye gazing is used in the communication of our sentiments. A person may look down as a means of communicating submission. It means they see the other person being of higher status who must not be looked at. It can also indicate an emotion of guilt. When a person feels guilty of their behaviour, they would be emotionally unbalanced and, as such, do everything possible not to maintain eye contact with the person(s) they have offended (Changing Minds 2019).

Psychologist World (2019) opines that when eye contact is persistent or constant, it is an attempt to intimidate the other person. The subject will feel they are overly studied and, thus, becomes uncomfortable.

Practical Illustrations

Case Study I: At the workplace, a colleague has been posted from another branch to yours some few months ago, and since then, you have been working on a project together. Since her arrival, you have seen the pretty lady as a good teammate; she stays with you most times after office hours to get things done, is always responsive, focuses on the vision of the firm, and has been indescribably productive in all realms. More so, she is jovial and approachable. So you have become so much used to each other that even on weekends, you decide to go out together and relax. Hence, friendship has started. Along the way, it seems you are developing some feelings for her, and you also notice that the topics she now discusses with you are very sensitive and emotional. You have tried to suppress your feelings so that it would not affect your friendship with her. However, both of you now discover that you watch each other more often. There is more eye contact than before, and whenever you exchange eye contact, it would be greeted with a smile and adoring look from each other. This is a show of interest and love from both parties.

Case Study II: Another scenario of this gesture can be seen on the home front. Your daughter is a Coke freak, and you have always warned her not to make it her only drink. You have just got some Coke, put them in the refrigerator, and counted them. When she came back from the school, after greeting you, resting, and having done her homework, she tiptoed to the refrigerator, took two bottles of Coke, and kept them while you were lurking behind the door. Late in the evening, you asked her if she took any Coke from where you kept them, and she denied vehemently, but upon checking her room, you brought out the two bottles of Coke, with one half-drunk already. From that evening till she slept, she was dodging direct eye contact with you. This expresses emotions of shame and embarrassment.

Case Study III: There was a case of a criminal who wanted to evade clearance at the border. Too many buses conveying people arrived together, and everything was in chaos already. It seemed the crowd was about to overpower the officers on duty, but after some reinforcements, normalcy returned to the location. In trying to clear the travellers, an officer discovered that there were some group of people who were trying to evade eye contact with him. After gazing at the officer, the suspect would break eye contact immediately. At first, he thought they were shy, but upon pestering them further, he discovered that they had no necessary documents for clearance and were looking for a way to evade the process.

6.13. Engaging Gaze

Generic Interpretations of the Concept

This is very unique because of what it seeks out to achieve. This gesture, which involves getting the attention of another person in a romantic and warm manner, is aimed at connecting deeply. The gaze of the person displaying this behaviour would be full of request, showing that they want to have a word, relationship, or even an affair with their subject. This behaviour is exceptional because the face is always calm, gentle, and soft throughout the period the person makes the gesture. Also, this is not the type of gesture whereby a person does it once and then focuses on other things; you do it consistently until you get the attention of your subject—that is, there is always a repeated attempt to connect with your subject eye to eye.

While the behaviour is being displayed, the face, eyes, and mouth are normally gentle—this portrays the person as a perfect gentleman or woman. Hence, this gesture is mostly seen in dating scenes where we try to win the heart of another person to ourselves by portraying ourselves as being responsible and romantic. It is a means of telling a person that you are interested in them. All the gestures is to make your personality likeable. With this, you want the person to draw closer to you in order to start verbal communication.

May I note that this gesture is even used by total strangers in broad daylight to subtly communicate their intents. Camps, bars, restaurants, and other social settings where people come in numbers are examples of places where the gesture is mostly put to use.

Scientific Explanations

According to Westside Toastmasters, when we explain and maintain eye contact in a comfortable manner with others, it serves as the foundation for successful communication. It gives the interlocutors a feeling of trust and well-being. The length of time and intensity with which the gaze is held tells us what it means. There is no form of gaze that does not communicate a message or another. Engaging gaze means that the person finds you interesting and attractive. Just like what I said under the section on pupil dilation, when one is happy and ready to connect with others, you would see them dilate their pupils. What is unique about this gesture is that it is made more charming just in a bid to getting into the heart of your target (WSTM 2019).

Christopher Philip (2015) notes that there are different ways in which the facial gaze is done, depending on the motive the person wants to achieve. In another article, the body language expert goes ahead to opine that we cannot leave out the eyes while trying to express sexual interest to a person. For a man to really establish an engaging gaze with a woman, he must ensure that there is eye contact with the woman, and immediately after that, it should be followed up with a smile. That is why the gaze must be done repeatedly until you connect with the person. After smiling, you can break the eye contact by looking downward. Sometimes, this gaze may require that you cover your eyes partly so as to make the sign glaring—people will always want to find out the reason for closing your eyes. So the message becomes clearer at that point.

One of the most common female sexual signals is for them to ensure that their entire face is romantic. They will look directly into the eyes of a man and lick their lips so as to make them glossy—no one is attracted to dry lips. However, I need to reiterate that these signs are not enough for a man to quickly jump in seeing that as an opportunity. It is usually risk-laden for a woman to ask out a man, and it can even be embarrassing if not well-managed. In other words, all these gestures can be given other natural interpretations. Hence, you must wait to see if these gestures are repeated before jumping to the *opportunity*.

Mind Tools (2019) explains that to make your gaze engaging, you must try as much as possible to hold the other person's gaze for a few seconds at a time. This is to show your sincerity. In conclusion, be careful that this does not turn out to be a staring match. This will make the other person uncomfortable and scare them away instead of endearing them to you.

Practical Illustrations

Case Study I: For instance, you attended the birthday party of a friend, and there were many other attendees too. Everywhere you look, there were beautiful young ladies prancing up and down. Finally, the party started. Everywhere seemed a little bit calm, and the food was yummy. At the other side of the mini hall was a middle-aged lady who seemed to be disconnected from other people. She had broken the proximity principle, but in her face, it looked as if she were yearning to speak with someone. Eventually, there was eye contact with her, and she smiled in a relieving manner. You smiled back, and she looked away. You thought this was just coincidental or innocent. And you continued with the conversation going on with those seated on the same table with you. After some few minutes, your eyes wandered back to her side, and the same gesture was repeated—a very pronounced one that cannot be disconnected or denied. At this moment, something registered into your subconscious, and you deliberately had to look at her direction the third time where the gesture was repeated. This means she was very interested in you.

Case Study II: You and your boss attended a strategic professional session from the office. The company executives were asked to sit at a place, while subordinates were offered another sitting arrangement. The session kicked off, and after some minutes, your boss began to look at you passionately. It is an indication that he wanted to communicate with you. Maybe the speaker raised a point that he wanted you to take note of, or something related to your firm was said that he needed you to respond to.

Case Study III: Criminal spies also use engaging gaze to communicate non-verbally among one another. For instance, Criminal A was sitting at a corner of the hall, while Criminal B sat at the other end. Their target committed a blunder they had earlier talked about, and Criminal A would look at his partner in an engaging manner to echo a 'Didn't I tell you' message. Ideally, it would be difficult for anyone to guess what the criminals are up to because you would think they are individually reacting to what the speaker is saying, but deep down, they are spying on someone, calling each other's attention to some vital issues so that there won't be disagreement after the whole process.

6.14. Staring versus Gazing

Generic Interpretations of the Concept

At different points in this book, I have tried to draw the thin line between gazing and staring. However, I want us to fully explore the concept here as a means of having a full understanding of it. Sometimes, in a bid to hold a gaze, some people end up staring at their subject, and that communicates the polar opposite of their originally intended message. In clearer terms, the difference between staring and gazing is huge. *Staring* tends to be more distant, impersonal, odd, alarming, suspicious, or even confrontational. In short, the staring gesture is used to communicate negative messages. This gesture itself is disgusting and makes others uncomfortable. This can either be intentional or unintentional. When it is intentional, it is directed at a person we are angry at; we really want them to know that what they said or did was not pleasing to us. When we stare, we are on alert to attack due to the disdainful attitude of someone else.

On the other hand, *gazing* connotes something positive. It means we take comfort in our subject. That is why it is considered as an inviting behaviour. This is an intriguing behaviour that communicates readiness to talk to other people and even tell them that we are ready for them. Gazing means we can be approached. We display this gesture to people we are interested in.

What is important is that we make use of the appropriate gesture at the right setting. This will prevent miscommunication. For instance, staring can be very offensive if done at a close range—on subways, on the bus, sitting at the same table, etc. Once you know the difference between the two, you would understand where to employ each.

Scientific Explanations

Changing Minds states that gazing at a person's eye while communicating is seen as being normal and even promotes the whole essence of the discourse. However, if the gaze is done to other parts of the body, it becomes irritating; it is considered as a sign of rudeness in some parts of the world. That is why some cultures urge their people to look away or focus on the ground. The body language platform further explains that gazing is a means of registration of interest—when you gaze at a thing or person, it means you have interest in such. Anybody looking at your eyes at that moment would be forced to follow the direction of your eyes. When you look at a person normally, the gaze is usually direct into the person's eyes.

When you interlock gaze with a potential suitor and the person keeps on holding the gaze, this is a sign of love. If the person should look downward, it may be taken as being lustful. It becomes staring if the person holding the gaze is a total stranger and unappealing. This may be a means of threatening us so that you would not look at their side any longer (Changing Minds 2019).

Christopher Philips (2013) identifies four forms of gazes—friendly, business, intimate, and face gaze. Each has the best context to make use of them. For the sake of space, we would not be able to explore each of them. What I want to bring out here is that gazing has specific social functions it performs while staring is mainly considered in the negative realm. Philip opines that lovers gaze at each other adoringly as a way of arousing sexual interest and deepening their love, while those indifferent about each other, oreven those who hate each other, will stare at each other. At the point of staring, if any of the parties does not budge, this is a way of challenging each other. It is confrontational, and each party is trying to prove their strengths.

The intimate gaze differs from one culture to the other. The gaze that deals with looking at the other person directly before focusing on the lower region of their body is predominantly a Western culture. In Japan, for instance, people who are sexually interested in each other will rather focus on the neck. Remember that Japan is a low-contact country that does not support eye-to-eye contact for people who are not of the same social status or age group.

Practical Illustrations

Case Study I: You were just employed in a company, and the management made it known at the point of the interview that they were bringing you in because of your exceptional skills, which none of their present employees possessed. Upon resuming duty, you were introduced to the person who was doing that job in a displeasing manner before the board of management was forced to bring you in. You noticed that whenever you were working, he would look away and wear a sober face. There were instances when you were expected to work on a job collaboratively, but he kept on postponing them until the verge of deadline just to paint you as bad before the management. There was a day you were faced to challenge him with the bid of clearing the air over every issue. However, since you started talking right to the point you ended, they were focused on you without budging their gaze for a second. This is a staring gesture which is employed to communicate his hatred for your personality.

Case Study II: You were the busy type who hardly had time to call on the teachers of your kids, but your children had been telling you how the parents of other kids were always coming to check the academic performance of their individual child. On a particular occasion, you promised to find time to come but could not make it due to other exigencies. When your children returned home, they were fuming that you deceived them. You took time to explain, but it seemed all your explanations were not tenable to them. You even called their teacher, yet they were not pleased. On the following day, you took time off your busy schedule, and surprisingly, you were at their school. After meeting with the management, you decided to call on their teacher in class. Immediately they (kids) saw you, and they rushed out of their seats to embrace you and kept on looking at you happily while you addressed their teacher. This gaze is that of satisfaction, and in most instances, it is accompanied with smiles.

Case Study III: The ideology of every criminal is that every normative person dislikes them, and they act this out; they tend to hate everyone they see as a potential danger to their ill ways. The hatred is much more for law enforcement officers. If as a law enforcement officer you see someone staring at you without any reason, you should know that this is an expression of their hatred for you. There was a particular case where a woman stared at me in an intense manner that I had to invite her to know if all was well with her. She answered in the affirmative, and I allowed her to go, but after five months, she was arrested in the community for spearheading an attack on someone.

6.15. Closing the Eyes

Generic Interpretations of the Concept

Except in prayer sessions for Christians, it is unusual to see people close their eyes in public. Hence, if you see a person do that, you should be alarmed that something has gone wrong. This is more so if the person closes their eyes for a long duration of time or if a person suddenly shuts their eyes. This is considered as a blocking behaviour, a category under closed body language. When a person does this, it would be difficult to speak with him or her—or how easy does it look like speaking with a person whose eyes are closed? This is an indication that the person is trying to reject any entreaty that can make them speak with others. Also, when the eyes are closed, understanding a person's body gesture becomes extremely difficult.

Some of the messages this body gesture communicates are worries, concern, disbelief, or dislike. This is an implication of being psychologically disturbed.

If the person delays in opening the eyes, it communicates deep concern. On the other hand, if this gesture is displayed in an intimate setting, it is an expression of trust. It means the person is purging out everything about themselves and connecting with the other senses. Come to think of it, you would not close your eyes in private if you do not trust the person you are with. Hence, this is normally done by lovers as a way of expressing trust.

I need to note that this gesture is subconscious. Even children who were blind from birth use their hands to cover their eyes when they hear something displeasing. Hence, context becomes crucial in the interpretation of this gesture.

Scientific Explanations

According to Changing Minds, 'Closing the eyes shuts the world out.' That is, it disconnects us from everything in our environment. The verbal translation of this gesture is, 'I do not want to see what is in front of me. It is so terrible.' That is why I opined at the other time that it is a closed body language gesture. The platform also suggests that this gesture is equivalent to avoiding eye contact. This means you do not want to give the other person the opportunity to speak. After saying your piece, you are shutting the door against them. This is like ignoring the person or taking them as being unimportant. Sometimes, people may even close their eyes while talking. This means they do not want to look into the face of their co-interlocutor so that they can get their message well-delivered; they understand that the emotions on the face of the other person may affect what they had planned to say.

This is also an attribute of visual thinkers. When they close their eyes, it gives them the opportunity to see internal images clearer and reduce distractions from the external world.

Ken Saladin, an emeritus professor of biology, says that when someone closes their eyes while speaking with us, it may be an indication of insecurity, lack of confidence, hypersensitivity, or being extremely afraid of the opinion of others. In other words, it is a means of escaping from what others have to say, especially when we consider the situation very threatening. Saladin concludes, 'This can be a very subtle, unconscious behavior borne from years of one's perception of approval or disapproval from others, maybe going way back into childhood.' That is, this behaviour is propelled by our past experiences. Our subconscious swings into action when it discovers that a past experience is about to repeat itself.

In his own submission, body language expert Joe Navarro (2009) says cognitive load can force a person to close their eyes. He gave an example of asking a person to multiply 56 and 89 without making use of a calculator. In this sense, eye closure is viewed as an aftermath of stress. He said this to debunk those who misconstrue every form of eye closure as a gesture of deception. In this context, the person is only processing information, which does not have to do with deception. Those who allude meanings to gestures without taking cognisance of the context are the major cause of misconception in the field.

Practical Illustrations

Case Study I: While in a board meeting of your company, there was a deliberation going on about a particular policy and how it had affected the fortunes of the organisation, and at some point, each member was asked to reflect on the issue and make their opinion known. Maybe one of you was asked to compare the policy with that of competitors and what was earlier in place in the firm. If the person closed their eyes for a few seconds at a point of speaking, this means he was trying to process a piece of information relevant to the point he was making. At this point, we cannot say he is lying because there was no situation that warranted that in the given context.

Case Study II: You are speaking with a friend about an accident that occurred while you were going to her house. Maybe the accident was fatal, and you had a full view of everything. While trying to relay the incident to her, you tried painting it vividly so that she could understand what exactly transpired at the scene, but at some point, she unconsciously closed her eyes. This means she did not want to hear it. Actually, your presentation was painting a picture in her mind which might be connected to a scene she was involved in times past. So your narration might be bringing back such old memories which she was trying to guard against with that action.

Case Study III: In your class, you were making a presentation about the same subject matter on an individual basis, and then after making yours, there was a thunderous applause from the whole class. If the next person to present after you would close their eyes by blinking for a while without closing their eyes before being invited, this is an expression of their fear. The person was overly afraid that he might not perform to your level, which would make people see him in a negative light.

Case Study IV: I never knew that drug traffickers were that fearful until I came across one. He wanted to sound deceitful when I told him that if he was found wanting, he was to die by hanging. He was shocked, and immediately I uttered this statement. I discovered that he closed his eyes as if something were about to splash into his eyes. He eventually opened them and looked pitiable, as if he were mourning. He could not make any denial again, yet he was reluctant to speak further on the topic. Fear was written all over him, and I had to deviate a little bit so as to calm him.

6.16. Closing the Eyes for Emphasis

Generic Interpretations of the Concept

To affirm what another person has said, we briefly close our eyes and nod in agreement. This means the person has aptly the thoughts at heart concerning the given issue. As noted earlier, context is central to understanding every body language gesture. The interpretation I have just given now is used in the positive dimension—that is, the context under which the discourse is taking place matches with this submission.

On the other hand, this gesture may be used as a means of expressing disagreement over what has just been said or done. When someone does something that is irritating, after condemning such verbally, some people may further close their eyes as a way of emphasising that the behaviour is really appalling. This gesture would be followed with other related ones like the wrinkling of the face and holding on to oneself to really show that we do not have anything to do with such attitude. When the eyes are closed, it calls the attention of your co-interlocutors to what you are trying to say. With this, no one can deny the fact that your message does not resonate enough. This, however, is mainly used among equals or colleagues. If used as a way of reacting to what a superior says or does, they may enquire that you explain the reason behind such a behaviour.

Scientific Explanations

Changing Minds says the essence of body language emphasis is to amplify what we have said verbally. Sometimes, this body language emphasis is not made consciously, and that is when it is in its truest form. Nodding the head, beating of outstretched fingers, closing the eyes, shaking the eyes are all means of displaying emphasis with the body. However, we will peruse closing of the eyes in this segment. If you pay attention to TV presenters, you would know how important the concept of emphasis is. They are aware that only their head is in view and, as such, must adequately deploy it to pass an array of messages around.

Emphasising with the eyes closed is a simple body language clue, but you need to be careful while employing the voice at the same time. A person who closes her eyes at the sound of something is saying that she does not want to see that thing. If at that point her voice is saying yes, then there is a mix-up already, and thus, people become confused of which to go for. The basic reason for using the eye closure for emphasis is for synchronization—that is, you are making your body agree with the other parts of your body for the essence of making your point more valid and acceptable. The issue of emphasis in body language is likened to an orchestra—if one differs from the rest, it produces a result that does not make sense (Changing Minds 2019).

The platform refers to eye closure as a 'big emphasis'. This is because the person displaying it is not hiding under anything. The point here is to defeat the other person with the power of your point. A person who closes her eyes as a sign of rejection of an offer may also shout, making use of powerful words. With this, their point will resonate in the head of their co-interlocutor. This body language gesture is always intimidating. When you close your eyes and make a gesture, people may conform to you temporarily due to the tone of coercion it carried, but it may signal the beginning of long-term hatred.

It should be noted that this body language emphasis gesture can also be employed to emphasise all that has been discussed earlier in the preceding subsection.

Practical Illustrations

Case Study I: You are speaking with your spouse at home, maybe discussing a new policy made by the government and what its likely effect may be, and after you have talked for a while, you see your spouse close his eyes while nodding his head simultaneously. This is an emphasis of his agreement with you. This gesture can also be seen while discussing a matter relating to any of your kids. This gesture by your spouse means you have really spoken out his mind and he has nothing to add than just to agree with your point.

Case Study II: At the workplace, you are having a short discourse with your colleague that is relating to work, and as you begin to talk, you discover that she is shifting her attention to other things rather than concentrating. You later end up winning her attention, and after making some few points, she closes her eyes, wrinkles her face, and probably turns against you. This is an indication that she does not agree with you on the point you just made. They may even express their dissatisfaction on the point through verbal means.

Case Study III: If your child is discussing with you and it seems your attention is on something but the kid thinks what he is saying is more important than what you are giving your attention to, he may suddenly close his eyes after making several appeals to give him your attention. At this point, you may be forced to pause every other thing you are doing and listen to him. This means he has emphasised his point with that body language gesture. After having your attention, he can now open his eyes and begin to say what he originally wants to discuss with you.

Case Study IV: You visited a friend at home, and there was a blast at a major point in time whose video was trending. Your friend had got it, and there was a discussion relating to that. Then he volunteered to show you the video as a way of making his point concerning the issue known and in order to allow you to have a first-class knowledge of the situation. You actually agreed at first, then it got to a scene where the terrorists were actually beheading their captives. At that point, you could not bear to watch it again, and you unconsciously had to use your hand to block the screen and then close your eyes. This gesture is used to emphasise the fact that you could not bear to watch the scene again.

Case Study V: There was the case of an overstayer who believed that he did nothing wrong. In fact, according to him, he was contributing to the growth of the country because he was hard-working and patronising local businesses. It was a sort of argument between him and the law enforcement officials. At some point, a senior officer had to step in to explain some things to him. He listened intently, but at some point, he closed his eyes, frowned his face, and shook his head. This was in disagreement with what the senior officer said. However, that did not deter the officer from making his point and meting out appropriate punishment on him.

6.17. Covering the Eyes

Generic Interpretations of the Concept

This is very glaring, and even people who are far away from us can easily notice this gesture. Anything that involves the movement of the hands or fingers across the face is not a hidden gesture. When a person suddenly makes use of their hands to block their eyes, this is a closed body gesture that is related to negative interpretation. When a person sees something threatening, they would cover their eyes as a way of showing that they do not want to see the scene again. Imagine being at the scene of a bomb blast or watching the event on your TV set where people were burnt; I will emphasise on this while giving the practical illustrations.

This gesture is also employed to express negative emotions. It may be an indication of worry; the person may be troubled by something, and they are doing so as a means of shutting themselves against the world. With this, you would not disturb them because you know all is not well with the person. On the other hand, a person suffering from inferiority complex or lack of confidence may display this gesture as a way of hiding their face from perceived threats to their status. Remember, I said that even congenitally blind children also cover their face when they hear something displeasing. That is why people refer to this behaviour as an ancient evolutionary one—it is an inexplicable one. Why would blind people cover their eyes when initially they do not see what is going on? This upholds the fact that their behaviour is subconsciously rooted in all humans. However, this does not mean that it cannot be feigned by criminals.

Scientific Explanations

Using the famous tale of the three wise monkeys as the basis of her article, Hanan Parvez explains that the eye-covering gesture is done when we do not want to see something. She said it is a childhood gesture and it is done unconsciously. However, as we grow older, we begin to modify this behaviour because it looks obvious and would not like people to see us cover our eyes with our hands. Hence, we make it sophisticated and less obvious. For instance, for an adult to cover the eyes, they will rub it or even scratch the eye area using just a finger. This means the person does not want to see what is being shown. The most commonly observed gesture of this clue is that the head would be tilted or turned away while a finger would be used to scratch the eyebrows (Parvez 2019).

Parvez notes that this gesture is common among men, and it is done when they feel embarrassed or angry or become conscious of anything that may make them hide their face. Sometimes, when a person tells lies, they may have to display this gesture as a way of hiding their eyes from the person they are deceiving so that the person would not get to read their non-verbal gesture. However, this is not a licence to label anyone as a liar just because you see them covering their eyes. It may just be a sign of nervousness. However, if you think the context of discourse does not call for lies or embarrassment, you can walk up to the person to ask them the reason behind that gesture. This will save you from needless incorrect assumption (Parvez 2019).

Giving a psychological illustration of this, Scott Rouse (2019) says this gesture is compared to when a person closes their eyes and look away when a truck is approaching them on a pedestrian. The fact is that you cannot fly away from such a horrifying scene in the twinkle of an eye. Hence, the brain takes over every activity of your body at that point. What the brain does is close your eyes and quickly turn you away from the impending action. Even though this is not realised at that point, you are performing an eye-blocking behaviour. Although the case study given here is extreme, but the approach is what we have in every circumstance. Parvez says that this gesture is built up in our genetics. Again, let me state that when you see someone display this gesture, do not assume that they are upset, frustrated, or offended; it is a mere suggestion that those things may actually be happening or, in simpler terms, something is wrong (Parvez 2019).

Practical Illustrations

Case Study I: You and your friend had worked on a project some six months ago. Your hopes were high while executing the project because you thought you had carefully carried out your feasibility studies before embarking on it. However, after putting your whole effort into it, it was yet to yield any tangible outcome since then. Your friend, who was in charge of processing the funds, was in your place for the third time after the project had been completed, and you thought he had brought good report, only for him to come and narrate the same old baffling story. Once you discovered that he was about to say the same thing, you might subconsciously use your hands to rub your eyes or even cover it. This is a signal that you were not interested in listening to the same old assurances.

Case Study II: At the workplace, you are dealing with a boss who is intolerant and does not have any iota of respect for his employees, and you must report to him. This becomes burdensome because he does not praise you but always attack for anything. More so, whenever he wants to deal with any employee, he does so in public glare. On a particular fateful day, you have misarranged the files, and he needs to get something out as quickly as possible. If he calls for you, then you are prepared that he wants to embarrass you. Once you get to his front, you may cover your eyes with your fingers as a way of saying that you do not want to see him. When the eyes are covered, it means you do not want to have anything to do with the person standing in your presence.

Case Study III: This gesture is mostly found among children; they do display gestures as it is with minimal conscious changes. Child A had confessed to his parents that he disliked the daughter of their neighbour even though they were attending the same school. On a Saturday morning, Child A and his mother were outside when their neighbour's daughter passed and greeted them. Child A's mother noticed that her son placed a finger on his eyes as if he wanted to rub it until the girl walked past them. She asked him if something was wrong, and he said something 'fell' into his eyes. It took some minutes for the mother to understand the drama her son acted with the girl; it was a representation of his dislike for her.

Case Study IV: Criminals close their eyes for emphasis too, but it is context-driven. Criminal A once duped a woman and ran out of the country with the hope that their path would not cross again. However, the woman eventually travelled to the country where Criminal A was a resident. Fortunately for him, he saw the woman first, but he knew that people present would suspect him if he abruptly took to his heels. So he unconsciously covered his eyes with two fingers as if he were hiding from the woman. It took him a few minutes to regain his balance after the woman had walked away. Those he was conversing with were not suspicious enough to know something had gone wrong.

6.18. Rubbing the Bridge of the Nose with Eyes Closed

Generic Interpretations of the Concept

This behaviour is obvious because two contradictory gestures are simultaneously done as one. For instance, eye closure is a blocking behaviour—a closed body gesture that is done as a way of preventing others from accessing our thoughts. It is always said that the eyes are the windows to the soul, and when a person closes theirs, it is tantamount to shutting the windows against people. If this body gesture is displayed, it prevents people from reading our thoughts. On the other hand, the nose rubbing is a pacifying behaviour. Remember that when the hands touch any other part of the body, it makes it warm and soothes the body.

On a general note, when you see a person rubbing the bridge of their nose while their eyes are closed at the same time, it means the person is worried or concerned. A troubled person does this to show that they are troubled and, at the same time, trying to assure themselves that all would be well. This gesture is primarily associated with negative emotions. There are various interpretations that such a negative emotion may connote. An anxious person may display this gesture. Concerns, dislikes, and insecurities are other possible interpretations of this gesture.

Scientific Explanations

There are many reasons that make people touch their nose. On a literal level, it means the person has detected bad smell and, as such, is trying to cover their nose. Some also believe that this is a sign you see in people who tell lies. However, it is just a hint that something is wrong. Also, it may be that the person is stressed and trying to pacify themselves. When you are stressed, there is dilation of the facial muscles which makes the blood in the vessels run at an increased level. At that point, you would discover that the nose has become swollen and reddish. The nasal engorgement then causes mast cells to release histamine, which makes the nose itch, and so it may lead to the person touching or scratching it (Changing Minds 2019).

This gesture has also been said to be a signal of disagreement. When a person closes their eyes and then rubs the bridge of their nose, this connotes that the person does not agree with your point. Further, it is taken as an evaluative sign. The person closes their eyes so that ongoing activities in their environment will not impede their thought process. The nose rubbing is a sign that what they are evaluating is usually something negative, and the person is somewhat frustrated by it. Sometimes, you should know that this may just be a habit of people when they are lost in thought (Changing Minds 2019). Philip also supports this submission as he listed the gesture as part of the common gestures of a person thinking hard or evaluating a given situation. According to him, when we see a person do this, it means he is trying to arrive at the best course of action. To come up with a satisfactory decision, he must shut himself off from the world in order to be able to think through.

Making a sign of disapproval or frustration is what Batul Baxamusa (2018) says about this gesture. She also notes that it is done when a person is contemplating. In short, we can say that this sign is mostly displayed when a person is confused. From the foregoing, it is glaring that all experts who contributed to this subject matter reached a consensus on the possible interpretations that can be given to it. It would amount to mere repetition to consider more when it has appeared that they are all saying the same thing.

Practical Illustrations

Case Study I: It has been a busy week for you, and yet there are still many appointments on your schedule that need to be attended to. Some of the appointments are conflicting, but you have been trying as hard as possible to get everything sorted. You have to visit two people—a friend at the hospital and a client. You have booked 6 p.m. for the client, and then the hospital where your friend is admitted would not allow in visitor once it is 6.30 p.m. At present, you are at the crossroad that leads to the residence of your client and also to the hospital where your friend is admitted. You are seated in the car, thinking hard of what you should do first—leave the friend for the night without delivering what he had asked of you to get for him or disappoint the client who is just new and must be given a satisfactory service to keep him or her. At some point, you may just close your eyes so as to enable you to jostle through these thoughts, and as a way of pacifying yourself, you would rub the bridge of your nose. Anyone who sees you at this point will understand that something is wrong with you, although they may not be able to figure out what exactly that thing is. It is a symbol of tiredness in this sense.

Case Study II: A terrorist who had been commissioned to bomb two different locations in the city would first have to do their background check and understand the peculiarities of the settings before unleashing terror. Maybe when he went there on two different occasions, he had the same view and, as such, concluded that that was how everything had always been on a daily basis. Upon getting there on D-day, he discovered that the first location—an embassy—was not open. His main target was to have foreign casualties so that it could be the talk of all media around the world. Upon getting to the second location—a shopping mall—everything was on a standstill. Surely, the mall had gathered from intelligence reports that there was going to be an attack. Now the terrorist was thinking if he should dare the security arrangement at the mall, bomb the empty embassy, change his location, or return to his hideout and restrategise. At this point, you can see the frustration on their face, and they may close their eyes, rub their nose, and sit depressingly.

Case Study III: Friends also display this gesture to register their frustrations. I remember when one of my friends wanted to marry a lady, and he sought my opinion about her, having known her for some months. True, the girl had some charming traits, but her Achilles heel was that when she becomes angry, no one can prevail over her. I was so confused on which way to direct my friend to on the issue, knowing fully that I would share in the blame if things should go wrong. I unconsciously closed my eyes and placed my hand on the bridge of my nose, lost in thought, until my friend tapped me to ask if all was well.

6.19. Crying

Generic Interpretations of the Concept

The functions of tears or crying are varied both on personal and societal levels. However, it is a universal gesture connoting the cathartic purgation of emotions. Some people believe that the hallmark of frustration is the release of tears, after which they think they will get better. Crying is a testimony that someone is really troubled. Crying is a gesture that is most pronounced and can be noticed from afar. When some people are crying, they make all kinds of signs that draw the attention of others to them. Those who cry while kicking objects or holding on to the next person beside them can create a scene out of every scenario.

However, this body gesture can be manipulated, and even children know how to use tears to blackmail a person. Hence, both adults and children feign this gesture as a means of escaping punishment or forcing others into doing something for them out of pity. From the foregoing, while you are reading a person's body language, you should not give this gesture prominence over others and conclude that someone is going through difficulties. In fact, you must look for other signals of depression, frustration, and negative emotions before concluding the person is going through some pains.

Crying should not be a regular occurrence. If it does, it means there is a need to pay medical attention to the person. It is a sign that the person is depressed clinically and is dealing with some form of psychological struggle. Crying is not a good means of understanding the innate feelings of a person, and if you are forced to deal with it, it must be perused logically in order to be sure that you are not being tricked with this gesture.

Scientific Explanations

According to Christopher Philip (2013), crying is also known as teary eyes, damp eyes, weepy eyes, or glistening eyes. Philip says a teary eye can be used to connote joy or suffering. When people are extremely happy, they may cry uncontrollably. This means they least expected such a huge positive occurrence in their life. Same thing goes for when people are deeply hurt. They cry and wish it had happened to any other person. The eyes are used as signals in showing that someone is undergoing intense emotions. Children use crying to reduce the level of punishment as they create sympathy in their parents and tutors.

Philip also notes that this gesture helps us bond with other people and gain sympathy of people when we go through physical and emotional pains. He says that women are the most likely to benefit from crying, especially if they are among men who love to pamper them. Potential suitors can go to any length to ensure that a woman does not cry. Ironically, women are the first set of people who cry when wronged or vice versa. Many of them are not emotionally strong and, as such, see tears as a common way of expressing their grief.

When facing authority or when one is being scolded or hit, it is a good form of eliciting the sympathy of others. It improves the outcome of such situation. However, men should be careful of how they make use of this gesture as it may portray them as being weak or not being emotionally stable. Men are only permitted to cry while mourning a loved one (Philip 2013).

Also contributing to this topic, Paul Chernyak, a licensed professional counsellor in the US, says that 'crying is considered to be caused by an explosion of emotion in most cultures'. He also backs up the view of Philip that crying is caused by both sadness and happiness. He affirms that crying is not a reliable means of understanding the emotions of people as it can be employed as an instrument of deception by criminals. That is why the colloquial expression 'crocodile tears' is now a common expression in the world.

On its own part, Changing Minds lists the gesture as a commonly seen one in emotional body language. However, it listed some other gestures that we should take note of before saying that someone is suffering from an emotion or another.

Practical Illustrations

Case Study I: There was an old woman who was a widow and only had one daughter who was in her middle age. The daughter was learnt, gainfully employed, and doing well in all aspects of her life, only that she had no suitor. This was a source of concern for the aged mother who wanted to see her grandchildren. She had always lamented that she did not want their generation to end abruptly.

However, nothing always came out of her talks because her daughter was not really concerned about that—bothered at times though. Eventually, a suitor came, who was very responsible and focused. In no time, they had fixed the wedding date, and she took him home to her aged mother to inform her about the wedding arrangement. When she found out the news she had yearned for over the years, she cried profusely. In this instance, the cry is considered as tears of joy; she was happy beyond words.

Case Study II: You told your daughter to wash the dishes and do other household chores before switching on the television to watch her favourite show. She grumbled as you told her. However, you feigned ignorance and decided not to pacify her or even look at her in a stern manner. After some few minutes, she came to meet you in the living room, crying profusely, and could not even manage to mumble words out of her mouth. You were disturbed and had to pacify her so that you could hear her out. She eventually told you that she had broken your beloved dish. You were pained to the marrow due to this because the action was mainly propelled by her reluctance to do her chores. However, due to how she was crying, you became weak of meting out punishment on her. Through this, she had elicited your sympathy to defend herself.

Case Study III: Criminals are perfect dramatists; they can act out just any scene they consider as the way out of their troubles. There was a case of a man who murdered his wife, but before he could tidy things up, some neighbours saw him. Immediately, he began to cry profusely as if he were truly bereaved. Neighbours were left confused as to the circumstances that led to the death of the woman. Even when law enforcement agents arrived, he was still shedding tears, but after completing the investigations, it was established that he murdered the woman. Some of them cry during confessions to show how they regretted their actions.

Case Study IV: Even though it is rare to see people cry in an office setting, I have witnessed some handfuls of this over the years. There was a case of two colleagues who were very close; they were a perfect combination on every given project. Their closeness was known to everyone in the organisation. At first, no one reacted as it was not negatively affecting their productivity. However, it got to a point where the manager was uncomfortable with their relationship, and one of them had to be transferred to another branch. They both shed tears to the point that people had to ask them if there was something secretive about their relationship. They were pained that they were to depart from each other.

6.20. Clutching Objects while Crying

Generic Interpretations of the Concept

As I have said in the preceding section, crying is the purgation of emotions—whether positive or negative. However, when a person cries while clutching objects on their body, it is a show of extreme purgation of emotions, and this is usually done when someone is really disturbed by some negative occurrences. Some clutch at their necklace, neck, or even shirt collar when they are crying as a sign of showing that they are extremely pained by an event. These people may injure themselves if nothing is done to salvage them; they need help because the gesture shows that the person cannot actually control their emotion any longer. This is very dangerous if there is a sharp object around. At that very point, there is a momentary suspension of their reasoning.

Anybody who sees them does not need to ask if anything is wrong because it is weird in any part of the world to see an adult cry while clutching at an object, whether in public or in private. When people who are emotionally weak are caught in the middle of an incident, they really need support in order not to 'misbehave'. Usually, this gesture is witnessed in informal settings—that is, people feel composed and suppress their emotions while in board meetings and at work. However, at home, in parties, and at the scene of ugly incidents, you can see people display this gesture.

Scientific Explanations

Philip (2014) gives the verbal interpretation of this gesture as 'I'm overwhelmed with so much emotion it's welling up and pouring out of my eyes.' He says that when a person clutches an object while crying, it is an expression of anguish, distress, and bereavement. These emotions produce additional moisture, which makes the eyes glisten. This gesture is related to deep expressions of grief or regret. The person is not trying to hide their loss over an action. A person who cries clutching an object has probably lost something that is invaluable, connected to their destiny. This is different from damp eyes where the person suppresses the emotion or makes it seem as though nothing is really happening. According to him, crying is a universal signal of sadness. This means you should not try attaching cultural interpretation to this signal anywhere you see it. Philip says that 'crying symbolises an overflowing of emotions such as sadness from emotional hurt, from pain due to physical hurt'.

Writing on Lifehack, Joseph Hindy also states that when you see a person crying, he or she is certainly upset about something. He says that while other body language gestures may not be obvious, this is undeniable. Glaringly, it is a sign of being uncomfortable or feeling shameful. Examples under the 'Practical Illustrations' section will widen your understanding of this concept.

This gesture is in response to an emotional state or pain that can no longer be suppressed. Coming from this point of view, we can define *crying* as 'a complex secretomotor phenomenon characterised by the shedding of tears from the lacrimal apparatus, without any irritation of the ocular structures'. Note that this is not lacrimation which deals with non-emotional shedding of tears; this gesture is emotion-laden and driven.

William H. Frey II, a biochemist at the University of Minnesota, proposed that people feel 'better' after crying due to the elimination of hormones associated with stress, specifically adrenocorticotropic hormone. This, paired with increased mucosal secretion during crying, could lead to a theory that crying is a mechanism developed in humans to dispose of this stress hormone when levels grow too high (Emotional Freedom 2015). Emotional tears have also been put into an evolutionary context. One study proposes that crying, by blurring vision, can handicap aggressive or defensive actions and may function as a reliable signal of appeasement, need, or attachment (Live Science 2019). A person who is crying in such a passionate manner does not think of harming or injuring his colleagues.

Practical Illustrations

Case Study I: As a law enforcement official, you come across different forms of temptations per day as you engage with suspects from various backgrounds just in upholding the oath you swore to. Let's take a particular instance. You were interviewing a female suspect, and from all indications, she could not absolve herself of the murder accusation. However, she was charming and undeniably attractive. After you were done interrogating her, she subtly told you of her availability and gave you the assurance of doing anything to satisfy you if you could change things in her favour. At that point, you looked at her lustfully, patted her back, and smiled. She thought this was in agreement to her request. After retiring home, you considered the request vis-à-vis the offence and the likelihood of upturning justice just in a bid to satisfy yourself sexually. All odds were against you, and hence, you decided to stand for the truth. When she was arraigned for prosecution, she thought it was just a formality, but when you entered the witness box, you began to reel out facts against her. At that point, she knew that nothing could save her from being convicted again. Immediately she started crying, and when the judge made her pronouncement, she held on to her collar, dragged it as if she were about to tear her shirt, and started crying profusely. This cry exemplifies shame and regret.

Case Study II: Another case is that of a young couple who got married just three weeks ago. The wife decided to return to her workplace in a neighbouring town after the honeymoon. Till that moment, the love was perfect, and neither of them could not dream of leaving each other. Before the young bride set out for the journey, they had kissed, discussed extensively about their future, and promised to make up time that would be lost during the week by the weekend. However, just fifteen minutes into the journey, the wife had a fatal accident, and she gave up the ghost. When the husband was called, he did not believe it until he saw the corpse of his wife. Then he started crying, holding his neck, and feeling restless. This means that he is truly bereaved.

Case Study III: Friend D received the news of the death of his close ally, Friend C, on the early morning of Saturday. He was with C at the hospital on Friday, and it appeared that C was getting better. So he had thought that C would soon be discharged and that things would return back to normal. In other words, Friend D was not expecting anything like the news of the death of his friend. But here was an undeniable reality staring at him in the face. He cried profusely and clutched to the wheels of his car for hours. All entreaties to him failed until he lost his voice to tears. Anyone who saw him in this state would know that he was truly mourning.

6.21. Darting Eyes

Generic Interpretations of the Concept

This is a form of a negative body language gesture. Eye darting is the movement of the eyes to and fro in a feverish manner. When you see someone's eyes dart back and forth feverishly, it means the person is fearful or has been taken over by concern. Someone who is afraid would become restless. Hence, they would focus on all sides as if they were on guard; they do not know the direction in which the 'harm' will come from. This also applies to a person who is bothered about an issue. A troubled person looks at all angles for a way of getting out of issues. They do not know where the solution of their problem is. So you see their eyes move at all angles, all in a bid to look for a plausible solution to the issue bothering them.

Another plausible interpretation of this gesture is that the person is trying to process some negative thoughts, doubts, or anxiety. In short, this behaviour is propelled by negative emotions and is mostly unconscious. A person who is processing negative information will not be comfortable—the darting eyes is evidence of what is going on in their inner mind. Also, a person who doubts a piece of information or concept they are being shown will look around as a means of confirming what they just heard. In order to accurately interpret this gesture as meaning of the interpretations I have given above, you need to look for other related ones, such as chin withdrawal and facial tension, which are also signals of negativity.

A person darting his eyes back and forth shows that he is analysing a situation or trying to make a decision having found himself in a dilemma. I have read different articles where the authors affirm that this gesture is a signal of deception. Inasmuch as this is not entirely wrong, I need to state that attributing meanings to this sign alone and out of context is wrong.

Scientific Explanations

According to Study Body Language (SBL), darting the eyes is categorised as a greater signal of stress than the simple avoidance of eye contact. Remember that I said earlier that avoiding eye contact is regarded as a sign of stress. However, when the eyes dart, its meaning goes beyond that. When someone's eyes dart, you will see them running to different angles—they want to look at every other thing but the person standing before them. According to SBL, '[This] behaviour usually appears when the emotional state of a person *is escalating with tension*. The eyes dart back and away to quickly find some solution or escape route from the current encounter.' This quote really captures the meaning of this gesture in apt terms. It means the eyes are in search of a solution. At that point, the person does not care whether the solution is worth working with or not. All they care about at the moment is an escape route.

Philip (2013) says that this behaviour is habitually related to deception and lying. However, as I have emphasised while perusing the gaze section, 'professional' liars tend to hold your gaze longer than honest people because they know that this is one of the most looked-out-for sign among body language readers. In a study carried out involving seventy-five countries, it was found that avoidance of eye contact is a sign of deception among both the young and the old. However, this is not all that reliable because liars are aware of that postulation, and they try as much as possible to defy that principle. From the foregoing, it can be said that taking this gesture as a sign of lying can be dangerous, but surely, it explicates stress.

'Looking away from complicated human faces helps us concentrate and so it doesn't really tell us much more than that thought is taking place' (Philip 2013). I am still establishing that this gesture does not necessarily connote that of deception. When an honest person is subjected to undue stress or put on the spot, they will lose focus and may begin to sweat because they never expected it.

Practical Illustrations

Case Study I: You and your friend attended a birthday party of another friend, and as a way of building your network and getting to know more people, you decided to sit on different tables. While you targeted the midst of girls, your friend sat with some guys with the hope that he would have the opportunity to discuss football with them and then have some chat about girls. However, upon sitting down there, he discovered that they were only discussing personal issues and fashion. Your friend could not follow with this discourse and does not want to react immediately, so he kept everything within himself. It got to a point that his eyes began to move to every corner of the room—he looked at every other place but the table where he was seated. This means that he is concerned about where he was seated; he was craving for more social interaction with like minds, which was not available at the moment.

Case Study II: As a teacher, you need to pay attention to all the students so as to be able to carry them along. On a particular Monday, you were introducing the students to a new concept which made the whole class be silent because it was a little bit tricky. However, there were two students among them whom you had been paying attention to; their eyes were darting back and forth. When you mentioned the name of the first student, he shivered before answering. This means he was not attentive; he was thinking of another thing while you were discussing the topic. When you called the second student, he answered as an informed person. You need not be deceived about this response. The darting eyes means that the topic was very confusing to him, and he was looking all around if he could gain some mastery of it and assimilate all that had been taught.

Case Study III: I had an encounter with a drug trafficker some time ago. He was an expert in doing transborder business, and he saluted my ingenuity, noting that for decades, no one had been able to stop him. Invariably, he owned up to the fact that he was a trafficker. However, I noticed that as I was speaking with him, his eyes were darting back and forth. Although he looked attentive, that was only at the surface level. I pushed a question to him and appeared lost. I needed to know why he had wandered away psychologically, and alas, he was thinking of another way to ply his trade after being released.

6.22. Eye-Accessing Gestures

Generic Interpretations of the Concept

The eye-accessing gestures explain the formation of the eyes while a person is trying to answer a question or process a state of mind. Before I move further, let me give a practical explanation of this gesture. When a person looks laterally downward or upward and face a particular direction, it is symbolic of trying to process a thought, answer a question, or deal with an emotional state of mind. This gesture is somewhat easy to identify in people. The non-verbal message that would be written on the eyes of the person is that of someone trying hard to get ahold of something—they are trying to access something and, as such, are focused at the side without looking to and fro. In the realm of scientific literature, this is referred to as the conjugate lateral eye movement (CLEM).

Without mincing words, this is one of the gestures that have suffered most from myths; for decades, people have made unsubstantiated claims about this facial gesture. Before now, the widely held belief was that when a person looks to the side or away while trying to answer, they are telling lies. However, over twenty studies have debunked this myth. What the researchers found is that when a person displays this gesture, it is only an indication that they are thinking and not trying to be deceptive. Being on a hot seat requires thinking hard, and not every instance of thinking hard should be taken as a sign of deception.

It is good that we debunk this myth in the simplest terms so that you would not end up arguing with facts, which can always be stubborn. Those who believe in this myth are among the people who make the whole concept of reading body language look unrealistic. Experience and scientific research should be the hallmark of body language interpretation.

Scientific Explanations

Different scholars contributed to this subject matter, and you can find a lot of information online. However, most bloggers maintain that it is used to exemplify deception, an unsubstantiated claim. We are not going to dwell on that. According to Ariel Lehrer (2019), the direction of our gaze alone reveals innumerable things about what is going on in our brain. He describes CLEM as 'involuntary eye movement to the left or right and can indicate whether a person is engaged in symbolic or visual thinking'. What I like about this submission is the use of the word *involuntary*, which means that this gesture is unconscious—people can hardly feign it. Research has shown that people cannot focus on both right and left directions at the same time. The study affirms that humans are predominantly left or right lookers. With this in mind, you would know whether you are dealing with a more analytical left-brain person who will most probably look to their right or a creative right-brain person who has the probability to look to the left (Lehrer 2019).

Philip also echoes the importance of eye movements in neurolinguistic programming and how they help in communication. This gesture also helps in the retention of thought. Through experiment, it was discovered that eye movements are dictated by the part of brain a person is trying to access. The brain does not process all information in the same hemisphere. 'It was found that right-handed people tended to shift their heads and eyes to the right during "left hemisphere" tasks such as logical and verbal processing and left-handed people had entirely opposite patterns' (Philip 2013).

There is a consensus between Philip and Lehrer that people tend to look at the opposite sides of their brain while in search for answers. Although there are controversies concerning this finding, it is also one of the most valuable discoveries. Changing Minds also lists some of the possible causes of lateral eye movement. It opines that lateral eye movement can be caused by literal events—a person looking at a big charming picture will turn to look at it even if they have walked past it.

Practical Illustrations

Case Study I: In an interview setting, an applicant was asked how to handle issues relating to his personal and professional life. In this context, the interviewer was expecting a specific answer, which the interviewee was also aware of. In order not to miss the opportunity of getting the job, the applicant had to think thoroughly and recall some past experiences in their life. During this process, the applicant had to avoid eye contact with the person at the other side of the table and faced their left side. This means the person is trying to think creatively.

Case Study II: In another scenario, an applicant was asked how to increase the rate of productivity of the company with its current resources. In this situation, any answer would not work—the panel must be made to see reason to buy into the proposed idea. Hence, the applicant must analyse the present resources of the organisation vis-à-vis his plans. While thinking about this, you may see the applicant looking at their right direction. This means the person is trying to engage in analytical thinking. This is what some regard as lying. In that context, there is nothing that calls for deception and so should not be taken as such.

Case Study III: A new product was in town, and almost everyone you know had been talking about it. Before you left home, it was the last discussion you had with your spouse. Upon getting to the highway junction, which was always busy because it served many routes, a billboard had just been mounted which captivated the attention of all passers-by. As you approached it, you discovered that it was bearing the label of the product you just discussed with your husband. Even after driving past it, you were still turning to where it was mounted to have a clearer view of it. In this sense, it is literal and not a way of avoiding eye contact with the person seated beside you in the car. So context is the key in understanding this gesture.

Case Study IV: A man forged some documents in order to allow him to gain entrance into a given organisation. He thought the security at the checkpoint would just flip through the documents and allow him entry into the place, but he was wrongly informed. He was stopped, and after a thorough scrutiny of the documents, it was obvious that he forged them. While being questioned on what led to such an action and his mission at the organisation, he looked away and focused on the sky, thinking of what to tell the law enforcement agents. After some few minutes, he could not come up with reasonable explanations.

6.23. Fluttering the Eyelids

Generic Interpretations of the Concept

Eyelid fluttering is an indication that something has gone out of hand. Ideally, the eyelids should be stable and work in consonance with other body parts in order to aid clear vision. From experience, when the eyelids begin to suddenly flutter, it means the person is struggling with something or even a medical disorder. When you mess up with an opportunity, you may flutter your eyes as a way of lamenting your loss. This is an unconscious facial expression that exposes people when all is not going in the right direction. The possible meanings of this gesture are truly numerous, and the context in which it takes place every time will help us in understanding better what its causative action is.

In public or during the moment of intense anger, people flutter their eyes when looking for the right expression. Looking for the right word at times can be troubling and intellectually demanding. The person will have to rack their brain and, at the same time, retain their concentration of the main issue at hand. Another possible place of occurrence of this gesture is when someone just heard something unbelievable or witnessed a ridiculously dramatic scene. Unwillingness to believe something is often associated with this action. The look on the person's face will seem as if they were demanding to know more about a given issue.

Scientific Explanations

Desire or interest can serve as the major propeller of eyelid fluttering due to excitement. This is most true in the world of romance. When people are sexually charged up, there is nothing they cannot do to communicate their interest to the other party. Eyelid fluttering is one of them. Since the face is what people target while looking at us, people who are romantically connected with another person will make a judicious use of it to communicate their intents. Without mincing words, this gesture has become a quintessential way of inviting a romantic partner (Gangwer 2011).

Navarro also speaks about this facial gesture while writing on the body language of the eyes. He sees this as an eye-blocking behaviour and categorises it

163

as one of the obvious things that every human does. According to him, when the eyelids flutter rapidly, it expresses our sentiment—it explains our state of mind at that particular time. Some of the possible emotions which this gesture expresses are frustration, concern, trouble, depression, or struggle. Just like I noted while giving the generic interpretation, all these emotional states are negative. A person who is depressed will not want others to see their true feelings, especially in a formal setting, where it is understood that the opposite is always expected.

Christopher Philip notes that when an eye flutters, it signals sexual arousal or heightened emotion. During this process, the eyelids would be open and close in quick succession. He gives the verbal translation of this gesture as 'I'm having an internal struggle and stress with what you have said, and it's causing me to flutter my eyes and eyelashes.' In the realm of romance, he says that it means 'I'm aroused sexually, and I'm drawing attention to one of my best assets, my sexy eyes and lashes, to evoke protective feelings.' The reason Philip's contribution stands out is that it takes cognisance of the two different interpretations of other experts. However, I need to add that this cue is mostly done by women in a dating context. So men, take note. What is important is that you pay attention to the context of the use of the gesture and see how it is related to the event at hand.

Practical Illustrations

Case Study I: A woman really loves a man. When they go out on their first date, it seems that the man is flirtatious by looking at other women at the venue instead of concentrating on the person he came with. The woman can draw his attention through the use of this gesture. She bats her eyes as a way of drawing attention to them. Most probably, she made use of eyeliner and mascara, which will visibly add sex appeal to the eyes. The message the woman is trying to communicate in this context is her availability by showcasing her 'window to the soul'. This gesture may be paired with other related cues such as brief eye contact then looking down and accompanied with a smile. In this context, the message is clear.

Case Study II: In another scenario, a daughter and her father went out, and while they were discussing her needs, she mentioned about the need to visit the latest eatery in town. But the father was reluctant, saying he needed to go home and rest. After some verbal appeals, it seemed the father would not budge. Then she decided to flutter her eyelashes. In this context, the daughter is trying to coerce her father into doing her bidding. If the gesture was done by her mother, it is a subtle means of telling her husband that she is interested in having intercourse with him.

Case Study III: In a public political debate taking place between two leading candidates, one of the candidates had just spoken and won the admiration of his audience. When the second person was given the podium, he started well, but while referring to a policy issue earlier raised by his opponent, the right word escaped his mind, and the context demanded that he mention the word so as to make people understand his point and show that he was well informed in everything relating to governance. At first, he made use of fillers to hold the attention of the audience, but when it seemed the word was not coming, he began to flutter his eyelids. This shows he was trying hard to remember something. This gesture would even increase if his own supporters ended up mocking him at the venue. In the context of the latter, it means the action was unbelievable—he never imagined that his own supporters could join the opponents in teasing him.

Case Study IV: Prostitutes also use this gesture to lure their potential clients to themselves. One thing about prostitutes is that they believe they can open any door with their body. If they are trapped in an issue, instead of them thinking neutrally and approaching such a case objectively, they will try to seduce the person in charge of the issue, especially if the person is in the opposite sex. A friend told me a case of a lady who fluttered her eyes to him, accompanied with a smile and other seducing gestures, when it was found out that she stole an item from a mall. Obviously, she wanted my friend to drop the case in exchange for sex.

6.24. Pointing at the Eyes

Generic Interpretations of the Concept

As I have always mentioned at different points in time, when a person uses their hands to touch any part of the face, it is an obvious body language gesture that can be seen by anyone within sight. More so, it is an attention-calling action because immediately you are moving the hands to the direction of the face, and everyone around would like to know the final destination of the fingers—are you going to bite it, use it to scratch the eyes, or use it in pressing down your hair? The possibilities are almost inexhaustible. However, the specific action will dictate what the person thinks of at that moment.

In the case of using the index finger to point at the lower area of the eyes, it has different interpretations among different cultures. Some believe that it is a way of expressing doubt or suspicion. Among many other cultures in the world, it is done by many people as a way of pondering on something that has just been said or even questioning a given event. The best way to understand this gesture is to ask locals what it stands for whenever you are out of your local setting. Let's take Romania as a case study. Locals interpreted this gesture as connoting 'Be careful. We don't trust everyone who is listening.' This can be extremely deep and may not be easily understood by someone who is ignorant of their culture.

However, remember that this gesture may not be in any way connected to metaphor—that is, the spot may just be itching the person, and thus, he or she has to scratch it gently just as a subtle means of pointing to the lower region of the face. That is why it is always good to establish a baseline before making your pronouncement.

Scientific Explanations

When a person points their finger at their eyes, it is a blocking gesture. When the finger points at the eyes, the eyes automatically close because of their delicate nature; the subconscious thinks the finger is attempting to gain entrance into the eyes, and as such, the eyelids come together to prevent it. In the context of deceit, this gesture prevents the liar from having a look at your face. This is a gesture that is common among men. If they think that the person is really trying hard to play on their intelligence, they would look away. With this, they would not utter any verbal expression that can collude them with the other person (Westside Toastmasters 2019).

This facial gesture is a subconscious action initiated by the brain as a means of blocking out the doubt a person is exposed to. If you doubt what someone is telling you, you may unconsciously do this gesture as a way of preventing it from getting into your brain—you do not want to process the information into your subconscious mind because you think it is unbelievable. Another point where this gesture is usually observed is when a person sees something distasteful and tries to prevent such from entering their eyes. If you see a young man maltreating or assaulting an elderly woman, due to your compassion for the woman, you may unconsciously do the signal. Women usually do the eye-pointing gesture in a tenderly manner due to their make-up (Westside Toastmasters 2019).

On its platform, Sonamics submits that when you see a person display this signal, it means they are not comfortable and is looking for every means to flee the situation. In a sense, it is seen as an interruption of eye contact in order to disrupt the communication process due to what they are hearing or what the other party is showing them. The verbal translation of this gesture is, 'Please can we talk about something else?' (Sonamics 2019). This paragraph surmises what Westside Toastmasters says.

Practical Illustrations

Case Study I: In a case involving a law enforcement official and criminal suspect, before the official started the investigation process, he created an atmosphere whereby the suspect was told to do anything he felt like. He offered him food and some drinks. While chatting with the suspect as a subtle means to know his baseline, the law enforcement official looked at the suspect in the face and informed him that he should not hide anything from him and that he was serving as a close friend to him (the suspect). This did not go down well with the suspect because of similar cases he had heard from people and how the same official ended up testifying against the suspects at the court. So he pointed at his eyes in reaction to that assurance. The meaning in this context is that he did not believe the enforcement official.

Case Study II: You just gave birth some few days ago, and your cousin came to felicitate you on the safe delivery. The baby was a little bit stubborn because he cried always, so you were easily worn out. As your cousin came, you saw that as a means to escape and to have some rest. As she took the baby from you in order to play with it, you told her to hold on to it for you so that you could get one or two things sorted in the room. You did not return until after an hour when the baby was already crying and the young lady had sung all the lullabies she knew. Upon seeing you, she started touching the tip of her eye. This is an indication that the situation was not comfortable for her. You should come and get your baby so that she could be out of the place as soon as possible.

Case Study III: Another setting where this gesture is normally seen is during negotiation. Take car dealers as an example. If you go to buy a car, as a way of telling you that the dealer is not going to make much gain from the deal, he may mention that he got the vehicle cleared for a particular amount and that his gain in the amount he had proposed to you does not go beyond 2 per cent. At this point, you may consider the statement deceitful and start pointing or rubbing your eyes.

6.25. Eye-Pointing Cluster

Generic Interpretations of the Concept

This body gesture is an extension of the preceding one. Here, apart from the eye pointing, there is also a noticeable eyebrow arching and compression of the lips. All these actions are done in clusters—they are simultaneously carried out. The message in this action can be a little bit complex. However, it is certain that the gesture is a representation of negative emotion or as a reaction to something unexpected. The first possible interpretation of the gesture is bewilderment. It means the person is trapped in an unexpected condition. The lips are compressed so as not to make the person utter wrong statements that can further fuel the negative action.

One can also display this gesture in an unbelievable situation. Seeing a student who finds it difficult to write his name lead in an essay contest written from home will spring up this action—the teacher will begin to doubt the originality of the write-up—because something unusual has happened at that point. Hence, incredulity, bewilderment, and doubt are the common propellers of this action. You can be more certain of these interpretations if the eyes are tucked in. When a person feels a negative emotion, they reduce in their physical shape—they keep to themselves and look smaller because something has eroded them of their confidence at that point in time.

Scientific Explanations

Arching of the eyebrow is seen in people when they are taken aback by an occurrence. Since the event is unbelievable, this happens as a way of opening the eyes wider, perhaps in order to see the action in a clearer manner. According to Changing Minds, 'The more the surprised, the higher the eyebrows are raised.' That is, if the event is really unbelievable, the eyes would be opened in their widest form. In addition, if the person points to the eyes and raises their eyebrows, it is a means of calling other people's attention to their face. It may also be a means of laying emphasis on a point (Changing Minds 2019).

Further, this gesture may connote submission. When you compress your lips, raise your eyebrows, and touch your eyes, it is a way of surrendering yourself to a particular situation. A compressed lip means that even though you have something you want to say, you are forcing yourself to keep it as a means of respecting or adhering to the status quo. As a way of expressing incredulity, it is only an eyebrow that would be raised. This can only be done by some people. It is like saying 'Are you sure?' when you discover that someone is not giving you the full fact about an event (Changing Minds 2019).

Joe Navarro says that this may be a means of self-pacification from stress. By pointing at the eye and raising the eyebrows and then compressing the lips, minor stress is relieved from the body. Navarro further states that 'when something more significant is bothering us, our limbic system, in reaction to events, will compel the lips to narrow and disappear if the stress is significant enough'. This is a means of expressing discomfort. He said he used to use this behaviour in getting the culpability or otherwise of suspects. The 'lip compression, eye pointing, and eyebrow arching' behaviour differs in levels; it is more pronounced in people depending on the kind of stress they are going through. When you ask someone a question they do not like, you may see them showcasing this gesture. It is a sign of submission on one hand and that of protest on the other hand.

Explaining this behaviour in one sentence, Philip notes that it is an indicator of negative emotion. He describes the gesture as a signal of disapproval. It means you do not like what someone just said or did, but you do not wish to express your dissatisfaction verbally. The body language expert also notes that it means someone is anxious or stressed. In some situations, this gesture is referred to as an honest cue. In this sense, you can use it to tell people that they should adjust their behaviour to suit your bidding. In general, when you see this behaviour, it means the person is holding back something (Philip 2014).

Practical Illustrations

Case Study I: Your marriage was by the corner, and you feel like you should inform your colleagues so that some of them would come and grace the occasion. After a general meeting on a Wednesday morning, you made the announcement publicly, and they all cheered for you and cracked some jokes. After that, a female colleague who is very close to you at work approached you after work on the Friday of that particular week to know more about the wedding arrangement and the would-be wife. You were very happy that some of them were showing concern for you. So you were quick to reel out the details with smiles all around your face. While talking about the bride, you mentioned that she was an eighteen-year-old lady just trying to lay her hands on some things in life. At this point, your colleague compressed her lips, raised her eyebrows, and slightly touched her eyes. This means she had some reservations about your fiancée. She might be bothered at her level of experience and your egoistic nature in relation to her age.

Case Study II: You were at home with your wife, and after she was done with her chores for the day, you called her to come over so that you could get some issues sorted out. When she came, you discussed the issue of your job security, age, state of the economy of the nation, and ultimately, the future of your children. You suggested that the three of them, including the last child who was five years old, should be moved to a boarding facility so that both of you could have the freedom to work for more hours, save up, and make investments. Upon making this suggestion, you discovered that your wife compressed her lips, pointed at her eye, and arched her eyebrows. This means she had a counter-opinion that forced herself not to say out.

Case Study III: Criminals also use this gesture when having a counter-opinion to what an enforcement officer says. A case of an illegal migrant readily comes to mind. She was frustrated with her country and, as such, tried to evade the hardship but did not acquire all the needed documents before coming on board. When she was stopped, she claimed that since she had no criminal intents, there was nothing wrong with her action. It took three senior officials to explain the implications of her action to her. While she was being offered the explanation, she pointed at eyes and compressed her lips as if trying to stop words from getting out. This action is a representation of her internal struggles.

6.26. Rolling the Eyes

Generic Interpretations of the Concept

Let me set the ground running on this by submitting that this facial expression does not have a place in a professional setting; it is only seen in an informal setting, among people who are close. That is why some regard it as being a familial gesture. Now let's talk about the interpretation. When a person rolls their eyes, it is a medium of communicating their dislike for someone or something. They are rolling the eyes as a means of taking away their real view from it. Eye rolling can be disgusting in many circumstances, and that is why people dare not make use of it in a professional setting.

Furthermore, eye rolling is an expression of contempt over somebody or something. When you speak with a drunk, you may not respect them, no matter their age, due to that malady. Whatever the person says, when he is confirmed drunk, would be taken with a pinch of salt. Rolling of the eyes is to show that something is valueless. When you are saying something serious and your co-interlocutor rolls their eyes and wears a feeling of indifference, this is to say that they are not attaching any value to what you are saying.

The third possible interpretation of this gesture is disagreement. A person who does not agree with your point will simply roll their eyes as a way of showing their opposition. This can be very fast and unnoticeable to unobserving fellows. If this is done immediately after raising a controversial point, it means the person is craving to have the floor so as to register their disagreement over what you just said. This gesture is mostly used by children while dealing with their parents as a means of expressing rebellion or contention. Children are generally perceived to be lazy when it comes to performing some defined cores and have to be put through by their parents. At this point, they may want to resist. However, they understand that doing such physically can be unethical. So they employ this non-verbal means.

Scientific Explanations

Tom LaForce (2019) laments that this body gesture is mostly misinterpreted. There is a consensus that the gesture is a depiction of negativity. However, where the disagreement sets in is when we begin to discuss the specifics. Some think it is a signal of disbelief, others align with frustration, and some others dismiss the idea and the person proposing such. While there is possibility that all these three would be correct in distinct contexts, what seems painful is that people tend to be rigid in their interpretation; they believe their view is the most accurate and that nothing can change it (LaForce 2019). The most important key to conquering this issue is to pay attention and dig deeper instead of making assumptions.

In the Western world, the eye-rolling gesture has undergone changes in interpretations. For centuries, it was read as a sign of flirtation. However, just about five to six decades ago, it was changed to mean disbelief or annoyance about what someone else did. History has it that this gesture is traceable to the time of William Shakespeare. However, for the sake of space, we would not be able to provide the full details of the history. These days, what is shared as a consensus among people is that eye rolling is a connotation of negativity. In fact, a community in the US, a town in Illinois, made a move to ban the eye-rolling gesture in 2017. But communication experts across the board still maintain that misinterpreting this gesture is common (Essilor 2019).

You should also note that there are cultural differences to its interpretations too. For instance, some African tribes use the gesture to signal male beauty. More weirdly, the advocates of alternative medicine are of the opinion that eye rolling has positive effects; it bolsters brainpower. Above all, this gesture is sometimes related to ocular health, and if it is involuntary, you should seek medical attention because it tends to be dangerous (Essilor 2019).

Philip (2014), while describing this gesture in one sentence, says that 'rolling the eyes says disbelief, contempt, sarcasm and lack of respect'. What he did in this interpretation is to give the possible interpretations in all contexts.

Practical Illustrations

Case Study I: A man and his wife were planning where to spend their next romantic vacation. The wife said he gave her husband an open cheque to make suggestions of where they should spend the holiday, hoping that he would mention a location that would suit her. While talking, the husband suggested that they should spend it in a rental lodge and take a four-day fishing expedition. She had thought that he would suggest spending it in the sun. Upon saying this, the wife rolled her eyes. This is to note that she was not satisfied with the decision made; the suggestion was ridiculous to her.

Case Study II: While in the midst of your friends, you were discussing the world economies and their effect on individual lives. Contributions were coming from everyone but you. Everything looked intellectual, and you felt that you should not be left out in the debate. As such, you decided to make your voice heard too. Your friends, who were very much aware that you were not good in issues relating to economics, all went deaf and dumb when you signalled to speak. Not minding the graveyard silence, you made your point, and the next reaction was your friends rolling their eyes at your direction. This is to downplay your contribution and note that it was out of tune with their discussion. If you are temperamental, this can be very painful, and you may react negatively. But if they are intimate friends, it becomes a shared joke.

Case Study III: You were joking with your kids at home, and then an argument ensued about the past and the present. You requested that they should allow you to explain what was in the past but was now missing, and they gave you the go-ahead. After making your point, they decided to roll their eyes. This is to show 'What's the big deal in that?'

Case Study IV: An employee tried to illegally engage his brother in the company where he was working. The illegality went on for some months before the management discovered it. Immediately, the boy was arrested and made to face an internal panel where he indicted his brother. The brother, not seeing anything wrong in his action, explained that since the boy was working, the money he was paid was legal. The committee became pissed off with this lame explanation, and while they tried to remind him of the company's policies, he rolled his eyes to look at each of them. This is a sign of disagreement, which angered the members of the panel.

6.27. Touching the Eyelid

Generic Interpretations of the Concept

This is basically a closed body language gesture. When you touch the eyelid, it prevents people from having a full view of your entire face. It is like shutting the window to the soul. Also, this gesture is seen as a means of relieving tension. This gesture is always displayed by people who are observant of the errors of others; touching the eyelid is a reaction to the verbal errors of another person. This can be done in both formal and informal settings. People who talk too much are liable to misfire—to say something wrongly. A wrong expression is an expression that is offensive to the listener, one-sided, unpolished, insulting, and ultimately, inappropriate for the given context.

In a way, we can say that this gesture is to hint the speaker that they have surpassed their boundary through their expression. This will help the person apologise, clarify what they mean, or even rephrase the whole construction. Scratching a closed eyelid shows that something uncouth has been said. This gesture is mostly found among politicians when they get ahold of the pitfalls of their opponents. If the person does not correct himself, his opponent will surely use the statement against them. In the political circle, this gesture is tantamount to saying 'I have a big catch against him already'.

Scientific Explanations

Eyelid touch is a blocking behaviour. According to Christopher Philip, 'Blocking is a term used to describe when a person wishes to distance themselves from a distressing stimulus. Blocking is a part of the fight or flight response and takes the form of the flight element because it creates distance between things we wish to avoid.' A person touching their eyelid is not ready to fight. Rather, they are hiding themselves through this behaviour. This partial coverage makes you see the person approaching, but it communicates a deep message to the person that you are not ready to entertain them. When you see a disturbing image in public and you do not want to scream so that you would not end up being the centre of attention to everyone present, you can make use of this subtle gesture. This is done especially by women (Philip 2014).

Further, when a person touches their eyelids, it may be a means of communicating disbelief. In verbal form, it would be 'Oh my dear, I can't believe what I'm seeing.' You know that when you touch the eye or any area around it, it is very delicate, and you do it in a gentle manner, hence the use of 'my dear'. Eye-blocking behaviour is not limited to physical things seen; it also encompasses what we hear. When you hear an undesirable thing, you touch your eyelid as if you do not want it to get to you. Just like when tiny specks or other particles enter your eyes, you quickly get them before they get to a deeper level (Philip 2014).

Touching the eyelids makes it appear that a person is thinking, but in the real sense, there is no thought going on; it is a mere desire to look away. When you hear something that is particularly distasteful, you close the eyelids longer than usual (Philip 2014). From the foregoing, it would be discovered that the body language expert is trying to emphasise his point using different scenarios, but the point is clear to a layman—touching the eyelids symbolises negative tendency for an event. This is the ultimate message being passed across by the expert.

Practical Illustrations

Case Study I: You have just arrived from work, and it was a hectic day for you had to prepare returns, take stock, and close the voucher. Your daughter earlier informed you that some of her friends would be visiting but would take their leave by five o'clock in the evening by the latest. You came back by 7 p.m., and upon entering the compound, you could hear the blaring music in your house. This annoyed you, but you kept that within yourself, walking briskly to the room. Upon opening the front door, you saw that the whole house was in dissarray, and you were supposed to host dinner for some family friends in the next hour. As a means of expressing your disbelief in what you just saw, you used a finger to touch your eyelid, closed it for a moment, and took a deep breath before walking out on them. This communicates your message to everyone around—you are displeased.

Case Study II: After taking a week leave, you returned to work early in the morning the following Monday. Upon getting to the office, you saw a letter on your table. Upon reading through, you discovered that you had been transferred from the branch to another. It seemed you were in a reverie and, as such, had to change your position, go through the letter again, and then recall some past issues before taking the leave. You had complained to a colleague that the branch manager was high-handed and lamented how you struggled to get your leave request approved. Could it be that your colleague, who shared the same view as you, had reported you, or was it just a coincidence? You had earlier thought that she was a confidante. You had to place a finger on your eyelid as a non-verbal form of expressing your dismay on this dramatic event.

Case Study III: You were in the interview room with an applicant who had a past criminal record, but he kept it because he thought it was the slightest offence anyone could commit, and after all, no one would know about it unless he told them. You were interviewing him for a high-profile job, and as such, you could not afford not to carry out a background check on him. Your discrete findings made you discover some mind-blowing facts about him. During the interview, after giving him the open floor to talk, you started reeling out facts about him and then told him to comment on them. Before speaking, he touched his eyelid as if he were thinking, *I can't believe this.*

Case Study IV: Many impostors do think that no one can unravel their identity. Some of them even go as far as doing plastic surgeries just to assume the shape of the person they are impersonating. Impostor J was stopped by a group of officials who questioned his identity at the airport. He was furious that they stopped him to ask him such questions. After scrutinising his documents vis-à-vis his real identity, there were glaring differences. In a civil manner, the differences were pointed out to him. He was bewildered. He couldn't do anything again; he only touched his eyelid and looked away, imagining what his end could be. This was a show of uncertainty and ill occurrence.

6.28. Tired Eyes

Generic Interpretations of the Concept

Fatigue is an expression of tiredness. And fortunately, the first place to notice this is in the eyes. When a person is tired, you need not look beyond their eyes before establishing this fact. Then how do you know that a person is worn out through the eyes? Their face will look puffy, weathered, strained, and may even change colour. I have given clusters of signals so that you do not misinterpret other body gestures as fatigue. Remember that we have spoken about similar concepts such as doubt, concern, and disbelief, among others, which also elicit negative facial signals. A person who is tired would obviously not look charming. Fatigue, in a facial expression, cannot be easily suppressed. No matter how hard you try, those who know you will enquire to know what has gone wrong with you.

Fatigue is caused by different factors. One of them is long duration at work. When a person does not plan to stay beyond schedule at work but was forced to miss out on some personal assignments to sort out some things at the office, the person would look tired due to long duration at work, coupled with the pain of not being able to make up with their personal items. Crying for a long period of time and other external factors such as stress can also weaken a person. I will expatiate on the examples under the 'Practical Illustrations' segment.

Scientific Explanations

According to Paul Coelho, 'The eyes are the mirror of the soul and reflect everything that seems to be hidden, and like a mirror, they also reflect the person looking into them.' This means that everything is encompassing in this look. Tiredness, depending on the context, is what many people like to feign. However, the eyes are a stubborn part of the body when it comes to non-verbal translation; it gives people out easily. The eyes have the ability to show if a person is tired or feeling refreshed. When a person is fresh and charged, their eyes will glow and shine naturally. On the other hand, someone who is suffering from fatigue will display a dull-looking eye, accompanied with dark circles (Pragya 2018).

For the umpteenth time, eye body language is not easily feigned. So when you are tired, it is better you give yourself rest and postpone all meetings in order not to send wrong signals to the person you are meeting with; the person will see through your tiredness and assume that you are disinterested in meeting with them (Pragya 2018).

One of the common signals of tiredness is squinting. Here, the eyes would be narrowed, and the person would feel sleepy. Changing Minds also expresses the same view with Pragya on this. The eyes would be unwelcoming as nothing interests it as of the moment but rest. Another related signal is dampness of the eyes. Women are known to be fast in releasing their emotions through tears. This may also be accompanied with redness of the eyes. However, men do suppress theirs in most cases, and as such, this signal can always be seen on them. When tears are too much, they also make a person look tired (Pragya 2018).

Philip also contributes to this subject matter by noting that the eyes would look weak and that the tired person may need to support their entire face with their hand. This means they cannot hold themselves high again, and as such, they release themselves into their hands to bear the weight. In conclusion, when looking for signals of tiredness, you should do that in clusters as a way of clearing your doubts—that is, you should not just focus on the eyes alone. As a good body language reader, you should note if the person is fidgeting, scratching the side of their nose, and tapping their toes. If you can see all these, it means you are accurate on your guess (Philip 2014).

Practical Illustrations

Case Study I: You were supposed to interview about five hundred people for a job within two days. You gave all the potential employees the same time of arrival, then you started calling them in one after the other. The last person for the day, a young lady in her mid twenties, was called in after you have attended to over two hundred people on the first day. When you began to engage her, she was not sounding as enthusiastic as the first set of applicants you interviewed. She had narrowed eyes, dampened and reddish. You might be tempted to conclude that she was not interested in the job or had lost hope due to the number of people she saw, but the real reason was that sitting down on a spot for hours had worn her out. Her speech might be slurred, and then you might notice the other accompanying signals I mentioned in the 'Scientific Explanations' section while making a conclusion.

Case Study II: A man was very close to his mother, but the old woman took her ill and later gave up the ghost. He was really pained by the uneventful departure of his mother; he cried uncontrollably as if all hope about his future were dashed. Meanwhile, before the demise of his mother, he had been transferred to another unit in the company where he worked. So he was informed to resume work in the office after the burial rites of his late mother. Upon assumption of duty, it was as if the unit was not as productive as before, which made the management doubt the ability of the new head of the unit. Upon inviting him to the CEO's office, the CEO saw his eyes dampened and squinted. This means he has yet to recover from the tears he shed while mourning his mother and this has affected his professional duty. If such a person can be given time, he would bounce back when he gets over the issue. Fatigue is the major cause of stress and can destabilise a person if not put under check. In the two cases shared here, what they both need are psychological support from the appropriate quarters.

Case Study III: A smuggler was apprehended at the border, and he presented fake receipts for the items he was about to smuggle into the country. His confidence could deceive just anybody. However, a cross-examination of the receipts showed that they were fake. This led to questioning sessions. The first session was based on how he got the receipts. At first, he was hesitant, but when drilled further, he spoke clearly and provided useful information. On the second questioning session, his eyes were tired already. So the officers had to stop and ask him when he last slept. It was then that he revealed that he didn't sleep for three consecutive days. So fatigue had actually taken over his life.

6.29. Far-Off Look

Generic Interpretations of the Concept

We all have our unique ways of thinking, and as a matter of fact, it is an issue of integrity for everyone to respect the personal modus operandi of individuals. Having said that, it is pertinent to note that some people are visual thinkers—they look into thin air to get inspiration to birth an intellectual response or idea. This is what they do while alone or even in the middle of a conversation with others. The far-off look is done by staring into the distance. This action prevents them from being distracted by things that are taking place in their immediate environment. It has been found that this gesture allows people to think thoroughly; they are not distracted by anything, and as such, the outcome of their thought is holistic. Such persons are able to contemplate more effectively as it appears that no chains are holding them.

When you see a person staring into the distance and seems to be disconnected from the realities of their present location, it is probably an indication of being in deep thought. This means you should not disturb them. A person trying to recollect an important event that took place in the past will also display this gesture. Any noise or undue interruption of any kind will break the line of thought and render the process futile for the person.

Scientific Explanations

Writing on body language of the eyes, Writers Write (2013) states that for a person to look far into the distance, their pupil must be dilated. This means that the person is interested in gazing into the distance or looking at something of interest far away. However, I need to remind you that alcohol, LSD, and cocaine, among others, can cause the pupil to be dilated. People under the influence of drugs too seem to look into the distance. So you need to take note of that variant.Apart from that, when the eyes of a person seem focused far away, it is an indication that the person is lost in deep thought or paying rapt attention to what another person is saying (Writers Write 2013).

Commenting on this, Simply Body Language (SBL) says looking straight into the distance is a good sign—it is a sign of interest which many people yearn for in every communicative context. When a person looks up, disconnecting a little bit from the person they were facing, it means they are thinking. If this straight, distant look tilts towards the left, it means the person is trying to process information in their thought; they are recalling past emotional experiences. If you are talking to this person and notice this signal, you may need to give them some space to process their thought without disruption. It is a good sign to you because it means the person is truly engaged in the conversation process and does not want to give bluff as answers. Again, do not buy into the myths that this signal is a symbol of deception (SBL 2019).

Some experts say that when a person looks into the distance and tilts towards the left, they are trying to make auditory recollection. This is like the literal attempt to look at one's ear. Again, context plays a key role in this interpretation. If the door is located at the left direction of the room and someone focuses on this side, it may also mean that he is trying to take his leave away from you. Hence, the person is calculating how to move out of the present location. If the person looks up without tilting to any side, it means they are carefully ruminating on what you are saying. The sign is particularly good when the hands are folded to the back and the arms are raised (SBL 2019).

Changing Minds also supports the postulation that upward look is an indication of thoughtfulness. Particularly, it means the person is trying to make pictures in their head—visual thinking. If this is done during speech presentation, it means trying to recall some prepared words.

Practical Illustrations

Case Study I: In a history class, a teacher is discussing colonial rule and tells the students the merits and demerits of colonialism. In order to make the class very practical, he tries to relate the topic to national development and how colonial rulers shaped the thoughts of nationalists. To further make the class engaging, he decides to ask questions that will elicit thoughtful responses from the students in the form of a debate. At this point, many of the students seem to be interested and, thus, raise their hands to be called on to answer the questions. Most of the students who first have the floor fail to give impressive responses. However, a particular boy who sits at the back, looking upwards and seeming to have been staring into the distance, stands up to address the posers in a very practical manner. Apart from the teacher feeling proud, even his colleagues applaud him without being asked to do so.

Case Study II: In the boardroom, there was a need to change some of the company's modus operandi and work policies for greater efficiency having discovered that the firm did not perform optimally in the outgoing year. All the decision makers and bigwigs in the company were present. For six hours at a stretch, a lot of ideas had been presented, and everyone could truly testify that the meeting was a gathering of intellectuals and industry experts. No one called for break; everyone was passionate about the growth of the firm. While everyone was speaking and making novel contributions, the CEO was focused, writing and listening attentively to different suggestions. At some point, he had to drop his pen, gaze into the distance, and keep mute for some minutes. Other members around were a little bit baffled about this, but they had to give him the honour of being the lead and just hear him out. This gesture means that he was lost in thought on the new model to adopt for the company.

Case Study III: I have seen criminals project this gesture too. It is a sign that they are lost in thought. There is no way a criminal would not be forced to think when properly drilled. A man was trying to launder his father's money. He had made every arrangement with his accomplice before we intercepted him at the airport. As a mark of honour, I decided to interview him. He was all smiles until we got to the interview room and I threw the first question at him. He gazed into the sky and looked far off as if he were not with me. I gave him some few seconds to think before asking him what was wrong. His non-verbal posture depicted him as someone who was lost in thought.

6.30. Glazing of the Eyes

Generic Interpretations of the Concept

There are a lot of things that can cause the eyes to glaze—both physical and psychological. Basically, alcohol and drugs such as marijuana and other more dangerous substances do make the eyes look glazed. There is a crucial need to establish if a person is under the influence of drugs while dealing with them. The reason for this is that when a person is under the influence of drugs, it affects their psychology and makes them behave in a weird manner. You cannot predict what they can do at this point in time. For instance, those who go on a robbery operation or are hired to assassinate a person ensure that they take drugs that rewire their psychological settings so that they can do what is ordinarily considered an impossibility.

It is pertinent to note that those under the influence of alcohol or drugs can be found in any facet of life; they are not limited to an informal setting alone. As such, everyone must understand how to assess a person to know if they are normal or have been influenced by some powerful, harmful substances. Also, glazed eyes is not a self-sufficient gesture in assuming that a person is under the influence of toxic substances; you need to look for other related gestures while assessing in order to arrive at a more accurate conclusion. Other behaviours you should take into consideration are slurred speech or critical slowness to respond to queries. Toxic substances weaken the efficiency of the brain, and you can see it in the speech of a person.

Scientific Explanations

According to Philip, what can cause the eyes to glaze over is emotional downtime, which we all feel at some point or another in life. A study reports that on average, people 'slip away' every three seconds to be with their internal thoughts. This helps them to internalise what is going on around them. It is this moment that is technically referred to as downtime. This downtime gives the brain the time it needs to process the information of the activities going on in our vicinity. A person undertaking this action will showcase these characteristic body languages: pausing their breath, appearing blank in the face, brief freezing of the eyes, and subtle chewing of the lips. Ultimately, the eyes would glaze over (Philip 2014).

Describing a visual system processing, NLP Mentoring, a body language platform based in the UK, says that it is like maintaining a glazed look. Such people will look ahead in a defocused manner. In a related submission by Steve Hedger, a relationship coach, he explains that glassy eyes may be used to communicate romance in the non-verbal realm. In fact, the relationship expert describes this signal as 'a sure-fire way of attraction'. He explains further that 'when someone is aroused by another, their body creates moisture in the genital region. What you may not know is, this moisture also builds up in the eyes, giving a glassy appearance. If you get this, yes they are very attracted to you.' This explanation seems logical and sheds light on the romantic process in a scientific form.

After you have observed this, the next thing to observe is the movement of the eyes to other body parts and then to the face. With this, you can establish the specific feelings of the person towards you. If they focus on your mouth, it means they want to kiss; if they focus on the nose, they are looking for mere friendship; if they focus on the chest, they really want to explore you; and if they focus on the genital area, it means they are craving for a sexual intercourse with you (Hedger 2019).

Exploring this concept from the medical angle, Taylor Griffith (2017) mentions intoxication as the foremost cause of glazed eyes. Substances that can cause this are not only the illegal ones but even prescription drugs. The substances affect the body's central nervous system and, thus, slow down the rate of regulation. He opines that 'of all drugs, glassy eyes are most commonly associated with marijuana and heavy alcohol use. Other symptoms of intoxication vary widely but can include slurred speech, imbalance, drowsiness, and argumentative behaviour.' Time is the known treatment of intoxication. In this circumstance, glazed eyes make a person appear dull.

Practical Illustrations

Case Study I: After a date with a lady, you decided to return home, and she suggested that she spend the night at your place as a way of completing the fun for the night. You reluctantly agreed, and upon getting home, you were critically tired. You had to undress immediately so as to freshen up and sleep in order to be hale for the next day's job. As you were undressing, she sat at the other side of the room, glancing at you. She was elated at your six-pack. Your charming smile was another point of attraction to her. At this point, she was really aroused because she was half-dressed too. Her legs were shivering, and you could see the moist in her eyes. This is an indication that she is romantically ready to have intercourse.

Case Study II: You have a colleague in the office who is very calm and seems not the social type; he stays on his own, does his work at his own pace, and leaves once it is closing hour. Those who try to speak with him seem to be forcing themselves on him because he is not forthcoming, no matter how hard one tries. Then you decide to give him a try, study him from a closer range, and see what could have been the possible cause of his weird act and dull look. After learning some of his likes, you decide to play to the gallery. On a particular Friday, you propose to visit him at home, and he agrees. Upon entering his home, all you detect is the smell of marijuana and cocaine. You hate the smell and become afraid that he would attempt rape. So you decide to leave after thirty minutes. Hence, you now know the reason for the dull look; he was looking dull due to the harmful substances he had consumed.

Case Study III: Some group of men were stopped on the road due to their questionable behaviour. They flared up, saying they did nothing wrong, and the law enforcement officers calmed them down, emphasising that their action was in the overall interest of the society. However, they noticed a young man—very calm and dull-looking. The officer who noticed him pitied him and moved nearer to him to ask him if all was well. Upon getting closer to him, the officer could perceive the smell of cocaine on him. The dull-looking man was searched, and drugs were recovered from him. He was an addict, hence the reason for his look.

6.31. Looking Sideways

Generic Interpretations of the Concept

Some describe this gesture as 'looking askance'. In an ideal communicative context, interlocutors are expected to face each other. This demonstrates their commitment and passion to what is being discussed. However, when one of the interlocutors look away without any just reason, then this calls for concern. It means something is amiss, and the second party must fish that out or else their effort will be in vain. The interpretation of this gesture is primarily based on what is being discussed at the moment. However, I will try to give some possible interpretations here which will serve as a guideline to you in your conversations.

When a person looks askance when you are proposing a major idea, it is a symbol of doubt; they do not believe in the feasibility of your proposal but understand that if they should maintain eye contact with you, you would see doubt written on their face. In another sense, it is interpreted as reluctance to commit oneself to a course of action. Making commitment does not only involve verbal proclamation; the body too must be fully involved. If a person is boxed into a corner in making commitment that is against their wish, they may look askance as a way of communicating non-verbally that they should not be queried if the promise is not fulfilled because they are making it under duress.

There is no gainsaying that facial expression is an embodiment of messages to anyone who knows how to decode them. Looking sideways may also connote disregard. When a person is addressing you and you intentionally decide to focus on some other things, this means you are giving due regards to the person. In a way, this action may be said to mean contempt. Putting all these possible interpretations together, it raises suspicion; people become suspicious that you have something to hide. Universally, this facial gesture is used to express incredulity, disbelief, and concern.

Scientific Explanations

Writers Write also contributes to this body language gesture. The platform gives three major interpretations to people who are fond of looking sideways—distraction, deception, and nervousness. However, if you look away from a speaker in a formal or informal context, it is an indication of submissiveness. This is mostly true in a situation whereby you are dealing with a superior and in some low-contact cultures such as Japan, Latin America, Africa, etc. These cultures forbid maintaining eye contact with a superior or elderly person for a long period. This is opposite of what is achieved in most parts of the Western world. In another sense, it may indicate discomfort; some people are not usually comfortable looking at a person straight in the eyes. If it becomes a stare, they will not even assimilate what the person is saying. Generally, looking askance means the person is in quest for more explanation because they are not convinced about what you have said so far (Writers Write 2013).

Also commenting via his Medium account, Dr Jack Brown says maintaining an askance posture is not in the best interest of a speaker. He describes the gesture using one of America's figures of authority. He says the cue involves partial closure of the eyelids and elevation of eyebrows. In an ideal state, these adjacent tissues should not be in contrast to each other; it is not a default non-verbal status. It means the speaker is critical of his audience. This does not make the communication process flow because the speaker has inadvertently or intentionally created a feeling of distrust through the body posture. Brown puts it thus: 'Human beings do not look directly at those whom they do not like, do not believe, or do not respect.' Hence, people with this behaviour also get the same treatment from their audience.

Philip (2014) describes this body characteristic as a symbol of disapproval. It is done through the eyes in combination with the head. He notes that this trick is much more effective when put to use by women. Some of the verbal translations of this cue are 'You didn't just say that. You better start back-pedalling' and 'I heard what you said loud and clear, but I'm not buying what you're selling.'

Practical Illustrations

Case Study I: A mother had just bought some candy from the mall and arranged them in the treat shelf in the pantry. She specifically warned her son, who was a candy freak, not to go near the shelf because she was planning to use it for her visitors she was to host sometime during the weekend. He answered reluctantly and moved away from the shelf. However, his mom knew that with the way he behaved, if there was no one within sight, he could come back and walk away with some. So she was lurking around the house, keeping tab of his every movement. Not knowing that his mother was still very much alert, he tiptoed to the shelf, and as he was about to dash for some of the candy, the mother appeared, looking askance at the boy for a moment. He was taken aback, withdrew his hands hurriedly, kept to himself, and bowed his head as he walked away. Even though she was not pleased with her mother's action, there was nothing she could do about it.

Case Study II: In an interview room, a law enforcement officer was engaging some suspects. The investigation was tense because the lead suspect had been on the watch list of the agency for up to a decade; he was hardened and smart. The official had documented all the allegations against him. He first started with the other two people apprehended along with him; he wanted them to speak first so that he could get some facts about their gang leader from them. They were inexperienced and could fall for simple tricks. And truly, they did. Then the hardened criminal was brought in. At first, he showed readiness to challenge every issue brought up by the official, but at some point, the official mentioned that one of his boys informed him about the issue he just denied. Yet he was still insistent of not having knowledge of such a thing. Annoyed, the official looked askance, and at that point, he looked away and succumbed.

Case Study III: A teacher told his students to prepare for test the next day. However, he did not tell them the form the test would take. When he came in, they brought out their books to write, but he instructed them to return them. He told them he was to call them at random and ask them questions. The students were gripped with fear at this point because they knew that if they could not answer the question thrown at them, their colleagues would likely mock them. When the teacher looked at a particular direction to call a student, they all looked away with the aim of evading being called; they were not ready to answer any question.

6.32. Looking at the Sky or Ceiling

Generic Interpretations of the Concept

When there is an upward look at the ceiling or gaze into the sky, this is always obvious because you see the head tilted backwards, hanging in the air, and the person focused on the things above. While speaking with the person, you would notice that he or she is not maintaining eye contact with you or any other person around. This is done when it seems that a project is not feasible to implement. So it is like the person is looking up to the heavens for help or finding an inspiration from any angle in order to continue with that particular assignment.

Another point where people look at the sky is when they have a consistent run of bad luck. At this point, a feeling of disappointment will be written on their face; they would be dejected and worn out. The feeling of depression tells anyone near them that something is wrong. This signal shows as if we were asking a superior creature to have mercy on us and make things change for the better. In a way, it is as if the person were surrendering to a higher power. This is normally seen in sports—when a footballer misses a great opportunity or when a golfer misses a putt. All in all, this is a look of disbelief with the verbal interpretation 'Despite all my effort, this is where I could only get to.'

This body gesture has some usefulness. Stress brings about tension on the neck, and as such, this behaviour serves as a pacifying means; it relieves the neck of its pains. Looking upward makes the sternocleidomastoid muscles to be stretched and strengthened. Hence, we can conclude that this behaviour is somewhat good for our health.

Scientific Explanations

While discussing some of the poor body behaviours that give people away, Gary Genard (2017) mentions looking at the ceiling as one of these gestures. His article is primarily based on how public speakers can maximise non-verbal cues to their own advantage. He says looking at the ceiling or any other side apart from the audience is a clue that the speaker is trying to articulate their argument. Once your eyes are off the listeners, you are subtly saying that you are done with the audience. He condemns this behaviour, noting that it does not produce the desired outcome. When you are looking away, do not address people, as it will look like you are taking them from granted. Hence, they will feel like taking their leave.

Christopher Philip (2013) also talks about this gesture while discussing eye contact in business. Remember, I said that eye gesture is the truest indicator of a person's emotion. That is why business people—and, by extension, every other person—take it with a sense of importance. Analysing gazing at the ceiling as one of the seven patterns of eye movements, Philip says that it is an indication of conscious analysis—that is, when you see a person focus their gaze on the ceiling, it means they are consciously analysing something. This submission is not different from that of Genard, who also says the person is trying to articulate their thoughts. If one is not addressing a crowd, there is nothing wrong with this behaviour. For instance, during negotiations, a person may look at the ceiling in order to consciously analyse their gain or loss if they proceed with the deal.

Jackie Annesley (2019), writing on 'The Power of Looking Up', says that those who face up have positive behaviour. He notes that those who look up have a high probability of blocking negative thoughts from slipping into their minds compared to those who look down. When you look down, you become smaller and, as such, can be easily depressed. Note that this is a literal interpretation of the gesture, but we cannot deny the truth that comes with it.

Practical Illustrations

Case Study I: A man went to buy some items at the market in order for him to resell them to consumers within his local community. For decades, he had been a trader, but things appeared to be dicey for him lately. On the last occasion when he came to make some purchases, he ended up losing a huge amount of money because he operated in today's dynamic market with the use of yesterday's methods. While making the purchase, he decided to bargain on every price mentioned and ensured that he was making the best decision in the interest of his business this time around. When a wholesaler gave him the least price he could release an item, he had to look at the sky and then decided to go for the product. This means he has analysed everything and discovered that the price was right for him.

Case Study II: A terrorist had been commissioned to bomb a location in town. When he got there, things seemed complex, but he was able to make his way through. While on the premises of where to bomb, he discovered that there were two groups seated wide apart. He needed as much casualties, but the way in which the people were seated apart made it almost impossible. More confusing for him was that the two groups were almost the same in number. Now he had to take cognisance of other factors so as to know which group to eventually go for. Should he think of the properties close to each group or the age group? He had to focus on the sky for some few minutes as if he were seeking something. This means he was lost in thought, consciously doing the analysis of the situation.

Case Study III: A secretary was asked by his principal to get some documents typed. The words in the documents ran into thousands, and he had to get everything ready before the next day because his principal was scheduled to fly out of the country for an all-important meeting. Hence, he worked overnight and polished everything. He typed directly on his flash drive so that he could easily send it to his boss after work. Not knowing that his boss had updated his laptop for a while, upon inserting the flash drive in the laptop—it was infected by virus—in the twinkle of an eye, all the data were gone! He raised his head and looked up to the ceiling. This signalled depression and search for succour.

Case Study IV: A politician who had embezzled public funds got a hint that anti-graft agencies were about to come after him. He rushed to the bank to empty his accounts so that he could devise a way to launder the money in order to come out clean if the investigation is conducted. While the teller was working on his requests, he received a call from his aide that the airport officials did not receive his bribe. This means his items would be thoroughly checked before departure. He became troubled. He stood there, gazed at the ceiling of the bank, thinking of another way to go about it. This was an expression of worry.

6.33. Searching for Acceptance

Generic Interpretations of the Concept

There is a point in our lives when we crave for acceptance from some quarters. There is nothing wrong with this, but when it is laced with some negative tendencies, it becomes questionable. In most communicative context, people who lack confidence or are deceptive in their ways are those in search of acceptance from their audience. If a person who is not confident is speaking, they will look at the faces of their audience from time to time, scanning through them, in order to establish if they are being believed or not. The same thing goes for a person who is lying; he wants to be sure if people are really falling for his lies or if he has to change techniques in order to make them believe what he is saying.

I need to quickly add that whenever you see this behaviour, it does not necessarily mean that the person is deceptive; they are only in a quest of finding acceptance of their speech. People who do not believe in themselves or the intellectual taste of their presentation will look into people's faces to be sure if they are making sense or not. As I conclude this, let me remind you of the rule of thumb used in this realm: *Honest people convey their story, while liars try hard to convince.* In other words, a person who is truthful only tells you what they know about something, while someone who is lying will seek you to believe whatever they say, hence the reason for going the extra mile to seek for approval!

Scientific Explanations

People can go the extra mile to make themselves acceptable. Kendra Cherry (2019) states how the eyes play a key role in seeking approval from others. She implores us to always take note of eye movements, which ordinarily is an important and natural part of our making. Those who are seeking for approval will make their pupils look bigger so that those they are seeking to convince can have a clear look at their eyes. The subtle message they are trying to pass is that they have nothing to hide, and that is why they usually leave the eyes wide open. However, you need not be deceived by this assumption at all times. Cherry explains that the 'bedroom eyes' usually used to connote dilated pupils is used to attract other people to us. In other words, people seeking for acceptance can make use of the eyes in numerous ways to win our heart.

Contributing also to this, Travis Bradberry (2017) says that this gesture is always accompanied with exaggerated nodding. This is done out of fear. When you are conversing with a person and he is scanning through your eyes, accompanied with excessive nodding, it is an indication of seeking your acceptance in all ways. They want you to buy into their idea or show some form of admiration to them. Even if you are missing the point, they will not bother to call your attention to it so that you do not dislike them.

A person who displays this gesture has an interest in you. The interest, however, can either be positive or negative. If they look at you with passion, it means they are in consonance with what you are saying. When they develop hatred for you, they may also look at you in the face so as to convince you that what they are actually saying about you is the whole truth. If you should buy into this idea, they may end up creating in you a sense of inferiority. Those who are not proud of themselves do not just start at that. Someone instigated the feeling in them, and they bought it without questioning (Pragya 2018).

Practical Illustrations

Case Study I: A multinational company commissioned some of its experienced staff to go and work on some policy issues and also interact with people so as to know the feeling of an average person on the quality of its services. After the conclusion of the work, the committee that worked on it was informed that the findings would be presented to the major stakeholders in the firm. After the presentation was made, the member of staff who represented the fact-finding committee stood on the podium, looking into the faces of the decision makers of the company. The reason for doing so was to seek for their acceptance of the work. If it were just for the performance on the presentation, he would have focused on the other members of the committee and not the authorities.

Case Study II: An applicant had tried her luck in many organisations, but after submitting her curriculum vitae, she was not even invited for an interview, let alone know what she was made up of. However, she eventually submitted her details at an up-and-coming firm, and she was invited. During the interview session, she was a little bit composed and made some brilliant answers to the posers of the panellists. As the interview was rounding off, she kept her gaze at the head of the interview. She responded to questions and were expecting them to agree to the fact that what she was saying was the response they were looking for. Hence, the gesture was a searching look.

Case Study III: A woman and her husband needed to discuss the future of their children. The wife was concerned that she and her spouse had works that keep them out till odd hours. Yet she was not a fan of getting childcarers to take care of their three kids. After succeeding in booking appointment with her husband, she first appealed to his emotions by shedding tears at some point when she was talking. Then the husband was moved and asked for her suggestions on how to salvage the future of the children before they turn to juveniles. She made a suggestion of boarding facilities and other alternatives. Throughout the period she was talking, her eyes were on her husband's. She needed an approval to every point raised, and she ensured that she ended up convincing her husband on her feelings. The non-verbal behaviour was hinting her if she was right or wrong.

Case Study IV: A man was arrested for illegally attaching himself to a firm. When he was called to explain the reason for that action, he began to look tired and pitiable just to appeal to the emotions of the officials. He explained that he took the action out of frustration as he didn't want to die of depression. He also explained that the wages he was receiving were far lesser than the services he was offering. He told them of his great exploits in the firm despite being illegally engaged. While offering these explanations, he looked into the eyes of the officials, searching for acceptance, which didn't come. This left him disappointed.

6.34. Lowering the Eyes

Generic Interpretations of the Concept

Do not assume this to be the same with eye avoidance. In the lowered eyes behaviour, there is no breaking of eye contact; what happens is that a person looks down as a way of showing deference, contriteness, humility, or piety. During this process, the eyes would be lowered so that eye contact becomes indirect and not intense. This is not a universal body gesture behaviour though; it is culture-based. Also, some children are taught not to maintain direct eye contact with elderly people. Also, they are told not to look back at people in authority, especially when being chastised. They grow up with this consciousness and pass it on to their children.

This is the culture of the blacks and Latinos. As such, it should not be mistaken for an act of deception. If you take this as an attempt to deceive, you may be regarded as a racist because you did not take into account the cultural peculiarities. Let's take Japan as a case study. It is out of place for you to stare at a person you are meeting for the first time. This can create enmity between you. At the minimum, what is expected of you is to lower your eyes as a means of social deference.

At the literal sense, this behaviour may indicate that the person wants to look at something on the floor; maybe something fell, and the person wants to pick it up. Also, those who are fashion freaks may lower their eyes to see the kind of shoes the person they are conversing with is wearing. If they like the pair, it can serve as a topic of discourse between them. The reasons are numerous, and what is most important is paying rapt attention to the context and other clustering behaviours to make an informed decision.

Scientific Explanations

Linda Melone (2014) describes this gesture as one of the eye-blocking behaviours. Navarro opines that the manoeuvring of this body language is extremely right. In this sense, they equate it to a reaction we show when something has gone wrong with an interlocutor—that is, if you do not like what someone else is doing or saying to you, you may lower your eyes. Lowering the eyes in this context is related to closing the eyes, and we do it in the face of negative emotions. Also upholding the view of Melone, Navarro says that this behaviour is an inborn aspect of us—we learn to close or lower our eyes without being taught. Although this cannot be totally right if we are to take cultural context into view. Some cultures specifically teach their children to lower their heads while conversing with an elderly person.

189

Changing Minds exclusively discusses this sign under the eye gesture. The first point the platform makes is that anyone who makes this gesture is shy and submissive. Since the person is facing down, it means they are submitting to the wish of the other person. Further, the website explains that the person may be tired. So in order not to let people know how weak they are, they lower their eyes while interacting with other people. In some parts of the world, anybody who challenges their elder would be seen as an outcast. I will explore this concept further in the succeeding paragraph.

In Japan and some South American and other Asian cultures, extended eye contact is seen as being disrespectful and rude; it is regarded as an aggressive behaviour. The above-named cultures do look away or lower their eyes while speaking with other people. There is always a problem if they are interacting with Europeans or Westerners because in those parts of the world, it is expected that one maintains eye contact with their co-interlocutor for at least three seconds (Westside Toastmasters 2019).

Practical Illustrations

Case Study I: A Japanese lady was posted to an American organisation. It is an understatement to say that she epitomises beauty. Apart from beauty, she was also intelligent and smart about her work. Very soon, she became a source of attraction to the male employees. To put matters straight, she did not have anyone she was dating as of then. For the first few months, most of the male workers were only eyeing her, and due to the differences in culture, she did not even get to know the signs at most times. One of the male employees thought she should have got the signs and register her availability, but he did not took the bold step to ask her out. At this point, she was getting familiar with some of the American cultural traits. After some pestering, she decided to give him a try. After all, love knows no bounds. Throughout the courtship, it was a show of love galore. After some few months, they decided to make the relationship legal. They kept on living happily. However, there were times that the husband was heavily bothered. He discovered that the wife would lower her eyes most of the time he was addressing her. He was afraid that she was hiding something from him, but there were circumstances that did not call for such suspicions and she still did that. He did not want to approach her directly, so he decided to see some Japanese movies. It was then he discovered that it was a cultural means of showing reverence among the Japanese.

Case Study II: A black American child had just been enrolled in a school dominated by Europeans, the teachers included. As a school that was sound in educational doctrines, it was expected of the teachers to interact with every child in order to know their peculiar needs. However, all efforts of the teacher to know this black American kid were abortive; when in class, he hardly maintained eye contact with the teachers. When called by his teacher for a private discussion, the case was also the same. The teacher was a little bit bothered, and she had to call the attention of the management of the school to her ordeals. It was then that they explained to her how to handle him and respect his cultural peculiarities.

Case Study III: Apart from cultural settings, students also display this gesture on a general level. Students are very tricky and devise all means to evade questions they don't know. As a trainer, I do see my trainees lower their eyes when asked some questions. Any time their eyes are lowered, then I was sure that I would see no hands up. This was a clear message to me that they did not know the answer to my questions. Sometimes, to drill them, I would tell them to think, but most other times, I would answer the question in order to save time. When students have an answer to a question, they will look up, flashing their eyes on you to call them. This means they are eager to give you a response to your poser.

Case Study IV: Except con artists who do not have shame for their actions, an average criminal feels embarrassed when issues surrounding their evil acts are revealed. Some of them honestly regret their actions, while some feign it in order to be released. A common non-verbal gesture you will see in that situation is the lowering of the eyes; the criminal will look away from you. In addition, criminals who want to make things difficult for you will lower their eyes so that you will have no access to them. This means you will be left confused on their involvement in a crime since you couldn't read their eyes to understand their thoughts.

6.35. Sad Eyes

Generic Interpretations of the Concept

Sadness is what every one of us hates; it is a child of nobody. Except in the rarest of circumstances, we all try to suppress the feeling of sadness in us. However, some people feign it as a way of showing that they are 'truly remorseful' about a given development. Fortunately, Paul Ekman notes that a sad look is part of the universal microexpressions that cannot be feigned. This means that when we look in-depth, we will discern between a truly sad person and a fake one.

For a sad look, the person would appear dejected, with the eyes saddened. Also, they will look depressed when the upper eyelids droop; they would look fagged out with little or no energy. This look of sadness is always similar to a person who is tired—the eyelids of both droop. The causes of fatigue are different from sadness. Fatigue weakens some of the facial muscles, which make the person look dull and unappealing. In the case of sadness, the emotion is aroused in a negative manner.

What is important is that we are able to discern between sadness and other related emotions in any given context. This is evidence of our understanding of non-verbal communication, which is usually the main thrust of any given discourse. In the succeeding paragraph, I will provide scientific explanation of this concept in order to shed light on it.

Scientific Explanations

There is a consensus among experts that this gesture is one of the universal emotional microexpressions. Cherry (2019) lists sadness as part of the emotions that can be expressed through the face. He opines further, 'The expressions used to convey fear, anger, sadness, and happiness are similar throughout the world.' In other words, the feeling of sadness is almost the same thing across the world. Hence, if you can identify a sad face in your own culture, you can spot it on people from other cultural backgrounds too. The simple arithmetic is to interpret the emotion as you do in your culture.

Changing Minds (2019) discusses the gesture of sadness in two different articles. The body language platform upholds that sadness is an expression of depressive state—that is, when a person is emotionally depressed due to a reason or another, you will notice it through their facial expressions. If they manage to utter some words, their tone would be flat while their lips tremble. If the sadness transcends what they can suppress, tears would begin to flow from their eyes. This means they cannot keep it within themselves any longer. In any circumstance, tears are considered as an outburst of emotions. This means the person is really troubled and wants others to know about it. This is biologically aided by tear ducts, which ensure the secretion of moisture to the eyes.

On a general note, damp eyes is an indication of sadness. It means the person has probably suppressed tears or they have been crying secretly in recent times. There are people who cry in their secret place when they are emotionally down, although they do this primarily because they do not want others to know what they are going through. However, when the eyes are dampened, it is also a message in itself. The eyes of a sad person would be red. This means the muscles of the eyes have been stressed and, as such, reacting negatively (Changing Minds 2019). Taking all the cues of sadness into view, it makes the person look dull, unattractive, and concerned. If meeting a sad person for the first time, it may leave a sad impression about the person on you; they keep close to themselves and are not open.

Practical Illustrations

Case Study I: You just visited one of your relatives, and you saw your little cousin sitting down in an unfamiliar manner. You know her to be a cheerful young boy. Whenever you were at their house, he would be the first person to come and hug you, chat with you, and keep the place lively for you till you take your leave. But this time around was simply different. You made advances and brought gifts for him, yet he was not forthcoming. You saw that the smile on his face was a forceful one. You waited until the arrival of his parents and enquired to know what was wrong with him. It was then the mother explained to you that he had failed his professional exam for the fourth consecutive time. Then you encouraged him and assured him of a bright future. This means that you were right that your cousin was bothered by something, only that you were not certain of what the issue was. There is an array of things that can lead to sadness.

Case Study II: You and your spouse had a discussion over the need to buy some things at home. However, you were low on cash and promised her that as soon as you were reimbursed, you would cater for those needs. But it appeared that she did not believe you and thought you were only reluctant to do it because those things did not appear as pressing needs to you. After a few entreaties, she seemed to have understood you. Then you drove out to respond to some important appointments. When you returned, you saw your wife seated at the side of the room, eyes dampened and reddish. She kept to herself, feeling heavy, then she stood up to come and hug you. You walked to her, gave her a kiss, and went inside to undress. When you returned, she was still not herself. So you walked to her to know what was wrong, and before she opened her mouth, tears were running down her cheeks. She later managed to speak with a flat tone that she was not pleased with your inability to meet the needs she considered dire in the house. This means she was really emotional about your financial status.

Case Study III: You had promised your last child that you would buy him his favourite snacks while you were coming back from work. However, being engaged with so many other things mentally, it escaped your mind. Upon returning home, he rushed to meet you with the hope that you had bought the snacks, only for him to be disappointed. Immediately, his eyes changed—they were dampened, and his eyelids drooped. This means he was not happy with your behaviour at that given time.

Case Study IV: A man was about to move a huge amount of money from a public account into a private account, obviously for selfish reasons. He had made arrangements with people who would help him fast-track the process. Unknowingly to him, the appropriate agencies had been intimated of what he was up to. When he got to the bank and was trying to process the documents for money to be released to him, some law enforcement officers who were lurking around suddenly showed up and arrested him. He could not put up any story. Immediately, his countenance changed; he wore a sad face and buried his eyes in shame. Almost everyone was asking him if something was wrong.

6.36. Looking Away

Generic Interpretations of the Concept

When a person looks away from their co-interlocutor, this embodies different messages to someone who understands it. However, let me quickly chip in that one of the few body language gestures that have been subjected to unsubstantiated and myopic interpretations is the looking away gesture. People erroneously assume that whenever a person looks away from the person(s) they are conversing with, such person is trying to hide something. Hence, that is why it is hastily concluded in many quarters that it is a signal of deception or lying.

Well, what matters most in this context—and by extension, in reading every other body gestures—is context. Basically, a context where a conversation is taking place can either make a person psychologically comfortable or otherwise. For instance, when a person is speaking with their friends where they are cracking jokes and relishing old memories, they are psychologically comfortable, and as such, even if they look away while speaking, no one tends to take it against them as a sign of deception. On the other hand, when this is done in a formal context where people are conscious of everything going on, they can assume that the person is trying to deceive.

There are a few points to note on this. First, there are people who are naturally shy—deception or not, they cannot maintain eye contact with people. This transcends cultural or tribal affiliations. So attention must be paid to such people. Further, looking away, especially while embarking on an intellectual assignment, is seen as a means of recalling. It has been discovered that when people look away, they find it very easy to recall an event than when they look into the eye of the person they are conversing with. In addition, some people are easily distracted; the slightest form of noise or interesting chat has diverted their attention. Taking cognisance of all these, you would agree that establishing the context of communication is very important.

Scientific Explanations

Writers Write expatiates on the concept of looking sideways in a conversation. The platform opines that 'people who look to the sides a lot are nervous, lying, or distracted. However, if a person looks away from the speaker, it could display a level of comfort or indicate submissiveness.' This submission is balanced and self-explanatory. People who are naturally nervous do look away while conversing with others. Generally, a person who is fond of looking sideways is not convinced about what the other person is saying.

Another contributor to this topic is Vanessa on Science of People. According to her, looking away is an indication of uncertainty. In a sense, it means the person is in search for more information. This means you have to speak more, ensure you get the person's attention, and convince them on the subject matter. This submission aligns with the point of Writers Write. Vanessa continues that a person looking away will always have a furrowed brow. In this realm, it is an indication of suspicion or critical feelings.

Changing Minds explains this gesture in its very depth. Mostly, our field of vision is in the horizontal plane; hence, when people look sideways, they are taking their vision off the person standing in their presence. This disconcerting look may indicate a conscious effort not to look at a person or one is being distracted by something. If the looking away is very quick, this means the person is only trying to assess a source of distraction which serves their interest or threatens them. Further, it can also be interpreted that what the person is seeing is irritating to them. As I have earlier explained in the introductory part of this gesture, a person who looks away may also be trying to recall something. In some rare instances, it is an indication that the person is lying and, as such, taking away their eyes from being assessed.

Practical Illustrations

Case Study I: Some files were missing in the office, which made the CEO bothered; he had to work on some of them and send them out for approval on some vital assignments. He checked the central system to see if he could retrieve the documents, but his efforts were futile. Then he called the man in charge of the files and electronic documents in the office. He remembers that he (CEO) left the employee in the office the day before. He seemed to be busy, and the CEO had thought that there were files on his table to clear. So he did not bother to disturb him before the boss took his leave. When asked questions on the whereabouts of the files and what he was doing at work after office hours, he kept mute and looked away. The CEO probed further, and still he was keeping his eyes away from him. At this point, the boss knew that something had gone wrong and that his employee was actually guilty.

Case Study II: You had assigned a work to some of your employees. They met and worked as a team. Then they sent you the report through one of their members. After glancing through, you appreciated their effort in a lukewarm way. Then you began to pass comments on the whole work. At some point, you said something about the composure of the group, and immediately the member looked away. This means he was trying to tell you that what you said was actually disgusting to him.

Case Study III: A man just came across a lady in the train while travelling for a holiday. They clicked immediately and found friends in each other. While discussing in the five-hour journey, their talk later revolved around past memories and how they had lived their lives. At some point, the lady had to look away for some minutes before talking. The man erroneously thought she was trying to be smart. However, when she later narrated the story she was trying to recall, he saw that there was no need to disbelieve her. Their bond grew more.

Case Study IV: A con artist hurriedly played on the intelligence of salespersons in a shopping mall. After pulling his tricks, he behaved as if he knew nothing about the occurrence and was prepared to walk out of the mall. However, the account officer who noticed the error called out to him. Instead of the con artist turning back and answering the call, he looked away and feigned ignorance. His pace became faster. It took the efforts of the security agents on duty to get him arrested and made him pay for the items he had carted away. His body language did not betray him. Thanks to the alertness of the account officer.

6.37. Long Stare

Generic Interpretations of the Concept

A long stare can be threatening to a person who does not understand the way it works. This gesture is mostly witnessed during moments of silence. While conversing with a person and they become silent, this would be accompanied with a long stare. Depending on the context, some stare into the distance, while others stare at the person they are conversing with. It should be noted that these two are situation-specific. While addressing a group of people, it would be out of place to stare at just a person; this would be threatening to the person and even give you an overall poor image. Ideally, stare into the distance when you meet yourself in this situation. Also, while dealing with a superior or elderly people, you will rather look away instead of staring into the eyes of the person. A superior can stare at your face, and you may later be forced to look away.

The first possible interpretation of this gesture is that the person is lost in deep thought. When you are thinking deeply, everything within your immediate environment does not really bear value to you. It seems you are blind to them and, as such, make you gaze into the distance. Another possible interpretation is that the person is processing a piece of information. In this case, the person does not want to mix things up and even reconnect with the past so as to be able to work with the information in an unarguable manner.

Scientific Explanations

According to Changing Minds, the eyes are always wider than usual when one stares. It is done when we maintain prolonged attention to a thing, and it drastically reduces blinking. In general, it is an indication of interest in someone or something. When the long stare is directed towards a person and done at a close range, it means the person is shocked or lost in disbelief. The long stare is mostly seen when someone hears bad news and does not know how to suppress the negative emotions that come with the news. Furthermore, when a person stares into the distance, it means they are defocused from their external environment, battling with their internal thoughts. Hence, what they stare at has no significance to them. In fact, they may not have a full physical view of the item or distance they are staring at (Changing Minds 2019).

The body language platform notes that when the eye contact is prolonged, it also signifies aggression, deception, or affection. However, the case of the latter is rare. The website submits that 'staring at another's eyes is usually more associated with aggressive action'. Looking is different from staring. So a long stare can be intimidating to a person. The website says further that 'when a person stares at another, then the second person may be embarrassed and look away. If they decide to stare back, then the people "lock eyes" and this may become a competition with the loser being the person who looks away first.'

As a means of deviation from the conventional interpretation, Mark Manson (2011) explains that a long stare accompanied with smiling is an indication of love. This is in line with the affection mentioned on Changing Minds' platform. If this is done by a man to a woman in the Western or European setting, the woman may think that the man has sexual interest in her. Addressing love seekers and his audience in general, Manson says that this gesture is arguably the most pronounced love sign anyone can get from a potential suitor. This means the person is not withholding any intention about their love for you.

Changing Minds concludes that 'the length of an acceptable stare varies across cultures, as does who is allowed to stare, and at what. Babies and young children stare more, until they have learnt the cultural rules.' The point echoed in this conclusion is very crucial and would like you to hold on to it at all times.

Practical Illustrations

Case Study I: You were travelling on an official assignment with your colleague, and while on the vehicle, you were having a nice time; it afforded you the opportunity to discuss other issues apart from official matters. For hours into the journey, it seemed both of you were just getting to know each other because that kind of intimate discussions had never happened between you both.

However, after you said some things, you discovered that he did not respond, and more worrisome, he was staring into the distance. After some minutes, you had to tap him, and he shook as if something unexpected came to him. He apologised that he could not respond to you immediately. He was lost in thought, which was probably propelled by what you said; he was worried by what he heard.

Case Study II: You went to chill out with your friends. It was on a Friday, and you had thought that hanging out was one of the ways to ease out the stress of the passing week. Being two ladies, when you got to the club, you decided to take some drinks and dance together. After that, you sat at a table, smiling and discussing a topic of interest with your friend. There was a charming, gorgeously dressed man seated adjacent to you. He seemed to be disconnected from people seated close to him. You had noticed the stare from him at first but did not bother to look at his place. So as not to make him uncomfortable, you subtly looked at his side again, and this time around, his stare was accompanied with a smile. He kept on with this gesture, and at some point, you had to call the attention of your friend to it. In this case, it was an expression of sexual pleasure.

Case Study III: You were addressing a meeting, and suddenly, there was a need to make reference to someone or something. The concept was so much relevant to what you were saying that you could not afford to move on to the next item without making reference to the name. You began to stare into the distance and scratched your head a little. This means you were trying to recall that piece of information.

Case Study IV: The identification of a man was checked, and some inconsistencies were noticed. The enforcement officers on duty called him to defend the inconsistencies noticed, and as usual, he argued that there was nothing wrong with the document. The officers decided to ask him some questions, and there, he seemed to answer them all. The question that gave him out was when he was asked to sign on a paper. Obviously, he seemed not to have paid attention to the structure of the signature on the document. After a long stare into the sky, he scribbled something on the paper, and when compared, the differences were glaring. The stare even depicted him as someone who was deeply confused.

6.38. Squinting the Eyes

Generic Interpretations of the Concept

One of the easiest ways to register displeasure or concern is through squinting of the eyes. This is most especially true when you are doing it in the presence of those who you converse with very often. Squinting the eyes is an indication that something has gone wrong with the person. When we see or hear something that does not augur well with us, we squint our eyes to register our displeasure.

It is the attribute of some people to squint any time they hear a disturbing or bothersome news. In this sense, this is good and encouraging as it reflects the true state of their emotion at that point. The reaction comes in real time, and you can always see it on people if you are observant enough.

There is also a literal meaning to this signal. When a person wants to have a close look at something or someone, they will squint as if they were blind to every other thing but what they were focusing on. In the same vein, when we are trying to make sense out of what we hear, we can display this gesture too. This means that we are processing that particular information and would not want to be distracted by other external factors. Hence, context is as important as the gesture itself. A well-thought-out response normally comes from this gesture.

Scientific Explanations

Christopher Philip (2014) says another name for this gesture is narrowing eyes. Other names given to this gesture are furrowing eyes, compressed eyelids, wincing eyes, eye constriction, eye blocking, eye shield, shielding the eyes, and squinting. This gesture occurs when the eyelids are compressed together, which constrict the eyes. This gesture appears in the twinkle of an eye. The main cause of this body language gesture is emotional or physical pain. When a person does not like what is being said or seen, people will narrow their eyes. This communicates your disdain to the other person. Although this gesture is a microexpression, if displayed, there is a high probability that the person will still get the sign being made. Philip gives the verbal translation of this sign as 'What I'm seeing is causing me emotional or physical pain, and to prevent all that negativity from coming into my body, I'm going to squint and block to resist.'

Squinting is an eye-blocking behaviour. It is done to show one's distaste for an image or thought. So the behaviour prevents the person from having a full view of the image. Hence, this gesture is an indication of anger, contempt, or distaste. Also, it may be a result of the sudden approach of projectiles and the sun's glare. When a print is too small, we squint our eyes in order to see it clearly. Hence, it is performing a functional purpose in this realm and emotional. According to Philip, 'A delayed opening or prolonged eye closure can be due to negative emotions or displeasure. A full wince with the eyes closed tightly signifies the desire to totally block out information.'

In the view of Changing Minds, narrowing of the eyes is a sign that someone is evaluating a situation. It also means uncertainty. In a way, this gesture can be used by liars so as to prevent others from detecting their deception. When the eyes are squinted, you are unable to see properly, and at that point, you may be rejecting a negative thought within. You should note that tiredness can be a major cause of squinting. However, if the eyelids are lowered and focused on a potential suitor, it means the person needs a romantic affair.

Practical Illustrations

Case Study I: A secretary had just finished preparing some documents and presented them to the manager for proofreading and approval. The manager told her to wait so that she could return with the documents after they had been duly treated. While going through them, at some point, he had to use his glasses so as to see the lettering of the documents. Before reaching for his glasses, he had to squint his face so that he could see clearly. When he squinted his face, the secretary had assumed that he was doing that in relation to the appropriateness and professional nature of the documents. However, her doubts were cleared when the manager told her to rework some portions of the documents. She had made a mistake while formatting the documents; those portions had a font size of nine, which was ridiculously small for people to read through. The gesture was made due to the tiny nature of the font size.

Case Study II: Some employees had just been accepted into a company, and the person who was in charge of their orientation programme had been on leave for about three weeks. It was also the culture of the firm to ensure the new workers report back to one of the experienced member of staff who would guide them and put them through whenever there was a need for that. Since the person handling that was not on ground, there was a need to appoint another person to man the post. There was an infamous story among the employees that the firm does not pay well for the position. As such, there was no one willing to fill in the gap. Finally, the management team later made a decision to bring in Mr AB to tentatively take up the post. When he came to his table and saw a letter, he was bothered about what it could possibly be about. After opening the letter to read it, he learnt of his appointment. For a moment, he was sad, and his eyes began to narrow. The entire eyes looked stressed and tired.

Case Study III: The break system in a model school had just been changed as part of its new policies that would contribute to the growth of the educational institution. When this decision was announced to the students, some of them were indifferent about it while many of them frowned at it. Of particular interest was a boy who stood in front when the principal was addressing them. At some point, he began to narrow his eyes, almost closed them totally, and looked pale. This is an indication that the decision did not go down well with him.

Case Study IV: Mr A had always used land transportation for his transborder business, but recently, some of his friends told him that he could dodge clearance if he used the seaport. They even explained how he could go about that to him. Without making further enquiries of his own, he decided to try his luck via the seaport. When his goods arrived, he went during the busiest hour to pick them up. He had thought that officers would be too engaged to notice him. Since it was his first time there, he did not understand the modalities of the place. He squinted his eyes under the scorching sun, looking for his goods. His behaviour was somewhat strange, and that drew the attention of an officer to him who asked him to present the necessary documents so that he could help him locate his items. Mr A became short of words, and that was when he was picked up. The squinting of the eyes depicted that the man was concerned or worried about something.

6.39. Slight Squinting

Generic Interpretations of the Concept

This is not as pronounced as the previous gesture discussed in this book. There are moments that we burn of excessive anger within but which we try as much as possible to suppress. This subdued anger, not withstanding, still subtly show up externally. When a person is trying to subdue anger, they will slightly squint and lower their eyelids. You must consider narrowing of the slits of the eyes in context. Some other related behaviours that point to the fact that someone is trying to suppress their anger are facial tension and, in some extreme situations, clenching the hand into a fist. When you see these clusters, it means the person is brewing within and something is wrong somewhere.

People think flaring up in some circumstances is not good enough. Also, many cultures across the world do not allow young or junior workers to look into the face of their senior colleagues or elderly ones and register their grievances. So in instances where they are really offended, they will try to subdue their anger in order not to utter statements they will end up regretting. In the same vein, when you are new to a place, it would be inappropriate to start showing your negative sides. So if you are offended, you will still need to learn how to subdue the anger so as not to be seen in a bad light.

Scientific Explanations

The Exploring Your Mind website, in a 2017 article, describes this body language gesture as an expression of anxiety. A person subduing anger is obviously not comfortable, and this is shown through the face. The touching words of Mabel Elsworth Todd is worth recalling at this moment: 'For every thought supported by feeling, there is a muscle change. Primary muscle patterns being the biological heritage of man, man's whole body records his emotional thinking.' The muscle-change claim is what I want to emphasise on at this point. When the muscles are changed, it means there is a thought ongoing in our minds. Those who are nursing negative thoughts have theirs in the form of anxiety or anger. At this point, their face becomes furrowed and stiff. The person looks irritated, and people may tend to take them as being overly serious. The slight squinting is also capable of communicating aggressiveness in some contexts.

Peter McLaughlin (2015) says that this gesture also represents stress. Other clustering behaviour he mentions that may accompany slight squinting is the disappearance of the lips. When you squint, it means the eyes and nose are wrinkled. If this happens, it also affects the size and shape of the lips as the nose tends to be longer than the lips in length. The lips become more tightened and pulled back.

Many people do not know that when you squint your face, you also grind your teeth. Although the lips are compressed, but there is also an internal grinding of the teeth. Philip (2014) states that this gesture connotes internal struggle. When you flex the muscles of the jaws, it sends a message to others that you are frustrated and that pressure is building up in you. Philip goes ahead to submit that 'you might consider using this signal as a way to have others take your aggression more seriously or as a warning that you are about to lose your cool. Often, demonstrations of aggression lead others to submit and placate. This can work in your favour.' If you see a person trying to subdue their anger through squinting the face and other related gestures, this means they can set loose at any point in time—that is, if the person can no longer suppress the anger, there may be an open demonstration of their anger.

As I have said earlier, there is a need to consider this gesture in relation with other clustering behaviours I mentioned. With this, you will know the true feelings of a person and what you can do as a way of preventing an ugly scenario.

Practical Illustrations

Case Study I: A terrorist was sent to one of the leading banks in town to make enquiries, survey the premises, and determine how feasible it was to launch an attack. When he got to the bank, he decided to follow every protocol but was observant of every activity going on at his target place. His unusual look and slow movement caught the attention of the security operatives at the bank. For a while, they kept watching him as he moved from one section of the bank to the other. When it was obvious that he had some ill intents and was not really in the banking hall for the purpose of any legal transaction, a security guard decided to challenge him. As a way of feigning that he was there to make a transaction, he raised his voice against the guard, calling his attention to the fact that he was 'wrongly challenging a client'. Still unmoved by his antiques, the guard queried further, and suddenly, the terrorist began to squint his face in a slight manner. This means he was trying to suppress his anger at the location.

Case Study II: A husband called his wife and informed her that they would be moving out of their present residence soon. This came as a surprise to the wife. However, she composed herself to ask some few questions on what propelled the action and why he waited too long before informing her. The husband mumbled on and on. He later used 'insecurity' and 'high rent rate' as some of the key excuses. He concluded by noting that there was a need to change environment after years of living at that particular location. The excuses were not tenable to the wife. From an economic point of view, their workplace was close to the present residence, and more so, she assumed the husband did not see her as a major stakeholder in the house and that was why she was not duly carried along. As the husband was speaking, she slightly squinted her face and looked away. This means she did not buy into the idea of the husband.

Case Study III: Friend A and Friend B were arguing over a topic. The argument seemed interesting as they were both lost in it. The voice of Friend A appeared to be dominating that of his friend's. Friend B had to appeal to him to lower his voice as they were not fighting. However, Friend A took this appeal personally and saw it as a mockery on his person rather than a call to correction. As Friend B was talking, Friend A slightly squinted his face and looked sideways. This was an affirmation that he was not pleased with the words of his friend. Apart from this non-verbal display, he also changed his countenance and the topic of the discourse that his friend was forced to ask him what went wrong. The gesture signals someone who is troubled.

6.40. Aggressive Staring

Generic Interpretations of the Concept

The combination of the two words *aggressive* and *staring* shows that this body behaviour is nothing but a representation of negative emotions. Without an arousal of negative emotion in a person or other primates, they would not stare aggressively at others. In most cases, this gesture serves as a prelude to altercation. This behaviour can be intimidating. The gesture is demonstrated through a laser-like focus on the eyes. The primary purpose is to send fear down the nerves of one's target.

When a person is staring at you aggressively, they will not blink or look at any other things. For a moment, they are focused on you and nothing else. This action usually births the flight or fight response in others. If the person stares at you and it becomes unbearable for you, you will look away and may even take your leave from that vicinity. This is a flight response from you. It means you are afraid the person may harm you. On the other hand, if a person stares aggressively at you for long and you also stay unmoved, focused on the person, and waiting for the person to look away first, this is a fight response—that is, you are challenging the authority of the person and questioning them on the reason they are staring at you. In some cases, this can lead to physical confrontation. This is also common among primates when they are about to pounce on potential preys.

Scientific Explanations

Any form of staring is an expression of aggression. However, when it is intentionally done with aggression, it becomes very threatening. Research reports that aggressive stare lasts for more than ten seconds aimed at creating anxiety and discomfort in another person. This is mostly done by superiors to subordinates. 'When done on more dominant individuals, it can lead to feelings of aggression and, in extreme cases, even physical altercations' (Philip 2013). When you hold eye contact in a way that is slightly longer than usual, it sends a potent message to one's subject. Aggressive staring is more pronounced when you look at a stranger and keeps the stare for a while. As a common courtesy, one is expected to look sideways once there is eye contact with a stranger so as to make the person feel comfortable. Aggressive staring is only permitted when a person is focused on an inanimate object. When you stare at a person aggressively, it is an indication that we do not attach any importance to them.

Eye contact and staring are different things to both men and women. 'When the sexes stare at each other, it's usually due to competitiveness or envy, as in sizing up the competition, and other times out of pure curiousity. When the sexes stare at each other, it's usually driven by sexual interest, however, women are far less prone to staring in any case' (Philip 2013).

Shelagh Robinson (2009) says that aggressive staring is used for visual violence. She submits that the look is not accidental; it is violently and intentionally done with the aim of making the other person submissive. There are four basic functions that this gesture is employed to achieve: to punish, to set boundaries, to establish dominance, and to warn someone. Hence, this gesture is used all over the world as a social gesture in regulating a behaviour from a distance. The fact is that if the aggressive staring is deployed rightly, it has its place in society. Although being on the receiving end of a nasty look can be so painful and depressing, it looks somewhat tamed when compared to physical aggression. Humans are highly sensitive to social threats and, as such, reacts to this gesture very quickly.

This gesture is perceived as being negative all over the world. The reaction is usually fear or confrontation. An aggressive stare will make some people shiver to their marrows, while some others may consider it as an affront and thus launch a counter-attack. Sometimes, aggressive looks may be an indication of stress (Robinson 2009).

Changing Minds also opines that when a stare is prolonged, it becomes aggressive. The interpretations can be diverse in different contexts. What is important is that this social gesture can either be used for correction or intimidation.

Practical Illustrations

Case Study I: A student had just been enrolled in a school, and as a norm to many humans, he was still trying to learn the ropes and know-how to best navigate the school, whom to walk with, and when to move closer to them. On his third day at school, he decided to move out during break so as to watch the students play and see if he could develop interest in any of the plays. As he stood outside, a group of three boys walked past him, and he seemed not to have taken a conscious notice of them. Then the young boys returned, and while they were in front of him, one of them, the well-built one among them, gave him an aggressive stare that he almost ran away. The scenario repeated itself the following day, and it was almost like that every other day. The new student discovered that many of the students were running away from them. He needed to ask about them, and someone informed him that those guys were bullies. The aggressive staring is intended to create fear in the minds of the subjects.

Case Study II: For some weeks, there were reported cases of banditry in town, and the heads of enforcement agencies had to launch a special operation to fish out the criminals. The first week was brutal for the uniformed men as the bandits fought them in an unexpected manner and left some of their men dead. The following week, the law enforcement officials were able to nab some of the bandits. While addressing his men and the bandits, the commander in charge of the force stared at the bandits aggressively. He looked at them without piety and ordered his men to be brutal with anyone who failed to cooperate with them. In this stance, it is used to show dominance.

Case Study III: Friend C and Friend D went to a party. They were both of age but had no suitors. This was a source of concern for both of them. However, during this outing, they sat at a table with a handsome, gorgeously dressed guy. The guy seemed to be more interested in Friend D. This was glaring with the way he was chatting with her. This, obviously, did not go down well with Friend C. She began to flash smiles at him and did everything just to divert the guy's attention. Friend D got to note this and had to aggressively stare at her friend, but Friend C looked resolved on her mission. The aggressive stare was meant to serve as a warning sign here, but it didn't serve its intended purpose.

6.41. Angry Look

Generic Interpretations of the Concept

All over the world, the only non-verbal means of identifying anger in a person is through the eyes. This is why Paul Ekman listed it as one of the seven universal emotions displayed through microexpressions. There are constellations of facial cues that show that a person is angry. This begins with the narrowing of the eyes near the nose region (the eyes look like the 'greater than' or 'lesser than' mathematical signs). In addition, the nose would be wrinkled or dilated, and in some rare cases, the lips would be pulled back in order to display the clenched teeth. Taking cognisance of all these facial cues, one would discover that the person is really tense.

An angry look can hardly be feigned because it is not a stand-alone behaviour; there are other gestures apart from the narrowing of the eyes, which is the prominent gesture. Anger is used as a means of registering one's grievance and displeasure against a person or something. You really want the person to know that you are displeased with their behaviour towards you. This can elicit the same response or compassion from the person. A compassionate fellow feels sorry for you and looks for all means to make you happy. On the other hand, when a person does not feel sorry for what they do, they care less about how you feel.

Scientific Explanations

Confucius, as quoted by Westside Toastmasters, said, 'Look into a person's pupils. He cannot hide himself.' This means that when a person is telling lies that he is not angry at a circumstance or a person, you can get to know the truth with their facial expression. Westside Toastmasters explains that in a given light situation, a person's pupils either dilate or contract as the person's attitude or mood changes from positive to negative and vice versa. When interacting with an excited person, you will see their pupils dilate four times as much as the size of the original. However, when a person is angry, you will discover that their pupils contract and give them the shape of snaky eyes or beady eyes. An angry person is not attractive or appealing to other people.

Deane Rosenberg (2019) also discusses the relationship between anger and body language. He notes that body language serves as the most potent way in establishing the true intent and feelings of a person. Rosenberg says that a bulging eye is an indication of extreme anger. In a confrontation, the body language of those involved shows the form of their psychological disposition— that is, you know how the person feels immediately after uttering a word or reacting to what another person says. At the moment of confrontation, there are clusters of body language cues pointing to that psychological disorder. There are gross changes in the facial look of a person who is angry. If you are dealing with such a person, expect the show of force and negative reactions. The best way to deal with a person with an angry look is to directly comment on their behaviour (Rosenberg 2019).

Philip (2014) says that an angry person's eyes always become narrow and may even squint. This means the person is pained by something. When the eyes are narrowed, it means the person is raging within, and you can see the outcome on their face. All in all, an angry look is used to show that one is not pleased with the behaviour of a person or the outcome of an incident.

Practical Illustrations

Case Study I: A family was preparing for Christmas and, as such, had to renovate their home and mop and clean everywhere, all in the spirit of the celebration. Also, they would be playing host to many family friends and professional colleagues. When the mom told her two children that they were going to clean the whole house the following day, they protested against the initiative, noting that their parents had the financial buoyancy to hire people who would professionally do the cleaning. However, their mom told them that since they were on a holiday, they should do it as a means of building up their sense of charity and giving back to the community. After all, charity begins at home. With this, they grudgingly agreed to help out in the cleaning service. The last child was told to wash the dish in the sink after doing some other chores. After washing them, the mother brought out other plates to wash; she had forgotten them in the first place. At this point, the young girl narrowed her eyes, looked sober, and bowed her head. It was a display of anger which could not be fully expressed against her mother.

Case Study II: A group of experienced law enforcement officials were supposed to engage a suspected murderer in a session. Ideally, the process was billed for ten o'clock in the morning. However, the third member of the team did not arrive early. He had some personal emergency issues he was supposed to attend to. More so, the traffic was unusually heavy that day. As a way of respecting the suspect, the two other members kept on apologising and assuring him that the process would start as soon as their colleague came in. Eventually, the third person arrived, and he was obviously looking disturbed, but the suspect had no pity on him. After shaking hands with him, the suspect focused on him, stared at him for more than ten seconds, wrinkled his nose, narrowed his eyes, and clenched his teeth. He maintained that gesture until the interview began. Anyone who saw him would notice that he was really furious.

Case Study III: A teacher had been engaged with her school management for hours on the need to get some official assignments done. After doing everything, she was tired but still had to take some classes before the end of the day. As she entered the class, the students were a little bit disorganised. She arranged them and then commenced the lesson. Just a few minutes into the lesson, one of the students known for being troublesome raised his hand and asked a question that was not in any way related to the topic under discussion. The rule of the school was that every question must be attended to, no matter how odd it was. Before responding to his poser, the teacher looked at him with a furrowed eyes, compressed lips, and wrinkled nose. She was angry, but as a professional, she mustn't display her wrath before the students.

6.42. Stiff Widening of the Eyes

Generic Interpretations of the Concept

Inasmuch as it is not good to keep the eyes narrowed at all times, it is also crucial to submit that keeping the eyes wide open for a long time shows that something is wrong with the person. The ideal way of looking at a thing or person is to moderately keep the eyes open and even narrowed in the right circumstances. An eye that remains stiffly wide open is an indication of being affected by some external stimulus. Having said that, there are many possible interpretations of this gesture!

First, it may indicate that the person is stressed. When a person is stressed, you can expect any form of weird behaviour from them. Some close the eyes, while others keep it open in a wider form. The person who keeps it open is craving for space and breeze just to be relieved. In addition, surprise makes a person display this gesture. You further open the eyes so as to have better view of the unbelievable situation. Sometimes, this is accompanied with the use of the hand to close the mouth because it is left open too.

Furthermore, fear can induce this gesture from a person. If you assume that something uncouth is about to happen to you, you will keep the eyes open so as to see where it would emerge from. Although this gesture may not be able to salvage you from the imminent attack, but it is a physical form of expressing that you are on guard. And finally, when you see a person widen their eyes, it is an indication that something huge is happening to the person. You may have to move closer, observe, and even ask some few questions in order to know what the person is going through.

Scientific Explanations

Most of the experts who contributed to this discourse uphold that the mere widening of the eyes is a positive gesture. However, it becomes a negative display of emotion if the widening is done in a stiff way. In a research by Keating and Keating, it was revealed that both humans and several apes make use of the same gesture to show dominance, aggression, and submission. In order to show aggression and dominance, people will lower their eyebrows, while they will raise it to show submission. If a person intentionally raises their eyes, it is seen as a sign of submission. However, the sign becomes disturbing if it's done with force or if it's stiff (Westside Toastmasters 2019).

When a woman raises their eyes in a stiff manner, it makes them look babyish and appear unattractive. Looking babyish in an odd manner does not draw people to you. Rather, they see you as a person who is not mature enough and, thus, should not be related with (Westside Toastmasters 2019).

In the same vein, Changing Minds says that eye widening that is not accompanied with a smile makes a person look weird. It means someone is trying to emphasise that the message he or she is passing across is meant for a particular person. Further, the website submits that if the stiff widening of the eyes is done without blinking, it may be an indication of aggression, dominance, or show of power. The person is subtly saying, 'My eyes are wide open, and there is nothing you can do to me.' The eyes are one of the most delicate parts of the body; people lay importance on it and go to any length to protect them. However, if a person widens them, remains unmoved, and is stern, it means the person is challenging the situations around them.

Philip (2013) opines that the mere widening of the eyes is a positive body language cue induced by some positive stimuli which causes them joy and happiness. From the foregoing, we can safely conclude that the stiff widening of the eyes is a self-pacifying behaviour. It is done when a person is stressed as a way of arousing the positive emotion in them. This body gesture is gravity-defying and only done when there is a need to show some innate, true emotions. This gesture means the person is in a dire search of true contentment and happiness. The wider the eyes, the more passionate the person is about the subject being discussed (Philip 2013).

Practical Illustrations

Case Study I: Mr J is a factory worker, and today was tedious for him at work. Some of his colleagues were not at work, and the company had to deliver some works in the next two days. So he practically worked out himself by ensuring that they did not lag behind in delivering the orders. Upon getting home, he decided to sit in a cool place and left his eyes wide open in a stiff manner. His children did not move near him as it was rare for him to sit in such manner, especially the stiff eye-widening gesture. He maintained the gesture until he was somewhat OK and Mrs J informed him that food was ready. This was a gesture used in depicting tiredness and someone under pressure.

Case Study II: It was almost closing hour, and many of the employees of B & D Enterprise were already taking stock for the day. Unexpectedly, a truck full of goods just arrived, and they had offloaded the goods and sorted them before going home because the next day was a Saturday, and it would be a busy shopping day in the establishment. They were busy with the job till five hours past the closing hour. When they were done, the manager wanted to address them in a short meeting, but those seated in front widened their eyes in a stiff manner and kept it open in an unblinking manner. The manager became incoherent and had to postpone the meeting till the next day. The display of this gesture was to send fear down the nerves of the speaker and show him that they were not interested in what he was saying.

Case Study III: The management of a hotel had just upgraded their services and warned that the prostitutes and drunks who used to make their premises and its environs rowdy were no longer tolerated. To those concerned, this was just one of the usual warnings that would not be followed up with the right actions. After a week, it appeared that the drunks and prostitutes were not going to vacate the hotel. So the management of the facility had to employ the services of security agents. The security agents strategically positioned themselves at different areas of the hotel, and when the prostitutes and drunks were gathered, they rounded them up. Upon seeing the unexpected, the nuisances widened their eyes in a stiff manner. This means they were taken by surprise.

6.43. Adorning the Eyes

Generic Interpretations of the Concept

Beauty and fashion has been a major part of our existence for a while. In fact, since the inception of Egyptian pyramids, both men and women across the world have been adorning their eyes for the purpose of aesthetics. In order to make it aesthetically appealing, they make use of different colours. Some of the major parts of the eyes usually adorned are the sides of the eyes, under the eyes, and the eyelids, among others. The reason for making the eyes attractive varies among people. To some, it is merely their culture, and they are trying to be socially acceptable. Some others see it as a means of being sexually attractive to potential suitors, while some also do it as a means of fitting into their profession.

The major items used for eye adornments are oils, minerals, and dyes. To those who see it as a part of their culture, they pass it on to incoming generations, and that is how the tradition has been sustained. One of the reasons why this culture has not been forgotten is because it works for us. We are naturally attracted to the eyes, and the chances of this attraction are raised when they are adorned. Hence, people have always succeeded in making themselves a symbol of attraction through this gesture. Also, we are attracted to befitting thick eyelashes that are mostly worn by women. On the other hand, men do accentuate so as to make themselves appealing.

Scientific Explanations

Collins Dictionary defines *adornment* as 'something that is used to make a person or thing more beautiful'. Hence, eye adornment is primarily done for the purpose of beauty. Philip (2014) says adornment is an elective non-verbal trait—that is, those who do adornment is not made compulsory but a matter of their choice. Hence, adornment is done for the purpose of creating a desired impression. People use adornment in a way that fits their personality. Philip makes a cogent point that is worth recalling here: 'When using adornments, be sure to understand that while you may seek to create an individualized personal impression, you will be ascribed traits common to the group you will subsequently fall into.' Although there is liberty or freedom of personal adornment, you must always take cognisance of the world view of your immediate society. For instance, those who tattoo their eyes or any part of their body are said to be drug users and risk-takers.

Eye adornments add colour, shape, and texture to our eyes. In fact, it has the capability of changing our look. Adorning the eyes also alters their size. Adding mascara and other eye-adoring items will alter their shape. That is why people look very different after adorning their face (CNS 2019). An understanding of this concept is very crucial to the way we peruse the concept of body language. The general concept of adornment is interlaced with the understanding of body gestures. In some instances, it becomes a little bit complex, but those who want to be on top of their world must understand how to simplify it. For example, when a person adorns their face, it changes some natural facial features. This impedes the seamless reading of eye gestures—that is, we have to stress ourselves or, in the case of criminal instances, ask them to wipe off their adornments in order to have a full view of their face. Eye adornment can make you see a sad fellow as being excited because some of the materials used in adorning the eyes make them bigger and dilated more than they should be. On the other hand, eye adornment can help us better understand the emotions of a person; the kind of adornment used points to their state of mind, cultural beliefs, religious affiliations, and fashion taste. With that, we can make a somewhat accurate prediction about their life and thought.

Practical Illustrations

Case Study I: Mr M and Mr K were invited to a debate on national television, and while they were preparing, both of them were looking for the best way to appear more intelligent than the other. They were going to talk about a national issue. Hence, both of them wanted to fight with all their might to appear appealing and sound to their audience. While Mr K was only focused on appearing neat and portraying the colour of his political party, Mr M, on the other hand, was thinking of how his dress code could work in his advantage. So about a day to the programme, Mr M went to the salon and shaved his head like a skinhead. From there, he proceeded to where he could have his face tattooed. The primary purpose for this was to devise a way of creating fear in his opponent.

Case Study II: Two female friends were in their middle age with no suitor. They had been accused of not being friendly enough and not mixing up with people. They had tried to work on some of their shortcomings that people mentioned. Yet it seemed men were simply blind to their existence. They had tried asking men out on their own, but it seemed weird, and even the guys took them for granted. Hence, they resolved to hung out at restaurants every weekend. From there, men began to move closer to them, and it appeared that the 'chains' were beginning to break. So they stepped up their game, dressed in a variety of colours, and added glamour to their appearance. They had to shave off their eyebrows, draw an artificial one, paint the upper parts of their eyelids, and fix their hair. The purpose of this adornment was to make them more attractive and charming. Also, their eyes would be more dilated and shine more to anyone they maintain eye contact with.

Case Study III: There is no gainsaying that one of the distinguishing factors of every human is the shape of the eyes. Criminals are very well aware of this fact too, and over the years, I saw how they cunningly adorned their eyes for the sake of evading justice. There was a case of a human smuggler who adorned the eyes of his victims as if they were natives for the sake of evading arrest. What gave him out was that he used almost the same style for his subjects, and that called the attention of law enforcement officers to them. He was secluded from them, and it was glaring that they could not speak the language he had claimed on their behalf. The purpose of the adornment here is to deceive.

Case Study IV: I was also told the case of two colleagues. It was learnt that they were very close and did almost everything together. There were times they would sleep in each other's home. Since their company brought up a policy that they all must be in uniforms, the two colleagues came together and brainstormed

212

on what they could do to still stand out from their peers. Their conclusion was to adorn their eyes. Not too many people were expecting them to go that far. However, almost every worker in the firm appreciated their uniqueness and made further enquiries on how they could adorn their eyes too, but they were not ready to disclose that to anyone. The reason for the adornment here was to look good and bond.

The case studies shared in this section are very powerful and insightful. They showcase different instances where the eyes can be adorned to achieve different purposes. This means the essence of the gesture should not be trivialised.

CHAPTER 7

The Ear

There are various forms of ears—deformed, cute, sagging, adorned, perforated, big, or little. In the case of the first type (deformed), it may be a result of a birth defect, an accident, or other biological factors that may not be necessarily captured in the article. The other ones are also based on natural causes, except for adorned and perforated ones, which are results of a human's conscious effort. Our ears communicate an array of non-verbal messages during conversations that we dare not overlook. Also, they perform practical functions, such as collection of information through sound waves. They also help us to dissipate heat. Before I go into the metaphorical functions of the ears, I will spend time to explain its biology, formation, and usefulness.

Joseph Hawkins (2019) submits that 'the human ear, like that of other mammals, contains sense organs that serve two quite different functions: that of hearing and that of postural equilibrium and coordination of head and eye movements'. From the point of view of anatomy, there are three distinguishable parts of the ear—outer ear, middle ear, and inner ear. The outer ear is the part that we all see (located at the side of the head), which is called pinna or auricle. It has a short auditory canal and one that is close to the inner part known as the eardrum. The primary role of the outer part of the ear is to collect sound waves and guide them to the appropriate parts of the ear.

On the other hand, the middle ear is a narrow air-filled cavity in the temporal bone. It is covered by three small bones—incus (anvil), malleus (hammer), and stapes (stirrup). They are all collectively referred to as auditory ossicles. What the ossicular chains do is to conduct sounds gathered by the outer ear from the tympanic membrane to the inner ear. On its own, the inner ear consists of two functional units—the vestibular apparatus, consisting of the vestibule and semicircular canals, which contains the sensory organs of postural equilibrium, and the snail-shell-like cochlea, which contains the sensory organ of hearing (Hawkins 2019). It is important to note that the most striking difference between the human ear and that of other mammals is the outer part of it.

There are two basic functions that the ear performs—hearing and provision of balance. For the former, sound waves gathered by the outer ear are regulated and modulated by the middle ear before being passed on to the inner ear (to the vestibulocochlear nerve). The nerve sends the information received to the temporal lobe of the brain. At that point, it would be registered as a sound. When the outer ear receives sound waves, the eardrum vibrates. The pinna ensures that the ear is focused on the sound being heard and it is processed appropriately. The inner ear contains all the necessary tools needed to change the sound waves gathered by the outer ear to process information. During vibration in the eardrum, there are two tiny muscles—stapedius and tensor tympani—that help in the modulation of noise. They dampen to ensure that the vibration is not in excess for the ear (Hall et al. 2005).

The human ear can generally hear sounds with frequencies between twenty hertz and twenty kilohertz (the audio range). Sounds outside this range are considered infrasound (below twenty hertz) (Greinwald et al. 2002).

The second function of the ear is provision of balance; whether we are standing still or moving, the ear provides balance for us. This balance comes in two forms—static balance, which allows us to feel the effects of gravity, and dynamic balance, which gives us a sense of acceleration. All the functions that we have so far discussed happen in the twinkle of an eye.

There are also societal and cultural dimensions to the ear. For instance, for thousands of years, the ears have been an object of different kinds of ornaments. Both in ancient and modern cultures, people place ornaments on the earlobes as a way of enlarging and overstretching them. That is why it is fairly common in our world today to see the earlobes being torn by the weight of heavy earrings (Sarnoff et al. 2002).

Further, injuries to the ears have long been dated to the Roman times as a means of punishment or reprimand from wrongdoing. 'In Roman times, when a dispute arose that could not be settled amicably, the injured party cited the name of the person thought to be responsible before the Praetor; if the offender did not appear within the specified time limit, the complainant summoned witnesses to make statements. If they refused, as often happened, the injured party was allowed to drag them by the ear and to pinch them hard if they resisted. Hence the French expression "se faire tirer l'oreille", of which the literal meaning is "to have one's ear pulled" and the figurative meaning "to take a lot of persuading". We use the expression "to tweak [or pull] someone's ears" to mean "inflict a punishment"' (Florin 2004).

From the foregoing, there is a strong link to the fact that the ears are an embodiment of non-verbal messages, whether in the ancient or modern times. When a person holds their ear in certain circumstances, it means they do not want to hear what is being said. That is why people refer to this as the 'hear no evil' sign. This is done when one disagrees with what is being said. The ear body language behaviour has been a part of us since childhood. That is why you see children block their ears in an obvious manner as a way of rejecting what is being said. For instance, we normally see this in children when they are being reprimanded by their teachers or parents or even when being teased by anybody. As we grow up, this becomes obviously childish, and that is why it is replaced by the pulling of the ear. We will expatiate more on this later.

7.1. Massaging or Pulling the Earlobe

Generic Interpretations of the Concept

When a person is stressed or contemplating on a thing and pulling their earlobes at the same time, this gives a soothing effect to the person. It is a self-pacifying act. Remember that this is another hand-to-body gesture which has been established at various points in time in this book to be a pacifying act. When a person is at crossroads, you are obviously disturbed, and this will increase if you should focus on the issue alone. So the earlobe massaging is a means of distracting you from the serious thought. This gesture is soothing and, as such, does not make you feel the burden of the issue bothering you.

Also, earlobe massaging is associated with hesitation, weighing of option, and expression of doubt. A person who is weighing two or similar options is obviously confused and lost in the labyrinth of their complexities. In the same vein, when a person is hesitant in making a decision about something, you will see them rub their earlobe. All these should be considered in their context of appearance. For instance, many people understand that scratching the earlobe aggressively in public is unethical. So they can subtly rub or massage it when there is a need to. In this sense, it is not attached to any of the interpretations given above.

In some cultures of the world, when you are talking and your co-interlocutor is pulling their earlobe, it is an indication that they have some reservations about what you are saying; they do not totally agree with you. It means they are pondering on what you have said and seem not to have a point of convergence with you. Not that the person is angry with the point you made, only that they are not truly convinced on its appropriateness in that context.

Scientific Explanations

Bob Whipple (2019) describes this behaviour as a common one that people do not necessarily take note of in their daily interactions. The life coach states that there are different interpretations of this gesture. He also warns that we should be patient enough to get additional information before ascribing meaning to the ear-pulling gesture of people. One of the interpretations Whipple gives to this gesture is that when a person does it unconsciously while listening to another person, it is an indication that the person who is speaking has the floor and, as such, can keep talking. Sometimes, they may exaggerate this by cupping the hand behind the earlobe as a means of preventing the sound waves from escaping.

He moves on to state that another interpretation of this gesture is the exact opposite of the first one he gave—that is, earlobe pulling is seen as a subtle means of blocking what is being said from gaining entrance into one's ears. This means the person involved wants to hear no evil. The extreme form of this behaviour is seen in children when they use their whole palm to block their ears or insert their index finger into their ear. In this sense of negative interpretation, it signals increased stress, which the person is trying to avoid. They think you are exaggerating or telling lies. This increased stress makes more blood to flow into the ear, which is triggering the person to pull their earlobe. He gives the third interpretation of this gesture as meaning physical itch or eczema (Whipple 2019).

Christopher Philip also submits that this gesture is a subconscious desire by a person to hear no evil. This gesture is done when you hear or say something that is disagreeable. This idea of earlobe pulling as a way of preventing an undesirable sound to reach the deeper part of our brain means we do not want our brain to process or work with it.

Another interpretation given to it by Philip is that it may be a representation of anxiety or nervousness. Hence, it can be regarded as a defensive posture in this regard. This gesture is not only used at the end of another person's lies but also at the end of ours too. That is why it is said to be the 'hear no evil' signal. Philip submits that 'the gesture used at the conclusion of our own lies serves to reduce what is called "cognitive dissonance" which is the uncomfortable feeling that comes from holding two contradictory ideas simultaneously'.

Practical Illustrations

Case Study I: Mr Z went to a salesman dealing with used cars. The salesman told Mr Z that the particular car he wanted to get works as perfect as a new one. In fact, he told the buyer that the used vehicle had no fault before the owner decided to sell it out. As he finished saying this, he subconsciously used his hand to pull his earlobe and rubbed the edge of this ear. This means that the salesman told a lie which seemed justifiable to him in a way.

Case Study II: The general manager of a company was addressing his employees and other stakeholders of the firm. There was a need to appraise the performance of some of the employees who had worked in groups on a particular project monitored by the assistant general manager. As the GM said that a particular group performed better than others, his assistant touched his earlobe and rubbed it for a while, looking empty and thoughtful at that given time. This is an indication that he did not agree with the presentation of the general manager.

Case Study III: After a preliminary investigation had been carried out over a suspected murderer, he was later arrested. The law enforcement officials to drill him went through the preliminary report and then fixed a date for the interview. In the interview room, the suspect was given the opportunity to narrate his story while the officials listened with rapt attention. At some point, his story became contradictory, and they were even implicating in some instances. The law enforcement officials looked at him sternly, and yet he still continued with his fabrications. At some point, one of the officials rubbed his hand over his earlobe. This was an unconscious way of registering his disagreement with what the suspect was saying; he believed the suspect was being deceitful.

7.2. Blushing or Flushing of the Ear

Generic Interpretations of the Concept

There are many things that cause the sudden flushing of the skin of the ear. In most instances, this flushing also affects the face and the neck. This behaviour is technically referred to as hyperaemia. People do not have control over it. Hormonal changes, anger, embarrassment, fear, reactions to drugs, or autonomic arousal may be the cause of skin blushing. When this happens, you will discover that the skin covering the ear will change to pink, purplish, or red. Also, the skin may become very hot when you touch it. This can be very embarrassing to many people.

When there is an arousal of the hormones in the ear region, it increases the rate of blood supply to the ear, and that is why the skin turns red without being under scorching sun. Also, when people are embarrassed or uncontrollably angry, all their body system charges, and one of the ways this is evident is through the blushing of the ear. It means the person is really charged and ready for an attack. The same explanation goes to a person suffering from anxiety or fear. When a person becomes fearful of another person or a given situation, all their body systems would be on alert—for the flight or fight mood. Blood moves to every part of the body in a fast rate. If it is as a reaction to medicine, this means the person needs to report to their doctor before it complicates.

It has been discovered that even if the personal space of a person is violated, it can lead to the flushing of the ear. The concept of personal space is relative across cultures. Overall, the blushing of the ears is a reaction to a negative occurrence; it is seen when someone is not feeling as they should.

Scientific Explanations

Wikipedia defines *blushing* as the reddening of the entire face propelled by psychological reasons. Ear blushing is an involuntary action that is engineered by emotional stress. This stress is usually associated with passion, embarrassment, romantic stimulation, or anger. Severe blushing is commonly seen among people suffering from extreme social anxiety. In this case, the person experiences persistent and extreme anxiety in performance and social situations. Health-related website Healthline notes that flushing is the severe form of blushing— that is, it extends to other parts of the body. If the redness does not disappear after some time, it is considered as an early sign of rosacea (Healthline 2019).

Blushing is mostly seen in people who are sensitive to emotional stress. If a stimulus such as anger or embarrassment is activated in them, their sympathetic nervous system will cause their blood vessels to open wide that the ear's skin and other body parts would be flooded with blood, which will make the ears become red. Apart from redness, the affected areas become really hot (Stekel 2013).

Summarising this gesture in one sentence, Philip (2014) says that 'ear reddening is a sign that someone is experiencing nervousness, stress, embarrassment, excitement, or is being physically active.' This submission tallies with what we have been saying since the beginning of this segment. This gesture is linked to the release of cortisol and adrenaline that courses through the body. When the hormone rises, it diverts blood from the digestive system and redirect it to some major muscle groups, which makes the muscles burst in energy. So the side effect is seen in this blood vessels being dilated—that is, they are open or relaxed and thus make blood get to the surface of our ears and ultimately cause them to turn red. The verbal translation of the ear-blushing behaviour is, 'I'm getting worked up, and blood is rushing to the periphery of my body in an effort to produce a cooling effect.'

Practical Illustrations

Case Study I: In an international high school where students are taught with world-class curriculum, Ms P had divided her students into groups four weeks ago. She gave each group a topic to work on. She reiterated that apart from submitting a mere written version, she could call on anyone to present. Hence, everyone was encouraged to participate. She also made it known that whatever the performance of a presenter was, she would judge the whole group based on that. This made most of the students take the project seriously. Many of them did it as if it were their final examination. Yet some of the students were lukewarm in their contribution. On the day of presentation, the students thought she was going to start calling the groups chronogically, but she surprised them by calling the fourth group first. This made many of them shiver and sit tight. When the members of the group came out, she called on the students hiding at the back of his colleagues to present on behalf of the group. It was disastrous. Ms P scored them low. When the second group was invited, she called the person standing at the front, who was obviously prepared, and their presentation was applauded by the whole class. When the next group was invited, a young lady standing at the middle was invited, and when she was called on, her heart began to race and her ear turned red due to nervousness; fear was registered on her face.

Case Study II: It was the nationwide marathon for students and teachers across schools in the country. Many people were enthusiastic about it due to the fun fair and other cheering that comes with it. A newly employed teacher in one of the popular schools in town had boasted how he was the best runner while in school. On the day of the marathon, he joined; and just thirty minutes into the race, he collapsed with his chest, face, neck, and ears blushing. This was due to physical exhaustion.

Case Study III: A company had fixed its annual general meeting to four o'clock, and people were around before the slated time. However, the secretary of the gathering came about an hour late, which delayed the commencement of the meeting. When he came around, the CEO, who was obviously angry, talked to him ruthlessly before the hundreds of people gathered at the venue. The secretary bowed his head, with his heart beating so fast that people near him could hear it. Also, both ears blushed as a show of his embarrassment. This means he was not proud of what he did.

7.3. Leaning of the Ear

Generic Interpretations of the Concept

When we turn or lean our ear towards a speaker, this can be interpreted in many ways depending on the context. The first possible interpretation of this body language behaviour is that the person is listening attentively. When people move the part of the body through which they hear towards you, it is an indication that they admire what you are saying and want to hear it more. Note that this gesture is like the opposite of the first one we discussed under this section (the 'hear no evil' gesture). If the discussion taking place between the two people is solemn, this gesture will encourage the speaker to keep talking because their co-interlocutor has demonstrated interest in listening to them.

Another probable interpretation of this gesture is that the person did not hear very well what was earlier said and, as such, was expecting the person to repeat himself. In other words, this gesture means 'Please come again.' In this sense, the eyes would be squinted as if the person were trying hard to get something done. Also, the person's hand would be used to guard the back of their ear in a way that looks as if they were trying to prevent any word from escaping them. The hand is cupped in a way that reflects a person willing to collect more sound. This gesture is very obvious for the person whom this action is intended for to see.

This gesture is also commonly seen in dating. We give people we admire the opportunity to do anything to us, including moving closer to our ear, especially if the ear is extended for the sake of the person. Remember that lovers mostly whisper to each other. This means they have to listen intently to each other so that no word will pass them by. That is why lovers are capable of hearing the heartbeat of each other.

Scientific Explanations

Changing Minds (2019) says ear leaning is a sign of interest in what is being said. If one does not like what another person is saying, one will detach oneself or move away from the person. However, moving closer to a thing or person is a show of interest. This is seen in dating scenes. Changing Minds states that the verbal translation of this is, 'I am interested in you!' When you are at parties or nightclubs, you see this gesture made by men towards a particular lady they love. This makes them move farther from other people and connect with the person they are interested in.

Furthermore, ear leaning can be an indication of curiousity, query, or uncertainty. In this way, the head would be pushed forward as if the person wants to hear something—that is, they are acting as if what the person earlier said was not heard properly. If someone says something that you never expected them to say, you would lean your ears towards them in surprise and tell them to repeat themselves. This is an expression of uncertainty. In this situation, you may look at the person in a disappointing manner with a short scream. According to the body language platform, 'The greater the tilt, the greater the uncertainty or the greater the intent to send this signal.'

If the leaning is supported by the hand in a cupped manner, it may indicate tiredness or a show of further interest. In the case of tiredness, the hands are used to pacify the person; it rubs through the back of the ear. The leaning in this instance is a form of defensive behaviour.

Whipple (2019) also says that ear leaning is an indication of interest in what one is saying. People may exaggerate this signal so as to draw the attention of others to it.

Practical Illustrations

Case Study I: A young lady and a charming young doctor met in a shopping mall and had eye contact like three times before the medical practitioner took courage to walk up to her. They exchanged contacts because the young man was running late for work. At the work, they both had time to spare. The man called the lady, and they fixed an appointment for that Saturday evening. They went to one of the best restaurants in the city. They sat at a corner, with cool music playing in the background. Then they began their conversations. Sometimes, they smiled together and leant towards each other in order to hear each other well. The person closest to them could hardly hear what they were saying. The leaning here is an indication of love because no one was trying to avoid the other.

Case Study II: A middle-aged European don decided to go and spend his sabbatical in an African country. He was accepted by a university, and his first day in class was traumatic for himself and the whole class. As he started introducing himself, almost all the students leant their ears towards him and echoed, 'I beg your pardon.' Then the young man had to repeat himself. At different points in time, he had to be called back to repeat himself. The whole class was silent for the two hours that the class lasted. All the students leant towards him throughout the class. This form of gesture is used to seek clarity.

Case Study III: The management of a firm was briefing its major stakeholders of a novel discovery they just made which will set them apart from their competitors. So they wanted to present the ideas before the stakeholders before the implementation of the programme. As the managing director was briefing them of the discovery, the whole boardroom was silent. Everyone followed with rapt attention. At some point where the director was reeling out the distinguishing factors of the policy, many of the stakeholders further leant towards him and watched with keen interest. In this case, it means the listeners are pleased with what they are hearing.

Case Study IV: A drug trafficker was in a public transport with some law enforcement agents who were coming from a meeting. The focus of the meeting was on how to wage war against drug traffickers as they were fast becoming an epidemic to the society. The two officers were discussing the outcome of the meeting and the role they have to play in its implementation. Since the drug trafficker overheard what the discussion was centred on, he leant towards the officers while looking away to eavesdrop into their discussion. The purpose of his action was to understand the trick of the officers in order to come up with a counterplan.

Hence, all the four case studies considered gave us different insights of how the ear-leaning gesture can be used.

7.4.   Listening Gesture

Generic Interpretations of the Concept

Anybody can hear, but not everyone listens—that is, listening is a skill that is possessed by some people. This is why sometimes when you say something, someone around you misinterprets your intentions. This means that the person only heard you but did not listen to you. Hence, active listening is a crucial part of both personal and professional settings. When a person listens actively to what you are saying, it communicates three basic things—empathy, reception, and interest. A person who is receptive to your ideas will do everything possible to listen to you. This explains the reason some audience arrive at the venue of a programme about an hour before the commencement of the event just to sit in front, which will aid their active listening.

In the same vein, if someone is empathetic or interested in what you have to say, they will listen actively, no matter the medium you choose to relay the message. Active listening means that the person is not distracted in any way; they are focused on the speaker alone. There are three basic attributes of good listeners: they do not exceed their speaking time, they wait patiently for a person to finish speaking, and they wait till they are called on. This means they do not interrupt while others are speaking; they give the person the opportunity to express themselves fully before responding appropriately to what the person says. Also, if they are speaking and saw through the facial expression that the other person is agitating to speak, they stop to listen to the counterargument of their co-interlocutor. This makes a conversation orderly, respectful, intellectual, engaging, and flowing.

In order to be an active listener, you need to face the person who is speaking to you. This will prevent all forms of distractions and ensure that both ears are listening at the same time. If you face sideways, it means only one ear is listening actively to what the person is saying. This is a passive listening style.

Scientific Explanations

According to Mind Tools content team, listening is one of the most important skills anyone can have. It has an impact on everything we do, even the kind of relationships we build. There are four basic functions of listening: we listen to

223

learn new concepts, we listen to acquire information, we listen for the purpose of enjoyment, and finally, we listen to understand something. You can see that none of the four functions can be wished away.

Also, the Global Listening Centre (GLC) says that being strategic in the use of our body plays a key role in communication. It listed seven ways that show that a person is truly listening. According to the revered platform, those who are truly listening do not do any other thing; they do not multitask. Their concentration is a means of encouraging the speaker to share their ideas with them. An active listener leans forward, faces the person speaking, and concentrates fully on what is being discussed. In every discourse context, what is most important is to first establish the fact that you are ready for the discussion. Readiness matters through active listening.

Also, an active listener maintains an open body posture. This makes them receptive to new ideas. They do not use anything to block their ears. Rather, they make them very visible for everyone to see. Also, they do not cover them with headgears or caps. People are subconsciously discouraged if they do not see your ears while conversing with you. Apart from keeping the ears open, you can accompany it with the occasional nodding of the head. With these related clusters, the speaker is sure of your attention (GLC 2019).

Alan Gurney (2016) also agrees with what the other experts said on this. According to him, the ultimate proof that one is an active listener is one's ability to understand what another person has said.

Practical Illustrations

Case Study I: A troublesome student was told to invite his parents to school for a crucial meeting with his teacher and the members of the school management. The parents came a little bit behind schedule, so the meeting started immediately but ended five minutes after the teacher was supposed to be in class. Upon getting to the class, she apologised to the students and told them to put everything in order. Those who were playing with each other quickly moved back to their respective seats. Also, those who were eating packed their plates, and in the twinkle of an eye, there was decorum in the class for the teacher to begin her lesson. Each of them was focused on the teacher and made jottings at the appropriate time till the end of the lecture. This means they all listened attentively.

Case Study II: A young woman was sent abroad by her company for an official assignment. She was in that country for the first time in her life. She stayed there for two weeks. After she completed what she came there for, she headed home. After typing her reports and submitting the same to the authorities, she was relieved and took some rest. Then on a Friday, she decided to give her husband the gist of some 'weird' and 'surprising' things she saw while away. When she was about to start the talk, her husband was busy with some files. However, when she began, he immediately closed the files, adjusted his seat, and raised his head to focus on her. This means the husband was giving her his full attention. This was to encourage her to speak about her experiences. In this context, it can also be perceived as a symbol of love.

Case Study III: The only child of Mr and Mrs W had just returned from school looking askance. The mother noticed this and asked him what went wrong. After dropping his bag and eating his lunch, he said, 'Dad, Mum, I saw something strange today at school.' When his parents heard this, they both moved closer to him, looked into his face, sat beside him, and asked what the issue was. The action of both parents showed they were attentive, and invariably, it also means they were interested in what he had to say.

Case Study IV: Some criminals are great listeners, and you can easily see this in the manner they engage investigators—they will always have something to say! I once interviewed a con artist who got me engaged for eight hours. And the only spectacular attribute he had was his listening skill. Any time I was talking, he would look me in the eye, pick every word, and study my non-verbal gestures; and then he would reply along the same line. This made us drag an issue for too long. Even though it was a tiring process for me, I learnt a lot of things no book could teach me. Here, it was also a symbol of interest from both parties.

7.5. Adorning the Ears

Generic Interpretations of the Concept

There are various ways in which the ears can be adorned. However, I need to state that this behaviour is mostly culture-specific; people adorn their ears according to the dictates of their culture. Before I talk of the different ways in which people employ the use of ear ornaments, let me chip in that this gesture is used to serve a clear purpose—it is used to communicate social status, to identify oneself with a given group, or to register courtship availability. In most parts of the world, it is uncommon for a woman to first approach a man for a relationship or love affair. So women do employ subtle means such as ornamentation of the ear to communicate their intent or give a man the go-ahead to ask them out.

Furthermore, ear ornamentation has the ability to give us an accurate insight into the background of a person. We can even guess the occupation of a person through their ear ornamentation. Social status, personality, and heritage of people are some of the other insights which ear ornamentations give us.

Now talking of the ways in which ears can be adorned, some people prefer it being perforated so that they can insert earrings or other heavy materials. It may also be deformed, coloured, or plugged in a unique way due to cultural guidelines or individual taste. Sometimes, some cultures even change the entire natural look of the ear so as to look different. However, it should be noted that when a person defies cultural dictates in the ornamentations of their ears, they may be regarded as being sociopaths. Some intentionally do their ornamentations so as to look like their celebrity models. The means of modelling has changed over time, with people doing them to conform to contemporary times and job demands.

Scientific Explanations

While giving the generic introduction, I made it very clear that ear ornamentation is culture-specific, and those who do not align theirs with culture-specifics are seen as outcasts. David Howes, a lecturer at Concordia University, discussed ear ornamentation in South America. In his findings, in the pre-Colombian Andes, Inca men were distinguished through the wearing of large gold ear ornaments. The don explains that 'these ornaments were bestowed on adolescent boys at the end of an elaborate puberty rite. During this rite, Inca boys were required to listen to a series of lectures on Inca tradition and morality given by their elders. The piercing of their ears and the insertion of ornaments at the end of the rite served to ensure that the lessons the boys had received would "penetrate" their hearing and be remembered.' After this, they would perform many other activities so as to 'open up' the participants' ear to the voice of the divine. Then, it was common to see Inca men boasting of their superior sense of hearing over other people in the region. They also kept their hair short as a symbol of this superiority.

Another group of people distinguished for their ear ornamentations are the Suya of Central Brazil. In this culture, they would paint wooden disks and insert them in their ears and lips. Just as done for the Incas, the disks are accorded to the youth after puberty. This represents their initiation into adulthood. So anyone with this ear ornamentation is regarded as an adult. Both men and women are allowed to wear the disks on their ears, while women are prohibited from wearing those of the lips. The Suya believe that the ornamentations lay emphasis on the two basic sense organs—hearing and speech. Hearing among the people is related to the right social behaviour. They also place high emphasis on public oratory, and that is why they expect their men to wear the ornaments on their lips. Men are accorded much social value than women among the Suya (Howes 2019).

There is also a religious dimension to this discourse. In an article posted on the website of Christian Churches of God (CCG), it is claimed that the use of ear ornamentations is against their religious doctrines. However, things have changed in this contemporary time as Christians, even church leaders, use ornaments to the place of worship. There seems to be no stand against it in most parts of the world.

Practical Illustrations

Case Study I: A man from Europe travelled to South America for a project, and upon getting there, he saw that the people adorned themselves in different manners. This baffled him, but he was still focused on what he came for. When he had the time to rest, he spoke with some few people who told him the meaning of some of the ear ornamentations. At that point, he fell in love with the ornamentations. He did not know that they were filled with such deep messages he could not interpret on his own. He began to respect those he had cunningly mocked. Then the locals also started moving closer to him and explaining some of the secrets of their traditions to him. In this context, the ornamentation of the ear is a form of cultural expression.

Case Study II: A young woman had been attending the Orthodox Church right from infanthood where they were warned against the use of any facial ornamentations. She had the opportunity to visit her aunt one day who attended a Pentecostal church. She followed her aunt to church and discovered that almost those in attendance used earrings and wore make-up. She asked how this was possible, and her aunt had to lecture her on the doctrines of their church and belief system. Then she became enlightened about what had initially appeared to her as a sin. It served a religious and educational purpose in this context.

Case Study III: A young lady was preparing for her wedding and was very elated. One of the key preparations she made was to look indescribably beautiful. On the D-day, she invited a beautician who came over to do her make-up. She used some earrings that required some other parts of her ears to be further perforated. When they were done, she became a cynosure of all eyes. In this sense, the ear ornamentation is basically used for the purpose of beautification.

Case Study IV: While the ornamentation of the ear is known for its beautification purpose, criminals rather use if for their selfish intent; it is a means of changing their appearance in order to deceive people. I once engaged an impostor who had ornamentation on her ears. Obviously, that was not the first time she had applied ornamentation to her ears. However, the lady in the passport only had one. What she did was adjust her ornamentation to match the one that was in the passport. So I questioned her on the old ornamentation and why it didn't appear in the passport. She wanted to give a confusing response before I made it clear to her that the other one was old and should have been captured in the passport, taking cognisance of the date of the issuance of the passport. The ornamentation here was primarily designed to deceive law enforcement agents.

7.6.   Damaged Ears

Generic Interpretations of the Concept

There are different causes of damaged ears. When the outer parts of the ears are damaged, the person would still be able to hear, only that they would become physically deformed, but when the inner part is scarred, there will be a problem, and this may require surgery if it does not lead to total deafness. Chemicals, heat, or trauma are some of the major substances that destroy the ear cartilage and tissue. This accounts for the reason many unformed men and tutors are told not to touch people around the ears. Even heavy sounds such as bomb blasts or continuous gunshots, among others, can cause damage to the ear. If you have ever lived with a soldier who spent most of his life in the war front, you would have a better understanding of this.

Those who are highly susceptible to damaged ears are wrestlers, judokas, and rugby players. This form of damage is referred to as cauliflower ears. The ear is part of the five sensory organs of humans that should be protected. If it stops functioning, this means a part of the brain has been affected. Apart from the eyes, the ears are arguably the second-most-important part of the head. Not too many people can communicate with deaf people seamlessly. That is why you need to be on guard at all times. Items such as broomstick and sharp objects, among others, can also cause damage to the ear. People who want to keep others totally deformed do target their eyes and ears during conflict. Those who work in dusty areas such as factories or sweep streets do use ear covers because of the negative effects of dust to the ears. Once one understands how to keep the ears safe, the job is half-done, only left with the implementation.

Scientific Explanations

William Blahd (2018) submits that ear problem can be triggered by different health issues. In children, it is mostly caused by inflammation, fluid build-up in the external and internal ear or infection. This does not mean that elderly people are also excluded from this issue. The medical doctor notes that 'ear problems caused by an injury to the ear can occur at any age'. That is why we must all work hard to ensure that this sense organ is kept intact. Some of the causes of injuries to the ear include falling directly on the side of the head or being hit forcefully with a blow. This can cause the eardrum to burst or even cause damage to the tiny bones of the inner ear that conduct sound to the brain. Also, contact sports are capable of causing injuries to the ear. Wrestlers are the number victims of this situation.

Further, loud noises or explosions—acoustic trauma—can cause damage to the ear. Those who are constantly in the arena of noise may suffer from this in their old age, if not early enough in life. In the same vein, changes in atmospheric pressure is a potential cause of injury to the ear. They are capable of destroying the Eustachian tube of the middle ear by trapping air in or keeping air out of the middle ear. 'Middle ear problems can be severe [for example, the eardrum can burst or the middle ear can fill with blood or pus] or mild and only be felt as changes in pressure' (Blahd 2018). Those who clean their ear forcefully with the use of cotton swabs or sharp objects can cause scar on their ears.

Mayo Clinic posts that ageing is one of the major causes of hearing loss. And unfortunately, most of the hearing loss cannot be reversed. So the most important thing is that it should not even happen in the first place.

Mayo Clinic, in its article, details the causes of hearing loss as follows:

- *Damage to the inner ear.* Ageing and exposure to loud noise may cause wear and tear on the hairs or nerve cells in the cochlea, which sends sound signals to the brain. When these hairs or nerve cells are damaged or missing, electrical signals aren't transmitted as efficiently, and hearing loss occurs. Higher-pitched tones may become muffled to you. It may be difficult for you to pick out words against background noise.
- *Gradual build-up of earwax.* Earwax can block the ear canal and prevent conduction of sound waves. Earwax removal can help restore your hearing.
- *Ear infection and abnormal bone growths or tumors.* In the outer or middle ear, any of these can cause hearing loss.
- *Ruptured eardrum (tympanic membrane perforation).* Loud blasts of noise, sudden changes in pressure, poking your eardrum with an object, and infection can cause your eardrum to rupture and affect your hearing (Mayo Clinic 2019).

Practical Illustrations

Case Study I: Wrestler A and Wrestler B fought for the golden belt some three weeks ago. It was the talk of the day among wrestling enthusiasts. Many couples had to force their partners in joining them so as to see the match together. The fight lasted incredibly for three hours. Wrestler A later emerged as the winner, but not without suffering injuries. When he was declared the champion and his fans were hailing him, he could not hear what they were saying properly because Wrestler B had hit him hard at the left side of his head. For a while, he was turning the right ear to people and thought it was just one of those things.

When the pain persisted for days, Wrestler A had to be taken to the hospital. It was at this point it was confirmed he had lost the left side of the ear due to a damage caused to the inner bones. This only bears literal meaning—damage caused by physical injuries.

Case Study II: A beautiful attendant was on duty when multiple explosions rocked their hotel. That was the first time she would be witnessing such a traumatic event. After a few weeks, when the hotel reopened, the terrorists targeted it again and were successful in throwing multiple explosions. This time around, she was very near the venue of the explosion that the sound affected her hearing. This impairment was caused by the explosion.

Case Study III: Most human traffickers are wicked and can do all sorts of despicable things just to get their victims to their destinations. Most of them use land borders because that provides them with the opportunity to take illegal routes. A human trafficker was trying to bring in some ladies into the country when border officials nabbed him. Of particular interest were two of those girls who had their ears severely damaged. It was learnt that the trafficker did that to them for the purpose of claiming that the girls were seeking asylum in the country. However, the girls couldn't put the drama together. The damage was for the purpose of deception.

CHAPTER 8

The Nose

Another important part of the face is the nose, which is meant for breathing, smelling, and other functions. At birth, our nose seeks our mother's milk for the purpose of survival—that is, we detect the location of our mother's breasts through our nose. This is not exclusive to only humans; all mammals do it as well. This function does not elude the nose as we grow older; our nose keeps detecting the location of food, and we go for it. It is like a signal that gives direction to our lives. It is highly protective—with the nose, we know the kind of food we should go for and what we should avoid. If not, we would have ignorantly consumed foods that are harmful to our health. The nose also filters the air entering into our lungs. Apart from this, the nose is crucial to understanding non-verbal messages. Before that, let us explore the biological and scientific explanation further.

The human nose is described as the most protruding part of the face and the first respiratory system. It is also the primary organ of the olfactory system. The nasal cartilages and nasal bones are the determinants of the shape of the nose. The nasal septum also helps in the separation of the nostrils into two equal parts. On average, a male's nose is said to be bigger than a female's nose. Olfaction and respiration are the two major functions of the nose.

Let us quickly consider how the olfaction works because it is more related to the concept of body language, which this book centres on. All the three passages into the nose cavity share the flow of air. However, only the superior meatus has the smell-sensing hairs and cells. The air goes through the nasal passage in a very quick and fast manner so that the sense of smell can work in details. Note that the air mostly passes through the two lower passages, but the long hairs of the upper passage reduces the speed of airflow, thus giving the smell sensors more time to work appropriately (Markgraf 2018).

In the words of Markgraf, 'When a substance that triggers a smell is present in the air, it is absorbed by the mucous lining the walls of the upper passage.' The nerve cells of the nose are positioned beneath the mucous lining and are very sensitive to an array of substances. When a nerve cell is propelled by the presence of substance molecules in the mucous lining, it sends a signal to the brain, which is later interpreted as a smell. Most smells are said to be composites. Hence, they take the signals of many other cells reacting to various substances and interpret the signals as a particular odour. For instance, the smell of smoke may encompass a lot of impurities in the air, but they are combined to be known as smoke. It is similar with the smell of sweart, which contains different components, but the brain has learnt how to interpret it as one. This principle goes to every other thing in life (Markgraf 2018).

When the nose is working as it should, it safeguards the respiratory system and delivers important sensory signals. With this, one will be warned of something harmful beforehand or can hint you of pleasant experiences ahead. For instance, you came home tired and fagged out, but as you entered, you perceived the smell of delicious food being cooked by your spouse. At that point, you would be relieved and happy. This is the positive nature of the nose. I will expatiate on this as we move on these studies.

According to Healthline, 'The most common medical condition related to the nose is *nasal congestion*. This can be caused by colds or flu, allergies, or environmental factors, resulting in inflammation of the nasal passages. The body's response to congestion is to convulsively expel air through the nose by a sneeze.'

Let's talk of the social uses of the nose apart from the areas highlighted above. It is mostly used in the romance and dating context. We build intimacy with the help of the nose; our noses have the ability to pick up on the pheromones of others. This makes us draw closer to them and subconsciously establish whether we like the person or not. That is why I said that all the sensory organs work together while processing information.

Also, the nose is seen as an object of adornment, and this is done in a cultural perspective. Ornamentations are capable of changing the shapes of the nose. With the use of make-up, one's nose can look bigger than usual. Some even pierce their nose and insert earrings and other forms of cultural adornments in it. Sometimes, this causes injuries to the nose. Ornamentations of the nose makes some thinner, more petite, less curved, or even wider. In the modern era, some go for surgical operation on the nose. Apart from the sake of aesthetics, some also hide under beautification of the nose to perpetrate crime. For instance, if a person wants to impersonate another person and discovers that the shape of the nose will easily give him or her out, the person will go for surgery or use make-up until it looks the same with the person's nose they want to impersonate. Hence, noses help in distinguishing among people; you can use the shape of the nose of a person to identify them.

The muscles surrounding the nose are very sensitive and, as such, get to work once one perceives an odour one dislikes—they will contract, therefore making the nose wrinkled. This is used to communicate disgust, and people around you can clearly get this message without an interpreter. When the nose is wrinkled, this is an indication that something has gone wrong with the person or that they are stressed. From the foregoing, it can be seen that the nose is, no doubt, essential in understanding the thoughts of others concerning us or our actions. You will understand this better as we proceed.

8.1. Covering the Nose with the Hands

Generic Interpretations of the Concept

When a person uses their two hands to cover their nose in a sudden manner, it also affects the mouth. This has so many interpretations, but none is related to any positive outcome. It is mostly related to apprehension and shock. People use their hands to cover their nose as if they were trying to block the nose from breathing in a particular event. When we find ourselves in shock or in any given unexpected situation, we breathe more rapidly. So covering the nose and mouth with both hands is to prevent people from knowing our true behaviour. Also, it is a form of relieving the stress we are going through. The reason the mouth is also covered is that if the nostrils are blocked, the mouth becomes an alternative for breathing. So the mouth is always open when we are in apprehension, but people do not actually get to know this due to the covering gesture.

Doubt, surprise, fear, and insecurity are some other factors that can lead to this body language gesture. It would be noted that all these features are stress-inducing factors, and as such, the body reacts immediately to them. This is normally witnessed at tragic events, such as accident scenes, and where natural disasters take place. Also, a person receiving horrible news may display this gesture. Covering the nose and mouth with the hands is a blocking behaviour which will prevent others from having full access to our reaction to an event.

One 'good' thing about this body gesture is that it is witnessed universally— that is, there is no part in the world where another meaning apart from which I have analysed here is given to the gesture. It is part of this reason that evolutionary psychologists opine that the behaviour may have been adapted as a means of preventing predators from hearing us breathe. Once a predator sees that you are tense, you become an easy prey in its hand.

Scientific Explanations

Changing Minds (2019) states that detection of bad smell may be one of the primary reasons why people cover their nose. Sometimes, some people even make use of handkerchief as a way of blocking out the bad smell. The platform also submits that people who are being deceitful also cover their mouth and nose. In some other times, this may just be the habit of a person when in deep thought. During this time, two of the fingers may be used in rubbing the bridge of the nose as a way of pacifying the muscles that are already charged due to the intellectual rigours.

Westside Toastmasters also contributes to this topic by noting that this gesture is subconsciously done as one is trying to suppress one's real feelings. Even if the person talks while displaying this gesture, you will not hear them audibly well because they have covered their respiratory organs. If the person uses this gesture while talking, there is a high probability that what they are saying is criminal. The website also supports the submission of Changing Minds that the person may be deceptive.

Christopher Philip (2014) says that this gesture represents shock, disbelief, or mischief. According to the body language expert, 'It is useful to show others that you can't believe what you just heard or saw.' That is, if you cannot verbally disagree with a situation or person, you can do that with the use of this gesture. Even if you say something that you were not supposed to say, demonstrating this gesture is an indication that you are ready to retrieve your words. When you are deeply hurt and understand that your utterances at that point may not be helpful to the situation, you can display this gesture.

Practical Illustrations

Case Study I: Mr K was supposed to board a commercial vehicle from the park to a neighbouring town, but when he got there, he was informed that the bus filled up and, as such, would have to wait for the next one. He was pained and depressed because he was running out of town for an official assignment at his destination. Fortunately, immediately after the bus left, he saw a friend of his passing by. He flagged him down, and after brief conversations, he learnt that his friend was heading to the same town. Then he opted to ride with him. A few minutes into the journey, they came across a bus that just had an accident. Upon coming down to rescue the passengers, Mr K discovered that it was the same bus he was supposed to take. For a moment, he was gripped with shock and used both hands to cover his nose and mouth, with his eyes widely dilated. This gesture means shock, surprise, and nervousness.

Case Study II: Ms Q was attending an interview for a high-level job. When she got into the lift, she met some people, but she did not bother to exchange pleasantries with them for reasons best known to her. Even those in the lift who were obviously older than her tried greeting her, but the response was incredibly low. Upon getting to the venue of the interview and she was called in, as she entered into the office, she used her two hands to cover her nose and mouth due to the shock she witnessed. She had just set her eyes on two of those people she ignored while coming for the interview. So she thought her chances were gone. This gesture is a demonstration of hopelessness, unpleasant surprise, and nervousness.

Case Study III: A bicyclist was rushing to the place of his friend who was supposed to travel out of the country within the next few hours. On high speed, he darted through the intersection and uncontrollably ran head-on onto oncoming traffic, smashing onto the hood of a car. Everyone around was stunned because they had thought that it was impossible for anyone to survive such an accident. As an expression of her shock, one of the women standing at the place where the incident took place covered her nose with her hands. This means that the woman was really shocked, and she expressed that through her non-verbal cue. In this sense, it means she was sympathetic towards the course of the boy.

Case Study IV: A man was in love with a prostitute for three years. She had always deceived her husband that she was a medical practitioner, and it appeared that she was on night duty always. Three years after marriage, there was no child, and she seemed to be comfortable with it. When the husband suggested that they should go for a check-up, she reminded him of being a medical practitioner. Since she wasn't always available at nights, the husband became wayward and decided going to nightclubs with his friends. On a fateful night, the husband ran into his wife dressed in an indescribable manner at the nightclub. Upon sighting her husband, she covered her nose with her hands—she was shocked and gasping for breath. Anyone who saw her could notice her nervousness.

8.2. Wrinkling the Nose

Generic Interpretations of the Concept

Nose wrinkling (in an upward direction) is usually an expression of disgust globally. This is also known as bunny nose. When the nose wrinkles, the skin will contract along the underlying muscles. Remember, I earlier said while introducing this segment that the muscles of the nose are highly sensitive to negative emotions. That is why they contract easily when a person is undergoing something traumatic. When the nose wrinkles, there is no way the corners of the eyes would not become narrow also. The whole idea is to make the entire face look rough, unattractive, and disturbed. This means that the nose-wrinkling gesture is not sufficient in its own self; it relies on other clusters in order to rightly communicate its message in a very pronounced manner.

This body language behaviour starts right from infancy; babies who are approximately three months old will wrinkle their nose whenever they perceive a bad smell. Some even say that children begin to wrinkle their nose before turning three months old. This cue remains a part of us throughout our lives. One particular thing about it is that when a person does it, people at the other side of the room or within sight will perceive it. The nasalis muscle (the underlying muscle of the nose) contracts involuntarily immediately after we hear, feel, or see something that we do not like. This helps us communicate our true emotions to people around us. With this, what others around us would be left to figure is the source of disgust.

It should be noted that this gesture is a blocking behaviour because when the nose is wrinkled, the nostrils are subtly blocked by the raising of the lips. This further communicates our intents. In the same vein, the eyes are squinted and the chin drawn in.

Scientific Explanations

Zawn Villines (2018) refers to this gesture as nasolabial folds. He considers it wholly from the medical point of view. He describes it as the indentation lines at either side of the mouth, extending from the edge of the nose to the mouth's outer corners. He explains further that these folds have the tendency to deepen as we grow older. One of the reasons alluded to this gesture is excessive exposure to the sun, which causes wrinkles and changes our facial texture. However, this does not really explain the core of our discussion.

Christopher Philip (2013) describes this gesture as a part of microexpressions. According to him, the display of disgust is a manifestation of a universal facial expression. This falls in line with what I said while giving the generic interpretation of the gesture. In his submission, each universal facial expression 'involves three independent parts of the face, the forehead and eyebrows, the eyes, eyelids and upper part of the nose called the "root" and the lower part of the face including the lower part of the nose, cheeks, chin, and mouth.' Explaining the show of disgust, Philip notes that this expression bears numerous meanings in the eyes and lower part of the face. Here, the nose becomes wrinkled, and either the upper lips or both are raised in a way that they block the entrance of the nostrils. The cheeks also move up, the lower eyelids rise, and lines show up in the skin beneath them.

Also lending its voice to this, Changing Minds (2019) states that when the nose is wrinkled, it pushes up the cheeks and mouth. This is noticed when a bad smell is perceived. Bad smell in this sense also encompasses a metaphorical smell—a bad or disgusting idea initiated by a co-interlocutor. Even when a person is not satisfied with their own thoughts, you may see them wrinkle their nose.

Practical Illustrations

Case Study I: Mrs Y travelled for a seminar and spent four days abroad. She thought she had informed the nanny to warm the remaining soup in the pot and consume it when she came around. However, the nanny did not go near the kitchen as a means of not surpassing her boundaries. When Mrs Y came back, she went to the kitchen to prepare some delicacies for herself, but she discovered that the pots and every other thing were still in the position she left them about a week ago. She rushed to open the pot to see what was going on. Upon opening it, she discovered that the stew had fermented and was oozing out a bad smell. She jammed the lid back on the pot, wrinkled her nose, and rushed out of the kitchen. This means she was not pleased with the smell she perceived.

Case Study II: A man went to the hospital to visit a friend of his who was very sick. The friend was so sick that he could not do anything on his own. Upon getting to the hospital, the friend had just defaecated on himself, and his relatives were trying to undress him so that he could be cleaned up. Such things looked disgusting to him, and he would have ordinarily turned back. However, for the sake of being a friend, he looked on but did not know when his nose wrinkled and his lips were pressed together to the nostrils. This reveals his state of mind to others at the venue; he did not like the offensive odour he perceived at the health facility.

Case Study III: Terrorists were training some of their recruits on the need to kill, bomb, and severe their victims. They were made to know that each technique or system had its own usefulness. Particularly, severing the heads of their captives while the media team captured it was a way of sending fear down the nerves of people; they would post such videos on their social media handles, which would trend and cause psychological trauma to people who saw the videos. So a particular boy, a young graduate of technology, was told that he would be in charge of the video capturing of the process. Even though he was ready to be a suicide bomber, he could not stand the process of watching a person's head being severed. During the training process, the tutor noticed that the young man was wrinkling his nose as the axe hit the neck of their victim. It got to a stage where he had to practically close his eyes. At that point, he was dropped from the role because the video quality was low and was sent to another department where he could function optimally. Here, it means the boy was afraid.

Case Study IV: Something about overstayers is that they cannot openly express their feelings on certain issues, especially issues that can bring them across law enforcement agents. Due to this, they live in slums and other areas where figures of authority do not frequent. Overstaying in a country means you have lost your means of identification and every right enjoyed by citizens. There was a case of an illegal stayer in the country. Some citizens decided to mess up his place when he went to carry out some tasks in order to survive. Upon coming back, the odor oozing out of the room was offensive, and he had to wrinkle his nose unconsciously while he cleaned up the place. One could perceive a dislike, unsatisfactory, and displeasing look on his face.

8.3.   Unilateral Wrinkling of the Nose

Generic Interpretations of the Concept

As I have rightly explained above, crinkling upward or nose wrinkling is the perfect indicator of disgust, displeasure, or dislike; and it appears on both sides of the nose. However, it has been noticed that there are people on whom wrinkling only takes place at one side of the nose—unilaterally. This gesture is not a stand-alone signal; you have to look for other clustering signs in order to interpret it accurately. It should be noted that this behaviour is different from sneaking from the nose that would soon be discussed in this book or even stroking the nose.

As a form of hint, nose wrinkling is not really associated with a positive body language. So your interpretations should be in the line of negative thoughts. When the nose is wrinkled unilaterally, a side of the mouth will move upward while the other moves downward. Unilateral nose wrinkling is not usually easy, and as such, people do it once in a while. Maybe the person is thinking and failed to arrive at a satisfactory conclusion. A person who is stressed or concerned about something may also display this gesture.

This gesture is sometimes called Elvis effect. Let me conclude that when a side of the nose is wrinkled, it is the same thing as a full nose wrinkling which is used to signify dislike.

Scientific Explanations

Knowing that language also uses bad-taste metaphor will help us in our understanding of this gesture in a better way. Unilateral nose wrinkling is used as a connotation of bad emotional state of mind. If you do notice the reaction of card players when they are being dealt with a bad hand, you will have a better understanding of this concept. This gesture is also displayed when you are trying to process the bad suggestion of a person. This cue is made more prominent in people who still have their conscience intact. This means the person is struggling to match the ill thought with their emotions (Changing Minds 2019).

Alvin Ng (2016) also submits that the wrinkling of the nose is a sign of disgust. Since the nose makes us feel the sense of taste in our environment, it would be unimaginable that someone will intentionally stiffen it out of its natural roles. Instead, we all try to activate it to its fullest so that we can have a better perception of our surroundings. The platform also notes that this gesture can be displayed in many ways. A typical disgusted person would have their nose wrinkled and their eyebrows pulled down. Another indicator of disgust you should focus on while interpreting this gesture is the pulling up of the lips, although they generally stay loose. This cue changes the look of the entire face, even though it is unilaterally done.

When the nose is unilaterally wrinkled, it means a side of the face is primarily affected. Vanessa Van Edwards describes this cue as a show of contempt. Of all microexpressions, contempt is considered as the most powerful. It means disdain or hatred for a person or thing. When the nose is unilaterally wrinkled, many people have erroneously misinterpreted it as being a half-smile signalling half-happiness, but in reality, this is far from it. When next you read the non-verbal message of contempt on a person's face in a discourse context, it means they greatly dislike what you just said or what is going on in their vicinity (Van Edwards 2019).

Also, this gesture may be used by a person to show class—that is, the person is trying to state that he or she is better than you are. In this respect, they are expecting you to respect them and give them due honour. As an aside, let me state that some people show contempt in their photos unknowingly. This means you are telling everybody that you do not want to be connected with them (Van Edwards 2019).

Practical Illustrations

Case Study I: Two general managers of rival companies met at an event. After being recognised by the organisers of the event, they were both called to the high table. When they were about to greet each other, the general manager of Company A unilaterally wrinkled his nose with the side of his mouth raised high. Those at the event thought it was a half-smile to greet his colleague, but in reality, this was a show of superiority by the head of Company A over that of Company B. It is an expression of dominance and show of pride.

Case Study II: A busty, young, and agile boy had just been enrolled in a school. The new boy being well-built was a source of concern to the troublesome students of the school. They thought he would threaten their position as the known bullies of the institution. For the first few days, the boy kept to himself, but many of the students who had been bullied and tortured by their colleagues started running to him. He was seen as a source of refuge to them. In no time, he had made many friends and were walking in their group. This further served as a source of threat to the bullies even though he appeared harmless. The students that had been bullied before the arrival of the new boy began to taunt the old group, and this was another issue the bullies had to battle with. On a particular occasion, both groups met at the corridor of the school, and the old group was expecting the other one to wait so that they would take their leave first. To their disappointment, the new group did not wait. This pained the old group to the marrow, and their leader unilaterally wrinkled his nose, smirked at the new baby, and passed. Upon looking at his face, you would know that he was displeased and unhappy with the boy.

Case Study III: A very intelligent man had just been sacked from his work for no just reason. So he applied to another firm, and fortunately, he was invited for an interview. Upon getting there, he discovered that those who would interview him were young and behaving like novices. More so, they were not organised in their questioning process. It got to a point that even members of the panel could not comprehend his responses, and he just wrinkled a side of his nose, praying the interview would come to an end soon. This was a show of nervousness and lack of confidence.

Case Study IV: A secretary had issues with his boss and thought of the crudest way to get back at the boss. He managed to gather all the facts about the company's account and then devised a way to withdraw a large sum of money from the account. He made all arrangements, forged the necessary documents, and presented it to the bank in the name of his boss. Since all the documents were intact, the bank granted the request without a long questioning session. While the money was being disbursed, he wrinkled the side of his nose. The banker thought he was smiling, but in reality, he was displaying a superiority gaze over the financial institution and his boss—that is, he was trying to prove that he was more knowledgeable than anyone he had encountered.

8.4. Twitching of the Nose (Caribbean)

Generic Interpretations of the Concept

This behaviour is very much related to the disgust gesture discussed above. However, this gesture occurs on a faster rate compared with the nose-wrinkling behaviour—1/25 of a second. This means that all eyes must be opened in order to be able to detect it. When a person looks at you directly, their nose muscle will rapidly contract and wrinkle the nose, the only difference is that the eyes would not squint as in the case of the disgust gesture discussed above. Some of the verbal translations of this cue are 'What happened?' or 'What is going on?' or 'What are you in need of?' This is a popular non-verbal behaviour among people in the

Caribbean—Puerto Rico, Cuba, and Dominican Republic, among other nations. It is also a popular culture in US cities with a large population from Caribbean. For instance, anyone who has ever been to New York and Miami would notice this gesture among the locals.

Scientific Explanations

Nose twitching is the involuntary contraction of the muscles of the nose. This twitching is always harmless to the person. However, it is a subtle means of distractions and may be a source of frustrations to the people experiencing nose twitching. The contractions of the muscles of the nose can last for a few seconds to a few hours. Stress, dehydration, and cramps are some of the major causes of nose twitching. In some rare circumstances, it may be a signal of a medical condition. When there are mineral and vitamin deficiencies in the body, it can lead to twitching. The human body needs the right amount of vitamins and nutrients in order to function properly. Minerals and vitamins ensure that blood circulates properly throughout the body, to help in muscle toning and nerve function (Anthony 2018).

There are some certain medications that can trigger nose twitching. Some medicines that can cause twitching are asthma medications, diuretics, high blood pressure medicines, and hormones and statin medicines. That is why people are always encouraged to contact their doctor immediately when they experience nose twitching while on medication.

Nerve damage is also a potential cause of nose twitching. When you sustain an injury in the nerve, you may also feel twitching of the nose. In some situations, nose twitching may be a symptom of facial tics. This disorder is much more prevalent among children but can affect any other person. Some other clustering behaviours of nose twitching are blinking eyes, tongue clicking, eyebrow raising, grimacing, and throat clearing. When you see all these, they are all pointers to the fact that something is wrong. Recent change in diet can even cause nose twitching. If twitching becomes severe or associated with tics, there is a need to seek medical attention before it turns to something threatening (Anthony 2018).

On a social interpretation, Mentalizer Education (2019) explains that this cue expresses distaste towards a literal odour or thought. It may show on one side of the nose or both. According to the website, this behaviour can be complemented by touching, which is interpreted as a deceptive act. Remember that when a person is generally under stress, their blood vessels around the nose region dilate, and this brings about the reddening of the nose. It itches and ultimately causes irritation to the person.

Discussing this cue, Philip (2013) refers to it as an evaluative gesture—that is, people turn their nose sideways as a means of revealing disbelief or dislike. He

241

opines that this gesture probably has its origin from trying to avoid a particular odour. He advises that this cue should be interpreted in the context of other clusters. Most times, this cue is signifies reserved disagreement, which affords us the opportunity to prepare better a case against a person. With this, the person will know that we are not taken by surprise. In conclusion, Changing Minds also opines that nose twitching may connote disgust or displeasure.

Practical Illustrations

Case Study I: Mr W was visiting a particular country for the first time. When he got there, the culture looked strange to him right from the airport, but he tried to play along. In most instances, he had to ask for clarifications. Upon returning to the country for the second time, he encountered the same issue. On the third occasion, he could match the people's action with their words. By the time he was there for the fourth time, as the official at the airport greeted him with a nose twitch, he understood that the person was trying to say 'What can I get you?' And as such, he placed his order without hesitation, and to his greatest surprise, the official did his bidding. He was taken aback at the meaning of the gesture.

Case Study II: The supervisor of a security agency told his subordinates to get some things done and man a dangerous zone, but none of them were ready to take on the duty. So for some minutes, the two camps were shifting the responsibility to each other. The supervisor came back on an impromptu visit and discovered that they were still at the same spot when he left. Visibly angry, he twitched his nose, and one of the leaders of the team had to offer him an explanation. Even though he did not utter a word, all of them seemed to have understood that he was trying to ask 'What is happening?' and so they offered an explanation before he would take a drastic action against them.

Case Study III: The kid of happy young couple had just arrived from school, but with a deviation from the usual culture, after dropping his bag and greeting his parents, he did not come out of his room. His parents called him out, and upon responding to them, he still sat far away from them. His father seemed baffled and subtly tipped his mother to find out what was wrong with him. The mother recalled that whenever he was behaving in such a funny manner, he needed something urgently. So when there was eye contact with his father, the father twitched his nose at the kid, and at that point, the kid moved closer to whisper something to his father. This gesture was to depict attentiveness and care.

Case Study IV: Two human smugglers were trying to partner together in order to smuggle their victims in without hassle. Smuggler A was more experienced than Smuggler B, someone who appeared in the business due to frustration. Smuggler A was coordinating the activities while Smuggler B was to go in first with the first batch of smuggled people. The process appeared tedious for Smuggler B, and he lost control at some point. He couldn't give feedback to Smuggler A as planned. Smuggler A became angry and twitched his nose at the people around him. His countenance changed, and those around him had to move backwards. This expression of anger was clear to all those who were around.

8.5. Touching the Nose with the Index Finger

Generic Interpretations of the Concept

Sometimes, people place their index finger on the side of the nose or under it for a period of time. When it is placed under the nose, it is made to cross the entrance of the nostrils. This gesture disrupts the breathing pattern of the person; air struggles to get in and out of the nose because the nostrils have been subtly blocked. The same thing applies to placing the index finger on the side of the nose. The gesture is obvious and calls the attention of people to you. Before I give possible interpretations to this gesture, let me state that it is not a stand-alone cue; you have to look for other clues along the same line in order to accurately interpret this gesture.

Having said that, a person who places their index finger on their nose may be concerned about something. This means the person is thinking very hard and has yet to arrive at a conclusion. In most cases, they would gaze into the distance with their eyes looking vague. This signals disconnection from their immediate environment.

Another possible interpretation of the gesture is pensiveness. A person who is saddened by an occasion in an unexpected manner would display this gesture. For instance, if someone offended their boss and had taken every step to appease him or her but the boss still took the issue up and meted out punishment on the person, they might display this gesture to reflect on their past relationships with the person and how things went wrong. Before I move to this next section, let me state that this gesture is different from the nose-stroking gesture (which will be explained later). This deals with concern and negative thoughts, while the stroking behaviour is a pacifying act, maybe from this kind of issue that makes the person sad.

Scientific Explanations

In his scholarly submissions, Philip (2013) expertly submits that 'when people are stressed, blood flushes into the skin. Our hands are then drawn to the areas most affected due to increased sensitivity and heat so we tend to point out our stress. Enlarged capillaries in the nose can induce our hands in its direction to sooth it. As blood flows to the nose, it enlarges, giving credence to the "Pinocchio effect".' This lays the foundation for the understanding of this concept. The body language expert describes the index finger touching the nose as a quick but purposeful one. He says that during the display of this gesture, the finger grazes the sides of the nose, while it may be brief, almost not touching the base of the nose, in some other times.

Touching the nose can be propelled by two reasons—one, it serves as a real function of alleviating itch on the face, and two, one that is propelled due to negative emotions, which make a person feel stressed or uncomfortable. The latter is not related to any physical reason but the need to suppress emotional feelings. For anyone to appear honest, trustworthy, and unconcerned before others, they must learn how to be natural by not touching any part of their face. With this, no one will accuse you of an act of deception.

Contributing to this, Farouk Radwan (2017) opens his essay by saying that 'a person will touch his nose if he believed that something negative has happened'. This is not only apt but also complements the submission of Philip shared above. Since many of us face many negative circumstances every day, this gesture is no doubt one of the most common body language signals. Further, this gesture is registered in our subconscious, and that is why people display it without knowing that fact. Many people have always attributed this gesture to lying. While I would not like to discard this opinion in its entirety, let me state that it is only those who believe that lying is bad who will display this cue while being deceptive. Also, when a negative thought enters the mind of a person while speaking, you will see them display this gesture.

Practical Illustrations

Case Study I: For the past seven months, Mr Q, who was an estate consultant, did not have any client. He had almost become frustrated with life and was thinking of doing something else. Fortunately, an old client who was known to be much disciplined gave him a call to come over to his office for a deal. On the day he was supposed to meet his client, he was a little bit weak, and his doctor told him to rest for a while. When he was relaxing, he slept and was only awoken by his wife when she did not see him go out. Already dressed, he immediately rushed out of the room. Upon getting to his car, he discovered that he did not take the key to his car. Checking his time, the distance to his destination, and the nature of the client, he placed his index finger on his nose for a moment and ran back in to get his keys. This was an expression of frustration; he was fed up at the moment.

Case Study II: Sir M had been battling with some marital crises for the past few months. His wife was a psychologist who had brought her career into her matrimonial home. So Sir M always tried to appear perfect in all things so as not to invoke her wrath. He had always loved her in all situations and respected her decisions. On a particular day, the wife was off to a seminar in another city, and Sir M's friends called him to come over to a nightclub. He went not knowing their intentions—they were ready to link him up with an old lover for the night. He rejected the suggestion, saying that it could backfire and destroy his marriage. But they prevailed over him, saying that it was only for the night. He eventually took the lady home for the night. When the wife returned, she saw some strands of female hair in their shower, and that was the beginning of the problem. Without saying anything, the wife showed him the hair and drove out immediately. Not knowing what his fate was, Sir M sat at a corner of the room, slouched on the chair, and his index finger touched his nose. This means he was lost in thought, uncertain of what could possibly befall him.

Case Study III: Mr U decided to practise as a consultant without properly registering with the appropriate agencies. The government had ordered that all unregistered consultants offering services were illegal and should be closed down. However, Mr U defied this order and was still operating. He had placed spies near his office to inform him if the monitoring agencies were coming so that he could abruptly close down. Unfortunately for him, the monitoring agents came in a disguise. Before he could unravel their identity, they had got all the necessary pieces of information from him. He became confused that he unconsciously used his index finger to touch his nose. Apart from confusion, this gesture also symbolises an expression of regret.

8.6. Brushing the Nose

Generic Interpretations of the Concept

This gesture is very distinct out of all nose behaviours discussed in this book and is even experienced all over the world. Both high-ranking members of the society and those in the lower cadre who care about their worth make use of this gesture. It is very subtle and fast. This makes it ideal in a public setting. However, it does not change the meaning from being negative. To display this gesture, you will see people brush their nose several times with the use of their index finger. From the literal point of view, it may be an indication that the place is itching, and as such, the person is trying to scratch it. They understand that the straightforward scratching in public will portray them in a bad light. Also, maybe they are trying to remove something from the surface of their nose. A person who works in a dirty environment may have cobwebs surrounding their face at the end of the work.

Apart from these literal interpretations, there are other metaphoric representations of this gesture. First, it may be a signal of psychological discomfort. Someone who is not fit psychologically will have their facial muscles dilate, and if the blood nerves move very high so much around the nose, they can subtly brush it off. A person trying to be deceptive may experience this discomfort, and as a way of maintaining their respect at the venue, they will brush their nose with their index finger for as long as they keep on with the lies. That is why you may notice this for several times. Stress is another possible propeller of this gesture. When someone is stressed but does not want others around them to know about their emotional state, they can make use of this gesture to pacify themselves.

This cue can also be seen in a person who is trying to be dubious or embark on a questionable adventure. This means they are still trying to figure out how to go about their plans.

Scientific Explanations

The nose is an embodiment of non-verbal cues. Being located at the centre of the face makes it pronounced and, as such, directs people's attention to it. If a person detects bad smell and does not want to use a handkerchief to cover their nose, they may just brush it several times. For instance, if you are in the office with your superior and he farts, it may be cruel of you to start wrinkling your nose and covering it, say, with a piece of cloth. Even though the smell is not pleasant, you will subconsciously brush it off as a mark of respect (Changing Minds 2019).

Also, the body language website alludes lying as one of the reasons for this gesture. The dilation of the nose may cause it to itch, and brushing it with your hand multiple times will not really call people's attention to this psychological discomfort compared with scratching it with three fingers. Further, this gesture may also be a signal of disagreement. This means you are not comfortable with the point someone just raised, but you are suppressing your feelings at the moment due to reasons best known to you.

While reeling out some of the ways of identifying deceptions, Nick Babich (2016) lists this cue as part of it. Remember, I earlier aligned myself with the submission of Joe Navarro that there are no signs of deception; rather, we have signals of stress that may be pointing to deception. Taking a stance from that philosophy, let me state that what Babich is trying to state is that nose brushing is one of the signs of psychological discomfort. He describes this sign as being the most common gesture of emotional instability. Nose brushing is fast because adults are aware of their actions, but since the clue is subconsciously registered, they will move their hand to their nose before it consciously registers that they are giving themselves away and, as such, will withdraw it as quickly as possible.

As I drop the curtain on this segment, let me drop a hint on how to distinguish between a normal nose itch and psychological discomfort. In a normal itch, the person will be satisfied with scratching or rubbing it without fear, while in the one signalling emotional stress, the hand will move very fast.

Practical Illustrations

Case Study I: A motivational speaker was billed to make a public presentation for an hour. When he mounted the podium, the listeners were expectant, but ten minutes into the speech, he discovered that the zeal was fast waning down on the part of the audience. So he decided to tell them a story of his laudable impacts in life. Even though he bought a rickety car to the venue, he spoke of how he became a multimillionaire in his early thirties, even though he was not specific about the job he ventured into. While telling them this story, he was always using his index finger to brush the top of his nose and looked restless to indicate that he was psychologically stressed.

Case Study II: A man got home late because he went to greet a female friend. He knew his wife would not tolerate that because the standing rule at home was that no one should visit an opposite sex without the approval of the other party. More so, the female 'friend' whom the man went to say hello to had always been suspected to be in love with him; the wife had held on to incriminating evidence against them. When he came home and the wife sought to know what kept him late at work, he waved it off with an explanation of 'Nothing much', which was not convincing to the wife. When she demanded a better explanation, he told her that he was working on some important files in the office because they needed urgent attention. While saying this, he made use of his index finger to brush his nose for at least seven times, which hinted the wife that all was not right with her man. Here, this gesture depicted the man as a liar; he was deceiving his wife.

Case Study III: Mr D impersonated someone to get into Country H. He appeared calm and composed. Upon presenting his passport to the immigration officer, he looked away. This was the point he betrayed himself as he was expected to look into the face of the officer so that the officer could run a quick scan of his face, but looking away hinted the officer that he was hiding his face. So he was given specific attention. At this point, Mr D knew that he was in for a big thing. When he was asked to give a brief description of himself, he used his index finger to brush his nose while talking simultaneously. It was a sign that he was not psychologically balanced. Many thoughts were going on in his mind, and he was looking for a way to play on the intelligence of the officers.

8.7. Holding the Nose High

Generic Interpretations of the Concept

This is an intentional tilting of the head which makes the nose point to an upward direction. It is also called a high nose profile and is an open body gesture. This is like making the nose more pronounced—that is, the entire face is lifted up without any part of the body blocking it. Hence, this cue is regarded as a show of confidence. In a classroom situation, when students or participants do not know the answer to a question and know that the teacher can randomly pick anyone, they would bow their head so as not to have eye contact with the person. But holding a high nose profile is an indication that one is truly confident.

In some situations, this can be interpreted as a show of superiority. When someone lifts their nose to look at you, it is a means of saying that you are beneath them. If the person is truly a superior in terms of status or age, it means they are trying to affirm their superiority. However, if this is not the case, it means the person is simply arrogant. An arrogant person thinks that every other person is lower in status to them and would want to demonstrate that in every given situation. In some other contexts, this gesture may be interpreted as indignation.

I need to state that this gesture is more a cultural display than a universal body language gesture; it is observed more in some countries than in others. Italy and France are some of the countries where you can always notice this cue. For instance, the infamous Italian dictator Benito Mussolini is known for the use of this gesture. So is General Charles de Gaulle of France. If you have ever seen the ceremonial guards of Kremlin in Russia, you will notice that they are also fond of the nose-high gesture.

Scientific Explanations

Vanessa Van Edwards (2019) simply describes this gesture as 'I'm better than you' cue. When a person intentionally tilts their head, it makes them vulnerable and less threatening. This means they are challenging whatever situation they find themselves. If you intentionally submit yourself to a situation, this means you are aware that it cannot do anything negative to you. Van Edwards reveals that the forehead of the person demonstrating this gesture would be tilted back so as to make the nose clearly seen.

Before moving forward, let me state that this gesture is different from tilting the head sideways. According to Westside Toastmasters, tilting the head sideways is a show of submissiveness to a situation. This is unlike tilting the head directly backwards, which is a form of challenge to the other person in the communicative context.

The nose-high gesture ensures that the person sees their nose—that is, you are able to see the tip of your nose when you raise your head high and tilt your forehead backwards. This is a show of superiority over your co-interlocutor or audience. It means you are looking down on them.

However, if this gesture is displayed in a love context, it means another thing entirely. This posture is a reflection back into childhood, and it means the person is seeking the approval of the other person. Lovers make their entire face more revealing. Raising the head also makes the neck and throat more revealing, and this suggests that the person is submitting themselves to the will of their partner. This is more so if the love is just brewing up. This posture is basically used in gaining sympathy from others; they see you as being harmless, non-threatening, and submissive and, as such, should be helped (Philip 2013).

Practical Illustrations

Case Study I: Professor J was an internationally revered researcher. In one of his field missions, he went to an unfamiliar environment and, in one way or another, missed his way. He needed to ask for directions so as to continue with his assignment. Out of curiosity, he managed to get the attention of a passer-by, raised his head, and tilted his forehead backwards before asking for directions. When the passer-by discovered that he was harmless, he took his time to give him a detailed description of the direction he asked for. This gesture is a demonstration of openness.

Case Study II: Company QKY usually held a review meeting every Friday before work ended. The meeting was usually chaired by the CEO or general manager in the absence of the former. Workers were more composed and orderly any time the CEO was physically present. On a particular Friday, the GM was the one to chair the meeting because his boss was away for another meeting. The workers dragged a little bit before assembling themselves for the meeting. Before going into the details of the meeting, he raised his nose high and tilted back his head in a direct position to gaze at the employees. This means he was trying to assert his authority as being the one in charge of the gathering.

Case Study III: There was an extraordinarily brilliant student in the class of Ms V. Any time none of his colleagues could not answer a question, he was usually the perfect bail out for them. Thus, he had won the admiration of all his teachers and most of the students alike. Showering him praises very often seemed to be affecting his psyche, and he now sees himself above others. During students' community duties, he would stay back and expect his colleagues to handle everything. On a fateful day, Ms V adopted the interactive approach to teach a topic she had considered a little bit technical for her students. During the session, the boy was asked to make his contributions. Instead of sitting down straight and talking, he opted to stand, raise high his nose, and look into the eyes of his teacher before making his contributions. In this case, the boy's action is considered as being arrogant because he considered everyone, including the teacher, as being inferior to his intellectual ability. This can be said to be childish but also seen in some adults.

Case Study IV: Twin A forged the documents of Twin B without his consent. Twin A had wanted to travel out even though he had no passport or financial capacity to bear the cost, but Twin B had always warned him against such risky adventure. One day, Twin A secretly took Twin B's passport and other documents, forged them, and decided to travel out. Twin B needed to use the passport for something important, but alas, it was nowhere to be found. He knew his twin brother was the culprit. He reported the case to law enforcement agents who swung into action immediately. Twin A held his nose high and tilted his head back at the point of arrest to display superiority, but with damning evidence against him, he buried his face shamefully. He wanted to cover up with a show of superiority, but there was an overwhelming show of real feeling.

8.8. Tapping the Nose

Generic Interpretations of the Concept

When you overtly tap the nose with the index finger, this is known as signalling, and it is an embodiment of non-verbal messages. However, let me quickly chip in that it is culture-specific. In many cultures of the world, this gesture is used by people to show that something is oozing out bad odour. In doing this, the index finger touches the tip of the nose on a very fast rate multiple times. Also, the person would breathe out more than they would breathe in at that point because they do not want to inhale the unpleasant smell. The verbal interpretation in this sense is, 'This stinks a lot.'

This gesture may also mean lack of confidence. If you do not believe what a person is saying but you are consciously suppressing your reaction against them, the body will reveal you. The facial muscles will be activated and make the blood nerves run on high speed. As a way of pacifying yourself, you will make use of the index finger to overtly touch the nose. What you are trying to tell the person is, 'I don't trust you.' If this gesture is done against you, this means you have to really convince the person.

In some other instance, it may be interpreted as 'all eyes on you'. This means the person is watching every one of your actions, and as such, you need to exercise caution in all that you do. Further, it can also mean 'I notice you.' If you place a file before your boss and instead of him reacting, he kept mum and tapped his nose, it means he is aware of your presence, only that he is busy with other things.

The gesture may also be used in acknowledgement of a person's brilliance. If you are making a public presentation and someone asks a very brilliant question, you may make use of this gesture involuntarily to mean they are very clever before providing answers to their question. We have given different meanings to this gesture, many unrelated interpretations for that matter. What matters most is that you understanding the context of its usage and look for other gestures pointing to the direction of your interpretations.

Scientific Explanations

When you perceive that a person is telling lies to you, you become internally agitated and feel like challenging them, but if the person is higher in rank than you, you may not be able to call them to order. However, this does not mean that your internal agitations have been conquered. So you may overtly tap your nose as a means of pacifying yourself. This also sends a message to the person that you are aware of their deceptions. In the words of Philip (2013), 'Pacifying behaviours happen automatically, our brains send a message to our bodies that we need to be pacified and out go our hands to serve the purpose.'

The TV Tropes website also offers explanations about this gesture. According to the website, when a person taps their nose, it is an indication that they 'know' something. The website opines that this gesture is more of a Western thing. For instance, in Asia, when you point to the nose (or face in general), it is equated to the Western non-verbal behaviour of pointing at one's chest to indicate that one is talking to oneself—that is, the unconscious gesture that follows your words whenever you ask 'Who, me?' So we need to take cognisance of these cultural differences while making our interpretations. The website also cautions that 'nose tapping is almost always dependent on the context in order to make much sense at all what it is'. The surest message is that whenever you see a person tap their nose, it means something.

Laure Gawne (2013) also gives an in-depth interpretation of this gesture after consulting different materials. She submits that almost all experts who did fieldwork on this gesture across Europe agreed that it means 'sniffing out trouble'. Hence, she submits that 'it can be used as a way of signalling knowledge, that someone is clever, or a threat'. This submission is in line with the generic interpretations I earlier gave. This means the person is ready to 'sniff' out whatever trouble their co-interlocutor is up to.

Practical Illustrations

Case Study I: A clerk came into the office of his boss to drop some files to be worked on. As usual, he would wait to receive some orders on when to come for them and get some other things done. The boss was known to be a fast responder; whenever the clerk would come in, he would respond to the clerk's greetings and then give him the instructions for the day. However, it had been over five minutes that the clerk had been standing, and there seemed to be no word uttered by his boss. He was baffled and had to greet his boss again. At that point, his superior looked at him sternly and continued with the documents he was working on. The fact is that immediately after the clerk entered the office, the boss had tapped his nose twice and looked away as a means of communicating non-verbally that he was aware of his presence, but the clerk did not catch up on that.

Case Study II: A company wanted to extend its tent of services to another province. So the managing director thought it was best to brief the management team of plans first before sharing it with the whole house. During the discourse, he told them the province they were targeting and the reason for making it their potential destination. After he was done with his presentation, he asked if anyone had a better understanding of the topography of the city beyond what he had said. A member of his team seated at the back was already tapping his nose even before he had finished talking. Then he quickly raised his hand to make his intentions known about the proposal. People were surprised about his contributions because it looked as if he had gone ahead to make enquiries about the place for the purpose of that meeting. The gesture here symbolises impatience and display of knowledge.

Case Study III: A smuggler was directed into my office some time ago. I was somewhat busy, and when he came in, I could not drop what I was doing to attend to him immediately. But I tapped my nose twice to acknowledge his presence. Obvious that he did not get my gesture, he muttered some words to show that he was around. I raised my head to look at him and kept on with my work. He still murmured some words, and at that point, I had to wave to him to sit down. Before the interview, I knew he knew almost nothing on the interpretation of non-verbal gestures. If he could not understand that I was acknowledging his presence, then what would he know?

8.9.   Flaring of the Nostrils

Generic Interpretations of the Concepts

The nostrils are technically referred to as nasal wings. We normally flare them while preparing to do something physical. When we are agitated, there is almost nothing that we cannot do. In the circumstances of war, you see people jumping fences and undertaking journeys they would not have dared under normal circumstances. This means their hormones have been alerted to avert evil.

Also, we oxygenate during such physical exercises; our nostrils become wider so as to enable us to breathe better.

In a violent situation, the fight or flight response comes to the fore. If you suddenly raise up your head and see a big stone rolling to your side, the first point of action is to guide your head with your hands as you run away. This is a flight response. But if someone you consider a minor is running towards you, you maintain your balance and wait for them so as to confront them. During these processes, the nostrils flare to ensure your breathing is not impeded at any point in time.

In law enforcement duties, flared nostrils may be an indication that a person is about to take to their heels. On an interpersonal level, it shows that the person needs time to calm down. If you just finished your early morning exercise, your nose will flare so as to help you calm down and get back to normalcy.

Scientific Explanations

Changing Minds (2019) submits that 'when the nostrils are widened, it allows more air to be breathed in and out and readies the person for combat'. In a sense, this may be an indication that the person is going through severe displeasure. A person who is not satisfied with their psychological state of mind can do anything as a means of liberating themselves. Furthermore, flaring of the nostrils may indicate that a person is trying to make an internal judgement about a concept. When you are undertaking an intellectual assignment, especially one that is expressed within, you become hot, and as such, you need more intake of air. That is why the nostrils open wider for you to inhale air.

Philip (2014) says that when the nostrils flare to a point, they remain fixed in a permanent fashion. Giving a one-sentence summary of the gesture, he opines that 'flared nostrils signals a negative thought pattern and aggression'. This means that when you see the nostrils of a person flared, it means all is not well with him or her. It is used to tell people that you do not approve of their idea or presence. If someone responds to you with flared nostrils, it means they disagree with what you have just said. This gesture is close to the signal of disdain, and that makes it a potent tool in expressing disagreement when something inappropriate is heard or done. When you see the nostrils of a person flaring, it is an indication that their aggression is building up. This means you have to correct your behaviour, run away, or be ready for combat before the person lashes out at you.

According to Philip, the verbal translation of this gesture is, 'We've probably got a problem on our hands. Time to load up on oxygen as we might need to fight or take flight!' Hence, this cue is part of the fight or flight response. During work, our body consumes more oxygen, and when the brain alerts us that there is major work to be done in the meantime, the nostrils will flare so as to load our body with hemoglobin—the carrier of oxygen molecules. A related cue to show you that someone is ready to fight is that their chest will begin to expand and contract on a rapid rate that you may even hear them panting.

As I have earlier said, remember that nostril flaring may also be a result of physical exercises not necessarily connected to the psychological state of mind.

Practical Explanations

Case Study I: A young lady secured a job with a private individual, and she opted in because she wanted to build her level of experience. She just graduated from school and needed to start her career from somewhere. However, her boss turned out to be a high-handed person. Because of the end goal, she endured everything and did all his bidding. One day, the boss came down hard on her and prodded her until she almost reached breaking point. Her fist balled up and nostrils flared. Every reactionary system in her body became tense, and it was obvious on her face. She only waited for the boss to further take a wrong step so as to enable her to act out her aggression. This was a display of anger.

Case Study II: A man was rushing his wife to the hospital, and a policeman flagged them down to check his vehicle particulars. The man handed over the documents to him and put on the emergency light of his car just to hint the law enforcement officer that he was in a hurry. Undeterred by the actions of the driver, the policeman began to question him further on the documents. At this point, his aggressive emotions began gathering cloud. He looked at the policeman in the face for a few minutes and failed to respond to his questions. As the policeman opened his mouth to speak, his nose flared and hands almost shivering on the steering wheel. When the law enforcement officer became aware of this, he simply directed him to go. This was a display of impatience and nervousness.

Case Study III: It had almost become a habit for Mr J to return home late. More irritatingly, he did not consider it good to offer explanations to his wife. The wife gave peace a chance for the first few months by not questioning him in an annoying manner, but he did not respect the decision of his wife. When the wife asked him to come for a round-table discussion, he turned down her 'call to peace'. Then the wife also started staying back late outside. He was annoyed and decided to punish the wife. When he called the wife to come and offer explanations for her sudden change in lifestyle, she looked at him sternly, hissed, and flared her nostrils. He retreated immediately. He knew the non-verbal display was a show of anger, and he was not ready for such confrontation.

Case Study IV: A community reported the unwholesome activities of some drug addicts and other miscreants troubling them at night. The police had to mobilise their men to their community, and on the first day, some arrests were made. As expected, the drug addicts considered the arrest out of order and challenged the authority of the police to carry out the raid—it was obvious they had psychological issues. When it was time to interrogate them, the first person to come into the interview room flared up his nose; he was obviously angry. But that did not stop the interviewers from doing their job. A show of anger did not deter the investigators from doing their job.

8.10. Fiddling with the Philtrum

Generic Interpretations of the Concept

Not everyone seems to know what philtrum is. It is the grooved area between the upper lip and the nose. It is like the bridge between the mouth and the nose. As tiny as it appears to be, it is the centre of playfulness for many people. Sometimes, some people do have hair growing at their philtrum, so they can play with it by plucking at it. Most times, this is done subconsciously. Other people may scratch or even pull on it. When you see people doing this, it is a sign that they are really stressed, and that is why you may see them pulling at the philtrum energetically.

Little did people know that the philtrum gives them away; sweat tends to gather there when we are stressed. So playing with it is a form of a pacifying act. Those who do not know about this may wrongly assume that that part of the person is only itching him or her. In fact, the person may subtly use their tongue in pushing it out by placing the tongue in front of the teeth, behind the philtrum. When they push the philtrum out very well, it moves to the entrance of the nostrils. With this, they would not touch it again; the air coming out of the nostrils is meant to do the pacifying job.

When the philtrum is stimulated with the tongue, people easily spot it because it makes the grooved area look protruding. Most people know that this is a pacifying act.

Scientific Explanations

Study Body Language (SBL) submits that many gestures are interrelated in meaning but can only be different in terms of the names we give them. The website notes that this gesture is used by people to show displeasure. It is related to the lip-pouting gesture normally seen in children. This is also done by adults, but in a very subtle manner so that we do not appear childish. When someone is displeased by an attitude, they would be stressed, and one of the means of pacifying themselves is to play with the philtrum.

In the same vein, Alvin Ng says this gesture represents disgust. When the tongue is used to pull up the philtrum, it blocks the nostrils, which hinders free flow of air. This means the person does not like what another person is saying or what they are hearing. Because they do not want to express this disgust in an obvious manner, they make use of this gesture.

On its own part, Westside Toastmasters notes that hand-to-face gestures serve as the origin of deceit among humans. When we hear something that is unpleasant or untruthful, we may likely cover a part or the entirety of our face. The person playing with their philtrum is doing it in a subtle manner so as not to distract the person talking. If a person is also saying something that seems deceptive, they may use this gesture. Remember that children do this openly; they cover their mouth with one or both hands as a way of preventing the falsehood from falling off from their mouth. But since adults do want to appear mature and respected, rubbing the index finger through the philtrum makes the other four fingers block the mouth.

This gesture also signals thoughtfulness—the person is thinking about something bothering them and has yet to arrive at a conclusion. So it may be an indication of uncertainty, doubt, or exaggeration. If you doubt what someone is telling you, you can just play with your philtrum. If you feel the person is exaggerating their story, you can fiddle with the philtrum and shake your head along. This tells the person that you do not agree with them.

Practical Explanations

Case Study I: Criminal O had been on the wanted list of the nation's law enforcement agencies for over a decade. He had perpetuated all forms of crimes ranging from armed robbery, murder, and terrorism. He was an infamous criminal who was fast turning himself to an important personality through negative means. He was eventually nabbed by a high-powered patrol team of the force given the duty to fish him out. After initial investigations, he was to face a team of experts who would interview him, gather evidence against him, and then arrange him in court. It should be noted that Criminal O operated on an international scale; he had been apprehended in neighbouring nations but manoeuvred his way out. So he thought this was business as usual. Thus, he sat confidently, smiling, and expected to play on the intelligence of the officials and return to his trade. When the session started, he was catching up, but before the dot of an hour, everywhere had become hot for him. He was obviously stressed due to the intellectual rigours he was being put through. He began to play with his philtrum. This was a symbol of stress and boredom.

Case Study II: A young man was employed as the secretary of a start-up. Expectedly, he had to work more than what his primary responsibilities were. He endured everything, hoping that he would soon hold a high position once the firm grew. However, the CEO did not see things from this angle; he was concerned about his present gains and, as such, worked out the young man. There was a week they were seeking the approval of one of the national agencies for their services. So he gave the young secretary the duty of getting everything ready within three days so that he could go through the documents and make corrections. Obviously, there was a lot to do that working on it during office hours would not be enough. So he decided to go home with some, even though there was no extra payment for working extra hours. On the third day, he was supposed to deliver the work, but he could not work at home because he had to settle some issues with his wife. His boss arrived at work earlier than usual to ask if the work was ready, which he dared not reply in the negative. He was really troubled on how he could finish the work on time. When his boss asked for it, he began to sweat beneath the nose and used his index finger to rub the philtrum. This was a show of nervousness, embarrassment, and fear.

Case Study III: One of the most demanding part of a professional gathering is to work in groups. While some can be enthusiastic about the job; others may drag you down. The case of two colleagues came to mind. They were given a job to do that they need submit to the supervisor within three days. Colleague A wanted to get everything done within a day or two, while Colleague B was postponing it, assuring Colleague A that they would finish in due time. At the end of the day, he could not deliver his own portion on the agreed date. When Colleague A approached him to make enquiries about the work, Colleague B started fiddling with his philtrum. This was a clear sign of failure to Colleague A; he knew his colleague did not carry out the task.

8.11. Subtle Touching of the Nose

Generic Interpretations of the Concept

There are some pacifying touches that are done in a very subtle way; if you do not pay attention to them, you would miss the signals. This form of gesture is done by rubbing the index finger on the nose. This means the person does not want you to know that something is wrong with them. Usually, when a person is psychologically unstable and is looking for a way to suppress it, they would slightly rub their nose with their index finger. This is usually the indication of tension. Tension can make a person lose their self-worth. People do not want to appear weak in certain circumstances. Take for instance, someone has always been known to be a strong, agile person whom people look up to, but suddenly, that person breaks down in the presence of those who have always eulogised him. Media personnel are the perfect example in this realm. No matter what they are going through, they must always be strong while anchoring a programme. We will expatiate on this at the 'Practical Illustrations' section.

Poker players are another set of people who try to bury their emotional feeling so as not to give themselves out to their opponents. When trying to hide their weak hands, they would slightly rub their nose.

Stress is normally induced by many things, but usually negative. In the case of poker players, it is defeat or fear of it that makes them psychologically stressed. When a person is also trying to be manipulative, they would be stressed. Fabricating experiences is usually energy-consuming, especially when done in the presence of those who are eager to expose you. All these factors raise the stress hormones in people.

Scientific Explanations

Changing Minds (2019) states that slightly touching the nose may be an indication that the person is frustrated. Someone who is evaluating negative situations would definitely be frustrated if they do not know which situation looks less threatening to them. As a way of wishing off their frustration on the outside, they would slightly rub the top of their nose. This pretence even works more for those who wear glasses; they would pretend as if they want to adjust their glasses. This is distractive and may not make you understand their real issues. Women who do not want to smudge their make-up are fond of performing this gesture with a discreet stroke.

According to Magical Apparatus (2019), the nose-touching gesture shows that as a negative thought enters the mind, the subconscious instructs the hand to cover the mouth, but in a bid not to make this gesture obvious, the hands pull away and had to think about this. In essence, this gesture is a complicated, disguised version of guarding the mouth. According to Magical Apparatus, 'It may consist of several light rubs below the nose or it may be one quick, almost imperceptible touch.'

Another explanation given for the occurrence of this gesture is that deception and other stress-inducing activities bring about the tingling of the delicate nerve endings of the nose. So a touch of the nose is aimed at satisfying this feeling. Again, do not confuse this with a person who has an itchy nose. In the case of someone experiencing itchy nose, they would deliberately scratch or rub it until they are satisfied. The sneaking nose touch can be used by both the speaker and listener. A speaker uses it to disguise their deceit, while a listener employs the gesture to express their doubts about what is being said (Magical Apparatus 2019).

Practical Illustrations

Case Study I: A popular political television anchor was billed to interview the president of his country. While driving down to the station, he received a distress call that his beloved mother, the closest person to him on earth, slumped and was in critical condition at the hospital. The interview with the number 1 citizen was to be held thirty minutes from that time, and the traffic was hectic. Not only that, the entourage of the president was already on ground. After thinking for about a minute, he concluded to go on with the interview due to many reasons. The president arrived on time, and the interaction kicked off as scheduled. He was obviously stressed and managed to forget about the incident for a while, but it was always recurring. He made use of his glasses to disguise and prevent people from noticing his troubled eyes. Yet he made use of his index finger from time to time to rub the surface of his nose in a slight manner. This was to cover up his nervousness.

Case Study II: Officials of the border patrol team arrested a man who was trying to sneak into the country through an unapproved route. When he was apprehended, he pretended as if everything was OK with him and that he was a resident. A few questions revealed that he did not know some basic things about that particular environment where he had claimed he was using for farming. Real trouble brewed for him when he was asked what he wanted to do with some of the sophisticated materials in his bags. While talking, he was almost shivering but was trying to show strength of an 'innocent mind'. When he almost started sweating, he began to touch the tip of his nose in a slight manner and then would continue with his fabricated stories. This depicted him as a liar.

Case Study III: A team of five people were selected to travel for an official programme by a company. One of them had longed for that trip and used every cunning means to get himself into the team. However, he began to feel weak from the inside just two days to the journey. He was supposed to take leave, but if he should apply for the leave, his name would be replaced by the committee. So he forced himself to be at the office for two days. He became weaker, and on the day they were supposed to travel, he delayed others because he was resting at home. When he came, he gave the excuse of traffic but was always touching his nose from time to time during the journey; he found it difficult to communicate with others. Those who were observant enough knew that he was telling lies.

8.12. Inhaling by the Nose

Generic Interpretations of the Concept

There is no culture that celebrates bad news. In other words, bad news is usually a source of sadness all over the world. That makes it herculean for people to deliver to another person. If not well-delivered, it can be a source of another tragedy to the person concerned. For instance, in Africa, elderly people are armed with the duty of delivering bad news. It is believed that they know the best way to portray the occurrence to a bereaved.

On a general note, when people are about to deliver unpleasant or bad news, they rapidly inhale through the nose. This is usually loud to the extent that those around them will hear the sound before they would eventually speak. Maybe it is a source of gathering internal strength so as to enable them deliver the news appropriately.

In some contexts, I have seen people display this gesture when they are faced with a difficult question. When a person is bothered by a question, they inhale rapidly through the nose as a form of taking deep breaths. This is just like the gesture displayed by a person who wants to try something that seemingly appears impossible. This gesture is also seen among liars in some rare instances. After thinking through the kind of lies they want to tell, they inhale rapidly through the nose so as to dispel all fears before releasing it.

The nerves and the hairs in the nose are incredibly sensitive to moisture. The same thing applies to touch and air movement. The rapid inhalation is known for stimulating the connected nerve endings and the hairs. Through this, the stress that the person is undergoing is momentarily mitigated. In other words, this gesture is a pacifying behaviour that is employed to deal with psychological stress.

Scientific Explanations

Sometimes, the rapid nose inhaling is interpreted as a sign of contempt. Changing Minds notes that the literal cause of rapid nose inhaling is a cold. Apart from that, every other meaning is seen to be metaphorical. It may happen to just a side of the nose. In this case, the mouth will also twitch up. Disgust and displeasure are some of the possible interpretations of this gesture. When a person is displeased with a question, scenario, or concept, they would sniff rapidly.

Eliot Hoppe (2019) extensively discusses this gesture while talking about how to detect liars. Remember, I earlier said that this cue can be seen in a person before they lie. Anxiousness or deceit makes people uncomfortable internally, and as such, their blood pressure will rise unimaginably. Due to the increase in blood flow, the small blood vessels at the earlobes and tip of the nose become engorged with blood, which makes the two places feel itchy at that moment. This is subconsciously done, so no one can exercise control over it. Before you know it, you would have put your finger into the nose to scratch or rub it. Most often, the quick inhalation accompanies this sequence of events. Sometimes, the blink rate may increase simultaneously. This gives the person away without much ado.

Mentalizer Education also lends a voice to this topic. It describes it as a body language 'expressing distaste towards a thought or literal odor and may show on one side of the nose, paired with a twitching mouth'. When rapidly inhaling by the nose is accompanied by touching, it is usually interpreted in many quarters as a display of falsehood. Stress causes the dilation of the blood vessels located in the nose.

Practical Illustrations

Case Study I: Neighbour J was returning from work when he saw that there was an accident on the other side of the road. He decided to wait while the emergency team was busy on the scene. He saw that one of the cars involved in the incident was a familiar one. So he decided to move nearer in order to see properly. Alas, the vehicle belonged to one of their close neighbours. He followed the accident response team to the hospital where they took the victims. After that, he quickly drove home to see if his neighbour's wife was at home. He saw the wife preparing some delicacies. Obviously, her eyes looked innocent and expectant, maybe for the return of her husband. Neighbour J called her to the living room and rapidly inhaled through the nose and then informed her of the accident. This was an expression of distate for what he was about to say.

Case Study II: A man was stopped by security operatives at the airport. At first, he frowned at the law enforcement officials who confronted him, because out of the thousands of people at the airport, why was it that he was the only one whom they approached? But when he discovered that the security operatives meant business, he became submissive. He did not know that his look, appearance, and dressing gave him away. They quickly located his baggage and took him to a room for questioning. He was in the country for the first time. In his papers, he had claimed that he came to visit a relative, but a preliminary search showed that they were not related with the person he mentioned. When he was asked to defend himself before he would be locked up, he rapidly sniffed through the nose, used his index finger to slightly touch the nostril, and then gave his explanation. At the end of everything, he was later detected to be a terrorist on a suicide mission to the airport. The gesture depicted him as someone who was not comfortable with what he was going through.

Case Study III: A particular girl had always prided herself as the most intelligent in her class. Sometimes, she arrogantly dared her teachers. She had been suspended from school for about three times for her arrogance. So many of the teachers had set a boundary for her. Yet it seemed she was not learning her lessons. One day, one of her teachers decided to ask her a simple but tricky question. Many of the students knew the answer because they were taught when she was suspended. She stood for minutes, rapidly inhaling and playing with her philtrum. She later said something that was out of context, and it made her an object of ridicule in the hands of her classmates. With the display of the gesture, the teacher knew that she was uncomfortable due to not knowing the answer to the question.

CHAPTER 9

The Mouth

Essentially, the mouth is fundamentally used for eating, biting, breathing, and drinking. It is also the part of the body through which we make verbal utterances. The mouth is very sensitive to temperature and touch. It is incredibly surrounded by over ten intricately reflexive muscles. The muscles are not built for touch alone but also to aid us in our sentiments and thought processes. Apart from the eyes, the mouth is the next facial part to focus on when trying to understand the emotions and the true state of mind of a person. Before we fully explore the concept of the mouth in non-verbal context, let's understand its anatomy first.

The mouth is also known as the oral cavity. It is the hollow opening that allows food and air to gain entrance into the body. The mouth houses many other organs, such as the tongue, teeth, and ducts of the salivary glands. They all work in unison to ensure that food is properly ingested and digested. The tongue, lips, cheeks, and teeth work together to ensure speech production (Barclay 2018).

Anthea et al. (1993) describes the mouth as the first opening of the alimentary canal that receives food and produces saliva.

The boundaries of the mouth are defined by the cheeks, lips, hard and soft palates, and the glottis. Basically, the mouth is divided into two main segments— the oral cavity proper and the vestibule. The section between the teeth, lips, and cheeks is referred to as the vestibule, while the oral cavity proper is primarily dominated by the tongue (Gillian 2006).

Explaining the concept and usefulness of teeth, Barclay notes that 'teeth are hard structures specialised for the biting and grinding of food [known as mastication, or chewing]. They form a continuous row in the bottom of the mouth surrounding the tongue on the lateral and anterior sides, as well as another nearly identical row extending from the roof of the mouth. Teeth form deep roots into the bones of the maxillae and the mandible, but grow out through the gums of the mouth to form biting surfaces. The gums, or gingiva, are soft mucous membranes surrounding the teeth, protecting the roots from decay and helping to hold the teeth in place.'

According to Kara Rogers, 'The chief structures of the mouth are the *teeth*, which tear and grind ingested food into small pieces that are suitable for digestion; the *tongue*, which positions and mixes food and also carries sensory receptors for taste; and the *palate*, which separates the mouth from the nasal cavity, allowing separate passages for air and for food.'

Let me lay more emphasis on the tongue due to its relationship with speech production, which is our major concern. It is the inferior portion of the mouth but has the ability to move to any region of the mouth. Hence, it can occupy whatever space that pleases it. Many people do erroneously assume that the tongue is a muscle, but in reality, it is an organ of the body. It is made of epithelium, several skeletal muscles, nerves, and connective tissues. The tongue contains many small ridges known as papillae that help it to grip and move food around the mouth. Taste buds are hidden in valleys around some of the papillae and produce the sense of taste by detecting chemicals found in food (Barclay 2018). The tongue's ability to stop or alter the flow of air helps in the production of speech and many consonant sounds.

Rogers continued that 'the oral cavity and vestibule are entirely lined by mucous membranes containing numerous small glands that, along with the three pairs of salivary glands, bathe the mouth in fluid, keeping it moist and clear of food and other debris. Specialised membranes form both the gums [gingivae], which surround and support the teeth, and the surface of the tongue, on which the membrane is rougher in texture, containing many small papillae that hold the taste buds. The mouth's moist environment and the enzymes within its secretions help to soften food, facilitating swallowing and beginning the process of digestion.'

Another important part of the mouth is the orifice. When the mouth is shut, it is the orifice that forms a line between the upper and lower lips. In the submission of Cassidy et al. (2000), 'In facial expression, this *mouth line* is iconically shaped like an up-open parabola in a smile, and like a down-open parabola in a frown. A *downturned mouth* means a mouth line forming a downturned parabola, and when permanent can be normal. Also, a *downturned mouth* can be part of the presentation of Prader-Willi syndrome.'

Now let's shed light on the social interpretation and usefulness of the mouth as a way of ushering ourselves into the non-verbal messages of the various gestures made with the oral cavity. As earlier said, the mouth has the power to reflect our thoughts and sentiments. More so, it works in real time—that is, once your emotion changes, the mouth reveals that immediately. So it is not what you have to wait for and notice after some minutes.

The mouth can serve as a source of seduction. Lovers know the best way to twist the mouth in order to arouse each other. Apart from the genitals, the mouth is also fundamental to lovemaking. In the same vein, when a person is sad, you can get to know that by looking at the shape of their mouth. A sad mouth is always motionless, unattractive, and dry. When a person is excited, you can know through how they carry their mouth. Even when they are in pain. From the foregoing, you would see that the mouth reveals the emotions of people every time. Once an emotion gives way for another, it registers immediately on the mouth. That is why you are able to see a child crying now and the same child laughing in the twinkle of an eye. Let me state that you would become most accurate in reading body language if you can match up all the gestures discussed so far together and interpret them as one.

9.1. Short but Loud Exhaling

Generic Interpretations of the Concept

The brevity of this gesture sets it apart from others. However, this form of exhaling is somewhat loud. This gesture is done by slightly opening the upper and lower lips and then breathing out. The literal interpretation of this gesture is that the person is tired and is trying to get back to normalcy. Breathing out in a short but loud manner is normally experienced after a person has finished running, especially one that is against the person's wish. For instance, if something is chasing you and you end up escaping the predator, you would exhale in this way. This is also seen in dogs after they have chased prey. In short, this cue indicates high stress.

When a person is also frustrated about something, you may see them display this gesture. When people are told something that is saddening, they normally display this gesture. It also works for those facing a threatening, difficult situation. All these incidents are energy-consuming; they demand internal rigours in order for you to be able to cope with them. For instance, a person who is being told bad news would have to think of the good memories they shared with that person or thing they lost, and this would foreshadow the future of how they would live without that person or thing.

To surmise it all, the short but loud exhaling is a great pacifying behaviour; it helps to relieve stress in threatening circumstances. This is especially true when we are angry. Short exhaling during our moment of anger is like purging out the anger and inhaling peace at the same time.

Scientific Explanations

Ideally, the nose is the part of the body dedicated for breathing, but there are situations when we resort to the mouth, especially when we need the oxygen in high proportion. Changing Minds (2019) refers to loud but short exhaling as stressed breathing. Sometimes, the person breathing this way may be hot. Maybe the person just moved away from the scorching sun or did something that was energy tasking. If care is not taken, this may be mistaken to be a signal of anger. Changing Minds also submits that this gesture may be an indication of sadness. When you are sad, you blow out more hair than you inhale. Another interpretation the website gave to this gesture is frustration. A frustrated person is obviously stressed and uses this gesture as a pacifying behaviour.

Mentalizer Education also commented on this gesture. According to the website, this gesture may connote hopelessness or sadness. A person who is expectant but ended up being disappointed by their source would display this cue. In this sense, it means they are resigning to fate. Keeping faith over an issue for too long can be tiring. While we still hope that something may eventually come to pass, a person will exhale in a short but loud manner. The website concludes that we also emit a deep breath with an audible sound as a sign of relief to mean that our troubles are over. Maybe you did not expect the problem to end as quickly as such, so you would exhale in an audible manner as if you were relieved.

Christopher Philip (2013) says this gesture is seen in the freeze, fight, or flight response. He observes that the gesture is more pronounced in animals that do not have verbal means of communication. He uses white-tailed deer to illustrate his point. This animal reacts to the threat from predators in different ways. To identify the distance of a predator, it would tilt its head backwards and take a deep breath through the lungs. If the deer discovers that it is in a safe position, it would exhale through the mouth in a short form to signal to the predator that pursuing it would be fruitless. Hence, this gesture is used by both humans and animals.

Practical Illustrations

Case Study I: Man H had never been fascinated to a lady like he did to Woman C. He approached her, and they discussed at length how to become lovers. Although the lady was indifferent throughout, he implored her to give things a try, and she opted in with a nod. They fixed a meeting for the evening of the next day, which was a Friday. The appointment time was seven o'clock. By 6.30 p.m., Man H was ready and hoping that thirty minutes from that time, they would be on their way. It was already eight o'clock, yet the lady was not around. Her line was not connecting, and he had yet to know her residence. He kept on waiting till nine o'clock, and still, not even a fly showed up. At that point, he began losing hope and decided to return home. When he stood up from where he had sat for hours, he exhaled in a short but loud sound and then headed home. This was an expression of hopelessness. He pacified himself of the sorry state he found himself in before taking his leave.

Case Study II: A young man had failed his final-year examination twice. At first, he appeared to be unserious, but on the second occasion, after his mates had graduated, he seemed to have rededicated himself to his studies. Yet the result ended up unfavourable. At some point, he wanted to call it quits, but his parents encouraged him to try once more. During the third attempt at the paper, he was psychologically depressed because those he was sitting the examination with were his juniors. He struggled to write some things and moved out before the others. When the results were released, he was afraid of checking it because he had lost hope in the whole process. Upon checking the results, to his greatest surprise, he passed excellently. Before logging out of the portal, he took a loud, short exhale. This was to celebrate the end of his 'suffering'—that is, he was trying to display how relaxed he had become from the initial frustrating situation.

Case Study III: The wife of a young man had just put to bed. She delivered through a caesarian section, and as such, she was admitted for days. The husband did not want to apply for a leave at work because he just resumed from one. So he was shuttling between hospital and work. When his wife was not dismissed on the scheduled day, he became frustrated with the whole system and exhaled in an audible manner when he was told. He took a deep and audible breath as a way of breathing out his nervousness and returning himself to his normal, confident position.

Case Study IV: A drug addict was arrested for the third time in a month. At that point, the officers in charge of his case decided not to release him but, instead, take him to a rehabilitation centre so that he could be worked on. The idea of a juvenile home or rehabilitation facility means that he would be losing a larger chunk of his freedom. When he was briefed of the next step about his case, he knew things were out of order for him. He exhaled in a short but loud manner. However, it was late for him to convince the officers that he could work on himself. So he only pacified himself on his misfortune with this non-verbal gesture.

9.2. Cathartic Exhaling

Generic Interpretations of the Concept

This gesture takes more duration to perform compared with the cue just discussed above. Cathartic exhaling is the puffing out of the cheeks and keeping the lips sealed. This gesture is more pronounced and attention-drawing. When you puff out the cheeks, this is a glaring sign of stress and thoughtfulness. It means you are really disturbed by something. This may also be a signal of regret. This is common among footballers. When the person loses a huge chance, coupled with the stress of running around the pitch, they would puff out their cheeks and exhale the air while the lips are pressed together. So the air is released in a whispering manner, as if the tyre of your vehicle were punctured.

Also, this gesture may be an indication that one has overcome stress. When you have just come out of a testy or challenging situation, the fear that has been built up would be released immediately. The air at the both sides of the cheeks is describing how high the stress was before coming to pass. The ideal locations to see this feeling are in a test venue, after the conduct of an interview, or after an accident nearly occurs. This exhale is very audible because it is done with some sort of vibration, causing the cheeks to shake after air has been exhaled. A person who escapes an accident through a whisk; they have almost zeroed their mind that the accident was going to occur before they were fortunately delivered. So they are puffing out every ill feeling that had gathered within them.

Scientific Explanations

Improve Your Social Skills, a website based on self-improvement and making people lead standard lives, states that cathartic exhaling is a gesture for showing discomfort—that is, when you see someone puff out their cheeks and exhale through the mouth, it is a signal that something is wrong with them. The website opines that this gesture may also be accompanied by the rubbing of the face—that is, they are calming their rising nerves down through the pacifying behaviour.

In the opinion of Changing Minds (2019), puffing out of the cheeks with sealed lips is a means of expressing uncertainty on the next line of action. The body language platform hints that the eyes of the person may also become rounded while their eyebrows are raised. It means the person is either tired or really confused. The blowing of air from the mouth is a means of exaggerating the whole thing. Exhaling calls the attention of others to him or her that something is really wrong with them. Another interpretation given by the website for this gesture is exhaustion. Tiredness can be psychological or physical. If it is induced by physical tiredness—exercise and hard work, among others—the face will be sweaty and red. However, if it is a result of psychological unrest, the person burns from within and exhales out the used energy.

In the submission of Mentalizer Education, it notes that this gesture may be the aftermath of anger. People first hold their breath in horrible situations as a means of conveying the message of fear. However, if he exhales with sealed lips, this means he is purging out his emotions. The person may flare up immediately after that by shouting at the person or situation they are angry at. You will also notice this in a person who is shocked. It means they are trying to comprehend the unbelievable situation. Note that if this breathing comes in a very rapid and heavy way, it means the person is afraid of something.

Practical Illustrations

Case Study I: Team A and Team B are playing the final match of a historic league. Team A parades a team of young but passionate guys, while Team B has experienced and fulfilled lads. The match has been tough as no team has yet to see the back of the net of another, and they are deep into the second half. The ninety minutes of play ends without a winner, and they have to proceed to overtime. Twenty-eight minutes into the overtime, the striker of Team A has an opportunity to give his side the much-needed victory, but his effort hits the bar. He goes down, puffs out his cheeks with his lips sealed, and exhales deeply. This is to express regret over the loss and also to show a sign of exhaustion.

Case Study II: Medical students across the land were taking a crucial professional exam that would determine whether they were eligible to practise or not. The exam was divided into different segments. When the first segment came to an end, the students were given some few hours to rest and then revise for the next examination. The expression of mixed feelings was written on the faces of most of the students when they came out of the examination hall. Many of them rushed to take their research materials to verify the accuracy of their answers. One of the girls standing at the front was seen with a red face, raised eyebrows, puffed cheeks, and sealed lips, exhaling loudly. This was to show that she almost missed out on the right answer.

Case Study III: Four cars collided at a T-junction, and the fifth one managed to dodge the scene. He was a little bit far from the four, so he could control his wheel without running into the other four vehicles. After parking, he came out of the car, and the casualty rate was indescribably high. Almost all the people in the four affected vehicles gave up the ghost immediately. As he rushed out, examining the environment again with his shivering hands and legs, he puffed out his cheeks and exhaled. He was trying to puff out his nervousness and ill feeling engineered by the accident.

Case Study IV: A young lady just came out of an interview room for an international job, sweating and tired. She took out her phone, going through some pages of the materials she had used in preparing for the test. She was saved by just an edge. She was seen exhaling deeply. This means she was trying to puff out her fears, and an observant fellow would know that she triumphed with just a bit of luck.

Case Study V: A con artist who had always boasted that no law enforcement agent could arrest him was nabbed and made to face the best investigators in town. Yet he didn't lose his confidence. However, when too many unexpected questions were being thrown at him, he knew that he was in for something he didn't envisage. At some point, he became psychologically disturbed as issues were muddling up, and it was glaring that he was fast losing the war. At some point, his eyes became red, his flushed cheeks pumped out, and he exhaled loudly. When the investigators saw that he could not control his anger, they had to go for a recess—that is, they were able to decode his psychological feelings through his non-verbal displays.

9.3.   Inhaling Affirmatively

Generic Interpretations of the Concept

Affirmative inhaling is not a body language gesture that is experienced all over the world; it is region-specific. I need to establish this fact from the start so as not to bother your mind, wandering around, in search of this gesture in your environment. It is mostly found among the Scandinavians and some parts of the United Kingdom and Ireland.

The affirmative-inhaling gesture is a sudden loud inhaling of air, which is done to make a distinct sound used in many communicative contexts. The verbal translation of this gesture is 'Yes' or 'Yes, I agree.' I know this seems weird in some parts of the world, but it is good that you understand it now so that any time you have the opportunity to travel to any of the aforementioned places and someone inhales affirmatively to your utterances, you would not be lost in the discussion.

This body language gesture is considered as a linguistic shortcut where your co-interlocutor does not need to utter any word. When demonstrating this gesture, the inhaling is done quickly and loud enough to produce sound that the other person would hear. It will appear as if the person were gasping for breath. Then they would exhale slowly after that. The 'Practical Illustrations' segment would shed more light on this.

Scientific Illustrations

Body language gestures dealing with breathing and breathing pattern in general have the ability to reveal a person's mood and emotions every time. Due to this, the link between breathing and body language must always be subjected to contextual interpretations. On a general note, deeper breathing, which deals with the use of the diaphragm and abdomen, is usually interpreted to mean relaxation and confidence (Stephen et al. 2006). This is why you cannot really be amazed by the decision of the Scandinavians to use affirmative inhaling as a medium of expressing agreement with another person. A nervous or anxious person will rather breathe rapidly and in a shallow manner. So someone who inhales affirmatively is trying to say that all is well with them.

When you are discussing with a person who chooses to use this medium of communication to express their affirmation to a request, you need to learn how to mirror their body language so as to create a feeling of mutual understanding in the discourse. Neurolinguistic programmers have promoted this concept at different forums (Andrew 2006).

On its part, Changing Minds opines that affirmative inhaling may lead to relaxation or meditation. If the person closes their eyes, they become hardly aware of what goes on around them. This means they are lost in their own thought and not really concerned about what goes on around them. It is pertinent to note that the context for the display of this gesture is different. If done in public, or at least when talking with another person, the Scandinavians make use of the affirmative inhaling to mean 'yes', while if done when a person is alone, it means the person is meditating on something, a concept that does not create a sense of fear in them. That is why they can afford to close their eyes in spite of is going on around them.

In a rare interpretation, Mentalizer Education (2019) states that this can be a gesture of attraction if it is done to an opposite sex or to a potential lover. When you breathe deeply to an opposite sex, the ultimate aim is to make a nice impression. For instance, if it is done by a guy, it makes him look broader on the upper side of the body, and his stomach becomes smaller so as to appear handsome to a woman. So context is key in giving meaning to this gesture.

Practical Illustrations

Case Study I: Some few years ago, I was in Sweden for a programme and had to rent a car from the airport to the venue of the event in order for me to meet up with the time scheduled for its commencement. Obviously, I was new to the country and was unfamiliar with the place. More so, I did not want to disturb the organisers of the event because they would have been busy putting things in place. So when I saw the driver parking in front of a building, I asked him if we were there already, and all that he did was to affirmatively inhale with a slight nod. Before travelling back to my base, I intentionally asked questions that would propel an affirmative response from the locals, even from those who invited me to the programme, and I noticed the same body language demonstration from them, then I got the clue! It was really an affirmative gesture from the people.

Case Study II: Man F was still trying hard to win the heart of Lady I. He always wanted to impress her with every given opportunity. They were on a date on a particular evening, and as per his custom, after some moments of deliberations, he would begin whispering, confessing his love for her and what his plans were. On this particular occasion, he decided to step up his game by making use of his body to aid him in passing the message across. After professing his love for her, he looked into her face and inhaled affirmatively. At that point, he appeared more handsome, huge, and comfortable. This was a confirmation that he meant what he said and was trying hard to make himself more attractive to the lady.

Case Study III: Mr X was a well-known businessman; his calling cut across different fields with thousands of employees. He made it a custom to meditate on the success and growth rate of his business once in a while. On a fateful day, he locked himself in his study and decided to reminisce on how he started, his first source of finance, and how he had managed to rise to such a high level in business despite the unfavourable world economic situations. After thinking through, he breathed a sigh of relief, looked at himself in the mirror, and inhaled affirmatively. This means he was in a relaxed state. And this bolstered his confidence.

Case Study IV: Ms Q impersonated another person in order to gain entrance into a country to commit some atrocities. She had submitted her documents to the immigration officers for checking when it occurred to her that she missed out something very vital. She thought to herself that it was the end of her. She was deeply troubled throughout the cross-checking session. When it was her turn, she kept mute, kept still, and tried to smile when possible. When she was finally released by the ignorant officer, she breathed a sigh of relief and inhaled affirmatively. This was a display of confidence and positive attitude.

All the case studies shared above are different instances where the body language gesture can be deployed to communicate our intents.

9.4. Intake of Air through the Corners of the Mouth

Generic Interpretations of the Concept

One thing that makes this gesture very unique is that it can both be seen and heard. So it is a non-verbal gesture that when demonstrated, there is no one who can feign ignorance of it. Those who display this gesture will suddenly open the corners of their mouth in a slight manner and inhale air in a quick manner, such that it makes a sucking sound. The message this cue passes across is clear and reliable.

It is a negative body language which is categorised under the closed body gestures. One of the interpretations of the cue is that the person is afraid. When one is gripped by fear, one looks for pacifying acts, especially an act that can cool the internal frustrations one is going through. So slightly opening the sides of the mouth enables the person to take in more oxygen to calm down their nerves. In the same vein, this gesture may reveal anxiety. When you are anxious, you are charged, and as such, the body will be demanding for rest at all times. Furthermore, if you see someone display this gesture, it means they are concerned about something. A concerned person is troubled, and their facial muscles do rise because blood is rushing speedily through their nerves.

For the fact that majority of the mouth is closed is a hint that the person is restricting free movement of the lips. This action suggests that the person is stressed or pained. For instance, when someone steps on your toes with their high heels, you know it would be childish for you to start shedding tears, so what you do is display this gesture and likely squint your face. People around will get the message that something is really wrong with you and may come to your aid.

Scientific Illustrations

Stacy Sampson (2017) rightly opines that breathing gives the body the oxygen it needs for us to survive. In the same vein, it gives us the opportunity to release waste and carbon dioxide. There is nothing wrong in using the mouth to breathe; in fact, it is a sign of healthiness. However, breathing through the mouth is propelled by allergies or cold in the nasal. Breathing through the mouth at all times is not good for our health.

Sampson categorically states that stress and anxiety are some of the factors that can cause a person to display this gesture. According to the health expert, 'Stress activates the sympathetic nervous system leading to shallow, rapid, and abnormal breathing.' So when you are stressed, either by a physical or psychological reason, it activates the sympathetic nervous system for you to breathe in a sudden manner. Although there are health implications for this, but this is not the focus of this book.

Nick Babich (2016) also notes that deception can induce stress in people, which may cause them to inhale through the corners of the mouth. He states that this action is a reflex; it is not subjected to human control. Babich based his assertion on the findings of Desmond Morris. Morris had found that lying brings about tingling sensations to the delicate parts of the face, and as such, we need to either rub or scratch those parts so as to be satisfied. This causes the blood pressure to increase, which requires other forms of pacifying acts such as more intake of air in a painful manner.

In conclusion, Changing Minds (2019) states that this gesture is a signal of stressed breathing. The worst form of this gesture is for the person to hyperventilate. The body language platform goes ahead to mention anger and fright as other causes of this gesture. The person may be trying to pacify themselves before they take to their heels or face what they consider as as threat in that context.

Practical Illustrations

Case Study I: A terrorist was commissioned to go and bomb some major locations in a city, which can cause an uproar and media coverage worldwide. Since it was not a suicide mission, he was expected to go back and give account of the assignment. While he was on the train, moving to one of his targeted places, he sat beside two people who were conversing about the recent heroics of the law enforcement agencies of the country. They talked about how they were able to foil attacks on some places and even kill the suspected terrorists involved. He decided to disconnect himself from what they were saying so as not to create fear in him. He plugged in his earphone and listened to radio. Unfortunately for him, it was the same discussion going on. To make matters worse, the presenter on the radio added that the security agencies were battle-ready on a 24/7 basis to ensure the safety of the whole country. This really baffled him. He became stressed and tightly pressed his lips together while sucking in air through the corners of his mouth as a way of pacifying himself.

Case Study II: In a particular year, the world witnessed a recession that really shook many firms, including multinational outfits that were believed to be dictating the waves of the economy. Many of the companies began to lay off a large chunk of their workforce so as to be able to meet up with the realities of the day. When the management of Company LXS called a meeting, the head of the firm frankly told his employees that many of them would have to be laid off in order for the company not to fold up. This announcement made many of the employees develop a headache that Friday afternoon, and it was the talk of the day. A particular employee, Mr C, had just taken a loan for a project and had a six-month period for repayment. Already, there were many issues against him at the company even before the recession issue came up. So he knew he was going to be sacked once the letters were released. Upon getting home, he collapsed into a sofa and started thinking of the next step. Without knowing, he closed his mouth, with the corners slightly opened, and inhaled loudly that his wife, seated at the other side of the room, heard him. He was nervous and disturbed about his situation.

Case Study III: Friend A is married, while Friend B is still a bachelor. Friend B would tell Friend A that since he was married, he had become confined to his wife. In other words, Friend A could not explore other ladies again, lest he is accused of infidelity. However, it seemed that Friend A could not stop his urge to have affairs with other ladies. So Friend B decided to teach him a lesson in a hard way. One day, during his affair with a lady, Friend B texted him that his wife was around. He lost his breath and left the lady immediately, rushing out of the room. He began to inhale air through the corners of his mouth before his friend eventually told him it was a mere set-up. His non-verbal gesture depicted him as being fearful; he had lost his confidence at that given point in time.

9.5. Breath-Holding Gesture

Generic Interpretations of the Gesture

Those who make use of polygraph in the detection of lies are very much aware of this gesture. This is not to endorse the use of polygraph, just making an illustration. I have always maintained that polygraph is pseudoscientific and must be backed by human efforts before its outcome can become tenable. Having said that, holding one's breath is one of the gimmicks that people employ in playing over the polygraph test. Some people have learnt to hold their breath when they are stressed. This helps them to perfectly contain their nervous breathing. A person who was supposed to be breathing rapidly would hold his breath, and those around him might be fooled to believe that all was well with him.

In most cases, a person who holds his breath would to be told to breathe before they do that. The situation can be baffling to someone who is not used to it; the person would wonder how it is possible for someone to intentionally seize their own breath. This gesture is a closed body gesture categorised under the *freeze, flight, or fight non-verbal response.* Mere fear of public speaking can induce this gesture. A person who is known to be outspoken, when made to come and face a larger audience, may lose their confidence, and as a way of hiding it, they would hold their breath.

In simpler terms, those who hold their breath do not want others to know that they are experiencing negative emotions. Hence, when next you see a person holding his or her breath, make sure you examine the context so as to figure out what is wrong with them. But on a general note, fear or apprehension is the major factor that can induce this gesture in a person.

Scientific Explanations

Many body language platforms and experts contribute to the interpretation of this gesture. Unfinished Success, a platform dedicated to inspiring people, describes the act of holding one's breath as a show of frustration. The website explains that when a person is frustrated by something, it takes them out of their normal self. Hence, the breath-holding gesture is considered as a means of survival in a threatening context. For a person to undergo a change and feel relaxed, they have to breathe out deeply for a few times. This would change their mood as their brain releases endorphins when the person exhales slowly.

In his own contribution, Philip (2013) says this gesture is related to the emotion of fear. He opines that this gesture is actually employed for the sake of covering up stress. Other clusters that may be passing the same message include 'a pale face, dry mouth, damp eyes, avoiding eye contact, trembling, speech errors, voice tremors, varying speech tone, increases in sweating, tension, and jerky movements'. All these are pointers to the fact that something is wrong with the person. People also use fake smiles to cover up their negative emotions; such smiles involve more of the mouth than the eyes. A person who is holding their breath will do everything possible to change the topic that is making them uncomfortable. When a person is being investigated and it seems you are hitting the nail on its head, he would look for other things to distract you.

Mentalizer Education also stresses the explanation of Philip. The website notes that this gesture is one of the breathing patterns in the world. People who hold their breath eventually release it through a deep breath. So you would not notice the obvious nervousness in it. According to the website, 'If a person suddenly holds his breath in a horrible situation, he is sending a message of fear.' This interpretation is clear and authoritative. It may also mean that the person is angry and is trying to hold their anger through the gesture.

Practical Illustrations

Case Study I: A man was driving to his workplace while listening to a sonorous music. Suddenly, a billboard mounted beside the road caught his attention. He believed that he was used to the road, so he was looking sideways to read the inscriptions on the board while driving slowly. It was the continuous shout of passers-by and other motorists that made him face front—he almost drove into the drainage! As he saw the danger ahead, he quickly turned the wheel, and fortunately, he was delivered. As he parked, he held his breath for a moment before coming out of the car. Even though he was not really breathing nervously, fear was written all over his face as he was sweating profusely.

Case Study II: The class captain of the final year class was called by their mathematics teacher to answer a question. By the virtue of his position, people had always respected him and believed he was brilliant. He also went about with this consciousness. However, he had no idea how to answer the question he was asked, and saying an outright no would somewhat portray him as a dullard. As he stood up, all eyes were on him, and he subtly trembled. He held his desk firmly so that people would not notice his trembling hands. He also held his breath because the class maintained a graveyard silence, which would have made his breathing very obvious. This means he was apprehensive.

Case Study III: Two groups were sent out on different missions by a company, and they were to make their presentations on the same day. When the first group made theirs, the other group was jittery because it was obvious that the first group did an extensive research and were clear on their mission. As the presentation was going on, the members of the second group began to stare at one another. The leader feigned sickness and urged any other group member to take up his role, which none was ready to do. To make matters worse, when the first group was done with its presentation, the head of the company still pointed out some loopholes. So the thought was that if they could criticise what they had considered as being perfect, how much more theirs? As the group leader was making his way to the podium, he bowed and walked slowly, holding his breath, pretending as if all were right with him. But in reality, he was engulfed in fear.

Case Study IV: A man and a woman arranged a marriage of convenience for the purpose of gaining entrance into a territory as husband and wife. They dressed in the same attire in order to clear all doubts. However, when they were stopped by immigration officers, they could not pull things off in the perfect way. One essential thing that gave them out was the distance they maintained; it was too wide to be considered intimate. Then the officers threw dozens of questions at them. While the man was still trying to cover up and answer the questions, the woman was apprehensive already, and this was seen in her breath-holding gesture—she was trying hard to hold her breath so that she would not breathe out loudly for anyone to notice.

9.6. Dry Mouth

Generic Interpretations of the Concept

The clinical term of this gesture is called xerostomia. There are different reasons that can cause our mouth to dry out. When the mouth is dry, communication does not flow as it appears that the person is being forced to speak. A literal cause of dry mouth is when a person has not spoken for long. For instance, if you have locked yourself up in the office for hours and have to receive a call or communicate with someone in the afternoon, you would discover that your mouth, and even your throat, is dry. In addition, those who are into illicit drugs may experience this. Sometimes, some prescribed drugs that do not work with the body system of the person using them may bring about dry mouth.

Apart from these biological or literal interpretations, there are also social aspects to this gesture. When a person is stressed, they may experience a dry mouth. This means the saliva that is supposed to moisten their mouth is not secreted. In the same vein, when a person is afraid, their body system automatically switches to the flight or freeze response. During this response, the body is only taking in but not releasing anything. When you are afraid of a person, you do not have the strength to speak up against them; you rather keep to yourself, and that is why the mouth is dry. Apprehension is another possible cause of dry mouth.

An erroneous impression I need to correct at this point is that dry mouth does not necessarily indicate a sign of deception. I have heard this sentiment in different quarters that when the mouth is dry, it means the person is telling lies. As you can see, there are different causes of dry mouth, and you must, as a matter of fact, establish the context of gesture before giving meanings to it. Basically, dry mouth is an indication that someone is anxious or stressed. So what should be looked for is the cause of the fear or stress.

Scientific Explanations

According to Mayo Clinic, dry mouth 'refers to a condition in which the salivary glands in your mouth don't make enough saliva to keep your mouth wet.' The famous health centre lists ageing, effects of medications, and radiation therapy for cancer as some of the major causes of dry mouth. In rare instances, this is caused by a situation that has direct effects on the salivary glands. Mayo Clinic further gives a detailed list of the causes of dry mouth, which include nerve damage, tobacco and alcohol use, recreational drug use, and other health conditions. Injury around the head or neck can affect the salivary gland, which will ultimately result in dry mouth.

Philip (2013) says dry mouth is as a result of fear. When you are apprehensive, saliva seizes to flow in your mouth and speaking becomes a herculean job or you. He says that the lips may be stretched across the face when one is experiencing dry mouth. Charles Darwin also shares the sentiment that dry mouth is caused by fear. In fact, he said this gesture is seen when a person is under extreme fear. The legendary evolutionary researcher puts it thus: 'The hairs also on the skin stand erect; and the superficial muscles shiver. In connection with the disturbed action of the heart, the breathing is hurried. The salivary glands act imperfectly; the mouth becomes dry and is often opened and shut.' He goes ahead to explain that all the muscles in the body may begin to tremble, and it is first noticed from the lips. Due to this trembling of the muscles and dryness of the mouth, 'the voice becomes husky or indistinct or may altogether fail.'

On its own part, Changing Minds attributes fear, nervousness, and anxiety to dry mouth. When our basic needs are under threat, fear occurs. This causes some parts of our body to be restructured, which includes dryness of the mouth.

Practical Illustrations

Case Study I: A high-paying firm was doing its annual recruitment, and as expected, people from all walks of life applied for the job. The interview started in earnest on the scheduled date. The first few people who came out were not smiling. Some could not resist the temptation of asking them how the session was. One of those who were not disciplined enough was a lady who had hoped that she could secure the job by all means. She was eventually called in. She first met the stern faces of the panellists, and this was enough to send fear to her nerves. As she sat down, a member of the panel threw a question to her, and she was asked to introduce herself simultaneously. This seemed mountainous to her, and suddenly, she lost her voice. Hence, she started by mumbling out words before she later regained herself, which sent a bad impression to the panel members. She was nervous, and no one was willing to risk someone who does not reflect confidence in their establishment.

Case Study II: A man was arrested at the immigration section of an airport. He was almost done with the clearing when he was nabbed. This was unbelievable to him. in the twinkle of an eye, he reflected on what could have possibly led to his arrest; he was well-dressed, good-looking. In fact, he had read up about the country and dressed like a citizen. So what could have possibly given him out? This sent fear to his heart because he did not know how to prepare his defence for the questioning section. He was later taken to a place where he was to be interrogated. The mere question of what his name was left him searching for his voice. His mouth was dry due to the apprehension he had nursed in his heart.

Case Study III: A child stole her mother's meat from the deep freezer, thinking her mum did not count them. When the mother was about to cook the meat, she recounted them, and three was missing. She knew no other person capable of doing that save for her little daughter. When the child heard her mother complaining, she had started shivering even before she was called. When she was called, she found it difficult to respond due to the stress she was undergoing. Stress as a major cause of dry mouth could be noticed on her.

9.7.   Saliva Balls in the Mouth

Generic Interpretations of the Concept

This is somewhat related to the gesture that we just finished discussing. When the mouth becomes dry due to illness, medication, or stress, it can cause saliva to become clumpy. Clumps of saliva do look like cotton balls. You will see them gather at the corners of the mouth. This can be irritating to a lot of people, and when speakers quickly notice them, they wipe the 'balls' out with their handkerchief. If they should use their bare hands, nobody (who saw them doing it) would be ready to exchange a handshake with them.

There is no gainsaying that this cue is quite distracting to both the speaker and the audience; the speaker has to think of how to clean it up without calling the attention of others to it. This adds to the thoughts going on in the speaker's head simultaneously. Also, the audience who are irritated may look away or see how the speaker is going to clean it up. This has automatically distracted them from the topic which is being discussed. Saliva balls in the mouth is usually noticed among nervous speakers; due to the dryness of the mouth, saliva is pushed to the sides of the mouth because the person is speaking, which makes the mouth moist.

Nervousness can be controlled but cannot be totally eliminated. So if you are a nervous person and speaking in public or official settings is indispensable to you, adopt the habit of pinching and wiping the corners of your mouth in order to avoid saliva balls. This will ensure that saliva balls do not clump at all, let alone having to clean them off. In addition, always drink water. Water makes the mouth moist. In some rare instances, the person who constantly experience this cue may need to seek medical attention.

Scientific Explanations

Saliva balls is technically known as mucous cysts or mucocele. Some also call it salivary gland stones or salivary duct stones (Ratini 2017). Melinda Ratini says that this can block the flow of saliva in the mouth. In her words, 'The majority of stones affect the submandibular glands located at the floor of the mouth. Less commonly, the stones affect the parotid glands, located on the inside of the cheeks, or the sublingual glands, which are under the tongue. Many people with the condition have multiple stones.' Giving the medical reason for this, she says that mouth balls form when chemicals in the saliva accumulate in the salivary gland. Although the exact cause has not been medically established, but factors contributing to less saliva production and/or thickened saliva may be risk factors for salivary stones. Some of the factors include poor eating habit, dehydration, and use of some medications such as blood pressure drugs, antihistamines, and bladder control drugs. A trauma to the gland may also raise the chances of the occurrence of mouth balls.

Noreen (2010) expresses regret that this topic is not widely discussed among scholars. He says that those who frequently experience this may also experience bad breath. He submits that 'the strong unpleasant odor is caused by a build-up of sulfur-producing bacteria that feeds on the tonsil stones collected in the crypts of the tonsils and is a combination of hydrogen sulfide, methyl mercaptan, and other stinky substances that form in it'. This is fairly common in adults and children. Noreen concludes that the simplest solution to mouth balls 'is to use a cotton swab or toothbrush so you can push the nasty little things out and rinse your mouth free of them.'

It seems body language experts do not discuss this topic on its own; it is usually subsumed under the dry mouth concept earlier discussed. However, from the various medical literature considered, we can conclude that mouth balls are caused due to discomfort engineered by fear.

Practical Illustrations

Case Study I: Mr T had just been employed by STE Royal School to teach sciences. He looked composed during the short interview conducted for him. Mr T was truly intelligent as demonstrated on the written test conducted for him and on how he was able to engage the panels who did the oral interview for him. However, when he was told to face a whole class, he became frightened—maybe due to the fact that he was told the students were extraordinarily intelligent and he did not want to disappoint them. After speaking for twenty-five minutes, it was discovered that some whitish elements began to gather at the corners of his mouth. When it seemed that the students were beginning to give one another a ridiculous glance, he had to use his thumb and index fingers to clean them. Then it was glaring to the students that he was overwhelmed by fear.

Case Study II: A man was arrested in a case connected to the death of his wife. He was a civil servant who looked innocent in all forms. However, the condition of the death of his wife called for suspicion, which he could not be totally said to be innocent of. The corpse of his wife was discovered on the early morning of a Tuesday on their matrimonial bed. They were the only two people who slept in the house that fateful day. He claimed that he did not sleep in the room that night; he had worked on some files overnight in the study. But this did not look tenable to law enforcement officials. What really made him nervous was that he had recently read on how some people were wrongly implicated in the murder/suicide cases involving known ones. So he was afraid that his own case was intimidating, and there was no way he could explain his innocence to the law enforcement agents. When he was called into the interview room and he was told to explain everything he knew concerning the death of his wife, he was gripped by fear. What he had been thinking for the past few hours had made his mouth dry. So when he started recounting his story, he was not really audible, and the panellists had to encourage him to speak up. Some white balls started forming at the corners of his mouth some few minutes into his narration. They were so obvious that the enforcement officials engaging him ordered him to clean them. This further confirmed the message to the officers that the man had some things he was hiding.

Case Study III: Just like teachers, students too do form white balls in their mouth, and I have witnessed a handful of them in my sojourn in the academic world—either as a teacher or a student. When they are gripped with fear, students will form white balls in their mouth, and some of them are even too anxious to clean them up. I remember when I asked one of my trainees to narrate his conventional duties at work, and he seemed lost. Upon standing up, he tried hard before he could make any pronouncement, and it was obvious to everyone in the hall that he was apprehensive. The white balls were just a physical confirmation of this. I had to ask him to clean them up because I was getting irritated.

9.8. Gum-Chewing

Generic Interpretations of the Concept

Chewing a gum is not a natural part of human behaviour; it is done as a reaction to a certain unfavourable situation. That is why it is widely regarded as a pacifying act. It is only a pacifying act when it is done subtly—that is, when the gum is softly chewed, it is a means of releasing stress. As explained at different points in time, stress is caused by an array of things, and it is felt in some parts of the body than others. So much effort is usually devoted to areas where the person is feeling uncomfortable the most. When a person is chewing a gum, they do not want to use their hand so that it will not become so obvious that they are pacifying themselves. When someone is chewing a gum, it means the muscles around the cheeks are really risen and the blood is gushing on a high rate in that region, so they chew the gum as a way of pacifying themselves. All they need at that moment is to make sure that the mouth is actively moving. Some may bite their finger if there is no gum in their mouth.

However, if the chewing is so vigorous, it means the person may be expressing anxiety or concern. If someone is anxious about a situation or something, they will chew the gum very hard as if the problem would just disappear in the twinkle of an eye. When a person is chewing a gum, it debars you from knowing their real state of mind because the movement of the lips do distort the facial look of people. It would be noted that the act of gum chewing has become the habit of some people; even if there is no gum in their mouth, they would still do it out of their habit whenever they are stressed.

Scientific Explanations

Philip (2013) categorises this gesture under emotional body language. He describes emotional body language as a direct response to negative occurrences. When we talk of negative events, you should understand that it cuts across an array of issues; even cruel, sexist, or silly jokes can cause the arousal of negative emotion. When you are being put on the spot or someone asks you a difficult question in an unimaginable situation and also having to make a presentation before an audience are also some of the issues that can propel negative emotions. I am taking time to explain it so that you would not think that chewing a gum is limited to a particular situation. Philip states that the act of chewing a gum is a form of emotional manipulation, which is engineered towards reducing blood pressure and lowering heart rate. An anxious or aggressive person becomes normal when their blood pressure or heart rate is reduced.

The body language expert notes that apart from exhaling air forcefully through compressed lips, people can also chew a gum as a form of oral pacifier, especially if the rate of chewing becomes aggressive. Sometimes, gum chewing is also referred to as a displacement gesture. When people become emotional and they resort to gum chewing, it means they want to orally pacify themselves.

Jeff Haden (2015) also contributes to this subject matter. In his own interpretation, he says chewing a gum makes people become more alert and puts them in a better mood. Although this is not professional, but there are situations when people make use of it to bolster their emotions. In some way, we can see that this is related to what Philip has said. A person who is using a gum for the purpose of changing their mood shows that they are not really feeling all right. So the gum is used to bring them back to normalcy. Haden also submits that chewing a gum improves reaction time and disposition and ensures that one's attention is sustained on a course of action.

Practical Illustrations

Case Study I: Mr R was an up-and-coming rapper. He was so dedicated to his music career that he saw every other thing as secondary. He was always in the studio, trying to record a song or another. One day, he saw an advert calling for auditions. The organisers were bigwigs in the music industry, and he knew that if he were picked, his music career would receive an eternal boost. So he filled the form and was preparing aggressively. On the day of auditions, he was taken aback by the sea of heads that he saw; he had thought that just a few people were interested in his kind of music. This first sent shivers into his heart. When they had all gathered, one of the organisers of the event came to address them in the hall, giving them the rules of the game and how they needed to compose themselves. This was another issue that frightened him. As a way of pacifying himself orally so that he did not lose his voice at the crucial moment, he quickly went to get a packet of gum and started chewing some.

Case Study II: A law enforcement officer was to interview a suspect. As an experienced officer, he made it a point of duty to establish the baseline of each of his subjects before they eventually move into the interview room. While interacting with this suspect on a casual level, he invited him to come and have coffee, and they discussed life generally. It got to a point that it was obvious to the officer that the suspect was becoming stressed and fearful. He tried to control this, but it seemed the suspect had just lost himself. As a way of covering up his anxiety too, he asked the officer to get him some gum. At this point, the officer confirmed his doubt. After providing him with what he requested for, he chewed it vigorously that the officer was becoming irritated. After the whole process, the officer noticed that he was returning back to his normal self. After allowing him to relax, he ushered him into the interview room.

Case Study III: The professional setting is believed to be a place where decency thrives, but the truth is, there are a lot of unimaginable things going on in that space. I have seen people treat their colleagues as enemies and vice versa. A lady was brought on board by a firm. She was not all that good; she got the job through recommendations. Hence, she was naturally nervous. As a means of covering up her nervousness, she would come with loads of gums and start chewing them while she did her work. This was irritating to her colleagues who had to warn her, but it seemed she was not giving up on that soon. Instead of her working on her confidence level, she was pleased with covering it up with an easy way out, which was not pleasing to other people around her.

9.9. Vocal Tics

Generic Interpretations of the Concept

Apart from Tourette's syndrome (TS), there are some other disorders that contribute to vocal tics. I will explore them further in the succeeding segment. Vocal tics is the sudden projection of clicks, noises, and chirps or throat clearing. This can be irritating and alarming to someone who is not acquainted with it. Anxiety and stress have been identified as the major cause of Tourette's syndrome. There are not too many explanations to give on this other than to say that it is not subjected to human control—that is, the person experiencing this disorder has no power over it. Knowing this fact will help you in your relationship with the person.

Another common feature of vocal tics is, the arm of the person experiencing this cue moves erratically. In this situation, you can always be of help to the person with TS by telling others who are oblivious of the fact I have shared here not to stare at them. If nobody stares at the person, you are helping them with the sense of belonging as they feel that nothing awful has actually happened. Without mincing words, Tourette's syndrome can be very embarrassing, and you need not add to it by looking at the person in a ridiculous manner.

Scientific Explanations

Cedars-Sinai (2019) defines *vocal tics* as 'sounds uttered unintentionally'. It should be noted that vocal tics is different from motor tics, an involuntary movement. The definition given by this health website has helped us clarify issues from the scratch—that is, the sounds are not intentionally uttered even though they appear as being intentional. This calls for an in-depth understanding of the concept so as to know vocal tics when you hear it. Tics are normally sudden and repetitive. According to the health platform, 'A person may be able to suppress a tic for a short time, but the tic movement or sound will recur as the urge becomes stronger.' This gives a scholarly backing to the point I earlier shared that vocal tic is uncontrollable.

Jayne Leonard (2017) says that a chronic tic can last for more than one year. She observes that if a chronic tic appears early enough in children, be it transient or chronic, they have high chances of recovery—that is, the affected children can recover within six years. However, if it continues after age eighteen, the symptoms may not be resolved any more. Explaining Tourette's syndrome

(TS), Leonard opines that 'Tourette's syndrome (TS) is a complex neurological disorder. It is characterised by multiple tics—both motor and vocal. It is the most severe and least common tic disorder.'

Reeling out the symptoms of vocal tics, Cedars-Sinai states that they can either be simple or complex. Simple vocal tics involve sounds made by moving air through the nose or mouth, including snorting, sniffing, throat clearing, hissing, grunting, and barking. On the other hand, complex vocal tics may include words, phrases, and sentences. In the words of Cedars-Sinai, 'Patients with a complex vocal tic may repeat their own words (palilalia) or other people's words (echolalia), and may use obscene words (coprolalia). These vocal tics may interrupt the flow of a normal conversation or occur at the beginning of a sentence, much like a stutter or a stammer.' I understand that communicating with a person with tics can really be frustrating, but you just need to tolerate them because it is beyond their personal control. The website also supports the submission of Leonard that if the tic should begin in early adulthood, it may be with the person throughout their life. If the tic is not severe, it may not be interruptive to the everyday life of a person witnessing it. If it is, however, complex and severe, the person may need to seek medical attention where they would be provided with medications that can manage the situation.

Gabrielle Garon (2019) describes this body language gesture as a negative body language. According to her, tics 'wordlessly communicate negative emotions like anxiety, stress, anger, and disengagement'. She notes that negative body language does not encourage one's co-interlocutor in every discourse context. This is important to note at all times.

Practical Illustrations

Case Study I: Mr T went to buy a car, and when he got to the dealer, they began conversation on the qualities of his choice car. The conversation seemed to be flowing well before the dealer started behaving funny. Mr T was angry that he was being taken for granted by the dealer. Suddenly, the dealer began to repeat the words uttered by Mr T as if he were stammering. This was done repeatedly that it became irritating to the client. The car dealer appeared jovial right from the start of the discourse, and Mr T thought he was only trying to mock him because he also stammers a little bit. He had wanted to confront him and maybe inflict injury on the dealer for daring to mock him before moving out of his stall. As he was approaching the dealer, that was how someone who was conversant with the situation of the dealer came and stopped him. He explained it to Mr T, and yet he seemed unconvinced. But he had to walk out of there, feeling annoyed.

Case Study II: An assistant supervisor was asked to pass some instructions to select workers. The workers were on probationary services to the organisation and were not performing to expectations. So the update by the assistant supervisor was to inform them on their performance so far and make them know where they were lagging behind and what could possibly follow if there were no improvements. As an assistant supervisor who wanted to assert his authority, he addressed them as if the decision reached by the management were his. Already, this did not go down well with many of the employees. Unfortunately, there was one of them suffering from Tourette's syndrome. Suddenly, as the assistant supervisor finished addressing them, he began to hiss endlessly. The AS heard it and thought that was in reaction to what he had told them. He took up the issue, and the employee was almost fired before the end of his probationary period.

Case Study III: A prostitute was hired by a client to a hotel. The prostitute was trying to get serious with her life and, thus, was looking for someone to marry. Hence, any time she had a client, she tried to convince them on the need to marry her. She would go extra miles to satisfy them on bed, but that seemed not to be working for her. On this particular occasion, after having an affair with her client, she sought to have his audience in order to discuss some issues with him. Having understood her body language, the client claimed he had an important appointment and, as such, needed to leave immediately. This angered the prostitute, and she began to hiss endlessly until the client left the hotel room.

9.10. Mouth Stretching

Generic Interpretations of the Concept

Mouth stretching is a form of gesture made to express regret; people stretch their mouth as an expression of regret over an action having realised their mistake. Mouth stretching has to do with exposing the bottom row of clenched teeth which makes the corners of the mouth to stretch substantially downwards and to the sides. This gesture is always done aggressively that people around will know that something is surely wrong. The teeth are tightly clenched as if the person were preventing the entry of any particle into the mouth. This widens the corners of the mouth than usual and makes them look as if they were sloping downward. Note that this gesture is different from the advertisement of many toothpaste companies where subjects are made to display their white teeth. In the case of an advertisement, the subject of the advert would be smiling and would show the teeth in a charming manner.

In the Western culture, this gesture is usually used when someone is reminded that they forgot to come along with a vital document. Through this, they express regret. In some other cultures, the meaning is not that different. Africans use it when they miss out on something nearly or when an unfavourable event occurs.

In the world of sports, this gesture is mostly seen when players miss out on great opportunities.

Scientific Explanations

All the experts who contributed to this subject matter maintain a consensus that the mouth-stretching behaviour is an expression of negative feelings. Changing Minds (2019) says when the teeth reclenched, this is a primitive expression of readiness to bite. This is potentially scary to the other person in the discourse context. Although actual biting is very rare, but this gesture means the person has reduced himself or herself to a base position. In simpler terms, it means the person is not thinking rationally at that point in time.

In her own contribution, Hanan Parvez (2019) says that this gesture hints the world that someone is extremely angry. When the mouth is stretched, we are able to expose the lower teeth to those who are watching us. Literally, the lower jaw is meant for biting, so if a person exposes them in the moment of extreme anger, this is to threaten the opposing party. She notes that this 'sends a very primitive, threatening, nonverbal message to the unconscious of the other person'. It would be remembered that right from evolution, our teeth has always been seen as the most primitive weapon we possess. Even now that we are fully mature, this thought is registered in our subconscious. When a person growls at you and exposes their teeth, you feel threatened. Even though you may not be the cause of their agony, but being in the same environment with them makes you nervous.

Christopher Philip (2014) says that the teeth may be compressed aggressively and ground back and forth as a means of expressing how pained one is. Because the muscles of the mouth are pulled, that makes the corners of the mouth widen, and the bottom of the mouth becomes more revealed. The body language expert says that this gesture is an indication of internal struggle. Sometimes, this cue means that the person is mounting pressure or frustrations. The variant of this gesture is that the jaw would be held open 'where muscles both work to keep the jaw open yet clenched at the same time. This causes pain at the edges of the jaw which people register as stress.' Also, the verbal translation is, 'I'm angry or frustrated, and I want to speak out but feel that it's inappropriate, so my teeth are clenching down to bottle myself up and prevent me from saying something I might regret' (Philip 2014).

Practical Illustrations

Case Study I: Ms G was attending an important screening conducted to streamline the workforce of the government. Those without necessary documents and qualifications were to be laid off. The screening was scheduled for eight o'clock in the morning. However, her aged mother was critically ill on that morning. So she decided to put things in place so that a capable hand would handle the emergency situation. She rushed out of her home ten minutes before the time and drove speedily to the venue of the exercise. They have started counting those on ground even before her arrival. Then the list of all the documents needed to be verified were pasted on a notice board. Ms G went to the notice board with her file to see the list and arranged all her documents appropriately, waiting for her turn to be called in. At the point of arranging the documents, she discovered that she had left a document in her study. Without the document, she would not be screened. Immediately after she got to know this, she clenched her teeth and widened her mouth, which made her friend approach her to ask if all was well with her. This non-verbal display was a show of nervousness; she was really disturbed.

Case Study II: A wife and her husband were conversing in their usual style after the day's activities. The wife was the one leading the conversation that night. She told her husband about everything that happened in her workplace. The conversation looked like there was not going to be another one as it extended into the middle of the night. The husband was known to be a jealous person, and as such, the wife was always careful with whatever she told him. During the course of the discussion, however, she had told him of how a guy in the office was eyeing her and how she had also fantasised about him before returning to her senses. Even though the husband did not react immediately, he took note of that aspect of the discussion. The following day, the wife returned late from work due to the need to work on some files. As she was just coming in, feeling tired, and was expecting her husband to show her some love, the first statement the husband uttered was to ask about the man she had talked about the day before. The wife regretted ever confessing everything to him. She stretched her mouth and almost went down in tears. This was a show of regret and pain. She was psychologically disturbed by her husband's action.

Case Study III: Mr PI was illegally connected to an industry. As a way of ensuring that he would not be fished out, he attached himself to the deepest and busiest part of the industry with a mass of workers. Those in this section were paid daily wages, and supervisors hardly come there to have a headcount or even supervise the works there. However, the factory came up with a new policy which required that every sector be supervised daily. Since this was unknown to him, he was surprised to see a lanky old man show up the next day asking them to fill a form with the company code written beside their name. Having heard this, he clenched his teeth and stretched his mouth wide open, thinking of the next move. He could not think properly due to the incident; he was thinking of a way out of his predicament, but none was coming.

9.11. Yawning

Generic Interpretations of the Concept

All over the world, people see yawning as a means of relieving stress; it is only when people are stressed that they yawn. It is seen as an excellent pacifier. Yawning helps in the stimulation of the nerves in our jaw—this is specific to the *temporopmandibular* joint. When you yawn, you open the mouth and relax every muscle on the face. If the yawning becomes excessive, it means the person is really tired and may need to sleep in order to truly relax. Also, when we yawn, we rapidly take in air, which has been observed to have the capability to cool the blood moving around the mouth. This is likened to our car radiator where water is poured to help regulate the heat rate of the engine. Hence, the air we inhale while we yawn is meant to cool the blood around the palate going into the brain.

In addition, yawning may signal severe stress or excessive heat. When someone is hot, they will yawn as a means of calming themselves. That is why you often see children who are wrapped too warmly yawn before sleeping. However, yawning can be interpreted differently in varied contexts. One thing that is certain is that it cannot be disconnected from stress.

Scientific Explanations

Describing yawning, Philip (2014) says that it is an 'exaggerated opening and stretching of the jaw with inhalation or exhalation of air'. Although he described the action as being 'exaggerated', but this does not disconnect it from the fact that the action is mostly unconscious. You would definitely know if someone is trying to feign it. So the word *exaggerated* as used by Philip in this context is to mean that the mouth is excessively opened wider than a person's imagination. People have always used yawning to their own advantage in many instances. If you are making a presentation and your listeners are yawning, this is an indication that they are either bored or exhausted. So you have the duty to speed up your presentation or restructure it to make it interesting for them. When a person wants to excuse himself or herself from a gathering, they may also yawn.

Hence, Philip opines that yawning can be interpreted to mean boredom, stress, or exhaustion. This is in tandem with my earlier assertion that this cue is a negative emotional gesture. He gives the verbal translation of this gesture as 'I'm bored, exhausted, or stressed, causing me to take an exaggerated inhalation of air, stretch out my jaw, and ease some of the discomfort I'm experiencing' or 'I'm yawning because I saw someone else do it, and I'm mirroring them.'

Little did people know that yawning is contagious; you would have witnessed this, only that you did not take conscious note of it. It is one of the most pronounced form of mirroring. When someone begins to yawn excessively beside you, you would join the person in no time. 'Yawning in one person can even set off a chain of yawns within the rest of a group, even if the members don't know each other' (Philip 2014). Fatigue is what we normally associate yawning with, and there is no cause for argument that this widely held sentiment is true. However, in some high-anxiety situations, it means pressure is getting to the person concerned. A yawn can help alleviate the dry mouth that is common when people are under pressure because it stimulates salivary glands (Philip 2014).

In his own contribution, Farouk Radwan (2017) states that there are numerous reasons why people yawn. Lack of attention, being bombarded with a lot of information, tiredness, and boredom are some of the factors he enumerated. What all these factors have in common, including those highlighted by Philip, is that they signal unwillingness to take in more information from a particular source. A person may start a relationship or an adventure on an exciting note, but they can lose interest along the line as the relationship unfolds.

Concluding on this, Philip (2014) admonishes people to watch for associated cues before affirming that yawning signals stress, fatigue, or mirroring.

Practical Illustrations

Case Study I: An interrogator was to engage a suspect for the fourth time in a week. All the previous three gatherings had not been productive as expected, yet all available evidence pointed to the fact that the suspect knew something about the crime being investigated. The interrogator handling the issue was very experienced and reputed for that. So it was baffling that the suspect could be having a field day under him. On this fourth occasion, he had known the suspect's baseline and understood some things better, which he was earlier oblivious of. On the start of the interrogation, he put a lot of pressure on him so that he would not have the opportunity of concocting unrelated stories. He started yawning excessively. In this sense, it means the suspect was stressed.

Case Study II: An expert was invited by a leading company in the textile industry to provide manpower training for its workforce. The training was scheduled to take place for three consecutive days. The first two days were short and practical. However, on the third day he was meant to conclude the lesson, he discussed more theories, and the session continued for an unimaginably longer time. The audience was obviously tired, and it seemed the speaker cared less about their feeling. At some point, the workers started yawning from different corners of the hall. At that point, he got the message that it was time to go, and he began to wrap up. The audience was tired and had lost interest in all that the man was saying.

Case Study III: Mr K had worked on some business documents. It was midnight, and he was left with a few more documents to go. He was yawning but seemed unperturbed; he was focused on the work he was doing. At some point, the yawning became so excessive that he could not control it. When he started dozing off, he left the work and headed to his bedroom to sleep. With this, it means fatigue had set in.

9.12. Smoking

Generic Interpretations of the Concept

Nothing just happens out of the blue. When you see someone smoke, something must have led to it. This is not to discountenance the fact that some people do it out of mere fun. It has been discovered that those who smoke often do that when they are stressed. In other words, they see smoking as a means of escapism for whatever they are going through. Before you can categorically state that a person is smoking for the sake of relieving stress, you must first note of that smoking habit. If there is any deviation, this means something is fishy; it is an evidence of how stressed the person may be.

Different people react to stress differently, even among smokers. When some smokers are excessively stressed, they may even lose count on the number of cigarettes they have lit—that is, as one is burning out, they are also resorting to another. Even if they are given a pack, they may finish it within an hour or two. In circumstances where they do not get cigarette to smoke, you would see them compress their lips and make air pass out through the corners of their mouth.

The air they exhale when smoking is like washing off the waste in their body. When smoking becomes excessive, you will discover that the fingers of the smoker becomes stained with tobacco. And also, you will perceive the stench in their hands. It is pertinent to note that there are consequences of smoking, and it is discouraged in many quarters as a means of escaping from stress. The health aftermath of smoking is so pronounced that not too many people will like to make use of it as a means of getting better.

Scientific Explanations

Efficient Technologies (2019) explains that the time a person smokes also reveals their inner conflict. According to the website, 'Smoking is an attempt by someone to explain away relaxation without putting forth the efforts of conforming to the normal strategies.' That is, smokers have a nervous disorder which they are trying to hide through their action. Explaining smoking gestures, the website submits that 'while non-smokers try to cover up their anxiety through acts like nail biting, head scratching, playing with their tie or a pen or pencil, finger tapping or foot tapping, a smoker smokes his way in a similar situation. Pipe smokers are often seen cleaning, lighting, tapping, filling, packing, and puffing their pipes to make themselves tension-free at what time they are under pressure' (Efficient Technologies 2019). What I want to draw out of this quote is that smokers do not only rely on the internal effects of the cigarette to cover up stress; they also make use of the methods of smoking to distract people from their actual feeling.

Philip (2014) supports the assertion of Efficient Technologies that the method(s) in which cigarette is being smoked reveal(s) the hidden thoughts of the smoker. That is why the body language expert summarises this gesture in one sentence: 'Smoking body language may give off cues of underlying emotion depending on how it is done.' Philip goes ahead to describe smoking as an addictive habit employed by some people to orally fix their discomfort. Some assert that smoking is a replacement for the comfort brought by thumb sucking. That is why Efficient Technologies opines that stress pacifiers in both smokers and non-smokers are similar.

Philip tries to explain some of the interpretations of different methods of smoking. When a smoker inhales deeply, it is a suggestion of the person's desire to be calm and sedated when they find themselves under pressure. When the person quickly puffs the smoke, it means they want to stimulate the brain and get down to work. You may see the person putting off and dropping the cigarette as if he or she were agitated. When the smoker exhales quickly and the smoke blows upwards, this means the person is nursing positive thoughts. Conversely, if the smoke is blown downwards, it means the person is battling with negative emotions. If the exhalation is done slowly, it means the person is increasingly considering something. Smokers are always conscious of the direction of the smoke. Most of them know how to blow smoke that it would not waft into the face of nearby non-smokers. Those who do this really show that they care for others, especially those who take extra efforts to study wind direction.

Practical Illustrations

Case Study I: An artisan had been trying work on a particular product that he had to deliver the next day. He had given all his efforts to ensure that the product was ready before the workday ended. He skipped his break and left other works just to concentrate on that particular one. Upon checking his time, he discovered that he had about thirty minutes before the end of his shift. Pressure mounted on him in an indescribable manner. When he returned to work, for about five minutes, he could not do any significant thing. He then reached out for his cigarettes. When he lit it, he inhaled the smoke deeply as a way of calming himself before returning to work. To him, this was serving as an energy bolster—he was optimistic that he would function better after smoking.

Case Study II: Student A had been smoking for almost an hour in his dormitory while most of his colleagues were at the library because it was examination period. He appeared unmoved by anything because he sat in a relaxed manner. The smoking seemed like a soothing pain relief to him. Immediately he remembered that he was to sit the toughest course the next day, he puffed quickly and dropped the cigarette. He rushed to get his books and then began to run to the library. At that point, he was caught up with reality, and the truth descended on him that there was no way he could alternate cigarettes for reading.

Case Study III: A terrorist group had just finished their permutations on how to attack the next target, and it seemed everything was perfect; they had all the resources and links needed to make the operation a huge success at their disposal. Then most of them reached for their cigarettes, lit them, and smoked. They exhaled quickly and blew the smoke upwards. This was to bolster their confidence. They were of the opinion that smoking would psychologically heighten their feelings.

9.13. Eating Too Much

Generic Interpretations of the Concept

Anxiety can make people do many unimaginable things; there are just a few people across the world who are truly disciplined when it comes to taming their weird demands in some given situations. I have seen people overeat not because they were hungry but because they need to deal with one form of anxiety or another. It is the habit of some people to consume food more than their usual intake any time they are stressed. To them, this is a pacifying act. Ideally, when you eat more than you were supposed to do, this will cause physical discomfort to you as you would not be able to walk well, breathe well, or even sit properly. For about thirty minutes, the person will become restless. So in a way, the overeating may be a way of diverting the person's attention from the threatening situation to another thing.

I have seen people consume a vast amount of food when results were not tilting towards their favour until they become sick. If you do see football matches on a regular basis, you would understand this point better. When some football fans become anxious over the status of their favourite team, they would divert it to their appetite, and this would make them consume food more than the ideal rate they were used to. At that point, they eat all forms of junks and drinks.

Scientific Explanations

What we refer to as overeating is actually an eating disorder. If we do not see it as something evil, we may encourage it in some other forms. When the food you consume is greater than the energy you expend, you have overeaten, and this usually leads to obesity and excessive weight gain. A source puts it that 'compulsive overeaters depend on food to comfort themselves when they are stressed, suffering bouts of depression, and have feelings of helplessness'. This affirms my earlier postulation.

Harvard Medical School provides in-depth explanation on why stress causes people to overeat. Known as stress eating, stress unleashes some hormones which pushes people to overeat. The foods people usually eat during this time are high-fat, sugary 'comforting foods'. Researchers have been able to link stress to weight gain. The website notes that stress has the ability to shut down appetite—that is, 'The nervous system sends messages to the adrenal glands atop the kidneys to pump out the hormone epinephrine [also known as adrenaline]. Epinephrine helps trigger the body's fight-or-flight response, a revved-up physiological state that temporarily puts eating on hold' (HMS 2018). However, if the stress persists, it becomes another story entirely. The platform explains further that 'the adrenal glands release another hormone called cortisol, and cortisol increases appetite and may also ramp up motivation in general, including the motivation to eat'.

The medical platform also proclaims that there is a relationship between stress and food preferences. Different studies—many of them carried out on animals—show that emotional or physical distress increases the intake of food high in fat, sugar, or even both. Some system restructuring such as high insulin levels with high cortisol levels may be behind this urge for those kinds of food. Some other researches opine that ghrelin, known as hunger hormone, may have a role to play. Once ingested, fat- and sugar-filled foods seem to have a feedback effect that dampens stress-related responses and emotions. These foods really are 'comfort' foods in that they seem to counteract stress—and this may contribute to people's stress-induced craving for those foods (HMS 2018). You need to know that overeating is not the only stress-related cause accounting for increase in weight—loss of sleep, alcohol, and inability to do much exercise are other factors.

Some research outcomes suggest that there is a gender difference in stress-coping behaviour. It was reported that women are more likely to turn to food while men turn to smoking or alcohol. A Finnish study that included over five thousand men and women showed that obesity was associated with stress-related eating in women, but not in men. What is most important is that you know how to manage this situation before you become addicted to it. Resorting to food as a means of escaping stress is like causing more havoc to the body.

Jillian Kubala (2018) lists different ways in which we can deal with overeating. To avoid overeating, you must learn how to get rid of distractions. When you are eating while distracted, you would not know when you would eat more than you should. If your overeating is as a result of stress, meditation, regular exercise, and social support are the best ways to deal with it.

Practical Illustrations

Case Study I: Mr F had finished school for the past three years and had been unable to secure a job. At first, he joined a firm on internship and later had to leave when it was not economically possible for him to continue. He pitched his tent with another for five months with the hope that he would be absorbed into the system along the line. But as days were passing by, there was no inkling of such, and he had to leave. Since then, he had been applying to one company or another without any fruitful outcome. On the latest one that he went for, he was rest assured that he would be considered due to his qualifications and level of experience. As he was seated in his living room watching his favourite television show, a message came in that his services were not needed in the firm. He rushed to the refrigerator immediately and brought out some high-fat foods and began consuming them even though he was not angry. This was done on impulse so as not to make him think negatively or of his loss.

Case Study II: Mr E was one of the diehard fans of Club TRZ, and fortunately, his team made it to the finals of a coveted league. While on the final match, the opposing team had got an early goal which was caused by the mistake of the goalie. They all had thought Club TRZ would equalise, but it was on overtime, and no other goal was scored. Many of them lost hope and started trooping out of the stadium. On his own, Mr E ordered for some sugary 'comforting food' and started devouring it at that spot. Even though he knew this was not good for his health, he wanted to consume it still as a reaction to the unimaginable loss his team suffered. This was an aftermath of anxiety.

Case Study III: Criminals too do eat too much as a way of dealing with psychological issues. An interesting case I witnessed was when a subject became obviously psychologically disturbed during investigation. I hinted at my colleagues that we needed to go on a recess in order to allow the suspect to calm down and recall issues vividly well without mixing them up. During the recess, some junior officials had to engage him in a jovial manner so as to calm him down. At that point, he requested for all kinds of delicacies, and in the twinkle of an eye, he devoured all. While this was unbelievable to many of them, I knew the possible cause of it—he was psychologically stressed and wanted to cover up this discomfort through his unappealing eating habit.

9.14. Tone of Voice

Generic Interpretations of the Concept

The way we use the tone of our voice every time can either send people away from us or endear them to us. In other words, our tone of voice can either make our co-interlocutor comfortable or uncomfortable. If you have ever heard of the expression 'It is not about what he said but how he said it that pained me', then you have had a practical experience of what voice tone is capable of doing it. Voice is uttered through the mouth; that is why it is categorised as a mouth body language. What I have been saying so far is that we can make use of our voice tone to make good impressions about ourselves. With the way you speak, you can win the admiration of people from all walks of life.

With your tone of voice, people can see you as being nice, knowledgeable, well-cultured, loving, sweet, and nice. If, however, you do not put it into proper use, you may be seen as arrogant, indignant, uncaring, rude, and suspicious. From the foregoing, you can see that the tone of voice matters a lot, and it plays invaluable roles in our everyday affairs.

If you want to get the attention of people in an ideal context (I mean in a peaceful atmosphere), the best thing for you to do is to lower your voice and speak with them. Lower the voice is indescribably sweet. Parents use this technique in putting their babies to bed. On the other hand, if you want to send someone off from your environment, you would need to employ a harsh tone. There is no one who wants to be ridiculed. If you shout at a person, it is humiliating, and that may be the end of your relationship. In some situation, the person may react back in the same manner.

Scientific Explanations

Merriam-Webster Dictionary simply defines *tone of voice* as 'the way a person is speaking to someone'. What is emphasised here is the medium and manner in which the person conveys his message and not even the actual message delivered. Skills You Need, a website that focuses on body language and other social issues, states that the tone of voice can make people know our feelings—that is, when a person is pained and he or she speaks, you would know their true emotions at that point. For instance, a shaky, low, shivering voice tells you that all is not well with the person. The website also goes ahead to explain that the use of a particular tone of voice will determine if there is a need to reply to the speaker or not. For example, in English and other non-tonal languages, a rising tone at the end of the sentence can indicate a question (SYN 2019). Tonal languages such as English do not play with the manner in which a person makes use of his or voice while speaking.

In her own contribution, Maria Pellicano (2017) says that thetone of voice can be used in four different ways to achieve various purposes. According to her, tone of voice can be used to motivate, educate, coach, and chat. In all these four instances, you must learn how to use them in a way that they would produce the needed results. According to the *Wall Street Journal*, having a charismatic tone is considered more important than the actual words you speak. Knowing how important the voice tone is, legendary Margaret Thatcher had to hire a vocal coach to help her in developing a voice of leadership and authority. Pellicano reports a research outcome which states that doctors who make use of the wrong tone of voice are likely to face legal consequences.

Pellicano moves further to explain that it is impossible for us to hear the sound of our own tone of voice. What is actually registered in our head is not what every other person hears when we speak. The only way we can listen to our voice tone is to record it and listen back to what we earlier said. What is important is that you speak with an honest voice at all times. This makes your communication standard, and people will like to relate with you.

Practical Illustrations

Case Study I: Wife B needed to get some amount of money from her husband, but her spouse has been proving stubborn. He had explained to her that he was not financially buoyant to afford the amount she requested for. However, she knew that was a pure deceit. So she decided to make use of force to get her demands. When her husband returned from work that day, she shouted at him and told him how she was being maltreated. She made her husband realise that she had other options. Her voice was so high that even their neighbours could hear her speak. This became very irritating to the husband, who had to move out of the house immediately. For three days, the man did not return. She called, but he did not answer her calls. When the husband returned after the third day, she was calm and, instead of shouting, showed him love. When she discovered that her husband was getting back to his normal self, she decided to approach him peacefully, spoke in a lowered voice, and explained what she needed the money for. Her husband gave her the money the morning of the next day. The calmness of the tone which represented love and compassion won her husband's heart in this context.

Case Study II: In its usual routine, Company TDC had just finished with the transfer of its top management from one branch to the other. The one who was brought to the headquarters seemed to be having inexplicable issues with his workforce. Since his arrival, rate of productivity had drastically dropped, and he thought it was a gang up against him. So he began to shout at the employees more. He was not attentive to explanations from anyone of them. When it seemed that matters were getting worse and his job was on the line, he invited one of the employees to help him. It was the employee who told him that nobody liked being shouted at. When he changed, he began to see strange results within a week. Here, the harsh tone of voice was a representation of aggression and hatred.

Case Study III: A young man was paraded by immigration officials due to some questionable segments of his passport. He appeared decent and responsible, and no one could think of him being a criminal on the surface level. So he was ushered into a private room for questioning while forensic investigation was being carried out on his documents. When he was asked the first question, he appeared to have lost his voice because the officials engaging him could hardly hear what he was saying. He was later appealed to speak louder, but all fell on deaf ears. The many thoughts going on in his mind had affected his voice. This means he was nervous and disturbed by the unpalatable thoughts he was going through.

9.15. Pitch of Voice

Generic Interpretations of the Concept

This is like the other side of the coin of the preceding gesture. Just like tone of voice, voice pitch is also important in communicating our intent in a discourse context. Maintaining our normal pitch of voice shows that all is well with us—that is, our words are understood by people without being laced with an iota of suspicion. Rise in the pitch of voice has been said to be as a result of nervousness. When a person becomes nervous and is compelled to speak in that situation, their voice would begin to crack, and they have to raise it so that you can manage to hear the information the person is passing across.

Insecurity is another possible cause of a rise in the pitch of voice. If you are insecure, tension rises in your body, and your muscles become charged. This reflects in the way you speak. Stress is another possible cause of this. Anything that makes us uncomfortable can reconfigure some parts of our body. The muscles of the human body are very sensitive, and they react to the slightest of emotions. What causes a voice to crack and pitch to raise is tension in the vocal cord. The vocal cord is at its best when we are relaxed, without harbouring any fear. This explains the reason musicians record their songs when they are in their best state of mind. This gives them the opportunity to sing with their sonorous voice.

Scientific Explanations

According to *Encyclopaedia Britannica*, pitch of voice is 'the relative highness or lowness of a tone as perceived by the ear, which depends on the number of vibrations per second produced by the vocal cords.' It is the primary acoustic correlate of tone and intonation. Explaining pitch, Tonya Reiman (2019) describes the human voice as a magical tool. Just like fingerprint, we all have a distinct voice. The body language expert defines *pitch* as the rate of vibration of the vocal folds. As the rate of vibration varies, the sound of the voice will change. So if the number of vibration per second increases, so will the pitch of voice. Faster rates form higher voices or higher pitches, while slower rates elicit deeper voices or lower pitches.

Explaining how vibrations and pitches are created, Reiman submits that 'the vibrations, and the speed at which they vibrate, are dependent on the length and thickness of the vocal cords, as well as the tightening and relaxation of the muscles surrounding them'. Now you understand why women have higher voices than men—women have shorter cords. Apart from the length and thickness of the vocal cords, our emotions, mood, and inflections are some other factors that affect our pitch. According to Reiman, 'When people become frightened or excited, the muscles around the voice box (or larynx) unconsciously contract, putting strain on the vocal cords, making the pitch higher.' However, not all pitch change is unconsciously done. When we do not want to scream even if the situation warrants it, we consciously exercise control over the pitch of our voice. As we express different feelings, thoughts, and emotions, the pitch of our voice tend to move up and down.

In a study conducted by Collins, Missing, and Feinberg et al., it was discovered that men admire women with higher-pitched voices while women are fond of men with low-pitched voices.

Christopher Philip (2013) also lends a voice to this subject matter. He contributed more to the emotional aspect of the discourse. He supports the assertion of Reiman that our voice varies with our state of mind. With the use of our voice, we are able to portray different feelings. For instance, a father can make his voice sound like that of his wife just for the purpose of grabbing the attention of their kid. In the same vein, a woman can lower her voice so that it takes the semblance of a man for the purpose of scorning their children. A noticeable bad habit among women is the tendency to raise the pitch of their voice at the end of every sentence. This makes every one of their sentence looks like a question and can have detrimental effect in the business world. According to Philip, 'People read this inflection as a signal of insecurity and believe that you are unsure about what you are saying.' So acting with conviction is the best means of commanding respect from people.

Practical Illustrations

Case Study I: An interrogator was engaging a suspected terrorist who had proved difficult for law enforcement agencies to gather evidence against. Whenever he was being interrogated, he had an excellent excuse or narration to escape the wrath of the law. What made it much more difficult for enforcement officers to nail him was that he was an educated terrorist. So the most experienced interrogator in that country who recently retired was brought back to come and engage him. The interrogation session was very lengthy as it was nothing less of 'jaw and intellectual war'. At some point, the interrogator threw one of the most potent accusations at him in the face, and that broke the camel's back; he became insecure and knew that his end had come. So he raised the pitch of voice in a trembling manner, defending himself, while the interrogator remained calm, looking at him in a bizarre manner. His trembling voice was a further confirmation of his nervousness and psychological disturbance.

Case Study II: Mrs O had a hectic day in the office today; she worked for eight straight hours dealing with some issues that needed urgent attention. Her pregnancy is in its fourth month. She left the office and headed to the market to get ingredients for cooking tonight. After getting home, she had to rush to the kitchen because her four-year-old kid was obviously hungry, and she did not want to feed her with junks. After cooking, she fell back to some other chores. Stress was already building up in her, and she was just looking for the best opportunity to rest when her husband came home to accuse her of what she knew nothing about. She raised her voice in anger and shouted at her spouse.

Case Study III: There are some temperamental students, and once they are angry, they care less of who they are addressing; they would raise the pitch of their voice in a trembling and disrespectful way. One day, I was teaching some participants from different organisations how to be productive and stand out in their job. At some point, I cracked a joke which was not intended to mock anyone. I never knew the scenario I painted was referring to one of the participants. Immediately she flared up, raised the pitch of her voice, and started making her rebuttals. It took me an extra display of maturity to bring the situation under control. Everyone who was there knew there was a real show of anger.

9.16. Wrong Tonal Inflections

Generic Interpretations of the Concept

This is also known as uptalk. The wrong use of tonal inflections can mar the meaning of our talks. As explained in the preceding section, this is more noticeable in women than in men. Uptalk is the act of inflecting one's tone up at the end of a declarative sentence, which makes it sound like a question. When you express yourself as if you were asking a question, the other person is usually thrown into confusion as he or she would not know how to respond to your 'question'. This impedes the free flow of communication. The wrong use of tonal inflections can create bad impression about you.

The use of uptalk is more pronounced when speaking over the phone. Even a single use of uptalk on the phone will create a bad impression about you. Apart from women, it has been noticed that this phenomenon is also common among the youth in general. Little do they know that it erodes them of their confidence. When you sound tentative, people are always expectant, and if you keep mum, they become disappointed in you. Language is dynamic, but that does not mean that it is subjected to arbitrary use. No matter our background or level of education or even philosophy of life, we must ensure that we abide by the laid principles of communication.

Scientific Explanations

Although the origin of this gesture is not certain, but it is agreed in many quarters that it probably originated from New Zealand. It is unclear whether the American English varieties and the Oceanic varieties had any influence on each other regarding the spread of uptalk (Alan 1990). While this phenomenon seems to be very old in Europe, it is somewhat new in America and very common among young speakers of English. The gesture has been portrayed badly in the media and among many other experts, yet it seems to be spreading like wildfire. In a 2010 article, Hanky Davis condemned uptalk in strong terms even before explaining what it is all about, but it seems that people are not willing to drop it from their expressions. According to him, when people make use of upward inflections, it makes them appear as if they were not assured of the truthfulness of what they are saying.

In other words, they are looking for approval of their own assertions from another source. This can be very irritating in many instances. Acceptability is another possible interpretation that can be alluded to this speech style—that is, you want to know if what you said is acceptable or not. There are many other meanings that can be given to uptalk. However, what I must note is that none of the meanings is intentionally intended. In the words of Davis, 'It's a nasty habit. It is the very opposite of confidence or assertiveness. It's got all out of control.' Davis is obviously angry about the whole process; maybe this is partially due to the fact that he teaches in the university and has to engage with young minds more often. He laments that students' speech lack confidence these days, a sharp deviation from what was achieved a few years ago.

When a person making use of uptalk speaks, you may likely think that every one of their expression is a question. Davis said he had noticed this pattern of speech since 2000, and it was prevalent among women. To his amazement, when he called them to question them on the rationale behind that pattern of speech, none of them were aware that they used to uptalk. When he called it to their attention, they tend to stop it for about three minutes before switching back to it. Concluding his article, Davis says that uptalk has become a normal speech pattern, and everyone must see it as a point of duty to point it out in people's speech.

Peter Khoury's article seems to be solution-driven; he proffers ways in which uptalk can be reduced in our expressions so as to gain the confidence of others. Every leader wants to sound certain, sure, and assertive. As such, the use of uptalk is a no-go area for any serious-minded leader. In order to fight this phenomenon, we must develop awareness around how we make use of it. 'Change happens after self-awareness. If you don't think you uptalk, then you will never work on improving it' (Khoury 2019). There is no better way this can be expressed. If you do not discover, it would be difficult for you to recover. It is pertinent for me to note that being self-aware should not be mistaken as judgement. So only take cognisance of your use of uptalk, and you should not condemn yourself. Another solution proposed by Khoury is that those suffering from uptalk epidemic should consciously practise the use of declarative expressions in private. When you speak to yourself again and again, it becomes a physical part of you; you would begin to utter declarative sentences without issues.

Imperative expressions are commands. So this is clearly different from the use of uptalk, which denotes uncertainty. Finally, he suggests that everyone who needs a sharp deviation from this speech pattern should work on how to develop their sense of certainty. If what you are saying does not sound convincing to you, who else are you expecting to believe you? If you think about this question at all times, you would do everything humanly possible to always sound convincing. Khoury implores that people should build their beliefs in themselves before seeking to lord it over external bodies.

Practical Illustrations

Case Study I: Students were supposed to make seminar presentations as a way of fulfilling all the requirements for a course. When one of the female students came up to make her presentation, she said, 'My name is Ms Q? I want to speak on food technology and modern requirements?' Many of her mates were lost, and the lecturer, who was visibly angry, asked her if she had changed her name or she decided to work on a different topic. This means she made use of uptalk in her presentation, which was wrong in that sense.

Case Study II: In the office setting, workers also make use of tonal inflections, and this has bad effects on the entire organisation, especially if the person being fed with the information did not seek clarification on the issue before acting on it. A manager was reported to have made use of the wrong tonal inflection while speaking to a junior staff. Afraid to ask for clarifications, the junior colleague went to do the wrong thing, and before the manager could made corrections, they have suffered more than a million-dollar loss. Even though the junior worker was eventually sacked, everyone knew the fault was with the manager.

Case Study III: Criminals are intentional about their wrong use of tonal inflections; the purpose of doing this is to confuse either their target or law enforcement officials. While fielding questions from law enforcement agents, a high-profile criminal, instead of supplying the needed answers, would respond as if he were throwing back the questions at the enforcement agents. At some point, the chief investigator lost his patience and had to warn the suspect to cooperate or face the dire consequences of his action. In some other contexts, they use wrong tonal inflections to prolong discussions—this is usually done to targets in order to give them time to further survey the target.

9.17. Stammering or Stuttering

Generic Interpretations of the Concept

This arguably seems to be the most pronounced form of body language that we witness in some people. Some people pathologically stutter; they unintentionally repeat syllables as they try to converse with you. This can be painful to them and irritating to you too. When a person stutters, you see them struggling to pronounce some syllables multiple times. In severe instances, they may even close their eyes and hit their head with their hands, all in the name of trying to utter a particular syllable. If you are conversing with a person that stutters, you need to exercise patience until they eventually express themselves.

On the other hand, some of us do not stutter pathologically, but going through stress can make us stutter or stammer in some given circumstances. When we become really tense and our emotions rise beyond a level we can control, we temporarily stammer. In such situations, it means we are really angry and psychologically abnormal. People going through such intense form of anger need help or at least be monitored because they can do anything. The person may even close an eye just in a bid to utter a word. This is normally seen in people when they are expressing their displeasure concerning a given issue.

Scientific Explanations

The World Health Organization (2014) defines *stuttering* as 'a speech disorder in which the flow of speech is disrupted by involuntary repetitions and prolongations of sounds, syllables, words or phrases as well as involuntary silent pauses or blocks in which the person who stutters is unable to produce sounds.' I so much like this definition because it takes cognisance of every detail. The definition makes it known that this speech disorder disrupts the flow of speech and is involuntary. These two concepts have answered the questions we need to ask on stuttering. According to Watkins et al., stuttering is a disorder of 'selection, initiation, and execution of motor sequences necessary for fluent speech production'. For many people who stutter, repetition is the primary problem. The term *stuttering* covers a wide range of severity, encompassing barely perceptible impediments that are largely cosmetic to severe symptoms that effectively prevent oral communication. In the world, approximately four times as many men as women stutter, encompassing seventy million people worldwide, or about 1 per cent of the world's population (Carlson 2013).

The British Stammering Association (BSA) states that some stammers do dodge some words and expressions in their conversations. This makes them go to extra length in expressing themselves over issues they would have used a word for. It should be noted that stammering differs from one person to the other, and the rate at which it appears and disappears in people is also different. Most people who stammer are of the consensus that there are many things they undergo that are not revealed to other people on the surface level. An American speech therapist called Sheehan, who himself stammered, described stammering as being like an iceberg. Only the tip of the iceberg shows above the surface while the bulk of it is hidden under the water. The hidden aspects of the stammer include avoidances such as those mentioned above, fear and anticipation of stammering, and other difficult—often strong—feelings about stammering such as frustration, anger, sadness, embarrassment, and shame (BSA 2019).

Stuttering is generally not a problem with the physical production of speech sounds or putting thoughts into words. Acute nervousness and stress do not cause stuttering, but they can trigger stuttering in people who have the speech disorder, and living with a stigmatised disability can result in anxiety and high allostatic stress load (chronic nervousness and stress) that reduce the amount of acute stress necessary to trigger stuttering in any given person who stutters, exacerbating the problem in the manner of a positive feedback system. The name 'stuttered speech syndrome' has been proposed for this condition (Irwin 2006).

It should be noted that the disorder is also variable—that is, there are certain conditions (such as discussing over the phone or in a large group) where stuttering may be more severe or less. This is dependent on the self-consciousness of the person who stutters. Stutterers often find that their stuttering fluctuates and that they have 'good' days, 'bad' days, and 'stutter-free' days. The times in which their stuttering fluctuates can be random (Bowen 2015).

Talking of the causes of stuttering, there is no single cause that can be pointed out to be responsible for this disorder. Studies show that there are different factors involved in this. However, stuttering has its root in neurological disorder. Studies have shown differences in the anatomy and functioning of the brain of those who stammer compared with most other people. In the same vein, we cannot discard the place of genetics. When someone has it in a family, there is the likelihood that it would reoccur on the long run. Because this disorder affects speaking, it may have a deep and lifetime psychological impact on the person experiencing it (BSA 2019).

There are different ways in which stuttering affects people. Some of the factors accounting for this include whom the person is talking, how they are feeling about themselves and their speech, and what they want to say. Environmental factor is another issue that determines how dysfluent a person may be. In situations where people lay high expectations on stammers, they can worsen the person's situations because while struggling hard to meet your standard, they become more conscious of their disorder. Sometimes, the person himself may put himself in such tight corners—while speaking on telephone, attending an interview, wooing a lady, saying one's name and address, etc.

Practical Illustrations

Case Study I: Man U was attending the wedding of a friend but missed his way at some point. So he parked to seek the help of passers-by conversant with the environment. He demanded from a man who, fortunately, knew the venue. As the man was about to give him the description of the place, he stretched forth his hand, and for about a minute, he could not manage to pronounce a word. Man U was troubled and almost got infuriated before he looked at the man in the eye and saw the passion written on his face and the difficulty in his mouth area. Then he waited patiently until he was able to make the utterances; he was stammering and, as such, had to be waited for so as to regain his speech.

Case Study II: Wife A had told her husband that he should not stay long outside again as she was beginning to feel lonely. However, the husband is finding it difficult to adapt to the new lifestyle that marriage is imposing on him. For the first three days after his wife's appeal, he was back home earlier than before. On Thursday, he stayed back at work to settle some issues, and it seemed the wife understood and didn't talk. However, he went to a nightclub on Friday and drank himself into a stupor before returning home. The wife was obviously angry, and this made her stammer while talking. Seeing the anger on the face of his wife, the husband begged passionately.

Case Study III: Student A was just enrolled in EGF High School. He came from a rural area. He had never seen such a standard school and his peers speaking fluently like that. So he decided to stay on his own. However, one of the teachers noticed this and decided to call him to answer questions in order to build his confidence and make him integrate with his mates. On a particular day, when Student A was called to answer a question, he didn't know anything about it, and in his bid to wash away the attendant shame that came with it, he began to stammer without saying anything in particular. However, the stammering did not come as one that was done on impulse, and his facial look only confirmed that he was not remorseful. Hence, it was observed that his non-verbal gesture was fake.

Case Study IV: There had been reports that illicit arms were being imported to Country VBD, and as such, law enforcement agents at the borders and other important areas were given the marching order. Just three days after the order came, a smuggler was apprehended, and when a check was conducted on the items seized, bullets and other harmful weapons were found on him. This was a direct indictment. So the officers asked him to explain where he got them and for what purpose he was bringing the ammunitions in. Seeing the seriousness on the faces of the officers, he lost his voice and began to stammer, but that was not enough for the determined officers; he was eventually arrested because the field officials did not trust him.

9.18. Delay in Response Time

Generic Interpretations of the Concept

When people delay in responding to a query, some erroneously assume that they are telling lies. This interpretation is not only hasty but also harsh. If a person is deceptive, the response time is not the best way to fish him or her out. There are many reasons that can make a person delay in answering a question. This is not to discountenance the fact that liars use the tactics in buying time for the sake of putting up a credible response, but all I have been trying to establish is that both the honest and dishonest do delay in responding to a query. From the angle of the guilty, they are truly thinking of what to say in order to wash themselves clean of an accusation, while an innocent person is thinking of how best to say their response in order to convey their message.

From the foregoing, a delay in response time should call our attention to the intents of a person, but we should not zero our minds towards the negative right from the beginning. I have travelled around the world, and one of the things

I have taken note of is that a delay in responding to a query is not uncommon among many cultures. People primarily delay in answering as a means of studying the nuances and complexity of a question. When a person responds to your question immediately and what they say is out of context, you would become angry because their response does not tally with your question.

In the same vein, fatigue and stress are also capable of slowing down the response time in people. This means that the person is still trying to muster strength internally before being able to respond to your queries. A stressed person is intellectually and physically weak, and we do not expect them to respond to our questions as if nothing were wrong with them.

Furthermore, a formal enquiry may also cause delay in responding to a question due to the seriousness and likely consequences attached to the issue. So the person would have to think of every one of their intended response before uttering it.

Scientific Explanations

A whole lot of people are normally concerned about how to detect lies—law enforcement officials, parents, teachers, and professionals, among others. It is usually very painful to later discover that someone has played on our intelligence without being detected. This has made a lot of people paranoid, making them think that even the slightest of all deviations from the conventional means of conversation is an act of deceit. Changing Minds (2019) opines that one of the best ways to spot deception is being able to identify how liars think differently.

The body language platform submits that delay in response to a question is a pointer to the fact that the person is thinking. This does not mean he or she is necessarily fabricating a story. People may be forced to replay the details of a story in order to know the best way to give response to what you have asked them about it. You have the right to be suspicious of a delay in response to your question if the question asked does not necessarily need long thinking—that is, you are certain that an honest person would be able to give a spontaneous, detailed response without having to brood over it.

Another indicator of deception pointed out by Changing Minds is that if after the delay, the person refuses to give you the needed details. This means he or she has consciously left out the details because they consider them implicating. Nicholas Miller (2014) also submits that when there is delay between words and expressions of someone while they are responding to your queries, it calls for concern.

In addition, the response time of a question may be delayed for the purpose of sustaining a story. If you do not want to end a conversation too soon, one of the tactics you employ is to delay how fast you respond to the queries of your co-interlocutor. In a way, this means you are relaxed and have nothing to fear. If, actually, the person was lying, he or she would be very fast to say whatever they want to say and move out of the frightening environment.

Practical Illustrations

Case Study I: Ms P was a young graduate and was very fortunate to secure an appointment with one of the best companies in town. However, the company was known to be disciplined—that is, they do not tolerate any act of unprofessionalism. Ms P was a lone ranger; she found it difficult to mingle with people. So while she was still learning the ropes in the firm, there were no people to put her through. This made her fall into many avoidable errors. In one of her offences, she was asked by the management of the company to appear before the disciplinary committee to present her case. Upon getting there, she was asked some few questions, and before responding, she would have to think through. She discovered that all the members of the panel were writing and, as such, was conscious of the kind of response she gave them. Her intentions were clear; her offence was propelled by ignorance and not the need to dupe the company. So the delay in response was to make her sound convincing to the committee, and she eventually achieved this.

Case Study II: A man picked up the phone of his spouse and saw many suspicious messages from a source. He became angry and called his wife to come and give him an explanation for those messages. When the wife came, she saw that her husband was tense, and if she was to make a direct presentation of the issue, she might lose her matrimonial home on that ground. So she remained calm and looked into the husband's eyes. Replying to his questions, she replied in a delayed manner, making sure that each potential response was well thought out before uttering them. This was to make sure that the situation did not get out of hand—that is, the non-verbal gesture was displayed to put the situation under control.

Case Study III: Suspect U was arrested during a robbery operation, and some bullets were found on him. After making his statement, he was arranged for investigations so that he could be arraigned in court. Due to the incriminating items found on him, he knew denial was not an option for him again. So he decided to be tactical about the whole process. One of his tactics was to play the delay game. Any time a question was being asked, he would go mute for some seconds before answering. In some instances, his answer would be to push the question back to the officials for clarifications. So all these helped him to delay the process but did not save him eventually as he was eventually fished out.

9.19. Silence

Generic Interpretations of the Concept

In some situations, silence serves as an embodiment of messages than verbal utterances or any other form of action. When a person intentionally decides to go mute in a conversation, this sends a strong message to the other party. Whether long silence or a pregnant pause, you need to know what each connotes in a discourse. Before going far, let me state that not every silence in a conversation is intentional. For instance, when we are trying to recall an important piece of information, we would unintentionally go silent; it is practically impossible to try recalling something when you are talking simultaneously. So the thought of recalling supersedes the need to talk at that point in time. In the same vein, when you are contemplating over an issue, you become silent because you do not want other thoughts to disrupt your thoughts at that moment.

In some other instances, silence may be well intended and employed as a potent tool to win an argument. For instance, when negotiating, a negotiator may intentionally go mum and leave the other party to fill in the void. If the other party falls into the trap by mentioning a price that favours him or her, they would seal the deal at that point.

Great actors and experienced interviewers do employ the use of silence to their advantage. In an interview context, a dead silence by the interrogator can send down fear into the nerves of a suspect. I will expatiate on this example during the course of our study. Silence may be used to communicate reconsideration, processing, recollection, or pondering. It may even mean that the person is nonplussed. What is most important is that people should know how best to make use of silence while the other party is able to decode the message effortlessly.

Scientific Explanations

Kurt Smith (2018) describes silence as a secret communication tool. He submits that silence is a very good tool for communication. Some people will obviously disagree with this fact. In fact, there are people who even share the sentiment that silence cannot be regarded as a component of communication. People under this category are greatly missing out on the effectiveness of silence in achieving their needs. Smith says that silence, sometimes, have the ability to convey our intended message than words. He goes ahead to list three reasons why people should consider the use of silence in their communication. According to him, silence helps us to communicate better. Many of us can be talkative, and this does not necessarily mean we are saying what is value-adding. So it is wise that we learn how to use silence in some circumstances. Further, silence helps us to hear what is actually being communicated. When you do not keep shut to listen to a co-interlocutor, chances are that you would misinterpret their intents when given the chance to respond to what they have said. Silence aids attentiveness, which is a major thrust in every communication. Silence also helps us to reach resolutions very fast. The major goal of every discourse is to ensure that each party understands each other and agree on a point. Silence helps in achieving this.

Jorma (2011) also upholds that silence can communicate much more than we can imagine. The body language expert lists three forms of silence—expressive silence, inviting silence, and reconciling silence. People can make use of silence to strengthen their bond. For instance, if you are on a date with a girl for the second time and the silence you are dropping is making her feel 'good' and even creating intimate moments between you guys, you would drop it more. Expressive silence can be used to show that one is in charge of a situation. A boss can make use of this over his subordinates.

Also, Adityan (2012) postulates that we can make use of silence to express a whole lot of emotions. If you are upset, you can decide to remain mute, which sends a strong message to the other party. Even in prayer, we do it in silence, communicating the intents of our heart to our deity.

Practical Illustrations

Case Study I: The general manager of DTW Manufacturing Firm was supposed to be off work for three days. However, he was able to finish up with his off-field assignment before schedule and returned to the office unannounced on the third day. Many of the employees were not expecting him. So some of them left their duty posts to engage in irrelevant things. As he stepped into the office, many of them were taken aback. As they rushed to welcome him, he waited for a moment, looked at them, shook his head, and walked out on them without uttering a statement. They all began to stare at one another, gripped with fear about what the next step of the manager would be. They all panicked because they could not guess what the decisive action of the manager would be.

Case Study II: Some group of interrogators were engaging a notorious armed robbery suspect. They asked him to narrate everything he knew about the issue. After fabricating stories for about twenty minutes, he stopped and was expecting the enforcement officials to respond to him immediately. However, for about three minutes, all of them did not say anything. He buried his head as he could not endure eye contact with the officials. He practically began to shiver to the extent that if he had had his way, he would have disappeared at that point. His silence means that he is engulfed in fear.

Case Study III: A man went on a date with a beautiful, charming young lady. He had the intention of marrying her. The date was the second one in a week. After the usual introduction and knowing each other better, he would hold the hands of the lady, look at her in the face, and make some confessions about his love for her. Sometimes, he would touch her cheeks. After each profession of love, he would be silent for some seconds, both of them would look at each other, and eventually smile. It was a strong bonding tool for them—that is, the silence makes whatever preceding action they had carried out to be more meaningful, impactful, and practical.

9.20. Silence and Freeze Response

Generic Interpretations of the Concept

Here is an African proverb: 'When a kid gets to a frightening place, he would be gripped by fear.' In other words, there are circumstances that can take our breath away in an unexpected manner. When you are used to a situation but it suddenly changes without any due course, you would be taken aback. This is what the silence and freeze response is all about. Unexpected, frightening situations make people suddenly go numb and stiff. Most times, it also alters the breathing pattern of the affected person.

So when you see this, pay attention to what is going on. This is usually the response to a negative and shocking event. The freeze response means the person does not want to risk the threatening situation. So they stay glued at a spot, grasping for breath. The person may even be physically shivering. Also, the freeze response is to give them the opportunity to reassess the situation so as to know what is actually going on. It is pertinent to note that the shocked person would have been used to the situation before the unbelievable incident occurs. So they want to know what has really changed. With this, they would be able to figure out the next step to take. Ultimately, the silence and freeze response is an expression of negative emotions.

Scientific Explanations

The silence and freeze response is the reaction to a specific stimulus that is most commonly observed by preys. A person who thinks he is powerful enough to face a threatening situation would not display the freeze response; rather, you would notice the fight response in them. Prey feign death with the use of silence, which will serve as a possible way of escaping the attack of a predator. Typically, this response changes the blood pressure and lengths of time of the crouching position of the prey. Other changes the silence and freeze response causes are shortness of breath, increased heart rate, sweating, or a choking sensation (Ressler 2009). Freezing is seen as the prior step before either fight or flight response—that is, before a person makes up his mind to either confront an unusual situation or flee, they would first make an assessment of it. Studies carried out on freezing behaviour shows that the basolateral amygdala and the hippocampus are the regions of the brain that elicit this feeling in people.

Leon Seltzer (2015) describes the silence and freeze response as a 'self-paralysing response'. He says that the decision to go into the freeze mode is made within seconds, or even milliseconds, when we are exposed to a frightening situation. To better understand how the freeze response works, paint a picture of yourself in a totally helpless situation; you cannot confront it, nor can you escape from it. Yet there is no one within sight to help you out. In this situation, your best mode of response is to act as if you were lifeless. To make this point clearer, imagine you are attacked by a ferocious dog who has sunk his teeth into your neck, and you are totally at its mercy. Shouting will make the dog think you wanted to launch a counter-attack, and at that point, you cannot even escape from it. So you become totally silent so that it would think you have given up.

From the foregoing, it means that a person who is displaying the freeze response is experiencing trepidation, horror, panic, and dread. All these are extreme feelings that are usually fraught with anxiety at its highest level. When you do not put a fight in such circumstances, your predator may lose interest in you and face another thing (Seltzer 2015).

Trauma Recovery (2019) lists increased or decreased heart rate, heart pounding, sense of dread, heaviness, stiffness, numbness, coldness, pale skin, and feeling stuck in some parts of the body as part of the symptoms of the freeze response. The most important thing is for you to know what best works for you when you are under stress of this kind.

Practical Illustrations

Case Study I: A new couple had just changed their apartment. The area looked bushy, and the person they contracted to clear the surroundings promised them the following weekend. Since they had cleaned the inner part, they decided to move in, hoping that by the time he came over to do the clearing, they would have been well settled. Since they fumigated the apartment before moving in, they used to leave the windows open so as to allow the cool breeze to enter. On the Thursday preceding the weekend the man was to come and clear the bush, both the husband and wife came back late from work. So the wife rushed to the kitchen while the husband was fixing some things in the living room. In the evening, when the wife went into their bedroom, she saw a snake crawling out through the window. When she set her eyes on it, she remained silent, compressing her lips tightly, and remained on the spot till it crawled out before she finally screamed to call her husband. She froze and remained silent at that particular point because she was engulfed in fear.

Case Study II: A high school girl unfortunately became a victim of rape. After the incident, she narrated everything that took place. She noted that her predator was lurking somewhere in the dark and held her from the back. She first tried to battle him by struggling to escape, but she could not match the man's strength. So the man later overpowered her and took custody of her body. At first, she was still trying to make some moves so as to prevent him from taking off her clothes, but when she discovered that the man was really charged and might injure her, she released herself to him. Her body became stiff, and after a round, the man was gripped with fear thinking that she had passed on. Then he quickly dressed up and took to his heels. She remained on the same spot until he was out of sight. That was how she was saved.

Case Study III: An area was notorious for being the abode of those with expired permits—overstayers. Apart from the massiveness of the illegal occupants of the country, it was reported by the citizens that they were beginning to constitute nuisance to the whole community. Thus, law enforcement agents decided to go for a raid at night. A lot of them were arrested. However, Overstayer G was not around when the officers arrived. On his way back home, he heard a noise coming from his residence. Intuitively guessing the issue at hand, he ran to the back of a tree, froze behind it, and remained silent for several minutes until the police drove past him. The fear of possible arrest informed his decision to freeze behind the tree and remain silent.

9.21. Interruptive Arguments

Generic Interpretations of the Concept

When people do not wish to continue a meeting and have no power to call it a day, what they do is employ non-verbal cues and other means to disrupt such meetings. These people may sound intellectual in their argument, but they do lack clarity of purpose. This leaves others wondering, was it the speaker who failed to make his points clear or the listener who was distracted at some point? This is the original intent of an interruptive person. If those who are arguing for the purpose of disrupting the meeting are up to two or three, this can be very problematic for the person in charge of the meeting.

Those putting forward interruptive arguments would not make use of their words but their body. They understand that if they employ the verbal approach, they would sound rude, arrogant, and indignant. So the subtle technique employed is to ensure that their expressions do not tally with their bodily actions. The non-verbal cues they display repetitively disrupts and antagonises the tranquility of the gathering. The primary purpose of this technique is to intimidate, aggravate, or even place a person on an emotional 'tilt'. The most common place where this occurs is during union meetings, where members try to disrupt the speaker.

Scientific Explanations

Interruption is a speech event in which someone or a group of people break in to interject when another person still has the floor. Ideally, a speech event is organised in a way whereby one person speaks after the other. So it becomes interruptive when another person takes the floor when it is not their turn to speak. In fact, Sacks et al. are of the opinion that the process of taking turns is subconscious; it is enshrined in our subconscious to allow others to finish up with their own argument before we say ours. It is only in the jungle that animals do not respect a speaker. So if someone intentionally adopts this jungle-like behaviour, it means they do not have a positive purpose to achieve.

Communication analyst Julia A. Goldberg says there are three forms of interruptions. Relationally neutral interruptions are interjections by the listener who seek to repair, repeat, or clarify something the speaker just said. During this type of interruption, the interrupter does not intend to exert power over the speaker or to establish rapport with the speaker. The act of interruption itself is understood as neutral in this instance. Another type of interruption defined by Goldberg is the power interruption, where the interrupter breaks in and cuts off the speaker as a way to display some social power. Power interruptions are understood as acts of conflict and competition and are viewed as rude, hostile, disrespectful, and/or uncaring about the speaker and/or what the speaker is saying. A rapport interruption is designed to display mutuality and generally conveys the impression that the interrupter understands and empathises with the speaker and/or the content of the speech and is interpreted as collaborative and cooperative (Goldberg 1990). What we are really concerned about in this book is the second type. Interruptive argument is done for the purpose of ridiculing a whole conversation. Those who interrupt in this manner seek to be socially dominant, and that is why it is usually seen in situations that are connected with power holding.

Temma Ehrenfeld (2017) states that instead of getting angry with those who intentionally interrupts a conversation, you should make use of their contributions and still talking. If they discover that you are not moved by their antics, they would soon drop the opposing view and exercise patience until you are done. You can also address the issue with your body language and tone. With this, the person would understand that you got their message and chose to neglect their view, especially since it does not come in the best way. Hostility cannot solve hostility. If you are trapped into believing that fighting those interrupting you is the best way to go, they will eventually win the war over you. Remember that their original intent is to end the meeting. So if it becomes confrontational in any form, you would later have to end of the meeting. Instead, learn how to use peaceful means.

Practical Illustrations

Case Study I: It was the annual reunion of STW High School students, and many of them, well established in their various fields, travelled from far and near to be part of the meeting. The new executives of the union had made some adjustments to the order of the programme. Some of them were not aware of this. So they had erroneously imagined that it would be business as usual—just come, sit anywhere, dine, and keep chatting with people till the end of the event. In the new order of event, there was a segment for discussing how they could contribute to the development of their alma matter and how they could be of help to those just graduating from the school. People were making contributions from different angles, but the discussion looked boring to some of them. So one of the bored people stood up, made his contribution, but was distracted throughout the period he spoke—he was using his hand to massage the hair of a female friend. So the attention of many of them were on the action rather than his words. His friend also stood up and did something similar. Before you know it, the meeting came to an end. This argument pattern was somewhat intentional due to the psychological feeling of the active participants at that given point.

Case Study II: A group of children were playing during break, telling one another stories and laughing to the funny ones. It was obviously an interesting session before a known bully came into their midst. He feigned cooperation, and when he demanded that he should be asked to tell a story too, he was given the chance. As he began his purported story, he subtly used his legs to pinch another student. As if it were not intentional, he also used his hand to hit another one when he was 'demonstrating' an action. The remaining students became fearful, and they began to leave one after the other. Apart from the interruptive argument, he was seen as a source of threat to others.

Case Study III: A man was arrested over the suspicious death of his wife. Even though he was the one who reported the death to the authorities, preliminary investigations carried out linked him to the crime. In his own argument, the wife died on her own, but autopsy reports showed that she was murdered. During investigation, the man decided to use interruptive arguments as a way of distracting the officers' attention. While talking, he would focus on a particular thing, use his hand to hit a part of his body, and do other nauseating attributes just to piss the officers off, but they were undeterred. His intentions of distracting the officials were well-known but was not productive due to the expertise of the law enforcement agents.

9.22. Cathartic Expressions

Generic Interpretations of the Concept

Sometimes, we would be on the verge of pronouncing some words, but we would restrain ourselves from doing it due for one reason or another. Expressions such as *ohhh*, *wooo*, or *fuuh* and a whole lot more, which are culture-specific, are pronounced but not completed. The reason they are considered as non-verbals is because we do not completely utter them. So we cannot claim to understand their meaning through the verbal context. Hence, we intuitively interpret them due to how the person feels and behaves while trying to utter any of those words but had to restrain themselves.

When actual words are not spoken, they do not mean anything to people, especially foreigners, but people who are conversant with the culture and idiosyncrasies of that particular society can intuitively make interpretations of them. In the real sense, these near words are used in relieving stress in a very mild manner. We do not offend people while trying to relieve stress. If a person had actually uttered those words, they may sound offensive and may be interpreted by other people as being angry. So not pronouncing them saves us from what might be the likely consequences and ultimately helps us relieve stress through the air we exhale in the course of trying to utter those words.

Scientific Explanations

There is no way anybody can understand this concept very well without knowing what *catharsis* is all about. Well, the word has its origin from Greece, which is defined as 'the purgation of negative emotions'. Thus, we can authoritatively assert that cathartic utterances are uttered for the primary purpose of purging out our negative emotions. Psychoanalytic theory states that, for example, experiencing stress over a work-related situation may cause feelings of frustration and tension. Rather than venting these feelings inappropriately, the individual may instead release these feelings in another way, such as trying to utter foul words but later restraining the attempt (Cherry 2019).

According to Cherry, 'Catharsis involves both a powerful emotional component in which strong emotions are felt and expressed, as well as a cognitive component in which the individual gains new insights. The purpose of such catharsis is to bring about some form of positive change in the individual's life.' Having established this, let me state that catharsis is connected to human psychology. Cherry says that cathartic expressions have gained a place in our everyday utterances. This is to emphasise how important they are. They are usually employed to describe the experience of finding closure or moments of insights. Cathartic utterances have the ability to heal our emotional wounds and make us move past our bad history. Apart from stress, people have also affirmed that they experience catharsis after ill health, job loss, accidents, or even the death of a loved one. Cherry concludes that cathartic expressions are used in describing emotional moments that translate to positive changes in our personal lives.

Mehmet Eskin (2013) also talks extensively on this concept. He describes catharsis as one of the most important change processes in psychotherapy. When we release negative emotions in psychotherapy, it removes the negative consequences of emotions. It is important to note that in order to free oneself from psychological inhibitions, cathartic expression should be done in a secure environment—that is, you should not express yourself in environments that will increase your chances of getting emotional.

For cathartic utterances to be effective, they must be propelled directly from within, not that someone hinted you to do it or so. 'What is important here is that the individual's own subjective experiences start the catharsis' (Eskin 2013). When it is driven from within, you may begin to feel happy and pleasurable, among others. The researcher concludes, 'If cathartic reactions are evoked by observing emotional scenes and processes in the environment, this is called *dramatic relief*. The individual's experience of catharsis by observing the scenes in the external environment and feeling a great relief as a result is as old as the history of humanity and it is very common.'

Practical Illustrations

Case Study I: Mr N came home from work feeling stressed out, but no matter what the feeling was, he would always find time to play with his family and watch news so as to know what was going on around the world. The tiredness of this night was simply incomparable, and with the situation he left the office, he knew that tomorrow would even be more demanding than today. Yet he relaxed on the sofa, watching the news. There was a bomb blast in a neighbouring city earlier in the day. Newsmen got there early enough to have a first-hand coverage of the event. As they were showing the scenes of the attack, there were many dead people, others heavily wounded, and some with minor injuries. These pictures further aroused his stress emotions, and as he shouted 'Fuuuh', he managed to stand up from the sofa, feeling a bit relieved, and went to his bedroom. Anyone who saw him could easily guess that he was bored and stressed.

Case Study II: Mrs D had always suspected her husband to be a cheater, but she did not want to confront him without evidence because she did not want to destroy her matrimonial home based on a mere guess. In fact, she had intended to block all thoughts along that line, but the inconsistencies of her spouse had made such an action to become inevitable. Time and time again, his deeds appeared suspicious. There were times she even thought that he was doing that to taunt her, but recent events showed that he might be seriously into another person. They both used the same brand of phone, same wallpaper, and same external design. But her husband did not even drop his phone carelessly again. While going to the toilet, he would take it along with the excuse that he was expecting an important call. On a fateful day, he left his phone in the room and went to the shower. A call came in, and the wife thought it was hers. She hurriedly picked it up, and it was the voice of a woman singing a love song specially composed for her husband on his promotion, which she was yet to be briefed about. She shouted 'Woooa' and dropped the call immediately, then she moved out of the house so as to regain her emotions. She was obviously destabilised, and the non-verbal gesture was a further confirmation of this.

Case Study III: Two smugglers planned on how to strategically get their goods into a country without the knowledge of the border officials. They were a little distance apart from each other. When the first person creeped in through an illegal route. He didn't know that border officials were lurking in front. As he looked forward to raise his head so that he could walk freely with some of the items, the officers who were lying in wait to ambush him stood up, and unconsciously, he shouted, 'Wooah!' The second smuggler wanted to run back, but he was rounded up too. They knew an end had come to their tricks. With the shout alone, an observant fellow would understand that it was a shout of defeat.

9.23. Speech Speed

Generic Interpretations of the Concept

Communication goes beyond mere uttering of words. There are many other component units that people do neglect, which negatively affect a conversation. Remember that communication has only taken place when those involved clearly understood each other. One of the most ignored aspect of communication is the speed of speaking. This is a good non-verbal indicator pointing our attention to various things. Let me submit that this gesture appears to have some cultural colourations—that is, there are some tribes who speak very fast while some are intentionally slow with their speech. In fact, this difference is noticeable in America, Asia, Africa, and some parts of Europe.

The speech of those who speak rapidly are normally clipped, and you have to listen well so as not to miss out on important words. While residents are used to this, strangers may find it difficult when communicating with a person who speaks fast and clips off some syllables in their utterances, especially if the foreigner is from a society where their speech is deliberately slow.

In short, the style adopted by an individual while speaking tells us a lot of things about them—it tells us their background, where they attended school, their philosophy, and even their age grade, among other things. However, if the change in speed of speech is sudden, it is an indication of stress. When your muscles are weak, you may find it difficult to speak the way you have always been doing. Reluctance to speak and provide answers to a sensitive poser is another reason that can bring about change to the speed of speech. After the person has spoken and you ask them to repeat himself or herself, they may not answer you again.

Scientific Explanations

Susan Dugdale (2019) defines *speech rate* as 'the term given to the speed at which you speak'. This is determined by the number of words uttered per minute. I earlier said that there are differences in speech rate across cultures in the world. So it would be inappropriate for me to give an ideal speech rate in this article. It would amount to trying to lord a culture over others. Hence, whatever I give here should be considered as being relative and to guide. Apart from culture, other factors affecting speech rate are the speaker's location, emotional state, audience, profession, fluency, subject matter, or gender. Taking all these variables into mind, there are some roughly acceptable guidelines:

Slow speech. This is less than 110 words per minute.

Conversational speech. On a slow range, it is about 120 words per minute and about 160 words per minute when it falls on a fast range.

Radio/podcast readings. They utter around 150 to 160 words per minute.

Commentators or auctioneers. They are usually on the highest speed with 250 to 400 words per minute (Dugdale 2019).

On a general note, we hardly take note of our habitual speaking habit, but if our listeners do not have issues with our speech rate, there is no cause to be bothered about it. However, outside of their normal environment, a person's speech rate may be considered as being too fast or slow. Again, if the person does not communicate with those finding his rate of speech strange on a routine basis, there is no cause for alarm. However, if you are changing your audience and purpose of speaking, you would need to work on your speech rate. For instance, if you move from Japan, which is known for its fast speech rate, to any region in Africa, which is known for its slow speech rate, through the response of your audience, you will know that you are habitually a fast speaker (Dugdale 2019).

Also, our job can draw our attention to our speech rate. A teacher who deals with a class of students from different regions of the world may need to speak slower so that his students pick every one of his words. So also is a person who deals with clients from different regions and who have to make presentations to colleagues. In fact, when it comes to public speaking, there is nothing like a 'normal' speaking rate. You must be flexible; you must possess the ability to mix and match the pace appropriately with the speech content and the audience's ability to comprehend it. If you discover that there is a need for you to change your speech rate in order not to be misunderstood, then you need to constantly train up yourself (Dugdale 2019).

Sims Wyeth (2014) writes an interesting article on how to slow down one's speech rate so as to connect with one's audience seamlessly. He gives a practical approach from an English perspective.

Practical Illustrations

Case Study I: An international expert was invited by a firm to conduct an in-house intensive training for its workforce. When the expert came around, he went straight to the hall and started his presentations. Most of his audience were squeezing their nose, and he thought maybe they were perceiving a bad smell which he was not due to his blocked nostrils. So he cracked a joke along that line, and none of his audience seemed to catch up. At that point, he knew something was wrong. He requested the attention of one of the management members who came to address the employees. It was then they made it known that they could not hear him properly. He smiled at their excuse because he was taken aback by the accusation and had to reduce the speed of his speech. After some minutes, he switched to his normal mode, and the workers frowned their face again. Then he got the message and became conscious of his speed again. That is, the workers were not pleased with the speed of his speech.

Case Study II: A teacher was employed during the holidays, and on the first day of resumption, he was assigned a class. During the interview, he had been told that the students of the school cut across cultures, but he did not know that implied the need to watch how fast he speaks. While taking the class, some of the students behaved unconcerned, and when he asked them what the issue was, he was told that they could not catch up with his speech rate. So he had to reduce his speech speed in order to ensure that the class was beneficial to them all.

Case Study III: Criminal J wanted to impersonate someone at an event; it was a masterfully planned crime in order to destabilise a country. Since the person whom he wanted to impersonate was a well-known figure to most of the audience, the impostor knew that he had to mimic his speech speed too. The person Criminal J was impersonating is a fast speaker. So he had to increase the speed of his speech. No one could pick what he said for the first five minutes. And also, he was not humorous. People became suspicious and had to cross-check if something was wrong. At the end of Criminal J's presentation, they found out he impersonated the invited guest—that is, it was later found out that he could not mimic the impersonated person perfectly.

9.24. Talking Incessantly

Generic Interpretations of the Concept

At some point or another, we have met people who can aptly be described as *talkative*. They are the set of people who do not get tired of talking. From every perspective, you would be made to believe that talking is their passion. The most painful aspect of it is that their speech is incessant; it does not add value to people. They are easily bored. Well, before painting every incessant talk as being bad, let me state that there is contextual connotation to this too. The first point of interpretation of this gesture is at the literal level—that is, there are people who just have interest in dominating every discourse context. They do not consider how others feel while they talk; they want you to listen to them all throughout while you keep your words to yourself.

In addition, talking incessantly is a show of nervousness. When people are nervous, they cover up their fear by talking endlessly. If you are not careful, you may not get to know what they are passing through. Accident can cause people to talk incessantly. In this situation, you do not need to blame the person but to serve as a support system to them. One of the aftermath of accidents is for people to keep rambling, talking non-stop. This is psychological and caused by shock.

If this happens at a party, it is a show of superiority. It means the person wants to show off. The person may be bragging about his achievements and other inconsequential things that you do not want to hear. If you do not cut them short, they may be the one talking till the end of the programme.

Scientific Explanations

Tarun Khemani (2019) discusses the psychology of talkativeness. He makes us understand that there are many reasons why people become too chatty. Most of the time, people who engage in incessant talks end up discussing themselves and nothing else. He makes it known that some people talk incessantly because they are nervous. It is their own way of coping with stress. Some people are just fond of talking of themselves without any good reason. Khemani suggests that those people may be afraid of silence. So they do everything possible to ensure that their environment does not remain silent at any point in time.

Another reason alluded to talkativeness is that some people want to appear smart. When a person who is chatty has a knowledge about a topic, they will go on and on discussing the topic because they are passionate about it and they want to show off their knowledge about it. It would be very difficult to interrupt a person of this kind. He also submits that women talk much more than men. On average, they make use of about twenty thousand words daily while men use about thirteen thousand words. A person who is outgoing will also talk more and more just in a bid to know more people and extend their chain of network.

Deborah Riegel (2018) lists ten reasons why people talk a lot. Many of the reasons she listed has been discussed by Khemani. Another reason she puts forward is that we talk incessantly with the hope of changing someone's mind. When you have facts at your disposal, you can easily convince people, but people who go to talk endlessly are those who want to persuade even when facts are against their standpoint. Further, people keep talking just to stop others from expressing themselves. This is common during staff meetings and during family holidays. Surprisingly, she notes that some people talk incessantly as a means of thinking—that is, they have to utter words before they can now ruminate on what they have said. In other words, these people are working out their mental process aloud.

Even if some people do not have anything to say, they will seize the opportunity to talk because they believe it is their turn. Their sentiment is that they should keep the privilege to themselves until they have something meaningful to say. Ideally, they should pass on this opportunity to another person in a meeting, but they do not believe in that process.

Marty Nemko (2015) states that another reason people are lured into verbosity is the illusion that others are appreciative of what they are saying. He goes on to list some of the body language gestures that show that your audience, in actually fact, do not appreciate your unending talks. Some of the gestures include sighing, tapping their feet, shaking the foot, tapping the finger, nodding impatiently, slightly turning away, and taking a step away, among other related gestures.

Practical Illustrations

Case Study I: A kid offended her mother by stealing from the pot despite the fact that she had warned her several times. The mother promised to inform her father who would mete out the appropriate punishment on her. She was always afraid of her father—no more gifts and other forms of pampering. When the father arrived from work, she was the first person who went to hug him. Funny enough, she did not allow him to rest when she started giving him the gist about what she saw in school and many other irrelevant things. When the mother came to greet her husband, after greeting him, the little girl did not allow her to say any other thing before she resumed her story. The mother stood there for an hour, and she had one thing or another to say. It was obvious her father needed to speak with his wife, but the little girl would not just let go. At some point, she had to be ordered to keep mute so that another person could talk. This was because her talk was not making any sense.

Case Study II: Man K had just won the lottery. When he got to work the next day, he wanted everyone to know what happened to him. During break, he was the first person to order for food and sat in a very pronounced place. The act, being unusual, called the attention of people to him. As he started chatting with his friend, he raised his voice so loud that every other person in the eatery could hear what he was saying. He was the only one who talked from the beginning of the break till it ended. Yet people could not make any sense of what he was trying to say.

Case Study III: Ms KL was a prostitute, and she had made it a point of duty to always connect herslf to high-paying clients, the opportunity her usual joint wasn't offering her always. So a friend of hers invited her to the party of a colleague at the office. It was a gathering of stars. Apart from her dressing, KL also ensured that she stood among men, a conspicuous place where she would be easily noticed. After an hour, she didn't see any sign of proposal coming to her. So she decided to step up her game—she started talking incessantly that the attention of everyone at the table was shifted to her. Their attention was truly shifted to her, but that did not make her wish come to fruition still.

9.25. Talking Incongruently

Generic Interpretations of the Concept

Incongruent talks can be irritating and confusing to the listener. However, the speaker does not even know that his talks are not making sense. Hence, this makes it more painful for the person listening to the talk. If this talk is orchestrated by a subordinate, you can easily stop them, but if it is done by a person you respect, you have no choice but to endure. One of the causes of incongruent talks is when the emotional side of the brain is stressed. This may be caused by an accident or a tragic occurrence. This is evidence that the ill event has overwhelmed the emotional side of the brain. Sometimes, the talks may be funny, and once people know a person for his or her incongruent talks, they would take the person for a clown—that is, they would not be willing to discuss any serious event with the person. This is an albatross to their spouses and loved ones.

Depending on the circumstances surrounding the tragic occurrence, the incongruence may be noticeable for hours or days. I have seen this in soldiers and refugees in a war zone. The usual traumatic events that they are always exposed to affects the emotional region of their brain. Sometimes, when they talk incongruently, you may be made to believe that they have gone mad, but after some days and help from the necessary people, they would get back to their senses.

Scientific Explanations

Carl Rogers was the first person who introduced the concept of incongruence in psychology in the 1950s. Although the usage of the term has now been generalised to mean inconsistent or incompatible action, Rogers was more specific in his description of the concept. In his words, *incongruence* is 'the matching of experience and awareness. *Incongruence* was therefore lacking congruence, or having feelings not aligned with your actions.' From the foregoing, we can contextualise incongruent talks as talks that do not align with the current realities of one's environment induced by psychological reasons (Fritz 2019).

Explaining the concept, Ron Fritz aptly states, 'Sometimes people say things that are contradictory to their non-verbal communication cues. The result is poor communication that leaves the listener wondering why the individual didn't say what he or she meant all along. When a person's words don't match what he or she is feeling or thinking, the communication is said to be incongruent.' If you cannot match a person's words with their non-verbal cues, it means their talk is incongruent. For instance, if a person who is obviously angry, maintaining a red face and a stern look, when asked 'How are you?' and answers with 'Fine', it means something is wrong with their utterance, making it incongruent.

David Puder (2018) rightly submits that incongruence did not start from birth; it is caused by some occurrences in life. When people cannot validate their inner experiences with outer realities, what they say becomes incongruent. For instance, as kids, we set lofty goals and pursue them, but when realities descend on us, we are forced to change them. When trying to match our childhood plans with the present realities, our talks may be incongruent.

Puder (2018) says there are five causes of incongruence. Trauma is the first on the list. A child who is perpetually exposed to its parents fighting may end up talking incongruently in life. Assigning meaning to traumatic events and establishing our beliefs around them increase our chances of being incongruent. If we do not make conscious effort in stopping it, we will end up living with it.

Having said that, Puder gives hints on how we can help people who talk incongruently to recover and get back to normalcy. Art is the first technique people can use to solve the issue of incongruence. Puder says, 'Art helps people bypass the logical areas of the brain and produce something raw and congruent to their inner experience. Painting, drawing, working with clay, or other forms of art help us connect with things deep down in our inner experience.' Then we need to dissociate ourselves from our body when we experience trauma, being true to ourselves and leaving out drugs out of the scene. People erroneously believe that taking drugs or alcohol can help them recover from their trauma, but they end up worsening it.

Practical Illustrations

Case Study I: A man was injured in an accident and had to be rushed to the hospital, and fortunately for him, his life was saved. There was nobody who saw the actual picture of the scene of the accident who would believe that those involved in the ghastly accident would survive. After some weeks, the man was discharged from the hospital and reunited with his family, where he was recuperating fully. However, the wife had noticed a change in his life. The way he now behaves and talks calls for concern but also amuses some people. Whenever he was in excruciating pain, he would be shouting 'All is well with me', yet he would be grinding his teeth, compressing his lips, pumping his cheeks, and keep the eyebrows dilated simultaneously. Hence, people wondered that if all was well with him as he claimed, why the negative body language cues? This continued for a while until he later returned to his senses with the help of his wife.

Case Study II: Recently, I met with a retired soldier who fought many wars in different regions of the world before he became incapacitated. He even had hearing impairment due to the heavy sounds he was exposed to at the war front.

Spending a week with him revealed to me that he was not emotionally stable. For instance, I remembered when speaking to him about cheating among spouses, and when he wanted to reply, he was giving political scenarios, talking of local politics that has no relevance to the issue that I raised. I also noticed this in other discussions that we had after that. It became tiring to me. I was frustrated to the extent that I never raised any serious issue with him again till I left his place. I was not used to people talking in such manner, and that would not make me be enticed to such people either.

Case Study III: A lady was stopped at the airport after discovering that her signatures were not matching—the one she signed at the airport didn't reflect the one on her passport. When the attention of airport officials was called to it, they raised a case of suspected forgery, and the lady was summoned immediately. They asked her why there were noticeable differences in her signatures, and she blamed it on *stress*, an untenable excuse. This further brought up some other questions. She began to sound incongruent and presented an obvious defective argument that could not bail her out of the situation she found herself in. Her incongruent talk and manner of presentation would easily tell any audience that she was being deceptive and could not even put up an intellectual argument.

9.26. Repetition

Generic Interpretations of the Concept

Repetition of words is not uncommon among people who are highly stressed. There are two reasons for the repetition of words: One, for the sake of emphasis. If you want to emphasise something, you would repeat the word over and over again until it sticks in the head of the targeted person. Two, words are repeated in a nonsensical manner—that is, repetition of words in a way that does not make sense. This is what I really want to expatiate on. Stress can cause people to unconsciously pronounce a word multiple times; they are just helpless about it, and that may be their own way of coping with the psychological situation. It is as if the person were stuck in a loop.

When a person is in this psychological dilemma, it may be difficult for you to help out until they are eventually relieved—that is, all your entreaties to them to say something more relevant may not get into their head at that point in time. For instance, a person struck by a car may repeatedly pronounce the word *metal* as a way of reflecting on the incident. Names of locations, items, events, people, and actions are some of the usual words repeated when people are in a psychological dilemma.

Scientific Explanations

Hazelden Foundation (2016) says that repetition of words in a nonsensical way is caused by obsessive compulsive disorder (OCD). This disorder affects a person's ability to process information without interference from any angle. 'It is often described as though the mind is stuck on "repeat" or on a loop with one constantly recurring thought or urge,' says the website. Someone who is suffering from OCD cannot let go of a thought despite all efforts to stop it. The thought ends up leading to excessive behaviour such as repetiting a word, repeatedly arranging objects, and making orders repeatedly, among other forms of obsessions. These behaviours become a ritual to the person suffering from this disorder.

Unfortunately, these behaviours have the ability to affect our relationships, work, and how we function in other spheres of life. Symptoms of OCD can be divided into obsessions and compulsions. Repetition of words fall under the latter category. The website concludes, 'People with OCD recognise the irrational nature of their thinking and behaviour but feel unable to control either.'

The repetition of syllables, words, or phrases involuntarily is known as palilalia (Critchley 1927). Palilalia is considered an aphasia, which is a language disorder and should not be confused with speech disorders. In palilalia, the person does not undergo any difficulty in pronouncing words, only that they repeat them uncontrollably. This is similar to stuttering or cluttering. Palilalia may occur in conditions affecting the prefrontal cortex or basal ganglia regions, either from physical trauma, neurodegenerative disorders, genetic disorders, or a loss of dopamine in these brain regions (Van Borsel and Tetnoswki 2007).

The number of repeats varies from an individual to the other. In a research outcome reported by Van Borsel and Tetnoswki, it was discovered that words may be repeated from a minute to about three minutes.

Ultimately, we can sum up the submissions of the scholars that repetition of words is caused by an anxiety disorder. Since it is a disorder, you must deal with people undergoing this trauma with care because it is beyond what they can control.

Practical Illustrations

Case Study I: Some terrorists were successful in their operation by carrying out a coordinated attack on three major locations in a city. One of the three locations bombed was witnessing an attack for the third time in a year. It housed about a thousand workers on a daily basis. One of the workers, a middle-aged lady, who was just arriving at work when the incident occurred was traumatised and started shouting 'bomb' repeatedly. She had escaped the second one by a whisk, and when this one happened, the old memory came up, which made her repeat the word uncontrollably. She was so scared that she did not know how the words were coming out of her mouth. Even when emergency workers at the site were calling her attention to what she was saying, she did not mind them. She was later taken to the hospital where she was given bed rest. The fact that she was not aware of all that she was saying means she was not psychologically balanced.

Case Study II: A university student was apprehended and accused of cultism by his school authorities. Although he denied this in his statement, but he was still informed that he would face the students' disciplinary committee of the institution where he would be explaining himself. As the norm is everywhere, he was to be in an academic gown any time he was to appear before the committee. The case lingered on for about four weeks. The committee is made up of professors and student leaders of the school. Any time he appeared before the committee, he would be sweating profusely within thirty minutes due to the intellectual rigours he was passing through. At the end of the sittings, it was discovered that he was indeed a cult member, but he was truly repentant, and that made the school pardon him, warning that if he should appear before the committee for anything again, he was to be expelled. Of particular interest was how he repeated some words. He repeated them to the extent that a member of the committee had to ask him what the words really meant, and it was that point that it was discovered that he used them in the sense of the idiosyncrasies used in their cult group. That was actually the starting point of his confession.

Case Study III: Because he renounced his membership of the cult group without informing other members of the group, which they considered as an abomination, they planned to implicate him. During the end of the semester examinations, one of them cunningly went to his desk and pasted some incriminating materials related to the course they were to write before the commencement of the examination. As the examination started, their invigilator was checking through when his eyes caught the incriminating materials. He went up to the student and asked him to explain the reason for bringing in exhibits into the examination hall, but he was taken aback by the wrong accusation until the invigilator pointed at it. He denied any knowledge about it, but the invigilator told him that he would appear before the SDC to explain himself. Immediately after he heard the name of the committee, he felt cold and started mentioning SDC repeatedly. This repetition was borne out of fear.

9.27. Speed of Response

Generic Interpretations of the Concept

There are different ways in which people respond to queries, and how we all respond to people's questions has something to say about our intent and ideology. For instance, some people will respond to your questions even before you utter the last word. They have an idea of what you want to know since you opened your mouth to speak. Depending on the context of its occurrence, this behaviour can be interpreted in different ways. For instance, if you are speaking with a superior and he gives you an answer before you finish speaking, what he is trying to say is that he does not have time to waste over the issues you are querying him about. So it is a subtle means of shutting you down. If this is done by your student, it is a means of showing you how smart they are.

Some others will take their time to respond to your questions. They will start talking, pause, and then continue with their talks. This means the person is relaxed and feeling confident. A person who does not have anything to hide will take their time to explain themselves. Conversely, this may also be a means of buying time. A person who does not want you to pronounce bad judgement on them will take their time to respond so as not to give you time to speak. So a slow response rate may be an antic of delay.

Ultimately, how fast a person gives answers to your questions shows their thinking pattern and how they process information. A fast thinker would respond immediately while a slow thinker will have to process information slowly before giving you a response. The issue at hand also plays a role in the response time of people. If it is just a mere conversation between friends, they will respond quickly because they know that nothing is at stake. More so, they are in a relaxed position, but if it happens to be an interview setting or a formal gathering, people will think thoroughly before responding to any question so as not to implicate themselves.

As you take all these factors into consideration, remember that speed of response is grounded on cultural affiliation of a person and their mental ability.

Scientific Explanations

According to Heather Walker (2014), one of the reasons for slow response is age. This is very intuitive in many people across the world. As we get older, our brain becomes weak, and it will be slow when processing information. Thus, if you ask an elderly person a question, they will process it more slowly compared with people in other age groups. Giving a scientific evidence for this, Walker says, 'Some compelling evidence suggests that such a decline reflects wear and tear of the white matter in the brain, which is made up of all the wires, or axons, that connect one part of the brain to another. Slowed information transfer along axons may impede processing speed.'

Other factors such as high blood pressure, diabetes, smoking, and other vascular risk factors can wear down the white matter in the brain, which can culminate into a slow response time. Walker explains further, 'In other individuals, slowed processing speed could be the first sign of a neurodegenerative illness, such as Alzheimer's disease. Head trauma, including concussions, may play a role.'

Providing a study guide to its students, the University of Leicester urges people to listen to all parts of questions before responding to it. If a person is brought up in this environment, their response time would be slow because after listening to a question, they would go ahead to process it adequately before giving you a response. This is to make sure that they understand you and do not respond out of context.

CogniFit, a website dedicated to improving the cognitive ability of people across the world, lists three factors that determine response time—perception, processing, and response. What causes delay between perception and response is the processing. How fast it takes a person to process a piece of information will determine how rapidly they will respond to their perception. If any part of the aforelisted processes is altered, it would affect response time.

Practical Illustrations

Case Study I: A man summoned his wife to their private room after their early morning prayer. The first question he asked her was, 'How was your night?' which she replied 'Fine' immediately without thinking. Then the husband asked, 'Where were you yesterday night?' She first opened her mouth and then closed it without any word coming out. She had to reflect on what could have possibly given birth to such a question in an unusual way. She looked at her husband in the eye and responded with 'Why the question?' which the husband encouraged her to provide holistic answers to. Then she thought of the events of the previous night again and replied to him. The reason the response time between the first and second questions differs is due to the likely implications of the two questions. For the first one, there was nothing to be afraid of, but for the second, it could end the marriage.

Case Study II: The chairman of a fast-growing company was about to employ another managing director after parting ways with the former one. In the process of interviewing the likely people to succeed the former one, he saw a bright mind who appeared to be answering all his questions adequately among the candidates. So he asked him the most important question which would determine his fate concerning the job. The question was, 'How do you merge your novel ideas with the current proven policies of the firm to birth an unrivaled company?' He looked at the chairman, sighed, and looked down. After taking a deep breath, he began his response to the question. Responding to this question took him more time than all that he had first answered because it was very technical, and he needed more time to process the information.

Case Study III: A young lady was found to have been on the services of a firm on illegal terms. When she was apprehended, she was too fearful to deny that fact. So the firm set up a panel to understand her reasons for doing that and for how long she had been on an illegal employment with them—this was to understand her modus operandi. She knew that whatever she said was to be used against her. When asked for how long she had been receiving wages from the company, it took her minutes to respond. She acted as if she were lost in thought for a question whose response she knew. This means she was extra vigilant of the responses she supplied in order not to indict herself before the committee.

9.28. Speeding through Comments

Generic Interpretations of the Concept

Patience settles all things and makes what looks impossible work without hassle. Unfortunately, patience now appears to be one of the rarest ingredients in today's world. In other words, being unnecessarily fast is not always the best while answering a question. For a question to be adequately answered, there are many things to consider, and if you decide to neglect them, you may be portrayed as being ignorant or foolish in some cases. For instance, if you write an apology to a person and he or she speeds through it, the apology will lose its value at that point—it makes it look mechanical and contrived. That is, doing it just for the purpose of doing it and nothing—no emotions evoked or pity on the person! This can be painful to the writer of the apology and render you useless, even after it has appeared that the person has accepted your apologies.

Just as in apologies, the same thing applies to showering encomiums on people or when you are welcoming others. If you rush to them, they lose their meaning. The simple message here is that the aforementioned actions derive their purpose through meaningful time spent in doing them and not the actual words uttered or written. Hence, you need to learn how to take your time when apologising, praising, or welcoming someone and vice versa.

There are many interpretations given to the action of speeding through an apology written by another person to you. One, it means we are socially anxious. There are people who exercise social anxiety for one reason or another. They may be shy or do not fancy meeting new people. This fear pushes them into handling social activities in a wrong way. Another interpretation given to this action is that the person is reluctant to carry out the action. If you apologise to a person and he or she rushes through your comments, it means they are reluctant to forgive you. In the same vein, a person who does it hurriedly may not be truly remorseful; they are just apologising for the sake of fulfilling all righteousness. And finally, such gesture may be taken to mean lack of conviction. If you are not convinced about an action, you would not do it committedly.

Well, we are able to arrive at all these possible interpretations through the non-verbal cue of the speed of talking. The action is tantamount to glancing over an important document. It means we do not accord the proper attention it deserves to it. Always remember that communication is a two-sided action. If the other party is not satisfied, communication has not yet taken place.

Scientific Explanations

Macmillan Dictionary states that hasty comments is evidence of 'not showing careful thought or good judgement'. When a comment is made in a hasty manner, it means it is done in a hurry without carefully planning or thinking about it. This makes the comment lose its value, especially when it is obvious to your co-interlocutor that you did not give their comment the attention it deserves.

Heidi Halvorson (2011) states it clearly that quick decisions create regret, even when they are good decisions. When something is done in a way where it is not given a careful thought, it would most probably backfire. All humans want to be loved and given the needed attention. If you do not do this to them when you have the capability to, when the table turns against you, they may repay you in the same coin; and that is when the regret comes in. Hence, our experience of choosing is tied to the quality of time. Halvorson warns against making comments based on little information at our disposal. He says further, 'But even if speedy decisions aren't necessarily bad ones, they still have a significant downside—they *feel* wrong. The popularity of blink notwithstanding, people seem to implicitly believe that a quick choice is always a bad one.' This quote explains my argument in clear terms—the feeling you create in others through how you make your comment is what matters most.

Practical Illustrations

Case Study I: A child offended his father, and as a way of showing the child that he was really pained by the behaviour of his child, the father stopped many things he used to do for him. The child was embittered, and after deep reflections, he decided to send his mother to help him apologise to his dad. But that did not seem to be effective. So when the father returned from his business trip the following day, he was the first to welcome him back. After the man had rested, his child went to meet him, very remorseful, and appealed to him, making him understand that his behaviour was triggered by childishness. Before he could finish talking, the father told him to stand up and go, that he had forgiven him already. But the whole scene did not make sense to the child; he was expecting his father to, at least, make some few comments and then hug him as a way of demonstrating that he had truly forgiven him. So he felt empty by his father's actions.

Case Study II: A young man went out with his date, and after some hours, they departed. They were just getting to know each other, and it seemed they were both sunk in love already. So when the lady got home, she was not satisfied with the quality of time they spent with each other. So she made up her mind to pass the night in the guy's place. She picked up her phone and gave him a ring, informing him of her decision. He told her that she was free to come over. She took a cab to the guy's place. Upon getting there, the guy was a little bit tired. After opening the door for her, he greeted her passingly and moved in to get some other things done. For a moment, the lady felt worthless and wanted to return to her house; the guy did not take his time to welcome her, despite giving him such a huge surprise treat.

Case Study III: An expert human smuggler had targeted a time when border officials would not be on duty in order to allow him to pass freely or, at least, with less drills. However, he ran out of luck this time around as the officials were still fully on ground when he got to the border with his victims. The way the passengers were seated was questionable. And when the first official who saw the sitting arrangement made a comment on that, he quickly interjected by saying that 'the passengers opted for such arrangement due to the economic situation of the country'. This was done in order to stop the official from asking further questions that could give him out.

9.29. Use of Filler Sounds

Generic Interpretations of the Concept

There are many forms of filler sounds across cultures. But for the sake of this study, we will adopt English ones so as to give us a common ground for discussion. Sounds such as *hum, ahh, ehh,* and *well,* among others are considered as filler sounds. The clearing of throat, hesitation, and coughing are some other actions considered to be filler sounds used by people while speaking to indicate that they are momentarily in short of words. When people are speaking and short of words, instead of keeping mute, they believe using sounds to fill the void is the best decision at that point in time. When you go mute, you may end up losing the attention of your audience. So filler sounds serve the duty of keeping the attention of your audience until the time you find the most appropriate word to express yourself.

I have travelled round the world and discovered that this concept is not limited to any particular culture; the sounds may be different, but almost every culture makes use of filler sounds. When you see someone make use of filler sounds, it means they are struggling for the right words to express themselves. So you are doing them a favour if you do not interrupt in what they are saying so as to help them think through.

Another possible interpretation given to this is that the speaker is buying time so as to enable them to recall an experience. The person does not want to present you with an inaccurate report. So while they are mentioning the filler sounds, they are also thinking simultaneously. The verbal translation of the filler sound in this context is, 'Wait for me while I try recalling the actual event.'

You may be wondering why we regarded filler sounds as non-verbals; they are considered a paralanguage because they are not actual words and are used in the expression of our heart in a subtle manner, which is a sharp deviation from what verbal utterances are used for.

Scientific Explanations

It is so unfortunate that people regard filler words as a sign of ineptness and stupidity. Linguists are not beginning to condemn that notion, noting that it is unfair. According to Olivia Blair (2017), people who often make use of filler sounds are conscious of the person they are talking to. Professor Michael Handford, a professor of applied linguistics and English language at Cardiff University says that discourse markers (filler sounds) perform two basic functions—interactional and cognitive. He explains that the interactional function deals with politeness— that is, if you invite a friend to an occasion and the person turns down your invite without the use of filler sounds, they may probably appear rude to you. For instance, if the person says 'Um, well, you know, sorry' and then make their intent known, it is much politer without the use of any filler sound. So the politeness function it plays cannot be wished off.

He explains that the cognitive use of filler sounds is when we are trying to process complex information. Handford notes that this is important for both the speaker and the listener. In actual sense, if we speak the way we write, we will not be able to process information, and that means communication may not take place in our discourse. When we speak too complexly, our co-interlocutor may find it difficult to understand, so we make unconscious use of the filler sounds in order to help them process what we have said before saying any other thing. Blair (2017) explains, 'This goes for ourselves as well, the reason we tend to over-fill these pauses is when we are not sure of what we are saying, think job interview or if a stranger stops you in the street to ask for directions to a place you are not too familiar with.'

To Richard Nordquist (2018), the use of filler words by some people may simply be a sign of nervousness. Such people are afraid of silence and, as such, will rather fill the void with mere sounds while they think of the next thing to say. A research carried out by experts from Columbia University submits that the use of filler words means the person is in search of words. Another reason put forward by Blair is that the use of filler words means the person will surely ask a question you put forward to them, even if they are pausing for a moment. This means the person has a bit of difficulty planning what they are going to say.

'Whatever the reason, the cure for filler words is preparation. You reduce nervousness and pre-select the right ways to say ideas through preparation and practice' (Timm and Bienvenu 2011).

Practical Illustrations

Case Study I: 'Hey, hey, *shh, shh, shh*. Come on. Be sensitive to the fact that other people are not comfortable talking about emotional disturbances. Um, you know, I am. I'm fine with that, but . . . other people . . .' (Owen Wilson as Dignan in *Bottle Rocket*, 1996). The use of filler words here is an indication that he or she is not psychologically in shape—that is, the person is mentally disorganised.

Case Study II: Pierce: 'About those *filler words* of yours. I mean, nobody wants to buy brownies from somebody who says "um" and "like". I have a method for fixing that. Start from the top.'

Shirley: 'Okay. These brownies are, uh—'

Pierce: '*Uh!*'

Shirley: 'They . . . um—'

Pierce: '*Um!*'

Shirley: 'These brownies are delicious. They taste like—'

Pierce: '*Like!*'

Shirley: 'That's not a filler word.'

Pierce: 'Whatever, valley girl.'

(Chevy Chase and Yvette Nicole Brown in 'Environmental Science', *Community*, 19 November 2009)

Case Study III: The general manager of SZT Vehicle Manufacturing Company needed to address his employees on an important issue. He started thus: 'I welcome you all to this all-important meeting. *Well*, as many of you have known that, *ah, I mean*, as many of you might have heard before, know that we are moving from this, *um*, location. *Well*, I think it is for the overall good of every one of us. *You see*, if we do not change, we would be changed.' The use of filler words in this sense is to help him select the right words.

Case Study IV: Child KH forged his father's documents in order to have access to his bank account. However, as he was hurriedly doing the forgery, he mixed up some things that were later discovered by the banker processing his request. When his attention was called to it, he became destabilised and opted for the use of filler words to cover up the shame. He said, '*Errm*, well, let me have a look at it. I think, *errrm*, the error was due to, *hmmm* …' The banker became suspicious at this point and said that except the corrections were effected, his transaction couldn't be processed. The child was incongruent throughout, and in such a delicate situation, an observant fellow would easily know that something was wrong, which the banker did.

9.30. Clearing of the Throat or Coughing

Generic Interpretations of the Concept

When we face some certain illnesses, we may cough and clear our throat. When some people are exposed to cold, they may also cough or experience a blocked throat. I have noticed that if we do not speak for a long duration of time and later have the opportunity to do so, what we first do is clear our throat so that we can be properly heard. Apart from these possible conditions, coughing or clearing of the throat has some roles to play in the non-verbal context. When we have to deal with something herculean and tackle a difficult question, we do clear our throat or cough. This is a subtle means of relieving stress before giving such task a trial. When a question is challenging, we would be careful about rushing into answering so as not to give a one-sided answer, especially if such is asked in a formal context. The time we use in clearing our throat gives us the opportunity to think more and approach the question from a safe side.

In some rare circumstances, I have also noticed that when some individuals are telling lies, they do cough or clear their throat. Let me quickly add that this is not a good or a reliable indicator of deception in whatever guise. After all, honest individuals also display the same gesture when they are tense or nervous. Nervousness affects the muscles of the nasal cavity and increases blood flow into the nerves. Before you can regard this gesture as a signal of deception, there must be more pointers to this direction. As I have always said, you should not take signs of stress as those of deception until you get the person to confess verbally. With this, you would be able to clear your doubts and be certain that you are not making wrong inferences.

Scientific Illustrations

Joseph Hindy (2019) shares the same sentiment with me as explained above. According to him, 'People clear their throat for a variety of reasons. Sometimes you may be ill and you have some stuff stuck back there.' However, if they do this in a perfectly normal social context, it is an indication of anxiety or nervousness. If you are used to watching stand-up comedy and after the comedian has cracked their jokes no one laughed at them, you would see them cough into their mic. Another use of this gesture is to show irritation. However, in most situations, it is used by people to mean they are not comfortable, and you would need to dig deeper so as to understand the cause of their discomfort.

Lauren Misak (2019) says that the gesture of coughing or clearing of the throat is caused by some thoughts, making the person uncomfortable. According to Misak, 'Coughing means you want to say something, but you're holding back.' In the same vein, Christopher Philip (2013) lends a voice to this discourse by aligning with the earlier submissions that throat clearing is a body language of discomfort. He categorises it under the closed body language where people hold some certain thoughts to themselves. He also expresses that the signs of discomfort can be a hint for discovering lies. When a person clears their throat frequently when they are not suffering any allergies, it means we must pay great attention to what they are saying. Being uncomfortable may make them hide their nervousness under this gesture.

The view that the act of throat clearing may be an indicator of deception is also shared by Trent Smith (2016). The scholar tries to distinguish between the throat-clearing gesture that indicates lying and one that points at stress. He opens his article by saying that 'throat clearing accompanied by an Adam's apple jump tends to signal deception. Throat clearing along with an Adam's apple jump indicates stress and anxiety. Liars experience cognitive overload and the fight-or-flight response.' He quickly warns that for us to determine if throat clearing signals deception or not, we must first establish a baseline of the person being interviewed when they have no reason to tell lies. This is very important so as not to make our effort futile.

Practical Illustrations

Case Study I: A lady from one of the low-contact cultures went on a date with a Westerner. They were becoming fond of each other, and that demanded them to talk and crack some jokes so often. However, the lady from the low-contact culture had not overcome the issue of maintaining eye contact for a while despite living in a Western nation for about three years. Ideally, she expected that when the guy looks at him, he should concentrate on another thing immediately but vice versa because the guy was also expecting her to look at him more so that they could communicate more intently through non-verbal cues. When the lady was become anxious due to the eye contact of the guy, she began to cough frequently in order to cover up her anxiety.

Case Study II: A group of interrogators were interviewing a suspected terrorist with the aim of gathering evidence against him so as to sue him. The suspect was exposed and learnt. Hence, he knew the likely consequences of his actions. The suspect had thought that many of his activities were hidden from law enforcement officials, but he was befuddled by the level of allegations raised against him, which he had to defend. At some point, it was very glaring that he could not mentally cope with the magnanimity of the allegations; he was obviously stressed, and he was losing his voice to the stress. He began to frequently clear his throat as a way of relieving himself of the stress. Despite this cover-up, when you observe some other parts of his body and facial appearance, you could easily establish what he was going through.

Case Study III: Not in his habit, a man came home later from work, which baffled his wife. Upon getting home, she asked him what caused his delay at work. Knowing his wife very well, he decided to cook up a story so as to not to put his marriage in danger. While feigning tiredness, he cleared his throat and managed to cough before fabricating his story, which did not sound convincing to the wife. The wife was convinced within herself that he was being deceptive.

9.31. Whistling in a Nervous Manner

Generic Interpretations of the Concept

This gesture is a form of *cathartic exhaling* earlier discussed in this section of our study. It is a great means of relieving stress. From experience, it has been discovered that this cue is a good means of self-pacifying, and that is why we tend to do it when travelling by ourselves through a desolate or dark area. It is as if we were gathering strength from within as a means of dealing with the situation in our hands. It is less surprising that we see people whistle nervously when they feel uncomfortable, even when they are alone. Whistling somewhat disconnects you from the realities of your environment and connects you with your inner vitality.

While whistling is a natural part of some people, it is a means of relieving stress to many others. If you do pay attention to characters in movies, you would discover that those who are portrayed whistling are those walking through a cemetery or undergoing difficult situations as a means of warding off their apprehension. Even when a husband and wife are having a disagreement, the former may take to whistling as a means of relieving the stress of the moment while feigning a carefree attitude; the fact is that he is feeling the heat of the moment, only that he does not want to accept it so as not to be painted as being weak.

Scientific Explanations

Christopher Philip (2013) defines *whistling* as 'blowing air over the lips and teeth to produce a high-pitched sound—often producing a "tune" with varying music notes'. Most times, the person who is whistling is trying to sing a known song, while in some other times, especially when they are highly stressed, it is just mere production of sounds. In the view of Philip, if whistling is done in an atmosphere where nothing threatens the peace of the blower, it is a show of contentment. When you do not have anything bothering your mind, you may decide to whistle in a relaxed state. However, if it is done nervously, it signifies the desire to be pacified. The body language researcher notes that these two parallel interpretations make the concept context-specific.

According to Farouk Radwan (2017), whistling connotes anxiety. He, however, states that we must find at least two other signals pointing to this fact before we can conclude that a person is anxious. He lists sweating, jiggling of pocket's content, fidgeting, fingernail biting, and tapping of the fingers as some other gestures to look out for in order to establish our doubt. Anxiety makes the mental resources of a person get occupied, and as such, the process power of the person's brain dwindles. This is why anxious people are lost in finding the right word or action to express themselves. So what they do is to unconsciously pacify themselves before returning back to what they were doing. Whistling anxiously is a pacifying act usually employed by people while going through dark moments, whether psychologically or physically.

Scott Tousley (2019), while explaining a practical, science-backed approach of dealing with stress and increasing confidence, mentions whistling as a proven means of getting this done in three minutes. Tousley notes that when people force themselves to whistle, it deals badly with stress and increases the confidence of the person. This furthers explains why people walking through a cemetery do whistle—they need the two ingredients of stress relieving and confidence booster. Passing through a difficult moment stresses you, while you also need inner confidence so as to be able to deal with a situation.

From what we have considered thus far, there is no gainsaying that whistling plays an unimaginable role in the affairs of men while going through issues.

Practical Illustrations

Case Study I: A man and his wife were having a disagreement over some critical issues. The issues seemed to be recurring, and right from the outset, he had always been known to be easy-going with the wife being otherwise. Everything playing out showed that the wife was taking the advantage of the husband's gentility to raise needless issues and push him out of his patience. On this particular occasion, the husband came back from work feeling tired and also thinking of how to augment his income so as to be able to give their kids the best education. Suddenly, the wife started her issues concerning some trivial things at home. She was prancing up and down as if she wanted to assault the husband. At first, the man wanted to react in a like manner but could not gather his inner strength for such an activity. So he went to the bedroom, whistling nervously, and locked himself in until the wife was done with her mild madness in the living room. Perhaps his wife also read the signals of nervousness on his face and decided to let it go.

Case Study II: A part of the country had been boiling for the past few months over terrorist activities. Apart from civilians, many law enforcement officials sent to the region had been killed. From all indications, it appeared as if the terrorists were better armed than the uniformed men. So no law enforcement official prayed to be deployed to that region for whatever reason. In its latest deployment exercise, more men were recalled from their duty posts in order to go and give reinforcement to their counterparts at the war-torn zone. Many of the officials deployed were gripped by fear. On their way to the region, they were recounting the ordeals of their counterparts, and this further sent anxiety down their nerves. Unconsciously, the soldier sitting beside the driver began to whistle nervously until they arrived at their destination. This means a lot of negative thoughts were flowing in his mind.

Case Study III: Mr S was the general manager of DTQ Enterprises. All his men had submitted their monthly report, and he was going through it one after the other. The entire report could be summarised as a sham, nothing different from the past month. The enterprise was fast losing its grip as a growing firm. Mr S had thought of every innovative approach that he knew, but they proved to be abortive or his men were simply not catching up. After thinking on the next line of action, he unconsciously began to whistle till he left his office that evening. This means he was not sure of the level of success of the step that he was about to take. In other words, he was afraid of the risk that was attached to his proposed next action.

9.32. Tut-Tutting

Generic Interpretations of the Concept

Tut-tutting can be described as the use of the tongue and teeth to make intentional noise as a means of showing disagreement. To do this, the tongue is placed against the back of the front teeth and the upper palate, and then the person inhales rapidly, which causes the person to make a sharp, quick sound audible enough for the targeted person to hear. In many societies of the world, it is used to show that a person does not share the same view with another. Also, it is used to call the attention of someone to something which is considered inappropriate. If you are outside with your spouse or kids and you think they are getting something wrong yet you do not want to shout or call the attention of others to that thing, you can make use of this gesture to get their attention and correct them.

In some other contexts, it is used to shame people. In the Western world, this gesture is usually noticeable in concerts with the waving of a finger as a means of showing that a transgression has occurred and has been noticed. In the home front, parents commonly display this gesture when their kids are about to misbehave as a way of calling them to order.

Scientific Explanations

Tut-tut is defined as 'an exclamation made for the purpose of showing disapproval or annoyance'. *Collins English Dictionary* puts it thus: 'Tut-tut is used in writing to represent the sound that you make with your tongue touching the top of your mouth when you want to indicate disapproval, annoyance, or sympathy. If you tut-tut about something, you express your disapproval of it, especially by making a sound with your tongue touching the top of your mouth.' However, we are not concerned about its usage in writing but how it is verbally used for the purpose of showing our state of mind at a given moment.

We cannot underplay the importance and essence of the tongue in non-verbal communication. Changing Minds (2019) expertly notes, 'With mouth closed and tongue inside the mouth, you can still sometimes see what it is doing, although this is a hidden action and often the person themselves does not realise they are doing this.' The use of tut-tutting is a little bit different as it is intentionally done to communicate an emotion. When the tongue is placed behind the teeth and made to touch the hard palate, the mouth slightly opens through which the person inhales air in a snappy manner to indicate that something is wrong. If what the other person is doing does not please them, it is a means of showing their annoyance. In the workplace where it is not very OK to get emotional, if a colleague is going through some turbulent times, it is a means of sympathising with them.

Mary Bond (2013) also tries to give the description of the right posture of the tongue. She notes that when the tongue is pressed against the upper palate, it flattens the tongue and makes the mouth become smaller, rightly positioning it to make the needed sound. Also, it would be noted that when this gesture is displayed, it gives the entire face a new look which suggests that something is wrong. It makes the person appear as if he or she were frowning—that is, it is widely assumed that the cue is employed to describe negative emotions.

It is pertinent to note that we cannot discountenance the lips from the whole process. In the words of Changing Minds, 'In emoting, the lips play a major role in creating visible shapes, with able backup from the teeth and tongue.' Whatever happens between the teeth and tongue, it is the lips that give the final outcome, being the outer part of the mouth. Without the lips slightly opening, it would not produce the rapid sound that sends the intended message to the target.

Practical Illustrations

Case Study I: Two friends were having discussions concerning some policies affecting their country and the world in general. They both shared different political views, which further made the conversation intense. At first, it seemed they were both frustrated about the policies due to how they were not making the needed gains in their respective businesses, but the point of divergence was created immediately. Friend A tried to compare the policies with those of the ruling party in their country, which Friend B was sympathetic of. Friend A pleaded that he should be given the opportunity to express himself. After his long talk, Friend B first placed his tongue at the back of his upper teeth and palate and then made a quick sound before registering his disagreement concerning what his friend said. With the making of the sound, his friend knew whatever he would say would not align with what he had said earlier—that is, he was envisaging the disagreement.

Case Study II: The mother of Kid V had just finished preparing a delicious meal, which V confessed to have enjoyed. She ate to the extent that she began to feel uncomfortable at the table, a behaviour the mother had always warned her against. The mother decided to overlook it at this particular time because the meal was truly delicious, and one could not totally write off those incidents from kids once in a while. However, she became furious when Kid V was going to the refrigerator to get some snacks when it was obvious that she was still struggling to breathe over the food she had just consumed. The mother looked at her, placed her tongue at the back of her front teeth and upper palate, and rapidly inhaled by making a sharp sound, which sent fears down the nerves of her daughter. V turned back and returned to the chair without the mother having to utter a word. V got the message that her mother did not approve her action; she knew this through her mother's non-verbal action.

Case Study III: A new employee in a company seemed to have only a confidante in the whole organisation. She was the only person who understood some technicalities of the firm, one of the main reasons she was employed. As such, she was always overburdened with work. It was becoming obvious to her, and when her confidante visited her desk, she opened up on her ordeal. Her colleague was really moved by her story and tut-tuts before telling her to take care, lest she was met at the wrong place by their boss. This means she was not ready for a long story that could possibly land her in a situation that she did not envisage.

Case Study IV: Criminal GV was stopped at the entrance of a company for allegedly providing the officials there with wrong information. At first, he argued vehemently, noting that it wasn't the first time he would be visiting the firm. However, the officials insisted that their checks showed that there were many things wrong with his documents. The senior official later invited GV to his office and pointed out all the inadequacies on his document to him. Noticing that he had no superior argument, he moved his tongue to the back of his upper teeth and then inhaled, making a quick sound before tendering his apologies. However, he was sent back all the same. The non-verbal gesture he made was to depict how he believed in the superiority of his argument.

9.33. Laughter

Generic Interpretations of the Concept

Universally, laughter is used to showcase bemusement, joy, and happiness. When we laugh, we hardly feel any pain physically and emotionally. You would hardly see someone who is emotionally down laugh. True laughter is a public exhibition that all is well with us. Laughter endears people to us as we communicate with them through the act that we are happy and welcoming. In short, laughing is a signifier of the fact that we are not stressed. There is little wonder some people postulate that the act of laughing may have risen in us a protective evolutionary benefit.

The above gives a general view about the concept. However, there are different types of laughter. Unrestrained cackles is the kind of laughter you see on people when they are being told a genuinely funny joke. This kind of laughter is not feigned because it was never planned. Everyone in that environment will laugh deeply because the joke is really hilarious. Another form of laughter is that of joyous laughter of children. Children are carefree, and little things amuse them. At their age, they have not been really exposed to feigning emotions for getting undeserved benefits. That is why you see them cry or laugh passionately. Whatever emotion they are expressing, they do it with their whole heart. That is why the joyous laughter of a kid is always contagious. The third form is the obsequious laughter. This is usually done with the intent of flattering a leader. The leader may not have said anything funny, but they really want to laugh as a way of making the leader feel good about himself. This is commonly seen among followers who want to get one thing or another from the leader.

From the foregoing, it would be discovered that the manner in which someone laughs matters a lot, and as such, we should try to examine each form of laughter as a means of determining the true depth of sentiment behind each. Also, taking cognisance of the context at each time will help us have a better understanding of emotions behind each kind of laughter.

Scientific Explanations

A consensus reached among scholars who contributed to this subject matter is that laughter is universal. According to Nathaniel Scharping (2016), 'From hearty belly laughs to polite chuckles, laughter underpins our more enjoyable social interactions.' That is, laughter is evidence of the fact that we are enjoying an interaction. Some people have always upheld that laughing is the extreme form of smiling, but their origins are quite different. While smiling is considered a submissive act, laughter is said to be somewhat aggressive. 'This is especially true to the kind of laugh that children use when ridiculing one another in the playground and when adults make hostile jokes against ethnic out-groups' (Wilson 2016).

Another form of laughter described by Wilson is tension relief, which he says is nearer to crying. This begins as an adjustment to the laugh that takes place when a kid identifies its mother and danger suddenly flies away. It is just like coming out of a crash unscathed. This emotion-laden event is making you laugh not because anything was funny but because of the relief that you came out without injuring yourself.

According to Westside Toastmasters (2019), a laughing face is not all that different from a tearful one. That is why some people, most probably women, shed joyful tears. Laughing is some people's method of reacting to shock or embarrassment. The website aptly submits that 'genuine laughter increases breathing, while lowering blood pressure and heart rate. Crying, as uniquely human as laughing, may accompany laughter and may be as much a sign of joy and relief as of shock or sadness.' However, many rules come to play as to the form of laughter that is acceptable across the world. In some societies, people are free to open their mouth wide and laugh hysterically while this is considered as rude and unethical in some given instances. In East Asia, for instance, many of them cover their mouth while smiling, let alone laughing. The website goes ahead to explain that there is a physiological evidence that laughter has positive effects on us.

Scharping (2016) says the way people laugh is enough to know their intent. In a research carried out by scholars from University of California, it was discovered that we can use the sounds of laughter to know if those interacting are friends or not. This is overwhelming when it comes to gender. The study was able to prove that our vocalisations differ depending on the circumstances we meet ourselves. Scharping reports an aspect of the outcome of the research thus: 'Acoustic qualities such as louder laughs and greater variations of pitch and volume were noted in laughter between friends, characteristics of spontaneity, and likely a result of greater familiarity and the accordingly lesser impulse to restrain our behaviour.' The study also outlines the difference in gender and how it plays out in our laughter.

Practical Illustrations

Case Study I: A young lady was celebrating her twenty-first birthday anniversary. With the help of her parents, the party turned big, and many of her friends graced the occasion. As a way of making the party more interactive, the master of ceremony compelled the celebrant to tell the gathering how she met the love of her life. Though very shy, she held the microphone and started thus: 'I was a young, innocent girl going about my normal businesses on campus when this serious-looking man started running after me.' She pointed at the direction of her fiancé, which made many people focus their attention on him and laugh. She continued, 'I thought there was war in the school and, as such, was confused at his action. Only for him to ask for my attention.' At this point, people began to laugh out loud. Smiling all through, she further said, 'I snubbed him and walked away, but this guy would not stop monitoring me both in the spirit, soul, and body.' At this point, the whole venue went wild, and the MC collected the microphone from her. This was a show of joy and excitement.

Case Study II: Mr JX was the director of his company. As the president of the firm, he didn't look down on anyone. He would also leave his door open for anyone to advise him on any issue affecting the firm. This means his employees could joke with him. One day, Ms KF, one of the employees, teased her colleague Mr YT, who came late to work that day that Mr JX said he should report to him. Gripped with fear, Mr YT rushed down to the director's office, and he was asked if it was his wife who gave him early morning 'tea' that made him come late. They both laughed heartily, and he went back to his desk. It was an undeniable sign of excitement between the interlocutors.

Case Study III: Child A had always boasted that he could ride a bicycle, but his mates kept on doubting him because they had never seen him ride any. One day, the parents of Child G bought a bicycle for him, and he brought it out, practising in the neighbourhood. When Child A came out, they all dared him to ride the bicycle to prove his expertise. Seeing it was an overwhelming dare, he grudgingly took the challenge. However, within two minutes, he was down on the turf, and immediately, his peers started laughing at him. The laughter was so loud that he had to join them—that is, instead of him getting angry with the mockery, he was rather lured into joining them; he could not resist the excitement on the faces of his peers.

Case Study IV: When criminals are on operation, you will think that they don't laugh, but in real fact, when they record victory, they celebrate it with laughter, champagne, and lots more. A repentant criminal once narrated a scene to me. According to him, they went for an operation one day, and their plans failed woefully. They stood in the mall and started laughing to each other. This was funny to the people around them, and it got the attendants in the mall distracted. While the attendants were distracted, the third person in the gang quietly and quickly carted away some items, and this time around, they laughed so hard and then bought some items to cover it up. This laughter was that of victory and mockery over those whom they successfully played on their intelligence.

CHAPTER 10

The Lips

Apart from making us beautiful and handsome through covering the teeth, the lips are full of messages. Being a part of the face shows that there is no way we can overlook them while trying to read meanings to cues. This means that we need to understand the structure, movement, and shape of the lips to have a better understanding of the non-verbal messages of the face. In order to make them more attractive, women paint them with lipstick, matching the colour of what they're wearing. We all purse our lips in front of our smartphones so as to take selfies. Some even go as far as injecting them with collagen so as to look younger than their age. And sometimes, we intentionally lick the lips just to keep them moist. All these actions are precursors to the fact that we can understand the emotions and intents of others by paying rapt attention to what goes round in the lips.

As it is our norm in this book, let's first consider the scientific aspect of the concept before streamlining it to body language interpretations. The upper and lower lips are referred to as the labium superius oris and labium inferius oris, respectively. The editors of *Encyclopaedia Britannica* define the lips as 'soft pliable anatomical structures that form the mouth margin of most vertebrates, composed of a surface epidermis (skin), connective tissue, and (in typical mammals) a muscle layer'. The outer skin of the lips contain sweat glands, sebaceous oil gland, and hair while the edges are covered with reddish skin referred to as vermilion border. They are generously provided with sensitive nerve endings. The editors explain that 'the reddish skin is a transition layer between the outer hair-bearing tissue and the inner mucous membrane. The interior surface of the lips is lined with a moist mucous membrane.'

The muscles of the lips are usually considered as part of the facial muscles. The muscles of the facial expression are all specialised members of the panniculus carnosus, which attach to the dermis and so wrinkle or dimple the overlying skin.

There are many functions of the lips. The first is food intake. Because they possess their own muscles in addition with the bordering ones, the lips are easily movable. We use the lips for eating; they can hold food or serve as passage into the mouth. In the same vein, they hold the mouth airtight shut. We need this to hold the cup firm to our mouth while drinking water or when we want to keep unwanted objects out of the mouth. When the lips are well compressed, it becomes almost impossible for anything to gain entrance into the mouth. Babies shape the lips into a narrow funnel to increase the suction of the mouth, which helps them in breastfeeding. We also make use of lips to suck items (Lip Book 2015).

Another function of the lips is to articulate sounds. The major sounds that we create through the help of the lips are bilabial, labial, and labiodental consonant sounds and production of rounded vowel. Hence, we cannot relegate them in the speech production process. We also make use of the lips to whistle. Remember that we explored the concept of nervous whistling in the preceding section of the book. Furthermore, we need the lips in articulating sounds for wind instruments, such as saxophone, clarinet, flute, and trumpet. According to Lip Book, 'Persons who have hearing loss may unconsciously or consciously lip read to understand speech without needing to perceive the actual sounds.'

Due to the many nerve endings that the lips have, they react as part of the tactile organs—sense of touch. They are very sensitive to cold, touch, and warmth. Therefore, it has been serving as an invaluable aid to toddlers and babies in exploring unknown objects. Furthermore, the lips are regarded as an erogenous zone. This is made possible due to their high number of nerve endings. Hence, they play an invaluable role in kissing and intimate, romantic affairs. Studies have also shown that a woman's lips is a clear expression of her fertility.

Lip Book (2015) reports, 'In studies performed on the science of human attraction, psychologists have concluded that a woman's facial and sexual attractiveness is closely linked to the makeup of her hormones during puberty and development. Contrary to the effects of testosterone on a man's facial structure, the effects of a woman's oestrogen levels serve to maintain a relatively "childlike" and youthful facial structure during puberty and during final maturation.' The studies was able to prove that the more oestrogen a woman has, the larger and fuller her lips would be. These two features are seen to be feminine.

In the same vein, surveys conducted by sexual psychologists reveal that men are fond of women with full lips compared with those with less ones. The reason women's lips are sexually attractive to their male counterparts is because the lips serve as a biological indicator of fertility and health in women. When women use lipstick, it tends to deceive us that they have oestrogen than they actually do. Ultimately, lip size is linked to sexual attraction in both sexes. Women are attracted to men with masculine lips, those with middle-sized lips—neither too big nor too small. Such lips are seen as being sensual and rugged. There is momentary swelling of the lips during sexual arousal due to the activeness of the blood nerves and muscles of the face (Lip Book 2015).

In conclusion, the lips contribute in no small measure to facial expressions. They glaringly show expressions such as frown, laughter, or smile. They can be pouty when we are about to get angry. In short, they are capable of communicating our mood every time. When we see something disgusting, we do not express this with only the nose but also with the lips. We cannot deny the fact that our lips are one of the things that distinguish us from other creatures. We step up our game as humans.

10.1. Fullness of the Lips

Generic Interpretations of the Concept

Our lips take shape according to our mood—the dimension and shape of our lips are determined by our state of mind each time. They tend to shrink or get smaller when we are going through stress and appear larger than they are when we are relaxed. When we have nothing to fear, this shows in our lips; we make them visible to everyone. When the lips are full and pliable, this is an indication of contentment and relaxation.

When we are undergoing stress, blood flows out of the lips to other parts of the body where it may be needed. This makes the lips look dry, pale, and unattractive. The moist that the blood was supposed to produce through the nerves would be diverted to other parts of the body. This communicates with other people that all is not well with us. Stress communicates nervousness, anger, depression, frustration, and anxiety, depending on the context.

From the foregoing, it is crystal clear that the shape of the lips at each given point can serve as a barometer of our state of mind. It reveals our emotions and what we are going through. The lips' fullness can be used to determine if a person buys our idea or considers it as being inconsequential. With this, we would know if we are to adjust or keep on with the track we are on. Those in a romantic affair understand the importance of understanding the mood of one's partner before demanding for anything so as not to be portrayed as being selfish and uncaring.

Scientific Explanations

Joe Navarro (2009) simply labels an article thus 'The Lips Don't Lie'. This means that when it comes to understanding of people's emotion in the most genuine way, we must take cognisance of the lips. He notes that we cannot discountenance the lips when it comes to emotions and feelings. In a rare manner, he states emphatically that 'they can even help us to detect deception'. He says that when we are stressed, the lips get smaller or even 'disappear'. Pay attention to people when they miss their flight or when watching a tense movie. This is also seen among politicians during debates and even in our everyday interactions.

Painfully, Navarro laments that most of the rich messages are ignored in our conversations with people. The lips are rich with nerves, making them highly vascular; this makes them react in real time to events taking place around us—that is, when you see the lips of a person disappear, this means what causes such gesture just happened. In the same vein, the event that causes a person to display fuller lips has just occurred—our lips react according to the emotions they are revealed to every time. When we are under extreme pressure, the lips may totally compress (Navarro 2009).

The former FBI expert says that 'in relationships, couples will immediately notice when their partner has issues because they notice the tightening or compressing of the lips. Even kisses will seem different under stress as blood flow is restricted which affects their fullness, warmth, and pliability.' He explains further that the lips' fullness is a universal gesture; it is controlled by the limbic system, which makes it reliable at all times. In other words, we do not determine the shape our lips take at each given time. We may not even notice it, but be sure others are aware of the shape of our lips.

The reason the lips become smaller when we are under stress is to give us the opportunity to bite them as a way of pacifying ourselves. Hence, we release tension through this means. Priyanka Arora (2015) also explains that the shapes of our lips reveal a lot of things about us. Arora states that flattened lips may be an indication of repressed desire to speak. This means the person disapproves what is happening in their environment, but they are restraining themselves from crying or speaking against the disapproved behaviour. He describes 'relaxed lips' as that which is not pulled to any direction. You see this in a person that is calm and at ease with the activities going on around them.

When the lips are turned up, they become fuller, which means the person is happy. This is the shape the lips maintain when we are smiling. On the other hand, when they are pulled down, it is a means of showing displeasure or sadness (Arora 2015).

Practical Illustrations

Case Study I: After work on Friday, Man B was called by his superior and handed a letter without any explanation. The expression on the face of his boss was indifferent, which made him more confused. He took the letter and quickly walked out. Upon getting into his car, he first read the letter before starting his engine. The summary of its content was either he settle for a pay cut or his appointment with the firm be terminated. He was lost in thought. What could have been his offence? Why was he the only one given the letter? Why did the letter come when he just tied the nuptial knot? His marriage was just a month old, and as such, he decided not to sadden his wife. Upon getting home, he thought he could feign perfection, but as the wife made her way to kiss him, she discovered that his lips were compressed and smaller than usual. She retreated immediately and asked him what went wrong with him. That is, she discovered sadness in the shape of the lips of her husband. This is what many couples do not take note of, and as trivial as you may consider the issue to be, it may be the foundation that will destroy the home.

Case Study II: Man G was never moved by girls, but when he met this particular lady in one of their outings, it seemed as though she was an angel sent to him from above. He asked her out, and fortune would have it, everything worked out very shortly. When they went out on a date, the last thing they did was give each other a deep kiss. Since they were both happy with each other, their lips always looked bigger any time they wanted to kiss, making the exercise more romantic. This is an example of an emotional or romantic affair that is working—both parties are happy and fulfilled.

Case Study III: XO was a human smuggler. He was so infamous that his name was mentioned in the wanted list of criminals in the country. He was eventually arrested in the most unimaginable circumstances. Expectedly, he was drilled for long hours. At some point, he became physically tired and exhausted. He was released to walk about the premises before the interview continued. However, he didn't seem willing to talk again. Perhaps, he saw the joy in the face of the enforcement agents engaging him. His lips became compressed and unyielding. The investigators had to divert his attention a little bit to get him to speak. Because with the shape of his lips, it was certain that he was not ready to speak of the issue at hand.

10.2. Touching the Lips with Fingertips

Generic Interpretations of the Concept

When you cover your lips with your fingers, it can be given different interpretations along the negative lines before being situated in the appropriate context. The fundamental meanings are doubt or insecurity. When you are insecure, you use the fingertips to cover your mouth as if you were protecting it from external attacks. In another sense, insecurity causes stress to people. So touching the lips may be regarded as a pacifying act—that is, you are trying to run your fingers through the charged nerves as a way of calming them. When it is interpreted as doubt, it means you are not sure of the next line of action or word to utter. So putting the fingertips across the lips is a way of restricting yourself from uttering any word. You are not sure of the aftermath of what you are about to say, and you think keeping it to yourself is better.

This gesture is mostly noticeable in people when they are asked a question that needs to be processed intellectually. So the gesture may be verbally interpreted in this context to mean 'Do not disturb. I'm in thinking mode!' This means they want to carefully ponder on the issue before giving any response to it. Most importantly, you need to be careful of some people who are fond of this behaviour; they do it in every given circumstance as a pacifier to the stress they are undergoing. This appears to them as the same thing as the thumb-sucking behaviour they were used to in their childhood.

Scientific Interpretations

Westside Toastmasters (2019) explains that this gesture is done when the brain subconsciously instructs the fingers to suppress what is about to be said. The website notes that this is most times a deceitful utterance, a sentiment that it shares with Christopher Philip (2013). Whether the fingertips or the entire hand is covering the lips, the meaning does not change. Some may feign this gesture by coughing. Criminals place their fingers on their lips in order to discuss criminal activities which they do not want others to hear about. If you do this while speaking, you are sending a wrong signal to your audience as they would believe that you are hiding something from them. This gesture is regarded as a subtle form of *shhh*, which is used by parents to tell their kids to be silent. The website concludes that anywhere you see this, it means something is being withheld.

Philip (2013) affirms that this gesture is a means of reducing the pain of being deceptive. This gesture is regarded as the 'speak no evil' sign. When we were small, we would cover our entire mouth whenever we said what we were not supposed to say, but as we grow up, we merely touch the lips with the tips of our fingers so as not to draw people's attention to our intents. Philip states that the gesture may be a representation of insecurity. He submits, 'Subconsciously, hand-to-mouth gestures lead people to distrust others and see them as less honest overall. The gesture can be done with a fist, a finger, or a "shushing" motion with the index finger vertically placed over the lips.' He compares this gesture with mouthing whereby a finger is placed on the side of the lips with the hope of gratifying the blood nerves so as to regain one's security.

IndiaBIX (2019) also shares the same sentiment with the two others considered above. The website also opines that it is the brain's subconscious means of instructing the hands to suppress something bad that is about to be said. If you subconsciously display this gesture while speaking, you need to ask the audience if they have any question in order to clear their doubts. If not, they will relate with you based on this wrong mindset that you have created in them.

Practical Illustrations

Case Study I: Two terrorists went to survey a bank. They were able to manoeuvre the security operatives and gain entry into the banking hall. In order not to be suspected, they first acted as if they had business at the bank by taking a number on different occasions and then sitting down, monitoring every activity of the bank. If they were not clear on anything, they would cunningly approach one of the bank workers and ask in a least suspecting manner. When one of the security operatives suspected that they had been in the banking hall for a while without doing any tangible thing, he approached them, and they claimed they were waiting for their partner who was coming along with the money they wanted to deposit. When they discovered that people might be eavesdropping into their conversations, they decided to cover their mouth, placing their fingertips on their lips. This made them more suspicious, which later drew the attention of the security head to them. They were eventually arrested. In this instance, they were withdrawing themselves from the larger group, which was very suspicious.

Case Study II: Two friends were planning to go to a nightclub. The first was unmarried, while the second married about a year ago. The husband of the second lady had begged her to minimise her outings and give more priority to building her new home. The argument over this one had threatened to tear their new home. So they later reached an agreement. On this particular occasion, the husband was to be on a trip for a week but returned home earlier than scheduled. The unmarried lady was around to pick up her friend for an overnight party, which the latter did not inform her husband about. As the husband knocked at the door, their mood changed immediately as it was certain that their plans for the night were disrupted already. The husband came in tired and needed to get something to eat. The wife was first feigning annoyance that she was not informed of the husband's decision to return earlier than planned, but when the husband offered his explanation, she kept quiet. She and her friend placed their fingertips on their mouth and started conversing. This made the husband suspect that something illicit was being planned. Despite his tiredness, he tarried at the living room, thereby destroying all their plans for the night.

Case Study III: Even though Ms IY was into prostitution, she decided to take up a job for two reasons—she believed that she would meet better clients in organisations, and then she wouldn't run out of money. The first reason was the motivating factor. In her job as the secretary to the managing director, she could do anything just to secure the favour of the MD. Despite the MD's simplicity and caring attitude, he never thought of taking advantage of IY. She thought things were being delayed. So she decided to dress in a way that would lure the MD to her. One day, she sat on the chair and used her fingertips to rub her lips. This was a glaring sign of being in the mood, but the MD still ignored her. She was later sacked. The head of the organisation saw her as someone who was primarily concerned about sex or romance than the primary assignment she was employed for.

10.3. Pulling/Plucking the Lips

Generic Interpretations of the Concept

When we pull or pluck our lips, this gesture is considered as a negative body language cue. Let me start from those who do it to pass the time. You may need to ignore people in this category because it is a pacifying act to them; they do it for no just reason other than the fact that it soothes them and they derive pleasure from it. So whether they are undergoing a negative emotion or not, you will see them pluck their lips.

However, if you see those who rarely pluck their lips do it, this is an apt indicator that something is wrong somewhere. The first probable indicator is concern. When a person is concerned about something which forces them into thinking mode, they may be pulling their lips subconsciously while thinking. This means they are not aware of anything going on in their environment again. They are lost in their thought and are digging deep to find solution by all means. In the same vein, a person who lacks confidence in himself or herself may display this gesture if asked to do something they are not certain of. This is to show uncertainty on the success of the assignment. It is a show of lack of zeal or commitment to get something done. So it can be concluded that someone who is plucking their lips is doubtful.

Furthermore, this gesture may be an expression of fear. A person who is afraid is insecure. The act of plucking the lips is considered as a pacifier to them. Other clusters you may see along with this gesture is that the hands would be somewhat shivering, the legs glued to a position or shrinking back, and the person showing a general lacklustre attitude. While they pluck the lips, they would rather move backwards or slouch on a chair instead of trying to confront what makes them fearful. This is considered as a freeze response.

Scientific Explanations

There are various ways in which the lips can be pulled or plucked. For plucking, it deals with the use of the index finger and thumb, while for pulling, it can be the use teeth to draw the lips inward. Changing Minds (2019) explains with the latter. The website notes that considering this gesture from all directions, it is a signifier of tension. The tension can be further interpreted as disapproval or frustration. A person who is lost in the labyrinth of an event may pull their lips as a way of showing that they are fed up. The body language platform describes this gesture as a classic sign of disapproval or anger.

In addition, it means the person is thinking of deciding between two possibilities—that is, the person appears confused on which to go for between two likely options. Disapproval or deciding are both evaluative actions commonly represented by the cue of lip plucking (Changing Minds 2019).

Christopher Philip (2014) gives an in-depth explanation for this gesture. He also refers to it as lip picking, a gesture he describes as harming oneself. Philip explains the cue in one sentence thus: 'Picking the lips is a way people self-harm as a way to retain perceived control over a world they see as working against them.' He advises against the display of this gesture because it is universally perceived as being negative. So there is not any positive outcome of it when deployed in any context. The verbal translation of this gesture is, 'I'm anxious and can't do anything about it or control it, so instead of acting outwardly, I'll pick my lip, causing me pain, but it is at least pain that I can control.'

Lack of self-confidence, vulnerability, embarrassment, anxiety, and insecurity are some of the possible interpretations of this cue. It is used by a person as an attempt to regain the loss of control, which is propelled by their anxiety. If this gesture becomes a habit, it may end up injuring the person, thereby leaving physical bruises, marks, cuts, and bleeding. In this case, it may be an indication of depression engineered by anxiety. The lips are highly sensitive, and if a person decides to manipulate them through pain, it reflects what they are battling with internally, which cannot be externally controlled. The clusters you can look out for in identifying this cue are the head being turned down, eyes turned in a downward direction, and slumped shoulders, with the body turning away (Philip 2013).

Practical Illustrations

Case Study I: It was exam time at a university as the semester was approaching its end. Ms E was a sophomore in the school. She was very close to her parents, and due to the academic demands of the semester, she could not go home. She was really missing her home, and her fear was that her mother might have travelled for a two-week seminar before her arrival. In the same vein, she was a lady who did not really like sitting exams. These two issues were the worst for her emotions. They had created inexplicable discomfort and anxiety in her. As a result, she had developed a habit of plucking her lips. One could easily read the signs of fear and nervousness on her due to this non-verbal action.

Case Study II: Man K took his annual leave, and before the end of the three-week leave, he fell ill terribly. He was admitted for about two weeks. He did not contact his workplace to inform them of his illness. When his office tried contacting him, he did not respond to his calls as he had warned his wife not to respond to any call on his behalf. All his mindset was that the medical report from the hospital would be enough proof for him. Upon assuming office, he was queried, which he responded to appropriately by attaching the medical report to his response. The management ignored it and referred him to the disciplinary committee. He was overwhelmed by the decision of the management because his highest point of defence had been refuted; he became anxious of what would be his fate. As the day of committee meeting drew nearer, he lost his confidence and became more anxious. As he went about his duties both at the office and at home, he plucked his lips subconsciously due these psychological feelings that had engulfed him.

Case Study III: Country A wrongly cleared Criminal VX, and their plane was already in the air before they discovered their mistake. They sent a message to Country G, his destination, to apprehend him at the airport. As their plane was landing, he was fished out of the passengers. When he was the only one invited to a secluded place, he had known that something was wrong. He became bothered, thinking of the excuse to give if called upon to explain his side of the story. While waiting, he began to unconsciously act out his mind—he was plucking his lips. He abruptly removed his hand when he saw two officers approaching him. This was an indication that he was thinking hard and trying to fabricate stories.

10.4. Biting the Lips

Generic Interpretations of the Concept

This is one of the most common body language gestures. Biting of the lips is reputed for its connotation of negativity—that is, it is a gesture that is used to show that all is not well with a person. It is a pacifying act which is employed by people to deal with stress. There is a high tendency that you will see this gesture on people when they have one concern or another. Lip biting is a replacement for thumb sucking. We understand that it is not socially acceptable for an adult to suck their thumbs, so the lip-biting cue is adopted as a subtle replacement for the childish thumb sucking. They both perform the function of the stimulation of nerves around the oral cavity.

Another probable function of this gesture is to serve as a self-restraint. When you want to say something but perceive that saying it may endanger your life or bear consequences that you may not be able to handle, you bite your lips so as to suppress the words from being said. In some cultures, it is forbidden that young people address elderly people in a disrespectful manner, no matter who is at fault. In such painful but helpless scenario, people may resort to lip biting. So we also notice this cue on people when they are angry; it means they are trying to calm themselves so as not to publicly vent their anger on people.

Scientific Explanations

Navarro (2009) likens the lip-biting gesture to lip compression; they are both means of pacifying ourselves whenever we are stressed. Lip biting helps in relieving minor or transitory tension. The former FBI intelligence expert notes that we can make use of this behaviour to determine our level of comfort or otherwise of those we are observing. Students preparing to take tests or individuals who do not agree with a stance may display this gesture. Navarro recounts how he made use of this gesture as an FBI special agent to determine a specific subject that stressed suspects, which used to give him the clue that they may be guilty concerning that particular subject matter.

In its own submission, Study Body Language (2019) compares lip biting with lip licking. The website states that the gesture is used to show nervousness and attraction; it is just another means of stimulating the lips. The lip-biting gesture is commonly displayed in three major forms. The first form is biting the upper lip. This is not a pretty gesture. Here, the lower teeth are made to bite the upper lip, which will leave some unfascinating marks on the lip. This is surely a show of nervousness and evidence that the person is dealing with an issue. When you show the lower teeth, it makes you ugly, which is another means of exposing your inner thoughts. The second form is biting the lower lip, which is considered as a sexy act if properly done, especially by females. This is used in the love context as a show of romance and to tell your partner that you are sweeter than they can imagine.

The final form of lip biting is the swallowing of the lips—both the upper and lower lips are encased between the rows of teeth. SBL describes the act of biting the lips as a 'trademark of insecure, shy type of people'. When a person feels insecure, they are battling with conflicting thoughts—the evidence of which is seen through this gesture. The website explains that lip swallowing is seen as the extreme form of 'tense lips'. This is usually a potent and pronounced indicator of self-restraint. That is, this may be regarded as a thought of anger. What is certain is that the person is trying to prevent something negative from escaping through the mouth. Again, this can be flirtatious and sexy for women; it brings out the childish tendencies in them through which they invoke the protective emotion on men. Those who do not want to appear sexy will not bite the upper lip.

Practical Illustrations

Case Study I: Man G decided to address his wife rudely in the presence of his cousin over the care of their children. The man accused his wife of suggesting the school which their children were currently attending. This was in a backdrop against a comment made by his cousin that the children were not academically sound as expected. So everything he was trying to say was to blame the wife for the choice of the school. Meanwhile, the wife had earlier noticed the academic deficiency of the children some months ago, but the husband said he was busy with a project which was consuming much of his income and promised that once he was stabilised, he would move them to a reputable institution. So the wife was taken aback and angry that he was now putting the whole blame on her. She wanted to reply to him in the same manner, but she thought they would be ridiculing each other in the presence of the husband's relative. Hence, she only looked at her husband, bit her lips, and shook her head subtly before going to the kitchen.

Case Study II: An investigator was interviewing a suspect for a high-profile case. The case was connected with the assassination of a top politician in the country. In what was believed to be a coordinated attack by a family on the deceased, his death shook his country, and it seemed most people wanted to know the truth behind the issue. So a preliminary investigation showed that the least expected person was involved in the case. Law enforcement officials got the suspects arrested, and as part of the processes of ensuring that the enforcement agency gathered enough evidence to defend its course in the court, the interview was instituted. It was a tough session as the suspect was trying to play round every accusation. However, when the investigator asked him where he was and his wife on the day that incident happened and the exact time, he became tense. He subconsciously started biting his lips, which hinted the interrogator that there was 'guilty knowledge' in the question—that is, there was a particular piece of information he would have wished that the interrogator had not said.

Case Study III: Politician K was contesting against Politician Y, an incumbent and well-performing administrator. Everyone knew K had no chance of winning against Y due to the latter's performance in the last three years, but he would not listen. During a debate, Y narrated all he had been doing for the people, what he intended to do, and what kind of country he wanted to leave behind. He was simply spectacular, and the whole venue went wild. Seeing this undeniable show of love, Politician K became intimidated that he didn't know what to say again. He began to subconsciously bite his lips before he was eventually invited to the podium. This illustrated lack of confidence and nervousness—he did not believe in himself that he could perform to the level of his counterpart.

10.5. Licking the Lips

Generic Interpretations of the Concept

This is just like the lip-biting gesture; it is done to pacify us. Lip licking is the act of rubbing the tongue on the lips—either one or the two lips. This behaviour is obvious as people who are around us can see that we are licking our lips. There are many possible causes of this non-verbal display. Starting from the literal point of view, it may be considered as a way of moistening the lips when they are dry. This is very common during dry season, popularly known as harmattan in some parts of the world—Africa to be specific. People will lick their lips so that they do not crack due to the high temperature. Most women go about with their lipstick so as to apply it whenever they feel their lips are becoming dry.

However, there are many metaphorical meanings associated with lip licking. Generally, it is considered as a display of negative emotions—that is, it means the person is having some hard times on the inside and is trying to cool the effect through the outside. Anxiety is one of the major emotions that can make a person lick their lips. It is as if the person is trying to assure themselves that all would be well; it is like patting oneself at the back when confronted with something herculean. In addition, a person going through some difficult moment may lick their lip. When people have something bothering them, they employ all forms of strategy to pacify themselves and maintain their balance.

For some people, this reliably shows that they are stressed. As a professional trainer for decades, I do notice this when trainees are not prepared for tests. The mere announcement of test disorganises them, and as such, you can see this when people are going through turbulent times.

Scientific Explanations

Study Body Language perfectly notes, 'Licking the lips is a very context-dependent expression because the act of touching the lip can be either comforting or stimulating at different times.' So we must bear this in mind before moving further than this. Christopher Philip (2014) gives the synonyms of the lip-licking gesture as frequent lip licking, lip wetting, moistening the lip, and excessive lip licking. He goes ahead to describe this cue in one sentence: 'Lip licking demonstrates a need for pacifying or, in the right context, sexual interest.' Those who want to make use of this cue intentionally must take cognisance of the context of its demonstration. If this is done habitually, it is considered as a sign of anxiety, especially with men. However, women can use this as a form of sexual attraction.

The sexual gesture is when a person intentionally places their tongue at the corner of the mouth, then licks first the upper lip before licking the lower part. This is done slowly so as to create a sensual feeling. This is a very obvious invitation to a potential suitor to see how juicy and colourful a person's lips are (SBL 2019). Philip says that it is an act of preparing the lips for kissing. Let me note that this bold move is for advanced courtship or relationship where both lovers are already into each other. Other cues to look out for are focused gaze and eye contact directly on the parts of the body that the person finds arousing.

Furthermore, this gesture may hint us that someone is ready to talk. When we want to communicate, we moisten the lips so as to have a smooth and seamless time talking.

Changing Minds (2019) opines that lip licking may simply be a desire to eat food. In this case, it means the food is in front of the person licking their lips. The body language website also shares the same sentiment with other experts that this may be a sign of stress, which reduces saliva flow to the mouth. Philip provides a clearer explanation to this by postulating that 'repeated or excessive licking serves to pacify and soothe negative feelings. In this gesture, the tongue can be seen darting out of the mouth, swiping the top lip on the way, and curling under to swipe the bottom lip as it reenters. A person that licks as part of his idiosyncratic behaviour is usually one that has underlying emotional turmoil.' This is a somewhat bad behaviour because it easily exposes you as someone who is not happy. People who are observant and use body language as the basis of their relationship with people may detach themselves from you just because of this perception.

Philip (2014) gives the verbal translation of the cue as 'I'm licking my lips to moisten them, to prepare for speaking or kissing, or to soothe myself.'

Practical Illustrations

Case Study I: Two friends were discussing, and one of them seemed to be leading the discussion. So the other person was practically reduced to be a listener in what was supposed to be a conversation. The second friend really had interest in the topic, but his friend would not just keep it shut to listen to his opinion. When it was obvious that he was not ready to let go, he licked his lips and parted them slightly before interjecting. The doggedness was noticed at this point.

Case Study II: Student H was busy preparing for his exams. As the day of the exam was approaching, the tension increased on him; he redoubled his effort due to the fear of failure. It got to a point that whenever he was reading, he licked his lips repeatedly in anticipation. This was in a bid to soothe his excited nerves.

Case Study III: A client—well dressed, handsome, and moderate in his overall appearance—had just walked into the bank. This was the ideal guy for the teller. Immediately after she set her eyes on him, she became hot and restless. She could not even resist the temptation of taking her eyes off him. Subconsciously, she started licking her lips while her eyes focused on his mouth and genital areas. All these are sexual gestures pointing to her readiness to clinch the client.

Case Study IV: Smuggler BJ had a stressful time on the journey that eventually led to his arrest—the vehicle he went with had issues, and he needed to dodge different checkpoints. However, he was apprehended at the only unavoidable and last checkpoint before driving to his home. He was physically stressed out. The officials who apprehended him saw this and first offered him something to re-enliven himself before going into the questioning session. When they questioned him on the legality of some of the items found in his vehicle, he had to first lick his lips and clear his dried throat due to the psychological stress telling on him.

10.6. Narrowing the Lips

Generic Interpretations of the Concept

Inasmuch as I would not like to outrightly state that most of the gestures associated with the lips tend towards negative emotions, our discussion so far has pointed to that direction. Narrowing, as you know, is a form of closed body language which implies that the lips shrink when we perceive something fearful. Fear makes us lose our sense of decency, and this is seen in how our lips become narrowed when we are afraid. Fear, as explained here, may be physical or psychological. The mere thought of something scary can make you narrow your lips subconsciously.

In the same vein, lack of confidence may cause a person's lips to shrink. Someone who is not confident will run away from speaking, even if they are given the opportunity to express themselves. They believe that other people are better than them. So they think whatever they have to say is inferior. Narrowing the lips is a subtle communication of the intent of their heart, which is, 'I don't have any tangible thing to say.' Anxiety is another likely emotion that can make a person demonstrate this gesture.

Furthermore, someone with negative concerns, which they are looking for every means to solve, will narrow their lips; they do not want to speak in order not to interrupt their thoughts. In other words, the person is saying that they want to be alone so as to think deeply. Someone who narrows their lips does not drink or eat. This confirms the seriousness of the emotion they are experiencing. It means the person is not available for anything trivial. For instance, if people want to kiss, they tend to push out their lips, but this person is saying that they are not in the mood for doing such a romantic activity. Thought processing tends to narrow our lips.

Scientific Explanations

Almost all the body language experts who contributed to this subject matter made it known that it is used to show negative emotions. In fact, Sarah Smith (2011) states that except in rare situations when a person is mad, trying to feign the lip-narrowing gesture is impossible. Joe Navarro, in his *Clues to Deceit*, notes that this gesture is usually observed when we are bothered by something significant. This concern is so bothersome that our limbic system is charged out of its original state. If the stress is significant enough, the limbic system forces the lips to narrow and disappear. Whenever you notice this in a person, it means the person is not finding it easy internally. If it is a loved one, it is high time you help them cope, and if it is in a formal context, this gives you a hint on how to deal with the person.

Changing Minds authoritatively submits, 'Lips which are pulled inwards from all directions are an indication of tension and may indicate frustration or disapproval.' A frustrated person who does not want to express themselves will pull their lips inward because they understand that their utterances may be out of ethics if uttered in that level of annoyance. The body language platform explains further that narrowed lips is a perfect sign of anger, even when it is suppressed. It is a perfect way of shutting the mouth against expressing itself. In another sense, it may indicate that someone is withholding the truth. Sometimes, people are always afraid of saying the truth due to the likely implication or harm that it would cause on them or others. Take for instance, if a friend does something bad and you know that telling people the truth will spoil your long-term relationship, you may decide to cover them up or force yourself to keep it shut, even though this is against your conscience. In the same vein, this gesture may indicate the possibility that someone is engrossed in a thought.

Paul Ekman, a professor emeritus at University of California, who is globally reputed for his research on microexpressions, says that when the red margins are narrowed, it clearly shows that we are angry. When all these experts' contributions are considered as one, it becomes very clear to us that those who narrow their lips do not just do it for the purpose of catching fun.

Practical Illustrations

Case Study I: Child D broke her mum's favourite dish while trying to arrange the kitchen and get everywhere cleaned up in preparation for an August visitor they were expecting. Not minding the little girl's effort in tidying up the home, the mother spoke to her rashly and still went ahead to report her to her father. Her dad was also pained and spoke out of annoyance. It got to a point where the girl was engrossed in the thought of which was valued more between the broken dish and her. She wanted to speak out in anger, but remembering that she came from a culture where elders must be respected, no matter what, she narrowed her lips, squinted her face, and went to her room. This means she was really angry but had to suppress it due to cultural demands.

Case Study II: An up-and-coming public speaker was invited to an event. Historically, the event was known not to be a crowd-pulling one. So he had thought he was only going to address a handful of people and move out of the arena. However, the organisers did an aggressive mobilisation, and the topic was timely enough that it drew people from far and near. He came earlier than scheduled. As he sat waiting for the right time to deliver his presentation, he saw people trooping in from all directions. At some point, he lost his breath; he narrowed his lips and rested his head in his palms. His confidence was gone! That is, he was nervous.

Case Study III: A man was arrested at the border of a country. He was used to smuggling and thought it was business as usual, but with the way he was handled, he sat up and cooperated with the law enforcement agencies. When he was asked some few questions, he knew that he had met his Waterloo. He could hardly utter a word because he narrowed his lips as an expression of fear.

10.7. Compressing the Lips

Generic Interpretations of the Concept

As we experience turbulent events on a daily basis, our body reacts and exposes them. One of the major ways through which we understand how a person feels every time is to observe their lips. Uncomfortable thoughts, negative events, anxiety, fear, lack of self-confidence, and horrible happenings do make our lips to be narrowed and tightly pressed together. This is known as lip compression. This body language gesture may be subtle or very pronounced. When it is glaring, the lips will change colour because blood has been forced out from the nerves. This makes the person displaying this cue become stressed due to the high rate of blood on the lips. They would employ other subtle means to ease the irritating effects of the blood on their lips.

The lip-compressing gesture is considered as a microexpression; it is fleeting and, in most cases, does not last more than 1/20 of a second. This invariably means that it is only those who are observant can catch a glimpse of this cue before it disappears. Those of us who are in a serious business of identifying people's emotions should try as much as possible to pay close attention to this cue. This is because it accurately points to the fact that something negative has happened to someone. Remember that I said it is a microexpression, and microexpressions are not only universal but also very accurate in revealing the inner intents and feelings of people.

Scientific Explanations

Navarro (2009) explains that the lips are the pointers to the exact feelings of a person; the shape of the lips each time tells us how a person feels and the kind of emotions they are going through. The former FBI agent gives different interpretations to the lip-compression gesture. On a general note, he opines that the lips are compressed under extreme stress. In relationships, couples are hinted that their partners are going through one ill emotion or another when they see them compress their lips. Even if their partner tries to hide their emotions with a kiss, it would still be made manifest because while experiencing stress, blood flow is restricted, which affects pliability, warmth, and fullness.

Navarro goes on to note that 'because disappearing or compressed lips are universal behaviors, controlled by the limbic system, these are behaviors that can be relied upon and are authentic'. That is, lip compression is a reliable gesture for you to understand a person. It is hardly feigned!

Jack Schafer (2018) also provides a detailed description of what lip compression is all about. He compares this cue to the lip-biting cue. He explains that lip compression obscures the lips. This gesture has a more negative connotation compared with the lip-biting gesture. Lip compression is evidence that a person has something to say, but they seal the lips so as to prevent the words from being uttered. He makes reference to his time at FBI while acting as the special agent of the agency that suspects used to compress their lips right before making any confession. He opines that empathic statements such as 'So you have something to say but you really don't want to talk about it' can prompt reluctant people to open their lips and express themselves. Note that this is only potent in a situation where the consequences of the self-expression is not grievous. For instance, if the person is shy, this empathic statement as suggested by Schafer will work perfectly, but in a criminal situation, it may prove a hard nut to crack.

Christopher Philip (2014) gives the likely verbal translation of this cue as 'I'm having a hard time with this, and so I'm going to suck my lip in and consume it while I deal with negative thoughts or while I am in deep concentration' or 'I'm biting back my words' or 'I'm holding something back with my mouth by pressing my lips together so no negative thoughts escape, which may get me into trouble.' A variant of this gesture is that the jaw is tense—this communicates additional negative thought. People can make use of this cue to their advantage. If you want others to know that you disapprove of what they said but that you are only keeping your reservation to yourself, you can make use of this cue.

Practical Illustrations

Case Study I: Mrs F visited one of their family friends. When she got there, she met the cousin of their family friend with her hosts. Among the many issues she heard them (her host and their relative) discussing was on an eighteen-year-old who was ready to get married. Even though she did not know the lady, she was bothered about the fact that she was not yet employed and was still failing in some etiquettes as they relate to marriage. At some point, she really wanted to speak out, but she maintained sealed lips and watched them discuss. This means she was worried and resisting all attempts to make herself utter a word.

Case Study II: The clerk had just brought some files to the manager of CAY Firm Ltd. Immediately after he received the files, he started working on them. They were about some major policies that needed revamping. Inasmuch as he was open to novelty, he was not of the opinion that the company should take some inconsiderable risks. With what he was reading, he was afraid that the firm was really taking risks that might backfire. The clerk stood at the side, watching with keen interest. From the manager's facial expression (compressed lips), the junior staff could establish that he was contemplating a thought and wanted to speak up, but instead, he kept it shut and focused on what he was reading. The compressed lips showed that there were a lot of thoughts going on in his mind.

Case Study III: A young lady left her beloved mother in a pitiable state at the hospital before proceeding to work on a Monday morning. What could have happened to her mother was bothering her. Throughout the day, she rarely held a full, relaxed lips even when her colleagues were cracking funny jokes; she was an embodiment of negative thoughts. A glance at her will tell you that she was overridden by negative thoughts.

Case Study IV: Prostitute OY had so much bills unattended to, and it was almost becoming a source of embarrassment to her due to the classy way she used to behave in the society. So she decided to flirt more in order to raise money to pay her bills. She fixed appointments with three different men at different venues. While she kept to time with the first and second man, the second man, not wanting people to see him with OY, lied to her that his car had issues, so she should look for other means to get home. Commercial buses weren't forthcoming, and this means she might likely miss the third man. While waiting for a bus, she compressed her lips to depict her sadness.

10.8. Slight Pressing of the Lips

Generic Interpretations of the Concept

This is like the minor form of the preceding gesture; it also has to do with lip compression, but not one that is full. This gesture mainly involves the upper lip where it is slightly pressed down. It is a means of showing that we are really annoyed with a person. In short, this cue is also associated with negative emotions. When we are angry, we would be tempted to speak to the other party in a hurtful manner, but considering other factors such as age, professional level, relationship, and other issues can deter us from uttering such expressions. So slight pressing of the lips is an indication of self-restraint. The lower lip is not involved because the person wants to inhale fresh air as a means of cooling their agitated nerves. Hence, this cue is seen as performing two functions simultaneously.

The movement of the upper lip from its original position communicates that something is wrong. Although the gesture is slightly done with the hope of not calling the attention of people to it, but an observant fellow should know that all is not well with the person. If you feel what you said was not supposed to be, you can take the bull by the horn by asking the person if they were offended by your action or words. This will make them register their grievances verbally. Also, if you consider this cue in relation with other gestures, you would be able to attach other meanings to it.

Scientific Explanations

Philip (2014) says that another name for the slight pressing of the lips is stiff upper lip. When it is seen in others, it means they are stressed or anxious. As explained earlier, when we are stressed, we look for ways of calming ourselves. The non-involvement of the lower lip means it allows the person to take in air. If you are dealing with another person and they see this cue, it is a message to them that you want them to change their tactic of relating with you. Philip submits that this gesture is a 'universal trait done to signify stress, anxiety, anger, frustration, and an overall negative thought indicator. The lips are tightened to contain and stifle emotion or signal deep concentration and internal turmoil.'

The stiff upper lip is the direct opposite of full expressive lips that are used to connote contentment. This cue is a subconscious communication for the mouth to close up so that nothing comes in—it should be bottled up so as to withhold information or feeling. Because this happens in real time, it is used to communicate a person's stress sentiments as it is taking place. Furthermore, slightly pressed lips is used to portray a person as being indecisive. This can be very useful for those in the business world as they can take cognisance of this while negotiating with a person. It would be at your own detriment to overlook this gesture. When you pay attention to these flashes, they tell you huge things about what is going on in the mind of your co-interlocutor (Philip 2014).

Other restraint gestures that you can look for in this context are hand clenching, head turned away, avoidance of eye contact, ventral denial, jaw clenching, and hand to the back of the neck.

Practical Illustrations

Case Study I: A criminal suspect was detained for an offence he truly did not know anything about; he was just unfortunate to be a victim of circumstances, and all effort to clear his name was abortive as the law enforcement officials who arrested him insisted that he must get to their station to write a statement of all he knew about the incident. The issue was latter dragged that he needed to be interrogated. He was a naturally calm person; that aided the reason for overriding him. The interview was handled by a junior officer who was still learning the ropes. He asked a question for three consecutive times, and the suspect kept on giving him the same answer. Still not convinced, he repeated the question; he was oblivious of the professionalism that he was supposed to reframe the question. At this point, the suspect became agitated, but instead of speaking, he slightly pressed his lips and avoided eye contact with the officer. The agitation was well pronounced that even the officer in charge noticed it.

Case Study II: A security guard was suspended because of laxity at the workplace. There was a criminal event in his duty post, and he had no inkling of how the event occurred. The reason for the punishment was not that there was an ill occurrence but that why he could not provide any explanation. This would paint the organisation he was working with in a bad light. So after his suspension, he was invited to face a panel so as to know if he was going to be sacked. Being at home for some weeks without payment had made him see the other aspect of life. So he became very anxious when he was handed the letter. At the meeting of the committee, when he was told to say everything he knew about the incident, he clenched his jaws, slightly turned his head away, and lightly pressed his lips. The committee chairman saw the anxiety in him and assured that, as humans, they would be fair to him. This calmed him down.

Case Study III: A teacher was meant to cover some two topics before he would present his students for an external examination. Due to unforeseen reasons, he could not teach those topics till a week to the examinations. So any time he went to class, the first thing he did was to implore all his students to cooperate with him for the sake of the examination at hand. For the first three days, they were very cooperative, even the known troublesome ones. However, the fourth day was terrible. It started with the bullies who did not recognise his presence and had the audacity to deal with their co-students in his presence. Then those who seemed to be intelligent were interrupting him throughout the study. He became visibly angry. Instead of speaking out, he just compressed his lips in a slight manner and walked out of the class for a moment. Even before walking out, the anger was so visible on him that the students were almost trembling.

10.9. Compressed Lips in a Downward Position

Generic Interpretations of the Concept

As humans, we are all prone to mistakes, and when these mistakes occur, we react in one way or another. One of the common reactions seen in people is the pulling of compressed lips in a downward position. This behaviour is a non-verbal acknowledgement that a person has made a major mistake. It is like entering into a fire before realising that it is one, and you quickly withdraw to keep to yourself. In doing this, the lips would be tightly held together while the muscles around the mouth will contract so as to slightly draw the lips down. This will stretch the upper lip away from the nose and pull the compressed lips towards the teeth. Now I do hope you have a mind picture of this gesture. When a person displays this cue, the message they intend to send to the world is that they are calm and all right. Nobody wants to be portrayed in a bad light, and this gesture is just in a bid to hide this obvious human weakness.

In addition, people also display this non-verbal message when they are caught red-handed doing something that is wrong. When someone catches you in the wrong act, what you want to prove to the person is that it was actually not intended. So you withdraw from the act immediately, hold your breath, and pray that it does not get out of hand. Note that this compression is very tight to the extent that nothing can gain entrance into the person's body; neither can any word drop out of their mouth. This is a means of detaching themselves from that particular act—that is, when people make mistakes, they do not want others to align or describe them in line with that error. This may look like a smart trick to them, but to a person who understands how to decode non-verbal gestures, this cue has actually given them away.

Scientific Explanations

Changing Minds (2019) tries to explain this gesture in the simplest way. According to the website, the clue may be a representation of displeasure or sadness. Displeasure in the sense that the person was caught in a state they were not supposed to be. This might be the propeller of sadness in them. Ideally, when a person is happy, they release their lips fully, but compressing it too tight is a pointer to the fact that something has gone wrong somewhere. Also, when a person is not interested in what is going on around them, you may see them display this gesture. The website sadly notes that some people are always miserable that they do not have any other gesture to display but this one at all times. This can be frustrating for a person dealing with them for the first time.

Christopher Philip (2013) is of the opinion that compressed lips pulled down is a signifier of stress. He states that the subconscious mind communicates with the body to close down once it is stressed so as not to allow anything in. This occurs immediately and honestly in order to show the real emotion of the person at that particular time. Philip describes this gesture as U shape—downturned smile. This means the person is highly stressed. Also, this gesture is displayed when a person is trying hard to birth an alternate idea. After realising that they have made a huge mistake, people will start thinking of the next step out of the mess they have created. In addition, this gesture may also signal that someone has an opinion that is different from yours.

Practical Illustrations

Case Study I: A man was driving in an area for the first time. This suggested that he did not understand the topography of the area. He was actually late for a gathering and decided to use Google Maps in locating his destination. He had his earpiece on, listening to music. He was later carried away by the music, and suddenly, he drove past where he was supposed to turn. This means he would have to drive for another five kilometres before he could turn back. When he realised the mistake he had made and how he was going to pay dearly for it, he held his lips tightly together and pulled the upper away from the nose while the lips were clenched to the teeth. This was a sign of regret and psychological torment.

Case Study II: There were some two bullies in Ms T's class. She tried to cut their wings and made them fit into the standard of the class, but they were simply too stubborn to see things from that angle. When it was obvious that no method would work on the bullies and they were even distracting their colleagues from learning, she brought the issue to the notice of the management. The management joined her, but the change was not evident. So Ms T was told to retrieve their names so that letters could be sent to their parents, inviting them for an important meeting. Meanwhile, there was a calm, knowledgeable, innocent boy who almost had the same name with the bully. The teacher made a mistake and wrote the innocent boy's name. Before she could reach the secretary, the letters had been signed and mailed to the parents of those they were addressed to. The issue now was how she would explain to the management and the next step she should take. She compressed her lips tightly as she reasoned on this.

She was in deep confusion and buried in thought of the way out, which was not forthcoming at that point.

Case Study III: A couple decided to get a nanny who would help them out at home and take care of their children while they were away—both of them were medical practitioners. Recently, the wife noticed that when she came back, the children were not really feeling happy. She called her husband's attention to this. After some few days, the couple decided to come home unannounced, and as they were entering, they saw that the nanny was assaulting the children. As she saw them come in, she was taken aback and suddenly compressed her lips, drew them away from the nose, and felt like shrinking at that point. This negative surprise was overwhelming.

Case Study IV: Industry FIR had thousands of employees, and yet they had a very standard system of capturing all their workers daily. They also measured the efficiency level of the workers. The way they do this still remained mysterious to outsiders. However, Criminal HD still found his way into the firm illegally. Unknown to him, all the wages he was receiving were being documented. When he was eventually found out, he lied about his duration at the firm. When the company later traced his name to the first payment he received right to the moment he was fished out, he compressed his lips, moved them away from his nose, and looked dejected. He felt ashamed of himself and knew there was no way out for him.

10.10. Unwillingness to Decompress Lips

Generic Interpretations of the Concept

I have explained the concept of compressed lips in about three different segments, and what I have always emphasised in each case is that the gesture is a microexpression; it appears and disappears in the twinkle of an eye. So it becomes a matter of special case if someone is unwilling to decompress their lips. This shows that the stress a person is undergoing is of high magnitude. In a way, the act of lip compression is a battening down of people's hatches. This is synonymous to covering our eyes with the use of our hands as a way of blocking out something negative.

When the tension or apprehension is greater, the more people will hold on to their compressed lips. This gesture is seen as a pacifier, and people will not let go of it if their fear is still within sight. Hence, when you see a person who is not willing to decompress their lips, it means they are still anxious. Even if after your entreaties they are still reluctant, this means that they do not trust your ability to safeguard against what is stressing them. The simple message here is that people will clinch to their pacifying behaviour until they feel secure.

Scientific Explanations

Any time I recall the message of Professor Albert Mehrabian, a UCLA psychologist, that most of what we do in communication is mostly influenced by non-verbal gestures, I am charged to explore the concept more. Today, miscommunication has, regrettably, managed to be the first issue that professionals battle with in the boardroom. Many people make their decisions based on verbal utterances, which, according to the don, only constitutes 10 per cent of what is being said. This is why many firms have folded up; making decisions without taking in all that are due to be considered always backfire. When we understand this, we become better informed and make things happen in the right manner. Remember that verbal utterances are always laced with lies and, as such, are always risky to work with.

Before you accuse me of being too generic about this gesture, let's get back to business. Randy Roguski (2008) describes the lips as the most emotional part of the body. He takes time to explain this cue in details. According to him, if the compressed lips is released immediately, it is an indication of slight resistance, stress, or negative feeling—that is, it means that the person is feeling the emotions in a way, but the stress or negative thought is yet to take over him. In simpler terms, it means the stress is minimal. You may notice this when a person is being accused of an offence which they truly did but are not ready to take on the blame publicly.

If the compressed lips tarry a little bit, drooping, it means the person is disappointed, angry, and sad. The slight drooping is a way of resisting the temptation to speak out their mind. Their reluctance to decompress their lips means what they are showing attitude against is still in progress. Maybe the person does not want their child to speak with a neighbour, but the child is looking the other way and having some good time with that person. This builds up the tension in them, and they will react by compressing their lips for a long duration, maybe until the child gets the clue and takes his leave.

Roguski explains further that unwillingness to decompress the lips is a way of showing disagreement. He says people keep on with this gesture when the disagreement is intensified. This communicates a message to your co-interlocutor that you still maintain your stance on that given issue. So they need to do more than what they are doing at present to convince you. That is why Schafer (2018) suggests in his article that when you see people with pursed lips in a conversation, you must try to change the person's mind. When you are confused on what causes this reluctance to decompress their lips, you can just take the bull by its horn by asking them directly.

Practical Illustrations

Case Study I: The wife of Professor G had just been taken to the labour room. She was due for the delivery of her second child. Professor G was present in the labour room when she delivered their first child but had to run when he saw the travails of his wife. This time around, he could not surmount the courage to enter with her; he was just prancing up and down at the entrance of the ward. It was over an hour, and he did not hear any news from the room. He became apprehensive. Then a nurse came out to inform him that his wife may be taken for surgery because it seems she cannot deliver on her own. As he followed the nurse to the doctor's office to sign the document of agreement, he almost turned into water. As he held the pen, he compressed his lips, and even after signing and the doctor made way to the theatre, he still compressed his lips, showing how tensed he was.

Case Study II: A first-time criminal was apprehended by law enforcement officials and needed to be interrogated. As a culture, the interrogating officials decided to play with the suspect so as to establish his baseline before going into business proper. Being an unfortunate criminal, he was apprehensive all throughout; he never had any successful outing before he was nabbed. Even when he was offered coffee and asked general questions he, ordinarily, should have been quick to react to, he was not. At the point of the interview, he still held on to his compressed lips. All entreaties for him to be well-composed met deadlock; he was further gripped with fear at the sight of the room.

Case Study III: A teacher came into the class and decided to test his students on an impromptu basis. Most of them were obviously not prepared, and as they heard him talk, they compressed their lips. As the teacher began to dictate the questions, they did not decompress their lips as one would expect. This means they were yet to recover from the shock of the unexpected announcement.

10.11. Withdrawal of Lips

Generic Interpretations of the Concept

Most times, people tend to mix up the lip-sucking gesture with the lip-compression cue as expatiated above; they are different but are used in the same context. Lip withdrawal is when a person unconsciously sucks their lips into their mouth as they are confronted with a frightening situation. Imagine a man, well built, sitting beside your crush. You know that if you dare challenge him, you would be beaten squarely. So the lips, the most emotional part of the body and object of kiss, subconsciously moves into the mouth, disappearing totally as a way of telling the person that you are not a threat to them. Remember, in the lip-compressing cue, much of the lips still remain visible after it has been compressed, but in this gesture, it is as if the lips had been cut off.

This cue is always portrayed when a person is deeply anxious or concerned about something. When we are confronted with an unexpected situation, we may display this gesture as a subtle way of communicating with others that we need their help. During moments of great concern, we can hardly hide our emotions. That is why you tend to see this gesture in a person who is shedding truly emotional tears. When the lips are sucked in, we also widen our eyebrows as if we want to have a clearer view of what is frightening us. The lip-compression gesture is very common compared with this.

Ideally, this behaviour is reserved for when we are undergoing severe stress or great emotional turmoil or feeling significant physical pain. That is why I opined that this behaviour cannot be feigned easily; it accompanies severe purgation of emotions. This means that without serious, severe, and threatening pains, you may not see a person display it.

Scientific Explanations

Matthew Ross (2017) describes the lip withdrawal as a behaviour that signals anxiety or discomfort. Discomfort can be propelled by different factors and, depending on individuals, can tarry or disappear immediately. Some people need the help of others to recover, while some others just need to be alone. The point here is not the reaction but what causes it and how we can identify one in people. Facing a huge crowd for the first time, attending an interview with the sentiment that panellists are always partial, making contributions in boardrooms, rushing into an accident scene, walking alone in the dark, and a whole lot more may induce the feeling of fear in us, which may be the cause of this body gesture. Before a person withdraws their lips, they will first compress them and then begin to 'swallow' them until they disappear totally. This gesture is very glaring because it takes more time than the compressing cue.

Ross notes that apart from stress, when a person is worried, they may display this behaviour. Concerns can make a person forget what goes on in their environment or how they even look like; all they are concerned about is how to pacify themselves and move out of the threatening condition.

Changing Minds (2019) explains that when the lips are withdrawn, there is no way anything can gain entrance into the body. In lip compression, it is very easy for the mouth to be opened, but in this, it means the person is not ready to speak at all due to what they are feeling. The platform explains, 'Lip swallowing can also indicate suppressed speech, where the person is preventing themselves from speaking when perhaps they know they should. This can indicate lying or maybe disapproval.' This means the person is intentional about their action;

they do not want to speak due to reasons best known to them. The website also explains that this behaviour portrays thoughtfulness. When you are uncertain about something—in most cases, bad events—you may unconsciously display this gesture. It makes you stare into the distance, looking blank and expectant.

Practical Illustrations

Case Study I: A man had drunk himself into a stupor and was heading home when he drove into a drainage. He slept at that spot, and on the dawn of the next day, his eyes were clear. He got out and saw the damage he had caused to his car. Taking the damage as secondary, his heart began to pound, thinking of what explanation he would the offer law enforcement officials if they should meet him at that spot. He started flagging down Good Samaritans to help him. When he managed to get three people, they decided to try if they could lift the vehicle out of the drainage. He was told to enter the drainage and push up the tyre from beneath. This was very frightening to him. He first compressed his lips as a means of acknowledging the magnanimity of the work ahead. When he got into the drainage, he swallowed his lips to show concern for himself. After some hours of work, they were able to take out the vehicle from the spot.

Case Study II: A woman was injured in a domestic violence and had to be rushed to the hospital by a neighbour. She was taken into the emergency ward upon arrival. Because she had lost much blood before she was brought in, the medical practitioners on duty started work on her immediately. As they were cleaning the injuries, she shouted in a wild manner before swallowing her lips, widened her eyebrows, and looked helplessly till they were done with the treatment. One would know without being told that she was in inexplicable pain.

Case Study III: Two young people had been in a relationship for a while, but it seemed the guy was no longer interested. He had been thinking of the best way to relay his intent to the lady but was very afraid of what she might do. So he began to withdraw and even disappointed her when she needed to see him. Now he hardly picks her calls. The lady still persevered and went out of her comfort zone to make things work. However, the guy later sought to meet her, and as he was about to speak, the lady was afraid of what he would say. She sucked in her lips, looked passionately into his eyes, and awaited his decision. She was obviously afraid as she was not ready to hear anything evil.

Case Study IV: A drug addict ran out of luck on a particular night after drinking and smoking himself into a stupor. He fell into a gutter and was found by law enforcement agents who were on patrol in that community. Since the most important thing was to ensure that he didn't give up the ghost, the officers administered first aid on him before taking him to the hospital. While the injuries he sustained were being treated, he withdrew his lips, looked pained, and eventually puffed out his cheeks as a way of demonstrating his feelings at that given time. After the treatment, he was taken to a rehabilitation centre.

10.12. Quivering of the Lips

Generic Interpretations of the Concept

When you quiver the edges of the lips, even in the slightest form, it is an indication that something is emotionally wrong with you. As it is my norm, let me begin from the literal point of view. Alcohol or neurological disorder may cause the quivering of the edges of the lips. So you must be sure that the person who is observing is not a drunk or suffering from any disorder.

In the absence of any of the issues raised, lip quivering is evidence of discomfort, fear, anxiety, concern, or other negative issues. Mostly, this gesture is noticed in young people when they are being questioned by their parents or someone who is in a position of authority. This means they have something to hide. Youthfulness inspires some people to participate in all forms of despicable acts. If you ask them questions concerning their involvement, their lips may quiver, which is a hint that you should probe further.

From experience, let me, however, note that I have seen this behaviour in honest people, those who have been drilled or questioned by law enforcement officers in times past. Some people are afraid of uniformed men even if they did not do anything wrong. That is why some of them are wrongly indicted; they wear the look of fear or discomfort even if there is no need for that. Further, my chats with some human resource personnel reveal that the lips of some young minds quiver when they are asked questions relating to the use of illicit drugs.

To surmise this, always remember that quivering of the lips is an attribute that is mostly seen in young people and fearful adults who have been to the den of law enforcement officials before. In these category of people, the behaviour signals stress, discomfort, fear, or anxiety.

Scientific Explanations

Christopher Philip (2013) takes his time to explain this non-verbal behaviour, relating it to the feeling of discomfort. He notes that when the lip compresses or trembles at the corners of the mouth, it is a means of showing that someone is eliciting negative attitude caused by an unfavourable event. On a general level, we cannot pinpoint a particular event that induces this feeling, but all that can be said is that the person is stressed. Quivering of the lips may lead to cracking of the voice. This is real evidence that the person is afraid and that they cannot control their emotions.

In his bid to draw the thin line between body language and microexpression, Joe Navarro (2011) states that quivering lips is a sign of tension and nervousness. This is in line with the submission of Philip. The former FBI agent notes that some other clusters that may accompany this gesture are furrowed forehead, quivering chin, and lip compression, among others. In short, the whole face shows that the person is stressed. The context will help you figure out what propels their uneasiness.

Changing Minds (2019) also shares the same sentiments with the two experts quoted above. The body language website explains, 'Small, lightning-fast movements of the mouth betray inner thoughts, for example, a single twitch of the corner of the mouth that indicates cynicism or disbelief.' This assertion gives us another point of view to the concept; all these while, we have been analysing trembling of the two corners of the mouth, but this talks about a corner of the mouth. This may be done in a formal setting by a subordinate to express their disbelief in what a superior figure has said. Also, this is very useful in the law enforcement setting. Liars sell themselves out through the fast trembling of the lips as their conscience stands against the conscious falsehood they are saying.

Practical Illustrations

Case Study I: The mother of K invited him to the living room. His father was around, so he answered the call immediately. When he came, he was told to stand erect and face both of them. His parents were not in town the preceding day, and they discovered that he came home late and even brought a lady in. It was his father who opened the questioning session. It went thus: "Where were you yesternight?" The question was enough to send shivers down his nerves. For a moment, he looked down and wanted to tell a lie, but the stern faces of his parents were enough clue for him that danger was lurking around. The mother re-echoed the question, and as he wanted to speak, the corners of his mouth started trembling. He managed to speak, but not too long into his explanation, his voice began to crack. That simply nailed him! He was lying, and there was no way he could muster the confidence to defend that brazen defeat which was glaring to the mother.

Case Study II: It was almost getting dark, and every office was expected to have closed business for the day. So the patrol team chattering by a business community was out on their usual duty. As they were checking if all offices were properly locked, they saw a man coming out from an office and looking distressed. As they did not want to assume he was a worker in the firm, he was invited for questioning, and he said that he was kept back by some urgent duties. The leader of the team asked if they could be briefed of what he was doing, but his mood changed immediately, and he lowered his eyes. When he discovered that the security team was serious, he decided to give them an explanation that would not expose the despicable act he was performing in the office. As he was speaking, one of the officers noticed trembling at the corners of his mouth. They were not convinced of his explanation and had to document his name so as to officially report him the next day.

Case Study III: During the weekly meeting of FSR Company, their manager informed them that the firm was ready to multiply the income of anyone of them who referred clients to them and also increased their level of productivity. That was not the first time for the workers to hear such promises. In fact, one of them saw a corner of the manager's mouth twitch while he was giving the assurance. So they quickly assumed that he was up to his old ways—he was being deceptive.

Case Study IV: Two forgers went to a bank to withdraw a huge amount of money belonging to a multinational company. They approached a junior staff and were putting pressure on her to hasten things up, probably so that they could get away before anyone noticed them. The junior staff needed to involve a senior staff who was conversant with the financial operations of the firm. Going through the document, the senior official suspected a foul play. He summoned the men who were about to escape immediately. When they were asked to offer an explanation on how they came about the documents, the lips of the first forger began to tremble, leading to a cracking voice, while his accomplice began to shiver in an obvious manner. That simply hinted that they were being deceptive.

10.13. Turning the Lips Upside Down

Generic Interpretations of the Concept

This can be a really ugly show of negative emotions. The lips are twisted in a way that they would form a U shape. To display this behaviour, the lips would be compressed, and then the edges of the mouth will turn downward. This is a signifier of discomfort or high stress. Faking this behaviour is like climbing Mount Kilimanjaro within ten minutes; it is very difficult, if not impossible, to fake. This means that whenever you observe it on anybody, it is an accurate communicator of the person's state of mind—usually a negative one though. Let me quickly sound this note of warning that you should be careful in your observation as some people have a naturally downturned mouth. So it would be rash and unfair of you to accuse such people of feeling uncomfortable.

This gesture can be likened to the sad-mouth cue discussed in (10.16). However, the difference is that in this gesture, the lips are either tightly compressed or they completely disappear.

Scientific Explanations

While not too many scholars specifically discussed this gesture, Christopher Philip foregrounds it in every aspect of it; he gives an in-depth explanation of the upturned mouth cue. He submits that this gesture can be seen in both the young and the old. Children turn their lips upside down if you want to feed them with what they do not like—that is, it is used to communicate dislike or disapproval by babies who cannot really express themselves through verbal utterances. However, this is a reflection of troubled mind among adults. It encompasses the true sentiment of the person's emotions at that point in time.

Philip encapsulates everything in one sentence thus: 'When the mouth becomes inverted in an upside down "u" shape [downturned smile], the facial expression turns into a high stress indicator.' It is like the person's smile has been painted with a cloud of ugliness, which is very obvious to the people around him or her to see. When a public official or even anybody is accused of an offence which they are seeking every way to deny, you may see this gesture in the person. It means the person wants to 'convince' you with their story without *conveying* their information. This makes the difference between honest people and liars. A liar wants you to believe them by all means even if their story is lopsided and obviously false, while an honest person will just inform you about everything that happens in an event. Believing it or not does not necessarily matter to a person whose conscience has adjudged rightly.

Apart from being a high stress indicator, this gesture may also signal anger, unhappiness, depression, and tension. If you are held for a long duration of time at a location, you become bored and depressed. Also, tension can be caused by varieties of things. A person who is unprepared for a test, someone who just escaped an accident, and someone who saw something frightening in the dark. All these are tension-inducing incidents. If you are angry, the shape of your mouth undergoes changes, and one of the common positions it assumes is the U shape. I need to remind you that this gesture does not last for more than a twinkle of an eye, so if you do not pay attention, they may elude you. It is usually more pronounced at the point where a person feels stressed the most. So watch out and see the traces so as to be informed about the discussion.

Practical Illustrations

Case Study I: After marriage, a man decided to move from his one-room apartment to a place that looked convenient and deserving for the new family. So an estate agent got him a place in his are of choice. There were two flats in the house. That means one was still vacant. After some few weeks when they had moved in, the estate agent brought in another person to check the place, and lo, it was an old notorious schoolmate of the newly wedded man. When he saw him, he first hid, but he knew hiding could not be a means of escapism for long. They later met and greeted each other. As the old notorious mate of his informed him that he was going to move in, in the next few days, the man became uncomfortable, knowing what he was up to. Responding, the man compressed his lips and turned his mouth downward. His 'friend' thought this was a smile, but in reality, it was a communication of discomfort.

Case Study II: Mr J had just been transferred from his duty post. This was the first time he was being moved out of his station since he secured an employment with the security company. His new role required him to be on night duty most times. This was against his lifestyle; he was a type who enjoyed staying late at night at clubs and going out with different women. With this, it meant he was going to disappoint many people. What was more troubling for him was the claim that the particular place he was posted to was considered as the most dangerous of all spots for his company. So apart from foregoing his lifestyle, his life was also in danger. When he was given the letter, it was as if life were taken out of him. He wanted to speak but resisted by compressing his lips and turning the corners of his mouth downward. He did not know what any utterance might lead to, so he thought it was just safe that he kept mute.

Case Study III: It was the policy of DWA High School to move their teachers from one class to the other at the beginning of every session. This was to fight against complacency or make people feel too comfortable with their present level. However, most of the teachers were always avoiding students in their year 5; it was the class preceding the final year. So there was usually much work for any teacher handling the class, and more so, most of the students in this class felt like they were on top of the world. At the beginning of the session, as Ms R received her letter, she discovered that she was posted to that class. She read through the letter again with compressed lips and downturned mouth. It was as if she were in a reverie. This is a sign of psychological turmoil and discomfort.

Case Study IV: It is not in the culture of Airport AR to keep travellers waiting due to clearance. However, there was an upsurge of new arrivals, and this meant more pressure on the clearing officials. Criminal H had forecasted this kind of traffic, and that was why he travelled at that given time. While the officials on duty were running up and down to answer everyone, Criminal H pretended as if he had been cleared and was about to walk away when a law enforcement officer looking at him quickly picked on him. He was shocked that someone was monitoring him. Not knowing what to say, he compressed his lips, turned his mouth upside down, and followed the officer who nabbed him—that is, he was confused and short of ideas that could liberate him.

10.14. Pursing the Lips

Generic Interpretations of the Concept

When you purse your lips, it forms the shape of a purse—that is, you pinch your upper and lower lips together in a very tight way; it is just like drawing your zipper. Just like the other closed body gestures discussed in this section, the aim is to keep the mouth closed and, symbolically, the mind too. On a general note, people are fond of pursing their lips when they do not agree with what someone is saying. Another context this behaviour is commonly observed is when we are thinking of an alternative. It is not usually easy for the brain to multitask at all times. So it subconsciously shuts the mouth against external factors when a rigorous thinking is taking place within. That is, when thinking of an alternative, we do not want the existing option to dominate our mind. So we shut our mind against it.

Also, when an audience do not agree with what a speaker has just said or they feel it is wrong, you will see this behaviour. If it is a one-on-one conversation, it would be better that you ask your co-interlocutor what they feel and try to clarify issues before moving further. If their guess is right, you can look for a way of convincing them. If not, you will need to correct their wrong notion.

If the pursed lips are moved outward in a glaring manner, this means the negative emotion or sentiment is very great. I have seen this in the game of poker when players do not fancy their hole cards. This behaviour is very reliable in identifying someone's dislike for a concept or another person. Note that the lip-pursing gesture distorts the shape of the mouth, and no one will choose to do it for fun.

Scientific Explanations

Many experts and platforms contribute towards the understanding of this subject matter. Study Body Language (SBL) states that when the lips are pursed, they create a round but tight shape. This gives the person a stern look, which in itself is message enough for a discerning mind. I mean, this gesture is intuitive to decode—it is used to connote suppressed anger or disagreement. When a person does not agree with you or is pissed off by your attitude, they will not laugh with you; their look becomes stern and unfriendly. When you see this from a superior, it is better if you cooperate with them before they fully express their anger. The website also explains that this behaviour may connote indecision—when a person is trying to weigh two equal options. The gesture gives a pictorial view of a person who is stalling the words in their mouth before eventually blurting them out.

In a persuasive context, this is an essential marker that hints you that this is the best time for you to hit harder and try to convince the person with your argument (the gesture means they are indecisive at the moment). So if you make your point clearer, you can easily win the person to your side. Once they verbalise their decision, it becomes very difficult to alter (SBL 2019).

Schafer (2018) also expresses the same sentiment with SBL that this cue is used to show dissension or disagreement. The former FBI agent submits, 'Pursed lips mean a person has formed a thought in their mind that is in opposition to what is being said or done.' Making decisions can cause tension most times. So if you allow them to articulate their opposition, the tension will dissipate, and this means you may not be able to change the person's mind on the issue again. At the other side of the coin, if you are the one displaying this gesture, you must be very articulate about your thoughts so that the other party will find it difficult to change your mind.

Changing Minds (2019) describes this cue as a 'classic sign of anger'. This means the person is tensed or frustrated about something. The platform explains that it is the unconscious shutting of the mouth to prevent a person from saying what they feel like saying. Liars can also decide to withhold the truth with the use of this gesture. The website also supports the submission of SBL and Schafer that the behaviour may be a representation of indecision.

Practical Illustrations

Case Study I: A family was having a meeting on Saturday, as it was their norm. The children raised concerns that the chores were killing them as they had to be engaged in them for a substantial part of the day once they return from school. This was in response to the reason behind their woeful academic performance noted by their father. So they all agreed that their work schedule should be revisited and adjusted appropriately. The children had thought that their parents would suggest getting a house help so that they could focus on their academics. However, their mother opined that they should first do their homework before doing any chores, and after that, they should quickly do their work and return to study to read in preparation for the next day. As their mother was talking, the children pressed their lips against each other, which gave their lips a round shape. They pushed their lips further as she continued. Noticing their disagreement, their father hurriedly chipped in that all they were doing was for their sake; he appealed to their emotions before they were allowed to talk. With this, he had won their heart and changed their perception of the whole issue.

Case Study II: Mr S was very tired and was on a high speed while coming home. Upon getting to their compound, he discovered that their neighbour had used his car to block the way. He was angered by this and had to wait for him to come and park the car well. As his neighbour walked towards him to apologise, he pursed his lips and drove past him in anger.

Case Study III: Mr LY was accused of forgery. He was taken aback by this accusation and became angry; he didn't remember when he did such a thing. So he was ready to challenge the law enforcement officials for wrongly accusing him. However, forensic analysis showed that there were inconsistencies in the documents. He requested that he should be given the documents so that he could go through them again. At that point, he noticed some weird things on the document. He became uncomfortable and pursed his lips while he thought on what could have gone wrong. It was later revealed that a colleague did it to intentionally indict him.

10.15. Pursed Lips Pulled to the Side

Generic Interpretations of the Concept

This is very similar to the lip-pursing gesture discussed above, the only difference is that the lips are energetically pulled to one side of the face in this case. So the attention and weight of the lips is felt on one side of the face. This alters the look of the face in every sense of it. Ideally, this is a microexpression that disappears in the twinkle of an eye. But when it is used in showing strong disagreement, it may tarry for some few seconds. This is very empathic, and it expresses the mind of the person concerned in a clear term. The verbal translation of this gesture is, 'I have a real issue here. I'm not pleased with the question I was asked, what you just said or where this is leading to.'

While some people may not be observant enough to catch the glimpse of pursed lips involving every part of the mouth, there is hardly any way this cue can be denied because attention is given only on one side. In some other parts of the world, this is used to label a co-interlocutor a liar. The verbal translation is given as 'I don't believe what you are saying. I know everything you've been telling me is a lie.' The longer the gesture tarries, the greater the sentiment shared by that person.

When people are asked questions which they feel should not be discussed, at least in public, they may display this cue as a way of telling you that you should overlook it and talk about something else. If you keep on with it, the response they will give you will surely be defective; they have forewarned you!

Scientific Explanations

Study Body Language (SBL) describes this gesture as 'quick and partial'. It is quick because it is subconsciously released, while it may be partial due to the fact that just a part of the mouth is involved. SBL alludes nervousness to this behaviour. The person may stylishly lick the side of the mouth in a self-comforting manner or as a means of releasing tension. Some people share the sentiment that pulling the lips has the capability of giving away their insecurities. Note that when the mouth is pulled to the side, the lips are pursed. So the licking is only accidental, which occurs when the tension is high.

Navarro (2011) also describes this gesture while differentiating between body language and microexpressions. The former FBI agent is not a fan of the overhyped role of microexpressions in the study of non-verbal gestures. He notes that when the 'corners of the mouth tightens to a side, dimples or pulls towards the eye or ear', this is a smirk that is used to express disdain or contempt. The body language expert was quick to add that contempt is not necessarily a sign of deception as it is noticed in both the honest and liars. He explains further, 'Contempt is often seen among the innocent when interviewed by those they deem to be of lower social status or whom they perceive as incompetent. You also see looks of contempt on the part of an occupied population toward their oppressors.' It is good that we try to make this point at this point so that whenever you see this gesture in a person, you will not be fast in labelling them as liars.

More weirdly enough, Westside Toastmasters (2019) says this gesture may be a cultural method of smiling; it is an English mannerism that those who are skewing up to the upper class maintain a stiff upper lip and should not appear emotional while smiling. Hence, they tend to hide their teeth and pull their mouth sideways rather than up due to cultural dictates.

Practical Illustrations

Case Study I: An old woman was arrested in a case connected to the death of her daughter. During interrogation, she was asked to explain the circumstances surrounding the birth of the child. She was taken aback by this question, feeling it was not necessary for such a question to be asked, but she explained everything. She was not aware that the question was only asked as a means of establishing her baseline before going into the interview proper. Long into the session, she was asked to explain how her relationship with her daughter went sour. She looked at the interrogating officer again as if she did not hear the question. Expectedly, the officer repeated the question, and she just compressed her lips and pulled it to a corner of the mouth for about three seconds, not knowing where to start her explanation. She was deeply confused and lost the appropriate words to capture what she could have said at that point.

Case Study II: In an unusual manner, Mr P came back home late the previous night. In fact, the whole family had slept when he sneaked in. He did not bother to call his wife to inform her he was going to keep long outside. Also, he did not return calls put through to his phone. When the wife woke up in the middle of the night to ease herself, she saw him sleeping beside her. She decided to let the sleeping dog be. On the next morning, she went to the dining to meet him after taking his breakfast. The only question that Mrs P asked was, 'Where did you spend the night?' Taking his head off the newspaper, Mr P looked around as if the question were meant for another person. Before he could look at his wife, she added, 'Yes, I'm talking to you.' This sent a deafening silence into the house. He squinted his face, looked sternly, and pulled his lips to a corner of the mouth before forcing himself to utter some incoherent words. It was certain that he just cooked up the explanation to dodge the wrath of his wife.

Case Study III: It was surprising to a teacher that one of the dullest students in her class did excellently well in a seemingly difficult test. She could not resist the temptation and, as such, had to invite him over to her desk. She asked, 'Young man, how did you do your test?' The poser sounded like a bombshell to him. Pursing his lips and moving them energetically to the side of his mouth, he went mute for a moment before explaining to the teacher. With the non-verbal gesture, the teacher knew that he was about to feed him with spurious lies.

Case Study IV: Ms GF was living with her elder brother who did not tolerate staying out late at night. However, it seemed that nightclubs were part of Ms GF's DNA—she took every opportunity to hang out with guys and do all forms of despicable things with them. Her brother was also bothered because he was a religious head in his local church. So he saw her behaviour as an invitation to ridicule to his personality. One day, he became so angry that he had to wait for her to return home so that he could blast her. After talking so hard to her, Ms GF had a dried throat. She pursed her lips and moved them to a corner of the mouth all throughout.

10.16. Sad Mouth

Generic Interpretations of the Concept

If the eyes serve as the windows to the soul, we can aptly submit that the mouth is the door through which we understand our emotional state. When I talk of a sad mouth, it is needless to further explain that this is used to describe negative emotions. Just like the eyes, we can accurately predict the emotional feeling of a person by watching at the shape of their mouth. For a saddened mouth, the corners of the lips would be turned downward in a slight manner. This is usually in concert with lowered upper eyelids. Seeing this cluster hints you that something is wrong with the person emotionally. Sometimes, people refer to this behaviour as 'grouper' mouth or face.

Let me quickly add that this is the natural look of some people—the corners of their mouth are always turned downward. To those in this category, this gesture does not have anything to do with the display of negative emotions. Apart from the eyes, the mouth is another expressive part of the face which gives us a detailed picture of how a person feels every time. A saddened mouth is always in consonance with the eyes and other parts of the face to express this feeling. In other words, it would be difficult for you to notice two opposing emotions on the face of a person every time.

Scientific Explanations

While explaining a lopsided smile, Westside Toastmasters (2019) says the downward movement of the mouth is an indication of sadness, anxiety, or any other form of negative emotion. If both sides of the mouth move downward, it means the person is angry, butbut if it is just a sad expression, it is an indication of sadness. A side moving slightly upward is to make the gesture non-threatening. What I am driving at in this paragraph is to differentiate between sadness and anger. When a person is angry, every side of the mouth turns downward in an awkward manner, which creates a feeling of fear in their audience, but sadness on the other hand, invokes the spirit of pity and sympathy. People are always ready to lend a helping hand to a sad person but is very fearful to move closer to an angry person. They do not know what the person is up to.

In the same vein, Changing Minds (2019) says flattened lips makes the mouth look saddened or frustrated. It notes that this feeling may be inspired by distress. Sometimes, we tend to hide our emotions by trying not to cry, but the fact is that there is no way we can do this in its entirety. The mouth will still communicate the fact that something is troubling us.

Kendra Cherry (2019) notes that the mouth is an embodiment of messages. A slight movement of the mouth is capable of communicating the intent of the mind to an observant fellow. Cherry particularly urges his readers to pay attention to the act of turning down the mouth by an interlocutor in any discourse context, noting, 'Slight changes in the mouth can also be subtle indicators of what a person is feeling.' He explains that 'a slightly downturned mouth can be an indicator of sadness, disapproval, or even an outright grimace'.

From the foregoing, it is very clear that all the contributors to this concept maintain the consensus that a slightly downturned mouth stands for sadness. And also, it is a universal sign that is noticeable anywhere around the world. This is the opposite of the upward movement of the mouth, which is used by people to denote a happy mood. This polar difference makes the behaviour easily identifiable.

Practical Illustrations

Case Study I: Mr H and Ms G had been lovers since their high school days, but they officially started a relationship when they got to university. Throughout their stay in school, everybody knew them to be fond of each other. Even after graduation, they ensured that they both secured employment in the same environment so as not to create distance between them. Everything seemed perfect, and they decided to tie the nuptial knot. All this while, they were oblivious of the genotype of each other. Eventually, they got to know that they were both AS. Their love had gone deep and were not truly ready to let go of each other. Mr H was of the opinion that they could decide not to give birth and go for adoption, but this was not tenable to Ms G—she had always dreamed of being pregnant and the kind of life she would lead for nine months. She was not ready to forgo that on that platter of anything or risk giving birth to a sickle cell. With a downturned mouth, she looked at Mr H tearfully and urged him that they should stop the relationship for the future benefits of both of them.

Case Study II: Ms U learnt that the results of their final exams were out, and she rushed to her portal to check. She was actually afraid of what her performance would be in literary studies because she fell sick on the day of the exam, and right from the onset, she was not a fan of the course. As she scrolled down on the portal, she discovered that she failed the course with just a mark. This means she would have to pay another tuition fee and take the exam again. Also, the provincial employment she had secured would be terminated. Things were not cool for her parents as they were striving to make ends meet. Slightly turning her mouth downward, Ms U dropped her device and slept off in thought. She was lost in sadness all throughout.

Case Study III: A suspected terrorist managed to gain entry into a shopping mall. At first, the security guard had suspected him but overlooked his suspicion and allowed him in. Within five minutes upon entering the mall, the terrorist opened fire on shoppers. And before he could be arrested, he set himself ablaze. The security guard at the entrance managed to escape the incident and sat at a corner, looking dejected, with his mouth turned downward. You will be moved if you should see the sight because he was soaked in sorrow.

10.17. The Oval-Shaped Mouth

Generic Interpretations of the Concept

Some also refer to this gesture as the *O*. When the mouth forms an oval shape, making it look like an *O* in communication, it means the person is either surprised or pained. It is an instinctive sound made in reaction to both positive and negative emotions. I have travelled around the world and noticed this gesture everywhere I have been to. In other words, this cue is a universal response to pain, pleasure, or surprise. Possibly, it can be a vestigial response we share with alarmed primates.

Because it is an intuitive response, the exact reason we do this is not established at the moment. However, we may try to infer. When a person is in agony, maybe after an accident, or a woman is in the labour room, the shouting of *O* gives the mouth an oval shape, which makes them release carbon dioxide fully into the environment. They are stressed and weakened by what they are actually going through, and the cue is to purge them of the pain. Also, when a person is surprised, this shout, when intuitively done, bears witness to the fact that they are not feigning their feeling.

Another possible context where this sound is made is when a person suddenly remembers that they left an important thing at home or at the office. The shout here means that they are pained by their act of forgetfulness. If they must get back to fetch that thing, you may see them frown as they make it to their car. They may pounce on anyone who offends them at this point in time because their emotion is charged already.

However, if the sound is made in the context of love, it is usually said in a sensational manner to arouse the feelings of the other person. Ladies mostly make this sound during intercourse as a replacement for the verbal utterance that 'I am enjoying it'. The *oo* sound will keep the man going. There is little wonder that most love song have the *oo* sound in them. Ultimately, remember that the oval structure gives the lips the perfect shape for kissing.

Scientific Explanations

Changing Minds (2019) states that when the mouth makes an oval shape, it is a show of desire. This is because it typically forms a kiss shape. The body language website explains that this hints on the reason most romantic songs do linger on the words *oo* and *you* in many parts of the world.

However, having formed the oval shape, if the person now uses their finger to touch their mouth, this is an indication of uncertainty. For instance, if the person leaves an important file at home, after making the *O* sound, they may put their fingers on their mouth, which means they are not certain of the next line of action—should they go home or wait until closing hour and work on the file after getting home? This thought may last for some seconds.

Practical Illustrations

Case Study I: Mrs E was in the mood of having sexual intercourse with her husband, but the man was delayed outside because his car broke down, which he had to fix. As a way of preparing for his arrival, Mrs E began to sing love songs. When he eventually came, she intensified her singing effort, making her mouth form a kiss shape. She rushed to her husband at the door, still singing with her sonorous voice, and she took off her husband's clothes and gave him a deep kiss, which aroused him. The shape of her mouth kept enticing Mr E. Once he finished eating, it was clear that his wife was ready for him, and in the twinkle of an eye, they were already on the bed. They were sexually aroused, and this was explicit in their non-verbal display.

Case Study II: Two people were trapped in an accident, but they were fortunate to have some Good Samaritans passing by who quickly came to their aid. They were both unconscious, and when they were being evacuated from the damaged car, the driver was shouting *ooo* with his mouth forming an oval shape. It was the same thing for his friend who was heavily wounded. It was a shout of agony which was really touching to the sympathisers. It made the sympathisers rush them to the nearest hospital instead of waiting for official first aid workers who might not arrive at that moment.

Case Study III: Ms R was the group managing director (GMD) of the firm where she worked. She took home some files the previous day so as to work on them in order to help her cover up lost ground before the end of the week. She had a three-year-old son who had been feeling not too well for some days. So her attention had been divided among many things. While taking care of her sick baby, she instructed her eldest daughter to help out in arranging the files in the study and drop them in her car. Upon getting to her workplace, she did not know that her daughter had mistakenly left out a sheet of paper where she wrote the agenda of the day for an executive meeting billed for the afternoon. It was just thirty minutes to the meeting, and she was much disorganised and would surely fumble if she was to chair the meeting. She checked her files again, and she unconsciously shouted 'Ooo!' with her face frowned. She stood up and sat on her chair again. If she should return home, the meeting would be delayed, a culture that was not tolerated in the company.

Case Study IV: A woman thought she would be due for delivery in two weeks but started feeling contractions somehow a week before the scheduled date. The husband was on a business trip, so she was alone. Suddenly, the pain came on her in a way she could not bear any more. Trying to get hold of her phone was like climbing a mountain. She later lay in the living room, screaming for help. It was the *ooo* sound that drew the attention of their neighbours to her. The people around knew that she was frustrated with her condition.

Case Study V: The uncouth attitude of some drug addicts in a particular community was reported to law enforcement agents. The agency sent their men to round up the building that was used for constituting nuisance in the society. Everywhere was barricaded while the enforcement officers sat somewhere. When one of the drug addicts came, he discovered that the entry had been blocked. He quickly made a move to gain entrance through another route, but it was still the same. Upon getting to the third gate and it was barricaded too, he unconsciously shouted 'Oooo!' with his mouth forming an oval shape as a means of registering his frustrations.

10.18. Mouth Open with the Jaw Moving to the Side

Generic Interpretations of the Concept

This is like the jaw-dropping behaviour that would soon be explored in the book. This gesture is usually done when a person realises that they have made a mistake or did something wrong. To display this gesture, one side of the mouth would be pulled to the side, which will cause the jaw to shift to the direction in which the mouth is pulled. This is done simultaneously with the clenched lower teeth on that side of the mouth being exposed. In simpler terms, this gesture is a sign of regret; it is done when we cannot shy away from the fact that we have done something wrong.

Because people understand that this gesture can easily give them out, they will not do it when they are in the presence of those who can punish them. As an educator who have interacted with students and participants across all levels, I have seen this behaviour in students when they fail questions that they were supposed to know. In a way, it means the students are accepting their own error or stupidity. Also, this is seen in employees who suddenly discover that they did not complete a task that they were supposed to before leaving the office, which might later backfire when their superior gets to know about it.

In some occasions, this behaviour is accompanied by the sudden intake of air via the clenched teeth. The air intake is to pacify themselves and reduce their breathing rate. If they fail to pacify themselves, the tension will increase to a level that may lead to tears, and some may injure themselves.

Scientific Explanations

Changing Minds (2019) states that pulling the lips back exposes the teeth, which is used to communicate aggression. The clenched teeth is an indicator that the person is showing a negative body gesture. If they were smiling, the teeth would not have been clenched aggressively. Also, a look on the eyes will tell you how the person feels. In the expression of aggression, regret, or snarl, the eyes would be narrowed. In the least, the person will also stare. When it is a smile, the corners of the eyes will crease. I will explain this better in the succeeding section.

Christopher Philip (2014) explains this cue in detail. He describes this gesture as, 'The jaws appear to be tightly compressed and the teeth can even be ground together back and forth. Sometimes the muscles connected to the temple can be seen flexing.' This is a sign of internal struggles. When we flex the jaw muscles, they make the mouth shift to the side. This tells your audience that pressure is mounting up in you; it means you are about to lose your cool. When you see this behaviour in others, you must take their aggression very seriously in order not to blame yourself at the end of the day.

This gesture may be a throwback to our primitive lifestyle, expressing the urge to bite someone. When the mouth is opened with teeth clenched, it 'is a non-verbal signal that indicates hidden or inward-directed grief, stress, fear, tension, anxiety, anger, frustration, or that aggression is being suppressed.' When the mouth is opened in a wild manner coupled with aggressive clenching of the teeth, which dictates the direction of the jaw, it is used to signal negative emotion or thought being held back. The obvious nature of this signal makes it frightening for people around us.

Let me state that some people are habitual teeth grinders or clenchers at night, so they make use of mouth guards as a way of protecting their teeth. People have always blamed this on high-stress occupations. Some go as far as developing pains in the muscles surrounding the jaw. However, when it happens during the day, it means all is not well with the person. In some other times, when the stress boils so high that the person cannot stomach their thought any longer, they speak through their clenched teeth (Philip 2014).

Eye rolling, eye darting, and snarls of the nose are the common clusters that do accompany this gesture.

Practical Illustrations

Case Study I: Mr W wanted to change his car and, as such, went to meet a car dealer with his wife. During the course of the conversation, the dealer analysed the features of the cars available and why he should go for a particular brand. As the dealer continued with his analysis, he sought to know the price of one of the cars, but the dealer told him to propose a price. He was too eager to have the car that he failed to obey the rule of negotiation, which states that 'seller first proposes while buyer beats it down'. With the price he mentioned, the seller was able to convince him to add more, which he knew he must do if he actually wanted to have the car. It was at this point that he discovered his mistake. As he opened his mouth to speak, his jaw budged to the side and he clenched his teeth.

The wife was also not happy with the attitude of her husband, but the deed was done already.

Case Study II: After a brief teaching session, a mathematics teacher gave his students an exercise so as to test their ability. The exercise was time-bound so that he would be able to do the corrections for them. The students were told to exchange their books with their partners so as to cross-check the work of each other as the teacher provided the corrections on the board. As the teacher began to work out the answers to each question, one of the students seated at the front opened his mouth, clenched his teeth, and pulled his jaw to the side. From the preliminary workings of the teacher, he was sure that he had missed a step that he should have done, but it was too late to withdraw his book from his partner. Not too long from that, another student displayed the same gesture. It was a show of regret having seen their errors. The teacher, being aware of the meaning of the cue, was smiling all throughout.

Case Study III: Trafficker UT was aware of the government's recent stuff policies against drug trafficking due to the harmful effects of drugs on its teeming youth. However, he was not ready to let go of such a lucrative business. So he decided to come up with another way of getting the drugs trafficked; he decided to smuggle the drugs in by using the cartons and items known for approved drugs to do a cover-up. On his next trip, after doing this, he didn't remember to package them in a least suspicious manner. His mere look at the border was enough to give him out. Upon checking how the drugs were arranged, he opened his mouth widely and unconsciously shifted his jaw to one side. He was overwhelmed by negative emotions, and there was no way he could stop it at that moment.

10.19. Smiling

Generic Interpretations of the Concept

Smile is a topic that is widely discussed among many body language experts. It is a source of concern to them because there have been reports of people faking it for the purpose of deceiving others. This can be very painful to an unsuspecting victim. That is why I have taken my time to explore the concept from different angles so as to make it easy for you to understand. When a smile is genuine and birthed unconsciously, it is a source of joy to people around us. That is why the cliché 'Bring smile to the face of people' is common around the world. In other words, smile is synonymous to joy. This is the first point that every reader needs to internalise.

For a smile to be genuine, it must be instant—that is, it must be displayed as soon as we feel the need to do so. If it is done later on, it is meant to be a cover-up and not true. When we smile genuinely, it is an irresistible way to communicate goodwill and friendliness. This approach works for both old friends and strangers alike. In the business world, leaders of the industry understand the role that smile plays in bridging the gap between people. If you think someone is not approachable, then you are saying that you have never seen the person smile before. Some firms have taken it as a point of duty to educate their security officials, front desk staff, and the entire workforce to learn how to smile while dealing with clients. In simpler terms, smiling is an incontrovertible marketing technique all over the world. We open the hearts of people with a smile, and if it is genuine, it is surely irresistible.

From the foregoing, you will notice that I have always emphasised the genuineness or otherwise of a smile and its effects. This suggests that there are different types of smile. A smile can be true, false, social, or tense, depending on the context and driving force behind it. We use the social smile to broker relationships with strangers; tense or nervous smile is the one worn by someone who is afraid—interviewees, students, etc., while the false smile is one engineered for the primary purpose of playing on our intelligence.

So it is always pertinent that you consider the intentions of people smiling at you before you open the door of your heart to them. Remember that if your heart is broken, it cannot be easily amended. This is an eternal caveat that I do leave behind in my trainings.

Scientific Explanations

Primarily, a smile is formed by flexing the muscles at the sides of our mouth. However, when some people smile, the muscles at the sides of the eyes are contracted. This is popularly known as the Duchenne smile. If a person smiles and their eyes did not contract, they may be taken as being insincere (Freitas-Magalhães and Castro 2009). Among humans, smiling is an expression that is used to denote pleasure, joy, amusement, happiness, or sociability. This is very different from the similar show of anxiety referred to as grimace. Cross-cultural studies have shown that smiling is an instrument of communication throughout the universe, but the differences among cultures are very pronounced with some nations using smiles as a means of expressing confusion or embarrassment (Izard 1971).

That a smile creates positive effects on others which makes us more likeable and approachable is not subjected to debate (Gladstone 2012). In the social context, smiling performs different functions. First, smiling is most times seen as the prelude to laughter, and secondly, it can be employed as a means of responding to laughter. There is hardly any advertisement where the subject of the event will not smile or laugh. The ultimate purpose is to endear products to viewers, and smiling opens the door of their heart to the advertised product(s).

In some contexts, it communicates sexual interest; this is more so when it comes from a female to a heterosexual male—it is very appealing to them. Smile increases the physical attractiveness of people. However, a recent study finds that a man's smile may not be the most potent tool in getting the attention of heterosexual women; it submits that facial expressions such as shame or pride tend to be more effective in this realm (Tracy and Beall 2011).

Not every smile has the intent of genuineness. Sometimes, it may be for the purpose of manipulation and reinforcement—that is, it can be employed for the underhand purpose of abuses (Braiker 2004).

It is pertinent that we discuss the cultural differences of smile. In most parts of the world, smiling is considered as an expression of positive emotions, but there are a few exceptions where it is seen as a means of expressing negative intents—such cultures see it as unwelcoming. When it is too much, it is interpreted as a sign of dishonesty or shallowness (Charles 2014). In some areas in Asia, people may take to smiling when embarrassed or in emotional pain. Some people simply smile to others as an indication of friendly greeting. That is why you see sportsmen smile at each other while shaking hands before the commencement of a game. In some parts of the world, a smile may be an exclusive reservation of close friends and relatives. For instance, a lot of people in the former Soviet Union consider smiling at strangers as weird and suspicious (RPI 2019).

In a large cross-cultural study carried out by Krys et al. (2016), it was discovered that a smiling person may be considered as less intelligent to their non-smiling counterpart in some cultures. The study also goes ahead to document that corruption of societal values has undermined the prosocial effects of smiling—that is, in societies where corruption is prevalent, people tend not to trust smiling individuals.

Despite all these issues and cultural differences, we cannot wish away the role of smiling in our society. In fact, Andrew Newberg concludes that 'a smile is the symbol that was rated with the highest positive emotional content'.

Practical Illustrations

Case Study I: Mr and Mrs UH were not pleased with the performance of their child. They told the management of the school, and they seemed helpless. At some point, they changed the child's school, and within a span of three months, they could see noticeable improvement on the child. They now engage him intellectually at home, and he responds in the same manner. One day, he decided to compose a song for the parents, and they listened intently. The message and lyric of the song were so funny that the couple smiled at their child. The child was unmoved by their smiles as he concentrated all throughout. The smile was a show of joy.

Case Study II: A middle-aged uneducated man walked into the bank to open an account. For the account to be opened, he needed to come with some documents and means of identification. The man first headed to the wrong section before he was redirected. Upon getting to the right unit, he was informed and taught the right steps to take, but it seemed he was in haste to get some funds transferred into his account. So he was suggesting an alternative method to the bankers. The bankers looked at each other and smiled. This was a way of mocking the man for his display of ignorance.

Case Study III: Students B and R liked group work so much, and they were both intelligent. This means that they also challenged each other any time they were learning. Another attribute of the young minds was that they study well ahead of time. In one of such interactive sessions, they battled with a mathematical problem. They both had different ways of solving the puzzle, but none led to the same answer. They were not ready to bow for each other. Since that was the topic to be taught the next day, they didn't ask the teacher. While the teacher was working it out on the board, they both looked at each other and smiled—they both got it wrong! It was more of teasing each other for being obviously wrong.

Case Study IV: A lady told his friend, an infamous prostitute, how a man in her workplace would not do without having an affair with ladies in a day. This was a good news to the prostitute. More so, the man was rich. So they planned on how to get the man connected to the prostitute. The lady fixed a date with his male colleague and promised she was going to come with a lady. Upon getting there, she allowed her prostitute friend to play the leading role, and within a few minutes, the man's manhood was standing erect already. The two ladies observed this and smiled to each other; they knew he was in their cage already—that is, they were happy that the man fell for their antics.

10.20. Genuine Smile

Generic Interpretations of the Concept

This topic has been widely researched by scholars. Today, our world is laced with deceits and betrayals. One does not know those who truly love one through their verbal utterances and modified body language displays. People can use fake smiles to lure you out of destiny. For a smile to be genuine, it must involve the corners of the mouth and muscles around the eyes. Without this collaboration between the two most expressive parts of the face, the smile is not true. Genuine smile is also referred to as the Duchenne smile. This name was given by Professor Paul Ekman, a renowned body language expert.

When a smile is true, the face would be visibly relaxed; you feel the ease on their face intuitively without being told—that is, the facial muscles portray joy instead of tension. This action is subconscious, and anyone who tries to feign it will still give themselves out at the end of the day. Those who cover up tension with a smile look weird and unattractive. I will explore this better in the succeeding section. True smile means that the person is without issues—nothing is bothering them at the moment as they are engulfed in the euphoria of joy due to a given event or thought.

From experience, I can boldly assert that a true smile can be very contagious in all spheres of life—personal, social, and professional settings. That is, when your smile is sincere, those around you will also smile back at you. This means they have mirrored your body language behaviour. There is little wonder that we attribute genuine smile with charismatic people—people with value, honour, and integrity. They are those whom we see as commanding respect in their areas of calling. A true smile is what we must always display. In other words, there is no need to smile forcefully if there is no need for that.

Scientific Explanations

In his research on the physiology of facial expressions, carried out in the mid nineteenth century, French neurologist Guillaume Duchenne identified two different kinds of smiles. A Duchenne smile involves contraction of both the zygomatic major muscle (which raises the corners of the mouth) and the orbicularis oculi muscle (which raises the cheeks and forms crow's feet around the eyes) (Drewnicky 2014). It is described in simpler terms as 'smiling with the eyes'. When a Duchenne smile is exaggerated, it is normally associated with deception (Davis 2014).

A Duchenne smile is believed to be propelled by the feeling of happiness. 'Research with adults initially indicated that joy was indexed by generic smiling, any smiling involving the raising of the lip corners by the zygomatic major [. . .]. More recent research suggests that smiling in which the muscle around the eye contracts, raising the cheeks high [Duchenne smiling], is uniquely associated with positive emotion' (Messinger et al. 2001).

Christopher Philip (2013) also explores this concept in a detailed manner. He describes seven types of smiles using the context-based categorisation. Philip notes that a true smile is a form of a broad smile—smiling without limits. During this process, the upper and lower teeth are very visible. This cannot be easily faked by anybody. 'The telltale sign of an honest smile is the appearance of crow's feet in the corners of the eyes. Crow feet make it seem as though the eyes are smiling. It is difficult to replicate these smiles without being truly amused or in good company as the muscles are usually out of our conscious control' (Philip 2013). He cautions that we should take cognisance of the places we make use of this gesture as it can be misinterpreted as being a sign of insincerity when displayed in the wrong context.

Kendra Cherry (2019) says smiling is one of the greatest body language cues. She notes that genuine smiles come easily, and the person does it in a relaxed manner—that is, you do not have to think of anything while displaying this gesture.

Practical Illustrations

Case Study I: As a way of encouraging every student to speak up and interact freely with their mates, a teacher decides to carve out the final five minutes of his teaching session to talk to students about life and crack jokes. This made every one of them look up to a session with him. After treating a seemingly complex topic, the teacher adjusted his trousers to his abdomen, which seemed amusing to the students. While adjusting the trousers, he also squeezed his mouth as if he were finding it difficult. Being on it for almost three minutes drew concern from the students at some point, but as he released back the pair of trousers to its normal position and breathed out, most of the students smiled at his 'victory' with their facial muscles contracting. In this context, they have nothing to lose if they fail to smile, but the action really appears funny to them.

Case Study II: In a football derby, the two teams had played out their skills, but it seemed the god of soccer would not just open the net to any one of them. They kept on manoeuvring each other till the last minute, but it was still a goalless affair. The referee added an additional five minutes, and it seemed this had charged the home team to go for victory. On the dot of the ninety-fifth minute, the attacker of the team found the back of the net of the opponents as the whole field went agog. Running to meet their coach, the goal scorer smiled with his mouth wide open, muscles around the eyes and mouth contracting. This shows real happiness.

Case Study III: As part of its recruitment process, SWR Company required its applicants to fill online questionnaires and take both numerical and verbal cognitive tests before the successful ones could be invited over for a face-to-face interview. Because the firm was one that many people wished to work for, their recruitment process was truly tedious. Two weeks after graduation, Mr L learned that there was an opening in the firm, and he put in his all for it. After the first test, he checked his email after three hours, and he received a congratulatory email to proceed to the next level of the application process. Reading through the mail, his face beamed with happiness as his facial muscles contract in a relaxed manner.

Case Study IV: A fact we need to establish is that not everything about criminals is fake. I have seen quite a lot of them smile genuinely. For instance, I once instructed a junior colleague to investigate a criminal case. I didn't know the criminal was a con artist; I only glanced through the report before calling on him to take charge of the case. He swung into action, and to my bewilderment, he could not hold the suspect to any crime or allegation convincible enough to give us a win in court. More so, the con artist came out smiling genuinely; this was in celebration of his cheap victory.

10.21. Fake Smile

Generic Interpretations of the Concept

This is the polar opposite of the gesture we just explored, and people smile falsely when there is something at stake. This is used for perception management; we want to deceive others that all is well with us. In a bid to convince them, we display this cue wrongly, which makes them form a bad impression about us. For the fact that fake smile is not contagious draws the consciousness of the person to you that all you are doing is a mere outward show of emotions.

A fake smile can be easily distinguished from true ones for those who are observant. In a false smile, in most cases, just a side of the face is actively involved; the other side will clearly depict negative emotions. In some other times, the smile tilt towards the ears instead of the eyes. Looking at these differences, you will discover that a false smile totally rewires the facial appearance of the person to depict falsehood. If it were a true smile, it engages the mouth, eyes, and entire facial muscles. It smoothens the face and sends away tension for the given time.

Nowadays, what we see in most parts of the world is a fake smile. People understand that happiness gives them access to you and, as such, will feign one even if it does not really come from their heart. Salespersons, contractors, students, junior workers, and sycophants are fond of this form of smile. They do it primarily because of their business or the favour they seek from you and not because it is an innate feeling they want to express. You also notice this when taking photographs; people are forced to smile for no just reason, and the photos end up looking weird than they could have imagined. The world is grossly corrupt that the situations where one uses a false smile cannot be totally captured in a short piece such as this.

Scientific Explanations

Some people refer to a fake smile as Pan Am smile or Botox smile. The zygomatic major muscle is forcefully contracted as a means of showing politeness. According to Harlow John (2005), 'It is named after the now defunct airline Pan American World Airways, whose flight attendants would always flash every passenger the same perfunctory smile.' Botox, which was introduced in 2002, can also cover up the wrinkles of the face when used in excess, thereby making a Duchenne smile an impossibility.

Philip also explains fake smile under different categories. He opines that this smile takes place when the lips are tightly stretched across the face without the teeth showing. Depending on the amount of lips raised in the corners of the mouth, this form of smile can vary in intensity. 'The low intensity smile has very little upward curl in the corner of the mouth and indicates a hidden attitude or thought, uncertainty, hesitation, or lack of confidence. In this smile, the lips are stretched toward the ears with no curl using muscles called the risorius. The risorius muscles are unable to raise the corner of the lips,' Philips notes. You will notice this smile in small babies while dealing with every other person except their mother. It means their true source of joy is their mother. A fake smile is used for the purpose of placating others or posing for photographs. This form of smile may also be used by strangers to greet each other while passing on the streets. This smile may also be a result of nervousness, so you may see people do it when they meet someone for the first time.

If the tight-lipped smile occurs with low intensity during a conversation, it is used to negate what has been previously said.

Another variation of a false smile discussed by Philip is an uneven smile. This is when a part of the face is employed in smiling while the other part is frowned or upturned. This showcases a state of mind where two opposite emotions are expressed. This is used by people to communicate sarcasm. It is mostly seen among friends. Let me add that an uneven smile is usually seen in the western part of the world.

A fake smile may also involve the raising of the upper lip, which will expose only the top row of teeth with the lower teeth hidden from the co-interlocutor. This signifies medium pleasure; the person is not totally happy. This is mostly seen in car salesmen who are telling you they are pleased with a certain price but will be happy to see you raise the bar (Philip 2013).

Practical Illustrations

Case Study I: A branch of DSR Dental Company was holding a send-off for the branch manager. Well, there were mixed opinions held among employees on the personality of the manager, but generally, he was seen in the negative light. When the news of his transfer came, most of them celebrated it privately. Some even went as far as organising a mini party outside of the workplace. So during the send-off programme, some employees were asked to share their thoughts on the behaviour of the manager. One of them stood up and submitted thus, 'He's a wonderful boss, a nice and caring man. I'm deeply pained that he is leaving us at this point in time. If he were leaving to establish his own company, I would have followed him, no matter the amount he is willing to offer me.' After making his comments, he ended it with a tight-lipped smile, which negated all that he had said—that is, he was being fake all this while.

Case Study II: A child offended his father and had been looking for every way to appease him. So he was always hovering over him, which did not move his father though. On a particular evening, the father thought of sharing his experience of the day with the family. Even before he commenced the story, he had started smiling. After telling the story, none of the family members smiled but only the child. Actually, nothing was funny about the narration, but he only forced himself to smile to create a false impression on the father that he admired what he said. This was a subtle lie performed to make his father feel better about himself.

Case Study III: Without being sarcastic, nurses are the group of professionals I have seen feign a smile in a perfect way. Check most of their smiles; they are not all that genuine. Their job requires that they should smile at their patients in order to birth hope in them. A friend who was a nurse once smiled to a patient who was not responding to treatment, and he turned back to me to confess that he 'only gave him false hope'. I was shocked he could say that. Even though the smile didn't look genuine, it still worked for the person in context—that is, he was able to deceive the person with his fake smile.

Case Study IV: A prostitute was looking for every way possible to gain the attention of a handsome man with the most expensive car who came to the gathering. The man seemed to be too much concerned about discussing politics than looking for good-looking girls. So she thought that the chances of gaining his attention through her mere looks was zero. Hence, she decided to feign interest in what he was discussing even though she never had interest in politics. Any time the man said anything, she would smile and try to ensure that there was eye contact. This fake smile became very obvious when she was the only one to smile at some point when there was no reason warranting such.

10.22. Nervous Smile

Generic Interpretations of the Concept

At some point in time, we all experience fear, but the way in which we handle it is what differs. Also, while some are habitually nervous, it is a once-in-a-while thing for others. Smiling is a means of escapism from stress in some people; they cover up their emotional feeling with a smile. What those who smile nervously want to achieve is to trick their audience into believing that all is well with them when in actual fact, they are cold within. All that some people care about is to see you smile and not the underlying meaning that conveys such a smile, hence the reason some people easily fall victim of deception.

Both guilty and honest people smile nervously in different contexts. For the guilty, they are trying to tell you that they are not afraid because they did not perform the offence they were 'accused' of. On the other hand, honest people who are habitually fearful of a situation or person will smile nervously for you to believe that they are happy seeing such a thing. For instance, some people are afraid of law enforcement officials even when they have never been arrested, maybe due to what they have heard about them in times past. So instead of shivering, they will smile nervously; meanwhile, their heart will pound till they take their leave from that vicinity.

From my own experience, I have noticed this form of smile mostly at airports or border entries. When visitors are being questioned by an inquisitive officer, they will smile as if they were enjoying the session. But if they are eventually released, the expression on their face changes, and they walk briskly so as to move out of sight of the officer.

Scientific Explanations

Philip (2013) explains the nervous smile in different forms—that is, smiling nervously is not done in a single way. For instance, the downturned smile is an expression of tension, stress, depression, sadness, and anger. This occurs when the mouth is inverted into a downward-facing U shape.

In another article, Philip (2014) describes a nervous smile as 'a fleeting smile that quickly shows and disappears, the eyes are tensed and darting and the lips may quiver in fear. Other times the smile is long-lasting—more than ordinary.' When a smile flashes at you and disappears within a twinkle of an eye, it is regarded as a nervous smile. Ideally, a smile should last till the other party mirrors it, but a nervous smile disappears almost immediately because it was never meant to be; it was only flashed to create a sense of normalcy, which is non-existent. A nervous smile is used to show that a person is undergoing emotional struggle.

People may decide to make use of this body gesture if they are looking for sympathy from another person. So we cannot say that this body gesture is entirely bad. If a friend is about to make a presentation or undertake a huge project and you see a nervous smile on them, you can walk up to them and give them a pat in the back, encourage them, or even give them a hug. In this sense, they have used a nervous smile to gain sympathy, encouragement, or care. The verbal translation of this gesture is, 'I'm scared and feel awkward, but I'm going to smile and try to put on a good face to mask my unpleasant feelings' (Philip 2014).

It should be noted that the motivation for a nervous smile is an awkward feeling or fear but which the person needs to wear a good look in order to draw the attention of others to their plight. The clusters to this cue are blushing face, sweating, paleness, fidgeting, cracking of voice, shortness of breath, inability to speak fluently, slightly turning the body away, lowering the head, or tucking the hands in pockets so as to hide their fidgeting hands (Philip 2014).

The variant of a nervous smile looks like a smirk, but they should not be confused. The smirk is usually accompanied by dominant body languages such as shoulders back, head back, and other open body language with excessive show of pride. You see this body gesture when someone is under verbal attack. Sometimes, the smirk is due to the stress of being put on a hot seat and not necessarily one's intent to question authorities (Philip 2014).

Practical Illustrations

Case Study I: As it was the norm in University of YTR, every final year, a student must make a presentation of their thesis in the presence of a large audience—students, researchers, internal and external scholars. Ms T was one of the students graduating this year, and her fear had been the random questions asked by the audience. If she failed to engage them as expected, she might be told to go and rework the whole project, which meant she would be left behind by her colleagues. On D-day, while making her way to the podium, she appeared as though she was a deer in the headlights. The corners of her mouth turned upwards as a way of hiding her anxiety.

Case Study II: It was Mr E's first time to travel to Liberty Country. As a researcher, he had been to many nations of the world, but he was never bothered by the law enforcement officers of those countries at the airport. It seemed that those at Liberty were different. The customs drilled him for several minutes, and while answering their questions, his eyes darted and tensed. He also slightly turned his body away as if ready to make his way out, coupled with his influent utterances. Ultimately, his mouth formed a U shape, which was a way of covering up his fear before the custom officials. When one of the officials noticed that Mr E was practically fidgeting, he told his colleagues that they should allow him to go.

Case Study III: Man KO impersonated his boss at a function, and he was almost perfect about it. He did everything in such an apt manner that none of the audience could notice that he was up to something. However, some of the audience began to have doubt on the personality when he began to fidget while smiling. The smile was so unreal that one of the top executives at the venue had to mention the boss's name again to be sure if he was truly the one. This was the point that he could not push further before his real identity was brought to light—that is, he could not hide the nervousness again at that point.

In the three cases above, we can see how people employed the nervous smile as a way of hiding their negative emotions. This can be seen in almost all facets of life.

10.23. Smiling as a Gauge of Feelings

Generic Interpretations of the Concept

Having discussed smiling under three different sections, this segment is to draw the curtain close on it by considering how smiling plays a role in revealing the emotions of people. I have strategically arranged the topics in a way that they will broaden your understanding and, more so, in a way that will give you the practical knowledge of all the concepts enunciated in the book. Having said that, how accurate do smiles reveal our inner intents? This is not a rhetorical question, so let me answer that smiles go a long way in telling us the true feelings of a person.

Research shows that sportsmen's smiles differ depending on the position they end their race with—first, second, or third. The person who ends up in the first position smiles with elation, while the second runner-up gives a pacifying smile. It is very interesting to note that this same assertion holds for congenitally blind athletes—those who have never seen a smile on another person's face since they were born. The smile on each of them reveals whether they are successful or not. This further confirms that a lot of non-verbal gestures are entrenched in our brains—that is, they are inborn. We have only used smile as a way of demonstrating that non-verbals are ingrained in our subconscious.

Scientific Explanations

Jessica Shirripa (2016) notes that the law of attraction can be used in explaining the act of smiling. We can either choose to focus on positive or negative thoughts, depending on the feelings that we want to invoke into our lives through intuition. In short, our smile plays a huge role in determining the perception of people about us. Without uttering a word, people can understand how you feel through your smile. Some studies attribute our smiles to our level of confidence. On the other hand, aesthetic experts define what a 'classic beauty' is through the kind of smile that people wear every time—supple lips, large eyes, and high cheekbones.

What we seek to establish at this point is that how we smile reveals our true feelings. Shortly, I will reel out different forms of smile and the emotions they connote. The first is the *no-teeth squint*. In this form of smile, the lips are tightly closed to form the curves of a crescent moon. This causes the eyes to scale shut effortlessly. In most cases, this cue is accompanied with a slight head tilt, which is used to show disgust for a person or a thing. With the picture I have painted, you will discover that this smile is not a good look for the person. So they are using it to tell their adversary to leave them alone. Even without opening their mouth, the message is clear enough for any discerning mind (Shirripa 2016).

Another way in which smile reveals our feeling is through the *awkward smirk*. A lot of people do this more than they would intentionally like to because their personality is unintentionally awkward. In the same vein, a smirk does not reveal the teeth, which is needed to make a real happy smile. When you see this smile on a person, it means they are feeling uncomfortable. This smile is seen on people when they make an accidental eye contact with a person on the street or if someone says a lacklustre joke but which you feel you should just maintain politeness.

The *fake grilling* portrays one as lacking emotions. This is also called Botox smile. It shows that the person is fake and lacks zero emotion. This is a tight-lipped smile which most of us display on a daily basis while dealing with our bosses and co-workers just to make them feel good even if there is nothing that warrants it from our mind; we do it to fulfil all righteousness.

However, the *gummy grin* is considered as being a genuine show of emotions. This form of smile occurs when your tooth-to-gum ratio is not as symmetric as you would have liked it to be. When we are legitimately happy, we cannot control the way we smile or laugh. A smile that shows a portion of our gum is evidence that the person is really happy and their intentions are genuine. This form of smile is often admired and easily mirrored by others (Shirripa 2016). Apart from being inviting, this smile also exudes sincerity and joy. The head would also be thrown backwards while smiling in a sincere manner (Lamberg 2019).

As reiterated at different points in time, some people smile as a way of hiding their negative emotions. This form of smile starts and ends quickly. This is like the nervous smile where we use facial muscles to regulate the smile expression. 'These include things like pressing your lips together or activating the muscles that pull down on the corners of the mouth. These muscles are under voluntary control' (Lamberg 2019).

Furthermore, smiles have the ability to expose people when they are under stress. Being under pressure makes people react in a way that is incongruent with the situations at hand. 'A common example of this is laughing when you receive bad news, freezing when you are in danger, or making jokes when you are uncomfortable. These incongruous responses are just a few of the brain's many ways of managing overwhelming emotional circumstances. An unexplainable smile may also be a signal of distress, especially when others are around,' says Shadeen Francis, a family and marriage therapist in Philadelphia. Francis also explains further that when people are under severe social distress, smiling is a more common action to them compared with when they are comfortable or in non-social contexts (Lamberg 2019).

Also, people use their smile to show how superior they are over others—a show of contempt. Here, you will notice a conscious disconnect between outward expression and the person's inner feelings. In some other cases, the disconnection may simply be unconscious, an outcome of pushing negative feelings to the side. In some cultures, they warn that a child's enraged feelings should not be practically expressed. In such situations, the child will suppress their anger with laughter (Lamberg 2019).

Practical Illustrations

Case Study I: Mr A was cracking a joke while the whole family was in the sitting room. The children found the joke really funny, and they laughed out their heart. However, Mr A discovered that his wife smiled in an unattractive manner and focused on some other things. He was bothered by this and had to ask her if anything was wrong. He wanted to know if he had offended her before supper time. However, after too much pestering, Mrs A later opened up that she had a bad day at work. She told him all that went wrong, and he sympathised with her. He was able to know her mood through her smile. The man was able to gauge the feelings of his wife due to how she smiled; it was different from what he was used to.

Case Study II: On the afternoon of a particular Friday, the bank manager of UCD Branch held a meeting with his employees and intimated them that the management was about to close down the branch but assured them that none of them would be sacked. Instead, they were to be posted to some other branches. Some employees only grinned at this news, while some of them frowned all throughout. Not pleased with their expressions, the manager asked them if something was wrong, and they said nothing. But in reality, they knew they would be somewhat demoted in their new branches. Because they didn't smile heartily, the manager was able to detect that they were not happy.

Case Study III: Teacher B was considered by students as a tough teacher. He didn't tolerate nonsense, and the students could not joke with him as they did with others. Also, he hated it when he was teaching and students were not responding. In such cases, he might spend extra time explaining the concept. On this particular day, most of the students were hungry and could not afford to lose a minute of their break time to him. As he was talking, most of them were smiling to encourage him. Because he had no knowledge of non-verbal communication, he thought they were impressed by his lectures, but in reality, this was not the case.

Case Study IV: Suspect AP had been investigated by different law enforcement agents, and he seemed to have understood how security agents function. He thought he could explore that and use it against me while I was interviewing him. When I was asking him serious issues, he began to smile as a way of dousing the tension in the room and indirectly appealed to me to 'tread' softly. He didn't know I had vast knowledge on this subject matter. His smile was not genuine, and there was no reason he could account for it. I had to let him understand he was only playing the role of a clown in that context.

10.24. Compressing the Edges of the Mouth

Generic Interpretations of the Concept

Merely looking at the corners of a person's mouth can reveal many things going on in the person's mind. For instance, when a corner of the mouth pinches tight and pulls in slightly or in an upward position, it can be interpreted as a feeling of smugness, contempt, dislike, or disbelief. In short, crimping the edges of the mouth is an expression of negative emotions. For the fact that a corner of the mouth pulled in hints you that the person is going through some difficult moments emotionally.

In the case where the contempt is glaringly overt, this gesture can be overhyped or dramatised, leaving no grey areas as to true sentiments. Mostly, crimping of the edges of the mouth is done at a side of the mouth, but in some instances, you may notice it on the two sides. Well, the meaning does not change either way.

In most cases, these feelings are expressed in subtle ways—that is, when you are expressing disbelief to someone who is superior to you, you know that doing it in a very glaring manner may put you in trouble. So you would rather use the corner of the mouth to subconsciously pass your message across. Same thing about dislike. Expressing negative emotion always changes our facial appearance to an ugly one; that is why we often use a part of the face to communicate negative messages.

Scientific Expressions

Joe Navarro (2011) speaks in practical terms about how this gesture plays out in the criminal world. According to him, when the edges of the mouth compress, it is an indication that the person is stressed. This is an outcome of years of observation while interrogating criminals. When a person is asked a question that they do not like, their lips compress as they prepare to answer the question or while providing an answer to it. The level of crimping is based on the kind of stress that the person is undergoing. For instance, you cannot compare the levels of stress of a child answering their parents with a murder suspect being interviewed.

Navarro practically explains, 'For example, when I would ask someone, 'Do you own a gun?' they would say yes, and then I would notice the lips would disappear or be compressed slightly. Then I would ask, 'Do you own a Smith and Wesson revolver?' Their lips would not react all that much. However, when I asked 'Do you own a 'Glock pistol?' knowing that this was the weapon found at the crime scene and unknown to the public, I noticed that the lips became really narrow and compressed and that the corners of the mouth would also turn downward.' With this, you can understand the involvement of the individual in the perpetration of the crime.

Although we need to be careful with our interpretations of the compressions of the edges of the mouth gesture because it is miserable that this is the natural state of some people's mouth. So we may be wrong to still read meanings to the cue in such people. Taking that aside, Changing Minds (2019) submits that crimping the edges of the mouth in a downward position is an expression of sadness or displeasure. This means the person is giving themselves up to the issue that weighs them down. If we do not like something or an idea, the sides of the mouth would be compressed as a means of deterring such thing from getting into our mind. If it were to be a feeling of happiness, the edges of the mouth will not draw to a particular position but will move up and down. So being static to either up or down shows that the person is eliciting negative emotions.

Practical Illustrations

Case Study I: It was a Saturday, and two female friends were relaxing at a bar as it was their usual norm. They used to talk about their activities during the previous week—home, work, spirituality, love, and the 'girls' thing'. Being childhood friends had made the journey a fantastic one for them. So on this particular day, Friend A narrated how a new person was employed in her workplace and how he had started looking for a way of dating her. She even demonstrated all the gimmicks of the said guy. She kept on talking about the guy for almost an hour. Putting things together and with the way her friend was hammering on the issue, Friend B was very sure that if what her friend said was not an outright deception, then it was grossly exaggerated. Knowing that her friend was a highly temperamental person, she only crimps an edge of her mouth to the side and sighed as a way of expressing her disbelief.

Case Study II: P and T were twins, and growing up together for decades had really made them very close to each other. Even after marriage and living at different places, they vowed to sustain the bond and inject it into their children. So one of the things they did was to send the children of P to T during summer break so that they could cohabit and play together. However, the youngest daughter of T did not really like the eldest son of P. She had made this known to her mother in times past, but she urged her not to create dislike for any human. As the children of P were driven in for this year's summer break, the children started greeting one another. When the eldest son of P stretched a hand to her, she shook hands with him with compressed lips and slightly turned edges of the mouth. This non-verbal gesture portrays her dislike for him.

Case Study III: It was the end-of-the-year dinner of Company TZD, and as usual, the employees were always in their best outfit, looking for a way to demonstrate that they were better than others. Mr G had always been known for his rudeness, and as such, many of his colleagues were always avoiding him. Upon entering the venue of the event, he sat at a table, subtly crimped the edges of his mouth to show contempt, before shaking hands with the others.

Case Study IV: Twin B impersonated Twin A in order to get into Country U. Being identical twins, their belief was that no one would find out the differences in them. They even deceived themselves that they found it difficult to differentiate each other. Upon getting to the airport, Twin B's documents were checked through the machines, and she was released. However, moved by his instincts, one of the officials at the airport told her to come back. Twin B thought it was for another thing, only for her to be told to bring out her passport. The official looked at it carefully and compared the passport image to the person standing. While he was doing this, Twin B compressed the edges of her mouth to show her disgust for the hard-working officer.

10.25. Raising the Upper Lip

Generic Interpretations of the Concept

When the corner of the upper lip is slightly raised, it is an indication that something negative is at stake. To display this gesture, the upper corner of the lip on the side of the mouth will rise subtly or 'tent' in an upward direction. This is usually employed to express disgust, dislike, disdain, or negative sentiments in general. Note that not all the sides of the mouth are opened; it is just a flip at the upper lip, which is to state that 'I don't like this' or 'This is awkward'. The opening is to let out carbon dioxide in a very slight manner.

However, when the sentiments are pronounced, the rise becomes very noticeable. This distorts the shape of the upper lip and pushes it to the nose, thereby exposing the upper teeth. This is similar to a snarl. Without mincing words, this represents utter disgust or dislike. It is pertinent to note that this produces a frown on the entire face which better echoes your message. You may notice this gesture when someone does not appreciate your presence at a location; they believe you are there to limit their chances. That is why it is common to see applicants do it when they see more people trooping in for an interview.

Scientific Explanations

Disgust is one of the six main universal facial expressions. In other words, I want to establish that this gesture is used universally. Philip (2013) explains that other cue clusters to the raised upper lip communicating disgust are inward turning of the eyebrows, wrinkled nose, and raising of the cheek muscles. All these come together to redefine the appearance of the face. It makes everything squeezed up as a means of showing that you do not like what you are actually seeing. A CBC article in 2017 also supports the view of Philip. The piece notes that apart from using this cue to show distaste, we also make use of it to protect ourselves—that is, when the upper lip moves closely to the nose, it blocks the nasal passage just as a way of protecting us from inhaling bad fumes. Most times, the eyes are also squinted when you make this gesture; this shields them from a potential damage. Sometimes, this can just be metaphorical—we do it to mean 'I don't want to see the idea you're talking about.'

In addition, you notice this gesture while people are displaying the smug smile—arrogant, self-satisfied, and evil-like smile. While portraying this cue, the lips would be pressed together and only a side of the upper lip will come up. The rising of the upper lip communicates the intended message. Interpreting this gesture, Study Body Language (SBL) describes it as a sign of doubt and attempt to wish off another person's opinion. It also means a sign of arrogance, self-satisfaction, and display of superiority. The rising of the upper lip also makes it a gesture of ridicule—that is, it is done in an attempt to mess up another person's life.

While I noted in the opening paragraph that this cue is use to signify negative experiences, it should be noted that the context of its appearance gives the specific meaning of what it stands for. We will have a better understanding of this under the 'Practical Illustrations' section.

Practical Illustrations

Case Study I: Dr P was a multibillionaire, and one of his cultures was to drop all protocols once in a blue moon and mix up with the downtrodden. This made him think of afterlife or, on the very least, the other side of the coin. On this particular occasion, he decided to board a train to another province, but the person seated beside him consumed different kinds of food simultaneously. Originally, he hated seeing people eating in public space, and he was even more irritated by the combination of the foods. Still, he made up his mind to respect the person's choice, not knowing what the person was going through. But subconsciously, he compressed his lips, raised a side of his upper lips, and moved it closer to his nose. This subtle gesture shows disgust.

Case Study II: Mr Q was the supervisor of CRA Security Outfit. He was known to be jovial, and as such, most of his subordinates opened up to him. But that did not erode him of discipline. He decided to make transfers and alter the duty post of his team in order not to make them complacent. Mentioning the name of one of the leaders of a unit, he said the unit lead was to be moved from the south to the north. He showered encomiums on him, noting that his new place would offer him the opportunity to acquire new skills and mastery of the job, but this did not really move the team lead; he was going to work with another set of people whom he did not know what they were made up with. As Mr Q ended his talk about him, he slightly raised his upper lip on the side of the mouth and squinted his face. This is to communicate his dislike for the new duty post.

Case Study III: Ms U was given a deadline by her manager to finish up a particular assignment. She knew the consequences if she defied the order. Since the order came, she disconnected her devices from social media and was focused. One of her colleagues came to make some verifications, and all she could do was to nod. During break, the colleague came back to crack jokes with her as usual, but she did not even respond to her prelude, so the colleague shifted her attention to the person beside Ms U. After murmuring, they both faced Ms U to know what was wrong with her; they did this in a mocking manner. Responding, she lifted up her head, raised a corner of her upper lip, and moved it closer to the nose in a way that exposed her teeth in an aggressive manner and simply said, 'Please, I'm not in the mood.' This was a resounding message for the due to stay aloof.

Case Study IV: A group of criminals were planning their next operation, and in their usual manner, the leader gave out the role each criminal would play. Their last outing was tough, and they were almost conquered by law enforcement officials. Most of them were afraid of the next operation because they were of the strong opinion that law enforcement agents would still be on the lookout for them. In fact, they had suggested that the operation be stopped, but the greed of their leader wouldn't. He told Criminal Y that he would play the same role as he did in their last outing. Y was almost killed in that operation. Immediately after their leader said this, he raised a side of his upper lip and moved it near the nose to display that he disapproved of the decision.

10.26. Licking the Upper Lip

Generic Interpretations of the Concept

From many instances, this appears as an expression of positive emotions, but not in all circumstances. When some people are happy with an event or the thought going on in their mind, they will lick their upper lip briskly back and forth. Their eyes will also be dilated as the entire face is expressing positive vibes. Their eyes will also gaze into the distance to connote that the person is thinking about something that is making him or her happy. For the fact that the tongue decides to go for the upper lip instead of the usual lower lip shows that the emotions the person is feeling is unusual—happiness is a transition from our usual feelings.

This gesture is unique from the usual lip-licking behaviour that is rampant. When the lower lip is licked, it is a means of relieving stress; the moist provided by the tongue is to reduce the effects of the stress that the person is going through. Let me simplify it by saying that when you see a person lick their lower lip, it means they are stressed, and when you see the same person lick their upper lip in another context, it means he or she is happy. So the feeling is like polar opposites.

Let me chip in that this interpretation is not absolute or all-situation binding; there are exceptions to this just like every other non-verbal cue. Some people prefer rubbing the upper lip when they are stressed. Some do it unconsciously while others do it as a means of deceiving others that they are feeling positive emotions. This can be very misleading, especially when you are in search of the truth, like law enforcement officials and business people. So the best way to know which emotion the action denotes is to look for other indicators before making interpretations. With this, you will make informed decisions.

Scientific Explanations

Study Body Language (SBL) describes the act of licking the upper lick as a 'sexual lick'. The website describes it as 'an intentional gesture where the tongue starts in the corner of the mouth, licking the upper lip and then the lower, in a slow-moving and sensual action.' This is an obvious way of enticing a potential lover. Licking the lips, especially the upper lip, emphasises their juiciness and makes the colour turn out brighter. Being an erogenous zone also makes it self-enticing. A person who is not in a happy mood will not be enticing lovers to themselves. If this behaviour is displayed by a woman, it is a courageous move, revealing the intent to 'taste' to a person who knows how to decode non-verbal messages. In some instances, this cue is only reserved for advanced relationship where both couple are readily deeply romantically nto each other. I must reiterate that this cue is slow and sensual; it is different from the self-pacifying licking which is done in a fast and partial manner.

Changing Minds (2019) explains various ways in which the tongue can be used in licking the lips and the meaning of each. The body language platform explains that when a person licks the upper lip, it is an expression of desire for either something that is said, a person, or even for food. You can know the specific thing that is arousing this feeling by identifying what is in front of the licker. If there is nothing in their presence, it means the person is elated by their own thought. If this is deliberately done, it is an expression of sexual desire meaning 'I will like to like you'. This can be very arousing for someone who has been expecting it and if it is accompanied by other clusters such as steady gaze and slightly lowered head. Hence, this gesture may be done as part of foreplay to intercourse or as a way of teasing a lover.

Christopher Philip (2014) notes that lip licking may connote a need to pacify or a show of sexual interest. Either way, habitual licking should be avoided as it does not speak well of you. If used to communicate a message and the person seems to not understand it, there is no need to keep dragging it. If you habitually lick your lips, it means you are always stressed, and that sends a bad impression to others.

Practical Illustrations

Case Study I: Student J was an attention-seeking person; he wanted everybody to focus on him at every occasion. They were given a group work, and he had been diligent just for the sake of winning the slot to represent the group during class presentation. When their group eventually met to rehearse and choose a presenter, J was the first person to arrive at the venue. In all realms, he had succeeded in creating an impression as the most serious group member to every other person, and after a few arguments and counterarguments, he was later nominated to present the project on behalf of the group. While accepting his nomination, he first licked his upper lip slowly before speaking. This is to show his happiness.

Case Study II: Every employee wanted to follow the manager of DAE Firm whenever he was going on a business trip due to the special treatment he dished out to them. Next week, he was to embark on a two-week trip and would be going with two employees. Since they got to know about the trip, most of them had been trying to outsmart one another and present themselves as the best qualified for the trip. The manager made it known that Employee R, who followed him from the last journey, would be going with him. When this was announced in the end-of-the-week general meeting, Mr R was very happy to hear this because it had never happened that an employee would go on two consecutive trips with the manager. He slowly rubbed his upper lip and tilted his head downward. The cue is a subconscious display of his state of mind—happy mood.

Case Study III: Man RT was a human smuggler. Before embarking on the journey, he had trained the smuggled people how to behave. He went with only two people so that he wouldn't have to deal with numerous people at a time. He taught them how to defend themselves when they get to the border, and he helped them with some forged documents as a means of identification. When they got to the border and the smuggled beings were being interviewed, they acted so perfectly that Man RT was unconsciously rubbing his upper lip with his tongue; he was indescribably happy at the display of knowledge by the boys.

CHAPTER 11

The Teeth

We do not really have much to discuss on the teeth, but the few messages herein cannot be ignored. Non-verbal messages are read in clusters, and leaving these out can mar the success of what we have done so far. As such, we are going to explore the concept of the teeth and relate it to other parts of the body. As it is our norm, we will use the substantial part of this segment to explore the scientific aspect of the teeth.

According to Matthew Hoffman (2015), 'The teeth are the hardest substances in the human body.' Apart from being used for chewing, the teeth also play a formidable role in the formation of speech. The primary role of the teeth is to mechanically break down items of food, cutting, crushing, and grinding them as a way of preparing them for swallowing and eventual digestion.

Like every other mammal, humans are *diphyodont*—that is, we develop two sets of teeth in our lifetime. The first set (called the baby, milk, primary, or deciduous set) normally starts to appear at about six months of age, although some babies are born with one or more visible teeth, known as natal teeth. Normal tooth eruption at about six months is known as teething and can be painful.

Briefly, let's consider the two sets of teeth:

Primary teeth. Among the primary teeth, ten are found in the upper jaw while there are ten in the lower jaw too, making a total of twenty.

Permanent teeth. In all, there are thirty-two teeth in the adult mouth. They replace the primary teeth when a child is about twelve years old. There a sixteen teeth in the maxilla and sixteen teeth in the mandible.

The maxillary teeth are the maxillary central incisor, maxillary lateral incisor, maxillary canine, maxillary first premolar, maxillary second premolar, maxillary first molar, maxillary second molar, and maxillary third molar. The mandibular

413

teeth are the mandibular central incisor, mandibular lateral incisor, mandibular canine, mandibular first premolar, mandibular second premolar, mandibular first molar, mandibular second molar, and mandibular third molar. Third molars are commonly called wisdom teeth and may never erupt in the mouth or form at all. If any additional teeth form, for example, fourth and fifth molars, which are rare, they are referred to as supernumerary teeth (hyperdontia) (Kokten and Buyukertan 2003). Hypodontia is when a person develops fewer teeth than the normal number of teeth.

There are a few distinctions between the teeth of males and females, with male teeth along with the male jaw tending to be larger on average than female teeth/jaw. There are also differences in the internal dental tissue proportions, with male teeth consisting of proportionately more dentine, while female teeth have proportionately more enamel (Sorenti et al. 2019).

The teeth have four basic parts:

Enamel. The enamel is the hardest and most highly mineralised substance of the body. It is one of the four major tissues which make up the tooth, along with dentin, cementum, and dental pulp (Ross 2002). It is normally visible and must be supported by underlying dentin. Ninety-six per cent of enamel consists of mineral, with water and organic material comprising the rest (Cate 1998). The normal colour of enamel varies from light yellow to grayish white. At the edges of the teeth where there is no dentin underlying the enamel, the colour sometimes has a slightly blue tone. Since enamel is semi-translucent, the colour of dentin and any restorative dental material underneath the enamel strongly affects the appearance of a tooth. Enamel varies in thickness over the surface of the tooth and is often thickest at the cusp, up to 2.5 mm, and thinnest at its border, which is seen clinically as the cementoenamel junction (CEJ) (Cate 1998).

Dentin. The dentin is a layer underlying the enamel. It is a hard tissue that contains microscopic tubes. When the enamel is damaged, heat or cold can enter the tooth through these paths and cause sensitivity or pain (Hoffman 2015).

Cementum. The cementum is a specialised bone-like substance covering the root of a tooth. It is approximately 45 per cent inorganic material (mainly hydroxyapatite), 33 per cent organic material (mainly collagen), and 22 per cent water. Cementum is excreted by cementoblasts within the root of the tooth and is thickest at the root apex. Its colouration is yellowish, and it is softer than dentin and enamel. The principal role of cementum is to serve as a medium by which the periodontal ligaments can attach to the tooth for stability. At the cement to enamel junction, the cementum is acellular due to its lack of cellular components, and this acellular type covers at least two-thirds of the root (Cate 1998).

Dental pulp. The dental pulp is the central part of the tooth filled with soft connective tissue. This tissue contains blood vessels and nerves that enter the tooth from a hole at the apex of the root. Along the border between the dentin and the pulp are odontoblasts, which initiate the formation of dentin. Other cells in the pulp include fibroblasts, preodontoblasts, macrophages, and T lymphocytes (Walton and Mahmoud 2002).

In the same vein, there are four types of teeth well-structured in the mouth. They are as follows:

Incisors. The four front teeth in both the upper and lower jaws are called incisors. Their primary function is to cut food. The two incisors on either side of the midline are known as central incisors. The two adjacent teeth to the central incisors are known as the lateral incisors. Incisors have a single root and a sharp incisal edge (Foster 2019).

Canines. There are four canines in the oral cavity. Two in the maxillary arch and two in the mandibular area. They are behind and adjacent to the lateral incisors. Their main function is to tear food. They have a single pointed cusp and a single root. They have the longest root of any tooth. They also serve to form the corners of the mouth.

Premolars. These teeth are located behind and adjacent to the canines and are designed to crush food. There are eight premolars in the oral cavity. There are two in each quadrant of the mouth. The one closest to the midline is the first premolar, and the one farthest from the midline is the second premolar. These teeth can have three to four cusps. The maxillary first premolar has two roots, and the remaining premolars have a single root. There are no premolars in the primary dentition (Foster 2019).

Molars. The most posterior teeth in the mouth are the molars. They have broader and flatter surfaces with four to five cusps. They are designed to grind food. Molars typically have two roots, although the maxillary first molar (behind the second premolar) has three roots. There are twelve molars in the permanent dentition with three in each quadrant of the mouth. They are named starting with the closest to the midline as first molars, second molars, and third molars. Although, some people do not fully develop the third molars. Third molars are often referred to as wisdom teeth. The primary dentition only contains eight molars (Foster 2019).

11.1. Flicking the Nails on the Teeth

Generic Interpretations of the Concept

One of the ways in which people release tension is flicking the thumbnail on the teeth. This is an obvious sign that shows that something is wrong with the person. Because some people are aware that this gesture is unethical, when they do it once, they desist so as not to call the attention of their audience to their stress. If a person does it repeatedly, it means they are trying to soothe themselves due to the anxiety they are currently feeling; it means the person cannot control the negative emotions that they display. Most times, you will see them clench their teeth and flick the nail on it. This can either be a means of expressing regret or forgetfulness. This is when the person does not want to shout 'Ooo'.

As an expression of forgetfulness, it means the person is really pained by the item they left behind. It may be important to the project they have at hand.

However, you need to note that a repetitive behaviour along this line may be their normal attitude, and as such, you just need to ignore it because there is not any metaphorical meaning that can be attached to it. You can only begin to take such people seriously if they significantly reduce this behaviour. In other words, those who display this behaviour once in a while are those who actually use it in communicating their innermost intent.

Scientific Explanations

Changing Minds (2019) states that when people sometimes tap their teeth with their nails, it echoes and makes noise. There are two possible interpretations to this—boredom and thoughtfulness. When people are bored, they can do the unthinkable; they can play with anything in the hope of livening the environment. If they think it is out of place to drum tables (which is an obvious childish act), they will take to beating the front teeth with their thumbnail. At least, they can use this to get the attention of other people. If it is as a result of thinking, it means the person is really disturbed about what they are thinking about and is yet to find a solution to it. The act of flicking the nail on the teeth is to tell the external world that they are pained about their inability to arrive at a decision.

The body language website also explains further that this may be a way of causing deliberate interruption or irritant to an event. However, this is not usually common and can only be done by babies and teenagers. If they think of frustrating the effort of their friends in a project or gathering, children can begin to tap their teeth, which will make irritating noise in the mouth. This can be very irritating to some people. If your friends know that you do not like it and they keep doing it in your presence, it is an intentional way of provoking you.

On her part, Tonya Reiman (2019) says the act of flicking a nail on the teeth is a distracting act. She explains that when you are in a gathering and you tend to pick your teeth, play with your hair and clothes, or even fidget in your seat, people will see you as being inattentive. This is capable of creating a bad impression on you. Once an opinion is formed about you, it will determine your future relationships—people may distance themselves from you or even tell other people not to have anything to do with you. Reiman (2019) specifically warns such distracting behaviours should be avoided in all realms.

Christopher Philip (2014) explains this cue in the simplest terms. She gives a synonym of this gesture as 'metronomic signals'. He interprets this cue in one sentence: 'Metronomic signals show a desire to release extra energy, that a person is anxious, or that thought is taking place.' This is in line with what I have earlier explained.

He explains that if this behaviour is not disruptively loud, it is not really negative as it can be used in communicating that a person is in the process of coming up with a solution. So this means you should give them space so that they will think it through. It is a subtle way of pleading with you to give them more time so that they will be able to ruminate more on what you are discussing. If this action is repeated, it is a means of putting the brain into action—relieving tension bolsters the brain's ability (Philip 2014).

Practical Illustrations

Case Study I: It was revision week in AEW International School. So the mathematics teacher was interacting with the first-year students. He asked a question on how to solve a mathematical problem having given them four methods of working such questions. Many of them remembered three techniques. So the teacher promised to give a previous gift to anyone of them who could recall the final formula. The prefect could be seen thinking hard. At some point, he used his thumbnail to tap his incisors repeatedly, and this was a further confirmation that he was deeply buried in thoughts. The whole class went mute as none of them could recall the formula. After about three minutes, the class prefect jumped up and shouted subconsciously, saying, 'Yes, I got it!' Everyone focused on him as he perfectly reeled out the answer to the teacher.

Case Study II: DTH Enterprises organised a manpower training for its employees. Many of them thought it would end at their usual closing hour on Friday. However, it dragged on and on, and none of them dared rebel. Mr D, one of the employees, had a date at six o'clock in the evening, and it was just ten minutes to the set time, yet the lecturer did not seem to have reached the end of his presentation. Many of them began to slouch on their chairs. Some even went as far as placing their head on their laps, but the lecturer seemed not to be moved by their antics. Mr D, sitting at the front, began to use his nail to beat his front teeth, which made disturbing sounds in the hall. At this point, the lecturer was forced to stop and apologised for shooting beyond time. Mr D made the interruptive sound with the non-verbal gesture because he was disconnected from the lecturer and subconsciously had to register his grievance.

Case Study III: Mr ZP had overstayed in Country Q, a nation that was known for its zero tolerance for illegal migration. He was cautious of the places he went and wouldn't drag issues with anybody so as not to be nabbed by security agents. However, someone angered him one day, and losing his self-control, he smashed a metal on the person's head. He was arrested for this violent attack, and it was at the point of taking a statement from him that the officials got to know he was staying in the country illegally. Discovering his mistake, Mr ZP flicked his nail on his front teeth as an unconscious expression of regret.

11.2. Baring the Teeth

Generic Interpretations of the Concept

When we are confronted with difficult situations, we are normally seen baring our teeth. This gesture is displayed by pulling the corners of the mouth back and holding on to it until their clenched teeth are shown. This is a blatant show of fear—that is, you see this gesture in people when they are gripped with fear. It is a primitive behaviour inherited from chimpanzees. Chimpanzees also display this gesture when they are afraid of another animal or a dominant male. Pulling the corners of the mouth back to show a substantial number of teeth in a clenched form is an apt demonstration that the person is fearful. Most times, when people display this cue, they will stand still because they do not want to move ahead due to the fear of unknown.

You also see this behaviour in people when they are caught doing what they are not supposed to. Hence, it can be said to be a show of regret. Another cluster that may accompany this is arching of the eyebrows, depending on the context on which the act is taking place. In whatever context this gesture is displayed, it is a show of negative action.

Scientific Explanations

Amy Bender (2011) uses dogs to explain the concept of the bared-teeth body language. Remember, I said that this body language behaviour is primitive and that we inherited it from our ancestors who originated from chimpanzees. Bender notes that a dog bares its teeth by curling its lips backwards— this reveals the teeth. She notes that this is a reflexive action that is propelled by some certain circumstances. When you see this gesture in a dog, it is often a warning sign; it is telling you to back off. The verbal translation of this cue is, 'I am going to make use of my teeth if you don't stop it.' In most cases, this behaviour serves as a prelude to other dangerous, aggressive acts. Some other clusters to this acts are snarling and growling.

Fear, resource guarding, and territoriality are some of the reasons that make a dog bare its teeth according to Bender. Let me state that the reasons are not different in humans too, especially the issue of fear. If you see some bare their teeth and you are sure you cannot stage a fight with the person, the best thing is to avoid eye contact with them and move away from their vicinity until they have fully expressed themselves.

Sometimes, a dog may bare its teeth without any attachment of aggression. This is more of a submissive grin that is used to calm a situation. Lip licking, relaxed body posture, averted gaze, or placing the ear flatly against the floor are other cues that show that the dog is not ready to attack. When humans also bare their teeth and it is non-aggressive, the accompanying body posture will tell you that the person is afraid of you.

Philip (2014) opines that the baring of the teeth is one of the ways of showing disgust. He also enumerates wrinkling of the nose, tightening of the eyelid, and lowering of the eyebrows as some of the clusters that go along with this behaviour.

In the contribution of Dr Michelle Callard-Stone (2017), he states that when you see the teeth-baring gesture in a person, it means they feel threatened. In most cases, it does not mean an offensive sign but hints us that somebody is dying within. If you see this gesture in an enemy, it is a sign that they are afraid of you. This means that the battle is half-won already.

Practical Illustrations

Case Study I: Country D made it to the final match of the most prestigious football league in their continent. This had become a source of joy in the whole country, and their president had promised to honour the team with unbelievable gifts. So the team coach and his team had doubled their effort. One of the things they did was to watch the clips of their opponents; they were watching all the matches their opponents had played for the past one year. After watching each clip, the whole team would analyse it. On the evening to the finals, they watched the semifinal match of their opponents from where they came from behind to clinch the victory in an unbelievable manner. But after seeing the clip, the coach downplayed their strength just as a means of encouraging his men. But the goalie of the team had become cold due to what he just saw. When the coach spoke of the strengths and weaknesses of their team, the goalkeeper grinned fearfully by moving back the corners of his mouth and showing clenched teeth. This depicted him as being nervous.

Case Study II: DQI Enterprises was established about five years ago, and for now, it is the only challenger of a fifty-year-old firm in the whole country in their sector. So they had been looking for ways to be taken seriously by clients from all over the country so that they could truly serve as an alternative to the old company. They were holding their board meeting in which they were brainstorming on the strategies that would be implemented in the coming year. After a power-filled five-hour session, the chief executive officer (CEO) said that with their conclusion, they were ready to go beyond the established company, but the decision they reached was not convincing enough to the head of administration. So he curled his mouth and bared his teeth. This was an expression of fear of the feasibility of the plan.

Case Study III: Mr R was the teacher who prepared his students for competitions. They were currently competing for an international laurel, and they had succeeded in the first three stages. And now the fourth stage would be taking place at the national level. The students were really frightened about their chances, which was obvious to the teacher. As he was jokingly encouraging them, the students moved the corners of their mouth back, exposing their teeth in a fearful manner. They were really afraid.

Case Study IV: Two men were trying to move some goods into Country D. While Man ZL had every necessary documents for the exercise, Man UT had none. ZL assured him that he could avoid clearance. He went on to give UT four different instances where he evaded clearance. Even though UT was not convinced of his chances, he decided to follow ZL. Upon getting to the border, they were stopped, and even ZL, who had all the necessary documents, went through some unforeseen rigors. Seeing this, Man UT knew there was fire on the mountain for him. He began to unconsciously bare his teeth where he was seated. His countenance changed, and anyone observing him could see fear overwhelming him.

11.3. Tapping the Teeth

Generic Interpretations of the Concept

Teeth tapping is one of the body language behaviours you see in people when all is not well with them. By now, you should have internalised the principle that the hand-to-head gesture is a pacifying act. In other words, we only move our hands to the head area when we are not feeling as we should. Although a lot of people see the hand-to-head gesture as an extreme form of showing emotions, but most of us are guilty of it at some point or another. This is because it is mostly a subconscious action. Hence, we would have done it before it comes to our conscious mind.

In the teeth-tapping cue, the jaw would be shifted slightly while the canines are tapped so as to favour a side of the mouth or another. This is a reactionary body language behaviour that is seen in people when they are bored, frustrated or generally stressed. There would be a slight gap between the upper and lower teeth through which the person exhales air. When the person taps the teeth continuously, it sends a signal to those around them that something is wrong. Hence, it can be used as a means of gaining sympathy.

The context of the appearance of the cue will determine the exact message that it conveys. A person who is tapping their teeth due to frustration will also squint their eyes and wrinkle their nose to give the entire face an ugly appearance. This tells their audience that the person is really troubled by something.

If it is boredom, the person will tap the teeth repeatedly until it causes a soothing effect on them. They are in search of a mood changer and what will bolster their feeling at that very point in time. In the same vein, tapping the teeth as a result of stress is to make us feel better and energised. The action ensures the secretion of more saliva in the mouth, which helps in easing the effect of the stress. Hence, the teeth-tapping cue sends repetitive signals to our brain that we need a soothing effect at that very point in time.

Scientific Explanations

Just like flicking the nail on the teeth gesture, which we earlier explored, the teeth-tapping cue also has the capability to cause some noise or echoing in the mouth. This action may be propelled by boredom or thoughtfulness. When some people are bored, they look for ways of getting the body charged, and the teeth-tapping gesture has been seen to be one of them. If it is in a context that does not warranty boredom, it means the person is thinking. If you care about their thought, you must respect that moment by not interrupting (Changing Minds 2019). Law enforcement officials need to always take cognisance of this while dealing with their subjects. It is wrong to often assume that any act of thoughtfulness is an avenue to fabricate falsehood; there are situations that are complex enough to warrant thinking. In some rare circumstances, tapping the teeth may be a means of interrupting an organised process.

On his part, Philip (2014) affirms that apart from the nail, people may decide to use other objects, such as pen and pencils, to tap their teeth. He notes that whenever we see this, it is an indication that the person is thinking. That is why it is common to see schoolchildren do this when they are solving a problem. In fact, it is also seen in the corporate world where leaders of industries will subconsciously tap their teeth with a pen before they can continue writing. It means they were stuck at that moment and needed to think through before furthering with what they are writing.

Philip furthers that the jaw-clenching cue is the variant of this behaviour, which indicates that there is an internal struggle going on. If this is done aggressively, it is a means of telling others that you are serious with the emotion you are displaying.

Practical Illustrations

Case Study I: Some students were taking their entrance examination for one of the best medical schools in their country, and as expected, people came from far and near. Hence, the battle became the survival of the fittest. The examiners set the questions in a very technical way so as to have a better rating of those who should be admitted. An applicant was seen seated at the left front row working assiduously, but at some point, he stopped and made use of his pen to tap his teeth in a gentle manner, and after about thirty seconds, he started writing again. This means he was trying to recall a piece of information while displaying the non-verbal cue.

Case Study II: Ms P needed a reference letter from her present place of employment before she could be admitted to a professional postgraduate studies abroad. She had already taken leave before she discovered that it was a part of the requirements. So she called her boss who told her to come for it. Unfortunately, she was delayed by traffic while heading there and, as such, missed her boss who had gone for a meeting. This meant she had to wait. After an hour of waiting, she became bored of everything around her, and unconsciously, she began to use her nail to tap her canine. This was an expression of her internal feelings and perhaps a way of trying to regain her lively self.

Case Study III: Mr H had just repaired his car, making it the fourth time in a month, and while taking his children to school, it broke down unexpectedly again. The management of his children's school was disciplined; they would not allow any child in once they were late. More so, he also needed to arrive at work early. He got down to open the bonnet so as to see if it was an issue he could easily fix, but his efforts proved abortive. He did not have much cash on him that could transport the children and him to their destination without being late. He stood still beside the car and was seen using the car key to tap his teeth repeatedly. This was an expression of negative feelings—a lot of negative thoughts were going on in his mind.

Case Study IV: Prostitute JG had just got a new client who told her to meet him at a spot by 7 p.m. JG kept to time, but an hour after the agreed time, the man was nowhere to be found. JG was not feeling comfortable due to the staring faces coming from passers-by. She tried putting a call through, and he promised he was almost at the spot. Waiting for another ten minutes was like forever to her. She became bored and had to unconsciously use her fixed nails to tap her teeth. The enthusiasm to meet a promising and rich client was gone. And her non-verbal behaviour was an expression of regret.

CHAPTER 12

The Tongue

Without the tongue, there is no way we can articulate our speech. Those who have speech impairment primarily have issues with their tongue—that is, if the tongue does not work properly, it would be difficult for a person to speak fluently. What I am trying to say is that the tongue is the mitochondria of speech production. Hence, we cannot relegate its place in the understanding of non-verbal cues. Some readers would be baffled on the possibility of paying attention to tongue movement, which is not all that visible, in understanding the intents of people, but by the time you are done reading this segment, you will see that you have been overlooking many things that are not supposed to be trivialised.

Let's understand the anatomy of the human tongue first. The tongue is a muscular organ that sits in the central position in the mouth of many vertebrates. Apart from being used for mastication, it is the surface through which food is grinded before being swallowed. Hence, it is indispensable to the digestive system. Also, it is the primary organ of taste of the five sense organs. Thus, if your taste bud is faulty, you will not know how something tastes like. The taste bud is the most sensitive part of the tongue, which is always kept moist by the saliva. It is richly supplied by blood vessels and nerves. Also, it is a natural means through which we clean our teeth (Maton et al. 1993). The tongue enables vocalisation and speech in humans and most animals.

The average length of the human tongue from the oropharynx to the tip is ten centimetres. The average weight of the human tongue for adult males is seventy grams and for adult females is sixty grams (Kerrod 1997).

According to Organs of the Body (2019), there are three major parts of the tongue—the apex, the body, and the root—while the surface is divided into the anterior and posterior. Let's explore the three major parts briefly:

The apex. The tip or apex of the tongue accounts for one-third of the anterior surface of the tongue. It is highly movable and rests against the incisor teeth in the mouth cavity. The taste buds for sweet are present on this part. The tip also plays its role in the production of labiodental and alveolar sounds (Organs of the Body 2019).

The body (main part). The two-thirds of the anterior forms the body of the tongue. The surface of the body is rough due to the presence of lingual papillae on the upper side. On the other hand, a layer of mucosa ensures that it is always moist. It is the part of the tongue that houses the taste buds for salty, sour, and bitter taste.

The root (base). The root is that part of the tongue which attaches it to the bottom or floor of the mouth cavity. It appears between the mandible and the hyoid bone. The primary job of the hyoid bone is to provide anchorage to the tongue. The dorsal portion of the root lies in the oropharynx. What is *oropharynx?* It is the part of the pharynx lying between the soft palate and epiglottis (Organs of the Body 2019).

It is important that we understand the tongue anatomy so as to know where it derives all the characteristics it uses in performing optimally.

Lingual papillae. They are small bumps on the surface of the tongue containing the taste buds. They are the projections of the lamina propria covered with tongue epithelium. Filiform, foliate, vallate, and fungiform are the four different types of papillae found on the surface. Different papillae contain different number of taste buds. For example, a vallate papilla may contain 250 taste buds, while the number of taste buds may reach 1,600 in the fungiform papilla. A taste receptor, edge, and basal cells are found in each taste bud. Meanwhile, several nerve fibers innervate each taste bud (Organs of the Body 2019).

Tongue muscles. The tongue contains four intrinsic and four extrinsic muscles. There is a fibrous septum that separates the muscles on each side. While the intrinsic muscles develop from the body of the tongue, the extrinsic muscles develop from outside of the tongue. The two forms of muscles work together so as to create all kinds of tongue mobility. However, they also have separate roles to play as well. For instance, the intrinsic muscle changes the shape of the tongue, while the extrinsic muscle alters its position.

Tongue nerve supply and vasculature. The arterial blood supply for the tongue comes from the external carotid artery. It branches off to join the lingual artery, which has three main branches, namely, the dorsal, the deep, and the sublingual arteries. The branches of lingual artery supply blood to different parts of the tongue. Turning to tongue nerve supply, the hypoglossal nerve provides most innervation for all the tongue muscles (Organs of the Body 2019).

As we unwind our discussion in this segment, let's conclude by exploring the functions of the tongue.

It is an organ of speech production. Let me reiterate that without the tongue, there cannot be speech. The mouth is the abode of a lot of organs of speech. Some speech organs are the teeth, lips, tongue, uvula, palate, etc. The tip of the tongue, the body, and the back significantly contribute to the production of vowel and other sounds. You can only understand the true value of the tongue when it is not there. The different parts of the tongue play their own part in producing and modifying sounds. For example, labiodental sounds are produced while the tip of the tongue touches the upper teeth. To produce the /k/ and /g/ sounds, the back of the tongue raises against the roof top. Being clothed with different muscles makes it easy for the tongue to move and assume different positions so as to produce the needed sounds at every point in time (Organs of the Body 2019).

Other functions of the tongue are chewing, biting, sucking, and tasting.

12.1. Chewing or Biting the Tongue

Generic Interpretations of the Concept

One of the major functions of the tongue is to bite or chew food. This is essential to ensure human survival. We eat to live, and as such, it should be done appropriately so as to keep us safe, hale, and hearty. However, the manner in which we chew or bite the tongue has its own connotations and can be an accurate reflection of what goes on in our mind at that point in time. This behaviour can be explained from two points of view—literal and metaphorical levels. If the person is eating and bites their tongue, this can just be accidental or a means of showing that the food is really delicious. When people get to eat their favourite food, they throw caution into the wind and may end up biting their tongue.

In addition, it may signal thoughtfulness. When you are thinking of something, maybe food, you may bite your tongue as an avenue for the consumption of the substance. Further, it may also be interpreted that you are troubled by something. When we are disturbed, we may bit the tongue while we think of the way out simultaneously. You also see this when people are expressing regret, thinking that they should not have said what they said. They are biting the tongue as a means of self-punishment. This gesture may be accompanied by the frowning of the face.

Some other times, people bite their tongue out of boredom. When you bite the tongue, you secrete more saliva, which moistens the entire oral cavity. Let me conclude by saying that this is just the habit of some people, and they should not be taken seriously when you see them display this gesture. It does not have any metaphorical interpretation. It is a bad habit which you must endeavour to discourage.

Scientific Explanations

From a biological point of view, once food enters into the oral cavity, two activities kick off simultaneously—mastication and grinding. During chewing, foods are broken down into smaller particles. Hence, these particles are easily mixed with the saliva to form a bolus. Mastication is the act of mixing finely chewed food with the saliva. That is why the process is also referred to as chewing. The tongue positions food between the teeth so as to be chewed appropriately (Organs of the Body 2019).

Changing Minds (2019) provides a sociological interpretation of the concept. When you see a person bite their teeth, it is an indication that they are going through severe internal struggles. It is like the tongue has been subconsciously tied down so that it will not express itself. In other words, it means the person has something to say but are being restrained by different factors. So they rather take to biting their tongue than express their ordeals. In some societies of the world, children are not allowed to talk to the elderly in a disrespectful manner. So even if they see an elderly person behaving foolishly, to say it would be a problem. They would obviously be pained by this societal limitation, but if they should go ahead to air their view, they may not be able to withstand its consequences. That is why they bite their tongue to caution themselves. Biting the teeth can also be done after one has spoken. This means they have realised their own mistake and are looking for ways to retract their statement, which is no longer possible.

Furthermore, biting the tongue means someone is finding it difficult to articulate their thought. Sometimes, you have an idea on your mind but lack the right and precise words to express yourself in a way that will really have an effect on others as you are internally feeling it. This is usually painful, especially in a debate or formal context when something is at stake. So you bite your tongue subconsciously as if punishing it to utter those words that are articulated in the mind (Changing Minds 2019).

Practical Illustrations

Case Study I: Child A had grown up to know his father as not really responsible. Most times, his father would not help his mother at home, and paying school fees was also an issue. One day, he took the courage to ask his father what the problem was and that he was not happy with his lifestyle. Instead of taking time to explain to the child, the father walked out on him and warned him never to ask him such a question again. Child A wanted to hurl insults at him, telling him that he was aware of his drunkenness and womanising acts, but he remembered that their societal rule required them to respect elderly people in all circumstances. So he bit his tongue painfully while tears dropped from his eyes. That is, he was lamenting the societal rule that placed the barrier to how far they could react to certain issues.

Case Study II: Ms L had been working with her principal in an establishment since her graduation from school. The establishment did not seem to be growing to the style of operation of the owner; he did not provide the tools to work and diverted profits to other sources. From all indications, the company was on its way to folding up if something urgent was not done. When this became glaring to the proprietor of the firm, he invited Ms L to his office to tell her how her level of productivity had dropped and its effects on the firm. He questioned her educational qualifications, noting that many other people had worked with him before her arrival and that the finances of the company were not in shambles. Really pained, she wanted to react in the same vein but had to bite her tongue quickly as a means of self-restraint. She then apologised and promised to get back through writing.

Case Study III: Law enforcement officials came to ransack the home of a woman due to the death of her husband. After checking through, they did not seem to have got any evidence linking her to the death, but their child knew that she was involved through proxy. He wanted to talk but remembered that he would be losing both of his parents at a tender age. So he bit his tongue and kept mute.

12.2. Tongue in Cheek

Generic Interpretations of the Concept

This body language cue has various interpretations in different contexts. The saying 'He spoke with his tongue in cheek' is another way of accusing a person of being deceptive. Hence, we can say that this action is seen in people who are trying to hide a piece of information from another person. Such people know the whole truth about an incident but will not say it due to their selfish reasons. When you push your tongue to the side, hiding it in the cheek, speaking becomes practically impossible. So this can be an intentional act of cautioning oneself from uttering a word.

Further, this behaviour is a great means of relieving tension for people who are stressed. When someone is getting away with something that they should not, their conscience will be against them and their brain may even be pushing for the uttering of those words. So their conscious suppression of this information makes them become disturbed. A way of dealing with the stress is to push their tongue to the side of the cheek, behind their teeth, which is also a moist place so as to generate enough softness to ease their tension.

Also, this cue can also be noticed at the literal level—those who are playing or being cheeky. If you want to mock a person with protruding cheeks, you can just use your tongue to push out your cheeks so that it looks like theirs. People play with this act when they are bored. In some situations, some use this gesture as a way of cleaning their teeth. When you place the tongue on the cheek, it lies directly behind your teeth. This can be used in evacuating some food particles that are hiding in the corners of the mouth, which you will eventually swallow or spit out.

Scientific Explanations

Changing Minds (2019) says the act of pushing the tongue against the cheek may be a sign of nervousness or deception. When people are afraid that what they have just said can end up backfiring, they become nervous and push their tongue to the cheek area so that they do not say another thing to complicate issues. Most probably, what they have just said is deceptive. Since there is no sure-fire way to point out lies in a person's speech, you need to look for other indicators toiling the path of your suspicion.

The body language website goes ahead to assert that 'pushing the tongue into the cheek can show pensiveness as the person thinks about something and tries to come to a decision'. When a person is in deep thought orchestrated by a sad event, they will push their tongue to the cheek. It means they do not want to talk at that moment; they want to give their full concentration to the event bothering them. Until the person gets a way out of the issue, they may not return the tongue to its original position. Sometimes, they will use their palm to support the other side of the face because the head is tilted towards that side.

There are some cultural points of view to this gesture too. Some Europeans believe that when a heterosexual woman presses her tongue against her cheek, it is a sexual invitation to the man around. If the feeling is reciprocated, it can serve as the beginning of their relationship. In fact, an interpretation states that the woman is trying to say, 'Come and feel my breasts.' However, this cue is not used for sexual acts in Asia, Africa, and even the Americas (Zarek 2015).

Practical Illustrations

Case Study I: Mr and Mrs AJ gave birth to twins, and they are now seven years old. The children were fond of each other and did almost everything together. Being identical twins also made it difficult for their teachers to know who was who. Hence, they had dodged several punishments due to this confusion. Even though this was not usually a problem for their parents, but covering up for each other when one did something bad had been a source of concern to them. For instance, Twin A took something from the fridge to hide it in their room, and Twin B was aware of it. When their mother was asking, Twin A was asleep, but Twin B, instead of saying the truth, simply pushed his tongue to his cheek and feigned seriousness on the novel he claimed to be reading. When you would look critically into his face, you would know that something was definitely wrong.

Case Study II: Mr B was being interviewed for the position of an assistant manager, and the panel wanted to know about his current workplace and what drove him to quit his current job to take up a position in a firm that was not as established as his current place. He talked on the need to change environment and explore other options. When asked of his salary, he mentioned an intimidating amount just to flatter his worth. After mentioning the amount, he quickly pushed his tongue to his cheek and looked away from the curious eyes of the panellists. His action aroused suspicions in them. So they repeated the question to focus on his non-verbal action and not really what he was saying.

Case Study III: A terrorist was nabbed after killing about twenty-five people in a shooting spree. Because he was not arrested on the spot of the occurrence, it gave him the gut to deny his involvement. After a few sessions of questioning with leading and experienced investigative officers, he later confessed to being the arrowhead of the massacre. Since that was secondary to the law enforcement officers, they asked about the group he was affiliated to and how he joined so as to give the agency a big picture of how to deal with the issue. Still unrepentant, he became inconsistent with what he was saying; he wanted to cover the others up. But it seemed the officers would not let go until he provided them with a satisfactory answer. He spoke briefly and pressed his tongue against his cheek, which hinted the officers that he was hiding something from them. They had to peruse further in order to unravel what was it that he was trying to hide from them.

12.3. Jutting Tongue

Generic Interpretations of the Concept

Tongue jutting is the sudden protrusion of the tongue between the teeth without necessarily touching the lips. This non-verbal cue is used in expressing two polar messages, depending on the context where it is used. First, when a person succeeds over an opponent, they will display this gesture. Anyone who is a sports lover will be used to this sign. Footballers, to be specific, make use of this sign after scoring against an opponent. It is a sign of proving superiority or telling others that you have triumphed over them. This can be very painful to the other party though. Hence, you need to be careful of whom you do this gesture to because if the person is an aggressive person, they may stage a confrontation.

In the same vein, when someone succeeds in deceiving you, they may display this gesture as a sign of victory. This can be very subtle, and you need to pay rapt attention in order to see what the person is communicating. As an educator and trainer for decades, I have seen this behaviour in students when they score higher grades and when they eventually pass a course they had earlier thought they will fail. The business scene is another common place where you'll see this cue. When someone thinks they succeeded in a bargain, they may display this gesture as a means of celebrating their marketing prowess. In short, the verbal translation of this gesture is, 'I got away with it.'

On the other hand, you also see this cue when someone is caught in a wrong act or when the person realises his or her own mistakes. In this realm, it is a show of regret. The person is trying to say, 'Oops, I am exposed.' They are certain that there is not any amount of cover-up they can use in bailing out themselves. So the gesture is a way of confessing their involvement in the wrong act.

Tongue jutting is a universal body language behaviour. Remarkably, it is also consistent in the messages it passes across. Once you are able to affirm the context, be sure that you will understand the essence of the gesture.

Scientific Explanations

Christopher Philip (2014) says the synonym of the tongue-jutting act is 'pushing the tongue through compressed lips'. He explains that when we stick out our tongue through compressed lips, it is a signal that we have got away with something. He says this behaviour may be a mere joke which has the ability to create a bonding effect by sharing what is being done. He proceeds that sometimes people subconsciously stick out their tongue in confession of an evil deed. It is also a means of showing disagreement with another person—that is, you are trying to tell them that you are 'rejecting' them or the idea they are presenting before you.

Some of the verbal translations of the cue are 'I'm sticking out my tongue through my lips because I've got away with this', 'I'm telling a cheeky joke or making a cheeky statement', 'I've made a mistake', or 'I've been caught trying to pull a fast one' (Philips 2014). He explains further that this cue can be seen anywhere at any given point, but that does not alter its meaning—that is, a person is involved in an act that is pushing the envelope of acceptability or they are being rejected because of being caught in an uncouth act.

If you notice this language anywhere, you should review what the person has just told you—maybe someone around has made the butt of a joke or you have been cheated or fooled. And finally, it means someone has realised their own mistake. The clusters to watch out for are smirk or goofy grin. If it is used to mean rejection, take cognisance of sneering, averted gaze, or body turning away (Philip 2014).

Navarro (2015) describes the tongue-jutting behaviour as 'the subconscious sticking out of the tongue, usually lightly clutched between the teeth, sometimes performed when someone is [1] caught making a mistake or a faux pas or [2] when they are getting away with something.' He moves on to note that he does not see any reason for it. Well, our point of concern is not to argue on the essence of the gesture or not but to have a clearer understanding of its meaning.

Practical Illustrations

Case Study I: Two close friends went to a bar to relax. Friend A asked for a non-alcoholic drink, while Friend B took an alcoholic one. Before the server could bring the drinks, Friend A sought to ease himself. Friend B spiked his drink before his arrival, knowing fully well that his friend could not withstand that rate of alcohol. When Friend A came and sipped his drink, he began to grow inebriated and stumbled at some point. So he confronted his friend who admitted that he added a bit of extra alcohol. Friend B followed his statement up by sticking out his tongue and quickly clamped it shut. He simply enjoyed watching his friend's reaction whenever he appeared drunk. In other words, he teased and even mocked his friend whenever he became drunk.

Case Study II: Mr A went on a professional training when he met a lady from another company. He was obviously into her and was looking for a way of speaking to her. The lady, however, was not moved by all his antics. Mr A would always sit beside her and smile at everything that was said, even if they were not funny. When the man later had the courage to approach her at the end of the training, the first thing the lady did was to jut her tongue to him. This was to show her distaste for him—that is, she was not interested in him.

Case Study III: A teacher gave his students an exercise and went out to attend to another need. He specifically warned them not to commit any malpractice. But one of them defied this order. Immediately after their tutor stepped out, he brought out his textbook to copy the answers. Not knowing, the teacher came in through the back door, and as the student saw him, he jutted his tongue nervously, which called the teacher's attention to him. The teacher moved closer to him and caught him in the act.

Case Study IV: A man decided that he was not going to rent out his apartment to unmarried people again due to his previous experiences with them. Two criminally minded people came together and did a marriage of convenience. When the man took them to the apartment, he decided to ask some few questions on the go. He began by asking them how their courtship period was. Then he went on how to ask them about the wedding date and something memorable they could remember the day for. They were taken aback by this question, and the woman jutted her tongue at this question. Even though her male counterpart tried to cover things up, but it seemed they could not just upturn things in their favour.

12.4. Insults through the Tongue

Generic Interpretations of the Concept

In many cultures of the world, people make use of the sticking out of the tongue to insult others. The exact way this is done can be slightly different from one region to the other, but on a general note, the tongue will be fully or partially stuck out as a way of communicating a person's dislike or disgust for a thing. This gesture is usually seen among children in a very tender age. If a child sticks out his or her tongue against another child who can deal with them, they take to their heels, knowing the consequences of their actions.

Even though this can be subtle among the elderly ones, but it still occurs. For instance, the Pacific Island warriors dramatically stick out their tongue and lower it as a way of intimidating and insulting others. When people stick out their tongue, their eyes become dilated, which makes the action somewhat intimidating. Till this day, this cue is still being used in Maori haka events.

Note that this gesture is like the pronounced form of the tongue-jutting cue we just explored. The tongue insult is used when people do not want to utter verbal insults. When conflicts break out, they can hide under the excuse that they were just displaying it for fun and not for the intention of intimidating or enslaving others.

Scientific Explanations

Changing Minds (2019) submits, 'A deliberate gesture of sticking out the tongue at a person is impolite, although considered rather childish and thus reflects as much on the person doing it. The gesture thus appears petulant unless it is done in an amusingly cheeky way.' In other words, when someone intentionally does the stick-out gesture, their primary aim is to hurl insults at you through the non-verbal means. To determine if the person is insulting you or they are being cheeky, you need to focus on the whole face. If they are cheeky, this action is normally followed with laughter and a smile.

If the sticking out of tongue appears at the side of the mouth, it means the person is thinking hard on an issue. In a romantic setting, it is a connotation of lust.

Leon Seltzer (2015) says that this gesture is one of the context-based body language cues, noting that in some contexts, it may mean nothing. He also submits that what the behaviour connotes in children is different from what it is among adults. To determine the meaning of tongue-sticking-out behaviour, you must first answer these questions: Is the tongue sticking straight out? To the left? Right? Hanging down? Or may it actually be curled? What's the accompanying facial expression and context in which it occurs? This is even made complicated when you consider the cultural differences that surround this cue.

Among the Europeans, the direct sticking out of the tongue is an expression of contempt. 'It would once have been more offensive than now, but because it is now mostly associated with children, it will often be taken as childish teasing rather than an earnest insult' (Hana 2013). However, those who are detail-oriented may not take this cue as teasing, especially when you do not have any relationship with the person before the display of the cue.

The origins of this behaviour are obviously lost but Levi-Strauss suggests that it may be traceable to babies rejecting breasts or food by pushing it out of their mouth with their tongue. Even though this submission is plausible, but proving or disproving it is complicated.

As noted earlier, this is purely a case of differences in culture. Among the Maori haka of New Zealand, this gesture is used to represent fierceness and has been adopted into their rugby team. In Tibet, it is used as a symbol of respect and honour. With these practical illustrations across cultures, it is safe to conclude that this gesture is not a universal one (Hana 2013). Many other contributors to this submit that this cue ends in childhood, save for those who are imitating children for the sake of humour. When we are guarded by these signifiers, we will not fall into avoidable temptations when we are out of our primary place of abode.

Practical Illustrations

Case Study I: During break, most of the pupils of SIG Primary School would rush to the playground to catch fun. However, there was one of them who had the features of a bully. Instead of playing on his own and with other pupils, he would be going about doing one negative thing or another against his mates. As such, most of the pupils avoided him. He had been warned by their teachers several times, but he did not seem to be ready for a change. With the last child he offended before moving back to their classroom, he stuck out his tongue and opened his eyes wider. This is to further taunt the person and make them look stupid.

Case Study II: Baby M was hungry, and the mother tried to feed him with a feeding bottle because she was trying to wean him, but he would not accept it. When he tasted it and it did not taste like breast milk, he would struggle to get ahold of his mother's breasts. Any time the mother put the feeding bottle in his mouth, he would push it out with his tongue and subconsciously use his hands to wave it off, and his legs would also move simultaneously. This is a symbol of rejection.

Case Study III: A man just arrived from Tibet and, as such, was a novice to the culture of the Europeans. His only mistake was that instead of him to take time to learn, he wanted to be social as soon as he arrived. So he secured an appointment with a manufacturing firm, and when he got to work the next day, he decided to greet his boss with a protruded tongue. This pissed his boss off because he saw no reason for such a gesture. His job was saved by another worker versed in non-verbal gestures across cultures.

Case Study IV: Woman XP is an infamous drug addict and was arrested at a nightclub which had become notorious for housing miscreants. She was unconscious at the point of arrest as she was indescribably drunk. On the morning of the second day, she was regaining herself and wanted to foment trouble in the cell. She questioned why she was brought to the place in the first instance. She looked resolute to cause a scene, and her mates seized the opportunity to make things go rowdy. The officers on duty swung to action. They calmed and warned her of the consequences of her actions. XP pushed out her tongue as a way of insulting the officers. And this did not end well for her.

12.5. Protruding Tongue

Generic Interpretations of the Concept

This gesture is like the tongue-insult behaviour we just discussed, but this has multiple meanings even in the same culture. The interpretation of the tongue-protruding cue, which is a sudden sticking out of the tongue, is dependent on the direction of the protrusion and the activity the person is engaged in at the moment of displaying the gesture.

Usually, when people are performing complex assignments, they stick out their tongue to a direction or another or they can even drape it over their lower lip. This is a means of fighting tension or stress. Having worked with a lot of people across nations and professions, I have seen this cue several times. For instance, an accountant was working with me some years ago, whenever he wanted to press figures on the calculators, especially huge data, he would stick out his tongue. Also, I notice this sometimes when I want to test my trainees after teaching sessions. This is more noticeable on the sponsored trainees who must present their certificate to their boss when they get to the office.

The tongue-protrusion behaviour performs two simultaneous functions. The fundamental function it performs is to pacify us when stressed. Also, it tells others that we are too busy; hence, we need our privacy for the time being. In other words, this is a 'Do not disturb' sign. While this may not really work among close friends with one's spouse, it will surely go a long way in the office setting. Renowned basketball player Michael Jordan was fond of this gesture while on the field of play. Whenever his tongue was out, more points would soon follow; he did concentrate more and win points for his team while displaying this cue. Hence, it is not an entirely negative body language gesture.

Scientific Explanations

Craig Baxter (2019) explains that the tongue-protruding gesture is always seen when children and adults need to concentrate on a given task. David Givens notes that we regularly show our tongue when performing tasks that involve precise manual dexterity (e.g., threading a needle), and this may well be a reflection of the neurological link between human toolmaking and speech. In the same vein, a research at the University of Western Australia opines that when a tongue is slightly protruded, it is a means of saying, 'Don't bother me at the moment!' If you see someone displaying this gesture, the best thing is to disengage any form of conversation with them so as to allow them to concentrate with what they are doing (Baxter 2019).

In addition, Givens writes in his *Nonverbal Dictionary of Gestures, Signs, and Body Language* that 'tongue-show is a universal mood sign of unspoken disagreement, disbelief, disliking, displeasure, or uncertainty. It may modify, counteract, or contradict a verbal remark. Following the statement "Yes, I agree," e.g., a protruded tongue may suggest, "I don't agree." Tongue-shows can reveal misleading, ambiguous, or uncertain areas in dialogue, public statements, and oral testimony and thus may signal probing points [i.e., unresolved verbal issues to be further analysed and explored].' For instance, among the people in Tibet and Southern China, the slight protruding tongue is used to say, 'I didn't mean it' (Morris 1994). In fact, Meltzoff and Moore (1983) state that a three-day-old child can imitate adult display of this behaviour.

In his own submission, Philip (2013) says that when this behaviour is displayed among friends, it would be laughed off as being cheeky, but if it is done in other contexts, it would be taken seriously. He also toils the path of other experts that when this gesture is displayed by an adult, it is a means of showing that they are genuinely focused on the task they are doing and do not want anybody to serve as a source of hindrance to them. Alternatively, he says, 'The tongue can also be seen moistening the lips more often when under stress or anxiety as the mouth dries up, or can be moved back and forth across the lips as a pacifying behaviour to soothe while under stress.'

He concludes that there are arguments about this cue as to whether it is cultural, innate, or learnt. While a lot of experts agree that most body gestures are not learnt, it is not yet clear whether it should be categorised as cultural or innate but dangles between the two.

Practical Illustrations

Case Study I: There were four female employees in GRS Company. Once it was time for their break, they would all meet at the desk of Mrs F to discuss. Most of the time, their talks revolved on their homes, spouses, and general women's talk. However, Mrs registered for a professional examination which would be held at the weekend. She was always engaged with chores and children's disturbance at home. So she had purposed to make the best use of the one-hour break at the office. Despite telling her colleagues her intentions, they seemed to be more interested in the gist than her success, so the 'encouraging' words ended up lasting for a whole hour. With the reality of the exam at hand and the need to cover more syllabus, before it was time for break, she had taken her book. So when they came over, they saw her focused on the book and her tongue slightly protruded. She only responded to their greetings with a nod, and they knew she was in for serious business. So they left one after the other because they knew they would not win her attention.

Case Study II: Boy T had always been fascinated with engineering since childhood. So his father had always taken his time to explain to him that he needed to be sound in mathematics and other science-related courses in order to stand a chance of being a successful engineer. This had subconsciously stuck into his brain, and he was deeply in love with all his courses. Their teacher gave them an exercise at school, but none of them could solve it. So he told them to take it home and try it again. T did not even eat when he headed to the study and was there for hours. When his father slipped in to check on him and saw that he was deeply focused with his tongue protruded, he retreated to the living room immediately. This was a display of seriousness.

Case Study III: Company ZOP had just got a new regional manager who appeared to be hard-working and creative. He seemed resolute to change the fortunes of the firm, and all his efforts were geared towards achieving this. So many times, his subordinates would see him do what his predecessor didn't care about. One day, he showed up unannounced at the production unit of the firm. Man QO, who was there illegally, was shocked to see him. Not wanting to show any sign of nervousness, he protruded his tongue and focused on the work as if he had been busy all day till the manager took his leave. That was how he saved himself.

12.6. Tongue Pressed against the Palate

Generic Interpretations of the Concept

This is a self-comforting gesture that is normally seen in people when all is not well with them. It is the act of pressing the tongue (usually the tip and part of the main body) against the roof of the mouth technically known as the hard palate. The mouth would be slightly open that their audience can have a partial view of their tongue. This allows air to come in and the person to breathe out the tiredness they are experiencing. In short, this cue means that someone is undergoing some internal psychological struggles.

You will see this sign in people who are being stressed or being intellectually engaged. When someone is filling out applications which need to be carefully done, such as documents relating to bank or employment, people will press their tongue against the palate. A cluster is that you will see them focused on that particular activity even if there are tempting distractions around. Also, students taking exams do display this gesture. It is an indication that they are fully concentrated and do not want to make mistakes.

In addition, you may see this sign when someone misses out on a great opportunity—a football player loses a goal or a basketball player fires a shot out of place. In this context, the person is certainly consoling himself. So when you see someone display this behaviour, it may be an invitation for you to come to their aid because they need to be comforted psychologically.

Scientific Explanations

Mary Bond (2013) says that when you press your tongue against the upper palate, it flattens the tongue and makes the mouth look smaller. However, when the front third of the tongue is lightly placed against the upper palate, the tip just touching the inside of the upper teeth, the back of the tongue becomes wide and soft. According to her, the best form of posture everyone should always maintain is the latter. She backs up her point by saying, 'The tongue's presence below the maxillae helps support the upper face, provides length for the throat, and tone in the entrance to the gut tube. It helps align the neck and head above the torso. It also helps support the nasal bones, making it easier to breathe through the nose.' From this submission, it means that when a person maintains the tongue posture of the former, it means something is wrong with them; nobody intentionally maintains a poor posture if their mood is not disturbed.

Sofie-Ann Bracke (2016) maintains the same view with Bond. However, Bracke provides a clearer explanation that when the mouth is not closed, the tongue should either be in the middle of the oral cavity or tilt downward.

However, if it is slightly open, as in the case of the cue we are considering here, and moves upward, it means the person is stressed. Maintaining a proper posture is important at all times, and a slight alteration communicates volumes.

Also, Tibetan School of Buddhism requires that its adherent press their tongue against the hard palate when meditating. Even though many of them do not know why the instruction was given, it has been explained that this cue is a 'thought stopping' gesture which blocks thoughts coming from the person's mind so as to enable them concentrate on their meditation. Some say that this gesture gives the person 'unremitting mindfulness'. That is, the person does not lose concentration at any point. The alternative explanation given is that it is to purge out external issues, stress, and exertion so that they can be internally refilled during the meditation. The preceding sentence gives a better explanation of the concept as it relates to body language. Even the act of meditation can be tiring to some people, and adopting that posture may be the only means of stimulation which they know to calm themselves.

Practical Illustrations

Case Study I: One of the organisational best practices that had made DKT Firms a cynosure of all eyes was that they conducted relevant tests for their employees before they could be promoted. In other words, if an employee did not pass a test, he or she could not be promoted to the next level, no matter the number of years they had spent at their present level. The aim was to ensure that the person understood the nuances of their next office; the firm did not want to learn its lesson in a hard way. This year's test seemed to be somewhat difficult as they were planning to extend their range of services to other places. One of the employees who was taking the test for the same level for the third consecutive year could be seen at the back, pressing her tongue against the roof of her mouth. This means she was finding the test difficult.

Case Study II: Parts of the requirements of OTC Company was for its applicants to fill some questionnaires about work culture and ethics. What they wanted to achieve was to ensure that whoever was coming on board shared the same ethics with them. The questionnaires were very tricky and could easily mar the chances of an applicant if care was not taken. Mr Y was an engineering student and was looking for an industrial training placement in the firm. Because of the rich history of the company, he purposed to do his IT with them, no matter what it would take him. While filling out their questionnaire, he could be seen pressing his tongue against his hard palate while the mouth was slightly open. This means he was finding it not easy.

Case Study III: Professor G was a renowned scientist who was always invited for paper presentations all over the world. On a particular occasion, he was to deliver a paper in his home university on a Thursday before flying out to deliver another one in another continent on Friday. Due to the question-and-answer session on Thursday, he stayed at the lecture venue beyond schedule, hoping that he would drive speedily to the airport, only for him to encounter minor traffic on the road. As he was getting to the airport, the plane he was supposed to board was flying out. He stood still and pressed his tongue against his palate and looked askance. He became tired and frustrated at the same time. He was engulfed in confusion because he did not know the next best step for himself at that point.

Case Study IV: I once stopped a drug trafficker who mixed some prescribed drugs with recommended ones. He did it in such a perfect way that no one would notice. When I flagged him down, he looked tired and psychologically weary. I thought something must have been wrong, and since his eyes were on the drugs and looking forward, I thought something was amiss. I ordered that the drugs be searched, and those prescribed drugs were found. I noticed that while the search was ongoing, he looked disturbed, pressing his tongue against his hard palate, and frustrated. That was enough reason for me to order the continuation of the search—that is, I clearly read the sign of deception and nervousness on him, and that was a bolster for me to carry our an in-depth investigation.

12.7. Licking the Teeth with the Tongue

Generic Interpretations of the Concept

Just as the lip-licking behaviour we discussed under the lips segment, we also lick our teeth when the oral cavity is dry. To display this gesture, the tongue would be used in rubbing the teeth and gums. This is done as a way of relieving stress. It is also a potential sign of dehydration. The stress causing this gesture may be propelled by fear, anxiety, or nervousness. When we are afraid of talking, for instance, the saliva in our mouth dries up. That is why you see some people open their mouth and no word would be uttered. It means they are stressed due to the fear they are nurturing. If it is essential that the person speaks at that point, they will moisten the teeth and lips with the help of the tongue.

When we exercise fear on an issue and we allow it to overtake us, it will show in our behaviour as we will become anxious to things that we could have calmed down and implemented. In a bid to cover up our fear, we may use the tongue to lick our teeth. In doing this, the mouth is slightly open so as to make the tongue move back and forth. Sometimes, the rubbing may extend to the surface of the lips too. Once the teeth and lips are moistened, we become relieved of our stress to a large extent. At this point, we can communicate fairly well.

This behaviour is a universal stress reliever. As a way of making it subtle, some people may decide to close their mouth, but the tongue track can still be seen under the lips, and the tongue pushes out the lips, which hints those around us that something is going on. Hence, when you notice this behaviour in people, it is an indication that the person is trying to pacify himself or herself because they are witnessing some negative emotions.

Scientific Explanations

While explaining the body language of the tongue, Changing Minds states that while lip licking is an obvious body gesture, licking the teeth is a hidden form of expressing the same desire. It states that this may be an indication of stress because tension effects reduce the flow of saliva, which make the mouth dry out. Since saliva is not flowing as it should, we make use of an improvised means, which is the conscious secretion through the use of the tongue.

Christopher Philip (2014) also expatiates on this concept. He gives the description of this cue as 'when the tongue is run back and forth over the teeth or lips either with the mouth closed or mouth opened [rare].' When the mouth is closed, it shows up as a bulge passing under the skin of the lips because it is forced out. In simple terms, running the tongue over the teeth shows the need to pacify because the person is feeling negative emotions. This cue can be very pacifying and has the ability to lift people out of their quagmire. If properly done, many people may not even notice you. Hence, it can always be covertly used to pacify the mind.

Because it is a pacifying act, teeth licking is normally done repeatedly, and the person will avoid eye contact while displaying the gesture. The soothing tactile stimuli provided by the tongue reduces anxiety to the barest minimum. However, if this behaviour becomes a habit, it glaringly communicates your discomfort to the external world; people will easily fish you out. The same principle applies to habitual lip lickers who are fond of sweeping their lips at every given opportunity. Philip submits, 'As the tongue sweeps, it serves the same purpose as running the palms over the thighs or rubbing the back of the neck, stroking the hands, rubbing the back of the head and so forth. These are all ways we pacify and soothe ourselves throughout the day as stress presents itself.'

The verbal translation of this cue is, 'I'm running my tongue over my teeth or lips in order to creating a soothing sensation because I'm in need of pacifying due to anxiety.' If you are not sure that a person is displaying this behaviour, you can watch for other clusters, such as stroking the thigh or arms, fidgeting, or rubbing the face.

Practical Illustrations

Case Study I: For the past two weeks, Mr S had not been patronised by anybody. The economic downturn was really telling on him. As he was about to pack in and go home, a man came to purchase some goods. With the look of the man, he thought he should be a big catch for him, and as such, he should be able to make the gain of about a week through him. When the man picked the goods, they started negotiating. When he gave the man the final price, the reaction of the buyer was not encouraging. The salesman formed a bulge under his front lips, which was an indication he was sweeping his teeth with his tongue—he was anxious that the buyer would walk away without making any purchase.

Case Study II: Dr H was a public official, and he was accused of corruption. So one of the best investigative journalists in the country scheduled an interview with him so that he would clear the air or otherwise. Appearing on the political programme, he first seemed to be calm and confident, but when the on-air personality asked him a question pertaining to a certain project and even mentioned the amount, he appeared to have lost his voice. After managing to speak, what he only told the journalist was to repeat the question in a clearer term. At this point, he was seen using his tongue to sweep his teeth, which created a track on his front lips. This is an indication that Dr H was stressed and was looking for ways to shelve off the distress. Hence, the request to repeat the question was a time-buying technique.

Case Study III: We were hinted of a crime by some of our men on the field. I led a team to lay ambush to the criminals. The team was only able to arrest one of them. He pretended in such a way that no one would link him to the crime. However, I noticed that he was stressed through his non-verbal gesture. He was not ready to exchange eye contact with law enforcement agents and looked to be in a hurry, but during our short conversation with him, I saw him lick his teeth with his tongue continuously in an obvious manner. For a second, I didn't believe we had apprehended the right person, and after all the processes, it was established that my guess was accurate.

12.8. Moving the Tongue

Generic Interpretations of the Concept

Those who dart the tongue from one side of the mouth to the other believe that they cannot be noticed. So they tend to hide their emotions while displaying this gesture so that you believe nothing is going on.

Those who move their tongue from a corner of the mouth to another (usually through the cheeks) are really worried about something. They do it playfully while they ruminate on the issue that is bothering them. To someone who is not observant, you will think they are all right, but the movement of the tongue within the mouth in a nervous manner says there is more than meets the eye. With just little questioning, the person will probably confess.

In simpler terms, the person who plays with his tongue in his mouth is afraid that something unpalatable is about to befall them. You may see this in students about to sit an exam, a worker who is to face a disciplinary committee, someone flying for the first time, a criminal about to be interviewed, and a person going to a competition. In all these contexts, those involved cannot predict the actual outcome of the exercises, especially if a giant is the opponent. We can aptly conclude that tongue darting is a self-comforting gesture.

Scientific Explanations

When the tongue moves from the corners of the mouth through the cheeks, the focus is not only on the tongue but also even the other parts of the body involved. For instance, when the tongue hits the cheek, it makes it bigger by protruding it. This is used to communicate uncertainty on the next line of action. It means the person is really lost on the next idea that can get them out of their state of quagmire. You may also pay attention to raised eyebrows and rounded eyes, which are the clusters in this sense. Note that the more the person uses the tongue to hit the cheek, the greater the emotions they feel. The gesture may also signal exhaustion. Hence, the person is trying to recuperate. You see this gesture in football players after they missed an opportunity and tried to run back to their normal positions (BLT 2019).

Christopher Philip (2014) says that this behaviour demonstrates the need for pacifying. When the tongue touches the corners of the mouth and cheeks, they release moisture in excess because those are the soft areas of the mouth. The saliva secreted is meant to pacify the body and keep them rightly activated against the nervous feelings.

T. J. Walker (2011) enumerates reasons why people dart their tongue. He condemns this among media personality. It can be very irritating to thousands or probably millions of people watching them. In all, he lists five reasons that cause the tongue-darting cue in the media space. First, being nervous makes people do things that are unusual. There is hardly anyone who will dart their tongue if it is not inspired by nervousness. Further, nervousness makes the mouth go dry. Since we are under obligation to speak in public—when being interviewed, at the workplace, anchoring a programme on the television, etc.—we will have to pacify ourselves, and the go-to method is to dart the tongue through the corners of the mouth so as to moisten them in preparation for speech-making. Furthermore, talking louder than normal or with more energy than usual forces air out of the mouth with greater velocity, drying the mouth further. Again, the tongue shoots out in search of water. And finally, when we talk under a bright light or the scorching sun, they can make us hot and thirsty, thereby putting the tongue into action.

Surprisingly, most people who dart out their tongue are not aware of this behaviour of theirs. In other words, people dart their tongues unconsciously. If you should call their attention to it, they would be shocked. The general conclusion on people who dart their tongues is that they are uncertain, nervous, anxious, or tentative. Ultimately, everything may be surmised as tagging the speaker as being dubious. Although this may not be fair on the part of the audience passing the harsh judgement, but if a person does not display the behaviour, they would not have had the opportunity to make such conclusions (Walker 2011).

Practical Illustrations

Case Study I: Mr O had been the general manager of GDW Manufacturing Firm for the past ten years. Within the last two years, it was discovered that things were not going as they should. The chairman, having trusted him, gave him the licence to sort out everything, not knowing that the general manager was behind the retrogressive movement of the firm; he had been cunningly diverting some materials for his own personal use. He wanted to establish his own company and had been looking for ways to run GDW aground before taking his leave. When there was no change, the chairman had to hire some auditors who did their investigations discretely. Then the manager was arrested. He was surprised that they got to know he was the one; he was afraid they would have all the evidence to nail him. When he was being interviewed, one of the officials noticed that whenever he was talking, he was always sticking out his tongue to sweep the corners of his mouth.

Case Study II: Mr L had just secured an appointment with BZL School. It was the norm of the school to hold a staff meeting daily, and the school leader could call on anyone to make suggestions or air their view on a particular issue. Mr L had witnessed two meetings and saw how the other teachers were logically arguing out their points. Thinking what one had said was very excellent, another one would stand up and counter it in an exceptionally unbelievable manner. Everything became intimidating to him, especially thinking of when he would be called on to make his own argument. Eventually, the day came, and Mr L felt like being buried alive. Before talking, he quickly ran his tongue at the corners of his mouth through the cheeks. That communicated his fear to others.

Case Study III: A man wanted to gain entrance into the country through an illegal means. When I saw him, I saw a person who was more frustrated than being daring; he wasn't that courageous. He thought his frustrations would come to an end if he got into the country. Although there was nothing wrong with this assumption, but he had no valid documents. He held some fake ones to deceive officers and prove his legality. Seeing the mass number of officers at the border, he became terrified of his chances of being let in. I could see his tongue cleansing the corners of his mouth. When asked to speak, he lost his voice for almost one minute before muttering some words. This was a display of nervousness.

CHAPTER 13

The Cheeks and Jaw

This is another dimension of our studies. Admittedly, there are not too many non-verbal messages related to the cheeks and jaw, but the little that are listed here are worth exploring. We think that the cheeks are merely a dormant fixture only meant for some pecking or decorations, while the jaw is meant for talking and chewing. It simply goes beyond that; it is loaded with non-verbal messages as well. One of the things that give humans our unique facial appearance is our cheeks and jaw. In fact, in many industries, having strong jaws is one of the physical attributes of leadership, while the fashion world is in constant search of people with high cheekbones for modelling.

The Latin name for cheek is *buccae*. It consists of the area of the face below the eyes and between the nose and the left or right ear. In humans, the cheek is innervated by the buccal nerve. The skin of the cheek is being suspended by the chin and jaws which form the lateral wall of the human mouth. It visibly touches the cheekbone beneath the eye. During chewing, the cheeks and tongue between them serve to keep the food between the teeth. The inside of the cheek is lined with a mucous membrane (buccal mucosa, part of the oral mucosa) (DMD 2019). The most common location to take a DNA sample is the cheek.

The jawbone is also known as mandible and is the strongest, lowest, and largest bone in our face. Forming the lower jaw, it is the one that holds the lower teeth in place. It is located below the maxilla. Tortora (2019) affirms that the jaw is the only movable bone of the skull, apart from the ossicles of the middle ear.

The bone is formed in the foetus from a fusion of the left and right mandibular prominences, and the point where these sides join, the mandibular symphysis, is still visible as a faint ridge in the midline. Like other symphyses in the body, this is a midline articulation where the bones are joined by fibrocartilage, but this articulation fuses together in early childhood (Fehrenbach and Herring 2012).

At birth, the body of the bone is a mere shell, containing the sockets of the two incisor, the canine, and the two deciduous molar teeth, imperfectly partitioned off from one another. The mandibular canal is of large size and runs near the lower border of the bone; the mental foramen opens beneath the socket of the first deciduous molar tooth. The angle is obtuse (175°), and the condyloid portion is nearly in line with the body. The coronoid process is of comparatively large size and projects above the level of the condyle.

After birth, the two segments of the bone become joined at the symphysis, from below upward, in the first year; but a trace of separation may be visible in the beginning of the second year, near the alveolar margin. The body becomes elongated in its whole length, but more especially behind the mental foramen, to provide space for the three additional teeth developed in this part. The depth of the body increases, owing to increased growth of the alveolar part, to afford room for the roots of the teeth and by thickening of the subdental portion which enables the jaw to withstand the powerful action of the masticatory muscles. But the alveolar portion is the deeper of the two, and consequently, the chief part of the body lies above the oblique line. The mandibular canal, after the second dentition, is situated just above the level of the mylohyoid line, and the mental foramen occupies its usual position in adults. The angle becomes less obtuse, owing to the separation of the jaws by the teeth. About the fourth year, it is 140° (Levin 2008).

In the adult, the alveolar and subdental portions of the body are usually of equal depth. The mental foramen opens midway between the upper and lower borders of the bone, and the mandibular canal runs nearly parallel with the mylohyoid line. The ramus is almost vertical in direction, the angle measuring from 110° to 120°. Also, the adult condyle is higher than the coronoid process, and the sigmoid notch becomes deeper (Marius 2012).

In old age, the bone can become greatly reduced in volume where there is a loss of teeth and consequent resorption of the alveolar process and interalveolar septa. Consequently, the chief part of the bone is below the oblique line. The mandibular canal, with the mental foramen opening from it, is closer to the alveolar border. The ramus is oblique in direction, the angle measures about 140°, and the neck of the condyle is more or less bent backwards (Romer 1977).

When remains of humans are found, the mandible is one of the common findings, sometimes the only bone found. Skilled experts can estimate the age of the human upon death because the mandible changes over a person's life.

The mandible may be dislocated anteriorly (to the front) and inferiorly (downwards) but very rarely posteriorly (backwards). The mandibular alveolar process can become resorbed when completely edentulous in the mandibular arch (occasionally noted also in partially edentulous cases). This resorption can occur to such an extent that the mental foramen is virtually on the superior border of the mandible, instead of opening on the anterior surface, changing its relative position. However, the more inferior body of the mandible is not affected and remains thick and rounded. With age and tooth loss, the alveolar process is absorbed so that the mandibular canal becomes nearer the superior border (Fehrenbach and Herring 2012).

When we take cognisance of the nuances of all these biological explanations, you will discover that the cheeks and jaws play an invaluable role in understanding non-verbal gestures of people. The face can express over a thousand emotions, and the jaws and cheeks are part of the process. In order to appear beautiful, people paint their cheeks with make-up, while others allow their hair to grow out on the jaw so that it fills up the face. When the cheeks flush, it is an expression of excitement or embarrassment, while the jaw shifts when we are nervous. All these are essential messages that cannot be overlooked.

13.1. Quick Facial Tics

Generic Interpretations of the Concept

Something about facial tics is that no one can predict where they can erupt on the face; you can notice them on the corners of the mouth, the forehead, the eyes, or even the cheeks. They are also specific to every human. A facial tic is a sudden, short convulsive or jerking movement on the face. It is an unconscious action that is always propelled by stress. Since this action cannot be controlled, it gives people out unexpectedly. However, it is crucial to also note that sudden a facial tic is a microexpression; it appears and disappears in the twinkle of an eye. This means if you are not observant, you may not notice this signal of stress in people.

Whenever you notice a sudden nervous twitch in an interlocutor, it is induced by anxiety or tension. It appears in real time in relation to an event—that is, the feeling shows up immediately after someone thinks something is at stake. For instance, if your co-interlocutor feels that what you have just said can later end up harming them or their plans, there may be a display of sudden facial tic from them.

Due to the tension aroused by this negative feeling, the flow of blood on the face is distorted, and one of the external reactions is the facial tic that can appear on any part of the face. The reason facial tics do appear on or near the cheeks is due to the interconnecting muscles that traverse the area. In other words, one of the regions that house the facial muscles is the cheek, and since the muscles are moved during tension or fear, this also affects the structure of the cheeks.

The gesture is also a signal that someone has ruminated on what you just told them, and they feel its outcome will not favour them.

Scientific Explanations

Philip (2013) says that a sudden facial tic is evidence that a person is thinking or trying to evaluate something. Also, it means the person is trying to come to a decision or arrive at a satisfactory conclusion. In other words, what is on their mind at present does not make them comfortable. In addition, he notes that if the twitching on the cheeks takes place very near to the nose region, it may signal disbelief or dislike. The nose works in conjunction with the surrounding regions to show dislike. Since the nose is the organ of smell, if we perceive something that does not seem favourable, even if it is an idea, the nose will move irritatingly, which will affect other parts of the body such as the cheeks. However, this latest cue should be paired with other evaluative gestures in order to be sure of the interpretations.

Some people are of the opinion that when a person is being deceptive, they may also display this gesture because of the psychological unrest that they are going through. Alex Denethorn (2016) submits that 'all humans constantly display body language that signals thoughts and feelings to the people around us'. Julia Yeckley (2016) notes that the sudden facial tic is an odd behaviour, but unfortunately, its appearance or otherwise is not within the reach of anybody. She compares it with breathing. Hence, it gives people away easily.

Denethorn explains, 'At any rate, the reason for your facial tic is an involuntary muscle movement (hence, micro-expression). Whenever you think or feel something, you will display this outwardly for others to see that: it's what

I tend to think of as a socially evolved behaviour designed to put others at ease. Humans need to know how to relate to each other, and if we display our thoughts and feelings in a way that other people can perceive or "read", they will have a much easier time to figuring out where they stand with you.' Even though many of us will not like people to know our feelings, especially when what we are thinking does not align with them. When you are at loggerheads with someone who can defeat you, you will rather want to suppress your emotions or keep them to yourself.

For instance, Psychologia, a website that is focused on understanding human feelings from the standpoint of psychology, notes that a facial tic is a signal of deception. HOWEVER, Westside Toastmasters is quick to caution that we should look for several other clusters that confirm our doubts on this issue.

Practical Illustrations

Case Study I: A notorious criminal causing mayhem in neighbouring communities was nabbed after over fifteen years of his nefarious activities. His apprehension was difficult due to his techniques of operations; he changed his facial appearance any time he was doing new operations. So there were controversies of his involvement or otherwise in each case. Many of those he impersonated were always arrested and released after proving their innocence. However, years of underground studies by experts connected most of the crimes to just one source. During his interrogation, he thought he was going to answer questions on the crime he was caught committing only for the interrogators to be making references to those he had committed for years. When the interrogator mentioned one relating to the murder of a family, he looked up and his face twitched. The evidence was too overwhelming to be psychologically discarded. The second interrogator noted the 'guilty knowledge' display.

Case Study II: Mr U had been an accomplice of some external elements who had perpetrated innumerable crimes on the firm where he worked. He did not seem to think of his being tied with the firm and possible apprehension, but with the way things had been going recently, he thought some people had been suspecting him. Hence, he walked about with that feeling and always wanted to prove that he was as innocent as every other person. One day, his boss invited him to his office, and the boss simply asked, 'Where were you yesternight?' And that tripped him off. Re-echoing the question, he twitched his face in a quick manner, which made his superior suspect that something was wrong. Meanwhile, the boss only wanted to compliment him for seeing him at his favourite bar. The twitching made the manager mark him up for some negative issues. He was later caught and traced to the dubious transactions against the firm.

Case Study III: The general manager of AIQ Supplies had noticed some clients using some dubious receipts to get goods from them. He ordered that forensic analysis should be carried out on every receipt tendered by clients, and it should be done secretly so as to fish out the bad eggs. When the receipt of one of the clients who had been the brains behind the atrocities was taken and he saw them taking it into an inner room, he unconsciously twitched his face. The manager, curiously watching him, knew he was up to something. After the analysis of his receipt, it was said to be fake.

13.2. Facial Denting

Generic Interpretations of the Concept

The face is literally dented when you use your finger to firmly press your cheeks against the jaw. This is a common gesture that is done by most people across the world. There is no need to emphasise that every hand-to-face gesture is meant to pacify the person. In other words, pressing the fingers against the cheek is a way of creating a sensation that will relief the tension being felt. In plain terms, when someone places their fingers on the cheek, it is evidence that they are feeling negative emotions.

Apart from the literal movement of the hands that make the gesture so obvious, the degree of stress being felt is determined by how firm the fingers are pressed against the cheeks. When the person applies so much pressure, it means they are really stressed and craving for rest in all front. One of the meanings popularly alluded to this gesture is that the person is thinking of something that has served as a source of concern to them. While displaying this cue, they may rest their elbow on their thigh or on a table. This is to support the tilted head. Also, the cue is seen when a person is wishing that something turns to their favour. That is why it is a common gesture in sporting events when the home team is putting up a disappointing show.

Facial denting can be displayed with one or two hands or even with the use of a few fingers on just a cheek. Sometimes, people pinch the cheek between their thumb and index or middle finger; they do this when they do not want you to know how they feel. Some will erroneously believe they are trying to play with pimples on the face. You need to be very observant in order to deal with such kinds of people.

Scientific Explanations

Joe Navarro (2014) says that facial denting is the act of distorting the face with our hands. Sharing his experience, Navarro says that people may opt to use other objects such as a pen in place of their fingers. He also attributes stress to this cue. High-stake interviews, students about to take tests, sporting events, poker players, and other demanding contexts are the common places where this cue is usually displayed. In fact, while parents are eagerly waiting to hear the results of their children at the hospital, they do show this behaviour. Explaining the reason this is done, Navarro submits that the action of pushing in our faces 'stimulates nerves on the face, in the facial muscles, and in the mouth which serves to pacify or soothe us psychologically'.

The former FBI agent proceeds that although not too many experts in the field have given their attention to this, but we cannot downplay its essence due to what it communicates—it means there are issues with the person or something is bothering them.

IndiaBIX notes that the facial dent is one of the few adult cues that is as pronounced as a child's. The website notes that if the hands cover the mouth, it is a metaphorical way of suppressing what the person wants to say. Maybe they wanted to tell a lie or say something that is against the established rules. However, if someone places their finger on their cheek when you are speaking, it means they do not believe you.

Stating that this cue is an evaluative gesture, Westside Toastmasters (2019) opines, 'Evaluation is shown by a closed hand resting on the chin or cheek, often with the index finger pointing upwards. When the person begins to lose interest but still wants to appear interested for courtesy's sake, the position will alter so that the heel of the palm supports the head as boredom sets in.' What this website does is that it opens our mind to the possibility that each technique of facial denting carries a specific meaning. To show genuine interest, the hand will slightly rest on the cheek without being used as a support to the head.

The website explains further, 'When the index finger points vertically up the cheek and the thumb supports the chin, the listener is having negative or critical thoughts about the speaker or his subject. Sometimes the index finger may rub or pull at the eye as the negative thoughts continue.' People tend to mistake this gesture as a show of interest, but the supporting thumb which is placed under the chin exposes their intent of being critical. Holding this gesture for too long means the person is very critical of the situation they are evaluating.

Practical Illustrations

Case Study I: Once in a while, the company president of SWA Enterprises would meet with the workforce of the firm so as to better communicate his vision to them and ensure they were on the right track. Apart from being lengthy, the president's speech was also boring and dull. However, as a show of respect, the top executives in the firm feigned interest. They understood that if they should openly communicate their lack of interest, this could lead to their being fired from the company. In the last meeting, the president was repetitive, boring, and uninspiring. The middle manager was extraordinarily tired. So he rested his hand on his cheek with the index finger pointing upward and gradually changed the position by using the heels of the palm to support the head. This means that boredom was setting in.

Case Study II: Mr J had just been fired from his workplace due to the global economic downturn. He vowed not to work under anyone again but to be self-employed. This was risky in every sense of it. As such, he decided to restructure some things within the home. He called his wife and two children to a meeting. During the meeting, one of the things he said was that they were going to move the children to another school because he could no longer afford what he was currently paying. This decision was not pleasing to the children. The eldest child used his thumb to support his chin while the index finger vertically pointed up the cheek. This means he was having negative view of what his father was saying.

Case Study III: Woman R was accused of impersonation, but she denied it and was insistent that every analysis should be done to ascertain the truthfulness of her identity—she was very certain that no officer would be able to unravel her identity. However, she became uncomfortable when the analysis was taking longer than expected. With a lot of thoughts running through her mind, she sat silently at a corner and used her hand to support her chin, making her facial appearance disoriented. The reason was to make it difficult for the law enforcement official to compare her facial look with the passport in their hand.

13.3. Cheek Massaging

Generic Interpretations of the Concept

All over the world, cheek massaging is used as a way of releasing tension or stress from the body. It is the soft and gentle rub of the cheeks so as to create a soothing and sensational effect. Depending on the context, facial massaging depicts various things. For instance, it may be used to denote that someone is thinking. When people are contemplating over an issue, they usually massage their cheek during the thinking process. This will not make them feel the load of the intellectual rigours that they are undertaking—that is, the cheek massaging positively distracts them from what they are contemplating on.

In addition, this gesture may also be displayed as a way of calming oneself. If you are in an official gathering and someone is saying something that is infuriating, you can just rub your cheeks to not react in a negative or unethical manner.

Further, cheek massaging may be a way of playing love. It can signal a prelude to intercourse between lovers. Due to the sensation this action creates, it has the ability to arouse people's sexual emotions if done rightly. Hence, a lover may employ it as a means of charging the feelings of their partner. This is usually subtle and enjoyable to both parties.

Meanwhile, some people just do it as a literal means of feeling the softness of their cheeks. Maybe they have had pimples in the past and are now feeling the cheek to know how smooth it has become. Ultimately, always consider this behaviour in the company of others in order to determine the message it is really passing across.

Scientific Illustrations

IndiaBIX opines that facial touch can either signal interest or boredom, depending on how it is done. For instance, when a listener places the whole palm against the cheek as a way of supporting the head, it is a hint that they are experiencing boredom. Hence, the behaviour is a way of holding themselves up so that they do not fall asleep. When the boredom is extreme, the head would be totally supported by the hand. On the other hand, it is a show of interest when a closed hand rested on the cheek, and in most cases, the index finger would be pointing upwards.

In its own submission, Changing Minds (2019) notes that the cheek is a wide area that can be touched without obstructing any of the functional organ. This makes it a go-to touch area for human beings. The platform explains that the cheeks are either touched as a show of surprise or horror. 'A light touch, along with an open mouth that says 'Oooh' indicate light surprise. Touching both cheeks with the flat of the palm is an exaggeration of this and may indicate horror' (Changing Minds 2019).

In another article, the website also explains that facial massage may be an indication of fear. This means the person wants to be relieved of their tension. Sometimes, you may see that they are physically sweating. Some people can deliberately exaggerate this gesture as a means of drawing the attention of others to their ordeals. Further, if the rubbing is done very slowly, it means the person is thinking. This has a literal meaning of massaging the brain so as to keep the intellectual process flowing. If the cheek massaging is close to the temple, it means the person is stressed and is trying to massage the headache away. And finally, it may be a means of propping up the face.

Practical Illustrations

Case Study I: Dr IBK was in the office—he stayed back after work due to some issues. His present work as the chief medical director was tiring due to the fact that many of those working with him were inexperienced. More so, the hospital was located in a strategic position in the city which made it easily accessible to a lot of people. So he had to work out himself. Even if he were supposed to be off, life-threatening circumstances do keep him back at work. Now there was an opening in another hospital that was well-established, and if appointed, he was going to be a subordinate under another—a known high-handed person. What was really serving as a source of concern to him was, to stay back and be a boss while garnering experience and working out himself or go to a place where he would work on lesser hours but may be at loggerheads with the boss at almost every given opportunity? As he contemplated on this issue, he subconsciously used his hands to massage his cheek, creating a soothing sensation. So even an outsider would know that he was psychologically stressed.

Case Study II: A terrorist commissioned to bomb some marked places in another province was aboard a train when he heard people discuss those places he was to attack. It was made known that due to fear of probable attack and state of the economy, a lot of people were no longer patronising those places. Hence, he knew that he might not really end up trapping down as many casualties as expected in those places. The train was actually filled up, and he thought of bombing it, but his point of concern was that bombing the train might not send fear down the nerves of people as expected. The primary reason in seeking to bomb those places was to create psychological trauma on people. While he was buried in this thought, he used a hand to rub his right cheek in a slow manner, with his eyes looking distant. He was really disturbed by this but was trying to keep himself composed with his non-verbal display.

Case Study III: Child G was extraordinarily brilliant, and due to that, the government of the land decided to award him an international scholarship. When this news came to him, to the disappointment of many, he received it with mixed feelings. He was attached to his parents, and accepting the scholarship meant he would be away from them for some few years. Further, he was weighing the differences between the standards of education of his home country and the country he was to take the scholarship. Upon telling his teacher, the tutor was also thrown into confusion. Sitting at the study, he found himself meditating on the issue again, but now with his hands slightly pinching his cheeks. Those who knew him before but found him in this state were taken aback because he did not appear to be his usual self.

13.4. Strumming the Cheeks

Generic Interpretations of the Cheeks

Musicians, especially those dealing with guitar, will understand the meaning of strumming better. But for the sake of those who are not into music, *strumming* is the act of moving the fingers across the strings of a guitar or a similar instrument according to *Cambridge Dictionary*. Well, I know you will be looking at the connection between a guitar and body language. When you run your fingers 'unskillfully' through your cheeks, it is referred to as strumming. Having given you a literal meaning, let's delve into the metaphorical interpretation of the concept.

In a discourse context, when you see someone strum their cheek, it is an expression of boredom. When people are bored, they incongruently use their fingers to lightly touch their cheeks as a way of getting themselves connected to the event at hand—that is, they are still managing themselves and want you to know that they have some level of interest in what you are saying.

Also, it means the person wants to move things along. This means they feel disconnected from what you are doing. Many speakers are guilty of this. When they have the floor to speak, they do not think of the interest of the other person. So they keep on discussing their own interest, not giving the other person the opportunity to express their own views. So if you see a person strumming their cheeks while discussing with them, it is a signal that you should give them the opportunity to speak. If not, they would be totally bored, and the essence of the discourse would not be achieved.

Like every other gesture, you need to confirm this behaviour by comparing it to other clusters pointing to the same direction. Looking bored, uninviting eyes, seat shifting, etc. are the common signs that do accompany this behaviour.

Scientific Explanations

When the hand finds its way to the head, it is surely on a mission of fixing things up—that is, it means the person is not feeling good and the hand wants to lend an emotional support by trying to create a soothing effect. In the case of cheek strumming, the hand is on the cheek in order to help emphasise the message that the person is bored. Your Dictionary, an online resource material, supports the view that hand in head can mean a lot of things. Boredom is one of the many meanings attributed to this gesture. The website also explains that it may signal anger—that is, the person is upset about something you have said or you were supposed to say but you evaded.

On his own part, Marc Chernoff (2019) sees the cheek-strumming behaviour as something that should be condemned—that is, it does not portray you well in many circumstances. Appearing bored in some situations, no matter how boring or selfish the speaker is, can dent your image. For instance, imagine the president of the firm you are managing addressing you and you wear this behaviour. He would simply interpret it that you are not interested in what he is saying, and you know the kind of impression he will hold about you from that moment. Chernoff explains that strumming will make people think that you disapprove of their ideas. If the strumming is near the nose, there is a high tendency that people consider you as being deceptive. While speaking or listening, the best thing to do is to ensure that your hands are off your face.

Fairfield Writers (2019) assume that the cheek-strumming gesture is an act of evaluation—that is, the person is thinking or trying to reach a decision, but the thought is going in a rash manner.

Practical Illustrations

Case Study I: Once in a while, the family of Mr and Mrs TQI would hold a meeting where they would consider the family progress and think of new things they could do. It was usually a wonderful moment for the whole family, but lately, it seemed the children were losing interest in the whole process due to the extensive talks of their father—he practically dominated everything while others only listened to him or made short contributions. On this last occasion, the eldest child informed them that he was preparing for his examinations, and as such, the family should be considerate in their discussions and make it snappy. Although they all seemed to think along what he said, the father thought within himself that there was no way he would read for the whole day, so the meeting followed the usual pattern. At some point, the eldest son slouched on his chair and began to shift. He also used his fingers to strum his cheeks back and forth; he was bored and disinterested in all they were doing.

Case Study II: A law enforcement official nabbed a man for breaking the traffic law which the driver was not ready to plead guilty of. He looked innocent and somewhat agitated. So the enforcement official decided to give him the benefit of the doubt so that he could explain himself. He kept on talking that he did not even allow any form of interjection from the official. Since he was only appealing to the emotions of the official, the driver first seemed to have the official's attention, but at some point, everything appeared like a mirage as the official could not get anything to hold on to in his explanations. He subconsciously began to use his fingers to strum his cheeks, which was a display of psychological stress and a means of keeping negative feelings in check. After some minutes, he had to assert his authority by stopping him.

Case Study III: Mr T was not really used to seeing movies, but his new job demanded that he watch movies as a way of inducting him and other newly employed colleagues into the system. The movies were recorded voices of the president of the company and other people in the top echelon, explaining the values of the firm. Thirty minutes into the first movie, Mr T was already shifting in his chair, maintaining a dull face, while his hands were moving incongruently on his cheeks. He was fed up and bored by the movie.

13.5. Framing of Cheek

Generic Interpretations of the Concept

Cheek framing can be used in different contexts to connote different things. Before reeling out the meanings, let's explain what it means: it is the act of resting the jaw on an extended thumb while the index finger is placed up along the side of the cheek. The thumb serves as the platform on which the entire head rests while the index finger supports it by holding up the cheek. Note that this is different from the cheek-rubbing gesture we earlier discussed. In any circumstance, the person displaying this behaviour usually makes use of just a hand. That makes the head tilted to the side of the hand used.

A common meaning alluded to this cue is that the person is thinking or pondering on something. Tilting the head to the side with the use of this gesture hints that the person is not thinking straight and that they are bothered by a particular issue. Sometimes, this cue can be deliberately used by a person who wants to appear pensive. As such, it is meant to invoke the feeling of sympathy or concern—that is, wanting to deliberately appear pensive is to appeal to the emotions of your audience. Imagine a person who was told a bad news but was not really moved by it. They understand that the person who relays the story to them would be disappointed if they fail to show the corresponding action.

Further, this behaviour is used by others to express doubt on what a speaker is saying. In other words, it means the person is critical of what the other person is saying. This may be accompanied by a short, deep breath.

Conversely, I have also seen people use the cheek-framing gesture as a means of aiding concentration—that is, they are holding on to themselves so as to be able to concentrate on the event at hand. This gesture disconnects them from every other activity going on within their vicinity. In the context of dating, it is generally considered as an effective pose for showing interest from afar. A potential partner who understands non-verbal messages will know that you are trying to register your availability. This can serve as the beginning of a relationship.

Scientific Explanations

Christopher Philip (2014) says the hand supporting the chin is a means of expressing boredom. With this, people can show disinterest which can compel their co-interlocutor to hasten up on what they are saying. Also, it means that the person is evaluative and that negative thoughts are being held. The amount of weight supported by the thumb helps in deciphering its meaning. He gives the verbal translation of this cue as 'I'm bored, so my hand is buttressing my chin with most of the weight so I don't fall over completely' or 'I'm lightly supporting my chin because I'm thinking, and my chin is my source of wisdom.'

Farouk Radwan (2017), while discussing the body language of the hands, notes that when the thumb touches the chin, it is an indication that you are evaluating something or you are engulfed in a thought. When you are trying to size up something, you use the hand to provide support to the head.

On his own part, Bob Whipple (2018) states that this cue can be better interpreted by understanding the context in which it takes place and the gender involved. As a teacher, he calls off his class when he sees his students display this behaviour—he understands that they are bored. Note that if this is done by just a student, it does not really count, as it may be a reaction of the student working all night to get a paper completed.

Conversely, he submits, 'When a male holds his chin between the bent forefinger and thumb, it usually means the man is listening intently.' He supports this submission with the assertion of Bill Acheson of the University of Pittsburgh. This may also be a means of holding the head. While you listen intently, it would prevent you from nodding in agreement. A point of importance is the direction of the chin. When it is raised, it signals positive intent—it represents alertness or pride. However, when it is lowered, it indicates negative action—it means the person is sad or worried (Whipple 2018).

Practical Illustrations

Case Study I: A man went to buy a car, and during the course of negotiations, the car salesman had to explain some things to him about his vehicle choice. Expectedly, the salesman seemed to have a firm grasp of the features of the car, laced with his sugar-coated mouth. With his introduction, the man knew the salesman was about to make some cogent points. So he decided to listen intently to all he wanted to say but did not want to nod in agreement to any point so that it would not be used against him during price negotiation. So he placed his thumb under his jaw and stretched his index finger over the cheek as a way of holding the head. This means he was trying to succumb his feelings.

Case Study II: A school invited a motivational speaker to interact with its students and inspire them to success. When the motivational speaker mounted the podium, he began by sharing a story of how he, as a student, succeeded tremendously. With the way he painted it, it sounded as if he were extraordinarily brilliant than his teachers. Ms H, a very curious female student, who was sitting at the middle row placed her thumb below her chin as the index finger pointed upward. This was an expression of disbelief in what the speaker was saying.

Case Study III: A leading firm in the building industry had just changed its manager. The new manager decided to address the house on what they should expect and the modalities with which he would work. A wonderful public speaker, he was able to get the attention of the hundreds of workers at once. The assistant manager leant forward and put his finger under his jaw as he listened with rapt attention. It was a show of interest which spurred that of his subordinates too.

Case Study IV: A money launderer was at a restaurant, sitting very close to two law enforcement officials discussing some of the prevalent issues in the world. One of the officers lamented that the menace of money laundering had been the source of other crimes. He seemed passionate about his suggestions that governments of different nations should come hard on such criminals. The second officer then started reeling out ways in which the crime could be curbed. After eavesdropping, the money launderer saw it was a topic of interest. So he placed his chin on his thumb in order to move his head closer to the discussants so as to hear them clearer. Noticing this, the officers changed the topic abruptly. They discovered he wanted to eavesdrop into their discussion, which wasn't a good idea.

13.6. Puffing Out the Cheeks

Generic Interpretations of the Concept

The gesture of puffing out the cheeks is visible to everyone, and that makes the message it carries very simple to interpret—worry. It is the act of pumping out the cheek in an obvious manner in order to express negative emotions. When you pump out your cheeks, it distorts your facial appearance, and people around you will simply ask the question 'What's the problem?' They understand that the behaviour signals something ill. It is a cue that is normally seen in people who are confused on the next line of action. Hence, the puffing out of cheek is to mean that they have explored all possible lines of action to no avail. In the same vein, you can also notice this behaviour in someone who is apprehensive. When they puff out their cheeks, they will not exhale as a way of holding to themselves.

In addition, the cue is also used to express caution, deliberation, or doubt. When someone is about to embark on a gigantic project, they may display this gesture as a means of expressing caution. They know from the beginning that the task is demanding and risk-laden, so they are playing the card of carefulness right from the beginning. Also, a person who does not believe in what you are saying would have thought about it before arriving at the conclusion that your story is not believable. This explanation covers up for deliberation too.

It is also not rare for you to see this cue in people while they are trying to find a solution to a problem. They hold this behaviour for a while which makes it quite observable to their audience. Remember that some people may use it to exaggerate what they are doing. They want to create an impression that they are really intellectually engaged, and as such, you should not distract them. This can truly be used to one's advantage if one is actually working on something that needs our full concentration. However, it may be an instrument of deceit in the hands of some other people.

Scientific Illustrations

Joe Navarro (2010) says that puffing out the cheeks is one of the body languages cues that we find difficult to hide. Sharing from his practical experience, he makes it known that when an interviewee hears a question that makes them uncomfortable, the limbic systems would be aroused by verbal cues which will make the signs of distress to manifest immediately. One of the signs is puffing out of the cheeks. This gesture is actually meant to pacify. Hence, it appears at the tail end of the show of discomfort.

Changing Minds (2019) relates blown-out cheeks to uncertainty on what to do next. This is always accompanied by rounded eyes and raised eyebrows. In short, the person wants their audience to know that they are confused. That is why it may sometimes be exaggerated by the person actually blowing air from the mouth. Another possible meaning to this cue is exhaustion. This tiredness may either be propelled by physical activities or some psychological unrest. If it is as a result of exercise, the entire face may also be red and sweaty.

In the same vein, Dr Georgina Barnett (2016) lends a voice to this concept. She notes that puffing out the cheeks is one of the known soothing behaviours of humans. She postulates, 'If a situation is making a person uncomfortable, the brain requires the body to do something that will stimulate nerve endings, releasing calming endorphins in the brain to restore equilibrium. Therefore, self-soothing behaviours show us that someone is going through discomfort.' In a way, we can assert that puffing out the cheeks is a distress signifier.

Practical Illustrations

Case Study I: Part of the rules given to applicants sitting an examination was that they must not make any cancellation while working out the answers to the questions. Making use of a pen made subtle cancellations impossible for them. R was a first-class graduate from one of the best universities in town. He had been finding it easy until he got to the matrix aspect, which required him to apply caution. He seemed to be getting the initial steps right until he almost missed a step. From that point, he could be seen puffing out his cheeks while working. This is a show of caution.

Case Study II: Mr A thought it was high time he settled down and got serious with his life. Before now, he had been going out with three different ladies. Two of them seemed desperate to settle down with him, while the third was obviously out for fun. Hence, his point of concern was how to deal with the two. Obviously, polygamy was out of choice for him. To make matters worse, both of them had the same educational qualifications and were earning almost the same amount with different companies. Every other factor worth taking cognisance of were clashing. So he decided to take a day out to be alone so that he would be able to think it through. For hours, he did not arrive at any logical conclusion. While still in the intellectual process, he puffed out his cheeks for minutes. This communicates to the external world that he was deliberating and needed his privacy.

Case Study III: Dr J had worked in both public and private establishments for about three decades. He thought of establishing his own hospital, but the fear of the unknown had always kept him away. His friends and relatives were now enjoining him to leverage on the networks and connections he had built over the years to get himself started. Since pressure was being mounted on him from every corner, he decided to think over the issue and analyse his chances. After some hours of thinking and paperworks, he puffed out his cheeks. His wife, who was very close to where he was, frowned immediately when she saw this gesture; she knew it connoted a negative outcome. She was reluctant to ask what his final decision was because of the expression of doubt which he had communicated.

Case Study IV: A public official who had a track record of corruption wanted to launder money to another country due to the alleged high-handedness of the antigraft agencies of his country. To make things easier for himself, the public official had established links with a banker who helped him in doing all the technical aspects of the job. However, on this particular occasion, it seemed the money was so huge that the banker thought being a channel to such form of corruption would expose him. When the public official came in, the banker informed him of the situation at hand. After thinking for a few minutes, he puffed out his cheeks and hit his hand on the counter—no way out. In other words, he could not think it through.

13.7. Rubbing the Cheek Slightly

Generic Interpretations of the Concept

When people do not want to call the attention of their audience to their feeling of discomfort, they make use of this gesture. It can be very subtle that it is only those who are very observant can decode that all is not well with the person. This cue is displayed by a slight rub of the index finger against the cheek. This behaviour is not pronounced because the person makes use of just a finger, which will make you think it is a mere rub, whereas it is a pacifying act used by authoritative and public figures when they are feeling distressed. This surreptitious form of cheek touch is often noticeable on people engaged on TV programmes or even on poker players.

When you see a person rub their cheek slightly with only an index finger, it means they are managing stress for the sake of perception—that is, they are conscious of the fact that if they should glaringly show that they are stressed in such contexts, they would be perceived in bad light. Someone appearing on TV is ordinarily expected to be bold and intelligent. Hence, their audience will be disappointed if they see anything less than this. Another concealing pacifier is touching of the inside of the nose.

Some of the possible interpretations of sneaking a cheek-touch behaviour are worry, insecurity, or anxiety. In political discourses, when journalists ask questions that are capable of throwing off their guests, they can become worried of how to answer those questions and, as such, develop stress. In the same vein, when a person is insecure in a situation, they pacify themselves throughout the time they are still within the vicinity of the occurrence. You can look for other signs of discomfort so as to better interpret this gesture.

Scientific Explanations

Depending on the kind of touch, there are different meanings attributed to hand-to-cheek cues. Philip (2013) explains this better by stating, 'Face touching can come in two forms, one that serves a real function to alleviate an itch, and one that is the result of negative feelings such as being uncomfortable and stressed. Face touching that is due to an emotion is meant as a fix behind the sensation, the emotion, and not due to any physical need.' The slight cheek rub falls under the second category—that is, it is a product of discomfort which is meant to hide the negative emotions people are feeling. If it were ordinary itching, it occurs as an isolated gesture, which cannot be linked with other clusters, and its time of occurrence is when it cannot be connected with what is being said. For instance, if you are discussing something on questionable honesty and then your index finger slightly rubs your cheek and moves to the side of the nose, it will likely raise suspicion in your audience. However, when you display this same gesture while describing a place, it will not be noticed.

You need to be conscious of the face touch when you know that your co-interlocutor has the tendency of tagging you as a liar. As such, you must endeavour to make gestures appear natural and unquestionable. At the end of every discourse context, it is your baseline that will expose your real intents. So you must be consistent with the behaviour you portray throughout a discussion. 'Most will find that their minds are more active and busier during lying, so it's easier to avoid gestures altogether instead of adding honest gestures. This makes eliminating face touching one of the easiest ways to appear honest with minimal effort' (Philip 2013).

We need to be careful with this gesture when it comes to some cultures. For instance, if the index finger forms a screw on the cheek, it is used to mean good, beautiful, or lovely in Italy, while it may mean that a man is effeminate in southern Spain (Steves 2019).

Practical Illustrations

Case Study I: A player was being accused of using drugs to bolster his energy, and that had always accounted for the reason he had defeated opponents in all competitions. The talk had become a debate among international authorities. So one of the best sports presenters on TV decided to bring the player in question on air so that he could explain himself and clarify bothering issues on the allegation. As a way of establishing his baseline, the presenter began with questions that were basic—his background, fantastic moments on pitch, and what inspires him. Then he moved on to the main issue. As he began to make prelude to the issue, the player began to shift on his chair which first hinted on his discomfort. Responding to the question, he adjusted his seat again and placed his elbow on the table while the index finger reached out to the cheek. He rubbed it slightly throughout the period that he gave his response to the poser. This means he was not feeling comfortable, perhaps due to the deceptive statements he was making.

Case Study II: All the unit supervisors in FTH Company had submitted their monthly progress report to the manager who was checking them vis-à-vis the report of the previous month. There seemed to be a marginal difference in growth in the last three months. Of major concern to him was the marketing unit whose result had been nothing short of failure in four consecutive months. He took his time to study the department alone. While doing this, he subconsciously used his index finger to massage his cheeks. His secretary detected that he was worried.

Case Study III: K was the first applicant to be invited in out of about a hundred of them jostling for thirty openings. As he entered, he saw the panellists on the other side of the table exchanging notes and giving one another signals. Then the man at the centre focused on him for about thirty seconds. Taking all these actions together, already with the tension on his body, he began to feel insecure. As a way of pacifying himself, his index finger found its way to the right cheek, and he rubbed it subtly before he tidied up himself for the interview.

Case Study IV: A human smuggler had made an arrangement that his smuggled beings should follow him an hour after he might have left so that if there was any reason to put a call through for them to stay a bit, he would do so. However, he misplaced his mobile phone on the way, and upon getting to the border, he met officers he didn't know before. He had to wait because there was no way he would call his victims to tarry a little bit. While waiting at the border, he thought of what he would tell the officers when the smuggled individuals arrived. He unconsciously placed his index finger on his cheeks and rubbed slightly as if he had pimples—he was disturbed.

13.8. Scratching the Cheeks

Generic Interpretations of the Concept

This is a more robust form of dealing with negative emotions compared with the slight cheek rub considered in the preceding segment. This is a technique employed to deal with stress in advanced form. In fact, interpreting the cheek-scratching gesture tends to be more accurate compared with the sneaking touch when we take cognisance of the hidden meaning. Before giving the metaphorical interpretations, let me note that this cue can also occur as a result of physical itching. When it is physical, it is done with the person's whole strength and will mostly be done once.

Having said that, when people want to deal with insecurities, worries, and doubts, they make use of four fingers to scratch their cheek. If you see a person doing this while you are addressing them, it most likely represents reservations—that is, they do not really buy the idea of the concept you are sharing with them. While a colleague can easily register their reservations, a subordinate will most likely keep it to themselves. If you see this, it is advised that you pause and ask if anyone has reservations as a way of addressing their concerns before moving forward.

Furthermore, this behaviour also indicates hesitation. Thinking that being too forward in a situation may backfire, you may decide to ruminate on the issue and consider your chances before delving into it. When someone is bewildered, they may also display this signal. In conclusion, I have seen people scratch their cheeks when they are apprehensive. It is as if they want to generate enough warmth through the action that will keep their body in the right shape as they deal with their insecurity.

Scientific Explanations

Let's start our discussion on this from the medical point of view. People have itchy faces for an array of reasons. Kathryn Watson (2018) scholarly enumerates this in an article published on Healthline. Dry skin, seasonal allergies, and skin contact with irritants are some of the major causes of skin irritation. Also, antifungal, antibiotics, and narcotic pain medications may lead to itchy face. 'Less often, an itchy face stems from an internal condition, such as liver disease, thyroid conditions, cancer, or multiple sclerosis. Nutritional deficiencies, such as iron deficiency, can also cause itching' (Watson 2018). While some itchy faces have a rash, some do not. The point I am trying to drive at is that when an itchy face is induced by a medical condition, the way in which it would be scratched will surely show that the person is feeling physical discomfort.

From the metaphorical point of view, Changing Minds notes that one of the reasons that can cause someone to scratch their face is surprise or bewilderment. When you are taken aback by the occurrence of an event, you may scratch your cheek as you watch or reflect on the incident again.

Mateo Sol sees the act of scratching the cheeks as one of the signals of deception. When people are deceptive, they feel the heat of the conscious rigours they subject themselves to. This creates stress in them, and then scratching the cheeks becomes a way of dealing with the stress. Hence, the behaviour can be seen as the aftermath of telling lies. Sol (2019) states that people normally use their writing hands in doing the scratching. And the scratches take place for about four to six times. He submits, 'This gesture is normally a sign of *uncertainty* or *doubt* and can be used by someone who is telling you they agree with what you have to say while secretly thinking something else, making up their mind or holding back their own opinion.'

Practical Illustrations

Case Study I: Mr GH was a businessman with international connections. It seemed his network of business allies was waxing and growing stronger by the day. While this was a source of joy to him, it appeared as the opposite to his wife and children. This was because he did not spend much time with them again. Although they had all they needed within their reach, but the love and warmth of a husband and father seemed to be missing in the house. For instance, there was a time he promised to be back home within five hours on a Monday, only for him to tarry till the third day. He obviously knew that things were beginning to go wrong at home, and he wanted to work round the clock to get them fixed. While going out, he called his wife and their three little kids and informed them that he would be back soon. Being his usual mantra, the wife also scratched her cheek, saying bye to him. This is a show of doubt.

Case Study II: Student R had obviously been distracted for a while, and his teacher had been calling back his attention to what he was teaching them, but all to no avail. Since he was not distracting another person, the teacher decided to continue with his lesson. After working out the formula, he scribbled a short exercise on the board and called on R to go and solve it while other students would confirm if he was right or not. When he heard his name, he looked up suddenly in an apprehensive manner. As he made his way to the front, he used his right hand to scratch his cheek, walking slowly. He was trying to look confident, but fear was glaringly written on him.

Case Study III: The general manager of GTX Industries was addressing the unit heads of the department, urging them on the need to work hard and give their subordinates a sense of belonging. Then he delved into the performance of each unit. This was the point that most of the supervisors had always been trying to avoid due to the way in which their boss used to handle it; they believed that he had his favourites and would always shower encomiums on them even in the face of obvious failure. As projected, despite the fact that the sales team could not meet their monthly target, the team was the first to be praised. The head of the production unit scratched his cheek with his four fingers and looked the other side. He wasn't pleased with what was happening.

Case Study IV: Madam IY was a prostitute but covered up with some menial jobs during the day. One day, a man saw her and fell in love with her. She comported herself and looked serious too. However, it seemed the man needed more than just love; he wanted marriage. In one of their dates, the man told IY what was on his mind, and while the man was talking, the lady scratched her cheeks with her fingers and disconnected eye contact. This was an expression of doubt on her commitment to such a relationship. Unfortunately, the man couldn't decode it. The relationship didn't last before it hit the wood.

13.9. Pinching the Corners of the Mouth

Generic Interpretations of the Concept

One of the great ways in which people relieve stress is the use of the fingers to tightly constrict the corners of the mouth. Some may even pinch it directly, depending on the level of stress being witnessed by the person. I have never seen people do this when they are relaxed or content. Usually, the person pinching the corners of the mouth will make use of their index fingers and thumb to constrict a portion of a corner just to soothe their cravings. Even though this can be a telltale sign that someone is going through a difficult moment, the person does not think of other people's perception about them at the moment due to the kind of feeling they derive from the action. Note that this cue is different from the facial-denting behaviour we discussed earlier, where the thumb and index finger are used to perforate the two sides of the face.

Pinching the corners of the lips simulatenously or one after the other is a clue that something is wrong. It is an indication that the person is trying to reach a decision over an issue that has been a point of concern to them. This behaviour does not make them really feel the weight of the thinking because the attention of the brain is mainly shifted to the pacifying act rather than the exhausting thought taking place. If there are people around the person, they will avoid eye contact with them because they do not want anything from the external environment to influence their decision. If you are conversing with them, be sure they are absent-minded or partially listening. Most times, I also discover that they slouch their back. This is also a show of negative emotions. It means the person is not receptive to ideas from their co-interlocutor.

Scientific Explanations

Lauren Guilbeault (2018) notes that apart from the Duchenne smile that has the ability to make the corners of the mouth pull up, which will squeeze the eyes to form a crow's feet, another thing that can distort the corners of the mouth is the subconscious pinching. While the former is used in expressing positive thoughts, the latter represents a show of negativity. When you pinch the lips, a portion of it pulls up into your hands. This will affect the entire mouth as it will draw every part to the side being pinched. While this is subtly done in most cases, when the person is feeling the emotions beyond what they can suppress, they will do the pinching consistently and with more show of force.

Also, pinching the corners of the mouth can determine the shape and direction which the mouth will face. If they are turned upwards, it can be interpreted as a grimace. They make the lips tenser and flatter. This means the person is witnessing a mixture of both positive or negative emotions. The person is actually sad but wants to cover up his or her negative feelings with a show of positivity.

In the same vein, Philip (2013) says that pinching the corners of the mouth is a demonstration of discomfort; it is evidence that the person is not feeling all right in terms of psychological fitness. I like the qualification which Philip gives to this cue. He describes it as a 'poor self-image', which is actually very apt. It is pertinent to note that pinching the corners of the mouth is not something that is suddenly done. So it is always glaring enough for others to see. Your sitting posture would be distorted, and this is also a message in itself. When you see people pulling, constricting, and pinching the corners of their lips, you would become concerned because it does not portray them well.

Practical Illustrations

Case Study I: A terrorist was to spy on three different locations within two hours before flying out of the country. To make his work very easy, he had read up on the cultures of the people and knew most of the basic things about the country. To some extent, this played a huge role in helping him out. However, his albatross was at the airport. The custom officer who checked him in saw how he was in a haste when he came, and while checking out too, the situation did not look any much better. At least, one would expect him to calm down after executing the assignment he came for. This tipped officers on duty to question him further on his aim in the country. Then he was set aside for the unit head to come and speak with him. He sat on the chair, looking around from time to time. He slouched on the seat and used his thumb and index finger to press the fleshy area of his cheek together. This expresses his nervousness.

Case Study II: Mr E, with his family, had just relocated from another province to their present abode due to a transfer and the need for his wife to explore new pastures. So he needed to enroll his children in another school in the province. After making findings on the quality of the schools around, he opted for one that he could afford and which he felt his children would appreciate. Part of the requirements of the school he chose was that applicants must score a certain percentage in their entrance examination before they could be guaranteed a place. When the children heard this, they became cold; they did not expect it. So while awaiting the examiner, the youngest child began to pinch the corner of his mouth as a way of pacifying himself.

Case Study III: Mrs D had some health challenges, and that had always affected her level of productivity at the workplace. While it seemed her boss was understanding, the present realities on the finances of the firm showed that the company could not cope with a liability like her again. So the firm gave her some compensation and fired her. Upon getting home, she locked herself in and thought if she should use her compensation to begin a personal business or apply to other firms. She used her right hand to pinch her cheeks in the mouth area while doing this reflection.

13.10. Wiping the Cheeks

Generic Interpretations of the Concept

When someone wipes off their face without the use of a handkerchief, it means there is something attached to it. Let me clarify that if the person is doing an exercise and does not have a piece of cloth with them, they may use their hands to wipe off the sweat. This can also be seen when someone undertake an unexpected demanding task which makes them sweat. For instance, having had to change a flat tyre under the scorching sun can make a person sweaty. In the two instances above, the meaning is literal.

Cheek wiping is normally done with the right hand will start right before the right ear and ends near the jawbone. If a person is not sweating or the situation does not demand sweat and they display this gesture, it calls for concern. This technique of wiping the face clean is seen when people are extremely stressed. It is as if they were cleaning the face so as to have a better view of what is making them uncomfortable. During the display of this cue, they will cover their eyes so that the stress they are 'wiping off' does not get into their eyes.

If this wiping tarries and is done in a hard way, it means the person is acutely stressed. Sometimes, some may even make use of a handkerchief to clean a sweatless face just to deceive you that all is well. I have always observed this behaviour in stockbrokers when the transactions of the day does not favour them. Also, sportsmen do this a lot when they eventually lose a competitive game at the second half. It is evidence that they are troubled by the outcome of the match. One thing you should keep at the back of your mind is that the cheek-wiping gesture is used to express negative emotions.

Scientific Explanations

All the experts that contributed to this subject matter share a consensus that those who touch their face while speaking are depicted as being deceptive and dishonest. According to Patti Wood, an Atlanta-based consultant, the cheek-wiping gesture means 'wiping away my worries'. That is, the person is trying to cleanse their face so that their stress will drop off. Wood puts it thus: 'Wiping the face in a downward motion suggests a desire to "wipe away" a problem or concern.' This message is simple and straightforward; it is only people with issues who use their hands to wipe off their face as if they were getting rid of the issues. This is a body language gesture that is very symbolic in the meaning it connotes.

Chernoff (2019) says that while wiping off the face, if the hand tarries on the nose, there is a high probability that people assume that you are deceptive. There is no part of the face that when touched will not denote you in a bad light. So the best thing for you to do is to ensure that you always keep your hands off the face.

In the same vein, RealMenStyle.com supports the submission of Chernoff. The website opines that cleaning the face can depict someone as being dishonest or anxious. When you place your hands on the face, it denies others the opportunity to read your real emotions. Also, if it denies you the opportunity to maintain the needed eye contact with people, this shows you are anxious or nervous. Touching the face is best understood when you think of small children that slap their mouth after realising that they have said something wrong. This same principle applies to facial-touch gesture. In adults, it is subtly done so as not to depict the person as being childish.

Practical Illustrations

Case Study I: Mr S and his wife had been having issues for years. Sometimes, they would appear as perfect partners, and other times, you would think they were arch-enemies. When they discovered that their lifestyle was beginning to reflect negatively on the children, they agreed to move them to a boarding facility. Yet it did not seem that they were getting along. The husband had actually filed for a divorce, but the wife was not ready to let go. This had frustrated the process, and the husband was really paying for it. Any time he was coming back home, he entered with the fear of the unknown of the next issue. After work today, he returned home to discover that his wife had gone out, most probably on a journey, because the traveller's bag was not at home. Thinking of how she could travel without telling him, he wiped his face off, trying to get the thought out of his head. And after that, he calmed down with a sigh of relief.

Case Study II: Today, Child F finished his examinations, and upon getting home, he did not even bother to eat before heading to the study. He wanted to confirm if the answers he supplied to the questions were right. He brought out his notebook, question paper, and workbook. Upon reworking the first two questions, he discovered that he made unpardonable errors in the examination hall. Gradually, he got depressed. So he wiped off his face and left the study to go to the dining. This means he cleansed off his 'worries' before eating.

Case Study III: Ms L was a teller in one of the leading commercial bank in the land. Monday was always a busy for them, and as such, she had learnt to deal with pressure. But it seemed this Monday was negatively different for her. She collected money from different clients so as to enter them into the system later due to poor network. When the network service became clear, out of pressure, she entered the wrong amount into different accounts. The owner of the account where she made an extra deposit withdrew the money before she could reverse the transaction. There was nothing she could do other than to just pay the balance from her own personal purse or face the wrath of the company. After a brief thought, she wiped off her cheeks and got back to work. It was a means of 'throwing everything off her mind' in order to concentrate on her work.

Case Study IV: Lady ER was illegally employed in a factory; she used the connection of one of her lovers to get the job even though there was no proper recruitment. Although she was reputed for being hard-working, but securing a job through illegal means was not tenable anywhere. One day, her unit supervisor who was always unavailable appeared out of nowhere and arranged a meeting with them. She couldn't walk out because the supervisor would see that as an affront and it would further expose her. She was afraid that the man could pick on her during the meeting. When the meeting eventually came to an end without any issues, she wiped her cheeks with her hand. It was a display of rest of mind.

13.11. Tensing of the Jaw

Generic Interpretations of the Concept

Whenever there is change of emotions from positive to negative, the jaws become tensed. Negative emotions do propel heat in the body, and this makes the entire body system to become reactionary. The shape of our jaws can reveal the emotions of people every time. Anxiety, anger, or fear are some of the factors that can make our jaws, which are near the ears, tense up.

When emotions are becoming heated or a person is stressed, you can focus on the jaws to see how tensed they are. If they tense up while the surface of the cheeks becomes red, it is an indication that the person is emotionally charged. If this tensed-up jaw is caused by anger, it means they may attack you because they may not be able to control themselves again. However, if the behaviour is propelled by anxiety, they may switch to the flight or freeze mood from any moment. What is important is that you understand what brings about this behaviour so as to be able to know how to react to it. We will flesh this out by considering the submissions of experts and practical case studies.

Scientific Explanations

Jack Brown (2014) submits that jaw tensing 'is a body language signal highly consistent with anger [although it can be seen in other settings depending on the other non-verbals with which it is clustered]. Additional non-verbal anger signs here include the eyebrows being drawn together as well as their downward-vectoring. Nostril flaring also accompanies anger [along with some other emotions].' This definition has given us an overview of what jaw tensing is. Apart from that, we have some clusters to fall back to in case we are confused on the meaning to allude to the gesture. If the posterior part of the jaw is tighter, this means the anger transcends ordinary level. However, when the anterior portion is the tight place, it means the person is not really angry. Hence, this can help us to determine the level of anger of an interlocutor and understand how to deal with them.

In his own explanation, Travis Bradberry (2017) says jaw clenching is a signal of stress. This is in line with the affirmation of Brown. Bradberry notes that what the person is saying is inconsequential to the reading of this gesture; no one will feel good and still subconsciously tense their jaw. There may be a probability that the conversation is moving to a point that is making them anxious, or they are probably reflecting on a negative emotion that is making them uncomfortable. Bradberry expertly concludes, 'The key is to watch for that mismatch between what the person says and what their tense body language is telling you.'

Philip (2014) also lends a voice to this. He notes that jaw tensing is evidence that the person is struggling internally. In other words, it is a feeling of discomfort. This means that many scholars in the field have a consensus on the meaning of this body cue. Philip traces this gesture to the primitive time when biting was considered as a way of defence. Jaw tensing is a body language that signals grief, tension, fear, anger, anxiety, frustration, or that the person is trying to suppress their aggression. This may also be induced by physical pain.

Jaw tensing is always an indication that someone is trying to hold back negative thoughts or emotions. When the jaws are tensed, the mouth is firmly closed. So this means the person is trying to ensure that their negative emotions do not spill out. It is usually a misnomer when it occurs at night, and there may be a need to see the doctor. When the jaw is tensed at daytime, it means all is not well with the person and they really want to voice it out but feels like the environment is not favourable for what they want to say, and as such, they bottle the thought up. If the stress boils higher than what can be suppressed, you see the person speak through their teeth. Philip (2014) gives the verbal translation of this behaviour as 'I'm angry or frustrated, and I want to speak out. But I feel that it's inappropriate, so my teeth are clenching down to bottle myself up and prevent me from saying something I might regret.'

Practical Illustrations

Case Study I: Mr D returned from work on a busy Monday and was expecting the usual show of love he used to get at the door, but his wife was nowhere to be found, and he was not informed she would be out. Concerned on what might have gone wrong, he put calls through her phone, but her line was not connecting. After trying all his best to no avail, he went to the shower to freshen up before returning to the living room to see his favourite TV show. After some hours, the wife came in and wanted to hug and kiss Mr D, but having seen his tensed jaws, she hugged him hurriedly and vanished from his presence. She knew he was to be avoided at the moment till he calmed down.

Case Study II: Suspect K was arrested in a terrorism-related issue. So he was to be interrogated in order to allow law enforcement officials to gather evidence against him so that he could be arraigned in court. Part of the rules of the agency was that an official would read out the allegations levelled against a suspect and then give him the opportunity to put up a defence. In the case of K, as the official was reeling out the issues, he became frustrated because cases of yesteryears were also mentioned. He was obviously agitated and would attack if he had a weapon with him. Since the rule required that he kept mum till he was given the floor, he tightened his jaw as a way of restraining himself from speaking. The enforcement officials were really sure that his negative emotions had risen. So they had to calm him down before he was eventually asked to talk.

Case Study III: The hospital is another place where this gesture is commonly displayed. Patients are really emotional, and their feeling is controlled by their state of health. This means that those with aggravated health conditions have the tendency to be more emotional. I once visited a hospital to check on my ailing friend. I noticed that one of the patients was very tensed, and she tightened her jaws in a noticeable way. I had to walk up to her and ask what her was wrong. She opened up to me, and everyone there was surprised that I could read her body language correctly.

13.12. Displacement or Shifting of the Jaw

Generic Interpretations of the Concept

Moving the jaw from its original position to a side or another is an apt way which people employ to deal with stress. When people are stressed, they shift their jaw from one side to the other. The purpose is to generate warmth that will bring them out of their state of nervousness. It is an indication that the person is suffering internally. Before moving further, let me chip in that this cue is simply a compulsive behaviour in some people; they do it without feeling any negative emotions. This can be troubling to a stranger, but those who have lived with them for long may not be irritated by it. The point is that you have to set a baseline first and then look for other confirming gestures before you can attribute meanings to this cue in a subject.

Having said that, most people shift their jaws infrequently and, thus, has a connotative meaning in this case—that is, you should not overlook the gesture when you suddenly observe it in a co-interlocutor during conversations. It is an indication that the person is nervous and is shifting their jaw so as to douse the tension caused by the nervousness. In the same vein, it is an indication that the person is thinking, most probably about something negative. Hence, the jaw-displacing action is to serve as a soothing relief to the daunting intellectual rigours.

From the foregoing, we can categorically establish that jaw shifting is an action that accurately points to the fact that a person is being bothered by something. This will help us in our decision-making and how we related to people every time. If you notice this gesture in a co-interlocutor and overlook it, the person will assume that you are not observant or you just decided not to have sympathy on their emotional feelings. In law enforcement, it helps in dictating the direction in which an investigation will take; observing that an interviewee is made uncomfortable by a question points to the fact that there is something he or she is hiding about that particular subject matter.

Scientific Illustrations

Navarro (2013) discusses extensively on jaw shifting, referring to it as a subtle stress reliever. Navarro recalls that the first time he encountered this cue was in 1975, while working as a police officer. He was accusing someone of shoplifting when he discovered that the person shifted his jaw from a side to the other during the questioning process. According to him, when he asked the question 'Have you been arrested previously for shoplifting?' after some consideration, the person answered, 'No.' But something struck him about the jaw-shifting behaviour that prompted him to ask a follow-up question, 'That's not accurate, is it?' The man did the behaviour again, shifting his jaw to the side, but this time, he smiled. And with that, he said, 'Yes, I have been arrested before.' Navarro notes that the shift of the jaw was the main thing that propelled him to ask the follow-up question.

Does it now mean that the jaw-shifting behaviour is a non-negotiable indicator of deception? NO! It is simply a cue that the person is stressed. Stress can be induced by many other factors apart from deception. When someone is caught in a wrong act, lack of self-confidence, anxiety over the possible result of an issue, an interviewee having difficulty with a question are some of the instances where the jaw-shifting cue has been noticed (Navarro 2013).

Hence, you may be forced to ask why people display this gesture in the aforementioned circumstances. Mainly, it has been observed that it helps to relieve stress. When you do this behaviour, the nerves in your jaw would be stimulated (you may try it out). When the nerves are artificially stimulated, it helps in calming and soothing us. Jaw shifting is not really a repetitive behaviour, but it has been noticed that it is done repetitively when a student is not prepared for a test. When done from one side or another or just to a side of the face, the function still remains the same, hence having the same interpretation (Navarro 2013).

Chelsea Ritschel (2018) says that jaw shifting is a subtle body language sign that somebody does not like you. Making reference to Navarro, Ritschel notes that if the feet or eyes are not giving us enough to make inferences about the thoughts of a person towards us, then 'lip compression, jaw shifting, tongue in cheek, and neck touching, especially at the base of the front of the neck' are the pointers to the fact that all is not well with the person.

Practical Illustrations

Case Study I: For the past one week, Mr H had been informing his students that there would be a test, but whenever he came into the class, he noticed general nervousness, and that had always prompted him to shift the test. However, examinations were approaching, which meant the semester would soon come to an end. Yet tests form an important part of the assessment. So he decided to conduct it today. Student F was not prepared because she had thought that it would not be conducted as scheduled, which made her watch her favourite TV show for hours. As Mr H began to dictate the questions, she shifted her jaws repeatedly. She was disturbed on how she would answer the questions; she was pessimistic about her chances of passing the test.

Case Study II: Suspect T was detained for a suspected shoplifting in a popular shopping mall. At first, he wanted to deny and challenge the security guards for harassing a 'customer', but the seriousness of the security men hinted him that he should better cooperate. When asked if he had been apprehended for shoplifting in times past, he hesitated for a while and said no while shifting his jaw. This hinted one of the officials that he was stressed and feeling uncomfortable. So he repeated the question, and with a grimace, he answered in the affirmative. He was only exposed by the jaw-shifting behaviour and hesitation, which means he was thinking of what he should not have thought of.

Case Study III: Friend A told his friend, G, to stop his waywardness because A considered it as a stain on his face. However, G seemed to be not disciplined enough to know what he wanted every time. On a particular occasion, they went to an event, and G drank himself into a stupor. He almost became a laughing stock at the occasion. Very disappointed in his friend, A sat on a spot, and unconsciously, he began to shift his jaw. He was down in spirit, and the shape of his mouth really depicted one who was angry. He later parted ways with Friend G.

13.13. Jaw Dropping

Generic Interpretations of the Concept

When the jaw suddenly drops, which leaves the mouth open and teeth exposed, it is an apt way of displaying a surprised emotion. This is usually done when a person is taken aback by the occurrence of an event. However, this surprise has always been noticed not to be pleasant ones. In other words, it is an expression of negative event that the person does not expect to befall them. Oftentimes, I have observed this behaviour in people when they are shocked. This means what happened is unbelievable to them, and they are grasping for breath. Opening the mouth allows them to release carbon dioxide and take in fresh air that will enable them to survive the present state of shock.

In the same vein, it is a cue you will see in people when they are confronted with an embarrassing revelation. Maybe their heinous secret deal is made public, so they are surprised that despite all they did to cover it up, people still ended up knowing about it. It should be noted that this action is mainly subconscious, which gives out the person. Ideally, people hate it when others get to know when they are feeling nervous or feeling any other negative emotions. Hence, the jaw-dropping gesture hints the other person that his or her subject is taken aback by the revelation they have made.

Although no one really understands the reason the jaw drops when people are confronted with a surprising event, but it has been an accurate indicator that the person was not imagining what is revealed to them. In law enforcement, this can be a good hint for you to know how to further question the person and get them to make verbal confessions. Also, it plays a huge role during negotiations.

Scientific Explanations

Westside Toastmasters (2019) discusses this gesture under the 'drop jaw smile'. The website notes that this form of smile is rehearsed, and that is why it is usually observed among politicians, celebrities, and movie stars. They are the set of people who believe they must smile in any given situation so that the public will not have a wrong perception of them. They understand that laughter is contagious, and as such, they want to induce amusement and playfulness among their admirers. When people laugh with the jaw-drop pattern, they also attempt to fake smiling eyes. This indicates that there is nothing that is truly making the person happy, only that they thought the situation needs it.

Another body language platform, Simply Body Language (https://www.simplybodylanguage.com), notes that the jaw-dropping gesture is an apt way of communicating surprise. When a person is surprised, you will see their eyes pulled up high, which makes the eyes open wide while the forehead wrinkles. Since the jaw muscles are relaxed in this context, the mouth is left open while the lower jaw drops. This is a glaring sign of communicating to the outside world that we are taken aback by an occurrence.

Christopher Philip (2014) also lends a voice to this concept. He describes a jaw-drop smile as a 'playful surprise.' It should be noted that if the jaw-dropping gesture is not accompanied with smile, it means that the surprise is not playful. Celebrities and politicians make use of this gesture to create a playful atmosphere. Also, it can help in calming people's mood when they are witnessing too much tension because it has been observed to have the ability to create positive feelings on people. Hence, the context in which a jaw drop smile can be used differs. That is why experts refer to it as an apt pacifier. That is, people make use of it when they are stressed in order to release tension. Philip gives the verbal translation of this cue as 'I'm laughing, or sort of laughing because my jaw is dropping and I hope you will see me in a positive light and see me as playful.'

When used in a non-threatening manner, people easily mirror this cue and thus, can create a tranquil environment for all forms of discussion to take place. Philip traces the root of this behaviour to appeasement and submission. Whether in the negative or positive display of the behaviour, this seems true because the person is openly confessing their surprise in an event, which means they are submitting to it.

Practical Illustrations

Case Study I: Mr U is a politician who has been tagged serial failure by his opponents because he had contested in the last three elections without emerging victorious, but he was not concerned about what his opponents say. He believed that he was in this race to win, and fortunately, he won the election. As expected, instead of his opponents congratulating him and move on, they decided to infer that he was only voted in due to sympathy and not on the basis of performance. While being issued his certificate of return, a reporter from a renowned television station asked if it was true that his election was propelled by emotions rather than intellect. Facing the camera, Mr U smiled with his jaw dropping and asked if there was any portion of the constitution that stood against 'emotional voting'. This elicited a smile from the reporter herself. This was meant to taunt his distractors.

Case Study II: Ms R made a mistake on Tuesday while solving a mathematical equation for her students. She was not sure of the formula and had to manipulate her ways with the hope that she would go back home and learn it and try to correct it on Wednesday. The students seemed to have agreed with her solution, even the intelligent ones did not question her. However, she did not know that there was a student who also doubted the correctness of the equation. So he had also noted it down in his book. It was the first thing he faced when he got home. Being able to solve it in the most appropriate way, the first thing he said on Wednesday was to call Ms R out. Surprised by this discovery, the teacher's jaw dropped while her mouth opened slightly. This confirmed that she was truly taken aback.

Case Study III: Two criminals were arguing of their chances of evading clearance. While Criminal D thought that was an impossible task, Criminal KO boasted that he could do it. So they decided to act it out. On getting to the point of clearance, KO was the first person to present himself. After some few minutes, he was cleared despite not having the needed documents. Criminal D's jaw began to drop unconsciously; he was surprised that Criminal KO could effortlessly play on the intelligence of the officers despite their display of seriousness and professionalism. When KO saw his accomplice's jaw dropping, he smiled and walked away. That is, he found it funny that his accomplice was taken aback by his action.

13.14. Pulsing of Jaw Muscles

Generic Interpretations of the Concept

When the jaw muscles throb, pulse, or become tight, it communicates an array of non-verbal messages, along negative lines though. One of the many messages it communicates is tension. When we are tensed, it is mostly communicated throughout facial muscles; our jaw muscles become tight as a way of reacting to an unfavourable incident. In a way, this might be an indication of 'fight, flight or freeze' response. If the brain discovers that we cannot combat the situation and win, it will switch to the freeze response, which makes the muscles tight and then instructs the person to take to their heels.

Furthermore, it may also signal impatience. When we are in haste to take our leave from a location due to fear of the unknown, our jaw muscles would pulse. This communicates to the person delaying us that we are no longer interested in whatever they are saying; we want to be at another place.

Also, it means the person is concerned about something. When you reflect on a given issue and it seems there is no way out for you, you may pulse your jaw muscles as a way of demonstrating apprehension. Hence, those who are observant around you will understand that you are worried about something.

I have also noticed the 'jaw muscles pulsing' gesture in angry people. Anger elicits negative feelings from the body, which charges the facial nerves. Hence, jaw muscles pulsing may indicate a person's desire to attack what they consider as an opponent. In general, when you see the muscles of the jaw throb, look inward—you will see a negative emotion or another that is being experienced by that person. As usual, do not forget to look for other clustering behaviours pointing to the same meaning which you might have that allude to this gesture.

Scientific Explanations

From the medical point of view, jaw muscles pulsing is referred to as 'temporomandibular disorder'. This means that medical experts believe that anyone whose jaw muscles throb is suffering from a disorder. According to Cigna (2019), 'The jaw joints, or temporomandibular joints connect the lower jawbone (mandible) to the skull. These flexible joints are used more than any other joint in the body. They allow the jaw to open and close for talking, chewing, swallowing, yawning, and other movements.' Headaches, muscle pains, joint pains, jaw locking, and trouble with opening the mouth are some of the symptoms of the disorder. In most cases, these disorders are usually mild and go on their own after a few days. Hence, you may not necessarily need a doctor's involvement. Injuries to the joint, how joints are shaped, and joint diseases are some of the causes of TM.

Considering it from the social point of view, Emily notes that stiffening of the jaw muscles is a signal of annoyance, irritation, frustration, and agitation. When someone is agitating for something or a concept, they stiffen their jaw muscles. If the agitation is against a superior figure, it is an indication of suppressed anger. That is, the person is not pleased with what the superior is saying but the context in which he finds himself makes it difficult for him to react appropriately. Hence, the muscle pull which is an indication of self-restraint. Also, when a person is frustrated, they become stressed and their utterances may not be well received by their audience. So the subconsciously believe that keeping mum, which is against their conscience though, is the best point of action for them. And when someone is irritated by an idea or something being done by another person, this may be their non-verbal way of registering their displeasure.

Christopher Philip (2014) notes that during the pulsing of the jaw muscles, one will discover that the muscles connected to the temple flex. This means they are forcefully moved from their original state as a way of communicating anger or any other negative emotions. This makes speaking difficult. Sometimes, this produces a bulge at the side of the mouth which is a good way of communicating to one's audience that one is gradually mounting pressure. When you see this cue, especially from a person who is not all that close to you, you have to take it very seriously because it is an indication that they are about to lose their cool. In other words, when they become aggressive, there is nothing that they cannot do against you. Others may simply use this gesture as a way of tricking you into submission.

Practical Illustrations

Case Study I: Mr I came to the former school of his daughter to get an important document which is needed for clearance in the foreign university she is attending. She should come to get it herself but due to its urgency, the father had to cancel a business trip. When he got to the school, he was asked to make payment and wait at the reception. It was after about two hours of waiting that a receptionist came to give him audience, apologising that the school is doing an open day. Not really angered by that, he made a formal request for the document, only for the same lady to return after over an hour to tell him that the person to append his signature was not around. Hence, he had to come back the next day. On hearing this, his jaw muscles throbbed immediately and looked at the lady with a snarl. He was frustrated and angered by the lady's behaviour.

Case Study II: There was an intelligence report that some bandits were about to attack a city. So law enforcement officials were strategically positioned around the city. This blocked some major sections of the city to conduct special checks before allowing passage of vehicles. Dr T was coming from work after closing from night duty. He was frustrated by what he saw on the road because he needed to go and drop his children at school when he got home. He would obviously be late and more annoyingly, he would still undergo the same checks. When he got to one of the checkpoints, his jaw muscles pulsed as he parked with frustration.

Case Study III: Even though doctors are expected to be patient, calm, and tolerant, there are times that some people other than their patients frustrate their lives. Since their profession requires that they treat everyone with respect, you will only notice this frustration in their body language. There was a time a doctor needed to get a man to sign an agreement that surgery should be done to his wife. He showed readiness to give his consent, but a few hours to the scheduled surgery, he withdrew his consent, insisting that there should be an alternative way to treat the sickness. On hearing this, the doctor's jaw muscles pulsed. This means he was frustrated by the unexpected attitude despite all that he was doing to ensure things work out well.

13.15. Jutting of Jaw

Generic Interpretations of the Concept

When we are angry, there is probability that we will move or jut the jaw slightly forward. This, in a way, distorts our facial look and gives us a stern appearance. The aim of all these is to communicate aggression to our opponents. Anyone who sees that our look has been changed will get the message that we are actually angry. Note that this cannot be easily feigned, and as such, there is no need for you to think of jaw-jutting when you are not truly angry. This body language behaviour is displayed effortlessly when the negative emotions are on the rise.

Usually, this cue is accompanied by tense lips and lowered upper eyelids. The ultimate aim is to ensure that the feeling is aptly communicated to our audience. If other parts of the face do not support this cue, this will make everything appear controversial and the person will not be taken seriously. They will rather being seen as deceptive type.

With this behaviour, it becomes extremely difficult for a person to hide their anger. In other words, those who want to suppress their anger may find it impossible due to the jaw-jutting gesture that is not subjected to the control of any human. This reflex action is a good indicator to observe while dealing with people in an aggressive situation.

Scientific Explanations

Christopher Philip (2014) notes that jaw jutting involves pushing the chin out and up by slightly tilting the head backwards. He explains in one sentence that this behaviour tells 'others that one is ready to confront rather than conform'. In some rare instance, the gesture is done as a means of greeting or showing acknowledgement. However, when it is not along the line of greeting, it is used to express pride, smugness, confrontation, and confidence. When the jaw is jutted, it exposes the neck to attack. This means the person is trying to dare the situation. During physical conflict, a quick jab to the chin often puts people unconscious because it compresses the nerve that runs behind the jaw (Philip 2014).

When used as a form of greeting, it is done as a means of acknowledging someone else and is usually observed among dominant individuals. In this sense, it indicates fearlessness, arrogance and superiority. Philip states that there are two possible verbal interpretations of this cue: 'I'm sticking my chin out to say "Hello there, I see and acknowledge you." Or "I'm sticking my chin out to tempt you into punching me and fighting me. It is a challenge as I'm not going to back down."' Hence, it all depends on the context of display of the gesture.

From the foregoing, it is seen that this cue is used to intimidate others or show dominance. The jaw-jutting cue can be employed in competition to taunt one's opponents and trick them into submission. Even in normal conversations, this cue can be used as a means of challenging the authority of a person. Philip concludes, 'As the cue is subtle, it is often registered under conscious awareness, but the message will be received as an insult against another person and their position.'

Changing Minds (2019) also discusses this gesture extensively. The website first establishes the fact that this cue is subtle and, as such, only those in the know are likely to notice it when displayed. It is used to dare the other person in a conversation to do something evil to you and see what will happen to them in return. Sometimes, it may be referring to a particular idea. Hence, it is seen as a signal of defiance. This is in line with the submission of Philip.

The body language platform also gives a gender colouration to this concept by noting that 'men with bigger chins have more testosterone (this has been correlated with those who reach positions of power). Thrusting out the chin enhances this, saying "I am an alpha male and easily become aggressive".' Feeling confident makes the jaw of a person jut out in a slight manner while the head is tilted backwards. Sometimes, this jutting is accompanied by exposed teeth, which means the aggression is taken to a higher dimension—the person is ready to bite.

When you point at a person with the finger, it is a threatening act. When you do it briefly with the jaw jutting, it is more covert and thus, always seen as an insult (Changing Minds 2019).

Practical Illustrations

Case Study I: Mr U asked his secretary to prepare him a coffee so that he could sip before attending an inter-organisational board meeting. While arranging files in preparation for the meeting, he discovered that there was a document he was supposed to attend to before the commencement of the meeting. He was obviously going to get there late, an attribute he was almost known for. Without much ado, he settled down to business. It was then that the secretary brought in the coffee. On placing it on his table, she was expecting him to offer some words of appreciation or make some comments but instead, he only stuck out his jaw. This was of way of saying 'I see and acknowledge you.'

Case Study II: It is obviously a busy Tuesday in one of the largest cities across the world. There is a traffic gridlock along the major roads but people have no choice than to get to their destinations. While some of them are patient enough to follow the traffic law and behave in an orderly manner, many others are impatient and giving flimsy excuses to disobey traffic laws. At some point, one of the few men that have been enduring the situation was about to make a turn when an impatient driver nearly hit him. The driver thought the law-abiding man would wait so that he would drive past him, but the latter only jutted his jaw and looking sternly. This was communicating anger to the other person.

Case Study III: A group of drug addicts had made themselves a force to reckon with in a community. They were constituting nuisance to the extent that there were reported cases of harassment of ladies and other innocent residents in the neighbourhood. Law enforcement agents thought such barbaric acts could become a culture if a swift action was not taken against those in question. A survey was carried out and officers learnt the best time when most of the drug addicts would be at the said venue. They targeted that time and arrested a host of them. One of them was about consuming his drug when he was nabbed, he was indescribably angry, and he didn't know when he jutted his jaw.

CHAPTER 14

The Chin

The chin is an embodiment of non-verbal messages and also an essential part of our face. Our existence as humans would be impossible without the chin. I know many people have never thought along this line, and you might have probably discarded the essence of the chin as part of our survival instincts. This is costly assumption and you would have been overlooking countless body language messages through that. There are array of reasons why you should not trivialise the chin in our communication. Also, those in the fashion world understand how the shape of our chin contributes to our beauty. The chin comes in varieties of shapes—dimpled, sagging, cute, squared, strong, scarred or baby chin are some of the different shapes noticeable across the world. The shape of our chin dictates our facial look. That is why beauticians pay attention to the shape of the chin before they reach agreement on the kind of facial adornment most appropriate for their clients.

In addition, the chin is also reputed for its protective functions. They help in the protection of the entire face, and if the need arises, they also secure the neck. For this reason, we have survived different stages of evolution due to the protective roles of the chin. As earlier noted, it also speaks volumes when it comes to the non-verbal world; but before then, let's have a biological understanding of this body part first.

The chin is also referred to as the mental region. It is the area of the face below the lower lip and including the mandibular prominence (O'Loughlin 2006). According to science, the chin is formed by the lower front of the mandible.

One of the most popular theories explaining the evolution of the chin seen in human beings is that it helps support the jaw against certain mechanical stresses. Ionut Ichim, a PhD student at the University of Otago published a journal in *Medical Hypotheses* in 2007 claiming that the evolution of the chin occurred as a response to the unique form of speech of human beings creating stress on the jaw from certain movements by the tongue muscles (Wayman 2012).

Nathan Holton, a scholar from the University of Iowa states that, 'In some ways, it seems trivial, but a reason chins are so interesting is we're the only ones who have them.' New research done by Holton shows that the evolution of this unique characteristic was formed, not by mechanical forces such as chewing, but perhaps from evolutionary adaptations involving face size and shape. Holton claims that this evolutionary adaptation occurred as our face became smaller compared to the Neanderthal-era human beings; the modern human head is approximately 15 per cent shorter. Therefore, through the change in size, the chin became a factor that balanced the shape of the face (University of Iowa 2015).

Research on the evolution of the chin was further continued by the University of Iowa through another perspective. Opposing to Holtons scientific methods of the examination of the evolution of the chin, Robert Franciscus tackled the issue through an anthropological lens. Franciscus believed that the evolution of the chin was formed as a consequence of the change in lifestyle that was seen in human beings approximately 80,000 years ago. This was an era when human beings started to communicate more, turning their hunter-gatherer societies into agricultural societies where they increased their social networks. This decreased territorial disputes, as it further incentified the building of alliances in order to exchange goods and belief systems. Franciscus then believed that this change in the human environment reduced hormone levels, especially in men, resulting in the natural adaptation of the evolution of the chin (University of Iowa 2015).

Another perspective on the evolution of the chin was built pointing that it may have been a cause of sexual selection. This is when certain traits and characteristics of a species evolve in specific ways because they are seen more attractive to the opposite sex. Zaneta Thayer, a graduate from Northwestern University, and Seth Dobson, a biological anthropologist at Dartmouth, examined the chin shapes of both sexes to inspect any differences in the chin. They found that the male chin was taller and more pronounced, whilst the female chin was smaller. They claim that this difference in the chin disproved theories of the evolution through mechanical stress, because if the chins were adaptations of mechanical stress both genders will have the same chin shapes (Wayman 2012).

Overall, human beings are unique in the sense that they are the only species among hominids who have chins. In the novel, *The Enduring Puzzle of the Human Chin*, evolutionary anthropologists, James Pampush and David Daegling discuss various theories that have been raised to solve the puzzle of the chin. They conclude that 'each of the proposals we have discussed falter either empirically or theoretically; some fail, to a degree, on both accounts ... This should serve as motivation, not discouragement, for researchers to continue investigating this modern human peculiarity ... perhaps understanding the chin will reveal some unexpected insight into what it means to be human' (Gauger 2016).

There is the concept of double chin. A double chin is a layer of subcutaneous fat around the neck that sags down and creates a wrinkle, creating the appearance of a second chin. This fat pad is sometimes surgically removed and the corresponding muscles under the jaw shortened (Larkin 2005).

Katie Nodjimbadem (2015) notes that there is no reason for humans to be shy of our chin because it is the symbol of our civilization.

From the sociological point of view, the chin can help in the accurate communication of our emotion and sentiments—whether positive or negative. When a person is displaying pride, it can be known through their chin while the shape of the chin also reveals a person who is suffering from shame. In the Western world, they usually say 'Chin up' when a loved one is down while the army salute the flag with the chin angled high. In conclusion, the chin has the ability to reveal our feelings per time, be it confidence, trouble or anxiety.

14.1. Chin Up

Generic Interpretations of the Concept

The common phrase 'chin up' is used to encourage people that are emotionally down. Hence, when you see the chin of a person pointed out, it is used in communicating confidence. When the chin is raised up, it exposes the neck, the most vulnerable part of our body. So it is a way of daring an opponent to launch an attack. Bosses usually display this gesture while addressing subordinates because they understand that the other party is expected to bow to their decisions.

Hence, it is intentionally done in this situation as a way of commanding the respect of others.

There are some contentious situations in which this cue is used too. I have noticed it during high delegates' meetings where everybody wants to prove superiority. Sometimes, when I hold trainings for industry leaders, I see the leaders of competing industries greet each other while raising their chin high. This means none is ready to bow to the superiority of the other person; each believes to be the best. While there is nothing bad in this, it sometimes blocks the realities of things—people are unable to seek help in the appropriate quarters because of pride.

The 'chin up' behaviour plays out mostly in certain European cultures. More specifically, the Germans, Italians, Russians, French, among others make use of this cue to portray confidence, arrogance and pride. In these situations, they intentionally raise the chin higher than its normal position so that it can be obvious for their target subject to see. In a way, it means the person is aware of their own insecurity or threat. So they want to use every available non-verbal means to deal with such threat. An employee who believes that their employer is not sound enough to lead him or her may arrogantly display this cue while in the presence of the latter.

Scientific Explanations

While discussing the head positions, Westside Toastmasters (2019) states that the chin up gesture is used to communicate fearlessness, superiority, or arrogance. The platform explains further, 'The person intentionally exposes their throat and they gain additional height which allows them to 'look down their nose' at you.' When you raise up your chin, you gain more height and this in itself gives you some sort of confidence over the other person. It has been observed that high testosterone levels are responsible for large chins which is why the 'chin up' cue is linked with aggression and power.

Hanan Parvez (2019) also explores this concept while writing on the various positions that chin take. All over the world, the neutral position of the chin is when it is set horizontally. Any time it rises above the horizontal level, it means the person is displaying superiority, fearlessness or arrogance. This is the same view expressed by Westside Toastmasters. The act of lifting up the chin is an attempt to increase one's height to be above others. In this case, the person is exposing their neck not in a submissive way but in a way that says 'I dare you to harm me'. From the foregoing, we can categorically submit that there is a consensus among scholars on the use of chin up cue. It should be noted that in most parts of the world, submission is rather demonstrated through bowing or looking down.

Kat Boogard (2016) lists the act of holding the chin too high as one of the seven gestures used by people to display their arrogance. She notes that those who want to express confidence with this cue should not take it too high so that their message would not be misinterpreted. There is hardly anyone in the universe who appreciates being looked down during conversation. Hence, those who want to display confidence should endeavour to strike a balance in order not to create wrong impression about themselves. To communicate in an ideal way, ensure the head is kept level. With that, you have no probability of muttering to the floor or take the confidence booster to a level where it would be negatively adjudged.

Practical Illustrations

Case Study I: Student T has been picked to represent his school in a national competition. Although he is intelligent, he has always been warned of his pride—both teachers and students see him as someone who is full of himself but he would not just listen. On getting to the venue of the competition, he started tracing out the representative of another school that has also been reputed to be one of the best. This particular school has always given T's school a run for their expertise and equipment. Eventually, he saw the student from that school, and T walked up to him as if he wanted to greet out of a pure mind. On shaking hands with him, he raised high his chin to mutter some words; he clearly wanted to show superiority.

Case Study II: Mr Y was contracted by one of the leading organisations to come and provide strategic training to its employees on workplace communication. He knew that the standard of the firm was high, and as such, anyone who was gaining entry into the organisation can truly prove his worth. This served as a source of fear to him because he did not want to make mockery of himself. Hence, he prepared beyond his usual method, but this could not totally send the fear away. On getting to the training venue, he slightly raised his chin so as to look at the trainees, starting from the head. This was a confidence bolster for him.

Case Study III: Mrs H is the president of a multinational company. She holds a meeting with the board once in a month. It is her usual trait to come about five minutes late. She may apologise or just get into the agenda of the day without uttering a word. In the last edition, all the board members were patiently waiting for her when she came in and raised her chin from the door till she had her seat. This was a demonstration of pride.

Case Study IV: A woman was deceived into believing that she looked identical with her neighbour, a highly placed person in the society. Being someone who wanted to travel at all cost, put machineries in motion and stole the passport of her neighbour. She went through the document again and was convinced that no law enforcement agent should be able to stop her. So she saved up money and travelled. On getting to the immigration point, she was asked some to submit her passport for verifications. She lifted up her chin while handing it over to the officer as a way of proving pride. She was humiliated when she was found out.

14.2. Chin Facing Down

Generic Interpretations of the Concept

As I have earlier hinted in the preceding segment, when people think highly of themselves, they raise their chin high and expose their neck, daring anybody to attack them; but if they are threatened, they look down so as to avoid eye contact with what is considered as a threat to them. Also, when the chin faces down, it is a way of protecting the neck; the person understands that they are vulnerable to an attack, and as such, they are trying to guard the neck.

On a general note, this cue is a demonstration of lack of confidence. We disconnect from a source that we think is too high for us if we have no confidence to match up with them. That is why students and trainees do drop down their chin if you ask a question they have no idea about. They do not want to maintain eye contact with you so that you do not get to read the expression of 'nothingness' or 'blankness' on their face. This is an accurate tell in many people. Another place I have taken note of this cue is during board meetings when a member seems to lack a good grasp of what is being discussed. The person will look down so as not to create the feeling of expectation on their head of the gathering.

In addition, I have seen people literally drop their chin when they hear bad news. The cue is a form of closed body gesture in which people employ to keep to themselves when they think there is nothing to hold on to in the external world.

You also notice this cue when a person reflects on a negative or painful event. It means they are focused on an event that is troubling their mind. Hopefully, they can find a way round it. They hang the head into the air and release themselves to whatever threat looms.

Scientific Explanations

Parvez (2019) explains that when the chin is positioned below the horizontal level, it indicates that the person is dejected, sad, or feeling shy. When you are faced with these negative trends, you unconsciously lower your head as a way of bowing to the pressure; you are accepting the superiority of the threat over your life. When you bow to pressure, it means you do not want to challenge it because you feel such situation is insurmountable. Hence, the chin looking down gesture is an unconscious attempt to lower one's status and height. That is why there is a saying that the head 'hang' in shame and not the head 'rise' in shame. This is to tell you that shame defeats the confidence of people.

The chin also points down in some instances when someone is deeply feeling an emotion or engaging in a self-talk. This is evidence that the person is overwhelmed with the emotions. People also talk to themselves when they are defeated. It may be a means of restrategising or trying to blame someone for the woeful outcome (Parvez 2019).

Further, when the chin is down and pulled backwards, 'it means the person is feeling threatened or judgemental in a negative way. It's as if they were being symbolically punched in the chin by the source of their threat and so have it pulled back as a defensive measure. Also, it partially hides the vulnerable front portion of the neck' (Parvez 2019). This gesture can be noticed in group when a stranger joins them. The person who feels that the presence of the new person will divert their attention usually portrays this cue.

Changing Minds (2019) also explains this gesture through the head nod and shake cue. The website writes that when the chin is tilted down while it swings, it is an indication of disapproval. The person is trying to say 'I don't even want to look at you'. However, if the head is tilted at an angle, it means uncertainty. In Southern India, it is used to connote 'Yes'.

Practical Illustrations

Case Study I: Player M would retire after this tournament due to age which has opened him up to injuries in recent times. Despite all his successes, he had never won the World Cup tournament. Hence, he decided to give it all his best so as to complete his list of laurels. From the beginning of the league to the quarter finals, his team crushed every one of their opponents. However, things were difficult for them at the semi-final stage; after a goalless draw, his team later lost on penalties. After the match, M sat on the pitch and pointed his chin downward. Before he could know it, tears were gushing out of his eyes. He was really sad and tired.

Case Study II: Mr D just arrived from another part of the world, and his skin colour, facial appearance, and other peculiarities simply give him away at any given situation. His strange look also made law enforcement officers to stop him at every given point. After some few weeks, he gained employment in the country. On the second day of work, he was stopped by the police on his way to the office. While trying to park his car, his chin pointed down. This shows that he was threatened by the action of the police.

Case Study III: Child F was planning a seventieth birthday celebration for his mother before her sudden death. In fact, he had put everything into motion and a date had been picked before she fell ill and before being rushed to the hospital, she gave up the ghost. The mother had been the source of his strength and inspiration. So he was deeply pained that she did not wait to eat the fruits of her labour. Anyone who sees F knows that he is still haunted by the memories of his mother. One day, while working at the office, he suddenly turned his head down and held the position sorrowfully for about five minutes. He shook his head pitiably while looking up to face his laptop. He was embittered and concerned about the incident.

Case Study IV: One money launderer wanted to subtly get some people to help him in moving his ill-gotten wealth out of the public coffers. He knew if he wanted to engage them directly, they would turn down the request and even expose him. He wasn't ready for such humiliation, yet he was hell-bent on laundering the money. He almost played on the intelligence of all those that were supposed to be involved in process before one of them suddenly discovered the danger of his action. He raised the alarm and the money launderer knew an end had come for him. Thinking of the likely consequences of his action, he turned his head down for several minutes; he was inattentive to all he did throughout that period. He was thinking of the likely consequences of his action.

14.3. Chin Withdrawal

Generic Interpretations of the Concept

More often than not, we do see this gesture, but we choose to overlook it. This has seriously backfired in many instances, but our inability to trace issues to the root has rendered us powerless in the face of challenges. Chin withdrawal is the instinctive movement of the chin very close to the neck. As you might have suspected, this is a closed body gesture where the chin closes up on the vital organs due to anxiety or fear. This is a subconscious action that controls our action when the brain analyses a situation and discovers that it appears more powerful than we do.

This is an accurate tell that a person is fearful, insecure, and doubtful of the outcome of an action. When we are insecure, we look for all forms of improvised means to keep ourselves protected; we want to ensure that if any evil should befall us, everything will still be intact. Also, having doubt on our ability to conquer a situation will make us think along the defensive line. That is why we have to shield the neck of any eventual attack.

If you notice the chin withdrawal after asking someone a question, it is an indication that there are numerous unresolved issues. You may just need to press further so as to know the truth about the situation. With my experience in the law enforcement, I have seen this while interrogating criminals; when they cannot own up to their actions, they withdraw their chin as if something is threatening their peace.

When kids are interrogated on an action that they should not have done, they suddenly withdraw their chin. This indicates contriteness. In the same vein, I have always noticed this response in adults. It is a subtle way of pleading guilty of their offence. Also, they do not know what will be the aftermath of their action, so, they put up the defensive posture as a way of getting ready for any eventuality.

Scientific Explanations

Parvez (2019) says pulling the chin backwards is an indication that the person is feeling threatened or trying to pass a negative judgement. It is as if their source of threat punches them at the chin which makes them withdraw it in a defensive manner. When the chin is withdrawn, it hides the vulnerable portion of the neck.

The feeling of disgust is another possible indicator that can make people withdraw their chin. This means they are judging the source of the disgust negatively and do not want to be aligned with it. You may try this out by informing someone that you had worms for breakfast. If the person believes this is the truth, you will discover that they will suddenly withdraw their chin and put on a feeling of irritation (Parvez 2019).

Changing Minds (2019) describes this gesture as a puckered chin. The website notes that chin withdrawal makes the chin appear wrinkled. The general meaning attributed to this gesture is a defensive move. 'This may be done at the same time as protecting the neck by holding the chin in. It may also be a part of a pouting cluster where the person is feeling hard-done-by or defiant,' the platform opines.

On his own part, Christopher Philip (2014) states that chin withdrawing is a means of expressing negative surprise. It may also show disapproval. Hence, you see people tuck their chin to register their divergence over an issue. That is why Philip hints that 'when you want to raise an objection without verbally stating it, quickly tucking the chin in shows others that you have been "punched" in the chin by their thoughts. Performing this gesture, therefore, may cause them to backtrack on their suggestion, or put them on their heels trying to justify what they have said. Regardless, it can make them act more conservatively.'

When chin withdrawal is combined with lowering of the head, it is an apt way of signalling submission. Hence, the verbal interpretation is given as 'To appear smaller, I'm tucking my chin and lowering my eyes so you don't hurt me.'

What is most important is that you understand the context of usage of this cue to achieve a given purpose. For instance, when used in courtship, it is a show of innocence, submission, and childlike behaviour; but in some other situations, it is an expression of disdain and anger (Philip 2014).

Practical Illustrations

Case Study I: M just joined the services of M & K Legal Services about three years ago. He was informed that before there could be a pay rise for any employee, that employee must take a promotional test and prove his abilities in other areas. What has always been a source of concern to him was that those who had been there for a decade were still in the same spot. Hence, he has been made to believe that the test is a ruse that nobody could pass but he saw some few people who actually passed it. When he was about to sit the examination, he tucked in his chin pitiably and looked down until he was told to start. He was pessimistic about the whole process even before its commencement.

Case Study II: Ms R has been looking for suitors, but it just appears men are blind to her beauty and calm attitude; no one was asking her out. Eventually, a new employee who is of age found out about her; within a few days, the relationship clicked. They started going out and smoothening everything. However, there was a particular day when the man was really offended by R's attitude. Knowing that she had offended him, she did not wait for the passing of the day when she went to meet him and apologise. While tendering her apology, she pulled in her chin in order to appear more submissive and childlike.

Case Study III: G was to prove to law enforcement officials that he was not aiding smuggling activities in his country. Knowing that he has been on the watch list for years makes it appear impossible for him to wash himself clean. While appearing before the panel, he tucked in his chin and lowered his head, trying to appeal to their emotions. That is, he wanted them to perceive him as being submissive and cooperative to all that they will say.

14.4. Hiding of Chin

Generic Interpretations of the Concept

Chin hiding is seen among children and adults but done differently. However, in both cases, it is employed to register negative emotions. Let's begin our discussion from the angle of the children. When children are embarrassed or displeased about the action of another person, they employ the chin-hiding gesture to make their grievances known. In some given contexts, you may notice this when they are upset. Apart from tucking their chin down, they will also cross their arms simultaneously and will resist lifting their chin up. This is more pronounced in children because they do not know how to hide emotions; they act it out exactly the way they feel. Dealing with children can be quite easy for this reason because they are sincere with us. So we are only left to reciprocate the gesture and get issues sorted out.

On the other hand, when used by adults, it serves as a means of displaying superiority and readiness to attack. This is why it is normally observed between males, who are standing face-to-face and yelling at each other; it means they are both angry at each other and none is ready to bow for the other. However, they are both conscious of the first move of each other. Hence, they hide their chin as a means of protecting the neck in case it yelling leads to violent confrontation.

This means that despite the yelling and excessive display of anger, they are still aware of the need to keep themselves secure. The neck is very vulnerable and simple rough handling of that region may lead to the death of a person. With this understanding, the chin hiding plays a huge role in ensuring human survival. There is little wonder some researchers assert that chin development is the last stage in evolutionary development.

Scientific Explanations

Explaining the reason the chin should be hidden, Changing Minds (2019) submits, 'The chin is vulnerable when fists are flying as a good upper-cut punch can knock you out. Even more vulnerable than the chin is the throat, where a predator might try to asphyxiate you or worse. Holding in the chin protects both it and the throat, and hence is a naturally defensive move that people use when they feel threatened.' I am tempted to say that the chin-hiding cue is a built-in gesture in us that preserves our lives. You may not really understand how protective it is until you physically witness where a violent confrontation is taking place.

When you hide the chin, it also lowers the head, which is used to pledge submission in some context. This is different defensive move where the head tilts down in a pronounced manner and the eyes are really downcast. This is used by lovers or those who are shy.

Chin hiding is a demonstration of disgust, anger, or disdain. Philip also expresses the view shared by Changing Minds that chin hiding helps in protecting us during a violent attack. He submits that 'as the profile of the chin is reduced, it eliminates the exposure it suffers during an attack. The chin is particularly vulnerable to injury and a quick blow can send someone unconscious.' So this might be an indication that an angry interlocutor is ready to back off from an argument that is tilting towards violence. Remember that in the chin up gesture that we earlier discussed, we affirmed that it is used to show arrogance, pride or disobedience. This means the person is ready to fight. But in the case of chin hiding, it serves as a means of protecting oneself. If it is done by just a person, it means they are not ready for any confrontation. Philip gives the verbal interpretation of this cue as 'I don't like what I just heard so I'm tucking my chin down in disdain.'

Some cue clusters you may pay attention to are averted eye gaze, looking downward, and sneering nose, but if it is used in a dating context, it may be accompanied by a coy smile and eyes cast upward (Philip 2014).

Practical Illustrations

Case Study I: K has been pestering his father to take him out for an outing. He reminded the father that the last time he was given a special treat was during his tenth birthday, and he was longing for another one, especially after performing brilliantly in his last examinations. The father is a businessman and does not have the luxury of time for such events at all times. He had suggested that he should tell his mother to take him there, but K would not just agree; he wanted it to be his father. So the father later succumbed to pressure and promised that the weekend to their resumption, he would make himself available. Just a day to the said date, he had an important trip to make and called K to inform him, but the young body did not want to know which business trip could be more important than the planned outing. After his father explained to him, he went to the dining and tucked his chin down while crossing his arms and refused to lift the chin. This was to communicate his annoyance.

Case Study II: In a busy parking space of a mall, two men hit each other due to lack of patience. Expectedly, none was ready to take the blame, and this was the real cause of the fight. So the first man came out to assess the level of damage made on his car; likewise the second man. Since they brushed each other at the side, there was no a clear-cut way to adjudge the issue. They both hissed at each other. But man A was really pissed off and had to yell at Man B who replied appropriately. Then, they started giving each other reasons why they were right. Security guards came there, but they could not douse the tension at once. The two men hid their chin and shouted at each other until the security guards were able to bring the situation to a rest. They were really annoyed at each other and did not give a dime about the concerns of people at that time.

Case Study III: The government of Country AOY held a meeting with all hotels, bars, and other concerned stakeholders that they should not sell drugs to the citizens again as the harmful effects of the consumption of such drugs was visible to all. Most of the drug addicts did not know that all the vendors would comply with this directive. Drug addict QY left for his usual joint that evening to purchase some drugs but was utterly disappointed to be denied. He got uncontrollably angry and hid his chin as he walked away from the premises. He uttered some violent words, which later got him arrested by the security agents within the premises.

14.5. Chin Dropping while Shoulder Slumps

Generic Interpretations of the Concept

Parents are very familiar with this cue too, because it is always displayed by children as a way of registering their hesitation to get something done. Here, children do hide or lower their chin while their shoulders slump. It is an effective way of saying 'I'm not interested in doing it'. If you discover that the child's arms are also crossed, this is very true; they truly do not want to get involved in that particular task.

Having interacted with children at different levels for years has given me the opportunity to understand them better. One of the most reliable means of studying body language cues is through children. This is because non-verbal communication is the primary means of exchange of information among humans. Even when we were all still babies that could not articulate words, our perfect means of expressing ourselves is through the non-verbal means. A hungry child will make use of both hands to point to the direction of her mother's breasts. If they do not want to go to a person, they will push the person off them while they cry continuously.

The point I am driving at is that the chin drop coupled with slumped shoulders and crossed arms perfectly mirrors an uninspired person. If the child is willing to do what you request them to do, the arms that serve as the main instrument for the execution of duties would not be kept to themselves. Also, the chin drop hints that the person is simply not willing to focus on any event.

Scientific Illustrations

We cannot have an apt understanding of this cue without reeling out the role of postures in our daily lives. Unfortunately, many people have underrated the role of posture in their communication with people. Looking at a chin drop with slumped shoulders and crossed arms, there is no way we can have an encompassing discourse without taking the whole concept as one. Philip (2013) says that 'Posture refers not only to the erectness of our bodies, but also to our body orientation, direction of lean, and the degree to which our bodies are open and inviting.' Let me not bore you with general explanations.

When the chin is dropped coupled with a slumped or rounded shoulder, it shows the inactivity of the person in the conversation. The addition of the arms crossing is evidence that the body has been closed off. Hence, we generally attribute negative thoughts to a posture like this. That is why Philip aptly submits that 'People that slumped over or habitually lean on their elbows while seated or against a wall come off as lazy and careless; sloppy. People with poor posture often come across as lacking confidence.' A child whom you are appealing to but is not forthcoming can simply be lazy or think they should not be sent on such errands.

I have been exploring the concept of chin drop, slumped shoulders and arms crossing together as one because it usually appears as clusters. Joe Navarro (2012) lays more emphasis on the shape of the shoulders. He notes that shoulders communicate vitality and strength and also have the ability to demonstrate hierarchy and dominance. Someone whose shoulders slump with the chin dropping communicates submissiveness. Navarro makes reference to how criminals had always told him during the course of investigation that the look of victims—looking frail, weak, and not being athletic were the major determinants in telling them who to or not to attack. Another issue they also made reference to is arm swinging. If a person is moving their arms vigorously, it means they are fully aware, and hence, criminals will desist from attacking them at that point in time. Slumped shoulders simply show that the person is not playing any leadership role.

Before I draw the curtain close on this segment, let me warn against some stereotypes. I have warned at different points in time that the gestures—chin drop, slumped shoulders and crossed arms—should be observed together because mere arms crossing may signal that the person is feeling comfortable but if observed in relation to other clusters, it may indicate anxiety or show of internal discomfort (Changing Minds 2019).

Practical Illustrations

Case Study I: Baby KJ is fond of her parents and she wants to be with them at all times. The nature of work of her parents requires that they stay outside. How to bring her up in a refined way has been a source of concern to her parents and the father had suggested that she should be taken to a boarding house when she is ten. They know she would not welcome this idea. So they have been devising all ways to make her live independently but seems it is not producing the needed results. For the past two years, the mother has been asking her how she would feel if asked to go and stay in one of the finest boarding facilities around, but the response has not been encouraging. So the last plan hatched by her parents is to make her go and spend her long vacation with granny. When her parents brought this idea, she dropped her chin with the shoulders slumped and arms crossed. This was to register her grievance over the decision—she is not willing to go to granny.

Case Study II: A group of law enforcement officials have been interrogating a suspect for the past three days. During each of those days, they ensured that they changed his sleeping place. After the interrogation on the fourth day, they insisted that he must sleep where he slept the third day. He decided to appeal their decision, noting that he did not enjoy the place; the officials discovered that he cooperated better than the first three days because of the discomfort he went through. Hence, it was wise that he should be remanded in the same location. As he was about to be moved out of the interview room, the suspect pulled his chin inward and slumped his shoulders as a non-verbal way of showing that he really did not want to return to the place.

Case Study III: Colleagues A and B do not agree on some basic professional issues. This is known to most of their peers in the office but the management is kept oblivious. There was a time the manager of the firm pitched them together on a particular task. Knowing the consequences of failing, they tried hard to shelve their differences and work in unison. However, it was a tough and difficult moment for both of them, and they both prayed that no group work should bring them together again. However, just few weeks after that, it was announced that they would have to work together again. Depressed by this news, Colleague A pulled his chin inward and slumped on his chair.

14.6. Touching the Chin

Generic Interpretations of the Concept

This is one of the obvious hand-to-head gestures which people tend to allude all forms of meaning to. While many seem to be accurate, some interpretations are given out of cultural stereotypes. But on a general note, when you see a person slightly place their fingers (usually two) on the chin, it is considered as an evaluative gesture; the person is ruminating over an issue. Some people tend to erroneously conclude that this is a sign of doubt; this submission is generic and does not reflect the truth of every situation. The behaviour simply means that the person is trying to process information. That is, it can either be on something positive or negative. Someone who wants to start a business but does not have an assurance of how successful it will be may maintain this posture while trying to analyse the risk factors.

When the fingers are used to support the chin, the head tilts forward and the entire body slightly leans to the front too. This is a non-verbal expression of being interested in the thought ongoing. That is, the person is solely focused on the piece of information they are trying to process. When you see cue in a conversation, you just need to respect the opinion of the person so as not to serve as a source of distraction to them.

However, if the chin-touching cue is accompanied by other gestures such as lip pursing, it is an indication that the person is thinking something along negative line. Pursing the lip is a symbolic way of stating that we do not want the negative thought to get into our body system. On the other hand, it means the person is thinking of an alternative to what has been discussed. That is, the person does not believe that the conclusion that has been reached is the best.

Scientific Explanations

Changing Minds (2019) explains that touching the chin is a signal that the person is thinking hard. It may also be a means of passing judgement on a concept or simple evaluation. This is very particular to conversations that offer people the choice to make a decision. This means the person wants to digest all the options at their disposal before they eventually pitch their tent with an option they consider as being the best for them.

In some other times, this cue may only be a literal means of supporting the head. The head becomes heavier when we are bored or tired and is held in a cup-shaped hand so that it does not drop embarrassingly, especially in public. Boredom makes people sleepy, and there are instances where sleeping will portray you in bad light, no matter how boring the place appears to be. Your audience may misinterpret this cue as a way of showing rapt attention. Further, holding the chin may also be a way of pinning down the head. That is, the person is lost between two contradictory decisions of moving the head and keeping it in its position. This is seen in situations when you emotionally agree with what a person is saying, but your intellect is demanding more information so you have good reason before eventually saying yes (Changing Minds 2019).

Philip (2014) maintains that this is a signal of boredom. He explains that it can be used to show disinterest, and an observant speaker will speed up their talk when they notice this signal. On the other hand, he opines that the person might be thinking over an issue. The two possible verbal interpretations given to this cue are 'I'm bored so my hand is buttressing my chin with most of the weight so I don't fall over completely', or 'I'm lightly supporting my chin because I'm thinking and my chin is my source of wisdom'. We must appreciate Philip for going further to clarify that when the fingers slightly touching the chin, it means the person is thinking (whether positive or negative); and when the chin is firmly pressed into the palms, it signals boredom. We can always be guided by this distinction as we try to read meanings to people's expressions.

Associated clusters that you can watch for boredom are slumping over, compression of the palms due to the extra weight it holds, drooping and closing of the eyes, staring and slow blinking rate, and the entire body may bob down due to the momentary sleepiness. However, if the hand is only bearing a part of the weight to indicate evaluation, you may look for clusters such as few fingers touching the chin, the head and body to be erect, titled at forty-five degrees, eye contact to switch from direct to thinking, down or up and the body to lean forward (Philip 2014).

Practical Illustrations

Case Study I: As the lecture dragged on, the student's head collapsed more and more into her palm. At first just her fingers touched her chin as the topic interested her. As the course dragged on, her fingers flattened and her chin fell into her palm. By the end of the lecture, she was slumped on her palm, and it was carrying most of the weight (Philip 2014).

Case Study II: Mr T has two business trips to make. The two trips are within the same continent. It would be economically wise that he merges the two journeys, but he has the wedding of a close friend to attend a week between both trips. More so, his wife would be due for delivery that same week. Now, he is lost on the next line of action that he should take. If he wants to attend one and return home before embarking on the second trip, it means the company will only be making provision for half sponsorship for the second trip. He has also promised to make himself available any day the wife would be putting to bed. Now, he is lost between tendering an apology to his friend beforehand and sorting things out with the wife and taking the extra financial burden. He sits on his chair and slightly places a few fingers on his chin as he ruminates over these issues. He was lost in thought, trying to find solution to the issues bothering him.

Case Study III: Prostitute OU has been having an affair with one of her neighbours before the arrival of another handsome guy. Apart from that, the new guy looks richer. However, she's lost on how to win the heart of the second guy and keep two of them without making them know she's into two of them. Both of the guys seem to have the same schedule as they go in and come out almost the same time. For three hours, she locks herself in to draft out a way to go about it but none of her proposed action looks feasible. At some point, she unconsciously placed her fingers on her chin while still in the thinking mode. It was a glaring display of frustration.

14.7. Brushing Chin with Back of the Hand

Generic Interpretations of the Concept

This cue is observed in many cultures of the world, and it can be considered from both the literal and metaphorical points of view. For instance, when your chin is itching, you will most probably make use of the back of the hand to brush it off; it looks irritating to scratch it continuously. Also, it is against the rule of personal hygiene to use the front of the hands (fingernails) to scratch the chin. Some also have aftershave infections and will prefer to brush it than scratching it.

On the metaphorical level, brushing the chin with the back of the hand is used to express doubt about what another person says in most cultures. The verbal translation is, 'I don't believe what you're saying and will wave it off from my chin because it's my source of wisdom.' This gesture is subtle and people may erroneously take it as a literal way of brushing off the beards. When you are addressing a person and they suddenly brush off their chin, it means they do not believe what you have just said. Hence, you have to device a way of convincing them or explaining yourself better until they come to the same point with you.

In most instances, this cue is accompanied by pursed lips or clenched teeth. That is, they do not want the disbelief they are waving off to get into their mouth, hence, the need to block all openings to the body. Depending on the style that suits them, some may prefer to brush the chin off at some point while others may do it from one side to the other. I have also seen people brush it from the back to front of the chin. No matter the variant you come across with, the mean does not change.

Scientific Explanations

This gesture is mostly used in Europe and some parts of Africa. Even though it is considered as being negative in those countries but its effects are milder compared with other nations of the world where it is not even tolerated at all. The Travel Galleries section of the Telegraph (2017) lists Tunisia, France, Belgium, and Northern Italy as some of the countries where the cue is mostly used. The website explains that 'In France, this gesture is known as *la barbe*, or 'the beard', the idea being that the gesturer is flashing his masculinity in much the same way that a buck will brandish his horns or a cock his comb. Simply brush the hand under the chin in a forward flicking motion. While not as aggressive as flashing one's actual genitalia, this gesture is legal and remains effective as a mildly insulting brush-off.' In the part of Italy where it is used, it means 'No'. In the other countries listed above, the gesture means 'Get lost'. This can be insulting to people, especially those who understand what it means, and they may be forced to react in the same way.

Sophie Forbes (2015) warns that this cue can land Americans into trouble when used outside of the home front. This is not only an American thing, but can be offensive all over the world, only that the degree of reactions varies.

Philip (2014) explains that this cue means someone is thinking or trying to evaluate something. He submits that 'When trying to come up with a solution, rubbing the chin can activate the mind to seek creative and profound solutions to problems. During negotiation you might use the chin rub to show that you are contemplating options and weighing the benefits. Rubbing the chin can buy you some time to think as it is universally seen as contemplation gesture.' People tend to respect your 'privacy' when they see this, by allowing you the time needed to think through an idea. Philip actually premised his interpretation on the cliché that says that 'chin scratcher is old, wise and bearded.' When someone is stroking, it means decision–making process has started and the person is yet to reach a conclusion.

I have given two contradictory views for this cue. If it is the mere abusive cue meaning 'get lost', the gesture would not be accompanied by any cluster other than a stern face or a grimace. However, if it is serving as an evaluative behaviour, clustering behaviours such as head tapping; rubbing the head, cheek, or temple; and even tapping the chin with a pen would be noticed. Other pacifying acts such as rubbing the back of the neck and head and brushing of the arms may also be observed (Philip 2014).

Practical Illustrations

Case Study I: A man went to get a second-hand car for his wife, and while speaking with the car dealer, he was informed that the car had not been used for more than six months before the owner decided to offload it. Looking at the appearance of the car, the man did not want to believe the dealer was saying the whole truth. So he asked him to open the bonnet so that he could assess the engine. It appeared neat but looked washed rather than new. He used the back of his hand to brush off his chin as he conducted the final evaluation on the car. This meant he was thinking of the truthfulness of the dealer's statement.

Case Study II: Mrs D went for shopping, and after buying every other item, the money left on her could not buy cookies cream and plain vanilla as earlier planned. Now she has to settle for one. For a moment, she was lost in which to go for. She moved to a side of the mall so as not to obstruct people's movement and stroked her chin with the back of her hand while she contemplated on the difficult decision. After some few minutes, she took off her hand and later settled for plain vanilla. Even though she picked and picked and dropped it numerous times, she eventually took the hard decision on which to go for. She walked out with a fast pace so as not to return to the evaluative mood. She had reached her final decision and was not willing to make a return to the disturbing state.

Case Study III: Smuggler BU has three routes through which he gets his smuggled items into the country. However, all the three routes are now under the supervision of one of the most experienced officers. He knows this is a hard knock on his illegal business and penetrating through corrupt officials has now become a herculean operation, but he is not ready to let go of the business. After buying the goods on this occasion, he is now engrossed in the thought of which of the three routes to try out. He is seen brushing his chin with the back of his hand, which exposes him as someone deep lost in thoughts.

14.8. Cradling of Chin

Generic Interpretations of the Concept

Chin cradling can have an array of interpretations. It is the act of placing the chin firmly on the palm of the hand. This can be considered as a variant of the chin touch earlier considered. However, this focuses solely on the palms and not the use of some fingers as explained in that context. When the chin is placed on the palm, it is often considered as a sign of boredom. This is usually accompanied by the relaxation of the facial muscles. When boredom sets in, we tend to lose our activeness and vitality, and that is why everything normally appear relaxed. Note that the chin will be firmly pressed against the palms because boredom makes the head weightier, and as such, the weight falls into the hands.

Considering it from the context of law enforcement, the cue may indicate a range of possibilities, depending on the events and circumstances surrounding its appearance. In other words, you cannot just read any meaning to this cue while investigating a person without taking surrounding happenings into considerations.

For instance, in a forensic setting, I have seen the guilty maintain this posture while sitting alone in a room just to create a deceptive perception about himself; he wanted the authorities to think he is innocent about the case. The guilty suspect wanted to use feeling of boredom to cover up his offence. However, with the aid of some few professional questions, he could not withstand the heated atmosphere. Hence, he later made confession.

On a general level, when someone keeps to themselves by placing their chin on their palms, it means they are closing themselves off to the ideas coming from other sources. They do not want to take in any other information because they are still battling with an issue at hand. If this is mere boredom, cheering of the person up with an interested talk or a topic that falls within their passion can ensure that they change their mood but if it is caused by an event involving crime or any other serious action, the person may not witness a mood change until they know the outcome of the issue. You do not expect a criminal to start cheering up when he does not know if he would end up at the prison or would be shot dead.

Scientific Explanations

Bob Whipple (2019) notes that the manner in which the chin is held can communicate different messages. For instance, chin touching may signal boredom for a male or the exact opposite. Chin propping has been explained to be a good listening gesture by males. Stroking the facial hair also means that the person is listening to you. Females too do stroke their hair but not as often as men.

Also, resting the chin on the palms is an unconscious way of protecting the throat. When you display this gesture, the wrist safeguards the throat. This means the person probably thinks he or she is vulnerable to attack in the environment they find themselves. This form of protection is usually symbolic and there is need to analyse the factors surrounding the context where the conversation is taking place. If you do not trust your co-interlocutor, you may wear this behaviour (Whipple 2019).

The expert explains that putting the chin in the palm of the hand is an outright expression of fatigue and boredom. The hand is used to contain the head so that it does not fall on the table.

This same view is expressed by Philip (2014). He explains that it is an apt way of expressing disinterest which can help a speaker hasten up on what they are saying. This simply means the person is tired and their emotions must be respected, if not, the speaker should not expect the best response from them. Apart from boredom and tiredness, it also means that the person is probably holding negative thoughts. He gives the verbal translation of this cue as 'I'm bored so my hand is buttressing my chin with most of the weight so I don't fall over completely'.

Changing Minds (2019) also expresses the fact that the chin on the hand gesture helps in protecting the throat, which may be a point of attack by an opponent. Note that this may not necessarily be a physical attack but a symbolic representation of disagreement between you and the other person. Also, dropping your chin into the palm lowers the head, which may be a submissive pose.

Practical Illustrations

Case Study I: Mr T just returned from a three-week business trip to another continent. It was his first time of being in that continent. While there, he saw many things that left him grasping for breath and had to take pictures at every point in time. Whenever his wife spoke with him, he would mention some of the 'wonders' he was seeing; and as such, the wife already prepared her mind that she would listen to numerous gest when he returned. As expected, the husband, started from the 'strange' culture of the people when he landed at the airport. At first, it was amusing and interesting to the wife. But when it seemed unending and, more so, the story was beginning to lack creativity, she began to lose interest. It was late into the night, and she had a busy day. Taking these two issues into consideration, one will expect her to be naturally tired. She placed her chin in her palm and leant towards her husband as she was listening to him. She did not want to shun her husband despite her tiredness.

Case Study II: Baby R decided to go out with her dad on a Saturday. While going out, the discussion was interesting as they discussed on issues concerning the child's welfare and academic performance. Also, the first place they went to was a restaurant and shopping mall where he got her many things. An elated R said she would follow her father to his friend's residence. When his father got there, he started conversing with his friend and they tarried for hours. She began to lose interest in the movie she was watching and could not connect with what his dad and his friend were discussing, she placed her chin in her palm and eventually slept off.

Case Study III: It was the first time of Man UC to impersonate another person. At first, he was excited about this criminal action and became enthusiastic of the prospects of what he could use the victim's identity to achieve. However, reality dawned on him while he was approaching the border of the country he wanted to escape to. While in the bus, he decided to feign tiredness by placing his chin in his palm. However, the officer that flagged him down knew he was being deceptive because he only looked nervous but not tired. This invariably means that he was not excluded from the identity verification process.

14.9. Perching Chin Angrily

Generic Interpretations of the Concept

This cue is displayed by placing the chin on the knuckles of the fists, while the elbows are wide and rest on the table while the person stares into a computer screen or distance. You will notice the grief on their face and disconnection from their immediate environment. The clustering behaviours that normally accompany this cue is furrowed forehead, squinted or narrowed eyes. This is always induced by momentary anger; something pisses the person and they want to react in the same manner. It is as if the person is getting ready to combat the situation that is making them feel unease.

Also, this cue may also be noticed when the person is pondering on something difficult. It means they have been thinking over the issue for long and there seems to be no headway. Hence, the feeling of frustration has been setting in.

Since this is normally evident in their look, the best thing for you to do is not to interrupt or fuel the anger; they will transfer the aggression on you. Some may think that appeasing them will be the best approach at the moment, but you cannot predict how the person will react. So stay afar and study their change in mood before eventually taking any safe step. Remember that every case requires a unique approach, and it would be better that you find out which will best soothe this situation.

Scientific Explanations

Mateo Sol (2019) notes that this is an evaluative gesture. When a person is paying genuine attention to what you are telling them, they will evaluate it to determine if it meets their standard or not; they want to be sure that you are expressing their viewpoint before they give a nod to your words. While they do this, the hands will rest on their edges of the chin. According to Sol, 'if what your saying is something they feel *negative* towards or don't agree with they will start *resting their head on their thumb or their hands lower palm* while still maintaining the index finger upwards and fist clenched to appear interested.' Sometimes, the person may use the index finger to scratch under their eyes as a way of reinforcing critical thoughts about what is being said.

Farouk Radwan (2017) also shares the same view with Mol. According to him, this cue means the person is trying to evaluate something or thinking over an issue.

Christopher Philip (2013) gives a detailed explanation of this gesture. He expertly opines that 'we can measure the level of interest or negativity our listeners have by how much pressure is held by the hand during a conversation'. When the body language is an average evaluative gesture, the index finger is placed to the side of the head and only lightly supports the weight of the head, or the hands are left and placed on the table with palms up or uncrossed to the front of the body. However, when the hands touch the chin and there is interest, the thumb and index finger form an L shape and the chin is placed in the crux of the L but is not supported by it (Philip 2013). The other emotions and gestures that surround this behaviour will determine if it signals anger or not.

I need to state that when a person is genuinely interested in what you are discussing with them, their hand will barely touch their face. The fact that the hands perch the chin in an angry manner shows that the person is only interested in doing something negative.

In other cases, the hand remains open with the fingertips of the index and middle finger gently resting on the cheek. As the listener becomes bored or tired, the hand will bear more and more of the weight and the body will seem to slump completely over the hand and be supported by it. As boredom sets in, the thumb will move under the chin to help the person hold their head even further, or the chin will seem to compress into the palm (Philip 2013). Note that if it is only the index finger that is rubbing the chin through to the corner of the eyes, it is used to express disbelief or fatigue and the movement of the eye should also be closely watched as it also expresses negative emotions.

Practical Illustrations

Case Study I: H is the clerk of GYS Firms, and the company is known for outworking its staff. That is why there have never been stable hands that will be committed to growing the establishment. On a particular occasion, H was given a huge file to work on. In order to complete it, he had to make himself present at the weekend. He ensured that he followed all the requirements of the file. After completion, he sent it over to the manager. Hoping that he would rest after days of marathon work, he received an email from the manager. Ordinarily, one would have hoped that it was a commendation email taking cognisance of the work H had done, only for it to turn out to be a rework email; the manager made a mistake by attaching the wrong instruction file. Looking at the effort he had dedicated to the work and where to start from again, H squinted his eyes and rested his chin on the knuckles of his fists and stared at the computer screen irritatingly. He was really frustrated.

Case Study II: A law enforcement official had apprehended a man that looked suspicious and brought him to his supervisor for further interrogation. After talking for some few minutes, the supervisor released him and pleaded for how he was handled by his subordinate. After about thirty minutes of releasing him, they got an intelligence report that anybody coming in from the country of the suspected man should be detained at the airport. Immediately, he gathered his men to go after him. When the law enforcement who had earlier apprehended him heard that he had been released and had to be traced again, he used his index and thumb to form an L shape and gazed into the distance while furrowing his forehead. He was irritated by the saddening news.

Case Study III: Politician U has bright chances of winning the forthcoming parliamentarian election because it is glaring that he is the choice of the majority. However, he appears reckless in speech and doesn't behave smart. In one of his private chats with associates, he said something negative about a particular section of the electorate, and unfortunately, the clip was released by his opponents with spies in his team. When he saw the devastating effect that release would do to his political ambition, he became restless. He sat on a couch and used his index finger to form an L-shape on his cheeks while looking at no particular direction.

14.10. Chin Shifting

Generic Interpretations of the Concept

This cue is used in communicating subtle disagreement. It is always used by adults and can rarely be seen in children. Chin shifting involves the movement of the chin from the left to right against the palm of the hands. That is, the chin rests on the palm of the hand while the thumb is placed on the right-hand side. This is subtle because the attention is always focused on the hand occupying the chin and not the underneath action. When you pay close attention, you will discover that as the chin shifts from a side to the other, the index and thumb also move along that way.

This behaviour is subconsciously used to express disagreement. If the chin had not rested on the palm, the person would have shook their head in a visible way. So the action is saying that 'I am not in support of this decision but I don't want to make it so obvious'. The person will also wear a frown on the face or may cover this up with a grimace; a close look of their face will show that something is wrong. Ordinarily, people are expected to put on a sigh of relief after reaching a decision that soothe them. Doing otherwise means the person only passively agreed with the decision.

Over the years, I have noticed this cue among decision makers in the conference room. Once they are not in alliance with a particular decision, they will bury their chin in their palm and move the chin from the left to right as a way of saying the decision did not match their thinking. Leaders in a meeting should always pay close attention to this cue after decisions have been made, especially those considered to be contentious. This cue is reliable because it is subconsciously done; it is beyond what the person can easily hide. Hence, it can help in making informed decisions.

Scientific Explanations

Whipple (2019) states that holding the chin prevents the head from moving. When you are paying attention to what someone is saying but you want to have a full grasp of where they are heading before you give a nod, you will use the index finger and thumb to clamp down the chin. In short, this means you are resisting yourself from giving your consent to an issue. Whipple puts it thus: 'Holding the chin would make it less likely for you to give out premature information on your state of mind. It adds a subconscious layer of security when you may be feeling vulnerable.' If after the information has been fully heard, the person shifts their chin from a side to the other, it means they do not agree with it. It is not rare to see people agree with what is said at the initial level but feel that the entire information does not reflect their standpoint. Like the example of conference room disagreement I earlier mentioned, I have seen cases where judges agree to the preliminaries of a case, but during the decision-making process, they ended up having split decision. If they had given their consent at the preliminary level, it would have been difficult to withdraw it when it matters most.

It is pertinent to note that this cue is different from the boredom or fatigue pose that we discussed earlier. The difference is the chin movement which is usually subtle. The chin shift cue makes the chin to be done which hints that the person has a negative mindset concerning the issue at hand. It means they are either sad or depressed by an action, which is making them to disagree with it (Whipple 2019).

Changing Minds (2019) states that only those in the know can notice this cue when it is made. That lays emphasis on its subtle and subconscious nature. Moving the chin from one side to the other expresses the notion that one does not agree with what every other person is saying. If they were having issues with just a member of the board, the chin would have moved to the person's direction and pause. Understanding all these minor but vital messages will help you in making informed decisions as nothing about another person's thought would be hidden from you.

Practical Illustrations

Case Study I: A student has been proving troublesome in ERS Schools. In fact, his colleagues have seen him as a bully and he seemed to be satisfied with this appellation. His issue has been discussed during staff meetings times without number but nothing seems to have changed about him. One day, the head of the school summoned all the teachers to specifically discuss the boy. They all agreed that the boy's issue is getting out of hand and it was good that an emergency meeting was called. After raising the preliminary issues which they all agreed to, when it was time to take decision over the boy's action, the meeting turned to a debating session. While some were of the opinion that he should be expelled, a section maintained that he should be put under close watch while the third group suggested parent–teacher alliance. The group that proposed that he should be expelled triumphed. The teacher who championed the parent–teacher alliance could be seen placing her chin in her palms while she shifted it from the left to right. This was to register her disagreement with the decision.

Case Study II: The board of directors of a firm were holding a meeting on how to swim through the recession period. After outlining how the economic downturn was negatively affecting the fortunes of the firm, they began to suggest ways to decisively navigate through the process. Some suggested that a portion of their workforce should be laid off while some others suggested a pay cut. At the end of arguments and counterarguments, they later settled for pay cut. The fear of those opposing this was that the employees would be demotivated to work. They should have just sent away the less productive ones. But since it was a majority decision, there was nothing they could do. Some of them only shifted their chin from a side to the other so as to subtly register that they did not go with the decision.

Case Study III: Two employees are trying to get one person aboard through illegal means. So the two employees, in addition with the person they wanted to 'help', decided to hold a meeting on how to go about it. What the person to be illegally employed just needs from the meeting is to receive instructions on how to go about it so as not to be detected by the management of the company. What seems to be a tug of war now is that the two employees cannot agree on the strategies to adopt. At the end, Employee A seems to overpower Employee B. B, not satisfied with their conclusion, shifted his chin from one side to the other.

14.11. Mustache or Beard Stroking

Generic Interpretations of the Concept

When you see a person stroke their beard or mustache, it is a way of pacifying stress. It is known as a great stress reliever. However, this can only be taken very seriously if it is done as a one-off sign. In other words, if it is done repetitively, then it is not worth being taken seriously and, as such, should be discarded. The reason being that I have noticed some people with facial hair who display this cue compulsively. Hence, it would be unfair to think those people are stressed.

If you suddenly see this cue in a person when you raise a topic and it persists as you discuss the topic in its depth, it means the person has issues with it; the topic is making them uncomfortable. Depending on the context, there are different causes of discomfort and you have to establish the reason and correct it, if need be. In law enforcement, this tells us that we have to investigate the topic deeper because the person has something, they are hiding about it. You may notice that the person is giving an evasive answer or avoiding eye contact as they display this cue. Although there is sole indicator of deception, but this points to the fact that the person is not cool with the discourse.

I need to mention that we must not leave out cultural context while trying to read meanings to the beard-stroking gesture. For example, I have observed that the act of beard stroking is common among men from the Middle East, especially when they talk while passing the time. In the same vein, a lot of men across the world see mustache or beard stroking as a soothing gesture as they pass the time of day. Each time you are interpreting the body gestures of people, you must pay attention to all these variables so as to ensure that you are not making a rash decision.

Scientific Explanations

Philip (2014) states that beard stroking signifies thought process and evaluation. When you are thinking of something and the solution seems to be far away, rubbing the beard can serve as a soothing action which will activate the creative region of your brain to think seamlessly. During the point of negotiation, people rub their mustache as a way of pacifying themselves after deep contemplation. Weighing the benefits of two similar things or trying to distinguish between things that looked exactly the same can be troubling, and we need to pacify ourselves in order not to break down. And beard stroking is one of the potent means people do this.

Philip notes that this cue was popularised by movies, cartoons, and shows, among others. In the old times, people used to believe that a chin scratcher is old and an embodiment of knowledge. Stroking the beards means one has started thinking but is yet to arrive at a desired conclusion.

Changing Minds also shares the same sentiment with Philip. The authors of the website opine that chin stroking is evidence that a person is thinking hard. This means they are trying to evaluate something and want to arrive at a decision that will be considered as being the best.

The website also notes that stroking the beard can be a mere preening gesture just to make a person appear more beautiful. That is, the person is trying to pass the message of 'I'm gorgeous' to those around them. Maybe, they have noticed a potential lover around and want to use the opportunity to market themselves.

However, Changing Minds rightly observes that 'beards and moustaches are sometimes controversial items, particularly in cultures where being clean-shaven is the norm. A beard may thus be an indicator of a nonconformist. A full beard is more likely to indicate a person who has no vanity needs and is confident and relaxed as they are. When the beard is shaped and neatly clipped, it may indicate a more vain and fussy person who is particular about how they appear and what they do.' It is good that we make these clarifications so that you would not just think the messages on beards and mustaches start and end with stroking. Some leave their beards unkempt and allow it to grow wild just to show their personality; they give less concern to what the external world thinks about them.

Practical Illustrations

Case Study I: A terrorist has been facing one of the best interrogators in town for the past five hours. Before now, he has been interrogated by three other people but appeared to be uncooperative. However, being under an interview session with this particular interrogator has made him realise that there is nothing done under the heavens that is hidden; what he had hidden from the three other interrogators have been unearthed. Now the interrogator is moving towards the case of mass shooting which he truly engineered but has been denying. He knows that if the interrogator should continue along the same path he had started, there is no hiding place for him. So he begins to feel stressed and even ordered for water at some point. As if that were not enough, he now strokes his unkempt beard as if something bit him there.

Case Study II: Mr Y has been suspecting the activities of his wife and there was a day that he even confronted her and informed her that things were gradually changing in their home, including the way she dresses and even the attention she gives him. However, she sternly denied every allegation, noting that her new role at work was time-consuming. She went ahead to accuse her husband that he was becoming insecure due to her new post and increased salary. So the husband let go of everything, especially when he did not have evidence to nail her. On a fateful day, the husband wanted to make use of her phone to send an urgent message. So she just pointed at it. As the husband was picking up the phone from the table, a message from one of her lovers came in. The husband just flashed it at her and asked her to defend herself but she just stroked her chin, looking for the best excuse to cover up everything.

Case Study III: Almost every teacher and student is complaining of the behaviour of Student B as being a bully. Almost every method known for taming such students have been applied to him but he just seems to be irresponsive. This serves as a source of concern to his class teacher because she bears the larger part of the issues. Feeling the resentment of others against him, Student B decides to pretend as if he has turned a new leaf. However, the teacher still places a close tab on him and one day, he tore the book of one of his mates. When the teacher asked him about it, he denied but when she brought the pieces out where B kept them, he was shocked and only stroked his chin without knowing what to say. He was dumbfounded and there was no explanation that could have changed anything at that given point.

14.12. Dimpling of Chin

Generic Interpretations of the Concept

People ordinarily think that a dimple is a thing of the cheeks alone, but during intense emotional moments, we do see it appear on our chin. Even though we may not pay attention to it, this does not change it from being real. When you see a dimple form on a person's chin, it is an indication that they are stressed. As I have always noted, stress can be caused by different things, and your surest way of being accurate is to ensure that you study the context in which an event is taking place. Physical stress due to long duration of work can cause a person to fag out.

Apart from physical causes, someone who is undertaking intellectual project that demands wide and extensive thinking may also experience stress. The furrowing of the forehead, squinting of the eyes and withdrawal of the whole face due to demotivation will also cause the chin to dimple. It is as if the chin wants to move out of public glare.

Another point where the chin forms a dimple is when we experience emotional turmoil. There are moments when we are down emotionally, and there is now how this can be hidden from those who sincerely care about us. The chin dimpling changes the look of the face and this may call people's attention to us. In the same vein, this cue is also seen in people when they are about to cry. When people are about to shed tears, the face gets broadened in a dull and uninspiring manner, which causes the sides of the chin to move inward before the eventual letting out of tears.

The act of forming dimples at the chin when we are experiencing negative emotions is true even for the most stoic of individuals.

Scientific Explanations

David Givens (2017) uses the belligerent chin of US president Donald Trump to explain this cue. He opines that the president experiences 'a chronic state of high emotional arousal' while he is in public. He explains further that the cue is always noticeable when he takes pictures at the White House. It reveals how he feels from a moment to the other. When made visible, a dimpled chin reveals a disagreeable state of mind. So when you ask the person any question during the period when they display this cue, the likely answer would be 'No'. This is different from a chin lift that is used in expressing superiority. A dimpled chin means the person does not buy your idea, and as such, you must look for a way to convince them. If you were lying to them, it is time to confess because they seem to have understood your intents before they materialise.

Leading Personality (2013) explains how a dimpled chin plays a crucial role in our daily activities, especially in the business world. The website notes that when you see a person with round dimple chin, it means they have interest in business along with discretion and caution. On the other hand, 'Square chin with dimples shows firmiess, stubborn and hot temper. The dimple always increases the ardor and affection.' Those who have natural dimples are said to be beautiful and adoring. Those who are temperamental will flare at every given mistake; it can be frustrating living with them.

Another body language expert, Jack Brown (2017) also uses Trump as his case studies in explaining the chin-dimpling body language. He notes that the gesture is only seen on him when he emerges as the president, as nothing traceable to such was observed in him while campaigning. Reading meanings to the chin-dimpling cue, Brown says that it expresses regret and bitterness. Apart from the dimpling of the chin, the corners of the mouth are also downturned. Sometimes, people refer to this cue as a *bitter smile*—this can be ironical to a lot of people as it does not assume any semblance of happiness or joy.

Brown explains further that if the chin dimpling is expressed through the front chin and accompanied by clenched jaw and forward movement of tissue just below the lower lip, it carries an element of frustration. Brown adds a caveat that 'In real-time, while people are displaying this expression, virtually everyone believes they are "pushing out" a slight smile (e.g., forcing a smile). However, if by some chance they could momentarily "freeze" their face—and immediately look in a mirror, they'd be very surprised to find their expressions are quite far from what they believed them to be.' This is universal human phenomenon. Any deviation from our emotional baseline distorts the entire facial appearance. Unfortunately, many people also become increasingly inaccurate in their interpretation of body cues at this point. In serious occasions such as law enforcement and business negotiations, this can have unimaginable disastrous effects on us. We simply need to read between the lines beyond surface-level cover-up of what is not.

Practical Illustrations

Case Study I: Mrs E's mother has taken ill for a while and she was taken to different medical facilities before she eventually gave up the ghost. Mrs E was optimistic throughout the period of her sickness that it was not yet time for her to die. The medical practitioners catering for Mrs E's mother also saw her passion and love for her mother. So when the old lady passed away, they had to devise a way to subtly inform her so that she will not break down in public. When the news eventually got to her by proxy, she held on to the news bearer in shock and shook him vigorously. Her front chin dimpled while she clenched her jaw all along. She was really saddened by the occurrence due to the love she had for her late mother.

Case Study II: A group of law enforcement officers have been combing a forest for days in search of terrorists. All the while, their search has not been productive, but they cannot retreat at that point without reaching the end of the vast forest. When they took a short break to eat, the leader of the team could be seen wearing the expression of frustration, with her chin dimpled and the lower lip bulging forward. He was disturbed that despite all their efforts, they have not recorded any success despite having intelligence report that the terrorists were there.

Case Study III: For some time now, SWQ Firefighters have been having issues with their equipment. Field agents have lodged complainants to the authorities but it seems those who are supposed to take action on that are putting up a lukewarm attitude. This is very disheartening because the firefighters end up exerting more energy on something that could have been done easily. This was the issue that the field agents were discussing when a case of fire outbreak was alerted. Firefighter RG while rushing into the vehicle dimpled his chin and looked pale. This was an expression of frustration and similar expression was seen on the faces of his colleagues.

14.13. Quivering of Chin Muscles

Generic Interpretations of the Concept

When the chin muscle suddenly quivers, it is an indication of negativity. It is a subconscious gesture that appears and disappears in the twinkle of an eye. David Givens explains that the mentalis muscle—the muscle that covers the chin and brings about skin quivering—is one of the facial muscles that aptly capture our emotional feelings per time. This means that if we can pay careful attention to its movement, we will get to know people's feelings better. In fact, there are times that the chin displays emotional turmoil even before the eyes are put into action. We rarely get to know this because we focus on only the eyes while important tells are being let out at other parts of the face.

Having said that, what are the messages that the sudden muscle quivering may be passing across? First, it may be an indication of fear. The feeling of fear can be triggered by either what we see physically or a frightening thought. For instance, if you reflect on the last time you were attacked by armed robbers, the feelings will play back as if it were happening real. This is more truthful if you are at the exact spot where you were robbed. So the muscle quivers as if you were experiencing the same emotion.

In the same vein, anxiety may arouse this cue in a person. If you are preparing for an arduous task and the feeling of failure sets in once in a while, this may be expressed through the quivering of the chin muscles. The reason the chin seems to be involved in most intellectual or brain activities is that it is widely regarded as the seat of wisdom. So it has direct connection with the brain. You may also observe this cue in a person that is apprehensive; exercising inordinate fear charges all the facial muscles into quick movement in form of shivering. I have also noticed this gesture in those who are worried about something. When the person's chin muscles quiver, it means they did not foresee a positive outcome about that particular incident. Sometimes, this behaviour may serve as prelude for those who are about to cry. Whenever you see this, be sure that the person is stressed and they are feeling negative about a concept.

Scientific Explanations

When the chin muscle quivers, it is medically referred to as tremor. *Tremor* is defined as 'involuntary, somewhat rhythmic, muscle contraction and relaxation involving oscillations or twitching movements of one or more body parts' (DMD 2019). It is the most common of all involuntary movements and can affect the hands, arms, eyes, face, head, vocal folds, trunk, and legs. Most tremors occur in the hands. Medical experts affirm that the most common cause of tremor is fear. Hence, this seems to be in line with our point. When the chin muscle quivers, it is an indication that there is a disorder in the part of the brain controlling its operation. Tremors can be an indication of hypoglycemia, along with palpitations, sweating, and anxiety. Tremor can also be caused by lack of sleep, lack of vitamins, or increased stress (Jim and Folk 2017). If the chin-muscle quivering is medically induced, there is no need of read meanings to it—it is an involuntary action caused by a brain disorder and not the person's will or an emotion they are going through.

Joe Navarro (2011), while debunking the myths of microexpressions, explains that the chin-muscle quivering is done as a means of dealing with tension in the body. Other clustering behaviours mentioned by the former FBI agent are uncontrollable blinking, thrusting of the jaw forward, uncontrollable trembling of the eyes, tongue biting, repetitive touching of the eyelid or nose to pacify the body, and jaw displacement to the sides. Navarro explains further that apart from the fact that these behaviours are repetitive, they may also increase under severe stress and can become indescribably fast. Incidentally, repetitive behaviours are soothing acts, and that explains the reason we display them in the first instance. It has been established that the brain benefits from the repetitive muscular movement which serves as a form of pacification to it. However, this can end up being pathological. Hence, it should be displayed within the right means.

Westside Toastmasters (2019) also discusses this cue briefly while explaining the reason it is difficult to tell lies. The reason people find it difficult to lie is that the subconscious mind acts independently of our verbal deceptions while the body gives us away. Hence, those who rarely tell lies can be fished out in no time. For instance, when people tell lies, they can deliberately suppress their major expressions which can give them out but have no power over the microexpressions. Flushed cheeks, dilation, contraction of the pupils, sweating, increased eye-blinking rate and chin-muscle quivering are some of the microexpressions that tell the other person that you are stressed.

Practical Illustrations

Case Study I: Ms T is in her third year in the medical school. Even though she likes medicine as a profession, she hates seeing blood but as a student, she needs to be taught every aspect of the course before she would later focus on a field later in life. She would be going to the theatre for the first time today. So the course tutor needs to address them on what they need to do when they get there. When she heard that they needed to be covered properly because they would be dealing directly with blood, her chin muscle quivered. Her mate who noticed this asked her what was the cause of her fear. The observant mate was able to decode fear in her face because she paid attention to the sudden change of emotions on T's face when the announcement was made.

Case Study II: TY is the one representing his school in a debating competition. He has survived the first two stages, and now, he is preparing for the regional level which will qualify him for the final stage at the national level. While catching the clip of his performance in the last edition, he was gripped with fear by the performance of his opponents. At this point, his chin muscles could be seen quivering. That is, he was afraid of his would-be opponents and their anticipated superb performance at the national level.

Case Study III: Smuggler ER was trying to relax at home when he turned on his television set and the station he tuned in to was showing a movie on the effects of smuggling and what law enforcement agents were doing to curb this menace. There was a scene where everything became violent, and some of the smugglers were eventually killed. At this point, ER was gripped with fear and his chin muscles quivered as if he had a cold. He eventually switched off the television set and moved into the inner room. He had a disturbing dream that night due to what he saw in the documentary.

14.14. Chin Touching Shoulder

Generic Interpretations of the Concept

Although this cue is rare, people do display it when the need arises. Chin to shoulder gesture is when a person places their chin on the edge of their shoulder, just like children will do. When you see this glaring gesture, it means something is amiss and the person does not have power over such thing. It is as if they were submitting themselves to that occasion. Those who display this cue usually look demure. This may be emotional blackmail engineered to draw pity from you so that you neglect the main issue at hand and focus on their feelings. My decades of experience in the law enforcement has exposed me to many things I could not have imagined at any point in my life; humans can be wickedly creative. After perpetrating evil and they discover that there is probably nothing they can do to get out of the problem they intentionally created, they would manipulate ways to refocus your attention and appeal to your weak point.

You should give special attention to this when a person does it while answering a question; it indicates their reluctance to talk. It means they are experiencing great difficulty discussing the subject matter you have brought before them. Most probably, the person is loaded with some pieces of information which they do not wish to reveal. If the person knows that saying such thing will end up haunting them, they will look for every manipulative means to dodge the issue. Also, I have seen this time without number in the interview room. This may be irritating to you but the person is passing a subtle message that they are not willing to talk much over the issue you are pestering them on. Most times, they face the direction of the door while displaying this cue and avoid eye contact with you. All these are reinforcements that they are not willing to continue with the discourse.

Scientific Explanations

Danielle Ann (2019) speaks clearly on the need to understand the meaning of touch before trying to rationalise the meaning. In order to have a full understanding of any kind of touch, you must first pay attention to location, pressure applied and duration it takes to occur. Beyond that, you need to pay attention to the context of how the touch should ideally be perceived. For instance, there is a difference between intrapersonal and interpersonal touch. The former is largely attributed to self-pacification while the latter may be a means of showing affection or establishing familiarity with strangers, depending on the context. However, the chin to shoulder cue as captured here is mainly focused on the former. Hence, it can be regarded as a way of dealing with stress.

Ann further explains that you also need to pay attention to some other ways in which the person acts and the manner of their speech in order to be able to strongly affirm what the gesture means. She states that if the chin is rested on another person's shoulders, it is meant to express comfort and familiarity, the urge to be closer and demand for affection. But if the person decides to do the gesture to themselves, it means seeking for self-comfort in a stressful or uncomfortable circumstance.

Westside Toastmasters makes it known that this behaviour is 'an unconscious outward reflection of our inner feelings.' That is, it reveals that the person craves for warmth from within and is being displayed through the outward means. Since the chin is aware that the hand is the most potent pacifying tool, so it defies all odds to move towards it at all cost, hence, touching the shoulder, being the closest portion.

Practical Illustrations

Case Study I: GH has been warned by her mother that she should not consume anything in the house which she does not know the source. In other words, she should always ask before taking anything or regarding such as her exclusive right. The aim is to discipline her so that she does not develop habit of covetousness. This seems to be working for some time, but there are traces that she still steals once in a while. In order to be sure that GH is really behind the once-in-a-while disappearance of items in the house, her mother intentionally placed her best food in the refrigerator and went out, knowing fully well that GH was coming back before her. Expectedly, GH consumed the food without bothering to seek her parents' opinion. When the mother returned, she first headed the refrigerator stand and discovered that food had vanished. When she asked what happened to the item she kept in the fridge, GH first feigned ignorance, asking how the item was dropped there. When she saw the seriousness on her mother's face, she subconsciously placed her chin on her shoulder as if she were dejected by an incident.

Case Study II: A man was arrested in a case connected to the death of his younger brother, whom they have always lived together. Ordinarily, no one would believe the man was connected to the death of his brother due to the closeness they maintained while the latter was on earth. So they only believed that the apprehension was to get statement from him. Unknowingly, they were expecting a huge sum of money as gain over a group project, but the man thought his brother should not have a portion in it. So he poisoned him at a restaurant so that the death would not be traced to him. However, few weeks after professionals handled the case, they were able to link it with the man 'fighting the course of his brother'. During investigation, he was asked what transpired between the moment his brother went to ease himself and returned to his seat. At first, he denied paying attention to the happenings around. When perused further, he contradicted himself by saying that he was not with him at the said time. When he discovered that the interrogator was not ready to let go on that subject matter, he placed his chin on his shoulder and looked away from the direction of the interrogator. He was dejected that he could not manoeuvre his way in that context.

Case Study III: Friends Y and Z have been together since their childhood. However, Y seems to be more fortunate as he is rich and well-known. Whenever Z is in need, Y is the go-to person. Recently, Friend Y has seen his friend's behaviour as being frustrating and uncalled for. While he has introduced him to many businesses, Z seems to be comfortable with just taking from his friend without rendering any service. A way Y has devised to run away from the troubles of Z is to avoid him these days. However, Z intentionally booked an appointment with him on a Sunday under the guise of wanting to see him for an important matter. On getting there, the matter was money-related. As Z was speaking, Y unconsciously placed his chin on his shoulder and looked away. This means he was not pleased with the discussion—it got him irritated.

14.15. Chin Pointing

Generic Interpretations of the Concept

There are various ways in which people point, depending on the situation they find themselves. Sometimes, pointing with the finger seems odd and may expose your intentions in a way you have not intended it. So the chin becomes a perfect replacement, through which the direction pointed at is subtly done. This behaviour is displayed by pointing the chin to any direction we want our co-interlocutor to focus their attention to. During this process, the neck is well stretched out so as to make the message resounding. To cover up what they are trying to say, the person may use the space between their index finger and thumb to brush off their chin starting from the neck area. So the other party may be deceived that their chin is itching and they needed to scratch it.

So the basic message the chin-pointing gesture does is to redirect the attention of people to a particular thing. If the chin is pointed at the door, the person is trying to tell you that they want to have their exit. You may also check the direction of their feet so as to establish the accuracy of your guess. In a conference room, if it points at the direction of a specific person, it means the person displaying the cue probably has issues with the focused person. Let me add that this gesture can be used for both positive and negative occasions. So you need to find out the underlying cause of their action before you read meanings to it.

This cue is noticeable in many parts of the world. Particularly, it is used throughout the Caribbean, in some areas in Spain, in Latin America, in the Middle East, and even in some American settlements. For each of these places, you need to know the ethnic peculiarity attached to the cue.

Scientific Explanations

Inspiring Leadership Now (2018) explains the concept of chin pointing. As earlier stated, the platform shares the same sentiment with me that the direction in which the chin is pointed at matters a lot. For instance, it notes that when it points to the ground, it is an indication that the person is stressed. It may also mean they are vulnerable or meek. This is polar opposite to the person who points it up to show confidence, power, and superiority. Taking note of the direction helps in solving the problem halfway. However, some people may point the chin down to show they are fed up with a situation. Just cast your mind back to those long, uneventful meetings to understand how this plays out. People question the rationale of being kept back at a meeting that is not productive. So the head pointing down may also express pretty boredom. It means the person is deriving more interest in objects than what the other person is saying.

Bob Whipple (2019) also makes his point along the same line as explained above. He aptly submits that 'jutting the chin in a specific direction is a kind of pointing motion that directs other people where you want them to look. It is a way to acknowledge a transfer of attention. The chin is raised in a quick jerking motion. This is less obvious than pointing with a finger, and it is less susceptible to being interpreted as a hostile gesture.' In some cultures of the world, if you point with the finger, especially at an elderly person or a superior, it would be taken as a sign of disrespect. So people now subconsciously make use of their chin if there is need for that.

Changing Minds also sheds light on this cue by saying, 'The chin can be used as a subtle pointing device and a small flick of the head may give a small signal that only people in the know are likely to notice.' The platform also backs up the viewpoint of Whipple that pointing with the finger can be threatening, and as such, people may prefer doing it briefly with the chin. In some contexts, this may be interpreted as an insult.

In what seems like a consensus among experts in the field, Study Body Language (SBL) says also that orienting with the head has a similar meaning with pointing. Where a person is headed is literally where they want to be.

Practical Illustrations

Case Study I: Mr Y is a public official but was accused of corruption which later led to his arrest. Before his arrest, the oppositions have said that the president and anti-graft agencies kept mum about the issue because Mr Y was used as an instrument by the number one citizen, not knowing that there were investigations going on underground. After his arrest, senior officials in the agency swung into action so as to be able to hear him and charge him to court. Mr Y had erroneously thought the interrogation would be like the interviews he had always featured in as a public office holder where the journalists would be treating him like a demigod; when the officials started throwing questions at him, he began to sweat excessively. At some point, he stretched out his chin as if he wanted to talk and pointed it at the door. Also, his feet were pointed at the same direction. It was a clue that he wanted to be out of the place.

Case Study II: Mrs TR was supposed to be out for an occasion with her friends. She was actually the one delaying her friends, but her husband did not want her to go. So he demanded that they settle an issue relating to their welfare before she leaves. After that, her child also needed her attention to get something done. Then, the husband came calling again before she was done with her daughter. She began to frown her face but was still doing the bidding of her family members. When she checked the time, she discovered that she was an hour late. At this point, she stood up and asked her husband to summarise his speech and keep it until she returned home. While saying this, her feet had turned to the door already while her chin faced the same direction. She was impatient and wanted to dash out of the home as soon as possible.

Case Study III: Mr IZ is an airline officer but recently, he has been facing some issues on a personal level which seems to be affecting his professional calling. Although he tries to make things up so that his colleagues will not notice but some of them have observed that he isn't as productive as before. One day, a case arose where his expertise was really needed. He pretended to be involved in it, but his feet and chin were pointing at the door. He truly wanted to be home because he received a call almost immediately after the occurrence of the case in office that his wife had difficulties in breathing.

CHAPTER 15

The Face

Now we want to talk of the entire face as an entity and see how far we can decode messages from it. I understand that research states that there are thousands of emotions that can be expressed through the muscles of the face. While it will amount to a self-deceit to try considering all those emotions, we will only consider some select gestures and how they feature in our daily transactions. Although we have covered all the individual portions of the face, some behaviours are accurately understood when taken as a whole. The first two places that draw our attention on people's faces are the eyes and the mouth. That is why I earlier said at some point in this book that if the eyes are considered as the windows to the soul, the mouth can be regarded as the door to the soul. However, this is not to downplay the essence of other facial parts, as you can see that we have expatiated on them all and the messages each bear in their respective areas.

The reason we focus on the eyes and mouth subconsciously when we look at a person is that they are an embodiment of countless messages. As our pattern has always been, let's have a biological view of the concept before breaking it down in sociological precepts.

The editors of *Encyclopaedia Britannica* define *face* as 'the front part of the head that, in vertebrates, houses the sense organs of vision and smell as well as the mouth and jaws. In humans it extends from the forehead to the chin.' To have a better understanding of the structure of the face, Dictionary.com divides it into five basic parts:

- The *forehead*, comprising the skin beneath the hairline, bordered laterally by the temples and inferiorly by eyebrows and ears
- The *eyes*, sitting in the orbit and protected by eyelids and eyelashes
- The distinctive human *nose* shape, nostrils, and nasal septum
- The *cheeks*, covering the maxilla and mandibula (or jaw), the extremity of which is the chin
- The *mouth*, with the upper lip divided by the philtrum, sometimes revealing the teeth.

We cannot downplay the role of facial appearance in human recognition and effective communication. Our facial muscles allow us to express the emotions we are feeling per time. In an article published on Face-and-Emotion.com (2011), it was revealed that 'The face is itself a highly sensitive region of the human body and its expression may change when the brain is stimulated by any of the many human senses, such as touch, temperature, smell, taste, hearing, movement, hunger, or visual stimuli.'

During the course of evolution from the prehuman *Australopithecus* to modern humans (*Homo sapiens*), the face became smaller in relation to the overall size of the head. While brain and braincase (cranium) tripled in volume, the jaws became shorter and the teeth simpler in form and smaller in size. In consequence, the face receded beneath the forehead. Thus, the modern human face exhibits an essentially vertical profile, in marked contrast to the protruding facial muzzle of the gorilla, the chimpanzee, and to a lesser extent, extinct hominids. The recession of the tooth-bearing portion of the jaws beneath the forehead left two distinctively human features: a prominent, projecting nose and a clearly defined chin (*Encyclopaedia Britannica* 2019).

What best distinguishes us as humans is the face. The shape of the face is influenced by the bone-structure of the skull, and each face is unique through the anatomical variation present in the bones of the viscerocranium (and neurocranium) (Moore et al. 2010). Facial shape is an important determinant of beauty, particularly facial symmetry.

As noted earlier, the face plays a central role in the expression of emotion whether consciously or unconsciously. A frown denotes disapproval; a smile usually means someone is pleased. Being able to read emotion in another's face is 'the fundamental basis for empathy and the ability to interpret a person's reactions and predict the probability of ensuing behaviors'. One study used the Multimodal Emotion Recognition Test to attempt to determine how to measure emotion. This research aimed at using a measuring device to accomplish what people do so easily everyday: read emotion in a face (Banziger 2009).

The muscles of the face play a prominent role in the expression of emotion and vary among different individuals, giving rise to additional diversity in expression and facial features (Braus 1921).

People are also relatively good at determining if a smile is real or fake. A recent study looked at individuals judging forced and genuine smiles. While young and elderly participants equally could tell the difference for smiling young people, the 'older adult participants outperformed young adult participants in distinguishing between posed and spontaneous smiles'. This suggests that with experience and age, we become more accurate at perceiving true emotions across various age groups (Murphy et al. 2010).

Talking about perception and recognition of the face, gestalt psychologists theorise that a face is not merely a set of facial features, but is rather something meaningful in its form. This is consistent with the gestalt theory that an image is seen in its entirety, not by its individual parts. According to Gary L. Allen, people adapted to respond more to faces during evolution as the natural result of being a social species. Allen suggests that the purpose of recognising faces has its roots in the 'parent-infant attraction, a quick and low-effort means by which parents and infants form an internal representation of each other, reducing the likelihood that the parent will abandon his or her offspring because of recognition failure' (Allen 2006).

Research has indicated that certain areas of the brain respond particularly well to faces. The fusiform face area, within the fusiform gyrus, is activated by faces, and it is activated differently for shy and social people. A study confirmed that 'when viewing images of strangers, shy adults exhibited significantly less activation in the fusiform gyri than did social adults' (Beaton et al. 2009). These days, cosmetic surgery can be used to alter facial appearance. Many disfigured individuals do go for total facial transplant.

15.1. Face Avoidance

Generic Interpretations of the Concept

At some point or another, we have had reasons to intentionally avoid eye contact with people and we will still do more of it as long as we live. This is done for variety of reasons. Sometimes, it may be positive but it is mostly inspired by negative tendencies. For instance, some cultures avoid direct eye contact with the elderly ones or superior figures. In that sense, this is positive and the person is trying to show him/herself as a conformist. Also, when you are thinking of an answer to an issue and you think looking into the face of the other person will serve as distraction to you, you may have to avoid their face. Furthermore, even cultures that allow eye contact do not approve staring at the other person. So as a hallmark of respect, you may decide not to look into the face of a stranger to give them the boldness and comfort they need to socialise and feel among.

On the other hand, the face avoidance is mainly used to connote that there is an issue between people. Even if those people are in their immediate proximity, they will still try not to look into the face of each other. This is seen when there is guilty knowledge with one of the parties. Having been to court countless times, I have noticed this between suspects and victims. The suspect has the unconscious belief that when he looks into the eyes of the victim, they may not be able to deny their wrongdoing; their conscience will prick them. In the same vein, you will notice face avoidance between couples during contentious and tense divorce proceedings. Definitely, if they should look into the eyes of each other, one may have to succumb for the other.

The avoidance is always obvious because it is quick and sharp. That is once the person who is trying to avoid the other person discovers that they are about to make a contact, he will quickly look to the other side. Also, they will become stiff by not moving their eyes about so that it would not make unwanted contact. If you see a person who intentionally dislodges eye contact and looks at a direction not connected to what is being said, it means there are issues.

Scientific Illustrations

Christopher Philip (2014) says face avoidance is the purposeful avoidance to make eye contact with another person. The body language expert gives a one-sentence description of face evasion: a person wants to avoid being called upon or they want to create an air of superiority. In a way, face avoidance can be powerful when employed in the right context. If someone wants to show their disdain for another person, they may simply ignore their presence by looking at the other side. Also, when people avoid eye contact, it makes them disappear in the sense that a speaker may not invite them to answer a question or make contributions.

On a general note, when there is face avoidance, it means the person submitting to the will of another person and feeling uncomfortable. When you avert the eyes, it plays two key roles—it makes you avoid conflict with the other party or makes you demonstrate your power over the person. Philip explains further that 'eye aversion is used to prevent others from resorting to an attack response and prevents others from seeing us as a threat. Subordinates commonly avoid eye contact with dominant individuals to indicate submission and respect. Eyes might wander to avoid being reprimanded. Eyes that avoid can serve to "flee" from an encounter, a protective response, as a person subconsciously tries to make distance between himself and his aggressor.'

This is normally seen in minor arguments where the eyes are quickly withdrawn to show that the person is not interested in continuing with the argument. The verbal translation given by Philip for this cue is 'I don't want to cause any more problems for myself, so I'm going to avoid making eye contact with other more dominant people so I don't draw attention and provoke people into attacking.'

Meghan Olsgard (2019) provides eight reasons why people may avoid eye contact. He mentions social anxiety as one of the major causes. Lack of interest in what is being said, show of love, lack of physical attraction, low self-esteem, trying to hide something from the other person and stress are the other reasons Olsgard gave as being responsible for face avoidance.

Practical Illustrations

Case Study I: While Mrs O was teaching, one of her pupils was playing with a paper airplane. Because she did not want to distract herself from the lecture, she communicated with him through eye contact, but he seemed to be deviant. At the end of the day, he eventually threw the paper airplane. Immediately after that, he buried his head in his desk, looking shameful and pitiable. Having got this message, the teacher decided to temper justice with mercy by handling him with ease. That is, the teacher discovered that the boy was remorseful already through his non-verbal gesture and decided not to mete out greater punishment on him.

Case Study II: Mr and Mrs HK went to bed angry; they had arguments over some domestic issues that could have been settled with patience which both of them appear to be lacking. Even though they slept beside each other, none of them behaved as if the other were in existence. Ordinarily, one would think that they would get over it the next morning but it seemed as though the fight had just kicked off; while preparing for work the next morning, they avoided facial contact with each other till they left the home. This means they were not ready to bow to each other, and this would make the fight to linger on.

Case Study III: Mr R is a known womaniser at the workplace, and that is what every new female employee is told on arrival. Not knowing that his illicit ways have been revealed to Ms E, who just secured appointment with his firm, he began to seduce her the very first week she started work. Since she was not game, she intentionally looked at the ground so as not to have a direct contact with him. She wasn't ready to give in to something she was not interested in, and this was aptly communicated through her non-verbal gesture of facial avoidance.

Case Study IV: Mr AD is a human smuggler who is on the wanted list of law enforcement agents but he has managed to dodge them through multiple identities. One day, he was at a public event which also had some law enforcement officers in attendance. Mr AD was really free at the event as he was interacting with people across board but when he heard that there was a law enforcement agent at a certain table, he immediately disconnected himself from looking at the direction of that table. He became evidently uncomfortable and had to take his leave before time due to fear of the unknown. In other words, he was afraid that the law enforcement official might later approach him and fish out his bad deeds.

15.2. Face Blocking

Generic Interpretations of the Concept

Even though this seems childish, the fact is that it occurs in adults from time to time. Face blocking is the act of placing the elbows on the table while hands are used to block the eyes as a way of denying the other person the opportunity to have a full view of their face. The face is central to understanding the emotions of people and when you see people block it, it means there are real issues. When you see a person block their face, they will not laugh or look cheerful because the emotions they are expressing is negative.

Probably, the person does not like what is being discussed and, as such, showing their disdain for the concept and the person narrating it. It is as if they do not want the negative idea to get into their eyes, so they try to block it by interlocking the hands and placing same on their face. This is very symbolic. Note that even blind children perform this task when they perceive something disdainful.

This may also be done as a show of lack of confidence. When asked a question which they think they have no proper grasp on, instead of them confessing verbally, they will use their hands to play over the face and may eventually end up speaking into them instead of addressing the person who asked the question.

In essence, this may be considered as a form of insulation due to the stress they are going through. When people feel uncomfortable with what is being asked, instead of them giving in freely to the threatening situation, they will instead employ their hands to massage the facial muscles as a way of dealing with the stress. Hence, the face-blocking gesture may be considered as an act of self-pacifying.

Further, when the eyes cover the face, this serves as a psychological barrier, blocking every thought or opinion by any other person. In the same vein, it suppresses incoming thoughts from getting out of the body. When a person is reluctant to unveil the face, this means there is a difficulty they are going through.

Scientific Explanations

When the hands cover the face, it is referred to as 'eye-blocking behaviour'. Philip (2013) explains that people display this cue when they do not like what they see or feel threatened by a situation. He gives the example of his wife who is fond of blocking her face and ear when the preview of horror movies suddenly appears on the television. This shows that she does not like it. While this gesture is being displayed, you will notice that the pupils will also constrict. This helps in emphasising the message that the person is not pleased with what they are seeing.

Face blocking has the ability to replicate itself in many other ways too. For instance, when you are having a meeting at a restaurant, there are some restaurants that place big centrepieces at the middle of the table. You may not shift it away. So you leaving it there may serve as a means of face-blocking tool for some of your employees or whoever you might have gone there with.

'Eye squinting or covering can be related back to a baseline to produce predictive powers. For example, while questioning someone about theft or vandalism, or any other event that brings back images that someone wishes not to recall, note when eyes become constricted. This will tell you which aspects of your recount makes them most uncomfortable. When vital information is struck, eye blocking in one form or another will surface. From there, it will be up to you to deduce the exact reason for eye blocking' (Philip 2013).

While explaining the face-blocking cue, IndiaBIX tries to reel out different ways in which it is done. For instance, some may guard their mouth, some may touch the nose, some may rub the eyes or ears while others may scratch the neck. Whichever way through which it comes, it distorts the appearance of the face and passes a psychological message of discomfort to the other person. The platform notes that these subtle cues can be used by people to cover up their deceit or in reaction to them. When people tell lies and they are not feeling comfortable about it, they may scratch the back of the neck. When you see the person rubbing the eyes vigorously, it may be an attempt to rub off their deceit or to block out doubts or lies. Note that if the discomfort appears bigger than what the self-pacifying gesture of face-blocking cue can achieve, they will look away—avoid the other person's face. They may even look at the ground or fix their gaze on the ceiling. What is important is that you understand the context of every behaviour so that it can be easy for you to deal with.

Practical Illustrations

Case Study I: Mr J is one of the conservative Christians that still apply their religious philosophy on everything they do; he likes people to appear natural without making use of any form of adornment. On the other hand, Ms G is someone who enjoys using make-up so as to look elegant and more charming whenever she is going for an occasion. So when she was sent by her company to deliver some documents to Mr J in his office, as she entered, J wore a frown. After the exchange of greeting, the man used his hand to rub his eyes continuously as he went through the documents as if he had pains in the eyes. This was an unconscious way for the conservative man to block his face from the 'abomination'.

Case Study II: Every Wednesday, Mrs U, the literature teacher at GHX School, has made it a habit to engage her students in open discourse so as to sharpen their reasoning and make them good communicators. While many of the students long for the day to come, those who are unprepared also pray that Tuesday stands still. On this Wednesday, Mrs U decides to ask the students about a novel which they all appear to know, but one seems to be ignorant of their discussions. So any time U's attention goes to her, she places her hands on her face as if she were looking for something. This was a stylish way of avoiding the teacher.

Case Study III: I saw a woman at a restaurant, and her look was suspicious. Even though I went with someone else, I had to focus on the suspicious woman. The person I went with almost took it against me, but I reminded her of the nature of my work, and she understood. The woman who was the subject of my attention also noticed that I was looking at her, and whenever my eyes were going to her direction, she would use her hands to block her face by placing her arms on her table. Six months after that encounter, she was arrested for impersonation. Her evil deeds had always made her avoid eye contact with people she ordinarily considered as 'enemies'.

15.3. Shielding of Face

Generic Interpretations of the Concept

Even though some people intentionally commit crimes and do things that can bring their names into disrepute, when the time comes to be shamed, they do everything within their means to evade the process of justice. This explains the reason people cup their hands to cover their face as a result of going through stress. The face-shielding gesture gives people the opportunity to hide their face so that others do not get to see how they feel during intense emotional moments. Apart from hands, some people may also use objects to cover their eyes just to serve the same purpose. They understand that making use of articles such as handkerchief achieves their purpose in a subtler way considered with the use of hands.

What makes this cue reliable is that I have witnessed it around the world. It shows that the person is embarrassed and does not want you to see their face. Feeling of shame makes people squint and look regretful, which may be giving them out that they are actually guilty of the issue being discussed. In the same vein, being anxious or apprehensive may make people display this cue. The entire facial orientation changes due to anxiety and apprehension which makes people feel uncomfortable. If the person wants to use stress as an emotional blackmail, they may not even bother to shield their face but if they want to keep it away from public glare, then, it can be shielded.

Fear of the unknown is another factor that has always led people to display this behaviour. When we arrest people and they are being paraded into the waiting police car, I have always observed this behaviour in them. You will think they are trying to wipe of their sweat with a piece of cloth or their finger but it is to cover the face because of fear that has taken over them. It is important that you pay attention to all these so that your investigation can be made easy.

Scientific Explanations

Philip (2013) notes that when the face is shielded, the eyes are constricted and squinted. This is regarded as one of the few eye-blocking behaviours designed to hide negative emotions. The expert notes that this is part of the brain's response to negative stimuli. That is, we subconsciously battle with negative emotions in various ways. When the face is shielded, it makes the person unattractive and their co-interlocutor finds it difficult to understand them. In situations such as law enforcement where it is cogent to take their facial look of the person into consideration, you may have to wait till the person takes off their hands so that you continue with the process.

Navarro (2009) also expounds on this process while discussing the body language of the eyes. He notes that the face-shielding gesture is naturally hardwired in us that you even notice it in children who are born blind. This is to explain the power of non-verbal communication in our world. A part of our brain has learnt to adapt to stress, and this has helped us in survival over the years.

Navarro explains further that face covering is one of the obvious non-verbal gestures that we display. When are emotionally struggling, troubled, or frustrated with something, we may cover our face as a way of reacting to it. You can pay attention to those close to you—see how they behave whenever they are witnessing negative emotions. Some of them may even hiss to show their open disdain for the concept or emotion they are witnessing. It does not matter for how long you have been together with person, people slouch in their seat and cover their face with their hands, thinking of the way out of their impasse or may serve as a cue of regret. Also, the blink rate of a person shielding their face may increase. This is often seen with liars and those undergoing stress.

Practical Illustrations

Case Study I: Mr G is an employee with one of the leading companies in town that treat their workforce well. But recently, he is walking with people who have introduced him to drugs and influenced him negatively. He now spends most of his income on things that do not really matter. He has abandoned his childhood friends and see them as those who do not understand life. His latest spree is robbing people and places at every given opportunity. Unfortunately for him, in one of their operations, he was eventually nabbed. While being taken to the police car, he used his hands to cover his face as a show of his embarrassment for the unfortunate act he was met perpetrating.

Case Study II: M was ushered into the interview room where the panellists were waiting for him to be interrogated on a criminal case. He had thought the interrogations would be handled by young or junior officials, only for him to meet the most senior and experienced officials with their grey hair on seat. He could not even withstand their look alone, remembering when he first met one of the panellists in the same context some few years ago. Before taking his seat, he placed his hand on his forehead as he was checking his temperature due to mild headache. This was due to the fear he was undergoing.

Case Study III: The general manager of GTC was addressing his senior employees in a meeting. He had given them some assignments to carry out in the previous meeting and was expecting a feedback. Since the meeting was not structured in any way, he took the feedback as he discusses related issues. One of the employees did not do what he was asked to do. Every one of them knows the manager for being mean on people who fail in their portfolio. However, his albatross is that he can be too forgetful. So the defaulting employee used his hand to shield his face as a way of not maintaining eye contact with the manager so that he would not be called upon. It was a perfect trick for him to psychologically make the manager not to think along his direction.

15.4. Facial Emotional Asymmetry

Generic Interpretations of the Concept

One thing we must be appreciative of this age is that knowledge increases on a daily basis. That is, more in-depth studies are being carried out in different fields which make us have a better grasp of our immediate environment. One of the areas in which this paradigm shift has affected us in the realm of non-verbal communication. It has been recently discovered that we can communicate multiple emotions at a time. Some decades ago, some people do not believe that we can express multiple sentiments at a time. So we had always looked for one while we neglected the others.

When you focus on the face, you can see a person who is struggling with multiple emotions internally. For instance, the face can sneer to show contempt and at the same time grimace to display social smile. This contradiction shows the internal struggles that the person is undergoing. It means that even though they do not like what they are seeing, for the sake of social acceptance, they consider it appropriate to smile. We have all had a reason or another to do this just because we think that expressing our stand on the issue can be painful to the person concerned, so we smile socially to dance to the tone of their music.

The fact that two contradictory emotions show up on the face simultaneously is evidence that there is an internal competition which brings about the 'leakages' noticeable on the face.

From the observations I have made so far, the left side of the face—the right side of the person you are facing—tends to give more accurate portrayal of negative emotions. You may watch it closely as from now so as to ascertain if my sentiment is right or wrong. *Emotional chirality* is the ability of the face to demonstrate opposing emotions on different halves.

Scientific Explanations

Navarro (2016) gives a detailed explanation of this cue. According to him, our face is much asymmetrical when resting. He notes that when both sides of the face do not express the same emotion, they end up betraying our sentiments. Explaining how we display true emotions, Navarro submits, 'When we smile, a genuine happy smile, there will be symmetry of emotion on the face even though our faces are not in and of themselves symmetrical. So even though both sides are slightly different, true emotions will be seen equally across both sides of the face—in essence emotional symmetry. In other words, when we are either truly angry or truly happy, both sides of the face reflect that emotion.' This is clear and concise.

On the other hand, when we simultaneously experience the same emotion or an attempt to hide an emotional feeling, the emotional asymmetry of the face betrays us. That is why in earlier referred to as emotional chirality. *Chirality* is a term that comes to us from the Greek language and is used to describe two objects that may appear identical, but when folded over on to themselves, they are not symmetrical (Navarro 2016).

Emotions such as fear, anxiety, animosity, and others freely appear on the face when we truly experience them. However, when we attempt to suppress these emotions, when there is an attempt to play on the intelligence of others on how we feel, or when there are issues we feel should not be expressed, most times, we see the emotion displayed on just a side of the face and not both sides. The fact that what you are seeing is a chiral emotional display, that should serve as a clue warning you that something is wrong somewhere (Navarro 2016).

It is pertinent to note that the chiral display is normally perceived through the subconscious means. Navarrro opines that 'when we see facial chirality as a result of multiple emotions, this lack of symmetry should make us more alert as to what is the cause for this behavior. Is there a substantive issue that is in conflict or is being suppressed?'

The former FBI agent warns that this emotional cue is not indicative of deception and should not be taken as that. The reason is that this emotional displayed has been witnessed in different instances outside of deception. For instance, if an abusive husband is being led away in handcuffs and the wife wears both the feelings of relief and fear, there is no iota of deception in this—it is only her feeling as it relates to the issue at hand. You may also see it where someone is tendering a verbal apology for a wrongdoing and a part of the face appears fake. I will emphasise on this under the 'Practical Illustrations' segment.

Martin Silvertant (2017) also shares the same view with Navarro. He goes ahead to share the story of one Drew Peterson who shares his image on Twitter, narrating his own account when he was accused of child abuse. He states that while a side of the face looks as if he were begging, the other looks as if he were scared. This hints that there is something fishy about his account of innocence.

Something about the emotional asymmetry of the face is that even if we fail to take conscious note of it, our subconscious mind is always aware that something has gone wrong with a person. This means that if we pay keen attention to the emotional display of people, we will not be easily deceived.

Practical Illustrations

Case Study I: Child M was supposed to wash the dish her mother left behind before going out and getting some other chores done before heading to the study to do her homework. However, she was engrossed in seeing movies that she did not end up doing any of the tasks till the return of her mother seven hours after she went out. Her mother was really annoyed by her disobedient act and planned meting out appropriate punishment on her. Seeing the anger on her mother's face, she went to tender a verbal apology with one side of her face looking unapologetic while the other was looking as if she were begging. This means that in the truest sense, she felt no remorse over her action.

Case Study II: Mr TC is notorious for defaulting in all the duties given to him. Due to that, his colleagues would protest hard whenever he was added to their group to execute a task. Many of them are of the opinion that they are better off being short-numbered than having him on board. A particular project was given to them, and he had to have a group or risk being sacked. One of his colleagues decided to help him to save his job after he promised to live up to his words. He eventually disappointed them as usual. The group leader became furious, but TC walked up to him to beg with a side of his face looking apologetic while the other betrayed his intents. He was not truly remorseful and only tendered the apologies to make peace reign.

Case Study III: A man was arrested at a checkpoint while he was scheming to smuggle some items into the country. Since he was caught red-handed, he did not bother to argue with the officers on duty. He was ready to lose everything seized from him. However, it wasn't certain if he would turn a new leaf because as he was begging, a side of his face looked so unmoved while the other looked pitiable. This cast doubts on the minds of the officials. The officers in charge of his case had to hand him over to higher authorities for further actions. This was a proactive measure to save them from regrets in the future.

15.5. Incongruence of the Face

Generic Interpretations of the Concept

Facial incongruence is a common gesture all over the world and is seen as the more pronounced form of the emotional asymmetry of the face discussed in the preceding segment. What is facial incongruence? Simply put, it is the contradiction of the face with what the mouth utters. The concept of communication goes beyond what someone says but HOW it is said and the ACTIONS accompanying those words. Until the three factors align, communication cannot be said to have taken place. Better still, your co-interlocutor will experience doubt on what is said.

A lot of scholars have emphasised that the non-verbal plays a huge role in aiding effective communication among people. If the face now expresses another thing different from what the mouth is saying, the person who is being addressed would be left confused in the sense that he or she will not know what to believe. From experience, we have always enjoined people to go for the non-verbal message because it is mostly out of reach of humans. So it cannot be easily feigned. Remember that words uttered are products of conscious thinking, and the person will only say what will soothe their selfish tendencies or make you happy, even if that is not the truth or what you were supposed to be told.

A person who is not happy to meet you may greet you with pleasant words while their face looks tense. This incongruence hints that something is amiss. Someone nearly caught in evildoing may also display the feeling of discomfort while they talk as if all is well. In any case, always dig deeper to understand where and what causes the incongruence.

Scientific Explanations

The concept of incongruence was introduced by Carl Rogers in the 1950s. He defined *congruence* as 'the matching of experience and awareness'. *Incongruence* was therefore 'lacking congruence', or 'having feelings not aligned with your actions'. These days, incongruence means something that is inconsistent or incomparable. To understand the meaning of incongruence in a better way, Ron Fritz (2018) gives this illustration: 'When you were a little boy or girl, did you want to grow up to be a firefighter, a movie star or a ballet dancer? At some point you probably gave up that dream in favor of something more attainable (unless you currently are a firefighter, movie star or ballet dancer). When our dreams appear to be out of reach, the result is often frustration, stress and anxiety. Many people wind up abandoning their dreams, believing they are impossible to achieve. These individuals have learned the pain of *incongruence*.'

Now let's move to incongruence in communication. Sometimes, people say things that do not match their nonverbal cues. According to Fritz, the outcome of such utterance is confusion and poor communication, whereby the listener wonders why the speaker decided to speak with their tongue in cheek. Communication is incongruent when what a person is saying does not match their thinking or feeling. You may be wondering, how do we know the thinking or feeling of a person and compare the same with their words? The answer lies on their face—the face is the home of human feeling, and there is no one who can totally suppress the emotions that ooze out of their face. Let me give this practical illustration to buttress the fact being made here: if a person is obviously angry to the extent that their face becomes red, if you greet them 'How are you?' and the answer they supply is 'Fine', with their face's appearance, the person is definitely not fine. Hence, their answer is laced with deception. So we say that their action and words are incongruent (Fritz 2018).

Jeremy Marchant (2015) also discusses the issue of incongruence but relates his with workplace. He notes that when the words of a person does not match their body language, there is incongruence. That is why someone might have put up a good defence and sold their proposal in a very laudable way but their look and action does not match those words. At the end of the day, without any tangible reason you can really point out, you end up not awarding them the contract. Well, what has just denied them the opportunity is face incongruence. Unfortunately, some people do not actually mean the negative emotions their body is communicating, only that they could not manage themselves well.

Practical Illustrations

Case Study I: Mr H has been seriously sick since Friday and resuming today being Monday, has been a sort of miracle. Beyond all odds, he actually forces himself to be in the office because of the fear of being sanctioned by his company. For the past one year, the firm has spent huge amount on his failing health, and he has gathered from reliable sources that if he should continue along the same path, he may be relieved of his duty. So he still wants to hold on to it. On getting to the office, his unit head sees the unusual, dull look on his face and asks if anything is wrong with him, only for him to wear a grimace, and reply 'Not at all, all is well with me.' The look on his face actually betrayed his verbal expression. Noticing this, the unit head says he should see him privately. And expectedly, he eventually confessed the difficulties he was encountering due to his ill-health.

Case Study II: IK returned home from school feeling tired. Before going to school, the mother informed him that they were to visit some family friends and go for shopping. However, he knew that if he should say that he was tired, his mother would tell him to stay back at home and rest. So when his mother saw him, she asked him what went wrong in school, but he quickly replied, 'Nothing unusual.' His mother proceeded, saying, 'Why are you now looking tired?' IK replied, 'I'm strong and agile.' The mother knew he was only forcing himself to look strong due to the outing. It was obvious from his facial expression that he was fagged out and needed rest.

Case Study III: Prostitute NB and Client XC fixed a meeting for 9 p.m. However, they both could not meet up with the time. While NB was with another client, XC had to attend to some pressing issues at the office before closing for the day. NB got to the meeting point about two minutes before client XC. She wanted to feign anger when her client tendered his apologies. She murmured endlessly about how she was delayed, but her facial expression did not express the same message. This was to play on the man's cluelessness. Since the man was ignorant of non-verbal cues, he was made to pay more for her services.

15.6. Strange Face in Crowd

Generic Interpretations of the Concept

Some people believe that identifying odd face in the crowd is an impossible adventure or will make us approach the wrong people. For some reasons, I share this sentiment with them. Profiling a crowd is obviously tasking, and there has not been any generally acceptable research that teaches how to spot an odd face in the crowd. However, from my personal experience and what other experts in the field have noted, the best way to deal with crime in the crowd is to always trust our intuitions. That is, while profiling a crowd and your intuitions tell you to engage someone, do not hesitate to. At the point of interview, you may be amazed by what you will eventually find out about them.

Having trained people in the security industry for years, I have come to discover that there is no need taking chances when you intuitively perceive that a face stands out. In simpler terms, what I am trying to say is that when you see an angry face in a location where everyone is looking joyous, then such person is worth challenging. Another instance is when you observe that the emotion of a person is fixed while every other person is expressing varieties of moods. If you look away, the person might turn out to be a suicide bomber or armed robber. That is why I said you must trust your guts, because you cannot be questioning the intents of everyone in a crowded area.

Also, I have trained airline security personnel for decades and have had reasons to work with them at various points in time. The sentiment most of them share is that it is usually the odd emotionally charged face—the one who does not align with others on the queue—that ends up being the most problematic at the counter. Their intentions are betraying them right in the crowd before getting to the point of committing their intended crime. In the case of the airport, the odd-faced person may end up being a terrorist sent to spy some places in the country or a human smuggler.

Scientific Explanations

Abigail Beall (2016) gives a summary of how to look for a face in the crowd. She begins by lamenting how herculean it is to find a person in a music festival or during a football match, where thousands of people are in attendance. Even if the person we are looking for is a friend and is waving at us, how do you identify the person among the multitude of the crowd? You may have to give up on them and hope that you meet at home or somewhere else, but not in the crowd. This gives a foundation to the difficulty that accompanies fishing out a particular person in a large gathering.

However, a recent study reported by Beall reveals that the human brain has the special ability to 'tune what our attention focuses on when we know what to look out for, meaning knowing what our attention should be drawn to makes the process much easier' (Beall 2016). In the case of looking for a criminal, the brain knows the qualities of the person—their facial look must be different from that of every other person in the gathering.

In our brain, it is reported that some areas of the visual cortex are used for spotting non-spatial features, like colour, shape or orientation. Other portions of the brain specialise in looking for the direction in which the person moves or how they are positioned. For instance, if the person is not following the movement pattern of every other person, it means they are alien to the place or they have an intention which must be carried out in a heinous way (Beall 2016).

In order to make this decision, the brain must first gather all the various inputs and then process them as one.

In a research championed by University of Chicago neuroscientists, both space-based and feature-based attention influence each other to help us find what we are looking for, like a face in a crowd. Professor David Freedman and Dr Guilhem Ibos scholarly examined how the brain can focus on the two features at a time. Being the first time, this kind of research would be carried out, they note that the region of the brain responsible for this action is very flexible and changes what it responds to, depending on what you focus on per time (Beall 2016). That is why I earlier said that you should not discard the place of intuition in recognising an odd face; if your intuition tells you to focus on the person, then the part of the brain is also put into action so as to help you identify the person.

The researchers report that the brain region responsible for this is called the lateral intraparietal area (LIP). They discovered the LIP gathers and processes visual information based on feature-based attention, like colour and motion. The new results show the LIP uses information gathered earlier in the processing system, and combines it with new information when a new kind of attention is used (Beall 2016).

Practical Illustrations

Case Study I: Country T is one of the most visited nations in the world due to its economic buoyancy, beauty and widely acknowledged incomparable level of hospitality. This is just the positive side of the story as the country has come under numerous attacks in times past due to the high influx of people. Hence, the security team at the airports have been told to beef up security so that people with heinous intentions do not go beyond the airport before being trapped down. On a particular day, while hundreds of people were lining up to be cleared in, having arrived from a country very close to the one reputed for terrorism, some of the officials were conducting their routine checks when one of them discovered one of the people looking 'odd'. At first, he looked away, but his intuition would not let him rest. After a minute, he looked at him again, and the man tried avoiding eye contact. Then, he walked up to him and asked him to step aside for questioning. It was later discovered that he was in the country to recruit people for terrorism.

Case Study II: Mrs PPE laundered money in her home country, and after successfully transferring it to her destination country, she looked for ways to withdraw the money from the account in order to make it untraceable to law enforcement agents and anti-graft agencies. She was not familiar with the country and did not make much enquiries so as not to make people suspect her. On getting to the bank, she stood on the wrong queue, and when she seemed confused, a security agent had to approach her to make enquiries on her purpose there. She sounded incongruent, and her face was very strange on the queue. She had to be taken out of the queue for some questioning. This was in a bid to unravel what birthed the suspicious non-verbal gesture.

Case Study III: Mr IG impersonated someone in order to gain entrance into Country DG. While standing on the queue to be cleared after arrival, he discovered that the officers were scrutinising every document with diligence. He quickly liaised with an accomplice that the moment he (the accomplice) submits his documents, he should immediately move out of the queue for him. They were to exploit the pressure on the officers to escape being cleared. However, as he was about to move to the front of the queue so that he could be freed instead of the accomplice, the officer noticed his strange face and ordered his arrest so as not to create a scene at the airport.

Case Study IV: The students of RQI High School have just resumed for a new session, and as such, they would be moving to new classes, depending on their grades. During the holidays, some students wrote applications and sat the exam of the school. Those who did well were picked. On the morning of the resumption, they gathered on the assembly ground to take instructions. However, many of the old students were moving away from a strange face standing with them. They were shocked to see him because he was not with them the previous session. It took the effort of their teacher to calm them.

Case Study V: There was a news story in town that some group of terrorists were to attack some health facilities. While law enforcement agents dispelled the rumour and assured that they were on top of the situation, many people were not willing to take the risk; some who were supposed to be in the hospital for a reason or another intentionally did not show up. Amidst all these, a man just showed up in one of the most crowded wards in DGC Hospital. The patients raised the alarm due to the way he was looking. Law enforcement officials got there in the twinkle of an eye to put the situation to rest.

15.7. Narcissistic Serenity

Generic Interpretations of the Concept

Let me simply put that this cue is 'serenity in turmoil'. Turmoil is a boiling situation where there is no iota of peace. In such an instance, what is always expected is that we should react in the same way. However, narcissistic serenity is when the face maintains an unusual calm in a circumstance where it is ordinarily expected to flare up. That is, it is when a person appears unmoved in a situation that will call for everything but calmness. In a way, we can boldly assert that this behaviour is incongruent to the event at hand and should be a source of concern to us. It is like when a child is beaten mercilessly, and instead of her crying, she begins to laugh. Would you not be taken aback when you witness such a situation? If you will, then narcissistic serenity must also spur you into action.

Although the look is serene, the context of its appearance makes it questionable. In American movies, I have observed this form of facial appearance on Timothy McVeigh, Bernie Madoff, and Lee Harvey Oswald when arrested for the hurtful part they play in committing some atrocities.

This look can be deceiving and make people overlook the guilty. For instance, there are people who are naturally fearful; any small thing related to law enforcement pushes them out of their comfort zone. Such people can be wrongly arrested in this situation while the person who maintains unusual calmness is ignored. Narcissists succeed in appearing emotionless, and this helps them in some given circumstances. What is important is that we look beyond suppressed emotion and engage people based on fact. In other words, if a situation requires that people should go emotional and there is someone who appears odd, they should not just be praised for their bravery; they should also be investigated for their weird attitude.

Scientific Explanations

Doug Hilton (2017), while explaining how people feign calmness and fake their emotions, notes that through knowledge, he takes charge of his feelings. According to him, 'All negative emotions evolved, because they generate an endless stream of dominant behavioral displays, which play a key role, in the selection of mates.' He believes that if we are always connected to positive emotions, there are so many hurtful things that will not get to us. He observes that reacting to emotions as they occur is part of our primitive setup, and those who do not react to situations have only learnt to live above the primitiveness. In other words, such people have trained themselves to live above the 'normal'.

In his own part, Joao Pedro (2017) says those who stay calm when the situation naturally demands them to be nervous or unsettled cannot really hide their emotions due to the potency of body language. The fact they are unmoved is itself a message. After saying that, he tries to give an insight into how those who remain calm in the face of provocation behave. According to him, they detach themselves from the event and then step back to take a deep breath and analyse the whole scenario and see what has gone. After they have a full grasp of what is happening, then they can behave as if the event does not take anything off them. Pedro adds that this may be hard as hell, but people end up obtaining this skill. When you react appropriately to a situation, people tend to see you as being rash in your actions. That is, a person who is panting nervously when law enforcement officials get to a murder scene has just given himself or herself out while a person who looks emotionless will make the officials look curious.

Adam Sicinski (2019) notes that those who remain calm in turmoil are always patient. Before they react to an issue, they would have thought of the consequences and what might be the way out. You will also observe that people who display incongruent facial expressions also let go of past regrets; they do not allow past occurrences to wear them down. So there is no accumulation of emotions to increase the stress or anxiety level in them. Being able to discard issues as they happen makes it possible for them to remain emotionless in the face of horror. They are also optimistic that they will surely overcome whatever stress they are witnessing now. It is just like a man losing his only child; he knows that tears cannot retrieve the child and, also, he cannot be buried with the child. So they will forecast into the end right from the beginning. All these qualities can be found in a person who maintains narcissistic serenity.

Practical Illustrations

Case Study I: A man had little misunderstanding with his wife before going out with the hope that when he returns from where he went to, they will settle the rancour. Petty disagreement was almost a culture in their family, an issue that was giving the wife sleepless nights. On the last occasion, the wife thought that her husband walked out on her, considering it as a mark of dishonour. This got her thinking to the extent that she thought that killing herself was the way out at that moment. Hence, she stood up and reached out for a knife, which she eventually used in terminating her own life. When the husband returned, he found her dead body in a pool of blood. He walked past her and returned and pranced about for a little while before sitting on a chair near the dead body to have a full view of everything without raising alarm or shedding tears.

Case Study II: Meting out corporal punishments at GAT School is not allowed, and this has always been emphasised to the teachers. However, Mr Y was angered by one of the troublesome students, and out of annoyance, he took off his belt to deal with the student. The school took it up against him, and after internal findings, he was handed over to the police. When he was being arrested, he looked emotionless and surrendered himself with ease.

Case Study III: Mr KA is a drug addict and smuggler. Even though he deceives people in his neighbourhood as being an international businessperson, the truth remains that he uses whatever he gets from his illicit smuggling business to buy harmful drugs and consume the same in large quantities. The wife, who knew all his criminal acts, warns him at every given opportunity that either of the two crimes would give him up to law enforcement agents soon if he does not turn a new leaf. He becomes adamant and almost files for a divorce. On the day he is to be arrested, he just finishes consuming drugs when he is rounded up. Throughout the period, he looks emotionless because he doesn't understand anything.

15.8. Odd Smirk

Generic Interpretations of the Concept

This is also referred to as 'duping delight' and was coined by renowned researcher Professor Paul Ekman. When someone is getting away with something they believed they should not have a field day with under any circumstance, they will wear a half smile or an odd smirk that does not match known or appropriate behaviours in the society. In a way, this is somewhat similar to the narcissistic serenity discussed above.

The name duping delight gives a hint into what this behaviour is all about. That is, the person is delighted that they have duped another person. This simple interpretation will stick better. That is why you tend to see this half smile in a person who thinks he or she has successfully played on the intelligence of another person. The half smile is to ensure that the person does not take note that something evil has been done against them. For instance, if you laugh in a situation where it looks absurd to laugh, the other person would be forced to do a quick analysis of issues. First, their mind will reflect on their physical appearance, if there is anything absurd in their dress that you are mocking them for, and then they think of the negotiations. So the smile was supposed to be full but suppressed because the victim is still within sight.

We also see this cue when someone succeeds in deceiving another person. The smile is like that of victory to congratulate themselves for being able to outsmart another person. In a way, they believe that they are more intellectually sound than the other person. Sometimes, an out-of-place smirk may be a pretentious smile; we may deceive others with our smile that we have all gained when in actual fact, you are aware that they did not make any gain.

Hence, you see this cue in a place and time when contriteness, humility, and seriousness are needed as virtues; it is a cover-up smile to match the above-mentioned virtues.

Scientific Explanations

Wiktionary defines *duping delight* as 'the pleasure of being able to manipulate someone, often made visible to others by flashing a smile at an inappropriate moment.' This definition has set the tone of our discussion under this segment. The owner of the coinage, Paul Ekman, describes duping delight as 'the near irresistible thrill some people feel in taking a risk and getting away with it.' He says that this sometimes includes contempt for the person who has been successfully and ruthlessly exploited. Ekman (2018) concludes, 'It is hard to contain duping delight; those who feel it want to share their accomplishments with others, seeking admiration for their exploits.'

He gives the example of Hitler and Chamberlain where the former succeeded in deceiving the latter that he had mobilised army for war against Poland when in actual fact, there was nothing like that. It ws reported that Hitler went into a room, after taking an excuse from Chamberlain, to jump for joy at being able to successfully deceive Chamberlain. Hence, Ekman states that 'the presence of others witnessing the successful liar typically intensifies the delight experienced and increases the chances that some of the excitement, pleasure, and contempt will leak, thus betraying the liar. Not everyone is likely to feel duping delight; some people are terrified of being caught. More manipulative individuals are vulnerable to this emotion; the third emotion that most often betrays a lie is fear–guilt about lying.'

On his own part, Philip (2013) explains that 'duping delight means that nearly any signal can be used during a lie to convey honesty, and the greater the pleasure felt by the liar, the more relaxed and honest they will appear. The converse can happen too, the duper can appear more excited and happy throwing a wrench in this signal as universal amongst liars. Signals of duping delight can include higher voice pitch, faster and louder speech, increases in nodding and smiles, and use of more illustrators.' The more a lie is being perceived as being truthful, the more the signals of duping delight appear because it is primarily based on the excitement of being able to deceive others without them detecting.

However, just because you saw some of the signals mentioned above does not mean that the lie is present or absent.

Changing Minds (2019) tries to state the giveaways that you can spot when it comes to duping delight. They are throwing the head back, creased eyes, and upturn of corners of the mouth. Apart from the body language, there are some transient signals that are combined to conceal this message. This makes the signal appear and disappear in the twinkle of an eye before they are eventually suppressed or quashed. That is why you see a person flash a smile very briefly, and then they return to the mask of emotion they were wearing.

Practical Illustrations

Case Study I: J was crying that he would follow his mother out. The mother had many places to go and felt his presence would further delay her. So he was told to wait at home, but he would not just stop crying because of that. Hence, his mother called him and explain that there were doctors on the road he would pass and he would be injected at every checkpoint. Apart from that, if he should cry due to the pains of the injections, then, he would be detained by law enforcement officials. Being an innocent, young baby, J was gripped with fear and when the mother asked him if he was ready for all that, he said 'no'. The mother smiled briefly and returned to her normal emotion before heading for the door.

Case Study II: Mr L stayed back at the office to tamper with some documents and do some other heinous things. On going out, he was sighted by the law enforcement official on evening duty. He was asked why he was sweating and decided to leave office late. He answered he was given an urgent assignment by the manager. When the officer was about to release him and take his leave, Mr L smiled and briefly cut it short when he discovered that the law enforcement officer was about to detect him. Except for those who were actually paying attention, no one could actually perceive the short display of emotions.

Case Study III: A human smuggler was able to smuggle two young guys in all in the name of his sons. Being an expert in smuggling, he played on the intelligence of the young officers effortlessly. He even went ahead to make friends with some of the officers, and they ignorantly apologised for all they 'made him go through'. Reacting to this, he smiled briefly and cut it short while approaching the supervisor in charge of the unit before taking his leave. He wasn't ready for any issue that the senior officer might raise. A smart move of some sort, but the official didn't really pay attention to him.

15.9. Face Touching

Generic Interpretations of the Concept

Face touch is one of the most known gestures around the world, most times, known for its negativity but seems to be unavoidable; we all find ourselves doing it at some point or another. It has multitudes of meaning, and we have to pay due attention to the part of the face that is touched before reading meanings to it. For the umpteenth time, let me state that context is key. Face touch is usually referred to as hands-to-face gesture. When the hand moves to the face region, it alerts everybody around us that something is about to happen. This behaviour can either be intentional or unintentional.

Oftentimes, we see models who touch their face used as the cover images of beauty magazines or even in advertisements. The intent of the brains behind the advertisement is to call the attention of the audience to the charming, beautiful face of the person. Most times, they might be advertising a beauty product that has to do with the face. In this realm, the touch is conscious and done for the sake of achieving a defined, economic purpose. So it serves the ultimate purpose of attraction in this sense.

On the other hand, the touch is subconscious, and that is the aspect I want to lay more emphasis on. When we are stressed, due to an activity or another, we quickly reach out to the charged nerves of the face in order to stimulate them. Students taking tests, applicants undergoing interview, a suspect being interrogated and law enforcement officials deployed to a war-zone will be stressed in a way or another. Also, those who are fabricating lies do undergo stress too because the brain is unusually charged and made to work on the spot. So when you see a person rub their hand on the face, it means all is not well with them, and they think pacifying themselves at that point is needed. Before you can understand the specific emotions that they are undergoing, you have to study the context of appearance of the stimulating act.

Scientific Explanations

Noting that touching is a common pattern in body language, Changing Minds asserts that touching the face is of high significance. The website lists fifteen different places in which the face can be touched and the meaning which each connotes. For instance, when people touch the cheek, it is always done in horror or surprise while stroke the chin while ruminating over something. Using a finger to cross the lips is to tell others to keep mute. When people cover or touch the mouth is silently, it means they are short of words and do not want to say what is on their mind. This is especially so when they consider the utterance very dangerous to their well-being. When we tap the teeth, it means we are either irritated or bored.

When you touch the forehead, it means you are saluting another person. This has its origin from the army and is being used all over the world. When you see someone tap their forehead with the palm or heel of their hand, it is an expression of regret. It is just as if the person is seeing himself or herself as being stupid. The subtle rubbing of the eyes is to take off the sight from seeing something or an idea (Changing Minds 2019).

The region that has proven to be the most sophisticated is the nose. Depending on the form of touch, the nose gives out different messages. For instance, when the nose is touched with a finger, it means the person is thinking and pacifying themselves all along, but scratching the nose is often taken as a symbol of deception in many quarters. This message is also resonated by Westside Toastmasters. Further, when you see a co-interlocutor pinch the bridge of their nose, it means they carrying out a negative evaluation. In addition, tapping the nose means that something is secretive. When we are feeling uncomfortable or disagree with what another person is saying, we do rub the nose. From the foregoing, it can be see that the nose is a bedrock of messages, and you must pay particular attention to the action and context before you pass your judgement (Changing Minds 2019).

Particularly, Marc Chernoff (2019) does not see the face-touching gesture as a positive act, and that is why he advises that we should try to do away with it during conversations so that we will not be misunderstood by the other party. So the hands should be kept away from the face while communicating.

Another coaching website, Improve Your Social Skills, notes that the face touch is a cue that is used by people to comfort themselves in a difficult situation.

Practical Illustrations

Case Study I: Mr K had just finished the theoretical aspect of his driving school lesson and needed to take the practical session in order to be given a driving licence. After some sessions on the field, his trainer told him that he was going to leave him alone in the car to have a driving session. This was very frightening to him. So he took the bull by the horn by pleading with the man to stay with him in the car. Before going to the driver's seat, he rubbed his face repeatedly. This was to pacify himself on the stress he was undergoing.

Case Study II: The management of FRQ Services demands that there is a weekly meeting among its staff where they discuss issues relating to the development of the workplace and then have a rotational training session. F has never been given a topic to handle. When this came to the notice of the unit head, he informed F to prepare for the next training session. On the D-Day, he could be seen behaving formal in all his approach and could not even laugh well. This was an indication that he was bothered about something. When it was time to deliver the lecture, before being called to the podium, he was seen using his handkerchief to rub his face continuously. It was a means of psychologically calming himself.

Case Study III: A politician was invited into a university community to come and tell them his manifesto during electioneering. Before going, his campaign team members had briefed him that he should address questions with caution as a lot of tricky questions will be asked in such an environment. He thought he was too knowledgeable to be caught unawares by any question, but on mounting the podium, some questions from the audience really proved tough for him. He was using his handkerchief to clean his face from time to time. This made his team members feel uneasy too, with them praying the programme would come to an end on time.

Case Study IV: A con artist was arrested in a crowded place and wheeled to station. From the point of arrest to the point they arrived at the station, he proved to be smarter than the officials that apprehended him; it was argument galore, and his words looked more enticing than those of the officers. On getting to the station, the senior officials recognised him as one of those on their wanted list. The best brains in the agency came together, and investigation started in earnest. At first, the con artist seemed to be on top of the world, but it got to a point where he was wiping off his face continuously—it was a sign of being stressed.

CHAPTER 16

The Neck

Gradually, we are moving from one segment of the body to the other, and our knowledge is being broadened on how people make use of their body during conversations. There is no gainsaying that the neck is the most vulnerable and weakest part of the human body. Everything that has to do with human survival—food, hormones, electrical signals, water, and blood pass through the neck. It is the channel that links the head to other parts of the body. That is why it is always the point of target of our adversaries during conflict. Now you understand why people hang themselves by the neck and not by the hand or stomach when they are about to commit suicide.

According to Healthline (2015), 'the neck is the start of the spinal column and spinal cord. The spinal column contains about two dozen interconnected, oddly shaped, bony segments, called vertebrae. The neck contains seven of these, known as the cervical vertebrae. They are the smallest and uppermost vertebrae in the body.'

The spinal column moves from the end of the skull to the pelvis. It safeguards and accommodates the spinal cord. The spinal cord is the long bundle of nervous tissue that transmits neural signals to the brain and rest of body. It runs from the back of the head to the small of the back.

The most commonly known external feature of the neck is the laryngeal prominence, popularly known as Adam's apple. It is more pronounced in men than in women. The thyroid cartilage that makes up the body of the larynx, or voice box, creates this prominence, and it develops during puberty. The reason the Adam's apple is more pronounced in male than in female is that the thyroid cartilage meets at a 90-degree angle in males, while it meets at 120-degree in female, which makes the bulge less pronounced (Healthline 2015).

Also, neck lines appear at a later age as a development of skin wrinkles. Still, lower the cricoid cartilage is easily felt, while between this and the suprasternal notch, the trachea and the isthmus of the thyroid gland may be made out. At the side, the outline of the sternomastoid muscle is the most striking mark; it divides the anterior triangle of the neck from the posterior. The upper part of the former contains the submaxillary glands, also known as the submandibular glands, which lie just below the posterior half of the body of the jaw. The line of the common and the external carotid arteries may be marked by joining the sterno-clavicular articulation to the angle of the jaw.

The eleventh or spinal accessory nerve corresponds to a line drawn from a point midway between the angle of the jaw and the mastoid process to the middle of the posterior border of the sterno-mastoid muscle and thence across the posterior triangle to the deep surface of the trapezius. The external jugular vein can usually be seen through the skin; it runs in a line drawn from the angle of the jaw to the middle of the clavicle, and close to it are some small lymphatic glands. The anterior jugular vein is smaller and runs down about half an inch from the middle line of the neck. The clavicle or collarbone forms the lower limit of the neck, and laterally the outward slope of the neck to the shoulder is caused by the trapezius muscle.

Muscles of the neck attach to the base of the skull, the hyoid bone, the clavicles, and the sternum. The large platysma, sternocleidomastoid muscles contribute to the shape at the front, and the trapezius and lattissimus dorsi at the back. A number of other muscles attach to and stem from the hyoid bone, facilitating speech and playing a role in swallowing. Without the critical structures within the neck, speech would be impossible. The larynx accommodates the vocal cords of vocal folds. Humans generate sound when the folds come together to produce vibrations. The movements of the folds also help in manipulating volume and pitch.

The larynx is located where the pharynx, the back of the mouth and the nasal cavity, divides into the trachea (the tube that carries air to the lungs) and the esophagus (the tube that carries food to the stomach). That branch occurs near the base of the neck near the collarbones (Healthline 2015).

Talking of the nerve supply, sensation to the front areas of the neck comes from the roots of nerves C2–C4, and at the back of the neck from the roots of C4–C5 (Talley 2014).

The cervical region of the human spine is made up of seven cervical vertebrae referred to as C1 to C7, with cartilaginous discs between each vertebral body. The spinal cord sits within the cervical part of the vertebral column. The spinal column carries nerves that carry sensory and motor information from the brain down to the rest of the body. From top to bottom, the cervical spine is gently curved in convex-forward fashion. In addition to nerves coming from and within the human spine, the accessory nerve and vagus nerve (both cranial nerves), travel down the neck (Frietson 1999). With this explanation, you can see that the neck is very vital part of the body.

Unfortunately, a lot of people do neglect the neck when it comes to non-verbal communication. Through this, we have lost countless messages passed by others to us. That is why many people end up in regretting missing these messages, saying 'I didn't see it coming'. Not that they did not see it, only that it was ignorantly ignored.

To those who care, the neck is an embodiment of messages. The neck can reveal our level of comfort, tell others whether we are receptive of their ideas or not, or determine if a person has interest in what we are discussing with them. Sometimes, the neck is touched, ventilated, or covered as a way of expressing our emotions alongside other non-verbal cues that tell the world our feelings or what we are thinking at that point in time. The vulnerability of the neck makes the messages it passes across very accurate and reliable. It is also used as an instrument of love due to its sensitivity to touch or caress.

16.1. Touching of the Neck

Generic Interpretations of the Concept

There are several reasons that can induce the touching of the neck. From the literal level, when our neck itches, we will reach out to it with our hands and scratch. This is normally done regardless of the environment in which one meets oneself. If the person is sensitive to the location where they are, they may simply rub the neck, but this may not soothe them as rubbing the specific point. Some infections may also lead to the itching. Such infections should be treated as early as possible before it leads to irritations.

Apart from the above-painted scenario, there are other meanings to neck scratching. It may be an apt indicator of insecurity, worries, anxiety, or apprehension. It shows that the person has issues. Due to the vulnerability of the neck, when we are faced with any threatening situation, it is the first place we reach out to as a means of protecting it or to massage it so that we would be emotionally strengthened to confront the situation. No matter how small the issue is, we tend to touch the neck when we are bothered by something.

In all its forms, I have come to discover that neck touching is often overlooked, and it is one of the most truthful repertoires of messages. When someone is feeling strong emotions due to the occurrence of a negative event, it can easily be revealed to others by the manner in which they touch their neck.

You have to pay close attention to how your co-interlocutor uses the hand to manipulate the neck, especially when you are discussing a sensitive topic. It means they are aware of the danger of such discourse. For instance, I have always observed the attitude of neck touch among suspects. This heightens at the peak of the interview. At that point, they are really confused and anxious because they have exhausted all their instruments of propaganda. It is as if they have a mental pictorial view of what is about to befall them.

Scientific Explanations

Joe Navarro (2009) stresses that when we are under stress (witnessing negative limbic arousal), the body looks for every means to be pacified, and one the potent ways in which this has always been done is through touching of the neck. He submits that pacifiers are always with us throughout the day, and they increase as we experience stress in high magnitude. However, some situations are not only stressful but also threatening and that is when the neck touch comes to the centre of all; it plays both protective and pacifying functions. Recalling when he first observed the significance of the neck touch cue, Navarro said that while he was a child, his grandmother was hit by a car at the beach and the first place she touched was her neck. Even when she was recounting the story later in the night, the old lady still reached out to her neck.

Another point where the former FBI agent observed this cue while growing up was during his university days when they had to perform experiments on animals in anatomy class. Those who were peering down smelly animals for the first time would touch their neck as they do so. Men always grab their neck more robustly while women are more tenderly with it. Navarro goes ahead to list insecurity, worry, concern, nervousness, and fear as some of the propellers of the neck touch behaviour.

Changing Minds (2019) also lists numerous situations that may warrant the neck touch. According to the platform, 'Touching the front of the neck may indicate concern about what the person is saying (via their windpipe). This may because they are lying or otherwise are embarrassed or uncomfortable with what they are actually saying or are thinking of saying.' Just like the nose touch I earlier explained, the part of the neck that is touched reveals a lot about what the person is thinking. Being uncomfortable with what is being said or thought about makes the neck muscles become tense. This affects the quality of the voice because the windpipe has been constricted. The vocal cords will also become tense. Also, when we fear an attack, we reach out to the neck; we prefer to use the hand as a protector to the neck than to allow anything untoward happens to the neck directly.

Apart from the front area of the neck, there are also some important muscles at the back and side of the neck that play an indispensable role in human survival. When you see a person touching or rubbing the back or side of their neck, this is an indication of anxiety or tension. Changing Minds concludes that 'Suddenly grabbing the back of the neck can be a displacement activity for anger, as if the person raises their hand to strike then has to do something to restrain it. A neck-grab can also be a sign of shock or surprise as if the person is pulling their head back and grabbing it to suppress the reaction. This may be done as a deliberate exaggeration.'

Practical Illustrations

Case Study I: T has just finished her housemanship programme after completing her degree programme in medicine. She submitted her CV to one of the leading hospitals in town where her uncle also works. Before the interview, the uncle had informed her that it was only the best brains that the hospital was looking for. This is so because of high remunerations and being concerned about the welfare of the staff. So this has created fear in the mind T. This is more so when she was reliably informed that the organisation was going to employ just three people out of the twenty applicants. While waiting for her turn to be invited in, she saw some of the interviewees that came out sweating even though the AC was functional. This further compounded her fears. She began to go through her CV again to be sure there was no item she could not defend on it. When she was eventually called, she touched her neck fearfully repeatedly before knocking at the door. She was afraid and feeling uneasy because she did not want to disappoint herself during the interview.

Case Study II: Mr RK was travelling by air for the first time, and the experience could be described as a mixture of good and bad. Good in the sense that he was enthusiastic about travelling through this means, and bad in a way that he was really afraid of a crash. On the D-day, he boarded the airplane, and after about nineteen hours, they arrived at their destination. He gave a sigh of relief, but this was not the end of everything, as he was informed that he would still board another plane to the state where he was to reside. While being called on to board the second plane, Mr RK was seen touching his neck repeatedly. This was a means of pacifying himself before continuing with the journey.

Case Study III: A human smuggler was nabbed and preliminary investigations revealed that he was the one behind numerous cases of smuggling reported. This meant he was going to face multiple layers of investigations. The officers started with him from the most trivial issue and then to more important ones. At first, he had explanations for his actions; but when it got to the third layer of the interview, he became stressed and confused. Anyone observant enough could notice this on his face. When the stress got to its peak, he began to unconsciously touch his neck repeatedly. This was a non-verbal communication of what he was experiencing inward.

Case Study IV: A hawker had been hawking for the past few hours, and there was no patronage. She doesn't want to return the food home as that would be a loss for her. Eventually, someone called her to buy food from her. She was a bit relieved but became dejected again when she discovered that the client was not going to buy much. As she was serving the food, she used a hand to touch her neck repeatedly. This was an expression of her state of mind; she was not psychologically stable due to the low patronage she recorded, contrary to her plans.

16.2. Covering the Neck Dimple

Generic Interpretations of the Concept

What I refer to as the neck dimple is also known as the suprasternal notch. The neck dimple is the indented area of the neck that is located immediately after the Adam's apple and just above the upper region of the chest. It is bordered by two muscles of the neck and looks as if pressed inward. When you see someone covering or touching this region, it means they have issues. Even though I earlier referred to the neck as the most vulnerable part of the body, let me state at this point that the suprasternal notch is the weakest point of the neck. Now I believe you have a mental picture of how delicate that portion of the neck can be. If a person inserts their finger into someone's neck dimple and then pushes it inward, they may terminate that person's life. That is why you can see some people commit murder without any weapon.

So when you see a person touch or cover this portion of the neck, it means they are insecure. The emotion of insecurity creates fear in them and there is no way they can hide it other than to reach for that weakest portion of the body. Some of them may try to subtly display this cue by rubbing the suprasternal notch but that does not change its meaning. Further, it might be an indication that the person is bothered about something. So while thinking about their source of concern, they will cover the notch with their fingers so that it is not exposed to an imaginary or real predator. Covering of the suprasternal notch is caused by negative emotions.

Men tend to grab the throat or neck with full force as they try to adjust their tie or collar. However, I have discovered that women touch this area much more than men, but they do it very delicately with the tips of the fingers. No matter the trick that is employed to touch the neck dimple, the overall message is that is something is amiss. The act of covering the neck when we feel threatened may be traced back to the past when predators go for the neck of their prey.

Scientific Explanations

The Young Entrepreneur Council (2013) refers to the suprasternal notch touch as calming non-verbal language. Being in a tense situation is never easy, especially when the situation relates to negotiation, business, interview, and personal affairs. So we need to non-verbal means of dealing with stress. The YEC submits that the suprasternal notch 'is actually touched when people are nervous as a way of self-soothing. Lightly massaging this area or the back of your neck can help lower your heart rate and make you feel more calm.' So it is used as an antidote to stress and nervousness.

Christopher Philip (2013) also explains that the suprasternal notch is touched or covered when people are under stress. This is because nervousness makes the neck tense and engorged with blood just as earlier noted while discussing the cheek body language. Philip states that the suprasternal notch touch is mostly seen among ladies but this does not mean that men too do not pull the collar when they are stressed. He authoritatively asserts that 'Covering the suprasternal notch is one of the non-verbal signals that is unmistakable and also reliable in predicting emotional distress, one that shouldn't be ignored.'

Apart from nervousness, the need to pacify the body also makes it touch the neck and, sometimes, the nose too. Pacifying behaviours appear on their own. The brain sends message to the body that there is need for pacification, and then, the hands switch into action automatically. It has almost become a cliché to emphasise in this book that you need to determine the emotion requesting the behaviour—it may be nervousness as a result of sweating or an underlying stress that is inducing the fear. The touching of the neck dimple is an indication that a person is feeling uneasy under the collar. If it is an interview setting, then you must try to find out the subject matter that is making the person feel hot.

Practical Illustrations

Case Study I: Here's a case study lifted from the article of Joe Navarro on this subject matter: 'Covering the suprasternal notch is one of the non-verbal signals that is unmistakable and also reliable in predicting emotional distress, one that shouldn't be ignored.

'However, when I inquired "Is your son in the house?" for the first time during that interview, she put her hand to her suprasternal notch (neck dimple) and said, "No, he's not." I noted her behavior, and we continued with other questions about her son's acquaintances. After a few minutes I asked, "Is it possible that while you were at work, your son could have sneaked into the house?" Once again, she put her hand up to her neck dimple and replied, "No, I'd know that." At that point, seeing this unique behavior relative to the question, I was convinced that her son was in the house or had been to the house recently.

'To make absolutely sure my assumption was correct, we continued to speak with her a while longer, as we prepared to leave, I made one last inquiry: "Just so I can finalize my report, you're *positive* he's not in the house, right now?" For a third time, her hand went to her neck as she affirmed her earlier answers that he was not home. Certain from her behavior that she was threatened by my specific question, I asked for permission to search the house. Sure enough, her son was hiding in a closet under some blankets and stuffed animals—unwisely sitting on a gun.

'Her body was talking to me more honestly than her words. The words "*son*" and "*house*" together were a threat to her' (Navarro 2009). This case study is so apt that it captures everything we have discussed so far under this section in the simplest language.

Case Study II: Teacher EJ has just been employed and posted to teach Grade 5. As an expert in the sciences, he teaches the science students. At first, he was jovial with the students and many of them saw him as their best teacher but he suddenly began to change and this was a source of concern to the kids who are in love with his teaching style. At some point, his indifferent attitude translated into a stern one and the management of the school was intimated at this point. The head of the school summoned Mr EJ to her office and while was talking, he could be seen covering his suprasternal notch. He was feeling stressed and had no better or justifiable way of defending himself.

Case Study III: Passenger AY lost her fiancé, and as a way of getting over it, she decided to travel to another country. She got all the necessary documents in order to have hassle-free journey. But the same could not be said of her co-travellers as two of them were impersonators. When they got to the border and the border officials had to conduct their routine check, she quickly presented herself to be cleared, but their vehicle was delayed by the impersonators, who were trying to argue. She really became emotionally stressed and began to unconsciously cover her suprasternal notch. An observant officer walked up to her and asked if all was well. She almost became emotional when she wanted to explain herself. This means she was engrossed in sorrow and negative thoughts.

16.3. Touching of Tie Knot

Generic Interpretations of the Concept

This cue is better and mostly witnessed in official settings where people are required to dress formal and make use of tie. Ideally, when you appear in public, you are expected to demonstrate a level of confidence and carry yourself with charisma. Part of this requires that you do not fiddle with any part of your body, including the clothing items you are wearing. If there is any reason that forces you to do that, it must be done once and for all. However, a repetitive behaviour shows that something is psychologically troubling the person.

The tie-knot touching cue is done by playing with or adjusting the tie knot, which is usually positioned on the suprasternal notch as if to safeguard it. Touching it means the person wants to reinforce security at the neck region. Also, it may be a way of relieving stress or anxiety. You are likely to observe this cue in men when they feel mild anxiety or awkwardness in public. Since tie-knotting is only a man's thing, you should focus on men alone when looking for this cue.

While some men display this cue as a one-off signal, others may do it repeatedly to show that they are trying to pacify themselves. This is likened to a woman playing with necklace when under stress (check 16.4). If the tie-knotting cue is for the sake of neck protection, the person will mildly do it and then focus on some other things, but displaying it as a repetitive behaviour shows that the person is really stressed and trying to soothe their emotions through this pacifying act. Sometimes, this cue is so subtle that you may simply ignore it; you would think the person is only conscious of their appearance, but it goes beyond that.

Scientific Explanations

Navarro (2009) rightly observes that men are robust in their use of pacifying behaviours; you would see them grasp or cup the front of their hands on the frontal part of the neck. This helps in the stimulation of the nerves of the neck. If the person is witnessing high beat of the heart, it would be slowed down and ultimately, calm them. It is considered as a psychological medicine to the body. Adjusting the tie knot perfectly helps to achieve this purpose. Other clusters mentioned by Navarro are adjusting the shirt collar, stroking the back or sides of the neck with fingers, among others. He hints that the method of pacification for women is different.

Jack Brown (2011) describes this cue as 'false tie adjust'. He makes use of Italian prime minister Silvio Berlusconi as his case study. He presents a picture where the prime minister was captured displaying this non-verbal cue. Brown states, 'It is performed at times of considerable anxiety, concern, emotional discomfort, fear, worry or vulnerability.' When the negative emotion rises to an unbearable level, you will begin to notice this cue in men. As said under the generic interpretation segment, the female counterpart of this cue is fiddling with necklace. Brown states that this form of touch plays three critical roles—adaptor, manipulator, and pacifier. Serving as an adaptive act, this cue will be used by people who are not feeling comfortable to adapt to the environment. They are doing this because they cannot take their leave from that particular location. When it serves as a manipulator, it shows one is navigating through a rough terrain of emotions. And it serves as a pacifier when the emotions are really charged and tense. This latter one is the most popular; people tend to allude all forms of neck touch to this. He advises that anyone who wants to be seen as being sincere should do away with this cue in public.

In the picture of Berlusconi displayed, the Prime Minster is wearing a sincere smile. However, in a situation where a signal of comfort clashes with that of discomfort, we normally take the latter as being the sincerest. So the true emotions of Berlusconi is actually experiencing anxiety compared with smile which he tends to have control over. So when people think they are professionals in masking some signs, the truth also has a way it slips out when it is least expected. Although people may not detect it, but it does not stop it from showing up.

Practical Illustrations

Case Study I: Mr L came in late into a stakeholders' meeting. This has actually turned out to be his behaviour lately. So many of the people attending the meeting with him have known him for this. In fact, there were times they had to put call through to him so that he would arrive for the meeting to begin. Another thing is that he usually has an excuse for his lateness. People have become fed up with his irritating talks. This was obvious to him in their previous gathering while trying to justify why he arrived behind schedule. Coming in five minutes past scheduled time, he thought there was no excuse tangible enough for him to defend himself. Hence, he was seen touching his tie-knot as he made way into the venue of the meeting.as he came in, all eyes became centred on him. When he could not withstand it, he had to look down immediately till he got to his seat. This was a nervous feeling.

Case Study II: R was supposed to be home four hours earlier; the wife had informed him that they were to go to congratulate a family friend that just put something to bed and then go for shopping in a bid to prepare for a family get-together billed for the weekend. Mrs R should have settled that, but her car was down. She expected her husband to understand the implications of this and run to her aid, only for him to go in his usual manner, without respecting the opinion of other people. Lately, Mrs R has been making him know his mistakes and the likely implications of each. So as he was making his way into the house, he knew he was going for reprimand. He adjusted his tie endlessly, as if he was experiencing a physical discomfort. It was both physical and psychological discomfort.

Case Study III: Recently, Mr RX has been witnessing a downward trend in his business. When he couldn't hold it again, he approached some of his friends doing the same business, and they advised him to include some prohibited items in his transactions, as those items were in high demand and people would pay higher for them. He was very skeptical about this piece of advice but had to go for it when he couldn't endure things again. He bought voluminous goods on that occasion with the aim to deceive border officials. While the officials were conducting checks, he grinned and simultaneously used his hand to touch his tie knot. This was a clue for the officials that something was wrong. That is, the official could read fear emotions on him.

16.4. Fiddling with Necklace

Generic Interpretations of the Concept

This is just like the female alternate of the cue discussed in the preceding section. Let me simplify our discussion by stating that when you see a woman playing with her necklace, it serves the same purpose with hands covering the neck dimple. That is, those who play with their necklace are feeling negative emotions which they are trying to deal with on their own. First, this cue may be considered as a childish act. It makes the person to lose concentration on important thing being done. In a classroom setting or where something formal is taking place, the tutor can easily recognise a distracted trainee or member of a team through this behaviour. Since this behaviour is subconsciously displayed, the person will become unaware of the place where they are displaying it. When they are suddenly called to order, you will see them shiver suddenly in an unexpected manner.

From the sociological point of view, the playing with necklace gesture can help a person to pacify their rising emotions. This is normally done repeatedly until it soothes the person and they derive joy from it. Playing with necklace or covering the neck dimple helps a person to be a little bit disconnected from a troubling issue. Shifting their attention from the issue bothering them to something that soothes them makes them recover from emotional stress and think straight.

Further, this cue is capable of protecting the vulnerable part of the neck—the suprasternal notch. When you play with your necklace with the use of about two or three fingers, those fingers sit at the central point of the neck, which nearly makes it impossible for another person to see your neck dimple. If any form of attack is coming against the neck, the fingers fiddling with the necklace will block them off.

This cue is more obvious than the tie-knot touching because females do their own in a very pronounced manner, while males may simply do it as if they are preventing the tie from appearing awkward.

Scientific Explanations

Being able to read body language should be one of the things you take very seriously, because in a thirty-minute conversation, an average of eight hundred non-verbal tells are let out. On the playing with the necklace behaviours, it seems experts in the field have different opinions on what its likely meaning may be. However, most of them make their interpretations in the context of love or dating. Navaro (2009) says that when couples are just beginning to know each other, you will observe a lot of neck-touching behaviour. He explains further, 'If the woman begins to play with her necklace, most likely she is a little nervous or timid. The man may do the same thing by touching his neck or adjusting his collar. As these individuals grow more comfortable around each other, you will see more head tilt and therefore more exposure of the neck.' With this, what is implied is that people first show feelings of nervousness when with each other for the first time, and after having the assurance that they can trust each other, they begin to become relaxed and open to each other. If it gets to a point where both sit facing each other with neck exposed and head tilted towards each other, it means they are certainly into each other. However, the moment any of the couple feels discomfort, he or she will straighten the neck and begin to touch it, explains Navarro.

However, in what seems to be a contradictory submission by Dana Burke (2015), he notes that when a lady touches necklaces, bracelets, or earrings, it sends a flirty invitation to the potential suitor around. The inside of the neck, hand, and hair are regarded as pheromone zones; they are the parts of the body that trigger attraction. Burke goes ahead to state that touching the neck is acceptable when on a date but has another implication when done among friends or colleagues. In the unrelated context of friends or colleagues, it would be taken as a cue of nervousness, stress, anxiety, and disinterest.

Brain Director (2015) also shares the sentiment that if a girl is in the presence of potential suitor and she is fiddling with her necklace, there is high probability that she is into the person. However, since this book is not only focused on a love context, I need state that you need to take all the indices into consideration when trying to make your judgement about the body language behaviour of a lady. Once you take cognisance of the location and issue being discussed, you should be able to make the right decision.

Practical Illustrations

Case Study I: Ms W just met with F, and after some few initial conversations, they decided to fix a date so that they would have time to discuss better. The first conversation they had did not leave W the same again; she began to long for the date and had to reflect on her chances of eventually being the wife of F. so, when they eventually went on the date, she ensured she was in her best dress and mood. As they started reminiscing on their past, the lady was moved to F the more but her fear was that she had trusted so many men in like manner in the past but she was later disappointed. So she was still unconsciously guarded by these past experiences. As they were talking, she subconsciously touched her necklace and fiddled with it all along. This communicates both interest and caution; although she is interested in the man, but she does not have absolute trust in him.

Case Study II: Mrs G made a wrong data entry, which had reflected on the central system of the company at the headquarters. This was the third time she would be making the same mistake in a month, and she had been warned the last time she did it that working in a financial institution requires caution. On discovering this mistake, she tried reversing it immediately, but it seemed the transaction was immediately approved. She also tried putting a call through to one of her close friends at the headquarters, but he was not picking up his calls. Immediately after that, a call came in, but before she could pick it, she first fiddled with her necklace as if she were getting confidence from that part of the body. The occurrence had eroded her confidence, and that forced her into fiddling with items.

Case Study III: Mrs EL impersonated another person in order to travel. She did this because of the story she heard that the officials at the border of Country RU were not professional in identity checks. She thought that was an easy way for her. Unknowingly, the system in the country has changed. When she got there, the kind of orderliness and systemic operation alone sent fear down her spine. However, she pretended as if all was well with her by playing with her necklace. This was a distractive tactic but people around her saw that as childish and something unexpected from an adult.

16.5. Playing with the Shirt Collar

Generic Interpretations of the Concept

At some point or another, we have all had course to play with our shirt collars for different reasons, but we may not have paid attention to the role the behaviour played in each context; this is because it was done subconsciously and to soothe that very purpose. When you see people touch the collar at the back, it is most probably meant to adjust the collar without attaching any other meaning to it, but if you observe that they are fiddling with the front shirt collar, then it is serving some psychological functions.

There are three basic meanings (of serving to relieve stress) that can be alluded to this cue, depending on the context of each. When a person plays with the front collar, it is a way of covering up the suprasternal notch. With this, they turn the back of the hand or wrist area to their co-interlocutor. Hence, the action becomes a protective one that is aimed at safeguarding the most vulnerable area of the neck. This is done when the person considers their environment as being threatening to their existence—when you see the person discussing with you or what they are saying as being threatening.

Further, it may serve as a tactile response to stress. This means the person is probably nervous and trying to seize that means to calm themselves down. Sometimes, the person may have to stylishly touch the neck directly if the stress seems unbearable. You may notice this in a person who is to address a high-delegate meeting for the first time. If they touch their collar repetitively, it means they are stressed and looking for a way to quash their fear.

And finally, it may be a means of ventilating the skin underneath. Slightly moving the collar enlarges it so as to let cool breeze. This shows that the person is internally hot and needs to be pacified by nature. If the person is obviously sweating, they will display this cue in a very pronounced manner. With that, you will see that they are not comfortable with the topic you are discussing or the atmosphere they find themselves. So these are the three roles that playing or touching shirt collar may be performing in any given society of the world.

Scientific Illustrations

Navarro (2009) notes that fiddling with shirt collar communicates discomfort or insecurity. He explains that this behaviour is usually noticeable among men when things are not going as planned. The alternate cue in ladies is stroking the back of the neck to lift their hair. What this behaviour seeks to achieve is to deal with the stressful and uncomfortable atmosphere. Navarro notes that if the stress level is within control, men only ventilate their shirt at the neck but when it goes beyond what they can suppress, then they pull at the ends of the collars so as to allow in air from both angles. The former FBI Special Agent added a caveat thus: 'Obviously you may see these behaviours on a hot day, but when someone is dealing with something stressful or they are asked a question that is bothersome, you may see this behaviour as a reaction.'

On his own part, Christopher Philip (2013) regards the act of pulling the collar as emotional body language. He hints that when observing emotional cues, it should be noted that men tend to touch their face more often while women favour the hair, jewellery, clothing, neck, and arms. Philip states that there are issues with a person when they touch or adjust their shirt collar when there is no reason to warrant such action. This indicates that there is a negative event that is making the person feel uncomfortable.

Mike Stoute (2019) notes that the act of pulling shirt collar shows doubt and uncertainty. When people feel insecure or nervous about the presence of another person or what that person is saying, they do display this cue. Whether at the literal level or otherwise, being in a 'hot spot' makes people pull their clothes away. Someone who is feeling exposed will begin to sweat and then will have to pull their shirt off so as to let in air.

Zoologist and body language expert Desmond Morris found that when we tell a lie, we get a tingling sensation in the face and neck. This is because the heart beats faster when nervous (which most people are when fibbing), the blood pumps harder, and the blood vessels dilate. As the skin on the face and neck is particularly sensitive, it's uncomfortable to have clothes rub against it, so we pull them away (Stoute 2019).

Practical Illustrations

Case Study I: Select law enforcement officials went to interview the elder brother of a wanted suspect in his home. They asked if they were related, and he replied in the affirmative. When asked about his childhood, he spoke without hesitation. Then, he was asked about the latest escapades of the suspect. At this point, he began to hesitate in his response, choosing his words carefully, and looking into the eyes of the officers for confirmation—he wanted to be sure if they were convinced of what he was saying or not. Then, the officers asked if both of them had anything they were working on together. At this point, he scanned through their faces and pulled his collar while simultaneously saying no. Observing this show of discomfort, another officer asked if he was aware of the means through which his criminal brother kept his stolen resources. He played with his collar again. At that point, a related question was asked which elicited the same response. This confirmed the officers' doubt that he was an accomplice. He was later arrested and during interrogation, he confessed of his involvement.

Case Study II: Some group of students were given homework which specifically requested them to do on their own but one of the students tricked his parents into helping him out. While marking it, the teacher did not see originality in the work and had to invite him over. When asked how he did the task, he placed his hand on his collar and started playing with it while conjoining words that do not match up together. His action depicted fear, and his manner of speech confirmed that he was being deceitful.

Case Study III: Two colleagues had been planning how to dupe the management of the company they were working with. However, it hadn't been easy due to the deployment of sophisticated technology in almost all the activities of the firm. However, they were resolute about their plans. At some point, Colleague B dropped out of the idea while Colleague A was insistent on it. Seeing the likelihood of its success, B eventually gave a subtle support. Unfortunately, Colleague A was caught at the last stage and he wasn't hesitant to indict Colleague B. When B was invited by the disciplinary committee, he was observed to have been playing with the collar of his shirt. This was a clue of his involvement to the committee, and they were smart enough to decode it and used that as a basis of their engagement.

16.6. Massaging the Neck

Generic Interpretations of the Concept

Nothing drops out of the blue on its own. In other words, there are factors and emotions that trigger the massaging of the neck. We tend to dismiss this behaviour by not reading any meaning to it, but whether subtle or pronounced, massaging the neck means someone is feeling uncomfortable. Neck massaging is the act of rubbing the sides or back of the neck slowly with the palms. Usually, the head is tilted to the other side in order to give the palm a full access to the neck. Women will stroke their hair backwards so as to directly lay their hands on their neck. I am taking time to provide an explanation of the full processes involved in this behaviour so as to emphasise the need to always pay attention to the context of discourse when you observe this cue for you to be able to interpret the message being passed to you.

Massaging the neck means the person is tense or hot. So when the palm of the hand touches the skin of the neck, it produces a tactile effect that helps in soothing the body. Through this means, stress is relieved. The behaviour dislodges the mind from the stressful event and connects it to the pacifying act offered by the hand. You may also notice this cue when somebody is thinking hard. The effect of the thoughtfulness is making them hot, which is felt in the neck area through the rise of the nerve endings. The neck may even become visibly red. At this point, the need to massage the area becomes irresistible.

Most of the time, when you see the hand tarry on the neck, it means something is amiss and you must diligently seek it out through deliberate discourse with the person experiencing the emotions.

Scientific Explanations

Navarro (2009) states that massaging the neck is a way of dealing with stress at different levels. Men tend to do it in a very obvious manner while women will touch and rub in a delicate manner. The aim is to soothe the emotions and stave off fear or nervousness. When people are confronted with an unexpected circumstance, this makes their blood level and nerve endings rise.

Philip (2014) notes that when a person is very stressed, this massaging can be done in a very vigorous manner and then pull the skin just above the Adam's apple to show the world that they are really feeling the heat of the discomfort that they are going through. He supports the stance of Navarro that neck massaging is usually a male thing because women prefer coverage of the suprasternal notch. He explains in one sentence that neck massaging is 'a sign of nervousness'.

Philip gives the verbal translation of the cue as 'I'm under stress, discomfort, or I am insecure, and I am pacifying myself by massaging my neck which is full of nerve endings.' The body language expert explains that neck massaging serves the dual function of pacifying as well as protecting the neck. When a person is also beclouded with uncertainty, you may see them rub their neck as they think of the way out of their state of confusion. Apart from the neck massaging, their entire face will also bear the message of hopelessness. That is, it would look empty, vague, and distant. This means the person is really searching and looking for solution to an issue but yet to arrive at a conclusion.

In a discourse context, when an interlocutor tells you something while massaging their neck simultaneously, there is need for you to examine and reconsider the authenticity of the expression. The massage might probably indicate that they mean the opposite of what they are saying. You must not overlook any show of stress, no matter how little it is because some may briefly rub the neck in an inconsequential manner but that does not change the fact that they are craving for soothing (Philip 2014)

In what seems to be a minor deviation from the stance of the duo of Navarro and Philip, Body Language Communication, notes that the neck massage can be both a male and a female thing—it can be observed in both sexes. The website explains further that it is a show of anger and frustration. This may be a reaction to what is said, a fight with another person or recalling of unfavourable event of the past. The website concludes that 'touching the neck area constantly might be a sign of stress, misery or maybe embarrassment.'

Practical Illustrations

Case Study I: Mrs R was the only one at home because her husband had travelled for a week-long training in another region. This put the burden of the entire household's chores on her. More so, her daughter was just recovering after a terrible illness. Her work schedule had been an issue these days because she had just been promoted and would have to work round the clock just to justify the promotion and pay rise. After a hectic work session today, she was rushing home so as to come and cater for her child. On getting home, she discovered that she did not take the key to her home from the drawer at the office. She would have to drive back—a journey of an hour! This made her feel frustrated of everything.

She reached for her neck, rubbing it delicately as she walked back to the car. Her entire face bore this negative feeling.

Case Study II: M became an unfortunate victim of terrorists. After being captured in one of their raids in a village, he was abducted to their hideout. After getting there, he was forcefully initiated into their group. They informed him that he would have to do their bidding or lose his life. Even though he was ready to lose his life, the terrorists thought of using him to achieve their purpose before his death. They first taught him the act of bomb production, which he joined reluctantly. The following week, it was agreed among top-ranking members of the group that he should be taught how to sever the head of their victims. M naturally hated watching horror movies, now he was to perform in it. On hearing that he was going to sever the head of people with an axe, his emotions changed. He looked at the horror site again and closed his eyes. As he stood up, he rubbed his neck slowly and walked as if he were a toddler. He was feeling nervous and never imagined himself doing such a dastardly thing.

Case Study III: Mr FH is a commercial bus driver and an expert in it. However, in recent times, his bus has been developing issues which are very inexplicable. For a whole week, he was with the technicians whom he had asked to service it. So he thought that he would be back to full operations this week, but the reality is far from it. On Monday, as he was about to go driving out, it developed an issue again, and after another two days with technicians, he decided to give it a try again. This time around, passengers were well-seated when it developed faults. FH alighted from the bus and began to massage his neck, confused on the next step to take. He was really frustrated and ashamed.

16.7. Massaging the Vagus Nerve

Generic Interpretations of the Concept

Let me first interpret the Latin word used in the title so as to rightly set the ground to take off. The word *vagus* means 'wandering' in Latin. This means it has to do with movement. Hence, the vagus nerve connects the brain to the vital organs of human body, the heart inclusive. When people are stressed, you may discover that they massage the side of their neck that is very close to the point we check our pulse. The reason for this is that when the vagus nerve is stimulated, it results in the release of acetylcholine. This is a neurotransmitter that sends signal to the heart in return. To be specific, it sends the signal to the antrioventricular node. This ensures that the heart rate goes down.

The nature of the vagus nerve painted above makes it very important, if not indispensable to human survival; it serves as the bridge between the brain and other parts of the body. So when the body is hot, massaging that portion of the brain can help in the stimulation of the nerve endings. This soothes the neck and calms us down. You may discover that people do it consistently. This is to show how stressed the person is. The person is rubbing vagus nerve so as to ensure that the important role it is playing in the body system is not impeded.

Scientific Explanations

Changing Minds (2019) states that rubbing the muscles at the side or back of the neck is used to indicate tension. Some other times, it may be a show of anxiety. When you see a person massaging their vagus nerve, be sure that they are experiencing something awful from within. This is expressed by the way in which they hold the neck and rub it. This tension stops them from thinking. If they were ruminating over a negative event, they would have touched the frontal part of the neck. Touching the sides means that they are really experiencing negative emotions and want to get a soothing relief from it.

Courtney Sperlazza (2019) speaks on how the vagus nerve can be strengthened for the sake of upgrading the whole body. According to her, the vagus nerve is a two-way network of communication between the brain and most major organs in your body. It regulates things like hunger, the immune response, feeling calm or anxious, and more.' This gives us a broader picture of what we have been considering since the beginning of the section. So when a person is hungry, they may grab their vagus nerve to rub, this is why I have always submitted that instead of accusing people of showing signs of deception, we must first of all understand the context governing the interpretation. Hence, it is always safe to assume that they are showing feelings of stress and not deception. Further, the definition also covers emotional feeling that has to do with anxiety and calmness. Fear of unknown or being exposed to an unfavourable situation may lead to rubbing of the neck.

Sperlazza continues that 'a properly functioning vagus nerve will improve brain-body communication, and in turn make your whole body work better. You can tone your vagal pathways with breathing exercises, cold blasts, maintaining a strong gut, and other easy practices. If you need extra help, you and your doctor can opt for a surgically implanted vagus nerve stimulator.' All these are medical suppositions. However, when there is need for stimulation due to being put on the spot, you cannot wait to see the doctor and take some careful processes in dealing with them, you make use of the palm of the hands to rub the side of the neck so that they can be soothed while they are still at the venue.

She observes further, 'When everything's going well, your brain maintains status quo. When an organ is struggling, it can signal to your brain for more resources. When it's time for your body to spring to action, your vagus nerve carries the signal from your brain to your organs to slow down. To make sure nothing is lost in translation, your vagus nerve needs to be in working order.' The brain depends on it to regulate anxiety, fear, stress, and flight-or-fight response, among other emotions. Even though this cue looks more scientific than others, it does not change the fact that it expresses tension or anxiety.

Practical Illustrations

Case Study I: Just five minutes after RD got his workplace—when he was still arranging and clearing his table for the previous day's work—when he saw people running downstairs, and flames rose everywhere. Some of them were shouting 'Fire!' as they ran helter-skelter. Immediately, RD left everything he was doing and jumped out of his seat and dashed to the ground floor. Remembering that his phone was on the table, he thought it was risky if the fire should eventually gut the place. He wanted to go back, but the strength of the flame was enough to send warnings to one's eyes and brain. He rubbed the side of his neck as he pranced up and down in shock till the fire was eventually put out by fire service. There is no gainsaying that he was very disturbed by this unpalatable experience.

Case Study II: As part of their initiative to prune down the number of applicants applying to their firm, the members of recruiting team of GWQ Technologies decided to test their candidates on diverse areas of life; it was unlike before when it was only focused on the course of specialisation of an applicant. Many of the applicants did not see that coming; they thought they were just there to take a mini-test and be offered a place without hassles. Many of them began to judge their performance based on how they were able to answer the questions. After the written session, it was announced that they would be doing the oral interview that same day too. Already tired and somewhat depressed, a lot of them thought that was the end of chances of securing job with the firm. While they were waiting for the oral interview to kick off, a lady slightly placed her hand on her neck and rubbed endlessly. That was a subtle means of dealing with her fears.

Case Study III: APV Factory engaged too many casual workers as a way of trimming down their expenses and getting the best out of those working with them. Even though they see this as a smart way of reducing expenses, it had its own shortcomings too—it's easy to bring in people illegally, and that was what a lot of the full-time workers did. When the management of the factory decided to engage some of its casual staff on a full-time basis, some of the illegal employees applied without hesitation. One was called LT, who even cited the factory as where he garnered his experience, and that was his weakest point. When asked how that was possible, he began to rub his neck continuously. He knew his illustration was wrong and would give him out. So he did the non-verbal action to pacify himself.

16.8. Pulling of the Skin of the Neck

Generic Interpretations of the Concept

When people are under stress, whether severe or not, you cannot imagine to what extent they can go in calming themselves. At that point in time, most of them do not give a dime about the location they are; when stress overshadows the positive emotions of people, they do not hesitate to show it, even in public. Pulling the skin is one of these shows of primitiveness among people under the influence of stress.

The part of the neck that is immediately after the chin is very fleshy and people do pull it when they are stressed. This is only seen among men. Sometimes, men's beards extend to the edges of the neck and they may hide under that pretext to draw their hair and skin. Pulling the skin makes them concentrate on the soothing event. Most times, they unconsciously forget that they are in the presence of another person keep pulling the skin till it comes to the conscious notice of the other person. Even if they are talking, you will discover that their speech would not be coordinated or fluent because they are not concentrated on that particular speech but the non-verbal act of soothing themselves. If they put up a defensive argument in their talk, be sure they are not comfortable with what they are telling you.

When the pulling becomes extreme, it means that the intensity and level of the stress is also on the high side. There was a time I came across a man under stress who pulled his skin with vigor and intensity that his skin became pale. When people do not expect a crude or negative incident to occur to them but it eventually happens, they react to the situation in an obvious manner. Skin-pulling cue with vigour exemplifies one of those scenarios.

Scientific Explanations

Navarro (2009) notes that touching the neck is one of the frequent means we employ in reacting to stress. This makes it very significant. Let me state that the hand does to the neck, what it does to the face. Remember I said that the hand only finds its way to the face when we are stressed. So when you see it playing around the neck, it means the stress is of high magnitude. The person pulling his neck skin is pacifying himself. Revealing the reason people pull that portion of the neck, Navarro explains that 'This area is rich with nerve endings that, when stroked, reduce blood pressure, lower the heart rate, and calm the individual down.' This sentence gives a summary of everything. The fact that both learned and illiterate pull the skin without being aware of this scientific explanation is evidence that the action is ingrained in our subconscious and we do it without our own conscious willingness; it is done as the situation arises.

Improve Your Social Skills (https://www.improveyoursocialskills.com) (2019) states, 'This area is rich with nerve endings that, when stroked, reduce blood pressure, lower the heart rate, and calm the individual down.' That is, when a person observes the feeling of discomfort in their system, they will quickly devise a way of fixing it before it becomes very obvious to their audience. In some situations, it is expected that you help your co-interlocutor to get back on track when they are feeling stressed while in some others, this is actually a cue that will help you get the truth in an event. For instance, when you are conversing with a colleague and you see him pull the skin of his neck repeatedly, it is your job to help them out of their stressful mood so as to keep the conversation flowing. But in the case of law enforcement, this is a cue for you to ask the perceived question making them uncomfortable again in order to help you confirm your doubts.

On its own part, Changing Minds (2019) says that a speaker pulling their skin may be indicative of concern about what he or she is saying. This means they are either embarrassed, deceptive, or uncomfortable with what they are saying or about to say. When their conscience pricks them, they become engrossed in thought about the appropriateness of what they are saying. This makes them uncomfortable, charging the nerve endings, which leads to the act of drawing or pulling the fleshy portion under the chin.

The body language platform explains further that discomfort makes the neck muscles become tense, and since they cannot have direct access to them, the person pulls the skin in a symbolic way of allowing in fresh air on the muscles. In addition, a person pulling their skin also performs the protective function of using their hand to guard the Adam's apple. This protective role means they probably fear an attack, and as such, thought they should be proactive in their action.

Practical Illustrations

Case Study I: Having noticed the dubious ways of a particular salesman on his street, Mr E decided to confirm his doubt and ensure that he does not fall prey of the uncouth actions of the salesman. So E sent a friend to the salesman's shop to make some enquiries about a product he had earlier purchased, which the salesman informed him would last for years but could not withstand the pressure of a quarter in a year. When Mr E's friend got there, he was given another description of the same item with different promises. Meanwhile, all his utterances were recorded. When Mr E listened to the recording, he became angry about the man's action and decided go back to the place, disguising his identity. The salesman, ignorant of who he was addressing, said things that were contradictory to what he earlier told him. While the salesman was speaking, Mr E was visibly becoming angry, and as a way of pacifying himself, he pulled the fleshy area beneath his chin repeatedly as if he was interested in what the man was saying. After the salesman's speech, he revealed his identity, and the salesman went dumb for a moment.

Case Study II: X and I are two close friends, and they have been tighter since their childhood. While X is calm, responsible, and easy-going, I is the direct opposite. What is more painful is that I would commit atrocities in the name of his friend. This has become common, and X has told him that it's either he readjusts himself or forget about the friendship. I behaves well for about three months, until he to picks some of X's high-valued clothes and sells them off. X notices this when he wants to attend a high-profile seminar. He gets angry, and as way of dousing his feeling, he unconsciously began to pull at the skin of his neck.

Case Study III: Prostitute XP is a high-profile one; she doesn't give consent to clients that appear poor and crawling through life. This means she scouts for her clients from select places, and it seems to be paying off for her. However, a client came under the guise of being rich and had an affair with her before changing their agreement. After satisfying the man, XP asked that her account be credited, but the man tendered an excuse that he had issues with his bank and this has been on for about a month. Visibly angry, XP started using her hands to pull off the skin of her neck—she was appeasing herself with this non-verbal gesture.

16.9. Ventilation of the Neck

Generic Interpretations of the Concept

We have our individual reactions to issues; what some people will flare up at, some others may consider as being nothing, depending on the circumstances. This makes our individual stress levels differ. Hence, if you are using your own psychological reaction to serve as a yardstick in passing judgement on others, you may never be accurate in any case. Whatever may have induced stress in individuals makes our skin become warm, and this happens in the twinkle of an eye—less than $1/250^{th}$ of a second; that is incredibly fast. This is a physiological reaction that is governed by the autonomic nervous system. This implies that we have no control over it. Hence, the warming of our skin under stress is not left to our own conscious control.

When the skin becomes warm, the next step is to devise a way of pacifying ourselves. One of the common approaches I have noticed is ventilating the neck. Since our skin craves for more air, we try to loosen ourselves up so as to ensure we are not totally distabilised. People ventilate the collar and neck area so as to relieve discomfort propelled by flushing of the skin.

This physiological reaction can be caused by different factors. For instance, someone caught on the spot may become warm in a millisecond. Finding yourself in shock requires that you let out many things at a time to ensure your survival—you do a quick analysis of what caused the shock, if you are safe, what the next step is, and how you prevent further havoc. All these thoughts take place simultaneously, and as such, the reaction becomes very noticeable on the skin, being the most vulnerable part of the body. Further, being caught in a heated argument can make your skin warm. A word or comment considered hurtful may also propel this feeling. In all, the hand switches into action by lifting the collar so as to ensure the intake of fresh air. When a friend thinks they do not get the respect they deserve, they may behave like this.

Scientific Explanations

Body Language Communication (2019) states that the act of pulling the collar to ventilate the neck signals discomfort and emotional tension. When you are interviewing a suspect and you see them display this cue, it means they are uncomfortable about the discussion. If they are the one talking while they displayed this gesture, it may be a signal of deception. Someone who is on a job interview and likes pulling his collar may end up squandering his chances of getting the job because the non-verbal message he is passing to the panellists is negative.

Navarro (2009) states that this behaviour communicates our insecurity to others. He also notes that men and women ventilate differently. According to him, 'Men will ventilate their shirts at the neck or sometimes by pulling at the ends of their collar. Women ventilate by stroking the back of the neck upward lifting their hair.' In either case, the meaning does not change. Navarro adds that we should not leave out literal causes while observing this behaviour. That is, a person may become hot due to a hot day, but you will know that the ventilation goes beyond normal when the person is dealing with something stressful or being asked a question that bothers them and you observe this cue. It certainly means they are having physiological issues.

Giving a sentence interpretation of the neck-ventilating gesture, Philip (2014) submits that 'pulling on the collar is a signal that a person is experiencing discomfort due to high body temperature or nervousness.'

Philip discusses the motivation for this behaviour as this: 'The collar pull is sometimes associated with liars, but it is more reliably associated with an overall increase in temperature and blood flow to the neck which may or may not be due to an increase in stress. When the collar pull cue is caused by stress, it is an attempt to reduce the pain caused by irritated nerves located in the neck which are being compressed by a tight shirt. When stress increases, our face and necks flush with blood and we pull our collar away as an unconscious indication of this process.'

In some other circumstances, this behaviour is an avenue to release heat created by the body while we're pressured or uncomfortable, which has made the neck moist due to excessive sweat. Sometimes, too, this is due to an increase in stress that causes more irritation as sweat creates additional friction. Other times, the collar pull has no meaning and is due to an uncomfortable shirt collar rubbing against the skin (Philip 2014). This ventilating behaviour is always accompanied by a tie adjustment or pull, blushing of the face, and scratching the face and parts of the neck and ear. When you see all these, it is an indicator that your guess about the discomfort of an interlocutor is right.

Practical Illustrations

Case Study I: Mr WT received an invite from the police to come for questioning over an allegation concerning bribery and corruption. He thought it was just an invite—he would write a statement and then walk out. However, after penning down the statement, explaining what he knew about the issue, he was delayed for investigation. When he wanted to challenge the jurisdiction of the police, they informed him that the invite states *questioning* and not statement writing. At that point, he became cold. When the investigation started, he began to show some signs of distress. The officials engaging him decided to calm him down so that he would not allege that he made any statement under duress. At some point, he started sweating from the neck area. Everyone was thinking he would just wipe off the sweat with his handkerchief and continue, but after about three minutes, he was seen fanning himself with the collar of his shirt. Everybody was expecting him to do it once and then focus on the interview, but he appeared to be overwhelmed by that exercise that his attention to the main issue became minimal. This made people understand that he was feeling uneasy, and it was a great glue for the law enforcement agents.

Case Study II: Mr and Mrs HW decided to have one week off work. They were to embark on a tourist visit, but the main issue was that both of them could not agree on the location to visit. The husband eventually manipulated his wife to follow him to his desired destination. Not really fascinated about the choice of the tour, Mrs HW got tired easily. Just an hour into their first site visit, she began to fan her neck. The site guide thought she was tired due to the long journey the previous day, but when he saw her repeat this non-verbal gesture in addition to the facial expression, he knew she wasn't excited about what they were doing. So he had to succumb to pressure to ask her what she wanted in order to make the place lively.

Case Study III: Mr XC is the principal of IDV Secondary School. And it is the culture of the school to hold an inter-house sporting activity annually as a way of encouraging the spirit of sportsmanship among the students. In one of their training sessions, a student sustained an injury; and after first aid was administered on him, he was rushed to the hospital. While the principal was being briefed of what happened, he could be seen using his collar to fan his neck nervously and impatiently. When he could no longer endure it, he told one of the teachers to lead him to the hospital where the boy was admitted. Anyone who saw him did pity him because he totally lost composure.

16.10. Placing a Fist in Front of the Neck

Generic Interpretations of the Concept

Although this is not a gesture that is commonly seen, when you observe it in a person, be sure that they are stressed to the extreme. All things being equal, no one will place their fist on the neck if they are enjoying a conversation or are pleased with their current location. When you see this, then you need to look closely so as to unravel what is really wrong with the person. In simpler terms, placing a fist on the front of the neck is a signal of negativity. Let me also state that this cue is mostly seen among men, but I have also seen it displayed by women in two or three instances when they were extremely stressed.

Having said that, let me submit that this gesture is not different from the covering of the suprasternal notch earlier perused in this chapter. In fact, this looks like an advanced and more primitive form of neck dimple cover. The reason being that the fist is the boniest part of the hand, which in turn makes it the strongest portion. If any physical attack is targeted at the suprasternal notch, it would be protected by the fist. The aggressiveness of this behaviour makes it more receptive among men than women who favour delicate things.

Furthermore, this cue is a subconscious and automatic response to fearful situations and threatening circumstances. You also observe this gesture when there are concerns. This is a defensive signal that can be categorised under the flight or fight response. In this aspect, the person is not ready to flee but to confront the situation by first defending the most vulnerable part of the body.

As noticed in different points in time, people tend to mistake this cue as a show of strength, but it is simply a sign of defensiveness, dislike, or anxiety. If the person were strong, as wrongly assumed, they will rather stretch out their hands to battle the person or dare the situation by exposing their neck (this would be discussed later). This erroneous notion should be corrected at this stage so that you do not misinterpret the weakness and fear of someone as a signal of strength.

Scientific Explanations

Skills Converged (2019) provides a clear and detailed explanation for this cue. The website explains that the act of covering the front part of the neck is common when we are threatened. As with every other body language signal, this behaviour is more meaningful and expressive when the person expressing it is emotional. The website also submits that this behaviour is done differently by both men and women. Holding the fist in front of the neck is an energy-consuming cue that is mostly done by men. Note that this is different from placing the palm on the neck in order to create a soothing or pacifying effect. The back of the hand does not possess the needed moisture to induce stimulation of the nerve endings. The platform notes that women, on their own, prefer covering the suprasternal notch instead of placing a fist on it. But they may be forced into displaying this gesture when the emotions are experienced in a very extreme manner.

The website states that this behaviour 'suggests doubt, feeling threatened, insecurity and deception' but adds a caveat that not every neck-touching cue is a signal of deception but a mere cue.

Business Insider (2013) states that about 93 per cent of communication is non-verbal, which makes every gesture very important in a discourse context. The fact that many business people and the world in general do not understand the place of body language in every discussion has made our world thrive on deception. The website explains that placing a fist on the neck is done when a person is uncalm. They think a situation appears threatening to them because they are fragile and seen as prey. So they put on this behaviour to non-verbally communicate with the person in the situation that they are also up to something.

Christopher Philip (2013) explains that nervousness is the main reason people place a fist on their neck. In a slight contrary submission to what we have said so far, Philip opines that 'women are particularly prone to bringing their hand up to the "suprasternal notch" which is the dimple just below the neck between the Adam's apple and the breast bone when nervous, distressed, threatened, insecure, fearful or uncomfortable.' The only difference in his submission from others is gender preference. However, the body language aligns with the interpretations of others.

When you see a person hold their fist in front of their neck, it is a reliable signal of distress that should not be ignored. When the emotion is at conflict with reasoning, there is no way this can be hidden from an observant person. The reason is that the emotional cues cannot be controlled by the person; hence, it becomes a reliable indicator to follow. When there is an underlying fear, you will get to know if you pay attention to this cue and how they employ other clusters to point to the same direction.

Practical Illustrations

Case Study I: A man came with to a bar with a date for the first time. Before now, he had been seen as a person who does not know what love looks like. This has always been the topic of crude jokes among his friends. At first, he was not mindful of the expression, but when it almost turned into the watchword of his friends, he became bothered. More troubling was the fact that he did not like most of the girls that he came across, and the few ones he passionately liked were not ready for him. So he became trapped between the devil and the deep blue sea. It became the thing that occupied his mind during his reflection time. Now he eventually got a lady, but he was still skeptical about her commitment to him. Another man came to sit beside her while he went to ease himself. When he returned, the lady was already flowing in discussion with the new man and behaved as if she was not aware of the arrival of her date. Getting pissed off but afraid of what the other man was up to, the man placed his fist in the front of his neck, hoping that the lady and the man would understand the feeling of threat and discomfort he was passing across.

Case Study II: Lovers A and B are a newly married couple, but things seem not to be working for them as envisioned; they are always at loggerheads. This situation is fast drifting into domestic violence. Sometimes they would come together with the hope of settling issues, but after few weeks, they are back to their arguing spree. There is no gainsaying that they have been a nuisance to the entire neighbourhood. One day, the wife was reporting her husband to one of their neighbours when the husband came in. The wife began to feel uncomfortable and placed her fist in front of her neck to depict discomfort.

Case Study III: Mr UF is a human smuggler, and he was one of the most experienced smugglers I had ever interacted with during my active years in service. His modus operandi was to make illicit documents for his victims and then liaise with some compromised officials who would run a false check on the documents and then clear the smuggled beings. This was going on for years until I apprehended him. I got to know his evil antics when while he was seated outside, waiting for his smuggled people to be cleared. When he set eyes on me, he was gripped with fear and then used his fist to cover his neck as a way of hiding his neck. This was a clear sign enough for me to work with!

16.11. Pulsing of Neck Veins

Generic Interpretations of the Concept

When we are stressed, it is expressed through our body in many unimaginable ways. The reason I have always said non-verbal communication is the home of meanings and revelations is that even those who claim to have a mastery of it do not know of many things, or better put, they would not be able to take cognisance of a lot of issues when truly stressed. One of those signals we do not always think of or try manipulating is the neck veins pulsing. Unfortunately, too, people do not always observe this cue while reading meanings to the non-verbal expressions of their co-interlocutors. It reveals a lot about the emotional state of a person.

Let me add that pulsing of the neck veins is not noticeable at all times. So when it becomes very noticeable in a person, it means they are really anxious or stressed. The veins vibrate in a very noticeable manner when someone is witnessing negative emotions. The rise in nerve endings, reddening or flushing of the skin, gushing of blood around the region, and muscular tensing make the veins of the neck throb in a pronounced manner.

There are two possible interpretations to this cue, depending on the context in which it is taking place. One, it may signal anger. When a person is visibly angry, their body would become hot, and the veins will pulse visibly. Also, fear can bring about this behaviour. When a person is frightened by an idea, a thought or physical occurrence, they will switch to the freeze or flight mood. The freeze mood makes them stay at a spot in a stiffened manner, thereby making the slightest of all bodily movement known.

Scientific Explanations

Most of the literature available on this concept are focused on the medical perspective. Carmella Wint (2016) discusses this concept under the 'bounding pulse'. He notes that during this process, the person will feel as if their heart is racing or pounding. Since the heart is covered by clothes, you may not visibly see this, but it is made manifest through the veins of the neck that can be clearly seen. Bounding pulse makes the pulse of the person witnessing negative emotions be powerful and strong. If it were not, it would not have been felt by their audience. That is why I earlier submitted that this cue is only seen when someone is passing through extreme stress. Medically, this may be referred to as heart palpitations—a term used to denote abnormal functioning of the heart.

Wint notes that most times, doctors do not really know the causes of this malady; and in the few cases where they know, it does not portend any danger to the life of those experiencing it. If this cue is basically triggered by medical condition, it means the person really needs doctor's attention because this can point to a severe health issues later in life.

Having said that, there are some causes that relate to both the social and physiological reasons. The first is anxiety. According to Wint, 'Anxiety is your body's natural response to stress. It is a feeling of fear and apprehension about what's to come.' So this feeling can really be the propeller of the pulsating of the neck veins. Some people cannot endure stress, no matter how little it is. For instance, if a person does not have hope of survival and their job is abruptly terminated, you may notice the pulsing of their neck veins during their reaction to the decision.

Further, Wint (2016) mentions stress and anxiety as the combined factors that also induce this feeling. The fact is that stress and anxiety are part of our existence but there are some people that cannot withstand any level of stress. They are distabilised when exposed to the minimum level of discomfort. If the discomfort heightens, they become totally disoriented, and the result becomes manifest in a glaring manner in public.

Heart failure, pregnancy, anaemia, fever, and hyperthyroidism are some of the medical factors that may engineer this feeling in a person. I have taken my time to explain the psychological and medical angle of this cue so as to let you know that there are literal causes of this gesture. With this, you will be able to dig in-depth before making a rash decision on what the neck veins pulsing is all about.

In a 2013 article by Emma Innes, pulsating neck veins led doctors to diagnose that someone experiencing this may be battling with deadly heart disease.

Practical Illustrations

Case Study I: R has always been warned of his I-too-know attitude, even while he was in school; his mates had always told him the need to exercise patience and ensure he takes cognisance of the opinion of others while making decisions, or at least, acknowledge them. However, his wanting to prove that the opinion of others does not matter or match his intellectual ability has made him to see himself as the island of knowledge. He took the same attitude to his first place of employment. His boss had called him to order about three times before finally serving him a query. Even after responding to the query, nothing appeared to have changed about his behaviour. His unit supervisor raised this issue during a management meeting, and they reached the decision that he should be sacked. He never believed his eyes when the letter was delivered to him. While opening the envelope, his hands began to shiver and anxiety could be felt throughout his body. After glancing through, he saw reality held in his hand. His neck veins visibly pulsed, and his face tension heightened.

Case Study II: Mr T left his key at home while rushing to work in the morning and, as such, informed his wife not to tarry outside that day so that he could gain entry to the house as soon as possible. However, Mrs T came back late and did not even show the feeling of remorse. Looking at her face, her husband's anger grew more than he could contain; his neck veins pulsed in a clear manner while he became literally hot.

Case Study III: Mrs PW was a drug trafficker, and she used to have hassle-free movement at the borders because she had perfected everything by bribing some officials, who gave her all the necessary information—when to come, who to approach, and how to behave. So she looked smart among her co-traffickers, who encountered various issues at the border. One day, the lead officer working with her asked that their kickback be increased, and she did that. However, the officer was transferred that very day; and when she arrived at the border, she got new arrangements should couldn't weather through. Engulfed in shock and anger, her neck veins pulsed visibly.

16.12. Hard Swallowing

Generic Interpretations of the Concept

Imagine being forced to swallow a stone—how do you think it would be? Hard, right? This gives you a better understanding of the concept we are about to peruse. The first hint I want you to hold on to is that it is a negative expression, and that is why it is seen as a hard pill to swallow. While this cue is mostly felt during meetings, it can be seen in other gatherings too. During official meetings or conferences where the venue is always as silent as graveyard, the drop of a pin will make an audible sound. The same thing goes for the hard swallowing. When people are stressed, they try to moisten the mouth through the tongue and other soft parts of the oral cavity so that they will be able to compose words and discuss with other people. When the saliva becomes accumulates in the mouth, the person will look irritating if they should speak. They will then decide to swallow it as if they are swallowing their negative thought. It is just like being forced to take something that is against your wish. Except for higher forces, you will reject it.

The hard swallow is usually very visible and audible to everyone paying attention to you. This is an accurate and reliable indicator of distress. If it is in the context of a meeting, it means you are not in tandem with the decision reached or finding it difficult to cope with it. The summary is that there are issues. Also, it means the person is finding something or an action extremely stressful. The feeling of stress makes you look for how to pacify yourself and move out of the state of discomfort. During this process, your action and inaction alerts the world that you are finding something really difficult. In addition, the hard-swallowing cue may be observed when someone considers something very dangerous to their survival.

The hard swallowing is an indicator that a person has thought about something and concluded that there might not be a positive way out. The swallowing is tantamount to acceptance of their fate. When a person is tensed and highly stressed, the muscles and ligaments surrounding the throat become tightened, as a result of that, bringing about the energetic movement of the Adam's apple up and down. This signifies stress in its extreme end; it means the person is even finding it difficult to express themselves as the mouth which is seen as an instrument of self-expression has been subconsciously locked.

Scientific Explanations

Many of the body language experts that contributed to this subject matter note that it might be a signal of deception. Dr Jack Schafer (2014) discusses 'hard swallowing' as one of the '9 red flags you may be speaking to a liar'. He compares this cue to the throat-clearing gesture. Schafer observes that when a person is stressed due to any activity, they will lack moisture in their throat due to the high stress level. Hence, this leads to hard swallowing that is often referred to as an 'Adam's apple jump.' The moisture that was supposed to be present in the throat would have been redirected to the skin, coming out in the form of a sweat. The don only states that when you notice the hard swallowing in a co-interlocutor, it *may* be a sign of deception—we can only have hints and probability and not an assurance.

Psychologia (2019) shares the same view with Schafer; the website submits that hard swallowing may be a cue to deception. The platform notes that hard swallowing of saliva is an automatic action that is used to show that someone is stressed. The website also adds that this behaviour is more noticeable in men than in women. However, this does not mean face-touching gestures will cease from showing up when someone is witnessing the hard swallow cue.

In his usual behaviour, Philip (2014), giving a sentence interpretation of this gesture, says that 'a hard swallow indicates stress'. This is very short, apt, and straightforward. The body language experts stresses the fact that this cue does not have any advantage nor is it welcomed in society. So the best thing is to avoid displaying the cue as much as possible.

The verbal translation of this cue as given by Philip is, 'I'm stressed and my swallowing has become conscious and controlled. I do a poor job of it due to stress induced dryness.' The hard swallow behaviour is usually involuntary and an embarrassment indicator, as saliva production is at its minimum when someone is ready to speak, maybe while defending themselves. Unlike many other contributors who have been making the categorical submission that this cue is a signal of deception, Philip (2014) postulates thus: 'In the right context, the hard swallow sometimes indicates that a lie is being told, but it is more reliably, a general signal of high stress.' Hence, context plays a key role.

Practical Illustrations

Case Study I: While making presentation, Mr Y's throat dried up. He tried drinking water, but there was no amount of water that proved potent enough to make his mouth wet. After making the presentation, the business leaders and the working team asked some questions which he did not really consider elaborating on. As the representative of his firm, he had been warned that he must secure the project. So when it came to the point of negotiation and to decide over the investment, his financiers were not convinced about his sincerity as presented in the proposal and, as such, were contemplating if they should pitch their tent with him. At this point, he was deeply and audibly gulping as he hard-swallowed.

Case Study II: A suspect was arrested by law enforcement officials and brought to the interview room so as to give him the benefit of a fair hearing and then gather evidence that would be used against him at the court of law. When given the opportunity to explain himself, he almost found it difficult to open his mouth and talk. When asked questions, he audibly hard-swallowed and slouched in his chair to feign false interest. However, this false show of interest and attention was not enough to swing the tide to his side.

Case Study III: Child A has been warned by his parents to be cautious of their neighbours. In fact, the instruction was that he should never be seen playing with their child. While A seemed to be obedient, he broke the rule one day while the parents were not around; he did not only play with the kid, he went as far as eating with him. Unfortunately, he didn't return to their apartment on time—before he got home, his parents were back. When asked where he was coming from, he became speechless, and he hard-swallowed as he forced himself to speak. His non-verbal gesture gave him away—he lost words because he went to the wrong place and whatever he wanted to say is a lie; he wanted to cover up.

Case Study IV: Politician A has always boasted that he is a man of integrity and the best man to be considered for the post he was contesting for. Instead of him telling the electorate what he would do for them, he would end up running down his opponent. He was fast losing credibility, but he seemed unmoved by the consequences of his actions. Unknown to him, his opponents had run secret checks on him; and just three days to election, they released instances where he compromised his integrity. A political journalist invited him to a programme and asked that he defend himself after playing all the clips to him. He did a hard swallow and looked dejected. Words weren't forthcoming for him.

16.13. Stretching of the Neck

Generic Interpretations of the Concept

Neck stretching can be seen in different places. From the literal point, we stretch our neck after waking up or during physical exercises to maintain body balance. When we sleep on the neck, it becomes very painful, and we will find it difficult turning from a side to the other. So the neck-stretching behaviour is to ensure that we maintain the needed stamina to go about our daily endeavours.

However, there are also times you see people stretch their neck involuntarily, and this is when you need to shine your searchlight on the person in order to better understand their intents and emotions. Neck stretching as used in this sense is the movement or turning of the neck in a circular motion; it is as if the head wants to be turned in a 260-degree angle. Even though this is practically impossible, you will see the person attempt the circular movement of the neck, which controls the head as a way of pacifying themselves when stressed.

When the neck is stretched, it obviously becomes longer than its normal shape. The aim of the person is to unburden the stress which has kept the neck in a lowly state. In simpler terms, the person is non-verbally communicating with you that they are truly stressed but would not allow that to make them totally uncomfortable.

Over the years, I have seen suspects and interviewees display this cue when asked a seemingly difficult question which they perceive should not be answered. This means they understand the implication of providing an answer to the question in such situation. Whenever I noticed this cue in a suspect, I used to repeat the question they were trying to evade so that I could confirm my doubt and know how the question is relevant to the overall goal of the investigation.

Scientific Explanations

Scholars who discussed this concept tackled it from the medical point of view. As usual, we will align with their position and thereafter infer from their submissions. Elizabeth Millard (2016) condemns the stiffening of the neck, which is fast becoming a phenomenon in the society. She believes that one or two cracks around the neck region will help in relieving the body. She explains that neck cracking or stretching is primarily done to ease the tension in the muscles and joints of the neck. In some circumstances, this tension is caused by physical stress such as engaging in a tasking assignment, while in some other times, it is propelled by psychological unrest such as the need to take on-the-spot intellectual exercise. When a person wants to be deceptive, especially to an authoritative figure, he or she will have to reason within themselves and see the viability of the lie before it is reeled out, and some other times, they may need to defend themselves against an allegation, which would require them to speak instantly. All these can cause tension to the muscles of the neck.

The reason the neck muscles and joints become tense during stress is that the brainstem runs through the neck. Hence, stretching the neck has an effect on the brain and spine. That is why Millard (2016) warns that it should be carefully done so that a pacifying act does not end up being a hurtful one. Repetitive actions build up tension in people. That is why you can see people become stressed after a long duration of work or doing a monotonous thing which does not in any way motivate the person. The building up of tension gets the person out of alignment. When this is not subconsciously controlled, it can lead to many other unimaginable things. Stressing the importance of neck stretch, Millard warns that people should be careful in turning this into a habit as it can end up being negative to the body; the neck would be overstretched, and this will bring about a lax, sore, and stiff neck.

On his own part, Tim Jewell (2017) explains the benefits and otherwise of the neck-stretching cue. He notes that cracking of our joints is a common habit, but not everyone does it to achieve the same goal. He simply makes the categorisation into two by saying, 'Some of us do it to release pressure that we're feeling in our shoulders or neck or as a reaction to stress. Sometimes it's just a matter of habit.' He explains that if the neck is stretched gently and occasionally, it would not do any harm to the body; it becomes problematic if wrongly, forcefully, and frequently done. That is why it should be done subconsciously. From the foregoing, it means that those who want to feign this gesture so that people will think they are stressed are doing themselves more harm.

Explaining what makes the neck crack sound, Jewell says that there are 'several sets of joints called facet joints in the neck. These joints are located on each side of your neck. When you crack your neck, the facet joints stretch, which lets fluid spread out in the joint capsule. Once the fluid becomes gas, your neck joints pop. This is what makes neck cracking feel like it's releasing pressure from your neck area.'

Jewell (2017) also reports a study which opines that cracking the neck in the right way has a positive effect on the brain. When the neck is cracked, the displaced joints and muscles are rightly repositioned, and this is seen in the release of pressure. In some rare cases, merely hearing the crack of the neck makes some distressed people feel better, whether the joint was successfully adjusted or not.

Practical Illustrations

Case Study I: Mr F had been on his desk for the past eight hours, trying to fix some issues and attend to seminar papers sent from around the world in preparation for the annual conference his company hosts. Many of the papers he went through did not meet the standard he was expecting. This was his first point of depression. The ones that seemed good had their owners coming from long distance. This meant it was either the company went for quality and paid more, or settled for wishy-washy ones and paid less. Taking off his eyes from the screen, he stretched his neck, and it cracked in a soothing manner before he stood up for his lunch. One would have noticed the frustration and disappointment on his face, which further expressed how disappointed he was.

Case Study II: Mr YI had a stressful day at school today. As a hard-working teacher, he is concerned about the success of his students, and since they are preparing for their exams, he now spends extra time with them, preparing them for the exams. Apart from that, he is in charge of many extracurricular activities and would teach some other classes too. He stood in for the school management today in a meeting and would have to prepare reports to the management. All these stressed him out. He completed work for the day at 6 p.m., and as he stood up, he stretched his neck and had a crack before going home. This was like easing tension on the neck so as to be relieved.

Case Study III: I once conducted a check on a bus at a border and had to delay the driver because there was someone without valid means of identification which could enable him come into the country. While the verification process was ongoing, the other passengers looked impatient. However, there was a man whose case was of interest to me; I discovered that all through the process, he buried his head, trying hard to avoid facial contact with me. When they were about to leave, he stretched his neck to ease tension. I asked him if all was well, and he nervously answered in the affirmative. Three hours after that, his load was impounded in another vehicle at that same spot.

16.14. Facial and Neck Flushing

Generic Interpretations of the Concept

Facial and neck blushing is an autonomic response to some stimuli that is out of the control of humans. This makes it a very accurate and reliable source of understanding the intent of those you are dealing with. Neck and facial flushing is when the face or surface level of the neck becomes glaringly red; it is flushed with blood that has been redirected to the surface level due to the negative emotion the person is witnessing. This behaviour practically changes the facial appearance of the person, and you can feel that is not well with them. Depending on the physique or build-up of the person, this cue can make them become threatening to people around them.

There are many possible causes of neck blushing. The first probable reason is insecurity. When a person feels insecure about being at a place or discussing a concept, it brings about disorientation of the body system, which makes blood flush on the facial and neck skin. Insecurity brings about confusion and makes people think in a shallow manner. This is made evident by their reactions to issues. In the same vein, the face and the neck become flushed when a person feels threatened. Threat births anxiety and makes people think less of themselves. Thinking that a situation is above them is the first point of submission that makes them appear fearful, which is demonstrated by the flushing of the face.

Also, in the rarest of circumstances, this behaviour can also be observed when a person is telling a lie or caught doing something out of bounds. In this situation, this gesture is a signal of regret. It means the person is regretting that they have been caught in an illegal act. I understand this is the only interpretation many people do allude to facial or neck flushing, but it only happens once in a blue moon. So you must understand the context of the issue before you assert that the person is deceptive.

What this behaviour does is that, it helps us to understand that someone is troubled—whether induced by innocent embarrassment or caught in a despicable act. In conclusion, let me remind you that some drugs and foods can bring about facial or neck blushing.

Scientific Explanations

According to Changing Minds (2019), 'a generally red face may indicate that the person is hot as the blood come to the surface to be cooled. They may heat up either from exercise or emotional arousal, for example when they are excited and energised.' But when it comes to blushing, the face and neck become red in different ways. The website notes that embarrassment causes people to blush in various manners. For instance, in some people, it is only the neck that will go red; in some others, it is the cheeks alone and in other instances, it may be experienced in the whole face.

Christopher Philip (2013) describes blushing as the 'colour of emotion'. The fact is that we have all had to deal with blushing at one point in time or another, but many of us do not understand the reason behind it. Science links blushing to adrenaline and cortisol, which are hormones that are released when we get excited, feel pressure, or are nervous. When the adrenaline hormone is released into the blood stream, it prepares the person for the fight or flight response—that is, the person either runs away or stays to confront a situation. The hormone also diverts blood flow from the digestive system and redistributes it to major muscle groups in the body, empowering them with more than enough power. 'As a side effect, our blood vessels that deliver blood to our faces dilate, meaning they relax or open, allowing more blood to reach the surface of our face causing them to turn red' (Philip 2013). This redness can be interpreted in different ways, depending on the context and the issue at hand.

Reading possible meanings to this cue, Philip (2014) states that blushing 'is a sign that someone is experiencing nervousness, stress, embarrassment, excitement, or is being physically active.' In short, when you see this gesture, it means the person is stressed. If the blushing is that of excitement, it would be accompanied with clusters such as smiling, looking radiant, and being opened. However, if it is a show of embarrassment, nervousness, or anxiety, clusters you should look out for include lowering of the head, shaking hands, turning of body away, avoidance of eye contact, shrugging of shoulders, freezing of the entire body, shaking of head, staggered speech pitch, and reduced voice volume.

The body language expert concludes that neck or facial blushing is not a cue that can be deployed to good usage, and more so, it happens autonomically; it goes beyond what we can control.

Practical Illustrations

Case Study I: S was the best runner during his high school days. But since graduation, he only ran once in a while, just to keep to shape. When he heard the announcement that there would be marathon race for people of all ages, he thought that was the perfect platform for him to prove himself to the world. On the D-day, he was one of the very first set of people to arrive at the take-off point. After three hours into the race, his face and neck were already flushed due to the physical stress.

Case Study II: An elder was to settle a fight between two women. In order to give them fair hearing, he said both of them should first narrate their own side of the cause of the fight. Woman A decided to take the lead. Even though her counterpart wanted to interject at some points, she was cautioned by the elderly man. After Woman A was done with her own account, it was Woman B's turn. When called upon, her heart started pounding, and her face with the neck turned red; it was obvious she was nervous. This, in a way, hinted to the elderly man who was at fault.

Case Study III: A woman thought she could perfectly impersonate her twin sister. When she got to the airport, she walked in boldly and submitted the concocted documents to be cleared. I looked at her and smiled. I had to run some further tests on her and was very certain there were discrepancies. Then, I needed to get some facts from her so as not to indict her unjustly. When she was told to talk, I noticed that her face to her neck immediately turned red. That was a clue that she was nervous, which I worked with, and it paid off at the end as she admitted impersonating someone!

16.15. Jumping of Adam's Apple

Generic Interpretations of the Concept

When the movement or positioning of the Adam's apple becomes inconsistent, it speaks volumes about the emotional feelings of a person. Before explaining the possible meanings attached to this body action, let's first peruse the concept further. The technical name of the Adam's apple is laryngeal prominence. The thyroid cartilage found around the larynx—the throat part which holds the vocal cords—gives the Adam's apple its protruding structure. This makes it very pronounced on the neck. Also, the fact that it sits very close to the chin makes it a point of attraction to people. It is bigger in men than in women, and that is why it is seen as a symbol of handsomeness in men. The Adam's apple is very reactive and highly sensitive to emotional stressors.

Having explained that, when you notice that someone's Adam's apple suddenly moves in an upward direction, there is high probability that he or she just heard something that puts them on their toes; they are rudely shocked by what they just heard or saw. Furthermore, it may also be an indication of apprehension. When you are caught unawares, the body reveals it to the world. Since the neck is a highly sensitive area that reacts to every emotion, the sudden surge of the laryngeal prominence is evidence that what the person is just exposed to frightens them. While they may try to suppress some other negative emotional cues, the jumping of the Adam's apple is an autonomic action that cannot be feigned. In addition, threat can cause this behaviour. While some people maintain their calm in the face of threat and provocation, many others often appear unsettled, thereby making their vulnerability pronounced. When you pay attention to all these hints, you will be able to factor that the emotional stressor making them reactionary in any given context.

Scientific Explanations

David Givens (2019) explains the Adam's apple jump cue in three different ways. Defining the concept, Givens opines that the behaviour is 'a conspicuous up-and-down motion of the Adam's apple' or 'a movement of the throat visible while gulping or swallowing, as in nervousness'. You will discover that the two definitions, when combined, perfectly capture everything that needs to be talked about. Sometimes some people use what they are drinking or swallowing to cover up their nervousness, but even at that, the visibility of the throat movement still reveals what the person is thinking about.

Explaining the usage of the cue, the renowned body language expert submits that this cue is an unconscious connotation of stress, anxiety, and embarrassment.

It is revealed when someone does not agree with the point made by another person. For instance, in a business gathering where you want to strike a deal with another person, if you see their laryngeal prominence inadvertently move up, it means they strongly disagree with what you have just said. The body language gesture appears in real time and cannot be controlled. There is no wonder that Givens (2019) states, 'I love the Adam's-apple-jump. Unconscious and uncontrollable, it gives an exquisite look into the sympathetic (fight-or-flight) division of the autonomic nervous system.' Aligning with the reflective preference of Givens, the fact that it is an autonomic action is what makes it reliable and accurate to work with.

Givens uses some of the political scenarios in the US to shed light on this concept. He recalls that the Adam's apple jump first gained its prominence during a 1988 vice presidential debate of the country when former vice president James Danforth Quayle's thyroid cartilage 'jumped' as his opponent Lloyd Bentsen pointedly replied, 'I knew Jack Kennedy. Jack Kennedy was a friend of mine. Senator, you're no Jack Kennedy!'

Apart from that, many other scholars have also conducted research on this subject matter. Ray Birdwhistell, Grant, and Guyton all submit that this cue is always observed when a person is nervous or experiencing any form of negative emotion. Fear, social discomfort (such as embarrassment), and anxiety are often visibly clear in unwitting, vertical movements of a projection at the front of the throat (Givens 2019).

As a concluding remark, Givens gives a neurological note that 'acting through the *vagus* nerve (cranial X), emotional tension from the brain's limbic system causes unconscious muscular contractions of the *sternothyroid*, *thyrohyoid*, and associated *inferior pharyngeal constrictor* muscles of the Adam's apple. Movement is evident as the muscles contract to swallow, to throat-clear, or to vocalise an objection which may be left unsaid. The Adam's apple is emotionally responsive (i.e., reflects visceral or 'gut' feelings) because its muscles are mediated by the vagus nerve, one of five cranial special visceral nerves.'

Practical Illustrations

Case Study I: Bank A and Bank B are having merger talks. The former has suffered some unimaginable losses in the recent past, which is leading to liquidation. So before they would be asked to leave the market by the monitoring body, they decided to have a merger talk with Bank B that was relatively doing well. During the process, it was the bidders (Bank B) that opened the floor. After an extensive presentation on how they work together as one under their common name, the CEO of Bank B made a proposal of financial commitment. As he mentioned the amount the bank was willing to pay in order to take over the administrative roles of Bank A, the CEO of Bank A looked at his counterpart curiously while his Adam's apple inadvertently jumped up. This action expresses his vehement disagreement with what his counterpart proposed.

Case Study II: The entrance examination into medical school was fixed for nine o'clock in the morning. D had forgotten the time, thinking it was to be held in the evening. When his mother reminded him, he raced out of home to catch a taxi heading there. When he got to the venue, his name had already been called; and as such, he had to wait for the invigilator to cross-check particulars; he did not bring it along while coming. Looking irritatingly, the supervisor asked him to stay at a side. He was embarrassed about himself, and his laryngeal prominence suddenly moved up.

Case Study III: Man A told Woman C that he wanted to marry her, but Woman C is a prostitute. Instead of her telling him that she wasn't ready for such an adventure, she thought she could play along. Over time, the man was not getting the satisfaction he needed in the relationship. He called her attention to this, all to no avail. After running some background checks on her, Man A discovered she was a prostitute. Determined to disgrace her, he liaised with Man B, his brother to woo her, and she fell for it. She booked a date with Man B. The two men agreed to meet at the venue, and when she got there, she met them sitting there. Embarrassed by her action, her Adam's apple jumped up uncontrollably, and she became dumbfounded.

16.16. Exposing the Neck

Generic Interpretations of the Concept

At different points in time, I have explained that the neck is the most vulnerable part of the body. As such, many human actions are aimed at protecting it during any form of threat or outbreak of violence. We have also established the way it serves as the bedrock of messages, revealing people's emotion as they encounter one issue or another. The high sensitivity and vulnerability of the neck makes it a reliable source of emotional expressions; we can accurately understand the intents of people through the neck's body language.

Having said that, if you see someone expose their neck by tilting the head to a side, it means they are relaxed and positive-minded. There is no gainsaying that this behaviour is one of the most used non-verbal cues, yet least understood. For instance, when we see a newborn, we instinctively tilt our head to its side. This is a symbol of interest and love for the child. Surprisingly, the child also recognises this show of love and tends to reward it as time goes on with a relaxed face and smile. When a newborn sees someone drawn to them, they tend to reciprocate this gesture. This instinctive action has bound them to their mother more than anyone else.

As we grow older, this non-verbal gesture grows with us. This is why you unconsciously tilt your head towards a lover during courtship. This act of neck exposure shows that you are drawn to them and relaxed when around them because you believe they will not harm you. Staring into your lover's eyes with the tilted head creates an inexplicable bond between you.

Apart from love context, this behaviour is also seen in professional and personal lives. When you are speaking with a person and they expose their neck by canting their head to a side, this is an indication that they are interested in what you are saying and, as such, listening intently.

This is a powerful disarming act that is very useful during moments of confrontations. If the neck exposure is accompanied with a smile, it serves as a potent tool to win people over your side; there is nobody that sees true love and resists it, whatever guise it may be under.

Scientific Explanations

Navarro (2009) discusses this cue while speaking on courtship behaviours. He submits that as couples are just learning about each other, you will see a lot of neck-touching behaviour in their discussions. This means that at the initial stage; they are not yet fully into each other and, as such, still nurse some reservations on what the other person is up to. He further says that 'as these individuals grow more comfortable around each other, you will see more head tilt and therefore more exposure of the neck. In fact, both may sit mesmerised looking into each other's eyes, head tilted, necks exposed.' This means that they have finally thrown caution into the wind and built trust to some extent.

Philip (2014) shares the same sentiment with Navarro, noting that this cue originates from women in dating and children in general. Explaining the behaviour in one sentence, Philip describes it as a 'submissive signal'. Men do not benefit as women in the use of this cue; when you see a woman tilt her head to a side, it means her willingness to submit. If used in dating context, this is alluring to men as it makes the woman look charming, especially when she wears short dresses. If a woman wishes to amplify this posture, she will brush her hair lightly, thereby directing the gaze of the man to that direction. If there is eye contact, it serves as a key to make the moment really become emotional. Just like women, children can also be a great beneficiary of this cue as it shows their harmless intent; this can propel help from adults.

The verbal translation of this cue is: 'I'm trusting and submissive of your dominance and am showing you this by exposing my vulnerable neck by canting to the side or removing my hair' (Philip 2014).

On the cluster to fix your eyes on so as to rightly interpret this cue, if it is displayed by children, you will discover that their eyes would also be lowered and they would show off the fat lower lip in order to draw the sympathy of those around. If it is a woman, she may seductively brush aside her long hair to make the neck more exposed, tilt the head to a side, and use her hand to carefully stroke and caress the neck skin. In some overt cases, this may be an invite to kiss (Philip 2014).

Practical Illustrations

Case Study I: T was going to visit her friends and needed to bring some amount of money in case she needed to get anything for herself. On going to meet her mum, her mother said she did not have cash on her. Then, T slowly walked to the dining room, where her father was eating. She knew that asking directly might not yield the needed outcome. So she craftily sat directly opposite her father. The father did not seem connected to her. She subconsciously tilted her head to the side, used her finger to curl her long hair so that her neck could be exposed, and then gazed at her father with doe eyes. Her dad was later forced to ask what was wrong with her, and she used the opportunity to make her request known.

Case Study II: A charming, gorgeously dressed young man went to a bank to make some transactions. On getting there, he became a point of attraction to the teller, a young lady. As she set her eyes on him, she could not concentrate on what she was doing again and was thinking of how she would get him. Hence, she tilted her head to the side and quickly twirled her hair with a finger so as to make her neck very revealing as she gazed at him with doe eyes. She was obviously ready for love and would do just anything to get this love.

Case Study III: Ms KV, an indescribably beautiful lady, impersonated her friend in order to escape from what she tagged the hardship in her country. She didn't look courageous, but she looked determined. When she was stopped at the border, she moved closer to the law enforcement officer who seemed thrilled at her beauty. Before the officer could ask her any question, she opened up a side of her neck to him and connected with him through romantic facial expressions. The officer almost lost attention because he had an erection before his supervisor stepped in to ensure objectivity. She later confessed that she adopted a romantic stance to lure the officer into overlooking her wrongdoing.

16.17. Stiffening of the Neck

Generic Interpretations of the Concept

Being retentive and receptive of another person's ideas makes us tilt our head to a side in order to expose our neck to the person. I explained in the preceding section that this is a cue of relaxation and shows that the person has trust in a co-interlocutor that he or she would not be harmed. However, when there is a sharp deviation from a relaxed mood to a rigid one, whereby the neck becomes much stiffened, it means a problem has set in. In simpler terms, a stiffened neck is a display of lack of comfort. If someone who was relaxed suddenly becomes rigid, it means an occurrence—whether physically or through thought—that does not match their perspective of life has taken place. When you observe a change in the mood of a person, always try to also check the positioning of their head and movement of the neck.

The fading feeling of comfort also negatively affects the neck muscles by charging them. When they are energised, moving freely becomes a herculean task.

A stiff neck connotes vigilance and hyper-alertness. That is, the person is very conscious of their situation—usually a threatening one. When you think a scene is capable of harming you, you become vigilant of whatever emanates from there. Your senses will be on the high side. However, this does not necessarily mean that the threatening situation is real; it may be just an imagination of the person. Also, you may observe this cue in a person when they do not agree with what you have just said. In this sense, it is an expression of shock; they were not expecting that from you. You may also notice the feeling of disappointment on their face.

Further, when someone suddenly remembers the need to discuss an important issue, they may wear this look. For instance, they had a reflection about a particular bad attitude of their spouse and promised to tell them when they are together, but it escaped their mind due to romance and love play. If the issue should suddenly come to mind, it will dilute the positive emotion and thus trigger the need to stiffen the neck so as to communicate the serious issue to their partner. Any time you see a person escalate from a relaxed state of mind to a quick stiffening of the neck, it means something is wrong somewhere.

Scientific Explanations

Anne Asher (2019) discusses the health implications of stiff neck. She notes that stiffening the neck is not good for our health. She lists muscle strain and herniated discs as some of the major causes of stiff neck. Even an infection may lead to stiffening of the neck. Although cases of stiff neck are not normally serious, if ignored, it can be hurtful or disruptive of our plans. She goes further to list seven things that we must avoid in order to prevent stiff neck. She starts with young minds, saying they need to stop overloading their backpacks. Students most especially load their bags with heavy books, and this ends up telling on them negatively in the future. In addition, we need to discourage the habit of wearing a shoulder bag over a shoulder. When a bag is carried on a shoulder, the weight of the bag would be felt on that part of the body, and this can actually affect the person's posture. If these issues can be resolved, it would be easy for us to understand the stiff neck at the societal level. For now, we make mistakes in our interpretations because of the misconceptions trailing it at different levels.

Those who cradle their phone with their shoulder are not left out in this issue; this is a surefire way to cause neck pain for themselves. Also, some people avoid movement breaks for reasons best known to them. This can complicate feelings of stress at the neck; people should take walk breaks regularly so that the neck can be strengthened and relaxed. When you fail to change positions for hours, this is called static posture and often leads to neck stiffness (Asher 2019).

Asher lists stress as another factor that causes the stiffening of the neck. She submits that 'stress often comes from what is known as the "fight or flight" response to a triggering event, where our initial reaction is to either get away from a perceived threat or to obliterate it in order to feel safe again.' The way our body system is built is that when we see anything that seems to be capable of endangering our health, it should either be avoided or confronted. Due to the vulnerability of the neck, this is felt in that region of the body. That is why the cue you perceive in that part of the body will be difficult to deny.

Due to the situation of things across the world, people feel it is not right to display physical or emotional reactions. Hence, they employ all means to suppress their feelings. Holding your feelings inside or employing wrong ways of expressing them can lead to chronic stress of the neck muscles. While stressed, the neck may become immobilised until it is relieved. Emotional therapy, massaging, and exercise are some of the ways to deal with stress in the neck region (Asher 2019).

Practical Illustrations

Case Study I: Lady R and Guy M are young lovers who have been fond of each other since they met. Both of them have purposed in their heart that they would marry each other. While on a date, they were enjoying the comfort of each other when Lady R asked M about his thoughts on polygamy and infidelity. Unconscious of the feelings of his fiancée, Guy M said he saw nothing ill with it. He went ahead to give instances of some of his friends who were doing it. He seemed to have a great grasp of the topic and also, displayed needless passion. This became baffling to Lady R because M was subconsciously passing the message that he can explore polygamy as an option. Before he ended his explanation, R stiffened her neck and slouched her posture, feeling uneasy to look at any other side.

Case Study II: There was supposed to be four nurses on duty, but three of them came late. This means there would be too much pressure on the only person on duty. As if this was not enough, one of the patients proved to be stubborn; after she pleaded with him to use his drugs and sleep, he remained adamant and was doing some other things. The nurse was attending to another patient when the disobedient patient started feeling uneasy. Determined not to attend to him, the nurse stiffened her neck with a frown and focused on the patient she was with for several minutes before eventually yielding to his request.

Case Study III: Ms QM was illegally employed by an ad hoc staff of TCD Company. One day, a seminar was organised by the management of the firm, and she decided to attend, thinking that there was no reason that would warrant her being called out. However, during the course of the lecture, the lecturer pointed at her to ask her some basic questions about the unit she belonged to. She tried to answer, and as a way of rewarding her, her appointment number was asked of her. Trying to feign deafness, she stiffened her neck and looked away from the man, but she was tapped by the person close to her. That was her end at the firm!

CHAPTER 17

The Shoulders

No matter the shape of your shoulders, it speaks volumes about your personality, thoughts per time, and disposition to an issue being discussed. Shoulders may be narrow, slim, broad, athletic, slumping, attractive, or beguiling. Variety is the spice of life, and this is aptly demonstrated with the individual structures of the shoulders. The padded shoulders of a business suit gives the person a sense of uniqueness anywhere they are. Swimmers always have broad shoulders. All these are factors that help us in understanding the intents of people and their background in any given circumstance.

According to Matthew Hoffman (2019), 'the shoulder is one of the largest and most complex joints in the body. The shoulder joint is formed where the humerus (upper arm bone) fits into the scapula (shoulder blade), like a ball and socket.'

The human shoulder is made up of three bones: the clavicle (collarbone), the scapula (shoulder blade), and the humerus (upper arm bone) as well as associated muscles, ligaments, and tendons. The articulations between the bones of the shoulder make up the shoulder joints. The shoulder joint, also known as the glenohumeral joint, is the major joint of the shoulder, but can more broadly include the acromioclavicular joint. Let's explore the shoulder joint the more in order to have an apt understanding of it.

The shoulder joint (also known as the glenohumeral joint) is the main joint of the shoulder (Free Dictionary 2019). It is a ball-and-socket joint that allows the arm to rotate in a circular fashion or to hinge out and up away from the body. It is formed by the articulation between the head of the humerus and the lateral scapula (specifically, the glenoid cavity of the scapula). The 'ball' of the joint is the rounded, medial anterior surface of the humerus, and the 'socket' is formed by the glenoid cavity, the dish-shaped portion of the lateral scapula. The shallowness of the cavity and relatively loose connections between the shoulder and the rest of the body allows the arm to have tremendous mobility, at the expense of being much easier to dislocate than most other joints in the body. There is an approximately 4:1 disproportion in size between the large head of the humerus and the shallow glenoid cavity.

The capsule is a soft tissue envelope that encircles the glenohumeral joint and attaches to the scapula, humerus, and head of the biceps. It is lined by a thin, smooth synovial membrane. This capsule is strengthened by the coracohumeral ligament, which attaches the coracoid process of the scapula to the greater tubercle of the humerus. There are also three other ligaments attaching the lesser tubercle of the humerus to lateral scapula and are collectively called the glenohumeral ligaments (Bogart 2017).

Apart from the shoulder joints, the rotator cuff is another important part of the shoulder. The rotator cuff is an anatomical term given to the group of four muscles and their tendons that act to stabilise the shoulder. These muscles are the supraspinatus, infraspinatus, teres minor, and subscapularis and that hold the head of the humerus in the glenoid cavity during movement. The cuff adheres to the glenohumeral capsule and attaches to the head of the humerus (Bogart 2017). Together, these keep the humeral head in the glenoid cavity, preventing upward migration of the humeral head caused by the pull of the deltoid muscle at the beginning of arm elevation. The infraspinatus and the teres minor, along with the anterior fibers of the deltoid muscle, are responsible for external rotation of the arm (Favard et al. 2007).

The four tendons of these muscles converge to form the rotator cuff tendon. This tendon, along with the articular capsule, the coracohumeral ligament, and the glenohumeral ligament complex, blend into a confluent sheet before insertion into the humeral tuberosities. The infraspinatus and teres minor fuse near their musculotendinous junctions, while the supraspinatus and subscapularis tendons join as a sheath that surrounds the biceps tendon at the entrance of the bicipital groove (Matava et al. 2005).

In addition to the four muscles of the rotator cuff, the deltoid muscle and teres major muscles arise and exist in the shoulder region itself. The deltoid muscle covers the shoulder joint on three sides, arising from the front upper third of the clavicle, the acromion, and the spine of the scapula, and travelling to insert on the deltoid tubercle of the humerus. The deltoid muscle covers the shoulder joint on three sides, arising from the front upper third of the clavicle, the acromion, and the spine of the scapula, and travelling to insert on the deltoid tubercle of the humerus. The teres major attaches to the outer part of the back of the scapula, beneath the teres minor, and attaches to the upper part of the humerus. It helps with medial rotation of the humerus (Bogart 2007).

Talking of the function of this part of the body, the muscles and joints of the shoulder allow it to move through a remarkable range of motion, making it one of the most mobile joints in the human body. The shoulder can abduct, adduct, rotate, be raised in front of and behind the torso and move through a full 360° in the sagittal plane. This tremendous range of motion also makes the shoulder extremely unstable, far more prone to dislocation and injury than other joints (Long 2019).

Having said that, there are some shoulder conditions that can affect the effective functioning of the body:

Frozen shoulder: Inflammation develops in the shoulder that causes pain and stiffness. As a frozen shoulder progresses, movement in the shoulder can be severely limited (Hoffman 2019).

Osteoarthritis: The common 'wear-and-tear' arthritis that occurs with ageing. The shoulder is less often affected by osteoarthritis than the knee.

Rheumatoid arthritis: A form of arthritis in which the immune system attacks the joints, causing inflammation and pain. Rheumatoid arthritis can affect any joint, including the shoulder (Hoffman 2019).

Shoulder impingement: The acromion (edge of the scapula) presses on the rotator cuff as the arm is lifted. If inflammation or an injury in the rotator cuff is present, this impingement causes pain (Hoffman 2019).

As earlier explained, the shoulders can reveal our inner feelings per time. You would be surprised about the ability of the shoulders in telling others what you think of them. In fact, the shoulders have the ability to predict your achievements. As we move forward in this chapter, you would be exposed to the different messages the shoulders are employed to communicate.

17.1. Raising a Shoulder

Generic Interpretations of the Concept

In any situation where you see just a shoulder raised, it means something is wrong because the person has unconsciously created an imbalance in the body which communicates their intent at the moment. When a shoulder is raised and moved closer to the ear as if they want to block their ears with the raised shoulder, it is a negative signal that the person is not ready to flow along with you in that discourse. Raising a shoulder gives a person poor posture, which is a symbolic representation that the person is not thinking anything positive.

If someone is talking and you observe this cue in them, it is a signal of doubt. That is, they are not really convinced of what they are telling; there are still some contradictory thoughts going on in their mind. So this obvious contradiction is making them feel uncomfortable and thus, demonstrated through the raising of a shoulder.

In addition, this gesture represents insecurity. When someone is insecure in an environment, you will get to know this through various body language cues displayed. Raising just a shoulder is an indication of a confused mind; the person is not sure if they should raise both shoulders or drop them in their natural state. Because they are stressed or threatened by an event or situation, they become psychologically unstable to think through at that given time.

To be sure that the person is insecure or doubtful of what he or she is saying, pay attention to other clusters such as hesitation in speaking, withdrawal of the arms into the body, trying to evade eye contact, and negative facial appearance, among others. If you notice a general closed body gesture, it means the person does not have confidence in what they are telling you. For instance, when negotiating with a client and you ask them that 'Is that the best price you can give?' and you observe this gesture in them, it is a hint that if engaged further, they will reconsider their stance and raise the bar; it means you still have the room to negotiate with them.

All things being equal, any time you observe this body language cue, it means the person is not convinced or fully committed to what they are saying.

Scientific Explanations

Joe Navarro (2012) notes that the shoulder is the most ignored part of the body, but it is filled with elegant messages. He notes that the concept of posture leans heavily on the shape and structure of the shoulders; if you carry your shoulders inappropriately, you would be seen as maintaining poor posture. Navarro shares his experience as a former FBI special agent after engaging thousands of interviewees. According to him, raising a shoulder is a symbol of outright deception or lack of confidence. Lamenting that this has not been captured in literature, he explains that whenever he sees this tell in a suspect, it was an opportunity for him to ask follow up questions. When people are not sure of what they are saying, they will shrug their shoulders. Navarro notes, 'We do it because it emphasises what we are saying. This quick gravity-defying behaviour (lifting up or shrugging of the shoulders) positively reinforces what was said.'

Navarro (2012) explains further that apart from law enforcement situations, this gesture is also a useful hint for clinicians while discussing with patients. If a doctor sees this cue, it means the patient is not sure of their response.

Hanan Parvez (2019) also expatiates on the partial shoulder shrug. Parvez shares the same sentiment with Navarro. She submits that shrugging just a shoulder is an indication that the person is insecure or not committed to what they have just said. Hence, it should raise some sort of suspicion in you so that you can question them further. This does not necessarily mean that the person is deceptive, but it is a sure sign that something is amiss. Parvez states, 'He might be hiding something important or he might simply have a nonchalant attitude about what you asked him.'

In what seems to be a consensus among the experts that contributed to this subject matter, Changing Minds (2019) also submits that a small and quick shrug of the shoulder means the person lacks understanding about a concept or uncertain about their thoughts. Note that this gesture is subtle and subconsciously displayed; this means the person is not aware that they are letting out the signal. The platform also explains further that shrugging of the shoulder partially may be a signal of deception. That is, the shoulder is speaking in a resonating manner instead of the mouth. This gives them away unexpectedly. The website concludes that 'a more prolonged and animated shrug can be similar to the circling shoulders that indicate readying for aggression and can thus signal a threat. In a smaller form it may indicate irritation or frustration.'

Practical Illustrations

Case Study I: This is a paragraph lifted from a piece on shoulder body language by Navarro. It is a case study situated in the context of a patient and a clinician.

When a doctor asks, 'Are you going to take your medications as I have instructed?' and they answer back with a slight shoulder rise, they know something is up. As one primary care doctor told me, 'invariably they don't want to come out and say what is on their mind: they don't like taking that medication or it causes them a stomach upset. So rather than speak up they answer with a shoulder up or slightly raised.' For the caring clinician this serves as a great opportunity to ask, 'What is your experience with this drug and has it caused you problems?' Observing the shoulders as they inch up should serve as a starting for even more questions to determine what are the issues. (Navarro 2012)

That is, the non-verbal gesture is a hint that there are lots of thoughts yet uncovered from the person.

Apart from a medical environment, this same technique can be used in the business world for negotiations. With this, a salesman can cart home more gain. This can also be used in law enforcement to better engage suspects.

Case Study II: Most times, I like buying items from a source. That is, I like being loyal to sellers, once I like the services being rendered to me. There was a day I got to one of my beloved salesmen and he advertised a product to me. Even though I didn't really need the product, I was forced to go for it due to how he well he spoke about it. However, when I eventually used it, it wasn't as potent as hyped. When I later returned to buy some other items, he inquired from me, if I found the product worthy and I unconsciously raised my shoulder. This was to mean that it was not useful as expected and, to be realistic, a waste of money. Unfortunately, he didn't get my message, and I wasn't ready to spoil his mood as there were other clients around him. So I just said yes reluctantly and took my leave.

Case Study III: Mr UY thought his neighbour's drug consumption habit was getting out of hand and had to report him. After that, he was arrested and taken to correctional facility. Mr UY had learnt that maximum care was being given to drug addicts and others in their shoes whenever they are taken to the facility. So he hoped he had helped his neighbour by reporting him. When the neighbour returned, Mr UY asked him what he felt about where he was taken to, and he raised his shoulders slightly. That birthed curiosity in UY, who asked him more questions to understand why he didn't enjoy the place. As a quality control agent, he needed to know if it was worth working on.

17.2. Show of Interest

Generic Interpretations of the Concept

The shoulder is capable of communicating both positive and negative emotions. So this makes it relevant in every given situation. The preceding segment speaks of how the shoulder is used to show uncertainty and lack of confidence but this talks on the usefulness of the shoulders in registering one's interest in another person. Using the shoulder to show interest has to do with an intentional, slow rise of a shoulder, accompanied with a head tilt towards the same shoulder while maintaining direct eye contact with the person in a stimulating manner. Whenever you see this, it means the person has personal interest in you.

I need to emphasise that this cue is intentional; it is consciously done. This means that after the person might have unconsciously picked interest in you, then they will switch to their conscious senses to make it known. The slow movement of a shoulder coupled with head tilt towards the direction is to draw your attention. So they maintain a dilated, wide, and charming eye contact with you to make their interest known. There is little wonder that this is mostly seen in dating contexts among women. Most cultures do not allow women to verbally approach men for love. So they use all forms of subtle and unconscious means to communicate the intents of their heart when they take interest in a person. When men who are in the know see such cues, it is taken as a green light to launch into action.

Let me state that although the shoulder interest gesture is mostly seen in dating scenarios, it is not limited to that. I have seen cases where female suspects display this cue as a way of showing their interest in a law enforcement officer so that the officer can be lenient towards them. This is taken as a seductive sign to distract the officer in the main assignment of investigation.

Scientific Explanations

Parvez (2019) describes the shoulder interest gesture as a show of submission. That is, you see the person as being superior and you are submitting to them. She aptly captures the whole context thus: 'Male-female attraction is all a matter of dominance and submission. Females are attracted to dominant males and males are attracted to submissive females.' Hence, that is why you observe this submissive gesture in females. The most submissive beings in the world are children. It is believed that the submissive cues of women are learnt from children.

When women put on this submissive gesture, it serves as bait to attract men who are unconsciously triggered through the rising of their paternal instinct to care for, love, and protect their kids. Probably, this accounts for the reason men say 'She's such an amazing babe' when they see an attractive lady. Parvez (2019) explains the gesture thus: 'The attraction shrug is a female submissive gesture in which a woman raises one shoulder, turning and tilting her head towards it, sometimes touching it with the chin or the side of her face. When children do this gesture, everybody finds it cute and when grown up females do it, they're trying to appear attractive.'

If you have never observed this cue in dating contexts, take time to check the profile pictures of ladies on your social media networks. They also display this childish gesture when they pose for photograph. In addition, when you compliment a woman for her dress, she may display this cue and verbally add 'Thank you' to spice it up. Parvez concludes on this that 'when someone she likes cracks a joke, you might notice a woman doing this gesture, smiling and looking at the person from the corners of her eyes'. The aim is to arouse the feeling of likeness in the person too so that they can start their relationship from that point.

Practical Illustrations

Case Study I: Ms T was invited to a wedding ceremony by her colleague. She never knew it was such a high-class event; she was wowed by the calibre of people she met on ground. In dire search for a rich, broad-shouldered, handsome, and light-skinned man, she quickly surveyed the whole venue. Not waiting for her friend to point to a seat for her, she quickly walked to a table where there was a vacant seat. In no time, she socialised with almost everyone on the table. But her target was clear; there was a handsome young man she has been trying to hook up with. When the man was speaking, she looked on with keen interest.

Her serious attention on the guy made other people to be suspicious of her. The man ended his narration with a joke which made Ms T slowly move a shoulder and tilt her head along the same direction while looking into the corners of the guy's eyes; this was a show of interest which was later decoded by the man. And that was the beginning of their romantic relationship.

Case Study II: Mrs Y and three other colleagues were sent on a manpower training in another city. The training had many people from other companies; it was a gathering of professionals, well-kitted and charming in every sense. Even though the programme was purely organised for the sake of practically building up the professional abilities of the attendees, many of them seized the opportunity to network and build personal relationships. Mrs Y, apart from having some issues with her husband, is naturally wired for promiscuity. Whenever she sees anyone handsome, she becomes distracted. She was emotionally moved to the anchor of the programme. So she found a way to connect with him after the second day. While discussing with the man, she intentionally and slowly raised her right shoulder and tilted her head towards the raised shoulder, then smiled charmingly to the man as she looked into the corners of his eyes. Even though the man was aware of this cue, he tried to resist it. She was not disturbed by the first resistance, so she tried again, and this time around, with other obvious cues, which eventually made the man succumb to her emotional needs.

Case Study III: Ms OA needed a favour from her boss, and she knew the only way that would be possible was to lure the man to have sexual intercourse with her. She made some administrative mistakes which required her to be sacked. She wasn't ready to look for job elsewhere. Before her sack letter was typed, Ms OA was always near her boss, pleasing him with everything. One day, when it seemed that the boss was relaxed, she sat directly opposite him and left her legs wide open while she raised her shoulders and slightly moved her head to the direction of the raised shoulders. She then accompanied the gesture with a radiant smile to the man. This was a glaring expression of love and emotional attachment.

17.3. Holding Both Shoulders High

Generic Interpretations of the Concept

Before now, we have been considering the use of just a shoulder in communicating non-verbally. However, this focuses on the use of the two shoulders to subconsciously get our intents known. Holding the head high is the polar opposite to holding the shoulders high. When you see a person holding their shoulders high, do not be tricked to assume that it is a show of confidence. In fact, it aptly illustrates insecurities of fears. To display this gesture, you will see people raise and keep the two shoulders high towards their ears. This non-verbal act is often referred to as 'turtle effect'.

Think of it or have a pictorial view of it: when a person raises both shoulders towards their ears, they become smaller, which communicates to their co-interlocutor that they are actually freezing out due to what is being discussed. While displaying this cue, the person will hold their breath due to the fear. That is why I refer to it as a show of the freeze emotional stimulus. In simpler terms, when you see a person display this cue, it means they are trying to hide in the open. If they had their way, they would have disappeared from that given venue. The general message in this is that the person is really disturbed by something—what is being discussed or the presence of someone.

The look on the person's face will betray their intent of deceiving you into believing that they are confident; they usually maintain an empty face, which is negatively thoughtful and laced with glaring regrets. When a speaker is asking for volunteers in a large group of participants and also when a student is not prepared for a test or question, you will notice this sign.

Scientific Explanations

Parvez (2019) says that a lack of confidence forces people into this mood. That is, when we lack confidence in what we are saying or what another person is telling us, this tends to make us submissive, thus switching into the 'protective' mood. When you raise the shoulders and lower the head, it slumps up at the neck, thereby offering a form of protection to the neck and throat, being arguably the most delicate part of the body. Parvez practically explains that 'we do this gesture when we hear a loud, banging sound or when we think that some heavy object is going to fall on us. Since our shoulders are strong, they can do a good job of protecting the neck should there be some kind of real danger.' This is very practical and you can try it out as you read this passage.

Let me give another example to shed more light on this cue: cast your mind on a person who is standing on a dark, creepy street, shivering due to fear of unknown. It is practically impossible to do this reflection without thinking of a person with raised shoulders and folded arms. That is why Parvez (2019) expertly states that 'people who feel tense and insecure keep their shoulders raised most of the time while those who feel confident have their shoulders spread out and relaxed.'

Furthermore, raising the shoulders simultaneously makes one appear smaller than one's size. This has both literal and figurative interpretations. When a subordinate is approaching their boss, their shoulders are usually high as a show of respect; the person is decreasing through that action so that their boss may increase by maintaining a relaxed posture. Also, this can be seen in the classroom situation when a teacher is rebuking their student; the said student would become insignificant and small by raising their shoulders. This aptly expresses their state of mind. In addition, you notice this cue when a group of people go to the theatre to see a movie. The person in front will display this gesture in order not to obstruct the views of those sitting behind (Parvez 2019). We will expatiate on these illustrations later.

Navarro (2012) says that when the shoulders are raised, it means they lack vitality. Reminiscing on his times as a special agent of the FBI, he notes that even criminals pay attention to the manner people carry their shoulders before an attack. That is, a person who raises their shoulders is telling other people that he or she is fragile and can be attacked without any form of reprisal attack; criminals hardly attack anyone who is relaxed and feeling confident because they do not know what they are up to. Hence, the look of our shoulders is a crucial factor to a person seeking to prey on us. One body language cue that all law enforcement officials, no matter their branch, seem to have in common is the look of their shoulders; they communicate power and leadership.

Changing Minds (2019) also notes that raising the shoulders and lowering the head is done when we fear an attack—whether real or virtual. The website concludes that 'shoulders hunched up, often with arms folded tight or crossed and holding the body, can be a sign that the person is cold (they may be shivering too). This may also be a sign of extreme tension, often from anxiety or fear.'

Practical Illustrations

Case Study I: In a training comprising of directors from different parts of the world, the trainer decided to make it interactive and practical so that he could know the different issues that they are passing through in their individual organisations. With this, it would be holistically discussed, and then others would know how to guard against such issues when they are encountered in the future. The discussion was actually stimulating as many of the participants were making insightful contributions. However, Mr H does not want to be called on because his promotion to the position of a director was politically influenced and, since, he has not lived up to expectations. He knows virtually nothing concrete about the job. So he was not willing to speak at the gathering. When the trainer asked for a volunteer from his side, he raised his shoulders and looked smaller than his size, while lowering his head. This was an unconscious way of hiding his entire body from being called.

Case Study II: One of those who really believe in the use of emotions in getting to the minds of people are salesmen. In fact, it is insinuated that a salesman who doesn't know how to appeal to emotions cannot make a headway. While I cannot confirm or discard this assertion, I have seen a few instances where salesmen appealed to my emotions while they could have done same to my reasoning. On a particular instance, a salesman approached me and instead of telling me what I stood to gain from his product if I made a purchase, he stood before me, raised his two shoulders slightly and buried his head as if he was dying of frustration. I just had to buy some amount to salvage his psychological situation. I later found out that he hadn't made any sales for sometime and urgently needed money to execute some projects.

Case Study III: There was a time I arrested a drug trafficker for the second time. On the first occasion, he appealed to me and made promises to turn a new leaf; and I had to let him go, even though that was at the risk of my integrity. However, when he was nabbed the second time, he accurately read the expression on my face, and he knew there was no escape route for him. Thinking he could appeal to my emotions, he slightly raised his shoulders and tucked in his head. This was a demonstration of nervousness and emotional appeal, but those gimmicks were not going to work on me.

17.4. Shrugging Shoulders Quickly

Generic Interpretations of the Concept

There is wide difference between a slow shoulder shrug and the quick shrugging of the shoulders. Like in the preceding section, we spoke on holding both shoulders high in a prominent and pronounced manner when people are asked questions and they have no idea of the answer. I said it is used to communicate lack of confidence. This is somewhat irritating, as the person presents themselves as someone lacking knowledge in an unexpected scenario. However, when the shoulders are shrugged and dropped in the twinkle of an eye, it is considered as gravity-defying behaviour, and it is usually associated with positive thoughts.

In this case, it means the person does not really know the answer to the question. Let me explain the difference between the two similar cues in clearer terms. For the former (slow upward movement of the shoulders), it is expected that the person should know the response to the question, but disappointedly, they do not know or they are unwilling to say the answer due to the likely consequences on their personality or profession. In the latter, the person does not sincerely know the answer, so instead of keeping you waiting, they communicate the intent of their heart through their shoulders. Hence, this is taken as a positive gesture.

Most times, the slow shrug is consciously done; the person is aware that they are letting out the cue while in the case of the quick shrug, it is subconsciously displayed to follow a verbal utterance. This creates a sort of alliance with the verbal utterance, hence, making their response more believable.

Scientific Explanations

According to Changing Minds (2019), 'The classic shrug, with one-off raising and lowering of shoulders usually means "I don't know!" and may be accompanied with raised eyebrows, downturned mouth, and hands held to the side, with palms upwards or forwards (showing nothing is being concealed).' This means the person has nothing to hide. The opening of the palms upwards is symbolic to the opening of their heart; if they were hiding anything from you, they would have kept their hands to themselves.

When it is performed in a quick and small manner, it means the person does it subconsciously, hence making it more accurate indicator of uncertainty or lack of understanding of a concept. This means the person is not happy that they are unable to provide an answer to the question but in order not to appear deceptive, they quickly communicated the intents of their heart to you.

Navarro (2012) states that we unconsciously make use of the quick shoulder shrug gesture in our daily affairs without paying attention to it. For instance, Navarro gives an illustration thus: 'When someone asks us, "Which way is it to the freeway?" and we immediately shrug the shoulders, elevating them quickly and emphatically, this is our way of saying "I really don't know".' The body language expert explains further that this cue is universal, thus making it reliable anywhere you see it. Further, if we were to answer the question verbally, there is high probability that we will make use of our shoulders alongside what is being said in order to potentiate our words. This is done because it lays emphasis on what is being said. When we make use of non-verbal cues to reinforce what is being said, whether positive or negative, we are viewed by others as being trustworthy. There is no gainsaying that we build greater confidence in others when we see them confirm their words subconsciously through non-verbal cues.

In the same vein, Christopher Philip (2014) notes that a shoulder shrug is an indication of lack of knowledge. He also agrees with Parvez that it may be a means of showing submission. When you are not ready to pursue a course further, you may indicate this with a quick shrugging of the shoulders. Giving the verbal translations of this cue, Philip submits that it can be one of two messages: When someone asks us, 'Which way is it to the freeway?' and we immediately shrug the shoulders, elevating them quickly and emphatically, this is our way of saying, 'I really don't know', or 'I'm sorry I don't know the answer and I'm shrugging to show others that I'm not a threat and wish not to provoke. In other words, I'm sorry I don't know, but please go easy on me. I'm not a target, I'm submissive.' Note that there are variants of the shoulders shrugging that can affect its meaning.

Practical Illustrations

Case Study I: Mr O is the secretary of the managing director of FDX Firms. One of the employees has been perpetrating some heinous crimes within the organisation. Some important files are being tampered with, and this is affecting the reputation of the company. The managing director was really disturbed by this, and he sought to handle issue without creating scene at any point in time. Knowing that the secretary is central to the administration of the firm, he invited Mr O into his office and recounted his ordeals to him, thinking that he would know something about the evil going on in the establishment. After telling him everything, Mr O really felt sorry for him and shrugged his shoulders in a quick glance to show his innocence on the question being asked.

Case Study II: Mrs Q was teaching her students on a topic pertaining to the society, and as such, needed to give examples that the students could relate with. During the lecture, she saw the needed to make the voices of the students heard because they were from different families with peculiar issues. So she decided to ask for their contributions by throwing questions to them in a technical way that will align with the purpose of the class. While many of the students performed excellently, some of them were lost and could not create a point of alliance between their raw experience and the requirements of the class. When Y was called on, as he was standing up, he shrugged his shoulder in a nano-second to show his lack of knowledge on the concept being asked on.

Case Study III: Mr IC is an illiterate, and when he wanted to get his passport in order to enable him travel, he approached scammers who only duplicated someone else's and gave it to him. The poor man only glanced through the document and kept it. When he eventually travelled, officers at the border checked the document and discovered it didn't reflect his personality. When they asked him how come he was going about with the wrong passport, he shrugged his shoulders quickly and threw the question back at the officers so as to be enlightened. At this point, the officers saw his ignorance, but that wasn't a tenable excuse.

17.5. Sinking into the Chair

Generic Interpretations of the Concept

When you see a person sinking into their chair, it means all is not well with them; this is a clear indication of a negative mindset as the person goes lower and lower as if they want to disappear from the presence of others. This has the same implication as the 'turtle effect' earlier discussed. In the turtle effect, both shoulders are held high in a slow, intentional manner so as to reduce the size of the person. Also, in this cue, the person gets lower and lower into their chair to the extent that their shoulders become lower in relation to the table. This makes the behaviour stand out. When you see a person looking smaller than their table, it means they are gripped by negative emotions.

There are different meanings that can be attributed to this gesture, depending on the place of its occurrence. For instance, it can be taken as a show of apprehension. When law enforcement officials arrest a suspect and are being taken to the station, they will sink into their chair because they are apprehensive of what their fate would be. The fear of the unknown is making them submit to the situation; this is a closed and submissive body language, telling their audience that they are not threatening. When a person is frightened, they will activate either the flight or the freeze response. In this case, the person is freezing and would have taken to their heels if the situation permits.

Further, it may signal lack of confidence. Not living up to expectations in a scenario where it is ordinarily expected can make people to sink into their chairs. When you do not have a full grasp of something, it erodes your self-esteem and confidence. Even though you may not verbally confess this feeling, your body language gives you out.

When someone sinks into their chair, it is a way of hiding themselves from the public glare. Hiding in the open means you are not ready to entertain anything from anyone. In a meeting, the person would be earnestly hoping that they are not called on. That is why this gesture is usually accompanied with the burying of the head. The person looks frail, and their negative mindset would be glaring to you.

Let me quickly add that there are moments this cue is seen as show of disinterest or indifference to what is being done. In this case, the person is neither apprehensive nor lacking confidence, only that they have no interest in what is being done. Hence, they are at the venue to fulfil all righteousness. This may be seen when a respectable member of the society is invited by youths to a programme and instead of them making it short and captivating, they decided to lengthen the event, thereby, making the person lose interest in what they are doing. Hence, the context will serve as the basis of interpreting the gesture rightly.

Scientific Explanations

Minocher Patel (2012) notes that even though sitting comes to us effortlessly, it should be done orderly so that people do not misinterpret our intents. The writer walks people through on the kind of sitting behaviour they should aim for and those they should disengage from. Patel condemns slouching or sinking into a chair because of what it communicates. When you see someone slouch into the chair, it means they are probably disinterested in what you are saying or doing. Also, it may be an indication of tiredness. When a person is tired, they will sink into the chair as if they should be taken off it to a bed. Their eyes will also look pale and uninviting. Sometimes, people might construe this cue as attitude issues. This wrong notion is usually difficult to correct, especially done to a person whom you might not see any time soon again.

Eric Ravenscraft (2014) also shares his opinion on this concept. He describes the 'sinking feeling' as a limbic response to negative occurrences. He gives a practical instance thus: 'Candidly tell a colleague about a drastic and costly mistake she just made at work and her shoulders and arms will sink down and droop.' Negative emotions have the power to bring us down physically. Apart from the fact that these limbic responses are sincere, they also occur in real time, therefore, betraying a person as soon as possible. Taking a soccer game as an example, when your team scores a goal, you will lift your arms up and shout, while you drop your shoulders and arms when you are being defeated or when the referee rules against your team. Ravenscraft concludes, 'These gravity-related behaviours communicate emotions accurately and at the precise moment we are affected. Further, these physical manifestations can be contagious, whether at a football stadium, a rock concert, or in a gathering of great friends.'

Christopher Philip (2014) describes the gesture as a casual attitude. He gives the verbal translation thus: 'I'm hiding in plain sight by reducing the size of my body and remaining motionless so that other people don't notice me.' When the body size is reduced, it means one is submissive. This is the exact opposite of what you will do to show dominance; to dominate, you have to take more space and broaden your shoulders, among other things, but this does not happen while sinking continuously into the chair.

Practical Illustrations

Case Study I: Professor JK did not mark homework in his office. He came to class with them, and then after providing answers on the board, he told his students to exchange their books and score each other. This was to breed a culture of discipline and honesty in them. Also, while providing the corrections, he would call on the students randomly to explain how they did their own. With this, he would be sure if the student relied on external support to get the work done or if they did it on their own. Student U did not complete his homework for Wednesday. So when Prof. JK came into the class on Thursday, he sunk down

Alan Elangovan

really low in his chair and buried his head in his desk so as not to maintain eye contact with the teacher; he feared being called on.

Case Study II: Mr AN was undoubtedly good and a man of many parts; he carved a niche for himself wherever he found himself. This made him very busy at all times. However, his Achilles heel was that he was shy of people; even when things weren't comfortable for him, instead of him telling you, he would keep himself in discomfort. A typical case was when he had so many things on his table with troubling deadlines, yet his colleague came to him to help him edit a voluminous content that was needed back within three days. He couldn't meet up with time, and when he saw his colleague approaching him on the promised date, he sank into his chair; he felt embarrassed for disappointing the colleague.

Case Study III: My colleagues and I were interviewing a con artist, and he really proved himself to be one. He didn't just answer our questions; he threw more questions at us at each given opportunity. When it was getting overwhelming for us, we had to go for a recess and used that opportunity to restrategise. When we came back, he could read our facial expressions and decode he was in for a big thing. Thinking of the way out of the ordeal awaiting him, he sank into his chair and looked tired. Since we were just coming from break, it would be unthinkable to close the process and proceed on another one. We later got a confessional statement from him, but it took painstaking efforts from us.

17.6. Rubbing of Shoulders

Generic Interpretations of the Concept

During intense moments, we are unconsciously led to do things we would not have done if we were in our relaxed state of mind. However, stress does not make us think in a normal way; we look for every means to deal with stressors. In this cue, when a person is stressed, they press their hand against their opposite chest, along the shoulder region, and rub the chest as they move their hands towards the clavicle in the chest. This is seen during interviews when an interviewee does not expect the process to be all that tedious, but it appears to be. It is a symbolic way of dealing with an increased heartbeat and to calm themselves down. I want you to cast your mind back to when a child is crying and you have to calm them by patting them at the back. By that you communicate, 'That's OK, calm down.' Since you cannot touch your back, you decided to touch the frontal part of the shoulders in line with the chest.

There are times that the hand will hover pressed against the chest, or it may be done continuously. When the action is repeated, it means the person is really feeling the intensity of the stress.

610

Remember that the hand-to-skin gesture is meant to increase the tactile effect and therefore pacify the person. By rubbing the shoulder and clavicle with the palm, it brings about a soothing relief engineered by the warmth generated via the action. Hence, people have always seen this cue as a good way of dealing with apprehension or stress. Although this may be a distorted posture in a formal gathering such as an interview, the need to pacify the body overrides the call to suppress the emotional feeling at that point. Thus, it becomes a reliable means for you to know that your subject is no longer feeling comfortable.

Scientific Explanations

Christopher Philip (2014) notes that this is used to pacify the body. He describes it as a self-administered hug. That is, when you feel that you should be shown love but the situation in which you presently find yourself does not permit that, you decide to show yourself the love because you are obviously stressed. Philip concludes, 'Hugs, done in this way, indicate a need for reassurance as a mother would sooth a child.' That is, the person is really craving for an assurance that all is well. Hence, the reason it is mostly seen in interview venues where things happen contrary to people's expectations.

Maria Maceiras (2013) emphasises the need to understand the baseline of the person before alluding meanings to the tell. She states this because the non-verbal tell of rubbing the clavicle and shoulders can be given an array of meaning, especially when noticed in a female. If the signal is seen once in a while, it is worth paying attention to, but if it is done continuously in every given context, then it should be discarded and not taken as nothing. That is, it is an idyosincratic tell just like people with ugly teeth who smile with the lips pressed together so as not to reveal the teeth.

Apart from that, shoulder rubbing is a reflex action; it is done outside of human control. Maceiras notes that we display this cue when we are nervous, worried, insecure, and uncomfortable. These actions make us feel as if we are in danger by increasing the heart rate and blood pressure. But the brain quickly evaluates the situation and communicates with the body that there is not any real threat that can warrant physical fleeing. So the hand is activated to touch the chest and clavicle so as to calm the body. So the body obeys and switches into action. We can really rub any part of the body, but we usually go for the clavicle or shoulders when the intensity of the stress is high, because the region is very sensitive and thus, can return the body part to normalcy in no time.

Due to the issue of context, we cannot categorically regard this cue as a show of nervousness. There is no tell that has the same meaning; it depends on different factors, with context playing the leading role. When you notice this gesture in a person, 'It could be she was nervous, it could be she was insecure talking about something she didn't know too much about, it could be she was in a hurry and worried about not getting there in time, it could be so many things. What's clear is when you spot this one, you should know something is going on with the person you're talking to, they're not comfortable' (Maiceras 2013). The best way to know the exact feeling of the person is to directly ask them. Questions such as 'Are you OK?' 'I feel like if you were worried about something . . . Can I help you?' 'Did I do something wrong?' and 'Do you disagree with me?' will help you in digging out the truth.

Practical Illustrations

Case Study I: Mrs G fudged some of the credentials in her résumé and thought that the interview she was going for would not be centred on the content of the résumé but issues relating to the job; she had attended about seven interviews where the panellists did not bother to question her so much about the résumé she submitted to them. Unfortunately for her, this present one did not take the same line as the previous ones; it was an all-round engagement. She became really stressed and felt danger was lurking around when it got to the stage of discussing her résumé. Unconsciously, she reached to her clavicle and rubbed it slowly downward across the chest region. This was her way of dousing tension.

Case Study II: Dr Y, the managing director of CYR Company, could not make it for a meeting and put a call through to Mrs L to help her coordinate the meeting. It was a high-delegate meeting, and she was obviously not prepared for it. She placed her palm on her shoulder as she rushed through the minutes of their previous meeting to have a clue what she was to discuss at the gathering. The massaging of the shoulder was to calm herself in order to be psychologically composed.

Case Study III: I once apprehended a man who was into smuggling for the first time. He appeared decent and responsible. And when he was apprehended, he had just three smuggled people with him. Starting from the first question, he appeared incoherent and confused. Also, he didn't give any outright denial to any of the questions thrown at him. This was an affirmation that he had something to cough out. Then, I asked that the office be arranged for interview proper. At this point, he began to rub his right shoulder with his left hand. He did it continuously that you could read the fear and regret on his face. And as an enforcement officer, I tapped into the opportunity to drill him until he owned up to the illicit act.

17.7. Widening of the Shoulders

Generic Interpretations of the Concept

If you want to be respected more than you are worth, then you have to carry yourself in an unusual manner. This accounts for shoulder widening. In other words, this body language gesture is a conscious and voluntary action that is done to appear bigger for the reasons best known to the person or as a situation warrants.

By widening the shoulders, they are moved from a relaxed state to a broad posture. This is the opposite of the turtle effect where the shoulders are raised from relaxed state to make the person look smaller. When you see a person widen their shoulders, it is seen as a perceptible display of authority and confidence. For instance, when a man is on a date with a lady and another man seems to be eyeing her, the former will widen his shoulders to non-verbally communicate with the other person that he is in charge. By this, the latter is expected to bow out. I have also seen this among military personnel; they make use of the shoulder-widening cue to communicate to an adversary that they have an authority over the enemy. With this, the enemy is expected to freeze out and cooperate with officials. Also, you may have observed this among athletes. Those who generally engage in competitive endeavours do display this gesture as a way of sending fear down the nerves of their opponents. It makes them feel bigger and better than they are. That is why I have always regarded it as a *power or ego bolster.*

There is little wonder that business suits have padded shoulders; the people who wear them are always in negotiations and, as such, must appear confident and authoritative. The shoulder-widening gives business people needed power and self-will to engage people from diverse backgrounds. If done at the wrong place, it would be seen as a sign of rudeness.

Scientific Explanations

David Givens, a famous anthropologist, and Desmond Morris, a renowned zoologist, both speak on the widening of the shoulders and its implications on every given communicative context. They note that when the shoulders are broadened, they communicate virility and strength. According to Navarro (2012), 'It is also something the Greeks particularly valued, as shown in their kouros statues with "V" shaped young men. There is probably a genetic component to this as Morris argues that we associate positive attributes to males who have that mesomorphic "V" look (wide shoulders narrow hips), we see on athletes.' In this perspective, widened shoulders represent vitality or health. Givens gives an evolutionary explanation that there are advantages to selecting a mate with widened shoulders.

Navarro (2012) explains that we are subconsciously attracted to this V shape due to the positivity it communicates. This explains why men's jackets are purposefully padded at the shoulders, to ensure that we take on this shape. Fashion designers purposefully add more padding to the shoulders for their clients if they want to look broader, more authoritative, and more powerful. If a person is pear-shaped, and they are asked if extra padding should be added, they will quickly concur because without it, they will look frail.

Apart from vitality, widened shoulders also communicate dominance. Navarro recalls that during the course of his career as a FBI special agent, he interacted with thousands of criminals, and he made it a point of duty to ask them what they observe in their victims before launching an attack. In all, they made three distinguishing factors—the look of the victims (frail and not athletic), situational awareness of the victim, and how they swing their arm. Hence, to a criminal, our overall look plays a key role in determining if we are a potential prey or not. That is why we see military personnel maintain a broadened look, because they have to non-verbally communicate with potential predators that they are aware of their environment. In other words, the widened shoulders communicate 'I am a leader'. Hence, that person expects others to follow them. There is no way we can achieve this posture by maintaining a slouch stance (Navarro 2012).

Practical Illustrations

Case Study I: Mr U is elected to represent his firm at the negotiation table with some other business partners. He has been in the service of the establishment for more than a decade and, as such, is believed to defend the best interest of the organisation when given the opportunity. The negotiation is on an international scale. So he decided to go online and do some research on the viability of the establishment he is to negotiate with. He discovered that they are known for being the best in their country. This serves as the first point of concern to him because he is not really used to making such interactions with people. He also decided to tarry in his study and rehearse even more because he knows that if he should maximise the opportunity given him, it would open more doors to him. Reflecting on his clothes, he decided to go for another suit that is well-padded. On wearing it, his shoulders become broadened, and that was a source of confidence to him; he put on an authoritative look.

Case Study II: A group of soldiers were deployed to combat in a place where intelligence reports had it that some terrorists planned to attack. Heavily equipped, the military men manned strategic points at the said location and diverted vehicular movements at different points so as to ease traffic at the location. Also, vehicles that had to pass through the route were subjected to scrutiny. Any time the military personnel saw any unusual face, they would puff out and widen their shoulders while they questioned the person. If the person looked uncooperative, they would bring him or her down from their car and interrogate them in a more sternly manner. At this point, they would spread their legs, stand with vigour, and further broaden the shoulders in order to appear authoritative and send the signal of readiness to the person. With this, they were able to foil the attack.

Case Study III: For a student to stand out among his peers, he needs to project confidence and demonstrate vast understanding of concepts being discussed. While many do not understand that the best way to practically display these attributes is through their body, I have seen a handful of them use it to my amazement. I was in a debate, and many of the students performed well, but the one who emerged winner was the one who broadened his shoulders while speaking. He projected authority through his body language and got the attention of everyone at the venue with his non-verbal cue.

17.8. Raised Shoulders, Palms Up, and Tilted Head

Generic Interpretations of the Concept

This is one of the most often seen shoulder body language gestures across the world. It is often used subconsciously to communicate the intents of our hearts. To display this cue, the shoulders would be raised (either both shoulders or just one) with the palms of the hands opened up, and the head would be tilted to a side, depending on the shoulder that is raised. While doing this, the person will face the person they are talking to. This may be accompanied with verbal utterance or not. When you see this cue, the simple interpretation is 'Please, why not?' or 'Yes, of course'. The raised shoulders are quickly dropped while the hands are also relaxed after sending this message. You may observe this signal when the person is either sitting or standing.

In some other times, this is used to question an unfavourable decision. In this realm, it may be interpreted as 'Why me?' or 'What did I do to warrant this?' Thus, it is regarded as a pleading behaviour, depending on the context of occurrence. This behaviour is not particular to any age grade or group—it is seen in both adults and kids. If you pay close attention to sportsmen, you will also observe this cue in them while trying to appeal a referee's decision against them.

In some cultures, it may be used to mean 'What else, haven't I done enough?' or 'What do you expect me to do in that scenario?' The fact is that the gesture is used universally, but the meaning is tied to the specific context of usage. So the meanings can be diverse. To have a right interpretations of the cue, you must pay attention to the topic under discussion and the words uttered at the point of displaying the non-verbal act.

Scientific Explanations

Parvez (2019) notes that raising the shoulders with the palms up is a submissive gesture used in subtly apologising to a person. Parvez explains thus: 'We shrug our shoulders when we want to communicate the message, "Sorry, I can't do anything about it" or "Sorry, I don't know" and when done along with a slight shaking of the head, "Sorry, I don't understand what you're saying".' So we need to pay attention to the variants and how they are used in communicating specific messages.

Howard Allen (2019) emphasises the fact that this is part of the most commonly seen cues among those who live around us. He describes this gesture thus: 'In the basic shrug, the head is slightly tilted, the shoulders are raised, the upper arms are held slightly away from the body, the forearms are pointed outward, and the palms are facing up.' Hence, we can state that this cue is a basic shrug; it is simpler and more common than those we have earlier discussed. On the premise of experience and general context, when you see this cue, it is a signal of helplessness and innocence. According to Allen, some of the verbal interpretations of the gesture are 'I don't know', 'I can't do anything about it', 'What's it got to do with me?' and 'It's not my fault', among others. These multiple likely interpretations buttress my point that there are different interpretations to this behaviour, and it can only be specifically determined when the context of its occurrence is understood.

Allen (2019) discusses this cue in broad terms. He notes that the shoulder movement is the bedrock of the gesture, and that is why it is regarded as a submissive gesture. Getting startled makes people instinctively raise their shoulders as a way of protecting the neck and throat. While this gesture is being displayed, the eyebrow is also raised. This is a natural movement during a shrug. When you lower the eyebrows, it looks confrontational. The canting of the head is also a show of submissiveness as it exposes the vulnerability of the neck.

From the foregoing, Allen submits thus: 'The central message of the shrug is powerlessness. This usually matches what the person is saying, and the context. It certainly seems genuine in these cases.'

Also, unlike many other gestures, this behaviour is very easy to perfectly display consciously. If a person wants to appear truthful or as if they are trapped in a situation, they may decide to accompany their words with a shrug. Hence, it would be at your own detriment to always believe this gesture hook, line, and sinker.

In some other times, this cue is unconsciously displayed when a person is hostile or aggressive. This means they are not committed to the negative emotions as they want us to believe. In the process of interpreting body language, what we are mostly concerned about are the unconscious clues that bear the whole truth. Obviously, the cues that contradict a person's verbal utterances are the most telling. 'The most submissive shrug has the head tilted and slightly lowered, raised eyebrows, and arms and hands in front of the body' (Allen 2019).

Practical Illustrations

Case Study I: Ms G just joined the services of KDT Enterprises. Being a too forward person, she behaved as if she knew everything. During their induction, she did not really pay attention to what was being said, thinking she did not need to be walked through. After being assigned a portfolio, she started making some unthinkable mistakes that no one would ever tolerate. The CEO had to summon the panellists who interviewed her to know if she lobbied her way in. Surprisingly, it was discovered that she did truly well. So they decided to give her benefit of the doubt by assigning an expert to her. Instead of her always consulting the expert, she would do things on her own. Noticing this, the CEO called her and gave her a stern warning that she would be shown the way out if caught in any unproductive act again. After falling into another issue, she rushed to the expert to inform him. But after hearing everything, the man tilted his head, raised his shoulders, and opened his palms to mean there was nothing he could do to amend the error. In other words, he was helpless.

Case Study II: A critical case was rushed to a private hospital, and the doctor in charge swung into action immediately. While the nurses believed from the onset there was nothing they could do to the situation, he was full of hope that the patient was going to live. For about five hours, the medical team battled to save the life of the man in question, but it seemed their effort was not yielding results. When he eventually gave up the ghost, the doctor raised his shoulders, opened his palms, and walked out of the theatre dejectedly. The message was clear to the family of the deceased as they were apprehended with fear and sorrow, even when the doctor had not said anything.

Case Study III: AB and CD are illegal migrants in Country AIG. They were so confident that they could not be arrested because they lived in the inlands. Even when they travelled to the cities, they walked with confidence, and this was, to them, an antidote to being arrested. However, they ran out of luck one day and two of them got into the hands of immigration officers. While on the vehicle of the officers, they looked at each other and raised their shoulders while opening up their palms in shame and regret. The message was clear; no way out for them again—they were to be deported from the country.

17.9. Kowtowing

Generic Interpretations of the Concept

This is the act of slightly bending the shoulders or upper torso forward. This can be done consciously or subconsciously. Depending on the location of its appearance, it is used as a symbol of respect. It has its variants across cultures. In some cultures, it is used in the presence of a higher authority. Hence, kowtowing is regarded as a submissive act. People who are naturally fearful and have low self-esteem will kowtow in the presence of a perceived dominant fellow. This is to tell the other person that they are not confrontational and willing to cooperate with them. In this situation, it is unconsciously displayed. However, if it is intentionally done for the purpose of honouring a superior, then this is a true mark of respect as the person is aware of their environment.

Bowing out of respect is a common phenomenon in many parts of Asia; the culture of respect is given a premium, especially among the Japanese. Even in Europe, the subjects of the queen of England bow to her any time they have anything to do with her.

The origin of this cue has been traced to primate legacy, where every other animal is expected to bend lower to the alpha male. However, in the case of humans, this is denoted by someone of higher authority. Some cultures of the world forbid looking at a superior figure in the eye; after a short eye contact, you look down as a symbol of reverence.

As a show of the universality of this gesture, when the conquistadores got to the New World, they discovered that Native Americans also kowtowed to their king, a replica of what they had done at the Queen Isabella's court. This cue is also more pronounced in Africa. It is societally forbidden for a child or subordinate to look into the eyes of a superior when being talked to. If they want to shake hands, it is expected that the elderly person or authoritative figure extends their hands first while the subordinate receives it with a bow. If not, the latter would be considered as being rude and challenging a constituted authority.

Scientific Explanations

The word *kowtow* is believed to have been borrowed from *kau tau* in Cantonese and is referred to as *ketou* in Mandarin Chinese. It is defined as 'the act of showing deep reverence to a person by prostrating to them', that is, by kneeling and bowing so low as to have one's head touching the ground. In East Asian culture, the kowtow is the highest sign of reverence. It was widely used to show reverence for one's elders, superiors, and especially the emperor, as well as for religious and cultural objects of worship. In modern times, usage of the kowtow has become reduced, but this does not mean that it is not used at all again.

In imperial Chinese protocol, the kowtow was performed before the emperor of China. Depending on the solemnity of the situation, different grades of kowtow would be used. In the most solemn of ceremonies, for example at the coronation of a new emperor, the emperor's subjects would undertake the ceremony of the 'three kneelings and nine kowtows', the so-called grand kowtow, which involves kneeling from a standing position three times, and each time, performing the kowtow three times while kneeling (Immanuel 1970).

As government officials represented the majesty of the emperor while carrying out their duties, commoners were also required to kowtow to them in formal situations. For example, a commoner brought before a local magistrate would be required to kneel and kowtow. A commoner is then required to remain kneeling, whereas a person who has earned a degree in the imperial examinations is permitted a seat (Immanuel 1970).

The Confucian philosophy requires that children should show reverence to their parents and grandparents. Hence, they kowtow to elderly ones and even their elderly ancestors during special occasions. For example, at a wedding, the marrying couple was traditionally required to kowtow to both sets of parents as acknowledgement of the debt owed for their nurturing.

Confucius explains that there is natural harmony between the mind and the body. Thus, whatever action expressed through the body is stamped in the mind. Because the body is placed in a low position in the kowtow, the idea is that one will naturally convert to his or her mind a feeling of respect. What one does to oneself influences the mind. The Confucian philosophy places a high premium on respect in society, and we cannot de-emphasise or discard that in its entirety at this point in time (Adler 2012).

In many societies today, the kowtow has been maligned. Pitiably, only vestiges of the conventional show of reverence remain these days. In many situations, the standing bow has replaced the kowtow; this involves the upper torso and shoulders bending forward. Even during wedding, the standing bow has replaced using the head to touch the ground. There are cases where the gesture is used to ask for forgiveness from a superior, to apologise, or to show an act of gratitude.

In English, kowtow is assumed to mean abject submission or groveling. The term is still commonly used in English with this meaning, disconnected from the physical act and the East Asian context. The behaviour is being used within and outside Asia for diplomatic reasons. While this may appear as bizzare to those not used to Asian culture, it is seen as a great diplomatic tool to those who understand it.

Practical Illustrations

Case Study I: Mr I just gained employment with an international firm. On resuming duty, he was placed under an elderly person. Humble to a fault, he thought showing respect to his superior would help him blend with the system and be accepted by all and sundry. Hence, for the first few days, not taking cognisance of the cultural differences, Mr I would kowtow for his superior. This was a point of concern for the boss, who was oblivious of that culture. He was later forced to ask I, who he explained to him that it was a sign of reverence.

Case Study II: Mr XZ just arrived in Country AIK for research purposes. He was to interact with hundreds of the citizens of the country, and his research focused on the unlettered. This means he would have a direct access to the culture of the people. Even though his research was science-based, he was forced to ask why almost everyone was kowtowing to him, and one of the educated people in the community explained that it was their culture. He was made to know that it was their own unique way of being respectful and honourable to others. That appeared strange to him, and it almost became the focus on his research. When he returned to his home country, it was the centre of his discussion.

Case Study III: Criminals who know that there is no way out of their heinous acts left for them will take to emotional appeals. While this could have been considered, a lot of them are pretentious; and once you release them, they would be back to their old ways. I remember arresting an impostor who seemed helpless. Even though we had not yet established that she impersonated someone, she was kowtowing any time I looked at her direction. The gimmick here was to make her look humble and, more importantly, hide her face from me so that I wouldn't take note of the distinguishing traits on her face.

CHAPTER 18

The Arms

Apart from protection, provision of balance, and helping us to lift items, the arms also serve as a great source of non-verbal communication. A lot of people concentrate so much on the face, leaving out the other parts of the body while trying to decode non-verbal cues. The fact is that both the subject and the co-interlocutor are taking cognisance of the fact that people are reading their face, so they will try to display the best body language gestures. Through this, the real emotions can be suppressed. However, paying attention to the use of the arms reveals a lot about a person's thoughts per time.

We just can't understand the prominent role played by the arms enough. When we are stressed, we hug ourselves as a means of pacifying the body. Also, when an athlete emerges first in a competition, they raise their arms in joy. And there is the outward reach of a kid who is passionately seeking a loving hug. Hence, our arms serve as an indispensable help for our daily endeavours, warming our body, attending to others on our behalf, serving as a source of assistance, communicating our needs and feelings per time. In short, the arms communicate far more than we can imagine at a glance.

From the biological perspective, in human anatomy, the arm is the part of the upper limb between the glenohumeral joint (shoulder joint) and the elbow joint. In common usage, the arm extends to the hand. It can be divided into the upper arm, which extends from the shoulder to the elbow; the forearm, which extends from the elbow to the hand; and the hand. Anatomically, the shoulder girdle with bones and corresponding muscles is, by definition, a part of the arm. The Latin term *brachium* may refer to either the arm as a whole or to the upper arm on its own (*Encyclopaedia Britannica* 2013).

The humerus is one of the three long bones of the arm. It joins with the scapula at the shoulder joint and with the other long bones of the arm, the ulna and radius at the elbow joint. The elbow is the hinge joint between the end of the humerus and the ends of the radius and ulna. The humerus cannot be broken easily. Its strength allows it to handle loading up to 300 pounds (140 kg) (Sam 2007).

Talking of the upper arm muscles, it contains of two compartments, known as the anterior compartment and the posterior compartment.

The anterior compartment is located in front of your humerus, the main bone of your upper arms.

The muscles of the anterior compartment include the following:

- *Biceps brachii.* Often referred to as your biceps, this muscle contains two heads that start at the front and back of your shoulder before joining together at your elbow. The end near your elbow flexes the forearm, bringing it towards your upper arm. The two heads near your shoulder help with flexion and adduction of your upper arm.
- *Brachialis.* This muscle lies underneath your biceps. It acts as a bridge between your humerus and ulna, one of the main bones of your forearm. It's involved with the flexing of your forearm.
- *Coracobrachialis.* This muscle is located near your shoulder. It allows adduction of your upper arm and flexion of your shoulder. It also helps to stabilise your humerus within your shoulder joint.

The posterior compartment is located behind your humerus and consists of two muscles:

- *Triceps brachii.* This muscle, usually referred to as your triceps, runs along your humerus and allows for the flexion and extension of your forearm. It also helps to stabilise your shoulder joint.
- *Anconeus.* This is a small triangular muscle that helps to extend your elbow and rotate your forearm. It's sometimes considered to be an extension of your triceps.

Your forearm contains more muscles than your upper arm does. It contains both an anterior and posterior compartment, and each is further divided into layers.

The anterior compartment runs along the inside of your forearm. The muscles in this area are mostly involved with flexion of your wrist and fingers as well as rotation of your forearm.

Superficial Layer

- *Flexor carpi ulnaris.* This muscle flexes and adducts your wrist.

- *Palmaris longus.* This muscle helps with flexion of your wrist, though not everyone has it.
- *Flexor carpi radialis.* This muscle allows for flexion of your wrist in addition to abduction of your hand and wrist.
- *Pronator teres.* This muscle rotates your forearm, allowing your palm to face your body (Seladi-Schulman 2018).

Intermediate layer

- *Flexor digitorum superficialis.* This muscle flexes your second, third, fourth, and fifth fingers.

Deep compartment

- *Flexor digitorum profundus.* This muscle also helps with flexion of your fingers. In addition, it's involved with moving your wrist towards your body.
- *Flexor pollicis longus.* This muscle flexes your thumb.
- *Pronator quadratura.* Similar to the pronator teres, this muscle helps your forearm rotate (Seladi-Schulman 2018).

The major function of the arms is locomotion; movement of the arm muscles. There are four basic movements of the muscles:

- *Flexion.* This movement brings two body parts closer together, such as your forearm and upper arm.
- *Extension.* This movement increases the space between two body parts. An example of this is straightening your elbow.
- *Abduction.* This refers to moving a body part away from the centre of your body, such as lifting your arm out and away from your body.
- *Adduction.* This refers to moving a body part towards the centre of your body, such as bringing your arm back in so it rests along your torso (Seladi-Schulman 2018).

In Hindu, Buddhist, and Egyptian iconography, the symbol of the arm is used to illustrate the power of the sovereign. In Hindu tradition, gods are depicted with several arms which carry specific symbols of their powers. It is believed that several arms depict omnipotence of gods. In West Africa, the Bambara use forearms to symbolise the spirit, which is a link between God and man. Symbolic gestures of raising both hands signal surrender, appeals for mercy, and justice (Tresidder 1997).

18.1. Hugging

Generic Interpretations of the Concept

In discussing the concept of hugging, one needs to be careful with the way the concept is handled because there are still some few cultures that are not receptive to hugging, especially between an elderly person and a kid or between a superior and a subordinate. Modernisation is fast making hugging a universal thing though. Having said that, hugging is used across the globe to denote closeness, cooperation, love, warmth, and good feelings. It is the act of opening the arms and interlocking the same with the body of your co-interlocutor. If there is no existing relationship between two people, they will rather stop at a handshake instead of a deep hug. When two bodies come in contact with each other, they create some warmth that further enhances the relationship of those involved.

The way the hug is done is itself a message. That is, it hints us on the feelings of the people about each other. If it is done by two people of opposite sexes, this is usually brief and sideways, except if the two of them are lovers. It is believed that hugging can arouse sexual feelings, especially with the sensitivity of female breasts or men who might eventually use their erect manhood to touch their female counterparts. So it is normally done using the side of the body. Hence, if the female freely gives a deep hug, there is a probability she is into the person or trusts the integrity of the person involved, depending on the context of such action is playing out. Also, culture plays a huge role in this; there are some cultures that forbid that action between men and women.

In some cultures, such as Latin America, a brief social hug usually referred to as *abrazo* is used as a greeting cue that has the same connotation as handshake. The way it is done can give you a hint on the feelings of the participants towards each other. If one is reluctant and the other is enthusiastic, then this communicates the entire message to you that one is forcibly doing it. You may also reflect on sportsmen exchanging a hug before or after a match; celebrities too. To determine their feelings about the action, you need to focus on their facial expressions, which in this case, is very reliable.

Scientific Explanations

Christopher Philip (2013) has a detailed descriptions of the forms of hugs in existence; he discusses eight types of hugs and their meanings. Explaining the body language gesture in a sentence, he observes that 'hug variations help define relationships'. For instance, the *abrazo hug* is done by pressing the chests together and engulfing the back of the other person with the arms. The verbal translation of this is 'I like you, so I'm pressing my chest against you'. However, the *bear hug* is a loving but firm one that can be done between a man and a woman, two men, two women, or an adult and child. The verbal translation is 'I really like you a lot and adore you and want to show how much I care by squeezing you tightly'. Then, there is the *buddy hug* that is normally displayed between friends where they pat the back of each other. This is verbally translated as 'We can be friends, but I don't want to date you'.

The *sleepy shoulder hug* is when two people cuddle up to each other and one person rests against the other's shoulder. The verbal translation of this is 'I like you, but more importantly, I feel safe in your arms, so I'm going to rest my head against your strong shoulder.' Then, the *quickie hug* is one that is brief, where one of the parties hastily removes their arms to speed off. It means 'I really need to be someplace else, so let's just hug quickly so I can get out of here.' The *unreciprocated hug* is when a participant is fully involved while the other person is passive. This means 'I'm not interested in hugging you. We don't see eye-to-eye, so I'm just going to let my arms go limply to the side as you hug me.' Further, the *cuddle hug* occurs when one person rests against the other's shoulder, usually while seated watching television, a movie, or at the park. The verbal translation of this action is 'I want to feel safe in your arms, so I'm snuggling up against you' (Philip 2013).

The body language expert also discusses the *squeeze hug*, which is not as pronounced as the *bear hug* but is still firmly done. This is interpreted as 'We have fun together. We should do this again.' And finally, the *waist hug* has to do with standing where one arm is wrapped around the waist of another. This means 'We are an item, attached at the hip, and walk as one' (Philip 2013). So the kind of hug exchanged tells us the feeling and thoughts of the participants towards each other.

Changing Minds (2019) lists different reasons why people hug to include greeting, comforting, affection, bonding, domination, romance, protection, and possession, depending on how it is done. For instance, if someone invades your body space by taking charge of your body easily without your permission, they are subtly telling you that they have authority over you and, as such, do not need to ask for permission from you; this is used to show domination.

Practical Illustrations

Case Study I: When T and D were reunited, they ran towards each other and hugged by engulfing each other with their arms. After that, they walked into the nearest restaurant, where they spoke lengthily about their past and what either of them was up to during the period they left each other. Although the meeting was unplanned for, they later ended up spending hours in the conversation. They were simply drawn to each other. And it was a pure show of love and attraction.

Case Study II: When Mr U got to his son's school to pick him, he discovered that he was looking pale and tired. So he got down from his vehicle to give him a huge bear hug to show he liked the kid and to cheer him up. Immediately, the countenance of the child changed as he moved to his father. He rushed into his father's car, and in the twinkle of an eye, he had started giving his father the gist of all that happened in school that day. This is the power of body language in display; the father got to read his non-verbal gesture accurately and employed positive non-verbal display through a hug to dispel the negative one earlier noticed. This is what non-verbal communication is capable of achieving to those who understand its usage.

Case Study III: Mr and Mrs W went to the beach to have some time out, and after the process, they decided to enjoy the charming, beautiful sunset by embracing at the hips. It was enjoyment galore, and embracing at the hips served as the peak of it all. This aroused their romantic feelings and got them into the mood of the holiday. It was a simple but a potent way of spicing up their relationship. All you need to do is to understand what works for you and implement it in your life.

Case Study IV: Criminals do come in the name of love and care to gain entrance into people's lives and mesmerise them afterwards. A subordinate once had an accident but wasn't injured in the process. While most people walked away, some stayed back to congratulate him and check if there was a way he could be helped. One of them went as far as hugging him as a show of love—he was happy that he didn't lose his life through the accident. It was later discovered that the man who hugged my subordinate was an illegal immigrant. He saw his action as a smart move so as to stop the officer from questioning his identity.

18.2. Hyperbolic Gestures

Generic Interpretations of the Concept

This is also known as animated gesture. This has to do with displaying broad gestures so as to portray us as being powerful to the other party. Hence, it is mostly done to grease our ego, bolster our self-esteem, and put on the look of a predator. This gesture does not only get us noticed while speaking, it also aptly reflects our state of mind. We cannot underplay the essence of animated gestures while speaking, and its dynamism to communication. Just imagine a person speaking without any accompanying display to back up their action. You may easily be bored, especially if the talk is an extended one. The dynamism hyperbolic cues add to communication is that it gives you a pictorial view of what the person is saying, and this is meant to keep your interest as the person expresses himself.

In many cultures of the world, it is expected that one exaggerates while laying emphasis. I have seen this a lot among people from different races and backgrounds; it is the exaggeration that draws the attention of the audience to what is being emphasised. Remember that I said in the introductory notes to this chapter that the primary role of the arms is locomotion. Hence, they become the go-to tools in making animated gestures; you see the person swinging their arms in different directions and hitting hard just to make a point clearer. With this, the attention of everyone else would be focused on what the person is trying to bring out from the point.

To a person who is not in the know or close to the speaker, they might assume that the speaker is about to stage a fight, especially, when the speaker accompanies their words and actions with a stern or serious look. However, this is simply just an emphatic gesture.

Scientific Explanations

The Silent Protagonist Team, in a 2016 article on animation and body language, postulates that 'body language and movement has always been a big part of visual media. The importance of this aspect of acting or animation can be traced back to visual media's origin in the Theatre. Actors had the ability to convey emotions across entire auditoriums without the need for the audience to see their face. Although when body language is used in the Theatre, it is often approached with broad gestures to make all emotions blatantly obvious, this of course helps members of the audience in the cheaper seats to understand the emotion of the scene when the actors don't specifically say what they are feeling, and help tell the story.'

Although their description is based on the theatrical performance alone, I want to note that it cuts across board. That is, our daily living is a replica of drama. Hence, we also use animation in communicating the deepest part of our heart. The main purpose of the use of animation is to emphasise a message with the body instead of verbal utterance. It is mostly seen in the acting world. For instance, when a person is sad, instead of telling you directly, they may slump their shoulders deeply to communicate their feeling. When you see an abnormally straight posture with the chest pushed out, this is used to communicate confidence. This may be a means of showing submission.

These days, overly exaggerated body language animation is one of the most common means of communication. Instead of explaining themselves over and over again, people resort to the use of their body gestures to exaggerate the message they are passing across in order to draw the attention of others to it. In the theatre, this is normally accompanied with music that furthers the message being passed across. Animated gestures make us see purely emotions; you do not seem to observe beyond the feelings of the person who is displaying those gestures. With this, you will be connected with the person through the mind and not just merely listening passively.

Practical Illustrations

Case Study I: Mr K has been the official secretary of FYD Enterprises for the past two decades. This means that he has had the opportunity to work with different managers. While some of them have been fantastic, others prove to be despicable. Well, the firm has made it a point of duty to always sponsor him on courses on human management, knowing the delicate nature of his work and it is connected to the growth of the firm. However, despite his professional trainings and patience, it seems that the present manager is simply from another planet; he has been working with him for the past five months, and they do not seem to agree on basic issues. On this occasion, he was told to prepare the minutes of a previous meeting and present the summary to him (the manager) only for the boss to return the file and ask him prepare the agenda for an unscheduled meeting when he was supposed to be heading home. He became extremely angry at the action of the manager. He kept his arms to his side aggressively while maintaining an aggressive stance with a red eye. The message was obvious to everyone, including the manager.

Case Study II: Lady K came to spend the weekend with her fiancé. She has always complained about the untidy attitude of her spouse, but the reply had always been 'You can't compare the neatness of a female to a male'. This was not pleasing to K because she knew how her brothers appeared neat and took care of their room. There was a time she contemplated calling the relationship off, but she was begged not to and assured of change. Now, on getting to his house, she saw that litter was everywhere, and she did not have the guts to stay in an untidy environment. So she decided to clean up everywhere without bothering to create a scene. On getting to her spouse's bedroom, she saw his underwear on the bed. On setting her eyes on them, she subconsciously frowned and maintained and a squeezed nose, looked disturbed, and kept her hands to herself to express her disgust for what she saw.

Case Study III: A con artist went to a shop to make some purchases. He intentionally went there at a busy hour. He was a regular client of the sellers, but they did not know that he was into crime due to his pretentious living. When he got there, he feigned striving to buy the items he needed to. Since he was not a stranger, the sellers thought he would understand and bear with them. When everything had subsided and they were to answer him, he looked so disturbed, dejected, and annoyed. Even a day-old child would know that something was wrong with him. He did this for the purpose of receiving undue compensation from the mall, which he unfortunately got.

18.3. Gesturing During Speech

Generic Interpretations of the Concept

Just like animation, the act of gesticulating while delivering a speech spices up what is being said. Even though people tend to neglect this important aspect of communication, its essence cannot be downplayed in any given circumstances. During my training sessions, I have heard people ask me the essence of gesticulation in communication, and as expected, I have always taken out time to explain to them. Myles Munroe states, 'When the purpose of a thing is not known, abuse is inevitable.' That is, people have either overused or have failed to take the advantage of gesticulation during conversations.

If properly used, gestures (made with the hands) help us to get the attention of our audience. There is no gainsaying that people are moved and glued more to pictorial images than mere words. That is why advertising agencies spend much effort and resources on putting out clear images with short words. Gesticulations make whatever you are saying sink into the head of the listener—if the person can recall your actions, they will easily remember your words. After getting and maintaining the attention of your listener, you can go ahead to highlight crucial points with the use of gesticulation. The more you gesticulate on a point, the deeper and more emphasised it appears to the audience.

Further, gesticulation ensures you maintain flexibility in your presentation. Instead of just being rigid and glued to the podium, when you move about and make use of your hands to demonstrate alongside the point you are explaining, it gives you the ability to be creative. With this, you will be able to recall the right words in the right context.

The fact is that gestures determine the receipt of our message by others and how much of it they can recall. For a moment, just picture in your mind a person who is delivering news and another one who is acting. Out of the two, whose words do you have higher probability to remember? The answer is glaring! Gestures serve as an echo to your messages, which make them substantiated and potentiated. The universal truth is that people want to see us gesticulate as we speak; they are fascinated by those scenes. If you notice the best motivational speakers, you will discover that they make the best use of gestures in communicating their messages.

Scientific Explanations

According to Kendra Cherry (2019), gestures can be some of the most direct and obvious body language signals. Waving, pointing, and using the fingers to indicate numerical amounts are all very common and easy to understand gestures. Some gestures may be cultural, however, so you need to pay attention to these peculiarities as you relate with people from across boards.

Westside Toastmasters (2019) talks about hand gestures in its extensive form. Research has shown that there are more nerve connections between the hands and the brain than any other part of the body. Hence, the gestures and portrayals we make with our hands serve as great insights into understanding the emotional state of a person. 'Our hands are usually positioned in front of our body, consequently these signals are easy to pick up and most of us have several trademark hand positions we continually use. Unconsciously, your hands reveal your attitude towards another person, place, or situation.' So instead of placing your attention on the face alone, give the hand movements close attention.

Observe the spontaneous movement of your hands as you communicate with people and see how they align with your thoughts. Even without your conscious awareness, the hands aptly depict your thoughts and communicate your mind to your co-interlocutor. Whether you're expressing love, anger, joy, or frustration, your hands hold the message (Westside Toastmasters 2019).

The body language platform explains that 'for thousands of years, the level of status people held in a society would determine the priority order in which they could hold the floor when speaking. The more power or authority you had, the more others would be compelled to stay silent while you spoke. For example, Roman history shows that a low-status person could be executed for interrupting Julius Caesar.' Things have changed considerably in today's societies. Hence, freedom of speech has been subject to abuse through the use of social media. In many countries, the hands have taken on the role of 'punctuation marks' to regulate turn-taking in physical conversation. A raised hands gesture has been borrowed from the Italians and French, who are the biggest users of 'hand talking' (Westside Toastmasters 2019).

Order-taking is very simple in a country like Italy where the person raising their hands has the floor to speak and the listener drops their hands or puts the hands behind them. When you see Italians continually touch each other in a speech context, do not assume that they are being intimate of friendly; they are restricting each other from speaking.

Proper use of the hands can bolster positive power reaction, and this is seen in TED Talks. With the use of gestures, you increase the attention of your audience, accelerate the impact of the discourse and help the retentive ability of your listeners. Westside Toastmasters (2019) submits that 'an analysis of TED

Talks found that the most popular, viral speakers used an average of around 500 hand gestures, which is nearly twice as many as the least popular speakers used. Other research has found that people who "talk" with their hands tend to be viewed as warm, agreeable and energetic, while those who are less animated are seen as logical, cold and analytical.' The advantages are simply innumerable.

Practical Illustrations

Case Study I: Mr and Ms P went out on a date one night, and the discussion that night bordered on the need to plan for summer vacation. Mr P led the discussion, while Ms P determined the plausibility of each point. As the vision and the plan for the holiday expanded and looked like something that can be materialised, Ms P smiled broadly and rubbed her palms together rapidly and exclaimed, 'I can barely wait!' That body language told us non-verbally that she expected the trip to be a high point of her year. Rubbing the palms together is a display of positive emotions.

Case Study II: Mr IO is supposed to be the lead presenter in a seminar. However, it was in his habit to arrive at occasions few minutes before their commencement. On this occasion, he didn't know he was planning for an ugly scenario. He had calculated that the venue of the seminar was just a four-minute drive, so he decided to leave an hour to the event. His car, however, broke down when he was about to leave. There was no way out. So he opted for public transit. While on the bus, he felt that the driver wasn't fast enough. As he was lamenting, he could be seen using his hands to make gestures as if he were driving. This was a non-verbal way of expressing his frustrations and heartfelt desire.

Case Study III: A suspected illegal immigrant was stopped on the street and asked to explain himself. He was confused with what to say because one could obviously read from his face that he was nervous. However, since he knew that failure to explain himself meant he consented to the accusation, he began to mutter some words, but with much gesticulation. He wasn't versed in the language of the land and only resorted to the use of gestures to explain himself. This hinted the officers that he didn't belong to the country, and when asked to present a valid means of identification, he was lost.

18.4. Pressing Arms against the Body with Flexed Hands

Generic Interpretations of the Concept

When you are happy and, for reasons best known to you, you decided not to show it openly, this is the kind of gesture you put on; it is referred to as restrained elation. That is, the happiness is suppressed because of some circumstances which your brain thinks may be detrimental to you if you show happiness openly. When people are satisfied with themselves and trying to keep the feeling away from others, they will tightly hold the arm against their body and then lift the hands at the wrist, with the wrist at almost ninety degrees, while the palm faces down. The palms may also be held tightly, as if they were preventing something from falling off the hands. This is very symbolic; they do not want to let out the elation at that point, so they are guiding it judiciously.

For instance, if someone succeeds in manoeuvring you despite all odds, they may suppress their feeling of elation so as not to call your attention to that particular event. Remember that lifting the hands is a sign of victory. So the hands want to subconsciously go up for the victory recorded, but the conscious brain is suppressing it due to the looming threat. The non-verbal cue cannot be totally repressed, thus, the reason the wrist is lifted.

If the arms are controlled, there are other things you can pay attention to ascertain your guess about the person. For instance, this behaviour may propel the rising of the shoulders. Of course, you need not neglect the face; there would be a display of joy. Since the person is overly concerned about suppressing the raising of the arms, their face will betray them. If the person does not frown or look sad, this tells you that they are experiencing positive emotions over a course of the action.

Scientific Explanations

A platform that is committed to human development, How to Get Your Own Way (2019) explains that 'Hand and arm positioning is one of the biggest giveaways to someone's thoughts and emotions. For example, when someone is happy (e.g., in an interesting conversation), he will move his hands and arms in an animated manner. A happy person will even have animated arm movements when walking. Conversely, if a person is feeling down, his arm movements become more suppressed as if his arms have suddenly become heavier, and they sink, reflecting his mood.' In the case of the gesture under discussion, the flexing of the wrists hints that it is a conglomeration of both positive and negative emotional states of mind.

The fact remains that there is no way a person can suppress this gesture, there would still be enough activities for you to work with. But again, remember – it's all part of an overall picture. It's not just a case of animated arms meaning happy or angry, and suppressed arms meaning sad or controlled (HTGYOW 2019).

The palm down behaviour is another thing that gives the person away. Usually, people think the palm-up is associated with positive emotions and honesty but research has shown that when people are dishonest, they may also maintain this stance; they want you to see them as being open when in actual fact, they are not. In the same vein, the person who is constraining their elation but trying to deceive you through the palms-down behaviour that they are sad would get caught through other clusters. That is why Farouq Ridwan (2017) states that 'showing the palms is considered one of the signs of honesty. Trained liars however can do it on intention to fool people.' So we need to be certain of the cues we analyse and process at every given time.

In conclusion, you need to pay attention to the context and culture of appearance. For instance, Westerners and Africans do not buy the idea of two heterosexual males holding their hands. Hence, the person may have suppressed their hands from moving due to this cultural influence. However, this cue may be common in other nations of the world. The author of How to Get Your Own Way blog recounts, 'During the war in Iraq, I was working with a colonel from an Iraqi Army intelligence unit. Mohammed was very professional and very personable, and we seemed to get on well. After a couple of months, we were walking outside discussing the day's work when he reached out and held my hand. I'd seen Iraqi officers holding hands before, and this flashed into my head just in time to stop me ripping my hand from his. However, my discomfort must have been written all over my face. Within a few seconds, the interpreter said: "He is holding your hand because he trusts you". If I had pulled my hand away, it would have been culturally extremely rude, and our professional relationship would have been damaged.'

Practical Illustrations

Case Study I: Mr H has been trying to sell an item for months because it would expire and it cost him a huge amount of money. While many people would have bought the item without issues of price, the nearness of its expiry date had been his albatross. So he kept on praying till another man came. After a brief negotiation on the product, the man made a payment without trying to check the expiry date. It had no warranty; hence, once taken out of the mall, it could not be returned again. More so, it had not expired at the point of purchase. As Mr H was trying to package the item for the man, he could be seen pressing his arms against the body and flexing his hands to show that he was suppressing his elation pending the time the man would take his leave so that he can jubilate as he liked.

Case Study II: While trying to wash a dish in the kitchen, Child U checked around and discovered that nobody was in sight when she headed for the stew pot and carted away the head of a fish. After he had consumed it, the mother came in to serve herself and seemed not to have discovered U's act. She had almost frozen when the mother came in, only for her not to have paid attention to the theft. As the mother was serving her own food, Child U pressed her hand against her body and waited for her mother to take her leave so she could celebrate her victory. She was really elated that her mother did not know.

Case Study III: Mr AT was in desperate search for jobs, and when one wasn't forthcoming, he decided to take to illicit means to secure one. He read an advert of a company looking for an expert in consultancy. Even though he had no knowledge about this field, he went to plagiarise another person's profile, backed it up with some concocted documents, and tabled the same to the recruitment team. His submission looked so charming that it was irresistible not to employ him. When he got the positive nod before leaving the interview room, Mr AT pressed his arm against his body and flexed his muscles, waiting impatiently to be told to take his leave so he could celebrate his undeserved victory.

18.5. Show of Elation

Generic Interpretations of the Concept

When a person is truly happy, there is no way it can be hidden from others. All over the world, people are receptive of joyous events and, in fact, will gladly join when invited. So if someone is sincerely elated and they display it, others will see this and may mirror their behaviour. Considering this from the non-verbal perspective, display of victory or elation tends to be gravity-defying. That is, it is shown through the upward movement of the body. A spontaneous show of joy has to do with a person flying up as soon as the positive occurrence happens.

There are times that we are forced to jump out of our seats and raise our arms and fingers in the air in celebration of a major victory. This is seen at sports events, especially tough ones where a team later manages to score a goal; their supporters will rise from their seats to cheer the players and show their joy for the triumph. The law of gravity requires that things should come down, but the show of elation defies this principle.

When you see a person raising their arms, looking interested, smiling broadly, and with eyes dilating, it means something great has happened to him or her. During this moment, they think all is well with them, and they want everyone around them to share in this joy. Save for the cases of enmity or where the other person hates the joyous person, the audience will easily mirror this cue by, at least, smiling in return. However, you do not expect an opponent who has just been defeated to smile or join you in celebrating your victory.

In the classroom setting too, if a student knows the answer to a difficult question, they will raise their hands and lobby facially to be called on so that they can be the star of the class.

Scientific Explanations

Changing Minds (2019) seems to differ in its explanation of raising of the arms. The platform explains that when the arms are raised rapidly, it is used in throwing things into the air. When it is done with both hands, it exaggerates the action. However, when the two arms are raised in typical form, it is used to signal frustration, according to the website. If this is coupled with a shrug, it means the person is telling you he or she does not know. The raising of the arms as explained by this website differs from the sign of elation in the sense that, in the show of frustration, the lifting of the arms does not really go up; just accompanying the shoulders in shrugging. But when it comes to elation, the arms are lifted beyond the air, with the fingers pointing into the thin air.

In its own explanation, Westside Toastmasters (2019) gives a clearer explanation of the raising of arms, describing it as a show of amiability. The website explains that 'open arms indicate a receptive, friendly, and honest attitude. This position says that you've got nothing to hide and are approachable and amenable. It draws people to you, making them feel comfortable and at ease in your company. By leaving your body exposed you're indicating that you're receptive to whatever comes your way.' When the arms are raised, coupled with the occasional jumping up to show elation, the entire body is left open, and this means the person has nothing to fear or hide. If they were afraid, they would have placed their hands on their genitals or the neck, these being the most vulnerable parts of the body.

Westside Toastmasters uses sporting events to buttress its point. It says thus: 'Go to any sporting event and watch the players. The moment the winner sinks his final putt, crosses the finish line, or scores the winning goal his arms open with the thrill of victory. The losers cross their arms in front of their bodies or let them hang dejectedly by their sides.' The fans and other admirers also mirror this cue by displaying the same gesture. It is an indication that they are committed to the victory.

If you are trying to persuade a person to see things from your own perspective, opening of the arms and holding them in an open position is the best way to go about it. This communicates your sincerity about the subject matter. Keeping the arms open shows that you are confident and have an impressive positive behaviour which lures others to your side. This gives others the perception that you are direct, trustworthy, and honest in your dealing, as long as other gestures point to this same direction (Westside Toastmasters 2019).

Practical Illustrations

Case Study I: Two rival high schools are locking horns in a debating competition. Obviously, both schools presented their best products as can be seen in the argument style of the students. For the first round, it was a square for both schools, and it was no way different in the second round too. So the panellists decided to use a spelling bee on the third round. Eventually, School A triumphed over School B by just a point. On announcing the results, the debaters, teachers, and students of School A went agog with jubilation by jumping up and raising their arms in a gravity-defying manner. They are also laughed and shouted with joy, with entire faces glowing.

Case Study II: A much-awaited table tennis competition was fixed on a Sunday in order to allow people from all walks of life easy access to watch the final. No one could easily predict the winner of event due to the expertise and track records of both players. Before the start of event, the stadium was filled to the brim. For the first few rounds, the players had a tie. This further aroused the feeling of suspense in the spectators. The game went on beyond what everybody had imagined, but everyone was still glued to it. Eventually, Player B smacked Player A at the final round, which gave him the much-needed victory. Player B dropped the bat and raised his hands into the air, jumping up and smiling with his admirers who also mirrored the same gesture. It was celebrations galore for them.

Case Study III: It is becoming increasingly difficult to get harmful drugs in Country WIO because the government has put in place high-level enforcement agents who arrest sellers and consumers of such drugs. However, one of them cunningly found a place in the outskirts of City UB to ply his trade. Within a short time, many of the drug addicts got to know about the place. They were indescribably elated on the first day they got there; they could be seen jumping, dancing, and shouting that they eventually discovered another 'hub'. However, their joy was short-lived as law enforcement agents trapped them down there after a few minutes.

18.6. Holding Arms behind the Back

Generic Interpretations of the Concept

This behaviour is mostly seen among royal authorities, and that is why it has been assumed to be a sign of royalty used by authoritative figures. However, this does not mean that arms held behind the back is the exclusive display of any specific class of people; the message does not change at any given time. When someone is exposed to a threat or feels that danger looms, they (especially men) block their genitals or cover their neck. However, when the arms are held behind back, it means the person has nothing to fear. That is why it is said to be a show of superiority and authority.

Two notable heads of England, Queen Elizabeth and Prince Charles, are renowned for the act of placing the arms and hands at their back while walking. Some other British royals later emulated them. They used to do this when they needed people (especially their subjects) to give them space. The message is clear: 'I don't want people close to me.' This demand for personal space is due to the reasons best known to the person demanding for it.

In the same vein, when we display this behaviour, it means we are telling others to stay aloof and give us our personal space. That is why this behaviour has been considered of being capable of sending people away from you; it does not endear others to us and vice versa. Remember that touch is associated with closeness and intimacy in most cases. So if the hands are psychologically tied to the back, it means the person is not receptive of others. This behaviour is not entirely bad; it is worth using during the moment of deep reflections when you do not want others to interrupt.

It is interesting to note that kids do not like it when their parents or guardians place their hands behind their back; it is communicating distance to them which they do not like.

Scientific Explanations

Farouk Radwan (2017) lists the act of placing the hand behind the back as a show of confidence. He submits that 'when you see someone standing with his hands behind his back, then know that he is probably feeling confident. He may be feeling confident because he is a confident person or because he believes he's on top of matters in a current situation.' For instance, if you are discussing a topic that the person has a good grasp of, you may observe this cue. When you are discussing unemployment and a person quickly assumes this posture, be sure that the person has a high-paying job.

Howard Allen (2019) also lends a voice to this subject matter. Allen goes in-depth by noting that there are two variations to this cue, looking superficially similar but different in its meanings. He surmises his point by opining that 'the standard version that we see most often is a dominant, confident pose. The second version is submissive and suggests insecurity.' So the question is, how do we differentiate between the two poses? For the standard hands behind the back pose, the person will stand erect with the feet at least shoulder-width apart and usually slightly pointed out, the shoulders are pulled back and the chest maintains a neutral position or expanded to make the person look bigger, the arms are behind the back with a hand over the other, the arms are in a relaxed state, and the hands would not be tightly clasped (the touch is normal) (Allen 2019).

On the other hand, the hands behind the back pose with arm or wrist clasp is displayed by a person who is standing up fairly straight with the feet closer than the confident pose, the shoulders are slightly forward, and there's usually a noticeable arch in the lower back. If displayed with a wrist clasp, both arms are held behind the back. If it is done with an arm clasp, one arm is behind the back, but the other is at the side of the body, slightly pulled back; then, you will observe tension in the person's arms (Allen 2019).

You begin to notice the difference from the standing posture; even though the person maintains a somewhat erect posture, the closeness of the feet than the standard version makes their balance inappropriate, thereby betraying their emotions. They are perceived as being smaller than their size. The slight forward placement of the shoulders also makes the person look smaller. 'The arch in the lower back is commonly seen from women when they're emphasising their feminine shape. This isn't a good look for a man. In either case it's on the submissive end of the scale but, strangely, it's even more noticeable when a man does it, probably because it plays against his natural shape' (Allen 2019).

When the palms are placed over a hand or made to face downward, it means the person is frustrated about something. This is different from the standard version where the palm is placed in the second palm. You need to take cognisance of all these while trying to interpret gestures, especially those that look similar, in order not to be deceived.

Practical Illustrations

Case Study I: Mr J was discussing with one of his brilliant students; the boy's brilliance resonates everywhere and many of the teachers try to dodge his questions because they do render them incompetent. The discussion taking place between the boy and Mr J only started on a casual note, if not, the teacher would have evaded it. However, if he should bow out at this point, his fear would be pronounced. So he cautiously continued in the discourse, trying to play the leading role; but once in a while, the boy dictated the direction in which the talk should go. They were standing at the corridor of the school. So Mr J stood fairly erect, closing the feet together, moving the shoulders slightly forward, with one hand clasping the other wrist. This is a self-comforting act which might be erroneously interpreted as a show of confidence by the boy due to the seemingly authoritative figure of the teacher.

Case Study II: There was a report of a group of terrorists trying to attack a facility, so soldiers were mobilised to the venue. While many soldiers were stationed at strategic areas considered as hotspots, just one was positioned at a spot that was X-rayed and had been found impossible for the terrorists to come through. Unfortunately, they came through that spot, and when the soldiers saw some people approaching him, he quickly held his arms behind his back to depict a sign of authority, which sent fear down the nerves of the attackers. He retained this posture until his colleagues were reinforced to the place. This was a smart move that later gave him victory where he would have been defeated.

Case Study III: Criminal CU and his accomplices decided to rob a woman of her possessions. He only coordinated the activities of his boys, and unfortunately for the victim, the operation was successful. Before the woman could raise her voice, they had disappeared into thin air. Knowing how risky it was for him to run too or even show signs of nervousness, he decided to cover up his fears by holding his arms behind his back and take an wider stance, which erroneously portrayed him as being powerful. And that saved him from being suspected. He later walked away freely when everything subsided.

18.7. Stiffening of the Arms

Generic Interpretations of the Concept

When any part of the body stiffens, it communicates a message of negativity. When negative emotions are being displayed, you should also pay attention to the movement of the arms to ascertain your guess. The stiffening of the arms means that something unexpected has happened to someone. During this process, the arms will lie dead at the sides of the body; the overwhelming event has made it very difficult for the arms to be moved. The arms move freely when a person is comfortable and expresses self-confidence, but when they become too heavy to be lifted, it means they have been weakened by a negative occurrence.

When the arms are stiffened, you will also discover that they look robotic or unnatural. The feeling of being artificial is an indication that an event has reconfigured the working of the arms. Once your instinct tells you that the arms are not moving as they should, pay more attention to them, and compare the body language behaviour with other gestures.

A fact that remains undeniable is that stiff arms is a potent indicator that something negative has just occurred. For instance, a person who has been defeated squarely in a table tennis game would be unimpressed to go further in the game when invited at that moment; their arm is communicating depression.

Also, when someone considers an action as being dangerous or threatening to their future, they will maintain a stiffened arm. Hence, stiffness of the arms in this sense means unwillingness to get something done. For example, if a board recommends sacking a lady who is a lover to the manager, you may notice the hands of the manager stiffen when he is about to sign the notice of termination;

he knows that the action may end their relationship. So the thought is weighing the arms down.

Scientific Explanations

Jill Avery-Stoss (2017) discusses this gesture under men's body language. He notes that movements of the hands and arms can be greatly revealing. Explaining the expression of negativity from this perspective, she submits, 'Negativity is signaled by crossing arms, leaning or turning away, stiffness and minimal eye contact.' When the arms are stiffened, it means a negative occurrence has sent the person into the freeze response mood. It is pertinent to reiterate that arm stiffening happens as an aftermath of an unfavourable event while crossing of the arms is mostly done during the conversation process, as a way of blocking out negative thoughts.

Practical Psychology (2019) discusses this cue as part of the body language of lying. Inasmuch as I would not agree outright with this because there is no sunfire way of spotting deception, there is a logical point in the fact that stiffness is used to denote something negative. So those who are being deceptive will make fewer arm movements and will remain tense as they spew out their fabricated stories. Again, you need to take cognisance of other cues before concluding on the truthfulness or accuracy of your interpretations. For instance, the stiffness of the arms does not stop the twitching of the fingers when a person is feeling uncomfortable. Hence, the little nervous movements of the fingers are pointers to the fact that the person is not in their normal mood.

In his own contribution, Christopher Philip (2013) describes the stiffening of the arms as a defensive posture. This occurs by thrusting the arm forward and away from the body with the palm face vertical in a 'stop' type signal. 'Another defensive posture is the curved arm, a variation of the stiff arm, where the arm is bent and locked at the elbow and thrust outward facing down or horizontally. As a cluster, the stiff arm and curved arm is accompanied by a step backwards to reclaim stolen space, which is the true intention of the stiff arm,' Philip explains. Both postures are seen as arm-distancing, as they are used to buy space. The common phrase 'keeping people at arm's length' is derived from this gesture. Taking a look at the cue from the broadest perspective, it is regarded as a closed body gesture.

At times, the arm fails to come up any higher than a few inches, or the hand might flip upwards slightly while being held at waist level; however, the message is the same. In some other times, we can make use of the arm-stiffening gesture to thwart closeness that we feel is unnecessary due to physical threats. When we don't want to get too close to people, we may intentionally keep our arms out. Also, the arms can signal the likeness or otherwise you have for another person based on the proximity you maintain with them. 'When someone is particularly turned off by someone else they will keep their arms away from them in-so-much as their bodies can maintain enough personal space and don't need to be thrown in arms way, so to speak, to serve as stiff arms' (Philip 2013).

Practical Illustrations

Case Study I: Here is a case study based on the context of a city slicker and farmer: A city slicker and a country farmer who meet for the first time. While exchanging pleasantries, the farmer accepted the handshake from the city slicker even though a wave would be more appropriate for the famer's comfort, and in order to keep his space, he had to push his arm forward, shoving the city slicker back. This sort of handshake can happen any time a person requires more space than their partner, and this isn't always people from the country (Philip 2013). This means the farmer is not comfortable with the proximity and needed to create more space through stiff arms.

Case Study II: Mr J had just been defeated in a novelty match where he served as the goalkeeper. After that, they were required to play table tennis. When he was called upon, he resisted, because his arms were heavy, not because of physical activity, but due to the physiological effect of the defeat. Thus, he became uninspired to play further. He was not willing to play again because the thoughts of defeat still pervaded his mind.

Case Study III: I once arrested an impostor who thought she could display higher intelligence than everyone that she comes in contact with. She argued vehemently that she did not impersonate anyone. Although the passport photograph and her real image were the same, there were some obvious inconsistencies in other pieces of information supplied. When the argument was unbecoming, I asked that she should duplicate her signature on a sheet of paper. She knew that any difference between whatever she signed and what was on the document in my hand would expose her. When handed a pen, she stiffened her arms as if she couldn't lift them. This depicted her as someone who was unwilling to participate in the action.

18.8. Revealing the Armpit

Generic Interpretations of the Concept

Due to many reasons, people across cultures prefer keeping their armpit from the public view; they do not expose it in the presence of others. However, there are some special times in which we reveal the inner arms, including the armpit, technically known as axilla. When you see a person revealing their armpit around you, it means they are comfortable being with you. Exposing the armpit has to do with lifting the arms, which will open the entire body to other people. So the assurance that we have in those around makes us maintain this stance, thinking that they cannot do any evil to us.

Women are fond of this behaviour if they want to register their interest in another person. To expose the axilla, they will scratch the back of the head which makes them reveal it directly to a person of interest. The head scratch is just a secondary way of passing their message. The armpit looks like the surface of the genitals and, as such, capable of arousing the interest of an opposite sex. If exposed slowly, with the licking of the lips, the message can be further pronounced. Hence, this gesture is used to get a potential suitor's attention and demonstrate our readiness to them.

On the other hand, when the armpits are exposed and a person walks near, we become uncomfortable; unconsciously, we will try to cover them. The place is delicate and very sensitive to touch; hence the reason we do not want others to have an unfettered access to them. We only use them to invite others, but keep them shut when the person decodes the message being passed across. Since they can easily be injured, the brain switches into action when it sees anything coming nearer to them by taking a protective action.

Scientific Explanations

Westside Toastmasters (2019) says the act of exposing the armpit very common to women. The website explains that 'when a woman sees a man she finds attractive she unconsciously tosses her head or runs her fingers through her hair. Whether her hair is long or short the gesture is a subtle way of showing that she cares about her appearance and is making an effort to look appealing.' However, the overall benefit of this gesture is that it reveals the armpit, a highly sensual part of a lady that most men across the world find irresistible. This allows her 'sex perfume' referred to as pheromones to waft to her potential suitor.

Jack Brown (2011) describes this cue as a classic display of sexual display. Brown explains that when a lady preens her hair to expose her armpit, it is an indication that she is attracted to someone in her immediate vicinity. He explains that this action is mainly subconscious in women; it is a strong signal of their biological sexuality. According to Brown, 'Such arm position puts the breasts on display in a prominent fashion while simultaneously exhibiting overall health and confidence.' All these virtues can be irresistibly enticing to an average man.

Before moving further, there is need to emphasise the fact that not every hair-touching gesture when the armpit is exposed is regarded as a sexual display. There are other similar gestures expressing the exact opposite of this meaning. So beware of hasty generalisation! In fact, there are instances where the preening is only engineered by an itchy head. That is why it is crucial to analyse all factors before arriving at a conclusion.

Also, the act of exposing the armpit is not only limited to women. It is also seen among men as the 'check me out' cue. That is, men raise their shoulders to pump their muscles in order to tell a potential lover that they are hot enough to date the targeted person. The basic role of the cue is to get the person's attention and then move the attraction signals to another level. That is why I refer to it as an inviting signal.

Sandra Prior (2009) also lends her voice to this concept. She notes that women often initiate touch than men—two-thirds of the time. Women are indescribably great in manipulating stuff to communicate their heart. For instance, you may discover that a woman begins to massage her neck out of the blue when she does not really have a stiff neck, the overriding effect is to reveal the armpit; she is aware that massaging the neck will expose her breasts, make them bigger, and help their target have a look at their armpit, a sexual hotspot for them.

Practical Illustrations

Case Study I: Ms K was feeling lonely and did not want to visit any of her friends due to some personal issues; they would talk about their spouses, and she was yet to have any. So she saw that as emotional torture. She had looked for ways of dodging such discussions, but they would still manage to raise it despite knowing how she felt in each occasion. Thus, she purposed not to call on or entertain any of them at the weekend. When the loneliness was becoming unbearable, she went to a restaurant to have some drinks and chill out for few hours. Just a few minutes at the restaurant, a man came in and sat directly opposite to her seat. She stylishly ignored him despite liking his physique. The man greeted her, and simple conversations ensued. When it seemed that she could not hide her feelings for the man and yet he was not hitting the nail on its head, she decided to arouse his feelings by releasing some pheromones; this would make her interest registered. Pretending as if she had an itch on her head, she began to preen her hair and, in the process, revealed her breasts and underarm. At first, the man turned his face away, but on looking at the direction again, they both smiled to each other, and this showed the message has been decoded; it was the starting point for both of them.

Case Study II: Lady U secured her job on controversial circumstances, and many people were of the opinion that she would not last in the firm. Little did they know that she had another plan as a way of sustaining herself. Within her first few days in the organisation, Lady U paid close attention to the men and how efficient each of them were. Then, she settled for two of them. She built a friendship with them, and whenever she was confused on any given assignment, she would rush to either of them, opened her armpit, and talk to them seductively. This was a smart way for her to survive in the organisation, as her deeds were often irresistible to the men.

Case Study III: Ms IB is an illegal immigrant, and when law enforcement officials were about to arrest her, she decided to changer her game and lure them to her instead. As the enforcement officer pointed at her, she did not bother arguing or feigning ignorance, she turned her side to the officer and raised her arms so as to reveal her armpit to him. Her dress was so revealing, and she then backed her non-verbal gestures up with a charming smile. It was glaring that she wanted to romantically lure the officer to herself so that he would lose focus on the primary assignment of arresting her.

18.9. Self-Hugging Gestures

Generic Interpretations of the Concept

When you see a person hug themselves, this communicates huge messages to those around. Hugging, in its natural sense, has to do with two people defying the need for personal space to touch each other. However, if you see a person performing the role of another person for themselves, it can be interpreted in different ways. For the umpteenth time, there is a tactile effect when the surface of the skin touches another. The self-hugging gesture has to do with crossing the arms and pressing them tightly to the body.

The first possible interpretation of this cue is the need for self-comfort. Maybe the person has been exposed to some discomforting events in times past and, as such, trying to hold themselves through the self-hug. In the same vein, people display this gesture when they are awaiting the arrival of someone. It is general human nature that we hate being delayed at a spot, doing nothing; this makes us feel bored. So the self-comforting act is to ginger the body so as not to look dull when the person arrives. Also it is to tell the body that the wait is worth it. I have always observed this cue while on plane; passengers, while lining up to use the restroom will cross their arms till it gets to their turn.

On simple interrogations with people, they reported an array of reasons for this. Some simply replied 'It's comfortable'. Some others believe it works effectively for them when the arms are weak. That is why you see yourself do it after hours of typing on the laptop. With this, the arms are stretched and pacified before going back to the work.

Weirdly enough, some ladies believe that this action hides their breasts. If they feel that their breasts are too big and do not want to be the point of attention, they will cross their arms, placing them beneath the boobs so as to neutralise the largeness. In the same vein, some people, especially men, use this cue to cover their pot-bellies. With this, you will focus on their crossed arms instead of the protruding stomach.

And some do it when they are curious or inquisitive. This may be accompanied by a slight scratch of the arms, communicating with the other party that you are a bit skeptical about what you have just been told. Some people mistakenly think that this cue is equated to keeping people off.

Scientific Explanations

Westside Toastmasters (2019) shares the conventional sentiment that arm-crossing is used to keep people out and create a barrier, whether physical or psychological. The platform notes that this gesture might be inborn because we display it unconsciously when faced with a threatening situation. The website explains that 'by folding one or both arms across the chest, a barrier is formed that is an unconscious attempt to block out what we perceive as a threat or undesirable circumstances. The arms fold neatly across the heart and lungs region to protect these vital organs from being injured.' Considering this explanation, we may be tempted to agree with the platform that arm-crossing is used to block people out, but I need to state that this is usually witnessed once in a blue moon. Monkeys and chimpanzees also display this cue when they feel they are about to be attacked.

Arm-crossing is the most discussed segment under arm body language by Changing Minds. The website describes the arms as the doorway to the body and self. Crossing them is like closing the gate of your house; you block out strangers from gaining entry into the house. In the same vein, arms crossing is very symbolic when it comes to being receptive towards other people's messages. When the arms are crossed, it serves as defensive posture in two ways—it helps in blocking an incoming attack or serves as a shield through which you hide so as not to be taken cognisance of. That is the case of those who do it for the purpose of hiding their breasts and bellies.

In a way, we may acknowledge anxiety as one of the possible interpretations of this gesture; if you do not have trust in the person addressing you or have a general sense of vulnerability, you may display this stance. For instance, childhood trauma may dictate how you feel and relate to people later on in life—if you observe something that once caused harm to you, you might cross your arms as a way of avoiding it. According to Changing Minds (2019), 'The extent of crossing indicates how firmly closed the person is. This may range from a light cross to arms folded to arms wrapped around the person. An extreme version which may indicate additional hostility is a tight close with hands formed as fists. If legs are crossed also then this adds to the signal.'

However, the act of crossing the arms is not totally negative. For instance, if a person is holding the arms in a folded position, it probably means the person is feeling comfortable, especially if there is some sort of tension in other parts of the body. Comfort means absence of fear and readiness to confront any form of attack. This can be seen when the arms are crossed among friends.

Hanan Parvez (2019) captures this in its very apt form in his introductory remarks thus: 'Crossing the arms across the chest is a classic gesture of defensiveness. This defensiveness usually manifests as uneasiness, shyness, or insecurity.'

Practical Illustrations

Case Study I: Mr O visited a long-time friend, and as expected, most of the discussions were about the past and how life had been treating each of them since their departure. It was a great reunion, as both of them took turns to talk and relay their experiences. At some point, Mr O was getting bored due to the endless tales of the friend. There was a particular account his friend gave which he was doubtful of, but he knew putting up a direct confrontation would affect the other person negatively. So he only crossed his arms, rubbed them warmly, and put on a little smile in order to comfort himself. Perhaps he would have a change from the present discomfort.

Case Study II: Student A didn't like reading novels. However, the school he attended mandates that they all must be part of the reading class. The aim of this was to inculcate in them a reading culture. Student A was easily bored whenever the class was ongoing. On a particular occasion, he felt tired because he didn't perform well in the sciences, his beloved area of interest. So when the reading class started, he felt like it was taking forever. After looking around, he hugged himself as a way of self-comfort. He looked so dull that the teacher in charge was forced to ask him if all was well. Although he lied to the teacher, he could not keep on this posture for too long as he eventually fell asleep.

Case Study III: Mr XO borrowed money to purchase some smuggled goods. He was lured into the illicit business by a group of friends who told him that the business was yielding high returns within the shortest period of time. He thought that was his chance to succeed without too much efforts. He ran out of luck, as he was apprehended before the delivery of the first set of goods. After giving his confessional statements, he knew the goods were not going to be returned to him. He looked dejected and hopeless after thinking about how he was going to make a refund of the borrowed funds. As a way of self-assurance, he unconsciously hugged himself. This was so comforting, but it did not take away the whole feeling.

18.10. Arm-Crossing for Protection

Generic Interpretations of the Concept

I briefly mentioned in the preceding section that the arms are sometimes crossed to prevent an external attack. Tracing it to evolution, it is discovered that both monkeys and chimpanzees do cross their arms when they see a signal of attack from the front. Our arms are very strong, and we will prefer using them as blockage other than exposing the body directly to all forms of attacks. In this sense, the arms crossing is tantamount to body guard.

The arm-crossing gestures are of different variants, and you need to pay attention to how it is done so as to know which is which. However, the most reliable way of distinguishing them is to understand the underlying meaning behind the cues. So in some instances, rather than being a self-comforting cue, it may be a defensive shield.

There is always the unconscious urge to shield the ventral side of the body (the body) when anything threatens us. Hence, the feeling of insecurity or discomfort can propel this cue in a person.

In the case of arms crossing for protection, you will observe that there are more tensions in the arms through their stiffening and a psychologically disturbed face. The negative emotion on the face, coupled with the force in which the hand is held, serve as a hint that the person is not just displaying the cue for the sake of fun but to serve an important purpose on the body. With this, you will be informed on the kind of interpretations you would make.

Scientific Explanations

Changing Minds (2019) sheds light on this concept from the viewpoint of psychology. The body language platform explains that when you see a person who is crossing their arms, there is high probability that they are undergoing internal discomfort. This may be propelled by what the other party is saying or being exposed to something that threatens their subconscious mind. This births a sense of attack and vulnerability. If you see yourself as being weak in comparison to an alleged threat, the body switches into a defensive mood, such as arm-crossing. Also, being a place where you do not have absolute trust in may make you a bit apprehensive.

Parvez (2019) emphasises the protective role of arm crossing. She explains that when we feel threatened by a situation, we cross our arms over our chest in order to create a barrier which helps protect the vital organs of the lungs and heart. It is an open secret that if anything affects any of those vital organs, it may terminate our lives.

When you are in a group and notice that someone crosses their arms, it means the person lacks confidence. If they feel that they may be attacked or asked something that will unsettle them, they may display this cue as a protective step. This is not different from a person who is told bad news and symbolically crosses the arm as if they do not want to be 'stained' by the news.

According to Parvez, 'Defence is a natural reaction to an offence.' So when someone is publicly criticised or humiliated, they may assume this defensive posture.

Westside Toastmasters (2019) states that the act of hiding behind a barrier when threatened is a normal response of humans; we learnt it from an early stage and tend to apply it all through life. The website recalls that as 'children, we hid behind solid objects such as tables, chairs, furniture and mother's skirt whenever we found ourselves in a threatening situation. As we grew older, this hiding behavior became more sophisticated and by the age of about six, when it was unacceptable behavior to hide behind solid objects, we learned to fold our arms tightly across our chests whenever a threatening situation arose.'

Research has shown that there is a downside to arm-crossing. About 1,500 seminar attendees were used as participants in an experiment where it was determined if arm-crossing affects attentiveness or not. It was discovered that those who crossed their arms had 40 per cent less retentive ability compared with those who did not fold their arms. Note that these experiments were carried out at different points in time and the results still appeared similar (Westside Toastmasters 2019). This says that apart from keeping people at bay, this gesture also has negative impact on our retentiveness.

Practical Illustrations

Case Study I: Y has been working with Mr P for some time now, so he knows what he is up to; you can barely predict his mood—this minute, he is jovial; and the next, he maintains a stern look. What seems most disturbing is the childish act of telling every other person the act of kindness he rendered to you in times past. On this particular incident, they were holding a meeting where every other employee was present; Mr P was baffled that some of the employees were not up and doing something. He wanted to know the reason behind their lacklustre attitude. During the meeting, he decided to give them the opportunity to explain themselves, but none of the employees were ready to argue against the boss. Then, he started mentioning names and good gestures he had done for them in the past, wondering why they could not reciprocate the gesture towards him. As he began to mention names, Y became uncomfortable because it was Mr P who paid his father's medical bills when he was last admitted at the hospital. Hence, Y crossed his arms tightly and looked disturbed throughout the meeting.

Case Study II: Mrs F is not used to horror movies; she does not join others in the family to watch them while at home. However, she is currently with her friend, after she went for a week-long seminar. Since it would be out of place for her to challenge the choice of her hosts, she decided to stay and play along with them on everything they did. On a night, they decided to watch a horror movie, and she decided to stay back a while before retiring to bed. Throughout the period, Mrs F sat in the living room, she crossed her arms as she watched the movie absent-mindedly. It was not appealing to her and, as such, made her uncomfortable.

Case Study III: One day, Mr AH, a drug trafficker, paid a visit to his friend, and he met them watching a programme on the harmful effects of hard drugs and what the government was doing to put an end to it. Since he had no authority to tell them to change the station, he reluctantly watched along. He became terrified when the presenter said the government had concluded plans to sentence drug traffickers to life imprisonment. He unconsciously crossed his arms as a way of self-protection. He was so down with the development that one would think he had been sentenced already.

18.11. Self-Restraint Arm-Crossing

Generic Interpretations of the Concept

Sometimes, we feel that some locations are not ideal to vent our anger. So even if we are offended and emotions want to get out of hand, we will try to suppress them. The foremost non-verbal way in which this is done is through arm-crossing. The person surely knows that if they should publicly display their anger at the given point, things will become messier. While this may not be easy because the emotions would have risen to its peak, the overriding urge to keep sanity still keeps the person within frame. When I notice this emotional struggle in people and they later ended up triumphing over the ill emotions, they do gain my respect eternally. The reason is that they are aware of the wrongdoing of another person against them, but for the sake of peace, they decided to embark on another internal discomfort.

As a way of having a practical understanding of this point, I want you to imagine being in an airport environment, and then a passenger is bumped out of a flight immediately. Do you think the person will be happy? Don't you think their reaction would be negative?

This cue is similar to the self-hugging cue earlier discussed. However, in the former, the pressure is mildly applied on the arms. In this, it is done with full force to connote the symbolic restraints of something trying to force itself out. The arms are the most mobile part of the body. Even if the person does not utter any word, the mere carriage of the arms can tell others around that they are pissed off. That is why the person is consciously suppressing the movement of the hands.

However, it is pertinent to note that for you to know if the arms-crossing gesture is for self-restraint or not, you must focus on their face too. If their face bears the message of animosity, it means your guess is most probably accurate.

Scientific Explanations

Humiliation or heavy criticisms are capable of making a person, especially if they think it was done in the wrong place. Hence, arm-crossing can be the aftermath of humiliation. Crossing the arms is symbolic of self-defence, with the person passing the non-verbal message that they will not take that from you any longer. In a discourse context involving two people if you see one of the discussants suddenly cross their arms, it means the second person has said something that does match their expectations. However, he or she is trying to repress the feeling of anger.

Note that the fists would also be clenched to display the attitude of anger. According to Parvez (2019), 'We clench our fists when we're angry and are about to punch someone, literally or symbolically.' This body language posture is negative and as an observant fellow, if you notice this, you should be able to ask your co-interlocutor what the source of concern is. If you choose to ignore them, the person may eventually burst out before the end of the discussion.

Changing Minds (2019) notes that arms crossing of anger deals with the two arms holding each other. This means the person is trying to keep themselves still. This is a sure sign that they are trying to suppress an emotion. The website mentions 'repressed anger' as one of the most likely emotions being suppressed. It gives the verbal translation of the action as 'I have to hold myself to prevent myself hitting you'. At this point, let me make a quick U-turn; there are some cultures that take this cue as a means of holding themselves still in order to pay greater attention to a particular person. In this sense, it is seen as a compliment instead of suppression of anger.

Practical Illustrations

Case Study I: Mr U is the official driver of HJK Firms. Even though the company has laid off a lot of people, he has always been retained due to his dedication to duty and expertise. Mr U is known to be principled, and some other employees have been taking that as pride, but the man seems to be unmoved about that. One day, he was supposed to drive one of the junior employees to a seminar in another province. Before the end of his shift the previous day, the junior worker had fixed a time and ordered that he should be picked in the front of his house. Mr U got there at the set time, only for the junior employee not to have taken his bath. He was conscious of the fact that they were outside of the office setting, so he only retired to his seat in the car and crossed his arms, while clenching his fists forcefully. This means he was trying to suppress his anger.

Case Study II: Baby M came home tired, and after few minutes, her mother called her to the living room to ask for her help to run some errands within the neighbourhood. Baby M thought that was the only thing she needed, only for her to come back and be sent to the same venue. After returning the second time, she was sent into the kitchen on four different occasions on a thing that could have been done once. After that, she took her seat at the dinner table and crossed her arms while her face was full of animosity. When her mother saw this, she walked up to her and asked if anything was wrong, and Baby M took the opportunity to vent her anger. She was really angry and would not feign peace that all was well; in actual fact, she was feeling tossed.

Case Study III: A group of law enforcement official came to a house to raid as it was connected to a crime they were investigating; the younger brother of the owner of the house was in their custody and he made some confessions linking them to the house. When they came, the man gave them the opportunity to search the whole house after being presented with search warrant. After hours of search, they could not find anything incriminating. The man, who was oblivious of everything, wanted to go out and was being delayed already. When they sought to search the rooms the second time, he became hot due to the official duty they were performing, he folded his arms and clenched his fists while standing aloof.

18.12. Arm-Crossing for Hatred

Generic Interpretations of the Concept

By now, you would have observed that the possibilities of expressing non-verbal messages through the arms are limitless. Apart from anger, there is a way for you to cross your arms to communicate with another person that you dislike for what they have just shown or done to you. Also, you will be able to decode this message when someone sends it to you.

If we are in the presence of a person making us feel uncomfortable or that we do not like for reasons best known to us, we may place our crossed arms on the belly as a way of creating some social space between us and them. Trying to create space between yourself and another, whether consciously or unconsciously, is a pointer to the fact that you are not receptive of the person's ideas. This behaviour comes to fore once you set your eyes on a person objectionable; this serves as the distinguishing factor between the cue and other related ones. Note that in other arm-crossing gestures, the behaviour may occur when something unfavourable occurs during a discourse. However, in this, you assume this posture immediately when you set your eyes on the person.

To a person who has an understanding of body language cues, this perfectly communicates your dislike to them.

This cue is somewhat similar to the self-hugging gesture. However, the feeling of dislike is accompanied by tense face. Your facial emotion will also move into the negative mood when you see a person you dislike, and also, the feet might turn away. Since your mind does not want to be with them, so does your entire body. Hence, the feet are ready to walk away from that location. Generally, the arm-crossing is also not tense; the pressure is the same as that of self-hugging.

Scientific Explanations

Ni'Kesia Pannell (2018) lists arm-crossing as one of the gestures used in showing dislike for a person. Before you form any friendship or relationship, impressions are based on the feelings people get from the other party. For instance, if a person is nice to you, you begin to imagine a long-term relationship and do everything with your means to ensure that the friendship works. And if they behave poorly to you, you would be caught in the labyrinth of thought of why they gave you such predisposition. Mostly, our assumptions are formed by the manner in which the person communicates with us with their body language. Pannell submits that 'though you can sometimes walk away not knowing that a person isn't a fan of you, it is common knowledge that people crossing their arms while speaking to you or looking elsewhere when doing the same are ways to know that your hopeful new relationships isn't going far.' The fact is that a person who does not communicate with you with an open language is either not receptive of your idea or person.

A 20th Century Fox television series, *Lie to Me*, spells it out well that when a person speaks with you, maintaining open arms, it means they are open and when the arms are closed, it means the exact opposite. Pannell explains that one of the biggest signs that someone does not like you is that they cross their arms while discussing with you. This happens more often than not, but we tend to neglect them at our own detriment. 'Crossing arms can be a sign that someone is closed off or not wanting to receive what you are giving to them,' says Ali Craig, an international speaker and consultant. There are other accompanying gestures that can further make this message clearer to you. Lack of eye contact, outward positioning of the feet, intentional creation of space, among others are some of the pointers to this fact.

Practical Illustrations

Case Study I: The home of Mr and Mrs YO can be described as a battlefield. The husband and wife fight at every given opportunity, and regrettably, their children are growing wiser to meet them in the same spot. This has been telling on the psychological configuration of the children. As time went on, the children began to take sides, anointing themselves as the judges over issues that pertain to their parents. Out of the three kids, two are for their mother, while the eldest son is suing for peace. These unending fights have created the feeling of hatred for the father in the minds of the kids. Child Y has made this confession to Child H. Any time the father was home, they do not feel comfortable and wait for the moment when he would vacate the home. One day, the three kids were having fun at home with their mother when their father suddenly showed up. As the father was making his way in, Child Y's countenance changed immediately. He became tense and looked fragile, maintaining crossed arms and turning towards the door of his room. After greeting his dad, he left the living room immediately.

Case Study II: Suspect A seems to be a professional criminal. He has been interrogated by a lot of law enforcement officials across nations, and weirdly, he has managed to escape. On the last crime that he perpetrated, the enforcement agencies were almost certain that he was behind it. However, no court would take certainty without proof of evidence to convict a suspect. Hence, the most experienced interrogators in the country and those of neighbouring nations were drafted to investigate him. After a few minutes of briefing by the leading interrogator, the officers were ushered into the interview room where Suspect A was waiting for them. On seeing the calibre of people filing in, he began to shiver, but he was still trying to suppress the negative feeling. As the last interrogator was coming in, he quickly crossed his arms and pointed his feet to the door, wearing a sad face. In one of his interrogations, he was engaged by the interrogator, and he only escaped by a whisker. Since then, he has created a sense of hatred for interrogator.

Case Study III: Friend A and Friend B are fond of playing with girls. They go about sleeping with any available lady. This, to them, is fun. However, there was a particular girl that came across, and both of them were willing to have her as a wife. After several hours of arguments and counterarguments, they couldn't reach a resolution. Meanwhile, Friend A has been speaking with the lady, and it seems the lady is ready to go for him. When B tried to make the same attempt, he was turned down. They seemed to have forgotten it, but B was still holding grudges. One day, the lady paid them a visit, and as she was coming in, Friend B crossed his arms and looked away. This means he was not receptive of her visit due to the ill feelings he had about her.

18.13. Arm-Crossing for Massaging

Generic Interpretations of the Concept

The fact that the arms can either be crossed at the chest or belly makes it have multiple likely interpretations. I have explained at different points in this book that massaging is primarily done to soothe the person. Hence, it is mostly not done out of fun, but on the need to relieve stress or arouse the feelings of a lover. In this case, the arms are crossed at the chest, which gives the hands the opportunity to reach the shoulders and massage them. Ordinarily, when the arms are crossed at the chest, it can be a sign of comfort for some people. However, when they begin to massage the opposite arm of shoulder, it means the person is experiencing some negative emotions.

When we are stressed and do not want others to know it, we may adopt this gesture to deal with the stressors. Massaging of the body gives us a pacifying feeling, and thus, you may see people display this cue continuously, depending on how stressed they are. In the same vein, massaging the shoulders through crossed arms may indicate that the person has some concerns. When reflecting on an issue that is bothering you, you may massage the body as you think along in order not to be weighed down by the power of the issue. With this, your attention is divided between the issue and the non-verbal act.

This body language gesture is mostly performed when the person is seated at a table with their elbows placed on the table, while the arms cross at the chest. However, I have also seen those sitting in a chair display this non-verbal cue; this is done as a form of self-hugging while they massage the opposite arm or shoulder.

I need to state that there are times that this gesture is propelled by mere cold. When someone is feeling cold, they can massage the shoulder and block the cold out symbolically through the crossing of the arms at the chest. When cold, massaging the shoulders or arms can make the body hot. Context is key.

Scientific Explanations

In his submission, Zaccheus Cacere (2018) notes that this body language gesture is used when a person is not comfortable. Discomfort makes us become aggressive, and as such, we look for decisive ways of dealing with it. Cacere notes that this gesture has two variants. The standard version is what I have been talking about. That is, the crossing of the arms at the chest with rubbing of the shoulders while the person looks uncomfortable. However, the variant is when the person does the gesture with a defiant look and leaning forward simultaneously. In the latter, it connotes aggression and not the act of pacifying. It may be a restraint to attack or explode at another person.

Navarro (2009) states that we massage the body when we feel threatened. He describes this behaviour as a frequent act of dealing with stress. The shoulders and arms are somewhat rich in nerve endings, and as such, we take the advantage of the arm-crossing cue to rub those parts in order to be relieved of our stress. When rubbed properly and continuously, we can be calmed down. This body language behaviour may be seen in men more than women; it is much more pronounced in women than men, and as such, females rarely do it.

Practical Illustrations

Case Study I: Mr AK has been working for seventeen hours without a break. He has a meeting with the president of the company where he works, and as the director, he needs to sound articulate and knowledgeable. The president expects him to have answers to every question concerning the firm without having to refer to any book. He has been living up to expectations, and the reach of the organization is becoming wider by the day. This means he has to work extra hours and get things fixed in order to be seen as the true head. However, he is still encountering different issues with one of their new branches. Many of their activities are not done transparently and despite all warnings, they do not seem to be catching. Since this was not an excuse to be offered before the president, he has to cover up by all means. For the better part of the day, he has been on their report alone. Deep down into the night, it seems he is getting to understanding it. He stood up from his chair, walked around the office and crossed his arms at his chest while rubbing the opposite shoulders. After some few minutes, he packed his items and went home. He was optimistic that since he had made a headway, his work would move faster the next day. So the non-verbal gesture was a way of pacifying himself for all the stress he had undergone.

Case Study II: Mr J is an external examiner and renowned teacher. This has opened the doors of nations to him. Of course, the reward of hard work is more work; there is hardly any day that he does not get invite for more jobs. Working all day on an essay prepared by some special students he was told to handle. He read all the essays and everything he taught the students did not reflect in their write-up. He called them one after the other and explained things to them, but it seemed they were not ready to turn a new leaf. For the third time, he adopted another special method to teach them, yet they were not impressive in their exercise. While marking the essays again, he became frustrated because he had never encountered such types of students. At some point, he dropped his pen and crossed his arms while he rubbed the opposite shoulders briskly to deal with the stress encountered due to the annoying work. He was visibly angry, and anyone who came to him at that point would notice this show of annoyance.

Case Study III: Ms R was to travel via air for the first time, and she was really afraid. This was very obvious in her behaviour, and she even confessed to one of her colleagues. However, the journey was unavoidable for her. On the D-day, while waiting on the queue to be ushered into the plane, she crossed her arms subconsciously and started rubbing her arms to ease the stressful feeling.

Case Study IV: Criminal AC was nabbed after the law spent three months going after him. He was not only an illegal immigrant; he was going about fomenting trouble in his neighbourhood. Before law enforcement officers went after him, he had been reported over a hundred times. When he was eventually arrested, he was interviewed and necessary statements that would be used in the court were extracted from him. The day he would be arraigned in court, he sat on a chair and looked sober. He crossed his arms and used crossed arms to massage his body continuously as a way of easing his psychological feelings until he was ushered into the court.

18.14. Holding the Wrist Gesture

Generic Interpretations of the Concept

When faced with an unimaginable issue, many people quickly reach to the opposite wrist, holding it as if it is the source of their strength. Ideally, if a person is told something damaging, they will grab the person standing or sitting next to them. However, in this case, which is mostly seen in a formal or semi-formal setting, the person cannot touch their co-interlocutor, so they use wrist-grabbing as an alternative.

This gesture is mostly seen in interview setting. For instance, when an interviewee is confronted with a damaging piece of information, they will stretch their arms across their stomach and hold the wrist of the opposite hand as if stopping it from slapping the person who made the accusation. If there is a block between you and the person, you may not have a full view of this gesture. Well, one of the possible interpretations is that this cue is symbolic. Conventionally, when a shocking revelation is made about you in an unexpected manner, your hands may begin to shiver. So grabbing it through the wrist may prevent this embarrassing action that gives you out. Hence, this behaviour is considered as a means of suppressing real emotions.

To spot this gesture in people, pay attention to it when a person is asked a difficult question or accused of doing something evil. The wrist is also said to be rich in nerve endings. So touching it with a hand might be a means of rubbing it in order to pacify the body. If the wrist is not massaged, it may serve as the first point of betrayal. Also, I have noticed this in poker players; they hold the wrist when they feel the hand is marginal or weak. This weakness may be induced by defeat or even physical activities.

All things being equal, no one will hold their wrist if there is not any special event or thought going on in their mind.

Scientific Explanations

Hanan Parvez (2019) notes that the hand can be clenched in three different manners: hands clenched in front of the face, hands clenched resting on the desk or lap, and while standing, hands clenched over the lower abdomen. The latter seems to be what I have captured in my explanation above. Anywhere you see any of the variants, it means the person is exercising 'self-restraint'. 'They are symbolically "clenching" themselves back and withholding a negative reaction, usually anxiety or frustration. The higher the person clenches his hands whilst standing, the more negative he is feeling' (Parvez 2019). This explanation is direct and concise. If the person thinks the consequences of the negative would be major, they would clench their wrist with more force. For instance, you cannot equate the feelings of a child caught stealing meat from her mother's pot and a man caught stealing at a shopping mall.

This gesture is usually displayed when it appears that you are unable to convince another person on a given issue or when you are anxious of what the other person is saying. When the feeling of anxiety rises to a level, then it births this behaviour. While discussing with a person and you suddenly notice this gesture in them, if the conversation is not revolving round any findings, you may have to change its direction in order to allow your co-interlocutor calm down. However, if it is situated in the context of law enforcement, then this is a huge signal for you to query the person further until he or she says the truth (Parvez 2019).

Westside Toastmasters (2019) describes this gesture as the feeling of frustration. The website differentiates between this behaviour and the palm-in-palm attitude which relieves a person of stress through the tactile effect. The wrist-holding cue may be performed through the back (wrist held at the back of the body). The platform agrees with Parvez that 'this gesture is a way of maintaining self-control, as if the hand is holding the wrist or arm to keep it from hitting out.' It is purely a symbolic action. If you observe that the hand is slightly moving beyond the wrist, this is an indication that the frustration is really building up. By the time the hand would have reached the arm, the frustration would have been turned to anger. Westside Toastmasters also agree that it is a sign of nervousness.

In what looks like a consensus among the contributors to this subject matter, Changing Minds (2019) states that holding the wrist is typically done to comfort oneself. This aligns with what I explained under the generic interpretation. However, when the hands are wrung, it is an indication of extreme nervousness. In the same vein, the body language website notes that this gesture may also be denoting self-restraint. This can either be to allow another person express themselves or stop an angry person from attacking their perceived opponent. 'The tightness of a holding group indicates the degree of tension the person feels.'

Practical Illustrations

Case Study I: A man had killed his child due to whatever reason known to him but believed that no one saw him. So after putting everything into order, he went to report to the police. So the law enforcement officials swung into action, even though he was subtly discouraging them from proceeding with the findings. After the extensive investigation, the officials accused the man of complicity in the case involving the death of the child. He denied outright, noting that he was the one who came to report to them. He was jailed and later arraigned for interview. During the point of interview, he was asked who went to drop the child at the point he was when he came to report the incident to the police. He claimed ignorance. Then, he was asked of his location twenty minutes before he came to report, and he fabricated another lie. The interrogator then asked him how he got to know about the death and location of the deceased so early, and immediately, he used his hand to hold his wrist, looking shocked and sounding inarticulate as he prepared to answer the question.

Case Study II: Dr MA gave his secretary an instruction to get some documents typed and to send them to the deputy managing director so that he could sign them on his behalf and dispatch them. They were important, and as such, he thought his absence shouldn't delay things. The secretary, who had headphones on, listened absent-mindedly and ended up doing the wrong thing. When Dr MA returned, he asked her if she had done what he asked her to do, she sheepishly smiled and said yes. When asked what the response of his deputy was, she became dumbfounded and unconsciously used her right hand to hold her left wrist. The manager knew there was trouble already! This was a negative sign that the work was not done at all.

Case Study III: An evergreen case was when I met a man who wanted to evade clearance because he was parading expired documents. He just held the documents for camouflage, but he knew that he would be required to sign and present the documents for close scrutiny before being granted leave. I noticed that when he was about to hand over the document to me, he was a bit reluctant, as his left palm was placed on his right wrist, as if metaphorically asking him not to extend the hand to me. When I saw this, I became enthusiastic to check the documents because I was almost certain something was wrong with them. And I was not disappointed by my instincts.

18.15. Spreading of Arms

Generic Interpretations of the Concept

For a bird to fly, they must spread their wings. The same thing is applicable in the human realm; those who spread their arms are the high flyers. That is, spreading the arms over several chairs or couches is an undeniable display of confidence. When a person is afraid, they will keep to themselves and even maintain a stance that makes them smaller than their size. They feel like cutting off their arms and sinking into the soil.

However, when the person is confident, they will flout the rule of space management and occupy more territories through the spreading of their arms. This is not only limited to sitting position but also the manner in which people carry themselves while walking—do they walk freely, leaving every body part to function freely, or do they walk as if they are carrying the burden of the whole world? Someone who walks with the arms spread appears smart, free, confident, inspiring, and reliable. People are naturally endeared to such a person because he or she is wearing an open body language. This is crucial for every serious-minded individual to emulate, especially businessmen who must convince people even before uttering a word.

You will notice this gesture in senior executives compared to junior employees. This is because their position is giving them the needed confidence bolsters. On the other hand, junior workers know that they must report to a supervisor, so they hardly think of expressing freedom through their arms. As from now, always pay attention to the position of the arms when someone of higher status or more respectable position walks into a room. You will notice that their arms are not pressed to the sides as if they are hiding them. This tells you that they appear somewhat vulnerable because they are not afraid of anything.

Scientific Explanations

The act of arm-spreading is categorised as a positive body language gesture. We all need to project positive image anywhere we find ourselves so that we can be easily mirrored by others. According to Kimberly Pendergrass (2013), 'Positive body language can be defined as these non-verbal movements and gestures that are communicating interest, enthusiasm, and positive reactions to what some else is saying.' There is no way you can display all the aforementioned gestures without spreading your arms, your foremost instruments of gesticulation.

The writer takes time to explain the need not to cross the arms while speaking with other people. When you cross your arms, this is a visual clue that you're disinterested in what is going on around you. This can be discouraging to the other party. Hence, Pendergrass proposes that you should 'Practise hanging your arms comfortably at your side or bringing your hands together in your lap to show others that you are open to what they are communicating.' The ultimate effect is to demonstrate confidence to the other person in the communicative context.

Study Body Language (2016) also emphasises the need to maintain openness through the arm-spreading techniques. The website explains that in order for us to build trust in any given relationship, we must prove to the other party that we do not fear them; neither do we serve as a threat. This cannot be achieved when the arms are unnecessarily folded. When we fail to maintain an open stance, it becomes difficult for others to approach us for any form of relationship. However, achieving positive or open body language is not something that can be done in the twinkle of an eye. So we need to understand that it takes a process. Spreading the arms is the final stage in the processe of displaying openness. The process speed is dependent on the context. For instance, you cannot compare a random party and meeting with a complete stranger in a formal setting as being the same. Also, the nature of the characters in question—are they introverts or extroverts?

Also, Changing Minds (2019) discusses the language of openness in the simplest language possible. In its opening sentence, the respected platform submits that 'the open stance has arms and legs not crossed in any way. They may also be moving in various ways.' In other words, the arms spread when you are positive. Apart from the fact that the arms are not spread, they move in line with what is being said; they align themselves to the words of the speaker. Further, the palms would also be in a relaxed state and show that nothing is hidden.

There are different reasons why having an open posture is sacrosanct. One, it shows that you are relaxed and comfortable. This gives people the confidence to approach you, noting that you are not harmful. In the same vein, it communicates a passive threat. Since this body gesture communicates confidence, if anyone wants to attack you, they would be afraid to because of the confidence displayed through arm-spreading (Changing Minds 2019).

Practical Illustrations

Case Study I: As a person that is known for his disciplined lifestyle, any time Dr R calls for a meeting, those who are concerned make it a point of duty to be there before time. However, twenty minutes into the time, he was yet to arrive for the meeting. The secretary put a call through to him, and he didn't pick up; his wife was sick and was going through issues. He had to cater for her first before leaving home. He later came in, holding his head high, with his shoulders at his sides in order to demonstrate confidence.

Case Study II: Every morning, after the teacher on duty has conducted assembly for the pupils of RYD School, the headmaster would be invited to address the staff and students; he would wait in the office till a member of staff comes to call him. While he was coming, everybody would maintain an absolute silence that the sound of his shoes would be heard by all of them. Also, he walked in full of confidence by carrying himself with respect and appearing simple. His arms were spread out, and he maintained the right proportion of eye contact while he passed his points across. With this, no one could look down on him.

Case Study III: A con artist who just supervised a robbery attack on a community decided not to go with his gang. He ensured there was nothing incriminating on him. He dressed responsibly and was walking on the street like every average person. He looked confident by spreading his arms. In fact, law enforcement officials didn't suspect him at first. However, an instinct told one of the officials to apprehend him. Even at that point, he still looked unmoved, but the officials decided to interview him before deciding to either release him or not. He was eventually indicted, and his members got arrested too.

18.16. Spreading out the Elbows

Generic Interpretations of the Concept

When you see a person spreading out the elbows, it means something up. This may be a negative or positive reaction, depending on the context in which the reaction is taking place. Just like the arm-spreading discussed earlier, when you see the elbows protrude, it means the person is confident. In fact, there is hardly a way you can spread out the arms without spreading out the elbows simultaneously. However, the elbows are usually more pronounced than the arms.

Elbows spreading out means that the person is aware of his or her environment. This serves as a passive threat to others around. The elbows are the instrument of attack due to how strong they are. When a potential predator sees that the elbows are spread out, then they will have a rethink before attacking you; it means you are aware of their presence and ready for them. One of the things criminals consider before choosing their prey is the person's consciousness of their environment. With this posture, you have gained a point over your adversaries.

In the same vein, this cue is a display of confidence; when a competitor sees you maintain the elbows spreading out posture, they will have to tighten their belt before confronting you. When junior colleagues notice this posture in you, they will definitely respect you. This non-verbal act makes you take up more space, look bigger than your size and more mature. All these depict positivity. People generally, especially ladies are moved to men that look confidence. This gives them a sense of protection being around that person. In the business environment, this posture works like magic too. It makes your business partner think highly of you, and this can end up making you negotiate better.

However, if the elbows spreading is done in a more obvious manner, as if you are guarding the body, this tells others that you are stressed or afraid and trying to use the posture to cover up your fears. With just a little bit of harassment, you would become unsettled.

Scientific Explanations

Westside Toastmasters (2019) did not mince words in making it known that spreading the elbows out is a sure sign of dominance. To better understand this gesture, the body language platform makes use of the hands-on-hips cue to explain it. Imagine a child ready to pick up argument with their parent, a boxer waiting for the bout to start, an athlete exercising in a bid to begin his game, and a man who is issuing a non-verbal challenge to other men that have probably invaded his space, you will discover that they are making use of the hands-on-hips cue to communicate their intentions. And according to Westside Toastmasters, 'this is a universal gesture used to communicate that a person is ready for assertive action. It lets the person take up more space and has the threat value of the pointed elbows that act as weapons, preventing others from approaching or passing.'

While the elbows spread out, you will discover that the arms would also be half-raised. This communicates readiness of the person to attack. If you are familiar with cowboys, this is the position they assume in a gunfight. The fact is that even if just a hand is placed on the hip, it still communicates the same message, especially if the elbow is pointed at the intended victim. This cue is used all over the world but carries stronger message of outrage or anger in Malaysia and Philippines (Westside Toastmasters 2019).

The elbows spreading out gesture is also referred to as readiness behaviour. That is, the person displaying it is set for an assertive decision. What cannot be argued is that the basic meaning of this cue carries subtle aggression in every given context. Westside Toastmasters concludes, 'It has also been called the achiever stance, related to the goal-directed person who is ready to tackle their objectives or is ready to take action on something. Men often use this gesture around women to display an assertive male attitude.' This is not to attack the woman or prove class to her, but to endear the woman to the man by assuring her that he has all it takes to secure her and cater to her needs. The woman's nature is generally fragile, and hence, she is always in search of an alpha male that will safeguard her.

Practical Illustrations

Case Study I: Boxer B defeated Boxer A in a final round of a much-cherished competition. Boxer A has been the holder of the title for five consecutive years, defeating Boxer B in two of those occasions to clinch the award. In the last edition, he thought it was going to be a walkover as usual, and this made him to be a little bit complacent mentally. Miraculously, Boxer B defeated him, and it seems the defeat overwhelmed his successes in the past five years. He was becoming infamous as every boxing lover was referring to his defeat. This made him go for more trainings and prepare himself well before asking for a rematch, which Boxer B later agreed to. On the D-day, while waiting for the bout to begin, Boxer A could be seen placing his hands on his hips and shifting from one side to the other. This was to non-verbally register his dominance over Boxer B.

Case Study II: Child B was always restrained from playing with the kids of their neighbours. For years, he has been obedient to the instructions of his parents. But it seems he is only harming his emotions to please his parents all this while. So he decided to confront them and get the issues settled with them. When he inquired from them, they told him that they had issues with their neighbours before his birth. He was irritated by the explanation he was offered, but his parents were unapologetic. Ready to challenge their decision, Child B put his hands on his hips, putting forward his argument. He looked assertive to the extent that his parents were later cowed to beg him.

Case Study III: A con artist wanted to take an undue advantage of a woman who appeared to be vulnerable. He saw how the woman was looking feeble, and he stylishly stood opposite the woman. He approached her at some point and asked if anything was wrong with her. Before the woman could open her mouth, he stood well, placed his hands on his hips and spread out his elbows, and then leant towards the woman. It symbolically looked as if he was protecting her, someone who was truly disturbed. The woman opened up to him, and he played along as if he had a solution until he milked her dry.

18.17. Narrowing of Elbows

Generic Interpretations of the Concept

This seems to be a little bit disconnected from the body; it is usually displayed when a person is seated on a chair and they rest their elbows on a table in front of them. We all do this every now and then; hence, there is nothing wrong with it inasmuch as it is not covering your face. However, it becomes an issue when you observe that the person's elbows become narrow all of a sudden.

One of the likely causes of this sudden narrowing of the elbows is insecurity. When you feel that a discussion is not favouring you or tilting towards your side, it becomes an issue for you. For instance, you are in a restaurant with a new date. All of a sudden, she seems to be focusing on another man and is responding passively to your discussions. You may become insecure due to her action, thereby subconsciously narrowing your elbows placed on the table. This is a form of closed body gesture, which is expressing the intent of your heart to close up due to the fear of something evil happening to you.

In addition, you may observe this cue when a person is threatened. Our reaction to every issue is revolves around freeze, flight, or fight responses. When the emotion is negative, there is high probability that it would be either a freeze or flight response. Being threatened by a situation will make you freeze and then take to your heels. When a concept being expounded seems to be a threat to you, without any benefit, you may likely narrow your elbows. The topic under discussion can help you determine this feeling. For instance, if it is a business dealing and the person thinks their money will go down the drain, they may display this cue to register their fear.

This metric can help you to determine the commitment and confidence of others to the issue you are discussing. It is accurate and reliable because it happens unconsciously. However, remember that the need to adjust position while the arms are placed on a table may also propel this kind of non-verbal action.

Scientific Explanations

Discussing the common gestures in non-verbal communication, Westside Toastmasters (2019) explains that when the elbows are taken in with the head tilted, it is used to express submission. Submissiveness is mainly propelled after a situation has been analysed and you discover that you have no chances of overcoming the situation. The elbows become narrowed because they are communicating their readiness to surrender to the threatening situation. Also, the head of confident people are held high in a balanced state. When it tilts to a side, it expresses a negative message. In simpler terms, elbows narrowing coupled with head tilting makes one look pale, uninspiring, and submissive.

Reacting to this, Philip (2013) describes the gesture as mild cocooning. According to the body language expert, 'Cocooning is a term used to describe the body language which shows others that we wish not to be bothered.' For example, when you see someone wearing a set of headphones while in public, it is a clear message that they are not interested in socialising. Talking of the elbows-narrowing cue in the sense of cocooning, it has to do with communicating with others non-verbally that you are not ready to have any form of discussion with them. 'This posture occurs by placing both elbows on the table and drawing the hands up to the forehead so as to put "the blinders up." The intention of the blinders is to tell others that we are under stress and are trying to block out the rest of the world so we can deal private matters.' With this, we can deal with our issues without the interruption of anyone. Sometimes, stress is best dealt with alone, without the complicated stance of the outside world.

Changing Minds (2019) laments how we overlook the elbows while trying to interpret non-verbal cues. Although they may communicate lesser messages compared with the conventional body parts we do focus on, whether individually or in clusters, the messages they bear are always potent and straight to the point. The body language platform explains that when seated and we put our elbows on the table, it is an indication of relaxation. Hence, you may see the head propping up by the cupped hands. However, if threat or insecurity sets in, you will notice the elbows being narrowed gradually on the table. This means the person is no longer feeling comfortable.

Practical Illustrations

Case Study I: Guy J and Lady H went on a date. They just got to know each other, and as such, they still have some fears about each other. Guy J just lost his girlfriend to another man. Although he knew the girl to be promiscuous, he never expected her to call the relationship a day at that point. This has created a feeling of fear in him; the consciousness of this probability is seen in his dealing with Lady H. This does not stop him for caring for her and living up to his responsibilities on her. Yet, the conviction is not just there. While on the date, another man came in and sat at his back, making him face Lady H directly. The lady's attention seemed to have shifted to the man that just came in because she was looking through the shoulders of Guy J instead of exchanging eye contact with him. This made J lose stamina and become insecure. His elbows that were on the table suddenly became narrowed, almost touching the cup of drink in front of him. All these were pointers to negative signals.

Case Study II: Mr U is a reputable businessman but does not know anything about foreign exchange. He has always heard people say it is profitable. So he scheduled a casual meeting with an expert at a restaurant in order to be briefed how it works. As the forex expert explained, Mr U maintained an absolute silence and followed suit, smiling at the advantages of the business, however when the man added a caveat that 'just an error can make you lose all your investment', Mr U became threatened and, subconsciously, his elbows narrowed. This was an expression of fear.

Case Study III: Before now, what law enforcement agents used to do to smugglers was to only seize their goods, take down their details, and then, release them. This was not all that impactful, as many of them were not feeling it. So it was promulgated that any smuggler caught henceforth would be imprisoned. However, Smuggler XI didn't hear of this new development before embarking on his journey. When he was arrested and he was informed of the new development, he became nervous and lost his right reasoning. His elbows were narrowed while he buried his head in thoughts, thinking of the possible losses he risked for his action.

18.18. Elbow Flexing

Generic Interpretations of the Concept

When you flex elbows, it means you want to display power at will. That is, you want others to notice your strength and give you the respect you deserve. This gesture is displayed by placing the hands on your hips, making the arms akimbo and then, flex the elbows forward as you make your points in a given communication. The elbows will form the shape of a butterfly flapping its wings. This can be very enjoyable to the person displaying this cue as it shows that they are relaxed. The elbows are very pointed at both sides, and it means readiness to safeguard the person. When you take up space with your elbows, if anyone intrudes into that space, it means they are fully prepared for a fight with you.

The elbow flexing makes you bigger than you are and since you are flapping them, it means that you are not stressed or undergoing any negative emotions. If the stance was rigid, it would have been communicating tension. The power to make your point in this manner is a testimony of your display of confidence. When people observe that you are confident, they will trust you and do many things with you without exercising any fear of you harming them. Once people see you as being sincere and trustworthy, you can only imagine how far this gesture will take you to.

Also, the elbow-flexing cue is used to emphasise a point. For you to sound convincing while making a point, your body must also align with the point. Displaying confidence while reiterating the point upholds its truthfulness. Senior managers, military officers, and coaches are the people that commonly make use of the elbow-flexing cue to emphasise their point and reiterate their superiority. With this, they gain more respect and admiration of the person they are addressing.

Scientific Explanations

Comparing this body language gesture to a display like a peacock, Christopher Philip (2013) notes that this cue makes people take up more space, thus appearing larger for the sake of asserting dominance. 'All the fingers also curl inward so that they point towards the crotch drawing attention in that direction which punctuates the point even further. The thumbs might also be tucked into the belt or into belt loops serving to "frame the genitals." The message said is "There are issues here", "Things are not right", "I'm standing my ground" or "I'm a virile male so check me out!"' (Philip 2013).

This gesture is also noticeable among women, but it is done once in a blue moon. When they hold their hips, their fingers would point to the direction of the buttocks. The pointing lays emphasis on the best assets as we present our case to another person. When the fingers are pointed backwards as women display this cue the more, it is taken as a sign of inquisitiveness rather than expressing authority.

Used by both men and women as explained above, this cue is used to seek the attention of others. Just like most life's issues, attention is competition-based, and that is why people go extra mile to ensure that they get the attention of their targeted person. 'We compete both against our own sex and for attention from the other sex. This seems like one in the same, but it is not. For example, appearing larger, heavier, taller or more muscular can serve to pique the interest of women, but also to repel nearby rivals' (Philip 2013). Hence, men puff out with this cue in order to appear more dominant and repel competition from other men wanting to lure their lover away.

Howard Allen (2018) also expresses the same point with Philip. He mentions threat, dominance, and challenges as the major messages that the elbow-flexing communicates, depending on the context. Apart from maximising perceived size, this cue is also open and direct. Opening the front body communicates with onlookers that we are not afraid of any threat. This may give an impression that you are daring someone to try something. In this sense, the person displaying this cue will directly face the person whom they have issues with. This is simple: cast your mind back on two people fighting, whether in movies or real life, you will see them face each other.

Also, this stance is somewhat threatening. You may not really understand this point until you find yourself in a crowded room where you have to make your way out. Instead of pushing people with your hands in a more aggressive and obvious manner, you can make use of the elbows to do it in a subtle manner. Seeing a person displaying their elbows registers to your subconscious that they are up to something physically. And finally, this shows that the person is ready for action; the pose looks challenging and alert. The person can quickly get their hands to an offensive or defensive state (Allen 2018).

Asserting the popularity of this behaviour, Parvez (2015) aligns with the submission of Allen that it is used to express readiness for action. So there is probability that the person assuming this posture is irritated or angry. She concludes, 'Sometimes this gesture is taken up by a person simply because he's too tired to rest his arms on his sides without support. You may notice this in runners when they are tired after a long run. So keep the context in mind when you interpret this gesture.'

Practical Illustrations

Case Study I: There was a report by residents that drunks in a nearby hotel mess up their neighbourhood after they might have been drunk and even disturb their peace at night. When the police head heard this, he mobilised some of his men to always patrol the place and bring anyone who is caught to book. Two police officers were asked to stay at the hot spot while others patrolled, in case the drunks wanted to mess up another location. The two police officers stood alert, maintaining an erect posture, with the chin up, while they put their hands on their hips, non-verbally communicating that they would bust anyone who messed up at that vicinity.

Case Study II: Friend XA and Friend BZ are very close and wherever you see one, you are most likely to see the second. They solve each other's problems and in simple terms, they are friends indeed. Recently, they were out with their lovers, and it seemed two other guys at the other end of the hall couldn't resist looking at the girls. Their attention was so much on the ladies that XA and BZ saw the need to take action. They sat in a relaxed manner and put their hands on their hips, flexing out their elbows. This was a clear message that the ladies were no-go area.

Case Study III: Human Smuggler GA is an expert in smuggling people in and out of the country. According to him, he has been in the business for the past twenty years and has built network of partners through an illicit manner that he is now fearless. He knows that if he has issues, in the twinkle of an eye, he knows the right people to call, and he would be released. When he is eventually arrested by some group of officials different from those he has connections with, he was seen flexing his muscles about, only to try all his illicit ways, but no one responded to his calls.

18.19. Interlocking of the Elbows

Generic Interpretations of the Concept

When you have a very close or intimate relationship with another person, you tend to do things that are extreme; uncommon relationships produce uncommon attitudes. The interlocking of the arms at the elbows is one of such attitudes. Some parts of the world where physical touches are not that encouraged, such as Japan, may see this as weird or unacceptable, but it cannot change the fact that a lot of people do it in some other regions of the world.

When you see people interlock their arms at the elbow as they stand, walk, or sit, it is a show of love. That is, they are really free with each other and want to show it to the world. This gesture helps people to bond more. I saw a church in Africa where members are encouraged to display this cue as they sing their family song. This is to create a sense of love and oneness among the members.

When you see this between people, it means the discussion they are having is very private. They are moving very close to each other because they do not want a third party to eavesdrop or hear what they are saying.

Also, this non-verbal act makes the hips come very close, suggesting that all is well with the discussants. This cue is very popular in the Mediterranean nations and even in South America; both men and women walk on the streets with their arms interlocked.

Scientific Explanations

According to Brian (2018), the body language of attraction in both men and women does not change. Hence, knowing the body language of attraction can be of great benefit to you. When someone is attracted to you, expect him or her to give you a lot of positive body language gestures; the person will often lean towards you and break into your personal space at will. This is the bigger picture of how attraction works.

Touch is a fundamental way that people use to communicate their attraction to other people; the least of touches is a signal that someone is feeling comfortable around you. Whether playfully, accidentally, or intentionally hitting you, it means the person has an irresistible interest in you. The trick to know if the touch is a truthful expression of attraction or not is to look at how she touches others and how she touches you. If there are differences, it means the person is really into you.

Kristin Canning (2018) explains the elbow-interlocking cue with the use of a picture depicting it. This body language gesture speaks volumes about how they feel about each other. The way people communicate non-verbally makes us understand most things about them. Canning notes that many couples do the arms-interlocking gesture to show to the outside world that they are in love. 'Touch symbolizes intimacy, emotional closeness and happiness in a relationship.' Hence, if you are not really close with your spouse, they may reject the offer to interlock elbows with you. This means they are not pleased with you at the moment.

The holding of hands should not be done just any way, as they way you do it also communicates rich messages. 'Most people have a radius of about a foot and a half around us that is our personal space, and if you let someone into that it indicates intimacy. Holding hands fully clasped, while walking close enough for your shoulders to brush, indicates more happiness and closeness than say, having a big gap between you and your partner and loosely holding hands or holding a few fingers. When there's a big gap between people, even if they're holding hands, I think of them more as friends' (Orbuch 2019).

A business platform in Turkey also explains this body language gesture and how it is used in the country. Handshakes are not the most popular form of greeting in the country; people kiss one another (whether with the opposite sex or not) while greeting. This means that the Turkish culture is rich in the non-verbal act of touch. However, if this involves two religious people, they will not touch each other.

'It is very common in Turkey to see two men holding hands or arm in arm at walking on the street. This does not mean they are homosexual, they are just good friends' (BWT 2001). Turks tend to touch more than people from other parts of the world. You need to respect them for their culture while going there to do business so as not to be seen as an outcast. In the same vein, they stare at strangers a lot. When you see this, do not assume that they single you out; it is their way of life, which gives them their unique nature.

Practical Illustrations

Case Study I: Lady H and Man O were in a bar to flex and wind down, having laboured tirelessly in their various places of work. After chit-chat, there was a need to discuss some private issues, and they did not want to leave the bar. So they sat at a corner, where there was a little bit of sanity. They were sitting very close to each other that their arms were touching each other. The person seated next to them could not hear what they were discussing as they murmured for some few hours. Although there was a vacant seat at the table where they were, out of respect, no one sat there; their posture communicated the need to have their privacy from the external world.

Case Study II: Child A and Child B are siblings and they are very close. People have always been amazed at the display of love and care by these two siblings. Any time they were together, you will find it difficult to hear what they were discussing. While coming home from school, they would hold each other arm in arm, walking down the streets. Those who do not know them take them as young lovers. More so, they smile at every given occasion, as new lovers will do. The message is still the same—there is strong cord and bond between them.

Case Study III: Man PC and Woman ZL arranged a marriage of convenience for the purpose of perpetuating their criminal activities. They wanted to move to another country and were perfecting their papers. They had an insider among the law enforcement agency that told them to work on their non-verbal communication. As a way of preparing for their epic journey, they went out and interlocked their elbows while walking in the neighbourhood. They asked someone to watch them and comment on their performance. They repeated the process for several times until they appeared perfect. After that, they went on the journey but didn't scale through as they appeared nervous when they encountered law enforcement agents. The officers relied on this show of nervousness to engage them in an interview which later led to their arrest.

18.20. Wrist Exposure or Hiding

Generic Interpretations of the Concept

Most of the times, we neglect some of the vital body parts that communicate huge messages when trying to translate non-verbal actions. For the umpteenth time, let me reiterate that most people are usually conscious of the conventional parts that you focus on while trying to read them. So they do everything possible to manoeuvre their feelings. If you work with those parts alone—the face and hands, you may end up working on feigned cues. This is not to state that you should neglect those body parts in their entirety, but you need to start taking an encompassing view of everything in order to make informed judgements at all times.

The wrist is one of the silent parts of the body that can open up the windows of the mind to you at will. Being a subconscious movement, even those displaying the cue do not pay attention to what it communicates, making it a good source of understanding people's emotions. Apart from being the joint between the hands and the arms, the wrist is also used to express our thoughts about people.

When the underside of the wrist is exposed to people around you, it means you like them. Note that the veins that go through the hands are easily visible at the underside of the wrist and, as such, can be easily be a point of target to a predator. When we now expose that side at will or subconsciously, it is an indication that we are comfortable being around those people. Women, while holding a cigarette or glass of drink, may expose their inner wrist to a person they are interested in. This means they are comfortable with the person and will like to spend more time with him or her.

The moment a person loses interest in you or feels you are becoming a burden to his or her comfort, they will rotate the wrist and turn the outer side to you. With this, they have unconsciously shielded the sensitive parts of the body from an impending danger. This is the same thing that is applicable to belly and neck, being very vulnerable parts of the body. This aptly communicates our dislike for the target person.

Scientific Explanations

The scholars that contributed to this subject matter made it known that the wrist exposure body language gesture is used mainly by women. That is, it is a female body language. One of those who discussed this concept in detail is Christopher Philip (2014). He gives the description of this cue thus—*Removing clothing, stroking the wrist, turning the palms up, or playing with an earring that causes the wrists to be exposed.* In one sentence, this is an expression of submission by a female. Possibly, you may observe this cue in gay men too. 'The wrists are a vulnerable part of the body and like the neck, when displayed, signal that a person is willing to heed to the dominance of another' (Philip 2014). Women may decide to flash the wrist to the person they are willing to submit to by turning the palm up or by lightly stroking the wrist with an index finger. It has been discovered that this does not particularly draw the attention of men, but if done rightly, it will elicit an appropriate response from him—there would be an unconscious attraction to the female. The body language expert gives the verbal translation of this gesture as 'I wish to submit to your dominance, so I'm exposing my delicate and vulnerable wrists.'

This cue is usually displayed in a dating context where the female is subconsciously communicating to her partner that she has trust in him. It is a visceral response displayed when women are in love. 'In men, flashing the wrist or loosely bending at the wrist is an effeminate signal. Thus, men and women share a similar submissive origin for this non-verbal signal' (Philip 2014).

Vanessa Van Edwards (2019) also notes that this body gesture is an expression of submissiveness. She explains that women do it in a room when they want to sexually attract a potential suitor. This tells you why women hold a cigarette in a hand, expose it, and make the inner wrist visible. However, this submissive act is not driven by fear, rather it is propelled by trust and the need to do the bidding of the person they are attracted to.

As you know, it is not advisable that you read this cue alone. Other pointers to look for in order to be certain of your guess are: batting eyelashes, self-grooming or fiddling with the hair, eyes cast in upward direction, head bowed, giggling, head tilting, shoulder shrugs, self-stroking, among other clusters along this line (Philip 2014).

Practical Illustrations

Case Study I: Lady K came across her first love, and in an inexplicable manner, the love ignited in her again. Although she had another lover, her moral justification was that since she was not yet committed to him in marriage, she could taste other people; more so, this person was her first love. Expecting the old friend to come and meet her, she sat in close range after exchanging pleasantries, but she was disappointed that the man did not talk along that line. So she decided to calm herself and subtly register her interest by fiddling with her earring and playing with her wristwatch, which exposed her inner wrist to him. This shows her excitement being around him.

Case Study II: Ms B was the secretary to the director of GHC Firms. A new director had just been employed after the retirement of the former one. The new boss was young, beautiful, and attractive; he was just a perfect man for her. However, she was lost in the labyrinth between love and professional calling. After deep analysis and she discovered that she could not control her emotions, she decided to take the advantage of being the closest worker to him. One day, when the director invited her to discuss some issues relating to work, she subconsciously exposed her wrist by trying to adjust her wristwatch from time to time and also bowed her head to win his attention; she believed that her beauty had a role to play, and she did not hesitate in revealing the sensitive parts to the man.

Case Study III: Mr HG has just assumed duty as the managing director of CZO Firms. He did not know that his secretary was a prostitute; she was also studying him to know the kind of person he is. When she discovered that he was the type that liked ladies, she changed the way she dressed and would look for every other way possible to lure him to herself. It seemed Mr HG was beginning to crack jokes with her already, and she saw it as a means of implementing her plans. One day, when the manager invited her to brief him on something, she locked the door and continuously adjusted her wristwatch for the purpose of exposing her wrist to him. He got the clue, grabbed the opportunity with all hands, and that was the beginning of their love story.

18.21. Goose Pimples

Generic Interpretations of the Concept

This is also called goosebumps or gooseflesh. It is an unconscious reaction to cold. When you form goose pimples, this causes hair to stand on the surface of your skin. This can also be induced by fear. The fact that we have undergone different evolutionary stages have made us lose much of our skin hair. That is why this may not be as pronounced as those you see on other primates. Perhaps, the arms and legs are our hairiest parts, and you can pay attention to the hair in those parts when someone is cold or being fearful.

Note that when we are cold or entertaining fear over an issue, the rate of blood flow in the body increases; the blood gushes to the surface of the skin, which usually makes the skin become obviously red. This leads to the standing of the skin hair. Whenever you see this, you should observe that something is putting the person on their toes.

Getting goosebumps is an involuntary action that makes a person or even primates look larger than their actual size. When the person wears clothes that cover the entire body, it may be difficult for you to see this gesture. More so, our evolutionary development has denied us the opportunity to see them in a pronounced manner, so this cue can only be used as the basis of making your judgement once in a while, after reading other gestures in the same manner.

Scientific Explanations

Christopher Philip (2013) says that this body language gesture is a response to negative emotions. Some may scratch the back of their neck in order to make their hair stand when feeling something negative. It is said to be response to arrector pili muscles. 'The arrector pili are a microscopic band of muscle tissue that connects hair follicles to the skin. When stimulated, the muscles contract and cause the hair to turn upward and perpendicular to the skin surface, or stand on end. While the purpose of the muscles in humans is vestigial, meaning they are an evolutionary throwaway, they were once used to trap air next to the skin to help keep the body warm' (Philip 2013). That is why you observe it when you are cold or overtaken by fear. In some other contexts, you notice this reflex action when competing or during displays so as to appear more threatening and larger to the opponent. Since this gesture is not as pronounced in humans as in primates, let's take the example of a cat. You will discover that the hair of a domestic cat turns up when challenged by another cat.

However, in porcupines, when you see their muscles contract, it brings the hair or quills up so as to serve as a defence. In humans, it serves the dual purpose of heat retention and defence. This may seem laughable at best, but it is a reflex action that our bodies still adopt in reacting to cold and fear. It also works for aggression by stimulating the muscles. 'When we reach for our scruff, we are showing an evolutionary throwaway to a time when our hair would have stood on end!' (Philip 2013).

Exploratorium.edu (2013) explains that 'goose bumps are the bumps on a person's skin at the base of body hairs which may involuntarily develop when a person is tickled, cold or experiences strong emotions such as fear, euphoria or sexual arousal.'

The term *goosebumps* derives from the phenomenon's association with gooseskin. Goose feathers grow from stores in the epidermis which resemble human hair follicles. When a goose's feathers are plucked, its skin has protrusions where the feathers were, and these bumps are what the human phenomenon resembles. It is not clear why the particular fowl, goose, was chosen in English, as most other birds share this same anatomical feature. Some authors have applied goosebumps to the symptoms of sexually transmitted diseases (Roberts 2004).

In animals covered with fur or hair, the erect hairs trap air to create a layer of insulation. Goosebumps can also be a response to anger or fear: the erect hairs make the animal appear larger, in order to intimidate enemies. This can be observed in the intimidation displays of chimpanzees (Muller and Mitan 2019).

In humans, goosebumps are strongest on the forearms, but also occur on the legs, neck, and other areas of the skin that have hair. In some people, they even occur in the face or on the head. Goosebumps are accompanied by a specific physiological response pattern that is thought to indicate the emotional state of being moved (Kaernbach 2011).

Some can deliberately evoke goosebumps in themselves without any external trigger. Such people tend to have the ability to increase their heart rate and describe the event as a chill from the base of their skull down the body, that causes the increase in heart rate and concurrent goosebumps on the skin, especially the forearms, which varies in duration. Further research is needed to discover more on such people (Benedek et al. 2010).

Piloerection or goose pimples is also a classic symptom of some diseases, such as temporal lobe epilepsy, some brain tumors, and autonomic hyperreflexia. Goosebumps can also be caused by withdrawal from opiates such as heroin. A skin condition that mimics goosebumps in appearance is keratosis pilaris. So you need to take cognisance of this health condition while reading meaning to this gesture.

Practical Illustrations

Case Study I: Ms UI has always lived in an environment known to be hot in temperature but due to the need to acquire more education, she needed to change her place of residence. Before embarking on the journey, she decided to make some research on her new 'home', and she was baffled by the temperature rate in the region. So she got thick clothes for herself. On arriving her hostel, she undressed to put things into order and the hair on the surface of her skin stood erect. One could easily notice that she was not used to the environment even without being told.

Case Study II: Mr IV was into private business before he ventured into politics. While he was in the business world, he was in control of his life, but when he came into politics, he discovered that things were not the same again. That is, he was forced to do some things out of his own will. One such thing was travelling to some parts of the country. He was the kind of person who doesn't like very cold temperature, but he was told by his political associates that if he needed the people's votes, he must be ready to reckon with them through physical visitations in order to share his plans with them. When he eventually travelled to the riverine areas, the hair on his skin stood erect. He was shivering but tried very hard to conceal this feeling so that he wouldn't look alien to the residents.

Case Study III: Criminal CA didn't make right enquiries into the country he wanted to illegally migrate to; he was only desperate about leaving his home country without thinking of what awaited him in his destination. He was the kind of person who didn't like cold environment but unfortunately for him, he illegally migrated to Country XYE, a country renowned for its coldness. On getting there, he was caught unawares. The hair on his skin would stand erect whenever he was out of his room. In fact, he would be practically shivering. This was what gave him away; he didn't seem to be a part of the people, and law enforcement officials picked him up for some questioning.

18.22. Hair Erection—Piloerection

Generic Interpretations of the Concept

This is the advanced form of the goose pimples considered in the preceding section. When we are exposed to certain emotions, the hair on the back of the neck, forearms, and torso will stand erect. This is also a reflex action but can be manipulated in some given instances to serve our purpose. The hair stands visibly on the parts of the body that are hairy that you can visibly see them. It is more pronounced in people that are hairy.

From an evolutionary point of view, this gesture is said to be a vestigial response that humans share with other primates. We tend to display this behaviour when the situation we see ourselves in requires us to feel larger than we are. It is as if we are pumping our surface level to give us a shape that is bigger than our normal look. We may take on this look when we are fearful, frightened, or scared about something or an idea. When you conduct a subconscious assessment of a person, a situation considered to be dangerous, a place that appears to be threatening to your peace, or an idea that appears too risky to work with, you may notice that the hair of your skin stands erect, this is a feeling of fear induced by the rise in your temperature due to the heavy thought you are having.

David de Becker in his *The Gift of Fear* emphasises the need to take cognisance of these ill sentiments or feelings while dealing with people; they should not be ignored because the behaviour is subconsciously aroused to tell us the true state of our mind concerning the issue under consideration. In the same vein, you should not look the other way when you observe this feeling in a co-interlocutor; it means the discussion is not working in their favour, and you have to do something about it, depending on the context.

Scientific Explanations

David Huron (2006) makes it known that this behaviour may be a reaction to hearing nails scratch on a chalkboard, listening to awe-inspiring music, or feeling or remembering strong and positive emotions (e.g., after winning a sports event, or while watching a horror film). Also, being under intense emotion can bring about this feeling. That is why you hear people say they 'feel their hair standing on end' when they are gripped by fear. 'In an extremely stressful situation, the body can employ the 'fight or flight' response. As the body prepares itself for either fighting or running, the sympathetic nervous system floods the blood with adrenaline (epinephrine), a hormone that speeds up heart rate, metabolism, and body temperature in the presence of extreme stress. Then the sympathetic nervous system also causes the piloerection reflex, which makes the muscles attached to the base of each hair follicle contract and force the hair up' (George 2003).

Music is another factor that can propel piloerection in humans. This was revealed by Canadian researchers. They made it known that humans are moved by music their brains behave as if reacting to delicious food, psychoactive drugs, or money (Salimpoor et al. 2011). The pleasure experience is driven by the chemical dopamine, which produces physical effects known as chills that cause changes in heart rate, breathing, temperature, and the skin's electrical conductance. The responses correlate with the degree to which people rate the 'pleasurability' of music (Craig 2005). Dopamine release is greatest when listeners had a strong emotional response to music. 'If music-induced emotional states can lead to dopamine release, as our findings indicate, it may begin to explain why musical experiences are so valued' (Salimpoor et al. 2011).

Medications and herbal supplements that affect body temperature and blood flow may cause piloerection. For example, one of the common reported side effects of the intake of yohimbine is piloerection (Smet et al. 1997).

Also, there are some people that have conscious control over this behaviour, although their proportion is unknown. These people can consciously initiate the sensation and physiological signs of piloerection. The phenomenon is discovered spontaneously, appearing to be innate, and is not known to be possible to learn or acquire. Those with the ability frequently are unaware that it is not possible to everyone. The ability appears to correlate with personality traits associated with openness to experience (Heathers et al. 2018). Note that these people are rare, and in some situations, they have no reason to believe that this gesture is not possible for us all.

Practical Illustrations

Case Study I: Mr K is quite doing well in his profession and, as such, was invited by TED Talk organisers in his community to come and inspire young minds in the neighbourhood. Despite his professional successes, Mr K does not buy the idea of public speaking; he is always afraid of speaking to a large group of people. However, he decided to accept the invite, hoping that he could prepare well and quash his fear through this means. Any time his mind went to the occasion and the likely people to grace the occasion, his heartbeat raced faster than usual. During that time, the hair on his forearm and back of his neck would stand on end. This means the whole idea was scary to him, and he didn't believe in himself.

Case Study II: An infamous wanted to criminal was eventually apprehended by a security patrol team in an unexpected manner. He was taken to the nearest police station, and the criminal was expressing an internal joy that he would surely beat the officials at the station when it came to making statements and during investigation. However, he was later informed that his case would be transferred to the regional headquarters, a place known to be a home to police experts and experienced individuals. When he got to know the date he was going to be moved to the headquarters, he was gripped with fear. There was nothing that he could do to salvage himself due to his past records. Any time he was lost in the thoughts of what his fate would be, the hair on the surface of his skin would stand erect, displaying his fear.

Case Study III: Doctor VD is one of the most qualified doctors in town, and whenever people had critical cases, he was the go-to person. Usually, he works beyond time in order to attend to people from all walks of life. But there was a critical case that was referred to him after every other doctor had tried their best. He was the last hope of the patient; if he couldn't do anything, the patient wouldn't survive. After studying the case, he became terrified of the person's chances but he decided to give a try. On the day the surgery was to be performed, the hair on the surface of his skin stood erect; an expression of fear and nervousness!

18.23. Excessive/Abnormal Sweating

Generic Interpretations of the Concept

The reason I tag this section 'abnormal sweating' is to make you understand that not every form of sweating should be read meanings to. In other words, not everyone you sweating is guilty of an offence or another. Having said that, when you see a person sweating excessively in a situation that does not warrant that, it is time for you to pay closer attention and fish out the likely causes of the behaviour.

Those who are under stress do sweat profusely. This is autonomic response propelled by the brain to cool the body temperature due to the high rate of heating coming out from it. Excessive sweating is a way devised by the body to ventilate itself through evaporation of water. Stress makes us become hot, and when this situation is not put under check, it may affect the normal functioning of the body. Hence, the reason the body switched into action itself.

To an observant person, you can easily fish out people with issues by relying on this cue. For instance, law enforcement officers have had reasons to stop people who appeared to be the only ones with sweat rings around their armpits at the borders and their neck glistening with moisture as they moved closer to the officers on duty. In most cases, they ended up being drug traffickers. When you notice this obvious oddity, it means something is wrong somewhere. At least, all the passengers were coming from the same place, so why is it that it is only one person who is sweating excessively? I am not trying to rule out the probability that when someone is sweating out of many people, it does not mean they are stressed due to a criminal event, but that surely serves as a clue for you to engage them and establish the truthfulness of your guess or otherwise.

All things being equal, when you see a person sweating abnormally, it means they are hiding something from public glare, which is causing them fear. In the case of drug traffickers, hiding the substance from customs officers makes them become fearful, which makes them stressed. Another likely probability is that the person is about to commit a crime. The feeling of whether they would be caught or not makes them sweat profusely. Again, this is not a guarantee of the accuracy of your thought, but it surely points to the fact that something is wrong with the person.

Scientific Explanations

Morgan Griffin (2019) makes it known that the very least cause of excessive sweating is hassle while it may sometimes be as a result of medical condition. Griffin says that sweating more than other people while working out ourselves when it is hot is never a signal of trouble. Sweating is a normal reaction of the body to cool itself down when you are stressing it. Dee Anna Glaser, MD, vice chair of the dermatology department at St. Louis University and president of the International Hyperhidrosis Society opines that some people begin to sweat more easily than others. I am taking time to give the medical dimension so that we can take cognisance of it while trying to make interpretations of this behaviour in people.

'True excessive sweating goes beyond the normal physical need to sweat. If you have hyperhidrosis, you may sweat heavily for no reason—when it's not appropriate to the circumstances' (Griffin 2019). For instance, given that the temperature is not hot and things are all right with you—you are not anxious, you are not sick or feeling feverish—and right there in the living room where you are watching a movie with your family members, you start sweat profusely, this is not in any way normal.

Basically, there are two forms of excessive sweating: localised hyperhidrosis and generalised hyperhidrosis. The former has to do with a form of excessive sweating that has its origin in childhood or adolescence, and it affects 1 per cent to about 3 per cent of the entire population. Even though experts are not sure of the specific cause of this, it was agreed that it may be as a result of slight malfunctioning of the nervous system, while the latter is a less common form of hyperhidrosis which brings about sweating on the entire body. It is referred to as secondary hyperhidrosis because it is caused by an underlying health condition (Griffin 2019). The telltale sign of the generalised sweating is excessive sweating at night-time.

Christopher Philip (2014) discusses this body language behaviour in details. He gives a sentence description of the gesture thus: 'Sweating is a universal signal of stress or of the body's attempt to regulate a high temperature.' This is very apt and captures everything that we have been discussing since the start of this topic.

Generally, sweating is not seen as a positive behaviour but is accepted in people undertaking physical exercise. Apart from that, if done in a formal setting (such as a business meeting) where no physical exercise is taking place, it can put other people off. This is not working in your favour.

In dating context, this behaviour has been linked to primitive animal conditions and, as such, can be said to create positive impression. Late-night photoshoots and even heat created during sex scenes may cause excessive sweating (Philip 2014).

Philip gives four possible verbal translations of this cue thus: 'I'm emotional and my body is releasing sweat due to the increase in stress.' Or 'I'm suffering from a medical condition which forces my body to sweat independent of context or stress' or 'I'm lying which is causing my body to increase it's metabolism resulting in a higher body temperature inducing sweating.' Or 'I'm hot, so my body is producing sweat to cool me off.' All these four possible interpretations have their unique contexts where they fit in appropriately.

Practical Illustrations

Case Study I: Out of twenty men boarding a bus to another province, it is only Man J that appeared to be sweating profusely, even though the AC of the bus was in proper condition. This called the attention of the officers on duty to him. After brief questioning, it was learnt that he was a drug trafficker hiding under the pretext of being a businessman.

Case Study II: A suicide bomber was sent to destroy a shopping mall—a big one whose collapse would result in numerous casualties. He had spied on the place and was confident that he would be victorious. As a way to confront the task headlong, he didn't hold any means of communication. Hence, he couldn't be told that law enforcement agents had blocked off the venue. When he ran into them unexpectedly, he lost his psychological balance and began to sweat excessively. His nervous look hinted to the officers at the venue that he was a terrorist, and they rounded him up before he could explode the bomb.

Case Study III: Ms YU doesn't really fall sick, but a strange sickness suddenly came on her, and she had to be rushed to the hospital. After they ran a series of tests and she was given some medications, the doctors said that she would have to undergo surgery in order to be totally healed. She detested surgery like the plague. On hearing that it was the only way out of her ailment, she began to sweat abnormally. When the doctors perceived the fear in her, they had to encourage and assure her that she was in safe hands. After numerous admonitions, she reluctantly agreed to do it.

Case Study IV: Ms IN impersonated her twin sister; they were so identical that it took extra expertise to spot their differences. More so, they grew up together. This invariably meant that there was virtually nothing they didn't know about each other. She thought she could use the counterfeit passport without any issue. She had tried it in some places, and it worked perfectly. However, she was taken aback when I called her out when she was about to come into the country. At first, she wanted to defend herself but when I started pointing out her differences to her sister, she went mum and began to sweat excessively—she thought the end had come for her. And that was the reality of her issue. Any time I apprehend a criminal with evidence, I would not let go. This is the simplest definition of integrity.

18.24. Self-Harm

Generic Interpretations of the Concept

The fact is that the structure of the world is not fair to anyone, but then, it is sometimes worse to some select group of people. Why am I sounding so generalist and a bit vague in this section? There are people who are created with some mental illnesses that they have to battle for the substantial part of their lives. In some others, it is caused by their own lack of discipline and self-control.

If you see individuals that are not stable mentally or emotionally and those who are suffering from borderline personality disorder, you may notice some scars on their body. This is a result of self-inflicted injuries caused by their instability, depression, or mental imbalance. When people are depressed or overtaken by some mental disorders, they may cut, slash, or intentionally burn themselves.

When you observe this cue in others, it is not time for you to look the other way but to rise to the occasion and get them the much-needed help. They might not open their mouth to demand help themselves, but what you have seen is a non-verbal communication of the fact that you should lend a helping hand to them. The reason being that they might not know that they are injuring themselves.

If you ignore such huge mental health needs, you are not only being selfish but also doing bad to the society as a whole, because those people may gradually move from inflicting harm to themselves to attacking other people who are either close to them or not. Anyone who becomes their victim would be afraid of relating or moving closer to people in the future, thereby creating more gaps in human relations.

Scientific Explanations

Self-injury or self-harm is said to be an intentional, direct injuring of body tissue, done without suicidal intentions. Other terms such as *cutting* and *self-mutilation* have been used for any self-harming behaviour regardless of suicidal intent (Klonsky 2007).

The most common form of self-harm is using a sharp object to cut one's skin. Other forms include behaviour such as burning, scratching, or hitting body parts. While older definitions included behaviour such as interfering with wound healing, excessive skin picking (dermatillomania), hair pulling (trichotillomania), and the ingestion of toxic substances or objects as self-harm, these are not considered along the same line in current trend (Klonsky 2007).

According to the psychologist, behaviours associated with substance abuse and eating disorders are not considered self-harm because the resulting tissue damage is ordinarily an unintentional side effect. So the definition is simple and straightforward; it must be intentional in order to be considered self-harm. Although suicide is not the intention of self-harm, the relationship between self-harm and suicide is complex, as self-harming behaviour may be potentially life-threatening (Farber et al. 2007). There is also an increased risk of suicide in individuals who self-harm, and self-harm is found in 40–60 per cent of suicides.

However, generalising individuals who self-harm to be suicidal is, in the majority of cases, inaccurate (Fox and Hawton 2004).

There are four basic causes of self-harm—mental disorder, psychological issues, genetics and drugs, and alcohol.

Mental Disorder: Although some people who self-harm do not have any form of recognised mental disorder, many people experiencing various forms of mental illnesses do have a higher risk of self-harm. The key areas of disorder which exhibit an increased risk include autism spectrum disorders, borderline personality disorder, depression, bipolar disorder, conduct disorder, phobias, and dissociative disorder (Johnson and Myers 2007).

Schizophrenia may also be a contributing factor for self-harm. Those diagnosed with schizophrenia have a high risk of suicide, which is particularly greater in younger patients as they may not have an insight into the serious effects that the disorder can have on their lives. Substance abuse is also considered a risk factor as are some personal characteristics such as poor problem-solving skills and impulsivity (Fox and Hawton 2004).

Psychological Issues: Abuse during childhood is accepted as a primary social factor increasing the incidence of self-harm, as is bereavement, and troubled parental or partner relationships (Rea et al. 1997). Factors such as war, unemployment and poverty also play a crucial role. Other predictors of self-harm and suicidal behaviour include feelings of entrapment, defeat, lack of belonging, and perceiving oneself as a burden, along with less effective social problem-solving skills (Hawton et al. 2012).

Self-harm is frequently described as an experience of depersonalisation or a dissociative state. The onset of puberty has also been shown to be the onset of self-harm, including the onset of sexual activity; this is because the pubertal period is a period of neurodevelopmental vulnerability and comes with an increased risk of emotional disorders and risk-taking behaviours (Hawton et al. 2012).

Genetics: The most distinctive characteristic of the rare genetic condition, Lesch-Nyhan syndrome, is self-harm, and it may include biting and head-banging. Genetics may contribute to the risk of developing other psychological conditions, such as anxiety or depression, which could in turn lead to self-harming behaviour. However, the link between genetics and self-harm in otherwise healthy patients is largely inconclusive (Skegg 2005).

Drugs and alcohol: Substance misuse, dependence, and withdrawal are associated with self-harm. Benzodiazepine dependence as well as benzodiazepine withdrawal is associated with self-harming behaviour in young people. A study which analysed self-harm presentations to emergency rooms in Northern Ireland found that alcohol was a major contributing factor and involved in 63.8 per cent of self-harm presentations (Bell et al. 2010). A recent study in the relation between cannabis use and deliberate self-harm (DSH) in Norway and England found that, in general, cannabis use may not be a specific risk factor for DSH in young adolescents (Rossow et al. 2009). Smoking has also been associated with self-harm in adolescents; one study found that suicide attempts were four times higher for adolescents who smoke than for those that do not (Hawton et al. 2012).

The motivations for self-harm vary, as it may be used to fulfil a number of different functions. These functions include self-harm being used as a coping mechanism, which provides temporary relief of intense feelings such as anxiety, depression, stress, emotional numbness, and a sense of failure or self-loathing. There is also a positive statistical correlation between self-harm and emotional abuse (Meltzer 2000). Self-harm may become a means of managing and controlling pain, in contrast to the pain experienced earlier in the person's life of which they had no control over (e.g., through abuse) (Cutter et al. 2008).

Practical Illustrations

Case Study I: There was a marching order by the CEO of AHU Company for an action committee to fish out all those who were illegally working with the firm. The committee was fierce and action-driven. While most of the illegal employees had stopped coming to work, some others would come and flee whenever they learnt that members of the committee were approaching their unit. GV was caught unawares in one of such visits. Thinking of how best he could save himself, he quickly intentionally injured himself with a tool. So he had to be rushed to the nearest hospital without questioning. And he fled from the hospital bed. Tracing him was a big issue, as he was not ready to undergo any investigation.

Case Study II: MG and Guy UT have been lovers since their high school days. They promised each other marriage. During and after high school, Lady MG had numerous suitors but turned them down because she was deeply in love with Guy UT. Even in her workplace, she wouldn't welcome any man. However, she was utterly shocked when she heard that UT had impregnated another lady and was ready to settle with her. All entreaties to her failed as MG became dejected. She eventually committed suicide before the next day. She was really hopeless about her future with someone else, and this made her take such a hard decision.

Case Study III: Passenger IH was flying for the first time. She wasn't expecting such a cold temperature. While every other passenger seemed unmoved and were busy with one thing or another, she was shivering, and when it got to a point that she couldn't bear it again, she began to pinch herself to the point that she was bleeding. Flight attendants had to approach her and asked what was wrong with her because she was almost creating a scene with her actions, as her co-passengers found it irritating. After so much explanations, her seat was changed. It was a drama of some sort.

Case Study IV: Student OS was a well-known bully. All his peers ran away from him because they knew that his victims were not well-treated; he would injure them before releasing them. After so many talks from all the teachers and school counsellor, his parents were informed that any time their son attacked any other student again, he would be shown the exit door of the school. The new tactic he now adopted was to deal with his victims and thereafter injure himself. So he played the victim before the school management. In fact, he would run to report the case before the real victim got there. This was to have an edge over the battered people.

18.25. Needle Tracks/Track Marks

Generic Interpretations of the Concepts

Just like the self-harming cue discussed above, when people injure themselves due to one reason or another, especially at the arms, when these heal, the injuries have effects on their arms. However, this has been discovered to have been primarily caused excessive intake of heroin and other intravenous drugs. So needle tracks are not necessarily caused by external injuries; they are the aftermath of hard drugs. You will observe the scars tracking the veins on the inside of the arms. If they fail to desist from the consumption of the hard drugs, the needle tracks would become more obvious.

There are many effects of having needle tracks on your arms. One, it distorts your beauty. Those who have scars on their arms or in any other parts of the body look different from their usual selves. Also, needle tracks irritate some people, so they may lock the doors of opportunities against you on the long run. Most importantly, when people see these scars on your arms, it gives them negative thoughts about you. Many people surely know this is an effect of consuming hard drugs. So they will detach themselves from you, thinking that you are a drug user and might end up pouncing on them as their relationship with you develops. The negative effects of alienation are better imagined than experienced.

Organisations are most likely to turn down your applications if they see this evidence of intravenous drugs on you; there is nobody that wants to entrust his or her life investments in the hands of a person who will eventually squander or misbehave with them. The negative effects are almost innumerable. On the other hand, this should guide your relationship with people. If you notice needle tracks on a person, take time to study them and be sure that they do not smoke or consume other hard drugs before building a lasting relationship in order not to be trapped in the web of regrets.

Scientific Explanations

According to DrugRehab.org (2018), 'injection drug abuse is one of the most dangerous ways of administering a drug. Intravenous injection delivers the drug rapidly into your system, creating what is nearly an immediate and very intense high. Because of this, it's the most popular way to inject a drug.' The fact that it is popular makes it easy for you to identify its effects on people. As of 2004, in a report published by Washington DC National Academies Press, there were 13.2 million people worldwide who used injection drugs, of which 22 per cent are from developed countries. This is to tell you how serious it is.

A wide variety of drugs are injected, often opioids. These may include legally prescribed medicine and medication such as morphine, as well as stronger compounds often favoured in recreational drug use, which are often illegal. Although there are various methods of taking drugs, injection is favoured by some people, as the full effects of the drug are experienced very quickly, typically in five to ten seconds. It also bypasses first-pass metabolism in the liver, resulting in higher bioavailability and efficiency for many drugs (such as morphine or diacetylmorphine/heroin, roughly two-thirds of which is destroyed in the liver when consumed orally) than oral ingestion would. The effect is that the person gets a stronger (yet shorter-acting) effect from the same amount of the drug. Drug injection is therefore often related to substance dependence.

The most frequently used veins are those in the crook of the forearm, though other locations may be used. If a person injects into their arm, it's typically the one opposite from the hand they write with. This makes it easier for them to inject the drug themselves. To work around this, some people may have a fellow drug abuser inject the substance for them into their dominant arm. There are other locations which may also be used, including the hand, foot, groin, or leg. Some individuals choose different sites so that they can more easily hide the track marks. Others may be forced to move to a new location once their primary site becomes too inflamed or scarred to continue injection (DrugRehab 2018).

When drug abusers keep shooting up intravenous drugs, it leaves scars on the spots. The needle tracks are as a result of:

Chronic abuse: Prolonged and repeated use at the same injection site increases the odds of a track mark developing. Over time, as a person continuously injects in the same spot, the vein becomes damaged and scars build up (DrugRehab 2018).

Used needles: If a person keeps on using the same needle, the tip will become blunted and dull. Upon injection, this places excess pressure on the vein and damages it even more (DrugRehab 2018).

Contaminated drugs: It's very rare to find a pure drug on the street. Instead, the majority of illicit drugs have some form of contamination. These impurities may result from poor manufacturing processes or because the drug was purposely adulterated or 'cut' with other substances. The build-up of these toxins is often responsible for the darker colour of the track mark (DrugRehab 2018).

Can you spot needle tracks on your own? There is no gainsaying that the tell-tale signs that someone is an intravenous drug user are needle tracks. Technically, as noted above, they are scars. However, due to the variations in use of the drugs, they appear differently on drug abusers. The marks look differently depending on the healing stage of each. What this means is that some people may have fresh marks layered upon or alongside older scars.

When they are *recent or new marks*, these lesions may look fresh, having not yet had time to heal. Shortly after injection, they may appear as puncture marks, scabs, or bruises. However, if they are *older marks*, you will notice that as the drug progresses, the skin may crack, bleed, and even become infected. Track marks and scarring run the length of the vein and appear slightly raised and discoloured (darker) in comparison to the rest of the skin (DrugRehab 2018).

Practical Illustrations

Case Study I: There was a marching order by the CEO of AHU Company for an action committee to fish out all those who were illegally working with the firm. The committee was fierce and action-driven. While most of the illegal employees had stopped coming to work, some others would come and flee whenever they learnt that members of the committee were approaching their unit. GV was caught unawares in one of such visits. Thinking of how best he could save himself, he quickly intentionally injured himself with a tool. So he had to be rushed to the nearest hospital. He took to his heels from the hospital bed without anyone noticing him. It took hard work and concerted efforts of law enforcement agents that track them down after a week.

Case Study II: MG and Guy UT have been lovers since their high school days. They promised each other marriage. During and after high school, Lady MG had numerous suitors but turned them down because she was deeply in love with Guy UT. Even in her workplace, she wouldn't welcome any man. However, she was utterly shocked when she heard that UT had impregnated another lady and was ready to settle with her. All entreaties to her failed as MG became dejected. She eventually committed suicide before the next day. She was really hopeless about her future with someone else, and this made her take such a hard decision.

Case Study III: Passenger IH was flying for the first time. She wasn't expecting such a cold temperature. While every other passenger seemed unmoved and were busy with one thing or another, she was shivering, and when it got to a point that she couldn't bear it again, she began to pinch herself to the point that she was bleeding. Flight attendants had to approach her and asked what was wrong with her because she was almost creating a scene with her actions, as her co-passengers found it irritating. After so much explanations, her seat was changed. It was a drama of some sort.

Case Study IV: Student OS was a well-known bully. All his peers ran away from him because they knew that his victims were not well-treated; he would injure them before releasing them. After so many talks from all the teachers and school counsellor, his parents were informed that any time their son attacked any other student again, he would be shown the exit door of the school. The new tactic he now adopted was to deal with his victims and thereafter injure himself. So he played the victim before the school management. In fact, he would run to report the case before the real victim got there. This was to have an edge over the battered people

CHAPTER 19

The Hands and Fingers

Immediately after the arms are the hands. And permit me to say that the human hands get no equals. They are very useful, and without argument, they are the most mobile part of the body. This invariably means that the hands serve as the engine room for body language gestures. So get prepared to learn many unimaginable functions of the hands and fingers as they relate to non-verbal acts interpretations. We will dissect every bit of them and see how they relate to our daily activities. The hands are so much cherished because there is no duty that they cannot perform—they are the life-saving part of the body. With the hands, doctors perform surgeries, lawyers argue out cases by demonstrating their points, artists mould and carve adorable images, we write and sign cheques. To better appreciate the hands and fingers, reflect on the innumerable uses of the hands and then, for a second, imagine a world without hands.

What I have been trying to drive at since the beginning of this chapter is that the hands are indispensable to human affairs. Whether at work, during play hours, or in the need to protect ourselves, there is no way we can overlook their role. With the hands, we exchange information and interact with the world around us on a daily basis.

The effective usage of hands in communication is unrivalled. For instance, when stopping traffic in school crossings, we make use of the hands. In addition, if a loved one suddenly slumps on the road, we will use our hands to flag down a taxi or a Good Samaritan. Further, those in the music world make use of their hands to conduct orchestras, which ends up ensuring orderliness in the play of classical music. When you want to call a person to come over or signal to them to keep going without wanting to raise your voice, you make use of your hands.

With the hands, we constantly communicate our passion, abilities, desires, concerns, and most importantly, through an appropriate touch, love. You can see that the uses of the hands are almost as endless as the world. Whatever idea the mind thinks of, without the cooperation of the hands, it cannot become a reality. Hence, the hand is the means through which we achieve all our desires. Before digging in-depth into the body language of the hands and how they communicate our emotions, let's briefly consider the biological explanation of this part of the body.

The areas of the human hand include:

The *palm*, also known as volar area, is the central region of the anterior part of the hand, located superficially to the metacarpus. The skin in this area contains dermal papillae to increase friction, such as are also present on the fingers and used for fingerprints.

The *opisthenar* area (dorsal area) is the corresponding area on the posterior part of the hand

The *heel of the hand* is the area anterior to the bases of the metacarpal bones, located in the proximal part of the palm. It is the area that sustains most pressure when using the palm of the hand for support, such as in a handstand.

There are five digits attached to the hand, notably with a nail fixed to the end in place of the normal claw. The four fingers can be folded over the palm which allows the grasping of objects. Each finger, starting with the one closest to the thumb, has a colloquial name to distinguish it from the others:

- index finger, pointer finger, forefinger, or second digit
- middle finger, long finger, or third digit
- ring finger or fourth digit
- little finger, pinky finger, small finger, baby finger, or fifth digit

The thumb (connected to the first metacarpal bone and trapezium) is located on one of the sides, parallel to the arm. A reliable way of identifying human hands is from the presence of opposable thumbs. Opposable thumbs are identified by the ability to be brought opposite to the fingers, a muscle action known as opposition.

The skeleton of the human hand consists of 27 bones: the eight short carpal bones of the wrist are organised into a proximal row (scaphoid, lunate, triquetral and pisiform), which articulates with the bones of the forearm, and a distal row (trapezium, trapezoid, capitate and hamate), which articulates with the bases of the five metacarpal bones of the hand. The heads of the metacarpals will each in turn articulate with the bases of the proximal phalanx of the fingers and thumb. These articulations with the fingers are the metacarpophalangeal joints known as the knuckles (Tubiana 1998).

At the palmar aspect of the first metacarpophalangeal joints are small, almost spherical bones called the sesamoid bones. The fourteen phalanges make up the fingers and thumb, and are numbered I-V (thumb to little finger) when the hand is viewed from an anatomical position (palm up). The four fingers each consist of three phalanx bones: proximal, middle, and distal. The thumb only consists of a proximal and distal phalanx (Saladin 2007).

There are numerous sesamoid bones in the hand, small ossified nodes embedded in tendons; the exact number varies between people: whereas a pair of sesamoid bones are found at virtually all thumb metacarpophalangeal joints, sesamoid bones are also common at the interphalangeal joint of the thumb (72.9 per cent) and at the metacarpophalangeal joints of the little finger (82.5 per cent) and the index finger (48 per cent). In rare cases, sesamoid bones have been found in all the metacarpophalangeal joints and all distal interphalangeal joints except that of the long finger (Schmidt and Lanz 2003).

The fixed and mobile parts of the hand adapt to various everyday tasks by forming bony arches: longitudinal arches (the rays formed by the finger bones and their associated metacarpal bones), transverse arches (formed by the carpal bones and distal ends of the metacarpal bones), and oblique arches (between the thumb and four fingers). Of the longitudinal arches or rays of the hand, that of the thumb is the most mobile (and the least longitudinal). While the ray formed by the little finger and its associated metacarpal bone still offers some mobility, the remaining rays are firmly rigid. The phalangeal joints of the index finger, however, offer some independence to its finger, due to the arrangement of its flexor and extension tendons (Tubiana et al. 1998).

19.1. Conditions of the Hand

Generic Interpretations of the Concept

The condition of the hand is like an identity card that is used to describe us. Yes, I mean the hands can perform the job which our ID cards perform; to tell others the kind of work we do. Calluses, scars and grooming on the hands are the indicators to the kind of work someone does. For instance, you cannot compare the hands of an office worker with that of a cement mixer or farmer. For an officer worker who only types or writes with a pen, the hand or palm seems to look soft, charming and warming. These people are not always intimidated to shake hands with other people because they understand and know how smooth their palms are. However, when you exchange a handshake with a person, and their hand looks rocky or very rough, it means they are probably factory workers.

This can also make us understand the experiences of people. No matter the nations of the world, when you see people who are trapped in the hands of fate, you will see experiences written both in their hands and on their face. For instance, a person who does not have a father or mother to care for them may have to engage in menial jobs and hard ones in order to make ends meet. When you see them, you will perceive the hardness of their hands. This means they have faced the wrath of life in times past or are still undergoing same.

Also, arthritis as well as neurological disorders can be well separated from the conditions of the hand as explained above. We can also chart a course between finger movements and agitation by the condition of the hands. When we are agitated, the way we move our fingers is different from how we move them when we are relaxed.

Scientific Explanations

Joe Navarro (2010) states it clearly that the hands speak louder than words. In other words, with what the condition of a person's hand expresses, you may not need him or her to tell you about themselves with their mouth. The hand is an embodiment of the messages that can be decoded by anyone attentive enough to listen to its echoes. The HarperCollins Dictionary of Body Language (2018) notes that despite the acquisition of spoken language over millions of years of human evolution, our brains are still hard-wired to engage our hands in accurately communicating our emotions, thoughts, and sentiments. That means you cannot decide to overlook what the condition of the hand communicates per time. On the premise of the foregoing, Navarro (2010) explains that whether people are uttering words or not, we deserve to give hand gestures our attention in order to understand the feelings and emotions of people through non-verbal communication.

Changing Minds (2019) also notes that reading palms is not just about the lines in them; the hand as a whole is most probably the richest source of non-verbal communication. No matter how small the condition of the hand signal is, it is capable of betraying the subconscious thoughts of a person. For instance, not too many people understand that the 'length of the index finger compared with the length of the ring finger is related to masculinity'. With this, you do not need anyone to tell you the gender of anyone again. Changing Minds reports that high levels of testosterone in the womb brings about longer ring fingers. Testosterone is also related to other masculine characteristics, including strength and aggression, and spatial and musical ability. Hence, by looking for long and short ring fingers, as compared with the person's index fingers, you can determine the tendency of the person's masculine or feminine behaviours.

Furthermore, Nicolas Fradet (2019) also sheds light on how the condition of the hands can communicate the thoughts of a person. For instance, when you see a person with clenched fists, it means they are firm on their resolve. That is, it signals unyieldingness. You can better understand this by thinking of a person ready to play a football match or engage in a fight with another person. In a related instance, when you see a person with a clenched fist and thumbs tucking in, it means the person is not comfortable. The person may be anxious about something, but they are thinking about how they want to deceive you into believing that they are firm.

When the hands are squeezed or clasped, they also bear huge messages. They are self-pacifying acts, and invariably, a person who does this is feeling uncomfortable. The person is probably fearful or nervous about something and, as such, trying to reassure themselves that all is well. The verbal translation of this cue is 'Everything's going to be all right.' When the hands are clasped with interwoven fingers, it means the person is really anxious, fearing that things might probably go more awfully than envisioned. When you spot this, you need to get yourself fortified because anything can happen (Fradet 2019).

Practical Illustrations

Case Study I: Ms J and Guy B met in a restaurant, and after exchanging pleasantries, Guy B decided to take things further by asking for some minutes out of Ms J's time. They got down to business, and it seemed J was gradually liking him too. So he she decided to ask what Guy B was doing for a living, and after about two seconds, he replied that he was a senior official in one of the leading banks in town. Ms J replied with a slight frown before adding a grimace. She did not believe him because of the condition of his hand—when they exchanged handshakes, Guy B's palms were obviously rough and thick enough that she felt the coarseness in her palms. So Ms J wondered what a senior bank official could be doing with his palms to make them so rough and hard like that. In reality, Guy B was a junior worker in a factory, where they had to work for an average of eleven hours in a day. The condition of his hands betrayed him in this context.

Case Study II: While Friend U is a medical doctor, Friend V is a factory worker. As a medical doctor, U doesn't handle things that can easily damage his hand, and he uses the right drugs that will fine-tune his skin texture. However, Friend V doesn't seem to care so much on his appearance. One Saturday, they both visited a business partner, and when he exchanged handshakes with them, the man was forced to look at Friend V in the eye. The expression on his face was glaring—he was shocked by the texture of V's hand. He later subtly asked what job V was into and when he mentioned 'Factory worker', the man shouted 'No wonder!'

Case Study III: Man B and Woman C arranged a marriage of convenience and forged some documents where they alleged that they were the managers of their personal firm. They claimed to be running only administrative duties. Of a truth, the man was only a labourer, helping people out in their gardens and doing other energy-demanding jobs. He had to wear a pair of gloves in order to cover up the texture of his hand. When the officers interrogating them saw no need to wear a pair of gloves, he was ordered to take them off, and all his secrets were exposed to the officers!

19.2. Grooming of Hands

Generic Interpretations of the Concept

There is a cliché all over the world that cleanliness is next to godliness. This denotes how important being healthy or hygienic is to our world. There is nothing that endangers our world today as much as dirtiness. In order not to sound too generic, let me state that the cleanliness or otherwise of a person's hands can tell you what they are made up of. We tend to make conclusions of a person's social status, belief systems, and concept of life based on their appearance. First impression goes a long way in determining our relationship with them. This sentiment is shared by almost everyone across the world and cannot be changed, not any time soon.

When you see a person with properly groomed hands, it is a signal of high sense of personal hygiene; it indicates healthiness. Such person will maintain proper nail length and clean fingers. This is evidence that the person cares about how they look. So in order to give a good impression of themselves, they spend time in appearing neat, smart, and socially fit. For instance, in many sporting activities, it is a general rule that all participants must keep well-groomed hands in order not to injure other people. This invariably tells you that there is no field of endeavour where uncleanliness is seen as a virtue.

When you are meeting with a person that has dirty, irritating long nails, unkempt cuticles and chewed or intentionally distorted fingers, most probably, you would be pissed off at the beginning of the meeting and will do everything within your means to detach yourself from them as soon as possible. Unkempt hands connote negativity and can have an ugly impact on your personality. In a business deal, you would not be taken seriously, and no one would be ready to stake their funds on your ideas, no matter how feasible and profitable they appear to be.

In dating, sports, business, and casual relationships, we make our conclusions on people based on how well-groomed their hands appear. This is to tell you how important this concept is.

Scientific Explanations

Many platforms emphasise the need to keep the hands clean and healthy. What particularly caught my interest during the course of my research is a caveat by Bevel Code that 'where grooming and lifestyle intersect, they unlock a better you.' This simply summarises the point I have been driving at since the start of the section. There is no way you can disassociate well-groomed hands from an acceptable lifestyle. Brickell Men's Products, a platform that is focused on meeting the daily needs of men, makes it known that the hands pass more messages than we all think they do. They said in their opening sentence thus: 'Having well groomed hands is important in the business world. Think of a rough, scratchy hand shake. Doesn't inspire confidence or respect, does it?' This is obviously not a rhetorical question, as we all know what the obvious answer it.

Beyond the business world, it is also important to look clean for the sake of our personal lives too. In dating context, touch is an essential part of the process; you want the partner to feel the touch and react to it appropriately. However, if your hands look unkempt and rough, the person will subconsciously shy away from it. Love dwells where all things work out well. The website enjoins people to devote time to their hand-grooming routine. After all, when meeting a person for the first time, after a look of your face, the second point of contact is a handshake, which will determine what they think of you without anyone uttering a word.

The first point of start in hand grooming is nail care. Without shocking you in any way, you have to keep the nails well-trimmed. This means they have to be clipped once in a week. The best time to cut them is immediately after a shower, when they would be soft. 'Be careful not to trim down too low. Rest your nail clippers on your finger tip and don't push down in towards your nail. That will prevent an overly zealous trim that ends up causing irritation' (BMP 2019). With this, you would be able to follow you nails' natural curve, making them appear charming and attractive at the end of the exercise.

The cuticles, the tissue that connects your nails to your fingers, also deserve your attention. Push them back to prevent fraying or a scratchy texture on your nail. Keep them hydrated with the best hand cream available. With this, you will not get them caught or ripped. Bloody, torn cuticles is not a good sight to behold (BMP 2019).

Also, appropriate hand washing can keep your hands well-groomed. 'Just like the face, hands need to be regularly cleansed to remove grit and grime. An added item that necessitates washing is the need to eliminate the pesky germs and more that lead to infection, etc. Quality hand washes are recommended for use and are usually less drying and harsh than regular soap' (Grooming Lounge 2019).

In addition, you need to use moisturisers. No matter the job you do—whether you work in a factory, office, sing, or what have you—the hands have a role to play in it, and this makes them take a pounding through hard work or other elements. 'Restore the vital nutrients hands need to stay healthy and looking good by generously applying a quality hand cream several times a day. Nobody wants to look at or shake 'alligator hands'' (Grooming Lounge 2019). Alligator hands communicates ill of you, and the best way to deal with it by moisturising your hands.

Bevel Code (2019) concludes its article on this subject matter thus: 'There is no universal law that says your hands have to age faster than the rest of your body. If you treat them well and take preventative measures, your hands can stay smooth and healthy for a very long time.' When you operate with this nugget in mind, you will send the right messages with your hands at all times.

Practical Illustrations

Case Study I: Lady PJ understood the need to be neat and healthy as a prostitute. She knew that nobody would approach her if she didn't look attractive. She was into prostitution on a full-time basis. So the spare time that she had was often channeled to cleaning and treating her body. Of all her body parts, one thing usually stands out, and that is grooming of the hands; her hands are always well-groomed. This ensures that when she is shaking the hand of a potential client, she doesn't wound them with her long nails. More so, the palm of her hand should not look so coarse and rough that people would not be willing to exchange handshakes with her. Whenever you see her, you will notice the elegance and attractive beauty on her.

Case Study II: Also, in professional settings, experts are expected to be neat and orderly. Handshakes are now a universal culture, and this means that you should give due importance to your hands as much as you give to your face. As a professional, if you are exchanging handshakes with your colleague, you must not injure them with untrimmed nails. I remember extending a hand to someone, and I regretted exchanging pleasantries with him; he injured me with his nails. Although he apologised profusely, that could not undo the deed that has been done. Since then, I used to pay attention to the hands of people before shaking them. I cannot afford another ill experience.

Case Study III: Mr JI believes in growing his nails; he would leave them so long that you might be made to think that he fixed them artificially. That was an expression of fashion to him, but when he travelled to Country CXB, he discovered that there was no one with such type of nails, and people were hesitant to exchange handshakes with him. He was later forced to ask someone why people were not willing to shake hands with him, and the person told him to groom his hands. Since he needed to interact with the residents, he eventually groomed his hands, which made him appear healthier. And truly, there was a change of attitude of the citizens towards him. He was shocked by this experience.

Case Study IV: One of the most cherished gifts at XIT High School is for the neatest student. It is an annual award sponsored by a health institution. Almost all the students covet the award because apart from the public presentation of the gift, the awardee would also have an opportunity to intern at the health organisation with a high remuneration. Hence, all the students usually groom their hands as an expression of their neatness while their uniforms are well ironed. When they file in line, it is usually a beautiful sight to behold. Also, it is a custom for their teachers to check their fingernails weekly to know if they unkempt or not.

19.3. Touch Rate

Generic Interpretations of the Concept

You can love without touching, but you can hardly touch without loving. The main instrument of touch all around the globe is the hand, and the manner in which we use it matters a lot. I am not going to dwell on how we touch in this segment, but I want to explain the frequency of touch and its implications on our relationships with people. Touch is a very sensitive issue across every culture in the world. So it must be approached delicately in order not to flout the rule of some. Some cultures encourage touch, while it is a sacred thing in other cultures of the world. It would be suicidal for us to begin perusing this concept on basis of each culture. But on a general note, some Asian cultures such as the Japanese, Filipinos, and Indians are low-contact cultures, while many societies in the Western world buy into the idea of touching people on a high-contact basis.

How frequently you touch other people communicates your feelings to them. If you do not admire a person or they look irritating to you, you would hardly touch them. If you see a person avoiding a touch with you, it means they are not comfortable being around you. The concept of touch is interwoven with personal space; when someone admires you, they will step into your personal space and touch you often, keeping the cultural dictate at the back of their mind.

There are other factors that determine the frequency of touch. In dating context, it is expected that couples touch each other often. Since they are comfortable being around each other, they will touch each other as a way of arousing their feelings. This is usually very delicate, sensual, and purposeful. In a business setting, touch rate is expected to be moderated; business partners are not expected to touch one another carelessly. However, if the person admires you and your idea, they will exchange a handshake with you at every given opportunity, hesitating to let go of your hand. If the person is in a hurry to take off their hands, it means they do not admire you.

Scientific Explanations

Changing Minds (2019) discusses the relevance of touch to non-verbal communication. When you see someone touching themselves frequently, it expresses uncertainty and discomfort. It is as if the person is giving himself or herself reassurance concerning a given issue. Their hands are made to represent that of an absent parent or friend. In some other times, it may be an affirmation of identity. This verbally translates thus: 'Since I can feel myself, therefore, I exist.' When you touch a friend, it affirms the identity of the person and, therefore, forms a physical bond between the two of you. Also, when you hold them close, it also emphasises this message.

The body language explains further that when someone touches a person that they are not comfortably familiar with, it is considered a show of power. Invariably, they are daring the person touched that they can break social rules and there is nothing the person can do about it. This may be used by a boss over a newly employed subordinate. The website concludes thus: 'Touching varies greatly across cultures, for example, in parts of South-East Asia, the head (particularly of others) is considered to contain the spirit and hence must not be touched. Touching in greeting rituals also varies hugely across cultures.' This backs up the point I earlier made under the generic interpretation segment. Study Body Language (2016) also shares the same opinion. The website submits that 'different cultures have different codes when it comes to the amount of touch that is socially acceptable and how it should be done. That's why it's important to check the local customs when visiting foreign countries to avoid offending or be offended by the locals.'

SBL (2016) goes ahead to explain the dilemma confronted by the female gender when it comes to touching. For instance, if women in powerful positions 'touch their male employees there's a chance that this would be interpreted as sexual advance, and not a display of authority and confidence'. If the touch becomes too frequent, there is hardly anything that the woman can say to wash herself clean of that allegation. The website also explains that touch is very frequent among couples, especially young ones, who have the probability to cling to each other too often.

Navarro (2009) emphasis the importance of touch. He notes that babies touch their mothers too often because of the bond that exists between them. Touching makes children grow up feeling safe and nurtured; when they touch an elderly person, they feel secure because they know that a shield is over them and the person will cater for their needs when they call on them.

Practical Illustrations

Case Study I: Ms D and Guy T just met each other about three months ago. Now, their love has grown to an incomparable extent. Being fond of each other, Lady D will wait for Guy T to come and pick her up immediately after work. After alighting from the car, they will hold each other arm in arm as they walk into a restaurant or their room. Even while sitting at a bar, they would find a reason or another to touch each other and smile charmingly. The touch arouses them, and that is why they do it more often, in order to keep the love burning.

Case Study II: Mr G and Mr K were meeting for the first time in a hotel, representing their individual companies in a business negotiation. Mr G, being the host, arrived the location before the set time and made preparations for the arrival of his partner. Mr K arrived on time, and this was the first positive signal that endeared them to each other. After exchanging handshakes, they got down to business, and the discussion was fruitful beyond the imaginations of both parties. Mr K extended his hand for another shake before standing up while Mr G offered him a hug before K was eventually driven off to the airport.

Case Study III: Criminal AV was not only a drug trafficker but also a drug addict. Usually, when he was about to transport the drugs from the point of purchase, he would ensure that he consumed a large proportion of the hard drugs in order to build his confidence level. His aim is that with a heightened feeling, he would confront law enforcement agents without fear. This has worked for him for some few periods of time. However, on this particular occasion, it seems he consumed more than he could bear. In order to assure himself he was still within his senses, he touched himself several times. Apart from self-assurance, this was to also comfort himself from the not too good experience he had.

19.4. Manner of Touch

Generic Interpretations of the Concept

Apart from touch frequency, another thing that matters in the realm of non-verbal communication is the way in which you touch. There are defined ways of touching, depending on the profession, culture, and occasion. Once you deviate from those set principles, you would be seen as being unfit. This will create negative impression about you on others. In short, the manner in which you touch another person tells them a lot about your feelings for them.

Depending on how it is done, a touch can be respectful, caring, palliative, tenderly, loving, sensuous, and playful or reserved. It all depends on the way you touch the other person, what the discussion revolves round, and what you seek to achieve with the touch. For instance, when a parent smacks their kid at the buttocks or the back, this is a corrective touch aimed at punishing the child for an alleged wrongdoing.

A light touch on the skin by the right person is capable of sending shivers down our spine, igniting sexual desire. That is why you see lovers caress each other in a sensual manner. Also, they are intentional about touching the sensitive parts of the body so as to arouse their partner. Hence, the reason you touch the neck area, cheeks, breasts, and other parts where you know are capable of arousing the sexual feelings of your partner.

When someone falls or is in deep pain and you pat them on the back while dragging them up in a gentle manner, this is a caring touch. You match this with the appropriate sympathetic eye contact, potent enough to give the person the needed relief at that point in time. A law enforcement officer would rough-handle a criminal because they believe that the culprit does not deserve their respect. In a symbiotic business relationship where the respect is mutual, business partners will shake each other appropriately without one sounding more authoritative with their hands.

When you touch a person with your full palm, warm in the presence of blood and placed on the surface of the skin of your co-interlocutor, this sends the message of love to the person touched; it makes them warm. This is the kind of touch is exchanged between babies and their parents and lovers alike. However, when a superior gives you a pat on the shoulders with the use of their fingertips accompanied with a 'Good job' utterance, the skin does not respond appropriately because the touch is dead; the gesture is simply not right and laced with deceit. So the manner of touch plays a huge role in our daily endeavours.

Scientific Explanations

Navarro (2009) highlights the importance of touch and how it should be done. For instance, it is said that premature babies should be stroked in order to improve their circulation and immune system. The elderly also thrive on physical touch; some people's day is not been made if they do not exchange physical touch with someone, even if it is their dog that will rub its body on them. Once the touch is appropriate, its benefits are numerous to all and sundry. If it is not done appropriately, it can be seen as an intrusion on the personal space of a person or mistaken as sexual advance.

Navarro opines that 'people can use their arms to demonstrate warmth and, in so doing, increase their chances of being viewed favourably by others. When approaching a stranger for the first time, try demonstrating warmth by leaving your arms relaxed, preferably with the ventral side exposed and perhaps even with the palms of your hands clearly visible.' This communicates a positive, welcoming, and loving message to the stranger. This behaviour is verbally translated as 'Hello, I mean no harm'. This will put the person at ease and help you facilitate interactions without much ado.

In South American, Mediterranean, and Arabic cultures, the rate of physical contact is high. Touching is an important component of communication and social harmony. When you travel down there and see people touch you at the arm, don't be shocked or taken aback. It is their own way of communicating non-verbally, 'We are OK.' In Latin America, the males use *abrazo*—a slight, brief hug to greet one another. 'In performing an abrazo, the chests come together and the arms engulf the back of the other person.' However, there are people, even in Latin America, who will not display this cue because it is assumed they are dancing with their grandmother.

Danielle Anne (2019) lists different touches and their meanings. According to her, when a person pats you on the back, it is a 'commendation, showing sympathy, an expression of pride, or an act of comfort'. However, when you are hugged, it is a form of greeting which signals intimacy, love, and comfort. When someone grips you on the arm, it means they are in search of security and guidance.

Rubbing the arm is a sign of 'for more physical closeness, wanting to be warmer, showing sympathy, or a gesture that requires complacency from the receiver' (Anne 2019). Anger, panic, shock, fear, or surprise can make a person hit you. However, if the person pushes you off, this is an expression of disgust.

Putting of the arm around the waist of another person is a cue displayed by lovers or people who are very close. It means the person is craving for affection and protectiveness. If you want to convince someone to buy into your viewpoint by being persistent, you will place your two hands on their shoulders, but if complemented with handshake, it becomes anger (Anne 2019).

Practical Illustrations

Case Study I: Guy L is a very shy person, but Ms R always craves for the need to display their love for each other openly. While walking on the streets, she wants them to hold each other at the waist, but Guy L always feels uncomfortable doing that. When it seemed R was about to get frustrated, L succumbed to her wish. While they walked, he would grab her by the waist from time to time till they get to their destination. Although L was indifferent about this gesture, it was a source of joy to R.

Case Study II: Teachers are often warned to exercise caution while touching their students due to the sensitivity of their job. However, Mr KH feels he is excluded from this call to honour; he likes two female pupils in his class and will always find a way to touch the sensitive parts of their body—specifically, he would touch their waist, chest areas, and buttocks. At first, the students thought those touches were unintentional, but they later discovered that he was indeed very purposeful about them. He was later reported to the management, and after investigations, he was shown the exit door.

Case Study III: A man and a woman were arrested for cooking up a marriage of convenience for criminal actions. They looked so perfect because it was learnt that they hailed from the same ethnic background. However, there was never a time they were romantically drawn to each other, let alone married. Law enforcement officials were able to easily fish them out due to their manner of touch—the distance between them was much and then, their consistent touches were at the arms, and not even near a sensitive part. This shows that all they were doing was artificial. Using that knowledge as a foundation for their questioning, the truth was later unraveled.

19.5. Touch in Relation to Social Status

Generic Interpretations of the Concept

Understanding how social conventions play out in every culture is very important in order not to be trapped in the web of regrets. There is a relationship between touch and the social status of people. If there is any non-verbal behaviour that is culturally governed, then it is touch. Whom you can touch, how you can touch, and when you can touch are dictated by the context in which you find yourself.

From my experience and what the literature says, almost all the world cultures expect somebody of a higher status—in age, achievement, profession, and other ranking system—to touch someone who is of a lower status. If your boss touches you, there is no big deal in it, but if it is the other way round, it becomes an issue for the society as a whole; people will take that as being disrespectful. So when a superior gives you a pat on the back, it is taken as a commendation, but if you should do that to him or her, it is seen as an insult. The best you can do is to verbally express your commendation while you shake them gently.

Although I have established that most cultures allow elderly ones and those of higher social status to touch the young and their subordinates, let me quickly chip in that this cannot be done at will; they must also respect the conventions guiding the principles of touch. For instance, the boss needs to be aware of when it is proper to touch the other person. If you do it at the wrong time, it would be taken as harassment and that can end up backfiring. Also, you need to take cognisance of the appropriate place to touch. Ideally, in a casual or formal setting, the arm, back, shoulders, or elbows are the most appropriate place to touch. For instance, touching the opposite sex around the neck, cheeks, forehead, genitals, or breasts communicates sexual advances. The issue of where to touch should be approached with caution because it can end up tarnishing your image. Then, be sure if the touch would be appreciated at that point in time. If the person is not feeling any emotions, whether positive or negative, and you touch them, it may be seen as bizarre and inappropriate. So the proper touch should be given at the most appropriate time.

Scientific Explanations

Julie-Ann Amos (2013) talks on the use of body language to convey status, hierarchy, and dominance. She opens her discussion by stating that 'body language and the power of non-verbal messages are quite noticeable when used to convey status, hierarchy, or dominance. Many people consciously develop and use their skills in these areas as a way to advance careers, improve their lives, or just generally exert all kinds of control over other people and different situations.' So apart from the fact that the concept of touch is being predominantly guided by culture, it is also consciously used by people for the sake of achieving a set goal.

Amos observes that people make use of height and size to convey status. That is, when a person is tall, there is probability that they would be looked up to in terms of status. However, this does not mean that those who are not physically tall cannot gain this respect. Maintaining the right posture, standing erect, 'holding your shoulders back and square, and holding your head upright are all ways of making yourself appear taller and bigger', she submits. However, we are not concerned about the use of height in this segment. In many situations, people make use of touch to convey status.

On a general note, during interactions, the person with higher status or position is most likely to be the one to initiate any form of touch. This may include placing hand on another person's shoulders, extending the hand for a handshake, patting the other person at the back, or rubbing a point of pain, among others. 'The power of touch to convey status even extends to observers of the same interaction, because if you are observed to initiate touch then you are most likely to be perceived by the observer as having a higher status' (Amos 2013).

Explaining high-social status body language, David Gershaw (2014) aptly opines that 'the higher your social status is in a group, the more likely that others will submit to your wishes. The lower your social status is, the more likely you will give in to the wishes of others.' In other words, others are likely to respect you and submit to your wish when your status is high compared to when you are a mere subordinate.

Apart from pre-established social status, we also reveal our status unconsciously through the use of non-verbal communication pattern. To make a higher status impression, you must display 'a non-verbal message of certainty, self-control and authority' (Gershaw 2014). One of the ways this is done is by initiating touch between you and your co-interlocutor.

Practical Illustrations

Case Study I: A group of workers were selected by their CEO to work on a particular project and present the outcome to all the stakeholders of the firm. It was a high-powered committee, and they did their work diligently. On the completion of the work, a date was picked for its presentation. Hundreds of people were around, and it was such a high occasion that other stakeholders that were not of the firm also came around. A team member was chosen to make the presentation. After the process, the president of the company called him, stood up to shake his hand, and patted him on the back. The action of the president demonstrated he was someone of higher status.

Case Study II: MT is a professor of literature in one of the leading universities in the world. He was invited as an external supervisor to grade one of the masters' students in another university. The internal supervisor of the student is a PhD. As Prof. MT arrived his office, he was the first person to extend a hand to the internal supervisor for a shake. This is to communicate with the doctor that he was of a higher status due to his academic qualification.

Case Study III: A con artist wanted to prove that he was better positioned in the society to a helpless man. He had promised the young man that he had connections that could help the young man get employed. Since the young man just graduated and was not ready to waste more time at home, he looked ready to do anything required of him by the con artist. He demonstrated he was of higher status through the manner of touch—he would use his left hand to pick any item from the job seeker. Also, if he didn't stretch out his hands, the young man dare not. This was how he put the unsuspecting youth under him for years.

19.6. Flesh-Pressing

Generic Interpretations of the Concept

This term is very common among the political class, which is used to denote handshake in its varied forms and the meaning each bears. For the sake of these studies, let me state that 'politicians are opportunists'. This means that whatever opportunity comes their way, they make the best use of it. They understand that politics is a game of chance, and they are not willing to misuse any given opportunity. When you hear the phrase 'pressing the flesh' among politicians, it means arm grip, shaking the hand, a hug, kissing, or holding babies. This term is gradually gaining a general usage among many English speakers across the world.

Handshaking is an avenue for politicians, businessmen, and people from other human endeavours to establish physical bond with their co-interlocutor. While shaking hands with the person, they will accompany the action with the appropriate eye contact, all in a bid to make the person like them. Politicians and businessmen seize every opportunity to sell themselves. When it comes to handshakes, the connection is basically chemical. When we touch others, there is a release of oxytocin, a potent hormone that intends to social bind humans. That is why you see people who constantly exchange handshake and other forms of physical touches develop attraction towards one another than people who only talk. Hence, 'pressing the flesh' is like igniting your love in others. That is, you want to unconsciously plant your love in the hearts of others through physical touches you exchange with them.

Scientific Explanations

Hanan Parvez (2019) notes that before we develop spoken words, our instruments of communication were the hands, and that is why they are embodiment of messages today. Of all the gestures communicated by the hands, what seems to be the most popular is the handshake. 'It is believed that the modern handshake is a refined version of an ancient practice in which people grabbed each other's arms and checked their hands to ensure that no weapons were being carried. The arm-grabbing then turned into hand-grabbing in which one person clasped the other person's hand in an "arm-wrestling" type position, commonly observed in gladiators of the Roman Empire' (Parvez 2019). This gives account of the various stages that the handshake gesture has passed through. The current version of handshake is not in any way aggressive, and it bears the message of harmlessness, telling others that you are not carrying anything that can serve as a source of harm do them—you are looking for friendship.

The double-hander is the favourite of politicians due to its effects on people. They understand that physical touches create bonds among people, so they make use of both hands to intensify this feeling. According to Parvez, the double-hander form of handshake is 'initiated by a person who wants to give the impression that he's trustworthy'. Notes that Parvez makes use of the expression 'wants to give the impression', this means that the person might not be necessarily be trustworthy. Parvez (2019) continues that this form of handshake is the favourite of the political class because 'they're desperate to appear trustworthy for obvious reasons. Businessmen and friends also sometimes use this handshake'.

When someone presses your flesh through the double-hander handshake, it makes you feel good because they have successfully aroused your oxytocin. There is probability you return this cue by placing your hand over theirs. When someone who barely knows you gave you this form of handshake, you should ask yourself some questions: Why does he want to appear trustworthy? What does he have to gain from this? Is he contesting for an elected position? Does he need my help at some point in life? Is he desperate to win the contract I'm about to award? Depending on the context, all these questions will guide you and help in determining the underlying reason for this handshake. With that you will not make decisions that will end up putting you in the web of regrets (Parvez 2019).

Mateo Sol (2019) shares the same view with Parvez. He describes the 'flesh pressing' as a hand hug. Noting that it is mostly used by politicians, he submits that if used in the appropriate context, the person is 'being *warm, friendly, trustworthy* and *honest*, and sometimes this handshake is reciprocated creating a pile of 4 hands'. This handshake, which takes the form of body hug, is expected to be done genuinely only by those who maintain close bond. However, if done by someone who is barely known to you, it is taken as an invasion of intimacy and may not be rightly received.

Kyle Wang (2017) says if this form of handshake is displayed by a party placing the hand on the other instead of maintaining a vertical structure, it is a show of dominance; the person wants to prove superiority. Such people usually stands on the left side because it gives them the advantage to place their hands over that of their co-interlocutor.

Practical Illustrations

Case Study I: Elections were approaching, and political gladiators had to put preparations on a top gear in order to win the hearts of the people. Being a media guru himself, Gladiator J knows the impact of the media, so he took advantage of it by using it as a medium to bear his messages to the electorate. After a radio interview, he ensured he shook hands with all the presenters on duty. At each point, he would place his left palm on the hand of the other person in order to create the feeling of honesty, trust, and admiration.

Case Study II: The director of HUY Construction was one of those people who came to bid for a project advertised by the government. The contract was worth billions, and many of the contracting firms have been lobbying to win the job. Even though the director could have sent his subordinates to defend the proposal, he decided to make himself available. After the defence, he exchanged handshakes with all the people on the other side of the table, making use of double-hander style. This was a show of confidence and honesty.

Case Study III: When Forger XH arrived at the destination where he wanted to use the forged documents, he discovered that the faces of the security agents at the venue were friendly. So he thought that was a plus to him. The first thing he did when he got there was to shake the officials with his two hands—he wanted to create a feeling of honesty, admiration, and trust so that he wouldn't be suspected. However, the handshake looked so artificial and unreal that the officers had to check his documents multiple times, and that was the point he couldn't overcome—he was eventually fished out, and he could not defend himself.

19.7. Placing Hands on Hips with Arms Widely Apart, Thumbs Facing Back

Generic Interpretations of the Concept

The act of placing your two hands on the hips, with the arms widely apart while the elbows point out and the thumbs face backwards (pointing to the buttocks) is popularly referred to as arms akimbo. When you observe this cue in a person, be sure that there are issues; nobody does that when there are no issues. On a general note, this is taken as a display of dominance. When you take on the posture, you look bigger than your normal size. So this self-pumping style is to challenge what is considered as a threat to your peace.

This stance also signals alertness. Someone who is not aware of their environment will not take on this stance. As a cluster, you would also observe that the legs are somewhat apart in order to give the person the needed stamina and prepare them for physical attack. It would be difficult for someone who maintains this stance to be attacked by another person. Other than that, the behaviour also means that the person has some issues they want to discuss, most probably a complaint or negative issues. From the experience of airline agents, they note that when a passenger does this while waiting in line, you should be certainly sure that they have a complaint or another.

The arms akimbo is an authoritarian look that gives people a bigger posture. Apart from aggressive situations, such as when a paid service is not rendered well, this posture should not be used in a social setting, especially when speaking with family members; it hinders communication as they are made to see you as an aggressive fellow who is intolerant of other's ideas. How do you feel when your children tell you that you look like a military drill instructor? It simply means that you are frightening they do not feel easy while speaking with you. Being a disciplinarian should not turn you to a terror among your people.

Scientific Explanations

Hanan Parvez (2019) notes that the arms akimbo body gesture is very common and seen on a daily basis in the Western world. Of course, using it intuitively is not the same thing as having the core knowledge of what it represents. Parvez submits, 'This gesture is taken up by a person who is "ready for action", typically an assertive action. We only take assertive action when we feel the need to assert ourselves and we only feel the need to assert ourselves when our rights have been violated or we encounter an unpleasant situation that requires us to set things straight.' That is why I gave the example of airline agents and passengers who placed their hands on their hips when they have a complaint or another. It is safe to conclude that the person displaying this cue is either angry or irritated. So it is good and appropriate when used to communicate annoyance; the person who offended you would take you seriously because they understand that they are ready for action.

Sometimes when we display this cue and open up the feet to take up a wider stance, this helps us to look bigger and take up more personal space. Anyone who wants to break into our personal space will think twice before doing so, knowing fully well that we are at alert and can have a reprisal attack. According to Parvez, 'When you see two people arguing, the person who takes up this gesture is the one who feels more offended and is more likely to be the one who strikes the first blow in case the altercation turns physical.'

Christopher Philip (2014), while giving a sentence interpretation of this cue, says that 'arms akimbo is an expansive posture used to make the body appear larger and taking up more space thereby creating dominance'. This is the same view expressed by Parvez. This posture can be used to your advantage while preparing to make an important presentation. According to research, when you take up a posture as this, it 'helps boost testosterone and simultaneously lowers the stress hormone cortisol'. Also, it makes you take up a bigger stance, giving you a dominant shape. Since it is classified as 'ready posture', the arms akimbo also communicates to others that you are eager to get down to business and get a deal struck. Those who want to take up leadership role and its corresponding responsibilities will definitely go for this posture.

Philip (2014) gives the verbal translations of this as: 'I'm much bigger than I appear, so you must respect me when I puff out like this', 'There are issues here', 'Things are not right', 'I'm standing my ground', or 'I'm a virile male so check me out!'

The body language expert traces the root of this gesture to evolution. Just like the peacock, when you place the hands on the hips, it makes you look bigger; thus, it can be attractive to men seeking leadership or a woman in search of a healthy mate. If the cue is used in the appropriate context, it can be very helpful and communicate our intended message in a clear, apt, and concise manner.

Practical Illustrations

Case Study I: 'Mom is in a good mood until her 6-year-old is caught eating sweets from the cupboard. She had earlier warned the little boy not to touch the sweets but he flippantly disregarded her order which made mom so annoyed. Mom strides to her child, puts her hands on her hips, then begins lecturing him about the harms of junk food. Mom went over to junior, put her hands on her hips, and spoke gently to him. With this posture, Junior knew he had better cooperate as the mother could do just anything to him.' (Philip 2014).

Case Study II: D was one of the contestants in a dating show. He was thinking of the way he could stand out from other contestants. Suddenly, he thought of placing his hands on his hips. After doing that, he discovered that he had taken up more space, making him feel bigger and superior to others. This further bolstered his confidence and made him a cynosure of all eyes.

Case Study III: Mr VR secured a job with forged certificates. He easily scaled through the screening process because there was no defined system put in place to checkmate those illicit acts. However, after some few months, the president wasn't getting the results he had imagined. He then relieved the manager of his job and brought in another person. The new manager could call on anybody to ask of his educational background before giving him or her a task to execute. VR will always sit with his palms placed his hips and the thumb turned backwards. His elbows would be turned out, making him take up more space. He thought this could send fear down the nerves of the new manager not to ask him such questions. However, since it was more of a conscious approach to cover things up, it didn't work out for him as the manager had suspected a foul play right from the onset.

19.8. Arms Akimbo with Thumbs Pointing Forward

Generic Interpretations of the Concept

This is like the variant to the preceding issue. Well, the only difference is the position of the thumbs. You might think that where the thumb faces is inconsequential to the overall message that the posture bears but this will amount to an ignorant comment. While the thumb pointing to the back posture is taken as a sign of dominance or show of superiority, when it is pointing forward, it is used to display curiosity. You can just practise these two postures and see the thought that slides into your mind in each given occasion.

When people are taken aback by the occurrence of an event, they will place their hands on their hips, with the elbows pointing outward while the two thumbs face front as they assess the situation or damage. The rough verbal translation of this cue is 'Wow! So this thing happened when we least imagined.' This shows that the person is not ready to take any action over the event other than just to analyse and walk away. This is different from those who are expected to take action—law enforcement officials, traffic control agencies, firefighters, among others. Those in the latter group place their hands on their hips, with their arms akimbo and thumbs pointing backwards while they do quick analysis of the situation and then, jump into action.

As from this moment onward, you can begin to pay attention to this stance, and those who display them in order to understand how significant the direction of the thumb is in expressing our feelings and intended actions per time.

Scientific Explanations

In a 2010 article by Jack Brown on this subject matter, the body language expert begins by noting that 'when accessing or using the "Arms Akimbo" stance, it is very important to note whether the thumbs are facing forward or the fingers are forward as these two variations have dramatically different meanings'. This emphasises the point I made under the generic interpretation segment.

Brown (2010) goes ahead to opine that 'when someone's thumbs facing forward, this indicates a supportive, friendly and inquisitive emotional tone'. This is dependent on the contextual code of the posture. For instance, if done on the playground, it is used to connote friendliness. You will also observe that the person is not necessarily frowning or putting up a shape that is capable of dissuading others from them. In a supportive context, it might be done when a friend is fighting or defending your course. This is to challenge the other party and demonstrate that they are for you. Ultimately, the inquisitive instances seem to be the most common. It is done to question an unbelievable event or something that seems to occur beyond what you had expected.

Brown observes that this cue is very common among the female gender and mostly used by mothers when they are on playground as a means of supporting their children or showing curiosity on how their child gets something done. A woman may even be curious at the leadership tendencies of their child while playing with his or her peers. We will expatiate on this while considering the case studies.

The Center for Nonverbal Studies also sheds light on this concept. The center explains that the thumbs-forward gesture is when 'hands-on-hips is made with hands in the supinated (i.e., palm up) position of the shoulder-shrug display. This more "effeminate" posture is less apt to signal aggressiveness than to telegraph uncertainty or thoughtfulness.' So the center also expresses the sentiment that the thumbs forward cue is not as aggressive as the typical hands on hips cue where the thumbs are facing back. To make things simpler, let me state that the standard version of the arms akimbo with the thumbs facing back is a typical gesture that is mostly noticed among men (it is rare to observe this among women except in cases where they are really irritated and they want to react in the like manner), while the arms akimbo with the thumbs pointing in a forward direction is used mainly by women. It is considered a feminine posture as the stance takes in their breasts and gives them the opportunity to ruminate better on the event at hand.

In another article published on Medium by Brown in 2017, he uses the photo of an actress (Emma Stone) displaying this posture to explain his point. In the piece, Brown describes the actress as being 'confident, open-minded and supportive' emotionally due to the thumbs forward arms akimbo posture that she displayed. He quickly adds that 'depending on the other non-verbal signals present, there may also be an inquisitive component present too'. So there appears to be a consensus in the interpretation of this body language cue in almost every given context.

Practical Illustrations

Case Study I: Ms U is a renowned actress, and the outgone year was a real fantastic one for her; she featured in many movies where she did excellently well. Her name has become a household name on the lips of both the young and the old. So it was not surprising that she was nominated for different categories of award spanning through the year. While emerging as the runner up in some, she clinched many of those awards. In one that appeared to be the most coveted, when called to mount the podium, Ms U placed her hands on her hips, arms akimbo, with the palms facing upward and thumbs pointing forward, took a deep breath before making her way to the podium with cheering from people present at the event. She won their hearts with her non-verbal display which portrayed her as being powerful, confident and unique.

Case Study II: Mrs L took her three-year-old boy to the playground. After dropping him off so he could have fun and play with his mates, the mother kept a close eye on him so that he would not go beyond his boundaries. The boy quickly got to know how the system worked. More surprising to the mother was a toy car which she had assumed he could not operate on his own; he operated the car effortlessly, which took the mother aback, Mrs L placed her hands on her hips with her thumbs facing forward and watched him as he moved the car without the help of anyone. She was pleasantly surprised that her child could do all that without being helped.

Case Study III: Con artist AE went for a job interview; the purpose was to get into the system in order to understand the internal workings of the company before setting up a team to attack them. Even though he was a qualified engineer, he added many other things he couldn't do perfectly for the purpose of securing the job. He also used his non-verbal gesture to back up his explanations. For instance, when he was about to leave the room, he placed his hands on his hips, with the thumbs facing forward, and then stood authoritatively. It looked so real that the interviewers thought they had got the best candidate for the job. And this deceived them into giving him the job, but just few weeks after he resumed work, he was shown the way out.

19.9. Displaying Territory with Hands

Generic Interpretations of the Concept

People can make use of the hands to buy more space and take charge of their territory. When the hands are stretched out, it ensures that a person covers a distance that could not have been ordinarily covered. This is considered as a form of mild intimidation and done when someone wants to appear aggressive. The subtle message being passed across is that no one should come nearer because they want to show themselves up to someone who offended them. When you see someone stretching their hands out than usual, you should look at their facial expression in order to determine if it is a mere relaxation or show of aggression. With this, you will know the best way to intervene.

Those who claim territory with the use of hands usually splay them on a desk or table, hoping that no one challenges their authority so that they do not pounce on the person. The most common place where this cue is normally displayed is at return counters. Here, you will see irritated customers take more space as they argue with a customer representative over the item sold to them. If the representative decides to challenge them, this may increase their emotional status which will make them throw their hands apart the more. When you see the hands growing further, this is an indication that they may likely attack if the argument continues along the same line.

Scientific Explanations

Christopher Philip (2014) discusses this concept under two categories. First, territorial display as an act of showing possession and then blocking or cornering body language. For the first one, it is done by putting parts of the body on objects. He gives a sentence interpretation of this cue thus: 'Putting any part of the body on an object (or person) signals ownership and ability or desire to control it.' When you put your hands or arms on a chair next to you, it is a means of increasing your territory through an expansive posture. This shows others that you have special rights to take up more space than normal. If someone is sitting on that particular chair, it means you own a part of them too; they cannot freely move their body because they are conscious of the presence of your hands on the chair which they will not want to push off.

When a person wants to show that they are relaxed or comfortable in a friend's house, they may place their hands or feet on the coffee table. This behaviour would be taken as dominance or ownership. Philip advises that you should 'use ownership gestures when you want to show other people that you control things or people and that you are dominant enough to state your claim'. The verbal translation of this cue is 'I own this so I have the right to put parts of my body on them and control how they are used'. In some other contexts, instead of putting the hands on an object, it may just be touching them in order to show that you own them. The verbal translation of the action in this sense would be 'I'm touching you because I own you and can do whatever I want' (Philip 2014).

Discussing the motivation behind this cue, Philip submits, 'Territoriality is a big part of the human repertoire. We rarely think about ownership of people, but placing an arm over someone, playfully messing up their hair or guiding them to where we want them to go by placing a hand on their back, as a parent would his child, are just a few ways that we show others that we own and control them.' When we walk with this consciousness, we will know the best time to touch and how to do it.

Also, the scholar also makes use of cornering or blocking to discuss the act of territorial display. With this, a person uses his or her hands to block exits so as to prevent others from going out. This territorial display is carried out when you want to get something from the other person. For instance, a lady who wants to get an item from her husband or does not want him to go out and drink may deploy the use of this cue to prevent him from going out. In a sentence, 'blocking the exits such that people cannot escape is a signal that one wishes to control and dominant a person'. When you see someone placing their hands on an entrance or route you were supposed to take while going out, you became restrained, feeling controlled.

When you prop yourself against the door while a stranger visits you, this is a clear signal that you are expecting them to take their leave as soon as possible. With the proper use of arms and legs, you can create boundaries and private space that you do not wish others to transcend. The verbal translation here is 'I'm going to stop you from exiting the situation with my body until I'm through with you', 'I'm trying to intimidate you by blocking you in' (Philip 2014).

Practical Illustrations

Case Study I: Ms K has been dating Guy W for years. K has always raised the issue of marriage, which W downplays or covers it up with things that do not add to that subject matter. When it was obvious that her spouse was not taking her seriously, Ms K became glaringly frustrated. She put a call across to him and W said she should come over to his home for discussion. After about an hour of speaking on the issue, she was left dejected still, so she decided to take her leave and go and plan with another person. Not wanting her to go, Guy W wrapped each arm around her and pinned her against the bar in order to prevent her from leaving. With the physical barrier set for her, she also decoded the message even without looking at him in the face.

Case Study II: 'She was set to confront her husband about his work around the house. She cornered him while he was sitting at his desk with her arms akimbo in the doorway. She used the posture to make it clear that she was prepared to barricade his exit' (Philip 2014).

Case Study III: Prostitute AQ got a client she never thought was that rich and good in bed—the man didn't look it. After having an affair with AQ, he gave her a huge sum of money, something she could have got from five men. Seeing that, she was determined to keep the man for a long time. When it seemed he wanted to take his leave, Prostitute AQ used her wrapped her body around him, making the man move closer to her. This made her message clearer—she wasn't ready to let him go. Signalling to her that he had no more funds, she volunteered to offer a free service.

19.10. Moving Arms Away From Table

Generic Interpretations of the Concept

While discussing at a table, it is a normal custom that people rest their arms or elbows on the table. Usually, the arms are spread out between a glass of drink. The shape and manner in which the arms is carried matters to us; they are capable of revealing our emotions. So it is pertinent that you pay attention to arm movements during a discourse.

When the arms suddenly become stiff and move away from the table, this is an apt indicator of issues. It means something negative has happened. Remember that nobody will keep to themselves when things are going well. The stiffening of the arms is a transition from a relaxed state to freeze mood. Stiffening the arms means the person is gripped by fear by what you have said. This means they were not expecting such utterance from you. It is a subconscious signal of disagreement.

Depending on the context, the person may not verbally open up that he or she is not in line with your suggestion. They might even accompany this cue with a grimace, meaning they are smiling at the 'illogicality' of your opinion that you may probably misinterpret as being a show of acceptance. When you see that there is a sudden change of mood during a conversation, it would be in your interest to clarify issues before moving ahead.

Another probable interpretation of this behaviour is that the person is threatened by what you have just said. When a thought, picture, or verbal expression creates the feeling of fear in a person, they may move their arms in a symbolic manner. Moving them away from the table is a symbolic way of defending themselves against what is considered as a threat to them. In other words, they are freezing themselves against what is threatening their comfort.

The speed at which the arms are moved or stiffened should be paid attention to. If they move them in a rapid manner, it means they are more concerned. The motion determines how threatening the issue is to them.

Scientific Explanations

Adam Dachis (2011) notes that the act of moving away from a co-interlocutor is a negative body language. He says that this may be complemented by the crossing or stiffening of the arms. The expert quickly warns that 'crossed arms falls under the category of negative body language and can suggest that a person is physically cold, closed off, or frustrated. It can even indicate that they've simply had too much to eat. It's necessary to pay attention to multiple behavioural cues as a single one can be misleading.' So this is the starting point. You should beam your searchlight on other cues and the context of occurrence. What every singular cue does is to help you understand the comfort level of the person but in having a deeper understanding of what makes them uncomfortable, you need to dig in-depth.

Philip (2014) says moving away from a co-interlocutor is a signal of disinterest. When you are conversing and notice that the other party is leaning away from you, this is an indication that they are not interested in what you are saying. Also, it might mean that you are breaking into their personal space and, as such, making them uncomfortable. You can observe this in dating, business, casual discourses, and other forums. Ideally, lovers move close to each other and speak in low voices, but the moment one of them begins to stiffen their arms and move away from a table is an indication that the game is almost coming to an end. The same principle is applied in business. In a business meeting, when an idea looks charming to you, you move closer to the proponent of that idea and sit in a relaxed manner in order to take in everything that the person is saying, but by the moment you begin to close off, it means you are not receptive of what they are saying. The body language expert notes that similar cues can be done when standing.

Reeling out the clusters that follow this body language gesture, Philip (2014) submits that 'leaning back, and disengagement should find itself with lack of eye contact, lack of nodding, deadpan face, stuttered conversation and head-on rather than head tilted'. When you see these gestures, then you can be certain that your guess is probably correct, but in order to be very certain, you can verbally engage them until they make confessions.

Practical Illustrations

Case Study I: D was really into S. Working in the same unit has given him the opportunity to develop interest in her the more. He seized every chance to speak with her, make her laugh, and present himself as the perfect man for her. However, he has not gathered the confidence to make his intentions known to her. On a particular lunch, D ensured that they both sat at the same table; he thought that could be a good avenue to make his intentions known to her or at the very least, fix a time to go out on a date. In actual fact, S only has a platonic attraction towards D, taking him as a clown that eases her day at work and nothing more. At the table, when D started talking along the line of love, S quickly withdrew herself, leaning out of the table. This was enough message for D to caution himself. That is, she had communicated her disdain for him non-verbally.

Case Study II: Mr U is a certified trainer whose services have been contracted by leading firms within the country and beyond. On a particular occasion, he was hired by the government to train workers from a particular ministry; the ministry's output was low beyond expectations. After doing his background checks, Mr U understood that most of the problems were traceable to the uninspiring attitude of the workforce. So this guided him while preparing for the workshop. During his presentations, he talked on the need for the government to appreciate the works of its workforce and how that could be achieved. They all seemed glued to him, but by the moment he started reeling out ways in which the workers have failed their employers, majority of them leant backwards with a frown, disconnecting eye contact and looking tired. The statement was not appealing to them, and they saw it as an indictment on them.

Case Study III: Smuggler AK was determined to have a friend among border officials in order to ease his illegal business; he thought that if he had a compromised official, the official would supply him necessary pieces of information. So when he went on a holiday and was returning home, he lied he was into international business and got the contact details of one of the border officials. After some few days, he asked that he and the officer should hang out. They did and while conversing at the restaurant, he demanded the officer's opinion on the activities of smugglers. The officer unconsciously frowned, withdrew his arms from the table and readjusted himself before condemning it. With this, he knew the officer wasn't ideal for his job.

19.11. Fiddling with Items

Generic Interpretations of the Concept

This is a very common behaviour that is seen all over the world. We have also had a reason or another to display it in times past. Even though it is a negative behaviour, it does not mean it has any affiliation with criminal inclinations. When you see someone playing with objects—pen, pencils, jotters, bag handles, among others, or body accessories such as jewellery, wristwatch, collar of shirt, earrings, fingernails, and other items, this is an indication that they are uncomfortable and saw the need to pacify themselves. The act of playing with items is said to be a great means of relieving stress. At least, it disengages you from the stressful act and refocuses your attention on the item you are fiddling with, which soothes your emotions at that point in time.

Shy people are also fond of this behaviour. When they meet themselves in an environment that makes them uncomfortable, instead of covering their face, they will want to show their confidence by moving their hands towards an object. Playing with that object pacifies them and keeps them in shape for a while. You will observe that such persons find it difficult to maintain eye contact in the most appropriate manner. All that they need is to be released from that location.

If they should go with another person, they will tell the person to hasten up as a way of getting out of the threatening circumstance. Hence, they are just passing the time with this behaviour.

Also, this behaviour is usually observed in interviewees waiting to be called in. Since they are not certain of what awaits them in the interview room, they are always gripped by fear. In order not to be lost in this negative thought, they will play with any item within reach to pacify themselves. When you are talking with a person and you observe them playing with an item, you can get them back to the discourse by asking them what is wrong. If it is a lecture context, this means the person has probably lost interest in what you are saying or has become bored. So you have to call it a day or find a way of rejuvenating their interest in what you are teaching them.

Scientific Explanations

Here are some of the synonyms given to this cue by Philip: 'Giggling Change, Opening And Closing Glasses, Running Fingers Over Zippers, Running The Hands Over Stubble, Playing With Keys, Rolling A Ring Around The Finger, Object Play.' So anywhere you observe these gestures, they are communicating the same message. The body language expert notes that playing with objects 'is a way to pacify'. That is why the verbal translation is given as 'I'm uneasy, insecure, bored, and need to pacify myself by keeping my hands busy.'

When you see someone playing with an object, this is a hint that they need to be pacified because they are suffering from an outright boredom or something is making them uncomfortable. When people have inner turmoil, there are external ways in which they reveal that to people around them. Playing with objects is one of those ways. Philip (2014) observes that 'most are rooted in infantile actions such as playing with a favourite toy, hugging a blanket, sucking a soother and being comforted by mom or dad'. The object within reach ensures that the hands are busy and through that, helps in burning out the excess negative energy that has overwhelmed the person. 'Playing with objects creates a soothing touch over the fingers or palms helping to release positive hormones further reinforcing the behaviour' (Philip 2014).

However, if another person owns the object, this is an indication that the person playing with the object wants to be with the owner of that object. Hence, it can be seen as a non-verbal way of building closeness with the person. For instance, if someone loses a loved one, you may see them playing with a necklace given to them by the deceased. Also, it might be an indication of insecurity; hence, they are subtly seeking the support of the owner of the object. Again, the context of display of the action becomes important in making your interpretations.

While this act gives others negative impression about you, there are some instances where it plays a key positive role. 'It provides busy hands with an outlet to release emotional tension or placate boredom. A set of keys in a pocket can be manipulated to give the hands something to do while releasing stress relieving hormones through tactile stimulation' (Philip 2014).

On his own part, Mateo Sol (2019) notes that when a lady is playing with an object, especially jewellery which is around the neck, while in the presence of a guy she has emotions for, this is a classic signal of showing interest in the guy. In this case, you will observe her laugh or smile at the guy as she plays with the object.

Practical Illustrations

Case Study I: The last gift that the wife of Mr L gave him before her death was a wristwatch. The couples were married for forty years before the death of Mrs L; they were fond of each other and eased the sorrows of one another. When she passed away, Mr L could not find succour in anyone else. So whenever he was facing a stressful event, he played with the wristwatch; that provided him with a sense of comfort. He does for a long duration of time until he regains his composure.

Case Study II: In an unusual manner, the staff bus came late today. So while Ms O was waiting for it, she subconsciously rolled her ring around her finger and looked fed up, with worry written all over her face. This means she was bored; she hated being delayed at a spot without doing any tangible thing.

Case Study III: 'She always felt awkward on the subway and made a habit of placing her handbag on her lap. When someone she didn't approve of sat near her, she opened her purse and sorted through her belongings to displace her negative feelings' (Philip 2014).

Case Study IV: Mr SA wanted to evade clearance, but with the strategic positioning of the officers on duty, there was no way he could sneak out of the venue without being stopped. He sat at the back and looked away from the officers. He was becoming bored and knew that exchanging eye contact with the officers might warrant being called on. So he developed interest in his wristband. He began to play with it for hours, yet no clear chance was coming for him. At some point, he began to drum; and when the noise was calling people's attention to him, he dipped his hand in his ears, pretending as if he needed to clean it up. All these are ways of playing with items due to the feeling of discomfort the person is going through at that point in time.

19.12. Placement of Objects

Generic Interpretations of the Concept

When someone decides to surround themselves with an object, then you should know that there are issues. This can be caused by different reasons. Every now and then, you see people placing pens, pencils, books, and other items on a work desk in order to prevent others from a having a full view of them. The symbolic representation of the objects placed is to serve as a barrier between the two parties. For instance, if you do not want to speak with the other person and think that their relationship with you does not bring any benefit, you can symbolically pass this message by using objects to create a hindrance between you. When you see someone doing this to you, be very well certain that your ideas or even you yourself are not welcome.

Also, someone may decide to place their jacket on a theatre chair or sprawl their hands over it. This is a subtle way of establishing territory. The extent at which they place an object is the connotation of the amount of personal space they need. If you tend to cross this boundary, they may begin to frown, thinking that you did not respect or obey the instruction that has been non-verbally passed across.

Another probable implication of the placement of object is to show that a relationship is suffering from issues. Ideally, when everything is going on well, people will take off objects and free to have a full view of each other. This is applicable in every form of relationship—casual, business, dating, among others. Taking the dating context as an illustration, when you are at a restaurant with your companion and everything is going well, you will move away objects from the table; but the moment there are issues, you will begin to place a bottle of drink, flowers, bags, and other available items in your line of sight so as to serve as a barrier between the two of you. This is usually more pronounced when done by the person speaking. When you see this, it is time to swing into action.

Scientific Explanations

While listing the twenty-five body language cues to avoid, Marc Chernoff (2019) mentions the act of holding objects 'in front of your body' as the first one to do away with. Items such as a cup of coffee, notebooks, handbags, etc. are capable of creating needless barriers among people. 'Holding objects in front of your body indicates shyness and resistance, such that you're hiding behind the objects in an effort to separate yourself from others' (Chernoff 2019). All over the world, this is the message that you communicate when you place items at your front. Imagine a person hiding behind a gigantic pillar when they are being looked for. This is the same message that you communicate when you hold items in front of your body. People who do not want to create a barrier between themselves and other interlocutors place items at the side instead of the front.

Study Body Language (2016) describes this as a form of defensive body language. The body language platform explains this point by referring back to children. The website notes, 'Little children who feel insecure often hide behind a piece of furniture or their mother's skirt, seeking refuge and protection. As they mature, however, they cannot use these obvious and inappropriate means to cover their lack of confidence, so they create other artificial barriers to help them feel more secure.' This is very apt and tells us the evolution in which the human mind undergoes from childhood to adulthood. The act of placing objects in front of the body is an act of trying to conform to the social environment and express our attitudes and emotions with much subtlety and self-control.

SBL (2016) observes that crossing the arms is the most common defensive posture among adults. However, people who are very much aware of their situation and status will not cross their arms (public figures for instance). So they use an 'advanced' subtle means of 'holding different items in front of the body—a book, a bag, an umbrella, the podium, among others.'

In the same vein, Carol Kinsey Goman (2019) shares the same sentiment while writing for the American Management Association. She notes that barriers are detrimental to collaborative effort. She then encourages thus: 'Take away anything that blocks your view or forms a barrier between you and the rest of the team. Even during a coffee break, be aware that you may create a barrier by holding your cup and saucer in a way that seems deliberately to block your body or distance you from others.' She narrated the story of how a senior executive told him how he was able to evaluate the comfort of his team through the way they were holding their coffee cup. Those who were insecure held their cups very high. If the hands were at the waist level, it means such a team member was comfortable but those feeling uncomfortable would hold their cups at the chest level.

Practical Illustrations

Case Study I: Mr K hosted his team members to a lunch in order to allow them discuss issues pertaining to a crucial project to take place in the next couple of weeks. At first, they were all relaxed as he started by showering encomiums on them, and painting the project in a way that they would all gain from it. However, when he started reeling out the roles of individual team member in it, some begin to feel disgruntled, thinking the responsibilities were not evenly shared. What was more appalling to them was the way Mr K was communicating with them.

They began to feel uncomfortable and raised their coffee cup along the line of their sight to serve as a barrier between them and Mr K.

Case Study II: Two young couples went to have a nice time at a restaurant. They discussed casual issues about life for the first hour before switching to the modalities on which their family would be run. The lady was not feeling comfortable with what her husband was saying and he appeared to be adamant about it. So she unconsciously placed her hand bag in front, moved the bottle of drink to also serve as a barrier, and reduce her eye contact with him.

Case Study III: There was a time I arrested an impersonator. The lady was actually fear-ridden, but she still tried to find her voice whenever I asked her any question. So the verification process was without noise. However, I discovered that she employed some non-verbal gestures to make my work harder; she had a handbag that she placed on the counter in order to create a barrier between us and blocked my view from having full access to her face. When I needed to do my full forensic analysis on her, I quietly shifted the bag to one side, and immediately, she greeted me with a frown. It was a clue for me that she was hiding her face, which I needed to see at that point!

19.13. Hand-Steepling

Generic Interpretations of the Concept

This seems to be a rare gesture in our society as it is seen by those who are confident of themselves. Before giving the possible interpretations of the cue, it is worth noting that hand-steepling is displayed when someone places the fingertips of both hands together and then spreads them out in a flexible manner and thereafter arches the hands in order to give the joined fingertips the shape of a church steeple. The fact that this looks playful is evidence of the fact that hand-steepling is a demonstration of positivity.

Universally, it is an expression of confidence. It means the person is not exercising any fear or does not feel threatened by what their co-interlocutor is saying. It is done in a way that does not serve as hindrance to the other person so that it is not mistaken for defensive posture; the hands are placed at the sides. The hand-steepling cue is common among those holding leadership positions. Being symbols of authority, they do not necessarily fidget at the sight of any issue. Hence, with the use of this cue, they are communicating to the world, 'I'm taking my time to ruminate over the issue and share my thought with you.' German chancellor Angela Merkel is the most famous person known for the use of this gesture.

Let me quickly chip in that the fact that someone displays confidence does not mean they have an accurate knowledge on what they are saying. That is, the person might be wrong in their display of confidence. However, this behaviour is a potent way of convincing others that you are committed to what you are saying or ruminating on. Thus, whether right or wrong with your fact, your co-interlocutor will believe that you have only expressed the sincerity of your heart. This is very important in building trust among people.

Scientific Explanations

Christopher Philip (2013) discusses the hand-steepling cue in a detailed form. According to him, 'The hand steeple happens by propping up the fingers of on hand, with the finger of the other hand, to form a bridge.' This is very short and easy to comprehend. Note that while displaying this posture, the fingers are not interlocked and the palms of the two hands would not touch each other. The word *steepling* as used here is reference to the similarity of the pointed roof of a church; when you display this cue, pay attention to the shape of the middle finger.

There are different ways in which this cue is displayed; the steepled hands may be placed low on the person's lap or hover over the lap. In some other instance, you may have a full view of it when the person props up their elbows on the table. Some may even decide to hold it so high that they have to look at their co-interlocutor through the space of the steepled hands. Philip (2013) notes, 'Hand steeples frequently occur by themselves as stand-alone cues, and don't require additional body language in a cluster to have predictable meaning.' This makes it very easy for you to make conclusion about the thought of the person without having to necessarily refer back to any clue.

The person displaying this cue is surely confident, sometimes, overconfident, filled with air of authority, power, genuineness, and may even be evaluative of those around them. Confidence as expressed in this realm is rooted in the control and power they possess over others in their environment. Hence, steepling is expressing the verbal message: 'I have access to hidden information (and life experience) and this is the source of my power and control over you.' From close observation, it has been discovered that steeplers display this cue when they are around subordinates or when it is obvious that they have an upper hand over their counterpart. There is no gainsaying that this gesture is more potent when the person displaying it has a legitimate authority over others or wants people to believe so. However, this would be felt as awkward in team building as others would easily assume that you are arrogant (Philip 2013).

Bosses normally steeple their hands while heading a meeting or when giving orders to their subordinates. The higher the steepled hands, the more arrogant or confident they feel. 'A more subtle version is the hidden steeple of which the sender could be trying to hide or shelter their opinion from view by keeping the steepled fingers below the table. The lower steeple is more often used by women and when someone is listening rather than speaking' (Philip 2013). When you observe that this cue is hidden, it means the person is trying to suppress their confidence and look more open and acceptable.

Westside Toastmasters (2019) shares the same sentiment with Philip. The website premised its submission on the study of body movements by Ray Birdwhistell. Because of the self-assured attitude of this gesture, it is also referred to as 'power position.' In what seems to be like a consensus, the body language platform also notes that this gesture does not come in clusters. The website concludes by cautioning that this body gesture should be carefully used because it can either connote positive or negative message, depending how it is used in any given context and what you want the other party to think about you.

Practical Illustrations

Case Study I: In what seems like a morning ritual, all the employees of GTC Security Services would have to report at the station so as to be addressed by the head of the firm. After that, the unit supervisors will take charge and reel out the duties for the day. Any time the CEO of the security firm was to address the gathering, all those present would be silent. So he would maintain a firm stance, speak slowly, completing each sentence and then steeple his hands to give instructions and his expectations of the workforce. Sometimes, he raises the steepled hands so high that he views the employees through the steeple. This means he was feeling more authoritative.

Case Study II: Politician A normally feels that since he governs a more populated region than his colleagues, he is more important than they are; he sees himself as a star and any time they have a meeting, he wants to prove this greatness. Apart from shaking his co-politicians with his two hands, he would also raise a steepled hand during the course of the meeting so as to address them. While some of them seem ignorant of this non-verbal display of authority, some others pick fight with him and that serves as the foundation of his political downfall but he doesn't seem to understand this on time.

Case Study III: Con Artist AI was being investigated by a group of renowned enforcement officials but he seemed to be unmoved by the experience and expertise of those on the other side of the table. Since the commencement of the interview, he had more answers to give to each question. More so, his display of confidence could make a naïve official doubt his rightness of arresting the con artist. At some point, AI formed a steeple with his hands and raised them so high that he was seeing the officers through the steeple. The officers considered that as an insult and this made them to come very hard on him.

19.14. Adjusted Steepled Hands

Generic Interpretations of the Concept

Let me put out straight that this just a variant of the hand-steepling cue. Here, all the fingers interlaced except for the index fingers that meet at the finger tips. The index fingers stand erect while the other four are interwoven and lowered. This makes the erect fingers very pronounced and portrays it as a replica of a church steeple. The adjusted hand-steepling looks more contrite than the typical gesture but the meaning does not change; it expresses confidence and assurance.

Variety is the spice of life and people take new dimensions to express their emotions in the most convenient manner. The modified hand-steepling makes the other four fingers to rest on one another, providing a form of warmth, while the index fingers symbolically connotes, 'I'm holding my head high because I'm authoritative and powerful.' Also, this adjusted gesture gives the person a firm grip of their hands while passing across the message of confidence.

Unlike the conventional hand-steepling cue that has the probability to block the view of the steepler, since the fingers are interlaced in this form, the person undoubtedly has a full view of the person being addressed, no matter how high the hands are raised. In a way, we can cautiously conclude that the adjusted steepled hands behaviour is displayed when someone is more confident of themselves. In the same vein, this form of steepled hands can be moved easily from one side to the other, giving the steepler, the flexibility to engage their co-interlocutor.

Scientific Explanations

The interlaced fingers should be carefully used as a small variation is capable of changing its meaning. I will try to balance the two in this segment. The interlacing or interlocking of the fingers which is sometimes accompanied with the rubbing of the hands may serve as a pacifying act, denoting that the person is less confident. In this sense, 'Interlaced fingers are an indication of frustration, hostility, self-restraint and other negative thoughts' (Philip 2014). However, this is also in line with the concept of confidence; when the entire fingers are interlaced, it is used to steady nervous hands so that the person appears somewhat confident.

In the words of Philip, 'By locking them together, it will provide security and comfort. This sign goes mostly unnoticed by others so it is unlikely that they will read your frustration, instead confusing it with self-control.' Context becomes the distinguishing in this realm. When this is displayed by an authoritative figure who has nothing to fear, it is taken as a show of confidence and assurance but when it is seen in a subordinate who is afraid of something evil happening, then it is a means of comforting themselves. The joy about this cue is that most people do not pay attention to it and the few ones that do, they assume it to be a means of self-control. Note that if the fingers are not interlocked, it is unarguably a demonstration of confidence.

The verbal translation of this cue is: 'My fingers are interlaced together because I'm holding frustration, hostility and other negative thoughts. I need to entwine my fingers so I keep them under careful restrained control.' The misconception about this posture is that it is a restrained and controlled posture but it is not. If it were to be a display of confidence as in the case of the adjusted hand-steepling cue, the index fingers would be pointing up while the interlaced fingers would not be rubbing one another because the person is not feeling any negative emotion. This difference, as insignificant as it appears, is the distinguishing factor between the two gestures.

Philip (2014) gives a detailed explanation of the concept thus: 'When the fingers massage the palm or the fingers are interlaced then gently rub up and down as the fingers stroke the inside of the other, it indicates a person who is in doubt, has low confidence, or is experiencing stress. As tension escalates, the gesture will move from palm stroking into more rigorous interlaced finger stroking making the two a progression of intensity. Thus while palm stroking is due to mild doubt or slight confidence issues, interlaced fingers that rub up and down is to do a higher level of anxiety.'

In all, what is important is that you pay attention the structure of the gesture in order to know which is which. With that, your interpretations would be informed and would not be trapped in the ignorant perception of taking a show of timidity for self-control.

A body language platform known as Unverbal, in a 2013 article shares the same opinion with Philip. It notes, 'Low confidence displays of the hands involve *finger interlacing*. If during the course of a conversation a person switches from steepling to interlaced fingers, you should take note–whatever that person just thought, said or heard made them lose a bit of confidence. The reverse is true for a person who changes from interlaced fingers to a steeple display.'

Practical Illustrations

Case Study I: 'In a meeting involving all the cadres of workers of a company, the junior associate made sure he was obedient while the senior ranking member said his piece; he understood that there was a need to give honour to whom honour is due. He interlocked his hands on his lap and sat quietly so as not to disturb the presentation. Once the floor was opened up to the rest of the associates, the junior associate unlocked his fingers and began to gesticulate as he showed the various shortcomings in the plan' (Philip 2014). This means he was authoritatively pointing out the errors to them, even though this was done to a senior colleague.

Case Study II: In a case that has to do with murder, a man was called in to be the defendant of the alleged, knowing what could likely be the lot of his close friend. So he chose to testify for him. At least, that were be an incontrovertible evidence of his help towards the course of a friend. He waited patiently on stand as he was cross-examined. His fingers interlaced neatly on his lap. On closer inspection, one could see his fingers moving up and down and his knuckles tightly pressed together (Philip 2014). This means he had no confidence and had to depend on body language to keep himself within shape. Except for those with adequate knowledge of this subject matter, you will not know that something was wrong with his attitude.

Case Study III: A group of employees were arrested for allegedly forging the signature of their boss that led to the stealing of millions of dollars. They were arrested based on their suspicious past activities. So the chances were high that some of them were only trapped in the controversy. The five employees were asked to sit on a bench and face the investigators that were on truth-finding mission. One of the investigators who had an expertise in non-verbal communication noticed that one of the suspects interlocked his fingers when they were asked to provide their signatures. This was a hint that he was not willing to provide his signature.

19.15. Hands Positioned Actively

Generic Interpretations of the Concept

Public speakers are surely conversant with this non-verbal gesture because they use it from time to time. To demonstrate this gesture, the hands are held about fourteen inches apart, right in front of the belly. The palms are made to face each other while the fingers are spread apart, positioned at the waist level. Being in the direction of the genitals calls the attention of people to the cue. Also, it is done in a way that it does not block the view of the interlocutors. The hands are moved inches away from the belly and genitals in order to demonstrate that the person is not actually afraid of anything but displaying the cue to pass a positive message.

During important speaking sessions, speakers use it to capture the attention of their audience. Putting the hands in a 'ready position' makes audience become curious of what the speaker wants to achieve with it at that point in time. It is pertinent to state that this is not the rogatory stance (to be discussed later) where the palms are facing up. In this context, the palms are made to face each other as if the person has a beach ball in their hands.

For those who want to build up on their public speaking skills, this is a useful one to learn; it portrays you as an experienced speaker who understands how best to grab the attention of his or her audience. From history, those who end up being successful public speakers are those who understand how best to make use of non-verbal cues. The fact is that the primary mode of communication still remains non-verbal means. Hence, it is those who have come in tandem with this truth that are seen as being exceptional in their presentations. Aligning your life with this universal truth will serve as a turning point in your life.

Scientific Explanations

Nicolas Fradet (2016) discusses the hand gestures and how they are being used on daily basis to communicate the intents of our hearts. One of the issues referred to in the piece is how American politician Hillary Clinton outstretches her arms and spreads the fingers out while standing behind the podium. The context of display of this cue has given hint of its purpose—it is to aid her public-speaking repertoire. The fact that it is meant to convince the audience does not mean that everything that the person says is accurate. In fact, political figures around the world are known for their untruthfulness, and that is why they employ all forms of techniques such as this gesture to convince their listeners. Whether being sincere or deceptive, every public speaker is expected to be sound, engaging, and practical. That is what they do with the 'hands in ready position' gesture. You will also observe this cue in many preachers. A close observation will tell you that those who see themselves as public figures in any field of specialisation will make use of this behaviour as they communicate with a large group of people so as to sound convincing, sincere, honest, and professional.

Social Dynamics (2019) explains that this gesture is used to depict that all is well. Spreading the fingers apart while the palms face each other is an indication that the person wants to lay emphasis on a point. Hence, it is seen as a prelude to gain the attention of the audience. Maybe the speaker has earlier made the point and did not get the expected outcome. So before re-echoing the point, they employ this gimmick to hook the attention of the listeners to themselves.

Also, the fact that the hands are spread out and the fingers spread apart is a way of non-verbally communicating openness. It is like saying, 'Look here, I have nothing to hide from you.' Note that exposing the vulnerable parts of the body also helps in echoing this message. Through this, trust can be built between the speaker and their listeners. Most times, legal defenders also make use of this gesture while arguing their case in the courtroom. They understand how delicate their job is and, as such, seize every opportunity to gain the attention of the judge (Social Dynamics 2019).

Practical Illustrations

Case Study I: Mr Y is an experienced teacher; he has been teaching at different levels for more than two decades. Also, he had had the opportunity to chair external examination bodies. So he is invariably a hot cake for educational institutions who do invite him to prepare their final year students for their external examinations. During examinations season, the invites are too numerous that he has to reject some on the spot. On a particular occasion, while preparing a large class for their examination, he discovered that the students were really lagging behind as they were not responding to questions that they were ordinarily competing to answer. So he decided to extend the time he was supposed to spend with them in order to cover some vital aspects of their syllabus. At some point when he wanted to tell them on how to approach examination questions, it seemed most of them were tired and losing interest in what he was saying. Having got their non-verbal message, he held his hands about fourteen inches apart in front of the stomach, around the waist, and spread out his fingers so as to gain their attention before talking.

Case Study II: A lawyer was hired by a political figure who believed he was unjustly disqualified by the electoral body to contest for a particular position. At the court, it was really a battle of wits as the defendants have also lined up a group of experienced lawyers to uphold their decision; they knew that the only way they could stop the politician was to prevent his name from appearing on the ballot. After the defendants have argued their case, the litigant took time to quote different authorities; and when he was about making his submission, he discovered that most of the justices were not paying attention to him, so he held his hands apart, outstretched, and fingers spread apart which made all the judges to focus on him before he eventually made his submission.

Case Study III: Three prostitutes were in a hotel, wishing to have a client because they were in hard times. Prostitute A was dressed half-naked while others were a little bit covered. So when a man was walking towards them, Prostitute A thought that was her client, but she was disappointed that he approached another person. After an hour, another man was seen approaching them, seeing him from afar, she feigned more commitment to the conversation at hand and stretched her fingers and hands wide open so that she caught the man's attention with that. She ensured that they exchanged eye contact, and she smiled romantically at him so as to make herself irresistible to him.

19.16. Palms Facing Up

Generic Interpretations of the Concept

In many quarters, this is also referred to as 'rogatory hand position'. It has to do with stretching out the arms without slouching the shoulders and opening the palms up so that it becomes visible to everyone seeing you. Universally, this is a positive body language cue that is used to denote humility, cooperation or compliance. There are instances that we want people to see us as being humble and compliant to rules. So we open our palms to tell them that we have nothing to hide. It also means that you are at the person's command. When you turn down the palms or clench them, there is probability that the other party would believe you are holding something back from them. But with this gesture, you are most likely to be taken seriously. That is why you see people asking for a favour using it so as to appeal to the emotions of the other person.

In the same vein, someone who wants to be believed or accepted makes use of this gesture. What they are verbally communicating is 'My hands are clean'. You may see this when a law enforcement officer is challenging a driver for disobeying traffic rule. With this gesture, they are appealing to the officer to believe what he or she has been told. And from experience, this seems to work like magic; after some stubborn rebuff by the officer, he would eventually allow the person passage.

Also, this cue is also used during religious activities to connote piety and humility. While making supplications to their deities, people are fond of raising the palms of their hands up so as to tell the deity that he or she is helpless and, as such, needs supernatural backup. It also means the person is not proud to the deity. Religious gathering is believed to be a gathering of saints, the act of turning the palms up is to also demonstrate this assumed purity.

Scientific Explanations

The Center for Nonverbal Studies gives two descriptions to this gesture. One, it is said to be 'A speaking or listening gesture made with the fingers extended and the hand(s) rotated to an upward (or *supinated*) position' or 'A gesture made with the opened palm raised to an appealing, imploring, or 'begging' position.' The second description seems to be shedding more light on the interpretation of the cue. When the palms are uplifted, it is generally believed to be a non-aggressive or vulnerable pose that is appealing to the listeners as allies rather than an aggressive one that sees them as enemies.

The center observes that 'throughout the world, palm-up cues reflect moods of congeniality, humility, and uncertainty'. This means that you do not need to exercise any fear in the use of the gesture as you go about your daily engagements; it connotes positive meaning throughout the universe. The act of showing the palms means that there is high probability for our ideas, suggestions, and viewpoints to be patronised and taken as conciliatory rather than being seen as aggressive or rude. The center concludes that if the gesture is 'held out to an opponent across a conference table, the palm-up cue may, like an olive branch, enlist support as an emblem of peace.'

However, there are cultural insinuations to this. In North Africa, cradling one hand in the other 'with both in the palm-up position' means 'I don't understand'. In Saudi Arabia, the supinated *palms up* gesture--made with the upper arms held inward against the sides of the body, and the forearms extended and held forward, horizontally—is a religious sign imploring the deity to witness a user's non-verbal statement, 'I swear!' (Morris 1994).

The Social Dynamics website also lends a voice to this. It notes that when the palms and fingers are visible through the opening of the hands, it is used to demonstrate honesty and openness. Those who display this gesture are trying to tell you that they can be trusted. 'Many people find it difficult to lie when showing their palms. The gesture exposes vulnerable parts of the body. Thus, it shows trust in the other person' (Sonamics 2019).

In the same vein, Study Body Language (2016) states that this cue is a universal way of seeking cooperation among humans. SBL traces this non-verbal gesture to chimpanzees that use the palms up cue to beg for support and food from their colleagues.

You may not necessarily know why this cue is important and demonstrates serenity until you think of the olden days when our forefathers used to go about with knives, clubs and other harmful weapons on their hands. Hence, as of then, exposing the palms goes beyond just saying hello; it was an indispensable act of not being killed—the person revealed that they had no weapon with them and, as such, should not be attacked. That was probably the origin of handshakes too (SBL 2016).

Practical Illustrations

Case Study I: Mr U attended a bilateral business meeting to represent his company. Before leaving, he was reliably informed that those he was going to have meeting with find it difficult to trust people. So he must do all within his means to convince them of his proposal in order not to make the whole trip futile. At the start of the meeting, he discovered that the people were not receptive of his points but when he subsequently had the opportunity to talk, he added the non-verbal cue of outstretching the hands and opening the palms up in order to make his fingers visible for them to see as he made each point. At this stage, they began to nod to every point he made. This means they saw him as being truthful.

Case Study II: Ms J is a sales representative working with a multinational establishment which means that she could be called for job at any given time. On Wednesday evening, she was informed by her unit supervisor that she was going to travel to another region on Friday for an official assignment. Meanwhile, she had already fixed a date for that Friday evening. Before the end of shift on Thursday, she walked up to the supervisor and asked him if she was truly going for the trip while opening up her palms simultaneously as a way of appealing to him.

Case Study III: I once glanced through a woman's passport and asked her passively if she was really the one, she looked at me, smiled and nodded while opening up her palms simultaneously. Although to a novice, her body language was positive but I saw some inconsistencies in them. First, the smile was more of a grin than a truthful smile. More so, as she opened up palm up, she closed them almost immediately. This was a clear sign that the gesture was rather fake. Then, I asked her to have her seat so that I could confirm the truthfulness of her words and she frowned immediately, disconnecting her face from me.

19.17. Palms Facing Down

Generic Interpretations of the Concept

Not to belabour you, let me state it clearly that the palms down cue is the polar opposite of the palms up gesture considered in the preceding section. This is an affirmative cue that might be taken as a sign of arrogance or pride. There are different ways in which this cue is displayed. It can be done in the air or the palms placed symbolically on a table. Other accompanying gestures would shed light on the intentions of the person. Also, this can be made with either a hand or both hands, the meaning does not change. When the arms are widely set apart, it means the intensity of the emotions is really on the high side; it gives the hands the opportunity to slap down in a hard manner. This means that the person is truly committed to the emotion they are expressing.

I wouldn't want you to see this cue as a depiction of negativity. It may really be affirming something in the negative, but it is affirmative about it unlike the palms up cue that is used to seek the sympathetic feeling of the other party. For instance, if someone affirmatively declares 'I'm not aware about it' and makes use of the palms down behaviour simultaneously, there is high probability that the person is saying the whole truth. The stronger the downward movement of the hands, the stronger the validity of the emotions expressed.

In general, we can state that while the palms up gesture is used to beg and show humility, the palms down cue is used to expressed an affirmative stance over an issue. It is usually a herculean task for liars to perform this cue; the way the hands are moved does not match how their words are uttered, thereby exposing their instability—liars normally perform the cue too passively, making it unconvincing.

Scientific Explanations

Study Body Language (2016) states that this cue is used to establish dominance; since the palms up cue is used in depicting submissiveness, it is logical that this would be used show power, authority, and superiority. The platform notes that 'palms down is the way to say "shut up, let me do the talking" or "I'm in control, listen to me now". It doesn't have to be that assertive—the intensity depends on how inclined the palm is down and how forceful is the motion'.

This can actually be a potent way of debarring others from interruption when you have the floor. While speaking and you discover that someone is about to interrupt, raise your hand and turn the palms down to form a 'stop sign' which will non-verbally keep the person on the waiting list until you are done speaking.

Also, this may be a way of creating a wall between you and another person, subtly telling them to converse with your hands. However, this can be rude and very annoying, so beware of who you use it for. SBL concludes that 'the palm down gesture doesn't mean that this person is dishonest or unreliable as in the opposite of the palms up gesture'. It only means the person is dominant and feeling secure. And probably, they are annoying.

The Center for Nonverbal Studies also notes that this cue is used to display confidence, assertiveness and dominance. The center notes that if our words are adequately accompanied with the palms down cue, they bear more weight, validity, and conviction. The CNS observes that 'the palm-down cue is highly visible above a conference table, where it is raised and lowered like a judge's gavel'. However, this does not mean that it cannot be used in other contexts.

Just like the palms up cue, there are also cultural perspectives to this cue too. In Greece, the pronated *palms thrust* or 'double moutza' gesture, with the arms extended horizontally and thrust outward towards another person, is an insult with which to say, 'Go to hell twice.' In Saudi, it means 'contempt' and the Italian *forearm thrust*, which is used as a sexual insult (Morris 1994).

Women who are in the position of authority are known to be always assertive. In boardrooms, they will use the palms down cue to order attendees to keep shut. Mothers also use this gesture to back up their words while disciplining her children.

Practical Illustrations

Case Study I: Dr G is the CEO of AAR Telecommunications. From his outlook and talk, one would definitely know that he is someone who is thirsty for results. However, it seems some of his senior staff that should understand him better are the ones letting the ball down countless times. This has really angered him and purposed not to control his emotion while addressing them. During their weekly meeting, he said, 'As from this moment, I will not take late report from anyone and if anybody should flout this order, he or she will face the music.' This is accompanied with a stiffened hand-down gesture to accent his utterances. Seeing this, the employees knew that he actually meant every of his words.

Case Study II: Mrs W came into the boardroom, expecting everywhere to have been settled, waiting for his arrival so that the meeting could commence but she was disappointed to meet the board members still moving from one place to another, exchanging pleasantries. Even after taking her seat for about five minutes, some of them were carried away in their respective conversations. Becoming obviously angry, she slightly raised her voice and said, 'Attention, please' while she turned her palm down like a gavel. With this, every member ran to their seat for the meeting to commence. They didn't want him to react to them aggressively.

Case Study III: Baby P has been warned by her mother to minimise the intake of junk food but she would not listen. In the last one month, she has been admitted in the hospital thrice. So the mother became obviously angry that she was still consuming junks without restraints. While disciplining her, the mother turned her palms down in order to give validity to her words. She had hoped that this would make her daughter take her serious.

Case Study IV: I once glanced through a woman's passport and asked her passively if she was really the one, she looked at me, smiled and nodded while opening up her palms simultaneously. Although to a novice, her body language was positive but I saw some inconsistencies in them. First, the smile was more of a grin than a truthful smile. More so, as she opened up palm up, she closed them almost immediately. This was a clear sign that the gesture was rather fake. Then, I asked her to have her seat so that I could confirm the truthfulness of her words and she frowned immediately, disconnecting her face from me.

19.18. Spreading of Fingers with the Palms Down

Generic Interpretations of the Concept

This is another version of the palms down cue discussed in the preceding section. Note that this variation is not captured in many literatures. This has to do with spreading out the fingers after the palms are pressed down. When you observe this when discussing with a person, there is high probability the person is telling you the whole truth. Considering this gesture, it is very symbolic in every sense of it. The turning down of the palms is a way of showing affirmation while the spreading out of the fingers is to show commitment to what you have just asserted. This is mostly subconsciously and that probably explains the reason I have not come across anyone who has been able to successfully feign it.

For instance, if someone utters a formal declarative statement like 'I'm not aware of anything about it' with their palms firmly turned down and the fingers well spread out, there is high likelihood that their response is sincere. The reason liars have not been able to pull off with this gesture is that the cognitive part of the brain might not be in consonance with the emotional region. Ideally, for emotional display to be considered as being sincere, it must align with what the person is thinking. In other words, purgation of emotion is a replica of our inner mind. If the emotional display does not reflect what goes on in the thinking faculty, there would be contradictions and this is what is popularly referred to as *telltale signs of deception.*

What I have been trying to explain is that liars actually know what to say—I'm not aware of anything about it—but their Achilles heel is how to act it out with the use of non-verbal clues. This is because the emotional region of the brain is not committed to the issue at hand. Hence, liars can think it but cannot act it appropriately.

Scientific Explanations

According to Nicolas Fradet (2019) this cue is a display of confidence and shows that the person knows what or she is talking about. So having full grasp of the subject matter is probably what makes them confident. In the same vein, this also depicts rigidity; you are maintaining your stance and nothing can make you change it. This mean you are convinced about what you said and that is why you are standing by it. If it were a lie, some simple manipulative questions will throw the person off balance.

Fradet explains further that downturned palms with spread fingers is an indication of authority, defiance or dominance. 'When a person does this while talking to you, it means he is not going to budge and you might have to change your approach' (Fradet 2019). However, if this accompanied with a chopping activity, it expresses emphatic disagreement.

Westside Toastmasters (2019) observes that this cue is used to give order when there is little or no room for discussion; the person uses the gesture to assert their authority. If the fingers are not spread out, there is likelihood that this gesture is taken as a show of tyrannical power as it was renowned with the infamous Nazi Germany. Hitler was aware of the intimidation this salute gesture conveyed. If the person at the other side of the table felt they have equal right as you do, there might be resistance and this can lead to issues. However, when the fingers are spread out, it simply expresses the sincerity of your heart. The palm down with the finger closed is seen more acceptable where there is an uneven balance share of power.

The website observes that the downturned palms with fingers spreading out can also be used to douse tension. It submits thus: 'if you want to cool down a tense situation or ask for quiet, you can moderately alter the palm down gesture by holding out both your palms slightly pointed downwards with your fingers slightly separated and gently beat them up and down. Make sure that your fingers are relaxed or you will negate a good degree of the effect.' So this is to tell you that you can achieve unimaginable positive effects with the use of this gesture.

Jessica Leber (2008) observes that if this gesture is not done well, it may be used to represent awkward turtle. This means the person is not feeling well. If this is not what you intend to communicate, then do not place a palm over the other while turning them downward and spreading the fingers out.

Practical Illustrations

Case Study I: Mr M was secretly committing adultery which his wife was certainly aware of but she did not have the full fact and, as such, could not confront him to talk it out. However, there was a day Mrs M was privy to his phone and everything let out into her hands. When she casually challenged him, he denied at first and was even feigning annoyance but when she began to reel out the evidence against him, he was taken aback and buried his head in shame. Mrs M threatened a break-up, noting that he could not be trusted any more. This means he would have to let go of half of his properties and this would definitely eat into his just-growing business. So he tendered apology which was later accepted by the woman. After some few months, Mrs M noticed that he had started spending time with another woman on phone. In actual fact, this woman in question was only a business partner. When she confronted him, Mr M told her the truth but she did not believe. When she perused further, he simply said, 'She's my client' turning his palms down with the fingers spreading out. This means he was saying the truth.

Case Study II: Boy J has been warned by his parents to always come home first after school instead of spending the better part of the day with his friends before heading home. For the first few days, he was adamant and when his father discovered this, he decided to punish him. After the punishment, he turned a new leaf but there was a day which he got stuck at school and when he came home, he was asked what kept him long at school, he said 'The school bus suddenly became faulty' with his palms downturned and fingers spread out. This was to give validation to his words—he wanted to be believed and perceived as being sincere.

Case Study III: Human Smuggler BFG was apprehended with some two boys. After he has duly identified himself, the identity of the boys was questioned and he quickly stepped in to answer on their behalf. He claimed that they were his sons and that he was trying to move them away from his ex-wife after a divorce. A presented a divorce paper to back up his claim. As a perfect con artist, he was backing up his assertions with the right non-verbal gestures. For instance, when he was asked again when the boys were truly his sons, he nodded his head and firmly turned down his palms. He was rearrested after a year for human smuggling and that was when they discovered he had deceived them earlier on.

19.19. Restriction of Hand Usage

Generic Interpretations of the Concept

I have established at different points in time in this book that the hands are the most mobile and expressive part of the body. They are equalled to adverbs in the conventional parts of speech in English. However, when a person suddenly minimises the use of their hands, this is a hint that something has gone wrong with them. Note that this is usually consciously done; the hands are suppressed intentionally so that they do not move against the verbal expressions of the person. That is, someone who is deceptive might be gripped by fear that if the hands are given free movements, they may contradict what the mouth is saying. Aldert Vrij, among many other researchers, have noted that when people tell lies, they tend to minimise the use arms and hands.

There is no gainsaying that this is a potent behavioural marker that exposes liars when they least expect it. However, let me also add that this behaviour may just be indicative of shyness or discomfort. When people are shy of being at place, their body suddenly becomes rigid; and except if there is a forceful movement, they tend to be static. So also is a person who is not comfortable. Thus, it becomes unacceptable for you to arrogate deception to the minimal use of hands. This is the point where understanding the concept of baseline becomes crucial; if the person is not a naturally shy person, then, there is the probability that your guess about them is right. Also, the issue that is being discussed should also be taken into cognisance—is it one that requires the person to lie; is there anything at stake? With this and other clustering behaviours, you would be able to arrive at an informed conclusion.

In any given context, this is a behaviour that should draw your attention but does not necessarily mean that the person is deceptive; it only means there are issues which you must carefully fish out.

Scientific Explanations

Study Body Language (2016) observes that hand restriction, even in the literal form, is not easy; the author of the piece describes it as a frustrating experience, having tried it once. There is no way you will not slip in your non-verbal communication, as the barrier you put on your hands will take over your attention. Bringing out the symbolic meaning, the author notes, 'But besides the physical inconvenience, I found out that my interactions with others just felt "stuck", my conversations grew to be formal, cold and short, as if everything I said had a very short expiration date.' This is how liars also feel when they restrict their hand usage. So when you are not feeling the lustre in the hand movement, that should be a hint to you that the person is holding back the full components of the conversation due to a reason or another.

When the hands are restricted by whatever means, the impact is felt by both interlocutors; the person speaking to you will look practically dead, and this is a telltale sign that they are either uncomfortable, shy, or deceptive. At this juncture, you need to revert back to their baseline to make an accurate prediction. We use the hands to understand and manipulate the world around us, and this makes them indispensable at every point of our life. Hence, there is no reason good enough for it to be 'imprisoned' by anybody; such action connotes negativity. The person is closing up their body so as to make it difficult for others to understand them through non-verbal means. It is as if the person is killing an aspect of the communication, leaving you to make deductions only from their verbal expressions. This can be frustrating. Fortunately, their intentional lack of non-verbal communication is a form of communication in itself. So the game still belongs to you.

A report by Olivia Goldhill (2015) suggests that if we really want to catch liars, we should focus on their use of hands. A study by the University of Michigan researchers have revealed that liars maintain eye contact, even more than truth tellers. Hence, this becomes an unreliable means of detecting deception. Also, those who are conscious of the conventional knowledge that liars rarely move their hands do wave them than honest individuals. Liars move their hands in an animated manner.

Practical Illustrations

Case Study I: Ms R is a very shy individual but always free when among closed family members and friends. If you want to shut her up without giving an order, then take her to a new environment. One day, she went out with her dad, thinking that the father was not going to any other place after leaving the mall. On their way home, her dad informed her that he had an important call and needed to see a friend. She frowned at this development, but there was nothing she could do. On getting there, the father and his friend moved to the dining area to have a private conversation, while she greeted other family members, and glued her eyes on the television set even though she was not really following what was being played. When she was offered food and drinks, she only rejected it with a stiff shaking of the hands and could not turn to her sides because her hands had become heavy. Apart from shyness, it also demonstrates discomfort.

Case Study II: Suspect U was being questioned on his involvement in the explosion of a shopping complex. At first, he denied his involvement in the whole scenario; but when it seemed that things were getting hard on him, he began to make subtle confessions. Stating that after buying some items he wanted for the family, he left the venue immediately, he demonstrated this gesture with a hand gesture that denotes a person arriving at a place. When he discovered that his hand movement was becoming an issue to him, he consciously suppressed hand movement, interlocking them in a rigid manner and placing them out of the view of the interrogators while he made his narration. He was telling lies and would not let the hands to give him out.

Case Study III: Patient BA does not believe in drugs; any time he is sick, he would rather opt for an injection, no matter how trivial the sickness is. However, this present sickness defied all odds, and this meant that he has to do the things he claimed not to be used so as to be heled. After several injections, it became excruciating difficult for him to sit up. So the doctor opted that he should take pills instead of injections. Since this became unavoidable for him, he reluctantly stretched out his hand to get the drugs. Restricting the hands is an indication of unwillingness.

19.20. Hand-Rubbing

Generic Interpretations of the Concept

This is also referred to as *hand-wringing* in some quarters. This gesture is displayed by rubbing the two hands together as if you are cleaning them with a handkerchief. When you see someone displaying this cue, it means they have issues. The cue looks too distractive, very negatively glaring, and obviously unattractive for a person to be doing it without any given reason. Rubbing of the hands together is an indication that the person is concerned about something. If someone is overwhelmed by thoughts of something negative, they may display this cue in a symbolic preparation for what the negative incident to come through. Also, it might be an indication that the person is thinking hard, hoping to get a way round the issue.

It may also be interpreted as a sign of anxiety. Fear actually presents someone in a fidgety manner. So if the person does not want their hands to move in a way that will make their feelings pronounced to everyone, then, they may unconsciously rub them together. In a way, this can be taken as a pacifying act. Rubbing the hands together makes the hands warm, thereby serving as a soothing relief to the stressed person.

Doubt and insecurity are some other factors attributed to this cue. Uncertainty of the next line of action, especially when undertaking a risky project may corner someone in the fear zone. This also births insecurity. Once a person becomes insecure and there is no one within reach to pacify them or that they can lean on, then they gradually begin to work on themselves.

To know the degree of stress the person is feeling, pay attention to how tightly they wring the hands; the more stressed they are, the more they wring the hands with full force. When you also discover blotches of red and white skin on the fingers, this means the discomfort is on a high side. If the person becomes really stressed, they tend to forget their environment and pay attention to only the event at hand. That is why you see them rubbing the hands continuously, forgetting that others are paying attention to their actions.

Scientific Explanations

Changing Minds (2019) discusses this gesture in different forms, reeling out the possible interpretations that can be brought out of it. The first probable meaning is considered from the literal point of view. When you see someone rubbing their hands together, there is probability that it is inspired by cold; when a person is cold and they rub the hands against each other, it generates warmth for the body to be hot.

However, this can also be done when the person is feeling gleeful about something. For instance, if a shared benefit is going to be used in a conspiratorial manner, this sign is displayed. 'When they do this less obviously and more slowly, they might be thinking that they are going to benefit at the expense of someone else. Watch also for small smiles and defocused eyes as they imagine a rosy future (at least for them)' (Changing Minds 2019).

The website also notes that this may be a signal of stress or anxiety. This is done when the hands are somewhat tense. This is obviously seen when someone is caught between the labyrinths of inexplicable confusion. It is normally accompanied by other indicators of stress such as frowning, looking dull, unexciting attitude, among others.

Also, Fradet (2016) observes that when a person is rubbing their hands together, this is done in anticipation of something. Normally, people employ the self-rubbing cue to dissipate stress 'and being overly excited in anticipation of something to come is a form of positive stress', opines Fradet. Further, men use this cue to crack their knuckles, and this expresses their readiness for an action.

The view of Psychologia is not different from what Fradet and Changing Minds opine. It simply notes, 'In most cultures, rubbing the hands together would mean excitement and anticipation of something good to happen.' The speed of rubbing tells you how excited the person is and how soon they are expecting their 'good tiding' to come to fulfilment. The website places emphasis on 'most cultures', meaning that there are exceptions in some given ones. For instance, in South America, rubbing the hands implies that two women are homosexual.

Practical Illustrations

Case Study I: Y and O are colleagues at the workplace. They have always thought of their boss of someone who is inconsiderate and does not want their progress. This is because he hardly honours their request for leave or to get paid in advance. However, some other workers see this as being disciplined. Since they discovered that not too many people share their view about their boss, both of them decided to connive against him; they planned that during the course of work, Y would pretend to have fainted while O would be the first person to raise alarm, then after Y has been resuscitated, he would demand for some stipends for upkeep while he recuperates at home. Eventually, they planned it and seeing the script that was masterfully acted out, their boss played to the gallery and approved the money. While signing the cheque, Y began to rub his hands together while suppressing his smiles so that he would not be questioned on what triggered that. He wanted to hide his real emotional feelings with this non-verbal display.

Case Study II: Mr P is a drug smuggler, and for months, he has been on the wanted list of different enforcement agencies. Having been briefed of this, he decided to reduce his activities pending the time the watchful eyes of law enforcement officials will not be on every passenger again. However, he needed money to settle some bills, so he decided to disguise himself and then smuggle some drugs. On the first checkpoint, he was almost nabbed, but he eventually played on their intelligence. After some few hours into the journey, he was flagged down by a customs officer. Going through his particulars, it was obvious that the face on the document as different from what P looked like at that point. So he requested him to step out of his car and follow him for further questioning. Uncertain of what would befall him, Mr P started rubbing his hands together while he was ushered into the mini-office. This feeling of uncertainty further serve as a source of destabilisation for him.

Case Study III: Mr SAG has always heard different stories about travelling on air. While many were fascinating, some were terrifying, and the fact that almost all passengers in a flight do die during a crash was enough reason for the poor village man to be afraid. When the chance finally presented itself for him to travel, he had mixed feelings; the thoughts of excitement and fear engulfed him. When he was about to be ushered into the plane on the D-day, Mr SAG unconsciously began to rub his hands together with a confused expression on his face. This represents feeling of uncertainty.

19.21. Holding of Fingers

Generic Interpretations of the Concept

When we are gripped by fear, we can be pushed to do the unimaginable. Although some of these actions are normally laced with subtlety, they still end up exposing our anxiety to those who care about our look. Holding the fingers is one of the ways we tend to soothe our feelings when caught in a frightening circumstance. This gesture is displayed by holding the fingers together lightly in our front. What is really pacifying about is the tactile feeling that comes with it; when the fingers touch one another on the surface of the skin, it provides a desirable, satisfactory feeling of bringing us out of our fear. This cue is more acceptable and subtle with other obvious ones such as squeezing the hands, touching the neck or some other hand to face behaviours.

This cue is often observed by those who are conscious of their status and that of the person they are about to meet. For instance, I have noticed that when a group of people want to meet a company president or head of a nation for the first time; while they patiently line up to exchange handshake with the person, they will subtly hold their fingers lightly. The status of the authoritative authority they are about to meet is causing a degree of fear in them which must not be made glaring at that very point. So they are soothing themselves through that gesture before they eventually meet with the person. With this, the hands will not visibly shiver, which would have been a very awkward experience in any way.

Usually, a lot of people do not see this as a show of anxiety but rather, an anticipation to exchange handshake with a respected figure. That is why I opined that it is very subtle and unpronounced. It is worthy to observe that this cue is not only displayed when meeting with a figure of authority but when meeting with anybody for the first time; because you do not know what they are made of, you would be cautiously of your utterances and how you relate with them in order not to present yourself in a bad light. So this is made manifest in the manner in which you hold your hands while conversing with the person.

Scientific Explanations

Christopher Philip (2013) covers this cue while explaining the various signals of comfort and discomfort. When people are comfortable, they will carry their body with ease and walk with breath of serenity; the body moves with fluidity because it is held loose. However, if you see uncomfortable people, they will hold their body and this includes as a subtle gesture as holding the fingers. This cue is often overlooked in many quarters because we tend to focus on the face rather than what the other expressive parts of the body are communicating. When next you are conversing with a person who is meeting you for the first time, look at the way in which they bear their hands in their front—are the fingers wide spread apart, held in normal position or subtly held close to one another? With this, you would be able to know what their state of mind is.

Parvez (2019) also discusses this body gesture. The author begins by opining, 'This gesture has three main positions: hands clenched in front of the face, hands clenched resting on the desk or lap and, while standing, hands clenched over the lower abdomen.' The main point here is that the gesture can be displayed while maintaining any posture. Hence, whether sitting or standing, always pay attention to this behaviour.

Parvez explains further that when you see a person holding their fingers, it is a subtle means of exercising self-restraint; it is a symbolic action to hold themselves back due to fear of the unknown. Frustration may also birth this action; having to wait for too long before eventually meeting with someone may be a propeller of this gesture. While standing, the higher the fingers are held together, the more stressed the person is. 'This gesture is usually done when a person feels that they are failing to convince the other person or are anxious about what they saying or hearing,' Parvez claims. Again, this point boils down to what I have earlier stated. In most cases, while meeting someone for the first time, you may not know their baseline and you feel that you are not probably sounding convincing as you should.

Practical Illustrations

Case Study I: Mr O was selected as one of the delegates to meet the president of a multinational company; the man is known for his precision, discipline and high sense of focus. So Mr O and his colleagues have been warned to present themselves and ideas logically so that he could give them a listening ear. After series of meetings and rehearsals, O was chosen to be the spokesperson of the group when they meet with the man. There is no argument that Mr O is a classic and respected public speaker but standing before one of the richest men in the world to share a business idea that will look irresistible to him was the cause of anxiety. Since he could not reject the work, he decided to be manly enough to lead the delegates to him. On their arrival, the man just finished a meeting and ushered them in immediately. While exchanging handshakes with them, Mr O stood at the back in order to pay attention to every of his action. When the meeting started and O was presenting the proposal to the man, his fingers could be seen held lightly together. This means there was a degree of fear in him but was trying to suppress it so that it was not made obvious to the person they were meeting.

Case Study II: Suspect N was being interrogated by an experienced officer whose look and mien sends a strong message to every interviewee. When he was told to offer his explanation on what he knew of the case at hand, he offered a detailed explanation, with his hand held in his front. The fingers were lightly held; he was not sure if the official was convinced by the explanation he was offering him which was his aim—he wanted to drive home his point convincingly.

Case Study III: Mr SAG has always heard different stories about travelling on air. While many are fascinating, some are terrifying and the fact that almost all passengers in flight do die during a crash is enough reason for the poor, village man to be afraid. When the chance finally presented itself for him to travel, he had a mixed feeling; the thoughts of excitement and fear engulfed him. When he was about to be ushered into the plane on the D-day, Mr SAG unconsciously began to rub his hands together with a confused expression on his face. This represents feeling of uncertainty.

19.22. Jittery Hands

Generic Interpretations of the Concept

When the hands begin to shake uncontrollably, we say that they are jittery. There are many possible causes of this action. Starting from the literal angle, neurological disorders may lead to the shaking of the hands. These medical conditions is an aftermath of things that have probably gone wrong in the body system. I have seen people that were in this condition after a car accident. Also, some diseases may bring about jittery hands or even as a reaction of some drugs, self-medicated or recommended ones.

However, if you establish that the person is healthy and then observe this cue in them, this is a pointer that something is amiss. Jittery can either be a result of positive or negative action. Positive in the sense of excitement and negative in the sense of stress. When we are overly excited about something, this can be seen throughout the body; we become restless and prance about from one place to the other. Even when sitting, your body becomes positively agitated. For instance, you see sports lovers throw their hands into the thin air and stand to cheer their team up when they have desirable results. Someone who is relaxing at bar and just checks his email to discover that he has been promoted at the workplace may become jittery with the movement of the hands.

On the other hand, when we are enveloped in fear, this may be revealed by the shaking of the hands; the more jittery the hands are, the more stressed the person is. There are practical evidences of jittery hands as you may see jitters unintentionally knock down wineglasses in their front or even through physical shivering of the hand holding a spoon. If you are eating with someone and discussing alongside and suddenly, you observe the visible shaking of their hand, this is enough cue for you to work with. This means there is a topic you have raised that is actually making him or restless. In a law enforcement context, this is a good clue to work with as the person has non-verbally pleaded guilty through their action.

Scientific Explanations

Philip (2013) makes it known that an undeniable cue of nervousness is when the hands start shaking. The body language expert asserts, 'Since the hands are designed for fine motor control, they are easily affected by a surge of adrenaline stimulated from stress from nervousness or excitement.' Any form of stimulus, whether positive or negative, is capable of stimulating the muscles of the hands out of human control, thereby leading to shivering. Our limbic mind is controlled by fight or flight response which brings about hand shaking, making the cue predictive and honest.

As earlier explained, even good events can lead to shaking of the hands. When you see a person you have a deep crush on or a splendid hand in poker, you will notice that your hands begin to shake uncontrollably. However, this cue is more noticeable at the turn of negative events; it sends us into the fear response mood. For instance, if you are about making a presentation before an audience that are highly expectant, your hands may quiver as you reach for the microphone. Being a survivor of a serious car accident, swerving to avoid a crash at the last minute, while in confrontation with an opponent, among others are some other occurrences that are capable of triggering this behaviour. A mere look at the context of the event can help you determine if the stimulus is stimulated by either negative or positive event (Philip 2013).

People are fond of disguising this non-verbal cue because it can be exposing; you will see them grasp at objects such as drinking glasses firmly or clasp the hands together. In some other instance, they may decide to get 'busy'. If there is a relative around, they will hold the person hand-in-hand, thrust the hands in the pocket and enclosed under the armpits. On this, Philip states, 'People who suffer from pronounced handshaking will develop elaborate ritualised gestures to keep their hands from being noticed. They will play with the arms of eye glasses, twirl pencils, or fidget with clothing. To others it will go unnoticed because they will appear as a normal part of their repertoire – their baseline.'

If you have ever witnessed the joyous celebration of teenage girls at the sight of their adored pop singer, you will have a first-hand understanding of how the hands defy gravity and fly in the sky and clasp them together in excitement. 'Hand quivering is important only when it deviates from a person's normal repertoire of actions. For example, if hand quivering suddenly starts up or stops when discussing a particular event, we know that event is the root. It will then be our job to decide why the event caused nervousness or excitement' (Philip 2013).

A website committed to the improvement of people's lifestyle, Social Anxiety Shortcuts, says that quivering of the hands is usually so obvious that it cannot be hidden from people. There are many causes of this embarrassing act as explained above. This symptom of social anxiety can occur at any given place, provided there is communication of ideas.

Practical Illustrations

Case Study I: It was obvious to Mrs IO that Student L detested any form of presentation; at class, if not forced to make contributions, she would keep mute throughout the session. Also, she has never been picked by her colleagues to represent them during extra-curricular activities, even during official academic presentations, her lacklustre attitudinal display normally discourages group members to choose her as their representative. Mrs IO discovered that if she was not specifically trained in the act of public speaking, she would end up limiting herself in life. So she decided to give her special attention in this regard. When she gave the class an assignment to be presented on a later date, she made it known that she could call on any member of the groups to present. When Student L heard this, she was almost certain that the statement was directed to her. On the day of the presentation, she was dodging eye contact with her teacher but it seemed Mrs IO's searchlight was beamed on her. Having discovered this inevitability, L's hands began to quiver uncontrollably when it was her group's turn to present. It was obvious that she was nervous.

Case Study II: There is an unprecedented customer surge for Bank XYR. Since this was not planned for, it means there would be too much pressure on their workers, pending when another branch is opened or more hands are hired. On one of the busy days, Banker AW mistakenly posted hundreds of dollars to a wrong account and the account owner withdrew it almost immediately. On discovering this mistake, her hands become jittery; they shiver uncontrollably and she began to sweat profusely. For about one hour, she should not process a single transaction as the fear on her was obvious. When she couldn't bear it again, she ran to the manager to report herself. This was the best way out for her. If not, she might have ended up creating a scene at work.

Case Study III: When Forger WP wanted to leave his home, he was rushing so that he would not be late to catch his flight. Unknowingly, he packed some genuine documents with the ones he forged together. Since there was not too much scrutiny at the take-off point, he walked in confidently at the immigration point at his destination country so as to be cleared. He was smiling when the officer he handed over his documents to was unwrapping them. A paper fell off the officer's hand and when he limped to glance at it, it was the wrong document containing his real information. His mood changed immediately with his hand shivering. This is a demonstration of nervousness.

19.23. Anchoring with Hands

Generic Interpretations of the Concept

There are times that gentility would have to be accompanied with style and show of oneself in order not to be taken as a sign of foolishness; when you see someone anchors an object or person with their hands, this is a non-verbal message that others should keep off. Generally, when you see people use their hands as anchors, it means they want to show themselves as a proud owner of something. The way they will place their hands around the given object will dissuade you from going near it. This is a good way of showing ownership and taking charge of your territory when you discover that there are interlopers around. In short, using hands as anchors makes people know that a particular object belongs to us.

In the same vein, this behaviour may also be displayed while speaking with a person that we admire; when you like someone, you are naturally attracted to the person and would like to be with them. When the admiration is on a high scale, you will use the hands, people will use their hand as an anchor near the given person so that others will not disturb their interactions with their 'idol'. The hand serving as an anchor is a form of physical barrier to stop unwanted individuals from gaining access to a cherished person.

This is often seen at parties and bars with the alpha male showing protective acts over their female lovers. They understand that the heart of their lovers can be easily lured away during social gatherings, so anybody that places high premium on their spouse will use the hand as anchor near her; men usually pivot around the anchor point as if they are permanently attached to the person. This is a territorial display that is normally appreciated by the other party if the love is reciprocated. However, if it is the other way round, the person being allegedly protected will see act of denial of freedom to explore and make new friends. The expression on the face of the person tells you what they feel about the gesture.

Scientific Explanations

Those who contributed to this concept discuss it under the power body language which is apt and accurate, considering the message that it passes across. Without mincing words, the noise in the world today is much that we need more than mere words to get our messages across to the right audience. Using the hands as anchors is one of the defined and potent ways of doing this; hand cues are not just useful for survival but very expedient to communication in any given context. When the hands are used as anchors, they speak of your territorial rights that anyone who wants to violate it will have to think twice of the likely consequences. A research from University of Rome notes that this hand gesture helps us to communicate our emotional state to people around us.

Vanessa Edwards makes it known that confident people speak with more conviction because they make appropriate use of their hands. In the same vein, if we want to be taken seriously on the use of our hands, we must understand how to use them to bear the messages we had intended. Although Edwards discourages the use of hands beyond the body while speaking with other people because it tends to be distracting, what we stand to gain in using them as anchors makes an acceptable gesture in this realm. An article on Social Triggers, while buttressing on this subject matter makes it known that using the hands to show ownership does not change what we say but only helps in buttressing them. In other words, if you are guarding a lover with the hands and still go ahead to verbally communicate your disdain for them, the message becomes conflicting because what you are saying with your body is different from what the mouth is saying.

The writers of Skills Converged also explains how this gesture is used in showing dominance. Giving a general introduction to the cue, the website notes, 'A dominant body language is usually adopted by people who want to show that they are in charge. A person who expresses non-verbal signals indicating domination may not even be consciously aware of such signals. It may all be expressed as a result of their dominant attitude. Alternatively, some people may plan their behaviour carefully so they can give the right signals at the right time.'

Practical Illustrations

Case Study I: Student K has always admired the personality of the new teacher posted to their school and the way he lectures. However, it seems most of the students share the same sentiment with him. At break, before he could ease himself and take his food, many of the students would have rushed to the teacher's table, denying him the opportunity to speak with the teacher on a private basis. He decides to make out time to see him, so one day as the teacher was walking along the corridor, he ran up to him and fortunately, he was able to book an appointment with the teacher at a time when no one is likely to intrude. While speaking with the tutor, Student K used his hand as an anchor near him so that no one could interrupt their discussion. That is, he wanted to have the teacher to himself alone.

Case Study II: Lady J and Man B went for a party. It happened that many of the people at the occasion were bachelors, so Man B knew that if he was slack about his protective actions on Lady J who he met just few years ago, he might probably lose her to one of those well to-do, handsome guys at the party. Hence, he lost concentration on the main event and ensured he stayed with his lady throughout. When he discovered that one of the 'hungry-looking guys' was moving closer to their table, he used his hands to form an anchor around her; his message for every other person to stay off was clear.

Case Study III: My men once arrested a smuggler and while his goods were still being checked, he rushed to where I was standing and began to offer unsolicited explanations. I informed him that he should allow the officials conclude their findings so that we would know the next step to take about him. But he wasn't willing to let go; he continued with his explanations and when he discovered that another officer was about to walk towards me, he used his hands to authoritatively form an anchor round me; he was unconsciously telling the officer that he was not needed in that environment. In other words, the officer should stay off because he wanted to discuss something with me alone.

19.24. Thrusting Hand to Face

Generic Interpretations of the Concept

In the heat of argument, sanity is always thrown into the thin air while people imbibe unimaginable attitudes; it is a period when the most stinking aspect of a person's life is seen. Apart from shouting at each other in an inappropriate manner, people also make use of their hands to gesticulate during confrontations. This is to buttress their point. One of the universal outward show of confrontation is thrusting the hands at the other person's face; you point your hands at them as if you want to deep it into their face or prevent them from going further.

This action is symbolic and pronounced. When seen in an argument, it is taken as a last affront in a confrontation; after this, you should expect physical combat or one of the arguers backing off. When a raised palm is thrust at your face, this is to symbolically tell you to stop what you are saying. This means the person is not pleased with your utterance. In the same vein, it means you should proceed no further. That is, they can no longer bear your actions or words.

In most places, this gesture is commonly referred to as 'talk to the hand.' This can be very irritating, especially when done by a person who is considered lower in rank or social status to you; you feel the person disrespected you when it was least expected. Thus, this gesture is not acceptable in any given communicative context. In interpersonal communication, it may be the beginning of a sour relationship. In boardrooms, no matter how intense the argument is, parties are not expected to point at each other.

This gesture is always accompanied by other negatives such as frowning of the face, looking at the other party in a stern manner and a 'ready' body to attack the person whom the hand is directed to. In most parts of Africa, when a child or teenager stretches out their fingers and make the palms to face an opponent, it is a way of insulting the person's parents. This is usually met with stiff resistance or even physical attack from the other party.

Scientific Explanations

The 'talk to the hand' slangy expression was popularised in England in the 1990s. According to Oxford Dictionaries, 'It originated as a sarcastic way of saying one does not want to hear what the person who is speaking is saying.' Martin Gray (1996) observes, 'It is often elongated to a phrase such as "Talk to the hand, because the ears ain't listening" or "Talk to the hand, because the face ain't listening."' This can be very painful and insulting to the person whom this cue is directed at. In other words, you are trying to tell the person that they are not worth your attention. If the person is of equal status with you, it can be demeaning, so you need to be careful with how you make use of it. Without mincing words, this gesture is usually obnoxious and sarcastic.

Jack Rawlins (2001) observes that 'it is usually accompanied by the gesture of extending one arm towards the other person, with the palm of that hand facing the person being insulted, in the manner of the gesture to stop'.

Joelein Mendez (2013) gives a more workable explanation to this gesture. She observes that the meaning of this cue is dependent on the context in which it is taking place. She warns against the use of this gesture in Greece because there is likelihood that you end up creating more enemies. 'In Greece, this hand gesture is called a moutza, and is said to have originated from a time when criminals were shamed by having palm-fulls of cinder (moutzos) rubbed all over their faces. In modern times, this gesture is used to denote displeasure with the recipient' (Mendez 2013). The more the hand is displayed, the more displeasured the person is. This is not to scare you from travelling to Greece but to help you understand how important it is to master both the spoken and non-verbal expressions of a culture you want to interact with.

The body language expert explains further that this could mean the person is ready to exchange a high five with another person. In this sense, it is not offensive but rather taken as a complimentary cue. Unlike in situations where it is used to denote insults, if holding the hand out with the palm facing away and fingers being stretched out is used to connote greeting, you will observe the accompanying body gestures to be friendly, such as smiling, laughing and even, readiness to hug the other party. The high five–greeting gesture is only done between people that are very close and might have known each other for a while (Mendez 2013).

Practical Illustrations

Case Study I: T and K are twins and coincidentally, they belong to their school relay race team. Both of them have had courses to travel out of their region for weeks in order to represent their school. On this particular competition, it is a coveted one as it was widely reported and winners, well-rewarded. They did well in all the four preliminary stages and now, they were at the finals. Fortunately for them, they also put up a good fight on the pitch on the D-day. K, being the person to receive the baton last, ran to meet T after emerging the first position. As he was about meeting T, T raised his hands and stretched out his fingers in order to exchange a high-five as a way of celebrating their victory.

Case Study II: Two ladies had to clash over a man. Lady A believes that Lady B has been having an affair with her man but Lady B is of the opinion that the man was not the exclusive property of anyone. In what seems to be a choice between the devil and deep blue sea, the man decided to keep mute in order not to blow off his chances with anyone of them. After few minutes of arguments, Lady B raised her hand, turned her palm to Lady A and stretched out her fingers, meaning the lady should keep shut.

Case Study III: Two identical twins were accused of impersonation but they denied it, recounting all they had travelled around the world with the same documents without ever being stopped at any given time to offer any explanation on them. Little did they know that such blackmails were not capable of deterring the officials from carrying out their responsibilities. Determined to frustrate the efforts of the investigators, the identical twins would raise their hands close to their face area and give each other a high five without any reason. They would even exchange their seats, whenever they thought no one was paying attention. This went on for a long period of time until the officers invoked their authority.

19.25. Self-Touching while Responding to Posers

Generic Interpretations of the Concept

When you see a person turn their body to a keyboard or guitar which they play or stroke while answering questions, it means they have issues. At some point in this book, I have explained that hands gestures are used for emphasis; we use them to buttress our points. This means that we have to gesticulate as we talk, this will align the actions with what we are saying. Self-touching is a means of pacifying ourselves. When you ask someone a question and as they are answering it, you discover that instead of the hands to help in conveying their message, it is rather touching some specific parts of the body, this means they are less confident; they are actually stressed and in order not to be exposed, they pacify themselves along. Such persons would not provide detailed answers to your questions because they are not feeling confident about what they are saying.

People will touch themselves while conveying a message end up leaving their listeners confused; you would not know which to go for—what the person is saying or how the person is behaving. Making a distinction between these two contradictory points would leave you unconvinced about what the person has said. From my personal opinion and observations over the years, those who make use of their hands to gesticulate alongside their words end up making more sense than those who either consciously or subconsciously divert the attention of the hands.

If you pay close attention to those who touch their face or any other part of their body when speaking, you will notice that they are distractive; their attention is always divided between what is said and what they are doing. This makes the message less potent and unconvincing. The level of touch explains the degree of stress the person is going through.

Scientific Explanations

Christopher Philip (2013) "Auto contact' is a term used to describe any gesture such as stroking the beard, rubbing the hands, tugging the ear, massaging the throat, pulling the fingers, rubbing the back of the neck and so forth, which is meant to sooth the body and create comfort.' This has given us a clue about how the gesture is used and what we can achieve with it. The possibilities of self-touch are numerous and the choice of which to do in any given context is based on individual preference. What we are most concerned about is the intention of those who display this cue and according to Philip, 'is meant to sooth and create comfort.' Invariably, those you see display this cue are not comfortable. Hence, they use the 'pacifiers' to deal with internal tension and reassure themselves.

'It is believed that these mannerisms (the act of self-touching) stem from childhood sources when our parents would comfort us with touch. Grooming and self-touching stems from arousal but this arousal can be due to a variety of reasons. It might stem from anxiety, anger, stress or uncertainty' (Philip 2013). Through the context and the question which the person is answering, you will be able to determine what the root cause of their discomfort is.

It has been established that when you touch yourself or another person, you tend to release oxytocin which helps in calming stress, creating a feeling of contentment, trust and peace. Self-touching is channelled at fighting negative stimulus causing stress in the body in order to create a soothing effect.

Zach Stone (2016) mentions self-touch as one of the body language signals that make people look insecure. He aligns his explanation with that of Philip by noting, 'When people are nervous, insecure, anxious, experience negative or painful emotions they often engage in what is called soothing self-touch. This is when a person will touch or rub their arm, leg, face, or neck in effort to calm themselves down.' He likens this behaviour to the adult version of the thumb-sucking attitude that is common to most children around the world. He observes that there is no reason someone should do it while talking as it is capable of painting them in bad light.

Body Language Communication (BLC) tries to provide individual explanation to each self-touching behaviour. For instance, it alludes frustrations and anger to a person touching their neck while crossed arms holding is associated with lack of interest in one's environment. Whatever be the case, self-touch is used to denote negative attitude.

Philip (2013) concludes by noting different ways in which the self-touch can be done. He observes that women have different ways of creating comfort with the use of their hands. He submits, 'Bouncing a leg up and down and squeeze their upper thighs tightly together can sometimes result in orgasm but even if a climax is not reached, women still enjoy the benefits of stimulation. Women may also lightly brush the lower parts of their breasts as they crossing their arms, which is also an effort to self sooth.' On the part of men, they 'might resort to rubbing their temples and women might employ hair touches and grooming or stroking the sides of their arms.' The ultimate message in any given case is that there are hidden insecurities.

Practical Illustrations

Case Study I: Every teacher at STY Schools has been a warned that corporal punishment is not allowed and that, they should explore all techniques at their disposal before they resort to punishing a child. Being a high-tempered person, Mrs T cannot withstand any form of indiscipline but has always tried to control her temperament since she was informed of the development. However, there was a day that one of the students annoyed her to the extent that she gave him a stroke at the back. The child eventually reported at home despite her subtle apologies to him before the workday ended. The parents reported the case to the school management and threatened to take legal action against the institution. After numerous pleas, they dropped the issue. Then, Mrs T was invited by the disciplinary committee to give her account of the story. While talking, she was always rubbing the back of her neck, touching her ear and stroking her face; she was insecure and her distractive gestures made this feeling obvious to the committee.

Case Study II: A fatal accident occurred near AZO Hospital where just a person survived. The survivor was rushed to the health facility by some Good Samaritans. Doctor AH was about to close work when they arrived. Most of the nurses had gone home. Yet, he rushed to the theatre to see what he could do to ensure that the accident victim was safe and sound. He had never seen a person so injured. Having to work under such great shock, Dr AH would touch himself from time to time, just to confirm if the injuries were not on his body. His insecurity was obvious to the few nurses present because he had never seen him behave like that.

Case Study III: Mr IU was lured into forging the documents of his organisation by a colleague; the colleague promised him a huge amount of money if he could forge those items and convinced him that there was nothing wrong with such steps. Being naïve to such happenings, he played into his hands and when their secrets were blown, the colleague easily indicted IU. Since forgery was a criminal activity, he was handed over to security operatives. When he was being investigated, he unconsciously moved his hands to his ears, cheeks and entire face continually as if those areas were itching him. He was nervous throughout the interview.

19.26. Thumbs Up With Interlaced Fingers

Generic Interpretations of the Concept

Upward pointing of the thumbs is an indication of a positive outcome. When the hands are interlaced, pay attention to the structure and direction of the thumbs, it can either be made to face up or down. This gesture is often displayed when the hands are rested on the lap, desk or table. The location of the hands does not really matter in the message being passed across. The rising of the thumbs while this cue is maintained is show of confidence. Note that this cue is predominantly subconscious, meaning that those who display it may not be necessarily aware of it.

The gradual rising of the thumbs as a way of emphasising a point is a demonstration of the genuineness of what is being said; it is done to add value to what the person which will make other take them more seriously. It is pertinent to note that this is a fluid behaviour that can change as soon as there is a change in the emotional feeling of the person; once the person is no longer feeling confident, the risen thumbs will begin to drop, and this tells you to pay attention to their words afterwards. In the same vein, how well the thumbs are raised is an indication of how committed the person is to what they are saying. If it is a feeling of certainty, the thumbs would be fully raised but if it is that which is accompanied with little doubt, they would be slightly raised.

Scientific Explanations

Christopher Philip (2014) says another name for interlaced fingers is interlocked fingers. When the fingers are interlocked, they can be used in expressing different emotions, depending on how they are being used. Note that a slight change in their positioning is capable of changing the meaning of the cue. When they are rubbed together, it is meant to provide pacifying effect. However, mere interlocking of the fingers with the thumbs raising up means confidence. Note that during nervous moments, people can use this gesture to steady their fear, thereby covering up their inner feelings with it. This is the point that you need to pay more attention and look beyond the surface level. According to Philip, the best way to display full confidence is by keeping the fingers un-interlocked.

Philip observes that 'if the thumbs dart up while the fingers are interlaced it can turn a timid interlaced fingers gesture into a positive cue. Thumbs-out is a representation of ego, dominance, confidence, comfort, assertiveness and sometimes even aggressiveness.' The specific interpretation is based on how it is used in a given context. For instance, if someone who is speaking with another person for the first time was timid, probably due to the appearance of the person or status but later discover at some point in the conversation that the person he was afraid of does not know some basic things, the timidity might quickly move to ego or confidence; he believes he is better than the person, and as such, no fear should be exercised.

In the same vein, when making a point under doubt but it seems the person you are conversing with is unsure of the outcome of that particular thing, you can make use of this gesture to make your point more assertive, taking charge of the conversation.

Scott Tousley (2019) describes this cue as a display of power. He makes reference to an assertion by Joe Navarro thus: *'When movie critics give a film two thumbs up, it indicates their confidence in its quality. Thumbs up is almost always a non-verbal sign of high confidence.'* Navarro explains this without taking cognisance of the issue of interlaced fingers. This means that the issue of the interlaced fingers does not necessarily affect the message passed across by the thumbs up cue.

Tousley gives an encompassing and apt explanation to this cue by maintaining that 'a common display of power is interlacing our fingers and keeping our thumbs pointed up towards our face. This is a body language sign projects confidence and power.' This scholar has further given us a guide on the direction the thumbs are pointed at. The gesture is a common behaviour of Russian president Vladimir Putin. When figures of authority make use of this gesture, it further bolsters their confidence and make people around them revere them. They mostly make use of this gesture while explaining an important point in order to easily convince those at the other end of the table.

Practical Illustrations

Case Study I: Mr U has worked in different public and private sectors for decades before deciding to establish his own firm. As usual, people and even professionals usually look down on start-ups, thinking that they have little or nothing vital to contribute to them. He was undeterred by this; he channelled all his resources into building the company. On a particular day, he attended a business meeting with the directors of a well-established firm. He knew he had to sound convincing from the start of his presentation to its end in order to be taken seriously. So any time he was making a vital point, especially on an idea that looks novel, he would raise his two thumbs up while the other fingers are interlaced and well-placed on the table. This was to display confidence and assert his authority on the feasibility of the proposal.

Case Study II: M is a 'professional criminal'. He has been in the crime world for about two decades and in a way or another, he has been successful in manoeuvring his way round law enforcement officials. Any time he was caught, he knew how to beat them to the game. This has made him confidence that he no longer fears any form of arrest. On this particular occasion, there were about six officials interrogating him and he appeared unmoved by their questions as he provided answers to them in a perfect way. At some point, he interlaced his fingers, put them on his laps and pointed the thumbs up while explaining a point to them; this was show of ego.

Case Study III: Son AR is the only child of Mr and Mrs ZT. Seeing him as their pride, they are ready to spend a fortune on him so that he could stand out among his colleagues. When they were not pleased with his display of knowledge in his former school, they changed it without hesitation. He improved in all areas in the new school and he was told that if he could emerge first, he would be given whatever he needed. This gingered AR to be further committed to his studies. When he eventually emerged first, his parents were happy. While explaining his giant strides to his parents, AR interlaced his fingers, placed them on his laps and pointed his thumbs up. This was a show of elation which bolstered his confidence in his speech.

19.27. Interlaced Fingers with Thumbs Down

Generic Interpretations of the Concept

This is the polar opposite of what was discussed in the preceding segment. When you see a person's thumbs darting down while the others are interlaced, it is a classic show of lack of confidence; it means the person does not believe in what they are saying. Hence, that is why this body gesture is regarded as a show of negative instinct. When we are not proud of what we are saying, we tend to lock up the body, closing up every point in order to make the body smaller. The pointing down of the thumbs is to ensure that all the fingers provide a soothing effect on the stressed individual.

When the entire fingers are interlaced, this is an indication of negative emotions; the person is undergoing some internal emotional turmoil and, as such, pacify themselves through this gesture since there is no one to lend a helping hand to them at the given point. When we have confidence in our words, the thumbs would be subconsciously lifted up to give a feel of genuineness to our assertions but the moment we lose the confidence, the thumbs point down, meaning a blissful chapter is closed on what is being discussed. That is why I said at the preceding section that this behaviour is fluid; emotions can change in the twinkle of an eye, so you need to pay attention to the thumbs of a person with interlaced fingers. With this, you will make informed decisions in your conversations.

I have taken my time to explain the two sides of the coin in order to help you understand the genuine intents of people you deal with per time. These subtle body gestures are capable of exposing people when they least think of it; they themselves are not aware the cue.

Scientific Explanations

Philip (2014) submits that when the fingers are intertwined or interlocked, it is an indication of 'frustration, hostility, self-restraint and other negative thoughts.' The downward pointing of the thumbs bears a message of negativity. When we are frustrated by an incident, we tend to interlock the fingers and subtly rub the palms against each other in other to generate soothing feelings for us.

The eyes of the person is also downcast as they look hopelessly for the way out of their problems. In the same vein, interlaced fingers means we do not want to take an action against a given person; a person who is ready to attack will not interlock their hands. This self-restraint typifies lack of confidence.

The body language expert notes that this gesture can be positively used to steady nervous hands. By interlocking of the fingers, it gives comfort and security to the person. If this is well acted out, people might mistake it for self-control. This means you have managed your frustration well at that given point. Philip gives the verbal translation of this cue as 'My fingers are interlaced together because I'm holding frustration, hostility and other negative thoughts. I need to entwine my fingers so I keep them under careful restrained control.'

Unverbal, a body language website, in a 2013 post attributes interlacing of the fingers and downward pointing of the thumbs to lack of confidence. This is different from hand-steepling that is used in displaying confidence. The platform also emphasises the fluidity of this gesture by stating, 'If during the course of a conversation a person switches from steepling to interlaced fingers, you should take note—whatever that person just thought, said or heard made them lose a bit of confidence.' The reverse truth is someone who switches from this cue to pointing of the thumbs upward.

Describing it as *pacifying behaviour*, Navarro observes that the degree of tightness of interlaced fingers shows the level of anxiety that the person is experiencing. 'People who are feeling more insecure will press their fingers tighter than those who are less anxious,' notes Unverbal (2013). All these details may appear insignificant at this level but when you are involved in serious business, they can either make or mar you, depending on the attention you give to them.

Unverbal (2013) states that this gesture is often performed subconsciously but it can be used consciously in business and social encounters, depending on what you want to achieve at every given time. Finger interlacing at the appropriate time will make people understand that you do not have confidence in what is being discussed.

A renowned love coach, Patti Wood submits that if the fingers are interlocked with the palms loosely pressed against each other in a love context, it shows a desire to connect to a spouse. She warns that this might also be a non-verbal display from someone who is awkward with holding hands, so it is a subtle means of evading that exercise.

Practical Illustrations

Case Study I: Mr J was in an interview for the position of an assistant general manager. He wanted to quit his job with a start-up where he was acting as the head of the organisation. Believing that his experience of the years would make him secure the job he was eyeing; he went with confidence. During the interview, he was very articulate with his points and also made use of the hands to make emphasis from time to time. For most of the duration, his hands were interlaced with his thumbs pointing up but it got to a point where the interviewers needed to know how vast he was in managing people from different backgrounds and immediately, his thumbs pointed downward as he answered the question. This was clear to the panellists that he was less confident in his response.

Case Study II: Mrs K left home for a party without informing her husband and even abandoned the children alone at home. Mr K was devastated to meet his children in a lonely state. When he enquired about their mother, the kids informed him that she went out with her friends. At that point, he knew it was a group of friends that she just came across. When she eventually returned home, he asked her where he went for hours without bothering to inform any member of the family. Her hands could be seen interlocked with the thumbs pressed together as she offered an unconvincing explanation. This alone gave her out.

Case Study III: Ms TR was arrested with some other illegal workers in an industrial area; they had no official permit to work in the country but they liaised with some compromised elements to operate freely in the country. When she was being interrogated, just like many of her colleagues, she was uninspiring. The explanations sounded so boring that it would take eternity to make sense out of it. While TR was talking, she unconsciously interlocked her hands and pressed the thumbs so hard together, facing downward. This was a display of lack of confidence. After few minutes, she eventually confessed of her involvement in an illegal act.

19.28. Rubbing Thumb

Generic Interpretations of the Concept

Massaging is one of the most known acts of pacifying. We tend to massage some given parts of the body, knowing fully well that they soothe the entire body. The thumb is one of those parts. The subtlety that accompanies this gesture normally makes it go unnoticed most times. Thus, the reason it is referred to as a mild pacifier. When the hands are interlocked, pay attention to the thumb placement. If one is placed on the other, then the one on top is probably made to rub over the one beneath. Depending on the degree of arousal of negative stimulus, this action can be performed repeatedly. As the action soothes them, they tend to continue with this action; they may not even face the side so that they do not call people's attention to it.

This behaviour is usually observed when people await the occurrence of an event; this means they are enveloped in suspense because they do not know what awaits them on the occurrence of an event. For instance, the finalists in an event may display this cue as they wait on the judges to make the final announcement. This cue helps in calming the body while the person focuses on the event ahead. This is mild because not the entire hands are involved.

Also, people may display this cue as they talk. This is evidence that they are somewhat anxious or nervous. Since this gesture would look very awkward when displayed while standing, people tend to demonstrate it while sitting. However, the posture does not necessarily change the message of the cue.

Scientific Explanations

Philip (2013) observes that this cue can also be extended to the massaging of the palms. The body language expert submits that this cue 'indicates a person who is in doubt, has low confidence, or is experiencing stress.' These three can be noticed in different situations. Recalling the illustration I gave above, if the finalist does not really have the confidence that he would emerge the eventual winner, you will observe this gesture in them; it is more or less of a self-consolation cue in this regard. If the tension is very minimal, the person may also stroke the palms but as it grows further, it moves from being palm stroking to thumbs massaging. The position of the thumbs might even be interchanged so that both can be massaged from time to time. This means there is higher level of anxiety; the more anxious we are, the more intense we rub the thumbs together.

Philip states that whether palm or thumbs massaging, both actions indicate that there is an underlying emotional discomfort which the person wants to sooth. He concludes by admonishing that 'as conversations intensify watch for increases in soothing body language revealing the underlying anxiety'. This will make you informed throughout the conversation, at least, you tend to understand the person better than what they say verbally.

Westside Toastmasters (2019) says that this gesture is a symbolism for expectancy. Since the thumb is usually involved in counting of money, rubbing it means the person is expecting the inflow of cash or some other thing. If this is accompanied by laughter, it means the person is really high and excited about their expectation. However, this gesture is slightly different from the fingers-interlacing cue. So the meaning cannot be assumed to be the same in the context of the above.

Practical Illustrations

Case Study I: Student E is the representative of his school in an inter-school essay competition. The competition is organised by the government; it is given the needed media coverage and at some point, the organisers needed to add debate to it in order to thrill the thousands of audiences following the event. Eventually, Student E makes it to the final round where he has to prove himself among students from other revered schools. On the day fixed for the event, every television outfit in the nation hooked up to them. The essay was written in public and after some minutes, they were called for the debate. Then, they judge declared a ten-minute break so that they could compute the results. While many of those at the venue moved about during the break, the contestants sat glued to the chairs, looking expectant. Student E interlocked his fingers and rubbed the thumb repeatedly. While he was expectant, yet he was engrossed in fear.

Case Study II: Mr W was one of the three workers of FRQ Services invited by the disciplinary team of the firm to come and explain themselves in alleged unprofessional behaviour. Of a truth, Mr W was not involved in the theft at the beginning but the other two workers discovered that there was no way they could succeed in their assignment without his involvement. So they lured him into it through enticing promises. Even after they had successfully committed the crime, they abandoned him without giving him his own portion. But it would amount to self-accusation to confess his involvement in whatever respect. Since he was compelled to make a statement or plead guilty, as he was trying to carefully explain himself, he interlocked his fingers and placed the right thumb over the left, using the former to continuously rub the latter; he was really anxious.

Case Study III: Summer break is fast approaching and Child H wants to enjoy it all alone; he picked a venue that was not favoured by either of his parents. However, his parents were reluctant to let him go because he abused the opportunity the last time he was given—he travelled to another place without considering it worthy to inform them and even spent more than the number days planned. Being the only child of his parents, he is so precious to them that he himself does not know what do prompt their actions sometimes. On the issue of vacation, he was also aware of the fact that he had blew his chances when last he was given. So he was not confident to approach them. On a night, his parents were at the dining and he went there as if he wanted to eat too. Placing his hands on the table, he rubbed his thumbs as he appealed to them to grant his desire, promising not to disappoint this time around. While saying this, it was obvious that he was nervous too as he did not know what his parents' response would be.

Case Study IV: Prostitute EG has never been to GXR Hotel all through her ten years of being a prostitute. The little findings she made about the place was frightening but that was the only place her client suggested for their meeting. She would have let go, but she needed money urgently to settle some bills. The client came late and while she was awaiting him at the solitary hotel, many thoughts were flying on her mind which made her nervous. Unconsciously, she interlocked her hands and began to rub her thumbs against each other. When she contemplated leaving, the man finally showed up. Yet, this did not entirely wash the fear off her.

19.29. Thumb Twiddling

Generic Interpretations of the Concept

When you see someone rotate their thumb, do not overlook it or mistake it as a show off, especially when done in a context that requires seriousness. Although this might not count on the surface level, it is a signal that the person is going through some stress. When we are stressed, there are numerous ways which it can be dealt with. The twirling of the thumbs might be a means of passing the time while you await the decision of someone. So instead of being totally focused on the action or what your fate would be, you decide to play with the thumb by rotating it.

This may also serve as a means of dealing with stress. If you are anxious about something but you do not want it to weigh you down for different reason, you can decide to lift off your heart from it by focusing on other activities such as twirling of the thumb. This can be soothing when done repeatedly. I have seen people do it as they ruminate over an action. By so doing, the mind becomes light for stimulation of ideas as the stress has been taken off through the action of thumb twirling.

Although the two thumbs can be twirled simultaneously, most people do twirl one so as not to call the attention of those around them to their emotional distress. This is one of the most subtle ways of fighting stress; it is usually overlooked by people because it does not involve the act of touching any other part of the body, not even the closest finger. The fingers are somewhat spread out, giving the thumb the opportunity to rotate freely. If the person is talking while displaying this cue simultaneously, they may be a little bit distracted because this action may also be calling their attention. And if they are thinking, they will look into the distant.

Scientific Explanations

Christopher Philip (2010) simply states that thumb twiddling is 'A subconscious gesture indicating boredom where the interlocked fingers support the task of thumbs circling one another.' A point emphasised in the above quote is that it is used to showcase boredom. When we are bored and looking for the best way to deal with it without sleeping, we can make use of this gesture; it is soothing and can make the body active when done repeatedly.

Tip Hero (2019) shares the same opinion with Philip that this gesture means a person is bored. However, the platform goes ahead to explain that this gesture also connotes 'high anxiety'. This really makes sense and is symbolic too. For instance, this stressed out generation spends substantial time on their phones and other devices by mimicking this gesture; the act of scrolling the screen of your device is equivalent to twiddling of the thumbs. This generation greatly relies on phone to deal with stress; once they are connected to social media, they imbibe another life, thereby disconnecting themselves from what might have occurred offline. Different people have different opinions on this but that is not the focus of this topic.

According to Hayes Justin (2008), 'Thumb twiddling is an activity that is done with the hands of an individual whereby the fingers are interlocked and the thumbs circle around a common focal point, usually in the middle of the distance between the two thumbs. While it is an expression of at least a moderate amount of manual dexterity, thumb twiddling is frequently used as an example of a useless, time-wasting activity.' Well, if done for the purpose of dexterity, one will quickly agree with the postulation of Hayes that this gesture is of no essence but if we are to take the two earlier submissions into account, we cannot trivialise the role it plays in fighting boredom. In medical line, this can be used for the simple test of manual dexterity.

Soph Laugh (2016) says that this activity is common to those suffering from obsessive-compulsive disorder. He also notes that it may be an aftermath of anxiety, nervousness, or boredom. It may also be the habit of some people.

In casual or sporting situation, this may be a way of confirming that an action is right. Africans are fond of this; they would twirl the thumb and smile alongside in confirming that they like what someone just did. It is pertinent to note that this is not often a repetitive action as the one done when one is bored or anxious.

Practical Illustrations

Case Study I: Mr P was sent by his firm to make an observation in the marketplace and hear the comments on people on a particular product that their firm has just released. He hates going on fieldworks that have to do with walking around and communicating randomly with people. But he does not have choice than to bring a verifiable feedback to the office. While prancing about in an area believed to be discussion hotspot, he became bored when the people were discussing another topic and left that one out. Hopeful that they would later mention it, he began to twiddle his thumbs repeatedly in order to deal with boredom. He did this repeatedly until he got the piece of information he came for.

Case Study II: Student J dislikes calculation but at the elementary level, he has no choice than to take all the subjects so as to have prerequisite knowledge about them in case of the need to do related thing in the future. Any time a teacher teaching them calculation related subject comes in and spends more than thirty minutes, he begins to feel sleepy. He has been spotted and called out times without number he seems not to be ready to turn a new leaf. So he had to devise a way of dealing with the boredom so that he was no longer made an object of laughter by his colleagues. Whenever he felt what the teacher was saying was not meant for him, he would interlock his fingers and twiddle his thumb continuously till the end of the class. This was a distractive gesture that depicted someone who isn't attentive or elated about what is being said.

Case Study III: Drug Addict CT cannot do without consuming harmful drugs within an hour—his life is so given to the substance that he cannot survive a day without a specified amount of it. He was eventually picked up when he least expected. In fact, he had boasted to his colleagues that he could not be arrested. So when his arrest came so cheaply, he was unprepared for it. He was detained for about three hours in order to allow investigators prepare their questions and tactics to adopt. He became bored within an hour and pleaded with the officers in charge of his case he should be allowed to move around but he was denied this opportunity. So he sat at a corner and weaved his hands together before twiddling with his thumbs as a way of waging war against boredom.

19.30. Closing Fingers Together

Generic Interpretations of the Concept

When there are issues, the brain sends signal to every part of the body to close off. While the obvious ones are usually slouching or lack of eye contact, closing of the gaps between our fingers also communicate a lot about our emotional state. There are a lot of negative feelings that can cause the closing off the space between the fingers. One, when we are humbled, we tend to lessen the space in the fingers. Being embarrassed makes the body to become weak and slouching; we lose our strength and the hands which is considered as our major instrument of self-expression becomes very weak that it closes up itself.

Feeling of bewilderment may also lead to this gesture. When taken aback by the occurrence of an event, we tend to keep to ourselves so as to have a full view of the baffling incident. Stretching out the hands may pass the message of readiness which is not intended at the given time. Being bewildered makes us think beyond our present situations and we cannot do this when at the same time, our body is let loose.

Anxiety is another probable reason you may see this cue. Being gripped by fear will make you disconnect yourself from the outside world. When a person is scared, you will get to know by the way in which they carry themselves. Someone who is excited will be loose and ready to welcome you; their body language behaviour will attract you to them. However, if scared, they will rather look the other way, closing the fingers as if they are rejecting what you are about to offer them. In the same vein, being concerned about something, overwhelmed by thoughts and taken over by negative emotions may make the fingers to subconsciously close off.

When the stress or anxiety is on the high side, people tend to curl their fingers. By this, they will not stick out for the other party to see. Whenever you see this, it is evidence of the limbic brain at work; it does not want to expose our fingers to an alleged threat. This action is automatic and, as such, an accurate indicator of the emotional feeling of the person displaying it.

Scientific Explanations

All the scholars that contributed to this concept are unanimous in their submissions that closing the fingers together is a representation of negative stimulus. Hanan Parvez (2019) says that this gesture can either be displayed when the hands are placed on a lap, desk or even when held in front of the body. It signifies self-restraint; the person does not want to dip their hands into something or an idea that is considered threatening. Parvez notes that this is symbolic manner of holding a negative reaction back, usually frustration, anger or anxiety. When a co-interlocutor is subconsciously reducing the gap between their fingers during a conversation, this is an indication that they are no longer feeling positive about what is being said. When the fingers are eventually curled up, it means the negative feeling has considerably increased.

Parvez observes that 'this gesture is usually done when a person feels that they are failing to convince the other person or are anxious about what they saying or hearing'. If you really are about the feeling of the person—you are sympathetic to their course—you can step in by calming them down. With this, you will help them break the negative feeling.

Nicolas Fradet (2016) observes that this gesture is employed to deal with stress. Being overly in an anticipation of something, whether positive or negative can lead to stress. However, the closing off of the fingers is propelled by negative feelings.

Changing Minds (2019) tries to be more diversified in its interpretation of this gesture. It submits that 'fingers held together and curled upwards form a cup that can contain things more securely than the plate. Relaxed fingers form a loose cup, whilst tense fingers form a more closed cup.' So at the literal viewpoint, this is made to contain something more securely. When they are also tensed due to stress, they form the cup shape. This interpretation is balanced. When people want to plead for something, they tend to form this shape with both hands; it draws the sympathetic emotion of their target person.

Practical Illustrations

Case Study I: Suspect O is a naturally scared person; he gets on his toes on the slightest attack. He was unfortunate to be at a location where violence erupted and was nabbed by enforcement officials that went there to restore normalcy. Before being arraigned in court, they were all interviewed so as to gather evidence of their involvement against them. Before the interrogation started, a senior officer addressed all the suspect and told them on the need to cooperate with them so that they will not aggravate issues for themselves. With this, Suspect O thought that they had to plead guilty even if they knew nothing about the incident. When invited in, he was offered a handshake which he frighteningly received. While sitting down, his fingers could be seen closing together. This exposed him as being scared. So the officers had to calm him down before they eventually started the questioning session.

Case Study II: Ms TY had just graduated from the college and, as such had no work experience but she had always loved teaching. So she applied to a nearby school and fortunately for her, she was recruited. The interview process was a little bit tedious but students were on holidays, so she had a mock class with just five teachers within five minutes. On the first day of resumption, she learnt that there was an average of twenty-five students in the class she was to teach. The number was alarming to her and when she entered the class, the faces of the students looked 'intellectual'; suffering from low self-esteem, she looked down on herself at the moment. As she made way to the front of the class to address them, her fingers could be seen closing together. However, the students were oblivious of this body language cue. Hence, they could not seize the opportunity to ask her questions that could expose her weaknesses.

Case Study III: Mr YR is a greenhorn in politics. People who know him well attested to the fact that he is a quiet person and doesn't want addressing crowd. However, there is no way he can succeed in his new found love without being an astute public speaker. At first, he rejects TV interviews but as time for election draws nearer, he sees the inevitability of being on the screen. On his first day of appearance, he begins to unconsciously close his fingers. The presenter sees this and offers him water in order to calm him down a little bit before going into the programme proper. The presenter knew that the programme was not going to be an interesting one with an obvious display of nervousness by his guest.

19.31. Thumb Out

Generic Interpretations of the Concept

When the thumb stands out of all the other fingers, this is an indication of positivity. In many parts of the world, attention is always given to the thumb out of the five fingers; the way in which it behaves per time can tell us the feelings of a person. When the thumb moves away from the index finger, this is an expression of confidence. You will easily take note of this when the hand is placed on a table. Pay rapt attention to the distance between the thumb and index finger in order to know a person is feeling concerning a topic under discussion. This cue is subconscious and keeping tab on it makes you be in control of the discussion; the person might not even be aware of the behaviour.

To better confirm how confident a person about what they are saying, you can use the gap between the index finger and thumb as a gauge. I would not like this to appear as a gimmick or magic to you; our brain has always found the hands as one of the easiest means of communicating our feelings to the world. So expressing confidence through the distancing of the thumb should not be seen as something that is out of comprehension.

Also, paying attention to this cue will help you determine the level of commitment of a person to what they have just said. When the distance between the thumb and index finger is close, this means the person is somewhat sceptical about what you have been told. However, if the distance is wide, this means the person is truly committed to their assertions. We need to understand all these intricacies as we deal with people on a daily basis so that we would not always be caught at the odd side of life. If you can be a master of communication, your destiny is surely secure.

Scientific Explanations

Philip (2010) observes that those who normally want to appear important and respected are those who are fond of displaying the thumb. There is a sort of royalty that is attached to the thumb out cue. It is unusual for you to see people tuck their hands in their pocket and leave out only the thumb; this is to show the world how big and confident they are. Hence, Philip concludes that 'thumbs-out is a representation of ego, dominance, assertiveness and sometimes even aggressiveness. Denotes superiority.' Although the message might need to be adjusted in order to fit into a given context, it does not change from the aforelisted. The ultimate message is show of superiority; the person is trying to say that they are better than every other person within sight.

Changing Minds (2019) also lends a voice to this concept. The website asserts that marking out the thumbs out of every other finger is used to show approval. This means your thought aligns with what the other person is saying. Even when some parts of the body are crossed but the thumb stands out, this still expresses subtle confidence. This can also be an invitation for others to show enthusiasm in what you are saying. When you feel that someone is not fully committed to what you are telling them, this may be a non-verbal means of appealing to them, to consider the need to approve your submission as being right.

The body language platform further observes that this gesture means someone is in control or being relaxed. When you are not bothered about anything, you will freely distance the thumb or even all the fingers from one another, allowing space as much as possible; this is an open body language that accompanies positive behaviours. Also, when a person feels to be in control of an activity, they will demonstrate this cue; if there are people challenging their authority in the gathering, this is a subtle call to them to bow for the person. Hence, Changing Minds concludes, 'It can thus be both a sign of authority and also of friendliness.' The context determines which is which; if it is done among subordinates, it is a show of authority but if done in a family or among friends, it expresses friendliness.

Practical Illustrations

Case Study I: The general manager of TQC Enterprises was absent from work and had to tell one of the supervisors to take charge of their weekly meeting. Being the most senior supervisor makes most of the workers to respect but other supervisors do feel they are in the same cadre and, as such, does not deserve their respect. During the meeting, the supervisor in charge saw the uncooperative attitude of some of his colleagues and he had to put his hands on the table and distanced his thumb from the index finger as a mark of confidence and authority.

Some of them got this clue and quickly adjusted, especially when they saw the seriousness on his face.

Case Study II: Mr U was conversing with a colleague during break; they were reminiscing on their childhood days and educational background. Since Mr U was on his desk, it was his colleague that was standing. The former also dominated the discussion. At some point, he would hit his hand on the table and spread out the thumb in order to show the importance of the point he was making. He was able to hold his colleague's attention throughout the discourse with the aid of this gesture. The latter also expressed optimism in what he told him due to the unconscious display of confidence that got registered in his limbic brain.

Case Study III: A man was wrongly accused of a criminal offence. After some days in detention, he was taken to the interview room to be interrogated. He seemed undeterred as he had his seat gently and looked around the room with a breath of confidence. While answering the questions thrown to him, he placed his hand on his lap and spread the thumb out subconsciously, displaying confidence along the line.

19.32. Withdrawing of Thumb

Generic Interpretations of the Concept

This appears to be the polar opposite of the preceding topic. Unlike the thumb out cue that is used to portray confidence, dominance, ego and authority, when the thumb is withdrawn, it is used in passing a negative message; it is an indication that the person is witnessing some internal discomfort. Thumb withdrawal is categorised under closed body gestures—the body becomes smaller when it is closed off.

This cue is a subconscious action done when we are faced with a threatening or frightening situation; when threatened, the limbic brain feels that the thumb is too exposed and may become a victim of attack, so it quickly moves it from the open and tucks under the other fingers. Sometimes, it may be pressed firmly against the index finger, the message still remains the same. If the person is overwhelmed by the negative emotion, the thumb would be suddenly withdrawn. This means that you should also pay attention to how rapid or otherwise the thumb changes position so as to understand how the person is feeling exactly; if the threat is considered as being minor, the thumb will gradually move inward but if it is very scary, the movement would be sudden.

This is one of the flight or freeze responses; it is a survival tactic meant to secure every vital part of the body capable of being attacked. You will understand this better if you have ever seen a dog tuck its ear down in order to streamline itself in order to hide or prepare for a fight. To hide, it becomes smaller because the ears are his most exposed or pronounced body parts. Even if it would later fight, it would first of all have a comprehensive review of the situation before staging a fight. The act of withdrawing the thumb also provides us with the same opportunity.

Thumb withdrawal is a non-verbal way of communicating our reluctance to attack to a threatening situation. Keeping to ourselves is a form of submitting ourselves to the situation that is causing fear in us.

Scientific Explanations

Christopher Philip (2014) discusses the cue in details. He mentions the two ways in which this cue can be displayed thus: 'Placing the thumb of the same hand inside the clasped fingers, or placing only the thumbs in a pants pocket with the remainder out.' When you see either of these two gestures, it means the person is insecure. The verbal translation is given as 'I'm insecure, timid, or feel social discomfort so I'm hiding my thumbs from view.' In most regions of the world, this message is the same. When the biggest and most pronounced finger is tucked in, it is a sure sign that the person is not feeling good. It is the polar opposite to the thumb display cue. You observe this in people of low status who are not confident; they look down on themselves and feel intimidated by what the other person is saying or doing. This is the motivation that drives people which you must always take cognisance of when discussing with someone.

Although this is a negative cue that should be avoided by all means, I must add that it is not usually noticed by people. So if this is what makes you comfortable, you should feel free to do it. However, when you are in the presence of a large audience, this should be avoided by all means because it portrays you as someone who lacks confidence and uninspiring. In this sense, all things might be permissible but not all things are good. When you are within the circle of friends, there is nothing holding you back but while addressing wider audience, they want to see your hands and how you use them in conveying your message.

Practical Illustrations

Case Study I: Mrs D and K have been friends since their childhood days and even after marriage, they still kept their friendship. This made their children, Y and T to become friends too. Y, the son of Mrs D has always been around while T, the daughter of K went abroad for schooling. When she returned, she had already changed. On a weekend, she made out time to say 'hello' to the family of Mrs D. so, Mrs D reintroduced her to Y who could not recognise her again. Y blushed and stuffed his thumbs into his back pocket, put his head down; although they were childhood friends, T had grown up to the extent that he could hardly approach her again. The non-verbal act of stuffing the thumbs into the pocket is a way of expressing his mind that he has lost the confidence to commune with her the way they used to in the past.

Case Study II: As part of the activities marking the end of study programme at DTC College, students are expected to do presentation on their thesis. External examiners are always invited to assess the students and the quality of their thesis. It is usually a stiff, tormenting and troubling time for the students because their intellectual acumen is subjected to test and if they should fail at that point, they may need to spend extra years at the school. For this year, WS is part of the final year students. He is a nervous person and this has affected him in almost every area of life. When it was his turn to present, even though he had a spectacular work, his presentation was uninspiring and the panellists were not hesitant to inform him that he would do the entire presentation again. When he heard this, he balled up his fist and tucked his thumb inside his palm. This was a show of negative feeling—he was eroded of his self-confidence.

Case Study III: As a teenage boy approaching eighteen years of age, DU was about to approach a girl for love for the first time in his life. So he remembered the scenes in movies, coupled with his instincts, he decided to approach her; he tucked his thumbs in his pockets and leave out other fingers. Thinking he was cool with this, he did not know that his hidden insecurity has been revealed to those who understand how to decode non-verbal cues.

Case Study IV: Ms RK was deceived by her fiancé that he had legal residency permit in his country of residence, and as such, he could invite people over. Since she was in a haste to join him, she didn't bother to ask relevant questions. On getting to the said country, she was given a work that was demeaning to her status. He urged her to take it as it as things are often difficult for immigrants at first. She was later arrested and when asked to offer explanations, she tucked in her thumbs into her palms and looked dejected; she was naïve and lacking in confidence.

19.33. General Thumb Display

Generic Interpretations of the Concept

When you observe a general display of the thumbs in any form, it is an indication that the person is 'full of life'. There are different means in which people employ to make their thumbs visible. For instance, some may adjust the lapel pin on their chest just to make the thumb visible to the person looking at them. Some may hold on to pant suspenders. Whether this action is conscious or not, it shows that the person is open, which is itself a message to the audience.

If they were threatened by something, the thumbs would have been tucked into their pockets or hidden under other fingers. Even in the face of obvious necessity to adjust the lapel pin, they will ignore it.

I have always noticed this unrivalled display of confidence among attorneys while in court; they understand that before you can convince a person, you must be confident and prove that you have a grasp of the course you are defending. So the display of thumbs as a mark of confidence is more or less like an ingrained attribute to those in the legal field. I have also seen this among experienced teachers too. Once your work has to do with facing the public and establishing your point in a way that sends strong message to the other person, then, thumb display may be a part of you.

Note that the person will not display the thumbs in a distracting manner. The main purpose is to convey confidence and not to impede the primary message that the person wants to pass across. Having a full view of an interlocutor's thumbs will trigger you to believe what they are saying or doing at that particular point in time. In a way, I can say this is a confirmation of a person's thoughts as being real.

Scientific Explanations

Hanan Parvez (2015) also the importance of the thumbs. The expert observes that apart from an advanced brain, the presence of opposable thumbs in humans has made us record unprecedented achievements. This is to tell you how indispensable the thumbs are. Most primates—monkeys, chimpanzees and gorillas also have opposable thumbs but they cannot move them farther apart from the fingers as done by humans. Little did you know that through these superior thumbs, we have been able to make tools, construct complicated structures, and undertake other endeavours that would have been otherwise impossible. The thumbs are also instrumental to our ability to write, hence, birthing written form of communication. Being the most physically powerful out of all the fingers, the thumb display is used to convey the messages of power, superiority and dominance.

Parvez aptly submits that 'when someone displays their thumb in non-verbal communication, it is a clear indication that the person is feeling powerful and superior. Thumb displays are often accompanied by other body language gestures but they can also appear in isolation.' What makes this cue reliable in its interpretation is that it can be read in isolation. Anyone who displays their thumb is passing the message that they are better off.

The most ubiquitous of all thumb displays is the thumbs up cue. This is used to mean that one is powerful and one can undertake some assignments thought to have been otherwise impossible. Parvez states that fire fighters make use of this cue to reassure their colleagues of their readiness to attack a given territory. Depending on the context, thumb display may also mean that something is amazingly done. 'You will often see males displaying their thumbs when they want to give the impression that they are 'powerful' or 'cool'. They put their hands in their pockets and have their thumbs protruding out of them, be it pockets of the pants or a coat,' Parvez opines.

As earlier noted, thumb display may also include other clusters. 'For instance, when a person crosses his arms he's feeling defensive but if his thumbs point upward, it means he's feeling defensive but wants to give the impression that he's cool.' If this is actually done well, it would be difficult for those watching you to know that you are only displaying the gesture to cover up your insecurity.

In its own submission, Magical Apparatus (2019) refers to palmistry where the thumb is used to connote ego and strength of a person. The platform furthers by giving a practical explanation of the use of the gesture by saying thus: 'Thumb displays are positive signals, often used in the typical pose of the 'cool' manager who uses them in the presence of subordinates. A courting man uses them in the presence of a potential female partner and they are common among people who wear high-status or prestige clothing. People wearing new, attractive clothing use thumb displays more frequently than those who wear older, outdated clothing.' This has given you a clue of where you can become conscious of the use of the cue in your daily interactions with people.

Magical Apparatus notes that this gesture becomes most pronounced when the person displaying it gives a contradictory verbal message. I will expatiate on this under the 'Practical Illustrations' segment.

Practical Illustrations

Case Study I: To understand the illustration of the contradictory verbal message as explained in the preceding paragraph, Magical Apparatus gives an example thus: 'A lawyer turns to the jury and in a soft, low voice says, 'In my humble opinion, ladies and gentlemen of the jury . . .' while displaying dominant thumb gestures and tilting back his head to 'look down his nose.' This has the effect of making the jury feel that the lawyer is insincere, even pompous. If the lawyer wished to appear humble, he should have approached the jury with one foot towards them, his coat open, an open palm display, and stooping forward a little to show humility, or even subordination to the jury.' In this illustration, we can see how body language cue can be exposing, revealing the messages that we failed to communicate verbally, even though it is the innate desire of our heart.

Case Study II: Teacher AUT does not really understand the topic he is teaching—for years, it has proven to be a difficult topic but if he should confess his weakness, he would be axed. So whenever he is teaching the topic, he is careful, slow and most times, boring. In fact, it is usually a contrastive display of his original self. To make things appear real, he would use some open body language gestures to cover up so as to get the attention of the students. For instance, he opens his fingers widely and ensures that the thumb is far apart from other fingers. But instead of this to look real to the students, it appears more like a drama to them.

Case Study III: Mr UT is being investigated for suspected forgery and with the preliminary investigations carried out, there were high hopes that he indeed committed the forgery. While being questioned, he displayed his thumbs in various was. In fact, it got to a stage whereby the attention of the investigators was drawn more to his thumbs than his face. So one of them was forced to ask him if he had an injury in the hands or not. He said yes but shook his head. This was a sign that he was lying. They knew the incessant thumb display was to distract them. Also, it was a means of lying that his thumbs didn't sign the alleged documents.

19.34. Making OK sign

Generic Interpretations of the Concept

We need to be careful on the kind of interpretations we give to the 'thumb up' gesture due to cultural peculiarities. Let me put it out straight that it is in the United States of America that the gesture is used positively to mean approval for something done. I have also observed that it is used in some other countries for the same purpose. However, in the Middle East and other parts of the world where they share similar cultures, a raised thumb is considered phallic symbol and, as such, should be avoided like a plague in order not to put yourself in trouble.

Having said that, let's be grounded in the cultures where the raising the thumb is regarded as a mark of positive gesture. When the thumb is raised, it is passing a non-verbal message of positive feeling which is received in the same manner by the other party. If the sender was not happy with what their co-interlocutor said or did, they will hide their thumb. Even though this cue is a stand-alone gesture, you can look at reactions of other parts of the body in order to confirm if your conclusion is right or not. Genuine smile (that creates wrinkling of both sides of the face), relaxed facial expression, and general open body cues are some of the clusters that usually accompany this behaviour.

Note that when the thumb (usually, the right one) rises up, the other four fingers will curl up, making the thumb very obvious to observers. When someone is far off and you think raising your voice to give your approval may sound improper, you may use this cue to show your confirmation for their action. This behaviour is often seen on the football pitch where the coach uses it to praise the action of a player when the game is on. The person may smile or nod in return to show that they got the message being passed across. This behaviour can also be used in boardrooms and every other context that requires giving approval in a pronounced non-verbal way. It can even be used as a 'thank you' signal if you like something done to you by a partner.

In conclusion, this can be done either through conscious or subconscious means. When it is subconsciously displayed, it is evidence of the sincerity of the message.

Scientific Explanations

Oktent Arika (2013) observes, 'While it is not known exactly how the OK gesture and the corresponding verbal expression coalesced, the English professor Allen Walker Read dates the expression's rise in usage to an 1839 humor piece in the *Boston Morning Post* describing the expression "o.k." as meaning "all correct", suggesting comically misspelled initials, at a time when acronyms for misspelled words were in vogue.' Due to the brevity of this segment, we will not be able to explore the historical segment further.

Gayle Cotton (2013) warns that this cue should not be used in multicultural context due to the negative implications that it bears in some parts of the world. He notes that this can be one of the major causes of cultural faux pas. If you are an international business person and fail to heed to this, it can sabotage you in an unexpected manner. Cotton (2013) explains thus: 'People from every culture, including various country leaders and several U.S. presidents, have been guilty of unintentionally offending people from different cultures through the use of inappropriate gestures. When it comes to body language gestures, the wisest advice might be to *keep your fingers to yourself!*' This may sound impossible or not plausible enough but it is the wisest piece of advice; do not use cues that bear different meanings in different parts of the world when you do not know the meaning it bears across board. With this, you will perfectly play the preventive role.

Parvez (2015) gives an explicit explanation of the gesture. He covers different areas in which the gesture can be displayed by opining that 'in most cultures, this hand gesture means, "Everything's okay", "I have it under control", "I'm powerful". When a fighter pilot is ready for take-off, he makes this hand gesture to re-assure his fellow troops asking if he's ready to go for it. When a stand-up comedian concludes a brilliant act, his brother in the audience does this gesture to say, non-verbally, "Your performance was amazing and powerful."'

The body language expert is quick to re-echo the message that this is offensive in some Mediterranean cultures. Apart from that, it is only used to denote 'one' in some European nations as they begin their figure counting starting from the thumb. Men are fond of using this gesture when they want to show that they are cool or powerful.

This behaviour can also be part of a gesture cluster which also includes other gestures bearing some other emotions. 'For instance, when a person crosses his arms he's feeling defensive but if his thumbs point upward, it means he's feeling defensive but wants to give the impression that he's cool' (Parvez 2015). You have to pay attention to such contradictory but powerful contexts.

Practical Illustrations

Case Study I: Candidate C is one of the leading contestants for the position of presidency in his country. It was his third time contesting and it appears that his chances of winning stand brighter in each occasion. He ensures that he does not miss any debate organised by different outfits. In each occasion, he goes with his wife who assesses his performance. On this particular occasion, the wife, seated beside her husband's campaign director, was filled with excitement on her husband's performance. After Candidate C's presentation, he looked at the audience, and the duo of his wife and director raised their thumbs up at him to show how happy there were about his performance—he really made them proud.

Case Study II: Mr J was on ground the day Mrs J was taking the practical session of her driving class. Looking at the scenario from afar, he was really thrilled that his wife driving prowess within a short duration. As Mrs J was alighting from the car, he smiled at her and gave out the 'OK' gesture. This means he was proud of her.

Case Study III: Smuggler RW planned on how to escape with his smuggled guys at the border before leaving their destination. The plan was that RW would be at the back to monitor how smartly the guys behave while being questioned by border officials. On getting there, the smuggled guys truly displayed a high level of knowledge and confidence. A little bit afraid while the process lasted, Smuggler RW became relieved when the smuggled boys were given a free pass. When they exchanged eye contact, RW lifted up his thumb and gave them the 'OK' gesture. This was a way of commending the boys for their performance during the interview. However, he suppressed his smile so that no one will suspect him.

19.35. Surrogate Touching

Generic Interpretations of the Concept

There are times that culture and other environmental factors stop us from doing the bidding of our hearts. If we dare defy them, we would be seen as persons of easy or low virtue. Such cultural restrictions are most pronounced in emotional relationships. For instance, many cultures of the world expect that a man should approach a woman for love and if done vice versa, the lady is seen as being too cheap and may not be taken seriously by the man. In the case of surrogate touching, at the beginning of a relationship, one may be tempted to touch their partner in order to further entrench the bond but may be considered too early for that. Since one cannot totally suppress this gesture, it would be manoeuvred by transferring the hands to other objects. It is like touching by proxy.

One of the ways in which the surrogate touching is performed is by using a hand to stroke the other arm. You will see the person touching the arm as if they are massaging it. The feeling on their face will also be unsatisfactory because the action is just a make-do for them; they glance at the person they wished to touch from time to time. In some other times, the person may choose to play with an object. For instance, if there is a glass of drink in their front, they will rotate it or touch it repeatedly. Sliding the hand through a glass is transferring our feeling to the object.

Most times, this action is subconscious and is regarded as a flirting signal; if your partner is observant enough, they may quickly decode the message and make arrangements to ease your feeling. Also, being unable to touch someone we wish to, brings about stress, and as such, the surrogate touching is regarded as stress reliever. This is considered as a potent substitute for our original intent.

Scientific Explanations

Many experts and platforms explain how the hands reach out to objects to comfort themselves in times of stress. Changing Minds (2019) explains plainly, 'Hands may be used to hold items such as pens or cups, which may be used as comfort objects, for example where a person hugs a cup (the cup represents the person, so they are effectively hugging themselves). Holding an item with two hands effectively creates a closed position.' When you see the hands of someone on an object, take note of the degree of emotion let out to hold the item. When we cannot extend our physical love to an intended person, we shower it on an object within reach. When there is a contact with an object, the hand becomes pacified due to the tactile feeling. If the need to clinch to one's partner is high, we will hold the item with the two hands. If the relationship is in its early stage, this is a message of what you stand to 'gain' on the long run.

Philip (2014) also explains what this 'seemingly affectionate touch' may mean in a given circumstance. In a research by Rhonda Hadi and Ana Valenzuela published in the *Journal of Consumer Psychology*, it was established that 'positive meaning can be transferred towards a product by mere physical actions'. The fact is that with the mere touching of an object, even when we do not feel anything, shapes how our emotions, beliefs, and attitudes are created about that object. In a way, we can momentarily transfer our love for a person to an object. We tend to trivialise touch when considered at the surface level. However, you will understand it better when viewed from an angle of a consumer who wants to purchase an object; you tend to like the ones you touch compared with those touched by some other persons. This is psychological. That is why the researchers noted that their findings 'are supportive of embodied perspectives of psychology, which hold that higher order cognitions and emotions are based in, or scaffolded upon, more primitive perceptual systems.'

In a 2014 article by *The Advertiser*, it also opines that fiddling with an object by the opposite sex is an expression of love. The piece attributes playing with round objects as being common to females. It submits thus: 'If a woman is fondling a phallic-shaped object such as the stem of a wine glass or a dangling earring and giving you repeated glances, she finds you attractive.' This is also an indication that she can be approached, if the relationship is yet to start at all.

Describing it as body language at its most basic level, when people unconsciously touch themselves, *The Advertiser* says it is also a show of love. The website advises, 'Watch for a woman slowly stroking her neck, throat or thigh.' As a man, if you play along well, you may end up touching those parts of the body.

Practical Illustrations

Case Study I: Mrs R divorced her husband on flimsy excuses because she got attracted to another man at her workplace who is widowed. She was very sure that the widower would not give her a chance because she was married. So she found a way to end the marriage so that she could take what she considered as an 'opportunity'. Even after the divorce, it seemed the widower was still blind to Mrs R. so, she deployed all cunning means to register her availability. One day, the widower eventually took her out on a date and while they were seated, Mrs R was longing for a touch with him but thought it would be too early for such, so she grabbed the wine glass on the table and glanced at the man from time to time. This communicated her innate desire to have her hands romantically on him.

Case Study II: Ms Y was really moved by the charming posture of Guy Q and she did not hide this admiration right from their meeting point. However, she was not bold enough to ask him out for love. They had the opportunity to sit for about an hour to chat and speak about life generally. All this while, Y strokes her thighs and neck repeatedly to suppress the temptation to extend her hand to him. While she was struggling with this, the man also got the clue and keyed into it.

Case Study III: Drug Addict XR was arrested with some cocaine on him. With that, he knew there was no defence he could put up to cleanse himself.

However, he was insistent that he could choose a life that pleased him without anyone having the ability to question. He even referred to it as his fundamental human rights. The officers knew he had developed some psychological issues already. So they just left him to his drama. The cocaine seized from him was placed some distance away from. He still longed to consume them. Knowing that this was impossible, he grabbed the pen on his table and fiddle with it.

19.36. Touching Each Other

Generic Interpretations of the Concept

I love the cliché that 'respect is reciprocal'. That is, the fun of life is when you do to somebody what they do to you. This makes it a fair deal. So when two people touch each other, it can be referred to as reciprocal touching. Ideally, if there is no close bond between two people, they will not touch each other. If someone touches you and you fail to return it, then the touch is not reciprocal but if, as they are reaching their hand out to you, you are also returning the gesture in the same spirit, this shows there is social harmony between you two. When people see this, they believe that your relationship is working—whether platonic or emotional. Have you ever imagined a scenario where a suspect is touching an interrogator affectionately? It is just weird! But close friends, lovers and even formidable colleagues at work exchange pleasant touches at the right time.

Reciprocal touching is a perfect emblem of comfort and when it is not reciprocated, it means the other person is feeling uncomfortable being touched. If you do not desist from the act, they may become aggressive and thus, launch a fight instead.

If you have always been touching a person and they respond reciprocally but they suddenly stop touching you of a sudden, it is time to pay attention to and evaluate the status of your relationship with them. For instance, in a work relation, if a boss has made up their mind to demote or sack an employee, they will reduce touch with the person, few months to when they plan to execute their plan. Also, in an emotional relationship, if a partner is planning a breakup, they will reduce the rate of touch in order to detach themselves from all forms of feeling they had towards the person.

Scientific Explanations

Changing Minds (2019) notes that there are different ways in which the body can be touched. One of the ways in which touching becomes reciprocal is if it is done in a romantic situation. Some parts of the body can be touched to stimulate the desired outcome. Sometimes, people touch erotic parts so as to send signals of commitment to have an affair with each other.

On a general level, 'Touching the other person can be an act of domination or of friendship, for example a hand on the shoulder whilst telling them off adds authority, whilst a gentle touch on the arm when sympathising demonstrates concern for them.' Note that the feeling becomes reciprocal when the person acknowledges and returns the posture. For instance, after a football match, the losing team will condole one another by exchanging this form of touch—by touching each other at the arm.

Anna Sandfield (2003) laments that non-reciprocal touching was a gendered behaviour. 'Non-reciprocal touching' refers to instances where one person touches another, initiating the contact and *not* getting touched back. Due to the patriarchal nature of many societies, men find it easy to touch women while it is not so if the roles are reversed, even in love context. Although men are not usually conscious of their use of this gesture, it is used to convey dominance and control. Most women, except for the uncompromising feminists, have accepted the fact that for men to exert their will, they must touch them.

Due to the modernised nature of the world, the word 'touching' may create negative impact on people's emotions, thinking of harassment. However, the reciprocal touching as explained here is a subtle one that all parties will yearn for forever. Explaining this cue in practical terms, Sandfield (2013) states recalls, 'A male acquaintance, with whom I get on well, recently "tickled" me as a joke. It is hard to resist this kind of behaviour because it is not commonly acknowledged verbally—to speak of it is to make an issue if it and risk the "frigid" label. I see men "cuddling", lifting up, grabbing, touching and "tickling" their female friends and colleagues regularly. In these instances, they are taking a culturally sanctioned opportunity to touch women's bodies without their explicit permission.' Women can also seize the opportunity of the moment to touch the person. Even exchange of handshake is a form of reciprocal touching.

Frank van Marwijk (2019) explains the power of touch. He states that touch is very close to intimacy. 'Intimacy is often expressed by the frequency and intensity of touch in combination with other signals such as: physical closeness, eye contact, smile and content of conversation. This cluster of signals gives us information about the desired level of intimacy,' he submits.

Depending on your physical closeness and how you touch each other, we can predict how intimate your relationship with someone is. People do adjust the aforelisted factors in order to help them achieve their set goals of intimacy. For instance, people may be forced to avoid eye contact when the distance between them is too small so as it will not look as if they are staring at each other. If the person is not interested in touch, they will not move closer to you.

Practical Illustrations

Case Study I: Lady K and Guy W are new couples. They are still hot in love and this is demonstrated publicly; whether outside or inside, they kiss, romance and hold each other at the hand. When they are at the bar, they will display all kinds of love through affectionate touching. On a particular occasion, they were at a restaurant where cool music was being played. As they stood to dance to the music, K placed her hand on W's arms, while the latter held her at the waist. This was a touch of elation and joy.

Case Study II: I and O are twins who grew up to love each other. They were always seen together. Being the same gender, they even wear each other's clothes. While walking, they will hold each other at the hand and take their footsteps majestically. Even if they want to sleep, they would clinch to each other. However, if one feels offended, she would ignore the need for physical contact from the second person. So even without verbal communication of their heart, the message is perfectly passed.

Case Study III: Man W and Woman Q planned to arrange a marriage of convenience for the purpose of helping Woman Q get into Country ATO. She had tried her chances for several times but she was denied visa. Since W was in the country, she saw that as an opportunity to be accepted too. After the marriage, and they went for visa interview, the officials at the embassy discovered that Woman Q would touch Man W at any given opportunity just to publicly profess that they had a romantic affair but Man W would unconsciously frown at those touches before consciously 'smiling' to cover up.

19.37. Clinching on to Furniture

Generic Interpretations of the Concept

Every now and then, you see people hold on to the edge of a chair, podium, desk or table when about to make a decision or even at the point of making it. This means something is at stake; there are issues. While some will hold the furniture lightly, others will grab it with full force. The degree in which the action is performed explains the exact feeling of the person. Those who hold to furniture with a higher level of force are really feeling insecure.

This behaviour is often displayed when people are making declarative statements. What it reveals is that they are not committed to their words or lack belief in it. When people are insecure, there is probability that the hands will shiver and thus, expose them. In order not to find themselves in this disappointing situation, they hide their insecurities by holding the furniture nearest to them. In a public presentation, you may be tricked to believe that the person is making adequate use of the podium but in the inner level, they are clinching on to it for their own sake.

I have seen this play out in different scenarios. In interrogations, suspects will hold their chair as they make faulty declarative statements. Against the popular myth that liars tend to disconnect eye contact, in this scenario, they will look into your eyes in order to assess your opinion on what they have just said—they want to know if you approve what they said or express some doubt about it. Also, I have seen this while people append their signatures on contracts that they are not willing to but under compulsion to do that. As an observer with a stake in what is being done, you have the duty of finding out what is really driving their insecurity.

Scientific Explanations

Study Body Language (2016) says holding on to furniture is a defensive body language. Insecurity and hostile attitude is revealed through the holding of something within reach. You may not really understand the significance of this gesture until you reflect your mind back to your childhood days. 'Little children who feel insecure often hide behind a piece of furniture or their mother's skirt, seeking refuge and protection,' SBL notes. However, as we mature, we begin to discover that it would be inappropriate to display this gesture, so, we tend to hold the edges of furniture to pass the message of insecurity. This is a subtle means of creating artificial barrier which conveys our lack of confidence to those who are observant enough to decode it. Since arm holding seems to be the most pronounced form of self-comfort, people now disguise that with holding of desks, lectern and edges of chairs.

Jack Brown (2016) quickly adds that not all podium-holding cues should be taken as signs of insecurity. In fact, the right form of holding should be encouraged—resting the hands lightly at both sides of the podium. Note that when a person places the hands on the back edge in a way that it becomes close to the speaker, that is when it becomes an issue. As inconsequential as this distinction sounds, it makes all the difference. When the hands are placed at the back edge rather than the sides, it mounts pressure on the person's back, revealing their insecurity. When you learn how to properly place the hands on a lectern, you will benefit from it greatly as it portrays you as someone who is authoritative and have a full grasp of what you are saying.

Marc Chernoff (2008) says the act of touching furniture should be avoided while making a declarative statement. The hands should be used in making emphasis and not in holding an item at that point. When you hold an item, it is a symbolic communication of holding back your thoughts or real feeling on the concept being discussed. We may be oblivious of our body language gestures but this does not mean that those we interact with also share in our ignorance. Although the podium is meant to support you and place your documents while addressing a large group of people, it should not turn out to be an item you hide yourself behind. At least, you are expected to lift the hands once in a while to lay emphasis on your words. Chernoff submits that 'holding objects in front of your body indicates shyness and resistance, such that you're hiding behind the objects in an effort to separate yourself from others. Instead of carrying objects in front of you, carry them at your side whenever possible.'

Apart from holding, the style in which you sit on a chair also matters a lot. If you see someone sitting on the edge of a chair, it is a clear 'indication of being mentally and physically uncomfortable' (Chernoff 2008). Not only that, this also makes a lot of people around the person feel uncomfortable too. A confident person leans forward without making use of their bottom, instead they use their back.

Practical Illustrations

Case Study I: Mr G had been serving as the managing director of FWZ Firms for the past one decade, so he surely understands the workings of the organisation and field in general. However, there is a case of a contract to be awarded out and it seems the president of the firm has an interest in it. Mr G has gone through the proposal several times and knew there would be issues along the line but the president is unrelenting in his efforts to ensure that that particular contractor gets the project. It was later learnt that the contractor has an affair with the president. Knowing fully well that things might later backlash on him if he fails to append his signature, Mr G holds the edge of his table with a hand as he approves the project for the contractor. This is a non-verbal communication of his doubt on the success of the work with the given person.

Case Study II: Passenger AL is sitting at the front of a public bus. He plies the road daily, and as such, he is used to all the drivers in that environment. However, he has never set his eyes on this particular driver. So he decides to converse with him to know more about him. It is as this point that he discovers that the driver doesn't even understand their language. AL becomes afraid that he might not know how to drive well. He unconsciously grabs the leg of his seat as if trying to secure himself from an imaginary impending hazard. He remains in this position until they get to their destination. This depicted how fearful he was.

Case Study III: Ms WP was arrested for working illegally in Country AIW. She denies this fact, noting that she had student permit to be in the country and, as such, could work there. This explanation was demeaning to the officers in charge of her case because they believed that she should know better, being a learnt fellow. She gives other incoherent points to back up her decision but looking at the faces of the investigators, she was not sure if they were convinced enough to release her. She unconsciously held on to the leg of her chair as if she would fall without supporting it with her hand. This communicates her doubt and nervousness to the officers.

19.38. Holding Attitudes

Generic Interpretations of the Concept

Stress or fear can make people do the unthinkable. While adults have developed means of hiding their insecurities, children do react to them in a 'raw form'. That is, they do not know how to hide their insecurities. Once they are stressed, they look for ways to comfort themselves. One of the techniques they deploy is clinging or holding attitude. When you are walking with a child in the dark, he or she will grab your clothing to have assurance of your presence until they pass the thick forest; this is a comforting act. If it were to be home, some of them will hide behind chairs or other items they believe are strong enough to give them the desired protection.

It should be noted that children also take cognisance of the person to cling to. For instance, while stressed, they would not run to a stranger because they do not trust the person; at that point, they need a trusted relative they believe should be able to act as a guard to them. In the absence of a close relative, they will hold on to their clothing as if it were a security blanket—it is symbolically serving as such in this context.

What soothes them in this scenario is the tactile experience of exchanging thought with another person or even a piece of clothing item. This psychologically informs them that there is someone or something close by.

Sometimes, adults also get this tactile feeling when they are preparing for an interview or speech presentation. Preparing to undertake an official activity where much is expected from you usually induces fear in a person. As a way of dealing with it, some adults may decide to hold can handkerchief while they perform on stage. This may look meaningless to others but it is actually comforting the holder. A great artiste had said in several interviews that holding a handkerchief while singing before an audience gives him a sense of security and comfort. During stress, the body craves for clinging to a person or object in order to be pacified.

Scientific Explanations

Social Dynamics (2019) explains holding behaviour under arms/hands body language. The website notes that this can be done by either a kid or an adult.

Using desks or chairs as its example, Social Dynamics observes that this is used as a show of insecurity. When we are feeling uncomfortable, we tend to seek protection by all means. The verbal translation of the gesture is *'This situation is very unfamiliar.'* If you encounter an unfamiliar situation, you may have to re-assess it several times before making up your mind on what the next step is. The social platform explains that 'we cling to objects when we seek protection. They serve as a barrier and holding on keeps our hands under control. At the same time, this gesture takes the freedom to move. This gesture should be avoided in presentations, so the speaker remains flexible.' If you display it repeatedly, your audience will see you as being rigid and read negative meanings to your posture. This makes them lose interest and trust in your presentations.

Iris Goldsztajn (2015) notes that women tend to display this behaviour while in a relationship, especially with a guy they are too fond of. Describing this as 'cat-and-mouse dating game', the writer notes that it can be exhausting. Clinging behaviour makes partners look desperate in a relationship. This is different from being flirty. Ladies love to be pampered and cared for in a relationship. As such, they tend to behave in a way that makes them dependent on the man. If such a girl should text her man and he does not respond, she becomes nervous. Also, a clingy lady will follow her man around. 'Following a guy around is pretty much the definition of clingy behaviour,' states Goldsztajn. This may actually be harmless but can be annoying to their spouse.

Lisa Shield (2019) states that clinging attitude shows that one is less confident. Many people that are clingy can be uninspiring; they do not believe in themselves and only have hope of survival when they are close to another person. They have low self-esteem and take every behaviour personal. Even without anything pursuing them, you see clingy person taking to their heels. Until they get over this feeling, they will always feel negative about themselves and what they stand to represent.

Practical Illustrations

Case Study I: The parents J, K and R travelled, leaving them at home due to their schooling. J, 14, being the eldest child is believed be grown up enough to take care of her siblings for the three days the parents were on trip. At night, when R, the youngest of them wanted to ease himself, he heard the sounds of birds behind the home while everywhere was silent, he held on to himself for a minute but when it seemed the sounds were increasing, he was forced to wake J from her sleep whom she held tightly as she led him to the shower. This means the boy was really afraid.

Case Study II: M is an up-and-coming artiste. For the past three years, he had only had the opportunity to perform in the presence of small group of people.

However, he had an unexpected invite to perform in the most watched live performance in his country. Even though it was an invite he had always dreamt of, he was still engulfed in fear, especially when he saw how the crowd went agog after the performance of the first three artistes. When it was almost getting to his turn, he brought out his handkerchief and held on to it until he was done with the performance. During the performance, he waved it at the audience. The crowd thought this was to charge them up, not knowing it was to serve as a *comforter*. M revealed that the handkerchief provided him with a sense of security through the performance and stabilised him for concentration.

Case Study III: Man PZA impersonated a relative who is highly positioned in the society in order to allow him travel and have access to some rare privileges. Before setting out on the journey, he had rehearsed very well on how to defend the documents with him. He even had some photocopies with him, in case the original is collected at any given point. He went as far as injuring himself so as to look exactly like his relative he was impersonating. However, he could not pull through at the last checkpoint. When he was accused of impersonation, he quickly brought out the photocopied documents with him and held on to it tightly as if he had the final say on the issue. This was a show of nervousness and disbelief that he could still be fished out despite 'perfecting' everything.

19.39. Making Emphasis with Hands

Generic Interpretations of the Concept

The primary duty of the hands in communication is to lay emphasis on what someone is saying verbally. That is, hand gestures are expected to align with verbal utterances in order to pass across the right message. Let me state for the umpteenth time that when the hands do not agree with the mouth on what is being said, it is an indication that there are issues. This does not necessarily mean the person is telling lies but they may not be confident enough to express the wish of their heart.

When we are comfortable without being overtaken by fear or other threatening situations, we tend to gesticulate with the hands. This is a universal body language cue that sends a message of conformity, flexibility and sincerity. However, the hands are used more in some cultures over the other. For instance, in the Mediterranean cultures, they make use of the hands more than many other regions of the world. This is usually done more emphatically in order to show how they are committed to what is being said. The significance of the gestures is more pronounced when subjected to the right context.

Generally, it has been observed that celebrated public speakers are also good users of the hand gestures; they make use of the hands to lay emphasis on their message. This makes a discourse very active as audience have a pictorial view of what is being said through the defined and purposeful movement of the hands.

However, when lies suddenly set in during a discourse, you will notice a lesser use of hand gestures; they are withdrawing their use of hands in laying more emphasis in what is being said. They understand that the hands may bear contradictory message with their conscious verbal pronouncements, so they hinder its free flow when they are sounding deceptive.

Also, when the hands unexpectedly become passive, it means the person is most probably losing their confidence. Once someone becomes less confident in what they are saying, they restrain the use of hands in amplifying their message. It is now left to you to fish out the reason that informed their decision or feeling.

Scientific Explanations

Vanessa van Edwards (2019) talks extensively on how the hands are used in making emphasis. She makes reference to a research she carried out with her colleagues where it was discovered that 'the most viral TED Talkers spoke with their words AND their hands'. That is, the mouth and hands work together to birth an excellent presentation. In an 18-minute talk, it was observed that the most popular TED Talkers make use of hand gestures in 465 times, this is against the least popular speakers that use hand gestures 272 times. Hand gestures in laying emphasis is simply indispensable in making an acceptable and convincing speech in any region of the world.

The hand gestures are so important because we were given birth to so as to communicate with our hands. 'Researchers have found that infants who use more hand gestures at 18 months old have greater language abilities later on. Hand gestures speak to great intelligence,' submits Edwards. That is why we tend to use the gesture naturally when comfortable. Those who restrain its usage are intentionally limiting the functionality of their brain.

Further, Spencer Kelly, professor of psychology and neuroscience at Colgate University and co-director of the school's Center for Language and Brain, found that gestures make people pay attention to the acoustics of speech. It makes people drawn to you and through that, you can win them to your side. Kelly states that 'gestures are not merely add-ons to language—they may actually be a fundamental part of it'. This lays emphasis on the indispensability of the hand gestures I have earlier said. The open secret is that this cue comes to every human naturally, even blind people use this gesture while conversing with other blind ones. This may appear funny but you can pay attention to it in your immediate environment.

Apart from the fact that the use of hand gestures helps others remember our words, it also helps us to access our memories. Edwards reports that when we make use of the hands, it makes us speak more fluently and quickly. It is considered as a form of embellishment for our words. In this sense, we can compare the hand gestures to salt in a stew; without it, our presentation would not have taste. With the use of the hands in making emphasis, we tend to understand more of what is being said. There was a study where children were asked to gesture while solving a math question, it was reported that they were able to learn novel problem-solving skills than when they were not forced to use hand gestures.

Social Triggers (2019) says the basic function of the hand gestures is to emphasise an idea. The website also shares the same opinion with Edwards that this actually an important part of our overall body language. The social platform gives fundamental reasons to expatiate why it considers hand gestures as being important. More so, the messages echoed by the hands are usually reliable. They also relatively have the same meaning across regions.

Practical Illustrations

Case Study I: Suspect A was detained over the death of his son believed to have been killed by his wife. The interrogators believed that there was no way such incident would have taken place without the awareness of the husband, more so, he was at home when the incident occurred. Suspect A had read on different platforms that one needs to be convincing and speak fluently while being interrogated, if not, one can be made to pay for one does not know of. Since he was truly not involved, he really took his time to explain the details of the event and what he knew about it. At each point of his explanation, he uses the hand gesture to buttress his point. With this, he was able to clear his name. He was easily believed because his hand gesture aligned with his words.

Case Study II: Sir YA is the managing director of UBT Firms. The company only came into being some few years ago but the pragmatism of the director has made it a force to reckon with. His story is being said in positive vibes in both within and outside the firm. For instance, his employees have organised surprise appreciation party for him twice. Of all his qualities, one of the most talked about is the great use of non-verbal communication; whenever he speaks, he uses his hands freely to make more gestures and add emphasis. This keeps people glued to him, no matter how long the conversation lasts. People are moved to those who tell their stories in dramatic manner and that is what he does.

Case Study III: Con artist BR was arrested after five years of looking for him. During his arrest, the officials thought their problems with him had come to an end, until he got to their station and he failed to make any formal statement. Since he could not be coerced, the officials employed all tricks before he eventually wrote something that he could not be indicted for. During his investigation, he was masterful with his delivery—he used both verbal and non-verbal communications in a way that you will have to just listen to him. For instance, his hands were actively engaged throughout the interview. It took the investigators seven hours to get him to confess his criminal deeds.

19.40. Giving the Finger

Generic Interpretations of the Concept

The middle or longest finger is as useless as anything; psychologists and scholars have read negative meanings to the gestures displayed by this finger. This was first noticed by pioneering psychologist, Paul Ekman who opined that people give the finger only when the have issues with another person. Ekman says this sign is always subconsciously made to mean 'F*ck you'. There is hardly any other form of insults that pains as much as that. To display this gesture, you see the other four fingers buried while the middle finger stands out. The facial expression while bearing this message also depicts someone who is angry.

If done by someone of lesser authority to a higher-ranking individual, this is like questioning the latter's authority and can be very insulting. Attaching indecency with the middle finger has made it bear ill message in whatever circumstance that it is used alone. Before you give someone 'the finger', you must consider the context, their feelings and the likely consequences.

When you scratch the face with the middle finger and employs it in adjusting eyeglasses into its position, the meaning does not change; it is taken as a show of disrespect.

However, we cannot rule out the fact that that this can be a baseline of some people. This is where the need to master the context of event becomes crucial.

If it is the primary behaviour of a person, they will make use of the finger even when there is nothing that warrants anger in a given situation but if you are dealing with someone who just started using it when an argument ensued, it means they are probably employing it to tell you to go to 'hell' or 'get the hell out of their presence'. What is most important is that you do not give interpretations out of context.

Scientific Explanations

Christopher Philip (2013) describes this gesture as culturally specific; it meaning is particular to a given culture. The gesture, along with others in the same category are so much known that they can be used as words replacement in the given cultures. 'That is, the gestures have a direct verbal translation. Obviously these gestures will mean different things in different settings and can range from complimentary to offensive' (Philip 2013). In the case of giving the finger, it is an offensive remark. Studies have revealed that those in the lower rungs of life tend to gesticulate more while speaking compared with those of higher economic status. 'Usually this is tied directly to education, and those who have a higher level of schooling also have a larger vocabulary so instead of using gestures to express themselves, they use words instead,' Philip explains. Apart from that, those who are economically buoyant and well-respected in the society will find it difficult to use insulting gestures while communicating with other people.

Giving the middle finger is very popular in the Western world. It is used to hurl insults at people. The V-sign on the other hand, is known to be peace sign but can also share the same meaning (as being insulting) with the middle finger in some countries such as some parts of France, Australia, Ireland, and United Kingdom.

Nasaw Daniel (2012) simply describes this gesture as 'The Finger'. He describes it as 'an extended middle finger with the back of the hand towards the recipient.' This is obscene gesture that is well rooted in the Western culture. Many of the experts that contributed to this subject matter noted that it is used in the Western world. This tells you that it bears another meaning in other climes. In some regions, this may be employed to warn someone to keep off or desist from an act so as not to be attacked.

A website dedicated to body language discussions, Simply Body Language, also shares the same sentiment with the sources listed above. It passively discusses this cue while explaining the 'thumbs up' gesture. The website observes that the thumbs up clue may not mean commendation outside of the Western world; it may also bear the same meaning of being rude as in the case of extending the middle finger. Hence, we need to be careful on our use of some cues so that it does not communicate unintended message to the world.

Further, Simply Body Language notes that 'the middle finger is a *fallus* symbol, a sign mimicking a penis and testicles. In essence, what the person is communicating is "My Dick is Bigger than Your Dick!" and is a way to say that the other person is sexually inferior.' This can really make the other person furious and may lead to physical combat. In fact, you may end up regretting you do not make the gesture at all if the person is highly temperamental because they will fight you to the end.

Practical Illustrations

Case Study I: Guy R went to a club with a charming, beautiful lady. He had just met her and, as such, decided to show her love in an unusual manner. Being a popular club in town, it is always filled with people from all walks of life at weekends. So they got there earlier and got a comfortable place for themselves. While they were still chatting, R had an emergency call which forced him to leave the venue for about thirty minutes. By the time he returned, another person was already dancing and romancing with the lady. He was really pissed off and directed his anger at the man. He bumped into the stage and showed the intruder his middle finger while holding the lady by the hand. The other guy tapped him, and it almost led to physical combat before security officials took over the venue.

Case Study II: A man lay in the bush with gun hidden at the side; he did as if he was in need of help. So Mr E slowed down when he saw him from afar with the hope of taking him to the hospital, only for the man to be subtly reaching out for his gun. On discovering that he was up to something, Mr E gave him the middle finger and zoomed off in his bullet proof car. This means he was pissed off by the man's inhumane reaction.

Case Study III: Drug Addict DA didn't know that his neighbour is a law enforcement official when he was busy telling him his evil deeds—he told him how he consumes hard drugs freely, when he buys them and how is energised whenever he takes them. He thought he could influence his neighbour into it. However, the law enforcement official only arranged for his arrest. He was not expecting it when his neighbour led other officers to arrest him. Seeing who it was that masterminded his arrest, he gave his neighbour the middle finger before walking into the waiting vehicle. However, the officer was unmoved by his insulting gesture.

19.41. Pointing of Finger

Generic Interpretations of the Concept

From observations, it is almost a universal thing that people do not like being pointed at; you can offend them with this particular act. However, it seems practically impossible not to point at a person or an object. Thus, we have to devise an acceptable way of conveying this gesture in order to be seen as being courteous. In order to point at people, use the entire fingers, instead of just one; making use of only the index finger it makes somewhat insulting or directly unnecessary attention to the person which they might not appreciate at that point but if you point all the five fingers, it may be seen as mere stretching out of the hands while the message is passed all the same.

The full hand pointing where the fingers are slightly pressed together is very crucial in a romantic or professional setting where everything counts and the person at the other side of the table makes an impression out of every behaviour of yours. In a professional world, pointing a finger at another person, an authoritative figure especially, may be considered as being demeaning and insulting.

Apart from when dealing individuals, keep this in mind while pointing at objects too; if you want to direct a person to a chair, point with the entire hand so as to pass the message in an acceptable manner. The respect is not to the object but the person is expected to make use of it. Once the arms are stretched, everyone that it within sight will be focused on where it is pointed and this is more pronounced when a single finger protrudes out among the five. Pointing with the full hand distracts the attention of others and limits the communication to just you and the addressee.

Scientific Explanations

Simply Body Language (2019) says that most times when the finger is pointed at a place, the aim is to have people look at the direction pointed at. This may be accompanied with verbal expressions such as 'Watch this', 'It's over there', 'Look at that', among others. However, if the finger is pointed AT a person, it is most probably a signal of dominance. 'The back of the hand is pointing upwards (a clear sign of dominance), and the finger is casting blame . . . 'YOU DIDN'T KEEP YOUR PROMISES!' Even worse is when you're poking someone, as you violate their space,' explains SBL. The other person, if felt wrongly accused, reply in the same manner, thereby leading to an unwanted situation.

However, upward pointing of the finger is to caution a co-interlocutor. This is usually the sign made by parents to their kids. It can belittle the person as it warns them that their action may bring them danger. Since it is mostly done by a higher authority to a lower one, it is expected that the person the cue is directed complies without a challenge. It can also be used where there is no clear cut leaders and people are trying to lay claim to leadership by all means. In this sense, the action may be challenged by the other person aimed to be belittled.

Fradet (2016) also states that 'pointing a finger at a person while speaking is an authoritative gesture. People do this when imposing themselves.' That is why it is a common gesture among teachers, parents, bosses and traffic officials. It is a subtle display of aggressiveness and anger. So it is used in talking down the targeted person. The body language expert observes that when it is done to a peer, it is seen as a display of arrogance. That is, 'it's confrontational, invasive and offensive.' This can be made fiercer by jabbing the fingers. He adds that it is usually impolite pointing with a finger, hence, the use of the whole hand is often appreciated.

This does not mean that finger point is bad in its entirety. For instance, a playful 'finger-point with a wink however, is a pleasant expression of approval or acknowledgement,' says Fradet. Apart from that, when you point a finger in the air, it adds emphasis on what you are saying. Thus, bringing about conviction about your authority and confidence. Pay attention to this particular usage of the finger by preachers and politicians so as to add certainty to their words.

Philip (2014) opens our eyes to other uses of the finger-pointing gesture. He states that 'finger pointing is a way people distract others from things they are doing by refocusing the attention of others'. When you point the finger, people forget about you and face what you are pointing at. This may be a subtle cue by people when they think they have done a wrong thing that they do not what others to know about. The body language expert gives a verbal translation of the cue as 'I want everyone to look at what I'm pointing at and not at me.' 'I've sharpened my spear. It is my index finger, and it's extended and ready to thrust. It will jab at anyone or anything that might be in its path—so watch-out! I'm here to make a point.'

Practical Illustrations

Case Study I: B had a confrontation with her husband, H and during the process, she used her index finger to point over and over, sometimes using it to prod and stab her husband angrily as if the union was going to crash that day. This was to show her anger and aggressiveness. The husband knew that she was not going to budge her ground or plead guilty at that point. In fact, she laid in more and more blame any time she pointed the finger at H. This was a pure display of anger and frustrations.

Case Study II: Lady P is serving as an usher in an event attended by respected members of the society. As the guests arrived for the occasion, she welcomed them with a smile and pointing humbly with the whole hand, she would direct them to the seat prepared for them. Pointing with the whole hand makes her gesture looked respectable, making the guests to appreciate her kind gesture towards them.

Case Study III: Mr OD is an illegal immigrant and when he was stopped by law enforcement officials to ask for his means of identification, the first problem he encountered was language barrier; he could not express himself well. Also, he had no permit of residency. However, he was respectful throughout the conversation. For instance, when asked where he was living so as to know if he was harboured by another illegal immigrant, he pointed to the direction of his house with all fingers, instead of one that an average person will do. This gesture was repeated while answering similar questions. However, this show of respect was not enough to salvage him.

19.42. Finger Jabbing

Generic Interpretations of the Concept

Let me state that the height of finger pointing is jabbing. This is done when there are real issues. There are two premises in which people touch each other—when there is close bond or when there is a physical confrontation. In the case of finger jabbing, it is the latter. Usually, an aggressive or angry person will jab their finger at their victim's face or chest. Without mincing words, this is an antagonistic attitude that is not acceptable in any part of the world.

When you jab at a person, it singles out the person and others within the scene understand whom your anger is directed at. Also, it opens the floor for confrontation between the two people. When the jabbing is subtle, it means the person can still be calmed but when actual physical touch is involved, it makes the situation more threatening. At this point, the person being touched is expected to give a reply, whether in the like manner or by tendering an apology to the aggressive person. However, if the jabbing is done repeatedly, it may propel negative reaction from the other party too.

Finger jabbing is always as a result of uncontrolled emotional outburst. There is no situation or context where this show of negative emotions can be said to be acceptable. It is done to challenge another person's authority and embarrass them publicly which just few people can withstand. Even if this happens between couples at home, it may lead to physical exchange of blows.

The message in this cue is clear—negativity and aggressiveness. This is classified under the fight response stimuli. We tend to confront a situation we think we have power over when threatened by such. This is unlike the freeze or flight response where we take to our heels.

Scientific Explanations

The body language experts that lent their voice to this subject matter made it clear that finger jabbing is a show of aggression. Fradet (2016) says jabbing is the fiercer form of mere finger pointing. Through this, people take up space and challenge the other person's authority. Once someone takes up your social space and feels unapologetic about their action, this means they are ready to take you up to any extent.

Changing Minds (2019) also states that jabbing at a person is tantamount to using the prod which is often considered rude and threatening. No matter your social status, you are not expected to jab at a person, most especially in a professional setting. In romantic setting, if you see couples jabbing at each other, there is high probability that they are about to drop down the curtain over their love affair. The website add that 'people who are angry tend to point more, including at themselves (when they feel hurt or insulted) and at those who they feel are to blame'. The finger becomes hyper reactive when the emotions are charged. That is, it tends to work more than expected when we get angry.

Philip (2014) says that finger jabbing is a 'type of finger pointing but with added emphasis and direction, usually aimed at a person who is being spoken to, and repeated rhythmically. At times, a finger might actually physically make contact with another person to make the cue more salient.' This gives us an encompassing view of the concept. Without mincing words, this gesture is a rude cue, symbolising being poked by a spear.

This cue should be used when deploying non-verbal means to make your aggression known. When you jab the finger at every point you make, this sends a strong message to others that you better be taken seriously. This is a show of force and intimidation. 'In an emotionally charged debate one can use the finger jab to drive your point home,' hints Philip. This means that the gesture is not totally bad after all. However, making your point in this manner will make others think of you as being irrational. To appear otherwise, drop this gesture and make your point in a calm voice, using the hand gestures in the most appropriate way.

The verbal translation of the finger jabbing is given as 'I'm trying to make a point that I feel strongly about. I'm jabbing my fingers towards you like I would jab a spear. I really want to drive my idea home.' If you think the person is more powerful than you do, it is better you cooperate with them before it turns really violent.

Philip (2014) says when the situation really becomes heated, you may observe that the person feet are also jabbed towards you. The voracity and amplitude of the jab outlines the degree of emotion present. When a jab is done between relatives, saw a nephew and an uncle where one tickles the other to make him giggle, we say it is playful. Hence, the context gives you clue of what to think of this gesture.

Some of the clusters to look for during finger jabbing are violation of personal space, shouting and loud voices, erratic movements of the arms, chin jutting, arms akimbo, puffing of the chest, and wide focus intense eyes.

Also, MagforLiving.com (2019) says that when someone is talking and jabbing their fingers simultaneously, is evidence that they are aggressive by nature. In a discussion, this means someone is surely trying to dominate and display aggression.

Practical Illustrations

Case Study I: Mr and Mrs JU was having a heated argument concerning the lifestyle they both adopted in recent times that is really telling on their home. The wife felt the husband was having extramarital affairs and, as such, should be 'paid in the same coin' while the husband was challenging such assertion. The argument started from a calm, explanatory note to a ferocious one, to the extent that neighbours could hear their voice. It tarried for hours and when now, it was almost nearing blows. They were both enthusiastic and passionate about driving home their point and not ready to step down for each other. The action of the wife was more noticeable. At one point, she was shouting angrily and jabbing at close quarters and encroaching on his personal space as if she was going to stab something on her husband. This show of anger and uncontrolled emotions further worsened things.

Case Study II: Lawyer JG was defending a criminal case but it appeared that the accused had already been prosecuted by the agency that arraigned him because their own lawyer was so emotional about his presentation and almost blackmailed him. He held on to his presentation as if he was the only one to speak. When it finally got to the turn of Lawyer JG to speak, one could see that he was annoyed as his facial expression had changed. He was on top of his voice, jabbing his finger any time he faced his colleague as if he was ready for a world wrestling show. This was a non-verbal way of directing his anger to him for what he had earlier said.

Case Study III: Mr CH was arrested with some prohibited items. It took long for border officers to get hold of him because he hid the products in the least imaginable places. When he was asked, he feigned ignorance, saying that he bought the goods in bulk and they were packed like that for him like that from the companies he got them from. As a way of running background checks before handing him over to the appropriate agencies, the officials took more hours and he had becoming restless. When he later got to know what the officers were doing about his case, he became psychologically stressed and started shouting, jabbing his finger at an officer at a close range, accusing them of infringing on his privacy. All such displays were emotional blackmail that would not work.

19.43. Use of Finger as Baton

Generic Interpretations of the Concept

Using the finger as baton is not a universal clue and people tend to misunderstand it, especially when used outside of the cultural climes. It is a gesture that is popular in the Mediterranean nations used for the purpose of laying emphasis. When the finger is used as a baton, it wags up and down. Hence, if you do not understand the context and motivation behind it, you may take it as an antagonistic display.

During the display of this gesture, the index finger is used to maintain a consistent flow in speech, cadence and even, music. If this gesture is displayed immediately after making a point, it helps in emphasising the point made. It is like appending one's signature to a letter; it is a symbolic mark of approval of what is said. If it were another person talking and you want to give approval to what is being said, you nod the head but in this instance where you appear to be the speaking, you wag your index finger subconsciously to lay emphasis on what you have just verbally uttered.

What is most important on this is that you notice where to use the gesture. In the Mediterranean countries where it is domiciled, you will not have issues using this gesture but once you move out of the region, there would be a need to restrict the wagging of the index finger as you may arouse the wrath of your co-interlocutor who may feel offensive about it. The clue to get over this is to pay attention to how your partner feels when you first make an unconscious use of it. If they frown, this means they are uncomfortable with the use of the gesture. So you begin to repress its usage throughout the conversation. With this, you are most likely to impress your audience or co-interlocutor.

Scientific Explanations

Changing Minds (2019) says this is used to give an exaggerated hand movement. Liking it to a club, the website notes that the wagging finger of admonition beats up and down as if striking a given culprit. This may also be done with the whole arm. If done in this manner, it is a show of aggression. However, if it is employed to lay emphasis a point, it would be politer with the index finger pointing downwards, perhaps, it may be tapping a table.

Philip (2014) says that this gesture is 'A motion done with the hands to emphasise points in speech sometimes in rhythm with each word. It is made by balling up the fist and repeatedly and rhythmically batoning it against the palm of the other hand, or the table, as an axe would fall against a log.' This description has gone a long way in summarising the whole gesture to us—it is used to make emphasis and can be displayed in different manners. This gesture is usually displayed when an important point is made in speech.

Philip suggests that 'batoning is effectively used when addressing a crowd as it can provide emphasis to certain key words or ideas. By moving the hand up and down with each important point it serves to "drive the point home". Imagine the hand like the head of a hammer coming down as ideas are expressed. Use batoning when you want to show passion, be it in business, or in debate amongst friends.' This action is very symbolic and if used appropriately, will bear the right message universally. That is, it can be used across the world as a non-verbal tool of laying emphasis on important point if it is not subjected to arbitrary use where its meaning would be abused.

Due to the role the baton gesture plays, it is often referred to as the 'politicians' gesture.' it has been observed that many world leaders make use of it when making points. More so, it is a less offensive gesture that sends the message of conviction into people's mind, doing effectively, what the finger pointing would have been considered rude for.

Philip adds, 'It is designed to be a conversation ender—to be the last word spoken. It is highly authoritative in effort to add emphasis to a thought or idea. A baton or chop adds emotion to the words it is attached to. It is habitually done by powerful people who have the floor and are in charge. A person using a power grip wants to appear strong, serious, and forceful.' That is why the verbal translation is given as 'I'm going to hammer my point home by beating it into your brain … one, word, at, a, time!'

The body language expert concludes that this cue varies in culture and frequency of usage. For instance, Latin cultures use this gesture more than Anglo-Saxon cultures while the latter use it more frequently than Asian cultures. If used too often, it might be regarded as a lack of intelligence in Asian cultures.

Practical Illustrations

Case Study I: Philip recalls as real life illustration of this gesture thus: 'Bill Clinton made the batoning motion famous as he emphasised nearly each word in his denial speech against his involvement with Monica Lewinsky 'I did not, have, sexual, relations, with, that, women.' as his arm pumped up and down' (Philip 2014). Whether the above statement is truthful or not is not the focus here but that the speaker was emphatic about his point, attaching importance to every word in the statement.

Case Study II: Mr OP is the president of QZY Enterprises, a multinational firm with branches across the world. However, in recent times, he has been receiving uncomplimentary comments on the actions of his employees at different levels. For a few times, he had sent the GMD to address them but there seemed not to be the desired changes. So he had to summon all those holding executive positions to address them directly. The seriousness on his face and in his voice could be felt right from the start of the meeting. Also, he uttered every statement carefully, adding the batoning gesture at the end of every statement to emphasise their importance.

Case Study III: Mr CZ has been doing international business for about two decades. This means he is aware of the way things work at every stage of the business and one can see it in the way he carries himself. However, just like most of his colleagues, he knows how to evade clearance once in a while, with the help of compromised officials. One day, when he was nabbed for an alleged attempt to evade clearance, he went emotional by telling the officials for how long he has been in the business and could present all his clearance papers since the start of the business. He would add the batoning gesture at the end of each statement. However, the gesture used to come too late; it was only noticeable when he was about starting another statement. This made it more of a theatric than emphatic gesture. That is, the action presented him as someone who was being deceptive in all that he was saying.

19.44. Symbolic Two-Handed Push

Generic Interpretations of the Concept

This is when a speaker holds their two hands up in their front with the palms facing the audience as if they are trying to push something away with the hands. Imagine a person pushing a car or any other item that requires force to move; the two hands would be made into a formidable force in order to be able push off the item. This is also symbolic to pushing away an idea. When speaking and you form this gesture with your hands, it means you are blocking ideas coming from the audience. This can send a very negative message to the audience, thereby disconnecting from the entire discourse.

When you push the audience away through this gesture, they feel useless and unloved. It would be difficult for you to reconnect back to them. Once humans lose attention, before you can have it back, something unusual must happen. More so, this happens through your ill use of body language gestures.

This is a subconscious gesture whose meaning is registered within the mind of your co-interlocutor once it is displayed. It is like saying the person should keep all their ideas to themselves. This can be belittling, especially when done with a frown or other aggressive body postures. It kills the enthusiasm of the person to speak with you. This is a form of physical barrier that limits the closeness of your relationship with the other person. Hence, the two-handed push may be seen as 'road blocked' signal.

Once you give the 'Go away' gesture to someone who wants to stay with you, you end up losing them at the most inappropriate time. This can be permanent when the cue is repeated in a discourse context. Even the person displaying this gesture is not finding it easy, which makes the negative message being passed across more potent.

Scientific Explanations

Sandy Gerber (2019) notes that this gesture is used in expressing dominance. By displaying this cue, the hands are held up and the law of gravity expects them to come down few moments after that. So they would be turned down, symbolically covering up the person. This is a show of dominance and to exercise power over the person. In an interaction, it sends unconscious message to the person that you want to take charge. If the person feels it is your right, they will comply but if they think otherwise, they will only take as meaning that they should hang off. What matters most is that your feelings must align with the discourse taking place because your co-interlocutor or audience will always decode the message you send unconsciously.

An article on Forensics Community (2019) states that this gesture is not entirely negative. That is, we need to punctuate our words once in a while in order to give the audience the ability to digest our message. The website advises that 'the first thing to always be conscious of when performing a Declamation is to never leave arms hang for a long amount of time. It is perfectly fine and encouraged to let arms and hands remain by the sides at times. Not every line needs to be punctuated physically. However, letting arms dangle for thirty seconds to a minute is not recommended.' When the hands in the air for too long, it forms the two-handed push gesture where the audience think you do not want to relate with them.

This is not to state that you should not make use of gestures; lack of gestures is capable of killing a potential great piece. But the message here is that not all gestures must be huge and cheesy, but having some movement does look visually interesting and stimulating to the audience. The audience must be connected to you from the beginning of your presentation until you utter the last word (Forensics Community 2019).

Also, if the two-handed push gesture is displayed repeatedly, it may be taken as a show of nervousness. The way in which the hands are held will reveal the degree of stress the person is undergoing. Even if you have earlier planned this gesture to achieve a specific purpose, you must be careful on its usage in order not to overdo it, thereby making it appear superfluous. Forensics Community (2019) concludes by warning that you should 'aware that hand gestures, much like blocking, are meant to accentuate a word/part of a speech. Blindly throwing in gestures just to fill space is an easy way to detract from the importance of gestures and the very speech itself.'

Practical Illustrations

Case Study I: Dr J was invited for a seminar by a multinational firm with hundreds of workforce. In order to make the lecture very practical, the speaker decided to employ an interactive method to deliver it. At the beginning, it seemed to be going on well as the attendees were responding appropriately. Along the line, some of the employees that were not really interested in the process decided to distract the attention of Dr J by asking irrelevant questions. When this was obvious to him, he decided to block them out by not entertaining questions from the end of the audience. Although he did not tell them verbally, he held his two hands in front of him and turned his palms to the audience. He did this for several seconds and repeatedly. This unconsciously pushed the audience away from him and, as such, was able to double his speed for the few serious ones.

Case Study II: Suspect C as interrogated in a series of criminal cases. Being on the wanted list of different agencies for years, his arrest became widely circulated and the agencies decided to work as a team so as to get the desired information from him and ensure his arraignment without delay. During the interrogation, Suspect C discovered that the attention was too much on him and thought of a way to reduce it. As he was talking, he held his hands in his front and turned his palms to the interrogators thinking they would lose interest in him, he was warned to comply and maintain the right posture. This means that the officers knew what he was up to and they were ready for him.

Case Study III: NPL shared a business idea with his friend, UTR, and outlined the practical ways he was going to go about it in order to record gain and make a career out of it. He was fed up of his 9-5 job. Before he could raise money to start the business, UTR had gone behind him to get a loan and kick-start the business. This went on for months without the knowledge of NPL. He only discovered when he was ready to start his own and there were no potential clients within the surveyed area again. Considering this as a betrayal, NPL symbolically placed his hands on the table and opened his palms to his friend the next time they met, symbolising the need to create a distance.

19.45. Biting of Nails

Generic Interpretations of the Concept

Nail biting is an action that is not approved of all over the world across all age groups. Children have the tendency to suck or bite their nails but their parents and teachers ensure that they correct them early enough so that they do not grow with the bad habit. Biting of the nails involves chewing the nails or cuticles with one's teeth. This is the height of stress. From the health angle, biting the nail is unhygienic. Also, taking the fingers into the mouth is one of the hand to face cues that is very pronounced. This means the person can no longer hide their nervousness or insecurity.

The cuticles are known to have blood run on their surface. So when the nails are bitten, saliva from the mouth touches the nail surface and cuticles which produces tactile feeling, thus relieving the stress.

There are many possible causes of this behaviour. Worry stands on top of the list. When we are engulfed in worrisome thoughts, we tend to bite our nails as we think through the issues. This hints that we are not having an exciting thought; our facial expression also conveys this undeniable hopelessness. You will look into the distance as you reflect on the issue that is bothering you, making happenings in your immediate environment look inconsequential to you.

In the same vein, lack of confidence can make people bite their nails. It means they are thinking low of themselves and this act reveals their vulnerability to their opponent. This is like a subtle way of surrendering themselves to a situation they feel is above them. There are two probable outcomes in this context—either the opponent takes undue advantage of your situation or takes your show of lack of confidence as an appeal. Nail biting is an undisputable show of a person who is insecure.

When we are extremely stressed, we may find ourselves biting our nails even if it is not our habit. If this is not controlled, it can become pathological to the extent of damaging the skin of the fingers or even ulcerate the finger that can destroy the healthy tissues of the hands. Also, when you bite your nails repeatedly, the marks become obvious in your hands and people may lose trust in your ability when meeting you for the first time; they have a negative first impression about you due to the aftermath of the nail biting that is evident on your nails.

Scientific Explanations

According to YourDictionary.com, nail biting 'is a type of habit that can demonstrate stress, nervousness, or insecurity. Oftentimes people bite their nails without even realising it.' The three main issues are caught in this definition—stress, insecurity and nervousness. Those are the driving forces behind nail biting.

Hanan Parvez (2015) observes that people may decide to downplay the essence of nail cutter by making use of their teeth to chew their nails. However, when we see this, we must look beyond the surface level as there are more hidden meanings to it. Parvez states that the foremost psychological reason for this action is anxiety. When we feel anxious about something, we tend to bite our nails. Sometimes, the anxiety may be glaring such as a chess player trapped in a difficult situation while in some other times, it may not be apparent, for instance, someone who is thinking of what awaits them in the office while taking breakfast at home may suddenly begin to chew their nails.

Parvez (2015) postulates that 'anxiety is not always easy to detect because it's almost always related to some future event that a person believes he's incapable to deal with. In other words, the person is usually anxious about something that isn't happening but something that he thinks is *about* to happen.' You may be thinking how nail biting comes into this situation. Well, once a person is anxious, they believe they have no control over a dreaded event about to take place. So they begin to do everything that will calm the situation for them. And this is where nail biting features. The gesture is controlled, predictable and repetitive movement. 'This sense of control that a person achieves from biting nails helps him reduce the feelings of loss of control that were initially triggered by his anxiety,' states Parvez.

Philip (2014) also explains that 'nail biting is a sign of insecurity, anxiety, discomfort and lack of self-confidence'. Apart from that, he says this cue can be so severe that it leads to 'bleeding, disfigurement, or unsightly nails down to the quick'. Except in circumstances where you wish to feign anxiety, this gesture should be avoided because it paints you in a negative light. The verbal translation is given as 'I'm suffering from extreme inner turmoil and anxiety. I need to pacify myself by reverting to childlike suckling or mouthing of my fingers, as a substitute for my mother's breast.'

This habit may be replaced by other variants such as 'thumb sucking, sucking on pens, chewing on the arms of the glasses and sucking on a cigarette.' All these communicate the need to pacify. This is emotional body language and may become habitual due to the pacifying role in plays. Although it reduces anxiety, the fingers appear unsightly. This screams our insecurity to the world, thereby exposing our vulnerability. When our negative thoughts are not guided, they grow the more and may become overwhelming, leading to chewing of the nails.

Practical Illustrations

Case Study I: Mr Q has been working as an administrative officer for years in the same organisation. As such, he was part of the senior officials in the establishment. When the head of the firm was on sabbatical, he was asked to step in. Mr Q thought this was the beginning of merriment for him but spending a day in the office showed him that there were many other things that he needed to learn. He was overwhelmed by the numerous issues he encountered and had wished the post was not given to him. On the next day, while taking his breakfast, he was seen biting his nail as he reflected on what to do in the office that day. This means he wasn't concentrating on the main issue but engrossed in the disturbing thoughts of works at the office.

Case Study II: Child VT has always told his parents he needed a bicycle but they would not give him a listening ear. They are absentee parents; they leave home early in the morning and return late at night. So they do not have the opportunity to spend quality time with him. He craves for the bicycle because whenever he returns from school, he sees their children of their neighbours riding theirs while he has nothing to ride. Sometimes, when he surmounts the courage to go and meet the coveted kids but his requests would be turned down. Engulfed in this thought while returning home from school one day, he unconsciously dipped his nails in his mouth and bit them for a long duration of time. This is a sign of negativity and someone looking for a way out of a disturbing issue.

Case Study III: Human Smuggler HE was once arrested with those he was trying to smuggle in. He begged relentlessly, noting that it was his first time. Everything looked so real that he got to the emotional part of the officers. Since then, he doesn't move in the same vehicles with his victims. He recorded few successes with this new tactic and decided to stick to it. However, things went wrong on a particular occasion when his victims were detained before his arrival. On seeing them, he started biting his nails incoherently and was looking very disturbed. His countenance changed as he thought of the excuse he would give so as not to be slammed with criminal charges. He already knew he was in trouble!

19.46. Drumming of Fingers

Generic Interpretations of the Concept

The fingers are great instruments in doing an array of things; we find them useful in drumming. Just like the batoning cue earlier espoused, the fingers can symbolically connote sticks used in beating tables or even thighs. This is a repetitive behaviour that is used in passing the time. This can be soothing when done over time. When the fingers are strummed on a table, it can be distractive to the other people you are sharing it with. In a party, this should be avoided as you can spoil the fun of others through that action. In a casual setting, no deep meaning may be read to this action as people may just see it as a means of catching fun or subtly testing your drumming skills.

However, when displayed in a professional setting, there are a few probable meanings that can be attached to it. First, it may be displayed when someone is waiting for another person to show up. Maybe you went to check on someone in their office and due to some reasons, you missed each other, while waiting for the arrival of the person and boredom wants to set in since you are doing nothing, you may resort to this gesture to pass the time. Also, while waiting for your turn to speak, you may strum the fingers. But it should be noted that your co-interlocutor may read many meanings to such action; they may see it as a subtle means of hurrying them up or not really interested in what they are saying because you have something more important than theirs.

This is similar to cheek-strumming cue discussed in the cheeks section. The finger strumming is getting the body charged so that things do not turn awry. While displaying this gesture, you may be reflecting on some past events that keep the mind light or even articulate the point you are about to make in a better way. The goal is to ensure that you do not fall into the unrepentant hands of boredom which may make you feel weak before the actual event.

Scientific Explanations

Farouk Radwan (2017) says that 'when a person keeps tapping his fingers on the desk or his legs then this could indicate impatience or stress'. The job of what is really the cause is left for you to figure out. When we are in haste to get something done but some factors above us are stopping us, we tend to drum our fingers on a desk. This registers our impatience to the person at the other end of the table. A piece authored by Hypnosis Training Academy (2019) also observes that 'when you're bored or impatient, you might drum your fingers on the table or shove your hands in your pockets'. Called 'stress' by Radwan and 'boredom' by the HTA, the meaning is the same; unusual feeling due to strenuous activities make us bored. This means the environment is unfavourable to us.

In its own explanation, Westside Toastmasters (2019) notes that finger drumming is the same thing as tapping the feet on the ground. The platform differs a little bit with earlier submissions by noting that this gesture does not signal boredom but it is rather a connotation of impatience. The website advises, 'If you are addressing a group of people and see these signals, a strategic move must be made to get the finger drummer or foot tapper involved in the conversation to avoid his negative effect on the other listeners.' This is the best way you can get the person out of their impatience.

Since they want to be involved, giving them any kind of role to play or even actively involved in the discourse will help cushion the effect of the impatience. However, if the audience display both the signs of impatience and boredom simultaneously, this is a message to the speaker that time is up for the presentation. The body language platform concludes, 'The speed of the finger or foot tap is related to the extent of the person's impatience—the faster the taps, the more impatient the listener is becoming.'

Changing Minds in its own interpretation says that this might be an indication of frustration. Maybe the person drumming the finger wants to interrupt in what another person is saying because they believe that the speaker is making some fallacious statements against them. You tend to see this often where crisis is being settled and the judge—whether official or circumstantial—tells the parties involved to narrate their story. Also, it may be a signal that the person strumming wants to take their leave.

The website explains further that this gesture can be disruptive to the other person. The noise can be louder or mild, depending on the intensity of the person's feelings; if the drumming and noise is faster, the greater the emotional feeling of the person. In conclusion, 'Drumming can also indicate that the person is thinking, and that the frustration is with internal thoughts and perhaps that an easy solution cannot be found.' So the act can be considered as a pacifying act in this sense.

Practical Illustrations

Case Study I: Mr and Mrs QR are having issues in their marriage and when it appeared that they could no longer be internally handled, the wife had to tell a respected relative of the husband. The person summoned both of them to a meeting. They were told to narrate their individual accounts of the issues so that the intercessor would have a balanced view of the issues. It was the wife that first took the stage. She talked for a long duration, making many accusatory expressions along the line. Many of the expressions were considered wrong and deceptive and wanted to interrupt but knew that it was not his turn to talk. When the urge to correct some of the 'wrong notions' of the wife got to a point, Mr QR began to drum the desk with his fingers. This message was understood by the man seated at the other side of the table; he signalled to the husband to calm down while telling Mrs QR to hasten up on her narration.

Case Study II: A man had issues with his account and headed to the bank to sort them out. Obviously, he looked and sounded confused. Banker QY was handling his case. When he demanded for explanations on the recent transactions he did on his account lately, he was saying things that were off point. His words became irritating to the banker and since it would be absurd for him to shut a customer up, he unconsciously began to hit the surface of the counter. This interruptive noise was clear to the man that he needed to conclude his narration. He quickly rounded off and gave the banker the opportunity to raise some other issues.

Case Study III: Prostitute DU did not collect service fee before having an affair with Client QO. She had thought the client was very rich and could afford to pay any amount mentioned. More so, the man lied to be the CEO of a company when he in fact, he was merely a part-time factory worker. When she told him how much his fee was after everything, the man began to offer flimsy excuses on why he could not afford it, when the explanation was becoming unending, DU began to drum the table in the room. He appeared to be ignorant of the message. This was very unfortunate because despite the fact that his co-interlocutor had lost interest in it, he was still committed to his talk.

19.47. Tucking Hands in Pockets

Generic Interpretations of the Concept

There are many myths surrounding the act of putting a hand or both in the pockets. One of such unfounded submissions is that a person who puts their hand in their pockets is deceptive or trying to say something suspicious. In all the literature I read, there is no authority that made reference to this superstitious submission. So if you are one of those who share this sentiment, it is time for cleansing.

Having said that, tucking hands in the pocket may be a show of comfort and relaxation. Oftentimes, when people are comfortable with themselves, they dip their hands in their pocket as they listen to music or even converse with another person. This is also common in a romantic relationship where the man will put his hands in his pockets as he and his lover stroll down the street. This means he is open and fearless; if they were afraid, he would have used his hands to guard his genital areas or any other part of the body that that is considered vulnerable. When this gesture is displayed, it means the person is not threatened by anything. This is the hallmark of their show of love in their partner. In some other times, this may be a way of avoiding holding their partners at the hand; they are shy of holding their partners in public.

While a boss is speaking to his subordinates, he may put a hand in his pocket. This is to show his authority. In such a discourse context, without any further introduction, a stranger knows who is in charge of the establishment.

In many situations, this is considered as being too casual and thus, may be unacceptable, no matter the position that one holds. In other climes, it is simply seen as a sign of rudeness. In fact, it is not acceptable anywhere in the world that a subordinates put their hands in the pocket while addressing a superior or an elderly person.

And we should not rule out the fact that this is a subtle means of dealing with stress; when the hands find their way into the pocket, they may be used to rub the thighs, a part of the body that is easily aroused. This is comforting and helps in wagging war against stressors.

Scientific Explanations

Fradet (2016) explains that 'pocketed hands indicate unwillingness, mistrust and reluctance. If a person keeps his hands in his pockets, you will need to first gain his interest as well as his trust.' This is if you are meeting the person for the first time. Ideally, if you are having your first meeting with a person who believes in your goals and receptive to your ideas, they should be open to you exposing their expressive body parts. Remember that the hands are the most expressive parts of the body and once they are dipped into the pocket, they cease from performing any meaningful duty.

Even if someone tends to suppress the truth verbally, you can get to know their innate feeling through hand mobility. Your sensitivity to language of the hands will help you in making informed decision. The hands are influencers and should be left in their natural state in every given communication (Fradet 2016).

On his own part, Radwan (2017) says that people dip their hands in their pocket when they are not satisfied of their self-image. That is, our hands find their way into the pocket when we feel low of ourselves. For instance, while going out with friends and they all put on goo-looking, nice clothes while you could only wear an obviously old one. Unfortunately, there is a new person going out with you that day. You will unconsciously put your hands in your pocket because you are not pleased with your appearance. The expert alludes this action to the unconscious mind which operates in the primitive way that hiding the hands in the pocket takes us out of public view.

Radwan explains further that those who habitually dip their hands in their pocket may be lacking confidence and feel uncomfortable being around people. Before you pass any judgement on a person displaying this act, let your mind be active. For instance, a person may display this gesture because they are cold and not going through any internal emotional turmoil. Context is indispensable in making an informed outcome. For example, if someone is asked a question and they quickly dip their hands in their pocket before answering, look for other clues to be sure that their action was propelled by the question asked.

Camille Lawson (2018) also reels out different reasons why men may put their hands in their pocket. One of them is observation. Someone who wants to fully observe a scenario may maintain this gesture so as not to be distracted by some other activities of the hands. The writer also mentions cold, injury, twitch, and appearance of the hands as some other reasons for displaying this gesture. For instance, if someone is embarrassed of the appearance of their hands, they may see this action as the best way out of their embarrassment.

Practical Illustrations

Case Study I: Mr J had a physical combat with his wife the previous night and sustained a small wound at the back of the hand, near the index finger. He knew that many of his colleagues would like to exchange handshakes with him at work the next day and will definitely notice the injury. Since he was not ready to talk on the cause of the injury, he decided to dip his hands in his pocket and nod at everyone that greeted him. Even when their boss wanted to greet him, he feigned cold, even though that was unusual, being in a haste did not give his superior the opportunity to question Mr J further. However, towards closing hour, one of his colleagues later approached him and asked what prompted his 'new lifestyle'. He dismissed the colleague with a grimace which revealed his discomfort to the person.

Case Study II: Mr EWQ has just been promoted as the branch head of the firm he works with. Not many of his colleagues saw that coming and it seems he also hasn't believed the new reality. This has created a feeling of fear in him as he battles to live with the reality and demands of his new office. As a way of showing his subordinates that he is really above them, he will tuck his hands in his pockets whenever he is giving them orders. This eventually becomes his culture and whenever they are in a gathering, a stranger can easily spot the boss without any form of introduction; he was a clear leader through his non-verbal action.

Case Study III: Mr TU is the secretary to Dr SA. His boss had told him that he wouldn't be at work for three days due to the need to attend a conference in a neighbouring city. TU thought this was an opportunity to perpetrate all the evil missions he had been nursing. On the second day, he unscrupulously gained entrance into his superior's office and began to forge some highly important documents. Surprisingly, his boss showed up from the moon. Immediately he heard Dr SA's footsteps, he tucked his hands into his pockets and looked uncomfortable. However, he couldn't give satisfactory explanation on why he opened the office when there was nothing to do in it. And that was his Achilles heel that exposed his ill intents.

19.48. Rubbing of Closed Fist

Generic Interpretations of the Concept

Wherever you see a hand massing a closed fist tells you that there are issues. A hand would be clenched or clasped while the other will spread over it and rub (usually at the edges) gently. This communicates the need to pacify. When we are overwhelmed by stress but do not want to break down, we will use this subtle means to keep the mind in shape. Massaging of closed fist is a non-verbal action that is done unconsciously. It can be done while sitting or standing. In most cases, it is the left hand that is clenched while the right will massage it. The tactile feeling generated through the rubbing of the back of the hands helps to soothe the body.

Sometimes, this may be covered up with the crackling of the knuckles. How fast, consistent and long the massaging is helps in determining the degree of stress the person is going through. When you see someone displaying this gesture, it is an indication that they are going some internal turmoil. They may be thinking of how to manoeuvre their way out of the impasse they currently find themselves. That is why they seem to be disconnected from activities taking place in their immediate environment; they look into the distance as if their help is far away.

Poker players are the most common example of those who display this cue. Also, when stock traders are trapped in confusion and fear of what becomes of their lot, they switch to this behaviour. It seems to be a general attitude in places where fortunes might be instantly won or lost. That is why you tend to see it when a sporting competition is going on; if the result is not going the way it was predicted by the fans, they become engulfed in fear, hoping that things come out as predicted before the end of the game.

Scientific Explanations

To better shed light on this cue, Fradet (2016) gives an explanation of what clenched fists is all about. When the hands are tightly held, it is a connotation of firmness of resolve. Maybe the person is preparing for a competition—fistfight or football competition. It may also mean that the person is unyielding. However, the form of clenched fist that leads to massaging is the one done without the thumbs tucked in. Fradet submits that 'clenched fists with thumbs tucked-in indicate discomfort. This person is anxious and trying to harden himself.' As a way of dealing with the stress, they will massage the clenched fist with the other hand. The thumb is usually the target, being the powerhouse of the hand. So the thumb is placed on the clenched fingers so that it can be well massaged by the second hand. Whenever you see a hand spread out on a clenched fist, it means the person is battling with some internal turmoil.

In the submission of Parvez (2015), the speed at which the rubbing is done also bears a message of how the person feels; if the degree of stress is high, we tend to rub the clenched fist with more force and on a longer duration. Also, the person will rub slowly so that the tactile impact can really be felt at every angle of the hand. You can also look for concerned expression on the face of a co-interlocutor while expressing this gesture. If the stress is on the extreme, you will definitely feel the wave of their negative feeling and this will affect your discussion.

Sol (2019) says this subtle gesture is displayed to feign confidence or respect when in actual fact, it entirely represents negative ideas. He states that this gesture means '*frustration*, *restraint*, *anxiety* or negative thoughts.' By clenching a fist, the person is trying to restrain himself or herself while the other hand does the work of comforting. Also, a frustrated person loses interest in almost all the activities going on in their environment.

Sol explains further that there are different ways in which this cue can be shown: 'some have their hands clenched in front of their faces while sitting and resting their elbows on the table, others rest their clenched hands on the table or their lap while many simply clench their hands in front of their stomach or crotch while standing up,' he opines. The positioning also affects its meaning. The height at which the hands are held determine the level of frustration the person is going through. For instance, 'clenched hands in front of the face means more frustration than clenched hands on the lap.'

Practical Illustrations

Case Study I: K was introduced into robbery by a friend. He was struggling to make ends meet while the friend, someone he graduated with at school, is living large. It seems the friend looks smarter than he does. So he decided to approach him so that he would be tutored on how to make it in his friend's way. After months of pestering, the friend opened up to him. Although K was reluctant to buy into the idea at first, the way in which the friend portrayed it makes it look as if there was nothing wrong in it. After few weeks of training, K was given a location to go and rob. Unfortunately for him, he could not scale through that particular operation before he was nabbed by policemen. While being interrogated, his mediocrity was glaring throughout the session. He could also be seen stressed; he clenched a fist and subtly rubbed it with the other hand in an irritating manner. This communicated his insecurity to the interrogating team.

Case Study II: Student L was to be nominated for the position of the head boy of his school but before that, he needed to be interviewed so as to know how vast he was in leadership apart from academic prowess. Even though the panellists were his teachers he had always interacted with in class, the formality of the occasion almost took breath out of his lungs. He could be seen slouching and clenching his left hand while he used the right one to massage it as the interview went on. A teacher who noticed this cue of discomfort had to calm him down before proceeding with the interview.

Case Study III: Criminal TW was commissioned by gang to go to Country WQD to spy on some notable organisations; the aim was to secure an appointment with one of companies so as to have first-hand information about them. They knew it was disastrous for him to go with his real identity, so he impersonated someone else. On getting to Country WQD, his passport was questioned and this made him uncomfortable because he wondered why it took the officials seamless effort to easily notice the inconsistencies. He clenched his right hand and massaged it with left one as he tried fruitlessly to defend himself. The fact that his non-verbal cue depicted him as feeling uncomfortable gave him out as being deceptive in his explanation.

19.49. Speaker's Fist

Generic Interpretations of the Concept

Some people are unofficially known as 'action speakers'. They are the set of people that speak with action and unparalleled level of enthusiasm; they commit the whole of their body to what they are saying. Such speakers give a vivid illustration of every point they make and people are always glued to their words. This is because through the non-verbal dynamism employed in delivering the speech, they are able to create a pictorial view of their expressions. Research has shown that speeches conveyed with much gestures are easily remembered compared with those delivered without much action. This justifies why the most watched TED speakers are those who make use of gestures generously.

The speaker's fist and how it is carried matters to us. Making a fist is to allow the speaker 'hammer' his point. If you want to talk about something you consider as being important or central to all you have been discussing since the beginning of the speech, you may form a fist and gesticulate appropriately. This draws the attention of the listeners and also makes the point very dramatic. This also tells your audience that you are wholly committed to what you are saying. This is very common among established speakers across the world. Note that the fist would not be carried as if the person wants to attack their audience, rather, it would be demonstrated in a way that draws the attention of the listeners to the point being perused.

However, it has been observed that when some people are waiting to mount the podium or make their presentation, they form a fist with their hands. This is unusual and, as such communicates deep messages. This represents constrained energy and pent-up issues. When you notice, you should also be preparing for some physical responses. It is symbolic action; the person is holding back some energy for the action ahead of them.

Scientific Explanations

Edwards (2016) notes that the 'speaker's fist' gesture is used by people when they are determined about making an important point registered in the minds of people. She submits that 'any time you have a solid fist–shaking it at someone or punching it in the air, you are showing intensity'. This tends to be universal and your expression helps in adding value to the intended message. Edwards notes that this should be used when making VERY important point. That is, the point you are making is impact-driven and has something good to achieve in the lives of the audience. However, you need to 'be careful when using this gesture with an irritated voice, because it can come off as anger.' Cues work in clusters and, as such, must always align. If your fist is emphasising a point while your voice is echoing irritation, the message becomes disjointed and your audience are left in confusion. Hence, let your verbal passion match the non-verbal gesture. With this, people will take you more seriously and give a listening ear to what you are telling them.

Communication Theory (2019) discusses this gesture in a wider form. It states that this cue is important in enhancing communication; it adds flavour to our speech and makes what we say look concrete and acceptable. However, the platform is quick to add that this gesture is culture specific. While clenched fist is seen as a means of laying emphasis on points in the West and some other parts of the world, but it is seen as a gesture of disrespect in India. Thus, you would be considered as being rude if you clench your fist while making an important point; you would be seen as being too full of yourself based on what you think you know. The misconception is birthed due to the inappropriate place of displaying the behaviour.

Practical Illustrations

Case Study I: Mr U is a young man but very successful in his trade. Having grown up in the computer age, he took advantage of the Internet to publicise himself and his products. Apart from the fact that his products were ordered for from both far and near, he became a sought-after; he was invited by people from neighbouring regions and countries to come and help in training youths on how they can be successful entrepreneurs. The manner in which the invitations are flowing in makes it look he was even born to be a public speaker. While honouring one of the many invitations, he met thousands of attendees at the venue; most of them were looking expectant and ready for him. And fortunately, they were not disappointed. He was moved to speak in practical terms due to the cooperation of the attendees despite their number. Whenever he wanted to make an important point, he would clench his fist and threw it into the air majestically. This added flavour to what he was saying.

Case Study II: Student Y was to represent his class in a debating competition. The topic chosen was one that he was really interested in. So he was really elated that he was selected by his peers to represent them. To balance the game, the opposing class also nominated a person that was really interested in the topic. The competition was interesting and at the same time, fierce. Y watched patiently as his opponent argued her point. People were afraid that the girl was so intelligent to the extent that Student Y would not be able to tackle her assertions. However, when he mounted the podium, Y spoke beyond everyone's expectations. More so, he was dramatic about his presentation; any time he made an exceptional point, he would clench his fist in the air which appeared a symbolic way of 'hammering' the crucial points.

Case Study III: Lawyer A and Lawyer B were arguing for their individual clients. Lawyer A was defending a case while B was the prosecutor. So B was the first person to talk and he made a very brilliant submission. As he was talking, Lawyer A could be seen holding his fist as he prepared to counter his colleague's point. This means he was restraining energy. That is, he was keeping energy so as not to be aggressive and to also defend his point excellently. So it is a two-way thing.

Case Study IV: For the first time, Con artist WY doubted his ability to manoeuvre law enforcement. Perhaps, this thinking was birthed by his law encounter with some security agents where he was almost nabbed. On this particular occasion, as he was walking into the interview room, one could easily notice the nervousness on his face. When the interview kick-started, he had a stiff body but released it gradually as it proceeded. At some point, he would he would clench his fist forward after making a point. This was seen as a demonstration of authority and one of the officers who understood body language knew that WY was gaining ground through such non-verbal displays. So he had to hint his colleague to up their game so that the suspect wouldn't have a field day.

19.50. Massaging Hands on Palms

Generic Interpretations of the Concept

The palm is somewhat succulent, and as such, serving as a great source of comfort for us. It is our most favoured surface to touch and exchange pleasantries with people. This is because it gives us the ideal feeling and makes us cool. When we are stressed and there are no people to comfort us, we resort to self-comfort. In fact, there are instances where there might be more than enough to console us but it would be wrong to reveal our vulnerability in the first instance, let alone asking for help. Thus, we learn how to subtly handle those situations within our means.

Rubbing the hands on palms is one of ways in which we deal with stress. You will use the other hand to massage the palms. If you think bringing the two hands together may call people's attention to you, you may use the fingertips of the same hand to rub the palms; this is subtle and simple. It is more pronounced when you are standing and there is no barrier between the interlocutors but it may be less noticeable while seated as the desk between you and the other person will serve as a shield to you.

Pay attention to how the cue is displayed; if it is done repeatedly, this means the person is highly stressed. Also, when the anxiety is on the high side, the person will double the pressure of the rubbing. When the cue becomes rapid, those who would have overlooked it would begin to note that something is wrong. The continuous rubbing of the palm with the hand makes it warm as soon as possible, thereby answering the need of the person at that given time. You may see this acted out as soon as a person is saved by the whisker out of a dangerous situation.

Scientific Explanations

Parvez (2015) notes that fingers rubbing the palms can be given both positive and negative interpretations, depending on how it is done. It is always important to draw this thin line while making interpretations so as not to end up reading fallacious meanings to people's gestures. For instance, if the palm is rubbed rapidly, it is an indication of positive expectation. However, if it is done slowly, it connotes negativity. The latter is our concern in this section. Slow rubbing of the palm signals doubt. When someone wants to take a decision and does not know of its probable end, they might display this cue to express their doubt on the success of the proposed action.

Parvez explains further that when this cue is being displayed, the person may also wear an expression of concern on their face. This is a cluster that confirms your guess on how they feel. For instance, in a business transaction, if you see a person rubbing their palm slowly, wearing a facial expression of concern and seemed thoughtful with a dull appearance, this means they think the deal does not tilt to their favour. If you are at the other side of the table in such deal, it would be better you ask them questions regarding their thought on the whole process before they verbalise a negative thought. This is because 'once people have said 'no', it's hard to convince them and make them change their statement.

You might even consider withdrawing the latest condition that you made if you have to, just to save the deal,' advises Parvez. This is not only limited to business context but every other human endeavour. You cannot have a fair deal where the other partner sees themselves as being cheated. Detecting rejection through non-verbal means is one of the beauties of communication. With this, you would be able to sieve through the other person's thoughts before a 'concrete' decision is made.

The body language expert observes further that this gesture signals uncertainty. He gives the description of the cue thus: 'The fingers of one hand (usually the right) rub slowly in the upward and downward motion on the palm of the other hand. This gesture is often accompanied by the 'clenched hands' gesture that conveys self-restraint.' Since the hands are rubbing each other, they cannot be used for other activities at that very point. You may notice this cue on people when they are to make difficult decision but trapped in confusion. 'When you're asking someone to make a decision and they do this gesture and then clench their hands, you need to modify your approach immediately so that they can break their position of self-restraint' (Parvez 2015).

It has been observed that changing gestures is capable of leading to change in emotional state. So if you want to break this self-restraint noticed in your co-interlocutor, you can give them something—such as a coffee cup or pen, among others—to hold; this is effective in opening them up.

Practical Illustrations

Case Study I: Dr TW is the CEO of FZA Companies, with branches spread over different provinces. As big as his company is, he ensures that he is always present when a potential employee is being interviewed. This is a culture he is known for. In one of the interview sessions, after every other panellist had asked their questions, he sought to know the background and past escapades of the interviewee who had displayed unrivalled mastery of the job when earlier question. It was at that point that everyone got to know that the interviewee had an ugly past; he had criminal records that spanned through years. Although he was later taken to a rehabilitation centre and everything seemed to be well with him now, Dr TW thought that the work to be committed into his hands is one that requires someone with impeccable records, both professional and personal. Yet he had demonstrated an excellent knowledge of the job. For some few minutes, the CEO could be seen rubbing his left palm with his right fingers. This means he was buried in confusion on the best decision to make concerning the interviewee.

Case Study II: Politician EQ has just won his election into the house of parliament in a least expected way. The margin was so narrow, and with this, he knew if he failed to deliver, he would not be considered during the next election. So one of the things he first concerned himself about was to put up a good media team that would help him project his achievements to the electorates. He interviewed two great journalists, and they both performed excellently. At the point of making his decision, he became confused on who to go for. He dropped his pen and began to unconsciously rub his right palm with his left fingers. This meant he was having a difficult moment in determining who he was to pick. Their excellent performance was the reason for this.

Case Study III: Mr HU is an importer and used to all the ports in his country. Whenever he wanted to evade clearance, he knows the best port to use. Before leaving home, he had planned to follow due process but he met the goods he wanted to buy at much higher prices, so, he changed his mind on the port to use. When he arrived, there were two clearing points and, on a glance, he knew the two officers are compromised beings. However, he was confused on which of them will be so lowly to accept the ridiculous bribe he was ready to offer. Standing on a spot, he unconsciously massaged his right palm with his left hand. This means he was undergoing some psychological difficulties.

19.51. Teepee Finger Rub

Generic Interpretations of the Concept

This is one of the most unique, yet universally observed cues. The teepee finger rub has to do with rubbing a straightened interlaced fingers against each other back and forth. The hands are held together with the fingers slightly interlaced and then, they are made to move up and down. With this, the hands have been taken from their natural state to perform the role of pacifying. Invariably, this gesture is always displayed when people are experiencing negative emotions. The joining together of the two hands calls your attention to the person that something is up with them.

There are many emotional upsurge that can lead to this behaviour. They are all encapsulated in stress. When we are overwhelmed by negative events, you look for ways to comfort yourself. The interlaced fingers afford you with a greater surface area to stimulate as the hands as the fingers and hands are simultaneously moved up and down to ease tension. The inner parts of the hands are known for being great stimulators, when they rubbed the together, the effect is always soothing.

When you notice this gesture, it is one of the best indicators that someone is trapped in something negative; it is a sign of severe stress. It accurately reveals that someone is not in their normal sense. The feeling is purely negative and the hands are used as tools in wagging war against the source of the stress. Concern is one of the probable inducers of this feeling. When we are overwhelmed about the possible outcome of a case or project, we may become negatively concerned; instead of excitement, we will feel depressed and defeated. The feeling would be on the high side if the stake attached to the event is high. We tend not to think of any other thing but that particular issue.

In the same vein, fear or anxiety may force us into this posture. Fear squeezes out every hope in us and leaves us dejected. When we are anxious, we become unstable, therefore losing our rightful mind. This makes us take decisions our own best interest. When this feeling piles up, it births negativity around us.

Scientific Explanations

Top Ten Topia (2019) states that we often touch ourselves in any form when we are stressed. Note that this is an everyday gesture that is displayed in various ways. The platform explains that rubbing the hands back and forth is a soothing act that is done to relieve stress. A lot of things lead to distress in the body as expatiated above and to deal with them, the body mechanisms are put into action. The website states, 'This incidental distress mechanism is the body's way of forcing a change in position, removing potentially harmful substances, and otherwise taking care of necessary but subliminal functions that cannot be tended to without some deliberate action by the brain.' This explanation gives us a better understanding of the psychological role the teepee hand gesture performs; it is a deliberate mechanism commissioned by the brain to take off stress, anxiety and concern from the body.

The teepee finger rub is a form of self-assurance; when everything seems to be against us, we take solace in ourselves by boosting our inner strength. 'This kind of reassurance triggers that sensation of relief we feel when we remove something that is stressing our bodies. Self-reassurances help to calm our anxiety and give us resolve to carry through some action we are reluctant to complete.' Imagine a driver who had driven through a rough road for hours and must drive back. While going to take his seat, he may rub his interlaced fingers so as to give them strength. After displaying the gesture, he would faster to the car because he had just derive energy to execute an otherwise frightening one.

Using the back-and-forth movement of the hand is to enable us have a better view of something. That is, we want to move from a state of discomfort to comfort. The movement of the hands is symbolic—it shows that we are emotionally unstable. Stress makes look caged, and as such, we look for freedom in all ways.

Also, Fradet (2016) says we use the hand-rubbing cue to flush out stress out of the body system. When you are overly excited about something about to happen, you experience positive stress and that will make you rub the hands very rapidly, unlike the teepee hand-rubbing cue where it is slowly done back and forth.

In conclusion, we should not overlook the fact that this might be a means of generating warmth for the body. Changing Minds (2019) states that physical stress such as cold and not necessarily emotional stress may be the motivating factor for this gesture.

Practical Illustrations

Case Study I: Terrorist D was sent to go and spy on some specific areas marked for attack. He was to be accompanied by one of the new 'intakes' so that he would be able to learn the ropes. They set out on the journey at the right time and were able to spy on four of the seven locations successfully. However, when they got to the fifth one, the subordinate following him was distracted by the activities of those relaxing at the centre. He was looking very odd that people could easily fish him out as being a stranger. One of the security men at the venue who was on patrol noticed him and had to challenge him. He responded with fear by trembling when he wanted to answer the security man's question. This gave him out. Terrorist D, having seen what was at stake, decided to feign ignorance of the scenario and run away but the arrested subordinate pointed at him which made the security agents nab him too. Then, they were handed over to the police who interrogated them. Suspect D could be seen interlacing his fingers and rubbing them back and forth as he was waiting his turn to be called in for interrogation; he knew that the young terrorist would have made some confessions that would be difficult to refute. So this was a mild expression of regret and frustrations.

Case Study II: Student YT is a bully but likes to play smart; any time he does something ill for any of his mates, he would be the one to get to their teachers first to report. Hence, he has earned many undeserved victories and even boasts that many of his peers are not smart like him. So some of the students came together to team up again him. He fell into their trap by hitting one of them. Apart from having a video record of it, they also sped to their teacher to report the incident. Seeing that he had played into their hands, he unconsciously interlaced his fingers and rubbed them back and forth. It was a subtle way to battle psychological stress.

Case Study III: A man was looking for a way to evade clearance. So he had warned the off-loaders beforehand that they should not drop his goods in a particular place. With that, he could easily move them out with few kickbacks. However, the off-loaders mistakenly dropped the goods in the 'prohibited' place. He knew there was no way for him to play his game aright again. This became an issue to him because he would have to tender some old documents that are related to those goods. He became engulfed in thoughts. During this process, he unconsciously interlaced his fingers and moved them up and down. By mere seeing him, you will understand that he was going to sort out things on his mind.

19.52. Interlocking Fingers with Palms Either Turned Down or Up

Generic Interpretations of the Concept

When there are issues, we interlace our fingers and think of the solution in that context. It is a symbolic way of holding the body together. Invariably, it means the person is psychologically disorganised due to an unpalatable experience. Since there is no succour coming from an external source, they decided to take solace in themselves. To display this cue, you will see the fingers interlaced while the palms are made to either face up or down. When you see this, it is a reliable cue that the stress is on the extreme side. This is a variant of finger interlacing earlier discussed. The high intensity of the stress is the one putting the palms on motion.

This gesture is done to sieve stress out of the body. That is, the palms are either turned down or upward as a symbolic way of doing away with stress. That is why people assume that this is basically done when the stress is in the finger area. The gesture ensures the hands are pulled towards the face, ending up with an awkward-looking triangular shape. The elbows, the most powerful part of the arms would be pointing down, meaning that the person is metaphorically down in strength.

In the palm-down posture, the palms will face down while the fingers are interlocked at the crotch level as if the person wants to crack their knuckles. This is both psychological and emotional. When the fingers are interlocked and the palms made to face a particular direction, depending on how the gesture is displayed, the arms and fingers form a contour through the stressing of the muscles, tendons and joints of the hands, a process renowned for relieving stress.

As earlier noted, this cue is displayed when one is at the ugly side of life. For instance, you may see this when a teenage boy who deferred his parents' order and drove out their car which he later crashed, then summoned the courage to call them to come and pick him up after the incident; he did not know what would be their decision on what he had done.

Scientific Explanations

Psychologia states that this cue can mean varieties of things, depending on how it is used. One of the meanings ascribed to the gesture is nervousness. Referencing body language experts Alan and Barbara Pease who co-authored fifteen books on body language, the body language website explains, 'The height at which the hands are held reveals the degree of the person's frustration. If the person holds her hands clenched and fingers intertwined in front of the face while sitting, she might be really difficult to deal with.' We need to understand these peculiarities before we start ascribing meanings to people's behaviours. Someone who holds the hands really high is suffering great difficulties and are not trying to hide it. The intertwined fingers portray a person who is yearning for comfort at all sides. If you have to converse with the person and you want it to flow without hindrances, you have to unlock the interlaced fingers by offering them drinks or activities that will break the yoke. With this, the person is likely to become more open to what you want to discuss with him or her.

Patti Wood (2016) discusses this gesture from the perspective of romance and dating. She observes that when someone interlocks their fingers while the palm is facing up, it is an indication of the desire to connect. This is a form of self-restraint from their obvious desire. Wood 'warns there could be some holding back from a person who arches their palms or is awkward with holding hands.' So you have to ask some few questions or pay attention to the context further in order to bring out the truth of the situation.

In his own part, Philip (2014) does not mince words in correcting the notion that people think this gesture is contained or controlled posture. According to him, the behaviour exemplifies 'frustration, hostility and that a person is harbouring negative thoughts.' When we are in doubt, not confident of our ability or stressed, we tend to display this gesture. As the negative experience increases, so also is the intensity of the behaviour. There is no gainsaying that this gesture is a representation of higher level of anxiety. Philip advises, 'As conversations intensify watch for increases in soothing body language revealing the underlying anxiety. The gesture feels comfortable to do because it closes up the body from the outside world preventing the hands from speaking (gesturing).' The symbolic nature of this cue should be taken note of. When people purposefully or unconsciously lock down the hands and figures from gesturing, it is as if the lifeblood of the conversation has been punctured. It is left in your decision to determine if the conversation is still worth pursuing.

Practical Illustrations

Case Study I: Guy P has been longing to connect with her lady and develop close intimacy with her but it seems he is not understanding the way she behaves; this moment she becomes happy and the other minute, she is moody. This has always been an issue that he thought should be settled before he makes the marriage official. So one day, he took the bull by its horn by asking for clarifications on some of those issues. The lady seemed to be in her right senses that day, making the discussion to flow. She was the first person to talk and she tarried in her explanation, giving instances and references of how she would want everything to look like. To Guy P, it seemed he was painting an insurmountable future to him. He thought of his past sacrifices and where he would start again if he decided to go for another relationship and became depressed. He intertwined his fingers and make the palms to face up while the elbows looked downward. Even when he had the floor to speak, he still maintained this posture and his words were without power nor charisma. The lady detected his anxiety and asked him to go for a walk with him so that he could get back to his normal status.

Case Study II: Nurse YI had some marital issues that wanted to destroy her career; a once agile, intelligence and hard-working lady became a novice by the day. In one of the errors that almost gave her out, she was ordered to give a patient some prescribed drugs but absentmindedly administered the wrong pills on the patient. The poor man almost gave up the ghost. When she went to check on him the next day, she was emboldened in fear; she stood lifelessly and interlocked her fingers with the palms facing down. However, as the patient's condition changed, she became relieved gradually too.

Case Study III: Criminal AP has just been introduced into drugs and as way of proving to his colleagues that he was really into it, he became addicted to it; wherever he was, you could be sure that there were some hard drugs on him. In one of their notorious outings, they were stopped by law enforcement officials and AP was gripped with fear immediately. With his hands almost shivering, he unconsciously interlaced his fingers and turned the palms upward as if he was trying to tell the officials that he had nothing with him. This nervous attitude rather gave him out instead of salvaging him.

19.53. Crackling of Knuckle

Generic Interpretations of the Concept

Almost all of us do this but we tend not to pay attention to the message that it bears. It is a body language gesture communicating the emotions of a co-interlocutor. Without mincing words, when you see a person cracking their knuckles, it means they are stressed and trying to get relieved. This behaviour can be consciously or unconsciously done. In a formal setting, this might be considered as unacceptable. That is why you see people mostly do it when they are in an unofficial setting or places where their sensibilities might not be necessarily subjected to questioning.

There are different styles of displaying this cue; people may decide to crack the knuckles individually or rack the whole fingers at once. In fact there are times that people might call on others to help them crack their knuckles while some others see the involvement of a third party as a no-go area. The way in which it is done does not really tell on what the final outcome is. However, when the frequency of the stress increases, the behaviour also catapults. That is, someone who is stresses may do this gesture more rapidly or continuously as the stress level increases.

It has been observed that this gesture is capable of soothing tension; it deals a blow with stress. When we crack the joints of the fingers, it restores power to the hands in an unexpected manner. The fact that our hands are engaged during a stressful period means that we do not have to overtly be bothered about the issue. Also, this gesture is very potent for dealing with boredom. When you see someone cracking their knuckles while doing nothing, it means they are probably bored, trying to keep themselves busy. So the context is very crucial in unlocking the meaning of the behaviour.

Scientific Explanations

Dawn Dugan (2013) while giving the interpretations of some body language gestures notes that the act of cracking the knuckles is impolite. He uses an interview scenario to explain what body language is all about and how it should be used for the benefit of one. Two meanings are ascribed to knuckle cracking—high rate of nervousness and inability to control the impulses. This means that the person's inability to control their fear has made them lose their stand.

When being interviewed and you crack your knuckles, you have created a bad impression about yourself to the interviewer; the person sees you as someone who is fearful and does not have a full grasp of the concept being discussed. Also, it means if you are offered the job and issues arise in the future, you will not know how to handle them without spilling your personal emotions over to professional issues. Generally, we all want to deal with people that are socially aware and confident; someone you can vouch for and trust with your fortunes. Cracking the knuckles does not bring such virtues out of us.

In the same vein, Philip (2013) says this behaviour represents hostility. He explained that when we are hostile, we tend to do to ourselves, what we would have done to the person who offended us. That is why you see people pinch themselves bite a part of their body just to communicate their hostility. We are offering out these non-verbal displays to warn the person of what we are capable of doing to them.

However, if the person seems to be blind to the warning signals or decided to challenge our authority, then things will move to the combating stage where those involved in the conflict with face each other. At this point, you may observe the knuckles-cracking gesture that is used to signal readiness; we are ready for the action of combating the person. He concludes, 'Keep in mind that these signals are obvious and rarely mistaken for other signals and should be heeded for what they are; an early warning system.' I have always warned that nothing happens out of the blues. If you see this warning cues and decided to ignore them, this means you are exposing yourself to great danger. Ignorance is not an excuse in the face of the law.

Also, John Grohol (2016) says that we crack our knuckles because we are not physically comfortable. He submits, 'Pressure associated with gas bubbles within the joints is relieved by cracking them. Sometimes this evolves into a nervous habit that drives other people crazy but relieves the person doing the cracking.' There are people who feel disgusted for others cracking their knuckles around them. That is why I observed that this cue should not be displayed in the public setting. You may end up invoking people's anger more than the tension you claim to be relieving.

Practical Illustrations

Case Study I: Suspect A was brought of the cell to speak with the interrogator to interview and generally rapport with others at the location. The aim was to ensure his baseline was established before any other thing is done. After being offered tea and other items, the atmosphere was so friendly that he began to interact with those at the vicinity. However, he seemed to become bored of that location because there was no one who shared the same ideals of life with him. The interrogator was delayed by traffic. As he was 'patiently' waiting, he cracked the knuckles of the two hands so as to fight boredom.

Case Study II: Some policemen on patrol in a very dangerous area heard that robbers were operating in that environment. They strategised in the twinkle of an eye and distributed their men to man some places where they knew the armed robbers were capable of passing through. Then, some officials went to where the robbery was taking place. One of the men manning a strategic entrance could be seen cracking his knuckles. This was to show his readiness to combat the opponents. He also looked fierce and was at alert throughout the search period to ensure that the opposing team does not lay ambush for them.

Case Study III: Mr AV is not good with figures; he is easily fed up when asked to do anything relating to figures. However, there was a company assignment that required his inputs; he was to liaise with a colleague that would work on figures, listen to the colleague's explanations on the figures and then, he would put them down in words. While waiting for his teammate to codify everything before explaining to him, he became bored, but thinking that sleeping in that context wouldn't speak well, he began to crackle his knuckles as a show boredom and impatience. His colleague got the message and simply smiled at him, assuring him that he would soon be done with the mathematical aspect.

19.54. Interlaced Fingers Knuckles Cracking

Generic Interpretations of the Concept

You may be thinking of the possibility of this cue but it is what we all that from one time to the other, especially, when are really stressed. It is done by interlocking the fingers while the arms are stretched out to the extent that the knuckles of the interlaced fingers begin to crack. Also, you will observe that the thumbs are facing down. This means that something is really wrong with the person. When compared with the mere knuckles cracking discussed above, you will discover that this is the advanced form of the gesture.

While stretching the arms, the palms of the intertwined fingers may be displayed to the outer part, made to face the other party in the discussion. This is very similar to contorted display that reveals the high level of psychological imbalance suffered by the person. There is high probability that the person will even yawn as he stretches out the arms to crack the knuckles. Everything about him will portray tiredness, discomfort and instability. Even if you see someone display this cue when the context does not necessarily demand them to be stressed, it means they are physically uncomfortable. In other words, this gesture represents negativity in its entirety.

I said the act of interlacing fingers while cracking the knuckles represents high intensity of stress because it is two negative actions that are intertwined as one. Interlacing the fingers as discussed at different points in time, is used to represent self-restraint and holding back a negative thought; it perfectly shows a person that is highly stressed while on the other hand, knuckle cracking shows a person that is in search of comfort. When these two interpretations are merged together, it makes the negative thought experienced by a person becomes more glaring. Hence, the reason the person adopted a double pacifier to wage war against it.

Usually traceable to anxiety or fear, this behaviour is an attribute that is seen often among men. Due to the physical build-up of females, it may be considered an outright impolite act to stretch the arms while the fingers are interlocked; it pushes out their breasts in a way that might not look decent enough. All these bits should be taken together so as to always have a concrete interpretation at all times.

Scientific Explanations

Philip (2014) states that this might be a sign of repressed aggression. When the hands are interlaced with the finger joints being cracked, it means the person is going through emotional turmoil but trying to keep themselves within shape so as not to vent their anger in that context. The body language expert explains that when you see this, it is most probably an indicator that the person is pressurised. With this stance, there be a hindrance to blood flow, thereby increasing the stress level.

This gesture may also be used to signal resistance of the urge to strike. Note that if it were the act of knuckles cracking alone without interlocking the fingers, this is regarded as readiness cue (Parvez 2016) but when interlocking the fingers is involved, it translates to unconscious way of pulling down the readiness gesture. However, it is pertinent to note that this can be feigned as anger bluff for the purpose of receiving better treatment from a person or group of people. Interlaced fingers with cracking of the knuckles is telling others that your opinion should be better be respected lest your lash out on them. Philip concludes, 'Naturally, this non-verbal signal should be used with care as physical aggression, or even threat of physical aggression is strongly frowned upon.'

Robert Shmerling (2018) discusses this concept from the viewpoint of medicine. He observes that this might be a way of life to some people or a means of dealing with nervousness. That is, we release tension through this act. However, some do not see it beyond an annoying act that irritates them when done within their vicinity.

Generally, cracking the knuckles may be harmless but if done with the interlaced fingers where additional space is created among finger joints, it can lead to dislocation. The Medical Practitioner states that there have been 'occasional reports of dislocations or tendon injuries from overly vigorous knuckle cracking, such problems seem very much to be the exception and not the rule.'

Practical Illustrations

Case Study I: Mr R is doing fine in his present job, being the head of an up-and-coming establishment. He has worked with many other firms before deciding to move to the present company when he saw that their vision was clear and he had roles to play in ensuring the realisation of the goals. However, he was specifically sent an offer by a popular company who had just relieved one of their senior employees of his job. So he thought it was an honour and thus, decided to attend to their invitation but to his dismay, he was subjected to vigorous interview process when he got there. He had wanted to leave but thought that would be rude. He was so stressed by the process that he could be seen interlacing his fingers and cracking the knuckles simultaneously at the end of the interview. The message was also written on his face, clear enough for anyone who cared enough to decode.

Case Study II: Guy Y and Lady G has been lovers during their college days. They are always fond of each other and could be seen together at all times. Even some of their friends crack jokes with them that they are unmarried married couples. Three years after schooling, things seemed to still be going in the right direction for them. As the saying goes, life is not a bed of roses, lately, something went wrong with the relationship and seemed both of them could not just factor it out. When things were getting uglier by the day, Lady G could not cope with the whole thing again. So she decided to take the bull by its horn by summoning Y to a meeting where the issue was discussed for hours. It still appeared that they were not getting it better and would be better if they went their separate ways. At some point, Guy Y interlaced his fingers and cracked his knuckles. This means he was ready to take the bull by the horn.

Case Study III: Ms IH was illegally employed in a high-demanding firm. Apart from being in the most demanding unit, it was also required that she worked at every minute so that she wouldn't be questioned by any of the supervisors on duty. Apart from that, she dodges people and security agents while going home so that she wouldn't fall into the trap of law enforcement agents. She did not know the process would be that tedious and long. Whenever she got home, she would interlace her fingers and crack her knuckles. This was a means of non-verbally releasing stress off her body—she was relieved that she was not caught. When things were not changing, she had to leave before being caught by enforcement agencies.

19.55. Leg Tapping

Generic Interpretations of the Concept

In some situations, the hands find their way to the sides of the legs—near the pocket area— to express our emotions. Note that the hands are not dipped into the pocket but made to touch the outer part of the pocket. More often than not, we tend to use the palms and not the fingers in touching the sides of the legs. The reason being that palms touching the thighs produces a tactile experience that is capable of dealing with stress. When we are overtaken by anxiety, we tend to look for mild ways of keeping ourselves in shape.

One of the causes of this behaviour is impatience. The legs are our instruments of movement. So the hands hitting them is a symbolic way of urging them to walk past where they are. This means the person thinks being at some other place rather than their present location will do them; they do not feel there is a corresponding value in that location. In the same vein, we tend to display this attitude when we are getting aggravated. We believe that we are getting delayed unnecessarily and trying to be the lord of our time.

One place I have always observed this cue is at hotels when people are waiting to be checked in; we think things should move faster than the present level of how the workers are handling them. Also, you may see this at airports when passengers feel they should have been called in ahead of time. In general, when we become impatient at the turn of events, we will tap the sides of the legs to keep ourselves calm. This a metaphorical way of rubbing the legs at the 'head' for keeping them delayed at a spot when you should have moved on.

When we tap the legs, we tend to be distracted from an activity that should have otherwise be a source of frustration to us. More so, it is a very potent pacifier. All these combined, we are kept in shape.

Scientific Explanations

Almost all the literature that contributed to this subject matter made it clear that it tilts along impatience. An article by Joe Navarro (2012) sates that touching the leg is an indication that you are in a hurry or anxious to take your leave. This is likened to bouncing the legs that is used in communicating the same message.

Changing Minds (2019) gives detailed explanation of this cue from the perspectives of sitting and standing. According to the platform, 'When sitting, more of the leg may be reached, particularly in the figure-four cross-leg position, and in a more visible manner. Seductive stroking can thus be a strong sexual invitation.' This is often done by ladies, especially when they wear skimpy dress that exposes the thighs, a very sensual area of the body, just for the purpose of arousing the sexual feelings of their partner or a potential spouse. When the hands are rubbed over the thighs, it may become irresistible to the other person. It is like a trap which has often been well used by females to non-verbally lure someone who has interest in to their bosom. In the case of tapping, the website observes that it may be an indication of impatience or done in a reaction to music.

However, while standing, we may not be able to touch the sides of the sides of the legs compared with the sitting gesture. When the side of the leg is tapped with a hand (usually the right), it is used to express irritation at something; you will see it being slapped rather than a slight tap. This means the person is not uncomfortable with something being done at them. If they were sitting, they would have banged at a table. This may also mean that they are calling the attention of someone so as to take their leave together. This is verbally interpreted as 'Right, let's go'.

David Straker (2019) states that when the legs are tapped and bounced simultaneously, it is a show of impatience.

Also, Bob Whipple (2019) lends a voice to this concept. According to him, the implication of the leg-tapping cue is 'almost always impatience'. He gives the counterpoint at the airport as one of the most often places where this cue is played out. Also, you may see this in the class where a teacher repeats a point over and over again just for the sake of the slow members of the class. The smart ones might tap their leg to show their impatience on the need to move to another point. They are trying to non-verbally communicate with the teacher that they have got on with the point already.

Whipple states that if a speaker ignores someone who is tapping their legs, it is evidence that the speaker has low sensitivity. Seeing someone tap their legs means your attention should be drawn to them. With that, the person will pour out their mind without necessarily elongating issues.

Practical Illustrations

Case Study I: It was almost time for break and the teacher taking cultural studies was still in class. He seemed to be explaining a very important concept because he had 100 per cent class attention. However, he was going over a point repeatedly and some of the students could be seen frowning their face and looking at the teacher irritatingly. The teacher obviously saw this but was more concerned about the students that were still looking lost. So he decided to run over the concept again. At some point, one of the boys seated at the back began to tap his foot, showing his impatience; it was break time and many of them could not afford to spare five minutes out of the time for any other assignment on earth.

Case Study II: Mr K was to fly out by 2 p.m. for an important meeting but an emergency came up that kept him back till some minutes after the take-off time. By 2.15 p.m., he rushed to the counter to make enquiries on what he could do to meet up with the next flight but it seemed the lady behind the counter was busy entering some data on the computer. Mr K tapped his legs continuously as he was becoming impatient until she looked up. And they were able to take up the business from there.

Case Study III: Prostitute HJ met a client via virtual means and after chatting for some few moments, they arranged a meeting. Her expectations were high on this particular man and she did dress well so as to impress him on their first meeting. When they met, HJ was utterly disappointed, both in the dressing and manner of talk of the man. She knew the man was not an ideal client for her. Not wanting to conclude on his financial muscle, she named her price and the expression on the man's face alone was enough to pass his message. While the man was trying to negotiate with her, she became impatient and started tapping his leg. This means she wanted to be on her way.

19.56. Preening Gesture

Generic Interpretations of the Concept

When you hear preening, your mind tends to go to birds. While this is right and conventional, let me state that preening is not an exclusive attribute of birds, it is also used by humans at different points in time. Just as in birds, we also preen to look charming and attractive. In other words, this is done by those who care about their appearance. There are people, such as academics, factory workers, labourers, among others, who do not give an iota of concern to their physical appearance. However, some are so much concerned about their look per time that they go about with their beauty products. So any moments they are not pleased with their look, they will quickly do a retouch.

Before you assume that preening must be a ladies' thing, may I add that it is done by both males and females but it is surely more prevalent among the latter group. Also, it is done at different points. For instance, men tend to preen their body before the start of a relationship but ladies do display this cue when the relationship has actually started; during the course of the affair.

Repositioning of bracelets, tie readjustments, fixing of the hair, plucking of eyebrows, reapplication of lipsticks, smoothing out a real or imaginary wrinkle on the shirt, among others are some of the means people preen their body. We do all for the sake of bringing out our best look.

When our urge is driven by romance, the most common form of gesture we display in this context is hair preening. Also, stroking the hair repeatedly is an attribute that get us noticed. It may also interest you to know that when legal practitioners pull at their jacket as the jury enters the courtroom, they are unconsciously perceived by the judges as being more likable. The emotion or psychology that drives this is still unknown. Hence, preening can be used in many positive ways. In a romantic adventure, business, personal or professional life, this gives us a better image when we understand how to rightly activate it.

Scientific Explanations

The Art of Charm Academy submits that 'one sign of attraction that's far more likely to be seen through women's body language than men's is preening. When a girl is preening (subtly adjusting her clothing, jewellery, hair, etc. in order to appear more attractive) it's often a signal that the girl is interested. And if the girl starts preening *you*, it's an even stronger indicator of interest.' Even though I have been careful of pinning down an outright meaning to any particular gesture, this appears to be an exemption. If it is not dismissive preening (discussed after this section), then it is surely a sign of attraction. However, too much of ingredients spoil the stew; when preening becomes too much, it gives a negative message.

If someone who is preening is so much focused on the action that she is not giving attention to what is going on in her environment, this means she has totally lost interest in the person she was moved to. 'When you see this make a point to switch gears and change the topic of conversation – before it's too late,' admonishes the Art of Charm Academy.

Also, Hanan Parvez (2016) lists this as one of the seven signs of attraction that was discussed in her article. She states that we all strive to look good when we are in the company of those that interest us. So when you see someone preen when you enter a venue, this is an accurate indication that they are interested in you. Preening gestures as used here refers to any behaviour that reassures someone that they are beautiful and standard, at least for the target person. This may include even the slightest form of body adjustment.

David Straker (2019) notes that this behaviour is common and appears to be a courtship ritual, used in all animal kingdom. To back up this claim, Straker submits that 'birds pick at their feathers, chimps pick at fleas and humans tidy themselves to look good for their prospective partners'. Some of the actions you may always look out for in people are: excessive look of the mirror, straightening of clothes or ties, combing or patting down hair with fingers, curling lips so as to even out lipsticks, among other actions.

Practical Illustrations

Case Study I: Lady H is well to do; she secured a high—paying job after school and has been on it for half a decade. However, she has not met the 'best' of guys, as she would always say. She was approaching her thirties and the reality descended on her that she had to settle down and lead a more serious life. So she pruned down all those unattainable virtues she was looking for in a man. However, the knowledge that she could not date humans has trended among men and, as such, none within her vicinity is ready for her. One day, she was invited for a wedding in a neighbouring city. She knew that was an opportunity for her. So she went there, dressing in highly fashionable style. Fortunately for her, she sat at a table filled with men. She fell in love with one of them and after some few eye contacts, she began to stroke her hair and curl her mouth to make her lipstick look evenly. All these are romantic gestures to make her a cynosure of all eyes.

Case Study II: Mr U was sent to make transactions at the bank from his workplace. When he got there, he could not concentrate on the assignment given due to an adorable lady working with the bank. As he stood before her to begin his official work, he began to readjust his ties, ran his hand through his hair, smooth his clothes and wipe off imaginary wrinkles from his clothes, he was preening his body so that he could look handsome to the teller. It took some time for the teller to decode this gesture but after it came to her consciousness, she smiled at the man; she was already married. Her smile at the man's preening gesture was more of a teasing or mockery.

Case Study III: Smuggler GO was arrested for trying to import some hard weapons into her country. The country was going through some internal crisis that many pundits feared that it could lead to ethnic wars. So law enforcement agencies were at alert on all the possible ways that warring factions could employ to make things got worse. GO had allowed herself to be used by opportunists who deceived her that being a lady, there were not going to be too much checks of her loads. Seeing that there was no objective way to defend herself, she began to preen her body so that she could look attractive to the officer checking her loads. However, the officer was expert enough and would not allow that affect his objective sense of judgement.

19.57. Dismissive Preening

Generic Interpretations of the Concept

To help resolve this issue, let me state from the outset that this is the polar opposite of the preening gesture discussed above. I explained earlier that preening is used in love and other areas of life to show interest and affection towards someone. However, this is the other side of the coin where preening is done to dismiss another person; it is a show of disrespect. Without opening their mouth or even displaying an insulting facial expression, people can trample on our right and question our authority through some other behaviours, such as dismissive preening.

When we are being addressed by another person, we are expected to listen carefully and follow their every word. This shows we care about them and what they are saying; this is a show of love that is appreciated by every human. However, if instead, we tend to clean our nails or pick hair or lint from our clothes, this is considered rude. We are being inconsiderate of what the person is saying. We are metaphorically telling the person that they are not worth our attention and we look is more important than what they have to say; it is a belittling act expected to birth a negative reaction from the speaker. If it is a formal gathering where the person had prepared for hours, it would seem as if their effort is not appreciated.

At worst, this is considered as a contempt. If you are dealing with a highly temperamental individual who has authority over you, then you should be expecting same reaction along that line. If it were in school, a teacher may discipline their student for showing that kind of uncouth attitude. Parents shout at their kids when they seem not to be listening while being addressed. This tells you that there is a stimulus in us that craves for the attention of the addressee in every speech context.

Scientific Explanations

Marc Chernoff (2008) says that pint picking is an attitude that should be avoided by all means. He notes that 'if you pick lint off your clothes during a conversation, especially in conjunction with looking downwards, most people will assume that you disapprove of their ideas and/or feel uneasy about giving them an honest opinion'. And incidentally, this seems to be a universal perception of the gesture. If you do not buy into an idea, you will definitely not give any importance to it. Looking downwards means you are not moved to communicate with the person. Those who are cheerful about the conversation they are holding will maintain an appropriate eye contact level and leave their hands to move naturally so as to lay emphasis on whatever they have to say instead of engaging in a way that makes it less productive. If truly there is a lint on the clothes, just leave them alone to show that you are concentrated on what the person is saying.

Philip (2014) describes this cue as an act of breaking eye contact during a conversation so as to 'remove lint, smooth clothing, apply lipstick and so forth.' Hence, the lint picker is referred to as a person that is showing non-verbal distain. This cue can be used in dating and general context. For the general usage, Philip explains that the cue is motivated by the need to dismiss or disapprove what another person is saying. He puts it thus: 'A non-verbal displacement gesture indicating a difference of opinion, disapproval, dislike, contempt, and indifference or dismissiveness which is especially salient when lint is entirely absent indicating that the true purpose is to avoid eye contact.' When a person is intentionally distracted or avoids eye contact by hiding under the need to pick lint, then be sure that they do not value what you have to offer them.

In the context of dating, this is a signal of interest until eye contact is broken for a while, meaning the person is no longer interested in you. If preening is positive, the person will pick items or parts of the body that will arouse the emotions of their partner but once items such as 'picking the nose, picking the nails or pinching pimples' is the order of the day, there is high likelihood that the person is not moved by your presence. They are distasteful grooming, expected to be done in private. Philip concludes, 'Making others witness such grotesqueness is truly offensive and dehumanising.'

The verbal translation of this cue is given as 'I don't like you and what you are saying so I'm going to act rude and remove fake lint from my body until you shut up.' This gesture may be used when you want to hurl insult that falls below the conscious radar at a person. When you see a person removing lint where none actually exists, you should decode the message that they are insulting you.

Practical Illustrations

Case Study I: D came to M's desk when it was time for break with the hope that they would share some gist together as the case had always been. Unknowing to D, a colleague had smeared her name before M. without bothering to verify, M thought that what was said concerning D was the truth. So when D came to her, she was not even ready to listen to her. As D started a conversation, she observed that M was much more attentive to her task of removing cat hair from her jacket than she was to her. D got the message loud and clear, broke off the conversation early and carried on with her day.

Case Study II: Mr T was addressing his secretary, Y on the need to implement some new policies in the company. Y did not really believe in what he was saying but it would be rude of her to confront her boss verbally. So she decided to listen on with feigned interest but when it got to a point she could not bear again, she refocused her attention to picking imaginary lint off her clothes, disconnecting her eye contact from Mr T. After some minutes, he got this message that his presence was distractive and asked Y what was wrong. She seized the opportunity to tell him what she felt about the policies.

Case Study III: Criminal FT had tendered a forged document to an organisation for the purpose of duping them and accessing some private pieces of information. After he had presented the forged item to the person in charge, he watched his reaction for some time. When he discovered that the man was actually shaking his head instead of nodding, he quickly fetched his phone from his pocket and busied himself with it. Even when the man needed to confirm some things from the document he presented, he looked away and pretended as if he did not hear the man call out to him.

19.58. Placing Hand on Leg with Elbow Out

Generic Interpretations of the Concept

This is a great pose that you tend to see during discussions and at other places. It is the act of placing a hand (usually the right) on a thigh with the elbows pointing out. When people, especially young men, are about to take pictures, they do display this posture. It makes them look bigger and more confident than how they could have been if they had sat otherwise.

In the context of communication, when you see someone display this stance, they are communicating huge messages. First, it is an indication of unmatched level of confidence. When the person is seated with the back rested on a chair, legs not interlocked and a hand on the leg, it means the person is not threatened by anything going on in their environment. For a minute, I want you to demonstrate this cue in order to have a better understanding of what is being explained. If the person were not confident, they would have used the hand placed on the leg to cover their genitals, thereby expressing their insecurity.

This message becomes distorted the moment the person begins to slouch on the chair. We are unconsciously made to see them as closing up their body, thereby impeding the flow of discussion. Ideally, this behaviour comes and disappears during the course of a discussion. When the person's self-assurance waxes strong due to a point made, they will display this cue but if it wanes off over an unfavourable comment, they will drop this and display another one. At least, this behaviour serves as an illuminator, telling you what someone feels about your words per time.

Further, pointing the elbows out is a territorial display. When you point out the elbow, no one will be able to come near. This means you have your personal space. In a way, this is display of authority. People who are respected in the society are given their personal space; you cannot just move very close to them without any reason. So the pointing out of the primitive weapon of the body is to guard our space from likely invasion by opponents.

Scientific Explanations

Straker (2019) discusses this under the thigh body language. He notes that depending on the kind of touch on the upper part of the legs, it can bear an array of meanings. For instance, if someone places their hand on a leg towards the end of a discussion, this is an implication that they are getting prepared to take their leave. By the moment the two hands are placed the thighs, this is to support the person to stand up and leave the location.

Also, when a hand is placed on the leg, it is a mild widening of the body; it would have been full if both hands were involved. This can be threatening to the other party, depending on the topic that is being discussed. It may also be a mean of expressing displeasure.

Also Straker states that 'touching the thighs draws attention to them. As the thighs are near the genitals, touching can be very suggestive. The nearer the genitals the hands move, the more inviting it is. Touching the inside of the leg is more suggestive than touching the outside of the leg.' You need to take note of this. In a meeting, if someone is probably displaying this cue, it may be an invitation to sexual romance instead of show of confidence. Someone who is displaying confidence will most probably place the hand at the centre or outer part of the leg so as to make the elbow pointing out more pronounced but if it were sexual invitation. The hand will move inward, towards the genital.

Study Body Language (2016) provides another angle to this issue. The author makes it known that a leg can be crossed over the other while the dominant is made to be on top before a hand is placed over it. Females are fond of this habit because it reveals a lot about the leg features. This is more connected with habit and comfort. When some are seated in this position, they do enjoy themselves. And also, the person might be cold. You will take on any posture you think gives you the best comfort at any point in time. Also, women may be using the hand to block out their thighs from full view when they are on mini-skirts.

Practical Illustrations

Case Study I: Mr Y went to meet one of his friends to discuss a business idea; a novel one which he thought if they could partner on, it would be easily realised rather than he alone pursuing it. So the friend needed to be sure of the feasibility of the proposed project before he would commit his finances to it. The friend asked Mr Y different questions. Any time he was to answer a question he was certain of, he would place his right hand on his thigh and slightly lean forward towards his friend but if the question seemed to be somewhat hard, he would take off the hand from the leg. Unconsciously, the friend discovered that any time his hand was on his leg, Y sounded more convincing than when he had it off.

Case Study II: Lady T and Guy W went out to relax and have some fun. They were at a classy bar that is known for hosting best of fashion freaks around the world. Guy W knew that smart men who could snatch away ladies were always there. He wanted to turn down the offer to hang out at that particular location but T's pressure was overwhelming. While seated at a corner, he discovered that eyes were on them by hungry men; those who did not come with any lady. Hence, his intuitions told him to be on guard. While discussing with his lady, he placed a hand on his upper leg, with the elbow pointing towards the people he considered as a threat. This was a territorial display, warning others not to come near.

Case Study III: Mr PR is a serial killer; he has killed so many people that human life does not bear any value with me again. He perfected all those killings that no one ever traced the incidents to him. However, the murdering of his wife which is the latest of his killings almost gave him out. Although there were traces that could be linked to him to have been the perpetrator of the action, he wasn't ready to admit and no major evidence on the part of the enforcement agents. While being interviewed, he stood with courage by placing his hand on leg, pushing out the elbow, which gave the perception that he was saying the truth.

19.59. Curling of Fingers and Flicking of Nails

Generic Interpretations of the Concept

This is an attribute that we often see when people are moved towards a negative occurrence. Curling of the fingers is a closed body language that denies us of the privilege to understand how expressive the hands can be in a conversation. I see the fingers as the 'mouth of the hands'. So imagined that your lips are sealed, how will you be able to communicate fluently? The same thing happens when the fingers are curled up and nailed made to flick on the thumb. Most often, this is usually done on a hand—whether right or left. The person displaying this gesture may flicker just a finger or the four, depending on how they are feeling the emotions.

Stress is the major reason deduced to this gesture. Once the intensity of stress overshadows our inner ability, we become weakened and look for ways to lessen the effects. Agitation is another common reason that has been said to be capable of making people display this gesture. Our temperament can be tested in different ways at any given location. There are some locations that we believe we should rather respect those present rather than reacting to the situation as we are pained. Conventionally, agitation makes us flare up and rise against the status quo but any time we become constrained to publicly display the agitation, it would be suppressed in a way that people around us who are observant enough will understand that something negative is happening to us. The hands that was supposed to be the tool of demonstration are curled up so as to defeat the purpose.

Also, when people are nervous, they may curl up their fingers and flick their nails. Fear recreates us; it brings out our weakest part—we become vulnerable to the extent that our fingers might begin to shake but since we do not want others to be aware of this vulnerability we will curl the fingers up and flick them. Hence, those observing us are made to erroneously believe that we are probably flicking the nails at will, when in fact, it is an aftermath of a negative occurrence.

This gesture is primarily meant to pacify an agitated, stressed or nervous person. The cue looks very dramatic to the extent that it can be distracting to the person; they are distracted from the activity that is giving them difficult time. It is pertinent to state that this may be a source of noise to your co-interlocutor. This can distract from concentration.

Scientific Explanations

According to Straker (2019) curling up the fingers and drumming the nails is an indication of frustration. People flick their nails. The essence may be to make distractive noise so that the person may release. In other words, they are communicating the urge to take their leave. When they become distractive, the other party gets the message that they are no longer adding value to the person's life and must allow their wish to prevail. We do this when we think expressing our wish verbally can be problematic.

Apart from the urge to leave, when you see a person flick their nails, it might be a means of interrupting the speaker. Probably, they have something to say but the speaker is not giving them the opportunity to express themselves. So they think that this disruptive habit will make their frustrations known to the person; it is a subtle means of coercing someone to do our wish. Straker puts it thus: 'Non-verbal noise sends an audible interrupt signal to the other person. The louder the noise and faster the drumming, the greater the tension the person is feeling. Drumming with the nails makes an even louder noise and hence sends a more urgent signal.' When tension increases, the person doubles the drumming rate. If the person at the other end of the discussion turns a blind eye to their agitation, it may end up leading to physical or verbal confrontation.

Also, this gesture may indicate that someone is having some negative thoughts. This means the frustrations they are experiencing is caused from within. This is usually emotional and capable of depressing the person. When someone curls up their fingers and flick the nails while thinking, this means an easy solution is not in any way near for them. Casting your mind on an issue and things still appearing very difficult can take breath out of one's heart. Hence, the person displaying this cue may be undergoing one of the most turbulent moments in life.

Practical Illustrations

Case Study I: Child D was accused by his parents of bringing in his wayward friends whenever they were not at home. Times without number, they have such traces—everywhere was always scattered, items carted away and the entire room rearranged in an irritated manner. When he was warned, they observed that there were changes. After some few months, they noticed that some electronics and cash could not be found. That day, Child D was not at home too but they thought it was after he brought his friends in that he went out. Unknowingly, armed robbers had gained entrance when they were all out. Child D wanted to plead innocence and explain himself but the mother would not take things easy with him. The child really became stressed at some point and could be seen curling up her fingers and flicking her nails against the thumb, making loud, disruptive sound to his mother.

Case Study II: After three months of securing a dream job with one of the leading multinational companies in the universe, Lady R was shown the way out; she could not scale through the probationary period. She was engaged in menial jobs four years after graduation from school before fortunes tilted towards her. She had built her castles in the air; what she would save up to buy, where she would spend her vacation and how she was going rise through the ladder to lead the firm. Now, they were all gone and she had to start from the scratch, now, changing her goals to match those of any other firm that would consider her worthy. While thinking of the next stage her life would take, she curled her right fingers and flicked one of the nails against the thumb. This depicted someone bothered by something important.

Case Study III: Drug Addict AK was lost in the labyrinth of making some decisions concerning his illicit acts. Apart from being a drug trafficker, he was also involved in some criminal activities to make ends meet. So he sees law enforcement agents as his enemies and relates with them as such. On a particular evening, he was really craving for hard drugs and decided to drive down to where he used to buy them. On his way, he had an inkling that there were law enforcement officers along the route. After waiting for few minutes, he saw people moving along the route effortlessly but he was afraid of being flagged down. At this point, he curled his right finger and curled a nail against his thumb. This means he was psychologically stressed due to the kind of thoughts he was brooding on.

19.60. Shaking of Hands

Generic Interpretations of the Concept

I am always careful when discussing this subject matter because of its delicate nature and how it is perceived across the world. Without mincing words, this is the favoured form of greeting in the Western part of the world. In many parts of Asia, it was not fancied by social media, need for international businesses and global cooperation is fast making the concept of shaking hands a global phenomenon. Even though handshake might still be seen in a negative light in some cultures, the professional world is adopting it as the favoured form of establishing bond. Trending of videos and cultures of the West has made this concept a household phenomenon across the world. Hence, understanding how handshake works should be the concern of everyone.

Handshake forms the first point of physical contact between people and also while departing, it is the last action that is always taken. The way it is done always leaves people with either bad or good impression about you. That is why it is crucial for you to understand it before you go global. When a handshake is too wet, too long, too strong or soft, it is considered as 'bad'. When you receive such handshake from people, it leaves a bad impression about the person for a long time and in future time, you will not be enthusiastic about shaking the person; you are not ready for another gruesome moment.

One thing that should be on the back of your mind is that the custom of handshake is not universal. There are cultures that prefer a bow or kiss to shaking of hands. Notwithstanding, an ideal handshake starts with the right amount of eye contact, a genuine smile (if appropriate for the context), and slight bending of the elbow when the arms are extended towards the target person. As the fingers approach the hands of your co-interlocutor, they should be pointing downward while the hands should be clasped with equal pressure-do not press too hard; no one is interested in what you can do with the hands. Then, the hands should engulf each other so as to trigger the release of oxytocin hormone that is known for bolstering social bonding. Ideally, the handshake is not expected to last for more than a second or two.

However, there are different factors that dictate the duration of a handshake. For instance, while shaking with a higher status person, the person will determine how long the shake lasts. If the person wants to maintain a strictly professional or status relationship, they will drop the hand as soon as possible. However, if the person is interested in you, they may hold the hand and exchange some pleasantries with you before finally letting go of your hand. The authoritative figure also determines the pressure you apply in the exchange.

When shaking elderly people, the pressure should be minimal; their age and strength level comes to play.

Scientific Explanations

Radwan (2017) explains that it takes an average of five to ten seconds for people to form their opinion about us. While you may not have control over your look, one of the factors you can take advantage of is the manner in which you shake the person.

One of the general uses of handshake is to portray confidence. Let me give this illustration to shed light on this. While you are comfortably seated at home watching horror movie, you become afraid. The secret is that the subconscious mind thinks in the primitive way, thereby inspiring the fear even when it caused by external stimulus. In the same way, when you firmly hold someone while exchanging handshake, the primitive mind makes you believe that you are stronger than the person. 'So by making sure that your handshake is firm, without exerting extra unneeded pressure, you will be leaving the impression that you are a confident person,' urges Radwan.

If some want to make 'disciples' of others through the handshake, they will position their palms horizontally instead of the vertical position it is always known to take. There are two possible cases in this instance—the first is when the palm is parallel and facing the floor and secondly, it is when the palm is made to face the sky. Radwan explains that 'the first gesture reflects the desire to dominate while the other one represents a state of submission. The person who positions his palm so that it faces the ground while shaking hands will usually be doing so because of his unconscious desire to dominate the other person. On the other hand positioning the palm so that it faces the sky usually reflects the state of being submissive to the other person.' Always take note of this and know the best to use in every given context, taking the status of the person into consideration.

Parvez (2015) traces the use of handshake to the ancient times when our forefathers needed to check the hands of one another to be sure their opponents were not holding weapons. In today's world, it is also used to show openness but in a friendly and hospitable manner.

What matters most is that you understand what someone is thinking of you through their handshake. Someone who tries to shake you with their palms facing down is seeking to control you; they want to overshadow you. You can control this by simply holding the person's hand and then firmly return it to the vertical stance (Radwan 2017).

Practical Illustrations

Case Study I: It was regional managers' meeting of SXU Multinational Concepts. It is usually a gathering of brains where cerebral discussions take place. However, many of them are always not submissive. While some think seniority should be based on the largeness of the branch they head, some are of the opinion that it should be based on the years of service while the remaining group are of the sentiment that it should be based on educational qualification. So this obvious show of pride has made them to restrict their relationship to professional grounds only. During the last meeting, Manager A tried to exchange handshake with Manager B by making his palm faced the ground so as to give him room to dominate the process. However, Manager B firmly turned the hand to vertical position so as level things up. This was a smart move to ensure that no one dominates over the other.

Case Study II: Prisoner BT was wrongly jailed for another person's offence. So he believed that he was not part of the prisoners. In fact, he used to refer to himself as 'prisoner of conscience'. His relationships with the warders and other people simply distinguished him. However, a lot of people saw this as a show of pride. For instance, whenever he wanted to exchange handshake with anyone, he would make sure that his palm was facing the ground as a way of showing domination. It usually turned to an awkward moment when anyone with an understanding of non-verbal communication wanted to turn it to a vertical position.

Case Study III: Con Artist KT has been looking for all ways to influence the life of Man RE; he knew the man is financially buoyant but seems to be lacking in confidence. So he devises a way to exploit him through his insecurity. One of the tactics KT employs is to also present himself as a rich man with services to render to RE. Hence, whenever they are together, he would talk of various things and how they can help Man RE. Further, KT will sit with authority and exchange handshake with Man RE by turning down his palm as a way of displaying his domineering attitude. Man RE unconsciously began to tell him so sensitive things until he got hold of his life.

19.61. Tendered Handshake

Generic Interpretations of the Concept

As I have earlier observed, the wave of the Western and civilisation has made handshake a common phenomenon across the world. However, it seems each region is trying to domesticate the concept so that it would reflect their own cultural views. One of the places where such is pronounced is the African continent. Africans are known for revering their elders and those in high positions. Conventionally, they bow out of respect while some go on their knees or even prostrate themselves.

In the tendered handshake gesture, someone, usually a junior or younger person, will outstretch their right hand to greet an elderly or revered personality and support the underneath of the forearm with the left hand as if the right counterpart is being carried. Literally, the right hand is being tendered to the respected person as if it were something valuable. The person tendering the hand hopes that the other person accepts it. It is also pertinent to note that, most often than not, it is the elderly person that must first stretch out their arms for the handshake. It is usually a great honour for a young person or subordinate to exchange handshake with a superior or elder.

Those who are not from that region of the world may see the gesture as being odd and unfathomable. However, this does not change it from being a culture of high respect and show of deference. Hence, strangers must accept it as such. At least, that is one of the things that make their culture peculiar and unique to yours. Once you come in tandem with this reality, you may see it begin to play out with you; subordinates and those who consider themselves as being lesser to you may start offering you hands, as if the right hand is heavier than the left or reluctant to move.

Scientific Explanations

Parvez (2015) states that those who use this gesture always want to be perceived as being trustworthy. There are some societies that value trust, and as such, those from those part of the world will do everything in order to be seen in that light. Remember that, that the person wants to give an impression of being trustworthy does not necessarily mean they are. It is left for the person being offered the hand to look inward and see if they are truly trustworthy or not. In the Western world, those who are passionately in look of acceptance may also make use of this gesture. That is why it is somewhat common among politicians.

When this kind of handshake is given to someone who values being honoured, they do appreciate it and may also use the two hands to shake the person; the person offering them the hand. When you see this, apart from pure cultural grounds, a person's intention may also be subjected to questioning when you observe this—what is the person desperate for that is making them look sincerely humble? With that, you may spot their intentions before showering encomiums on them. With this, you will not regret making any decision in regard to the person's behaviour.

In his contribution, Radwan (2017) also observes that this form of handshake where the two hands are involved is a bit uncommon. He states that 'that person, who uses both hands, is putting more effort in the handshake than others. The two handed handshake in body language is like an exaggeration of the handshake process and this leads us to the conclusion that more emotions are involved during that handshake.' They are trying to create the impression that they are totally committed to the process. Since those offering a hand by supporting with another hand sees it as an honour to be shaking the other person, they want to prove that their feeling is sincere and motivated from the within.

When someone like you a lot, there is likelihood that they show extra emotion while trying to exchange handshake with you. Since the person might need some goodwill from you in the future and wants to establish rapport by all means, they might use this form of handshake to broker a relationship. We do not have to be pessimistic about everything; the person may truly feel elated or even fulfilled for meeting you and this is demonstrated in their exchange of handshake.

Further, Radwan submits that 'if a person feels guilty towards you or if that person feels that he should be overly nice to you because he didn't treat you well in the past for example then he might also use the two handed handshake to compensate for those feelings.' One thing that is undeniable is that this cue is a positive sign that shows a person who wants to improve their relationship with you. If they had treated you badly in the past, they are seeing this as an opportunity to correct their past errors.

Radwan (2017) sounded the warning that an enemy may also use this gesture as a way of getting into you; not all that glitters is gold and every offer must be considered critically. However, it is rare for you to see actors make use of this gesture. If there are no genuine emotions backing up the person, they will feel unpleasant, exposing their deceit. In the same vein, 'this gesture is usually common among males as it's not common for a male to shake hands with a female with both hands since it can seem awkward.'

Practical Illustrations

Case Study I: Despite being rich and well connected, Chief YT is reputed for his humility. As an African, he is known to give much attention to his culture. He serves as the president of ASQ and rarely goes to check on his workers. There was a day he paid an unscheduled visit to the office. He walked in, meeting the security official at the gate, he offered his hand and the security man, honoured by this unrivalled humility, outstretched his hand and supported it with the left at the forearm, bowing gently, so as to exchange handshake with Chief YT. This was a show of deference.

Case Study II: Mr QL hates his neighbour, Dr PY, a very rich folk. The assumption of QL is that his neighbour is too full of himself due to his wealth. However, he has never been to PY for help and come back empty-handed. Even when he tries to run the rich man down before others and they ask him what the man's offence is, he becomes confused, lacking any definite explanation. However, QL lives pretentiously; whenever he wants to exchange handshake with Dr PY, he would use his right hand with the left at the forearm and gently bow as a fake show of deference. His facial expression usually betrays him—he looks scornfully instead of smiling.

Case Study III: My men once arrested a man for being an illegal immigrant. After some few questioning sessions before he was driven down to our office, he had confessed that he came into the country through an illegal means. He begged my subordinates so hard that they almost became emotional about him. However, they informed him that I was the only one who could decide on his fate. So when he was showered into my office and I stretched forth my hand to him, he bowed simultaneously as he also stretched out his hand and used his left hand to support the forearm of the other hand. At that point, I knew the show of humility was for a sinister reason. And this ensured that I stood on the right path on the matter.

19.62. 'Indian Handshake'—Namaste

Generic Interpretations of the Concept

I tag this 'Indian handshake' because it is a prevalent gesture among them and used to serve the same purpose which the handshake serves in the Western world. I have decided to discuss this at this point so as to prove that handshake is a Western thing and people from other parts of the world have their own unique ways of greetings. India is one of the countries where respecting elders or superiors is of the uttermost interest of the citizenry; they pride themselves over their culture, just like Japanese and other Asian nations.

Namaste is a conventional Indian exchange of pleasantries. To demonstrate this, the palms would be placed together, positioned directly at chest level, fingers directed upward, the elbows spread out an may be sometimes capped with a little bow or leaning forward and genuine smile. This is usually seen in formal settings. When the palms are held together, this means the person cannot stretch out their hand simultaneously to exchange handshake with another person. That is why it is said that this cue is made to replace the handshake concept in the Asian country. It can also be used to connote 'so long'.

There is no gainsaying that this cue has deeper meaning than the Western handshake version in its physical display and metaphorical connotation. The physical display of the gesture looks like someone who is appealing to another person; it invokes emotion of the person whom this is directed to. There is little wonder that it is always received with respect. The joined hands are placed at the chest region to metaphorically state that the greeting comes from the deepest part of their heart—it is done wholeheartedly. On the other hand, handshake is common seen as a means of casual greeting. This is not an attempt to prioritise a form of greeting over the other but just to state the obvious.

Scientific Explanations

While trying to discuss the way various cultures meet and exchange pleasantries, Philip (2013) states, 'The namaste is a greeting done in India by placing both hands together palm to palm across the chest and bowing slightly. It's origins like the handshake and wave demonstrates that no weapon is present.' Spreading the elbow out also make the other person know that despite the fact that you are not holding any weapon, you are not fidgeting.

Singh (2015) states that this is a customary Hindu greeting. Thomas Burrow explains that Namaste is derived from Sanskrit and is a combination of the word *namah* and the second person dative pronoun in its enclitic form, *te*. The term *namas* is found in the Vedic literature. *Namas-krita* and related terms appear in the Hindu scripture *Rigveda* such as in the *Vivaha Sukta*, verse 10.85.22 in the sense of 'worship, adore', while *Namaskara* appears in the sense of 'exclamatory adoration, homage, salutation and worship' in the *Atharvaveda*, the *Taittiriya Samhita*, and the *Aitareya Brahmana*. It is an expression of veneration, worship, reverence, an 'offering of homage' and 'adoration' in the Vedic literature and post-Vedic texts such as the *Mahabharata* (Monier-Williams 2008).

According to the Indologist Stephen Phillips, the terms '*te* and *tvam*' are an informal, familiar form of 'you' in Sanskrit (much like thou and thee in archaic English), and it is typically not used for unfamiliar adults. It is reserved for someone familiar, intimate, divine or a child (Phillips 2009). By using the dative form of *tvam* in the greeting *Namas-te*, there is an embedded secondary, metaphorical sense in the word. This is the basis of the pragmatic meaning of *Namas-te*, that is 'salutations to the (divine) child (in your heart),' states Phillips.

In the contemporary era, *namah* means 'bow', 'obeisance', 'reverential salutation' or 'adoration' and *te* means 'to you' (singular dative case of 'tvam'). Therefore, Namaste literally means 'bowing to you,' state Douglas Harper in Etymology Dictionary. In Hinduism, it also has a spiritual import reflecting the belief that 'the divine and self (atman, soul) is same in you and me', and connotes 'I bow to the divine in you' (Lawrence 2007). According to sociologist Holly Oxhandler, it is a Hindu term which means 'the sacred in me recognises the sacred in you'.

The gesture is widely used throughout the Indian subcontinent, parts of Asia and beyond where people of South and Southeast Asian origins have migrated (Ying et al. 1999). Namaste or namaskar is used as a respectful form of greeting, acknowledging and welcoming a relative, guest or stranger. In some contexts, Namaste is used by one person to express gratitude for assistance offered or given, and to thank the other person for his or her generous kindness (Shaules 2007).

The cue is also part of the 16 upacharas used inside temples or any place of formal Puja (worship). Namaste in the context of deity worship, scholars conclude, has the same function as in greeting a guest or anyone else. It expresses politeness, courtesy, honour, and hospitality from one person to the other. It is used in goodbyes as well. This is sometimes expressed, in ancient Hindu scriptures such as Taittiriya Upanishad, as Atithi Devo Bhava (literally, 'treat the guest like a god') (Kelkar 2010).

Practical Illustrations

Case Study I: Dr A is an unrepentant conservative fellow; even though he had travelled across the length and breadth of the world, he still prefers his cultural way of greeting. There was an occasion he travelled to another continent for an official engagement and along the way met someone who also hailed from his tribe. While the fellow stretched out his hand to exchange pleasantries with him, Dr A joined his palms and positioned the hands in front of chest, bowed and accompanied it with a smile. The fellow did that in return in acknowledgement of his greeting.

Case Study II: Woman F thought she had stayed long enough with the family of her fiancé who was away for a fellowship programme. As she stood up to take her leave, those present urged her to honour them with her presence but she clapped her hands and placed them at her chest region to express the need to go.

Case Study III: Man QP just arrived in Country WOP where Namaste is their culture. At first, he was taken aback by this culture because he had never seen anything like that before he got there. So he saw it as fun than a mark of respect. When he started working, he began to hang out with people that eventually misled him; they introduced him to hard drugs and it didn't take long for law enforcement agents to arrest him and his cohorts. Thinking of what to do as a way of pleading for mercy as he had language barrier, he brought his palms together and raised them to his chest region before bowing to the officers but this had no effect on them.

19.63. Holding of Hand

Generic Interpretations of the Concept

It is an innate human behaviour to hold hand with those that we love or have some level of admiration for. Even as children, we start the act of holding hands by clinging to those of our parents. This gives us assurance of their protection and reciprocal love. Even as we grow up, we tend to reciprocate this gesture with our mates. This is most common among siblings; it is one of the shows of bond between them.

After growing up to maturity, we still display the hand-holding cue. This is often seen among romantic partners. The manner in which hands are held between lovers is a signal of their closeness. Some may just make it trivial by clasping the hands while some hold hands intimately by interlacing the fingers. The coming together of the palms produces a tactile feeling for the couples. This is the whole essence of the action; they want to have reassurance from each other that they will always be there.

Some lovers are shy and may be looking for ways to dodge holding hands with their partners. When they are forced to do it, it is done awkwardly, revealing their reluctance. This can send a negative message to their partner who may assume that his or her lover is not proud of them outside. This suffice to say that some romantic partners hold hands in public for the sake of show-off.

I also need to submit that this gesture is affected by some cultural and religious doctrines. For instance, some cultures frown at opposite sex holding hands when they are not yet married. They see it as an invitation to immorality. These are societies where the Islamic Sharia law is still being observed. If one is oblivious of what is in practice in those societies, one may fall victim of their ordinances. On the other hands, there are some countries where it is not unusual to see men hold hands while walking on the streets. Vietnam, Saudi Arabia, and Egypt are good examples where this can be found.

Scientific Explanations

Experts consider this gesture from different points of view and factors that can affect how it is perceived. For instance, Psychologia states that when you attempt to hold hand with a person, you are violating their personal space. It is now left for the person to determine if they are comfortable with it or not. Before you touch another person, you must confirm if they want to be touched or not. You can make this confirmation by subtly moving your items to their side and see their reaction. For example, if you push your handbag (serving as an extension of your body) into their personal space and they become uncomfortable, this is a warning sign that holding hands with you might not be their thing. Someone who is receptive of your items will definitely open up themselves to you.

There are different meanings attached to hand-holding gestures. The message is dependent on the person you are holding hand with—friend, family member, spouse, kid or stranger. Inasmuch as we will not be able to explore all these in details, we will try to espouse them passingly. Mercury (2016) submits that 'holding hands sends the message that you are proud to be with that person. But it is also a confirmation of union, and shows that you are together or bonded in some way.' There is little wonder our instinct tells that those holding hand are in a sort of relationship. Their gender does not matter in this sense. However, when they are adults, we may be quick to assume that they are romantically connected.

Mercury explains further when you hold hand with someone, it sends a message of interest to the person. It is an expression of an affection towards the person. This is why singles need to be careful while holding hands with people; if you do not have an interest in dating them, be cautious of how you frequently hold hands with them. You may end up arousing their feelings towards you. 'Women have been known to prefer cuddling and holding hands as a way of expressing their feelings towards someone, but it is a universal sign of intimate affection, along with kissing, massages, cuddling, and caressing,' notes Mercury.

Mercury also states that holding hands in an intimate relationship has a huge impact than anyone can think of. It may appear as being a simple gesture but its impact goes beyond the simplicity of its display. Mercury reports a study on 16 happily married couples where he observes that 'holding hands with someone you love can help to reduce stress'. Hence, we can conclude that this action is therapeutic. 'In the study, the wives were told they were going to receive shocks, and even were able to watch when the shocks were coming. It turns out that they felt more at ease when they were holding their husband's hands as opposed to facing the shocks alone. In addition, when holding a stranger's hand, they still experienced more calmness when they were not holding anyone's hand' (Mercury 2016).

Holding hands is symbolic in any relationship. For example, in a romantic affair, it has been observed that men usually place their hands over that of women. This is a dominant behaviour non-verbally expressing the need to protect the woman. In general, the person who perceives themselves to be strong will put their hand on top. I must state that when you already have a working, happy and enjoyable relationship with the person you are holding hands with, you will enjoy the most benefit of this gesture compared with someone who is not really OK with the person they are holding hands with (Mercury 2016).

Practical Illustrations

Case Study I: Mr and Mrs JR were going for a party and as they alighted from their car, they discovered that everywhere was agog already. In order to feel among and fit into the spirit of celebration, they decided to hold hands and walk into the venue in grand style to the admiration of those who focused their gaze on them—they presented themselves as the happiest couples in the gathering.

Case Study II: Today is the annual prize giving day at HRQ High School. It is a day of pride for parents whose kids had performed exceptionally during the session. Parent AW knows that her daughter would most probably lead her mates this session. Being a lover of such events, she holds the hand of her daughter after alighting from the car till they enter the venue of the event; she wants everyone to know that she is the mother of the child. And indeed, their guess works out. So immediately after the programme, she runs to her daughter and hold her by the hand again, commending her publicly before giving her a warm hug.

Case Study III: One great attribute I have noticed among criminals is their show of solidarity to one another; no matter the threat, they would hardly betray one another. In fact, I have had reasons to conclude that they are the most loyal group of people. For instance, there was a time we arrested some drug addicts who joined hand in clusters as if in a solidarity walk. And even after their arrest, they still held hands together till they were called in individually for interview. As expected, they all said similar things. It took a great deal of efforts to get them say the truth.

19.64. Precision Gesture—OK Cue

Generic Interpretations of the Concept

In our daily communication with people, we look for ways to emphasise our points through non-verbal means. This shows the accuracy and sincerity of our thoughts. One of such exercises is the precision cue that is popularly known as OK sign in the Western world. This has to do with holding the tip of the index finger with the thumb in a way that it forms a circle. When you see a speaker display this, it is a show of precision; they are not beating about the bush and have a full grasp of what they are portraying to you.

However, it is pertinent to note that there are cultural differences in the use of this gesture too. For instance, it is common in the Mediterranean where it is used to lay emphasis on a point. When people are conversing, they will use this gesture when they want to call their listener's attention to a specific point. Invariably, it is an indication that the point is somewhat important to every other one or serving as the thrust to the topic under discussion. In the US, this is used to connote agreement with what another person is saying; you are telling the speaker that your thought is in consonance with that they are saying. In some other times, it is used to mean that all is well. While you are in the United States and you see someone display this cue, this means you can relax because everything is in shape.

However, there are some other nations of the world where you should be careful about the use of this gesture because negative meaning is attached to it. For example, in Brazil, the OK sign is rather interpreted to be vulgar. Precisely, it is used to describe an orifice—the female genitals. Hence, it may be seen as an invitation to intercourse with the wrong person. This is the same in most African nations too.

Scientific Explanations

Tom Rothe (2015) gives a precise and clear explanation to this on Social Dynamics. He states that making the thumb to touch the index finger to form a circle while the three other fingers are spread apart is a means of saying that everything is OK in the Western culture or when a speaker intends to lay emphasis on a point. I have foregrounded this in the introductory section. In Japan, this means change (of money). That is, when you collect your balance after making a purchase. In France, this means nothing but 'zero'—the connotative meaning shares same with its literal symbol.

However, you may consider not using this gesture in Spain, Brazil, and Turkey because it is considered as inappropriate. This is a practical demonstration that body language may be perceived differently across the globe. For instance, a website that is focused on how to transact business in Turkey—BusinessinTurkey. com explains that in the country, displaying this gesture means that one is homosexual. So apart from being appearing offensive, it may also misrepresent your intentions to your listeners. This should not be confused with the act of holding hand with palm up where the fingers are brought near the thumb. In this case, the meaning is that something is good. It is a compliment, showing that we agree with something being done. 'It can be done when they like a food, a cloth, or any object. It can also mean they find a woman or man nice and handsome,' explains the website. Note that in this instance, the index finger will be pressed to the thumb instead of using it to form a circle.

Westside Toastmasters (2019) explains this gesture while discussing the cultural variations of gestures. It notes that the 'OK' sign originates from America but due to the influence of the American culture over others, we tend to imbibe their way. The website explains thus: 'Due to the wide distribution of American television and movies, the younger generations of all cultures are developing a generic form of North American body language. Most countries now recognise the ring gesture as meaning 'OK', even if it's not traditionally used locally.' This is to hint that you should not be surprise to see this cue even in the countries earlier mentioned that it is not acceptable, at least, among their younger generation. This is the effect of the social media and American technological revolution.

Practical Illustrations

Case Study I: Mr J was discussing some pertinent issues that have turned the world against itself, thereby giving it a dystopian look. It was a gathering filled with people from across the length and breadth of the world. So they were easily distracted whenever a debatable point was made. As an experienced speaker who understands how to keep the attention of large audience to a concept, Mr J would touch the tip of his index finger with his thumb to form a circle whenever he wanted to lay emphasis on a point. Even though some of those at the gathering were not really pleased with the gesture due to their cultural background, it was still potent in drawing their attention to what the speaker was about to say. With this, Mr J ended up making his point to thousands of listeners without having to verbally beg for their attention.

Case Study II: Mrs TO went to a place with her son. When they got there, she got busy with some other activities and had to tell her son to sit somewhere and enjoy himself. Since the boy was strange to the environment and known to be fond of her mother, Mrs TO was a bit worried about how he would feel being left alone but appearing to be between the devil and deep blue sea, there was no way she could abandon what she was doing to spend hours with him. When she had break, she quickly rushed to his son and asked if he was pleased being there, the boy formed a circle by holding his thumb and index finger together while the three other fingers stretched apart without uttering a word. With this, the mother knew that all was well with him. That is, he was having a nice time there.

Case Study III: Two criminals devised anon-verbal means of communicating so that people would find it difficult to understand them. They both forged some financial documents and went to the bank to present them. It was Criminal YD that approached a banker first. The banker, after a quick glance, approved his request. YD was engulfed with excitement but suppressed this feeling so as not to be suspected. So he simply formed a circle with his hand by using the tip of thumb to touch his index finger; this was to tell his accomplice that it had worked out and he should approach the same banker so as not to risk being caught.

19.65. Politician's Thumb

Generic Interpretations of the Concept

Let me clarify from the outset that this gesture also has a form of cultural colouration as it is more common in the west than other parts of the world. But beyond that, it is considered as *leaders' gesture*. The reason being that it is commonly used by political leaders while addressing a given audience. The politician's thumb is the act of pressing the thumb against the curled index finger so as to pass across a point. This is a symbolic way of making a precision.

In order to make this cue pronounced, the speaker will stretch out their hands, visibly to the person being addressed, or even point it into the air before pressing the thumb against the finger. This is a subtle emphasis to connote that they are making a strong point. Without mincing words, this is a modified precision body language act. Politicians hate being perceived as weaklings and, as such, will seize every opportunity to convince their listeners of their point.

They understand that the sentiment shared among the general public is that they are liars, so in order to live above this conventional belief, they tend to emphasise their points with their body gestures.

Some world leaders that are fond of using this cue are Barack Obama, Hillary Clinton, Canadian prime minister Justin Trudeau, and Bill Clinton. In addition, those who want to show themselves as being powerful and their point, cogent, will make use of this gesture. Remember I said in the previous section that this gesture may be complimentary among the Turks. So we need to take note of these cultural deviations in our interpretations of the concept.

Scientific Explanations

Leif Davenport (2015) asserts that world leaders are trained in the act of manipulating body language for their benefit. Explaining this gesture in particular, he observes that this is intentionally used by world leaders to make emphasis. He describes it as 'an emphatic gesture that helps to assert a point without being over-dominating.' This is very diplomatic; you make an assertion without sounding authoritarian. This endears your audience to you because you are appealing to their reasoning instead of the use of brutal force. Davenport states that this is not a coincidence as many politicians have been allegedly briefed by their handlers on the use of this gesture. 'Pointing a finger at someone and punctuating each assertion with vigorous hand movements is naturally received as a confrontational overture. World leaders wish to appear reasonable, even when they may not be, and therefore practise the appropriate accompanying hand gesture while rehearsing speeches and public appearances,' notes Davenport. Any gesture that will put the audience on the defensive or uncomfortable is normally avoided. However, when the situation demands this, you may see them display such form of body language cue.

Chris Weller (2016) states that this gesture is literally weird but surprisingly, politicians still make use of it. Describing the gesture in his own words, Weller states that 'in a kind of loose fist, the politician presses their thumb firmly into the middle joint on their index finger, curling their fingers into their palm'. While trying to make a point, they will extend the closed hand out as if wanting to hand over a sum of money to their co-interlocutor. In reality, this is not a natural posture to maintain but Navarro notes that it is a reflection of what the brain is communicating. The body language expert puts it thus: 'When we talk about one precise thing, we tend to do this. This is a modified precision grip.'

Weller explains further through reference to Navarro, 'Precision grips are used for a variety of fine-motor movements, including writing, eating, and drawing. If a politician makes a similarly precise gesture during a speech, Navarro takes that as a sign the speaker is trying to make an important or complex point.'

It is a symbolic way of guarding the point so that it does not exclude them. That is, it is a non-verbal way of placing importance on what is about to be said because it is considered crucial to understanding the whole speech. It displays focus and cognitive grasp of a content.

Navarro was quick to note that the fist-for-emphasis gesture is mostly North American in nature. According to Weller (2016), the tendency to make use of this gesture by other world leaders from other regions is 'to adopt a gesture closer to the one used by Donald Trump, in which he forms a tight 'A-OK' sign with both hands. Both are matters of preference.' That is, the slight change does not necessarily affect the meaning of the cue. For instance, Francois Hollande, former president of France, and President Mahmoud Abbas of Palestine are also fond of using the variant discussed above.

Both gestures is a hint that a speaker is about to make a cogent or crucial point. However, it is pertinent to state that if the cue is overused, it is capable of diluting its meaning from being a power gesture to a mere tic. That is, it becomes a means of describing the person rather than a means of conveying powerful emotion.

Practical Illustrations

Case Study I: Politician A was having a debate with Politician B in a university setting. Being aware of what possibly awaited them in that kind of environment, they both prepared well and had their best of appearance. When Politician A had the floor, he spoke calmly and ensured that a point sunk before moving to another one. At the point he was about to explain his main motivation for vying for the post, he could be seen pressing his thumb firmly into the middle joint on his index finger, curling their fingers into their palm. This drew the attention of the crowd further to him because they thought he was about to make a vital point.

Case Study II: Two regional heads were having a discussion on how they could collaborate and work as a team in order to achieve their set aims. Leader B, known for his pragmatic approach to issues, pressed his thumb into his index finger and curled other fingers into the palm to express what he considered as the most important point in his speech.

Case Study III: One attribute that Prostitute AU has used in winning numerous men to herself is her open display of knowledge; she knows how to sway the public to her side and since men are easily moved to such ladies, they would be the ones chasing her for love and through that process, fall into her trap. She was in a party of a colleague in office and there was a discourse she knew much about. In the twinkle of an eye, she had taken the central stage. While talking, in order to grab the attention of the handsome and gorgeously dressed men at her table, she would press her thumb into her index finger before making an important point.

19.66. Fiddling with Ring

Generic Interpretations of the Concept

I have heard many superstitious interpretations about the act of playing with wedding rings. People fiddle with it by twirling it or taking it off and on. One of the popular misconceptions is that people who are not happily married do engage in this act. There is no iota of truth in this.

When you observe this cue in a person, it means nothing but stress. As I have explained at different points in time, people react to stress differently and the environment in which they find themselves also determines how they let out their feelings. Someone who fiddles with their wedding ring probably does not have any other item in sight to play with or finds it most convenient. If you are waiting for an outcome of a test or even somebody and the feeling of boredom is beginning to set in, you may play with the ring in order to keep yourself active. This is soothing when done repetitively. Hence, it is a good way of passing the time.

However, apart from passing the time, this gesture is mostly used when people are experiencing negative emotions. As you touch the band and return it to its original state, the fingers also maintain a contact, creating a tactile feeling that is capable of calming the nerves. The more stressed a person, the longer the duration of displaying this cue. Also, when the stress is intense, they may also increase the speed of playing with the band.

Note that until this becomes a repetitive behaviour, you cannot necessarily assume that the person is stressed; if it is done once, that means the person only adjusted the ring and not stressed. It only becomes an issue when the person does the ring-playing cue over and over again. So take note of this seemingly insignificant but crucial point.

Scientific Explanations

The editors of *Reader's Digest* make it known that the act of playing with rings should be avoided because it communicates negativity. The editors say this is an indication of discomfort or shyness. Shyness can make people uncomfortable and as a way of keeping themselves together, they may decide to play with their ring. This distracts their attention from the unpalatable situation to the soothing act. In cases where they do not wear their rings, they may fidget with their button. When talking with someone and instead of them to face you, their attention is drawn to the ring on their hand, this means something is making them uncomfortable. Instead of ignoring their feelings, you may just seek for clarifications in order not to be lost in the conversation; someone who is uncomfortable will withhold crucial information from you.

Body Language Communication (2008) states that when people play with cellular phone, coins or their ring, it probably signals 'boredom, nervousness or disrespect.' This interpretation gives us a broader view of the possible meanings of this gesture. If the person is not bored or afraid of anything but still fidgets with ring, while being addressed by an equal or elderly one, this probably means the person is seeking to be disrespectful. Playing with your ring while someone addresses you is an indication that they are not worth your time or attention. This can be very painful to the speaker. It means they are not worthy of your attention. If this intentional, then it is a good way of making your grievances known but if it is not, you need to be cautious of how you carry your body in the presence of them so as not to create misconception about yourself.

On his own part, Sol (2019) states that this gesture may be one of the signs of attractions. He notes that this is common to women in love context. Repetitively taking a ring off and putting it back on may be a girl's means of teasing a man they have interest in. Come to think of it, this is very symbolic in the sense that the ring is representing a vaginal hole while the finger serves as penis. The repetitive dangling of the ring connotes a man inserting and removing his penis in female private part. This is it is done repeatedly, it is expected that the targeted person gets this message and act on it appropriately. They may also accompany this gesture with other cues such as portraying the mouth in a romantic way or fiddling with their hair to reveal the back of their neck. Most importantly, the location where this gesture is displayed also adds to overall message of the romance.

Practical Illustrations

Case Study I: Mr D is a coolheaded man and for almost a decade that he had been living in his rented apartment, none of his neighbours has ever heard is voice raised in anger. However, things seem to be taking ugly turns these days as he and his wife have been issues concerning some affairs at home. The wife is very temperamental. No matter how he appeals to her to lower her voice during the moments of argument that she would obey. This is almost becoming a shame to him because his respect among neighbours is fast fading off. Fortunately for him, the wife invited him to a round-table discussion on a particular morning. Even though he was supposed to be at a function, he decided to forgo that to ensure that peace returns to his house. When they eventually sorted themselves out, he rushed to the bus stop but there was none available; he had to wait for about thirty minutes before another bus would arrive. In order not to think over the unfortunate incident he just scaled through, he decided to play with his finger band till the bus arrived.

Case Study II: Ms P was really interested in the man seated next to her at the bar but it seemed the latter was blind to her beauty and show of availability. She opened her laps but the man seemed not to be looking beneath. So Ms P placed her hands on their table, in a very visible manner, and started taking off and putting back her ring repeatedly to the extent that the man's attention was drew to her. She was ready for love and would do just anything imaginable to send her message to the person she picked interest in.

Case Study III: One attribute that Prostitute AU has used in winning numerous men to herself is her open display of knowledge; she knows how to sway the public to her side and since men are easily moved to such ladies, they would be the ones chasing her for love and through that process, fall into her trap. She was in a party of a colleague in office and there was a discourse she knew much about. In the twinkle of an eye, she had taken the central stage. While talking, in order to grab the attention of the handsome and gorgeously dressed men at her table, she would press her thumb into her index finger before making an important point. Even though she eventually had the attention, she did not make full use of it.

19.67. Moving Away from Objects

Generic Interpretations of the Concept

Another way to break into someone's mind is to see how they behave with objects close to them. It would amaze you to note that if we loathe the idea behind an object, we will move away from such object. This is a subconscious behaviour that expresses our thoughts and feelings concerning any given thing. When you see a person distancing themselves from an item, this means they are nursing a negative feeling concerning such object. There are many situations this can be used to determine the truth of a matter. For instance, if a person is on a diet, they are likely to push a bread basket away from their reach in order not to be tempted to go for it. Also, they will limit their visit to the dining so as not to set their eyes on the foods they are trying to avoid. Those who dislike alcoholic beverages may even demand that empty wineglasses be taken away.

This has also played out in law enforcement situation in different ways. For instance, someone who was injured by a gunshot will dislike and take their eyes off gun whenever they see it; they see it as a negative object and threat to their existence. As a first-hand experience, there was a time surveillance photographs were passed to a criminal to see and make his defence against them but actually refused to touch them. Once he saw himself in the image, he quickly pushed them back to the other end of the table. This was accompanied with a frown and disconnection of eye contact. This was a useful hint for the interrogation; he had non-verbally pleaded guilty of his involvement in the crime. To confirm our guess, the picture was left on the table for some minutes and throughout the duration, it was discovered that the criminal was not looking at that side.

All these are crucial to take note of because you understand the thoughts of people through proxy; it reveals what is on the person's mind at that point in time. With this, you can make useful deductions on what is making the person distance themselves from such objects.

Scientific Explanations

Ni'Keisa Pannell (2018) mentions this cue as part of the gestures showing that someone does not like what they are moving away from. I also at different points in this book that maintaining bodily contact is evidence that love exists between people; the stronger the bond, the closer they would move to each other. However, when you see someone performing the opposite, it is an indication that they have hatred towards the person or objects they are moving away from.

Ali Craig, an international consultant, speaker, host, and best-selling author states, 'Believe it or not, the distance someone keeps from you, whether or not their arms are crossed, lack of eye contact, forced smiles and other non-verbal behaviours can and sometimes are indicators as to whether or not someone likes you.' This is a factual statement that does not derive its substance from your affirmation; it is a universal truth you must agree with in order not to be caught unaware. When interpreting distance in body language, you do not need to take cognisance of any other thing before you can arrive at your conclusion.

The golden rule is: *once there is a wide distance, there is no love or affection.* Have you ever imagined couples making love from two beds? Before you assume my illustration is weird, it is the same thing as moving close to a thing. When a thing interests us, it catches our attention and we are drawn to it but if after seeing such thing, we withdraw ourselves, it means there is something negative about it.

Craig (2018) gives a summary of everything thus: 'Typically the closer someone gets to you physically, the more comfortable they feel with you and around you. Likewise, the more distance an individual keeps between you and them says a lot, too. People who like each other generally don't have problems being in close physical proximity to each other. If you dislike someone, however, you are less likely to position yourself very close to them. You'll keep a 'safe' amount of distance between the two of you.'

Julie-Ann Amos (2015) states that the reason we create a distance between ourselves and objects that we do not like is create a visible boundary; we want to maintain a comfortable and safe distance from such thing—in case there is an 'attack', we will be safe.

Practical Illustrations

Case Study I: Mr K is a diabetic patient and, as such, has been warned to desist from anything that contains sugar. He seems not to be disciplined enough as he 'backslides' within a week of giving him the instruction. So the sickness took another dimension and after returning to the hospital, the doctor was emphatic about the fact that the only way he could live long and healthy was to detach himself from taking sugar. Unfortunately for him, this is the favourite of the rest of the family. After returning from work the previous day, he saw a packet of sugar on dining. Before going there, he yelled on Mrs K to come and take it off the table. This was to show the negative impression he has created towards sugar due to its ill effect on his health.

Case Study II: Suspect U was arrested after three days of perpetrating a crime that led to loss of lives and property. He never imagined he could be traced because he played on the intelligence of an innocent person to perpetrate the crime but his picture was captured by the CCTV. So investigators were able to link things up and he was finally arrested. While he was being interrogated, an image containing his picture where he was lurking around at the time of occurrence of the event was shown to him. As he saw himself in the image, he squinted his eyes and returned the picture immediately. It was as if he was shown something abnormal and this made him develop negative feelings. While he was told to explain the image, he looked away for a while before he could utter a word. This was in a bid to fabricate lies.

Case Study III: Passenger YR does not like long distance journeys but once in a while, he has no option than to embark on one when selected by his organisation. However, his experience with border control in his last trip has made him create a form of hatred for them; their vehicle was unnecessarily delayed when it was noticed that there were some people with no passport in it. He missed an important programme due to that. When they got there this time around, and people were asked to come down, he identified the officer that orchestrated their delay the other time and moved away from him as a display of his dislike for him.

19.68. Being Hesitant to Touch with Palm

Generic Interpretations of the Concept

The moment we fail to engage the palms in our touching activities, this is a hint that there are issues. Taking the hand as a whole, there is no part that can produce a tactile feeling like the palm; it is the powerhouse of arousing emotional feeling. So it is ordinarily believe that if there is any need to touch, it is the part of the body that would be stretched forth. However, there have been instances when this conventional perception failed. This suggests that the person has issues with their co-interlocutor.

If a parent consistently avoids touching their child with the palm, it is a significant issue that is worth discussing. Probably, this is a sign of indifference towards the affected child. Probably, they have been warning that child on a given issues and there seems to be no changes, so, they are trying to cut off feelings they have towards the child. This is psychological and can either be intentional or subconscious. For instance, if a parent is about to take their child to a boarding facility, they may resist themselves from touching the child with palms of the hands. This is to ensure that the child is not really fond of them so that he or she does not reject the hostel idea when the time comes. Also, the child will settle down quickly because the bond has been tamed for months or years.

In the case of couples, instead of them to touch each other with the palms, if they should employ the fingertips, this is a sure sign that there are issues in their relationship; the bond is gradually breaking off and instead of them to love each other, they are merely tolerating each other with the use of the fingertips to communicate. If this resistance continues for a long time, that might be the end of such relationship. This may be trivial or insignificant at the surface level, but we cannot discountenance its effect.

Scientific Explanations

Study Body Language (2016) explains that touch is an amplifier. That is, we ignite relationship through the act of touching. This is more so if the touch is serving as a complementary approach to what is being said. The website aptly notes that 'influential figures know that and they use touch in body language to emphasise their messages. They know how to push the right buttons at the right moments to amplify their message tenfold.' So if you see anyone avoiding touching through palms of the hands, this means they are probably aware of what is the likely effect.

When we touch with the palm, we amplify the already existing mood. That is why you see lovers or friends touch when the mood is in their favour. For instance, if you want to sympathise with a person, doing it with the hands touching the person tends to be more effective than merely uttering words. Touching them with the palms of the hands makes them feel your emotions towards them.

However, when people fail to touch, there are many possible causes of such action. Here is a case study given by SBL to shed light on this: 'Suppose a salesman is sitting with a customer and he wants the customer to trust him to make the sale. Our salesman should initially avoid touching his customer (beyond the initial greetings) until he established some basic connection with him. We don't want him to appear too 'pushy' and aggressive. If, however, he receives some positive reaction, then he can use a light touch (through the palms of the hands) to accent this mood while presenting the benefits of the product - to project the customer's positive reaction towards the salesman and the product, and therefore increase his chances of sell' (SBL 2016). In this illustration, we can see that the initial reluctance to touch is good. This helps in establishing trust. If not, the salesman would have been seen as harassing the buyer to do their bidding.

Some other scholars consider the act of resistance to touch as closed body language. That is, you are not enhancing the channel of communication between you and the other person if you fail to touch them. In fact, Sara Hendricks (2018) states that if this happens between couples, it is a sign that their relationship is doomed. The journalist notes that when you touch with the palm, this tells the other person that you love them—you share the feeling of intimacy, emotional closeness, and happiness in a relationship when you touch with the palms of the hands. However, this must be reciprocated. Hendricks concludes that 'not every couple uses physical touch to express affection. But suddenly losing a sense of ease when it comes to touch can point to trouble in a relationship.'

Practical Illustrations

Case Study I: Child H has been performing poorly in his academics despite the parents spending huge amount of money every term. The mother has called him several times to explain the reason for his failure and tell her where she could come in and straighten his curved lines. However, it seems H also does not know what is the reason behind his retrogressive performance. H's mother had to go to his school to confirm what was wrong. The teacher explains that H has made new friends who are distracting his attention from his studies. The mother was pained that he didn't open up to him when she demanded explanation in the least aggressive way. Since, then she has been avoiding a palm touch with him because plans were on top gear to change his school so as to make him stay in a boarding facility.

Case Study II: Mr Y is finding his wife less attractive due to advances to him from a woman in his workplace. So he has been looking for ways to break the bond between them, create issues and ultimately, orchestrate a divorce. So whenever the wife was around, Mr Y will focus his attention on some other things. Even when the wife was massaging him, he would only touch her with his fingertips. The wife was later fed up and had to demand explanation. It was at this point that everything went ugly with their relationship. The love was not a two-way thing and there was no way it was going to be sustained.

Case Study III: Prostitute GQ has made Man UR her regular customer due to his generosity; the man does not really last on bed and will still part with huge amount of money after the process. So she sees him as an easy access point. Of recent, he has been having issues with his business and this means he won't be able to afford what he usually gives. Being inconsiderate, Prostitute GQ becomes detached from him. In one of their sessions, while the man tries to massage her and make love, she only touches him with the tip of her fingers. When he does not feel the usually horny nature, he asks what the cause of such is and she becomes evasive about it. She didn't want to answer the question because she had no better and justifiable explanation of her behaviour.

19.69. Inconsistent Arm and Hand Movement

Generic Interpretations of the Concept

The hands should be seen as an instrument of stabilisation with the entire body. We are expected to see the hands as the main driver of our non-verbal movement. That is, with the way they move, we can reliably establish if all is well with a person or not. There are times that we meet people that who are inconsistent in their arms and hand movement—the motion is erratic. Instead of the hands to complement what is being said, it will express another message entirely, thereby creating confusion in the communicative context. This may look funny sometimes but it is not what we should laugh at. Firs, we need to establish if the person is intentional about the mix up or there is a psychological problem beyond their control.

When the hands and arms are out of synchrony with the rest of the body and a given person's environment, it means reading the person becomes difficult. As I have earlier opined, the best you can do is to identify the malady at work. If you do not discover, there is no way you can recover. The discovery of the issue wrong with the person will help you in making an informed decision concerning them—recognising and identifying the cause of the problem are crucial to lending invaluable help to the person concerned. Painfully, our world is deteriorating in value by the day. Instead of us to see a needy person as one, we rather look on as if we are spectators. If you are not concerned today, you cannot predict the form of help you might also need tomorrow. This is not to appeal to emotions but to state a reality that our society yearns for—being passionately concerned about the needs of one another. This is the hallmark of humanity.

Scientific Explanations

According to Mayo Clinic (2017), 'The term 'movement disorders' refers to a group of nervous system (neurological) conditions that cause abnormal increased movements, which may be voluntary or involuntary.' Most times, this movement is involuntary.

The American Association of Neurological Surgeons (2019) lists some common movement disorders. *Ataxia* appears to be the most common. 'Ataxia is a degenerative disorder affecting the brain, brainstem or spinal cord. This can result in clumsiness, inaccuracy, instability, imbalance, tremor or a lack of coordination while performing voluntary movements. Movements are not smooth and may appear disjointed or jerky. Patients may fall down frequently due to an unsteady gait. Ataxia also can affect speech and movement of the eyes.' The symptoms listed in this description are the common ones we notice in our interactions with people. So before we allege that people are deceptive in their use of body language, we need to establish if they have the control of their movement. Metabolic disorder is always alluded as the cause of this movement disorder.

Dystonia is another form of movement disorder. This 'is a neurological muscle disorder characterised by involuntary muscle spasms. Dystonia results from abnormal functioning of the basal ganglia, a deep part of the brain which helps control coordination of movement. These regions of the brain control the speed and fluidity of movement and prevent unwanted movements. Patients with dystonia may experience uncontrollable twisting, repetitive movements or abnormal postures and positions. These can affect any part of the body, including the arms, legs, trunk, eyelids and vocal cords' (AANS 2019). One thing about dystonia is that its impact can be felt beyond the arms.

The repetitive movement is normally dramatic and you be tempted to think that the person is acting out something funny or using that means to distract attention from a main issue. This is not the case; they are under an influence beyond their control. Usually, this normally affect the entire body. When it affects the hands, it is known as writer's cramp. Depending on what part of the body is affected, the condition can be very disabling.

The AANS proffers solution to this issue by observing that 'there is a three-tiered approach to treating dystonia: botulinum toxin (Botox) injections, medication and surgery. These may be used alone or in combination. Botox injections help block the communication between the nerve and the muscle and may lessen abnormal movements and postures. Surgery is considered when other treatments have proven ineffective. The goal of surgery is to interrupt the pathways responsible for the abnormal movements at various levels of the nervous system.' Hence, this can serve as a guide for you to help out someone you think is under the influence of this disorder.

Another movement disorder is *essential tremor*. This 'is an uncontrolled shaking or trembling, usually of one or both hands or arms, that worsens when basic movements are attempted'. This disorder affects millions of people in each country of the world. Research shows that the victims of essential tremor are aged people who are above sixty-five years. It is caused by abnormalities in areas of the brain that control movement and is not tied to an underlying disease. From all indications, this appears to be one of the most common movement disorders Krista O'Connell (2016). The AANS submits, 'This condition usually does not result in serious complications, but it certainly can interfere with daily activities and cause distress.' So it is not a disorder that can be totally trivialised.

At times, physical therapy or change in lifestyle may conquer essential tremor. However, if the condition affects a patient's ability to perform daily tasks and has a negative impact on quality of life, medication or surgery are considered. A large percentage of patients taking drugs have positive outcome concerning this disorder. But if it is so severe that it leads to disability, surgery may be the last resort.

And finally, one that appears to be above treatment is *Huntington's disease*. It 'is a progressive, degenerative and fatal disease caused by the deterioration of certain nerve cells in the brain. Onset most often occurs between ages 35 and 50, with the condition progressing without remission over 10 to 25 years. Symptoms include jerking; uncontrollable movements of the limbs, trunk, and face; progressive loss of mental abilities; and the development of psychiatric problems. The condition is hereditary – a child with one affected parent has a 50 per cent chance of developing Huntington's disease' (AANS 2019).

Practical Illustrations

Case Study I: Criminal UW was arrested in a crowd during a violent outbreak. He thought he would easily escape due to the large number of people at the location but was surprisingly nabbed by some eagle-eyed officers. After being asked to put down a statement, he was ushered into the interview room and one of the first things that gave him out was his inconsistent arm and hand movement; where he was supposed to raise them to emphasise a point, he would keep them to himself and this sent a message to the interrogators that he was faking it. His statement was also error-laden with numerous cancellations.

Case Study II: Mr RA does not really like talking but his colleague, Ms US can talk for hours with ease. Whenever she wants to raise a topic that can elongate their discussion, he would look for a way to evade it or even frown so as to make her know he is not up for that. In some instances, where she defies all odds to go ahead with such discussions, one of the ways her effort is being frustrated is through inconsistent use of arms and hands. At some point, she would be confused of what Mr RA is trying to say because his arm movement does not match up with his verbal expressions.

Case Study III: Salesman AJ knows how to convince buyers through every possible way—he would convince, go objective and then, cap everything up with emotional appeal. Thus, he is seen as the most active among his colleagues. However, some clients who have known him for this try as much as possible to avoid him because they might later part with what they never budgeted for. A client runs into him for the first time and after all his advertisements, the client becomes inconsistent with his talks; he consciously employs an inconsistent hand and arm twisting for the purpose of confusing him so that he would allow him go. It was such a funny scene he wasn't expecting.

CHAPTER 20

The Chest, Torso, and Belly

By mass, the torso is our largest body part and, as such, serving as an abode to a lot of our vital organs. This means it is a part of the body which we would not like to play with or expose to unnecessary risk. Without mincing words, the torso is the area of the body we are most likely to protect first whenever we are threatened. It is like a billboard to the body—it gives some insights, with the aid of clothing, about humans. When I say 'insights', the word is used in the strongest sense of it in that sentence. For instance, with a focus on the torso, we tend to establish how physically fit a person is, who they are, what they do for livelihood and the group they belong to. If you can unravel all these pieces of information about a person, there is no gainsaying that you have identified all the essentials of their identity.

In the same vein, the torso serves as the reservoir of almost all the essential organs of the body—the lungs and heart and others are found in this area of the body. Regrettably, most literature tend to neglect this aspect of the body when discussing body language. It is like throwing away the wheel of a car and expect it to move. In other words, this is a huge and rich source of information about people while interpreting people's non-verbal cues. If you pay right attention to its movement during discourse, you would be amazed at the amount of information you will get concerning your co-interlocutor. Through the torso, you can identify how a person feels and their thoughts towards you. Before we launch out into stage by stage interpretations, let's switch our light on the biological aspect of this part of the body.

According to *Dorland's Medical Dictionary*, 'The *torso* or *trunk* is an anatomical term for the central part or core of many animal bodies (including humans) from which extend the neck and limbs. The torso includes: the thoracic segment of the trunk, the abdominal segment of the trunk, and the perineum.'

Most critical organs are housed within the torso. In the upper chest, the heart and lungs are protected by the rib cage, and the abdomen contains most of the organs responsible for digestion: the stomach, which breaks down partially digested food via gastric acid; the liver, which respectively produces bile necessary for digestion; the large and small intestines, which extract nutrients from food; the anus, from which faecal wastes are egested; the rectum, which stores faeces; the gallbladder, which stores and concentrates bile; the kidneys, which produce urine, the ureters, which pass it to the bladder for storage; and the urethra, which excretes urine and in a male passes sperm through the seminal vesicles. Finally, the pelvic region houses both the male and female reproductive organs.

Many important blood vessels travel through the abdomen, including the aorta, inferior vena cava, and dozens of their smaller branches. In the front, the abdomen is protected by a thin, tough layer of tissue called fascia. In front of the fascia are the abdominal muscles and skin. In the rear of the abdomen are the back muscles and spine (Hoffman 2014).

Also, the torso also harbours many of the main groups of muscles in the body, including the: pectoral muscles, abdominal muscles, lateral muscles and epaxial muscles. The organs, muscles, and other contents of the torso are supplied by nerves, which mainly originate as nerve roots from the thoracic and lumbar parts of the spinal cord. Some organs also receive a nerve supply from the vagus nerve. The sensation to the skin is provided by:

- Lateral cutaneous branches of torso or lateral cutaneous branches
- Dorsal cutaneous branches

There are some conditions that affect the effective functionality of the torso. They are:

Peritonitis: This is the inflammation of the covering of the abdominal structures, causing rigidity and severe pain. Usually, this is due to a ruptured or infected abdominal organ.

Acute abdomen: This is a medical phrase doctors use to suggest that peritonitis or some other emergency is present and surgery is likely needed (Hoffman 2014).

Appendicitis: It is an inflammation of the appendix, in the lower right colon. Usually, an inflamed appendix must be removed by surgery.

Constipation: Having fewer than three bowel movements per week. Diet and exercise may help but many people will need to see their healthcare providers (Hoffman 2014).

Peptic ulcer disease: Ulcers are erosions and peptic refers to acid. Peptic ulcers are ulcers in the stomach and duodenum (the first part of the small intestine). The usual cause is either an infection with H. pylori or taking anti-inflammatory medications like ibuprofen (Hoffman 2014).

There are many more infections that may not be able to appear in this text. However, most of these conditions can be treated. Let's consider some:

Abdominal surgery: Surgery is often necessary for serious abdominal conditions like cholecystitis, appendicitis, colon or stomach cancer, or an aneurysm. Surgery may be laparoscopic (several small incisions and using a camera and small tools) or open (one large incision, what most people think of as a typical surgery).

Histamine (H2) blockers: Histamine increases stomach acid secretion; blocking histamine can reduce acid production and GERD symptoms (Hoffman 2014).

Proton pump inhibitors: These medicines directly inhibit the acid pumps in the stomach. They must be taken daily to be effective. There is, though, some concern about taking them for more than a few months.

Endoscopy: During upper or lower endoscopy, tools on the endoscope can sometimes treat problems (like bleeding or cancer) that are discovered (Hoffman 2014).

Motility agents: Medicines can increase contraction of the stomach and intestines, improving symptoms of gastroparesis or constipation.

Laxatives: Various over-the-counter and prescription medicines can help relieve constipation (Hoffman 2014).

Before admitting any form of treatment, there must be examination of the torso to ascertain what is wrong. The most known means of examination is through physical means. By listening with a stethoscope, pressing, and tapping on the abdomen, a doctor gathers information that helps diagnose abdominal problems (Hoffman 2014).

20.1. Heaving Chest, Fast Breathing

Generic Interpretations of the Concept

There are numerous reasons why the chest heaves and people breathe rapidly. In whatever context you observe this, it is a call to pay close attention to yourself and the person displaying this gesture. When we are confronted with tasks that seem insurmountable, the chest will heave and we tend to breathe faster than usual. In other words, fear is a potential factor that can make people breathe in an unusual manner. The saying that the 'heart race' is used to refer to faster breathing rate in the face of fear. Thinking that a situation will defeat us will make the brain programme the body into the flight or freeze response mode. Even if the person freezes at some point, you will still hear how hard they breathe, especially when the location is silent.

Also, anger can ignite chest heaving and rapid breathing. This is very common to temperamental people. Once they are angry, they yell at the top of their voice and this translates to fast breathing immediately they are done with their argument. They frown their face and will be ready for another round of argument if the other party does not keep mum. Excessive display of anger makes people breathe faster than their normal breathing rate.

In the same vein, being overwhelmed by a negative thought can affect our breathing. When we are concerned that something negative will happen to us, the moment we draw a mental picture of that particular event, the subconscious mind believes it has happened already and thus, leading to chest heaving. The same thing goes for excessive worrying. All these are pointers to the likely things that may cause the heart to race.

However, there are literal causes of chest heaving and heavy breathing. For instance, if someone just get themselves involved in a physical exercise or demanding job, they may display this cue. This does not mean they are worried about anything. Heart attack, anxiety and age are some other literal causes of this behaviour. What is most important is that you observe duly and unravel the cause of this behaviour so that you are not caught unawares.

Scientific Explanations

David Straker (2019) says that deep breathing makes the chest expand and move on than usual. With that, we can use it to thrust out our chest. 'It also increases the oxygen intake and readies the person for action, thus indicating such as fear or anger. We also breathe deeply when we are experiencing intense emotions such as love,' states Straker. One thing that this expert opens our eyes to is that intense emotions, and not necessarily negative ones lead to chest heaving. In the case of love, the person is really feeling high in positive mood but often than not, chest heaving and rapid breath is a way of preparing for a negative action. When we are bothered, we need more intake of air so as to maintain our balance. This is the reason the chest is expanded for oxygen intake to increase. To be on a safe side, you need to keep distance between you and the person displaying this cue. The reason being that they can attack at any given time.

Mentalizer Education (2019) says that when someone is breathing deeply, it is probably an indication of fear, anger, love, attraction or excitement. This is in consonance with Straker's submission. Mentalizer Education notes thus: 'Deep breathing is one of the most noticeable breathing patterns in terms of reading a person's body language. If a person suddenly holds his breath in a horrible situation, he is sending a message of fear. It may also convey anger when a person takes a deep breath to pull out his emotion followed by shouting out.' This means this form of breathing is getting the person charged. To know the difference between rapid breathing that signals positive or negative emotions, you need to pay attention to the facial expressions of people per time. For instance, one that is frowned, squinted or furrowed, is expressing anger, tension or anxiety while one that glows shows excitement or surprise.

Also, rapid breathing is said to represent fear or tiredness. For example, consider a person who has just ran after a robber, the person breathes rapidly and pants. 'It is because the heart beats faster and the lungs need more oxygen that's why he is like catching up his breath. Same as through with a person who is trying to escape something that is fearful, his breath is very rapid and heavy. So you can easily notice that a person has been running for some reason – after or from something – through his breathing' (Mentalizer Education).

Practical Illustrations

Case Study I: Boy T dreamt of snake in his; he dreamt that the snake bit him and he was rushed to the hospital where he was admitted. He woke up immediately after the dream, creating fear in his heart. His heart was still racing on the bed as he recalled the dream. When it seemed that he was getting over it, he decided to go and ease himself. There was a wet towel on the floor. As he stepped on it, his mind went back to the dream. He quickly withdrew his legs and reached for a lamp, thinking it's a snake. His chest heaved and he breathed rapidly, showing his fear. He stayed glued to his bed for some minutes before he later surmounted the courage to go and urinate. Even while heading to the shower, he was looking around nervously.

Case Study II: Mrs R was in the kitchen, busy preparing supper for the family while Mr R was putting some finishing touches to a proposal in the study. Their children went to visit their friends. This means there was no one in the living room. A robber crept in and was packing some valuables he wanted to cart away. Unfortunately for him, Mrs R was bringing some items to the dining at that time. As she saw the robber, the woman was shocked beyond description and yelled, drawing her husband's attention. At that time, the robber had taken to his heels. Mr R gave him a wild chase but could not meet him. At the end of the day, both husbands and wife were breathing rapidly. The wife's own was borne out of fear while that of the husband was due to physical exertion.

Case Study III: Human Smuggler TK decided to evade border officials by going through an illegal route with those he smuggled. He had always heard of the route but was yet to give it a try. It proved to be a difficult journey for him from the start of the journey as his victims were not cooperative enough. After numerous hours of going through the bush, he got to the border and that was where the herculean task lay ahead of him. Initially, he thought the illegal border was far away from the legitimate one, only for him to be hearing voices from afar. Afraid that he might be caught, he took to his heels for about an hour. When he finally stopped, his chest heaved and he breathed rapidly. This is a combination of both psychological and physical stress.

20.2. Shallow, Fast Breathing

Generic Interpretations of the Concept

When we say that something is shallow, it means it is not deep. That is, it does not exist beyond the surface level. If this is done with speed, there is high probability that there are issues. When we are faced with negative emotions, we tend to breathe in a very rapid and shallow manner. It is as if we do not want to lose any millisecond to not breathing. This show of tension is higher than that of rapid, deep breathing earlier explained. In this realm, it means the person has been entirely engulfed by stress. Take note of the shallowness of your subject's breath so as to establish their level of anxiety.

Someone who breathes as if they are told not is definitely afraid. They allow fear to take over their emotions, thereby tormenting them. The person probably assumes that breathing deeply may exposing them to what they are running away from. Imagine yourself being behind a sleeping lion; at this point, you will not shout because you understand the slightest form of noise can wake the dangerous animal and this means your life becomes a worthless gift in its hand. In such a threatening situation as this, we will maintain shallow breathing. Since breathing is an indispensable part of us, instead of not doing it at, it is done in a shallow manner.

The saying that a fearful man dies multiple times before real death comes to fore in this situation. Fear literally kill us. There are some events that will befall us, and instead of us to demonstrate great hope and unrivalled level of courage before such issue, we begin to shiver around, giving the problem an unfettered access to torment us the more.

At some point when the breathing becomes shallower and faster, this means the person is indescribably distressed. You can help the person to calm down by telling them to inhale on a long duration and then exhale for as long as they can (about 5 seconds may be OK). Repeat this process for some time and before you know it, the person is in control of their emotions; this helps in lowering breathing rate.

Scientific Explanations

Straker (2019) observes that when we are under intense shock, the body is held rigid (freeze mood), thereby impeding the free flow of breathing. When we find it extremely difficult to breathe, our breathing becomes unimaginably short. This is an expression of tension. Our body does not overlook what the mind is thinking of or experiencing per time; if the subconscious thinks that we are in danger, the body quickly assumes this shape and our pattern of breathing is affected. The shortness of the breath in this scenario is to state that all is not well with the person. Fear does not allow us to express ourselves in a normal manner; it changes the default setting of the human system.

Mentalizer Education (2019) states that there are connections between emotions and breathing; once the emotions change, our breathing patterns also do. In other words, they are complementary. To better understand this, for the next one week or so, take note of the breathing pattern you use while in the presence of a friend, suitor, boss, colleague, and family members. You will notice that your breathing changes according to the emotions you feel towards each of them. It tells you your exact feelings and situation that warrants it.

The platform explains further that shallow breathing may be a connotation of hopelessness or sadness. Our breathing is only felt at the surface level when we think that there are no more open doors for us concerning a given situation. Imagine a man who has booked an appointment with a date, told all his friends and colleagues about his adventures and the said date later disappointed. As the hope of the man fades on the likely disappointment awaiting him, he would find it very difficult to breathe because he is going through a conglomeration of sadness, disappointment and hopelessness.

Practical Illustrations

Case Study I: Applicant H had an interview with one of the leading firms in town. This means that a lot of people would be jostling for the opening. Before oral interview, applicants were expected to take aptitude tests on some relevant subjects. Applicant H had enquired from some past applicants who gave him a hint of how things were conducted at that stage. He was informed that the cognitive reasoning test would come before the departmental test. So H was busy preparing himself for the former at the expense of the former, with the hope that he would revise the departmental course during break. However, when the organisers of the interview came, the applicants were informed that they would first sit departmental tests first and that would qualify them for the next stage. H became destabilised because of lack of preparedness; he became anxious and started breathing in a shallow, fast manner. However, no one paid attention to him in the crowd as most of his colleagues were also caught unawares.

Case Study II: There was supposed to be a coordinated attack on a mall by some suspected terrorists. So as a way of preparing the ground for others, two spies were sent ahead of time. Unfortunately for them, the security agencies had had a wave of their plan and subsequently launched into action. As the spies were getting into the premises, various intelligence officers were on ground too and even uniformed men could be sighted all over the place. Seeing the obvious, the terrorists began to shiver because they were sure that their plan had been busted. More important to them was how they were going to escape the venue unscathed. As they made plans to behave 'normal' and move out of the location, they were intercepted by one of the military police on duty. It was as if life was taken out of them. They both looked at each other in the face and began to pant, breathing in a shallow and rapid manner. They could not muster the courage to answer simple questions. Through this, they gave themselves out.

Case Study III: Witness SU thought court is a place she could easily walk in defend her husband in a case involve robbery. Her love for her husband did not make her settle for the voice of reasoning. When she entered into the witness box, she looked confident and informed. However, when asked during cross examination by the prosecuting counsel of where the husband was the night the offence was committed, she was gripped with fear and before she could muster courage to proffer an answer, she started breathing fast in a shallow manner. This disrupted her talks as she obviously became nervous. She was disconnected and incoherent.

20.3. Fingers on Chest

Generic Interpretations of the Concept

If people want to pick lint off their clothes, they will use the thumb and index finger. However, in this case, pressing two or the finger fingers on the chest is a form of giving self-assurance; it is a pacifying act. When we are faced with difficult situations, we tend to press our chest or diaphragm area with our thumb and middle finger. This is a subtle form of massage. But if the intensity of the stress is high, we will press the five fingers against the chest. This is said to be a good way of relieving pent-up stress. People may disguise this by trying to adjust their buttons or the lapel on their clothes. However, such actions are expected to be a one-time off activities. Once it becomes repetitive, it means the person is undergoing stressful moments. This is mostly subconscious and the person is not even aware of letting out those gestures.

The chest is the powerhouse of the human body; it houses the heart which is our only instrument of breathing. Hence, pressing on the chest with our fingers is like greasing the engine of our life so that it does not break down at that given point. Apart from the face, hands hovering around the chest is to self-pacify the person involved. Hands are primarily meant for emphasis during communication. So when they are held close to the body, they are denied of their primary duty for the role of survival.

The fingers are pressed against the body near the centre of the chest which is known to be rich in nerves. This ignites good feelings in a person that has been feeling otherwise. The pressure applied is dependent on the feeling of individual involved. If the fingers are lightly pressed against the chest, it means the negative emotion is still within control but when it is on the extreme, there would be more application of force. I have always noticed this gesture on people receiving bad news. It is like a symbolic way of telling themselves to take heart or not to break down due to what they just heard.

Scientific Explanations

Parvez (2015) explains that the thumb is prominent when the fingers are pressed against the chest because of its symbolic connotation of power and dominance. As the most powerful finger, pressing it against the chest area is like supplying power to a weak heart. It may also show that the person is superior to the problem they are passing through.

In order to have an accurate interpretation of this cue, you need to take cognisance of other gestures. For instance, pressing the fingers on the chest is a means of exercising self-restraint. 'But if this hand gesture is accompanied with thumbs pointing upwards it means that even though he is restraining himself, he has got something powerful to say' (Parvez 2015). In a way, we can state that despite being overwhelmed in negative emotions, the person still has hope of positivity. So where the thumb points matters in determining the real feeling of a person. The person may even lean backwards as a way of having a better view of the events taking place in their vicinity.

In his own submission, Straker (2019) says that touching the chest draws attention of others to it. 'When a woman does this in front of a man it makes the man think of doing this and is thus a highly suggestive and flirtatious act,' he opines. Since the breasts are located at chest region, when females press their fingers against it, this can arouse the men present. It is like a subtle invitation to the breasts. When this particularly becomes repetitive, it raises the emotional feelings of a man who has interest in the woman. That is why it is regarded as a flirtatious act. Consider a man doing this, there is no one that will give such meanings to it.

The body language expert explains further that this gesture may also suggest discomfort and pain. The aftermath of tension and stress is, most times, felt in the chest. Those who have heart attack may not necessarily suffer from any physical injury on the chest but from emotional shock. So pressing the hands against the chest is to pacify ourselves from ill feelings.

Practical Illustrations

Case Study I: Mr R had just resigned his appointment with one of new schools in his neighbourhood and decided to seek greener pasture elsewhere. It did not take long that his yearnings materialised as he got an interview with one of the best schools in the city. The invitation was received with mixed feelings. One, he was elated that his application received positive review and on the other hand, the pressure of scaling through an interview with such a reputable school. As the scheduled day of interview was drawing nearer, the positive feelings began to make way for the negative perceptions. Despite preparing well, he was still somewhat anxious. On the D-day, he first had an aptitude test and then, an hour interview with some select panellists before he was asked to do a microteaching. Entering the class and seeing how the students were naturally composed, coupled with the stress from the previous sessions, anxiety took over the better part of Mr R. Before he was introduced to the class, he pressed his thumb and middle finger on his chest for about thirty seconds.

Case Study II: Dr L was attending a conference when he had a fatal accident that claimed his life. Meanwhile, he had just had an extensive discussion with his wife that morning on some future actions before embarking on the trip, where he was expected to be one of the paper presenters. Knowing the kind of bond that existed between the late don and his wife, those who were sent to inform her about the unfortunate incident were reluctant and thought of the best way to deliver the message so that it does not affect her psychologically. When Mrs L was eventually told, she pressed her five fingers on her chest, looking at the news bearers in an unbelievable manner. This means she was trying to gauge her shock and think thoroughly because the news has affected her flow of thought pattern.

Case Study III: Ms G's instinct tells her that law enforcement officials would soon be on a raid on the slum she lives; it is a community filled with illegal immigrants who were seen as a threat to the citizens due to the ridiculous rates they were ready to take for any job. After four hours of hiding, Ms G returned to her house and what she saw baffled her; everywhere was scattered and disorganised, perhaps, when people were running for their dear lives. Given to nervousness, she pressed her middle finger and thumb to her chest as if she was trying to calm herself. This lasted for a few seconds before she got restored.

20.4. Rubbing of Clavicle/Collarbone

Generic Interpretations of the Concept

Some have their clavicles very pronounced while some others have theirs covered up with flesh. Whatever the case is, there is no human without clavicle—a long bone serving as strut between the shoulder blade and the sternum or breastbone. It is popularly known as collarbone due to its location. The clavicle is the longest horizontal bone in the human body. This uniqueness calls people attention to it when we touch or rub it. There are many things that can motivate clavicle massaging. Most often than not, it is caused by negative emotions.

The clavicle is divided into two by the lungs. When people are stressed, they grab the clavicle at the opposite side and massage it so as to pacify themselves— that is, the right hand is placed on the left clavicle and rubbed gradually to create a soothing effect. When the hand is placed on the collarbone, the elbow points out, showing that the person is trying to guard their personal space. They do not want anybody to come nearer as they pacify themselves. Also, the arm drawn across the body is a protective approach. What this shows is that the person is very conscious of their environment. Most probably, their stress was inspired by fear. Hence, the thought that they may be attacked at any given time.

If the clavicle is rubbed once, we may assume that the person is feeling itchy but when it becomes a repetitive action, this means the person is feeling some negative emotions. An open secret is that this area of the body is highly sensitive to touch. This is why it is regarded as an erogenous zone. The feeling is always sensual when the clavicle is massaged. That is why couples may rub it along the neck so as to arouse the feelings of their partners.

Scientific Explanations

Philip (2013) states that when people rub their collarbone, it is crave for comfort. This is an emotional body language that hints that something is wrong. Massaging the clavicle is a direct response to negative occurrences. The negative occurrences spoken about in this context cuts across a range of things. When someone is put on the spot or made jest of, you may see them reaching for their collarbone. At this point, it is pertinent to note that women tend to do this gesture more than men. Men will rather touch the face more often than touching the neck or clavicle. Also, men are known to be aggressive in their ways but rubbing the clavicle is emotionally soothing, the more reason it is considered a female. Ultimately, both gender display the cue when they are stressed.

Men are particularly subtle about this gesture; they may start by adjusting their neck collar or tie when there is no reason for that and then move their hands to the clavicle. You may observe this cue more in an informal setting. On the other hand, women may begin to 'adjust' their necklace and from that point, begin to rub the clavicle back and forth. While doing this, they are distracted from the events taking place in the immediate environment. This connects their thoughts to the possible way out of their stress. Hence, the probable reason those massaging their collarbone look into the far distance. If you are able to effectively manipulate your emotions, it calms you down and reduces the flow of blood in that area of the body. This has an effect on the heart rate; it lowers it. This means you do not have to place your hands on your chest before the heart rate can be normalised (Philip 2013).

Reflecting on the effects and potency of this body language gesture, the body language expert states that like 'most emotional body language they serve to pacify the body to make it feel better by stimulating nerve endings to release calming endorphins.' While you are lost in deep thought, you may massage the clavicle so as to pacify you. People may also exhale air through compressed mouth simultaneously.

Navarro (2009) states that this is one of the frequent ways of responding to stress. A variant of this gesture is rubbing the back of the neck. The message is still the same.

Practical Illustrations

Case Study I: Preacher B was invited by a friend, Preacher A, to come and minister in his church. The former had always ministered to a small congregation and did not bother to train himself on how to face a large congregation; he was comfortable in his comfort zone. When Preacher B got to A's church, he was taken aback at the crowd in the auditorium. After being introduced and he took his seat, Preacher A informed him that he would soon be invited to deliver his sermon. Thinking of the coordination of activities and crowd, he became uneasy. From the moment he was informed that he would soon be called up, Preacher B's hand could be spotted around his clavicle. He would rub the horizontal bone and feign adjusting his collar. The initial stammering of his voice exposed his anxiety to the audience.

Case Study II: Guy T saw an attractive, charming lady at a party. At first, there were some other people at a table with the lady but the three people left, leaving the lady alone. So Guy T stylishly moved closer to her. The lady who was busy pressing her phone answered passingly when he greeted her. She would only look up once in a while and then smile to her phone. This sent fear down the nerves of Guy T; he thought she was probably chatting with her spouse. Also, her response was not inviting. All these were troubling him, yet he could not suppress his love for her. As he was thinking of the method he could adopt to break the barrier of communication, he could be seen rubbing his clavicle up and down. This shows that he was afraid of approaching her for love even when she did not say a word against him.

Case Study III: Man GT forged a document and was afraid to present it to authorities because she was afraid that he would be caught in the process. However, after consuming some hard drugs, he was overtaken by desperation which made him muster courage to approach the relevant authorities. He walked in with confidence, thinking that his frowned face would make them attend to him without cross-checking what he submitted to them. He got back to his senses when he saw the officials running a forensic analysis of the document. He became terrified and started rubbing his clavicle back and forth. This action shows that he was nervous.

20.5. Continuous Hand Raking of Chest

Generic Interpretations of the Concept

Just like the fingers pressed against chest body language, repetitive hand raking of chest is used for self-pacifying. This has to do with continuous massaging of the upper chest. The fingers would be curled up while the thumb moves back and forth like a rake. The curling up of the fingers hinders the palm from directly touching the chest. So the pacifying job is really done by the moving thumb that is reputed for being rich in nerve endings which caresses the upper region of the chest.

When you notice this gesture, it is a symbolic pledge to negative stimulus. That is, it is a strong indication that one is feeling bad about something. Insecurity is one of the possible causes of this gesture. So you rub the 'heart area' with the thumb to have the assurance that you are still alive. This assurance, couples with the soothing effect of raking gradually restores calm to the person. Insecurity can really make one be enveloped in fear for a long period of time. Dropping the hand becomes an issue because it serves as a protective shield for the person. The fingers are subconsciously curled up so as to make the finger joints point out in case of any attack. As in the case of clavicle rubbing, the arm is crossed on the body so as to repel an unexpected attack on the body. The person looks very nervous as their eyes are wide open, looking around as if their adversary is lurking around. You will observe that the general demeanour of the person is not positive.

Further, this might also be a hint that the person has issues bothering them. This might not necessarily be physical. Having psychological issues that you cannot probably fathom may make the heart weak that will warrantee raking the chest are with the thumb and fingers to get the body in shape. There is no doubt that this gesture is one of the most reliable indicators of anxiety. This also illustrates a pending panic attack. It is as if the person has a hint of something evil about to befall them.

This behaviour is unique from any other one due to how the fingers are curled in forming a rake-like shape. This is to ensure that the nails do not rub the chest or even maintain a direct contact with the palm. This makes the behaviour pronounced among non-verbal cues.

Scientific Explanations

Social Dynamics platform in an article on the interpretations of body language gestures makes it known that the fingers curled up on the chest is a symbol of insecurity. This shows that the person is probably arching of low self-esteem. If you do not believe in your ability, you tend to close your body up against the world. It would be hard to enjoy one's conversation with a person that crosses their body with their arm. This serves as a barrier, telling other people not to come near.

The website explains further that while displaying this cue, we are expectant of something, usually negative. The look may be unfocused for a moment, a symbolic way of imagining the event. In general, this gesture portrays a person that is stressed. The raking may be done rapidly if the person is really stressed but if it is done gently, they still a level of control over the situation. The platform is quick to add a note of caution that this might be an indicator of a cold person. The person, probably, does not want to clasp both hands to themselves so that people do not assume that as an extreme negative behaviour.

Philip (2013) also opines that this is an emotional body language cue that is targeted at calming the body. Philip notes that this is not the only pacifier but people decide to use this gesture because the stress is felt heavily in the chest area. It may also be a preference of some people in dealing with emotional turmoil. For instance, some have been known of speaking to themselves as a perfect way of get to back to normalcy in the case of emotional struggle. Hence, this has become their favoured way of pacifying themselves when psychologically or emotionally disturbed. I mean 'they will use the same ones each time when they become tense making it easy for us to read them accurately,' stressed Philip.

Chest raking is displayed in real time to the level of threat present. That is, people do not wait to keep calm before they massage the upper part of their chest; they do it as they feel the emotion. This makes the gesture reliable.

Practical Illustrations

Case Study I: Suspect Q is a dropout. He lost his father at an early age and the mother was not really available for him. So he lost the parental care every child yearns for at an early stage. Also, he was negatively influenced by friends he met in the high school. It was at this stage that he was introduced to an extravagant life. When he got to the college, the friends were no longer there for him, making him to take to cybercrimes. He began defrauding people under different pretexts. When his 'business' was expanding, he decided to quit school so as to give it full-time concentration. The straw that broke the camel's back was when he hacked into the central system of a leading bank. He was traced and nabbed by law enforcement agents. When he was arraigned in court, he stood in the box, with his fingers curled up against his upper chest, looking away from the jury and moving the fingers and thumb up and down. His anxiety was pronounced enough for people to notice.

Case Study II: Mrs Y failed a professional examination that was needed for her promotion. Without it, no matter the number of years spent in service, she was not going to be promoted. So she prepared for it well in the subsequent year. On the day of the exam, when all was set, she was anxious of the possible questions and if she could scale through. In order to pacify herself before the distribution of the question papers, she pressed her fingers to her chest regions and darts them back and forth in a sensual manner. This was a mild way of calming herself and assuring herself she would do well.

Case Study III: Mr and Mrs IR were trying to illegally migrate from their home country. They were very desperate on this trip as they looked for all ways to ensure the journey was successfully. They willingly submitted themselves to a human smuggler who showed them the 'best path' to follow. Unfortunately for them, they were nabbed just before entering their destination country. Since the border officers laid ambush for them, they were really shocked. While still trying to compose themselves before being asked questions, Mrs IR unconsciously used her hand to press her left chest region as if she was trying to reduce her breathing rate. This means she was trying to recover from the psychological shock and keep herself within shape.

20.6. Pressing Palm on Chest

Generic Interpretations of the Concept

This is one of the controversial body language gestures, not in its display, but the meaning which it connotes. In many cultures of the world, the sentiment shared is that when the palm of the hand is placed on the chest, it is a show of sincerity and honesty. Also, they believe that this is a gesture of goodwill when meeting people, especially for the first time. Maybe this accounts for the reason many people place their palm on their chest while reciting the national anthem or pledging allegiance to a particular organisation.

Let me state it loud and clear that from personal experience and having gone through different literature, both the deceptive and the honest are likely to put their palm on their chest since they are aware that the sentiment is that they are more likely to be believed when they display the cue. For the sake of objectivity, this cue should be treated as neutral.

The fact that this behaviour is offered as a claim of honesty or sincerity does not make it one. In a forensic environment, when a person makes a denial like 'I didn't know anything about it' and then places their palm on their chest, it should not be given much value or weight, no matter how apt the cue is performed. People are indescribably good in acting and feigning an emotion such as this is very easy. This is very important so that criminals and deceptive people do not hide under this to commit all forms of atrocities and go scot-free.

Having made this important observation, I have noticed over the decades that sincere ones normally press the palm against the chest with more force and ensure that the fingers are widely separated. On the other hand, those who are set out to deceive will mainly touch with their fingertips, without being forceful about it. It is a non-verbal way of not being committed to their words.

Yet, there is no single cue that is capable of spotting deception and this is not an exception. So do not base your conclusion about the sincerity of a person solely on this. The wisest thing to do is to merely consider this gesture, how it is performed and look for other behavioural cues before reaching any conclusion. With this, you will be most probably accurate in your interpretation of a person's sincerity or otherwise.

Scientific Explanations

CBS News is one of the many platforms that believe in the sentiment that hand on the chest is a show of sincerity. However, the website also notes that this is not absolute show of sincerity with the use of the word 'may'.

However, Philip (2014) gives a somewhat different interpretation of this gesture. He states that 'holding the hand over the heart is signal that one is thinking about the best interest of others'. In a way, this can still be related to honesty but it is better taken as a cue of commitment. The scholar makes references to researches that opine that holding the hand to the heart makes people make moral judgements in a better way. He advises, 'When you wish to have others make an honest confession, having them swear and make oath by holding their hands over their chest, will help produce desired results.' Again, this might not be the best way to determine the sincerity of an issue. However, once the two hands are involved, the meaning tends to change; it becomes a show of tender love.

Philip (2014) upholds that this is an appeal to honesty and sincerity or deep appreciation. In the west, when they want to show their condolences to a person, they will hold their hands to their heart, showing their sincerity of purpose. He concludes that 'our hand comes to our heart when we wish to be believed and show that it is us who cares deeply about another'. From the explanation of Philip, we will discover that he relates his stance to emotional moments where it would be difficult to feign your feelings. This is unlike situations where one may be required to plead guilty or not.

The Social Dynamics website also shares the sentiment that people use this gesture when they want to be believed. They are showing that they are trustworthy. Some may even place both palms on the chest. That is a height of desperation to get the approval of people concerning their behaviour or words. Sonamics (2019) gives the verbal interpretation of this cue as 'Let's be honest: You can trust me'. It is left to the person being addressed to take this cue hook, line and sinker without looking inward. Sonamics puts it thus: 'The gesture is easy to fake and it may be used consciously – for example by sales man. If the gesture is shown as a reaction, the person feels attacked and he wants to reaffirm his/her innocence. You cannot draw any conclusions about truthfulness from this gesture.'

Practical Illustrations

Case Study I: Child E did not wake up early for school because his parents were not around. The policy of his school is that once a child comes later than the stipulated time, he should be turned back. When he discovered that he could not meet up again, he decided to spend the time with another wayward friend because he knew the parents would arrive before the close of school and, as such, would know that he did not go to school. He played with his friend till late in the evening. He saw the need to go home when it was getting dark. By the time he got home, his parents had arrived. When asked where he was coming from, he said school, lying that he and some other colleagues were delayed by their mathematics teacher. When the mother looked at him scornfully, he placed a palm on his chest to show the sincerity of his narration. However, when the mother reached for her phone to call their school administrator, he begged her not to, pleading guilty.

Case Study II: Patient EY has been admitted in the hospital for a long period of time as his condition seems not to be improving. Any time he feels pain at the chest region, he would gently press his palm against it, doing as if he is massaging the place. The expression on his face will tell an observant fellow that he is going through pains. Also, EY presses his palm on his chest whenever the doctor doubts his response to a question—this is to prove that what he says is right. However, there are times that he does this just for the sake of rejecting injections or irritating medications.

Case Study III: Con Artist PZ was engaged by a group of law enforcement officers. It was really an interesting as well as a tedious session. Interesting in the sense that the law enforcement officials learnt some new ways of doing things and tedious in a way that he was uncooperative; the officers tried for several hours before they could master his tactics. For instance, any time he wanted to prove that he was being sincere, he would press his palm against his chest. He was so perfect about this that he was easily believed. His words were subjected to doubt when he told a clear lie, simple and obvious; they later got to know he had been faking the gesture all through.

20.7. Removing Clothing to Ventilate

Generic Interpretations of the Concept

No matter the circumstance, it is unethical to pull one's clothe to ventilate, whether in public or in our privacy. Our concern is how people publicly pull their clothing to ventilate themselves. This may be triggered by heat. Some people cannot withstand heat in any form. If they are in a meeting and there is abrupt disconnection of power, they may pull the collar of their clothes to ventilate themselves pending the time power is restored.

That apart, people pull off their clothing—by holding a shirt out at the collar for a moment away from the neck or continuously plucked at or pulled away—as a means of relieving stress. This is like every other ventilating cue. All things being equal, when you see a person displaying this cue, it is an insightful indication that all is not well with them. This behaviour is usually displayed subconsciously. This makes it very reliable.

Apart from the literal stress explained in the opening paragraph, there are many psychological factors that may cause increase in the body temperature. For instance, when you are faced with a tasking or difficult situation, you may begin to sweat, even when every environmental factor favours you. I have had instances where suspects sweat profusely in a room with four ACs. In such circumstance, we do not need to look far before establishing the cause of the heat. Also, in a testy board meeting, people may ventilate repeatedly when the discussion does not tilt to their side. This feeling tends to increase when there are punitive aftermaths to the person's behaviour.

Further, this ventilating behaviour happens suddenly. That is, it appears out the blues. For instance, the person was feeling good before you ask them a particular question when they suddenly begin to ventilate themselves. This means it is the question that unsettled them.

Men and women tend to ventilate differently. Females do ventilate their clothes by pulling on the midriff and front top while men reach for the collar. The neck is the most affected when the body temperature rises and that is why effort is always directed towards that part of the body.

Take note of this behaviour in a forensic environment. The manner a subject behaves when they hear or answer a question tells you what is going on within them. Ventilating oneself after answering a question shows that the person would not have answered the question if they had the liberty.

Scientific Explanations

Philip (2014) states that pulling the collar off or even loosening the tie is a way of allowing in air when we are tense. Giving a sentence summary of this gesture, Philip explains that 'pulling on the collar is a signal that a person is experiencing discomfort due to high body temperature or nervousness'. This is apt and encompassing. On a general ground, this gesture should be avoided as it paints one to be uncomfortable. However, if you wish to show others to give you needed privacy, you may think of using this gesture. The verbal translation is given as 'I'm getting a little bit stressed and hot under the collar so I'm pulling my collar away from my neck to let some of the heat escape.'

This is sometimes associated with liars but that can be a superstitious sentiment that this book has stood against since the very first page. To be on a safe side, we can submit that when there is an overall increase in temperature and blood flow within the neck region, people tend to pull on their clothing. This may be attributed to an increase in level of stress. 'When the collar pull cue is caused by stress, it is an attempt to reduce the pain caused by irritated nerves located in the neck which are being compressed by a tight shirt. When stress increases, our face and necks flush with blood and we pull our collar away as an unconscious indication of this process' (Philip 2014).

In some other circumstance, this gesture may be a way of releasing heat produced by the body while we were under intense pressure. The neck would have become moist due to this discomfort. As stress increases, the moist will also increase, leading to more irritation in the neck. The body language expert concludes that there are 'times the collar pull has no meaning and is due to an uncomfortable shirt collar rubbing against the skin.' This is where you need to confirm your guess before giving final verdict. With that, you will not make what is considered as fallacious. Other clusters you make look for are 'tie removal or tie adjustment, pulling at the sleeves, blushing or flushing of the face, perspiration, touching or scratching of the face and cheeks, front and back of the neck and ears' (Philip 2014).

WP Lie (2019) states that this cue is displayed when we are psychologically threatened. It tends to be most meaningful and expressive when the person is emotional. Lie explains that this gesture may 'suggest doubt, feeling threatened, insecurity and deception.' When people are trying to be deceptive, they sweat and become unnecessarily hot. This may lead to pulling on their dresses to ventilate. It is pertinent to note for the umpteenth time that this is just a clue and may not be an outright indication of deception.

Practical Illustrations

Case Study I: Mr G applied for a managerial position in a highly disciplined company. Out of desperation and as a way of ensuring that he secured the job, he forged some items on his curriculum vitae. He claimed to have held a high position in an establishment where he only interned. Unfortunately for him, one of the panellists knew a lot about the establishment in question. So the panellist purposively asked him the question at the peak of the session. Caught unawares, he shivered for a minute and then got himself in shape. Moist began to gather in his neck region and subconsciously, he pulled out his collar to ventilate the neck despite having cross ventilation in the room. Even a kid could recognise the fact that he was psychologically stressed.

Case Study II: Athlete WP thought being the best at the regional level will automatically place him ahead of others at the national level. So during preparations, he rehearsed for just a while and waited for the D-day. However, he was utterly disappointed in himself that he was nowhere to be found during the race; he came last. Spectators who had always seen him as being proud seized the opportunity boo and throw jibes at him. This made him to lose his stamina and courage. Immediately after the race, he removed his jersey so as to properly fan himself. Apart from defeat, this shows that he was tired.

Case Study III: Criminal TQ was trapped in job scam; she was interviewed and employed by an alleged recruitment agency. Since they have some insiders working for them in various organisations, it was easy to fix their victims into any organisation of their choice. Since TQ thought she got the job on a merit basis, when the company she was attached to wanted to do a staff audit, she went there with confidence. It was at this point the management discovered that she never came in through a legitimate means. Confused to hear this, moist began to gather at her neck as she shivered. She gently reached for the collar of her clothe to ventilate her body. This means she was not psychologically stable at that point in time.

20.8. Fiddling with Zipper

Generic Interpretations of the Concept

Instead of concentrating on a given activity, if we decide to play with our zipper, this is a distractive act that explains our emotional feelings. It is not uncommon to see people play with the zipper of their sweatshirt or jacket. This is said to be a reformed and acceptable form of lint picking. It is to ensure that the hands are actively engaged throughout a given process. One of the likely causes of this behaviour is boredom. When we are bored and think it is inappropriate to sleep in a given place, we may take solace in the zipper of our shirt. In some other times, being in a gathering that does not reflect our thought pattern may make us feel bored. Take for instance someone who is kept in a four-hour lecture may be indescribably bored and as a way of relishing the moment, they will reach out for their zipper, play with it in a soothing manner.

Further, this gesture is displayed when people are nervous about a given event. Nervousness can make people do some childish things that they would not have done when in a normal circumstance. When we are gripped with fear and do not want to reflect on the negative probable outcome, we may unconsciously play with the zipper. Even though this does not take away the original feeling, in some way, it pacifies the person from the intensity of the negative stimulus. It is not unusual to see students do this when they are about to take a test that they are not well prepared for; this is a non-verbal way of telling the world that they are concerned about the test they are about to take. Also, poker players do this when the game is not in their favour. This means they are concerned about their failing bank roll.

Generally, fiddling with the zipper is a way of pacifying oneself from stress, anxiety, nervousness or boredom.

Scientific Explanations

Eliot Hoppe (2009) regards playing with the zipper as negative body language. He urges people to pay attention to their co-interlocutor in a conversation so that they understand what the other party is communicating through their body. He observes that when your audience begins to fiddle with their zipper instead of them to listen to what you are telling them, they are bored. Note that they may be facing you but their mind is definitely off what you are telling them. Hoppe explains further that playing with a zipper is an attitudinal display of emotion. 'Jingling keys, preening with miscellaneous articles such as scarves, mitts and hats' are some other clusters you can look for so as to ascertain the accuracy of your guess.

Philip (2014) describes this gestures under the body language of playing with objects. He submits that playing with objects is a way to pacify the body. On a general note, fiddling with a zipper can give negative impression about you; almost everyone understands that this gesture is normally displayed when we are undergoing emotional turmoil. However, it has some useful purpose that it serves. 'It provides busy hands with an outlet to release emotional tension or placate boredom.' If not, we would have been moody all through, thereby increasing emotional feelings along negative lines. A clever manipulation of the zipper can get the hand engaged while stress is released from the body; this propels stress relieving hormones through tactile stimulation.

According to Philip, what this communicates verbally is 'I'm uneasy, insecure, bored, and need to pacify myself by keeping my hands busy.' When you see someone playing with an object, it is an indication that they need to be pacified because they are not finding it easy emotionally. It is also an indicator of discomfort and boredom, as earlier explained. The body language expert notes that this behaviour is rooted in infantile action; it is a childish trait that is 'recalled' in order to weather through the moment. 'The object keeps the hands busy and helps pacify by burning up some of the excess negative energy. Playing with objects creates a soothing touch over the fingers or palms helping to release positive hormones further reinforcing the behaviour' (Philip 2014). Apart from playing with the zipper, there are array of other forms of object plays. Some may take solace in the handles of their bags, wineglasses, necklace, and wristband, among others.

Practical Illustrations

Case Study I: F is not used to travelling alone. Over the years, he has always had the luck to have a known person going through the same route when he needed to travel but he was called by his research supervisor to come and get some things sorted out in school before he (the supervisor) goes on sabbatical. F tried to look for someone to accompany him on the three-hour journey but there was none. Since the journey could not be shifted, he decided to leave as early as possible on the next day. An hour into the trip, he became unimaginably bored. Making new friends is not his thing. Unconsciously, he began to play with the zipper of his shirt until he fell asleep. This is the ultimate effect of boredom.

Case Study II: Student R does not like sciences but since it is required that every student must take it at the elementary level, she decided to grudgingly participate in the class, earnestly waiting for the end of session when she would have the freedom to face the humanities alone. They were moving towards exam period and, as such needed to be assessed before the main examination so as to know the major areas the students were defective. When the science teacher came in, maintain a straight face, Student R became nervous, trying hard to remember all that she had read. When it appeared that all had flew away, she started moving her zipper up and down. She was disturbed by this ugly development and its likely consequences.

Case Study III: Beyond what many people could understand, the bus conveying workers to their workplace arrived late, forcing all the passengers to wait endlessly at the bus stop. S hates being delayed without any reason. Out of sheer boredom, he began to fiddle with his shirt zipper. She believed that was a good way to while away time and cure himself of boredom.

Case Study IV: Some smuggled individuals were arrested at border control. Since they were naïve, it was easy to get confessional statement from them. However, it was later discovered that their smuggler was still on his way. So they had to be delayed until their smuggler arrived. They thought he was driving just behind their own vehicles; they didn't know he was hours behind. Since they were not used to the location where they were and the officials there, they became bored. Out of the three of them, one began to drum, the second fiddled with his ring while the third played with his zipper.

20.9. Distancing Selves

Generic Interpretations of the Concept

In an atmosphere of love where we share the same world views and beliefs with people, we tend to mingle without restraints but by the moment we discovered that someone does not mirror our opinion or belief about a concept, we tend to subconsciously or consciously lean away from them. All over the world, there is nowhere where leaning away is viewed as a show of love. Rather, it is seen as an aftermath of discord and strained relationship between individuals.

By the moment you lean away from someone, you create a distance. This means you do not want to share in what they are saying. If you do not like something, you try as much as possible to avoid. This applies to speeches too. It is as if you do not want what the person is saying to get to you. To make it more practical, if you are seated next to a speaker and they utter an objectionable statement, unconsciously, you inch away from them. This is a form of mental disconnection, showing that you do not align yourself to the viewpoint expressed by the person. If you were in consonance with it, you would have nodded to the speech and moved closer to the person, as if you want to hug them.

Talk shows is a common arena where you can observe this gesture. Also, you may notice this when two leaders do not agree on a point. Pay attention to a manager and his assistant, especially when they do not reach a meeting point concerning a policy issue, the assistant will frown and subtly lean away from the boss if he decides to be adamant about doing away with the concept.

Most often, we are not conscious of how far we lean away from people when they say things that are considered as being contentious. Disagreeing with a person on a given point is, most times, emotional. This means that if care is not taken, we may end up creating dislike for the person and not just their words. This can have a detrimental effect on the personal relationship you maintain with the person.

Scientific Explanations

Philip (2014) highlights that leaning away from someone is a show of disinterest. Leaning in and out can be used in determining someone's level of interest in what is being said. When you lean away from someone, this means you have no interest in their personality, what they have to say and their ideas. In a way, this is a total rejection. Philip explains further, 'Dominant people will tend to lean back and take up space, but someone who lacks confidence or whom has a great interest in another person will try to engage them more by leaning in towards them. This tends to have the reverse result to what is intended.' So if you are smart, there is a way you can use this body language gesture to your advantage.

Sarah Smith (2015) states that there is nothing surprising about the fact that we lean towards people we admire while we pull away from those we do not like. From Smith's submission, this means it is possible to hate a person and their idea. The body language expert urges people on a date to pay attention to the direction of movement of their companions. If the person does not fancy you or what you just told them, they will lean away from you. Also, someone who has started developing likeness for another person at the venue may lean towards the person at your detriment. This is not only applicable to dating scenario but all areas of life. Once something caught our attention, we tend to neglect what another person is telling us.

Practical Illustrations

Case Study I: Mr U is the national chairman of GEX political party while he has Mrs E as his deputy. It was election period. This means that they had no time for frivolities as they were always holding meetings, strategising, attending campaigns and symposia, all in a bid to ensure that their party emerges victorious at the polls. However, it seemed crisis was setting in between the chairman and his deputy over the choice of candidates and how they were running their campaigns. To ensure that everything was centralised and to entrench party supremacy, Mr U was the opinion that every candidate should submit their manifestoes to the party headquarters and wait for approval before making such public while Mrs E believed that the process would be tedious and laced with bureaucracies capable of thwarting their victory. She opined that such innovative approach should be discussed after the election against subsequent ones but it seemed the chairman would not just listen. During a press conference, Mrs E was seated next to the party head who was reading the press statement. When he eventually made the decision of the 'party' public, Mrs E subconsciously leant away from him, making it so obvious that those around knew she was not in support of the idea.

Case Study II: Mr D is a conservative person who believes that familial ties should be kept, no matter the sacrifice to be offered for such. So he had always advocated that their children should spend a week of their holiday with granny but Mrs D was never pleased with this opinion. Any time the husband brought up the issue, she would find a way of distract his attention from it or even convince him to drop it. But it got to a point Mr D thought he must have his way. After supper that day, he informed the wife of his decision and called for their three kids. He addressed them on several issues and later told them they were to spend a week with granny. As Mr D was briefing them on this, his wife leant away from it, trying to detach herself from the decision. She also frowned at it, forcing their eldest child to ask if anything was wrong with them.

Case Study III: There was a time I arrested some people that engaged in marriage of convenience. From my conversation with them, I discovered that the woman was forced into the whole game. Although she did not speak this out, all her behaviour pointed to this direction. For instance, when they arrived at our station, I discovered that the woman stayed at the back instead of walking side by side with the man. Apart from that, whenever the man was giving any explanation, she would lean herself away from him, as if she was trying to detach herself from him. I knew that with a little drilling, she would say the truth. And I was right!

20.10. Sitting Back

Generic Interpretations of the Concept

This is another variant of the leaning away cue just perused above. Sometimes, you will see people push their chair back and lean away from other discussants at a table. This is to distance themselves and take up enough space for themselves. Also, this gesture gives the person additional insulation that they need in order to think and arrive at a convincing decision. It is a metaphorical way of pulling oneself out of the crowd so as to be able to have time to reason without interruption from the public. When someone sees you sitting back and pulling your chair backwards, they get the message that you are taking yourself off them. They may be forced to ask what informed your decision or simply respect the choice you have made.

When you want to contemplate on what someone has just told you and you do not want them to influence your thought about the issue, you may use this gesture to seclude yourself for some minutes as you ruminate on the issue. Taking a deep breath before sitting back will better communicate your message to them.

The message you are sending to the person or group is that you are not convinced on what they have said and, as such still have to consider it objectively on your own. If you do not lean away from them, they will keep talking and pointing your mind to different issues. If care is not taken, you may later take a decision that does not meet your standard. By the moment you move backwards, they would not want to raise their voice. This means they will keep shut till you utter a word.

Some may use this gesture to detach themselves from a decision. It means they do not want to be involved in it. Imagine a group of friends planning how they will lay ambush on a particular lady to rape her. The one who still have conscience among them may quickly take himself off such decision. This may weaken some others and if not, they were at least certain that the person did not endorse their decision. Pulling away in this sense demonstrates their unhappiness. Hence, this gesture can be used in communicating our emotions to people.

Scientific Explanations

Ileana Paules-Bronet (2019) states that when you sit back, it portrays you as an analytical person. That is, others see you as someone who is sieving through opinion or considering which decision might be in your decision. Be default, people tend to respect those who are analytical and curious—they see them as being cerebral. Paules-Bronet opines thus: 'Leaning back allows you to observe a situation without acting on it. It means you like to take in what you're seeing, but you're careful before getting involved.' This shows you are very careful and think through before taking final decision. People like are less likely to make mistakes or regret their actions in the future.

Also, sitting back to ponder on issues is an attestation that you are considerate. With this, you will not hurt other people's feelings and emotions at will. Usually, those people we claim to like are analytical humans; they do not offend us at all times. When there are misconceptions, they take time to study the situation and get things cleared before they become too messy. Sometimes, their action can be time-consuming and frustrating, especially when you are in haste but they are not moved. You can hardly subject those people to undue pressure (Paules-Bronet 2019). Analytical humans are not perfect but being thoughtful and considerate are the essential factors that make them unique.

Practical Illustrations

Case Study I: Mrs K was working in another country before her wedding to Mr K some few months when she decided to drop the job in order to close to her husband and build a tranquil home. Since then, she has not been able to secure another job. This means she is a full housewife for now. The responsibility of taking care of the home is solely on the man. Summer vacation was fast approaching and it seems Mrs K is good in making plans. She was the one who brought up the discussion and gave most of the suggestions on how to spend the break. It seemed the budget was becoming a burden to Mr K. When she sought his opinion on all that she had said, the man sat back and hanged his head in the air for about three minutes before speaking out. He was able to influence her to revisit some items on the list for the benefit of the family.

Case Study II: Mr S was just transferred to another branch of the establishment where he works. He was informed that the branch was not meeting up to expectations in terms of productivity and even spent more. So he is expected to overhaul the branch within few months. Known to be disciplined, the authorities were certain that Mr S would succeed in the task. Few weeks after his arrival at the branch, many of the workers, especially those that benefited from the corrupt proceed of the former manager began to develop hatred for him but he appeared to be unconcerned about their thoughts. When they discovered that he was not giving them the attention they deserved, many of the senior employees decided to come against him, manipulate figures and dent his integrity so that he could be axed by the company.

They fixed a meeting in a hotel where no one would notice them. As they were making the plans and distributing roles, one of them was not pleased with them. He was passive throughout the process. At the stage of role distribution, he pushed his chair backwards and leant away from them. This drew the attention of others to him. He told them plainly that he was not interested in the evil scheme. They knew if they should continue with it, he would expose them. They became dejected and regretted involving him at first.

Case Study III: A man was trying to evade clearance at the port. Unlike many of his counterparts, he did not look disturbed but rather jovial and no one could have guessed what was on his mind based on how he was behaving. At some point, he even went as far as getting a chair, pushed it back so as to have a full view of all that was being done at the port. He was in this position when someone noticed his display of authority. The junior officer approached him, listened to him, but lamented how it was difficult to render the 'help'.

20.11. Sitting Forward

Generic Interpretations of the Concept

In a way, we may regard this gesture as a 'ready posture'. After thinking through an issue and making our decision, we will sit forward in order to communicate our intentions to the person or group at the other side of the table. When you see a person lean in in their sitting position, this is an indication that they are ready to make their mind known to you. This does not mean that their decision would be favourable but most often than not, it does tilt towards the positive aspect.

Having given this general background, when you sit forward, it communicates your readiness to negotiate in good faith. That is, what you want to say is objective and aftermath of your thinking. The person will also develop interest in you and lean to you, making the feeling a shared one. With this, discussion takes place without shouting at each other. The parties involved are able to talk extensively when they maintain this posture.

Also, sitting forward may also signal compromise. The verbal translation of the gesture in this sense is: 'Have thought about it, I think your stance is right and am ready to go with it.' This may be followed with a sigh of relief so as to get the attention of the person who had been waiting for the reply. Someone who leans forward after sitting back for a moment telegraphs that they have reached a decision.

However, while displaying this gesture, you need to be very careful, especially when you sit at a desk or table that is narrow. This might make you lean in than usual, thereby intimidating the other party; the leaning should be moderate, just to invite the person's attention.

If it is a team negotiation, you have to ensure that all the members of the team are well seated. With this, the eagerness to concede to the opponents would not be conceded well ahead of time; some people lose stamina easily and may make people take slouching or literal leaning as a show of interest. With this, you make your mind known when it is time.

Scientific Explanations

Study Body Language (2016) states that sitting forward is equivalent to the leaning in body language; they are both used to confess likeness for a person. Having admiration for a person is like a magnetic pull which is used to draw our body to the person in question. While sitting at a table, you will move your body closer to them. SBL when you get closer, this shows how interested you are in the person. The website submits that 'leaning forward, especially when combined with nodding and smiling, it's the most distinct way to say non-verbally: "yes, I like what you're saying, keep going"'. So you should take note of the clusters mentioned here in order to ascertain your doubts. It would be difficult for anyone to feign nodding and smiling simultaneously while they also sit forward.

SBL states that while this body gesture is good, it should not be overdone so that it does not negate the message that it sought to communicate. For instance, if you overextend your leaning, 'you can inadvertently invade personal space and create discomfort for the other person. That's also the reason we lean forward when we try to intimidate our opponent, only this type of lean is much tenser and aggressive,' explains the platform. So if you do not want to make your co-interlocutor uncomfortable, then you should not lean too forward but if it is to subtly coerce them to do your bidding, moving too forward may be a potent tool.

As I have warned under the generic interpretation segment, 'If you nod, smile and lean all the time, with all people, you will always appear eager to please, and therefore you lower your status in the eyes of others' (SBL 2016). Even if a negotiation favours you in an unexpected manner, instead of lowering your status, keep it to yourself until you take your leave from the meeting. To better understand this point, I want you to think of leaning as driving—'the more you press on the gas the more engaged and eager you are, the less you push – the more relaxed and distant you are. So you don't want slip to the extremities, and you always need to alternate your 'speed' to match the situation,' explains SBL. You also need to pay attention to the direction—you subconsciously lean towards the person you like. You must make sure that you do not express positive expectation at all times so that it does not portray you as being a weakling. People tend to take undue advantage of your vulnerability.

Also explaining this cue, Sonamics (2019) says that it is used to show agreement and sympathy. As the person sits forward, the arms would be slightly open as if they want to hug the desk. If the person as the other side of the table mirrors this cue, this means there is harmony in communication. If you are not receptive of a person's ideas, you tend to do the opposite. Being on the same page with a person means you would not want to miss anything from them. Humans tend to carve out a god in everyone that they like.

Practical Illustrations

Case Study I: Mr D had just withdrawn his child from a school because the performance was not giving the value for the fees. So he had purposed that he was going to make his findings very well this time around before enrolling his child. He went to the first four schools and they tend to have the same story to tell. When he got to the fifth one, they were tilting towards the same path the other four had taken. He was almost preparing to leave when the administrator addressing him made a novel point he considered exceptional. So as to reflect on the point, Mr D leant back and after about three seconds, he moved closer to the speaker and at this point, discussions started in a dynamic way. This was a show of interest in the person for saying something similar to what he wanted to hear.

Case Study II: Mr RD is a stranger in Country WCU. Although he admires the culture and geography of the country, he was really finding it difficult to integrate due to language barrier. However, he knows that he must find a way to overcome this issue as he needs to get down to business and return home on time. In one of his conversations with one of the natives, RD leant forward at some point in order to better catch his expressions. The man misinterpreted this gesture as a sign of genuine interest. Although this was not the case per se, it served a good purpose in that context.

Case Study III: GW doesn't know the real implications of migrating illegally. When he was about to do it, he did not inform anyone in order not to be discouraged. Even he didn't inform anyone on the day he set out on the journey. However, he was not successful. When apprehended, he became nervous and was shivering. However, his real fear came when he was told that he could die in prison. On hearing this, he unconsciously leant forward and turned his right ear to the officer. When the officer re-echoed it, he became totally destabilised. At that point, he lost his voice and sense of reasoning.

20.12. Turning Belly Away

Generic Interpretations of the Concept

The position of the belly while communicating with another person matters a lot. Most times, we do not pay attention to it because we tend to neglect or even oblivious of the message this part of the body passes across. It is one of the few parts of the body that we can hardly manipulate to our favour. Hence, this is the reason we should pay attention to it at all times.

Being one of the most vulnerable parts of the body, we move the ventral away from people we do not have likeness for. Also, if we are not in tandem with their ideas, or generally feel uncomfortable being around them, we will turn away the belly side. The subconscious mind is seeing the person as a threat and, as such, hiding the stomach so that in the case of an attack, the place is protected.

When you meet with a person you do not have care for, you may be able to manipulate your facial expression to appear friendly, but the belly will subtly turn away from them. This is what is technically referred to as ventral denial. The whole essence of this is that while the eyes are open, focused on the person you do not have admiration for, the vulnerable part is not making itself available for the person.

Apart from strangers, this may also be noticeable among friends when there is disagreement. It is a form of disconnection that is orchestrated by the brain in a subconscious manner just to keep us safe. In times of physical combat, if a person is hit at the belly, they may not be able to weather through. Ultimately, there are two likely things that this gesture communicates—turning belly away means the person wants to leave; they no longer fancy their stay with you because it appears unbeneficial to them and it might also mean someone does not share the same believe with you on a given issue. This means 'count me out of what you just said.' We hardly pay attention to this and it affects in our discussions in many ways.

Scientific Explanations

Most of the experts that contributed to this subject matter maintain that this gesture is subtly used to distance oneself from another person that is considered as threat to him or her. Philip (2013) observes that since the torsos house many of the vital organs that keep us alive, we tend to guard it judiciously, knowing fully well that damage can be done to it in the twinkle of an eyes. So when we expose our ventral side, this is an indication that we trust the person we are exposing it to. For instance, we only lay on our back when we are at home because of how it exposes all the vital organs of the body and weakens us from self-defence.

Particularly, the body language expert observes that we tend to shift away our ventral side from those that we do not trust. The real-time occurrence of this behaviour means that it can be changed multiple times during the course of a conversation. For instance, if your co-interlocutor says something that you agree with, you will move your belly to them, and once they utter a statement that does not reflect your philosophy, you will deny them of your belly side. Philip explains further that 'in dating, as women are turned off by an approach they will first shift their feet towards the exit, followed by the torso. If they wish to remain polite so as not to offend, they might keep their faces oriented towards their solicitor, yet the rest of their body, the important parts, will face away.'

If people distance their ventral from you, this means there is no harmony between you. Lack of commonality during discussion will make people distance their belly side from you. Perhaps, they do not like what you are saying or the topic does not interest them.

In the same vein, Body Language Study (2019) states that ventral denial reveals the emotional feelings of people. The website notes that this cue occurs when someone does not feel comfortable with a situation or concept. The platform explains further that 'this is common with females who are uncomfortable in a male-dominated setting. This expression can be pictured as a female clutching her purse close, and turning her body away from any action. Ventral denial indicates discomfort, and extreme caution.'

Ravenscraft (2014) also shares the same opinion with the other two submissions given above. He states that when relationships turn sour and a topic of discourse does not favour us, we will engage in ventral denial by turning or shifting away from the person engaging us in the discussion. The limbic brain is at work in this instance because it sees the need to protect the crucial organs of the body from a perceived enemy.

Practical Illustrations

Case Study I: Ms W fell victim of rape of a known person, someone should would never imagine doing such despicable thing. So she was dumbfounded and could not muster the courage to report to the appropriate authorities. She also thought that she had no convincing evidence against the rapist. So the case would drag unnecessarily, thereby increasing her emotional torture. So she decided to nurse this pain within herself. However, she created an eternal hatred for the man in question. One day, she was at a party and suddenly, she saw the man entering the hall. Immediately, she turned her ventral side from the man. This was a display of hatred.

Case Study II: Mr Y and Dr Z are close friends and managers in their individual companies. They do make out time for each other at weekends to discuss both casual and important issues. One day, in one of their numerous talks, a topic linked to how high-ranking officials were using their position to take advantage of young ladies in search of employment opportunities. As the topic came up, Dr Z subconsciously shifted his ventral side from his friend; he was culpable of the allegation. And he wouldn't like the issue to be raised so as not to be indicted.

Case Study III: Ms TR has be developing affection for Mr HG, her colleague at the workplace; her own style of prostitution is laced with decency—she only scouts for them in select places and keeps them in private locations instead of rushing to hotels. She begins to show signs of attraction to HG and in the twinkle of an eye, he got the signs and keyed into it. Being criminally, smart, HG had a sexual intercourse with her once and failed to pay for her services. This makes her develop hatred for him; whenever she sees him at the workplace, she would turn her belly away.

20.13. Belly Fronting

Generic Interpretations of the Concept

This is polar opposite to the 'ventral denial' discussed in the preceding segment. Belly fronting is a signal of positive event. Moving one of the most vulnerable parts of the body towards a person shows our unrestrained trust in them. It is like selling ourselves out to the person. The limbic brain pushes the body nearer to someone we pick admiration in. So one of the most probable interpretations of this gesture is likeness. While at home with our spouse, we will lay on the bed with our ventral side facing upward. Also, we rest our back at a chair when feeling relaxed and expose the torsos to our co-interlocutor. All these are indicators that we like those in the communicative context. This behaviour can also be noticed in children; they turn their entire body to people they like and vice versa to those they are uncomfortable with.

Apart from likeness, this non-verbal cue communicates comfortable and relaxation. Belly or ventral fronting tells the other person that we are interested in them or what they are saying. This is subconsciously understood by the person too and thus, the floor for communication is made open. Ventral fronting can be done in both sitting and standing postures. While sitting, and you pick interest in someone and what they are saying, you will unconsciously move your shoulders and torso towards them. This is metaphorical gesture of readiness to hug or embrace the person. This is a variant of the leaning cue earlier espoused.

Ladies may use ventral fronting to arouse their partners. Through this means, the breasts are pushed out, thereby drawing a man's attention to them. When a lady turns the sensitive parts of her body to you, this is a 'ready gesture' that some men will never ignore. To surmise it all, this cue is employed to gradually communicate interest and admiration to people.

Scientific Explanations

Philip (2013) begins by noting that exposing our ventral side expresses our optimism that we will not be attacked. When you trust that a situation or person will not cause havoc to you, you will be free to expose the sensitive parts of the body. If there are more than one person you trust in a situation, you will turn your belly to the person you trust most. For instance, if a kid has her parents, close relatives and teachers at a place. All things being equal, she should feel relaxed with anyone of them. However, there is high probability that she would orient her ventral side to her parents in that context. Philip also observes that the topic under context will also determine their move. For instance, if her teacher is throwing their weight behind her in a discourse while her parents are scolding her, she would prefer the teacher at that point.

When you agree with people, you tend to move close to them and shrink any gap between you. This explains why you mostly observe this ventral fronting in situations where true positive emotions are displayed. 'When we are reunited with loved ones we take part in hugs which is intimate precisely because the torsos are sandwiched together. We even move our arms away from our fronts so that we can get even closer' (Philip 2013). You will not move closer to a person you are not sure of.

When you orient the torsos forward, it reveals the direction of your thoughts. For example, lovers in deep conversations will cover up gap and orient their belly towards each other. This means they have no desire to leave the conversation. You will also notice the ventral-fronting cue in business meetings where both parties agree to the deal. Philip (2013) concludes that by urging, 'To use ventral language best, lean forward and drop the arms to the side when you wish to project agreement.'

Lending its voice to this, Body Language Study also states that due to our high level of sensitivity, we will only open up our ventral side to people we are comfortable with and they are expected to reciprocate this gesture in order to entrench the feeling of harmony in the conversation.

Ravenscraft (2014) also states that 'when things are good, we expose our ventral sides towards what we favor, including those people who make us feel good'. This means there is a consensus among experts on this gesture. In courtship, ventral fronting is one of the most reliable indicators that a relationship is on good path.

Practical Illustrations

Case Study I: Business Partner Q and Business Partner R have been transacting business together for over a decade but there are still times that deals do not work out for them. In this particular one, Q was discussing a contract with R, how they could partner and deliver the work as fast as possible. Since R was reluctant due to the offer, he slightly turned away his ventral side while still maintaining facial contact. When Q discovered that unless he made a compromise R was not going to work with him, he improved on the offer and immediately, R turned his ventral side towards him. Also, his level of enthusiasm in the topic increased simultaneously.

Case Study II: Mrs T is a fun-lover; she does not joke with parties and other activities that would give her the opportunity to live out herself. Summer vacation was fast approaching and Mr T was mentioning anything about it, discussing other things that the wife did not really pick interest in. When Mrs T discovered that unless he compelled him to do something, the summer vacation was not going to be observed, she began to be moody at home. When the husband could not withstand her tormenting act, he decided to bring it up one night. Before he started the topic, she was lying down away from the husband but once the topic was raised, Mrs T stood up and moved closer to Mr T, turning her ventral side to him. This communicated her admiration and readiness to her husband.

Case Study III: Man IY and Woman OH did a marriage of convenience and since both of them were looking for one thing or another to benefit from the unplanned union, they cooperated with each other and did rehearsals numerous times before embarking on the execution of their plans. There was a time both of them went for an interview and when they were asked a seemingly difficult question, it was the man that answered. Woman OH was very pleased with the response he was giving and unconsciously turned his belly to him. This further boosted the potency of their message at that give time. There was a show of love and enthusiasm.

20.14. Covering of the Belly

Generic Interpretations of the Concept

One of the ways you know a person is vulnerable is how they expose or cover up their belly. As stated at different points, the torso is one of the most delicate parts of the body. We tend to guard it with our strength. The protective mechanism in charge of the torsos is controlled by the limbic brain. This means that we do not have to direct it before it swings into action. Having said that, you know that someone is lost to anxiety when they begin to cover their stomach with all kinds of items.

Once the person becomes insecure, the environment in which they find themselves and topic under discussion will determine how they display this cue. For instance, an insecure student will use book bag to guard their stomach. This is very subtle that the context might not really make you reflect of their nervous actions. Also, women tend to cover their belly with purses or handbags. Since they are always with their bags, they will quickly resort to them as a weapon when they are threatened. In a discourse, pay attention to how women place their bags. If they are pleased with the person at the other side of the table, they will place their bag at the side but immediately they lose interest in the person, they will subtly move the bag to their front. They may even use wineglasses. The ultimate interest is to ensure that whatever is coming towards the belly does not hit them directly. That is, they want to take the ventral side out of sight.

Even among couples, you will also observe this cue when arguments ensue; they will cover their belly with pillows. As the argument gets more intense, they will press the pillow against the belly the more. They know the consequences of allowing someone hit the place during physical confrontation.

Discomfort is another likely factor that can lead to this behaviour. When people are not comfortable being around someone, they may lift up their pet to the ventral region. This will not only distract their attention; it would also serve as protection to the person. In the weirdest instance, some people even use their own knees; they will place their feet at the edge of the chair, lifting the knees up to the chest region. However, this is mostly done in casual instances. We want to feel safe in an atmosphere that is charged.

In an official setting, you may observe that someone is slouching in their chair towards a table. This is to use the table as a cover for the belly. So the ventral side is buried under the table while the head and neck are the only parts revealed.

Scientific Explanations

Philip (2013) observes that this is a negative body language gesture; covering the ventral with objects prevents others from getting to your mind; when the person communicating with you does not have a full view of your body, especially the sensitive parts, it impedes the flow of discussion. However, the body language expert notes that you can make use of this gesture if you want to pass a message that you do not want to be approached. Sometimes, people might not use objects; they will cross their arms at their chest regions. This forms a 'road closed' gesture. There is no gainsaying that making friends with everyone is not in your best interest, especially when those people are malicious and unbeneficial. The best way to cut them off is to cover the belly. This tells them that you are not comfortable being with them. He concludes, 'Being courteous all the time, to all people is a misuse of proper body language so use the non-verbal language that is most appropriate for the feelings you want to convey.'

Also, Study Body Language (2016) describes this gesture as defensive body language. SBL states that the act of covering the belly with items is a childhood behaviour that is embellished with a form of subtlety and self-control. For instance, 'Little children who feel insecure often hide behind a piece of furniture or their mother's skirt, seeking refuge and protection' (SBL 2016) but as we mature, this becomes impossible or societally unacceptable and that is why we portray it in a more mature way.

Practical Illustrations

Case Study I: Lady R and Man H were on a date, the third in a week. Although they just met with each other, it seemed that they are both into each other. As a way of intensifying the relationship, Lady R sought to know Man H more—she wants to know his past, plans, escapades and thoughts on his viewpoints on some issues of life. Before then, she placed her bag at her side and the discussion was really flowing. She begged the Man H to open and be sincere. So H decided to heed to her pleas. After saying the sweet ones that wowed her, he made mention that he just returned from the rehab about seven months ago, recounting the evil deeds that made a candidate of rehabilitation centre for years. At that point, Lady R became vulnerable, almost shivering. She gradually reached for her bag, drew it to the centre of the table and tried to change the topic of discourse. She was afraid and, as such, looking for how to safeguard the sensitive parts of her body.

Case Study II: Man A and Woman B were negotiating a deal. They discussion appeared to be fruitful at the initial stage as both of them saw the advantage of engaging in the business. However, when they got to the aspect of financial commitment and viability of the business, it seemed Woman B would be paying more than she had budgeted and that the feasibility of the business was close to nothing. Man A could glaringly see the fear and doubt written on her face, he was trying to calm her down. When Woman B became more nervous, she moved the wineglass at the table to her front and also the bag she had placed at her left hand side. This unconsciously communicated to the man that his partner was feeling uncomfortable.

Case Study III: I once interviewed a man for forgery. The case was such a source of concern to the affected organisation that their leadership were present when I was treating his case. In fact, with the way the case was handled from the beginning, he knew that he had no hiding place. While the interview was going on, it got to a point that he felt like standing up and then walk out of the room but he knew the implications of this. He became obviously nervous and he eventually raise his hands along his stomach region and block it so that they might become inaccessible to me.

20.15. Mirroring

Generic Interpretations of the Concept

Mirroring is the soul of every non-verbal discourse. That is, it aptly explains what positive body language behaviour is. Mirroring is when another person assumes the posture of an interlocutor. That is, the two people assuming the same posture during a conversation. In a way, we say that they are reflecting the thoughts of each other. Technically, this is referred to as isopraxis. I said this posture is an emblem of positive body language because people mirror each other only if they are comfortable in all realms. If you do not like the environment, topic being discussed or even the person, you will not mirror them. Hence, mirroring is the aftermath of comfort and admiration.

It is pertinent to observe that you can echo the posture of anyone at any given situation; friends, strangers, colleagues, among others. While sitting with a friend, unconsciously, you might find yourselves mirroring the relaxed posture of each other. Any time this comes to your conscious mind, you would discover that both of you share the same sentiment on what you are discussing. That is why you are at ease with each other. If it were to be a tense situation, you would maintain different postures; you will assume a stance that will make you get your point across in the best possible way. You may even display a defensive posture, fearing the likelihood of attack from the other person.

Another context where people find it easy to mirror each other is dating. Since this is an emotional relationship, most times, the gestures displayed are accurate representation of what goes on within the parties involved. The person who admires their partner will lean forward and if their spouse shares the same feeling with them, they will also reciprocate this gesture. That is why you see lovers always move close to each other, even in sitting position.

Generally, mirroring is the most accurate way for you to know that someone agrees with you emotionally, temperamentally and physically. However, it is crucial to add that mirroring is not limited to positive events; negative events can equally be mirrored. The message mirroring passes is 'I share the same emotions with you—whether positive or negative'.

Scientific Explanations

Psychologia (2019) notes that the essence of mirroring is to bond and enhance understanding in a discourse. As powerful as it is, we use it instinctively without our own conscious awareness. The platform explains better by submitting that 'the most obvious forms of mirroring are yawning and smiling. When you see someone yawn, or even if you just read the word "yawn", you are likely to yawn immediately, or during next 30 seconds. Smiling is also pretty contagious— seeing a smiling person makes you want to smile too, and as a result you will feel better, even if you were not feeling particularly happy in the beginning.' This explains how potent this tool in influencing the way we think and behave in a given situation.

Some scientists explain that 'there is a neuron that affects part of the brain that is responsible for recognition of faces and facial expressions' (Psychologia 2019). It is this neuron that brings about 'mirroring' which makes you see smiling faces in different people at the same time. That is, the neuron makes you copy the facial expression that you notice in your co-interlocutor. The research shows that people who experience the same emotions are likely to experience mutual trust, connection and understanding. They will also begin to match facial expressions and body language. In other words, they will subconsciously mirror each other (Psychologia 2019).

Often, you hear people say that the vibes are around a given person, what they are referring to unconsciously is the act of mirroring. There is little wonder that in dating, lovers play romantic music so as to bring them to the same wavelength. Once you mirror a person, you begin to feel how they feel.

Practical Illustrations

Case Study I: Lady N and Man D were out on a date. They could not even explain how they clicked with each other. But the relationship has been fantastic, birthing numerous innovative ideas. So any time they decide to hang out, it is a means of celebrating their partnership in a unique manner. On this occasion, they decided to reminisce on their high school events. Luckily for both of them, their high school days were eventful. It was Lady N that led the discussion. As her narration caught the attention of the man, he subconsciously leant forward to her, as if he wanted to be swallowing her words. The lady, happy with this show of interest, also leant towards him that their discussion almost became a whisper because they were intimately close to each other.

Case Study II: Mr U is the management staff in charge of recruitment and related activities at FAW Schools. It was part of the institution's culture to take applicants on microteaching session in order to ascertain the person's level of delivery. During one of their recruitment session, he took an applicant to the final year class; many of them were intellectually mature because their exams were fast approaching. The applicant, very cool, intelligent and experienced, chose a topic and discussed it in a very practical manner. Many of the teachers, who used to be critical of applicants, listened attentively and started nodding to what the applicant was saying. Mr U also unconsciously joined in the nodding session because he was also impressed at the sagacity and expertise of the applicant.

Case Study III: Mr and Mrs HX were discussing their children after the day's work. They were both impressed about their recent academic performance, a paradigm shift from a session ago when they were in another school. Although they were never happy with the other school, financial incapability had always handicapped them. During their discussion, they were just reminiscing on their countless complaints and how they old school administrators could not do anything about it. At some point, they turned it to a mockery of sort. As the husband relaxed back to laugh and rest, the wife also laughed hysterically, leaning back flexibly on her chair too.

Case Study IV: I once interviewed a man for forgery. The case was such a source of concern to the affected organisation that their leadership were present when I was treating his case. In fact, with the way the case was handled from the beginning, he knew that he had no hiding place. While the interview was going on, it got to a point that he felt like standing up and then walk out of the room, but he knew the implications of this. He became obviously nervous and he eventually raise his hands along his stomach region and block it so that they might become inaccessible to me.

20.16. Sitting Rigidly

Generic Interpretations of the Concept

The way in which we sit tells others about our emotional feelings. When we sit flexibly, we are able to move about, listen attentively and express ourselves without tolerating any form of intimidation from any quarter. On the other hand, sitting rigidly is as if a glue has been used to pin down our buttocks to a chair; psychological glue makes sure we do not move away from our sitting posture even if there is an obvious reason for that. If you notice someone sitting rigidly at a spot for a long duration without moving, this is a sure indication that there are issues with them. Nobody fascinates sitting on a spot for long; at least, you move once in a while to give yourself the needed rest.

Sitting rigidly at a spot is one of the freeze responses. They think there are dangers surrounding them, so they tend to sit at a spot fearfully. If you look inwardly, you will definitely observe the fear written all over a person that sits rigidly at a spot; they tend to look hopelessly into the distance with empty expression on their face. Even when there is humour in their environment, they tend not to take note of it. This means they are lost in the realm of negative thought; they are reflecting on the situation that keeps them glued on a spot for several minutes or hours.

This is mostly seen in forensic settings where this behaviour cripples in subconsciously. Depositions and police interviews are other common places this can be found. Suspects do become fearful to the extent that they cannot move. They freeze on the chair as if a lion is lurking somewhere, waiting for them to show up to be pounced on. I have also observed this gesture in public settings among those who are shy. When the programme is ongoing and they feel the urge to stand up and get something done, they will resist it, thinking all eyes would be on them.

Rigid sitting should not be taken as a sign of deception but rather a clear indicator of psychological discomfort on the part of the person expressing this behaviour.

Scientific Explanations

Bud Smith (2019) states that when you see a person maintaining a rigid posture while sitting, it means they are either uptight or anxious. My usual expression is, 'Fear recreates you in a negative light, tormenting you until you stand against it.' Anxiety does not like you to have your freedom. This is why it keeps people glued to their seat even if that is against their wish. The person displaying this cue would slouching in their chair, looking like an old vegetable. Slouching exposes them as lacking confidence to face others.

Also, Narin (2017) explains that when someone sits rigidly on a spot for a while, this is an indication that they close-minded; there is no positive thought going on in their mind. Perhaps, they are confused and afraid that what they are thinking about would not work, so there is no need moving from their seat to trying implementing those plans.

Further, a body language expert who has authored 18 books in this field, Lilian Glass (2017) also observes that sitting rigidly is a symbol of negativity. When a person sits rigidly closing off the arms into the body, this means they are not receptive of any idea. That is why Narin states that they are close-minded.

Practical Illustrations

Case Study I: Suspect F was arrested in a case connected to arson. He is a smoke addict that anyone who moves close to him would notice this. He had been arrested several times for smoking at the wrong venues but he had always pleaded that he was working on how to curb himself. This time around the havoc caused by his cigarette led to loss of lives and property. The police had the video and other evidence to prosecute him. All they needed was his oral confession to hasten his arraignment. Having seen the obvious, Suspect F became helpless. He could not even muster the courage to put up a line of defence. While it was time for him to stand up, he sat helplessly for several minutes until one of the interrogators patted him at the back and helped him up.

Case Study II: In a public transport, a robber deprived a military officer of his expensive phone. Since he was not on uniform, the robber did not know that he had surpassed his boundary on this particular one. Before getting to their destination, the military officer got to know that his phone was not on him again. Immediately, he announced it to all passengers, imploring that whoever took it should return it before the person was fished out. Many of the passengers were compassionate towards him as they checked the floor and sides to be sure it did not drop off. However, the robber sat rigidly on a spot as if it was going to fall off his bag if he stood up. He became nervous to the extent that he almost lost his breath. The military officer's attention was later called to his defiance act and this made him to approach the robber. Some few questions and he was already cold, this exposed him and the phone was later retrieved from him.

Case Study III: Mr O is a very shy person; he feels uncomfortable being in a new place or among crowd. However, there was a particular training which he was required to attend, comprising about a thousand other attendees across the world. He sat somewhere at the middle so as not to call attention to himself. However, about three hours into the programme, he felt like easing himself but when he looked around, saw how everywhere was silent and the distance of the restroom, he found it difficult to stand up even though no one was holding him back. He remained in that uncomfortable state until the end of the event.

20.17. Ejection-Seat Effect

Generic Interpretations of the Concept

When someone clinches to their seat as if they are resisting a forceful ejection, this means they are battling with the effect of fear. This is nervousness at its peak. This sitting posture is very unique; the person sits as if he is ready to be ejected from a military jet but does not want to get down, thereby gripping the armrests with full force. Without having a pictorial image of this cue, you might not understand it; think of a person about to stand up from a chair but resisting it by holding the armrest tightly. They will not place their back on the backrest. This is very symbolic; they are not comfortable with their present state but also fear taking their leave from that location. Hence, they behave as someone who is lost between the devil and deep blue sea.

This is also one of the freeze responses used in depicting a distressed person. He or she is tired of situation but does not have power to revolt against it. In other words, we can safely assume that those who are displaying this cue are feeling threatened. Interview settings is a common place where you can see this gesture. Fear disorganises candidates, making them to sit in a very inappropriate manner. Since this behaviour is subconscious, they are not aware that they are letting out this cue. When questions become tough or the interviewing panel is making huge revelations against the interviewees, they would feel like leaving the interview room but since this is not possible, they slouch and use both hands to press tightly to the armrests to give themselves the assurance that they are still safe.

Apart from the posture, another thing that makes this behaviour stand out is how rigid those displaying this cue look; they look as if they are metaphorically hanging on for their dear life. They are engulfed in fear and this betrays their confidence as they are not able to make outstanding or convincing points in that state.

Scientific Explanations

In order to have a better understanding of this concept, we need to peruse it from the literal point of view before relating it to body language. In aircraft, an *ejection seat* or *ejector seat* is a system designed to rescue the pilot or other crew of an aircraft (usually military) in an emergency. In most designs, the seat is propelled out of the aircraft by an explosive charge or rocket motor, carrying the pilot with it. The concept of an ejectable escape crew capsule has also been tried. Once clear of the aircraft, the ejection seat deploys a parachute. Ejection seats are common on certain types of military aircraft. The purpose of an ejection seat is pilot survival. The pilot typically experiences an acceleration of about 12–14g (David 1958).

Just like in the scenario explained in the preceding paragraph, we also use the ejection-seat effect for the purpose of protecting ourselves in an unfavourable circumstance. It is like reinforcement against a threat. With this sitting posture, we believe that we should be able to weather through any storm arising from the camp of the 'opponent'. The rigid stance makes the body to pump up its whole power so as to grip the armrests tightly. With that, the person is sure that nothing can move him or her from the spot.

Practical Illustrations

Case Study I: Ms R was a renowned student leader while at the college. She was very versatile and respected. So she had the opportunity to be invited by different student bodies to help interview applicants for extra-curricular activities. Hence, she knows how it feels being on the other side of the table. However, with this, one would ordinarily expect her to be confident after school and face any interview panel but reverse is the case. Instead of her to think of her experience, she was thinking of how the student applicants used to shiver, thereby sending fear down her nerves. While on interview for a job, she was asked a tricky question at some point and she felt empty. She became ashamed of herself. Ms R felt as if she wanted to fall from the chair she was seated, so she held on tightly to the armrests, looked rigid and maintained a disconcerted eye contact as if her life was under threat.

Case Study II: Suspect E was arrested in a case relating to terrorism. The interrogators were clear to him, the likely consequences of his crime if found guilty at the end of the day. This unsettled him because he doubted his ability to manoeuvre the experienced interrogators. The interview started on a good note and Suspect E seemed to be having a field day until one of the interviewers played an audio-visual record to him, made references to some specific dates and the colour of the dress he wore. At that point, he knew he had reached his melting point. He felt as if the ground should open up and swallow him. He shifted away from the chair, gripped the armrests very forcefully and looked rigid. He could hardly utter a word until about a minute later.

Case Study III: Student A had been warned of his bullying tendencies over time but he would not listen. His disturbing activities had become worrisome some of the students informed their parents to withdraw them from the school. When this came to the notice of the management, they set up a disciplinary committee immediately. The committee invited Student A to give explanations for his behaviour and why he was unyielding. He thought he could behave anyhow without being subjected to punishment. After the session, the committee listed some of the consequences of his actions. As the secretary of the panel was reading out the statement, A held the arms of the chair he was seated on tightly as if he was ordered out of the room but resisting the attempt. His face was also rigid as his expression became undetectable.

20.18. Chair Distancing

Generic Interpretations of the Concept

A secret about emotional body language is that the higher the feeling, the more intense the non-verbal show of it. This means that we tend not to control our emotions when caught in unexpected circumstances. When negative emotional feelings rise beyond measures, instead of leaning away, people will practically move their chair away from the person or situation that is considered as a threat. The purpose of this non-verbal display is to distance themselves from an alleged threat. With this, the ventral side would be safeguarded. If it is lesser threat, people will rather lean away and guard the torsos instead of moving away but by the moment the limbic brain hints them that they need to widen the physical distance, they will shift their chair backwards. This is unconscious and they would have done it before seeing how weird the behaviour is.

This behaviour can be observed at any given place. For instance, there was a time when an acrimonious discussion was going on in the academia where a don moved his chair completely from the table very near to the window in the corner of the room where the discussion was taking place. To him, it was as if the behaviour was not wrong but others at the meeting were left dumbfounded at his behaviour. It was as if he was looking for cool breeze through the window. However, the underlying meaning is to protect his belly.

Note that this attitude is not only birthed by physical attack or threat, the cause of fear may be words or ideas shared by their co-interlocutor. In the case of the professor shared in the preceding paragraph, he was not pleased with what his colleagues were saying and decided to move away from them. The person may not necessarily carry the chair; they would use their buttocks and legs to gradually move the chair away from the table while their arms are closed.

Scientific Explanations

Westside Toastmasters (2019) states that a person that moves their chair away from the table is vulnerable; they have a feel that things are not working out for them and if they do not protect themselves, the person at the other side of the table may injure them. When they move their chairs back, it provides them with the opportunity to have a full view of everything. At least, they are certain that before anyone can rush to them, they would have taken flight. However, if the other party moves closer to him or her, this becomes unnerving to the threatened person. If care is not taken, they may even fall off the chair because moving into their personal space is like taking life out of their throat.

Further, Philip (2014) states that when you see a person moving away their chair, it is an indication that they are moving out of a situation—they want you to count them out of any decision you are about to make. Moving away reduces the overall profile people, making them look smaller than their normal size. This is a closed body language, aiming to shield the person from suspected adversaries. Whenever you notice it, think of something negative.

Practical Illustrations

Case Study I: Mr and Mrs GC with their three children where at the dining taking their supper. After they had all eaten, they decided to have a short family meeting. They started with general issues affecting the whole family. Then, they moved on to individual issues, starting from the parents. However, Child C, the last of the three seemed to be different—he was seen to be wayward, uncompromising, greedy, intellectually poor and disobedient. This was a point of concern to the whole family. So when it was time to discuss him, it was as if the other four members of the family had planned it; they all lamented bitterly, noting how he was constituting nuisance in the family and causing shame to the family name. He thought they were going to stop any time soon but as they were elongating it, he could not bear the psychological trauma any more. Subconsciously, Child C moved his chair away from others. When he seemed to be far away, the mother had to order him to move nearer.

Case Study II: A group of experienced interrogators were interviewing a suspect that had constituted himself as a nuisance in the society for years. He appeared to be master of the trick but the interrogators were not ready to take chances with him. Being one of the longest sessions of interrogations, it took the experts fourteen unbroken hours to dig deep into the issue. At some point, it seemed the suspect was being successful as he was beating about the bush without any definite confession that can be used in nailing him. At some point, about two or three interrogators had to engage him at a time. Then, he lost balance and could not do intellectual manoeuvring any more. When it appeared that the 'attack' through questions were flying from everywhere, he unconsciously moved his chair away from them. Before he could know what was going on, he had moved farther from them. Recognising this, he sighed and gradually moved it back.

Case Study III: An applicant was engaged by the recruitment team in a university. Due to the large number of applicants, each session was short so that they could take as many applicants as possible each day. However, the case of a particular boy who applied from one of the least expected regions caught their attention; his result was amazing, and as such, he was expected to be intellectually sound. So they wanted to confirm this through various questions. Truthfully, he committed exam malpractice to have such charming result and could not defend it. When the session was becoming intense, the applicant placed his two hands at the edge of his chair and placing his legs firmly on the floor, he shifted towards the door. The team got his sense of insecurity and allowed him to take his leave.

20.19. Slouching the Body

Generic Interpretations of the Concept

You will observe that I have made reference to slouching at different points in time, using it to explain some negative body displays. However, I want us to consider it in full so that we can know how it is effectively deployed when people are emotionally weak. There are different meanings that can be attached to body slouching, depending on where the gesture is displayed. It is a potent tool in the hands of children while dealing with their parents to show that they are not moved; they don't care what the decision of their parents is. They mostly use this when threatened and want to show indifference. For instance, if their parent says that if they fail to perform their chores, their school fees would not be paid, instead of begging or dispensing the duty, they would slouch their body in a chair, indicating that the threat does not shake them. This is a perception management technique which has worked for them at different times.

This attitude is also used by adults to pass the same message. However, it can be used in some contexts to project relaxation. You will see people shrink in their chair and disconnect themselves from other activities going on around them. This means they want to take rest from the hues and cries, typical of our today's world. Slouching makes the torsos to move in as the person shrinks in the whole body.

While this body language technique can be effectively deployed by children and adults in showing indifference to relax in casual settings, the case is not the same when used in formal setting; it passes a negative message on professional grounds. While in the office or during negotiation, when a party slouches, it means they are not impressed or motivated about the discussion. When people are bored, they tend to slouch in order to take rest. Slouching passes message of disinterest to your business partner and this may affect the outcome of your deal. In a formal setting, people are expected to sit straight and look straight in the eye of the person at the other side of the table while negotiation is ongoing. With this, informed decision would be made.

Scientific Explanations

Philip (2014) states that this body language cue is used to depict a casual attitude or someone who is relaxing. Giving the description, the body language expert notes that 'the posterior is moved forward towards the front of the chair so a person can slouch and drop down low. The feet are held tightly together, head lowered chin down, eyes averted and downcast, the shoulders hunch up, the arms are kept close to the body.' This gives a pictorial view of how people slouch in chair. You may observe this cue when someone wants to non-verbally communicate that they are withdrawing from a situation. Since their bodily expression has depicted someone who is not in the mood to talk, this will also dampen the spirit of the other party in the discourse. However, if you do not want to send the message of indifference, you should not assume this posture.

Philip (2014) explains that teenagers are effective in the use of this gesture, especially in educational setting. When they slouch their body, it reduces their overall profile, reducing the chances of being called upon. He gives two possible verbal translation of this cue as 'I'm hiding in plain sight by reducing the size of my body and remaining motionless so that other people don't notice me.' Or 'I have a relaxed attitude. I'm too cool for school.' So the context differentiates the messages from each other—whether indifference of relaxation.

Practical Illustrations

Case Study I: J's mother was going out to see her friends and promised to be back within two hours. She told J to wash the dish and clean the kitchen before she returned so that they could go out for shopping. However, J was engrossed in seeing movie until her mother came back. The mother was deeply pained that she did not obey her instruction. So she decided to punish her by not taking J for shopping that again. When she informed J of her decision that if she did not stand up at once to perform the chores, she would not attend to her needs again. J looked at her mother and turned away, slouching in the chair; she was feeling lazy and unperturbed of her mother's threat.

Case Study II: Mrs G is a medical doctor while Mr G is a teacher. This means that the latter is always more available than the former. So he mans the kitchen, prepares delicacies before the arrival of his wife, especially when she was on night duty. This has kept their matrimonial home strong as Mrs G does not take this rare gesture for granted. One day when she returned from the hospital, the husband had prepared food, waiting to usher her to the dining after she might have showered. However, the woman was sounding tired due to hectic sessions at work. After showering, she collapsed herself into the couch. All the husband's pleas to move to the dining were rebuffed as she relaxed herself for about an hour.

912

Case Study III: Mr L had just secured a job with a private firm in his area. The proprietor of the firm and other workers are reputed for the love for work and diligence but L was not ready to stress himself as he just wanted to use the opportunity to garner experience and build his curriculum vitae. His work rate was slow and uninspiring. The CEO was aware of this but only decided to keep him for the probationary period. Any time they were having a meeting, L will slouch in his chair, placing his elbow on the arm of the chair in order to use his hand to support his head. Unconsciously, he would contribute less and even irritate others when told to speak. He was shown the way out immediately after the probationary period.

Case Study IV: I had what can be called an evergreen encounter with a smuggler; he had wanted to play smart by travelling separately with his smuggled goods. He knew how difficult it is to get items smuggled in but he sees that as the best business idea on ground for him. Despite the threats to his life, he would not let go of the illicit job. When I arrested him, I told him that we were not going to start the interview until all the trucks containing his loads arrive. This means he would be waiting for hours. I offered him a chair and within few minutes, he started slouching.

20.20. Doubling Over

Generic Interpretations of the Concept

When you are anticipating something evil, you do not just sit back and wait while it comes to consume you; you either rise to the occasion or find a reinforcement that will protect any time the attack is launched. In the case of doubling over, we manoeuvre the body in a way that makes it fit for it to withstand emotional troubles. The body is doubled over by bending forward at the waist while seated or even in standing posture as if the person is suffering some intestinal unrest. Mostly, this is done by tucking the arms across the stomach. In overall, the person does not maintain an appropriate posture and appears pitiable. The weight of the body falls on a side while the hands are made to guard the stomach.

This is very symbolic; they are protecting the intestines so that the emotional distress they are going through does not affect them. One of the most common places you will observe this cue is at hospitals. Also, in locations that are fragile and prone to bad news, people will display this gesture. Invariably, people display this gesture when they receive shocking or bad news. I have seen people that developed stomach upset immediately after receiving bad news; they rushed to the toilet and after that, came to reflect on what they were told. If we are truly touched about someone's loss, we feel some pains around the ventral side and we double over to pacify ourselves. The arms are strong and can assure us of protection. So they are delicately woven around the stomach as we receive or grapple with the thought of something evil.

A key factor to spotting this cue is to observe if the person is bending forward to the waist while standing or sitting. This makes the body appear odd and sends a huge message to you; something is amiss and then, you can move ahead to determine what the problem is.

Scientific Explanations

Parvez (2015) states that doubling over is a classic sign of defensiveness which is made manifest through insecurity, uneasiness, or shyness. When a situation appears unpalatable, we become threatened and the subconscious mind first shields the ventral side by waving the two hands on it. When the stress becomes very intense, the person may also cross the legs. This is a reflection of awkward feeling. Imagine someone who has been waiting for hours and at the end of the day the person did not show up, feeling of awkwardness will set in which would make the person bend towards the waist. Even in a group, you will observe this awkward gesture in a person that does not feel elated.

Doubling over is also noticed when someone feels offended. Defence is a natural reaction to an offence. That is why you see people cross their arms in the ventral side when they are criticised or embarrassed by another person. This is a defensive mode meant to pacify and ensure that the person criticising them does not have access to their delicate area in case he or she decides to attend. In a communicative context, when all is going on well between the interlocutors and out of the blues, one of them doubles over, this means the second party had said something that arouses the negative feeling of the person. They may not get over this feeling till the conversation comes to an end.

Practical Illustrations

Case Study I: The school bus conveying three of Mr and Mrs WO had an accident on their way home which led to the loss of lives of many of the pupils in the bus. Unfortunately for the couples, they lost two of their children while the third one was dangerously injured. When they heard the news on radio, they became restless, putting calls to the school administration before the school sent a member of staff to them. When they were informed, Mrs WO held her head, ran out of the house and weep bitterly while the husband bet forward at the waist, tucking his arms across his stomach as he reflected on his unquantifiable loss.

Case Study II: A young man has been trying his effort to be admitted into a university after his high school but it seemed every time he tried his effort could not yield any productive outcome. So he decided to do some menial jobs for about two years before giving another trial. After the two-year break, he tried and things still looked unfavourable. When he did not get any feedback from the university he applied to, he had to go there in person. After meeting with the admission team, he was told to wait for some few minutes while they check the status of his application. A lady later came to the reception area to regretfully inform him that his application was not successful. Having heard this, the man sunk himself in the chair where he was seated and bent forward at his waist while tucking the arms across the ventral side. Depression and frustration could be read on his face.

Case Study III: Ms P was in haste and did not pay attention to the fact that people are not allowed to park at the place where he wanted to park. After rushing out of her car to drop an item with a friend, she discovered that men of taskforce were already at her vehicle. At first, she was lost, wondering what could have brought them to her car before looking at her side where it was clearly written that anyone who parked at the placed risked huge fine. She pleaded with them but they were unyielding. So Ms P followed them to their station and gave a statement. On the following day, she was arraigned and a fine was levied against her. As the judge was delivering his judgement, Ms P, standing in the witness box, could be seen doubling over by bending forward on her waist and using her arms as protective shield over her belly as if the pronouncement was going to pierce through her.

Case Study IV: A contract was billed to be given to couples that had been married for at least two decades. When Man YR heard this, he began to think of how he would have access to it even though he had no wife. The first thing he did was to think of a person he would do marriage of convenience with. He eventually got a woman who was desperate for money too. After all the formalities, they altered their wedding certificate and backdated it before applying for the contract. Unfortunately, the application was not successful. When the man heard this, he was overtaken by sorrow as he could be seen bending forward on his waist and using his arm as a protective shield over his belly.

20.21. Foetal Position

Generic Interpretations of the Concept

This is also called foetus position in some quarters. This suggests that in order for us to have an apt understanding of this gesture, we need to think of a pregnant woman. The body of the prenatal foetus has to be positioned well as it develops in its mother's womb. The womb is not really big that it can contain foetus anyhow they like. This means they have to be positioned in a defined way so as to stay healthy and comfortably in the womb. You may be thinking that what is the connection between a foetus in the womb and body language but I make bold to state that many people metaphorically maintain this posture even in their adulthood when they are threatened or faced with an opposition that they think they cannot challenge.

Often, people switch to the foetal-positioning gesture when they are undergoing emotional stress and other forms of psychological trauma. When displaying this cue, the head is bowed while the back is curved with the legs pressed together so that they can both be lifted up to cover the torso and serve as a pillow on which the head is placed. There are times that the person concerned will make use of real objects to pacify themselves while they are undergoing emotional turbulence.

This is mostly seen among couples while they pick up an intense argument with each other. Until one is tired, they will keep on being at the top of their voice. However, if one of the partners is able to win, the defeated fellow would feel dejected. At this point, the defeated partner has become overwhelmed with negative emotions—they will raise their two knees and sit in a foetal position while they try to protect the torsos and other delicate areas of the body.

If the person thinks that guarding the ventral side with their knees alone is not enough, they will use additional objects such as pillows and dresses to cover up their belly. This is a metaphorical 'bullet proof' that gives the person the assurance that their life is secure. Whatever level of stress the person might be going through, as they display this gesture, it begins to dissipate gradually.

I must state that once a person assumes this posture, they become silent; this will help them to deal with the stress instead of keep arguing intensely.

Scientific Explanations

Philip (2014) explains that this cue can also be referred to as 'Hugging The Knees, Pulling The Knees In, or Balling Up.' He describes it as a protective posture, revealing that a person needs to be comforted emotionally. The body language expert states that the verbal translation of this cue is 'I need to feel the comfort of being held to remind me of the protection I felt in my mom's womb or when she snuggled me, as I am suffering extreme discomfort and stress.'

From the foregoing, we can describe this gesture as a child-like display, reminding us of how we feel while in our mother's womb. Grief, fear, timidity, shyness, discomfort and pain are some of the emotional factors that can lead to this body posture. The limbic brain tells us that the body needs to assume a smaller shape and also find comfort simultaneously. 'As adults, we must provide comfort for ourselves so we are forced to use our own arms and legs to self-hug,' explains Philip. However, as we gain more maturity, we discover that this body cue, just like thumb sucking, is not acceptable in the society, so we tend to drop the extreme form of the gesture in favour of subtler cues.

Philip (2014) explains different places where it can be used in simple terms thus: 'In mild forms, it can be simply a posture one uses for comfort. When it appears in public it signifies that a person has an underlying motivation for pacifying and feels insecure. When done at home, can simply be a way to feel embraced and cared for.'

You may be tempted to think that people may not use this cue in public, and as such, you need not bother on the behaviour of your team members but it can be done in the subtlest form if there is need to comfort and secure oneself; it is done in a more acceptable adult manner where you may not really pay attention to it. 'While at an informal party, for example, a woman might find herself hugging her knees at the end of a couch. To her, this feels comfortable, which is why she does it, but it reveals her true emotions' (Philip 2014).

However, the most acceptable form of this gesture in public is when you pull the limbs in closer to the body and across the centre line as in the 'self-hug'

Practical Illustrations

Case Study I: Child W and her mother were arguing. They have been at loggerheads with each other for the past few months. So an event occurred which flamed up everything. Unfortunately, the head of the family was away for a business trip so there was no one to settle the issue for them. They argued for hours that at some point, one would almost think that it would lead to physical confrontation. When it seemed the mother had better argument and was upbraiding, Child W became weak and threatened. She sat on the ground, covering her belly with throw pillow and assumed the foetal position by bowing her head to meet with the raised knees.

Case Study II: Mr and Mrs YT were engaged in an unusual argument. In times of disagreement, the husband had always played the role of a peacemaker, overlooking the shortcomings of Mrs YT because he knew her to be highly temperamental but in this time around, none of them was unyielding. That made the argument tensed and unimaginably disturbing. In what looked like a defeat on the wife, she broke down in tears on the bed as she raised her two knees close to herself, blocking the ventral side and then, placed her chin on them as she thought on the issue. As she was thinking of the issue, she was also experiencing more negative emotions internally.

Case Study III: A group of drug addicts were once arrested with their drugs. In fact, some of them were still staggering due to the psychological effects of the drugs on them. But when they were brought to the station of law enforcement agents, the reality began to dawn on them that they were in real trouble. The first thing that was taken away from them was their freedom of movement. And then, they were asked to sit on the floor due to their unruly attitude. With fear birthed on most of them, they raised their knees close to themselves and block their ventral side with that action.

20.22. Sudden Cold

Generic Interpretations of the Concept

When the body is suddenly engulfed in cold, it is testament that the person is feeling negative. In an environment that is comfortable where everyone feels calm without any complaint, if out of the blues, someone in that same environment begins to shiver, it means you have to pay attention to an event that just took place or the topic that is being discussed. Usually, stress is the reason people feel cold in a tranquil environment. Invariably, be sure that the atmosphere is warm and the person is not sick before passing your verdict.

Feeling cold due to something awful being said about you or another person serving as a threat to you is an autonomic response geared by the body. During this process, blood moves away from the skin into the larger muscles, thereby making the surface level of the body weak. It is the blood flowing around the skin that makes our body warm and adaptable to the environment. That is why you see that people become red when arguing or at the slightest rise of emotions. However, once blood changes route, this is perceived in the body in the form of cold.

Threat is one of the most common reasons why the body suddenly becomes cold. That is why some people state, 'I became *water* when I saw the questions.' This means their body became cold. In a contest, if you see that your opponent is well-dressed, more built up and charming than you do, you can become threatened, thereby feeling cold. This is one the freeze or flight stimulus. If it is a physical combat, this may be preparing you to take to your heels.

Also, we become suddenly cold when we are worn out. By this time, the body becomes drooping. This passes message to your co-interlocutor that you are not ready for any activity again. When overwhelmed by anxiety, the body may become cold. The thought of something evil or extra-ordinary happening alone is enough to make you cold. In the same vein, when you cast your mind back on a terrifying event, you may experience this feeling. For instance, thinking of when a gun was pointed at you before the robber retreated.

Scientific Explanations

Dachis (2011) says body chill is a negative body language. He lists it as part of the cues that make people exposed to threat. Dachis observes that when the body becomes chill, the person may begin to move away from their potential threat as a form of flight autonomic response. Also, they will cross their arms like a person in search of warmth. The person may also rub their nose, eyes and the back of the neck as they look for warmth across the body. Dachis adds that we have to look at these displays in clusters before we can conclude that the person's cold is caused by stress, nervousness or anxiety as each gesture can signal a myriad of things. This is why you need to look deeper before making an assertion. If there is the opportunity, you may even throw some questions at the person in order to affirm or quash your doubt.

Philip (2013) states that the hands may begin to shake when body chill is at its extreme. A surge of adrenaline affects the body as whole when it is confronted with an unusual situation. Note that this can be triggered by either good or bad stimulus. However, more often than not, the body becomes cold in the face of negative occurrences. For instance, while making way to speak before a large audience for the first time, if you discover that you need to tighten up your preparation before you were called up, your body may become cold as if you are afraid that your listeners will notice your errors and mock you. Also, when one is being embarrassed by one's boss in the presence of others, one's body may become chill. The eyes would also become downcast and sudden frustration would set in but since it is impossible to challenge one's superior, one will repress this feeling. You may avoid speaking with any other person because the body is too weak.

Practical Explanations

Case Study I: A neighbouring country wrote a letter to Country Z asking for military assistance. Since the authorities of Country Z knew that if they did not lend a helping hand to their neighbours, the terrorists may soon find way into their country too, they took quick action over the issue by instructing the head of military to mobilise a sizeable number of his men to the country. Meanwhile, Officer X had always watched in the television how the terrorists laid ambush on both military men and civilians, severing their heads. More so, the terrorists seemed to be formidable with sophisticated weapons compared with what the military were carrying about. Praying that he should never be deployed to such a fragile area, his name was, unfortunately for him, mentioned as part of those going to the war zone. Immediately, he became cold, shivering as if he was dropped in a drum of water; he was anxious of what awaited him there.

Case Study II: Student O had prepared well for her final year examinations, having been warned beforehand that the questions were always technical. She read even beyond the syllabus, hoping to come out in fly colours. However, when she got into the examination hall, she saw all the invigilators maintaining a stern face as if they were bereaved. Also, they were warned that any student caught turning back the question papers when they had not been told would be sent out. It was as if the questions were specifically set to fail the students with the way the supervisors were behaving. For about thirty minutes, they were still putting things in place, arranging the students, fear of the unknown suddenly descended on Student O and she became cold without knowing what could have led to it. She was destabilised for the better part of the examination before she got her calm back. However, the better part of her time had been wasted to this negative feeling.

Case Study III: Smuggler AG has an insider among border officials that supplies him information on how to navigate his routes so as not to be arrested. This has worked for some few times but the last time the official did it, he was almost exposed. So he decided to walk out of the agreement without informing AG. So when the smuggler called him, he supplied him wrong piece of information that made him run into border officials. Since he was not expecting that, he was overtaken by shock and fear. Immediately, he began to shiver due to sudden cold as is he had been suffering from pneumonia before. That was the extent to which he was psychologically disturbed.

20.23. Clothing Choice

Generic Interpretations of the Concept

The clothes we wear mostly cover the torso. In a way, we can say that we are dressing the torso with our dresses. There is no culture where clothing does not play a crucial role in understanding the people and their thoughts; clothing style is an indispensable part of every culture. Smart people across the world take huge advantages presented by clothing to pass their message. With clothing, status is projected within a culture. For instance, there are some attires that are meant for the ruling class alone. Those in the lower cadre of life would wear cheap, unfascinating clothes. To them, all they need clothes for is to cover their nakedness.

Those who are class driven can be identified through their clothing; they spend huge amount of money on what they wear. Some of them can even borrow money to purchase clothing items just to look good and charming. Competition is usually high among women across cultures; they dress to outsmart one another. This is usually noticeable at workplace and even in the neighbourhood.

The society tends to share the sentiment to always respect those who wear expensive items; we believe they are well to do even if we do not know what they do as a means of livelihood. Invariably, what we wear gives people impression about us. That is why celebrities spend a large chunk of their earnings of accessories.

Inasmuch as this is the general belief universally, there tends to be differences in preferences across cultures. Brand names, colours, design, among others are the things that determine how we are perceived by others. Once the brand name is seen, people can determine if the clothe is of high quality or otherwise.

Depending on the kind of dress you are wearing, you either become more submissive or authoritarian. I have seen friends reject invitations to parties because they were unable to afford the clothing their mates were putting on. Sometimes, the odd person will not feel free among friends; they think low of themselves because they are not wearing something that matches the quality of other people. Hence, dressing can segregate people into classes. To better understand this, think of little children; when they wear something nice, they will keep looking at themselves from time to time and then call the attention of their friends to it but when their parents buy something they do not like for them, they will not be proud of themselves; they will stay indoors and look for opportunity to do away with the clothe.

Your dressing can determine if you will get a job or not as it forms an essential part of the grading process during an interview. Also, your clothing and dressing style tells others where you hail from. When you travel to other parts of the world, you will discover that your dressing style is different from yours; this is cultural peculiarity that helps in identifying people across cultural lines. There is no culture of the world where clothing is relegated to the woods. While reading people, you must endeavour to take cognisance of their dressing.

Scientific Explanations

Libby Pelham (2018) gives a detailed description of the relationship between appearance and body language. He laments that when we think of body language, we tend to limit to every other thing but clothing which is equally important as others. People often use clothing to signify four important things—age, economic class, political views and gender. Although you may not have paid conscious attention to this, you might have judged people based on their clothing alone in times past. Meeting a person for the first time, before you hear the person speak or make a point, you might have reached certain conclusions based on their appearance. Usually, we expect certain people to dress a certain way before we learn anything about their credentials. If they fail to meet our expectations, we become disappointed in them.

Through illustration, Pelham (2018) emphasises, 'If you have ever gone on a job interview, you have probably put much thought into what you wore. Most people try to pick out one of their nicest outfits to wear, so they make a good first impression before the employer ever asks them any questions. First impressions are very important and clothing is one of the biggest factors in first impressions.'

If you visit your doctor and he appears in a shabby, dirty and irritating lab coat, you may think of changing your doctor but if you see a painter or construction worker who appears very neat, you would think they do not have much to do or are probably lazy.

Practical Illustrations

Case Study I: Mr K and his friends where to attend a birthday party of one of the leading businessmen in town. People from other provinces and even nations were supposed to fly in for the party. Because Mr K and his friends wanted to sew classy items, they bought materials and dropped them with their individual tailors having agreed on style. However, Mr K's tailor could not finish with the clothes on the stipulated day. He became depressed and unmotivated to go for the party. Even all his friends' pleas to wear a dress of the same colour with the new one were rebuffed. He thought he would look indescribably odd and unattractive in that kind of meeting.

Case Study II: Dr R was prepared to receive some international investors at his office. Apart from preparing his proposals and rehearsing hard so that he could sound convincing, he also paid attention to his clothing because he knew that it was going to be their first point of impression about him. He got a new designer suit with a suit that matches it. On the day of the meeting, Dr R was very conscious of his dressing and that of others. Before offering the visitors a seat, he had gauged them based on their dressing and thought they sat down. With what he saw, he thought they were good business partners for him. This means they were not looking poor and tired as one would have expected them to due to the air travel among others.

Case Study III: I once had an engagement with an impostor who did not leave any stone unturned in his deceptive tricks; he went as far as doing plastic surgery just to have a semblance of the person whom she impersonated. Also, when she was caught, she wore the same dress as the one on the passport. Even though the dress did not really look good on her and was odd for the season, he still decided to go for it. That was why she flared up at first when accused of impersonation. However, she was oblivious of the fact that such an unnecessary display of anger only aggravates things in that condition.

20.24. Placing Hands on Belly in Pregnancy

Generic Interpretations of the Concept

I have often heard people say that that pregnancy recreates women. That is, it changes their lifestyle even without their approval. That is why you see women demand for other choices of food when they take in. They may also find their spouses irritating until they deliver of their baby. Another prominent way in which they change is how they react to stress and deal with vulnerability. Ideally, when threatened or overwhelmed by stress, women tend to cover their throat or suprasternal notch with a hand. They feel this is one of the most delicate parts of the body and should be protected during insecurity.

However, the code changes once they are pregnant. After taking in, women will raise their hand as if they want to reach for their neck but will quickly divert the attention of the hand to the belly when exposed to threat. This may look dramatic but it tells us what is important to the woman at that given point; all her attention is on the pregnancy and will not allow anything come to that region.

Hand covering the belly is to metaphorically protect the foetus. Pregnant women are unconsciously made to believe that any threat coming to their body is to let them have a miscarriage and thus, the need to protect the foetus in the face of any threat, whether real or imaginary. Although the hand would not be pressed on the belly, no matter the intensity of the stress, the main purpose is to safeguard the foetus and not suppress it. If you pay attention to pregnant women, you will discover that they touch their belly more than any other part of the body. Also, covering the belly provides warmth for the foetus. As a way to display this gesture, they may rub the hand down from the chest region.

Scientific Explanations

Straker (2019) states that when women take in, there are different thoughts going on in their mind but one thing that cannot control is the protrusion of the belly. Even if they had wanted to hide the pregnancy from the public, once the abdomen protrudes, even if they should wear big gowns, it would still expose them. 'This can be a point of pride, perhaps for feminism, perhaps as a signal of fertility or maybe just delight at impending motherhood,' notes Straker. However, that is not the thrust of our discourse per se. Our concern is how they touch and guard the pregnancy.

Straker (2019) reveals that the abdomen walls contain significant muscles and we can carry tension here. So when you see a pregnant woman or any other person holding them, this may be a signal of tension. This may be the aftermath of excessive worrying. Straker explains further, 'The gut is particularly vulnerable to attack and is a common area for punching and stabbing. If the gut is pierced, this can cause internal bleeding and a slow death. Holding hands across the tum can thus be a defensive act when we actually or literally fear attack.' Hence, covering the belly during pregnancy may be a reaction to an imaginary threat to foetus. The vulnerability of the belly coupled with the child being carried in it makes it a good part to defend in the case of an attack. Women and by extension, every human, prefer doing away with their hand than their incurring injury in their belly.

Jason Pham (2019) says that women tend to display this behaviour the more when they are carrying their first pregnancy. Apart from dealing with stress through this behaviour, this also reveals that the person displaying the gesture would be an enthusiastic and doting mother.

Practical Explanations

Case Study I: Mr and Mrs IO were having a slight argument about their home and some other things. Meanwhile, the wife had already taken in at that time. She only sat on a couch and could not muster the strength to stand up to the husband. When the argument got to its crescendo, the husband started threatening her and she could not process everything at that point in time. Feeling threatened, she raised her right hand as if she wanted to touch her neck but suddenly diverted it to belly, placing it dearly on her belly as if the foetus was threatened. When the husband saw this unconscious display of her vulnerability, especially, her protective action over the pregnancy, he was deeply touched. Immediately, he moved near to her, begged her and gave her a deep kiss.

Case Study II: Mrs DW had just taken in after waiting for about ten years after marriage. So one can only imagine how happy and elated she would be. Now, her face is always filled with smiles. Even her colleagues could not resist the attention she gives herself. She comes to work a little bit behind usual and does not engage in activities she was used to. One day, an unexpected incident occurred at work as one of the workers at the construction unit suddenly drop a heavy equipment that resounded all over the company. While everyone was moved, either holding up to their chest or covering their ears so that the effect of the sound could be felt less, Mrs DW covered her belly with her two hands, looking troubled as if that was enough to give her miscarriage.

Case Study III: During her teenage years and even as a lady, Mrs LK had always heard how pregnant women recounted their ordeals, especially during childbirth. There were times she was gripped with fear and thought giving birth was not her thing. However, she had also read up on how some women narrated their thrilling pregnancy stories. So she made up her mind to have a personal experience so that she would know how it feels like rather than imagining it. So when she eventually got married and had her pregnancy, she discovered that it was mixed feelings. One day, she was thinking of how the labour room experience would be and had to go and watch some videos. She became fearful to the extent that she used her hand to cover her belly unconsciously.

Case Study IV: Woman D got pregnant out of wedlock and, as such, was ready to do just anything with it. So it was not an issue when a man approached her and informed her that there was a business that could be made out of her pregnancy. After agreeing on how to go about it and share their gains if worked out, they hurriedly did a marriage of convenience. So they set out on the journey and tried their luck with the agency they wanted to deceive. To their bewilderment, they were exposed easily. When the official that exposed them were telling them the implications of their action, Woman D became fearful and unconsciously placed her hand on her belly, as if protecting the unborn child.

20.25. Rubbing of Stomach

Generic Interpretations of the Concept

We all rub our stomach at some point or another. Those who have protruding belly tend to do it more than others. That is why you commonly see this behaviour among pregnant women. There is hardly anyone who rubs their stomach for fun. So when you see it, especially when suddenly done, it is a sure sign that something is missing. From the literal point of view, when a person gluttonously consumes more food, they will become uncomfortable and this is made manifest through the belly and accompanying facial expressions. The belly would be so heavy that they would become restless, struggling to breathe. At this point, they will rub their stomach consistently as if they are pounding and pushing off the excessive food from their tummy. This produces a gradual soothing effect for the victim of over-feeding.

Apart from that, pregnant women rub their belly as a way of dealing with metaphorical discomfort. Subconsciously, this also helps in safeguarding the foetus. To better understand this gesture, consider a security patrol team in an area—can any evildoer move near the area? It is the same thing for a pregnant woman that shields their foetus by rubbing hand over their tummy.

Since this is a repetitive tactile action, it ensures calm over time. Rubbing the stomach generates the needed warmth for the body. When we are uncomfortable, we become cold because the body has probably given in to fear and anxiety and as a way of fighting back, we begin to rub the stomach for the intent of generating warmth that keeps us calm and focused. That is why you see people pacified after some moments of doing this cue. Some scholars even opine that the act of rubbing the stomach is capable of releasing oxytocin into the bloodstream.

If a man is doing this in a meeting, they may have some troubles with their stomach and do not be surprise when they ask for the way to the toilet; it is unusual to see people who are suffering from running stomach hold on to their belly.

Scientific Explanations

Straker (2019) opens his account on this body gesture by noting that 'the tummy area contains the stomach and the intestine, both of which are used to process food and which may be subject to assorted pains as we over-eat or consume substances that disagree with us. Rubbing the stomach can mean the person simply has a digestive problem.' So you must not always neglect this point when you are interpreting the cue. There would obvious feeling of discomfort written on the person's face. Also, the person would be distracted from every activity going on in their environment as they are concentrated on how to deal with their digestive issue making them uncomfortable.

Also, an article on CBS News states that when someone crosses belly with their arms, this means they are holding back; there are things they are keeping away from you. If their feet are pointing at the door, perhaps, this means that they want to take their leave. When someone is feeling uncomfortable being around you, they may rub their belly and look towards the door instead of looking at you as a way of informing you that they would like to go if you will allow them. The message is audible enough for anyone who pays attention to the body echoes of their subject.

Practical Explanations

Case Study I: Mrs DA who had just taken in was appointed by her firm to be its representative in a business talk. The parley started as scheduled and each party presented its proposal. Then, it was time to discuss modalities, price and how to sort things out so that there would be a common ground for both parties to work as a team on the project. It was Mrs DA that first made her presentation, citing different case studies to back up her submission. After hers, the other team leader was given the floor to speak. The man, instead of going straight to the point, resorted to criticising the Mrs DA's point. The woman was not feeling comfortable with all she was saying but knew it would be unprofessional to cut him off. So pending the time he would be done with his presentation, she was rubbing her hand over her belly repeatedly to deal with the discomfort.

Case Study II: Mr JF, who is known to be very selective in what he eats, travelled abroad for an important programme. One of the things he detests is having too much vegetable oil in what he consumes. However, it seemed this is the favourite of the people he visited. Since he does not want to appear selective or too demanding to the people, he reluctantly consumed the food he was offered. This, coupled with drinking water that was different in taste for a very long time, he developed stomach upset. Despite using the restroom before heading for his meeting, just thirty minutes into the programme, he was lost and could not comprehend anything again due to the way his belly was troubling him. The entire auditorium was silent as everyone was focused on the discussion. So he thought every eye would be on him if he should stand up. So he was rubbing his belly for some time until he could not bear it again when he had to rush to the toilet.

Case Study III: Mr and Mrs ST was on a journey; they did not make enquiry on the trip and thought they would be there within some few hours but five hours into the journey, they were yet to arrive at their destination. They became tired and fagged out. None of them could hide their disappointment as it was clearly written on their face. However, Mrs ST felt it more because she was carrying a seven-month pregnancy. At some point, she stopped speaking with her husband and subconsciously concentrated on rubbing her stomach as a way of dealing with the discomfort and probably, 'appealing' to the foetus for the stress she had subjected it to.

Case Study IV: Criminal HG was not feeling too well when he was called by one of his accomplices that there was a deal for him to smuggle some humans to another country. So he tried his best by defying the illness and setting out on the journey on time with the smuggled people. However, he did not know that his tricks were not going to work out well as usual. He was frustrated at every checkpoint but still tried to manure his way. Unfortunately, he was caught at the border control. The thought that all his sweats were gone further compounded his pains and made him uncomfortable. He started rubbing his stomach continuously before dashing to the toilet. This was the height of the feeling of discomfort.

CHAPTER 21

The Hips, Buttocks, and Genitals

One of the most obvious parts of the body is the hips supported by the buttocks and genitals. Any non-verbal guide that does not take cognisance of the area between the navel and the top of the legs, is not complete. This region contains both obvious and silent messages that can help us in understanding the intent of people towards us. Their movements may not be pronounced as other parts of the body but they are definitely involved in the show of our emotional feelings. The hips, positioned rightly for the purpose of walking or running on our two legs at a great speed, give the entire body the needed form and shape. Apart from the postural balance provided by the hips, they perform other social functions; through them, we understand something about another person—it is capable of telling us something about the sensuality or reproductive health of the person we are conversing with.

Renowned geologist, Desmond Morris, expertly points out in his *Bodywatching* that throughout the universe, the hips and buttocks are centres of attraction and enticement to people. This is more so to the female gender. If many men will confess, they will tell their wives that the foremost thing that drew their attention to them (the women) was the shape of their hips and buttocks. Even though men tend to make judgement of who they will date or marry based on other internal factors, it is the external features of the person that draws their attention first. Invariably, if a lady is not beautiful, no matter how outstanding her behaviour is, she might not be wooed by men. This may sound sentimental but it is what we are all unconsciously guilty of.

Furthermore, it is pleasing to note that the earliest sculpture of a woman to be discovered—the Venus of Hohle Fels—in more than thirty-five thousand years ago gives a masterpiece of the female form; it lays emphasis on the genitals, hips and buttocks—the most important selling point of every female. Many other

928

similar figurines have been discovered around the globe. This attests to the natural attraction that humans find these areas of the body. In fact, if a man has protruding buttocks, he is likely to be described in the feminine sense—people will claim that he has feminine features. Even for men too, the genital area generally serves as the point of attraction; it is expected to ejaculate if the person thinks of a sexual scene or sees something that moves them. If it does not, people will assume that the person is likely impotent. The attraction we have for this part is inexplicable and the feeling is the same across the universe.

In this segment of our study, we will explore this region of the body to unearth messages beyond the obvious. Before that, let's have a brief biological explanation of these body parts in order to strengthen our understanding of the concept.

In vertebrate anatomy, hip, refers to either an anatomical region or a joint. The hip region is located lateral and anterior to the gluteal region, inferior to the iliac crest, and overlying the greater trochanter of the femur, or 'thigh bone' (MediLexicon 2018). In adults, three of the bones of the pelvis have fused into the hip bone or acetabulum which forms part of the hip region.

The hip joint is a synovial joint formed by the articulation of the rounded head of the femur and the cup-like acetabulum of the pelvis. It forms the primary connection between the bones of the lower limb and the axial skeleton of the trunk and pelvis. Both joint surfaces are covered with a strong but lubricated layer called articular hyaline cartilage. The cuplike acetabulum forms at the union of three pelvic bones — the ilium, pubis, and ischium (Faller 2004). The Y-shaped growth plate that separates them, the triradiate cartilage, is fused definitively at ages 14–16. It is a special type of spheroidal or ball-and-socket joint where the roughly spherical femoral head is largely contained within the acetabulum and has an average radius of curvature of 2.5 cm (TAA 2006).

The acetabulum grasps almost half the femoral ball, a grip augmented by a ring-shaped fibrocartilaginous lip, the acetabular labrum, which extends the joint beyond the equator. The joint space between the femoral head and the superior acetabulum is normally between 2 and 7 mm (Lequesne 2004).

In the submission of Tim Barclay (2017), 'The hip joint is one of the most important joints in the human body. It allows us to walk, run, and jump. It bears our body's weight and the force of the strong muscles of the hip and leg. Yet the hip joint is also one of our most flexible joints and allows a greater range of motion than all other joints in the body except for the shoulder.'

Surrounding the hip joint are many tough ligaments that prevent the dislocation of the joint. The strong muscles of the hip region also help to hold the hip joint together and prevent dislocation. There are four main ligaments that reinforce the hip joints—extracapsular (left and right) and intracapuslar (right and left). The *extracapsular* ligaments are the iliofemoral, ischiofemoral, and pubofemoral ligaments attached to the bones of the pelvis (the ilium, ischium, and pubis respectively). All three strengthen the capsule and prevent an excessive range of movement in the joint. Of these, the Y-shaped and twisted iliofemoral ligament is the strongest ligament in the human body (Platzer 2004).

The *intracapsular* ligament, the ligamentum teres, is attached to a depression in the acetabulum (the acetabular notch) and a depression on the femoral head (the fovea of the head). It is only stretched when the hip is dislocated, and may then prevent further displacement. It is not that important as a ligament but can often be vitally important as a conduit of a small artery to the head of the femur, that is, the foveal artery (Davenport 2012).

In humans, unlike other animals, the hip bones are substantially different in the two sexes. The hips of human females widen during puberty. The femora are also more widely spaced in females, so as to widen the opening in the hip bone and thus facilitate childbirth. Finally, the ilium and its muscle attachment are shaped so as to situate the buttocks away from the birth canal, where contraction of the buttocks could otherwise damage the baby. The female hips have long been associated with both fertility and general expression of sexuality. Since broad hips facilitate child birth and also serve as an anatomical cue of sexual maturity, they have been seen as an attractive trait for women for thousands of years.

21.1. Buttock or Hips Shifting

Generic Interpretations of the Concept

When the buttock wiggles or hips swivel, this is a pointer to the fact that the person is going through issues. Under normal circumstances, people are expected to sit at a point and maintain decorum. This will facilitate the communication process as the parties involved are able to exchange information without rancour. However, when you notice that someone is shifting their buttocks, it means issues have set in; they are feeling uncomfortable. When you sit on a spot for too long, fatigue would set in and as a way of dealing with it, you may have to shift your buttocks. This is like a pseudo movement on a spot. Applicants delayed by a panel may display this cue. Since they would not want to be walking around the premises, they tend to battle fatigue through this means.

Similarly, this non-verbal gesture is noticeable during boredom. Watching a movie that is not interesting for hours can be boring. The same thing applies to listening to a lecture that is not as impactful as expected. If you have ever been addressed by a president of a company that is not inspiring in speech, you would understand this gesture better. It would be considered an affront to walk out on the president of the firm you work with, no matter the number of hours he spends addressing you. It is as if a military officer is watching over you. When you become tired, you shift your buttocks from a side of the chair to the other so as to make the hips flexible and relaxed. In general terms, stress is responsible for this behaviour.

Further, we tend to swivel the hips during contentious debates when our emotions have been riled up or immediately afterwards. During boardroom heated arguments, executives tend to shift away from the relaxed position, shifting towards the table as if they want to reach for the person they are arguing with. After making their point known, they will shift back their buttocks, disconnect eye contact and take a deep breath. When the emotions rile up and the person is displaying this cue, they may be pointing and raising their voice simultaneously. This is evidence that they are no longer in control of their emotions. The equation is simple: when a person is shifting forward during contentious debates, emotion is rising and when they are shifting backwards, emotion is going down.

You hardly observe this cue where things are working out well, especially in a romantic relationship. If it all, it would show up, it is when the couples have issues along the line. That is, when the affair goes sour.

Scientific Explanations

Smith (2015) states the shifting the hips or buttocks ensures that weight of the body is transferred from one side to the other. It may also be shifted from front to back and vice versa. The hips bear much of the weight of the body and how we feel as individual are different. However, the way a person shifts their hips reveals their attitude. 'Constantly transferring your weight from one foot to the other or rocking forward and backward is a comforting movement that indicates you are anxious or upset,' says Smith. Without mincing words, what you are acting out is what is going on within your head: Smith encapsulates it in these words 'You are betwixt and between many unsettling thoughts and can't stop moving from one to the other.' As the thoughts are unsettling you, so also is your body. Hence, the reason you move from a side to the other.

Straker (2018) says that this behaviour may be propelled by tiredness and disappointment. For instance, if someone says you should wait for him as they were going to show forth soon but tarried unexpectedly, you become disappointed, and thus, may be forced to shift your bottom from one side to the other. It may also be used as a pointer through this action, hinting on what someone wants. For instance, if a lady shifts away their hips from the chair, it may be to draw attention to them.

Practical Illustrations

Case Study I: AWZ Firms has made it a culture to always organise trainings for its employees and irrespective of your status, once you are under the payroll of the firm, you are expected to participate. Mr GU was just employed about three weeks ago as an engineer to lead the technical department of the organisation. He is not used to sitting at a spot for long duration of time. Even while working, he would stand up, walk around after few minutes and then returned to his seat. However, this training session was getting too long for him. At first, they went on two hours straight before giving them a short break but on the second segment, it is over three hours and the speaker is still very much alive on the stage. He lost interest in what the trainer was saying and subconsciously, he began to shift his buttocks from one side of the chair to another looking worried, praying earnestly that the speaker makes his concluding remarks. A glance through his face would tell you that he was bored and yearning to be in another environment.

Case Study II: XQS Enterprises has been suffering from inexplicable losses in recent times. When it seemed that the supervisors and other active heads involved in the daily running of the establishment could not give any substantial explanation for the downward trend of events, the CEO had to summon a meeting of the executives and stakeholders of the firm. It was a full house meeting as everybody concerned was present. After the CEO's briefing, the floor was opened for opinions and suggestions on how to push forward. Many of them lamented the unfortunate incident, noting that it was part of business while some stakeholders believe there should not be any loss at any point in time. This caused uncontrollable argument. Mr J, the leader of the latter group could be seen shifting his hips gradually to the table, pointing towards those having contrary opinion with theirs and shouting at the top of his voice. When he was done, he shifted back to his normal sitting posture, now with a calm disposition. His non-verbal gesture depicted him as being angry and trying so hard to defend himself.

Case Study III: There was a time I met a man in public transit. Perhaps, he noticed my badge and wanted to make friends with me. He thought I was one of those compromised elements he could easily use for his criminal activities. I paid rapt attention to all that he was saying. I mirrored his body language, making him endear himself to me the more. After saying all that he had to say, I then began to point out reasons why humans should not be trafficked into our country. Even though I did not issue any threatening statement, when he saw how I was vehemently condemning such illicit act, he began to unconsciously shift his buttocks away from me. This was a show of disagreement with what I was saying but that was not going to make me compromise.

21.2. Hip-Rubbing Cue

Generic Interpretations of the Concept

Overtime, I have always explained that rubbing is primarily done for the purpose of calming a tense situation or person down. This is not different in hip rubbing too. Hips can be rubbed, whether in standing or sitting position. However, it is often done when people maintain the latter posture. Rubbing is as a result of stress. When we are stressed, we employ this cue to pacify the body. The joints of the hips connect the upper and lower parts of the body together. There are also substantial amounts of muscles around the hip region. This means that there is nothing that goes on in the body that does not affect the hip region. When we walk, run or jump, the ultimate effect lies on this part of the body. That is why people subconsciously reach out to the sides of the body during stressful moments.

If a person is highly stressed, you will discover that they will rub from the hips down to the legs (this is usually possible when the person is seated). Sitting at the same spot for long duration can be strenuous. When you can no longer repress the feeling, you begin to rub gradually back and forth. Some people even do it more subtly by feigning to tuck their hands in their pocket, meanwhile the ultimate essence is to rub the hips. If you do not pay more attention, it would be very difficult to understand such individuals.

Further, this may also be the aftermath of nervousness. When we are highly threatened, the hands become sweaty and as a way of cleaning them up, we will rub them at the hips. Even we do this when we are comfortable; after rinsing your hands and you do not have handkerchief with you, you will dry them by rubbing them at the hips. People understand that using the lower part of the clothing is better than more pronounced parts. Students feeling nervous about a test may also display this gesture as they wipe off their hands.

Scientific Explanations

Straker (2019) says when the hands are placed on hips, it makes the elbows protrude, making the person look larger than they are. This means they are going through issues and keeping people off their personal space; as they deal with such issue, they do not expect interruption from anyone. The posture makes them appear aggressive and powerful as they battle with stress. People may be deceived with the big look to overlook what goes on within—the stress that the person is actually dealing with.

Hip rubbing in a romantic setting may lure the person at the other end of the table to do it too. In this sense, the gesture is flirtatious; it is inviting others for a romantic affair. This is particularly noticeable if it is accompanied by swaying hips and prolonged eye contact; with this, the message becomes very audible that the person is in for an affair.

Sonamics (2019) draws our attention to the specifics of this gesture; it notes that when rubbing the hips, if the fingers are pointing out (all visible in the front), it is an indication of aggression and dominance. This is different from a situation where the fingers are tucked in—this represents submissiveness and fear. It is the latter posture that people assume when they are stressed. It makes them look smaller and unyielding to external invitation. We need to pay close attention to this gesture as we give meanings to them.

Practical Illustrations

Case Study I: Mr IT had announced to his students that he was going to conduct an impromptu test for them and, as such, should always be prepared whenever they were coming to school. They thought he was only threatening them as usual, and as such, many of them did not make up time to prepare from home. Just the third day after the announcement, Mr IT came to the class with printed question papers. He told the students to do away with items that could implicate them and at that point, they all knew it was a reality. Many of them began to rack their brain to ascertain if they could recollect few topics taught during the course of the lessons. When the questions were later given to them, many of them could be seen sweating as they held their pen. So they dropped the pen and rubbed their hand against the hip so as to make the hand comfortable for writing. This was a subtle way of fighting psychological stress.

Case Study II: Suspect F was arrested in a matter relating to scam and allied matters. After some few days in the custody, he was interrogated so that the law enforcement officials could have undeniable evidence against him. The interrogative session was very difficult for F as questions were coming from every corner of the room for him. At some point, nervousness could be seen visibly as the hands were sweating. To cover this up, the Suspect would rub his hand against his side, at the hip region and then continue with his disjointed explanation. Any time he rubbed his hip, he used to lose focus as he had to start with his story from another angle. This means the fear was overwhelming for him.

Case Study III: Mrs HA is a naturally fearful person; any small thing, she was off her mind. One day, she travelled to another country for an official engagement. When she got to the airport, she discovered that the immigration service and security apparatus of the country could not be compared with hers; right at the airport, they were deporting people that had just arrived with her. As the queue moved closer to the customs, Mrs HA was thinking of many things—what could have led to their deportation? Why are the customs officials not lenient? Would she be deported too? And how she would defend herself? This defeating thought, coupled with the long duration of standing made her hips to become painful; she rubbed them slowly as she waited for her turn to be interviewed by the officials. This was like massaging them in order to do away with the physical pains she was witnessing.

21.3. Hip-Torso Movement

Generic Interpretations of the Concept

When stressed beyond verbal utterance, people may begin to move back and forth at the hips while in their sitting position. The movement is so real that you observe it while at some distance away from the person. It is as if the person is dancing to the tune of a favourite music while busy doing another thing. However, the expression on their face will betray this feeling as the person looks longing for peace; the face is expressionless, looking into the distance with fear and generally disturbed. This cannot be compared with someone who is dancing to a favourite music who is expected to be happy, filled with laughter and enthusiastic.

To better understand this gesture, just reflect on a person who is chained to a chair, trying to make a move; the more they try, the more they are drawn back by the fetters. At some point, the person is expected to be tired and give in to their circumstance. This behaviour is usually as a result of severe stress. For instance, if a person loses a loved one who is very dear to their heart, they may display this cue. You may see them crying simultaneously as they reflect on the beautiful moments they had spent together before the departure of the deceased. The primary reason of initiating this behaviour is to pacify themselves; the repetitiveness of this action creates a tactile motion that soothes the body. It is just like the sea-saw little children do; they become relieved when it is done overtime.

Further, you may observe this form of gesticulation from those suffering from mental instability such as autism. The brain becomes inconsistent in its operation and may choose to work haphazardly at any given point. This looks dramatic and may propel mockery in innocent ones but it is disturbing to their loved ones.

Scientific Explanations

Straker (2019) notes that 'swaying the hips from side to side is a common dance move and can indicate the person would like to dance'. This is at the literal level. All things being equal, if you see someone busy with work on their computer but on hearing the sound of music, they begin to sway the hips, this means they really want to dance but kept back by the work they are doing. Also, this gesture also draws people attention to the hips. In a romantic mood, this can be invitation to flirt. This is an opportunity many men would run at without hesitation.

On the other hand, if this gesture is displayed in a gloomy scene, it means things have really gone wrong. It is a repetitive action done to send away stress. This is highly pacifying as it stimulated the muscles and joints of the hips. It is done repeatedly for the purpose of arousing this soothing effect. This is autonomic response of dealing with stress; the limbic brain has stationed it that way to help the body overcome stressful moments.

In the same vein, Smith (2015) states that this action is comforting movement that exposes our anxiety. We are made to understand what goes on in the person's brain through this physical action; many disturbing thoughts are colliding at a time and this is making the person weak as they are unable to process one at a time. The gesture will last as long as the feeling continues.

Practical Illustrations

Case Study I: Mrs L got to the office on Tuesday, only to hear of the death of her partner, one of the closest persons to her both on professional and personal terms. Just the previous day, they had made time to talk on their future endeavours before they departed for their individual homes. The deceased, Mrs S, never made any complaint of any ailment to her despite being confidantes. So she was more disturbed on what could have possibly fuelled her death. Mrs L collapsed on her chair and for hours was paralysed; her eyes were filled with tears. At some point, she began to rock forward and backward at the hip in her sitting position. She kept on doing this while others stayed away from her until she was able to find some relief and cleansed her face.

Case Study II: It was end of the month, and as such many workers had been paid. Being a Friday, Mr PO goes to a bar joint to have some drinks and chill out with friends. Even though gambling is not his thing, he could not resist the discussion among his friends. He listened to them patiently as they did analysis of a team that could possibly win a tough game, considering their past encounters. The analysis looked plausible to him and more so, the financial gain was intimidating that he thought that was the best opportunity for him to augment his income. So he used a large percentage of his salary to bet, hoping that he would smile to the bank the next day. However, things did not turn out as predicted—his money was gone when the new month was yet to start! After his money prayers, he reached for his phone to check the results of the match, only for him to discover that he had lost it all. He looked up, dropped the phone and rocked forward and backward at the hips while still seated on the floor. At some point, tears dropped off his eye and he stood up to prepare for work. This was a display of frustration, pain and regret.

Case Study III: Guy C had some mental issues and that is why his parents had placed him on close watch. Even when they were not at home, they hired someone to keep tab on him while he received his medications. His actions became unpredictable. One day, while they were all seated in the living room, watching a movie, Guy C began to move back and forth at the hips in his seat. He continued this action for about two minutes before getting back to normalcy and then, the family was able to concentrate again. This means the medical condition had worsened at that given point. And they just needed to bear with him, hoping that he got healed in no distant time.

Case Study IV: Prostitute GE was really cash stripped and became desperate for clients. This means she would do just anything to have money. She eventually got one through an online medium and after chatting for few days, they agreed to meet at a given location. Although she demanded that the man should send her money for transport, he gave excuses that sounded genuine. So she borrowed money from her neighbour with the promise that she would return it later in the day. After getting to the venue, she placed a call through the man but he refused to answer. She became tired and confused as there was no way she would return home. She was seen moving back and forth on her hips. She was greatly disturbed and became nervous—imagining every possible negative occurrence that might befall her.

21.4. Hip Swaying

Generic Interpretations of the Concept

This gesture shares some attributes with the one considered in the preceding segment. However, the only difference is that while the former has to do with back and forth movement of the hips, this has to do with moving the hips from one side to the other. Hip swaying is best done in standing position. This may be done by athletes in preparation to run. Apart from moving back and forth, you see athletes or sportsmen in general sway their hips from one side to the other before the start of a competition to ensure that they are fully fit and ready for the contest. The thrust of every sportsman is the hips; it is the powerhouse that determines how well they jump and run. If the joints and muscles are not well stretched out, they might not be able to perform optimally.

However, hip swaying is mostly done as a reaction to stress. When bored, especially after sitting for long hours, you may stand up and sway your hips from side to side in a manner that is symbolic to rocking or cradling a baby to sleep. This action is stimulating as the movement seems to be coordinated. When done continuously, it suppresses stress and bring back life to a person. Teachers are fond of using this cue when dealing with their pupils—when they discover that many of the pupils are getting bored or tired, they will ask them to stand up and sway their hips from a side to the other. This looks dramatic and playful to them. So the students will gladly do it and after some few minutes, they would be asked to take their seat. They would have been relieved through this action and this will bolster their attention span.

Also, when you sway the hips, it makes the hairs and fluids in your inner ears to move, creating a soothing sensation. That sensation alone is enough to brighten the mind and restore lost vigours.

Scientific Explanations

Philip (2014) discusses this gesture in the romantic sense of it. He observes that this is particularly a female posture which is done for the purpose of emphasising their curves. Rolling the pelvis draws the attention of potential partners to it. Explaining how the gesture is made use of, Philip states that 'women may cant their hips to the side to showcase their fertility to men. In a dating context, dropping one hip emphasises curves that separate men from women. While walking, a hip sway is particularly effective in attracting or maintaining male attention. Girls are known to adopt this posture early in life which may be the result of modelling older women, or perhaps a genetic predisposition.' Hence, the verbal translation of this gesture is given as 'My hips are wider than yours and I want to draw male gaze so I'm going to exaggerate and draw attention to my wider, sexier hips, by titling to the side or walking with an exaggerated swing.'

Practical Illustrations

Case Study I: Mrs Y has been teaching her students a seemingly difficult concept for the past forty-five minutes. Despite the interactive and procedural approach she employed, she discovered at some point that many of the students were fast losing interest in what she was saying; they were only used to forty-minute lectures and more so, this was a bit demanding. However, the teacher had to finish explaining the concept so as to ensure they understood it at once. Hence, she was lost between the devil and the deep blue sea. Thinking of the way out, Mrs Y paused the lecture and asked all the students to stand up and sway their hips. About two minutes into this action, many of them forgot the toughness of the topic and were smiling due to the soothing effect of the non-verbal action. When they got back to the class activity, they were strong and willing to listen to the teacher again.

Case Study II: The members of staff of SOH and Co. were hosted to a meeting by their CEO. All the employees always feel sober whenever it was announced that they would be meeting with the head due to the boring way he speaks. More so, he does not have respect for time as a meeting scheduled for two hours can end up spanning into five hours. So any time they were to meet him, the employees would put every other activity on hold because they are not sure of when the boring meeting would end. On the last occasion, the meeting was extra-ordinarily boring that many of the attendees were almost sleeping off. Ms LD, seated at the back, was hissing due to the irrelevance of what the man at the front was saying compared with the work they were doing. Suddenly, the kid of one of the employees also seated at the back began to cry. Ms LD rushed to it as if she was a Good Samaritan, took the child from the mother and stood at the rear corner of the auditorium, swaying her hips as if to plead with the child to stop crying. This was rhythmical and engaging. It took her about five minutes to get the child to sleep and she was happy about that because she was relieved too.

Case Study III: Child X followed her father to his friend's place. She thought her dad was not going to take too much time there but for hours, they were still discussing. She was fed up with the movie they were seeing. Since it was not their home, she understood the place of courtesy. She was looking at the direction of her father, praying that they exchange eye contact so that she could plead with him. When this technique seemed not to be working, she stood on her two feet, swayed her hips from side to side and this caught the attention of her dad. The hip swaying was so pronounced and a bit irritating that everyone at the venue would have no choice than to pay attention to her. Immediately the dad looked at her side, she threw her leg to the direction of the door, meaning that she was ready to leave the place.

Case Study IV: A group of illegal employees were rounded up at a given factory. When they saw law enforcement agents, they became nervous and even from their facial expressions, one could say which was which as the legal employees were going about freely with their jobs, although some of them were shocked. Before the enforcement agents could move close to them and enforce their arrest, one of the illegal employees, abruptly changed his mood from that of psychological distraught to physical exercise by swaying his hips as if he was tired—he did it continuously to cover up the first uncontrolled show of psychological distress. He thought this could salvage him but he did not know that he his first reaction had been noticed.

21.5. Hip Tilted Out

Generic Interpretations of the Concept

Displaying the hips is a thing of joy as both men and women do this, especially during their youthful years. The major reason people tilt out the hips is to ensure that they get the attention of others. Since the hip region is a natural point of attraction when it is further pushed out, then it becomes irresistible for the other party to ignore it. This action in traceable to the Western world where the famous statue of David is drawn by Michelangelo. The statue shows David standing contrapposto, with a leg slightly bent, which makes the buttocks more prominent and inviting. These days, pushing out the hips and breasts seems to be the trending behaviour across the world, especially among those who are just coming of age.

How large the hips are is a reason enough for a man to run after a lady; this adds to her beauty and makes her charming, looking more mature than her age. Hence, people, even celebrities, have always used large hips to gain the attention of their subjects. For instance, Kim Kardashian is fond of this behaviour. Apart from doing it at every given opportunity, she does it with pride.

More than any other context, tilting out the hips is mostly used during courtship. At this point, the couples always try to be their best; they want their partner to know that there is not any other person like them on the planet. Also, they know that the human heart is flexible; it can be easily lured away by another person. So the hip-out display is to ensure that their partner notices them at all times. With this, their heart would not wander to any other person. There is little wonder that some ladies go for artificial buttocks or even perform surgeries on them just to make them look bigger and enticing.

Across the globe, the hips are emblem of fertility and youthfulness. Due to childbearing, it is bigger and becomes wider during pregnancy among women so as to ease delivery. In every circumstance, people confidently display their hips due to the sensual effect it creates on others.

Scientific Explanations

According to Philip (2014), this cue is a 'a feminine gesture meant to emphasis the allure of wide childbearing hips'. According to Philip, what makes the difference between a sexy individual and one that does not look charming is how they thrust out their hips. That is why women have always taken the advantage of the gesture to attract the attention of lovers. He concludes that 'the hip emphasis posture is pervasive in fashion and advertising. We see women slouching to one side forcing their hips out to emphasise their curves, or walk in an exaggerated way, bouncing their hips up and down as if on a pendulum.'

Straker (2019) states that when the hip is tilted out, it is a suggestive gesture that the person needs something. However, the context in which the action is displayed is what will tell you what message the person intends to pass across. For instance, if the legs are opened and the person tilts out the hip, this is a romantic invitation which is made to look very pronounced. Opening the legs exposes the genitals and it is an invitation to intercourse. However, the body language expert cautions, 'Pushing the hips forwards is difficult without losing balance, so this is sometimes done by leaning back against something like a wall to support the upper body whilst the hips are clearly foremost.' And that is why you see people do it where they think they are most convenient. It requires a level of confidence to push out the hip without losing stamina.

It is crucial to note that this gesture can be used among men alone; it can be tilted out to other men as a show of power. The verbal translation in this context is 'My penis is bigger than yours' or 'I am so powerful that you dare not attack my exposed and vulnerable parts.' This may be done under contentious grounds—maybe they are both eyeing the same woman and, as such, trying to prove superiority.

Practical Illustrations

Case Study I: Lady G is very attractive and beautiful and she has never failed to advertise her beauty and use it as a means of getting whatever she needs. On a particular weekend, she went to a party with other female friends. The event had people from all walks of life who were established in life already. Lady G, who wanted a change of job knew that this was her best opportunity to cling herself to one of the CEOs at the event. After thinking through everything, she observed that where she was sitting was not open enough. So she subtly moved to another table where she thought she would be able to market herself. Eventually, she saw a man, well-fed and obviously gorgeous seated opposite to her. When their eyes met, Lady G pushed out her hip. Thinking it was not intentional, the man disconnected his eye and looked back after some minutes in which the same gesture was displayed. They smiled at each other and signalled to meet outside of the hall. This was a mild proposal and registration of intent of love which was well decoded.

Case Study II: Ms FT is the secretary of FCB Worldwide. She has worked with different managers and has been able to manage them successfully well. However, apart from her professional duties, she cunningly gets them into romantic affair with her too. In a way, this has saved her numerous times when she defaulted professionally; due to the affair between them, the managers would be handicapped in sacking her when she misbehaved. Now that another manager has been transferred to the headquarters, she has been looking for a way to get into him but it seemed the manager is not getting her clues. So she decided to step her game. Whenever she heard the manager coming out of his office, she would push out her hip towards the door and lick her lips sensationally and then smile charmingly any time they exchange eye contact. Within a week, the manager asked her out on a date and that was the beginning of their relationship.

Case Study III: Woman EI begged and actually paid Man TF to engage in a marriage of convenience with her because she needed to indicate that she was married before she could access a huge grant. She went for the briefing with Man TF and while they were seated, it came to her consciousness that the gap between them was so much as the expressions on the grants officers' faces confirmed this. So she decided to push her hips out Man TF's side. On seeing this, instead him to move closer to her too, he started touching her. Everyone knew something was wrong! It wasn't a true display of love as everything looked automated.

21.6. Hands on the Genitals

Generic Interpretations of the Concept

You may think this is out of place or you have never done it but it is a blatant lie to share such opinion. Touching the genitals is what we have all done at a time or another while we were young. Invariably, this gesture is prevalent among kids. Teachers have always reported how young boys and even girls will attempt touching or even pulling at their genital through their dress. Most times, this is done unconsciously and that is why they do it in the presence of others, especially when they are carried away by their feelings.

Before you panic, let me quickly state that this is somewhat natural. So there is nothing to be overly concerned about, although they should be calmly corrected if you should observe this in your child so that they would not become addicted to it. Teaches have always do this but there is need for concerted efforts for parents too. That aside, it has been discovered that both the male and female genitals contain a sizeable amount of nerve endings. This means that when they are touched, they do not just calm and soothe a person, but also make the person feel pleasant. Hence, this kids' behaviour is borne out of sincere reasons to deal with stress at their own level.

However, there have been instances when adults also make use of it. Unlike children that will pull at it or touch their genitals, adults will only point at their genitals as a means of drawing attention to it. This may be a means of telling a potential partner of their availability. Anybody who calls your attention to their sexual organ is definitely ready for an intercourse. It may also be a means of telling you to see how big their private part is.

Scientific Explanations

Study Body Language (2019) states that we do not allow people touch the genital areas; we prefer giving people access to the head than allowing them come near the genital. This is due to its vulnerability, sensitivity and the role it plays. You see people guard this place with most vigilance as if it houses the heart. However, when we now touch it willingly on our own, it means there is something going on. Among children, it is an innocent and perfect way of dealing with stress. This is seen with their level of commitment to this gesture; they are always lost to the act of carrying out this gesture.

From the point of view of Westside Toastmasters (2019), it notes that we can be aroused at any given time—whether in private or in public. This means that our genitals are also charged. In the case of men, their penis would ejaculate and might have to use their hand to rub and adjust it in the trousers before it goes down. The situation can be very embarrassing in public and that is why you see men becoming uncomfortable. Unknown to some people, women too do get aroused in public. Unlike men that have to battle with just the penis alone, women will have the lips, breasts and genitals to deal with as the three become redder and itchy. That is why you may see them extend their hand to their underneath to scratch it.

However, SBL notes that this may be a defensive body language if the arms, rather than the hands are placed on the genitals.

Practical Illustrations

Case Study I: It's Monday and Child K can be seen to be very tired. She had just started schooling less than a year and, as such, was not used to the system yet. Even during break, she finds it difficult to mingle with her peers to play. On this particular day, as the lecture was ongoing, her teacher discovered that she was not looking up. So he decided to move closer to her. It was then he saw her pulling at her genitals. As he called her name, she was shocked, meaning that she had obviously lost touch with what the teacher was teaching. She did not look up for a while because she was enjoying the soothing effect of the non-verbal action.

Case Study II: It is break time at SOX Kiddies School. Almost the pupils are on the playground, displaying various skills while their caregivers were very near to monitor their activities so that they do not injure one another. It is always a pleasant sight to behold as the kids socialise joyfully. However, there are times that they try to manoeuvre and outsmart one another. In such instances, there are bound to be conflicts as those who look cheated would want to fight back. Sometimes, some of them would retreat immediately, acknowledging the superiority of the other person. The latter case describes Pupil M who was sent out of play and at once, lost interest in everything. Instead, he went to sit at a corner and was touching his genitals repeatedly until the bell was rung. This means he was bored and looking worried due to the unexpected defeat.

Case Study III: Mr SI was on an outing with his friend around a university community when he saw a beautiful, adorable lady. Immediately, he lost concentration on what he was discussing with the friend even when his friend reminded him of the importance of what they were at the location for, he only responded passively. The friend wondered what could have led to such a shameful act until he lifted up his head and saw the young lady walking in their direction. He was angry at his friend but there was nothing he could do at that point in time rather than just to wait till the lady was out of sight. As the lady moved closer to them, Mr SI widened his legs and touched the head of his ejaculated penis, looking at the lady with passion. Seeing this, the lady only smiled at him and walked past them. He became frustrated as his friend further subjected him to all manners of mockery.

Case Study IV: Prostitute MI visited Mr UY in his office. She went at a period she knew there would be no one with him. At first, she looked serious and presented some documents to him to look through while she took her seat. While the man was busy with the documents, she carefully and consciously placed her hand on her genitals, trying to pull the hair in that region. When Mr UY saw that she had buried her head for a while, he called out on her, asking if all was well but she failed to reply until the man curiously sneaked at her to find what she was really up to. Unfortunately, he could not resist what he saw!

21.7. Grabbing of the Crotch

Generic Interpretations of the Concept

Even though people used to display this gesture in an unnoticeable way, it became a public thing when first used by late American singer, Michael Jackson. Then, many people were shocked that a public figure would grab their crotch while performing. It became a subject of controversy for some time but today, this behaviour is not only a common attribute among entertainers in most parts of the world, but also a behaviour noticeable among the youths. Invariably, it is a non-verbal display that has come to stay.

There are numerous postulations as to why men display this gesture. One of the foremost submissions is that this to garner people's attention. Imagine the moment Jackson did this while on stage, even the person who was not paying attention to what was going on will look at him immediately. Also, the uncertainty of what the person would do next might make focused on him—will he touch his genital thereafter or even attempt bringing it out? Also, some are of the opinion that this is a manhood display; to show people how big their manhood is. It is learnt that ladies are always thrilled at the sight of seeing the shape of men's genital and finally, we should not rule out the possibility that this might only be a way of adjusting their trousers for comfort.

In whatever context, if this is done once, it would probably be overlooked. However, it becomes disturbing when done repeatedly and at a close range by adult males in the presence of females. While this may be part of the 'show' in a romantic environment, it is not usually the case in an official setting. In some cases, the targeted person may institute a case of sexual harassment against the person displaying this cue. So there is need for balance and caution.

Scientific Explanations

According to Philip (2013), 'There are a few postures that men use to display their prowess, but the jury is out as to whether or not women find them attractive per se.' one of such is crotch grabbing. If a woman is interested in the man, she would look at the crotch. However, it has been found that this does not make a man look attractive. There are different ways in which this gesture can be displayed but they all pass the same message. 'These signals are less of a sexual invitation than they are signal of their dominance over others in the room, which in and of itself makes them appear more attractive to women,' notes Philip. Perhaps this non-verbal cue explains why Michael Jackson was never short of female fans.

On his own part, Parvez (2015) states that if this cue is not displayed at the right place, it has the potency of offending people. He puts it thus: 'Penis display, symbolical or not, has come to be strongly associated with offending someone or showing dominance in the human psyche, thanks to its effectiveness.' A subtle form that is acceptable in many places is belt and crotch grabbing. Other subtle forms include wearing tight-fitting pants, small-size speedo swimming trunks or even dangling a large bunch of keys/chains on the front or side of the crotch. What is important is that you evaluate the appropriateness of the gesture in the context you find yourself before displaying it.

Practical Illustrations

Case Study I: M is an up-and-coming artiste with a fast-paced movement into stardom. He has been invited across the length and breadth of his country within the short time he kick-started his career. The biggest of it is the Christmas carnival which every artiste wants to perform at. Even those that are not invited still pay to go and watch their senior or experienced colleagues perform. So it was like a golden opportunity for M to share a stage with his mentors and perform at such great event. On mounting the podium, it appeared as if the audience were already tired as they were distracted from his performance. This almost dampened his spirit. All the techniques he used in getting the attention failed. At some point, he suddenly grabbed his crotch, held on to for about two minutes while dancing. This was irresistible to the crowd as that was the first time seeing that. Many of them brought out their phones to record the display while others wore their dancing shoes by jumping up to dance.

Case Study II: Man J was at a bar to chill out with friends and wind off a hectic week. He is known to be an unrepentant womaniser among his friends and it seems that after countless appeals from the wife, she has rescinded to fate because there is no iota of readiness to change. Man J has always used the excuse of inability to control his libido as the reason for being running after women. On this particular Friday, he saw an attractive, charming lady at the bar with a man. Scaling up the man, he discovered that he looked fidgety and small. Hence, he planned on how to snatch away the lady from him. He left his seat for another where it would be easy to exchange eye contact with the lady. After gaining her attention, J grabbed his crotch, made his legs wider that the lady could see his genital dangling in his pair of trousers. This was a spectacular display by the man towards the lady.

Case Study III: A woman paid an official visit to a firm and was hosted by the receptionist pending the time the CEO would be done with his present engagements. The woman did not maintain the right posture, making the receptionist have a view of her panties. This made him get emotionally out of hand. He thought the woman's posture was intentional and show of her availability. So he also grabbed his crotch, looking at the woman. It was at this point that the innocent woman became confused, she readjusted herself and looked away. When she later met with the head of the organisation, it was the first issue she reported to him which eventually led to the termination of the receptionist's appointment. This was a sexual display that went to the wrong person.

Case Study IV: Impostor YS once tried to come into Country GRT through impersonation but he was not successful. When he was asked to present his passport at the border, he handed them to the officers with smiles, probably just to camouflage. There were mainly female officials on duty. When the senior official noticed some inconsistencies in the document, she decided to conduct a forensic analysis. During this process, Impostor YS sat directly opposite her and grabbed his crotch, smiling at her. He thought this would sexually lure her to him but it rather infuriated her, making her check through the documents all over again until he was convicted.

21.8. Framing of the Genitals

Generic Interpretations of the Concept

Framing the genitals is just like the crotch-grabbing cue considered in the preceding segment. However, this is subtler and societally purposeful than the former. Men are very smart about using their vulnerability as a source of strength. The genital is one of the most vulnerable parts of the body and we only expose it as a means of daring opponents or to show somebody that we are relaxed being around them. Now, people are innovative about it, based on their intended message. Genital framing is done by placing the thumbs in one's pants or by hooking them on the belt while the fingers straddle the crotch region. It is a common display by cowboys while taking photographs or in movies.

Usually, men use this gesture to garner attention to themselves. If they want to be noticed but observe that people are not looking at their side, they will make use of this gesture to draw their attention. Maybe, it is to make others see how attractive they are or even the clothes they put on. Some men are fashion freaks and do want people to compliment them any time they spend a fortune to look good.

On a general note, it is a masculine display that men use to segregate themselves into classes. That is, this a show of dominance. Tucking thumbs into pockets and straddling the fingers around the genital is what a superior can do before a subordinate and not vice versa. While displaying this cue, the elbows are thrusted outward, making the person look bigger than their actual figure. This gives them a tougher posture too. With this, they take up more space and command respect from people—whether females or males. So that might be the sole reason for making this gesture. More so, ladies are easily attracted to men that huge and dominant—alpha males.

Scientific Explanations

Philip (2015) while explaining this gesture, notes that genital framing is 'a posture where the hands and fingers draw attention to the genitals. Men can genital frame by placing their thumbs in belt loops and aiming the fingers towards their penis and women can place their hands on their hips aiming the fingers in the same direction.' Although it is generally regarded as a male posture, this has shown that it can also be done by ladies, but on lesser rate. It is natural that we look at the direction where the fingers point out and this informs the reason we look at the genital area when the fingers are pointed there.

HarperCollins (2014) states this is one of the gestures that are hardwired in our brain; we display them unconsciously. It is a sign of love, showing the affection we have towards the targeted person. He states that the hands are pointing to where the person wants us to notice. This is a sexually aggressive attitude. This means he is ready for action. With this, the person has unwittingly revealed what goes on his mind; he does not need the woman in context rather than for sexual pleasure. This means he might not be in for any serious relationship after an intercourse with the person.

Practical Illustrations

Case Study I: Mr LK has always been mocked by his colleagues because he had not many clothes. As a factory worker, they believe that he should be able to cope with life to an extent but he is nothing near their yardstick. Unfortunately, none of them has ever considered it worthy of having a heart-to-heart discussion with him. Unknowingly to them, he was channelling all he had to the education of his children while many of them are irresponsible. So their mockery was not always an issue to him, even in instances where it was coordinated against him. Eventually, one of his children graduated from the college and got a good job. Out of his first salary, he bought his father a designer outfit which he wore to work the next day. So as to call the attention of everyone to himself, he thrusted his thumbs in his pockets and scrabbled the fingers around the crotch.

Case Study II: Mr HF has just been promoted as the new director of his workplace after serving as an assistant for about a decade. As an assistant, many people hated his discipline and how he used to carry himself. Also, he was not on good terms with the former boss. This means that he was always relegated in the scheme of things. Even when he wanted to mete out punishment on erring workers, the director would make a mockery of his efforts. Now that he had been officially promoted by the board of management, it means he now has the power he had always longed for. Even though this was against the wish of many of the employees who had trampled upon him, there was nothing they could do. On the second day of his promotion, Mr HF was moving about the firm, accessing the state of things, with his personal assistant at his back. He walked slowly while hooking his thumbs on his belt, while the fingers straddled the crotch region. This was a show of dominance.

Case Study III: A college student has been keeping an eye on one of his mates. The lady is very beautiful and stands out in every way. But it has been difficult breaking communication barrier; he has tried fostering a relationship but it seems the lady rejects all entreaties. However, he was not depressed, knowing fully well that she was worth pursuing with the last pinch of blood in his veins. Fortunately for him, they met at a college party and that was where he had the opportunity to start everything with her. He came in a little bit late, and walking to a seat at the lady's table, he thrusted his thumbs in his pants and straddled the fingers at the crotch area with an infectious smile, heart-warming to the extent that she could not hide her admiration for him. It means that the woman got the sexual gesture and keyed into it.

Case Study IV: A con artist once went to a bank and presented a fake document so as to cash out money from another person's account. He was really bold and interacted well with the bankers that no one would ever picture him as being a criminal. He even walked about and ensure that everyone had a contact with him. On seeing that the female banker attending to him was young and probably wouldn't have been taken, he inserted his thumbs in his pocket so as to frame up his genitals. She got this signal and when she later found out the document presented was fake, she told him courteously instead of calling the security agents to arrest him. At least, the non-verbal sign got him the respect of not being barked at.

21.9. Covering of the Genitals

Generic Interpretations of the Concept

There are times that we are engulfed in fear, no matter our level of confidence. Being overridden by anxiety makes us appear vulnerable before others. One of the ways that expose our vulnerabilities is covering of the genitals or crotch when standing before others. This is different from mere touching served to arouse our feelings. In this case, we guard it with both hands or arms as if we received an intelligence report that someone is coming to cut it off. The hardness of the body, how stern the face is and general rigidity at that point tells an observant mind that some negative is going on.

This non-verbal act can be noticed in every atmosphere where there is general feeling of insecurity. For instance, men are fond of placing their hands on their genital when in elevators while looking at the numbers or doors. Also, when a public gathering, where you feel shy or anxious about the presence of another person or even a thought, you will cover your genitals with your hands and cross your legs. You may find it difficult to stand up from your seat, even if there are countless reasons demanding that. With this behaviour, we effectively deal with social anxieties.

Further, you may notice the display of this gesture when someone who serves as a threat—real or imaginary—is closing in our personal space. When someone you do not like comes too close, you know that there is probability of attack from the person. So you cover the genital, being one of the most likely targeted places for a predator. Even the thought of a negative occurrence is enough to send you into the fidgeting mode. Imagine yourself at the matrimonial home of your concubine and as you are about to start intercourse, their partner shows up. Apart from being shameful, you cannot imagine what would be the likely outcome of such scenario. Whether sitting or standing positions, this gesture can be displayed once the feeling sets in.

Scientific Explanations

Westside Toastmasters (2019) observes that we feel safer by placing our hands on the genital when threatened. It is like a metaphorical representations of a child running to her mother when threatened by her colleague outside; she knows that is her surest safe haven.

Experts refer to the hands covering the genital as 'fig leaf' position. SBL (2016) explains, 'It's a self-comfort gesture that reveals vulnerability, as it protects another sensitive part of our body—our genitals. It's often seen in funerals or other somber events, when people feel uneasy, but know that's inappropriate to use the arms folding gesture.' A point made in the quote above is that people display this gesture when they are uncomfortable. The sensitivity of the part of the body is why attention is always drawn to it during stressful moments. It is a defensive body language meant to ensure that we are secure from the 'arrows of the evil ones' targeted at us.

This gesture can also reveal that a person is shy, introvert or innocent. People who do not fancy displaying their sexuality in public may also display this gesture. It is pertinent to note that it is the opposite gestures to this such as genital framing, touching or grabbing that show a person who wants to garner attention about their sexuality. The person covering their genital does not want to show who he is through sexual prowess (SBL 2016).

Westside Toastmasters (2019) says that the 'fig leaf' position may also be displayed by people who are ordinarily expected to appear confident but are not. The platform puts it thus: 'When a person finds themselves in a position where they feel vulnerable but are required to display confidence and respect, they may clasp their hands over their lower abdomen or crotch.' That is why it is a common pose among world leaders when they meet for photographs and videos.

Practical Illustrations

Case Study I: Mr RA was in the living room with the wife when an argument ensued. This was not the first of its kind, and as such, he was used to it but his albatross has always been the quick physical attack by the wife. He has done everything to curb her but after being remorseful for a while, she goes back to her old ways. And more so, her usual points of attacks are the vulnerable parts of the body. Since he was on shorts, he knew that she could jump at his manhood and rough handle it. So Mr RA placed his two hands on his genitals while he kept on watching his favourite series. However, he kept a tab on her movements. This was a protective measure which came in a proactive manner.

Case Study II: Ms KF likes watching health series where things pertaining to science and medicine are discussed in practical terms. Since she was considering furthering her education in medicine or nursing, she knew it was the best programme for her. However, Ms KF is easily irritated by things. On a particular night, a patient had infections in her private parts and the doctors were trying to clean the vagina up and then operate it. At first, she was enthusiastic of the action, filled with suspense of how successful the medical practitioners would be. When they began to dissect the crotch, she became frightened and irritated to the extent that she subconsciously placed her two hands on her genitals and pressed them harder as if she was preventing them to get access to hers.

Case Study III: Two men were standing by the roadside, discussing, but while one of them looked enthusiastic and concentrated on the discussion, the other looked disturbed. At the beginning of the conversation, they were both mirroring each other and seemed to share similar view but as Man B brought up another topic, the demeanour of Man A changed. Apart from being uninterested in the new topic, Man B was moving closer to him and unconsciously, his two hands were used to cover his genital. He did not change his posture until the discussion came to an end. Man A was afraid that anything could happen to him—perhaps, he would be attacked by his co-interlocutor.

Case Study IV: I remember an illegal immigrant who was arrested by border control agents. During his arrest, the officers discovered that he would not let go of his trousers; his hands were used to cover the genitals right from the point of his arrest. At first, the officers thought that he hid something there but when a check was conducted, nothing was found on him. Just few minutes after that he returned to that posture and an officer needed to ask him what informed the behaviour, it was then he confessed that he was afraid that the officers might hit him something at the genitals. They really laughed at such imagination and asked him to relax.

21.10. Sitting with Knees Spread Out

Generic Interpretations of the Concept

Because this behaviour is prevalent among men, it is also called *manspreading*. The gesture is displayed when a person is seated with their spread wide apart.

Note that when this is done in one's privacy, there is nothing wrong with it but it becomes an issue when done in the presence of others—where a meeting is ongoing and most especially in public transportation. You hardly see this behaviour among women but this does not mean that they do not do it. Some females, especially ladies of easy virtues, will also spread out the knees in public in order to call attention to their genital area. If they are wearing skimpy skirts, this means even their under-wears would be seen by those around. This can be very troubling, especially to an uninterested person. Ladies who are desperate about having an affair with someone can display this gesture. All over the world, women are known to close off the legs when they are seated and those who deviate from this universal culture is either not well cultured or she decided to make another being out of her own.

As said earlier, this is a male thing that also paints the person in negative light. People who do this are considered rude and inconsiderate. Widening the distance between the knees takes up more space. This means that the person is invading another person's space without any justification. If the person being affected by their action decides to react, then it can lead to an ugly scene or even a physical violence. It is blatant disregard for others and this should be avoided as much as possible as you do not know the status of the person as the receiving end of your behaviour. People who wield influence also board public transport and this may fetch you more than you had budgeted.

In the same vein, this behaviour is undiplomatic as it makes the inner leg and crotch public. There are contexts romantic actions should be displayed so as not to be seen as a reckless fellow. Displaying this behaviour in a professional setting only portrays you as someone who places pleasure over work; this is bad for your reputation.

Scientific Explanations

SBL (2016) states that this is a gesture that is used by men to show sexual interest just like the crotch display earlier discussed in this chapter. Such men are considered as being expressive. When a man or even a woman, is seated with the legs wide apart, it is a signal of availability and virility. The website explains further, 'These men usually signal that they feel dominant, strong and even a little smug—this position takes a lot of space and exposes their groin for the whole world to see.' While people may not really have any problem for the public display of this gesture, it becomes an issue when you begin to enter their personal space. Hence, it can either offend or entice people to the person displaying the gesture. Hence, the body language platform cautions that 'while it's good to show confidence, if you don't want to annoy anyone—mind the distance between your knees'.

Also, Ruby Mey (2019) opens his account of this concept thus: 'People who sit with their knees far apart appear to be self-centred, arrogant, and even judgemental.' This may sound harsh but it gives a sincere description of what such people are. Also, individuals that do this usually put on fancy items so as to bolster their profile and look.

Practical Illustrations

Case Study I: FS is the only child of Mr and Ms RT and as their only daughter, they lavish everything on her and also ensure that she fits into the society properly; they are training her to be an all-round child who is not defective in any segment of the society. The family has a friend that visits them with her boy, a teenager too, about the age of FS. From every indication, it seems the two children were getting into each other. Most times, while their parents were in the living room, they would be alone at the backyard for hours. On a particular weekend when the family visited, FS sat on a couch with her knees spread apart that anyone coming in through the door will have free access to her pants. Immediately the mother saw this, she roared on her to close up her legs. The way she was sitting depicted someone who lacked manners.

Case Study II: Mr KH, although very wretched and grossly irresponsible at home, is a man who feels larger than life; he does not think anyone deserves his respect. He behaves weirdly both in public and while at home. One day, he boarded a train while going to work and instead of him to maintain decorum as others, he decided to spread his knees far apart that the person seated next to him began to feel uncomfortable. In a gentlemanly way, the man informed him of his discomfort but he turned a blind eye to the glaring injustice. When the man got tired, he kept shut and engaged in other things. Unknowingly, KH did not know that the man is a police officer; he had sent a message to his subordinates to wait at the station and arrest KH for his unruly behaviour.

Case Study III: OL and his colleagues decided to discuss football and other common issues during after taking their lunch. The discussion, which is always laced with a level of friendly argument is always led by OL, even days when he was not in the mood of speaking, they would prevail on him to join them. However, it is now a culture for OL to spread his knees far apart while leading the discussions, an attribute many of them do not like. Many of them had told him subtly but he has always behaved as if he was above them. One day, his colleagues planned against him. As he took this posture, one of them threw an object at him, which almost hit his genital before he blocked it with his hands; he looked as if life was taken out of him. Since then, he had learnt how to maintain a proper sitting posture without being forced to.

Case Study IV: A man wanted to evade clearance of his goods but it seemed that all tricks he had lined up did not work. He was there for more than eight hours and nothing was forthcoming. He decided not to go home that day because anything could happen to his items and no one would be held responsible, especially since he was seen in the location a day before. So he decided to sit via walkway he knew the clearing agents could not afford. He spread out his knees in a way that anyone passing would have to appeal to him to adjust before passing. He thought with this, an agent would see the expression on his face and ask him what the problem was and through that, beg the person through emotional blackmail. Unfortunately, no one seemed to care about him or what he was doing.

CHAPTER 22

The Legs

Another part of the body that is mostly ignored by people when reading non-verbal cues are the legs; we tend to forget that they are crucial parts of the body and, as such, embodiment of messages. Once you look inwardly, you will see more than you could have imagined. More than the upper part of the body, the legs are sincerer and accurate in revealing a person's feelings. In fact, those displaying the gestures always forget to manipulate the lower part of the body. So it can serve as a good trap in nailing down insincere individuals.

Of all animals, our legs are very unique due to how they are pointed in at the hips. This allows us to walk, sprint, climb, bicycle, swim, hurtle, and kick. There are incredible functions that we perform with our legs. We may not pay much attention to them as other parts of the body, but they are the vehicles that convey us around as we go about our daily businesses. There are things they are used for—creation of dominance, locomotion, protection, and a reliable anchor for kids to hang on to when they are gripped with fear or shy of someone. In moments as such, the legs play more helpful roles than the hands because the kid would think that they are still exposed to some extent even when they held by the hand compared to hiding behind the legs.

There are various forms of legs just as there are varied people across the universe—stocky, long, and sinewy legs all tell us something unique about people. The shape and structure of the legs per time has power to communicate what a person is passing through—elegance, joy, or nervousness. In times of trouble, the flight mode is activated once the legs are ready to run. This has helped and saved us from untimely death or other fatal injuries. The reason we should all strive to decode the messages passed by the legs is the level of honesty and accuracy with which they bear a person's mind during communication. Before we begin to understand this concept more than the obvious, let's delve into the biological aspect of it.

According to the *Dorland's Medical Dictionary for Healthcare Consumers* (2009) gives a general definition of the leg as the entire lower limb of the human body, including the foot, thigh and even the hip or gluteal region. However, the definition in human anatomy refers only to the section of the lower limb extending from the knee to the ankle, also known as the crus (*Merriam-Webster Dictionary* 2019).

In human anatomy, the lower leg is the part of the lower limb that lies between the knee and the ankle. The thigh is between the hip and knee and makes up the rest of the lower limb. The term lower limb or 'lower extremity' is commonly used to describe all the leg.

Evolution has provided the human body with two distinct features: the specialisation of the upper limb for visually guided manipulation and the lower limb's development into a mechanism specifically adapted for efficient bipedal gait. While the capacity to walk upright is not unique to humans, other primates can only achieve this for short periods and at a great expenditure of energy. The human adaption to bipedalism is not limited to the leg, however, but has also affected the location of the body's centre of gravity, the reorganisation of internal organs, and the form and biomechanism of the trunk. In humans, the double S-shaped vertebral column acts as a great shock-absorber which shifts the weight from the trunk over the load-bearing surface of the feet. The human legs are exceptionally long and powerful as a result of their exclusive specialisation for support and locomotion — in orangutans the leg length is 111 per cent of the trunk; in chimpanzees 128 per cent, and in humans 171 per cent. Many of the leg's muscles are also adapted to bipedalism, most substantially the gluteal muscles, the extensors of the knee joint, and the calf muscles (TAA 2006).

The major bones of the leg are the femur (thigh bone), tibia (shin bone), and adjacent fibula, and these are all long bones. The patella (kneecap) is the sesamoid bone in front of the knee. Most of the leg skeleton has bony prominences and margins that can be palpated and some serve as anatomical landmarks that define the extent of the leg. These landmarks are the anterior superior iliac spine, the greater trochanter, the superior margin of the medial condyle of tibia, and the medial malleolus. Notable exceptions to palpation are the hip joint, and the neck and body, or shaft of the femur (TAA 2006).

Usually, the large joints of the lower limb are aligned in a straight line, which represents the mechanical longitudinal axis of the leg, the Mikulicz line. This line stretches from the hip joint (or more precisely the head of the femur), through the knee joint (the intercondylar eminence of the tibia), and down to the centre of the ankle (the ankle mortise, the fork-like grip between the medial and lateral malleoli). In the tibial shaft, the mechanical and anatomical axes coincide, but in the femoral shaft they diverge 6°, resulting in the *femorotibial angle* of 174° in a leg with normal axial alignment.

A leg is considered straight when, with the feet brought together, both the medial malleoli of the ankle and the medial condyles of the knee are touching. Divergence from the normal femorotibial angle is called genu varum if the centre of the knee joint is lateral to the mechanical axis (intermalleolar distance exceeds 3 cm), and genu valgum if it is medial to the mechanical axis (intercondylar distance exceeds 5 cm). These conditions impose unbalanced loads on the joints and stretching of either the thigh's adductors or abductors (TAA 2006).

Adolescent and adult women in many Western cultures often remove the hair from their legs. Toned, tanned, shaved legs are sometimes perceived as a sign of youthfulness and are often considered attractive in these cultures. Men generally do not shave their legs in any culture. However, leg-shaving is a generally accepted practice in modelling (Pretty Legs 2015).

22.1. Proxemics

Generic Interpretations of the Concept

The term 'proxemics' was coined by foremost anthropologist. Edward T. Hall to connote spatial distancing among animals. He advocates for individual personal space through this concept. How close someone stands to us and the relationship that exists between us determines how comfortable we will be. Generally, people are not expected to stand too close to each other. This means that one of them has invaded the personal space of the other which will bring about discomfort and resistance in the conversation. Two basic factors that determine our spatial needs are personal preference and culture.

On the former, we all have our individual preferences and do not want anyone to violate them. This is called privacy. It is expected that anyone who wants to communicate with us should respect how close we want them to stand to us. People who are highly social may not really care about the closeness but those who are very detailed will enforce the need to maintain personal space in conversation. To enjoy your conversation with people, make sure you understand their preference on how close they want you to stand to them. On the aspect of culture, this also differs. You need to understand what each culture preaches, especially if you are a stranger in such environment so as not to offend the sensibilities of your hosts.

Generally, people feel comfortable when the public when a distance of about fifteen to twenty-five feet is maintained. Since there is no close relationship among you, stand too close is considered inappropriate. However, in social gathering, a distance of four to eight feet would be considered OK while many people prefer a personal space that ranges from one to four feet. The closest of all is the intimate space which is less than a foot. This is reserved for the closest persons to us; we trust that they can shield us and will not do any harm to us. Romantic partners and parents are those who usually have free access to one's intimate space. Again, all these are approximations and the ultimate still lies within the dictates of one's culture and individual choices.

Also, location and time of the day determine our spatial needs. Our feelings at night are not the same with how we feel in the day. For instance, while we may find it easy to mingle with people—strangers and known persons alike during the day, we normally maintain a wider distance with people at night. Usually, we tend to feel uncomfortable walking in a distance of less than ten feet with strangers at night; in the case of an attack, we might find it difficult to repel. Remember that respect is reciprocal; what you would not want others to do to you, do not do unto others.

Scientific Explanations

Oxford Dictionary defines *proxemics* as 'the branch of knowledge that deals with the amount of space that people feel it necessary to set between themselves and others.' According to this definition, the concept of proxemics is based on feeling; you are expected to know what makes your co-interlocutor comfortable in a conversation. This means you should not just consider your own needs but that of the person you are discussing with too.

Emily Cummins (2019) defines *proxemics* as 'the study of how humans use space when we're communicating.' How close we stand to someone, whether we touch them, and how comfortable we feel are all part of spatial distancing. Cummins even reveals that colour is part of proxemics. For instance, some people are easily distracted by very bright colours in a room. In such case, it means the person needs to maintain wider distance or space with the colour. The don opines that when we miss the concept of spacing in communication, our discussion might not end up being effective.

Apart from personal space, how well we use physical territory also matters. Explaining this concept, Cummins (2019) submits that 'it's more about the ways that we arrange objects in space. For example, you probably have your bed set up so that you face the centre of your bedroom, instead of the wall.' If another person should come and rearrange them, we begin to feel uncomfortable.

Practical Illustrations

Case Study I: Lady K and Man Z just met about a week ago and have been on dates for about three times. The urge to talk to each other seems irresistible but

Lady K still believes that they are just getting to know each other, so the intimacy should have a considerable point of barrier. Z does not share this sentiment with her. Any time they were together, the man would always want to move very close to her so that they would talk at a whisper. However, Lady K would subtly resist this through a frown and tilting of the head backwards. When Man Z thought that everything was fast becoming absurd, he retrained himself until some few weeks after. Perhaps, the lady thought things were moving too fast than her imaginations.

Case Study II: Despite the hectic work schedule of his parents, Child E is fond of them and spends every minute with them by moving very close. Due to their work demands, the parents had to get him a caregiver with whom he stays till they are back from work. The usual routine is that after he was done with take-home assignments, he would watch movies and discuss with the caregiver till the return of his parents. One day, Child E and the caregiver were discussing with each of them sitting at the rear end of the couch but as his mother entered and took her seat, Child E rushed to her, sitting very close, while the mother welcomed him with a smile. This was a show of affection and love—he was more inclined to the mother than every other person.

Case Study III: Dr RT was in a medical conference with some of his colleagues from other countries. The sitting arrangement was professionally done for the ease of movement and sharing of ideas. They all took their seat and the conference started in earnest but at some point, Dr RT discovered that one of the participants seated at his left side was trying to shift his chair very close. This was unsettling him and was about to lose concentration at that point. So he was forced to give him a look of 'hope all is well' which was enough to curb the urge of the person; he needed no personal space with the person.

Case Study IV: A law enforcement officer once went to a restaurant to eat. As he was entering the place, a drug addict who had cocaine and other harmful substance on him quickly looked away. As if it was planned, the enforcement agent went to the drug addict's table to sit. The man felt more uncomfortable and had to excuse himself. This action made the law enforcement agent to become suspicious. He faced the direction of the drug addict went to. When he discovered that anything could happen with the suspicious development, he quickly dashed out of the restaurant. The enforcement officer later went after him and he was arrested with those substances.

22.2. Territorial Position

Generic Interpretations of the Concept

We use the legs as a means of creating territories to ourselves. If you do not want others to come into your personal space, then you must know how to create boundaries for yourself. If not, people will override you without tendering any apology. This can be painful but life is not meant to be fair to anyone, no matter your status and level of sincerity. The way you stand tells others what you are doing with your personal space. Those who take advantage of this non-verbal cue are the people who stand with the legs further apart. The wider the space between the legs, the more the territorial display. This tells others that you are confident and self-conscious. Those who are not aware of their rights will stand with the legs very close apart. This means others will intrude into their personal space and they will find it difficult to resist.

Also, this stance is affected by one's profession. Generally, law enforcement officials tend to stand with their legs wider apart compared with others—doctors, engineers, bankers, among others. The reason being that, as law enforcement agents, they understand how delicate their job is; they are dealing with criminals and, as such, should expect attacks from any direction. Standing with the legs further apart gives them stamina. For instance, it would be difficult to fall a person from the back when their legs are spread out compared with someone who maintains a submissive posture of closing up the legs. To have a better understanding of this gesture, draw a mental picture of a police or military officer deployed to a scene due to intelligence report that criminals are coming to attack the facility.

Apart from the subconscious claim of one's territory (and that of others when you want to intimidate them), this is also a glaring display of confidence. Note that spreading the feet apart also exposes your vulnerable part—your genitals. This means you are communicating the need for others to stay off or dare attacking you. It means you are fully prepared and not afraid of anyone.

Scientific Explanations

Straker (2019) states that territorial stance is a dominant body language. This is to ensure that the body looks bigger than it is. Generally, this gives the person an open posture. A person spreading out their feet may also place their hands on hips in order to make the elbows thrust out, making them take up more space than they could have done on a normal ground. The person would stand upright, erect, with the chin up and the chest pulled out. The overall body size becomes bigger and this is an unsaid way of displaying dominance over others in a given setting. The body language expert submits that 'by invading and occupying territory that others may own or use, control and dominance is indicated'. This is what many dominant people are set out to achieve.

When you own something that others covet, it automatically gives you a symbol of authority. A larger office, or displays of wealth or power, such as a Rolex watch or having many subordinates are some of the things that might drive a person into displaying this posture. Owning things is not the issue here but flaunting such through the use of territorial display. That is simply a show of power. That is why a senior manager will stand with the legs wide apart while they expect the junior workers to close themselves up while in their presence (Straker 2019).

Sonamics (2016) states that while talking a person takes this posture, it means they feel safe about what is being discussed and have a sense of superiority. The verbal translation in this sense is *'I'm smarter than you.'* The body is open and yet, the person still lay claim on territory. 'The gesture makes us look bigger and shows dominance,' states Sonamics.

However, we need to state that this might be disrespectful when you invade on the personal space of others (Straker 2019).

Practical Illustrations

Case Study I: It is the culture of students of DXC High School to assembly in front of their classes early in the morning to pray, learn some general things and recite their anthem before a teacher comes to pass any announcement to them. The process is always capped up by the principal of the school coming up to address the students and teachers alike. He would walk to the podium majestically to the wild applause of the staff and students and then, he would take his stance by spreading his legs far apart. Also, he uses the hands to demonstrate as he speaks slowly, paying attention to his diction. Everywhere is always silent as he addresses the gathering. Apart from his knowledge on what he says, his masterful use of body language also contributes to this unique delivery.

Case Study II: There have been several reports by the residents of a particular area that a bar was constituting nuisance to them; they blare music, and then, people drink late into the night, misbehaving as they return home. Unfortunately, many of the drunks do not even reside in that environment. So residents are normally forced to wake up late at night. In recent times, this drunkenness has been transforming into armed robbery. When the police were informed, they analysed the situation and discovered it was getting out of hand. So the authorities mobilised their men to man the area of a 24/7 basis. Standing in strategic positions, the policemen who wore stern face could be seen standing with their feet wider apart and their gun, within close range. Their stance alone sends fear down the nerves of people—they portrayed authority and dominance in their stance.

Case Study III: Two leaders of different rival nations were speaking on the sidelines of an international conference. Leader A seemed to be the one leading the discussing as Leader B did more of head nodding than speaking. Also, Leader A had his feet well spread out, looking as if he wanted to pounce on his co-interlocutor. This was a clear show of class and confidence meant to pass the message that he is superior to his counterpart.

Case Study IV: Three boys were smuggled from Country FAE but it seemed their smuggler had one on one conversation with them on their way which made them to cooperate with him. This made the process easier for him as they obeyed him at every given point but they were unable to manoeuvre their way at the toughest border. When the smuggled guys were brought down, they could not withstand the stern look of the gun wielding officers. While two of them looked away, the third person turned back and faced the direction they were coming from. He was about taking to his heels before he was stopped. This means he was overwhelmed by nervousness.

22.3. Invasion of Territory

Generic Interpretations of the Concept

When someone challenges your territory, you better get prepared or take your heels; it is a clear invitation to trouble. If you know you can withstand the person, then you brace yourself up and resist the attempt but if not, it may be the best time to appeal to them. Those who challenge your territory will move into your personal space at the wrong time when they do not have your consent. This is always intentional and happens during heated arguments.

The person will move so close that they will just be inches away from your face. This can take breath out of you because the closeness is never what you had expected or even a comforting one. Even if you will attack back, you will first tilt back your head to ensure your safety first. This gesture figuratively denotes 'in your face' and a gross display of disrespect for your person. The person appears glaring as they puff out the chest to look larger than they are.

This violation of your personal space is to intimidate you. Someone who wants you to lick their boot or accept them as your head on controversial grounds will look for implausible ways to prove themselves a master to you. Once you are intimidated, you would be forced into submission. This is the usual attribute of bullies; they take offence at little issues and make an unimaginable drama out of it just to prematurely announce themselves.

This may also be a prelude to physical assault. In such instance, you should not take chances. Safety first! Even if you think you can repel their attack, first retrieve yourself into a safe place where you can assess the situation before fighting back.

Scientific Explanations

Straker (2019) describes this gesture as a superiority signal that is meant to deprive others of their personal space. This is to disrespect the person and what they represent. If you hate an institution, through this behaviour on the person in charge of the institution, you can make a mockery of it. Imagine a parent shouting at and vilifying a school administrator. In the actual sense of it, what is being attacked is the school because if not for it, there would not have been any relationship between the administrator and that particular person.

Invasion of territory means that someone is moving too close to the extent that our body space does not belong to us again. 'Other actions include sitting on their chairs, leaning on their cars, putting feet up on their furniture and being over-friendly with their romantic partners' (Straker 2019). Territorial challenge is trying to say that 'what belongs to you belongs to me' and 'I can take anything of yours that I want and you cannot stop me'. Sometimes, if you wield a response at the appropriate time, you may be successful in stopping them but if you consent to their challenge, it means you have given them a seal to take charge of your life. This is not to mean that you should confront them headlong when your life or something precious to you is at stake.

Practical Illustrations

Case Study I: Two men were at a bar and a little argument ensued on the need to share a table or move away from each other. Man A was still sipping his drink while talking passively but Man B was boiling inside already, panting as if the issue was beyond what could be settled amicably. When Man A noticed the obvious unrest on his face, he jokingly said 'Calm down, man', and this was what flared him up. Man B stood up with full force and nodded his head at his counterpart as if he wanted to hit him with his head, questioning loudly, 'Do you mean I'm drunk?' 'Are you trying to say that I'm out of my senses?' Man A, a widely known gentleman, was already shivering, trying to understand what had really gone wrong. It was the security officials at the bar that prevailed on Man B not to beat Man A up.

Case Study II: The monthly board meetings of XYC Enterprises is always a tug of war and incessant show of superiority; every board member wants to prove their seniority and expertise during the meeting. Most times, this has been an impediment to the growth of the firm. The director had lamented to them a lot of times but it appeared that none is ready to step down for the other. During one of their meetings, they were discussing the need to change the modalities of the company. If the proposal scales through, this means most of the present supervisors would be axed in order to bring in new people that would fit in perfectly into the proposed idea. Member C would be affected by this decision as most of the present supervisors are his loyalists while Member D would benefit immensely if the proposal is approved as he would be the one to bring in the new people. So they were both arguing heatedly just to defend their personal interests. At some point, Man C jumped up and moved closer to Man D, shouting at him—he invaded D's territory with this action. It took the combined efforts of others at the meeting to curtail the situation from going physical. The meeting was called off immediately afterward.

Case Study III: Mr and Mrs DS were discussing on how to take care of their children. It was obvious that they were fed up of each other and did not want the court to take decision on their children when they officially file for divorce. So they decided to settle that amicably so as not to affect the future of the innocent kids. The discussion had been going on well before they find it difficult to agree on an issue. Still dragging the issue, the husband moved closer to the wife and gave her a stern look, they both stood still for about a minute before Mr DS later restrained himself from hitting her. By moving closer, the man was ready to attack the woman.

Case Study IV: Mr UY wanted to go into importation business but many people wrongfully discouraged him that clearance fee would gulp up all his gains. He then became confused and asked how those who were involved in it were making their profits and he was told that most of them do dodge clearance. So he wanted to understand that aspect of the business before starting. So he went to the port and confidently, moved very close to the point of clearance that he began to choke the officials working there as a way of laying pressure on the officials. When they could not bear it again, they demanded what he was there for and he lied that he missed his way. But he did not appear truthful and that birthed curiosity to drill him the more in the officials.

22.4. Posing to the Side

Generic Interpretations of the Concept

Even though we have vaguely encouraged speaking face-to-face as a means of displaying superiority and honesty, most of us still angle to the side while interacting with people as we find this posture very convenient in dealing with others. Being on a slightly angled position gives you a relaxed view of the person you are conversing with. This behaviour is unconscious and can be traced to our childhood. For instance, when children first meet with each other, instead of maintaining a direct stance, they will approach each other from an angle. This has been noticed to be beneficial to both—they are better received that way; one will not think of the other as being bully. If one of them was standing directly, it may be assumed to be a pose of attack, thereby shrinking out trust.

This behaviour grows with us into adulthood. If you can cast your mind on your recent discussions, especially with strange people, you will observe that you had a nice time when you maintained this pose rather than facing them directly. In the same vein, I have taken a conscious note among businesspeople that when they face each other at a slight angle, their discussion is always robust and more detailed than the other stance. When the amount of time businesspeople spend together increases, this means they are having a good time with each other. If not, they would have concluded abruptly so that everyone can go their ways.

Even in times of acrimony, this is always the best stance to display; it is preferable you stand angled, slightly away from your opponent. It has been discovered that this stance has a high probability of diffusing negative feelings. If the person does not have 100 per cent access to your face and vice versa, you tend to do away with negative emotions about each other. But if there is direct facing of each other, you get more irritated as you look into each other's eye and this flames up negative feelings.

Do not misinterpret my explanations here; I am not saying that you will not face each other, only that you look from an angle; slight view of the person you are conversing with.

Scientific Explanations

Philip (2014) refers to this gesture as *blading body language*. He explains that we turn our body to people or ideas that we agree with and vice versa. So if you see someone turning away from you, it means they do not fancy what you are discussing with them. The body language expert gives the verbal interpretation of this cue as 'I like what I'm hearing so my body is angling towards you so we're facing each other even more.'

Apart from the shape and direction of the legs, we need to understand that there are more important things attached to the angling of the body as Philip explains thus: 'Torsos house important vital organs that are responsible for keeping the body alive. Heart, lungs, liver, intestines and so forth are all easily accessible through a thin layer of skin, fat, muscle, ribs and a sternum and exposing our ventral side means that we trust we won't be attacked and is therefore a signal of openness and liking.' We orient ourselves to people we like.

This is natural but can also be feigned by people. Hypocrites may angle their side to you but in reality, they do not agree with you.

Smith (2015) also urges the use of this gesture while discussing with a friend or loved one as it gives them the assurance that you are listening to them. On a literal level, the ear is turned to them which tells them that you want to listen to their stories.

Practical Illustrations

Case Study I: Student W has just been enrolled in DTA Schools because his parents had a transfer to the region and since he does not want to be disconnected from them, he followed them down there to continue with his schooling. Student W is unarguably smart and intellectually charming. And he likes people who put him on hot seat and engages him in dynamic way. In his first class, he picked interest in one of the students, X, for his unrivalled display of understanding of what the teacher explained. So he made up his mind to meet him during break so that they could start their friendship from there. At break, Student W rushed to Student X and the latter was happy to give him his attention because it was rare to see a new student pick interest in an intelligent one within a day. Unconsciously, W approached him at an angle and vice versa. They spoke to the end of the break without even bothering about food. They quickly reunited at closing to further their discussion. One of the things that helped them was the posture they displayed—they showed interest in each other.

Case Study II: Businessman E was recommended to Businesswoman V. That means that it was the first time they would be engaged in a business deal. Looking for ways to keep each other for long, they both showed enthusiasm in receiving each other. When they eventually got to meet, they faced each other at a slight angle while discussing. This made them spend more time together as they were very free to each other without any feeling of intimidation from both parties. They looked into each other's eyes when there was a need to and break it at the appropriate time. It was a perfect communication style that worked out well for both of them.

Case Study III: HX is an intern in one of the leading engineering firms in town and heard that those who perform extra-ordinarily well during their internship are normally retained by the firm after their schooling. So he worked very hard on his first day at the firm that his unit head was full of his praises. At closing, HX ran to his supervisor who gladly gave him his attention due to his impressive performance earlier at work. Standing at the corridor, they both faced each other at a slight angle and talked for a long duration as the supervisor explained many secrets of the company to him and how he could succeed. Apart from the humility and quest to succeed, his posture was also an advantage in this context.

Case Study IV: Con artist AY was looking for every way possible to develop a relationship with Woman CD. He heard that she is rich and unless you have something to offer her, there was no way you could part with any amount from her. So he went with a well plagiarised business proposal to the woman which really caught her attention. When they were speaking, the con artist carefully and consciously turned an angle to her which made the woman also mirror him over time. They kept on with the discussion for over three hours and before it came to an end, he was able to convince her.

22.5. Walking Attitudes

Generic Interpretations of the Concept

The way we walk tells others what is going on in our mind or what we set out to achieve. Beyond the fact that our legs convey us to where we want to be per time, during the process there are a lot of things that they communicate to those who are paying attention to us. Some people are intentional about their walks; through walk, you can arouse the emotional feelings of other people. Ladies are fond of this and they know the appropriate place to use it. For instance, the way they walk while at party is different from the pace they maintain at work. If there is a potential partner at sight, they will walk slowly and throw waist at the person. This is to ensure that the person looks at their side and initiate a love process.

Some others walk to show how determined and strengthened they are. This is usually observed in a professional setting where vitality is the soul of business. We cannot give what we do not possess. An inspiring professional or entrepreneur is one that carries themselves with much charisma and power. Such person must wear a befitting outfit while they walk purposefully. To show determination, you see the person walk erect and focused in getting an assignment done. Strength is when the person keeps walking until the implementation or realisation of a given job. A person who droops, slouches or glaringly display laziness in their walking pattern is displaying negative behaviours to those that are observing him or her.

The way we walk tells others that we are on an important assignment. This means we are walking on a fast pace, leaving out every distraction. Even if there are things that should ordinarily call our attention, we will overlook it at that point. Some may exaggerate this so as to be noticed but this does not negate the original message that is being passed across.

Those who are not engaged in any serious business or adventure walk in a relaxed or casual way. They may even tuck their hands in their pocket as they take note of everything going on around them. This is mostly seen on weekends when people are not too engaged with their professional callings.

When you have an interest in someone, you walk past them frequently so as to let them have a full, charming view of your body. This takes place even in professional gatherings where ladies would get a man's attention by how often they walk by and smile charmingly at their target at each time.

Scientific Explanations

Jacqueline Delange (2012) discusses the walk attitude, by taking cognisance of the submissions of different body language experts. She begins by stating, 'Talk is often cheap, but the way you walk can speak volumes about you.' That is, most times, we pay conscious attention to what we say but when it comes to walking, we pay less attention to it but it reveals much more we can imagine at the surface level. How you walk reveals what you are made of, Patti Wood discovers this in her research. She uses the DISC acronym to describe the form of personality profiles we can unravel through the way we walk: 'Drivers (who display dominance) walk quickly with intent and don't like to stop once they know where they're headed; influencers often act emotionally, changing direction often; supporters who show steadiness walk politely with their arms close to their bodies and might stop to speak with others; cautious people, who Wood call can be referred to as 'correctors,' walk precisely and follow foot traffic rules' (Delange 2012).

Practical Illustrations

Case Study I: STZ Firm management are trying to get their company registered so as to give them more opportunities to tap into and build goodwill with being a registered firm. They knew that this was their chance and they should blow it, they have to wait for a minimum of two years before the approving agency can consider their proposal. So the day that was earmarked for the agency to visit was the most strategic and demanding the lives of the workers involved. Ms D, the secretary, who is known to be friendly with people suddenly changed as she passed by those people they used to crack jokes together without uttering a word. The people also watched her in amazement as she went back and forth, taking files to the manager's office to be treated and then dispatched before the arrival of the agency. She walked faster than usual and looked smarter than before. Her walking style confirmed her professional approach to work.

Case Study II: Ms FC was at a party with her friends and her eyes caught a man who appeared to be the ideal man she had always been looking for. She did not hide her admiration for the guy as she talked openly about him at their table, forcing other ladies to take a look at him. She thought a chair was going to be free any time soon at the guy's table so that she could move there but that seemed to be a dream. So she switched plans. She decided to stand up several times, walked past the guy, throw her waist at him and carried her legs so slowly that the man would see how large her buttocks and hips were. Particularly, when she was at the central point of the guy's table, she would pause her movement, behaving as if something fell off from her body. This was a subtle advertisement of herself.

Case Study III: The family of Mr and Mrs RD decided to take a walkout on a Saturday morning as it has always been their culture. During this exercise, they walk casually and talk about some things that are not important to their personal lives just to make the exercise enjoyable. A particular woman who was rushing to the grocery shop left them behind and to her surprise, they had not moved as expected when she was returning home. She looked at them as if they were going through issues but when she saw them laughing, behaving as if nothing was bothering them, she knew all was well and then, moved on a fast pace because she had a programme three hours to that time and she needed to eat before going. Hence, her fast pace means she was impatient.

Case Study IV: Illegal immigrants in Country GTD are finding it difficult to walk freely during the day because a special agency to fish and flush them out has just been commissioned. To justify their existence, officers of the agency work day and night. This actually takes away the freedom of movement of the illegal immigrants. One day, one of them was walking home after work and as he was approaching their base, he began to walk slowly. At some point, he would stop and look at his back to confirm if the agents were not coming after him. He tiptoed till he got home. This walking pattern depicted a person that is fearful and nervous.

22.6. Determining Pace of Walk

Generic Interpretations of the Concept

In every endeavour in life, the person who gives direction is automatically regarded as the master; people look up to him on what they should do next. The same thing is applicable during walk. When people are walking in a group, the person who determines how fast or slow others go is said to be the leader. Others are expected to abide by his rules and principles.

From another angle, the person who determines the pace might actually not be with those trekking. For instance, if a senior manager sends a subordinate on an errand, the junior staff will 'run' through fast pace movement because they do not want to appear in the sight of the boss. If someone who is not really older than they do or in the position that can influence their appointment, they will walk slowly, knowing that the person will have to be patient because he was never meant to be sent on the errands. A person who walks fast or courageously has an important assignment to deliver which must be done with full respect.

Situations also dictate the pace of walk of people. Imagine a person whose wife is in the labour room and told to go and get some items outside the hospital. Also, a man who receives an emergency call from home will drive carelessly and walk very fast into the house so as to quench their suspense and dispel fears. A student who is late for an examination will walk very fast, disengaging themselves from all forms of distractions that might occur on their way.

In every given endeavours, we walk according to the pace of authoritative image figure in the context. Even teenagers observe this among one another. However, they defer this clue by ensuring that they walk authoritatively as they like without being coerced at any given time. For instance, instead of taking the leading position, a teenage leader might stay at the back while others run, not minding what would be the implication of his or her actions. So while dealing with groups, we need to always remember that the person is in front might not necessarily be the leader.

Scientific Explanations

Carolyn Steber (2018) says that we cannot disconnect a person's personality from the pace of their movement. If a cautious person is leading a walk in a group, you will discover that the walk would be slow; they want to pay attention to every detail that caught their eyes as they walk and would not like to think critically of every step they take. This means they will not rush and those walking behind them have to obey and respect their decision, if not, it may lead to fracas. She puts it thus: 'Slower, shorter strides may mean you are more self-centred, though not necessarily in a bad way. It means you are cautious and are looking out for yourself. It is a measured kind of individual who walks that way. Introverts may be found walking like that, with their head sort of down.' Hence, the personality of the leader will always reflect the pace of movement of every other person in a given group.

Further, Smita Pandit (2018) notes that the walking pace is dictated by a person's mood, personality and intention. For instance, if you are following a person who has just lost a contest, there is high probability that the person walks with spring in their leg; they walk as if a heavy load has been placed on their legs.

Practical Illustrations

Case Study I: The car of Ms FV broke down unexpectedly while going for work. Unfortunately, her husband was out of town that day. This means she either have to rely on the unreliable public transport because it happened in an estate or get help from any other source. Her two children were with her. When she checked her watch, she was already getting late for work and could not further risk anything that had no guaranteed result. So she decided to walk with her children to the nearest bus stop in order to be picked up from there. The kids thought it was one of those days that they could influence how she walked; they were walking slowly but there she was, practically running to the station because she knew the kind of boss she had. At some point, the kids started jogging after her till they got to their destination. The pace of walk here was determined by lateness and the need to resume work on time.

Case Study II: Some military officers got an intelligence report that some infidels were planning to penetrate through their territory via a border. So the officers had to double their efforts and swing into action immediately. A major-general was commissioned to lead a team to the venue and block off other likely areas. As they got to the location, they parked their vehicle at a place where it would be difficult for anyone to notice them and then, the major began to walk very fast, trying to condone off the area before it was too late. The other soldiers that were assigned to him could also be seen walking at the same pace with him so that they would not be left behind. They were nervous and had to walk at the same space so as to combat any antagonist as a group.

Case Study III: Lady G is the personal assistant of Dr TR, a very dedicated and courageous entrepreneur. It was not up to three weeks with him that G knew that she had better braced herself up for work or else tender her resignation letter before she was sent packing. Fortunately for her, she was able to blend into the culture within the first few weeks. One day, Dr TR had a legal battle with one of their clients and he needed to go through some files before calling his lawyers to institute a case. At the point of making photocopies of the documents, the company's photocopier developed fault which means that Lady G had to go somewhere else to do it. Her boss told her to hasten up and she could be seen walking like a military officer in a bid not to disappoint her boss. If not for the superior's order, she wouldn't have walked in such a fast pace.

22.7. Sitting Attitudes

Generic Interpretations of the Concept

I have seen many people trivialise this gesture, thinking they can sit the way they like and still be accommodated by all kinds of cultures. A secret I need to let out at this point is that the way you sit tells a lot about your person—it reveals your emotions, mood at that given time and what your intentions are probably are. What is most important is that almost all the world cultures have their unique sitting style and once you are interacting in a new environment, one of the things you must know is how they sit. This helps you in quickly fitting into the culture of the host community. Again, you cannot download this and think those at the receiving end will welcome you warmly.

It would amount to a self-mockery to attempt explaining the various ways in which each culture sits in this short segment but we will consider some major regions of the world. In some areas in Asia, people are fond of squatting, with the buttocks nearly reaching the ground and knees in a high position as they wait for a bus. Some other cultures believe in the intertwining of the legs as they sit. A foremost example of this is Ghandi's sitting position while working a loom.

In Europe and many other cultures, people will sit with a leg draped over the knee of the opposite leg with the sole pointing downward. There are varieties of sitting patterns in America; some may sit, maintaining the figure four stature by placing their ankle at the topmost part of the opposite knee while the foot is obviously high.

The above-given examples are just few case studies given to illustrate differences in culture. Again, to be better received by a host community, learn their sitting pattern and demonstrate it effectively while with them. This tells them that you care for and value them.

On the other hand, the way a person sits is capable of revealing their mood. Some may slouch in their seat, look moody and find it difficult to smile while others are doing so. Some others may glue their buttocks into the chair while others will rest towards an arm of the chair, leaving a wide gap in the opposite side. All these patterns communicate a huge message to those who care to understand.

Scientific Explanations

Many experts that contributed to this subject matter notes that our sitting pattern can wither make or mar us in any given context. Minocher Patel (2012) tries to explain the behaviour that should be maintained while sitting both in formal and informal gatherings. Generally, women all over the world are not expected to leave their legs widely open or cross them while seated. She furthers that 'when sitting in a formal meeting or party, men/women should sit with an erect posture and with poise'. This is a universal behaviour that should be imbibed by all and sundry.

Practical Illustrations

Case Study I: A man saw an advert in his neighbourhood that a family driver was needed. Since he was not pleased with the factory where he was working, he decided to give this offer a try, hoping that it would connect him to many other parts of the country. More so, driving is nothing but fun to him. Note that he knocked at the gate of the house where he saw the advert while going to work; he did not want to lose the opportunity and yet, he must not get late to work so as not to be queried. So he thought the driving job discussion would be fast. However, when he got there, the father of the home was discussing with a friend and, as such, informed the applicant to spare him some minutes. The man sat impatiently but not resting his back on the chair. More so, his eyes were focused on the wall clock while his feet were unconsciously pointed towards the door. At some point, he became very much agitated by drooping as if he wanted to fall off from the seat. All these communicated the fact that he was being delayed more envisioned, making her bored and impatient.

Case Study II: Ms IR was in a conference with many of her professional colleagues; it was an avenue to meet with people from many parts of the world and exchange ideas. Since she came alone, this means she had no trouble of trying to sit down with another person. On the second day of the conference, she found herself sitting between two men. Her Achilles heel was that she cannot resist a tall, well-built, and gorgeous man. And this description aptly captures the man seated at her left and the exact opposite was at her right. For the better part of the conference session, she tilted herself to the left, smiling at everything that the man reacted to. She moved so near that she was almost choking up the man and the gap at her right could contain another person. The well-built man got her message of love and they picked things up after that particular session.

Case Study III: Mr MK was lured into stealing some items of the company where he works. The initiative was brought about four times before he bought into it. He was considered as a man of integrity, easy-going and one would not do any negative thing against the firm, considering his past encounters with top members of the firm. Unfortunately for him, the thievery later leaked and all those suspected were lined up to face a disciplinary committee to decide on their fate. Mr MK was utterly embarrassed with his action while almost everyone who heard of his involvement was disappointed in him. During the committee meeting with him, Mr MK sat fearfully on the chair, looking down and away to the door. Instead of resting his back and interact freely with the people on the other side of the table, he buried his head in shame, shifting repeatedly on the chair as if he was not balanced on it.

Case Study IV: An alleged impostor was delayed by a group of officials so as to find out if he really impersonated someone or not; it was difficult to establish at first because he impersonated his twin brother who is an identical twin with him. When the verification process was going on, he would look away from the officers. However, this sitting posture was not comfortable for him as a disconnection in eye contact signalled that he was looking directly into the sun.

Hence, whenever he discovered that no one was looking at his side, he would quickly change his sitting style. This was what he did throughout that period. He was really nervous and trying to dodge all eyes he considered as being threatening to him.

22.8. Sitting with Legs Held Together

Generic Interpretations of the Concept

There are many possible reasons that can lead to crossing of legs while on a seat. I need to remind you of the cultural aspect explored in the preceding segment. In other words, some people sit with the legs held together because it is culturally required for them to do so. In this case, we cannot allude any other reason to it; we will believe that the person is emotionally OK. In the same vein, in most parts of the world, women are expected to sit with the legs held together. If they were at loose and immediately, a man shows up from nowhere, they would suddenly revert their sitting position by holding the legs together. This is a social convention that must be respected.

However, if someone suddenly brings their knees together without being attached to the two instances given above, this is an indication of insecurity. Bringing the legs together serves as a means of protection to the person. Insecurity can be induced by anything. The thought of someone harming us or even seeing the person with an actual weapon can make us switch into this posture. This is an unconscious show of our emotional feeling.

When the legs come together, there is a tactile feeling, especially around the upper part of the leg. This feeling is highly needed by an insecure person to feel comfortable. When the legs come together, the body is kept in shape and if there is any need, the person can easily take to their heels. Also, sudden bringing together of the legs makes the body smaller. In a way, this is a symbolic way of hiding the body or trying to reduce one's profile so that a potential threat does not see one. This may also be a non-verbal way of pleading guilty. If you think a situation is greater than you, instead of challenging it which you know is disastrous for your person, you may consider surrendering to it as the most plausible thing to do in that situation.

To have an accurate interpretation of this gesture, you need to first understand your subject's baseline and then consider this gesture in line with other accompanying clues, pointing to the same direction.

Scientific Explanations

Patel (2012) states that when someone sits with their legs intertwined and very twisted, is a sign of nervousness or insecurity. This is more done by women. Since they know that the society expects them to close up their legs in a public function, they will hide under this to twist the legs when nervous. The best way you can fish such people out is to identify the level of force that accompanies the action. If it were to be in obedience to social convention, the legs would be held together lightly but as a reaction to an unfortunate event, there would be obvious application of force. Patel advises thus: 'Women shouldn't cross legs at the knees, especially if they are wearing a skirt or a dress, it can ride up. Instead cross at the ankles. For men, unless it is a deep lounging seat, should lean against the back and put a hand or an elbow on the arm.'

When the legs are crossed with foot kicking slightly, it is a perfect display of boredom; the person only needed something that will keep him or her warm and then play with without necessarily drawing attention to the hands or the upper part of the body as a whole (Patel 2012).

Practical Illustrations

Case Study I: Ms UH grew up in a conventional family that passionately believed in orthodox ways of doing things; for once, they never cherished modernism and all the changes that it brings. Even their religious beliefs are tilted towards the olden ways. UH was also brought up with this sentiment and would not change from it any time soon. One day, she was in her dormitory with other girls when she decided to sit in a loose manner since it was a girls' affair. She was not aware that one of her roommates would be hosting a male visitor that afternoon. Suddenly, the guy came in without even bothering to knock at the door. It was a clear lack of courtesy which she would react to but before doing that, she quickly held her knees together and changed direction. She was ashamed of her present state when the boy came in.

Case Study II: Student Q is a very nervous type, especially when you tell him to come and face a crowd; he melts. However, the structure of an average university system requires him to do presentations before his mates and dons across disciplines. Before the start of their seminars, a lecturer was in their class to teach them how best to do it and many of the errors that people make while presenting the outcome of a research. Q is guilty of many of the shortcomings listed by the lecturer. He began to feel insecure, thinking that those things 'were his nature' and there is no way he can evade them while presenting. Unconsciously, he gradually slouched on the chair he was seated and also closed up his legs as if someone wanted to shoot an arrow at his genital. This means he was psychologically stressed.

Case Study III: A suspect was nabbed in connection with an incessant robbery that had been taken place at a mall. Despite beefing up security at the mall, the 'invisible' robbers still find ways to cart away with valuables whenever they showed up. This suspect nabbed by policemen was a security agent with the mall before he was suspected to be a spy in the firm. Since his conspiracy to defraud his employers of their valuables was glaring, it became almost impossible for him to deny. When being interrogated, he was free at the beginning of the session, thinking they had no evidence that could convict him. But at some point, when one of the interrogators played an audio-visual record of some of his accomplices to him, he suddenly held his legs together and practically shivered. His countenance changed and his feet pointed at the door. He wanted to leave the location due to the negative feelings he was having there.

22.9. Sitting with Legs Spread Apart

Generic Interpretations of the Concept

This is the polar opposite of the legs being held together discussed in the preceding segment. Ideally, females are not expected to display this gesture, at least, not in an obvious manner. This suggests that spreading apart of the legs while seated is a cue that is mostly noticeable among and practised by men. As the mood of a person changes, their non-verbal displays also change. This is why there is congruence in people who are being truthful; you do not have difficulty in understanding people who do not manipulate their non-verbal displays.

If all of a sudden, someone changes their sitting posture from legs being held together with one that is spread out, it is an indication that the person has gained some sort of confidence. When you think things are working in your favour, you tend to display open body language. This means you have nothing to hide or fear. Someone who spreads the legs apart is invariably exposing their genitals which can be attacked. So this may be a way of daring those around them or communicating the message that there is nothing to fear. I have seen this in an interview setting; when interviewees think they are doing better or the questioning session is in line with their preparation, they will spread the legs apart in a courteous manner to show that they have everything within their ambit.

In the same vein, this non-verbal gesture implies greater comfort. Those who are comfortable or relaxed will spread out their body. If it were in an informal setting, the person may even place the legs on a stool or table. People spread out on couches when at home to rest and show that there is nothing to panic about, unlike in the office when they would be under pressure to get some tasks sorted out within a short period of time.

When the legs are spread out, we ordinarily take up more space. This territorial display is evidence of show of superiority. When someone decides to take up more space, this is a subtle way of stating that the space allocated to them can no longer contain them as such, they need more. In the process of taking more space, they can invade another man's territory and this may be taken as an affront on the person concerned. The farther apart the legs are, the more territory is being claimed.

Scientific Explanations

Westside Toastmasters (2019) begins the explanation of this gesture by noting that it is a predominantly male gesture and then goes further to describe it as a 'resolutely stable immovable posture.' In other words, this is a power stance. Spreading the legs while seated gives you a stable stance, making it difficult for anyone to displace you. This metaphorically tells you that the person is maintaining their ground and that is why it is a favoured gesture for those who wish to establish their dominance. 'It is used as a dominance signal by men because it highlights the genitals, giving them a virile look,' states the platform. Spreading the legs apart gives men the opportunity to prove their masculinity which is conventionally attached to power pose in most parts of the world. The website concludes by advising that 'if you're feeling defeated and want to change your mood, adopt the legs apart stance, with your head held high'. This can be complemented by resting the arms on the armrests. It has been observed that a change in non-verbal appearance is capable of effecting change in mood.

Similarly, Straker (2019) expresses the same view with Westside Toastmasters by submitting that 'a wider stance makes the body wider and hence appear bigger and is a signal of power and dominance. This also takes up more territory and shows domination.' When you feel you are powerful in a given situation, this means you are comfortable being there. You tend to lord yourself over every other person at the given place and display your superiority over them. If this is done between men alone, it may be a show of power through the genitals.

Practical Illustrations

Case Study I: Before now, Student N has been the unrivalled best in his class. However, a new student who is unarguably talented and very intelligent has been enrolled in his class and he seemed uncomfortable that he was going to be displaced from his comfort zone, or at least, he would have to work harder in order to retain his status as the most intelligent student of the class. To aggravate issues, a seat to the left of Student N was allocated to the new student. This means they would see every of each other's activity. During discussions, you would always hear the voice of the two students, trying to outwit each other. Any time N appeared as the obvious winner, he would sit by spreading out his knees so as to invade the territory of the new student as a way of proving that he is superior to his rival. Apart from the psychological feeling this attitude births, it also serves as a discomfort for the other student.

Case Study II: MJ is a fresh graduate from one of the leading universities trying to secure an appointment with a leading firm. Before the interview, he had read many frightening things about the company online; most interviewees' reviews on them was not encouraging and could destabilise even the bravest person. Instead of being depressed, MJ decided to read wider and assured himself that if the company was to go for a single person, he would be the one. On the day of the interview, he did not know how he became nervous but he tried to suppress it. When he was eventually invited in, the fear tended to increase. However, few minutes into the session, he was able to masterfully answer almost all their questions and even the panellists were forced to drop their stern look and relate with in a friendly manner. This further bolstered MJ's confidence and he then rested his back on the chair and spread out his legs, feeling comfortable.

Case Study III: A criminal suspect was arrested for the third time in a month and it was decided that he should be scrutinised so as to make him confess in order to be charged to court with those confessional statements for easy conviction. Hence, the best hands in the agency were brought in to handle the case. However, it seemed the suspect was not perturbed by this arrangement. When they started the interview, he spread out his knees and looked at the interrogators in the face. This immediately sent the message that he was confident and it would take a great deal of professionalism to get things corrected.

22.10. Interlocking of Ankles

Generic Interpretations of the Concept

Again, the fact that most people do not pay attention to the lower part of the body while interpreting non-verbal gestures has made it a safe haven for people to express themselves freely without being caught. People interlock their ankles every now and then but it is mostly done in formal gatherings. Before giving this gesture possible meanings, it is crucial to note that this might be a favoured gesture of some people; the feel comfortable doing it. Also, when the ankles are interlocked, it makes the body smaller, thereby giving a passer-by the opportunity to walk freely without stepping on us.

However, if the ankles are suddenly interlocked without relating to the two instances explained above, this means there are issues and you must not allow it go unquestioned. Due to my expertise, I have always paid attention to this gesture in public gatherings. To understand what actually births this behaviour, consider the topic that is being discussed at the moment and the person's earlier contributions.

During controversial or argumentative discussions, people are bound to take sides. When this happens and a side thinks they are being defeated, they may begin to feel negative by interlocking of the ankles. Also, if a point that does not reflect the world view of a person is adopted in a meeting, they may display this gesture. This means they have some reservations about the concept but are restraining themselves from speaking out. When the ankles are crossed, it forms a 'keep off' signal. Hence, they are keeping shut on what you have just said. The reason they are keeping to themselves is best known to them. To some, it might due to the fear of being condemned by others. For instance, a junior colleague is more likely to restrain themselves when they do not feel well about the point made by a senior colleague, especially if the latter is known for being intolerant. To some, it may be birthed by nervousness of speaking in an organised setting.

In the same vein, this gesture may also imply psychological discomfort or hesitation; the person is careful and wants to critically think about a concept before voicing out on it. Generally, people do not cross their ankles when feeling good.

Scientific Explanations

Alyssa Jung (2019) says that when someone crosses their ankle while seated, it is referred to as 'ankle lock'. She alludes different negative meanings to this gesture. It may be used to signal uncertainty. When a person is confused on which way to go, they may demonstrate this gesture; it is impossible to walk with the ankles crossed. Symbolically, it means the person does not want to take any further action until they are certain of what their eventual decision holds for them. It also means that the person is holding back; there are loads of unexpressed thoughts on their mind. And also, they may actually be nervous—of moving forward or continuing in a discourse. If ladies do want to appeal to men, the legs are better crossed at the knees.

Straker (2019) also states that this a representation of tension. This may be accompanied with clenched hands while the person leans forward as if they are slouching when the negative feeling increases. According to the body language expert, this is used to signal self-restraint. If the person was relaxed, they would have leant back, displaying an open stance.

Practical Illustrations

Case Study I: In a board meeting comprising of workers of different cadres which was headed by the CEO of the firm, they were discussing different ways in which the company can be innovative and take over the reins of power in the industry. Ideas were flying from every side of the room and a lot of them have reservations about the submissions of one another. Particularly, one of the senior officers in the establishment made a point that one of his subordinates did not agree with, drawing from what he had read and even experienced while interning at a sister company as a student. However, he knew that the senior colleague would shut him down for being inexperienced. More so, he would see it as an affront on his status and become reactionary after the meeting; the senior colleague was reputed for being self-centred and intolerant. In order to repress the urge to talk, the junior employee crossed his ankles and looked away from the person concerned. He didn't want to talk and every non-verbal behaviour depicted this—being evasive and symbolic crossing of the ankles.

Case Study II: Mr EX was teaching in one of the senior classes when a student called his attention to what he said, noting that it was controversial and to a large extent, untrue. Mr EX does not buy the idea of students correcting him even though he is not all that intellectually sound. The student had the backing of many of his colleagues, meaning that he could not say anything derogatory about the student without possibly facing the music. So he decided to overlook it and yielded to the demand of the students. However, he never gave the student any attention again even when he needed clarifications on some issues. This was obvious to many of his classmates. One day, he made another academic blunder and one of the students, GV, noticed it but having ruminated on what could possibly become his lot, he crossed his ankles and kept to himself. That is, he resisted the urge to speak up so as not to invoke the anger of his temperamental teacher.

Case Study III: Mr and Mrs HB were discussing on the need to change their apartment. The husband said he was fed up with that area and needed to move to another area. However, the wife thought since the place was peaceful and close to their workplace, they should keep living there but the husband would not buy into that idea. He said he did not want being too comfortable at a place and that they should change location so as to better expose their children. Mrs HB was not pleased with this idea but knew the personality of her husband; he might fail to renew the rent if she had insisted. She crossed her ankles as the husband spoke on endlessly. This means she would rather keep shut than raising a controversial point against the husband.

Case Study IV: A man was alleged of smuggling but he denied it vehemently. He even went as far as shouting at the officers. However, his goods were impounded while he was taken to the interview room to be drilled; they thought it was a stain on their integrity to keep him out while he kept on with his theatrics. On getting inside, he became unbelievably calm and crossed his legs at the ankles. When he was being asked questions, he would just look at the officers and wouldn't utter a statement. This further irritated the law enforcement agents who were looking for an amicable way to settle the issue.

22.11. Interlocked Ankles around Chair Legs

Generic Interpretations of the Concept

This is a more pronounced form of the interlocking of ankles discussed in the preceding segment. This is when a person interlocks their ankles and move them close to the leg of the chair they are seated on. This is the routine behaviour of some people. To such individuals, it would be difficult to determine the emotional state by looking at the pattern or the way in which the legs are structured. This gesture becomes a reliable means of understanding a person's emotions when it is done suddenly during discussion. This means something has propelled this behaviour and you must try to identify what has changed a person's emotional feelings.

During interviews, when the ankles are suddenly interlocked around the leg of a chair when a question is asked, it means the question has most certainly unsettled the person. This is a feeling of insecurity which I have noticed among interviewees when asked seemingly difficult question. This is a freeze response, keeping the legs in a 'safe' haven. While growing up as children, we run to the back of a chair or even the legs of our parents when confronted with something frightening. Hence, this non-verbal action is performing the same role that the chair and our parents did while growing up. When faced with uphill task, instead of running away in that context, we tend to hide our legs near a chair.

Furthermore, you may also observe this while discussing a sensitive issue. People are easily offended when you do not express their world views while discussing a delicate issue. Instead of shouting you down, they may interlock their ankles around the leg of a chair. This is an expression of concern; they are moved about what is being discussed but restraining themselves from making their point of view public.

Those who are afraid of embarking on a task may also display this cue as if the legs are chained down. When you notice any of the above, it is a good and potent indicator that something is wrong with the person. If you ignore this red light, you may end up being trapped in the webs of regret.

When the ankles are interlocked around the leg of a chair, the entire body becomes tensed, communicating the discomfort that the person is going through.

Instead of being enthusiastic, you rather see someone who is not motivated and uninspiring.

Scientific Explanations

Philip (2013) also refers to this gesture as scissor cross. He laments that this gesture is, most times, out of sight because desk or table can block you from accessing the lower part of a person's legs. He notes that this gesture signals that negative thought is present. According to the body language expert, interlocking the ankles behind the legs of a chair is a 'restraining-freeze-behaviour.' He observes, 'When the legs are wrapped around the chair they can't move, hence they are locked, and are also there precisely so they don't move, and are hence frozen.' Women, while wearing skirts, tend to use this behaviour more than men. Since it does not connote positive thing, it should be avoided. However, this is generally an unnatural position in men; your brain should switch to action any time you observe this in men.

Describing the message that this gesture conveys, Philip states, 'The ankle cross indicates that the person is holding a negative emotion, uncertainty, fear, feels discomfort or threatened, stress, anxiousness, insecurity or timidity. The ankle or scissor cross also shows reservation and self-restraint, due to withholding of a thought or emotion.' The feet express the exact feelings of a person. Pulling the ankles under the chair helps in amplifying or exaggerating the negative message.

Straker (2019) states, 'An ankle cross with legs tucked under the chair can indicate concealed anxiety. The concern may be more obvious if the person is leaning forward.' It is concealed because it is pushed under the chair instead of leaving the legs in the open for people to access them. Those who are conscious of their body language gestures will try their best to cover up their anxieties. Leaning forward means the person feels like leaving but are constrained by conditions.

Practical Illustrations

Case Study I: Mr DC went for an interview as an assistant executive position. Coming with a lot of experience, he was afraid that his experiences could not get him the job, so he should embellish his curriculum vitae in order to look more appealing and acceptable. So he decided to ask some fictitious items. Although the panellists did not dwell so much on his CV, its uniqueness and how he was not able to demonstrate this same level of excellence called the attention of the panel to it. So one of the interviewers decided to know what brought about the incongruence; was he a paper person without being outspoken or just overtaken by the fear of the interview. Immediately the interviewer asked a question pertaining to his fictitious issues, he became further tensed and his ankles could be seen interlocked around the leg of the chair as if it was a rope binding his legs from shivering.

Case Study II: Student L is fond of not doing his homework. Even though the school authorities have reported this case to the parents, they seemed to be unconcerned about it and this has been telling on the academic performance of the child; he is now lagging behind. Probably the root of the matter is because his parents are absentee parents. Mr IJ is not ready to go with that lame excuse he believes that there are many things that can be done to make the child stand out despite their busyness. One day, he gave the class homework, expecting them to solve the exercises on their own and report back to him on any issue encountered during the process. All the students did it except L. This angered the teacher, thinking he was trying to dare him. After marking through the scripts, Mr IJ walked majestically to the class and spoken sternly about 'those' who did not do the homework. Since L knew he was a victim, he began to feel nervous, thereby interlocking his ankles and shifting them into the chair.

Case Study III: A drug trafficker was arrested while trying to come in with the harmful substances. Since he was caught red-handed, he knew it would be difficult to defend himself. In fact, the expressions on the faces of the officers were enough message for him. Although he was tense, he looked for a way to appear physically fit. When ushered into the interview room, he decided not to talk or at best, censor all that he would say. However, many of the questions were unexpected which further unsettled him. He interlocked his ankles on the legs of the chair he was seated on. This he was psychologically disturbed.

22.12. Leaning Back with Knee Clasping

Generic Interpretations of the Concept

The sudden grabbing of the knee by people is a result of negative stimulus that has risen to its crescendo. When emotions rise to a stage, there is no way such can be repressed again. When such emotions are expressed in a subtle manner, you may overlook it, thinking they do not matter. Some people are taking cognisance of the fact that if they should hold the legs together or cross the ankles, the attention of people might be quickly drawn to that. So they think holding the knee is a good idea that takes semblance with the figure four gesture which is known as a show of confidence. However, what betrays their intentions is how the knee is clasped; it is held tightly with the hands as if preventing it from cutting off from other parts of the body. The rigidity is evidence that something is amiss. Also, the person leans back in a rigid manner which depicts the action as being forceful rather than being a display of comfort; a comfortable, confident person will lean back and make appropriate use of the backrest without necessarily producing a rigid force to get that done. Hence, the main issue with this non-verbal cue is anchored on the rigidity of its display.

This is usually a demonstration of stress; when exposed to an unfavourable condition for long, it leads to stress that is capable of destabilising the entire body system. High level of stress can make the legs to start shivering but pressing it down by clasping it at the joint (knees) can help in stabilising the condition.

A firm knee clasp usually signals self-restraint. Due to nervousness and fear of the unknown, people may side to keep to themselves in some given instances. Tight holding of the knees is symbolical; it is like tightening the legs so that they do not move. In the same vein, this may be interpreted as keeping words back. This subtle display of nervousness is a common non-verbal behaviour among job applicants during interviews.

Also, the palms directly touching the knees produces a tactile feeling. This may be a smart display by a person going through stress as a means of calming themselves. The hands placed on the knees for a while will produce a soothing effect which will gradually return the person to their normal state of mind.

Scientific Explanations

Study Body Language (2016) describes this gesture as a show of self-restraint. It compares it with the lip-biting cue when a person bites their lips so that a word does not slip off their mouth again. In the same vein, this may be a way of containing anger, fear, frustration and other negative emotions. Apart from clasping of the knees, men may also interlock their ankles as they display this gesture while 'females will usually close both legs and turn them to the side while their hands rest on their knees.' Although with noticeable differences in both genders, the meaning does not change while trying to give an overall interpretation.

Clasping of the hands on the knees is actually a means of reinforcing the body guard; you do not want to leave anything at loose as you restrain yourself from the demonstration of fear, anger or frustration. Metaphorically, the hand is serving as a clamp to the knee. When you see a person display this gesture, it would be difficult to get them to open up. Apart from interview setting, this is also very common 'to observe in subways where strangers sit in front of each other' (SBL 2016). Since strangers think it is absurd or odd to open up to each other on some certain issues, they keep to themselves and restrain the urge to discuss some peculiar issues.

On his own part, Straker (2019) observes that the knees are clasped because they are vulnerable to attack; a hard knock on the knee can unimaginably destabilise a person. In the case of imaginary or real attack while seated, we will quickly guard it off with the hands. Thus, this is a defensive act when someone is feeling anxious. Also, when women do it in the presence of a man, it means they are not ready to mingle with the man. Hence, the man is not worth having their attention.

Practical Illustrations

Case Study I: Some high school students were given some exercises to solve by their mathematics teacher. The tasks were challenging but the atmosphere of group discussion, not giving up and quest for intellectualism created by the teacher made it a thrilling one for the students; they were not discouraged from trying. After they were done, each of them would be called out to explain the techniques used and issues encountered while working on the tasks. They were not informed about the issue of presentation until they were done with the exercise. When Student P heard this, he became destabilised; he cheated by copying what his neighbour did. He even stopped at some point and never bothered to call the attention of the teacher to it. The enthusiasm among the other students was evident, and everyone knew he was prepared to embarrass himself. As the students filed out one after the other to work the exercise for their mates to see, Student P clasped his knees and leant back rigidly as if instructed not to cheer up. This was a show of nervousness as he gripped in negative thoughts.

Case Study II: A young lady attended an interview for the position of graduate intern. She thought it was something she would get with much ease only for her to be subjected to rigorous drilling. Since the company had the culture of retaining most of their interns, they pay much attention to the quality of graduate trainees they bring on board. She performed well at the start of the interview but as someone who could not cope with stress, she lost balance when the interviewers decided to throw multiple questions at her at a time. When she was about to break down, she clasped her knee and leant back rigidly, reducing the pace with which she talked and concentrated more on keeping herself composed rather than attending to the questions. This meant she was trying to quench the negative emotions through this non-verbal behaviour.

Case Study III: Two people that were involved in a marriage of convenience were arrested. The man looked undisturbed and was trying to play the role of a husband indeed, but it seemed that the woman did not trust his ability, so she became restless and wanted to be in the forefront of everything. This made the man angrily withdraw himself by being passive. When the pressure of defending herself dawned on her, she became really tense. At some point, she had to lean back on the man with her knees clasped. The indifferent reaction of the man at that point also confirmed they never had any emotional attachment towards each other. That is, everything happening there was merely theatric.

22.13. Leaning Forward with Clasped Knees

Generic Interpretations of the Concept

This is a ready position. Unlike the knee clasping while the body leans back that is used to portray rigidity and restraint, in this gesture where the hands are placed on the knees and the body leans forward, it is used to signal preparedness. Usually, the legs are structured in a starter position—a leg is placed forward while the other follows suit; both legs would not be placed on the same level. After all, while walking, we lift the legs one after the other. This is also done when displaying this gesture.

Usually, what this communicates is readiness to leave the place. While discussing with a person and you see them display this gesture, it is a signal that they are not mentally and psychologically with you again; their mind has been cut off from what you are telling them. This is a way of telling you to release them so that they can be at the place where their heart desires. Their face will also communicate this impatience as they will be looking around, expecting you to say the last word so that they can rise at once and leave the venue. If they are the one talking, you will notice an obvious incongruence in what they are telling you. All these are pointers to the fact that the discussion should come to an end.

That being said, it would be improper for you to do this in a formal meeting when you are not the most superior. It is considered as an affront and abuse of office of the person coordinating the process. People who pay attention to non-verbal cues may take it up against you, and that might be your last meeting with the person. Without mincing words, it is insulting to signal your readiness to leave when you are in the presence of your boss; this tells him that you feel what he is saying is worthless and not worth listening to. Courtesy demands that you listen attentively to what a superior is saying, whether you are content with it or not. You may now raise your objections afterward, and if there is a real reason to leave, this should be formally communicated instead of hastening them up with your body.

Scientific Explanations

SBL (2016) observes that leaning is the direct way to indicate interest or lack of it in a discourse. Depending on how it is done, this body gesture can either communicate positive or negative messages. While talking, if a person lean towards you and listens with rapt attention, with proper eye contact, this is an indication that they are interested in what you are saying. On the other hand, if the person leans forward, clasping their hands on their knees and rather focused on the exit with a disturbed facial expression, it means what you are saying is not as important to them as taking their leave. The website emphasises the need to pay attention to where the feet point at when this gesture is displayed. With this, you can determine if someone has interest in what you are saying or you better obey their opinion to leave.

Practical Illustrations

Case Study I: The parents of Student J had warned him not to tarry in school on Monday because they were billed to go out together and that would be impossible if he whiled away the time playing with friends after school. Since where they wanted to go was a place he had always pestered his parents to take him to, he was taking cognisance of their instruction. Unfortunately, it was a teacher who did not have respect for time that came to their class last that day. After closing period, he pleaded with the students to spare him some minutes to finish up with his explanations. Since everyone else agreed, he would sound odd to raise objections but his mind was already disconnected from the class, waiting impatiently for the teacher to move out of the class. Student J placed his hands on his knees and leant forward, looking worried until the class came to an end when he rushed out without waiting for any of his friends.

Case Study II: Mr AG came to his elder brother to solicit for money. After telling him what he came for, explaining what he wanted to use the money for, knowing fully well that his brother is mean and detailed-oriented, he waited patiently for his brother's reply. A slow speaker, the brother started off by beating about the bush, telling him stories that had little to do with his request, but since he needed his help, Mr AG pretended as if he was listening to him. At some point, his elder brother categorically said that he could not afford to give him the money, and then, he wanted to highlight reasons why that would not be possible. However, since AG heard that his needs would not be met, he clasped his hands on his knees and leant forward, waiting for his brother to finish talking so that he could leave his house. When the brother observed this, he had to excuse him. That is, there was no need further keeping him there when he would not be given anything.

Case Study III: In a board meeting comprising of managers from different branches, the CEO was addressing them on the imminent changes about to happen within the firm; many of them would be transferred while some would be fired and others promoted so as to reorganise the whole organisational structure. The first thing the CEO did was to announce the transfers—people being moved from a branch to the other. Dr LK was deployed from one of the biggest branches to one that was just coming up in a local area. This means he had to work harder and leave the bogus allowances he enjoyed for the latter. By the moment he heard the announcement, he became unstable and wanted to leave for a solitary place in order to reflect on his life. He hardly contributed to what was said any more and only placed his hands on his knees, leaning forward with his feet pointing at the door. This means he yearned to leave the venue because he felt useless there.

Case Study IV: Prostitute HT thought she could deceive Man KT into believing that she was a responsible fellow; the man informed her he wanted to settle down with her when he was yet to know she was the promiscuous type. However, he decided to carry out a background check on her, and the reviews were really bad. So he decided to play along on for a while. While on a date, she started counting all that she needed, and Man KT told her point blank he had no money for such. This really made her uncomfortable as she leant forward with her knees clasped. The statement changed her countenance.

22.14. Leg Crossing as Hindrance in Seated Position

Generic Interpretations of the Concept

When the legs are crossed in such a way that is obviously serves as a barrier to the person and others around them, this is an indication that something is amiss. Here, a leg is placed on the other with the knee of the upper leg pointing so high that it almost blocking the face of the person. Note that to display this gesture, the lower limb (usually the left) is placed on the knee of the other leg. This incongruence symbolically represents what goes on in the mind of the person. It is an indication that issues have set in. You may be tricked to believe that this is a sign of relaxation, but it is not, whether at home or workplace; it is a crystal red flag that must be heeded.

This is an accurate reflection of people's feeling and that is why it is regarded as emotional body language. In the same vein, it appears in real time; you notice it immediately a topic the person is not comfortable with is raised. This is a subconscious action. If the person observes that they are already giving themselves out, they may plan dropping the leg immediately but the message of discomfort has been passed already. Even the person displaying this cue is not feeling comfortable. This further reinforces the message of negativity being passed through this behaviour.

Also, you will observe this cue when a person has reservation concerning what you have just said. They may not want to challenge you, so crossing the leg is a subtle form of self-restraint.

It is pertinent to add that this gesture, when done in the presence of elders in some cultures of the world, is considered as a sign of rudeness; subordinates or junior colleagues are not expected to cross their legs while being addressed by a superior. In fact, some people frown at this to the extent that it might lead to the axing of such junior worker. While out of your home community, you need to pay attention to the non-verbal behaviours you show.

Scientific Explanations

Parvez (2015) discusses the concept of leg crossing in details. He states that this is a subconscious attempt for a person to be defensive. This might look like a silly way of protecting the genitals but the unconscious mind works in a way that we cannot fathom. 'When a person feels extremely defensive, he might cross his legs in addition to crossing the arms thereby achieving a complete sense of protection since all his ventral delicate organs are covered,' Parvez submits. When there are issues, our first point of concern is how to be secure with what is threatening our peace and that is why the subconscious mind swings into action by defending the most threatened part of the body.

This is a closed body gesture that shows that someone might not really be into a discussion as expected. Parvez (2015) explains further, 'During a conversation, it can indicate a "withdrawn" attitude and it has been observed that people who cross their legs in the seated position tend to talk in shorter sentences and reject more proposals and are more inattentive to what's going on compared to those who sit in a more "open" position.' since barrier has been created, the person does not want to welcome anything coming from the other side; it means they are closed off to any form of discussion.

In the same vein, Narins (2017) states that this gesture is a show of insecurity. Crossing the legs makes the body smaller, making you feel lesser than you are. This means you see the other person as threatening. Confident people will rather spread out instead of shrinking in when faced with issues. In a way, this might be a subconscious way of pleading guilty. Note that there are some exceptions to this gesture; a person feeling cold may also display this gesture as a way of making the body smaller and feeling warm.

Practical Illustrations

Case Study I: Guy RE and Lady TF went out on a date and they were really enjoying their time out when an issue came up which they felt is important for them to discuss if they were really serious about marrying each other. Guy RE led the discussion and was not apologetic in pouring out his mind on some issues he had noticed in the lady that could puncture their marital bliss. One thing Lady TF was not used to is being told the truth to her face; she could not bear what the guy was saying and at some point, crossed her legs to form a barrier.

Not deterred, Guy RE continued with his observations and at some point, the lady frowned and wanted to reply in the same manner before the guy cautioned himself. He had to apologise and appeal to her not to take his words against him, knowing that the appeal did not invalidate his observations.

Case Study II: Mrs IY is becoming worried about the recent lifestyle of her husband; he has changed for no obvious reason—he no longer returns from work on time, blaming it on his promotion and their bedroom has become a mere sleeping room, attributing that to tiredness during the day. Also, their communication is now suffering. All these issues were eating deep into the woman's heart and she has been keeping all to herself, thinking it is inappropriate to wash her dirty linens outside. But the husband has always found a subtle way to reject all entreaties to talk. However, she decides to hold a hard conversation with him on a night. She first showers encomiums on him, noting that she knows how tiring it can be to justify a new position and even surpass the expectations of one's employers in the highly competitive market. Mr IY smiles at these commendations, thinking the wife has been boxed to a corner and could hide under that pretext to continue with his waywardness. Immediately the woman raised the issue in their home, her husband crossed his legs, forming a barrier in his sitting position, accompanied it with a stern look, feigning tiredness. He wasn't ready for such talks as they hit hard on his behaviours.

Case Study III: An officer was strolling through the street when a man quickly walked up to him. The officer liked the friendly nature of the man and, as such, developed relationship with him. The officer did not know that he was an ardent criminal who only wanted to learn some tricks from him so as to keep having a field day. One day, they both hanged out and they were talking about general issues. The criminal was really free at first but when the officer began to speak on crime and the kind of punishments that should be meted to criminals, he quickly crossed his legs as if he was blocking those words from reaching him. And this is what he was metaphorically doing in the other realm of life.

22.15. Draping of Legs

Generic Interpretations of the Concept

Without mincing words, this is a clear show of class, superiority and dominance. Those who want to stand out and want their authority pronounced are always in the habit of draping their legs over tables, desk, stool, other objects within sight and even when at the extreme, on other people. Women do not necessarily like this behaviour but there is nothing they can do when it is displayed by someone who is superior to them. Note that this behaviour can be displayed both in a formal and informal setting and the meaning does not change. At home, it means the person is relaxed and feeling comfortable. However, parents are likely to scold their children who do this when being addressed; it shows they are being rude.

From the foregoing, it is clear that this gesture should not be displayed in the presence of a superior. This is a universal body language rule; you sprout out and look commanding when you drape your legs on an object. Also, subordinates are expected to stand when being addressed by their boss or even while talking to them. If peradventure your boss walks up to you to make a confirmation on something and you sit, draping your legs on your desk without considering to drop them on sighting them, this a challenge of their superiority and even the humblest of all bosses will not take that from you.

Hence, it is a regular attribute of some bosses. When subordinates see this, they tend to respect the person the more. It is an open, fearless posture that displays every vulnerable part of the body. This is an indication that the boss thinks there is no one that can harm them. Moving closer to them is like daring their authority.

Also, this posture is used to claim territory. If someone does not want another person to move very close, they are likely to use this gesture. Executives using expansive rooms as offices are fond of this gesture.

In the same vein, people do this as a sign of tiredness. Most probably, they are fagged out already from the day's work and relaxing just before they go home or start another work. It is a common behaviour of bosses during break. The aim is to stretch out the legs and relax well. The entire body feels relieved when displaying this gesture. Symbols of authorities prefer this non-verbal cue to massaging the body or other forms that make them look smaller than their stature.

Scientific Explanations

Study Body Language (2016) describes this gesture as 'feeling at home' and from all angles, that is exactly what it is. In an informal relaxed state, there are different leg positions that are used for people to communicate how comfortable they are. Since it is largely informal or one (the person displaying it) is a symbol of authority without being accountable to any other person in the given context, you are allowed to sit in the way you think is most convenient for you. SBL observes, 'Most informal positions have the tendency to be spread out and take strange forms.' Hence, the reason people drape their legs over objects. It is even reported that in ancient Africa, their royal heads could drape their legs on their servants as a show of class and royalty.

The ultimate feel good gesture is when the feet are placed on a table or other similar objects. There is arguably no more relaxed form than spreading the legs up and then put the hands behind your head—this is the extreme non-verbal form of enjoying life. That is why you hardly see this gesture among those still in the lower cadre of life; it is meant for people who have arrived and whose authority cannot be challenged if displayed at any given time or place (SBL 2016). To better project this behaviour, you have to sit on a chair that is lower than the object you want to drape your legs on or at the very least, at the same height.

Practical Illustrations

Case Study I: Mr S is the CEO of XCU Firms International. Within the short stay of the firm in the market, it has changed many things and added value to people. There is no doubt that Mr S is the secret behind these enviable successes and he does not want to relent in anyway. When it was obvious that he needed a break, the board of the company had to prevail on him to go on vacation lest he broke down. He heeded and was away for two weeks. When he returned, he was not pleased with the fact that many things were not put in their rightful positions; he got to work almost immediately. After working for eight unbroken hours, he decided to take a short break and then return for the second session. He took off his shoes and draped his legs on his table, pushing his chair a little bit backwards to relax his back. When his personal secretary was about to go home, she met him in this position and only stood afar off to address him. She saw tiredness written on him and the need for him to rest.

Case Study II: Mrs DC is a woman who wants everyone to bow at her feet; she can go to any length to prove her authority and make people do her bidding. While a lot of people have always celebrated her for this, some see it as an act of desperation and have been looking for a way to curb her but it seems nothing can make her turn a new leaf. One day, while at home with her kids, she draped her legs on the central table while seeing movies and sprout out on a couch. When one of her kids stood behind her to make an enquiry, she behaved as if she did not hear her until the poor girl moved forward, standing aloof that she responded to her. Even when her husband came in, she did not change position as she conversed with him, making the husband see her as someone not interested in what they were discussing. All these negative signals really affected the peace of her home as others could not bear with such behaviour for too long.

Case Study III: Mr YUT is not only a drug trafficker but also a drug addict. Before embarking on any journey, he would consume the hard drugs on a very high rate so as to wild and weird throughout the journey. He would also drive himself. Driving at a full speed, he was flagged down by some enforcement officers who wanted to conduct a routine check on his vehicle. When he stopped, instead of him to do the needful by cooperating with law enforcement agents, he removed his shoes and draped his legs on the steering wheel. The officers were first taken aback because they had never experienced such before. It was an affront on their status and profession and this pissed them off, making them to go cruel on him.

22.16. Rubbing of Legs

Generic Interpretations of the Concept

Any form of rubbing occurs when a person is stressed. When seated and feel uncomfortable in the leg area, we may subtly reach out to it and rub it—we rub the tops of the quadriceps when stressed. Running the palms on the lower limb has been proven as a potent way of dealing with stress. This is known as *leg cleanser* in some quarters; you do it as if you are washing the legs or performing ablution. This can be very unpronounced as the person places their palms beneath the knee joints and rubs back and forth. This why the sign is always missed by people. More so, it also occurs under a desk or table, preventing the person at the other end to see what is going on with their co-interlocutor. However, in cases where the stress is beyond what the person can repress, they will stylishly bow to rub the legs to the ankle area. Thus, when you see a co-interlocutor bowing with the arms moving back and forth, it is a red flag to pay attention to.

When under high stress, this gesture is a great pacifier. The tactile feeling generated by the palms connected with the hairy part of the leg or even smooth skin is capable of generating warmth to keep the body in shape. Overtime, it has been discovered that people mostly feel stressed at the legs when seated or while engaging in a demanding task in sitting position. The rubbing assures the legs that all is well; this self-assurance goes a long way to quench the feeling of fear or nervousness in the body. It is a metaphoric way of washing off all forms of negative feelings from the body. The leg is the downward exit of the body, when we take our bathe, water moves from the head to the toes. In the same vein, all forms of negative emotions can be pushed away from the body through the use of hands in the moments of discomfort.

Scientific Explanations

Smith (2015) describes the act of rubbing the legs as soothing action to the body. According to her, 'These soothing actions counter feelings of uneasiness or vulnerability.' Invariably, we rub the legs when we are not feeling all right. This is a way of providing the body with what it needs at that very moment so as to make us feel at peace. Smith gives an example of a student seated in the front row of a lecture hall and hope not to be called on. The feeling increases when you know that the lecturer is in the habit of calling students randomly to attempt an exercise. By rubbing the legs, you stroke the nerve endings which is capable of lowering heart rate and blood pressure. In moments of discomfort, your heart races while blood flow on the surface of the skin increases. All these can be dealt with by rubbing of the legs.

In the same vein, Silvia Del Corso (2017) testifies to the fact that we use the leg rubbing and other self-rubbing gestures to dissipate stress. However, he expertly notes that this is not use when we feel negative alone but even in the moments of positive stress.

Practical Illustrations

Case Study I: Mr UC is the group managing director of the firm where he works. He is reputed for being detailed oriented and focused in all that he does. Even when all his subordinates were out of office, he would stay back to verify and review the day's work. His position has been much of chief servant rather than being a chief executive. And fortunately, this has propelled him and the firm to enviable successes in numerous ways. On a Friday morning, he was going through a report of the week when he noticed some figures that could not be reconciled from the marketing unit. After checking through a few more time to be sure he was not the one at fault, he called for the supervisor of the unit immediately. After the friendly welcome, he gave the supervisor a copy of the document so that they could go through it together. Then, he was questioning the head of the department all along. At some point, the supervisor knew that what he thought was hidden from all men had been unearthed. He became highly stressed and his legs, almost shaking. As the GMD made his observations, he rubbed his legs back and forth as if he hit them on a stone. After getting his balance, he spoke well. However, the non-verbal gesture depicts a person looking for psychological calm.

Case Study II: Suspect D was being investigated on multiple crimes; there had been several reports traceable to him in times past that he could not be brought to book but when he was eventually nabbed, the law enforcement officers in charge of his case opened his book from the first suspicion made about him. This made the process tedious for both the officers and the suspect. Being a professional criminal, he was able to defend himself on some of the allegations but there were some that the officers had incriminating evidence against him which they began to present one after the other. It was at that point that he became stuck and could not manoeuvre his ways again. He began to feel weak and depressed, noting that he had come to the end of the road. He rubbed his legs from time to time that one of the investigators was forced to ask him if he was being bitten by insects. This feeling of weakness and depression was telling on him in form of stress.

Case Study III: One of the things that Ms, JG detests most is being called to speak in public, even though she is very fantastic in writing but she finds it difficult to articulate her points when it comes to public speaking. While she had always had her way at every other place, she met herself, it seemed that was not going to work in her new workplace; during meetings, all employees are called upon one after the other to make their submissions on the subject of discourse. On her first meeting when she saw this happening, she felt like running away from the venue but that is not psychologically possible. She was almost being overwhelmed by stress and as a way of stabilising herself before being called, she rubbed her legs from time to time. This means she wanted to 'wash away the stress'.

22.17. Scratching or Rubbing of the Knee

Generic Interpretations of the Concept

Just like the leg rubbing discussed above, we also rub the knee as a way of dissipating tension from the body. The knee, due to the joints present in it, contains more nerve endings than the lower limbs and, as such, is a good point to rub during the moments of stress. Rubbing the knee is also easier and subtler compared with the leg rubbing where you still have to bow a little bit for the hand to reach the lower part. People who are concerned and conscious about what other people feel about them are in the habit of rubbing the knee instead of the lower limb. Due to the subtlety involved in the performance of this gesture, it is most likely to be overlooked by observers when displayed.

Having said that, when you see people scratch or rub the area just above the knee, it is most likely that they are stressed. Consider their reaction in relation to other things that have been discussed during the course of your interaction with them. If the topic you are presently dealing with is a sensitive one, this is an indication that it is making them uncomfortable. Maybe, if you keep on with the topic, it would lead to a secret that they are keeping away from you. Employees who might have gossiped about you understand that when you talk about the person they gossiped together, he or she is liable to make reference to the issue, thereby putting themselves on the spot. In order to avoid such a baffling scenario, they will try as much as possible to change the focus of the discourse. If they lack power to do so, they will become stressed.

On the other hand, positive emotion may also cause people to rub the knee. We have all been at a stage when we are filled with suspense, expecting an exciting report or gift delivered to us; being overwhelmed by this feeling makes us positively uncomfortable or restless. That is when you will see people prancing about. If you are sitting, you will rub the knee to feel calm pending the delivery or arrival of your expectations. Unlike in the case of negative stress where there is general tension on the body, this is always accompanied with uncontrollable smiling and excitement; nothing hardly pisses the person off at that point.

The pacifying effect of this behaviour is felt when it is done repetitively; it assuages the feeling of tension or excitement as the case may be.

Scientific Explanations

Straker (2019) explains different ways in which the knees can be touched and the unique message each bears. If a woman rubs the knees, it 'may signal a desire that a nearby man does the same and is hence a sexual invitation or tease.' Mostly, this is seen in romantic contexts—at bars, parties, beaches, restaurants, among others. If this is done to the opposite sex when nothing is being discussed, it means the person is aroused and wants to connect with her targeted man.

During moments of anxiety, people rub the knees repetitively to be sure that they are safeguarded. In the moment of attack, a strong kick can destabilise the person. However, stroking it gives them the assurance that the vulnerable part of the body is secure (Straker 2019).

On the other hand, women may rub their knees as a means of communicating their disdain for a man. When you see them wearing skimpy dresses and appearing in attractive attires, you might be tempted to assume that they are attracted to you but that is a wrong assumption; most times, the nice attires are borne out of the need to align with social conventions rather than being an invitation to be picked up. Hence, when you see a woman rubbing their knees, be sure you see other gestures before taking it as a romantic invitation. With that, you will not fall into avoidable pits.

Practical Illustrations

Case Study I: Mr DZ is a married man but had to leave his children and wife in search of greener pasture in another country. For five years in the country, he tried processing his papers so that he could work legitimately and bring his family over but every attempt proved futile. He became depressed as he could not get high-paying jobs or move freely. More worrisome is the condition of his family he had earlier promised it would be a matter of months for them to reunite. After the fifth year, he decided to try for the tenth time and this time around, there seemed to be a positive report for him. His eyes shone brightly as he was informed at the agency's office that he would be handed his papers that day. As he sat, waiting for them to locate and do the final processing before handing the documents over to him, he was overwhelmed with positive excitement that he repeatedly rubbed his knee, feeling elated and laughing at every little joke.

Case Study II: Mr ET was invited into the school administrator's office due to numerous complaints received from parents. As the science teacher of the school, he is expected to liaise with other teachers and teach the subject in clear terms, using illustrations students can easily relate with and understand with little efforts but many of the students are complaining that since his arrival in the school, things have not been the same again; many of them who loved sciences as their best subject are fast losing interest in it and education in general. Knowing the long-term effects of this, the administrator summoned him immediately to question him on some specific issues. At that point, it was discovered that he uses examples meant for university students for high school pupils. The administrator knew it was time for him to show the teacher the way out. Seeing the expression on his boss's face, he began feeling stressed, praying earnestly to be released. He rubbed his knee repeatedly as he awaited the administrator's verdict. This means he was not feeling OK—he was disturbed by the thoughts of the unknown.

Case Study III: Mr MJ is a human smuggler but whenever he is stopped border control officials, he knows how to present a perfect lie that they were either his family members or new colleagues yet to be issued means of identification. However, it seems the officials have known him to parading different people for the same title. So the last time he tried to do that, they said he would be taken in for an interview. During the interview, he was able to manoeuvre his way again. Seeing that the officers were falling for his lies already, he rubbed his knees continuously in excitement. This was a non-verbal means of congratulating himself for the victory.

22.18. Scratching of the Ankles

Generic of Interpretations of the Concept

The level of stress we are witnessing per time will determine what we will do and how we behave. Even those who claim to be aware of the gestures they let out often default when it comes to unconscious body language signals let out in real time. They are uncontrollable and the gestures would have betrayed our feelings before it comes to our conscious awareness. One of such cues is scratching of the ankles. When the hand moves to the lower part of the body by bending, all eyes would be on the person, looking at what the person is about to do. Your action will give people the conclusion to make about you. If you pick up something from the ground, they may not necessarily think of anything concerning your action but if you scratch at the ankles, the joint, then there are arrays of meanings that can be attributed to that. Note that if this is done once, the place might actually be itching the person and thus, compelling them to scratch it.

However, repetitive scratching of the ankles means there are issues. This means the situation is tense for the person and cannot hide their uncomfortable feeling. One of the obvious functions it performs is to ventilate the skin; as you scratch, you open up the body for ventilation. It is as if there are particles that have probably blocked the ankles from feeling comfortable.

More importantly, scratching at the ankles helps in relieving stress. As you scratch, it soothes the body, giving you a feeling of satisfaction. This is why it done repeatedly for the body to be totally restored to its original setting. The level of the stress the person is passing through will dictate the degree of force applied to rubbing the ankles.

It is not uncommon to see this gesture in forensic interviews when difficult posers are thrown at the interviewee; they slightly lift up the feet and scratch at the ankles as if they were stepping on the answer. They may rub up the leg as they revert back to their normal posture. This tells you that there is something amiss; it is either they do not know the answer or are looking for way to fabricate something. Another common place where this happens is during large pot in poker competitions. You are most likely to observe ankle scratching in places with high-level of risk.

Scientific Explanations

Hoppe (2008) gives a detailed explanation of this body gesture. He observes that apart from the show of stress, it is also used to display interest in a sexual partner. People subtly seat in a figure four position and might pretend as if they want to remove their sock and through that process, touch the ankle. Slow rubbing or scratching of the ankle area while speaking with an opposite sex is a sign of sexual interest.

However, Straker (2019) states that the ankle area is mostly touched when we are stressed.

Practical Illustrations

Case Study I: A select law enforcement agents were investigating a woman for the death of her husband. The death occurred in a mysterious way that one would be made to believe that it was not orchestrated by anyone but came through supernatural means. However, a close view by experts revealed that the incident leading to his death was well planned. In the undercover investigation conducted, it was discovered that the wife had a role to play in. During her arrest, she was still claiming that she knew nothing about it. During the investigation, she was still playing the innocence card, wanting to appeal to emotion, but when drilled properly, she opened up. When a hard question which she must answer was thrown at her, instead of her to answer, she bent a little bit, stretched her hand to the ankles to scratch it. Then, she would raise her head to state one or two things and then, returned to the act of scratching, making her words to lose value. She was obviously stressed and there was no way she would detach herself from this feeling.

Case Study II: Mr KL was queried by his unit head on Friday after work. Meaning that he would be made to face the disciplinary council on Monday on resuming office. He was said to be lackadaisical in his duty and played a role by conniving with some other people to dupe the firm of its resources. Reflecting on all the allegations on the weekend, he knew they were true even though a part of him was not really ready to plead guilty. He had to think of the plausible explanations that would prove to the disciplinary committee, the reason he involved in some and how the situation of things made him to support the uncouth of actions of his colleagues. While thinking of this, he was gripped with fear, with the thought that his excuse might not convince the committee. He subconsciously scratched the ankles repeatedly as he ruminated on the way out of his ordeal. This means he was nursing negative feelings that he hoped to overcome.

Case Study III: Mrs WD withdrew some amount of money while coming home on Sunday because she had no cash on her to buy some petty items. She kept the money in her purse and dropped in on the dining, being an unrepentant careless person. Unknowingly, her daughter had stolen the money at midnight so that she could spend it at school with her mates. She later got to know this when she wanted to purchase an item and could not find the money again. Since no there was no visitor that came to their house the day before, she was certain the heinous act was perpetrated by her daughter. When she arrived from school, Mrs WD did not behave as if something was wrong; they joked together and everything still went as usual until later in the night when she called her to the living room and raised the issue. She wanted to deny but the expression on her mother's face frightened her. She scratched her ankle as she looked away, losing her voice before pleading guilty. This gesture gave her out.

22.19. Flexing of the Knees

Generic Interpretations of the Concept

The knee joints can be manipulated to function in different ways depending on one's feelings. Knee flexing has to do with bending of the knee forward in a rapid manner, causing the person to sink down in a noticeable manner. When this happens, it quickly registers into their subconscious and they try to readjust in the twinkle of an eye but this does not deprive their co-interlocutor of the message being passed across. So no matter how fast they are in readjusting themselves, the message still resonates. When this is done, it connotes something evil and negative; the person is depressed that something does not go their way.

That is why it is always assumed to be a juvenile behaviour that is akin to the starting of a temper tantrum. Teenagers do not have the spirit of tolerance; they react to issues as they affect them. This momentary reaction dictates how they relate to colleagues, parents and other people that come their way at that given time. The fact that it is common among young mind does not mean that it is not found among adults too. For instance, it is an act I have observed on adults overtime at car-rental counters when they are unable to find a vehicle of their choice. It is as their height is reduced because they are unable to find a car of their choice. This is noticeable in other endeavours too when people are met with disappointment. Since the person was standing erect, the knee shifts at the joint immediately they get to know that their expectations have been cut short. It is a metaphorical way of saying that something has been taken off them. The person recovers immediately because they do not want you to know how they feel concerning that particular thing. Apart from knee bending, their facial expression and general coldness of the body betray them too. Hence, all these should be taken cognisance of while reading a person's emotions.

However, I need add that the direction the knee points to when it bends determines what it is actually communicating. If it bends towards the exit, it means the person wants to leave because their expectations were not met but if it bends towards a co-interlocutor, this is an indication of interest, meaning the person is listening intently and will like to be fed more of what is being said.

Scientific Explanations

Straker (2019) observes that the knee is wired to function like the elbow in some ways. For instances, serving as subtle pointers in discourses. The direction the knee points communicates a huge message. However, if it does not flex, this pointing cannot be obvious. When it bends towards a thing or someone, this is an indication of desire. It is an unconscious action let out by the limbic brain to register our interest in a concept or person without our approval. When you desire something, you feel like moving very close to it and this is the function that the knee flexing does in communication. On the other way, instead of moving towards a thing, if the knee flexes in another direction, it is communicating its hatred for the thing it is moving away from.

Practical Illustrations

Case Study I: Guy DL is known for his fake lifestyle among friends; he comes from one of the poorest families in his locality but whenever he is among friends or at school, he wants to prove to them, what he is not just to gain an undeserved popularity or win the admiration of opposite sex. Many of his friends are aware of this ill living and that is why he does not have long-term friends so that they will not publicise his fake living to others. One day, he met with a girl, told her that he was the son of a CEO and his father was willing to let him come on board to handle one of the most important departments in his firm. The lady was obviously thrilled and was ready to mingle with one of the 'richest young minds' in town. In order not to disappoint her, the day they had a date, he went to the car-rental to hire a particular classy, luxurious ride, only for him to be disappointed, he went to another place and the story was the same. The third place was not different. On the fourth, while standing at the counter, his knee flexed awkwardly as he heard the same ugly experience. He frowned, conscious that he was becoming dejected, composed himself and moved out.

Case Study II: Woman A and Woman B were standing outside of their premises on a Saturday morning discussing some general issues of life which later led to a gossip about one of their neighbours who was not around. As the name of the neighbour was mentioned by Woman A, who reduced her voice volume and stretched out her mouth as if she wanted to kiss her counterpart so as to enable her whisper so that passers-by would not eavesdrop into their discussion, Woman B flexed her knee quickly in A's direction, turning her right ear slightly to her as if she does not want to evade a sound from what her co-interlocutor was about to say and listened intently. This was a show of interest.

Case Study III: Professor DM was scheduled to deliver a paper in an international conference and needed to read a book which was crucial to what he was about to do; the book was the main thrust of the conference and all he had seen online is mere summary whose authority could not be affirmed. He went to the library but could not locate it. Without much ado, he drove down to one of the best bookshops in the city and it was the same sad story. Looking dejected, he was told of another place and after some minutes of checks, he was informed that the book was not available. As he was about to turn out, his knee flexed forward, but he noticed this quickly and got himself back almost immediately—he wasn't ready to lose himself to dejection. He later got it through an academic colleague in a neighbouring city.

Case Study IV: Two law enforcement officers stopped an illegal immigrant on the road. She looked innocent and decent. This appearance deceived the first officer that she was a wrong suspect but the second officer insisted that the right thing must be done. While this argument persisted, the illegal immigrant's knee flexed to the first officer and when she was asked any question, he would be the one she would face. This was a demonstration of her likeness for him. However, the first officer became disappointed when it was eventually proven that she was an illegal immigrant. At that point, he could not apologise to his colleague.

22.20. Feet Dragging

Generic Interpretations of the Concept

We drag our feet at different points in time, depending on the message that we intend to communicate. I must also note that feet dragging is a universal behaviour that has different but similar meanings across the world. Also, it is an attitude that begins from our childhood. If you pay close attention to kids, you will see them drag their feet back and forth as they wait for someone or something. Once the mind of children is set on something, it cannot accommodate any other thing again. This is unlike adults that may leave their expectations to think of some other things. During the waiting process, boredom may set in for the kids. As a way of dealing with this, they will move their feet back and forth.

Once the feet are in motion, their thought will wander to this action, making them wield war against the boredom that would have made them inactive. This seems like the sea-saw on the playground to them. It is pertinent to note that the soothing effect of this behaviour is actually embedded in its repetitiveness; when down repeatedly, it calms the body and helps in passing idle time. In the same vein, adult too drag their feet back and forth while waiting for someone. It is an easy way out of boredom for them too, only that theirs is subtler than how kids display their own behaviour but this does not neutralise the message.

Further, dragging of feet is a way of dealing with anxiety. When people are anxious and do not want you to know, they may drag their feet, masking their real feelings. When people are overwhelmed by fear, you may notice them shivering, especially while standing still but once they begin to drag their feet, your attention is shifted away from the nervousness to the action of movement. I have observed this particular behaviour among shy, inexperienced ones on their first date; they do not know anything about the process, yet they do not want others to know about their ignorance.

In some parts of the world, when you see someone dragging their feet, it is an indication that they are unwilling to participate in an assignment; it is a clear show of interest.

Scientific Explanations

There are different expert interpretations given to this gesture that we would not be able to peruse in details due to space constraints. Radwan (2017) says that people's walking style reveals their personality. According to him, 'Some people walk slowly dragging their feet behind them as if they have no energy to move. The lack of energy is usually associated with sad feelings or depression but it could also reflect fear or uncertainty about what is lying ahead.' When you are burdened with negative feelings, this weigh you down; it is an emotional weight that is noticeable in everything you do.

If you see a once smart, cheerful fellow dragging their feet, it means they are trapped in one form of negativity or another which you must try to find out. In the same vein, fear of what lies ahead may make people display this gesture. If a presenter is mounting a podium, dragging his feet during the process, do not expect much from him; it is either they are afraid or have nothing fantastic to tell their audience. Repetitive feet dragging generates the motion needed to keep the body in shape and that is what they are trying to achieve with this behaviour.

Practical Illustrations

Case Study I: One of the busiest shopping malls in a city turns out to be one of the dangerous too; there are many criminal activities taking place there and it seems those committing the heinous act are overpowering the security agencies there. The crimes are perpetrated both within and outside of the mall; in car parks and other places. People who are forced to go there are always vigilant. Mrs DB had some valuables in her car and even official laptop when she got to the mall with her son. So instead of both of them entering the mall, she told him to wait so that he could keep a tab on the activities of people around the vehicle. She got the list of what her son would like to buy. While waiting for the mother, the son dragged his feet back and forth and looked towards the entrance of the mall from time to time. He was really bored for being kept waiting.

Case Study II: Ms AJ needed to get something from her neighbour but before she could arrive in her neighbour's place, she was told he had stepped out. Since she was in a dire need of the item, she decided to wait for him. Being a very popular person with admirable personality in the neighbourhood, he had about two to three people stopping him to discuss an issue or another with him, making him tarry more than he should. Ms AJ was becoming bored and losing interest in the movie being shown. It would definitely look absurd to sleep off at that point in time, so, she dragged her feet back and forth subtly, hoping that the man showed up any moment soon. Even though she was tired, this gesture would keep her from sleeping. However, anyone who sees her demonstrating this gesture would know that she is actually undergoing difficult times.

Case Study III: Child JX was sent on an errand by the mother but he does not want going to that route; he had offended some peers who have been bullying him since then. If he is to take another route, that means he would spend an additional thirty minutes on the road. However, he could not tell his parents that he was not going to run the errand because he does not want them to be aware of his escapades, lest they threw him into a boarding facility he detested so much.so, he could be seen dragging his feet irritatingly while heading for the door. The mother had to call him back to be sure if all was right with him which he answered in the affirmative even though every other part of his body denied that answer. So she was forced to probe further until he said the truth—he was not willing to go through that route.

Case Study IV: Criminal ED sealed a deal with a compromised clearing agent that he would help him clear his goods in the evening when most of his colleagues would have gone home. However, when Criminal ED came at the appointed time, he was busy as he was given an impromptu work by his supervisor. So ED decided to wait for him but the execution of the task was taking longer than usual. If the report for the day should be prepared without his clearance report being slotted in, it means their tricks might never work out again. When ED became excessively bored and worried, he started dragging his legs back and forth. This was to psychologically charge himself.

22.21. Ankle Twisting

Generic Interpretations of the Concept

This is a body language behaviour that is better performed when people are standing because the foot is slightly lifted up to display this cue. However, it is sometimes displayed while seated and in either case, it is always visible for observers to see. This is because when an ankle is twisted, the whole leg shakes visibly. When you see a co-interlocutor quiver their foot to the side at the ankle, it is time for you to pay attention to the cue and what the person says afterwards. With this, you can decode the direction the discussion is heading.

Usually, the ankle is twisted when one is engulfed in negative emotions. So you can know the direction to align your thoughts to when you observe the display of this gesture. One of the possible meanings is restlessness. The person does not want to stay at some point; they are feeling like moving about. Quivering the ankle which is the last joint in the body is a non-verbal way of stating 'I want to move away' or 'I feel like walking about'. The legs are the instrument of walking, and when one is kept by circumstances in a place, it becomes 'itchy', which is demonstrated by twisting it.

Further, it may signal agitation. If you want to confront someone or something for doing something that is unpleasing, you will need to move closer to the person. In a formal setting where it is rare for you to see such violent confrontations, observing a quivering ankle means the person is agitated and would have attacked you if it were in an informal context. Other non-verbal indicators may point to this fact to make it obvious; their voice may also shake while the eyes turned red, looking like a hungry lion. In the same wise, quivering ankle is a representation of animosity.

When people are irritated, they may also twist their ankle. This is unconscious way of saying that they do not like how something is being done. This irritation may be tempting them to turn away their eyes or leave the vicinity entirely. Again, this is perceptible due to the shaking of the entire body.

Scientific Explanations

Navarro (2012) observes that ankle twitching may be the direct effect of anxiety. Anxiety may not be displayed with the shivering or shaking of the hands or trembling of the voice but quivering the legs. You need understand that what determines this is what the source of anxiety is. In the case of public speaking, the voice will tremble while other parts of the body may also be used in passing the message. However, if the activity is mainly concerned about the hands, you may see the shaking very hard; imagine a person about to drive on a dangerous or busy highway for the first time. If it has to do with running, walking or even doing things pertaining to the legs, you may observe the twisting of the ankles.

Straker (2019) states that this twitch is a connotation of aggression. If done in the wrong place, it may be a source of embarrassment for the person. For instance, it is rare to see people actually strike another person they pick argument with but they may move in a bid to do so. This is when the twitch occurs. This may simulate kick.

Practical Illustrations

Case Study I: Mr UB had stomach upset; he went to party the previous day where he ate different things against his health. His boss is very disciplined; he could not just sit back at home and feign or claim any form of sickness. So he was at work because he was 'compelled' to. He was so much disturbed by the pile that he found it difficult to either sit or stand; it was as if something was hooking him at the buttocks. While standing, he was having a discussion with one of his supervisors when he became restless, feeling the urge to walk around or leave the vicinity for a while, but this could not be done due to the person standing before him. So he quivered his ankle so high that the supervisor had to inquire from him if all was well and he never replied in the affirmative. He could not verbally demonstrate his feelings and when the supervisor got the message through his non-verbal demonstration, he had to release him so that he would not defaecate on his body.

Case Study II: Governor DO has just be sworn in after winning the election of his province some few months ago. There were allegations of poor performance and gross misconduct against the former governor. So people are expecting the new governor to query and investigate his predecessor so that many of the items stolen can be recovered. In one of his tours to the province-owned hospitals, it was discovered that despite claiming to have spent billions on the facility, nothing seems to be working. Governor DO became visibly agitated as he addressed the newsmen that followed him to the inspection site. He could be seen twisting his ankle as if he wanted to throw a leg at the journalists interviewing him. Also, his facial expression turned sour, looking dejected because he never imagined such a high level of monumental fraud could have happened.

Case Study III: Mrs E hates any sight of drunks; she does not like seeing people drink themselves into a stupor and begin to display all kinds of madness. However, she is a field worker who has to go out in search of information. This means she might be forced to go to places beyond her wish. One of such cases happened when she went to collate data of an area with her colleagues. There is a bar in that area where people drink and do all kinds of despicable things. They were done with their data collation when a colleague needed to buy bottled water in a nearby shop, meaning others had to wait for her. While waiting, someone who had drunk beyond measures was displaying his madness on his way home; he would vomit, fall, stand and stagger on the street, on seeing this Mrs E became irritated, began to twist her ankle, earnestly craving for her colleague to show up so that they could leave the place. The person was irritating to her, thereby causing some psychological turmoil for her.

Case Study IV: Prostitute TR went to a hotel with a man, a strange man in the land. Since the man came on a visit just because of her, they stayed in the hotel for three days. However, whenever the man was ordering for food, he would order for his local delicacies. As a way of proving that he really 'loved' the man, she decided to order for the same food on the second day. An hour after eating it, she began to witness stomach upset. All that the man was doing had no meaning to her as she twisted her ankle before running into the toilet. The man was lost at her display as he didn't know what went wrong with her.

22.22. Self-Hugging with Knee in High Position

Generic Interpretations of the Concept

If you have ever paid close observation, you will notice that those who preach self-love do so when they are going through down moments; may be, they have been jilted by someone or feel lonely in life. Sometimes, things might truly be against them while some other times, they serve as the architect of their own problem. The point I want to bring out from this is that when people hug themselves, it is a means of self-comforting. This is true all over the world, only that the propeller of self-hug might be different from an individual to the other.

Among teenagers, you will see them raise their two knee to their chest level while seated, very close to themselves and hug the knees with their two hands as if they are tying them to the body. This can only be done in a sitting position. One of the possible reasons for this action is cold; when we feel cold, we look for a way of making the body smaller and bringing everything together in order to generate the warmth needed to keep the body warm. The hands around the lower limb massage it so well that when done repetitively, it makes blood run to the surface of the skin to keep us in shape.

Also, teenagers enjoy this posture while listening to music; it comforts them and further spurs their interest in the song they are listening to. You may see them moving their head to the sound of the music. In the same vein, it is a favourite posture for them while dealing with negative emotions. A child who has just been scolded by her parents or one bullied or frightened by his peers will quickly switch to this posture as they deal with these unfavourable incident all alone. This non-verbal behaviour is also a good way of arousing the emotion of pity in another person. For instance, my children made use of this gesture a lot when they were young. If I denied them any of their request, they will sit at the corner of the room, hugging their knees close to the chest and looking at me expectantly, thinking I will heed to their pleas through that and most times, I ended up doing them.

Apart from kids, there have been instances when I observed this cue among criminal suspects while being interviewed. Even though it looked informal or unthinkable, they could not control their emotions; they were overwhelmed. They deal with stress through this behaviour.

Scientific Explanations

Philip (2014) notes that this behaviour is a signal of the need to be comforted; the person is saying that he or she desires comfort. The body language adds that 'self hugging replaces the need for the comfort of another. Thus, it is to be used when one does not wish to rely on the care of others, but when one still wishes to receive a caring touch.' Sometimes, not that we do not need the touch of others, only that they are not available to us. So this is like a self-medication. Philip quickly points that this is a negative body language cue that should be avoided. You should only consider using it in situations where you want to appear vulnerable. Sol (2019) describes this cue as 'the ultimate act of physical self-reassurance.'

Practical Illustrations

Case Study I: Since Friday, Child V has been watching television, visiting friends and playing game without bothering to do his loads of homework brought from school. Now, it is Sunday evening and the parents are going out. As a way of punishing him, he is told to stay back at home and do the exercises in order to prepare for school tomorrow. He surely knows that his parents will go to the cinema to watch a favourite movie. He becomes mad at their decision, explaining to them that he would do the work in the evening after returning home but this does not sound plausible to his parents. When Child V discovers that his excuses are not working, he becomes really sober and moves to the couch, raised his knees to his chest level and hugged them to himself. The mother is moved by this but his father would not budge. This means he was really remorseful with his non-verbal display but the father was too cruel to see this emotional message.

Case Study II: Child CX and his siblings have been playing a game for the past two hours and at the end of the day, he was defeated. As it is the custom of kids, they mocked him, made jests at him and did not allow him to participate in the next round. He left them angrily, reached for his phone and earpiece, put on his favourite song and sat far away from them by hugging his knees to himself, feigning disconnection from his siblings but he was still paying attention to what they were doing, waiting for the next person to be eliminated so that he could join in the mockery too. Every now and then, he would look at them and then, focus on his music. He was only comforting himself through the posture so as to vent his anger on his siblings at that very moment.

Case Study III: Criminal F really had it in a very turbulent manner during investigation after his arrest. He is a kingpin who seemed fearless about his ways; he had tortured many people and had taken crime as a profession with accomplices and 'employees' in different parts of the world. It took the combined efforts of policemen from different nations to eventually arrest him before he was ferried to his home country for investigation. During the process, it was like a game as he dominated the first few sessions, trying to manoeuvre his ways. But at the peak of it, he lost his balance and look pitied. At some point, he raised his two knees up, high to his chest level and then curved the two hands around them as if binding the knees to himself. The experienced investigators were not surprised at his action as that would not be the first of such occurrence. His non-verbal display is a confirmation of the fact that he was not feeling easy due to how he was being drilled.

Case Study IV: There was a time a new smuggler was brought to me; it was his very first operation and he was unfortunate to fall into our hands. When I saw him, I knew he had no prospects in crime and if well-groomed, he wouldn't indulge in evil acts. So instead of the usual steps, I looked the other way—empathy! I spoke extensively to him about the consequences of his action to himself and the society as a whole. He became really sorry at some point as he raised his knees and hugged himself. Still, I continued with my admonition which made him cry bitterly. My aim was achieved—it was to call his attention to how he was wreaking havoc on the society.

22.23. Crossing Leg in Standing Position

Generic Interpretations of the Concept

Crossing the legs while standing is an apt portrayal of comfort. This is unlike the sitting counterpart that is mostly used to denote discomfort. The legs are usually crossed at the ankle while standing. Usually, the left is placed at the front. This is often done when we are standing alone or in the company of others that we trust will not harm us. When you cross the legs, you lose stamina; a simple push will throw you off balance. This is just like the open body language where you expose the vulnerable parts of the body by sprouting out. Military and other law enforcement officials will spread out the legs so as to stand confidently in the case of an attack but with this posture, one can easily be defeated by the enemies. In other words, we cross our legs while standing in our comfort zone.

It is a display of trust and confidence in the system and people in it. You may see a person display this gesture among close friends. This behaviour is capable of endearing others to you; they understand that you repose your confidence in them and will like to reciprocate the gesture. This is called mirroring and shows there is symbiotic agreement between you and the person.

However, the moment we become insecure, the person will uncross the legs. This is a real-time action. The reason is that you feel something or someone is about to attack you and you must stand actively in order to defend yourself or take to your heels, depending on what you feel about the adversary. For instance, if a stranger shows up while discussing with your friends, you will quickly uncross your legs because you do not know the intentions of the person towards you. In elevators, lone riders may decide to cross their legs but the minute a stranger shows up, they will uncross the legs as if the strangers will take offence in their action. Even if there is a topic of disagreement you are arguing on within your friends, you will uncross the legs due to the psychological discomfort; the limbic brain knows that the situation has changed and it is doing everything to put you under close watch. Spreading out your legs will make you balance and argue better.

It is crucial to state that you can only cross the legs while speaking to colleagues or people below your level; it may be taken as a sign of rudeness to cross your legs while addressing your boss. Hence, we should be guarded in our show of how we feel so that we do not end up feeling sour in the right place.

Scientific Explanations

Westside Toastmasters (2019) shares a view that is somewhat different from mine. In the submission of the platform, it notes that people cross their legs when they are in the midst of those they are not familiar with. An interaction with those in the group will reveal to you that one or two of them do not know each other well. When legs are crossed, it is regarded as a closed body language that shows that a person is not open. A person maintaining this posture will find it difficult to speak freely on a given topic.

Also, the website explains that it is a defensive posture; the genitals, which are vulnerable parts of the body, are protected when the legs are crossed. Depending on the legs that is placed on the other, it explains the direction in which a perceived threat is coming from. We can also state that it is a submissive attitude. When you guard your vulnerable parts before the real occurrence of an issue, this is an indication that you are afraid of that, thereby not willing to give it a challenge. Westside Toastmasters (2019) categorically notes that 'for a woman, positions like the scissors stance and the single leg crossed stance send two messages: one, that she intends to stay, not leave; and two, that access is denied. When a man does it, it also shows he'll stay but wants to be sure you don't "kick him where it hurts".'

Practical Illustrations

Case Study I: Mr AX and his friends were discussing during break at work. After taking their lunch, they would gather at a place and catch gist. It is always an interesting gathering as they discuss a range of topics. This time around, they were standing as it was almost time for them to return to work. Mr AX crossed his legs, feeling light and listening to what one of his colleagues was saying until about three minutes later when one of the newly employee who wanted to feel among showed up. Since they were not close to him, Mr AX quickly uncrossed his legs, moved backwards and crossed his arms. Even though this was an unconscious action that he did not pay attention to, some of his colleagues got the clue. This means he was not receptive of the idea of the new employee coming into their circle.

Case Study II: Student OB and his friends were discussing at school. They were chatting, mocking one another and gossiping their peers. They move together in cliques; if you do not belong to their group, it would be difficult for you to blend due to slangy expressions and other distinct communication forms they use. Student OB was not really into what they were discussing that day but only crossed his legs while listening to them. It was as if he was left out of the discussion. A friend had to ask if him he was sick and he said 'no'. So others did not bother about him again, noting that he would talk when a topic of interest was brought up. As they were still there, a student from another class came into the midst, they all readjusted their stance, thinking it was one of those bullies. Student OB quickly uncrossed his legs too and moved backwards. Meanwhile, the strange student was sent by a teacher to call one of them. OB's action showed that he was ready to take to his feels, or at least, defend himself in case of violence outbreak.

Case Study III: Mr C and Mrs UQ were discussing at work on some policy implementation of the government and how they were affecting their industry. Both of them shared the same view on most of the issues, lamenting bitterly on how they were losing clients on a daily basis. Even though Mr C was heading somewhere, he crossed his legs and listened intently as the woman poured out her mind. He complemented it once in a while by buttressing some of the case studies given by his co-interlocutor. However, the woman said something at some point which he did not really subscribe to. Immediately, he uncrossed his legs and stood firm, moved a step backwards and then, reeled out reasons why the woman's postulation is wrong. The closed body gesture is to register his dissenting view to what the woman said.

Case Study IV: Two criminals were having a discussion and anyone could easily notice with the ease with which they communicate. Although they were standing, their legs were crossed. In fact, an average person would think they had forgotten themselves at that spot. However, their standing position changed immediately they saw some law enforcement passing by; they uncrossed their legs in order to have the ability to run if the officers were to go after them. However, the enforcement agents only passed beside them without saying anything. They returned to their normal legs crossing position after they had gone. Their posture per time reveals the state of their mind. Their posture hints that they were afraid of the law enforcement agents.

22.24. Leg Kicking in Sitting Position

Generic Interpretations of the Concept

Of all the body language gestures we have discussed so far, I can, in a way, state that this is the most symbolic. It is displayed when seated and a person places a leg on the knee of the other, making the upper leg point out in a visible manner and then kicks it up and down after an uncomfortable incident. This is a gradual action that moves from twitching, shaking and then eventually, to kicking. This is a common attribute only that we do not pay attention to it; it happens to TV guests during interviews.

When a person is questioned and in the process of giving a feedback, they place their legs on each other and kick the upper leg, it means the question has unsettled them. Note that they will kick the leg back and forth and not from a side to the other. The latter is actually a demonstration of comfort but kicking back and forth means you are trying to kick something away from you. Invariably, you do not like that particular thing. Goat is noted for its stubbornness and we will kick our legs and wave at it when it surpasses its boundary. In the same vein, a difficult question is seen as a ball which is kicked back to the person who asked it.

The person does not want to talk about the concept being questioned on or the questioner is about to unravel something they do not want to discuss. The possibilities are limitless and what really determines the truth is the context in which the event is taking place but in general, it means the person is highly uncomfortable. They may smile to cover up their feelings as we see on television, but kicking the leg betrays them.

This is not in any way a pacifier, except it is what the person does regularly; it is part of their baseline. If not, it represents a subconscious act of kicking away something objectionable. This happens suddenly, meaning that the person was probably shocked by the question. It is an act of hiding the feeling that makes some of them to grin afterward.

It is a display of strong negative stimulus. It is a non-verbal way of saying, 'Go, I do not want to deal with you, lest you embarrass me in the process.'

Scientific Explanations

Philip (2013) explains that kicking is a substitute to walking or taking to one's heels, if the situation had permitted such action. The person may also look at the exit longingly.

In addition, Straker (2019) says that when we do not desire to see or hear something. Kicking, which is metaphorical in this sense, means the person would have kicked away the question if it were a tangible object. Hence, it is used to communicate disdain.

Practical Illustrations

Case Study I: Mr ER is a member of the parliament and was accused of raping a lady. The case has become an international issue as different organisations and agencies across the world are calling for thorough and objective investigations into the matter. It is the number one issue that is trending on social media. Yet, the law enforcement agencies in that country seems to be playing politics with it; they are yet to invite him because he is an ally of the president. However, one of the fiercest journalists in the country books appointment with him and now, he is live on the private television channel. The man crosses his legs as he entertains questions from the journalist, speaks carefully and sometimes, clips off some explanations. The session can be compared to an intellectual crossfire. When the journalist asks him if he has met with the lady in question anywhere, he frowns immediately before diluting it with a grin and simultaneously kicks his leg. He loses balance at this point as everyone knows of his relationship with the lady. He later surmounts the courage to answer in the affirmative. In other words, he had truly met the lady before and his non-verbal gesture is a confirmation of this 'guilty knowledge.'

Case Study II: B is a security officer, very respected by his colleagues and admired by his employers but he has been moving away from the path of honour in recent times. He now has a new circle of friends that influence him negatively, making him lose his virtues at work and home. His wife has tried to curb him, lamenting what his life could not turn out to be if he does not desist but he would not listen. When his waywardness gets to its crescendo, he would absent himself from duty post, leave his subordinates to their fate and would not bother to submit report to the headquarters. When this gets to the note of his employers, they carry out an investigation discover that B is no longer up and doing. In order to give him fair hearing, they serve him a letter to appear before a committee. He obeys by resuming on time. Meanwhile, he has been spending his time with a strange woman, who would drug him, making him sleep there overnight. He crosses his leg as he answers questions from the committee. At a stage, the leg begins to shake, twitch repetitively and then it kicks back and forth when questioned on his whereabouts during work hours. This gave him out—he was experiencing stress because he didn't do the right thing.

Case Study III: Teacher AV had been warned that on no ground should he mete corporal punishment on her pupils but she seemed not to be ready to obey the order. Although she does not do this in an obvious manner, she still finds ways to assault the students whenever she gets angry. Since this is always done on a controversial ground, it has been difficult to hold her to account until one day, she uses a ruler to hit a pupil which was captured by CCTV. Immediately, the management summoned her and asked her to explain what transpired in the class. She dodged the aspect until the CCTV footage was played to her and she was thereafter asked to explain the scene. She started kicking her leg as if the question should have never been asked. In other words, she was truly guilty and there was no explanation from her to depict otherwise.

Case Study IV: Prostitute AW has been defrauding Mr UT his hard-earned money all in the name of a non-existent relationship. The man had proposed to her but she still finds her way to sleep around with other men. One day, Mr UT had an engagement in a particular hotel but he forgot to inform her about it. As fate would have it, that was the same place that AW's client decided to hang out with her for the day. As she was moving out with her client, UT was driving in. Her legs began to shake uncontrollably as if she had paralysis. This was an expression of fear, depicting that she had something troubling on her mind.

22.25. Jumping for Joy

Generic Interpretations of the Concept

While the described the preceding gesture as being the most symbolic, permit me to state that this is the most action driven and it is used to connote the same meaning across the world. When people jump up, they defy the law of gravity, meaning that every natural law is suspended for the person to express his or her emotional feeling. Overtime, it has been discovered that this behaviour is driven by positive emotions. When you see people lift the two feet up at once and returned with elation, it means something big that cannot be kept as a secret has happened to them. There are some good tidings, that when they locate you, no matter how pretentious you are, people will still know. Imagine a person who has been trying university admission for years but his application was turned down but one day, he was fortunate enough to be accepted by one of the leading universities in the world. How do you think the person will react when he sees the mail?

Coincidentally, primates too jump for joy just like we do. This means the behaviour is evolutionary; it grows with us over time, right from the time of the first man, went with us through the stages of development and it is now an admirable behaviour all around the world. When primates sense they are about to get a good treat, they jump for joy. This is what kids do too when their parents promise them something fantastic that they have longed for over time. Such a kid may even lock himself up in a room to jump up several times as a means of displaying happiness what he or she is anticipating.

The limbic system, the emotional central zone of the human brain, is in charge of this behaviour. It directs it on its own; we do not need to be conscious of the fact that we are about to jump before doing it. This explains why sports spectators jump up in unison when their team scores a point against the opponent without being trained or taught how to do so; it is ingrained in our brain and we display it when we are uncontrollably elated.

Scientific Explanations

Cassie (2013) lists jumping as one of the emotions expressed through non-verbal cues. He observes that jumping is a literal way of showing our anticipation for joy and in other instances, it is a testament that something we have been anticipating has been delivered to us. This is always accompanied with a wide and easy grin, rubbing hands together, and vigorous pumping of the hands. When you see these clusters, it is an indication of excitement. People only throw themselves up when there is something to be excited about.

In the same vein, Marcello Mortillaro and Daniel Dukes (2018) notes that jumping is one of the means in which we can recognise someone who is joyous. The researchers observe that jumping is a stronger indicator of positive emotions compared with smiling and other conventional ones that can easily be feigned by people. It is difficult for people to fake this because it requires you carrying your body and negative emotions do make the body weighty.

Practical Illustrations

Case Study I: A team led by Mrs UF was handed over a duty by the management of their firm. Many other teams have been constituted by the management in other branches across the world. So the best team report would be adopted and used as the pilot study for the implementation. More so, the winners would be awarded and put in charge of the proposed project. Invariably, they would be promoted. Due to these remunerations, all the teams across the branches gave their possible best; they were up and doing just to stand out. While many of them were able to beat the deadline, some of them could not. This means those that could not submit have been weeded off. After going through all the submitted report, a message was sent that each of them should come for verbal presentations and questioning. At the end of the day, Mrs UF's team won the coveted awarded. As the CEO made the announcement, all of them, seated on a row, jumped up in celebrations of the feat.

Case Study II: It is the final football competition of the most coveted trophy in the game's history. The match is taking place on the largest stadium and people travelled from the length and breadth of the world and the stadium is filled up to the brim, with each fan cheering up their respective teams—Team A and Team B. The game in the first half is very tough and ends on a stalemate. The fans are still charged, singing, blaring trumpets and booing one another since the scores are still levelled. The second half starts in earnest but it also goes the same way as the first one. After thirty minutes' extra-time that both of them are shy to find the back of the net of each other, the game goes into penalty shootout. The first four players in each team score but the fifth shooter for Team B hit the bar while the skipper of Team A finds the back of the net. The whole field goes gaga. The thousands of Team A's supporters on the pitch that day jump up with cheers while the players also run near them to display to them. A wonderful sight to behold for the victors and vice versa.

Case Study III: Ms RQ submitted a proposal for grant with a world agency. She read that the grant is very competitive as people from all over the world do apply. She was about to be discouraged from those she knew that did it but brought bad news. However, she assured herself and thus, put in for it. One day, she just came back from work when got a mail that she was a part of the few successful applicants. As she saw the message, she jumped up and screamed that everyone's attention was drawn to her. She eventually composed herself to explain to them.

Case Study IV: For years, MU and MT had been looking for ways to go to Country EQT but they had no means to legally get themselves there. Even though they had heard several times that other youths were getting their way in through illegal means, they could not afford to take such risks. However, MU woke up one day and decided to take the illegal route. After a week, he called his brother that he was there already. MT unconsciously began to jump for joy; he knew that if his brother could successfully, then his too was as good as done. He did not know life is not a bed of roses; his did not work out as planned.

22.26. Incongruent Legs and Feet

Generic Interpretations of the Concept

When the legs are uncooperative or incongruent to what we are saying, it means something is wrong. We tend to overlook this action because the leg is the farthest part of the body to the brain. And the unpronounced rule in reading body language is that the farther the part, the less aware we are about its gestures. Both children and adults default when it comes to the use of legs. The most important thing is that it is more reliable for you to work based on the action of the legs than the person's words.

For instance, if kids and even adults do not want to go someplace, you see them drag their legs or kick them. This is a clear resentment for sending them on errands to that particular place. The legs become suddenly weight that they are unable to carry them. This may be covered up by staring at an image as if the image caught their attention but in reality, it is a way of showing their resentment towards that particular course. Your attention may be shifted to where their face is focused on but when you look at their legs, you will understand that it does not cooperate with their action.

I have seen the act of protestation with the legs by kicking, twisting, dragging and turning them into dead weight among adults when they are about to be arrest. It is a peaceful resistance of the action. The legs are unequivocally and audibly communicating the feelings of the person; if they had had their way, they would not have subjected themselves to arrest.

When we disagree with what an interlocutor is saying, we will also demonstrate this gesture. By twisting the leg, we are trying to state 'I do not go with you on that' or 'I hold a different point of view'. Such clues are mostly illustrated while dealing with people we think it is difficult to counter their stance. For instance, when talking with a boss, if you do not believe their directive on a policy will be productive, you may find it difficult to verbally state your mind so that you will not be seen as being rude.

In your dealings with people, one of the things you should start taking conscious note is the reaction and behaviour of their legs, most especially when a sensitive topic is brought up.

Scientific Explanations

Radwan (2017) states that people do not twitch their legs for no apparent reason. Although you may be made to believe so if you do not dig inward, there are numerous messages that can be unravelled through this gesture. 'A person can shake his leg if he felt, bored, anxious, worried, tensed or stressed,' states Radwan. They are the possible clues you should look for when reading people's legs. Worry about what lies ahead makes people twist their legs. This expresses their pessimism about what the future holds for them. Someone who is not willing to move forward is sceptical about their chances of recording positive outcomes in the future.

Also, anxiety about past events too is a factor that should not be neglected at this point. The subconscious brain is in charge of this gesture; it works based on past events, whether imaginary or real. If the past event recorded is negative, the limbic brain will work on that, making the person kick their leg (Radwan 2017).

Practical Illustrations

Case Study I: Child A has always been reprimanded for his destructive act but he does not seem that he is willing to change. Apart from their home, he also derives joy in spoiling the items of friends and neighbours. Just yesterday, he went to play with the kids of their neighbours when he spoilt a cable of their television. He left without bothering to inform them and when he was later accosted by a kid of the neighbour, he denied any knowledge of that. Today, his mother gave him an item to go and deliver to their neighbour but he has been very reluctant to go. While holding the item, he stood at the door, with his feet pointing inwards and focused on the movie as he was captivated by the scene when in actual fact, he is not a fan of the series. The mother later had to rebuke him and he dragged his feet out, not knowing what awaited him the next door. He was really afraid!

Case Study II: Mr HZ was engaged in a fight with another person at a bar the previous night. It was actually a free-for-all. So he thought there would be no consequences for his action as the security agents at the scene arrested those that were really violent before he and some others took to their heels. Many items of the bar were destroyed during the process. He was so frightened by the incident because he almost lost his life. Since morning, he tarried indoors, still trying to get over the incident. He heard a knock at his door and rushed to open it; there were security officials at the door. He looked baffled, asking them what their business was at his house; he did not know that the activity was captured by CCTV. As they tried arresting him, he resisted by pushing his legs backwards, twisting them and kicking as if the officials were something to really detest. This was to implicitly state that he was not willing for an arrest.

Case Study III: Mrs SP was discussing with her boss, Dr MP on some of the modalities to adopt in running their firm. Dr MP is known for his intellectual prowess and also prides himself over this. So it is always difficult for people to call his attention to his shortcomings because he would end up embarrassing the person. While majority of the issues raised during the course of the meeting were fantastic, Mrs SP had issues with some but she dared not call his attention to them. Whenever such points were raised, she would twitch her legs, subtly kick them and nod grudgingly in agreement.

Case Study IV: It is the culture of the border officials of Country WQU to tell all passengers to come down in order to enable them search the entire vehicle and affirm the identity of each of them before ordering them back to their various seats. The officers are always positioned at strategic points. The officer that was standing at the door noticed the incongruent movement pattern of one of the passengers. He took interest in his case and while others were being engaged by his colleagues, he rushed to him to know what was wrong which he said nothing but when asked to present his means of identification, he went blank.

22.27. Loss of Balance

Generic Interpretations of the Concept

There are many things that can cause us to lose our balance. Losing balance is not something that should be taken with levity due to its consequences on the victim. Even though this does not really communicate any social message, it ultimately shows that the person is not feeling well. At least, not too many of us will like to associate with a person that staggers or moves incoherently. Losing balance has to do with not walking properly. Medical condition is the first propeller of this gesture; when a person is battling with high blood pressure, it affects most of their actions. Such people can fall or lose stamina in an unexpected manner. Also, someone who stands up too quickly may lose balance and fall. Perhaps, the person wants to give something a hot chase or put some things in order and stand up without paying much attention to themselves.

We cannot trivialise the place of drugs and alcohol. There are some drugs that make the body weak. When you take them, they drain you of your vitality. Rapists do use this on their victims in order to give them free access to the person. It is not unusual to see drunks fall and rise again; they are usually objects of mockery because they lose balance after drinking themselves into a stupor. They will stagger all over. This paints the person as being undisciplined, careless and irresponsible. If you meet them in such state, you will be discouraged to have anything to do with them; relating with them means you are not serious about the business. Even those who take drugs, apart from rare cases, most of them do that to arouse an effect in the body.

Furthermore, age is capable of making people lose balance. Old age weakens the bones and makes the body fragile. This is the stage of life where people need to be tenderly and affectionately catered for. Your eyes should always be on your elderly ones because they can be affected by anything at any given time. It is often disastrous when elderly people lose their balance due to frail bones. In the case of that, you should swing into action immediately.

When you see a person lose their balance, the first action that is required of you is to render help to them. With your assistance, they can bounce back to life without going through down moments.

Scientific Explanations

Chitra Badii and Marijane Leonard (2016) states that 'balance problems cause dizziness and make you feel as though you're spinning or moving when you're actually standing or sitting still'. Considering this description, if care is not taken, loss of balance will interfere in our daily business. Also, it can lead to unimaginable falls, leading to broken bones and other grievous injuries.

The Mayo Clinic (2019) notes, 'Many medical conditions can cause balance problems. However, most balance problems result from issues in your balance end-organ in the inner ear (vestibular system).' Some of the symptoms of balance issues are feeling a floating sensation or dizziness, confusion, feeling of faintness or light-headedness (presyncope), loss of balance or unsteadiness, vision changes, such as blurriness and Sense of motion or spinning (vertigo). When you notice any of this, do not hesitate to contact your doctor before it gets out of hand. Migraine is capable of leading to balance issues.

Practical Illustrations

Case Study I: Pa. FN is an eighty-five-year-old man who lived the better part of his life working in the factory. This means he dealt with a lot of heavy equipment during his youthful years. This did not spare him in old age as it now looks as though he has stroke. He has been to the hospital different times and treated but it does not seem to be returning to his normal state. So his movement is confined within the house. On a particular day, as he was about to stand up from the couch and get something done at the backyard, he fell staggered and eventually fell on his left hand. Fortunately, one of his sons was at home. He quickly rushed the father to the hospital where he was adequately treated.

Case Study II: Mr SA works in one a leading financial institution in his city. He is very smart and co-employees love working with him because he makes their work move faster and make them gain more accolades from the management. However, his out-of-work life is nothing to write home about. People who revere him at office are fast losing interest in him. Apart from being chronic adulterer, he spends most of his time at the bar, drinking with people of the lower radar in the society; factory workers, cleaners, among others. More so, he does not know when to call it a day; he drinks to the extent that he would not be able to drive himself home. On a particular Friday, he did drink more than his capacity—he drank irresponsibly, and as he was about standing up, he lost balance and hit his body at the table, breaking all the bottles of drinks on it. He was forced to pay for them by the management of the bar. He returned to his senses when slammed with the bill!

Case Study III: Mrs DT is a young widow; she lost her husband eight years into their marriage after giving birth to their third child. They were fond of each other and had planned how to lead comfortable life, providing the best education for their kids and helping people. Ten years after his demise, the woman cannot just get rid of the memories shared together. More so, she now has the burden of the children to bear all alone; she works for longer hours, deprives herself of gratifications and lives a life she never imagined for herself just to make sure that her children get the best out of life. Being overly burdened with negative, disturbing thoughts is now making her to suffer from high blood pressure. One day, as she got home from work, making to alight from her car, her mind had wandered away, and she suddenly fell. It took the help of neighbours to salvage her.

Case Study IV: Drug Addict AH had drunk himself into a stupor when law enforcement officials ransacked his community. At first, when all his colleagues who were still in their senses were trying to run away, he staggered around as if he was about to give up the ghost. But when reality descended on him, the officers were already at a close range. With the way he was staggering and smelling, he appeared irritating to the enforcement officers. In fact, before they could grab him and cart him away, he had fallen like three times. It was not a scene many of the officers like to be reminded of. He was seen as nothing than an irresponsible and reckless fellow.

CHAPTER 23

The Feet

Our discussion is incomplete if we leave out this part of the body, although I have mentioned it briefly while considering the legs but it is crucial that we understand it as a concept in order to know its role in non-verbal cue interpretations. Let me start with the indelible words of Leonardo da Vinci: 'The human foot is a master piece of engineering and a work of art.' He said this powerful statement after years of working on the human body. This means the foot has always been charming to him, leaving him baffled at every point in time. There is no exaggeration in the fact that foot defines us. To understand how important the foot is to your survival, let it be injured and see how you feel throughout the body.

Although smaller to other parts of the body, the feet serve as the powerhouse to the entire body; it bears our weight and carries us about. The pressure we put on the feet surpasses any other part of the body. There is hardly anything we do without its involvement. Also, we subject them to punishments at all times through wearing of tight shoes and endless trips. Once our brain tells us to go somewhere, the feet must be ready to, whether willing or not. Through our carelessness, we hit them on stones and other items, cause injuries to them and have to nurse them for some time.

They are also indispensable in the sensing of motion, humidity, cold, heat and vibrations. In moments of doubts, we consider it safe to put our feet to test than other parts of the body. That is why you dip your feet into the beach to feel the temperature of the water before diving in. We also rely on them to know how deep something is. So they are subjected to all forms manipulations by the brain.

When we want to hit a person rather hard, we will consider using the feet. Although this may cause injury to us too, we consider that relatively safe compared with the vulnerable parts of the body. It is a tool for those are involved in karate. The feet are very sensitive to touch—it reacts to the slightest touch. This makes it a very sensual part of the body. By massaging it alone, it can arouse the feelings of sexual partners.

Just like every other part of the human body, the feet carry out their functions adequately. If they default at any given time, it causes breakdown in the body. With the feet, we get to balance the body, walk and climb mountains. Anything that has to do with movement is connected with the feet. Beyond all these, they are also capable of revealing people's emotions to us; with them, we can understand how a co-interlocutor feels, what they fear and their intentions. This is also applicable to us. Being the farthest part from the brain, we are not always conscious of the numerous messages being passed across by this part of the body. Even those who tend to control their non-verbal cues are not always of the displays in this part of the body. Hence, this is one of the major points of betrayal of liars and insincere people. Beyond looking at the upper part of the body, beam your searchlight on the feet and unravel countless things about people's emotions.

Before navigating through the messages, let's briefly take a leap into the scientific submissions on the feet.

According to Matthew Hoffman (2019), 'The feet are flexible structures of bones, joints, muscles, and soft tissues that let us stand upright and perform activities like walking, running, and jumping.' Another definition states that 'it is the terminal portion of a limb which bears weight and allows locomotion. In many animals with feet, the foot is a separate organ at the terminal part of the leg made up of one or more segments or bones, generally including claws or nails.'

The human foot is a strong and complex mechanical structure containing 26 bones, 33 joints (20 of which are actively articulated), and more than a hundred muscles, tendons, and ligaments. The joints of the foot are the ankle and subtalar joint and the interphalangeal articulations of the foot. An anthropometric study of 1197 North American adult Caucasian males (mean age 35.5 years) found that a man's foot length was 26.3 cm with a standard deviation of 1.2 cm (Hawes and Sovak 1994).

The foot can be subdivided into the hindfoot, the midfoot, and the forefoot:

The *hindfoot* is composed of the talus (or ankle bone) and the calcaneus (or heel bone). The two long bones of the lower leg, the tibia and fibula, are connected to the top of the talus to form the ankle. Connected to the talus at the subtalar joint, the calcaneus, the largest bone of the foot, is cushioned underneath by a layer of fat (Podiatry Channel 2019).

The five irregular bones of the *midfoot*, the cuboid, navicular, and three cuneiform bones, form the arches of the foot which serves as a shock absorber. The midfoot is connected to the hind- and fore-foot by muscles and the plantar fascia.

The *forefoot* is composed of five toes and the corresponding five proximal long bones forming the metatarsus. Similar to the fingers of the hand, the bones of the toes are called phalanges and the big toe has two phalanges while the other four toes have three phalanges each. The joints between the phalanges are called interphalangeal and those between the metatarsus and phalanges are called metatarsophalangeal (MTP) (Podiatry Channel 2019).

Both the midfoot and forefoot constitute the *dorsum* (the area facing upwards while standing) and the *planum* (the area facing downwards while standing).

Humans usually wear shoes or similar footwear for protection from hazards when walking outside. There are a number of contexts where it is considered inappropriate to wear shoes. Some people consider it rude to wear shoes into a house and a Maori marae should only be entered with bare feet. Foot fetishism is the most common form of sexual fetish (ABC News 2010).

23.1. Dead Feet

Generic Interpretations of the Concept

There are times that our legs become frozen; I mean when they are practically dead. At that given point, it seems does not run in the feet again. This is an aftermath of some occurrences. When you observe someone's feet suddenly get 'punctured' and fail to move, it means there are issues. It is a perfect illustration of insecurities. When you are insecure, you will never think of the way forward, rather, you would be concerned about what how to take away that thing that is causing you the turbulent feeling. At this given time, you will freeze at some point while the subconscious brain processes all forms of information related to your present experience in order to come out with what you consider as the best way out.

Also, we freeze our movement when someone threatens us. This is more so when we believe that the person is able to defeat us. This means our feet have become 'cold'. Moving towards an actual or imaginary danger is tantamount to signing a treaty with death. When our movement is frozen, we have the opportunity to analyse the situation and know what our stakes are—should we flee, attack and remain on the same spot. For instance, if you are walking in the dark and something crypts in the bush, instead of running at it or away, you will stand on the same spot, keep your breath and listen more intently to know the direction of movement of the thing and what actually it is.

Being worried too can make the feet dead. During moments of concerns, many thoughts collude in our brain. Since the thoughts are negatively inclined, they may birth the feeling of fear in us. For instance, if you have ever seen a scene of fatal accident before and probably weeks after, you were delivered from a similar occurrence. If you are to embark on a journey on that same route, and thinking of the journey, once the thought slides into your mind, you will become frightened because everything is playing out clearly in your mind. Lifting your feet forward would become a herculean task at that given time.

Even scary discussions at a meeting can sentence the feet to death; you will not feel like leaving the venue even after the meeting until you get your balance. Feet freezing is a freeze response displayed in moments of intense fear. It is an evolutionary response that shields us from being observed or seen by predators. When you keep your breath and stall your movement, even a lion is likely to bypass, unlike those animals that scamper for safety and end up running into its mouth at its roar.

Scientific Explanations

Philip (2014) states that dead feet is an indication that someone is lacking power in their legs; they are very weak due to an occurrence that has got rid of their power. Stress is known to drain people of their strength; you have to think, manage fear and put forth a way to safeguard yourself. All these activities take place in the twinkle of an eye. So the brain is subjected to unimaginable level of stress by being overstretched. In such a given situation, the part of the body that is most affected is that which is directly concerned to the event at hand. If it has to do with walking or moving out of the present location, the legs become frozen but if it has to do with lifting an item or writing something scary, the hands would be impeded. When the legs become frozen, it is a message to you that they are not willing to move beyond their present location.

Practical Illustrations

Case Study I: It is two o'clock in the midnight. Guy CX stands up to ease himself. He does not sleep with the lights on. As he is just waking up, trying to reach for the switch, he hears the sound of a reptile somewhere around the window. He becomes indescribably fearful, shivering at that point and almost urinating on his body. What he hates most is the sight of a snake. The bush around his house are overgrown and he has been procrastinating when to mow it. For about a minute, he cannot do anything; he maintains the same posture, expecting the reptile to make another sound to know his fate. However, when it seems the reptile is more, he switches on the bulb, looks around after urinating and returns to his bed when he does not see anything. However, it takes him several minutes to find sleep as the negative thoughts still occupies his mind. This expresses his anxiety over the issue.

Case Study II: There is a deadly corner along route C leading to a major commercial city in Country CX. Being a sharp corner, those who are driving along the route for the first time are always victims of death. The government has not been responsive in ensuring that there is a turning point in that given location. One day, Mrs F and her colleagues were plying the road, heading for a business in the cosmopolitan city. When they got to the deadly bend, they discovered that an accident had just taken place, claiming the lives of three people out of five. The vehicle was really destroyed beyond recognition. There is nobody with human feelings that will get to the scene of the occurrence without sympathising with those involved in the incident. Mrs F became very much afraid and felt like walking to where they were heading to. On their way back later in the evening, they were saved by chance as their own vehicle nearly had accident at that same spot. Until they got home, the woman did not open her mouth to talk as the fear was still very visible on her. After about three weeks, she learnt that she was to lead the team to the neighbouring city again. She really became disturbed by this and her feet were frozen until she thought it through in the meeting.

Case Study III: Criminal AO was becoming worried of his ways, having the instincts that some people were after him. Ideally, one would think that he would turn a new leaf with this but far from it; it only made him cautious and conscious whenever he had an operation. For instance, there was a day he was trying to smuggle hard drugs into his flat despite being warned several times to desist from such criminality. While he was about entering, one of the managements of the apartment came out. This made him to stick to a spot; his legs got frozen while he awaited the next move of his alleged tormentor. This was the effect of fear which was glaring in his reaction even when the person did not see him.

23.2. Withdrawal of Foot

Generic Interpretations of the Concept

Sudden movement of the feet backwards or out of public view is a testament to the fact that something has gone wrong. When we 'see' or imagine danger running towards us, we tend to gradually withdraw our feet and tuck them under a chair in order to safeguard them. Sometimes, this is done in a noticeable manner and it is usually displayed in a sitting position. You may have difficulty seeing this behaviour if you are at the other side because of the table serving as a hindrance to the lower side of the body. However, if it is a glass, or transparent table, you have no issues. Further, there are times that their shoes make audible sounds while withdrawing the feet. Even if you cannot see the action, the sound is a confirmation that something is ongoing.

This has always played out during job interviews. When interviewees are hit with difficult questions, they feel like reducing their profile because they are gulped by fear. When you notice this, it means the person does not want to answer the question. We evade questions due to different reasons. From experience, I have seen criminal suspects evade a question because they understand that it would lead to a more difficult one and probably, to an eventual confession which they are not prepared for. Job applicants who are not ready to provide sincere answers to some questions will also withdraw their feet at some point in an interview. For instance, if asked, 'Have you been fired by an employer before?' If the answer is in the affirmative, this will lead to other numerous discussions which they are not ready for.

Apart from the official settings, this behaviour is also noticeable in the home front. When a spouse or kid thinks it would be unfavourable for them to supply truthful answer, they will tuck their feet in a chair and keep mute for a w while. This is to enable them think of the appropriateness of their response or even find ways to 'polish' their response in a way that will augur out well for them. A child who is asked 'Where were you last night?' might display this behaviour before giving a response, depending on past events in relation to their location.

Scientific Explanations

Carol Kinsey Goman (2019) states that sudden withdrawal of feet is an indication of negative feeling. According to her, when the feet are tightly wrapped under the legs of a chair, it means the person is withdrawing and disengaging from a discussion. Taking in the feet is symbolic to blocking or withholding one's thoughts. The shifting of the feet is a hint that the person does not want to make any contribution to the topic you have brought up. Goman encourages that if you observe this cue in a co-interlocutor, you should pause for a moment and consider your own body language—is there any alteration? Or have you raised a topic that is very sensitive for the person? This will help you to determine the next line of action.

Practical Illustrations

Case Study I: Lady X and Guy T are really having it very good. Their relationship has been superb and both of them behave as if they are from mars; since they have met, there has no be any reason for them to argue or witness any controversy. They fantasise about the future and the numerous things they will do as couples. In summary, their relationship has been operating on a superficial level. One day, Lady X just feels like Guy T behaves like an angel, so why would it take such a fantastic lover many years to find someone 'unworthy' like her. So she decides to ask of his past. She brings up the topic when they are both relaxed, sipping their favourite drinks at a restaurant. When she asks if Guy T has ever dated another lady, he answers in the affirmative. She then proceeds with 'What led to the breakup?' this question is rather greeted with a frown which is quickly dissolved into an unpleasing grin and the feet tucked into the chair. After about ten seconds, he begins by beating about the bush, hinting the lady that the guy might really be acting at this early stage. That is, he is not sincere in his dealings.

Case Study II: A group of interviewers engaged a man who was billed for one of the top posts in their organisation in an interactive session. And fortunately, the man did not disappoint; he answered all questions to the satisfaction of the panel. This further aroused their interest in him and out of curiosity, one of the panellists demanded, 'If you are such an embodiment of wisdom and innovation, why have you changed four jobs within five years?' He could have said that out of the zeal to explore but he had earlier told them that he liked being committed to an organisation for too long in order to enable him materialise his plans for such a firm. However, there are contradictions with his lifestyle over the past five years. With the question, he knew 'blood has been drawn out of his veins.' So he subconsciously withdrew his feet into the chair and then summoned the courage to reply them. His non-verbal cue testifies to the fact that he is overridden by negative feelings due to the unwanted question. So this accounted for his change in countenance.

Case Study III: Child HC has been warned several times of his wayward tendencies. His parents are religious leaders in their community and very revered across the nation due to their numerous successes across many fields. So it would be despicable for any of their children to exhibit juvenile delinquency tendencies. The child, although always remorseful at the point of scolding him but whenever he leaves their presence, the moral lessons fly out. It has recently been discovered that he spends his night at hotels and nightclubs, smoking, taking alcohol and sleeping with different women. The parents had a vigil the previous night and expected him to be at home but when they came back, he was not around, so the father decided to query his whereabouts the next day, seated opposite his father at the dining, Child HC tucked his feet in the chair and shook his head, stammering that he slept over at his friend's place. This was a show of nervousness which is birthed by sense of guilt.

Case Study IV: A man once came to me to report the death of his wife. He looked so disturbed but a bit composed. I felt sorry for him at first but with the way he was talking, it appeared as if he that he needed was to cover up everything. Then, I had to take my time to ask some pertinent questions. I discovered that instead of him to answer my posers, all that he wanted to prove was to tell me the kind of love that existed between him and his wife. I eventually hit the nail on its head by telling him to recount the last moment of his wife. I noticed hesitation, a frown and tucking in of his legs in the chair before he carefully chose his words, then I knew something was wrong. This means he was telling lie and as an expert, I was not going to be derailed by that.

23.3. Playing Footsies

Generic Interpretations of the Concept

While the preceding segment talks about feet withdrawal, this has to do with moving our feet closer to that of the person we are endeared to. In other words, it is a positive body language gesture which is used to register what goes on in our mind. If you do not like people, you will be naturally withdrawn from them. The limbic brain believes that such a person can injure you and that is why you try as much as possible not to have anything to do with them. On the other hand, we show admiration for people by moving towards them and what represents them. While playing footsies, the feet subconsciously move towards those of the other person under the table. Sometimes, they may even have a contact.

This is mostly seen in romantic scenes and at the beginning of a relationship when both partners still look like angels to each other. When the feet subconsciously come in contact, the person will not think of withdrawing them immediately because it arouses their feeling and sends a positive message to the other party too. When this action comes to their conscious knowledge, they may accompany it with a laughter; it is like a secret has been revealed to them.

The touch, although playful and appears insignificant, is very potent means of connecting our spirit with the other person. It is like a bridge through which we ride into the heart of the person we admire. This is both scientific and sociological. Neurologically, when the feet are touched, it makes an impact of sensory strip along the parietal lobe of our brain, this is very close to where the genitals also register. That is why I said that this behaviour is best for romantic situations.

Also, you must be sure that the feeling is symbiotic; play footsie with a person you have established some sort of relationship with. That is, you need to be sure that the person also admires you. If play footsie with a potential suitor, it may lead to an ugly scene you would not want to witness—the person may flare up and allege that you are intentionally matching on them. Also, limit the use of this gesture to informal situations as it may be considered inappropriate for a professional setting.

Scientific Explanations

All the experts that wrote on this gesture made it known that it is related to romance. In fact, one of them describes it as a 'common flirtatious practice'. According to Syncrat (2005), 'Someone is said to be 'playing footsie' when they are touching and rubbing their legs against another person's in a sexual manner, often under a table. More often than not, a lady will initiate it. It cannot be done with shoes on as it needs skin to skin contact to work the best.' That is why I earlier opined that displaying this gesture in a professional setting might be out of hand because you are not expected to remove your shoes in such atmosphere.

The platform explains further, 'A game of footsie is often incorporated into movies, where a lady with a stocking covered foot with start running her foot against a guy's leg while they are both in a restaurant (or diner). She starts touching her toes against the lower leg and then rubs her foot up the leg. It is often accompanied by a playful, sexual stare and direct eye contact is made.'

Practical Illustrations

Case Study I: Man H has vowed that he would lead a life of celibacy after being jilted by three different ladies. He is a careless lover; whenever he is in a romantic relationship with a lady, he opens up his heart and life to the person—they would know all his secrets. So it would be very easy for the lady to do evil to him. Even he does not hide his bank details from them. It is not as a show up, he does that because he is the only child of his parents. So he believes that anyone coming into his life should be ready to play the role of a sister before being a wife. With his past experiences, he made the affirmation that may be, he is not destined to marry.

However, he met a lady one day and the urge was irresistible. No matter how hard he tried, he kept meeting the lady at different points of the location. More so, the lady's smile is enticing and charming. He cannot just delete her beauty from his head. So man H decided to give it a shot and fortunately for him, it worked. In one of their outings, he narrated all that he had gone through to her. The lady pitied him and promised to be the 'chosen one'. And from all indications, she is. The love began to wax stronger, making them to ask of each other every minute. One day, as they were chilling at a bar, Man H's feet subconsciously moved towards the lady's. When she became conscious of this, she left them at the same spot for about a minute, making the feeling intense— it adds flavour to their love as their faces become more romantic and enticing. Conscious of their action, they both looked at each other and smiled. This was a confirmation of the romantic feeling.

Case Study II: Mr and Mrs VN were doing fine for years and their relationship was a cynosure of all eyes in the community before a misunderstanding which they could not handle very well set in and made them to separate for some years when it seemed they were about abusing each other. When they both could not cope with their state of loneliness, they tried exploring other people but the satisfaction was not just there for them. One day, Mr VN was courageous enough to give her a call and they scheduled a meeting. After about two to three meetings, they were getting used to each other again—the memories poured in massively and they both decided to sheath their swords. While sitting, Mrs VN stretched out her feet under the table which later had contact with that of her husband. The feeling was sensual and the husband felt it should just remain like the forever; he further moved his feet towards her as they talked, creating a romantic scene in the process. It was a pure show of love.

Case Study III: Man RS and Woman TQ did a marriage of convenience in order to help the woman travel with him. The agreement was that if it worked out, the woman would give him a given amount as monthly allocation. Immediately after the wedding, they headed to the embassy for interview. They were both smiling when the interview started. However, the session was taking longer than envisioned, so the man became disinterested in it. Seeing that Man RS was unconsciously distancing himself from her, the woman stretched her foot to his direction. Instead of him to understand the language of love, he rather got irritated. So he kept his foot to himself which was an obvious way of saying 'I am not interested in you.' The officials interviewing them got to know about this abnormality and after series of questioning, they were denied.

23.4. Rocking of Foot

Generic Interpretations of the Concept

We rock the feet for different reasons, all in a bid to ensure that a situation does not overcome us. When we rock the foot, we shift it from the heels to the toes and then move it back and forth. This is a repetitive behaviour that is action-laden; anybody that is in sight will know that our foot is engaged in an activity. Both positive and negative emotions can inspire this gesture. So it is one of the cues that you cannot just assume to know their meanings until you critically consider the circumstances surrounding their display.

Foot rocking is done repetitively for the purpose of pacifying the body. Moving the foot back and forth and raising and lowering it from the toes to the heel leaves a satisfactory feeling in us when done over time. It distracts our attention from something that has been giving us hard feelings. For instance, if you are waiting for someone to hasten up, you might find yourself doing this gesture; it is a metaphorical implication that the foot is ready to move. If you are really in a hurry, you may subconsciously involve both feet in this behaviour. Instead of your eyes to focus on the person alone, you would shift them from the person to the exit. You are monitoring the person to know what is delaying them and looking at the exit longingly as if you should have been walking through it.

Also, you may find yourself displaying this behaviour while alone but thinking about something difficult. Schoolchildren do rock their foot while working on a particular exercise without a headway. With this, they are able to midwife through the difficult feelings and set their minds on something less bothersome. That is why it is seen as a pacifying behaviour that is meant to soothe the body and relax the brain.

Apart from alleviating boredom, people use this behaviour to tell others that they are in charge. As you rock your foot, it makes other people conscious of your presence. This is unlike the 'dead thinking' where people gaze into the distance, looking disconnected from their immediate location. With this behaviour, an adversary would have a second thought before making up their mind to attack. So it is a good tool to inform others of your awareness and strength, even though you may be feeling otherwise within.

Scientific Explanations

Foot rocking is a show of masterpiece. Smith (2015) says that the way we move our body is a reflection of our attitude. According to her, 'Constantly transferring your weight from one foot to the other or rocking forward and backward is a comforting movement that indicates you are anxious or upset.' In other words, we rock the foot when something has gone wrong with the system as a way of stabilising the body. This is a physical representation of what goes on in our brain; we are torn between two unsettling thoughts and trying to locate our focal point so as to deal with the issue appropriately. Navarro (2014) also states that this behaviour aids in 'soothing or pacifying and help us deal with stress.'

Practical Illustrations

Case Study I: Mr MB and his wife were supposed to be at a function together. He had dressed up and even washed the car, took his breakfast and was waiting for the wife to be done so that they could move out together. He hates going out with the wife most times due to her lateness; he is a time conscious person, expecting every other person to be disciplined as he is. However, ten years into their marriage, the wife seems not to be meeting up to his standard in this regard. On this particular day, he was really pissed off with the attitude of the wife because he relieved her of most chores just to ensure they did not get there late. However, he decided not to talk, knowing what could be the consequences of his outburst. So Mr MB stood midway, looking at her wife impatiently as she made up. He rocked his foot back and forth and from the heels to the toes, gazing at the exit simultaneously. He was impatient and his mind was not inside again!

Case Study II: Mr DX and his son went out and then had to branch a popular eatery to refill their stomach before going home. When the son demanded for food, he was taken aback at the amount of food requested for, asking him if he could finish it, he answered in the affirmative. Even though he was sceptical about his answer, he did not want to go against his son's opinion publicly. Before he could finish up with the food, he was already showing some funny signs of unrest. Mr DX feigned ignorance, behaving as if he was not paying attention to him. After finishing up with his own, he told his son to hurry up as the time was far spent. At some point, the son shouted 'Dad, toilet,' left the table immediately and rushed to the toilet. It was a mixture of frustration and comedy for the father. The son tarried in the toilet beyond the duration he had expected. Waiting for his arrival, Mr DX moved his right foot up at the heels and dropped it at the toes and then back and forth, alleviating boredom till his arrival.

Case Study III: Mr SE just relocated to another country. Before his relocation, he did well by learning the basic mode of communication of the people. After three weeks in the city, he decided to have some fun at a nearby bar. He looks obviously strange. The people seated next to his table discovered this and wanted to seize the opportunity to play on his intelligence. He heard them while planning. He simply rocked his foot back and forth as one of them made his way to his table to broker communication and nodded in addition. Through this, it was clear to the people that he was aware of his environment, making it difficult for them to go on with their plans.

Case Study IV: Criminal AF is an international businessman and has built connections at every chain of the business, including among clearing agents. This invariably means that there are times that he would not pay the right dues and still get his goods easily cleared. It seems he now does this recklessly and all eyes have been on him and his accomplices. On a particular occasion, he expects his goods to be promptly cleared having bribed some officers but they are careful of going ahead due to the need to still keep their job. He begins to back and forth, feeling impatient about the whole process but he cannot report to anyone. Hence, this movement is propelled more by psychological stress.

23.5. Foot Facing Outside

Generic Interpretations of the Concept

When you see a foot moving away from your direction to the exit, this is a symbolic way of communicating 'game over'. This behaviour can be both conscious and unconscious. When communicating with someone and the person suddenly or gradually move away a foot and point same at the door, it means they are no more interested in what we are telling them. They are fed up of the gathering. Whatever you discuss after this gesture has been shown will amount to mere waste of time because the person is psychologically disconnected already.

This gesture non-verbally communicates 'I have to take my leave.' I have always implored people to obey this subtle gesture due to many reasons. One, the person is respectful; instead of cutting you short, he or she decides to use non-verbal means. More so, the gesture is largely subconscious. This means they are not mentally connected to the discourse. Even if you physically keep them in the discussion, they will not focus on what is being done. Communicating is a two-way thing. If the other person is not responding as they should, it means you are merely talking. Hence, this 'intention signal' should be taken note of.

Once it comes to your conscious awareness that a foot is turned away, and you do not want the person to leave, you may do well by pausing to find out what informed their decision. Some people do not like staying at a location for too long. To such persons, they love being in their comfort zone. So if you are taking too much of their time outside of where they feel comfortable, no matter how interesting your story is, they want to leave. Some others may be in haste to get something more important settled. Imagine meeting a colleague at the corridor and holding them to ransom in a discussion without bothering to ask where they are heading. Further, some will turn away their foot once you raise a topic that is considered offensive or that will put them on 'hot spot.' So be sure you know what is wrestling the attention of the person with you in order to know how to gain them back or release them.

If someone displays this gesture and you decide to look the other way, it can be so irritating to them; it means you are not caring. Hence, be mindful of it in your daily endeavours.

Scientific Explanations

Straker (2019) explains how one can decode the various messages passed by the foot. He notes that when the foot is swung towards a particular direction, it is equivalent to pointing. We point to where we want to be. Pointing at a direction other than where a co-interlocutor stands is an indication that the person wants to move away from their present location. Our urge to take our leave from an uncomfortable location increases as the reality of being hurt shines brighter at us. This is a subtle means of communicating our mind's intent and can get more pronounced if the person fails to cooperate with us at the initial stage.

Practical Illustrations

Case Study I: Mr DZ and Mrs KV are high school mates, very fond of each other then. But life happened along the line and they lost contact. Mr DZ was recently transferred to another city to manage a branch of the firm he works with. Unknowing to him, Mrs KV also lived in that same town. One morning, as he was going to work, he bumped on her high school mate on the walkway. He grabbed her at the arm and drew her closer. The woman was pregnant and was heading for an antenatal appointment. She was very happy to meet him too. They hugged and exchanged contacts again, lamenting how they both made efforts in reaching out to each other. After few apologies, the woman thought that would be the end so that they would call each other later on to fix a date in order to discuss better but Mr DZ looked relaxed, he started recalling memories that would take hours to discuss. At some point, Mrs KV turned a foot away and looked into the distance—it means she was disconnected already. When the response was not encouraging again, the man brought the discussion to an abrupt end. Although pained, he knew this was the most honourable thing for him to do.

Case Study II: Student CX is extremely intelligent; he is a cynosure of all eyes in his school and has warned many laurels for the institution. He is a source of pride to some teachers while others see him as a threat because they dare not make a mistake while teaching his class. Mr D just arrived at the school and within three days, he has discovered CX to be a genius. So he decided to hold a private talk with him because he had never seen such display of knowledge by any student in his twenty years of teaching. At closing hour, CX went to D's office to honour his invitation. He thought it was to be a brief discussion but thirty minutes into the meeting, they were still discussing the obvious and the student had a reality show he wanted to catch up with at home. He began to frown, hoping that the discussion ended. At some point, he subconsciously turned his right foot to the door and looked away from his co-interlocutor. Mr D got this message of disinterest and told him to leave and see him the next day.

Case Study III: A and B are colleagues at work. They are also friends and always seen together any time they had break or even when there is a team work to carry out. Others have tagged them as twins due to the obvious bond between them. They discuss virtually everything together but B does not like discussing her relationship. A has noticed this overtime and tried bringing it up one day but her effort has always been rebutted. In their last discussion, she still made efforts to discuss it but once the topic was mentioned, B's foot turned away from her, accompanied with a frown. She knew it was time to quit the discussion. That is, B was not interested in the discussion and there was no way she alone could be talking about that.

Case Study IV: Prostitute AR and Man UT met in a hotel room and had sexual intercourse. The initial agreement was that they would be together for an hour. So the lady had fixed an appointment with another client somewhere else. All her thought was that she should finish up with him and dash out to the second place. However, it seemed Man UT enjoyed the first round so much and would like to go for another round again, so he employed delay tactics by not paying on time. AR wanted to play along but the fact that her foot was facing outside expressed her innate desire. That is, she wanted to leave and nothing else!

23.6. Turning Away of Feet

Generic Interpretations of the Concept

While turning away of a foot is a signal of disinterest or tiredness, turning the two feet away is a clear demonstration of dislike. In other words, we swiftly turn the body away from those we do not have admiration for. There are people that we would have had preconceived thoughts about before meeting them, if you later cross path with that person, you may turn the feet away from them. This communicates the thought that goes on within you that you do not want to share any moment with the person. This is usually more pronounced and noticeable than a foot being turned away.

When a person turns their two feet away from you, it means they are not ready to share a thought with you. They are usually turned at the exit, meaning the person wants to 'fly' out of your presence. The two feet are in ready mode to move once you release the person. Looking solely at the face may not allow you understand the intentions of people towards you. For instance, someone might carry feigned expression on their face while the feet are not turned towards you. If you work with the upper part of the body alone, you are certainly rubbing minds with someone who does not share same values with you—a person who does not like you and what you represent.

This can happen at any given context—both formal and informal. There are people that hate their boss; they do not want to have anything personal to do with them. If situation now calls for that, they may smile at the boss but their feet will not align with the message that other parts of the body is passing across. This showcases their resentment to the boss, which most times, they do not pay attention to.

Also, it has come to my notice through close observations for the past few decades that when jurors do not like a witness or attorney, they turn their feet at the jury room immediately that person wants to speak.

In social gatherings, you may see two people smile and hug each other while their feet are turned away, this is an expression of mutual dislike; they both did it just for the sake of exchanging pleasantries.

Scientific Explanations

Heather Cichowski (2016) notes that this gesture is reliable because the feet do not lie; to look for accurate body language signals, you have to look at the feet. He notes that during discussions, we should always glance at the feet every now and then to know if the person we are discussing with is still interested in the discussion or their mind has wandered away. This stance is also supported by Vanessa Van Edwards. She explains that when the toes are pointing away, the person does not like you or what you are saying. The best way you can maximise this technique is to make conscious efforts in keeping an eye on the feet as conversations proceed. Someone who moves their feet away from you is closing the chapter of their interaction with you and you must learn how to strictly adhere to this.

Parvez (2015) aptly captures it thus: 'In any situation where we are involved with some other person or a group, be it standing or seated position, the direction in which our lead foot (the right one, mostly) points, reveals the direction in which we want to go.' He notes that before we orient the body to where we want to go, we first orient the feet. The feet move before any other part of the body since it is the medium of movement.

Practical Illustrations

Case Study I: Lawyer B is known all over the country; apart from court cases, he has also been invited to many functions to deliver lectures, making him very popular. More so, he says a runs pro bono for some people in the society. This makes some people refer to him as human rights activist. However, he is hated by judges and many of his colleagues, not because of his intelligence but what most of them refer to as hypocrisy and pride. Due to his fame, he does not seem to respect anyone again and while arguing in courts, he quotes past cases he had won rather than citing more relevant examples from other sources. He also lost some cases due to this but there was no one to hint him. In his last appearance in court, he was arguing for a politician who was suspended from his party due to alleged anti-party activities. As he stood up to present his case, the juror turned his feet towards the jury room while still facing him. This communicates the latter's disdain for the lawyer.

Case Study II: Mr PZ had worked as the secretary of Dr XV some three years ago before the former was transferred. During that period, it was a tug of war between them as they never aligned in principles and policies. Being the manager, Dr XV would always have his way. This was a point of pain for PZ. So he was filled with happiness when he got his transfer letter, noting that he was out of 'hell.' Lo and behold, three years after, they seemed to be reuniting as Dr XV has also been transferred to the branch where PZ currently works. When PZ heard this, he felt like tendering his resignation letter; he recalled their ill memories and had always prayed not to have anything to do with him again until he got the letter. As the job demands, he had prepared his office and put everything in order before his arrival. When Dr XV finally arrived, he was also surprised to see his former secretary. He composed himself and stretched out his hands to him while PZ received them warmly with smiles on the faces of the two but their feet were not pointed at each other. This is a show of mutual dislike.

Case Study III: Impostor FY is both social and confident; it takes him just a few minutes to make friends wherever he finds himself. So he counted this trait as one of the things that would work for him while trying to impersonate another person. When he got to the checkpoint, he looked for a way to make friends with the officials but none was ready to relate with a total stranger under whatever guise. He knew he might not survive the scrutiny at the venue. Even before his name was called on, he had felt like fleeing the place. His feet were turned to the direction of the exit door while awaiting the decision of the officers. This is show of low self-esteem and loss of hope, culminating into disinterest.

23.7. Pigeon Toes

Generic Interpretations of the Concept

The emotional stability of people is determined by how they react to difficult situations. To know people and what they represent, let them be confronted with a troubling situation and see how they handle it. Those who make lasting decisions are known as strong people. There are people that when something threatens their peace, they quickly turn their toes in. This is referred to as *pigeon toes*. It is a negative body language that is displayed in reaction to an unfavourable circumstance.

There are a lot of reasons that can propel this behaviour in people. What mostly causes this is insecurity. When you think something or someone will defeat you, you curl in your toes to look smaller and secure. This is symbolic; it is as if you are throwing the toes into your pocket so that they are not injured.

Imagine walking on a bushy road and a snake just runs past the same route. Even though it has gone, you will still point in your toes as if it climbs them. They are the most pointed part of the body and it shares in almost everything happening to the feet. Also, if you have ever nursed the evil thought of a gigantic object falling on you, you will observe that the first thing you do is to point the toes inward so that the heavy object does not fall on them.

Those who are shy are also fond of this behaviour. It means they do not want to move beyond their present location. The person might be shy of changing their seat so that all eyes are not focused on them. Toes that move inward illustrate resistance to walk. The same thing goes for introverts. To a shy or introverted human being, this gesture means discomfort. They are trying to hide from public glare and would not want to take anything that will expose them beyond their present comfort.

Pointing the toes inward is a behaviour that we display when are particularly vulnerable. When you see this, it means the person is afraid of something—real or imaginary. A mere thought of something defeating or putting us to shame is enough to arouse this cue. We display fear when it appears real to the limbic brain that it can occur. This behaviour is often seen among children and sometimes displayed by adults too. When you observe it, it means the person is emotionally apprehensive and needs your help.

Scientific Explanations

Philip (2014) states that this gesture is also known as *tibial torsion*. The body language expert surmises that this gesture connotes submission. It is used in general and dating context. He opines, 'The pigeon toes posture is most effective when used by children and women as it is submissive in nature.' This does not mean that men too cannot make use of this gesture but the challenge remains that no one might be sympathetic towards their course. This gesture is used by children and women to invoke the favour of people. When they point their toes inward, it means they are submissive and needs the other person's help. The verbal translation of this gesture is given as 'When I point my toes inward, I'm shrinking my body profile so as to appear more submissive and docile.'

Practical Illustrations

Case Study I: Child X is a very shy kid; he is only free and happy when with his family members. While many people think he is reserved, they do not know that he can speak for hours while with his parents. This behaviour has been affecting him negatively academically because he finds it difficult to ask questions even if he does not understand a concept. Sometimes, he is forced to whisper his questions to a mate. His teachers have called him several times on that and his parents have always warned him but he does not seem to be getting over the attitude. One day, they were given a group project by one of their teachers. This means they had to meet and liaise on how to do the presentation and present the best work. When they gathered and everyone was suggesting modalities to adopt, Child X stood straight with his toes pointing inward, finding it difficult to raise his voice like others. He was later forced to talk. This is an act of cowardice, portraying himself as being inferior to others.

Case Study II: Mr RD is an introvert. Although he has a few friends that he moves with, he finds it difficult to make new friends. Maintaining eye contact for too long is another issue he has. His colleagues at work knows him for this and many of them will actually have to force him to voice up on some issues so that he would not be taken for granted. Among his close friends, he is always mocked that he cannot woo a lady. Whenever they were walking together and see a beautiful lady, they would dare him to go for her, but he would smile at their mockery, even such crude jokes get into him sometimes. When he eventually got a wife, people were surprise, thinking it was arranged by friends through a match-making medium. The day he went to know the lady's parents, while in their living room, he pointed his toes inward as if he was asked not to stretch out his legs. This was a clear depiction of nervousness and fear.

Case Study III: Mrs FG needed to spend some time with a man-lover outside of her duty post because the man was billed to travel out of the continent the next day. She knew that if she failed to meet with him that day, he was not going to drop anything for her. However, she did not know the excuse to present at work because of the strict discipline there and non-tolerance for unprofessional attitudes. She decided to take the bull by the horn by making herself absent without informing anyone. She switched off her phones throughout the day so that no one would reach out to her from the office. When she resumed work the next day, she was queried and, as such, needed to appear before the CEO. On her appearance, she sat with her toes pointing inwards and was almost shaking, seeing the anger on the face of her boss. This means she was fearful as the reaction of her boss would definitely be negative.

Case Study IV: Before Man TE was illegally brought into Country DQO, he was expressly told that illegal immigrants find it difficult to find work and live freely. Yet, he agreed to the terms and paid the agent huge amount of money to be helped out. In his first week of arriving the country, he could not move out of his room due to the proactive nature of law enforcement officials in arresting illegal immigrants. Then, he knew he was into real trouble; he started regretting his action. Sometimes, the raid looked like war as the illegal immigrants would run to save themselves. Whenever at the window to sneak at them, his toes would unconsciously point inwards. This means he was engrossed in fear.

23.8. Pointing Toes Up

Generic Interpretations of the Concept

We point our toes up to tell the world that we are feeling good. When people are elated or comfortable being in a discussion, they will point the toes of a foot up, while the heel is rooted firmly on the ground. This can even be done when the person is on phone. Anywhere you notice it, rest assured that the person is feeling at home. I have maintained at different points in time in this book that gravity-defying behaviours are used in displaying positive attitude and this is not an exception.

When you root the heel on the ground and raise the toes up, this behaviour opens up the underneath of the foot. This is metaphorical; it shows that the person is open. People will not display open behaviour when they feel threatened. Hence, this gesture can be taken as a symbol of comfort. This is a reliable indicator that the person is sincere and honest in their discussion with you. If the person were talking with their tongue in their cheek, they will not point the toes up; everything about them would be close. You will also observe that people who point up their toes will feel relaxed and use their hands in demonstrations while talking. They do everything to add credibility to their message without sounding rude.

The toes pointing up cue may be as a result of the topic being discussed. There are times that we do not necessarily like people but agree with them on certain issues. This is seen in politics and business world. Even while in public transport, when someone who does not know you is receptive of your ideas, they will open up and may point their toes up to tell you that they share the same opinion with you. This increases trust between the discussants, making them to keep on with the discourse for long duration.

When good friends run into each other, this gesture is not rare between them. A person who displays this gesture can easily be wounded by an adversary. It is an indication that they trust their co-interlocutor that nothing evil will come through them. Once they do not feel comfortable with each other again, they will quickly release the toes, making them stand more firm to argue and fight, if need be.

Scientific Explanations

Parvez (2015) states it clearly that when people point their toes upward, it is an indication of positivity. He puts it thus: 'When the toes point upward, it means the person is in a good mood or is thinking or hearing something positive.' Just the thought of something negative is capable of truncating your good feelings, so also is having positive thought is capable of arousing your emotions along the right path. The limbic brain processes every piece of information as real. For instance, if a teacher announces a camping trip to the class, the especially excited students will point their toes upward.

If someone is on phone and you see them pointing their toes upward, be sure that they are either hearing good news or enjoying the conversation with their co-interlocutor. You can confirm this by the ceaseless smiles that appear in the conversation. They will be generally feel relaxed and hold on to the call for as long as the person keeps saying what excites them (Parvez 2015).

How To Get Your Own Way (2019) also aligns itself with the explanation of Parvez. The website states that when someone points their toes upward, it is an indication of happiness. It is encoded in the root of the term 'jump for joy.' We move up to show that we are delighted about something.

Practical Illustrations

Case Study I: Guy V and his spouse, Lady K, are discussing on the phone. The latter is not in town; she travels for a professional course in a neighbouring city. Before leaving, she promised her lover that she would always make out time to speak with him for hours on a daily basis. As expected, the discussions are not based on nothing serious apart from being briefed on their respective activities during the day and then play love on phone. Running a hectic schedule at work, Guy V would sit on a couch, place the heel of his root foot firmly on the ground and point up his toes. He smiles to himself and in the relaxed mood, will speak for hours with his lover. They had no reason to doubt each other. Hence, this non-verbal gesture is a depiction of positive vibes—they are excited and feeling great about each other.

Case Study II: T and Y are very close friends. In fact, some people have labelled them as being gay due to the intimacy they share. Their individual spouses are even sometimes jealous of the time they spend together and how they do not get tired speaking for a long duration of time. T had to try for a work-related assignment for two weeks. The two weeks was really a tough period for both of them even though they were speaking on phone. When T arrived, Y rushed to his house and the reunion was done as if the former had been out for a year. They surely have many stories to tell. After eating, T placed his heel firmly on the floor and pointed up his toes and started dishing out the things that amazed him during his trip. This is a show of comfort. That is, he did not have anything to fear.

Case Study III: A head of an organisation and his assistant are discussing some of the ways to improve on their service delivery. They are very close and their relationship trends beyond official lines. This has positively affected the firm as they make decisions without trying to outsmart each other. A lot of people have envied them, noting that such show of true brotherhood is rare in today's world. Even after every other employee might have left, they will still stay behind to discuss important issues pertaining to the growth of the organisation. On this particular occasion, the head of the firm places his heel on the floor while pointing up his toes, relaxing and exposing his vulnerable part while he chats with his colleague. This means he is really relaxed and excited about the discussion.

Case Study IV: Con artist QI was looking for every means available to develop relationship with Man RC, an international consultant. He was particular about the friendship because he knew the man had link to some of the organisations he wanted to gain entry into. While they met at the eatery for their first few encounters, he volunteered that he should visit the man at home in their next meeting. Man RC agreed to his suggestion and he was surprised at the way he felt at home on his first visit; he took off his shoes, placed his heel on the table which made his toes to point upward. This is a positive body language.

23.9. Exposing the Soles of the Feet

Generic Interpretations of the Concept

This is laced with mixed reactions and interpretations across cultures. As such, you need to understand your host community before attempting to display this gesture. When you expose the sole of your feet by rest the ankle on your knee it is taken as a symbol of relaxation in the Western world; they do not see anything being wrong in it. However, there are other regions of the world where it would be inappropriate to display this gesture.

Africa, Middle East and some parts of Asia are the major parts of the world where this gesture should be avoided. It is considered as an insulting gesture in the aforementioned regions. It is believed that the soles of the feet are meant for stepping on the ground, you now raising it to them is tantamount to rubbing shit on their face. To these communities, it is a forbidden act to show them your soles. We challenge people's authority by exposing the soles of the feet; you are non-verbally telling them, 'You are beneath me.' If you say this to someone higher than you in profession or age, it is truly insulting and you should be prepared for the same measure of reaction. Some other times, this is also interpreted to mean that someone is not worth the least of our time.

This is rude. When talking to someone higher than you in rank, you are expected to be on your feet and address the person respectfully. Even if the person is a colleague or a junior, they also deserve some respect. So sit right and respond to their posers. This portrays you as a responsible and caring human.

To be on a safe side, do not expose the soles of your feet while in public. When both feet are kept on the ground, it gives you the opportunity to defend yourself if the need arises. Better still, you can drape a leg over the opposite knee in order to make the sole point downward.

Scientific Explanations

Straker (2019) warns that we should understand the individual demands of each culture before displaying some cues. The best form of feet placement is for it to be down on the ground. With that, they are usually unnoticeable and subtle in the message they pass. However, when you place your ankle on the knee, it exposes the sole of the foot to others which is considered unacceptable in some regions of the world. Straker encodes it thus: 'In some cultures the feet are the lowest part of the body and exposing them to others is an insult, particularly the sole of the foot.' Hence, you need to exercise caution in your display of this gesture, especially when in a location comprising of people from different cultural affiliations.

Practical Illustrations

Case Study I: Mr UI went for a programme in another continent. He lives a careless lifestyle; he easily socialises with people and break barriers in communication, especially when dealing with those he thinks are good for his future endeavours. While a lot of people have commended him for this, some think it was getting too much and should be curbed. On this particular trip far away from home, he actually reaped the negative side of his behaviour; he did not bother to learn some specifics of non-verbal cues of the people. After one of the days' activities, he decided to chill out in a restaurant near him. Of course, due to his open-mindedness, he quickly made friends. While discussing with the natives at the restaurant, he felt like relaxing himself by placing his ankle on his left knee. Immediately, the person his sole was exposed to wore a frown, dropped his glass of wine and withdrew himself from the conversation. Others became passive too and Mr UI wondered what went wrong until he readjusted his posture and then, they came back to life. This amazed him but he learnt his lesson. That is, he did not know that this gesture was an insulting one before he used it in public.

Case Study II: FM has been looking for a way to disassociate himself from one of his foreign friends who has been nothing but a locust to him. He has tried helping him out of his lack in all ways, but it appears that the friend is just a lazy folk who wants manna to drop for him from nowhere at all times. When it was becoming obvious that until a drastic step was taken, he would not desist from his annoying act, FM decided to find out what is most painful to him and he said being looked down upon. Hence, FM decided to use non-verbal means to pass his message. One day, when he came, he served him food and sat adjacent to him. While the friend was eating, he placed his ankle on his knee and the friend seemed not to be perturbed but when FM maintained the same posture for too long, he dropped his spoon and rushed out, claiming to have an urgent appointment. That was his last day there. He thought FM was not willing to see, and as such, he should maintain a distance with him.

Case Study III: RD always feels bigger than everyone else and does not believe in reciprocating respect accorded him by others. This has made him lose important people in his life but he does not look like someone who is willing to turn a new leaf. More so, he surrounds himself with sycophants who are only concerned about what they can get out of him and not how to make him loved by others. He has a political ambition and believes that his wealth and connections will endear him to the people at the polls. However, this is far from the truth with fillers from the populace. In one of his interview series with a man believed to be the gateway of journalism in their abode, RD looked down on him, perceiving that journalists are poor and he cannot be questioned anyhow. During the course of the interview, he placed his ankle on his knee and exposed the sole of his foot to the journalist to insult him for his seemingly difficult questions.

Case Study IV: Impersonator FB made his effort a do-or-die one; when he submitted his details for the immigration officials to verify. Instead of standing at the counter, he went to sit on an available chair as if he cared less of what was being done. He looked away and when he wasn't being cleared, he had it in mind not to leave the place—he told them he was really the one, trying to prove the authenticity of the image on the passport to them from his seat. He got angry when no one was giving him attention. As a way of hurling insults at them, he removed his shoes and revealed the sole of his feet to their direction but none cared.

23.10. Bouncy Elated Feet

Generic Interpretations of the Concept

When we are happy, the feet are not left out in the demonstration of this. They begin to bounce and become very light to carry. This means the person is excited about something. We use this to register emotional high. When the feet become animated and jumpy, the person is experiencing some positive emotions. There are times that people might feign sadness just to elicit the feeling of pity and sympathy from you. They may even use this means to dupe you of your resources. If you feel a situation should not warrant negative emotion and someone is trying to display such, leave their face and focus on the feet. If they feet are jumpy in a gravity-defying manner, it means they are actually happy but trying to lure you into doing their bidding by appealing to your emotions.

Jumpy, happy feet are very pronounced in kids when you tell them something they want to hear. For instance, informing them of your intention to take them to theme park or cinema to see a favourite movie. Kids hardly hide their emotions; they display them according to the situation at hand. This behaviour is also seen in adults too. For instance, poker players are also fond of feet bouncing whenever they have a monster hand.

While displaying this behaviour, the feet might be out of sight but the effect of the bouncing feet makes the entire leg to shake or tremble, hence perceiving the gesture through the clothing, even to the point of the shoulders. When we hear good news, the feet are always ready to jump in elation, shaking the clothing and the body as a whole. It is only dull feet that will remain in the same spot for long without any movement. Also, the expression on the face will either be genuine smile or laughter to complement the appropriateness of the gesture. This means lines are falling in pleasant places for the person and they will like to swim in the positive feeling for as long as it can last. This is a special feeling that we all love being attached to. When people are truly happy, they want others close to them to know about it. While this might not be verbally expressed, our non-verbal cues point in that direction. We must learn how to decode this in order to mirror them and help them keep the unique feeling. With that, we will endear them to our heart.

Scientific Explanations

Goman (2010) is clear about the fact that our feet do not only react to stressors but are also very audible in the projection of positive emotions. She affirms that 'dancing for joy, kicking up your heels, walking on air and staying on your toes are all familiar phrases for a reason. Bouncing, tapping, wiggling feet are what professional poker players call "happy feet".' In poker game, when you notice this gesture, it means the player has a strong hand in the game. This also extends to business world where we see happy, jumpy feet when a negotiation works in the favour of one of the negotiating parties. As a result of this gesture, you will observe a bounce around the shoulders.

Philip (2014) describes happy feet as those that 'bounce up and down with joy, point upwards when standing, or seem to have a spring in their step when walking. Other times happy feet are feet that point or move in the direction of something they like.' This is apt as it gives instances where this gesture can be demonstrated. To tell others that you are happy, healthy and feeling confident, this is a good posture to use. People who see you display this gesture see it as a sign of good fortunes and are likely to relate with you based on that. Hence, the verbal translation of this cue given as 'I'm happy with joy so my honest feet defy gravity by bouncing, toes rising and pointing.'

Practical Illustrations

Case Study I: T has always begged her parents to take her for a hangout but their busy schedules have been a point of denial for her. At school, when her peers are recounting their enviable, charming experiences at different forums, she is always kept in the dark and feels alienated. Inasmuch as she understands the nature of her parents' job, she thinks it has been coming too much because they still made out time for other things. In a way, she is trying to infer that they are not making her their priority. To every child, this can be unimaginably painful, especially when such attitudes are done without any iota of remorse from the offending side. Hence, she begins to act funny. When the parents can no longer bear with her 'weird behaviours' at home, the father calls her on a particular Friday to assure her that he would dedicate the whole of the following day to her. Immediately, T feels unusually happy, becomes indescribably light and her feet bounce in an elated manner.

Case Study II: One technique that Mr AX has consistently used in keeping his class in the right shape is his ability to make it interactive. Even the shy ones among the students whisper their feelings and opinions to colleagues seated beside them. This means no one is ever left out in the process as the class goes on. This has ensured passing of knowledge in the best way; at least, each student has something to learn in his class. For almost a decade, he has been winning the prize of the best teacher. Students that come under his tutelage have also improved dramatically, making him a cynosure of all eyes. One of the students, MB, has always looked for ways to win his prizes but always missed out on the verge of doing that. One day, Mr AX came into the class and informed them that he was not only going to award those who got his answers right but also those who had always been participating overtime. MB knew it was just his time to be celebrated. Unknowingly, the teacher had written a list to be announced at the end of the class. When his name was eventually called by the teacher, MB's feet became jumpy and he bounced out of his seat.

Case Study III: When the luxurious bus moving from Country RDE to Country FQY was stopped, some of the illegal immigrants among the passengers thought an end had come to their journey because they heard that that particular checkpoint is the toughest. However, it seemed the officials were focused more on drug traffickers and human smugglers than illegal immigrants this time around. After the whole search process, Illegal Immigrant QY was not found out. He was very happy as they were asked to return to their seats. His feet became light and bouncy and the general feeling of excitement engulfed him. He couldn't share his story with anyone so as not to be exposed.

23.11. Tapping of Foot

Generic Interpretations of the Concept

Tapping of the foot against the floor is done in different instance, meaning that the message each bears is peculiar to the context in which it is displayed. I will run through at least three different contexts in which this can be done and the likely message it communicates in each. Before that, it is crucial to note that the foot can either be tapped with the heel in a static position while the front of the foot moves up and down while some people actually make use of the heel, drumming it against the floor. The case of the latter is often more pronounced and audible due to the fact that the heel is strong and hits the ground more forcefully compared with the front of the toes. Hence, the case of which part of the foot to use is based on preference or the force of the emotional feeling at that given point in time.

Having said that, foot tapping is a classic way of dealing with boredom. If someone does not want to appear bored while passing the time, this is a fantastic way out for them. The action directs the attention of the brain to this rhythmic action. It produces a soothing effect which overrides the otherwise negative feeling that would have set in. For instance, if you were waiting for someone, instead of being disturbed by the delay caused by the person, this behaviour calms you down and diverts your attention from the ill feeling against the person.

In another context, tapping foot is in a bid to keep tempo with music. Some people are music freak and they demonstrate it from all indications—whether in public or in private settings. In a public transport, you may see someone plug in their earpiece or headphone, get distracted from the activities going on in their immediate environment while they tap their foot to the tone of the music they are listening to. This means the person is really into the music may even use both feet in demonstration of this when the feeling overwhelms them. I have a musician friend who is fond of foot tapping as if he was beating drum set at all times. Sometimes, I get irritated with this but I must remind myself that he is overwhelmed with passion.

Another instance you may notice the tapping of the foot is when someone is becoming impatient. It is like the finger strumming earlier discussed. If a person has been kept waiting for long, and they begin to tap their foot, this is an indication that they can no longer bear it. They are non-verbally telling you, 'My legs are in motion; they want to move.' This may also be feigned to hasten people up. If the person is truly impatient, their face will also bear this message as they would become destabilised.

Scientific Explanations

Parvez (2015) states that shaking the feet is an indication to run away from a given place. 'We shake or tap our feet when we feel impatient or anxious in a situation,' the expert notes. However, he quickly adds that foot tapping may actually connote excitement. This is where the place of context comes in. If there is nothing making the person impatient while they also smile and keep their body open when demonstrating this gesture, it is actually a sign of positive emotion.

In the same vein, Whipple (2019) states that finger and foot tapping bear the same message but there are instances where the latter can be complicated to decode. People tap their foot to deal with impatience and fight boredom. Classroom, presentation arenas, airport counters are some of the places where this gesture always plays out. Whipple states that when you observe this gesture in a person, instead of looking the other way or behaving as if you do not care, you should acknowledge it with a modified cadence. This makes the person feel important and somewhat attended to, even though there has not been verbal communication.

Trying to state the cases where we need to be careful in our interpretations, the body language expert submits that 'when women sit with legs crossed at the knees, they will sometimes bounce the upper foot (the one that is not currently on the floor). They will also often dangle their shoe as they bounce the foot. This gesture can indicate a number of different things, so it is wise to exhibit care with interpreting what you see.' One, it may mean impatience if it is accompanied with finger tapping and also, it may be readiness on the part of the woman to share some information with you. We should not also rule out the likelihood of stress. Tapping the foot also makes the shoe of a woman dangle, this may be a flirting gesture. Hence, you need to look for other clusters along the line of your guess in order to determine the accuracy of your guess.

Practical Illustrations

Case Study I: Mrs DW was supposed to pay a visit to a family friend who was delivered from a ghastly accident. She put a call across to her husband to inform him of her schedule, should he come home and did not meet her. Since the person was well-known to the husband too, Mr DW suggested that she should wait for him so that they go together as he was not used to such occasions. The wife told him to hurry up before nightfall and he promised that he was almost through at the office. Mrs DW decided to quickly prepare food before his arrival. After cooking, she sat at the living room, dressed and hoping that the husband would show up soon. But an hour after that, she did not see him. She called him again, and he informed her to lock the door wait outside as he was a stone throw away. Ten minutes after that, Mr DW did not arrive. The woman began to tap her foot as she looked across the road longingly till his eventual arrival. The impatience could be seen in her eyes as she dashed off into the car immediately.

Case Study II: Doctor HW gave much of his attention to Patient DQ due to the peculiarity of her sickness. This means that he worked outside of his duty time just to ensure that she responded well to treatment. She had been rejected in about five other places before she was referred to him. So he knew her hope was dependent on him. At first, she was cooperative by doing all that was required of her but it got to a point she started selecting drugs by herself without anyone's knowledge. When the nurses got to know and informed HW, he became infuriated and was unconsciously tapping his foot continuously. This means he was stressed by the occurrence.

Case Study III: Man TW is an illegal immigrant in Country TSA. This means that he doesn't have the legal requirements to work or even live in the country at all. So he only takes menial jobs and has specific times that he goes out so as not to fall into the hands of enforcement agents. In one of such outings, he finished the job at hand late and instead of the woman he worked for to have prepared his payment beforehand, she was not responsive and while he was waiting, he became impatient, began to tap his foot as if he should have got home before the start of evening raid. Apart from the leg tapping, the frown he wore would tell any observant fellow that he was disturbed by something.

23.12. Wriggling of the Toes

Generic Interpretations of the Concept

Just like happy, bouncy feet, when we begin to wiggle our toes, it provides us with unique and exceptional feelings that is capable of making us stay positive throughout the day. Toe wiggling is actually inspired by the occurrence or thought of something exciting happening to us. When you see a person wiggle their toes, chances are high that things are working out favourably for them. It is an indication of lack of negative feelings. Someone who was probably thinking that something will not work out but to his surprise, later worked out than they had envisioned will wiggle their toes in demonstration of joy. It is just a state of mind where the toes become happily restless because something fantastic has happened to a person.

Further, I have noticed this gesture in those who are eagerly anticipating something. The toes twist and turn very rapidly as if they are about walking to meet their expectations. For instance, if your spouse promises you something you long for on their way from work, once you begin to expect them to arrive home, your toes may wriggle in display of your suspense. The same thing goes for a long-time friend who tells you he or she is in town and coming to see you. You begin to feel excited that you want to set your eyes on a beloved friend. This is demonstrated through the whole body, the toes inclusive.

The quick movement and twisting of the toes is connected to the proper functionality of the brain; the process stimulates nerves which aid in dealing with stress or boredom. Our feeling per time is dependent on the event at hand. A thought of something exciting which appears real to the subconscious brain is worthy of lifting us out of a depressing thought. I have heard of instances where doctors treated patients based on confessions when their condition defied all forms of medications. Hence, we may observe this feeling when we move from a depressed state to an exciting one.

Scientific Explanations

Philip (2014) observes that when the toes wiggle, they move up and down in a bouncy manner. Sometimes, toes may wiggle in the direction of a thing that interests a person. The twitching is usually very pronounced as the toes make effort in communicating the heart desire of a person. The non-verbal communication expert submits that toe wiggling 'signals happiness, confidence, and good health.' When we are elated, the body is charged and we are bound to display this gesture in various manner. If you want to communicate with others that all is well with you, twitching or moving your toes in a rapid manner bears this message. When people perceive happiness or general positive emotion on you, they are likely to relate with you in a more open manner. The natural law of life is that like poles attract while unlike poles repel. If you behave like an excited, happy person, you are more likely to attract people with the same feeling and mindset into your life.

Wiggling of the toes keep the body in motion. This prepares them for an action. If you are elated about something you are expecting, the toes are set in motions through this gesture. Metaphorically, the toes are set to accompany you to where they think your happiness lies. I have seen people who bluff with this gesture while playing poker. Those who are attuned with this behaviour will think that they actually have a strong hand, when in actual fact, they have none. Hence, toe wriggling maybe a mere camouflage in some instances. The non-verbal translation of this gesture is given as 'I'm happy with joy so my honest feet defy gravity by bouncing, toes rising and pointing' (Philip 2014).

The body language expert concludes that the toes may also wiggle as a way of dealing with boredom or stress, especially when we want to take our leave from a given place.

Practical Illustrations

Case Study I: Child CJ is a sport lover but his school does not encourage sporting activities. This has really affected him negatively as he was beginning to lift off his heart from anything sports. However, no matter how hard he tries, he still finds himself running towards the television any time there is a major tournament being broadcast. He has complained to his parents about this and they have made his intentions known to the management but the school does not appear to be proactive about it. Due to that, they planned withdrawing him from the institution but he is already at the final year. Hence, such a decision would have a devastating effect on him. Towards their end of high school activities, the parents received an email from the school on a particular Saturday which revealed that CJ and peers would play a football match with a neighbouring school. When CJ was informed of this development, he knew he would be one of the participants and immediately, his toes began to wiggle uncontrollably as he anticipated the event.

Case Study II: Ms UY and Mr DP graduated from the same university. They were very close during their university days as they were always seen together— they were reading partners, attended party as couples, hanged out on weekends and sat beside each other during lectures. At some point, they began to develop emotions for each other and it later worked out in an inexplicable manner. However, the lover was not really solidified before their graduation and eventual departure. Life happened and each had to pursue their visions but they kept checking on each other. Any time they planned visiting each other, something will come up and scuttle the plan. One day, DP had a conference to attend at the city where UY lives. He gave her a call and fortunately, she was off work for those three days. Invariably, she could play host to Mr DP without any issues. When she heard this, the lady became inexplicably excited the reunion that was about to happen. Her toes wiggled as she awaited his arrival. This shows she was anticipating something good which was actually coming her way.

Case Study III: Man RD and Woman FD did a marriage of convenience in order to enable the woman travel abroad. On her scheduled day of interview, the man was there to give her moral support. In fact, he held her bag just to camouflage that they were indeed in love. Since the man had good reputation at the office, they just asked them few questions and gave them the nod. When it was sure that she would be issued that visa, Woman FD's toes began to wriggle as she smiled unreservedly at Man RD before making for the exit door; she was really excited at her success.

23.13. Feet Agitation

Generic Interpretations of the Concept

When we are agitated, the feet are not left out in demonstration of this. In fact, they play a leading role as other parts of the body may be afraid to show our divergence, especially if the opponent is seen to be more powerful than we do. Generally, when we are agitated, it means we are not pleased with something. Hence, we either have the option of moving nearer to put things in order or moving away from what is irritating us. In either case, the feet serve as the object of movement in fulfilling our aspiration. Their indispensability makes them an object of focus in non-verbal communication. This is not limited to a particular age grade as it can be seen across all strata in the society.

As parents, we all identify the agitated feet of our feet when they are about leaving the table to play. While working their school exercise with them or trying to teach them something, once they become bored or their attention is diverted, they will begin to agitate for a break through their feet. You will see them dragging the feet in a noisy manner so that you would not feign deafness. More so, they will tilt their head backwards to look at you in a pitiable manner, trying to evoke your sympathy emotions. It would be clear to you that the child has lost concentration and the movement of their feet is telling you that he or she would prefer to be at any other place but with you. If you eventually heed their pleas, you will see them move briskly out of your presence because the feet are already in motion.

Even in a gathering comprising of only adults, you will observe agitation through the feet when someone wants to take their leave. Our feet telegraph our desires per time. For instance, if we want to leave, the movement becomes noticeably uncomfortable. The toes may also point at the door. In a boardroom, if someone draws our interest through their submission, we tend to move closer to them by pointing at their direction. In the case of a negative reaction, the feet become restless as they seek to fight or fly, depending on the instruction of the limbic brain. In either way, the discomfort becomes excessive that those on the other side of the table may be forced to call off the meeting.

When we are not in tandem in what a co-interlocutor is saying, we demonstrate our dissatisfaction through the movement of our feet; we begin to move them from side to side, shift them repetitively, move a foot inward or hide both feet, and continuous raising and lowering of the heels.

Scientific Explanations

Study Body Language (2016) observes that it can be very annoying when people display agitation through their feet because it irritates the mind. It is just like the foot tapping that was earlier discussed. People become agitated when bored and impatient. The continuous shifting of the feet is to deal with nervousness and put the body in motion so as to resist every form of attack. Even though this habit can be controlled but people may rather intensify it as a means of passing their message across. To make the agitation more pronounced, the shifting and movement becomes more rapid and shaky. The faster the rate, the more agitated the person is. Interestingly, as the boredom or nervousness fades, the feet become slower and more relaxed. Hence, this is a good way to measure someone's level of discomfort or unrest.

Westside Toastmasters (2019) also opines that feet agitation is one of the most reliable means of understanding the intent of people. According to the platform, this gesture is 'revealing an evolutionary base frustration at not being able to escape a situation.'

Practical Illustrations

Case Study I: Child TF is very playful and despite being scolded at different points in time, he is yet to turn a new leaf. The parents first blamed his attitude on the caregiver taking care of him but after some close monitoring, it has appeared to them that the boy is simply unserious. Being the only child, they understand that something drastic needs to be done before he is lost to negative occurrences. After series of meetings, the mother decides to resign her time-consuming job and begin to offer freelancing services so that she would spend more time with the kid. Three months after her resignation, the family can see some improvements as he pours out his mind to the mother than other person. The parents now ensure he does his homework on Friday before switching on television. However, this does not mean that TF is totally reformed. On a particular Saturday, he and his mother were solving some mathematics questions when he discovered that it was time for his favourite team to play, he began to shift his feet from one side to the other and yawned uncontrollably that even the mother began to feel tired. So she was forced to release him. He was only feeling tired because he was kept in a place against his wish.

Case Study II: In a boardroom filled with people from different departments, they were discussing how to block leakages in their firm and be innovative about creating other channels for making money so as not to be adversely affected by the world economic downturn. Before talking of any form of novel idea, the CEO suggested that they should first do a review of their present performances and individual participation in the overall interest of the firm. Many of them know that any time their head makes such insistence, heads are about to row and this time around, no one can predict who would be affected because they were not briefed beforehand. They began to fidget and looked for a way to shelve the situation report aside. One of the supervisors brought the suggestion while a lot of them backed him up but it looked as if the CEO was not going to buy into their idea. Many of the disgruntled people at the meeting began to shift their feet from side to side, looking worried and withdrew the feet at some point. Yet, the CEO did not succumb to their wish. It means the employees were stressed.

Case Study III: Man TD almost got his goods cleared through the backdoor with the use of a compromised agent; when the clearing agent was about to push out his goods, there was an order from their supervisor that no one should be attended to that day again. This was a dent on his image as some other officers would take over the next day and his goods would be the first to be attended to. This means the rot he was covering would probably be blown up on this given day. He became agitated on hearing the order of the supervisor; he shifted his feet from one side to the other in protest of the order. It was really baffling and one can easily notice this agitating spirit on his face.

23.14. Anxious Pacing

Generic Interpretations of the Concept

We all have our unique ways of dealing with stress. This means you should not be myopic or too relaxed in pinpointing a particular behaviour to people as a sign of stress. Doing that will make you miss out on the indicators of stress as you meet more people in the course of life sojourn. One of the means some people have consistently demonstrated their anxiety is through nervous pacing. When gripped with fear, the effect is felt on the feet and this is displayed through the walking style imbibed by the person at that given time. It should be noted that the level of stress we are confronted with and what is the source of the nervousness will dictate our action. In the case of freeze response, we will not move at all; we will stay at some point, losing our breath, shielding ourselves from what is considered as the source of fear.

However, nervous pacing is regarded as flight response. After analysing a situation and considering our chances of winning in the case of violence and discover that our chances are slim, we tend to take to our heels. This is common on the playground among kids. If they see one of their peers as a bully and there is a disagreement, before the bully gets to them, they would have dashed for the road and run home, usually on a high speed. This is to flee from all appearances of danger. While running is acceptable among kids, this may look weird among adults. Hence, walking on a fast speed being a subtle form adopted by adults. As we walk on a steady speed, we will look at the back once in a while to be certain that the adversary is not following us. Note that nervous pacing, most times, is a directionless form of walking; the person does not have a particular location in mind, only for them to dodge what is perceived as danger and stay in safe distance.

When you see a person pacing up and down in exasperation, you can look for other clusters in order to confirm their nervousness. They are usually restless; they are afraid that what they are walking away from might still be within reach or something may show up to further destabilise them. Further, the person is generally not composed. The pacing about is meant to pacify their emotions and until the person is pacified, they will still give themselves out.

Scientific Explanations

Oxford Dictionary defines *pace* as walking 'at a steady speed, especially without a particular destination and as an expression of anxiety or annoyance.' There are two important factors we should take cognisance of in this definition— no particular destination and expression of anxiety. Those who are anxious are not particular about where they go rather than for them to get out danger. It is usually safety first and any route that appears safe to them would be taken whether it leads to where they are going or not. And secondly, it is done out of anxiety. The two points definitely link up to each other. If not for anxiety, people will not walk aimlessly.

Philip (2014) maintains that the essence of nervous pacing to burn off excessive energy from the body. Without argument, it is a sign of anxiety—a negative body language signal. He gives the verbal translation as 'I'm uneasy and full of stress so I'm walking back and forth to burn off some of my excess energy and provide a self-soothing feeling.' Imagine a person whose spouse is wheeled into the theatre for a surgery, they will look disturbed and pace up and down as they await the outcome of the process. Philip concludes that 'pacing is a classic full-blown signal of anxiety, and falls into the energy displacement category because it gives us something to do and burns extra calories in a slight, but controlled fashion to make us feel more relaxed. It is the burning of energy that provides a release of soothing neurochemicals.'

Practical Illustrations

Case Study I. Terrorist FFC is an expert in suicide-bombing planning, an educated terrorist. He was brainwashed during his university days when he met with one of the adherents of the doctrines of the terrorist group. Since then, he has even become more committed to the group than the person who introduced him. Being educated makes him one of the most valuable tools in the group. Immediately after his induction, he was made to join the intelligence unit of the group. So he helps in feeling the pulse of the public about their activities and what different law enforcement agencies were doing to track them down.

Due to his zeal and many unimaginable feats within his short stay, he has been promoted as the head of the unit. This propels him to do more and even subjects his life to needless threats. He and his group decides to attack an economic hub to a city, knowing that if it works out successfully well, there would be numerous casualties and it would trend throughout the continent. He was the one who went to spy on the targeted hub himself. However, there had been security reports before he got there. So everywhere was already rounded up and everyone thoroughly searched. Seeing this, he knew if he should attempt going further, that might be his end, he paced nervously out of the hub, looking disturbed until he got a cab out of the area.

Case Study II: CB brought in his friends to their home when his parents were out and had a party. They were about twenty. So they had to rearrange the living room so that it could give them desirable shape. Many of them did not just stay at the living room, they moved about freely and did whatever they wanted to without any fear of being caught. Some of them went into the inner rooms to smoke. Somehow, one of the room caught fire. They quickly put it off and knew it was time for them to leave or else face the wrath of CB's parents. Without telling their friend of what had happened in the inner room, they dashed out immediately the party came to an end, pacing nervously, with the hope that they would have gone out of sight before the return of CB's parents. As they paced up and down, they kept their eyes on each route and coming vehicle. This means they were really afraid, and as such, their spirit is high so as to keep watch on everything that might serve as a threat to them.

Case Study III: Mr HX forged a document of an organisation demanding that the receiving organisation should send a piece of confidential information to a different address from where they had often sent it. Since such letters are to be submitted during official hours, he deceived his boss that he was sick on the day he was to submit it; he took a day off. However, while approaching the place, he was engulfed in fear due to the possible questions that would spring up in the course of submission. This thought slowed down his pace of movement in order to think of all possibilities. This is an ideal portrayal of someone engulfed in negative thoughts.

23.15. Legs Indicating Desires

Generic Interpretations of the Concept

If all other parts of the body compromise in the display of an intent of a person, the legs will not join them. They are always reliable and accurate in revealing the desires and intentions of people per time. The feet indicate the desire of a person even when we may decide to feign such with the upper part of the body. The direction our legs point to bears the message of the heart. If the legs are pointing away from a person, meaning that we are not fascinated about them or the idea they are discussing. Invariably, the legs try to register dislike in that sense. Even if we try to fake leaning towards them, our mind is definitely disconnected and whatever the person says might not bear the intended fruits.

However, when we point towards a person, this is a positive gesture. It means our heart is drawn towards the person and will like to share in their philosophy. Once we find someone admirable, our legs get into action; they want to close the gap that exists between us and the person. Even if we look the other side so as to avoid public backlash or draw people's attention to our desire, the legs would still be pointed to the person. In a gathering, if you see an attractive person you would like to have a romantic relationship with, your legs will give the signal that you want to get closer to them, even though you may seriously be concentrating on a paper you are treating. I have often observed this in a professional setting where it might be out of hand or considered inappropriate for you to approach people for love. Hence, if your mouth is conditioned not to state it, your legs will inadvertently express your desire.

Direction of legs may also be pointed at something—so, it is not all time human. For instance, the legs of my daughter often gravitate towards the windows of a shop displaying candy because she so much loves it, despite having warned her numerous times consuming a lot of candy is not good for her health. Some are fashion freaks; they can spend the last cash on clothing just in a bid to look good. If they see an item that interests them but have no money to purchase same, their feet and legs will gravitate towards that item. This means they desire to have it, only that they are financially incapacitated.

Sometimes, we are torn between two conflicting options whereby we have another appointment somewhere else but are enjoying our conversation in our present location. In such case, the person may be leaning away while their legs remain frozen and pointed to their co-interlocutor. This means we do not want to leave our present location because we like the person we are conversing with.

Scientific Explanations

Cherry (2019) reports that legs, just like many other parts of the body, are useful in communicating the desires of a person. For instance, if you see someone crossing their legs, it is most probably an indicator of discomfort and defensiveness. It is their desire to be comforted at that given time. It may also be a need for privacy. We close off when we do not want others to intrude on our thoughts.

Westside Toastmasters (2019) notes that how we carry our feet per time indicates what our heart desires. The platform notes that when we first meet with strangers, we may cross the legs as if we do not want to open up to them but as the rapport develops, we change our stance gradually. 'The procedure follows a predictable pattern that entails uncrossing their legs first and placing their feet in the parallel pose,' states the website. Particularly, if we admire the person, our feet will be slightly apart and point at them. On the other hand, we tend to withdraw the feet from someone we do not like or share the same opinion with.

Practical Illustrations

Case Study I: Mr KL is the accounting officer of the firm he works with; he is in charge of the financial management of the firm. Hence, he is seen as the bridge between the company and the banks they transact business with. He is a popular face in the major banks in town. So he has a working relationship with many of the employees at the banks. One day, on a Monday, he went to a bank to balance his company's account after he was unable to do that before the end of shift on that Friday. To his surprise, a new face had resumed duty in the bank that day. While that was not his business, the charming beauty of the new employee is a temptation that seemed mountainous for him to overcome. Even though he was standing before another teller, his legs and feet gravitated towards the newly employed lady. The person he was transacting business with saw that he was not really concentrating, smiled at him and urged him to say hello to the lady he was fascinated to in order to concentrate on what he came for. He was romantically drawn to her and this could be seen in his non-verbal behaviour.

Case Study II: Child LJ is an unrepentant lover of candy. At first, no one stopped her but when she later fell sick and the family had to spend huge amount of money in treating her, she had been warned to desist from taking it or minimise its intake to the barest minimum. Her parents' eyes are now o her and what she consumes. Whenever they were walking past a candy shop, her legs would be directed at the window of the shop as if that is where she was heading. There was a day she made this obviously glaring that her mother was forced to ask her if she had changed route. The direction of her legs expresses the innate desire of her mind which is to have some candy.

Case Study III: Mrs UH knows that her husband does not tolerate coming home late. The man is of the opinion that staying back out for long is a hallmark of irresponsibility. However, Mrs UH is having some catch-up chats with one of her childhood friend. They are so engrossed in the conversations that she did not remember to keep track of time. Before she knew it, it was sunset. She began to lean her body away from her childhood friend but her legs are still frozen on the same spot and pointed at the person. She actually wanted to be with the friend but being mindful of her husband. So she grudgingly had to leave.

Case Study IV: Lady AL went on a date with Man HT. Although that was their first date, she was hopeful that it might yield into marriage. So when they were together, she was conscious of the topics she raised; she wanted to know more about the man and his ideologies on certain issues of life. She liked all the answers she got, and her mind connected with him the more. But her mood changed when the man revealed to her that he was a human smuggler. At this point, she leant away from her but her legs, in a frozen state, still pointed to his direction. This means that despite the fact that she frowned at the job the man was involved in, she still loved him for every other thing.

23.16. Leg Outburst

Generic Interpretations of the Concept

Do not forget that the legs are also good communicators of emotions. Housing the largest muscles in the body, they are usually a great source of understanding the emotional feelings of the people we deal with; when the legs communicate emotional feelings, they do so with a maximum effect, making them resounding and audible for those concerned to understand how they feel. Hence, that is why I tagged this subsection 'leg outburst.'

When we do not like what someone did to us or a situation where we find ourselves, we will communicate this unreservedly with the use of our legs. This is a common gesture found among kids. Remember that kids show it as they feel it. In other words, they do not feign what they feel per time. When angered by their parents or peers, children will move, twist and energetically stomp their legs and may accompany it with zigzag shaking of the head and other parts of the body so as to make the person who offends them understand how they feel. This gesture requires that they move about as they display it. This is a negative body language that communicates disdain or dislike. If the child is truly at fault, the person at the other end may not appeal to them but if otherwise, you know that it is time to tender an apology.

This is not only limited to children as adults also flare up with the use of their legs when angered beyond control. In the case of adult, this may be accompanied with the shout of 'Gosh!', 'Ohh!', 'What nonsense!' and other language of anger peculiar to an individual. I remember once banging my leg on the floor when an executive was 'unjustly' bumped out of a flight. Leg tantrum is an emotional outburst that is mostly found among people who cannot control their anger. While this may be an expression of sincerity of their heart, they should be feared because in some cases, the person can attack when the anger is on the extreme.

In all, what this gesture reminds us is that we adequately demonstrate emotions through the use of legs.

Scientific Explanations

Toddler Sense (2019) authoritatively states that tantrum is a common behaviour among kids between the ages of 18 months to three years. However, you need not panic about this as they are regarded as a normal part of development. This manifests itself in different ways among children—some have a high prevalence of it while others have it less. 'Children with strong wills and high emotions are more likely to fall into tantrum behaviour than those with milder temperaments,' states the website. This is why the gesture is normally attached with people with high temperament. Some of the reactions you should always expect are 'full-blown screaming, hitting, kicking, pushing and pulling outburst to a milder response that includes whining or crying.'

Depending on the child, some may display this behaviour once in a day or immediately they are overtaken by an unusual emotion. While some people display their anger and put an end to it immediately, some may last for about twenty minutes. If this is noticed frequently in a child, it is high time their parents swung into action in order to teach such child self-control skills. It is absurd for an adult to kick and twist their legs very often in public. However, if self-control skills are not learnt from childhood, it would be difficult to prevent such behaviour later on in life (Toddler Sense 2019).

When you see either a kid or an adult demonstrating this gesture, do not argue, scream or get angry with them as this will only escalate issues instead of dousing it. A party involved needs to prove maturity to put the situation under control.

Practical Illustrations

Case Study I: Child CJ was sent to a grocery store by his mother. After buying what he was sent, he was able to cunningly cart away an item. So he left the premises hurriedly so as not to be caught. On getting home, the mother discovered that she needed to get more items from the store in order to prepare stew that would last the family for days because she needed to embark on a journey in the course of the week. When she informed CJ that he was to return to the store to get the needed ingredients, he became indescribably annoyed—he moved from one place to the other, banging, twisting and moving her legs as he wanted to cut them off his body. The head was also tilting from one end to the other. The mother was also angry at his behaviour, noting that she was only caring enough to have decided to help him and his siblings prepare stew before travelling; she did not understand the source of the boy's anger. The boy blamed her for not thinking through before sending him in the first place but in the deepest part of his heart, he knew his protest was borne out of the fear of being apprehended on his return to the shop.

Case Study II: Mr MX just got sacked from his workplace while the wife's salary was also slashed in order to keep her by her employers. This means their financial fortunes are in danger. Many things are affected and with the way things are going, except a drastic step is taken, the couples knew their end would be ill. So Mr MX called his wife for a hard conversation that took them hours. They outlined all their expenses compared same with their income. It appeared to them that pending the time things get better, they need to adjust their budget to reflect the current realities. One of the decisions reached was that their first child be withdrawn from the school he is currently attending to one closer to home and where they pay lesser. The child is already used to school and likes everything about it. When informed, without giving a thought to the condition of his parents, he twisted his legs, moved them about and stomp them energetically in protest of the decision. However, the parents are not perturbed by his action.

Case Study III: There are two layers of verification for people coming to Firm GTV. Most times, if there are no controversies with a visitor's identity, he would be given a pass after the first verification process but if some things are under doubts, then it would pass through more scrutinisation. When Impostor GX got there, he was politely asked to proceed to the second verification platform. He was angered by this as he knew the implication. He could be seen twisting his legs, moving them energetically and stomping them just to protest the decision but he could not make this known through verbal means, so everyone pretended not to have understood his agitations. This made him to endure this frustrating circumstance for long.

23.17. Foot Stomping

Generic Interpretations of the Concept

This is related to the cue discussed in the preceding segment. More related to children but seen in people of all ages. Stomping is when people walk with heavy steps due to anger. You feel this because everywhere vibrates as if the person is heading for war. Each step is always resounding and aimed at sending fear down the nerves of the opponent. Someone who is happy will walk lightly; their steps may be fast but their legs would not hit the ground heavily as if they are trying to dig the grave of an adversary. Children are fond of this behaviour. Their frown, wrong posture, throwing of the arms around and blatant disrespect for anyone who comes their way at that given point in time are all pointers that such a child is overwhelmed with negative emotions. There is no amount of appeals that can work at that point in time because the child is bound to display their feeling. Most times, this behaviour is also fuelled with childishness. Hence, you should probably expect them to go beyond their boundaries.

What makes the child angry is also a factor in judging the display of this gesture. If a teacher allegedly offends them and also their parents, you should not expect the stomping to be the same. The former is a formal setting while the latter is informal. Thus, they will act out their aggressiveness more with the parents than their teacher. If they want you to punish a pair who offends them, they will continuously stomp their feet until you notice this action and take the needed step. Invariably, this can be exaggerated for the purpose of tricking others into doing their biddings.

Apart from kids, this often plays out among adults too. When we have outstretched the limit of our patience, we begin to react angrily to people that cross our sane lines. Hitting the feet against the floor or walking heavily passes the message of aggression to people that care enough to understand it. When you are on a line and it moves slower than you had planned, you may unconsciously begin to stomp your feet in protest against whoever is behind the slowness of the line.

Among adults, the foot is often stomped once for the purpose of calling a person's attention to you. So it is not done for the purpose of disorganising things or making a location uncomfortable for others. This differs from how children display theirs in a continuous manner until they are emotionally calm.

Scientific Explanations

According to *Collins Dictionary*, 'If you stomp somewhere, you walk there with very heavy steps, often because you are angry.' From the foregoing, one of the foremost causes of stomping is anger. This means the anger is uncontrollable and we want to vent it as we feel it. This may be the direct outcome of anxiety. Nervousness is an emotional display that is not easily controlled. Foot stomping may be a way of hiding how we feel; a shaking leg is bounced on the floor to connote anger instead of the original attitude of fear.

Joseph Hindy (2019) notes that both kids and adults can be found stomping their feet. He explains that 'it's usually done as an expression of anger, and that's how most people associate it'. Hence, his position aligns with the dictionary meaning given to this gesture. Another reason people stomp is to frighten an opponent—something that is considered as danger. This can even be an animal. There are times you see dog owners stomping towards their pet just in a bid to scare them away. I have seen frightened friends who even stomp at my dog, not because they are confident but are really afraid of the pet.

In its own, contribution, Study Body Language makes a submission that 'stomping the feet is one universal sign for hostile attitude or frustration. In the animal kingdom the bull stomps his hoof as he prepares to ride down his target. In humans it simply shows that something is gone amiss, so we express that anger in a physical way.' This makes the concept clearer and more understandable. When you see someone stomping their foot, be sure that they are boiling of anger inside. Hence, their foot aptly communicates how they feel.

The website notes that because foot stomping is a childlike gesture, it holds some form of curiosity when an adult displays this behaviour. It is an evolutionary behaviour; that is why we still display the gesture, well after we have frown into maturity. Hence, whenever we allow our feelings to overwhelm us, you begin to notice this gesture. This hints those around that something that is beyond our control is happening to us.

Practical Illustrations

Case Study I: Child FC is charged with the duty of looking after their garden—taking care of it and ensuring that the flowers flourish to the admiration of all. At first, he did not see as something herculean but along the line, it appears to him that he has to give more than he had budgeted to meet the expectations of his parents; he now wakes up earlier than usual to water the garden and he does same in the evening. This has taught him discipline, an attitude the parents planned imbibing him through that duty. However, Child FC is beginning to get fed up because before his return from school, their dog would have lain in the garden and scatter many places he had earlier arranged. The dog was not properly trained and now, he is suffering from that deficiency. Any time he sees the dog in the garden, he would stomp his foot to send it packing.

Case Study II: Mr VG just arrived Country XZ for an important conference he is expected to deliver the opening address. They had a wait over in another country beyond the expected duration. So they arrived four hours behind the time scheduled. He needed to rest for about an hour and change his clothing before heading for the venue but it appears that immigration line was moving too slow. Very often, he would stretch out his neck to the front to see if there is any pandemonium but it seems everything is all right. Thus, he becomes baffled at the possible cause of the slow movement of the line. At some point, he stomped his foot in a way that draws the attention of most of the people there to him. It was an agitation sign that took people by a surprise in that situation—no one was expecting an unruly behaviour there.

Case Study III: Man CU in the company of his smuggled beings decided to walk through unapproved border. There were claims that Country FVI is known for its porous border system and CU and his co -criminals would not desist to take advantage of this porosity in bringing in people. While on this journey, there were fears that some law enforcement agents would have laid ambush for them due to the pressure on them recently to get illegal routes closed. So after walking a few distance, Man CU would stomp his feet so as to know if there was anything lying ahead of them or not. This was an expression of fear.

23.18. Pulling of Sock

Generic Interpretations of the Concept

In a formal setting and generally, due to the high rate of modernisation and how civilisation is fast taking over the world, wearing socks is now seen as a part of our culture and people who not wear them as seen as incomplete. In fact, you dare not attend a job interview without trying to wear socks. Before now, it used to be predominantly a white culture but the story has rapidly changed over time. The point is that as inconsequential as this may appear, we dare not overlook it in trying to explain non-verbal cues.

Since it is part of our dressing, touching or pulling it is an unacceptable behaviour—it amounts to undressing in public or in the very least, fiddling with clothing item (which is itself a nervous body language gesture).

When we are stressed, blood gushes to the surface of the skin and makes it very warm. The parts of the body in which individuals mostly experience such uncomforting warmth differ. To some, it may be the face while some have their hands on the arms. However, this psychological discomfort may also be felt in the lower part of the body. The rise in temperature will make us feel uncomfortable in our feet. If this discomfort persists for a while, it destabilises us and diverts our attention from whatever we are doing. At this point, we tend to leave everything and devise a way of dealing with the stress.

One of the most common techniques which people use is to ventilate the ankles by pulling the socks. If it were in an informal context, they person would have taken off the socks in its entirety but since it is absurd in a professional or formal gathering, the person will pull it in a subtle manner. Usually, people do not pay attention to this non-verbal signal which is used in expressing discomfort.

The degree of distress the person is passing through will dictate how often they pull the sock. Those who do it repeatedly are definitely greatly distressed. If you look beyond the surface level, you will discover that the person will be destabilised in an obvious manner; they will no longer be composed with their primary assignment and will bend every now and then as if trying to pick up something from the floor. Once they leave the presence of the person making them uncomfortable, they may first do away with their pairs of shoes and socks just to get calmed very rapidly.

Scientific Explanations

Locke (2019) and many other sources that contribute to this subject matter explain it along romantic line. She compares sock pulling to preening. 'Fiddling with his socks and pulling them up indicates he preens for you. You make him nervous, so he checks that he looks presentable for you too,' she notes. There are two issues to take note of in this explanation. One is nervousness. The person who is pulling his sock is actually nervous of something. In this case, a woman. There are times that guys see a woman they are drawn to but are afraid if they are really up to the person's standard. This fear is making them feel warm at the feet and thus, trying to ventilate it through the pulling of the sock. And on the other hand, it is a call to action; the man is trying to adjust himself and be bold enough to make his intentions known to the woman. This may be a preening gesture which many women, unfortunately, overlook.

In the same vein, Michael Martinez (2019) tries to explain this gesture along romantic context. However, he cautions that we should not be in a hurry to conclude that it is a preening gesture. 'Men pull up their socks when they are alone, no one can possibly see them, and there is no hope of anyone seeing them with straight socks,' Martinez submits. A factor that has always rendered many body language interpretations impotent is to assume that a signal bears the same meaning in all contexts.

Martinez states that we pull the socks 'because we feel uncomfortable and we want to feel more comfortable. While discomfort can be associated with a stressful or emotionally charged (or hormonally charged) situation, when it comes to socks, the most common reason we feel discomfort is that they've lost their elasticity. They just sag around the ankles and they feel uncomfortable.' We can see that a point that is emphasised throughout the above quoted text is 'discomfort'. Psychological discomfort can arise from any event and not really attached to a romantic scene as many platforms have always painted it to be. This gesture may be displayed out of the mere need to adjust the sock without any hidden meaning attached to it.

Practical Illustrations

Case Study I: Coach BV has an agreement with his employers that if he does not win the tournament they are competing in, he should be axed. He has been the gaffer of the side for the past five years and they have always reached either the final or semi-finals of the tournament. So many fans are of the opinion that providence is probably against him and someone else should be brought in who would not suffer them emotionally on final days but help in winning silverware. The final match of the competition is currently ongoing and Coach BV is obviously restless; he moves from a side to the other, trying to ensure that his guys play according to set out plans. On the dot of the seventieth minute, the attacker of the opponent finds the back of Coach BV's net. He feels like getting into the pitch to play himself and change things. He quickly calls his players and changes the pattern of play. Fifteen minutes after, there is no goal yet. He is tired and tries to rest for a while. While on his seat, he pulls his sock repeatedly, focusing on the pitch. He takes off his hand from the sock when one of his players later scores an equaliser in the closing minute. Holding on to the socks shows that he was tensed and looking for what would flush out the stress in him.

Case Study II: Politician YB is a grassroots' politician; he understands the language, needs and desires of the average person on the streets. So his party sees him as the best fit to present for the forthcoming election. The campaign team becomes complacent with the hope that they would be handed victory easily. However, they are shocked to see the level of acceptance of the candidate of Party B he is contesting with. On the day of their debate, YB also marvels at the knowledge and delivery style of his opponent. He pulls his socks continuously throughout the presentation of his opponent due to nervousness.

Case Study III: Man GJ murdered his wife and was still the first person to report the incident to law enforcement agents. However, he had taken away all the items that could indict him from the scene before calling the officers to come. According to him, he met his wife's corpse in the living room while their main door was left opened; he was instigating that an outsider could have been behind it. He even said he would be willing to help the officers in any capacity to bring the culprit to book. He was with the senior officer in charge of the case when the preliminary report was submitted, as the officer read through, he would take his time to look at the man again. He became fearful of the content and unconsciously pulled his shocks.

23.19. Dangling of Shoe

Generic Interpretations of the Concept

When we are comfortable, one of the things we do is to dangle our shoe. This is a behaviour that is very common among women. You will see them shake their shoe from a side to the other near the instep of the foot. This is against the rigid posture that fearful people normally display. Making the foot move back and forth like children playing on a seesaw is a childish act that shows that the person has no issues to deal with; there is no heavy negative issue on the back of their mind that can actually weigh them down. The person may also smile subtly. If the person were fearful or anxious, they would have positioned their feet in solid, defensive manner that can make them combat whatever is coming to face them.

Since it is women's behaviour, you are likely to notice it in romantic contexts. When a woman is really into a man, they will dangle their shoe. This is a symbol of comfort and rest. Dangling the shoe may make the whole shake. A shaking body keeps the entire body warm and thus, makes the person active throughout a conversation. A frim or rigid person can easily lose interest in a discourse. Also, you might not find it easy discussing with such person because the body seems locked against ideas and interactions. In other words, shoe-dangling gesture gives the body a dancing-posture that makes you admire your partner.

Next time you see a woman dangling their shoe around you, this is a non-verbal pledge of their total belief in you; they believe that you will protect them. This is the hallmark of trust—if you do not trust a person, you will not feel relaxed around them. That is why you may not see this gesture in the early days of a relationship when the partners are still studying each other. It would be a grievous error to be at ease with someone who you not really know. This does not mean you should be paranoid but you need to look before leaping.

Once the context changes from comfort to danger, the shoe would be slipped back immediately. This means the person is either ready to switch into the flight or freeze mood. It may also signal preparedness to fight. Slipping back of the shoe happens in a very sudden manner and the entire body also readjusts because the foot posture has been modified. Apart from dislike for a person, it may also be a symbol of disagreement with what is being said. You need to be observant and relate with interlocutors on the basis of how they use their body language per time in a conversation.

Scientific Explanations

Philip (2014) states that removing the shoes signals comfort. He also aligns with the submission that it is a cue made by women in romantic context. There are times that women remove the shoes entirely just to feel comfortable. When you are conversing with someone and she removes or dangles her shoes, this is an indication that she is not ready to leave any time soon. This is a common practice among friends; you remove or dangle your shoe because you are with someone you love and trust. However, this can be interpreted as being disrespectful in business setting. In a formal context, you are not expected to take off any of your clothing items.

'In a dating context, woman can remove their shoes as a symbol of their trust in their partner. Dangling a stiletto from the tip of the toe is a great way to show arousal and trust at the same time,' states Philip. That is why the verbal translation is given as 'I'm comfortable in this environment and not going anyway so I feel safe enough to remove my shoes.'

Practical Illustrations

Case Study I: Ms FC went out on a date with a colleague at work. They have been colleagues for the past three years, cracked jokes together and gave many subtle signs of love but it appears that they are both not courageous enough to approach each other. When Mr DB discovered that he might later lose the lady to another employee who is very confident and could woo all the females in the firm without bothering if they end up telling one another about his antics or not. Since Ms FC had been expecting him to come, she did not belabour him before agreeing to be a lover to him. Having known each other for a while works for them because many of the issues they would have battled with in the early days of love are not there. In other words, they started their relationship on a highway of emotional pleasure. On the date, Ms FC dangled her shoe as her hobby whispered to her. It was after work and she feigned tiredness as she displayed this gesture all in the bid for her spouse to pamper her. To some extent, we can say that this is a display of romantic gesture.

Case Study II: Mrs NG has always had a soft place for Mr RC, her neighbour. They have been living in the same neighbourhood for years without a day of rancour. Any time she sets her eyes on Mr RC she felt some regrets within that she did not marry him. To her, apart from his handsomeness, he is also responsible, caring and loving. Her decision is borne out of the way Mr RC relates with her wife. Even though she relates to the wife well, Mrs NG has always prayed for an intimate moment with Mr RC. Whenever she has the opportunity to display her body to the man, she does so without hesitation. However, it seems

Mr RC appears blind to all her antics. One day, Mrs RC was out for a meeting in another country and the husband was obviously bored because the person who keeps him company every weekend was not around. Mrs NG decided to take this opportunity to further her personal gains. Dressed in a tempting attire, she knocked at Mr RC's door and entered, and in no time, conversation ensued. She sat facing the man and dangled her shoe as she led the discussion. It was a way of displaying her interest to him and make him succumb to her tricks.

Case Study III: Ms RD has been looking for a way to make love with her boss in order to earn unmerited accolades but it seems the opportunity is not coming as all her gimmicks failed. There were times she would approach him when they are both the only ones at work and induce him into wooing her but it seems the man is just too disciplined to do such. So she changed her tactics. One day, she sat on her chair and kept on dangling her shoe with a feigned expression of tiredness, she was expecting the man to ask her what was wrong in order to be taken out for a treat, yet, it failed.

23.20. General Agitation of the Leg and Foot

Generic Interpretations of the Concept

In general, we tend to display some behaviours that betray our confidence and courage. When the legs generally become agitated, there is no way people will not observe this, not because of the cue itself but what it leads us to do. Agitation means restlessness; the feet become restless and uncontrollable—it itches for movement. That is why you will see some people moving about against their wish. If you should accost such person and ask them what they are heading, they will not give you a definite answer because they sincerely do not know.

In displaying this gesture, the feet will race and pace. The heavy movement is to give the person the certain of the floor they are matching. You will have a pictorial image of this by thinking of someone who is under the influence of drug or alcohol. Even if the person is seated, their feet will shift from one end to the other. The whole body vibrates as the person agitates to stand up and walk away or at least, express themselves in another way. He or she may keep bouncing the feet on the floor. By this time, they are totally disconnected from what you are saying. They might look attentive to you but their thought is concentrated on their psychological feeling and not whatever you are telling them.

There are many possible causes of this psychological imbalance in people. One, it may be traceable to a diagnosable occurrence such as a reaction to shock, intake of illicit drugs, bad effect of prescribed drugs, among others. When you consume a drug that reacts negatively in the body, it may make you to become restless and agitate endlessly. Panic attack is another possible foundation of this behaviour. When some people are frightened by an incident, it takes them long duration to get calmed. They may also place their palms on their chest to gauge how their heart is racing and open their mouth in order to breathe well. The person agitates with their feet as if they should stay on a spot, the source of their fear will catch up with them.

Other clusters you can pay attention to when you notice feet agitation are lip biting, fidgety hands, eye twitching, and clenched fists. When you observe most of this gestures in a person, it is a pointer to the fact that all is not well with the person. More so, it means the person is struggling to deal with their psychological distress.

In a moment like this, the least you should expect from the person is to behave normal—think and speak with coherence. They might need psychological counselling or medical assistance while some will get back to normalcy after some periods of rest. No one is exclusive to this behaviour; there are times we have all met ourselves at the odd side of life. Also, while dealing with an agitated fellow, you need to exercise caution, thinking of the likelihood of attack from the person.

Scientific Explanations

Crystal Lassen (2018) notes that we experience agitation in different forms. One of the reasons why people become agitated easily is that there was no one to curb them in their childhood. If you notice that you are becoming agitated, the best way to curb it is to stop whatever you are doing immediately and walk out of the uncomfortable environment. We become restless when the environment is not favourable and tense. Most probably, the person has denied themselves of good rest. The feet react easily to stress because they are our vehicles of movement. If they need rest and you keep on denying them, it may turn out a subtle protest through the shifting and uncooperative actions.

Further, this may be an obvious sign of anger. People who get angry at the slightest offence are normally agitated. When the person prances about, he or she becomes very dangerous because they can resort to violence at any given time. When you notice an agitated person, it is better to let them go their way as bothering them may translate to transferring their emotions on you (Lassen 2018).

Practical Illustrations

Case Study I: Mrs HV normally drives her children to school before returning home to take her breakfast and then dress up for work. The reason being that her kids' school and her workplace are parallel to each other. This morning, the routine is not altered. After dropping them on the premises and waving at them, she zooms back home but hardly had she got home when she receives a call from the school administrators. She rushes back to the school. One of her kids has fainted and rushed to the hospital when it looks more complicated than what the school clinic can handle successfully. When Mrs HV hears this, she becomes destabilised and confused. Her feet become agitated as she does not know what really next she should do; she walks towards the school clinic, returns, and then paces to the car before driving to the hospital where the child is.

Case Study II: The management of GZO Shopping Mall do leave the mall open for all and sundry every Thursday; the security checks are normally minimal and people are allowed to snap pictures at places that would not have been allowed on every other work day. This is an initiative that most customers appreciate and has translated into more sales for the mall authorities. Hence, their resolve to keep the process ongoing for a long time. Unknowing to them, terrorists have marked it out as one of the places for an attack. So the spies are always there on Thursdays to evaluate their chances and set out modalities to adopt in attacking the place. After months of planning, they eventually attacked the mall successfully. Many people were trapped in the incident. Meanwhile, Mrs IB was just alighting from her car when the incident happened. She lost her breath as she did not know where to run to. She moved in the direction of others and turned back when it seemed a sound was coming from the direction they were running to. She was later taken to the hospital for medical attention.

Case Study III: Human Smuggler OH was kept in a room after being interviewed while his suspected smuggled boys and girls were taken to another room to be interviewed. The reason for this is that so that he would not interrupt the process or give them signals of what to say. He thought it was a process that will last for just few minutes, only for it to be running into hours. He became agitated due to fear of the confessional statements those people might have made. At some point, he began to move his entire legs back and forth, looking as if he wanted to walk into the other room where his people were being held but he knew the implication of this. He was obviously nervous and concerned but he is not permitted to break any known or unknown rules.

CHAPTER 24

The Colour

In a way or another, we are all familiar with colours and understand its importance to the society. Even if we claim not to have a societal understanding of it, one thing that is unarguable is that we all have our colour preferences. Sports lovers consider colour while making their decision on which team to support. There are people that will never wear certain colour because they think whenever they put such on, they normally record bad luck. While this may be regarded as personal sentiment, we cannot blame the person or talk them out of their personal wish which is not harmful to us.

Even societies too attach invaluable importance to colour. You need to take note of societal peculiarities whenever you are leaving your culture for another. To some, wearing a particular colour may be an insult to the deity of that particular society. There are people who will or decline helping you solely based on the colour of your cloth. This may sound odd but it is reality of our world which we must learn how to deal with. The best way to get the best out of this lesson is to first assimilate and digest this fact—that people and societies have colour preferences.

From the foregoing, we can authoritatively assume that colours are embodiment of meanings. Before a person can detest or admire a particular colour, it means a lot of interpretations has been given to such colour. A colour can either signal something positive or negative. Although there are no universally acceptable definitions given to any colour, we can find a common ground in explaining each based on the large acceptance of such among people. For instance, when you see red, you are most likely to conclude that it is a symbol of danger, blood, struggle or call for caution, depending on the context of its usage.

Because of how important colours are in the world, there is hardly any gathering, firm, nation or group without their official colour. Many elementary and high schools across the world have their own colour preferences that they expect both workers and students to wear. This is popularly referred to as 'uniform'. I have witnessed situations where firms wielded the big stick on their employees just because they fail to comply with their colour selection. In that sense, it is a means of identification that people who know how crucial identity is will not joke with. Today, this culture is also prevalent in the informal context; there are colour codes for each occasion and if you do not want to look odd, you will try your best to have the colour or stay back; not wearing the recommended colour may make you look depressed, especially when you are one with a low self-esteem.

Without mincing words, there is no way you can dodge the effect of colours in your daily engagements. Even if you are the type that does not care about colours, you need to be careful with those you deal with in order not to offend them. People communicate with colours and it is to your own advantage that you understand the message they are passing across so as not to be caught unawares when you are required to take decisive steps. For instance, if there is a red flag hoisted on the road, it might be a message that danger lies ahead if you ignore it, there is high probability that you will end up in regrets. While you point accusing fingers there was no one to inform you beforehand, you would not understand that you were warned only that you were too ignorant to decode the message.

Colours are used as a show of patriotism. During sports tournaments, you will see people adorn their national colour just in a bid to plead loyalty to their country. It is usually a sight to behold as people celebrate and hold high the colours of their nation, no matter what may. Whenever you see red, black, green and white, then the person is probably from Afghanistan. Armenia will adorn red, green and orange while China is known for red and gold. For Iran, it is green, white and red. Singapore subscribes to red and white while the football team uses blues. Due to space constraints, I would not be able to mention the primary and secondary colours of each nation of the world. You can always act smart by finding out the national colour of the country you are travelling to in order to wear and feel accepted. This is a show of love which no patriotic citizen will take for granted.

To be specific, Asians do not joke with red colour because it is used to denote good luck. In its 2015 blog post, Shutterstock emphasises the differences in colour interpretations around the world just like the case of red given above where it is known for good fortunes in most Asian cultures and danger or bad luck in other cultures of the world. 'For instance, the Bassa people in Liberia only have two words for classifying colours (*ziza* for red/orange/yellow and *hui* for green/blue/purple), while the Inuit reportedly have 17 different words for white alone, which are modified by different snow conditions' (Shutterstock 2015).

Oxford Dictionary defines *colour* as 'the property possessed by an object of producing different sensations on the eye as a result of the way it reflects or emits light.' Another definition states that colour is an indication of one's race. In this regard, it is believed that there is no colour that is more important to the other—wither white, black, albino and other colours of people of the world.

Colours also have the ability to affect our emotions and moods in a way that many other things cannot. That is why you see some people become suddenly depressed when nothing is done to them. This means they have probably sighted a colour that they do not like. 'Colour meanings may have something to do with your past, your experiences or your culture. For instance, while the colour white is often used in many Western countries to represent purity and innocence, it is seen as a symbol of mourning in many Eastern European countries' (Olesen 2019). Briefly, I will explain each colour and what they connote in general terms.

24.1. Black

Generic Interpretations of the Concept

There is no colour without its own positive and negatives. In this generic section, I will explain them in general terms while I make national and societal differences in the preceding segment. Having said that, black is seen as a symbol of protection. When someone is putting on black in some places, it gives them confidence and stops others from moving nearer to them. Probably, this informs the reason many nations adopt black as the official colour of their police officers. Black passes the message of being strong to the subconscious when not mixed with any other colour. It makes the wearer appear firm and resolute. If you see action police in their uniform, you may tremble at their appearance alone.

Furthermore, it is a signifier of formality. When you are going for an interview, you either put on white, blue or black. Any other colour might be counted against you even if that is what you prefer. Many leaders of the world and industry captains put on black suits. This means the person is not out for any frivolity but strictly business. For instance, if someone is wearing purple or pink, you might be tempted to believe that they are going for a social function because such colours do not fit a professional context. Black can also absorb dirt unlike other colours where it would show once you rub your body against some particles. And also, we use black to denote something classy.

On the other hand, black is used to mark evil. Racists believe that anything that is black is of no good value, while this is an ill sentiment that should be condemned, it does not change the fact that a lot of people relate with colour with that degraded mentality. In many part of Africa, when people are mourning the departure of loved ones, you will see them in either black or red. Hence, it is used to connote death in that context. When you see a group of people wearing black and wear a sober face, this is enough to change your mood as you feel sympathetic towards their course even though you do not know the person they lose. That tells you how powerful and transferring colour can be.

Black colour is also used to denote mystery. If you do not understand a concept or person, you may adorn them with black. That is why phone users put some contacts they consider unworthy under 'black list'. Till date, people still seek out to understand the strength of black colour in the wheel.

From the psychology point of view, black has two basic meanings—unhappiness and evil. This seems to give life to all I have explained in the preceding paragraphs. Pay close attention to those wearing black, especially where it is less expected, you will notice other negative gestures in them.

Scientific Explanations

Shutterstock (2015) in its opening statement captures all that relates to this colour thus: 'In many cultures black symbolises sophistication and formality, but it also represents death, evil, mourning, magic, fierceness, illness, bad luck, and mystery.' This further affirms explanations given above. Sophisticated people wear black in order to make it difficult for you to read them; you will most probably blank while trying to read wearing black, especially if the person's behaviour differs from what you expect. For instance, someone who appears happy and undisturbed but putting on black. You are lost in making your assumptions between their action and what he or she is wearing.

The platform explains further, 'In the Middle East black can represent both rebirth and mourning. In Africa it symbolizes age, maturity, and masculinity.' While in these two continents, you need to pay close attention to the locales and see how they make use of black in every given context before making assumptions. This is very essential for multinational companies that will indispensably interact with people across cultural divides. By knowing the symbolism of different colours around the world you'll be able to speak to your audience in a way that's both culturally appropriate and effective.

Olesen (2019) also explains that black bears the same meaning as reeled out by Shutterstock. He adds that it may depict anger, remorse and technicality too. People who work in factories mostly prefer black because it denotes technicality in that context. He opines further that 'in colour psychology, the colour black relates to protection against emotional stress. It creates a barrier between itself and the outside world. It provides comfort while it protects its feelings and hides its vulnerability, insecurity and lack of confidence.' Psychologically, we tend to prefer black above others because it covers up our vulnerability and makes it difficult for adversaries to understand us. This colour holds on to information, thereby shielding us from communicating our fears with strangers.

As laudable and interesting as the above sounds, you need to be careful where you wear it. Due to the power it radiates, it makes you unapproachable, unfriendly and intimidating. Maybe, this is why the public never take the police serious any time they confess that they are our friends. I mean, how does an unfriendly person becomes a friend to us? Hence, it can prevent two-way communication because of the negative impact. A salesman, who is dressed in all black, will definitely sell a lot, but he will not have many friends. He radiates authority and power, but also creates fear along the way. Black involves self-control and discipline, independence and a strong will (Olesen 2019).

Practical Illustrations

Case Study I: Mr TP is vying for a contract with one of the top organisations in town. Before submitting his bid at all, he had prepared his mind for bureaucracies but he never knew it would get that far. When he went for the briefing in white, he discovers that the management did not really take him serious. So he went back home to think on areas he did not sound professional but could not figure any out. He decides to wear black for the second stage. Although the jokes reduce drastically this time around, the discussion is fruitful in every sense of it. The colour signals fruitfulness and productivity in this sense.

Case Study II: Mr VO was a hard-working and committed staff of GHT, a multinational firm before he gave up the ghost. Since he died in an accident while on the course of official duty, the firm thought that he should be given a befitting burial. To show that they were mourning, all the workers, starting from the top management were asked to wear black attire on the day he was to be buried. This added more meaning to the event as anyone who came across them knew they lost someone important. Also, the expression on their faces buttressed this important message on their heart.

Case Study III: A group of armed robbers were going for an operation in a particular community filled with rich people. Since they were aware that there would be a high presence of security operatives in the area, they went there prepared with bullet proof clothes. Also, they wore black attires so as to blend with the colour of the night. This also included the mask they used; they believed that black is a bit dull and too thick for anyone to see their face through it. In addition, the colour of their clothes communicated the message that they were in the community for a serious business—to steal and kill anyone who dare to stop them.

24.2. White

Generic Interpretations of the Concept

In many parts of the world, this colour is often related to something positive. For instance, it is seen as a symbol of purity. Many religious people share the sentiment that their deities appear in white because such does not sin. This is why every picture of an angel you see is usually in white. An evil-intended fellow will probably not wear white because they understand that it can easily be stained. Imagine red oil being poured on helm of a white cloth, it would be glaring. Hence, people believe that those with 'white heart' are pure and holy. This is a sentiment that is shared throughout the world. Thus, we can safely conclude that this meaning is universal.

White is unarguably outstanding. From all colours, white stands out. Hence, it is regarded as a gesture of cleanliness. If you see someone wearing white and they appear very neat, especially late in the day when you would ordinarily expect them to look dirty and rough but are still very OK and clean, you will easily assume that the person is hygienic. We even tend to salute the cleanliness of kids more in this situation because they are expected to play with their peers at some point in the day.

Furthermore, white is used to connote innocence. When white is used as the symbol of a thing, it means such firm or thing is open-hearted. Companies that are risk-laden or which you might doubt before committing yourself to are more probable to use white as their logo. This is to tell you that they are safe to transact business. It is the hallmark of honesty and that is why most banks across the world see white as the most preferred colour. This is symbolic and people are likely to deal with them based on this confession.

In the same vein, white means that a person is easy-going. Imagine going for an important function and you adorn white. You would not like to offend anyone or pick fight with anybody until you get to your destination due to the colour of your cloth. In the outbreak of violence, you know that you will be at the losing end. Hence, you will rather resolve issues amicably than stoop so low to fight anyone who disagrees with you.

In addition, white is used to depict freshness and goodness. There is the superstitious belief shared in some quarters that when you meet people wearing white along the way, it means something good awaits you. Even though this is not scientific, we must acknowledge it as an opinion which has thrived among many cultures. Whenever you are wearing white, you are more likely to pay attention to your body than when you appear in any other colour. Colour psychology also believes that white is the symbol of purity and innocence.

Scientific Explanations

According to Shutterstock, 'In Western cultures, white symbolises purity, elegance, peace, and cleanliness; brides traditionally wear white dresses at their weddings.' To many people, especially ladies, the happiest day of their life is usually their wedding day. Hence, putting on white on that day means they are happy. Historically, a bride who is qualified to wear white on her wedding day is one that has not been defiled. This is where the purity and innocence comes in. Someone who has had sexual intercourse with men can no longer claim to be innocent. Hence, the white colour is very symbolic in its use in religious and Western contexts. However, 'in China, Korea, and some other Asian countries white represents death, mourning, and bad luck, and is traditionally worn at funerals' (Shutterstock 2015). In this continent, people tend to wear white while mourning a loved one. We need to pay attention to this sharp contrast while moving from one continent to the other. Further, this colour possesses another meaning in Peru. It is interpreted as a sign of time, good health and angel.

Richard Brooks (2016) opines that white is mostly used as a background colour without any significance on its own. In other words, this is expressionless. However, he goes ahead to state the possible meaning the gesture may denote in each continent of the world. He states that white is a connotation of purity and mourning in the Middle East. In Latin or South America, white is interpreted as peace. He concludes that 'in Africa, white symbolises peace, purity, goodness and good luck. However, in Ethiopia it also indicates illness.' However, it is pertinent to note that all these are mere guidelines, in business and other interactive situations, it is essential that you understand your audience better so as to reflect their mind in your discourse.

Olesen (2019) is also not left out in this. He suggests that white is used as a symbol of reverence in some situations. That is why it is used as the colour of royalty in some places. It is also a sign of youthfulness. Youth are more concerned about their look, pay attention to details and what others say about them and that is what this white represents.

In colour psychology, white is the colour of new beginnings – wiping the slate clean. The colour white is a blank canvas, just waiting to be written on. Although white does not stimulate the senses significantly, it paves the way for the creation of something that the mind can imagine. White contains a balance of all colours in the spectrum that represents both the positive and negative aspects of all colours (Olesen 2019).

Practical Illustrations

Case Study I: Ms AJ goes on a date with Guy TA. The place is unusually filled up on their arrival and she is not ready to undergo the stress of considering other options. She dresses in white, making her look charming than before. TA later manages to spot a table with two empty chairs. He tries offering her a seat but she rejects it because it looks somewhat broken and does not want it to dirty her cloth. Hence, Guy TA moves to the chair while she takes his own which looks much better. Here, white signals purity or cleanliness.

Case Study II: Woman ST and Man GY met each other at the workplace and love happened. When they decided to knot the nuptial tie, Woman ST said she would wear a white gown for different reasons. First, it serves as a mark of purity. According to her, she had never had any sexual intercourse and wearing white is a symbol of her innocence. Also, white was picked as the favourite colour for the guests. This is a symbol of joy and excitement. They were of the thought that a conglomeration of white colour in a given place would further beautify the wedding venue and it was really a talk of the town. Hence, it stands for beautification here.

Case Study III: Another attribute of white is that it makes people appear responsible and respected. This is why Con Artist CX will put it on whenever he wants to deceive people with his appearance. For instance, there was a time he deceived a lady that he was a businessman and when he was going to meet her, he wore a white attire just to look neat and presentable. He was so charming in the clothes that the lady had to compliment him especially on it. Hence, his choice of dress serves as a foundation through which he gets to his targets and it really works for him.

24.3. Red

Generic Interpretations of the Concept

Red is a symbol of love. All the emojis I have come across on every social media platform has red as its colour. The reason for this is not far to seek; rose flower which is normally used for love proposal is red. The flower is attractive and charming. No matter how far a person is, the colour calls them out. Having a colour that speaks for itself can only fit aptly into the love context. In other words, if you see the person whom you truly love amidst hundreds of people, you should be able to fish him or her out without issues, either by voice or through look.

Further, red is used as a symbol of energy. Those who want to demonstrate power adorn themselves in red. What gives us strength is our blood which is red in colour. So it is a symbolic connotation of power and strength. Firms also make use of the colour to show that they are passionate about their service. At this juncture, let me submit that you should not just pick any colour for your brand design; do not be concerned about the beauty alone but whatever colour you are picking should represent your values and promote the business. There are a lot of people that pay attention to such things which you might erroneously wave away, thinking it is not important.

On the other hand, red is also used as a warning sign. During my many travels, anywhere I see red flag or cloth tied somewhere, I pause to understand the reason behind the action and if it is appearing incomprehensible to me, I seek the attention of a locale. All 'be warned' signs are normally written in red. This passes a huge message to you on the meaning of the colour. In other words, if you do not heed the warning, something unpalatable awaits you. In many parts of the world, red is used as a sign of danger—fire has red as its colour. Places where there are wild dogs, they make use red colour to call the attention of people to this obvious danger.

In the moments of anger too, red is the go-to colour, hence, the statement 'I turn my red eye at him.' This means the person is angry. If a parent warns their kid, 'Don't see my red eye,' it means the kid should not provoke them. Soldiers who are always on war front wear red.

Scientific Explanations

According to Shutterstock (2015), in the Western world, red connotes excitement, energy, passion, action, love, and danger. In that part of the world, it is used more as a positive symbol than being negative. However, in Russia, it is the colour of the communists and used to signal revolutionary. Most times, revolutionary actions are violent and lead to bloodletting. Thus, the reason red is considered a perfect colour to warn that evil looms.

'In Asian cultures red is a very important color—it symbolizes good luck, joy, prosperity, celebration, happiness, and a long life. Because it's such an auspicious colour, brides often wear red on their wedding day and red envelopes containing money are given out during holidays and special occasions' (Shutterstock 2015). To be more specific, red is a symbol of spirituality, sensuality and purity in India. However, the story is not the same in Africa. Many countries associate it with death. When they mourn, many of them are likely to wear red and in some other cases, black. In Nigeria, it is used to represent vitality and that is why many adverts demonstrating strength comes in that colour and used as a sign of aggression in some other instances. In Iran, red represents courage and good fortune and a hallmark of luck among the Egyptians.

Brooks (2016) describes red as an 'attention-getter' in all cultures of the world. According to the BBC, 'Wearing red can change your physiology and balance of hormones and alter your performance in a football match.' That is how powerful the colour can be. However, attention as used in the sentence above is generic; the kind of attention this colour draws to you is dependent on the situation you find yourself. In South Africa, it is a symbol of mourning and sacrifice. In the Middle East, it is sometimes laced with threatening overtones, danger and call to order. In Latin America, red means passion, but can also symbolise Christianity when used alongside white.

Olesen (2019) draws our attention to important occasions where red is indispensable—Valentine's Day and Christmas. This further solidifies the claims that red is used to represent love as the two aforementioned events depict. Discussing the positive interpretations of the colour, Olesen submits, 'The red color is a warm and positive color that is associated with our physical needs and our will to survive. Red radiates a strong and powerful masculine energy. It is a sporty color, that many automakers choose to showcase their showroom cars. The color red is energizing and it provokes the emotions and motivates us to take action. The red color expresses pioneer spirit and leadership qualities, and promotes ambition and determination.'

The expert concludes, 'Being surrounded by too much red can make us irritable, agitated and ultimately angry. Too little red can make us cautious, manipulative and afraid. In Eastern cultures, such as China, red is the colour for good luck. Although times are changing and many Chinese brides today are dressed in white, red is the traditional colour for weddings.' Hence, we need to take note of this changing trend in our interpretations too.

Practical Illustrations

Case Study I: It's Christmas season and Mr HC has ordered his employees to ensure that every part of their company is decorated with red. After the decoration, the showroom appears more beautiful and colourful. When he returns to work the next day, he was dumbfounded at the creativity of his employees. He informed them that even after Christmas, red would be the official colour to be used in the showroom and since then, this has bolstered their market rate as even clients found it adorable and pleasant.

Case Study II: Firm HTR holds an annual dinner for its workforce. According to the management, the purpose is to bond the employees and create a sense of importance among them—it is always a time to celebrate hard work. In order to add glamour to the event, there is usually red carpets for the VIPs and the general workforce. The one designed for the VIPs is more colourful and attractive and there is no way you will not like to have some shots while walking on it. VIPs are those invited outside the rank and files of the firm, and as such, they are of the opinion that they should be treated with more sense of importance. Hence, red is seen as a mark of honour and attraction in this regard.

Case Study III: As said earlier, colour has a way of impacting on our psychology and criminals do take cognisance of this in their dressing. For instance, there was a time I was interrogating a man who allegedly murdered his brother due to what he tagged as 'irreconcilable differences'. When it came to the question of the colour of the clothes he wore, he said 'Red', and I furthered by asking him what informed the choice of the colour. According to him, in case there was blood stain, it would be difficult for people to know, and it also spurred him psychologically to commit the atrocity; he said it gave him a feeling of fire and wildness. In this context, it is considered as the favourite for criminals as a bolster for their psychological feelings.

24.4. Blue

Generic Interpretations of the Concept

Blue is one of the most popular colours used around the world and interpreted in multiple ways, depending on the context in which it is used. Blue is used as a symbol of love in some instances. People use blue to denote love due to its calmness and attractiveness. Unlike some other colours that appear flamboyant, this colour is creates a feeling of serenity in one's mind. In the same vein, it is considered a perfect emblem of tranquillity. If you have ever been to a flowing river early in the morning, away from the hues and cries of the world, you will understand the real meaning of tranquillity. Beaches and oceans we go for hangouts and holidays are in blue colour. This metaphorically communicates the peace of mind related to the colour. The skies are predominantly blue which is believed among many people as serving as a cover to heaven where there are no troubles and sorrows. This further buttresses the fact that blue is made for tranquillity.

In addition, this colour is seen as a symbol of trust and loyalty. Some nations that had undergone turbulent moments in the past use this colour to pledge their loyalty to the national entity. Also, I have seen many companies use this colour to reaffirm their loyalty to their customers and other people they transact business with. In relationships too, some use this colour as the foundation of their love. Blue is one of the best colours to wear to an interview; it tells your potential employers that you will be committed to the goals and ideals of the firm if you are eventually employed, just like white tells them the purity of your mind.

Security and intelligence are some other meanings that have been attributed to blue. It is used in depicting security because it is not flamboyant and somewhat thick. Just like in the case of stream or ocean referred to above, when people have challenges and need somewhere to think through, they normally go river bank. Great writers across the world are also known for this behaviour. The serenity and orderliness achieved in this environment births knowledge.

On the other hand, the colour is used in some climes to mean coldness, masculinity and fear. It is in the times of trouble that people look up into the heavens for help. When you see a person standing in a disturbed manner, with the eyes focused on the skies, it is mostly a means of communicating their fear.

Scientific Explanations

Shutterstock (2015) states, 'Blue is considered the safest colour choice around the world, since it has many positive associations. In North America and Europe blue represents trust, security, and authority, and is considered to be soothing and peaceful. But it can also represent depression, loneliness, and sadness (hence having 'the blues').' This gives us a clue of how to interpret the colour when in that part of the world. Those who have 'the blues' are not in the good book of life— they have issues they are battling with, which make them depressed and sad.

Brooks (2016) explains from the business perspective that blue is the most cherished colour of international brands. He states further that blue is one of the few colours with predominantly positive meanings. He stresses that blue is a representation of authority, tranquillity, trust and sadness among the Westerners. In many Asian cultures, it connotes immortality, relaxation and healing. In India, it is the colour of Krishna and denotes strength. In Mexico and many parts of the Middle East, it is used to mean mourning. However, the Middle Eastern nations also interpret blue as depicting 'Safety, protection, and spirituality.'

Olesen (2019) sees blue as a calming and cool colour that is used in depicting creativity and intelligence. Due to its meaning, airline operators and hospitals are some other common places in which this colour is prevalent. Among men, there is no doubt that blue is a favourite colour. The sincerity, quietness and reserved nature of the colour makes it outstanding; it does not attract unnecessary attention to itself. The colour is unique and values doing things on its own. 'From a colour psychology perspective, the blue colour is reliable and responsible and radiates security and trust. You can be sure that the colour blue can take control and do the right thing in difficult situations. The blue colour needs order and planning in its life, including the way it lives and works.' It seems Olesen is trying to personify blue in this sense. That is to tell you how spectacular the colour is.

However, be careful with your use of blue colour when it comes to food. There are not too many foods in this colour, hence using it in this context is capable of suppressing people's appetite. This is a cogent point for those that deal in food selling. The colour is renowned for its one-way communication system—it likes being the voice rather than being one that is being addressed.

Hence, public speakers and teachers may see this colour as a favourite. The colour blue is your helper, saviour, your friend in need. The blue colours success is defined by the quality and quantity of its relationships. It's a giver, not a taker. Blue likes to build strong, trusting relationships, and is deeply hurt if the trust is betrayed (Olesen 2019).

Practical Illustrations

Case Study I: Mr KX is a renowned public speaker in his locality, but his name was not heard at the national and international levels. Even though he has an event or another to attend every week, he is not happy that he is being limited to just his immediate environment. He laments to a friend and the idea of setting up a website and social media platforms came. He buys into the initiative and now, he has many open doors. On his first invite outside of his domain, his performance was not sterling. This was very depressing to him. When he had the second opportunity, he did not just think of what to say but even what to wear. After reading and watching numerous outstanding speakers, he decided to go for blue. He was dumbfounded at his performance this time around as everyone was showering encomiums on him. Blue signals intelligence, brilliancy and exceptional productivity in this context.

Case Study II: These days, I see people go for blue colour when they want to paint their homes. I thought it was particular to a country until I toured the world. So I had to ask some of them and it seemed they agreed on similar reasons. One of the common factors mentioned is serenity; painting a home blue makes it serene—it does not produce too much heat in the afternoon. Also, it beautifies the home, especially at night when the lights are switched on. Unlike white, when you have kids and they stain the wall, it is easier to clean it off. This is an advantage many other colours don't have. So blue stands for endurance. It endures just anything and this is why it is also known for stability.

Case Study III: One of the reasons criminals use blue is for inclusion. Blue has a reputation of being inclusive because it is the colour of the sky. According to one criminal, he chooses blue because it makes him comfortable with other people and makes him blend with them easily. He said people do not question him whenever he comes to their midst. And through this, he gathers pieces of information easily from them. Another criminal I once interrogated said he chooses blue whenever he wants to cart away some items in the crowd. He recounts how this works for him several times. That is, he uses the inclusiveness of blue to appeal to the emotions of his targets.

24.5. Green

Generic Interpretations of the Concept

One of the most common expressions around the world is that people are looking for 'greener pastures' elsewhere. From the foregoing, it means that people are in search of a better life elsewhere. Invariably, green represents fertility. You only search for greener pasture when you believe that you are not productive enough at your present level. This is a sentiment that is shared among many cultures of the world. Green is fertile and represents agility. Farmers have a better understanding of this concept. When the grasses on a particular land are not green, there is high probability that if the same parcel of land is used for farming, nothing good will come out of it. Loamy soil which is best for agriculture is in green colour.

In the same vein, green is used to depict freshness. Coming out to relax early in the morning in your garden is capable of curing you of any depressing thought. Many people who care about their health eat green food—sea fish, vegetables and other supportive supplements. Red meat has been preached against by medical experts due to its side effects. This has given green foods an upper hand, especially among the elites. Also, we can safely assume that green is used as an instrument of healing. We walk in gardens and other places filled with green plants when we are psychologically troubled in order to be relieved. Fresh and assuring ideas are birthed at this moment and are capable of redefining one's experience. Diabetes and other chronic illnesses also give way in the face of green leaves.

Money and growth are other interpretations given to this colour. In some climes, green is used to represent money and if something is increasing, it is also qualified with green. That is why the statement 'ever-green' is used to mean something that is relevant, no matter the location and timing.

There are some negative meanings attached to this colour too—guilt, envy and jealousy are the predominant ones. A colleague may decide to wear green to work just to show how jealous or envious they are about your success. Green is somewhat dull and when you expect someone to actually be on something nice for an occasion but end up wearing green, it probably means they are not happy about the event. This can be very subtle but it reveals what goes on the mind of the person. However, you need to be careful about making generalisation of this point as some might not actually wear the colour for such occasion out of their love for the outfit or even a mere coincidence.

Scientific Explanations

Shutterstock (2015) explains this from the Western point of view. The popular website states that green 'represents luck, nature, freshness, spring, environmental awareness, wealth, inexperience, and jealousy (the 'green-eyed monster')' in that part of the world. However, it is very emblematic in Ireland which earned its nickname 'the Emerald Isle' from its lush green landscapes. It is the mark of independence in Mexico. Hence, it is their primary national colour. While travelling to Indonesia, you need to be very careful as green is a conventionally forbidden colour in that country.

Brooks (2016) says because green is the colour of grasses and leaves, that is why it used in denoting nature. It is very calming as many people do not get irritated by it. Brooks opines, 'The line between blue and green can be difficult to draw, though, and in some languages, it's not named as a separate colour.' This is to state that there are some similarities between the two colours such as calmness, serenity, and tranquillity. The language expert states further that since green is used to depict 'go' in traffic light, we can assume that it is a colour of progress. Green is also used in marketing to indicate environmental awareness. Those who preach the need to go back to the serene nature of some centuries ago do use green colour as their template.

In many Asian and Eastern cultures, 'green represents nature, fertility, and youth.' In some way, we can conclude that green is one of the few colours that enjoy universality in its interpretations. However, it may also connote infidelity among the Chinese. In the Middle East, too, green indicates fertility, money, and good fortune. Equally important, it's also the colour of Islam. In Mexico, it is an emblem of patriotism. People who relate to this colour are always admired, especially by those that know what it took for them to be freed from the shackles of colonialism. If your audience are Mexicans, it would be an advantage for you to wear green as it gives them a sense of belonging and shows how you cherish them as a people. However, in some Latin and South American nations, green is regarded as the colour of death (Brooks 2016).

Olesen (2019) associates green with health. Because of its pleasing nature, it relaxes the body and possesses healing power. The language expert states, 'Many pharmaceutical and nutritional companies use green colour meaning in their logos and their material to advertise safe and natural products.'

'Dark green is often associated with the military, monetary, financial and banking businesses. The colour green is full of balance and harmony. From a colour psychology perspective, it's the colour green, that puts heart and emotions in balance, and equals head and heart. The green colour is an emotionally positive colour, which gives us the ability to love and care for ourselves and others unconditionally' (Olesen 2019).

Practical Illustrations

Case Study I: Mr AF and his friends are trying to set up pharmaceutical company and one of the issues they are concerned with at the start of the firm is how they would be able to communicate their values, ideals and vision through the use of logo. They understand that their brand is their identity and, as such, should be duly promoted along the right line. After arguments and submissions of different opinions, they decided to settle for green as a background colour due to its connection to nature and health.

Case Study II: The students in sciences of TXO High School are divided into groups on an annual basis to undertake a unique project and thereafter do a public presentation of those ideas. It is usually a gathering of executives as they come to hunt for talents. Group A is working on a project that they expect to last for a minimum of one hundred years if implemented. So they choose green as their favourite colour to portray the durability of their work. During the day of their presentation, apart from the uniqueness of their projection, the colour depiction is also the talk of the town. That is, it adds value and standard to their work.

Case Study III: Impostor FP left home prepared for whatever might end up being his lot that particular day; he was fed being in his home country and wanted to leave by all means. He was assured by the person who fabricated that passport for him that he was safe because he had done similar things for people in the past and they were not caught. So after putting everything in place, he discovered that he had no green dress. He had to buy one due to what he read about it; he believed that if the immigration officers eventually caught him, his colour would calm them. Green as a representation of calmness cools the head and puts the mind at peace.

24.6. Yellow

Generic Interpretations of the Concept

Arguably, there is not any other colour as bright as yellow. It is also the colour of the sun. That is why it is regarded as the colour of brightness. People who want to stand out are fond of wearing this colour. In a large gathering where people are wearing other colours with you being on yellow, you will easily be fished out because of the flashy nature of the colour. It announces itself, no matter how far away it is from the target. Without mincing words, yellow is not the colour of introverts because it would expose them when they are least prepared for it.

Due to the universality of the sun, this colour is regarded as a connotation of light. Those who want others to believe they have come to make a difference will appear in yellow. Some religious gatherings are known to favour yellow as a colour because they want others to see them as the 'children of light.' Hence, this makes the colour very symbolic in many parts of the world. From the perspective of nature, yellow is considered as a source of energy—the sun propels the process of photosynthesis through which plants derive energy. Hence, those who want to show that they are powerful may decide to appear in yellow. There are some automobile companies that prefer this colour solely on the basis that it is used in communicating strength—they want their clients to believe that their products are strong, durable and reliable, just like we are certain of sunshine daily.

Happiness, intellect and creativity are some other interpretations given to this colour. Those who are not happy will prefer some gloomy colours. By now, we should have understood that the colour we are exposed to or wear is capable of affecting our mood and psychological feeling. Because yellow is naturally bright, it is capable of changing the mood of someone who has been feeling depressed. During mourning and other solemn occasions, people avoid this colour because it would depict them as being insensitive to the plight of others.

On the other hand, yellow is also seen as a mark of instability and irresponsibility. There are some contexts whereby this colour will depict you as someone who is irresponsible. That is why I have always emphasised the need to understand your audience. If it were a business setting and a partner sees you as being irresponsible just because of the colour of your cloth or badge, this will portend a great havoc to your chances of securing the contract.

Scientific Explanations

Among the Westerners, it is believed that yellow represents 'happiness, cheeriness, optimism, warmth (as the colour of sunlight), joy, and hope, as well as caution and cowardice,' opines Shutterstock. Egypt is an African country that shares a similar meaning with the Western nations. Egyptians associate yellow with good fortunes and happiness and sometimes, a colour of mourning. However, it is a symbol of envy among the Germans.

Brooks (2016) mentions respected brands like IKEA, Lipton and McDonald's that use yellow as a symbol of identity. The reason being that they want to communicate happiness, vigour and optimism through the colour. Brooks adds that this does not reflect a universal world view. That is, not everyone sees yellow in the light of their own interpretations. In the west, you are likely to see more of yellow in the summer. And there are times it is used as a colour of hospitality.

Among Asians too, this colour is mostly associated with positive meanings. In Japan, it is a royal colour that represents courage and prosperity. In Thailand, it is a lucky colour associated with the recently deceased King Bhumibol. However, in China, it is associated with pornography. Generally, among the Middle Eastern residents, yellow is interpreted as a positive colour. In Latin America, it is used when people mourn. In Africa, it is used in depicting status and wealth (Brooks 2016).

Olesen (2019) regards yellow as the brightest colour we can see as humans. Due to its cheerfulness and energy, it is used as the most preferred colour for children toys and dressing. The language expert furthers that 'yellow is the best colour to boost enthusiasm in your life and can contribute with greater confidence and optimism. It loves challenges, especially the mental kind. In colour psychology, yellow is known as the colour of communication. It is a great speaker, networker and journalist, who all work and communicate on the mental level. The colour yellow is the scientist, who constantly analyse things and look methodically on both sides of a case, before making a decision. Yellow is also the entertainer, comedian and clown.' Yellow does so many unimaginable things to the brain; it affects numerous things going on in the human brain when we are least conscious of them. You may do yourself good by adopting this colour when you project a hectic day ahead as it refreshes you and ensures you stay refilled throughout the day.

When lost in the midst of decision making, yellow makes your thoughts clearer to you and births new ideas. Yellow also helps us focus, study and remember information. This can be useful under examination situations. This is another lifestyle you can adopt. You may not really count this as being significant, but the effect it leaves on us are always huge. However, due to how it moves rapidly forward in life, it may easily provoke nervousness in people (Olesen 2019).

Practical Illustrations

Case Study I: Student TF likes yellow out of all colours because of what he learnt about it in his elementary school that it aids academic excellence by helping people study, focus and remember information. Since then, he has been conscious of the use of the colour. In fact, he would not attend a high school that does not have yellow as its uniform, despite all entreaties from his parents. During examination periods, you should not expect him in any other colour than yellow. This ended up making him a distinction student. Yellow represents excellence and people who long for such results align themselves with it.

Case Study II: Among prisoners and ex-convicts, yellow is a positive and adorable colour. To prisoners, it gives them hope that they will regain their freedom but it has much more metaphoric interpretations among ex-convicts. To them, it symbolises rebirth of hope. An ex-convict once shared his story with me about how he got a job unexpectedly due to the yellow ribbon project. He was emotional about it because he never had hope of such a high-paying job again. Since then, he has made yellow his favourite colour. In fact, there is no amount that a favourite yellow shirt is sold that he would not afford it. The experience also made him more passionate about the yellow ribbon project.

Case Study III: Two couples that got wedded via a marriage of convenience because they wanted to access a loan meant for married people were rehearsing their appearance; they did not want to leave any stone unturned because they both needed the loan for some nasty things though. One of the items they gave priority to is the colour of their clothes. For instance, when they were going for the interview for the loan, they settled for yellow despite it was never part of their favourites. They went for yellow because they wanted to portray themselves as happy couples and to also instil the culture of laughter in each other so as to cover up their weirdness.

24.7. Purple

Generic Interpretations of the Concept

Purple is one of the primary colours that are rarely used due to its importance. When you see purple, look inwardly, there is something special about to happen or going on. Those who are colour blind are most likely to take purple for blue. This is something I have witnessed in different places. In other words, purple is also a calm, cool colour. That is why it is used as a symbol of nobility in some parts of the world. Those of noble background with so much honour and integrity do not use flashy things; they do not believe in self-announcement. That shows that nobility is in the blood and a culture to them. Those who are fortunate to be a little bit wealthy are the ones that lead flamboyant lifestyles just to let others know that their fortunes have changed. This is not to condemn any form of living but to state the kinds of people you can find in most human societies in our contemporary times.

In the same vein, this is also used as a mark of royalty. Apart from being decent, purple is also classy. In some way, it regarded as the rare form of blue. Hence, royal heads use this colour to show class and difference, while still communicating their allegiance to the people they govern or rule.

Further, those who are fond of this colour are always seen as being ambitious; they can go anywhere to ensure the realisation of their goals. The sky is blue and seen universally while purple is the thicker form of blue colour, this metaphorically means that those who subscribe to this colour are resilient in the face of struggles and temptations to relent on their goals.

To some, it is an emblem of spirituality and others interpret it as a mark of luxury. From the psychological viewpoint, purple is a mark of wealth, mystery and wisdom. When wearing this colour, you can be mysterious in your actions and thoughts which other people may take as a sign of wisdom. You will even be dumbfounded by the ways in which things work out for you. This may lead to wealth as people begin to relate with you the more in the business world.

However, since the colour is not flashy, a conglomeration of it in a given place can make you feel moody. For instance, if you walk into a firm and all that the employees put on is purple, this may be depressing to you as the colour does not appeal to a happy person. If you are dealing with people from different backgrounds, this may not be the best colour to adopt for your business.

Scientific Explanations

Shutterstock (2015) states that purple is a colour that is often associated with 'royalty, wealth, spirituality, and nobility around the world.' This means that these interpretations are not limited to any part of the world. Historically in Japan only the highest ranked Buddhist monks wore purple robes. Purple is also associated with piety and faith, and in Catholicism, penitence. This tells us that purple is an adorable colour in the spiritual realm. However, in Thailand and Brazil, purple is the colour for mourning. In the US, this is a colour of honour— the Purple Heart is the oldest military award still given to US military members.

Brooks (2016) opines that purple is often associated with wealth because it is historically expensive to produce. In many parts of Asian cultures, it is a mark of nobility. In Africa and Middle East, it is also a show of wealth and royalty.

According to Olesen (2019), 'Purple combines the stability of the blue colour and the energy of the red' and that is why it has always been attached to prestige and royalty. It is a colour that involves the combination of two predominant ones in the colour wheel. Purple colour meaning is often used to portray rich powerful kings, leaders, magicians and even sorcerers. Purple combined with gold can be flashy and portray wealth and extravagance. 'Bright purple and pink are good as feminine designs and is popular among teenage girls. Light purple together with the colour yellow is commonly used in advertisements for children's products. It gives the impression of something that is fun and easy to deal with' (Olesen 2019).

If you want to get to the deepest part of your thought, then you need to be a companion of this colour; it is related to spirituality and imagination which makes people get to the hardcore of their thoughts. Olesen also goes ahead to enlighten us on the difference between violet and purple by saying that 'the difference between violet and purple is that violet is displayed in the visible light spectrum, while purple is simply a mixture of red and blue. Violet vibrations are the highest in the visible spectrum. Although violet is not quite as intense as purple, their essence is the same.' On a norm, the names of both colours can be interchanged. They both derive their energy from red colour and spirituality and integrity from the blue colour. The colours symbolise the union of body and soul, which creates a balance between our physical and spiritual energies (Olesen 2019).

If you are in search of spiritual fulfilment and meaning to your life, look not beyond this colour. It connects us to higher level of consciousness through the expansion of our horizon. 'From a colour psychology perspective, purple and violet ensures harmony of the mind and the emotions and contributes to mental balance and stability, peace of mind, a connection between the spiritual and physical world, and between thought and action. Violet and purple promotes meditation' (Olesen 2019).

Practical Illustrations

Case Study I: AD is a comedian and as one of the best in his city, he was invited by one of the moneybags in town to come and officiate a get-together. He knew that the gathering would be star-studded as rich and well-to-do people from all over will make it to the occasion. Thinking of how best to dress, he ensured that whatever he was going to conclude on must have a touch of purple as a mark of nobility. And when he did it, it really portrayed him as a noble being.

Case Study II: Mr RC was into importation business but was not making headway for years. He almost became a frustrated man before he met a woman who told him some other things he could be doing to increase his income and have a firm grip on the business. He got loans and implemented the ideas as stated by the woman. He was diligent with it and within three years, he became super rich. As a way of demonstrating his riches, he would wear purple to most events, especially those with average persons in attendance so as to be distinguished among them. The manner he carries himself also communicates this message. That is, both his behaviour and non-verbal gesture complement each other to buttress the message of riches.

Case Study III: Mrs EV forged the financial documents of her husband in order to withdraw funds from his account illegally; they had a quarrel and she believed that that was the best way to get back at him. She brought in an accomplice to help her with the background works so that she would not be caught at the bank. After everything was set, she thought of the colour to wear. After few minutes of thinking, she settled for purple. It communicates three basic messages she needed at that point—mystery, respect and wisdom. She wanted to feign respect so as not to be questioned at the bank and it is a product of wisdom. Even though he actually looked wise, this colour did not impact what was written on the forged documents.

24.8. Brown

Generic Interpretations of the Concept

Brown is a combination of red and green in the colour wheel. Thus, drawing its meaning from the two colours. Brown can be interpreted from both positive and negative angles, depending on the context and audience in view. It is the colour of the earth. This speaks of its universality. The earth is the most conducive for humans to live in, without it, we would not have been in existence. Invariably, this tells us that brown is the most accommodating colour. Through it, we derive meaning for our existence and it also empowers us to go for our goals. It is the platform through which we find fulfilment and make plans about our future.

Further, brown is interpreted as friendliness. Most parents prefer brown shirts for their kids in their early stage because it has ability to contain dirt; people do not easily notice it when it is dirty. Further, it is the best colour for outdoor events. It takes away all your worries of your decorations getting tainted before or during an occasion. Also, it is a representation of conservative due to its relation to green. Whatever plant you see around today surges from the soil, which is brown in colour. If you want to appear original and uncompromising to others, brown should be your favourite colour. It is a symbol of respect as it naturally tells people about your firmness.

Durability and longevity are some other charming attributes of brown. There are some parts of the world where this colour is seen as a symbol of long life. Organisations that deal with aged ones or anything that has to do with health do use this colour as a representation of their brand.

On the other hand, some cultures do not subscribe to the idea of conservatism behind this colour. These are the class of people that believe that you should not hold the same opinion over time; your stance and beliefs should be influenced by things happening around you. Such individuals are unrepentant believers in technology and change. Even if things seem to be static, they move the hands of things for the sake of newness. However, this newness does not necessarily mean that it is a better version of what has been in existence before. Anyone who does not believe in conservatism will definitely hate brown because it does not help their philosophical sentiment. Also, some see brown as a mark of dogmatism. To them, brown is thoughtless, powerless and reckless—it believes in what it is being fed without questioning.

Scientific Explanations

'The colour brown is serious and very down to earth, with properties like stability, structure and support. The brown colour stands for protection and supporting the family with great sense of duty and responsibility. Brown colour meaning calls for high priority, a strong need for security, belonging to a family and having lots of good friends' (Olesen 2019). Those who love to acquire material things and desire security for such will be in this lane—that is exactly what brown represents. Brown is encompassing. It opens the heart up for caring for others and think of the needs of others in whatever you do. This is the truest definition of friendship—being selfless in all your endeavours.

The colour brown finds quality in everything – a comfortable home, the best food and drink, as well as loyal friends or a partner. It is a colour that exudes physical comfort, simplicity and quality. From a negative perspective, the colour brown may also, under certain circumstances, give the impression of stinginess (Olesen 2019).

Brown is the hallmark of friendliness, reliability and hospitality. It tells you how to relate with others in a practical and feasible manner. Brown does not subscribe to theories in its dealings. 'In colour psychology the colour brown is referred to as honest, genuine and sincere. It refers to the hard-working, diligent and reliable, with both feet planted firmly on the ground. Brown is sensual, sensitive and warm, and gives one a sense of calmness and comfort. It is a practical and sensible colour, indicating common sense. The colour brown is associated with healthy, natural and organic products, and everything related to the outdoors' (Olesen 2019). Brown is simply a different breed whose source is undebatable. This sense of difference is acknowledged by most people across the world.

Being a scarce colour, it is not in any way related to waste or abundance. That is why it is valued and cherished by those who understand what connotes. It prides quality over quantity. Some brown colours may show a degree of sophistication, depending on what other colours they are connected to. For example, the colour brown, with a soft white or ivory, looks elegant and classic, but still more casual than black combined with the same colours. If you want to suppress your negative feelings, this colour is the best for you to rely on. It invokes haven from the outside world, restoring your comfort and peace in an unimaginable manner. The colour does not require you to be perfect but maintain orderliness and appreciable sense of organisation in your dealings (Olesen 2019).

Olesen concludes that 'the psychological significance of the color brown may vary slightly, depending on the colors that are mixed together to create the brown color. Brown may arise from a combination of black, yellow, orange, red, gray, green, blue, pink and purple, and each of the colors add a variation to the brown color meaning.'

Practical Illustrations

Case Study I: Ms VG decides not to take up any paid employment after her college; she is an ardent believer in entrepreneurship. She likes being a boss of herself and believes that one of the most potent ways to find solutions to lingering issues of graduate unemployment is to start small and nurture such goals into fulfilment. However, the journey has been rough for her and she does not know where she is at fault. After working on other things, she shifts her attention to her dress code and colour. This serves as turning point in her business life as she discovers that she is always more organised, orderly and focused whenever she is in brown.

Case Study II: Various security agencies subscribe to the use of brown due to its relationship with the profession. On the surface level, brown is accommodating; it does not easily get dirty and it is easy to wash. Apart from that, it symbolises security. That is why many security outfits ensure that their uniform has a touch of brown. Brown is the safest colour that guarantees protection and since law enforcement job deals with that, it calms the nerves of officers, especially during violent reactions. For countless times, I have looked at the colour at difficult moments for reassurance of success and it has never failed.

Case Study III: Criminals use the colour to represent accumulation of material possession. If someone is building a suspicious relationship with you and you discover that they like wearing brown whenever coming to you, it is a metaphorical message that they are after your material wealth. A criminal once shared a similar story with me of how he uses the colour to position his psychology for the operation. As a con artist, he built the relationship on phantom promises just to get the person to cooperate and after few months, they victim let down the guard and he got free entry into his life. He had carted away with the man's millions of dollars before he was apprehended. This is a testament of material accumulation depicted through this colour.

24.9. Orange

Generic Interpretations of the Concept

Orange is a familiar fruit universally. Even though it has always been reported that it is acidic, we still consume it to some extent. This means it cannot go into extinction, especially when we consider its usage in industries where it is used in producing drinks and wines. Our focus here is the interpretation of the colour among different people on the surface of the earth. Orange is a symbol of friendship. People who value true friendship see it as a fruit that must always be nurtured to fruition. It means you are committed to a course.

Orange is also a symbol of success. Success is not a myth; it comes through practical efforts and consistent commitment to a given course. That is the philosophy of orange colour. Whatever is worth doing is worth doing well. Orange does not back off from an assignment easily; it makes sure you stay on course till you achieve your end goals. If you want to embark on an assignment that you think is really demanding, it would be a great advantage for you to involve orange from the start. This colour gives you the needed energy when you are fagged out. The colour has proven itself as an engine oil that drives people to success when it matters most. When you see people who have orange as their favourite colour, there is high probability that they are success-minded; they are driven by the need to break new grounds, achieve breakthroughs in uncommon tasks and leave indelible impacts wherever they find themselves.

In addition, orange is a symbol of courage and confidence. If a task seems daunting and unapproachable, then orange is the most appropriate colour to engage in such situations. Orange does not believe that any task is insurmountable. Even when others are thinking that something might not work out well, orange colour is always optimistic to the last point. It is a colour that sets the pace for others to follow. It gives energy and refuels your mind to stand up where others are fainting.

However, there are some negative meanings to this colour too. Some are of the opinion that it is sluggish. That is, it takes slow pace when getting something sorted out. Maybe, this is due to the fact that it does not want to commit too many errors that can end up ruining the assignment with fatal errors. Further, ignorance has been attributed to this colour. Other people are likely to see you as being unknowledgeable when you wear orange colour. The colour does not represent wisdom to people who share the sentiment. Hence, they will relate with you based on their thought towards you; they may likely override you or even spit at your face, believing that you do not understand all that is going on.

Scientific Explanations

Brooks (2016) states that this colour has a variety of meanings across the globe. In the Western cultures, 'Orange is the colour of fall and the harvest. It also symbolises affordability. In Northern Ireland, though, it's the colour of the Protestants. It's also the national colour of the Netherlands, where it's associated with royalty. For brands, it's a kid-friendly, fun colour that appeals to impulse buyers,' notes Brooks. In most parts of the West, orange is an adorable colour that they want to relate with—both kids and adults.

In Asian cultures, saffron orange is sacred among the Indians and other cultures that believe in Hinduism or Buddhism. In Japan and China, it symbolises courage, happiness, prosperity and good health. However, in the Middle East, it is laced with negative interpretations such as loss, danger and mourning. In Latin America, it is a representation of the earth and sunlight (Brooks 2016).

Olesen (2019) says orange is a combination of red and yellow. This is where it derives it warmness and brightness. Orange is considered a fun, light colour with appetising and delicious qualities. It also increases the oxygen supply to the brain and stimulates mental activity. It is one of the few colours that are not just concerned about our emotions but also about the efficiency of our mental ability. It is related to healthy, strong and appetising food. Such foods are great and nourishing to the body and bolster our mental health. The orange colour radiates warmth and joy, and combines the physical energy of the colour red, with joy from the colour yellow. Orange is related to our intuition, as opposed to the colour red, which is related to the physical reaction, or yellow, which is related to the mental reaction. The colour orange provides emotional strength in difficult times. It helps us get through disappointments, despair and grief. In your down moments, you can always count on this colour as a confidante and companion (Olesen 2019).

Olesen encourages that 'in color psychology, the color orange is optimistic and uplifting—it lifts our spirits. In fact, orange is so optimistic and uplifting, that we all should find ways to implement it in our daily lives. Using an orange colored pencil or a pen may be enough. The color orange adds spontaneity and a positive way of looking at life. It's a great color to use in tough economic times, to keep us motivated and help us look at the bright side of life. With great enthusiasm, the color orange calls for adventure and risk-taking, physical confidence, competition and independence. Those inspired by orange are always on the go.'

Practical Illustrations

Case Study I: There is global economic downturn and many organisations are making decisions they consider best for their survival. Part of such decisions was to sack workers or reduce the salaries of those that are active and committed to their service. Dr LB's firm is also not left out in this action. However, after doing everything, he still discovers that he is not getting the needed satisfaction; he still panics and the results are not encouraging as expected. Then, he plans leading a new life which includes changing his stationaries to orange colour. This ends up stabilising him and helps in birthing creative ideas.

Case Study II: Schools and childcares are fond of the use of orange colour for its symbolic representation. Orange is a common fruit loved by most people and children can easily relate with it. That is why it is used at the elementary levels. Beyond that, schools use it in their logo to symbolise brightness. This depicts the kind of impact they make on their students. A friend once told me that he cannot allow his child attend a school without a touch of orange in their logo. Orange means the school imparts quality knowledge on their students and that is the most essential thing in such environment.

Case Study III: Employee DX was indicted in a fraud case and had to be suspended for six months. He would have been dismissed like the principal actor of the crime but he pleaded that he was trapped into ignorantly. On resuming duty after serving the suspension, his colleagues noticed that his colour preference has changed; before his suspension, he wears clothes at random and even confessed that he had no preferred colour but after the suspension, it was noticed that he was always on orange. This was to communicate the message that it was a new dawn for him—a representation of new behaviour.

24.10. Pink

Generic Interpretations of the Concept

Due to the fragile appearance of the colour, it is mostly attributed to feminine look. When you appear in pink, people might take you as being coolheaded and easy-going. This is more so if you are a female; the sentiment is high among females because some see them as being naturally weak, although recent occurrences around the world have proven otherwise. Pink is cool, calm and unassuming. It is a colour that thinks critically before taking any decision for the fear of meeting up with deadlock along the way. People with feminine look do not like encountering difficult issues in the process of carrying out a task. They are more likely to give up if the challenge is overwhelming. Hence, instead of starting abruptly and stopping midway, they would rather think well, consider their chances and critically evaluate the proposed project before launching into action. This has earned some of them appellation of pessimist but I think it is better that way. In this sense, I can refer to pink as a sign of wisdom; it looks before leaping.

Further, pink is a colour of happiness. Probably, it derives this from blue. Happiness is the bedrock of healthiness; those who are not happy are probably not healthy. Being moody at all times is one of things that can result into incurable illnesses. Pink lights up the mind and ensures that you are healthy and joyful in your sojourn in life. Pink tells you that nothing is worth the exchange of your joy; if a thing does not work out, let go of it instead of allowing same weigh you down and take away your happiness.

In the same vein, pink is playful. Those who are fans of this colour do not believe that life is war. They play out their minds and forget whatever negative issues they are battling with. This is why this colour is also associated with sweetness. Those who wear this colour are high-performers; they do not allow the bad event of a place affect the positive event of another. For instance, if they have a bad day at work, they will not transfer that aggression on others at home. They are at peace with their neighbours, kids and spouses. Transferring aggressions will make you a perpetually moody fellow and pink does not believe in that.

Further, pink is a symbol of compassion. Ordinarily, it is expected that something that is feminine should be compassionate. That is, you should care for others and be reliable to them in times of need. Pink does not overlook people's needs or feign ignorance; it rises up to the occasion and offers whatever help it can.

However, some believe that pink is a symbol of weakness and immaturity. Pink does not show the needed agility and strength in tough situations. It would rather back out rather than try to give more effort in getting something done. Life is not fair and will not give us what we deserve on the first call. This means we have to be strong and unrelenting. This is one quality that is lacking in pink.

Scientific Explanations

Jennifer Bourn (2010) defines *pink* as 'a delicate colour that means sweet, nice, playful, cute, romantic, charming, feminine, and tenderness, is associated with bubble gum, flowers, babies, little girls, cotton candy, and sweetness.' This definition is encompassing as it gives us a view of all the possible areas in which the colour can feature. Universally, it is a symbol of love for oneself and others. It is love that is both experienced and shared. Hence, it displays friendship, inner peace, approachability and affection. Pink does not pick fights with people at every point of disagreement. It is a colour that is more concerned about its peace; it does not flex muscles with negativities. Thus, it is a natural symbol of peace and compassion.

Whenever you think of anything nice, also think of pink. According to Bourn, 'Pink is the sweet side of the colour red. While the colour red stirs up passion, aggression, and action, large amounts of the colour pink can actually create physical weakness.' Both red and **pink** represent love. The colour red represents heat and passion, while the colour pink represents romance and charm. Hot pink is used to communicate playfulness, while light pink is used to communicate tenderness (Bourn 2010).

It is believed in many quarters that pink gemstones bring relaxation, serenity, contentment, acceptance, and discard all forms of frustrations.

Empower Yourself with Colour Psychology (2018) explains pink from the psychological viewpoint. According to the platform, it is a symbol of hope. This colour assures you that everything will turn out fine and should not lose hope in the midst of troubles. It comforts and births a warm feeling that gives you strength. It appeases the brain and upholds it through its reassuring feeling that nothing will go wrong with it. The platform submits that 'studies have confirmed that exposure to large amounts of pink can have a calming effect on the nerves and create physical weakness in people. Violent and aggressive prisoners have been successfully calmed by placing them in a pink room for a specified amount of time. Exposure for too long can have the opposite effect.'

This means pink has been scientifically certified to be a colour of peace and selflessness. When things seem to be getting out of hand, this can be an adequate means of escapism for you. You do not have to fight everyone to prove your masculinity; this creates more enmity than friendship which is not good for your health and destiny.

Practical Illustrations

Case Study I: Mr AO is the CEO of CQO Enterprises. It has come to his notice that one of his workers is very temperamental; he suddenly becomes violent and aggressive. However, he is very instrumental to the growth of the firm. Hence, he is finding it difficult to show him the exit door. Mr AO knows that if he does not curb the worker of his excesses, it would affect others too. Hence, he demands that the aggressive worker's office be painted pink. At first, the man does not know the implication of this but whenever he picks fight with anyone, he is asked to return to his office. After some few minutes, he would calm down without anyone urging him to do so. The effect of pink is at work.

Case Study II: Gone are the days when pink was disliked among women as it is now seen as a favourite colour among them. Pink is now the most favoured hair colour among women. When I discovered that this is fast becoming a culture among the female gender, I had to ask some of them what drives them to the colour and the consensus answer I got is 'beauty'. Pink gives rare and charming beauty to women's hair. Also, it adds more substance and texture to light-coloured hair. These are some of the reasons why some women spend more to have pink on their head.

Case Study III: A drug addict was arrested at a bar when he was constituting nuisance. Even on the point of his arrest, it was obvious that the drugs have been affecting him psychologically as he was making jest of everything, not minding the presence of law enforcement officers. When he was matched into the vehicle of the officers, he was still perverse in his behaviour. At first, he was thrown into a yellow cell; but when his response was more aggressive, he was moved into the pink cell, a colour known for its ability to calm very tensed situations. And truly, it suppressed his aggressive tendencies.

CONCLUSION

What propels me into writing this book is to see a change in people's conscious in relation to their immediate society. You should not just be concerned about what lies ahead but also about things that you are surrounded with. The best way to understand the world around you is to pay rapt attention to events and people you interact with on a daily basis. My aim is that, through this book, you understand people's intents and appreciate them or take appropriate actions by relying on non-verbal communication. I'm always humbled when I see people fall prey of circumstances that are glaringly against them. That is why I have taken painstaking efforts in listing out some of the issues you can be confronted with at any given point in your life.

The first step is that you read about non-verbal communication as expertly reeled out in this book and then, implement what you have learnt by testing it on others. They are practical enough for you to assimilate at a go. Case studies given are daily illustrations that caught across board which you can relate with. Through personal verification of these skills in your daily endeavours, you will unconsciously develop the skill sets to read human behaviours without hassle. This gives you an untold advantage in every communicative context. The more you pay attention to these skill sets and verify through this book, the better you become in reading other people. Many a time, you will see what others are overlooking.

Humans are social beings; we interact with others on a daily basis, no matter our profession. To be attuned with others is to unconsciously tell them that you are concerned about them; it portrays you as being carrying and loving. We are all leaders in our own right. However, every leadership position comes with its own responsibilities—you should be able to communicate your goals in clear terms and understand the feelings of every of your team members. Body language is an indispensable part of this enormous task.

Communication is a two-way thing; you listen and speak. If one of the parties does not understand what the other is saying, communication has not taken place. Effective and focused leaders have an apt understanding of this fact. You should listen to both the verbal and non-verbal utterances of the person you are conversing with.

Regrettably, the world is gradually being overwhelmed with digital conversations, depersonalising interactions, but this does not mean that face-to-face communication is being relegated to the woods; if you want to build a lasting, truthful and solid relationship, you must still refer to this method. Physical interactions create empathy in you and makes you understand others better. You see their feelings; it tells you where your boundaries are and if you should make your aspirations known to the other person. You are likely to talk carelessly without an apt understanding of non-verbal communication.

There is no gainsaying that technology is of great importance to us; it has made the world a village, opening unimaginable opportunities to us and eases our works but it obviously has its own detriments too—relying on it to choose a best friend or marriage partner is very risky; you do not know if the person truly shares the same principles and ideals with you. In this aspect, we non-verbal cues we drop and those we notice in others are very crucial in understanding each other.

No matter how voluminous a book is, it cannot encompass everything about human behaviours. This is to acknowledge the fact that this book may not discuss some behaviours in details as you would have expected. There are other books that will focus on such aspects and contribute to knowledge beyond my experience and scope in life. My dream in life is to share my decades of experiences with people and give them a guide that will help and prevent them from making avoidable mistakes in life and it is an indescribable joy that I'm finally able to achieve this feat. I hope you will make it a flowing stream by also sharing with others, what you have learnt in this book or about body language in general. May you be richly blessed to the point that you will become a channel of blessing to others, sharing your stories about life and making this world a better place for us to live in. Thank you for your time.

REFERENCES

ANS (2019) 'Movement Disorders' Retrieved from https://www.aans.org/en/Patients/Neurosurgical-Conditions-and-Treatments/Movement-Disorders.

Adityan, V (2012). 'Silence as a Means of Communication'. Retrieved from http://voiceofadi.blogspot.com/2012/12/silence-as-means-of-communication.html.

Allen, H. (2019). 'What Does the Hand behind the Back Pose Mean?' Retrieved from https://owlcation.com/social-sciences/What-Does-the-Hands-Behind-the-Back-Pose-Mean.

—— (2019). 'What Does the Hand on the Hips Pose Mean?' Retrieved from https://owlcation.com/social-sciences/What-Does-the-Hands-on-the-Hips-Pose-Mean.

—— (2019). 'What Does the Shoulder Shrug Mean?' Retrieved from https://owlcation.com/humanities/What-Does-the-Shoulder-Shrug-Mean.

Amos, J. (2013). 'Body Language to Convey Status, Hierarchy, or Dominance'. Retrieved from http://www.bodylanguageexpert.co.uk/bodylanguageandstatushierarchydominance.html.

—— (2015). 'Body Language and Personal Space'. Retrieved from http://www.bodylanguageexpert.co.uk/bodylanguageandpersonalspace.html.

Andrew, B. (2006). 'Talking Body Language'. In *Develop Your NLP Skills*, 3rd edn, 54. London: Kogan Page.

Ann, D. (2019). '20 Types of Physical Touches and What Each Touch Means'. Retrieved from https://www.lovepanky.com/my-life/relationships/types-of-physical-touches-meaning.

Annesley, J. (2019). 'The Power of Looking Up'. Retrieved from https://www.victoriahealth.com/editorial/the-power-of-looking-up.

Anthony, K. (2018). 'Nose Twitching'. Retrieved from https://www.healthline.com/health/nose-twitching#causes.

Arangua, M. (2018). '18 Examples of Female Body Language'. Retrieved from https://www.betterhelp.com/advice/body-language/18-examples-of-female-body-language/.

Arora, P. (2015). 'The Shape of Your Lips Reveals a Lot about You'. Retrieved from https://www.speakingtree.in/allslides/the-shape-of-your-lips-reveals-a-lot-about-you.

Asher, A. (2019). 'How to Put an End to Stiff Neck'. Retrieved from https://www.verywellhealth.com/stiff-neck-things-to-stop-doing-right-now-297173.

Avery-Stoss, J. (2019). 'How to Read a Man's Body Language'. Retrieved from https://healthfully.com/79238-read-mans-body-language.html.

Babich, N. (2016). 'How to Detect Lies: Body Language'. Retrieved from https://medium.com/@101/how-to-detect-lies-body-language-5a184e90337b.

Badii, C., and M. Leonard (2016). 'What Causes Poor Balance?' Retrieved from https://www.healthline.com/symptom/poor-balance.

Baidya, S. (2015). '20 Interesting Body Language Facts'. Retrieved from https://factslegend.org/20-interesting-body-language-facts-part-ii/.

Bänziger, T., D. Grandjean, and K. R. Scherer (2009). 'Emotion Recognition from Expressions in Face, Voice, and Body: The Multimodal Emotion Recognition Test [MERT]' [PDF]. Emotion 9/5: 691–704. doi:10.1037/a0017088. PMID 19803591.

Barclay, T. (2017). 'Hip Joints'. Retrieved from https://www.innerbody.com/image/skel15.html.

—— (2018). 'Mouth'. Retrieved from https://www.innerbody.com/image_digeov/dige28-new.html.

Barnett, G. (2016). 'A New Take on Body Language'. Retrieved from http://www.seventy-thirty.com/blog/2016/11/a-new-take-on-body-language-part-2-what-behaviour-tells-us-about-the-intentions-and-feelings-of-others.

Baxamusa, B. (2018). 'A Complete Guide to Interpreting Gestures and Body Language'. Retrieved from https://socialmettle.com/body-language-gestures.

Baxter, C. (2019). 'Tongue Protrude Gestures'. Retrieved from http://www.all-about-body-language.com/tongue-protrude.html.

Beall, A. (2016). 'How We Find a Face in a Crowd: Our Brains Use Special Tricks to Pick Out Certain Features from Busy Scenes'. Retrieved from https://www.dailymail.co.uk/sciencetech/article-3810227/How-face-crowd-brains-use-special-tricks-pick-certain-features-busy-scenes.html.

Beaton, E. A., L. A. Schmidt, J. Schulkin, M. M. Antony, R. P. Swinson, and G. B. Hall (2009). 'Different Fusiform Activity to Stranger and Personally Familiar Faces in Shy and Social Adults'. Social Neuroscience 4/4: 308–316. doi: 10.1080/17470910902801021. PMID 19322727.

Bender, A. (2019). 'Dog Body Language: Bared Teeth'. Retrieved from https://www.thesprucepets.com/dog-body-language-bared-teeth-1118207.

Benedek, K. (2011). 'Physiological Correlates and Emotional Specificity of Human Piloerection'. Biological Psychology 86/3: 320–329. doi: 10.1016/j.biopsycho.2010.12.012. PMC 3061318. PMID 21276827.

—— et al. (2010). 'Objective and Continuous Measurement of Piloerection'. Psychophysiology 47/5: 989–993. doi: 10.1111/j.1469-8986.2010.01003.x. PMID 20233341.

Bevel Code (2019). '5 Tips to Keep Your Hands Healthy and Ageless'. Retrieved from https://getbevel.com/bevelcode/grooming-tips/5-tips-to-keep-your-hands-healthy-and-ageless.

Blahd, W. (2018). 'Ear Problems and Injuries, Age 12 and Older'. Retrieved from https://www.uofmhealth.org/health-library/earp4.

Blair, O. (2017). 'When We Use Discourse Markers and Filler Words'. Retrieved from https://www.independent.co.uk/life-style/um-like-filler-words-discourse-markers-why-use-er-you-know-a7665721.html.

Bogart, B. (2007). Elsevier's Integrated Anatomy and Embryology, 246–260. Elsevier

Bond, M. (2013). 'Posture, Mobility, and Tongue Tension'. Retrieved from http://healyourposture.com/blog/2013/10/2797.

Boogard, K. (2016). '7 Common Body Language Habits That Are Making You Look Arrogant'. Retrieved from https://www.inc.com/kat-boogaard/7-common-body-language-habits-that-are-making-you-look-arrogant.html.

Bourn, J. (2010). 'Colour Meaning: Meaning of the Colour Pink'. Retrieved from https://www.bourncreative.com/meaning-of-the-color-pink/.

Bowen, C. (2015). 'Information for Families: Stuttering—What Can Be Done about It?' speech-language-therapy.com.

Bracke, S. (2016). 'Where Is Your Tongue?' Retrieved from https://sofieannbracke. be/en/position-of-tongue/.

Bradberry, T. (2017). '8 Ways to Read Someone's Body Language'. Retrieved from https://www.inc.com/travis-bradberry/8-great-tricks-for-reading-peoples-body-language.html.

Braiker, Harriet B. (2004). Who's Pulling Your Strings? How to Break the Cycle of Manipulation. ISBN 978-0-07-144672-3.

Brian, M. (2018). 'Decoding Body Language of Attraction'. Retrieved from https:// theartofcharm.com/art-of-dating/decoding-body-language-attraction/.

Brooks, R. (2016). 'Colours and Their Meanings around the World'. Retrieved from https://www.k-international.com/blog/color-meanings-around-the-world/.

Brown, J. (2010). 'Thumbs Forward Akimbo'. Retrieved from https://www. bodylanguagesuccess.com/2010/12/business-body-language-secret-33-thumbs.html.

—— (2011). 'Body Language and Emotional Intelligence'. Retrieved from https://www.bodylanguagesuccess.com/2011/02/negotiation-secret-97-false-tie-adjust.html.

—— (2011). 'Romance and Dating Secrets: A Classic Female Sexual Display'. Retrieved from https://www.bodylanguagesuccess.com/2011/09/romance-and-dating-secret-231-classic.html.

—— (2014). 'Body Language and Emotional Intelligence'. Retrieved from https:// www.bodylanguagesuccess.com/2014/08/nonverbal-communication-analysis-no_17.html.

—— (2017). 'Body Language and Emotional Intelligence' Retrieved from https://www.bodylanguagesuccess.com/2017/04/.

—— (2017). 'Non-Verbal Communication Analysis'. Retrieved from https://medium.com/@DrGJackBrown/nonverbal-communication-analysis-3897-roger-stone-donald-trump-body-language-and-emotional-6b20c43f6188.

BSA (2019). 'Basic Information of Stammering'. Retrieved from https://www.stammering.org/help-information/topics/what-stammering/basic-information-stammering.

Burke, D. (2015). 'The Body Language Mistakes You're Probably Making'. Retrieved from https://www.huffpost.com/entry/the-body-language-mistake_n_8547454?guccounter=1&guce_referrer=aHR0cHM6Ly93d3cuZ29vZ2xlLmNvbQ&guce_referrer_sig=AQAAAN06bUMZWIk5p1gF1Xz0sYEHQFPZEnYsarwzeL2WzYzoCdUCW0xbsz4movWzq3_ciHwRc1ssKqHKfZTPSXr0yp4pOIYjOaoCLSjMxPX0bVcb1VM2mvOqV6q_3ccABmLVo-gQBl7y0EGhknEw0qrgYK1ueGPed17-9ZlVuWOpsFAi.

Butler, T. (2019). 'How Eyes Convey the Body Language of Love'. Retrieved from https://dating.lovetoknow.com/Eye_Body_Language_of_Love.

Cain, A. (2018). 'Eleven Horrible Body Language Mistakes That Are Hard to Quit'. Retrieved from https://www.independent.co.uk/life-style/body-language-mistakes-confidence-playing-with-your-hair-fidgeting-distraction-slouching-eye-contact-a8291431.html.

Callard-Stone, M. (2017). 'Baring Teeth Is Often a Sign of Aggression in the Animal Kingdom'. Retrieved from https://www.quora.com/Baring-teeth-is-often-a-sign-of-aggression-in-the-animal-kingdom-How-do-our-pets-adjust-to-our-use-of-it-as-a-sign-of-friendliness-happiness.

Canning, K. (2018). 'This Is What Your Body Language Says about Your Relationship'. Retrieved from https://www.womenshealthmag.com/relationships/g19131151/body-language-relationship/.

Cassidy, B., E. Dykens, and C. A. Williams (2000). 'Prader-Willi and Angelman Syndromes: Sister Imprinted Disorders'. American Journal of Medical Genetics 97/2: 136–146. doi: 10.1002/1096-8628(200022)97:2<136::AID-AJMG5>3.0.CO;2-V. PMID 11180221.

Cedars Sinai (2019). 'Motor and Vocal Tics'. Retrieved from https://www.cedars-sinai.edu/Patients/Health-Conditions/Motor-and-Vocal-Tics.aspx.

Changing Minds (2019). 'Arm Body Language'. Retrieved from http://changingminds.org/techniques/body/parts_body_language/arm_body_language.htm.

—— (2019). 'Cheek Body Language'. Retrieved from http://changingminds.org/techniques/body/parts_body_language/cheek_body_language.htm

—— (2019). 'Chin Body Language'. Retrieved from http://changingminds.org/techniques/body/parts_body_language/chin_body_language.htm.

—— (2019). 'Duper's Delight'. Retrieved from http://changingminds.org/explanations/behaviors/lying/dupers_delight.htm.

—— (2019). 'Elbow Body Language'. Retrieved from http://changingminds.org/techniques/body/parts_body_language/elbow_body_language.htm.

—— (2019). 'Emotional Body Language'. Retrieved from http://changingminds.org/techniques/body/emotional_body.htm.

—— (2019). 'Eyebrow Body Language'. Retrieved from http://changingminds.org/techniques/body/parts_body_language/eyebrow_body_language.htm.

—— (2019). 'Eyes Body Language'. Retrieved from http://changingminds.org/techniques/body/parts_body_language/eyes_body_language.htm.

—— (2019). 'Face Body Language'. Retrieved from http://changingminds.org/techniques/body/parts_body_language/face_body_language.htm.

—— (2019). 'Finger Body Language'. Retrieved from http://changingminds.org/techniques/body/parts_body_language/finger_body_language.htm.

—— (2019). 'Forehead Body Language'. Retrieved from http://changingminds.org/techniques/body/parts_body_language/forehead_body_language.htm.

—— (2019). 'Forehead Body Language'. Retrieved from http://changingminds.org/techniques/body/parts_body_language/forehead_body_language.htm.

—— (2019). 'Hair Body Language'. Retrieved from http://changingminds.org/techniques/body/parts_body_language/hair_body_language.htm.

—— (2019). 'Hand Body Language'. Retrieved from http://changingminds.org/techniques/body/parts_body_language/hands_body_language.htm.

—— (2019). 'Head Body Language'. Retrieved from http://changingminds.org/techniques/body/parts_body_language/head_body_language.htm.

—— (2019). 'Lips Body Language'. Retrieved from http://changingminds.org/techniques/body/parts_body_language/lips_body_language.htm.

—— (2019). 'Mouth Body Language'. Retrieved from http://changingminds.org/techniques/body/parts_body_language/mouth_body_language.htm.

—— (2019). 'Neck Body Language'. Retrieved from http://changingminds.org/techniques/body/parts_body_language/neck_body_language.htm.

—— (2019). 'Nose Body Language'. Retrieved from http://changingminds.org/techniques/body/parts_body_language/nose_body_language.htm.

—— (2019). 'Shoulder Body Language'. Retrieved from http://changingminds.org/techniques/body/parts_body_language/shoulder_body_language.htm.

—— (2019). 'Teeth Body Language'. Retrieved from http://changingminds.org/techniques/body/parts_body_language/teeth_body_language.htm.

—— (2019). 'Thinking and Lying'. Retrieved from http://changingminds.org/explanations/behaviors/lying/thinking_lying.htm.

—— (2019). 'Tongue Body Language'. Retrieved from http://changingminds.org/techniques/body/parts_body_language/tongue_body_language.htm.

—— (2019). 'Touching'. Retrieved from http://changingminds.org/techniques/body/core_patterns/touching.htm.

Chernoff, M. (2019). '25 Acts of Body Language to Avoid'. Retrieved from http://www.marcandangel.com/2008/07/07/25-acts-of-body-language-to-avoid/.

Chernyak, P. (2019). 'How to Read Body Language'. Retrieved from https://www.wikihow.com/Read-Body-Language.

Cherry, K. (2019). 'The Role of Catharsis in Psychology'. Retrieved from https://www.verywellmind.com/what-is-catharsis-2794968.

—— (2019). 'Understanding Body Language and Facial Expressions'. Retrieved from https://www.verywellmind.com/understand-body-language-and-facial-expressions-4147228.

Chris, P. (2013). 'Agreement Indicators'. Retrieved from http://bodylanguageproject.com/the-only-book-on-body-language-that-everybody-needs-to-read/tag/head-nod/.

—— (2013). 'Body Language of Eye Squinting or Narrowing of Eyes'. Retrieved from http://bodylanguageproject.com/nonverbal-dictionary/body-language-of-eye-squinting-or-narrowing-eyes/.

—— (2013). 'Dilated Pupils'. Retrieved from http://bodylanguageproject.com/the-only-book-on-body-language-that-everybody-needs-to-read/tag/constriction-of-the-pupils/.

—— (2013). 'Eyebrow Flash: The Social Greeting'. Retrieved from http://bodylanguageproject.com/the-only-book-on-body-language-that-everybody-needs-to-read/eyebrow-flash-the-social-greeting/.

—— (2013). 'When and How to Use the Eyebrow Flash'. Retrieved from http://bodylanguageproject.com/the-only-book-on-body-language-that-everybody-needs-to-read/tag/eyebrow-flash/.

—— (2014). 'Body Language of Chin Stroking'. Retrieved from http://bodylanguageproject.com/nonverbal-dictionary/body-language-of-chin-stroking/.

—— (2014). 'Body Language of Eyebrow Knit or Oblique Eyebrows of Grief'. Retrieved from http://bodylanguageproject.com/nonverbal-dictionary/body-language-of-eyebrows-knit-or-oblique-eyebrows-of-grief/.

—— (2014). 'Body Language of Forehead Rubbing'. Retrieved from http://bodylanguageproject.com/nonverbal-dictionary/body-language-of-forehead-rubbing/.

—— (2014). 'Body Language of Furrowed Forehead'. Retrieved from http://bodylanguageproject.com/nonverbal-dictionary/body-language-of-furrowed-forehead/.

—— (2014). 'Body Language of Interlaced Fingers'. Retrieved from http://bodylanguageproject.com/nonverbal-dictionary/body-language-of-interlaced-fingers/.

——(2014).'Body Language of Sweating'. Retrieved from http://bodylanguageproject.com/nonverbal-dictionary/body-language-of-sweating-or-hyperhidrosis/.

—— (2014). 'Body Language of Tense Face'. Retrieved from http://bodylanguageproject.com/nonverbal-dictionary/category/confused/.

—— (2014). 'Body Language of the Eyebrow Cock'. Retrieved from http://bodylanguageproject.com/nonverbal-dictionary/body-language-of-the-eyebrow-cock/.

Cichowski, H. (2016). '6 Body Language Movements That Show That Person Is Totally Flirting with You'. Retrieved from https://articles.aplus.com/a/body-language-of-attraction-poses?no_monetization=true.

Cirino, E. (2018). 'Why Do We Have Eyebrows?' Retrieved from https://www.healthline.com/health/why-do-we-have-eyebrows#1.

CNS (2019). 'Palm Up'. Retrieved from http://center-for-nonverbal-studies.org/htdocs/palmup.htm.

CogniFit (2019). 'Reaction Time'. Retrieved from https://www.cognifit.com/science/cognitive-skills/response-time.

Cole, J. (2013). 'Botox Silences Women's Faces and Freezes Out Empathy in Body Language'. Retrieved from https://www.theguardian.com/commentisfree/2013/may/22/botox-silences-womens-faces-empathy.

Coleman, K. (2019). 'When He Runs His Fingers through His Hair'. Retrieved from https://love.allwomenstalk.com/ways-to-decode-your-dates-body-language/10/.

Corso, S. (2017). 'A List of Body Language and Their Meanings: Arms and Legs Positions'. Retrieved from https://junior-broker.com/life/careers/list-of-body-language/.

Cummins, E. (2019). 'What Is Proxemics?—Definition and Examples'. Retrieved from https://study.com/academy/lesson/what-is-proxemics-definition-examples.html.

Cutter, D., J. Jaffe, and J. Segal (2008). 'Self-Injury: Types, Causes, and Treatment'. HelpGuide.org.

Dachis, A. (2011). 'How to Read Body Language to Reveal Underlying Truth in Almost Any Situation'. Retrieved from https://lifehacker.com/how-to-read-body-language-to-reveal-the-underlying-trut-5852572.

Darwin, C. (1872). 'Body Language'. Retrieved from https://www.laphamsquarterly.org/fear/body-language.

Davenport, L. (2015). 'World Leaders Are Trained to Manipulate Their Audiences with Body Language'. Retrieved from https://www.

wakingtimes.com/2015/10/14/world-leaders-are-trained-to-manipulate-their-audiences-with-body-language/.

Davis, H. (2010). 'The Uptalk Epidemic'. Retrieved from https://www.psychologytoday.com/intl/blog/caveman-logic/201010/the-uptalk-epidemic.

Delange, J. (2012). 'What Your Walk Says about You: Quick Study'. Retrieved from https://www.huffingtonpost.ca/2012/05/08/what-your-walk-says-about-you_n_1497198.html.

Denethorn, A. (2016). 'Why Does Our Face Twitch When We Lie?' Retrieved from https://www.quora.com/Why-does-our-face-twitch-when-we-lie.

DrugRehab (2018). 'What Are Track Marks?' Retrieved from https://www.drugrehab.org/what-are-track-marks/.

Dugdale, S. (2019). 'What's Your Speech Rate?' Retrieved from https://www.write-out-loud.com/speech-rate.html.

Efficient Technologies (2019). 'Body Language Smoking Gestures and Signals'. Retrieved from http://www.efficient-technologies.com/bodylanguage/smoking.html.

Ehrenfeld, T. (2017). 'How to Deal with People Who Interrupt'. Retrieved from https://www.psychologytoday.com/intl/blog/open-gently/201709/how-deal-people-who-interrupt.

Ekman, P. (2009). 'Duping Delight'. Retrieved from https://www.paulekman.com/blog/duping-delight/.

Encyclopaedia Britannica (2019). 'Face'. Retrieved from https://www.britannica.com/science/face-anatomy.

Eskin, M. (2013). 'Catharsis'. Retrieved from https://www.sciencedirect.com/topics/psychology/catharsis.

EYWCP (2018). 'The Colour Pink'. Retrieved from https://www.empower-yourself-with-color-psychology.com/color-pink.html.

Fader, S. (2018). 'Using Eye Attraction to Build a Relationship'. Retrieved from https://www.betterhelp.com/advice/attraction/using-eye-contact-attraction-to-build-a-relationship/.

Forbes, S. (2015). '18 Gestures That Can Get You in Trouble outside the US'. Retrieved from https://nypost.com/2015/03/24/18-gestures-that-can-get-you-in-trouble-outside-the-us/.

Foster, V. (2019). 'An Overview of Dental Anatomy'. Retrieved from https://www.dentalcare.com/en-us/professional-education/ce-courses/ce500/types-of-teeth-and-their-functions.

Fox, C., and K. Hawton (2004). Deliberate Self-Harm in Adolescence. London: Jessica Kingsley. ISBN 978-1-84310-237-3.

Fradet, N. (2019). '13 Revealing Body Language Hand Gestures'. Retrieved from https://nicolasfradet.com/hand-body-language/.

Fritz, R. (2018). 'Incongruence in Psychology: Definition and Overview'. Retrieved from https://study.com/academy/lesson/incongruence-in-psychology-definition-lesson-quiz.html.

Fuller, C. J. (2004). The Camphor Flame: Popular Hinduism and Society in India, 66–70. Princeton, NJ: Princeton University Press. ISBN 978-0-691-12048-5.

Gangwer, T. (2011). 'Body Language and Eye Contact—Explained'. Retrieved from http://visualteaching.ning.com/profiles/blogs/body-language-and-eye-contact-explained.

Garon, G. (2019). 'How to Make Sure Your Body Language and Verbal Cues Align'. Retrieved from https://www.topresume.com/career-advice/how-to-make-sure-your-body-language-and-verbal-cues-align.

Gawne, L. (2013). 'Secret Meanings of the Nose Tap Gesture'. Retrieved from https://www.superlinguo.com/post/62861551556/secret-meanings-of-the-nose-tap-gesture.

Gershaw, D. (2014). 'High-Social-Status Body Language'. Retrieved from https://puadatingtips.wordpress.com/2014/06/17/high-social-status-body-language/.

Givens, D. (2017). 'Trump Decoder'. Retrieved from http://center-for-nonverbal-studies.org/htdocs/10101.html.

—— (2019). 'Adam's Apple Jump'. Retrieved from http://center-for-nonverbal-studies.org/htdocs/adajum.htm.

GLC (2019). 'Body Language of Listeners'. Retrieved from https://www. globallisteningcentre.org/body-language-of-listeners/.

Goldberg, J. A. (1990). 'Interrupting the discourse on interruptions'. Journal of Pragmatics *14*/6: 883–903. doi: 10.1016/0378-2166(90)90045-f.

Goldhill, O. (2015). 'To Spot a Liar, Look at Their Hands'. Retrieved from https://qz.com/572675/to-spot-a-liar-look-at-their-hands/.

Goldsztajn, I. (2015). '7 Signs You're Being Too Clingy'. Retrieved from https:// www.hercampus.com/sex-relationships/7-signs-you-re-being-too-clingy.

Goman, C. (2010). 'A Body Language Secret: Look below the Belt'. Retrieved from https://www.forbes.com/2010/07/15/body-language-feet-leadership-managing-legs.html#43ea2b0f26e6.

—— (2019). '10 Powerful Body Language Tips'. Retrieved from https://www. amanet.org/articles/10-powerful-body-language-tips/.

—— (2019). 'The Body Language of Disengagement from Head to Toes'. Retrieved from https://www.amanet.org/articles/the-body-language-of-disengagement-from-head-to-toes/.

Griffin, M. (2019). 'Medical Causes of Excessive Sweating'. Retrieved from https://www.webmd.com/skin-problems-and-treatments/features/is-your-excessive-sweating-caused-by-a-medical-problem#2.

Griffith, T. (2017). 'Causes and Preventions for Glassy Eyes'. Retrieved from https://www.healthline.com/health/glassy-eyes.

Grooming Lounge (2019). 'How to Nail it'. Retrieved from https://www. groominglounge.com/best-hand-nail-care.

Guilbeault, L. (2018). '22 Body Language Examples and What They Show'. Retrieved from https://www.betterhelp.com/advice/body-language/22 -body-language-examples-and-what-they-show/

Guptha, A (2014). '10 Body Language Love Signals to Keep in Mind Next Time You're on a Date'. Retrieved from https://www. adelaidenow.com.au/lifestyle/body-language-love-signals/news -story/da6bf2ad8bda9380d9b4ebd27c7b4fa1?sv=e55a84a594d72 4d86954cb3b0ff95664.

Gurney, A. (2016). 'Body Language for Active Listening'. Retrieved from https:// learn.filtered.com/blog/body-language-for-active-listening.

Haakana, M. (2010). 'Laughter and Smiling: Notes on Co-Occurrences'. Journal of Pragmatics 42/6: 1,499–1,512. doi: 10.1016/j.pragma.2010.01.010.

Haden, J. (2015). '10 Body Language Secrets of Highly Successful People'. Retrieved from https://www.inc.com/jeff-haden/10-body-language-secrets-of-highly-successful-people.html.

Hana, J. (2013). 'What the Gesture of Sticking Out the Tongue Signify as Body Language among Native Speakers of English'. Retrieved from https://english.stackexchange.com/questions/139171/what-the-gesture-of-sticking-out-the-tongue-signify-as-a-body-language-among-nat.

Harlvorson, H. (2011). 'Quick Decisions Create Regret, Even When They Are Good Decisions'. Retrieved from https://www.fastcompany.com/1758386/quick-decisions-create-regret-even-when-they-are-good-decisions.

Hawes, M. R., and D. Sovak (1994). 'Quantitative Morphology of the Human Foot in a North American Population'. Ergonomics 37/7: 1,213–1,226. doi: 10.1080/00140139408964899. PMID 8050406.

Hawkins, J. (2019). 'Anatomy of the Human Ear'. Retrieved from https://www.britannica.com/science/ear/Anatomy-of-the-human-ear.

Healthline (2019). 'Nose'. Retrieved from https://www.healthline.com/human-body-maps/nose.

Heathers, James A. J., K. Fayn, P. J. Silvia, N. Tiliopoulos, and M. S. Goodwin (2018). 'The Voluntary Control of Piloerection'. PeerJ (preprint). doi: 10.7287/peerj.preprints.26594v1.

Hedger, S. (2019). 'Reading Body Language! What's Really on Their Mind?' Retrieved from http://www.life-coach-tips.co.uk/relationships19.html.

Hendricks, S. (2018). '9 Ways Your Body Is Telling You Your Relationship Is Doomed'. Retrieved from https://www.insider.com/body-language-red-flags-in-relationship-2018-5.

Hindy, J. (2019). 'Top 20 Body Language Indicators'. Retrieved from https://www.lifehack.org/articles/communication/top-20-body-language-indicators.html.

HMS (2018). 'What's the Constant Headache Pain in the Temples?' Retrieved from https://www.health.harvard.edu/diseases-and-conditions/whats-that-constant-headache-pain-in-the-temples.

—— (2018). 'Why Stress Causes People to Overeat'. Retrieved from https://www.
health.harvard.edu/staying-healthy/why-stress-causes-people-to-overeat.

Hoffman, M. (2014). 'Picture of the Abdomen'. Retrieved from https://www.
webmd.com/digestive-disorders/picture-of-the-abdomen#1.

—— (2015). 'Pictures of the Teeth'. Retrieved from https://www.webmd.com/
oral-health/picture-of-the-teeth#1.

—— (2019). 'Pictures of the Shoulder'. Retrieved from https://www.webmd.
com/pain-management/picture-of-the-shoulder#1.

Hope (2013). '10 Common Facial Expressions Explained'. Retrieved
from https://listverse.com/2013/07/05/ten-compelling-origins-of-
our-facial-expressions/.

Hoppe, E. (2008). 'Body Language: Your Feet Say a Lot'. Retrieved from http://
www.eliothoppe.com/articles/20080825-feet.html.

—— (2009). 'Body Language—5 Secrets to Get What You Want'. Retrieved
from https://ezinearticles.com/?Body-Language---5-Secrets-to-Get-
What-You-Want!&id=3187956.

—— (2019). 'Body Language: How to Spot a Liar'. Retrieved from http://www.
eliothoppe.com/articles/20071029-body_language.html.

Howes, D. (2019). 'Body Signs: Body Decorations and Sensory Symbolism
in South America'. Retrieved from http://www.david-howes.com/senses/
Howes.htm.

HRF (2019). 'Meaning of Twirling Hair Body Language'. Retrieved from
https://healthresearchfunding.org/meaning-twirling-hair-body-language/.

IITGYOW (2019). 'Reading Hands and Arms in Body Language'. Retrieved
from http://www.howtogetyourownway.com/body_language/hands_and_
arms_body_language.html.

Immanuel, H. (1970). The Rise of Modern China, 152. New York: Oxford
University Press.

IndiaBIX (2019). 'Body Language: Hand to Face Gestures'. Retrieved from
https://www.indiabix.com/body-language/hand-to-face-gestures/.

Irwin, M. (2006). 'Terminology—How Should Stuttering Be Defined? And
Why?' In J. Au-Yeung and M. M. Leahy (eds). Research, Treatment, and

Self-Help in Fluency Disorders: New Horizons, 41–45. The International Fluency Association. ISBN 978-0-9555700-1-8.

iVillage (2013). '18 Body Language Clues That He's Interested—Definitely'. Retrieved from https://www.today.com/health/18-body-language-clues-say-he-s-interested-definitely-t72476.

Jewel, T. (2017). 'Neck Cracking: Is It Safe or I Should Stop?' Retrieved from https://www.healthline.com/health/neck-cracking.

Jorma, D (2011). 'A Silence Can Say a Lot'. Retrieved from http://www.bodylanguagefordummies.com/silence-can-say-alot.

Joseph, S. (2007). *Deep Culture: The Hidden Challenges of Global Living*, 68–70. ISBN 978-1847690166.

Jung, A. (2019). '8 Secrets Your Body Language Is Revealing about You'. Retrieved from https://www.rd.com/advice/relationships/reading-body-language/.

Khan-Panni, P. (2019). '20 Tips on Body Language'. Retrieved from http://phillipkhan-panni.com/free-stuff/20-tips-on-body-language/.

Khemani, T. (2019). 'Psychology of Talkative People'. Retrieved from https://discventionspsych.wordpress.com/2016/08/22/psychology-of-talkative-people/.

Khoury, P. (2019). '3 Ways to Reduce Uptalk to Boost Your Credibility as a Leader'. Retrieved from https://magneticspeaking.com/stop-uptalk-boost-credibility-leader/.

Kokten G, H. Balcioglu, and M. Buyukertan (2003). 'Supernumerary Fourth and Fifth Molars: A Report of Two Cases'. Journal of Contemporary Dental Practice 4/4: 67–76. PMID 14625596.

Kozarsky, A. (2017). 'How Important Are Our Eyes?' Retrieved from https://www.webmd.com/eye-health/qa/how-important-are-our-eyes.

Krys, K., V. C. Melanie, C. A. Capaldi, V. Lun, M. Bond, A. Domínguez-Espinosa, C. Torres, Ottmar V. Lipp, L. Manickam, and S. Sam (2016). 'Be Careful Where You Smile: Culture Shapes Judgments of Intelligence and Honesty of Smiling Individuals'. Journal of Nonverbal Behavior 40/2: 101–116. doi: 10.1007/s10919-015-0226-4. ISSN 0191-5886. PMC 4840223. PMID 27194817.

Kubala, J. (2018). '23 Simple Things You Can Do to Stop Overeating'. Retrieved from https://www.healthline.com/nutrition/how-to-stop-overeating.

Lamberg, E. (2019). '13 Secrets Your Smile Can Reveal about You'. Retrieved from https://www.rd.com/culture/secrets-smile-reveals-about-you/.

Larkin, Dimitrije E. Panfilov (2005). Cosmetic Surgery Today. Trans.Grahame, F. Stuttgart: Thieme Medical Publishers, 64. ISBN 1-58890-334-6.

Lassen, C. (2018). 'Signs and Symptoms of Agitation'. Retrieved from https://careertrend.com/info-8205639-signs-symptoms-agitation.html.

Lawson, C. (2018). 'Body Language: What It Means When Men Put Their Hands in Their Pockets'. Retrieved from https://www.rebelcircus.com/blog/body-language-means-men-put-hands-pockets/2/.

Lehrer, A. (2019). 'How to Read Eyes—Eye Body Language Cues'. Retrieved from https://www.blifaloo.com/reading-eyes/.

Leonard, J. (2019). 'Tic Disorders'. Retrieved from https://www.medicalnewstoday.com/articles/317950.php.

Lie, W. P. (2019). 'Body Language of Lying'. Retrieved from https://www.skillsconverged.com/FreeTrainingMaterials/BodyLanguage/BodyLanguageofLying.aspx.

Linda, W (2019). 'Body Language: Saying without Speaking'. Retrieved from https://www.ecellulitis.com/body-language-saying-without-speaking/.

Lip Book (2015). 'The Functions of the Human Lips'. Retrieved from http://www.lipbook.com/education/the-functions-of-the-human-lip/.

Maceiras, M. (2013). 'When a Woman Touches Her Neck While I Talk to her, Is She Nervous of Me or Attracted to Me?' Retrieved from https://www.quora.com/If-a-woman-touches-her-neck-while-I-talk-to-her-is-she-nervous-of-me-or-attracted-to-me.

Magical Apparatus (2019). 'Nose Touching'. Retrieved from https://www.magicalapparatus.com/body-language-2/nose-touching.html.

—— (2019). 'Thumb Displays'. Retrieved from https://www.magicalapparatus.com/body-language-2/thumb-displays.html.

Marchant, J. (2015). 'Noticing Body Language: 14 Tips'. Retrieved from http://www.emotionalintelligenceatwork.com/resources/noticing-body-language/.

Markgraf, B. (2018). 'How the Human Nose Works'. Retrieved from https://sciencing.com/human-nose-works-5477127.html.

Martinez, M. (2019). 'The Other Side of Body Language Tips'. Retrieved from https://blog.michael-martinez.com/the-other-side-of-body-language-tips/

Marwijk, F. (2019). 'The Power of Touch'. Retrieved from http://www.lichaamstaal.com/english/touch2.html.

Matava, M. J., D. B. Purcell, and J. R. Rudzki (2005). 'Partial Thickness Rotator Cuff Tears'. American Journal of Sports Medicine *33*/9: 1,405–1,417. doi: 10.1177/0363546505280213. PMID 16127127.

Maton, Anthea, Jean Hopkins, Charles William McLaughlin, Susan Johnson, Maryanna Quon Warner, David LaHart, and Jill D. Wright (1993). Human Biology and Health. Englewood Cliffs, New Jersey, USA: Prentice Hall. ISBN 0-13-981176-1.

Mayo Clinic (2019). 'Dry Mouth'. Retrieved from https://www.mayoclinic.org/diseases-conditions/dry-mouth/symptoms-causes/syc-20356048.

—— (2019). 'Hearing Loss'. Retrieved from https://www.mayoclinic.org/diseases-conditions/hearing-loss/symptoms-causes/syc-20373072.

McLaughlin, P. (2015). 'Body Language That Reveals Stress'. Retrieved from https://www.linkedin.com/pulse/body-language-reveals-stress-peter-mclaughlin.

Melone, L. (2014). '10 Ways Your Eyes Give You Away'. Retrieved from https://www.msn.com/en-us/health/wellness/10-ways-your-eyes-give-you-away/ss-AAcWAp#image=3.

Mendez, J. (2013). 'Talk to the Hands: Body Language'. Retrieved from https://www.languagetrainers.co.uk/blog/2013/09/09/talk-to-the-hand-body-language/.

Mentalizer Education (2019). 'Learn Body Language: What's with the Nose?' Retrieved from https://mentalizer.com/learn-body-language-whats-with-the-nose.html.

—— (2019). 'Learn Forehead Body Language'. Retrieved from https://mentalizer.com/learn-forehead-body-language.html.

——— (2019). 'What Does Your Breathing Pattern Mean?' Retrieved from https://mentalizer.com/what-does-your-breathing-pattern-means.html.

Mercury, L (2016). 'The Many Meanings of Holding Hands'. Retrieved from http://www.ilanelanzen.com/personaldevelopment/the-many-meanings-of-holding-hands/.

Mey, R. (2019). 'These 11 Sitting Positions Can Reveal Your Personality'. Retrieved from https://www.theepochtimes.com/these-11-sitting-positions-can-reveal-your-personality-4-shows-your-are-a-leader_2797270.html.

Millard, E. (2016). 'Why You Think Twice before Cracking Your Neck'. Retrieved from https://www.self.com/story/why-you-should-think-twice-before-cracking-your-neck-or-anyone-elses.

Miller, N. (2014). '10 Sure-Fire Ways to Spot a Liar'. Retrieved from https://mind-hacks.wonderhowto.com/how-to/10-surefire-ways-spot-liar-and-tell-better-lies-yourself-0155036/.

Mind Tools (2019). 'Body Language'. Retrieved from https://www.mindtools.com/pages/article/Body_Language.htm.

Misak, L. (2019). 'Coughing, Sneezing, Sparked by Certain Thoughts'. Retrieved from https://www.empowher.com/mental-health/content/coughing-sneezing-sparked-certain-thoughts.

Mohney, G. (2013). 'Why Surprise Looks the Same in Every Country'. Retrieved from https://abcnews.go.com/Health/emotional-responses-country/story?id=19893909.

Moore, Keith L., Arthur F. Dalley, and Anne M. R. Agur (2010). Moore's Clinical Anatomy, 843–980. United States of America: Lippincott Williams & Wilkins. ISBN 978-1-60547-652-0.

Morgan, N. (2019). 'How to Decode Other People's Body Language'. Retrieved from https://publicwords.com/2012/05/26/how-to-decode-other-peoples-body-language/.

Mortillaro, M., and D. Dukes (2018). 'Jumping For Joy: The Importance of the Body and of Dynamics in the Expression and Recognition of Positive Emotions'. Retrieved from https://www.ncbi.nlm.nih.gov/pmc/articles/PMC5962906/.

Murphy, S. (2011). 'What His Body Language Means'. Retrieved from https://29secrets.com/relationships/what-his-body-language-means/.

Narin, E. (2017). 'What Your Sitting Style Says about Your Personality'. Retrieved from https://www.cosmopolitan.com/health-fitness/a8976967/body-language-sitting/.

Navarro, J. (2009). 'Body Language Secrets of the Neck'. Retrieved from https://www.psychologytoday.com/us/blog/spycatcher/200911/body-language-secrets-the-neck.

—— (2009). 'The Body Language of the Eyes'. Retrieved from https://www.psychologytoday.com/us/blog/spycatcher/200912/the-body-language-the-eyes.

—— (2009). 'The Body Language of Touch'. Retrieved from https://www.psychologytoday.com/intl/blog/spycatcher/200912/the-body-language-touch.

—— (2009). 'The Lips Don't Lie'. Retrieved from https://www.psychologytoday.com/intl/blog/spycatcher/200911/the-lips-dont-lie.

—— (2010). 'Body Language of the Hands'. Retrieved from https://www.psychologytoday.com/us/blog/spycatcher/201001/body-language-the-hands.

—— (2010). 'Some Things You Just Can't Hide'. Retrieved from https://www.psychologytoday.com/us/blog/spycatcher/201005/some-things-you-just-cant-hide.

—— (2011). 'Body Language vs. Micro-Expressions'. Retrieved from https://www.psychologytoday.com/us/blog/spycatcher/201112/body-language-vs-micro-expressions.

—— (2012). 'Cool Body Language'. Retrieved from https://www.psychologytoday.com/us/blog/spycatcher/201202/cool-body-language.

—— (2012). 'What the Shoulders Say about Us'. Retrieved from https://www.psychologytoday.com/us/blog/spycatcher/201205/what-the-shoulders-say-about-us.

—— (2013). 'Jaw Shifting'. Retrieved from https://www.psychologytoday.com/us/blog/spycatcher/201311/jaw-shifting.

—— (2014). 'Body Language of Jaw Drop Smile'. Retrieved from http:// bodylanguageproject.com/nonverbal-dictionary/body-language-of-jaw-drop-smile/.

—— (2014). 'Facial Denting'. Retrieved from https://www.psychologytoday. com/intl/blog/spycatcher/201407/facial-denting.

—— (2015). 'Tongue Juts'. Retrieved from https://www.psychologytoday.com/ intl/blog/spycatcher/201506/tongue-juts.

—— (2016). 'Chirality: A Look at Emotional Asymmetry of the Face'. Retrieved from__https://www.psychologytoday.com/us/blog/spycatcher/201605/ chirality-look-emotional-asymmetry-the-face.

Nemko, M. (2015). 'What If You Talk Too Much?' Retrieved from https://www.psychologytoday.com/intl/blog/how-do-life/201501/ what-if-you-talk-too-much.

Nick, B. (2016). 'How to Detect Lies: Body Language'. Retrieved from https:// medium.com/@101/how-to-detect-lies-body-language-5a184e90337b.

Nigel P., F. Derek, and S. Roger (2006). 'Head and Brain'. In *Anatomy and Human Movement*, 5th edn, 645–646. Elsevier Health Sciences. ISBN 9780750688147.

Nodjimbadem, K. (2015). 'Why Do Humans Have Chin?' Retrieved from https://www.smithsonianmag.com/science-nature/why-do-humans-have-chins-1-180955299/.

Nordquist, R. (2018). 'Filler Words Definitions and Examples'. Retrieved from https://www.thoughtco.com/what-is-a-filler-word-1690859.

Noreen, D (2010). 'What Those White Chunks That Sometimes Come from Your Throat Are'. Retrieved from http://www.todayifoundout .com/index.php/2010/09/what-those-nasty-white-chunks-that-come-from-your-throat-are/.

O'Loughlin, M. M., and D. Valerie (2006). Human Anatomy, 400–401. Boston: McGraw-Hill Higher Education. ISBN 0-07-249585-5.

Olesen, J. (2019). 'Color Meanings'. Retrieved from https://www.color-meanings.com/.

Organs of the Body (2019). 'Human Tongue Parts, Functions with Details, and Diagrams'. Retrieved from https://www.organsofthebody.com/human-tongue/.

Pandit, S. (2018). 'What Does Your Walk Reveal about Your Personality?' Retrieved from https://socialmettle.com/what-does-your-walk-reveal-about-your-personality.

Pannell, N. (2018). '10 Subtle Signs Someone Doesn't Like You'. Retrieved from https://www.insider.com/body-language-signs-that-someone-doesnt-like-you-2018-6.

Parvez, H. (2015). 'Body Language of Crossing the Legs'. Retrieved from https://www.psychmechanics.com/2015/05/body-language-crossing-legs.html.

—— (2015). 'Body Language: The Crotch Displays of Men'. Retrieved from https://www.psychmechanics.com/2015/05/body-language-crotch-displays-of-men.html.

—— (2015). 'Meaning of Hands on the Hips Body Language Gestures'. Retrieved from https://www.psychmechanics.com/2015/05/body-language-hands-resting-on-hips.html.

—— (2015). 'Nail Biting and Other Anxiety Behaviours'. Retrieved from https://www.psychmechanics.com/2015/05/nail-biting-and-other-anxiety-behaviours.html.

—— (2015). 'Psychology of the Different Types of Handshakes'. Retrieved from https://www.psychmechanics.com/2015/05/when-we-shake-hands-we-dont-just-shake.html.

—— (2015). 'The Truth of the Pointing Foot'. Retrieved from https://www.psychmechanics.com/2015/06/body-language-truth-of-pointing-foot.html.

—— (2015). 'What Do Seated Legs and Feet Gestures Reveal?' Retrieved from https://www.psychmechanics.com/2015/05/body-language-seated-leg-and-feet.html.

—— (2015). 'What It Means When People Display Their Thumbs'. Retrieved from https://www.psychmechanics.com/2015/05/what-it-means-when-people-display-their.html.

—— (2016). '7 Body Language Signs of Attraction'. Retrieved from https://www. psychmechanics.com/2016/03/7-body-language-signals-of-attraction. html.

—— (2019). 'Body Language: Crossing the Arms'. Retrieved from https://www. psychmechanics.com/2015/04/body-language-crossing-arms.html.

—— (2019). 'Body Language: Gestures of the Head and Neck'. Retrieved from https://www.psychmechanics.com/2015/04/body-language-gestures-of-head-and-neck.html.

—— (2019). 'Body Language: Hands Touching the Head'. Retrieved from https://www.psychmechanics.com/2015/05/body-language-hands-touching-head.html.

—— (2019). 'Body Language: Shoulder Movements and Their Meanings'. Retrieved from https://www.psychmechanics.com/2015/04/body-language-shoulder-movements.html.

—— (2019). 'How We Threaten and Express Disapproval with the Mouth'. Retrieved from https://www.psychmechanics.com/2015/07/how-we-threaten-and-express-disapproval.html.

—— (2019). 'The Three Wise Monkeys and Body Language'. Retrieved from https://www.psychmechanics.com/2015/05/the-three-wise-monkeys-and-body-language.html.

—— (2019). 'Why Do We Raise Our Eyebrows to Greet Others?' Retrieved from https://www.psychmechanics.com/2015/07/why-we-raise-our-eyebrows-to-greet.html.

Patel, M. (2012). 'The Way We Sit and What It Means'. Retrieved from https://economictimes.indiatimes.com/the-way-we-sit-what-it-means/articleshow/12211700.cms.

Patel, V. (1993). 'Crying Behavior and Psychiatric Disorder in Adults: A Review'. Comprehensive Psychiatry *34*/3: 206–211. doi: 10.1016/0010-440X(93)90049-A. PMID 8339540. Quoted by Michelle C. P. Hendriks, A. J. J. M. Vingerhoets in 'Crying: Is It Beneficial for One's Well-Being?'

Paules-Bronet, I. (2019). 'The Way You're Currently Sitting Reveals Everything about Your Personality'. Retrieved from https://www.littlethings.com/sitting-positions-personality-test.

———

Pelham, L. (2018). 'Clothing as a Form of Non-Verbal Communication'. Retrieved from http://www.bodylanguageexpert.co.uk/clothing-form-non-verbal-communication.html.

Pellicano, M. (2017). '4 Essential Types of Tone of Voice in Communication'. Retrieved from https://mariapellicano.com/four-types-tone-of-voice-in-communication/.

Pendergrass, K. (2013). '10 Positive Body Language Techniques to Help You Succeed'. Retrieved from https://blog.udemy.com/positive-body-language/.

Philip, C. (2013). 'Additional Emotional Body Language'. Retrieved from http://bodylanguageproject.com/the-only-book-on-body-language-that-everybody-needs-to-read/tag/holding-breath/.

—— (2013). 'Blushing: The Colour of Emotion'. Retrieved from http://bodylanguageproject.com/the-only-book-on-body-language-that-everybody-needs-to-read/blushing-the-colour-of-emotion/.

—— (2013). 'Cocooning'. Retrieved from http://bodylanguageproject.com/the-only-book-on-body-language-that-everybody-needs-to-read/tag/elbows/.

—— (2013). 'Comfort and Discomfort Body Language'. Retrieved from http://bodylanguageproject.com/the-only-book-on-body-language-that-everybody-needs-to-read/tag/lips/.

—— (2013). 'Duping Delight, Eye Contact, and Training'. Retrieved from http://bodylanguageproject.com/the-only-book-on-body-language-that-everybody-needs-to-read/duping-delight-eye-contact-and-smiling/.

—— (2013). 'Eye Blocking'. Retrieved from http://bodylanguageproject.com/the-only-book-on-body-language-that-everybody-needs-to-read/eye-blocking/.

—— (2013). 'Eye Contact in Business'. Retrieved from http://bodylanguageproject.com/the-only-book-on-body-language-that-everybody-needs-to-read/tag/eye-movement/.

—— (2013). 'Eye Direction, Thought, and NLP'. Retrieved from http://bodylanguageproject.com/the-only-book-on-body-language-that-everybody-needs-to-read/tag/eye-movement/.

—— (2013). 'Freeze, Flight, or Fight'. Retrieved from http://bodylanguageproject. com/the-only-book-on-body-language-that-everybody-needs-to-read/tag/ deep-breaths/.

—— (2013). 'Hand Steepling'. Retrieved from http://bodylanguageproject. com/the-only-book-on-body-language-that-everybody-needs-to-read/ hand-steepling/.

—— (2013). 'Hand to Mouth Gestures'. Retrieved from http://bodylanguageproject. com/the-only-book-on-body-language-that-everybody-needs-to-read/tag/ hand-to-mouth/.

—— (2013). 'Looking Up through the Forehead'. Retrieved from http:// bodylanguageproject.com/the-only-book-on-body-language- that-everybody-needs-to-read/tag/head-tilt/.

—— (2013). 'Neck and Nose Body Language'. Retrieved from http:// bodylanguageproject.com/the-only-book-on-body-language- that-everybody-needs-to-read/tag/suprasternal-notch/.

—— (2013). 'Neck Rubbing'. Retrieved from http://bodylanguageproject.com/ the-only-book-on-body-language-that-everybody-needs-to-read/tag/ goose-bumps/.

—— (2013). 'Nervous Hands'. Retrieved from http://bodylanguageproject. com/the-only-book-on-body-language-that-everybody-needs-to-read/ nervous-hands/.

—— (2013). 'Nonverbal Language of the Eye'. Retrieved from http:// bodylanguageproject.com/tiny-book-of-body-language/nonverbal- language-of-the-eye-face-gaze-friendly-gaze-intimate-gaze-and-the- business-gaze/.

—— (2013). 'Nose Language'. Retrieved from http://bodylanguageproject. com/the-only-book-on-body-language-that-everybody-needs-to-read/tag/ index-finger/.

—— (2013). 'Other Emotional Body Language'. Retrieved from http:// bodylanguageproject.com/the-only-book-on-body-language- that-everybody-needs-to-read/tag/breast-bone/.

—— (2013). 'Other Evaluative Gestures'. Retrieved from http:// bodylanguageproject.com/the-only-book-on-body-language -that-everybody-needs-to-read/tag/twitching-muscles/.

—— (2013). 'Reading Posture'. Retrieved from http://bodylanguageproject. com/the-only-book-on-body-language-that-everybody-needs-to-read/tag/ rounded-shoulders/.

—— (2013). 'Shifty Eyes'. Retrieved from http://bodylanguageproject.com/ the-only-book-on-body-language-that-everybody-needs-to-read/tag/ shifty-eyes/.

—— (2013). 'Shirt Collar'. Retrieved from http://bodylanguageproject.com/ the-only-book-on-body-language-that-everybody-needs-to-read/tag/ shirt-collar/.

—— (2013). 'The Ankle or Scissor Cross'. Retrieved from http:// bodylanguageproject.com/the-only-book-on-body-language-that -everybody-needs-to-read/the-ankle-or-scissor-cross/.

—— (2013). 'The Ear Grabber'. Retrieved from http://bodylanguageproject. com/the-only-book-on-body-language-that-everybody-needs-to-read/tag/ ear-lobe/.

——(2013). 'The Male Crotch Display'. Retrieved from http://bodylanguageproject. com/the-only-book-on-body-language-that-everybody-needs-to-read/ the-male-crotch-display/.

—— (2013). 'The Most Common Types of Smile'. Retrieved from http:// bodylanguageproject.com/the-only-book-on-body-language-that- everybody-needs-to-read/tag/true-smile/.

——(2013). 'The Stiff or Curve Arm'. Retrieved from http://bodylanguageproject. com/the-only-book-on-body-language-that-everybody-needs-to-read/ the-stiff-or-curved-arm/.

——(2013). 'Tonality and Voice Depth'. Retrieved from http://bodylanguageproject. com/the-only-book-on-body-language-that-everybody-needs-to-read/tag/ voice-pitch/.

—— (2013). 'Tonguing Language'. Retrieved from http://bodylanguageproject. com/the-only-book-on-body-language-that-everybody-needs-to-read/tag/ tongue-protrusion/.

—— (2013). 'Universal Facial Expressions'. Retrieved from http:// bodylanguageproject.com/the-only-book-on-body-language-that- everybody-needs-to-read/tag/wrinkles/.

—— (2013). 'Ventral Displays'. Retrieved from http://bodylanguageproject. com/the-only-book-on-body-language-that-everybody-needs-to-read/ ventral-displays/.

—— (2013). 'What Do Hugs Mean? The Different Types of Hug Body Language'. Retieved from http://bodylanguageproject.com/nonverbal-dictionary1/ what-do-hugs-mean-the-different-kinds-of-hugs-body-language/.

—— (2013). 'What Does Hand on the Chin Body Language Mean?' Retrieved from http://bodylanguageproject.com/tiny-book-of-body-language/ what-does-hand-on-the-chin-body-language-mean/.

—— (2013). 'What Does Self-Touching or Auto Contact Mean in Body Language?' Retrieved from http://bodylanguageproject.com/ tiny-book-of-body-language/what-does-self-touching-or-auto -contact-mean-in-body-language/.

—— (2014). 'Body Language of Arms Akimbo'. Retrieved from http:// bodylanguageproject.com/nonverbal-dictionary/body-language-of- arms-akimbo/.

—— (2014). 'Body Language of Chin Stroking'. Retrieved from http:// bodylanguageproject.com/nonverbal-dictionary/wp-content/ uploads/2014/10/BodyLanguageProjectCom-Chin-Stroking-2.jpg.

—— (2014). 'Body Language of Compressed Lips or Stiff Upper Lip'. Retrieved from http://bodylanguageproject.com/nonverbal-dictionary/ body-language-of-compressed-lips-or-stiff-upper-lip/.

—— (2014). 'Body Language of Compressed Lips'. Retrieved from http://bodylanguageproject.com/nonverbal-dictionary/ body-language-of-compressed-lips-or-stiff-upper-lip/.

—— (2014). 'Body Language of Cornering or Blocking'. Retrieved from http://bodylanguageproject.com/nonverbal-dictionary/ body-language-of-cornering-and-blocking/.

—— (2014). 'Body Language of Crying'. Retrieved from http://bodylanguageproject. com/nonverbal-dictionary/body-language-of-crying/.

—— (2014). 'Body Language of Ear Blushing'. Retrieved from http:// bodylanguageproject.com/nonverbal dictionary/body-language- of-ear-blushing/.

—— (2014). 'Body Language of Eye Aversion'. Retrieved from http://bodylanguageproject.com/nonverbal-dictionary/body-language-of-eye-aversion-gaze-avoidance-and-wandering-eyes/.

—— (2014). 'Body Language of Eye Flutter or Batting Eye'. Retrieved from http://bodylanguageproject.com/nonverbal-dictionary/body-language-of-eye-flutter-or-batting-eyes/.

—— (2014). 'Body Language of Finger Pointing'. Retrieved from http://bodylanguageproject.com/nonverbal-dictionary/body-language-of-finger-pointing/.

—— (2014). 'Body Language of Hand Covering or Cupping the Mouth'. Retrieved from http://bodylanguageproject.com/nonverbal-dictionary/body-language-of-hand-covering-or-cupping-the-mouth/.

—— (2014). 'Body Language of Hand on the Chin'. Retrieved from http://bodylanguageproject.com/nonverbal-dictionary/body-language-of-hand-on-the-chin/.

—— (2014). 'Body Language of Hand over the Chest'. Retrieved from http://bodylanguageproject.com/nonverbal-dictionary/body-language-of-hand-over-the-chest/.

—— (2014). 'Body Language of Happy Feet'. Retrieved from http://bodylanguageproject.com/nonverbal-dictionary/body-language-of-happy-feet/.

—— (2014). 'Body Language of Hard Swallow or Swallowing Hard'. Retrieved from http://bodylanguageproject.com/nonverbal-dictionary/body-language-of-hard-swallow-or-swallowing-hard/.

—— (2014). 'Body Language of Interlaced Fingers'. Retrieved from http://bodylanguageproject.com/nonverbal-dictionary/body-language-of-interlaced-fingers/.

—— (2014). 'Body Language of Jabbing the Fingers'. Retrieved from http://bodylanguageproject.com/nonverbal-dictionary/body-language-of-jabbing-the-finger/.

—— (2014). 'Body Language of Jaw Clenching or Jaw Tightening'. Retrieved from http://bodylanguageproject.com/nonverbal-dictionary/body-language-of-jaw-clenching-or-jaw-tightening/.

—— (2014). 'Body Language of Leaning In and Leaning Out'. Retrieved from http://bodylanguageproject.com/nonverbal-dictionary/body-language-of-leaning-in-and-leaning-out/.

—— (2014). 'Body Language of Lip Licking'. Retrieved from http://bodylanguageproject.com/nonverbal-dictionary/body-language-of-lip-licking/.

—— (2014). 'Body Language of Looking Askance'. Retrieved from http://bodylanguageproject.com/nonverbal-dictionary/body-language-of-looking-askance/.

—— (2014). 'Body Language of Nail Biting'. Retrieved from http://bodylanguageproject.com/nonverbal-dictionary/body-language-of-nail-biting/.

—— (2014). 'Body Language of Nasal Wing Dilation or Nose Flaring'. Retrieved from http://bodylanguageproject.com/nonverbal-dictionary/body-language-of-nasal-wing-dilation-or-nose-flaring/.

—— (2014). 'Body Language of Neck Scratching or Neck Massaging'. Retrieved from http://bodylanguageproject.com/nonverbal-dictionary/body-language-of-neck-scratching-or-neck-massaging/.

—— (2014). 'Body Language of Ownership Gestures'. Retrieved from http://bodylanguageproject.com/nonverbal-dictionary/body-language-of-ownership-gestures/.

——(2014).'Body Language of Pacing'. Retrieved from http://bodylanguageproject.com/nonverbal-dictionary/body-language-of-pacing/.

—— (2014). 'Body Language of Pigeon Toes or Tibial Torsion'. Retrieved from http://bodylanguageproject.com/nonverbal-dictionary/body-language-of-pigeon-toes-or-tibial-torsion/.

—— (2014). 'Body Language of Playing with Objects'. Retrieved from http://bodylanguageproject.com/nonverbal-dictionary/body-language-of-playing-with-objects/.

—— (2014). 'Body Language of Running the Tongue over the Teeth or Lips'. Retrieved from http://bodylanguageproject.com/nonverbal-dictionary/body-language-of-running-the-tongue-over the teeth or lips/.

—— (2014). 'Body Language of Self-Hugging or Double Arm Hug'. Retrieved from http://bodylanguageproject.com/nonverbal-dictionary/body-language-of-self-hugging-or-the-double-arm-hug/.

—— (2014). 'Body Language of Shoe Play or Removing Shoes'. Retrieved from_____http://bodylanguageproject.com/nonverbal-dictionary/body-language-of-shoe-play-or-removing-shoes/.

—— (2014). 'Body Language of Shoulder Shrugs or Shoulder Rise'. Retrieved from http://bodylanguageproject.com/nonverbal-dictionary/body-language-of-shoulder-shrugs-or-shoulder-rise/.

—— (2014). 'Body Language of Sinking in the Chair'. Retrieved from http://bodylanguageproject.com/nonverbal-dictionary/body-language-of-sinking-in-the-chair/.

—— (2014). 'Body Language of Sweating'. Retrieved from http://bodylanguageproject.com/nonverbal-dictionary/body-language-of-sweating-or-hyperhidrosis/.

—— (2014). 'Body Language of Tapping Fingers'. Retrieved from http://bodylanguageproject.com/nonverbal-dictionary/body-language-of-tapping-the-fingers-or-metronomic-signals/.

—— (2014). 'Body Language of the Chin Jut or Chin Lift'. Retrieved from http://bodylanguageproject.com/nonverbal-dictionary/body-language-of-the-chin-jut-and-chin-lift/.

—— (2014). 'Body Language of the Collar Pull'. Retrieved from http://bodylanguageproject.com/nonverbal-dictionary/body-language-of-the-collar-pull/.

—— (2014). 'Body Language of the Hip Tilt'. Retrieved from http://bodylanguageproject.com/nonverbal-dictionary/body-language-of-the-hip-tilt/.

—— (2014). 'Body Language of the Nervous Smile'. Retrieved from http://bodylanguageproject.com/nonverbal-dictionary/body-language-of-the-nervous-smile/.

—— (2014). 'Body Language of Tongue Jutting'. Retrieved from http://bodylanguageproject.com/nonverbal-dictionary/body-language-of-tongue-jutting-or-pushing-the-tongue-through-compressed-lips/.

—— (2014). 'Body Language of Wrist Exposure Displays'. Retrieved from http://bodylanguageproject.com/nonverbal-dictionary/body-language-of-wrist-exposure-displays/.

—— (2014). 'Body Language of Yawning'. Retrieved from http://bodylanguageproject.com/nonverbal-dictionary/body-language-of-yawning/.

—— (2014). 'Smoke Body Language'. Retrieved from http://bodylanguageproject.com/nonverbal-dictionary/body-language-of-smoking-body-language/.

—— (2014). 'The Hidden Meaning of Baton Gestures'. Retrieved from http://bodylanguageproject.com/nonverbal-dictionary/the-hidden-meaning-baton-gestures-or-hand-chop-gesture-body-language/.

—— (2014). 'The Hidden Meaning of Blading Body Language, Body Angling, or Ventral Displays'. Retrieved from http://bodylanguageproject.com/nonverbal-dictionary/the-hidden-meaning-of-blading-body-language-body-angling-or-ventral-displays/.

—— (2014). 'What Does Body Language of Chin Tuck Mean?' Retrieved from http://bodylanguageproject.com/nonverbal-dictionary/what-does-body-language-of-chin-tuck-mean/.

—— (2014). 'What's in a Non-Verbal Object Caress?' Retrieved from http://bodylanguageproject.com/articles/whats-in-a-nonverbal-object-caress/.

—— (2015). 'Non-Verbal Body Language Dictionary'. Retrieved from http://www.bodylanguageproject.com/dictionary/tag/gaze.

Pinkstone, J. (2018). 'Girls Don't Flip Their Hair If They Fancy You'. Retrieved from https://www.dailymail.co.uk/sciencetech/article-5713713/Girls-DONT-flip-hair-fancy-reveal-experts-studying-body-language.html.

Practical Psychology (2019). 'Body Language Basics—How to Read Someone'. Retrieved from https://practicalpie.com/body-language-basic-how-to-read-someone/.

Pragya, T. (2018). 'The Eyes Convey Things Unsaid'. Retrieved from https://socialmettle.com/eye-body-language.

Prior, S. (2009). 'How to Interpret Female Body Language'. Retrieved from http://www.articlesfactory.com/articles/sexuality/how-to-interpret-female-body-language.html.

——

Psychologia (2019). 'Body Language of a Liar'. Retrieved from https://psychologia. co/body-language-of-a-liar/.

—— (2019). 'Body Language of the Hands: Common Gestures and Their Meanings'. Retrieved from https://psychologia.co/talking-with-your-hands/#rubbing.

—— (2019). 'Mirroring in Body Language'. Retrieved from https://psychologia. co/mirroring-body-language/.

Psychologist World (2019). 'Eye Reading [Body Language]'. Retrieved from https://www.psychologistworld.com/body-language/eyes.

Puder, D. (2018). 'How to Fix Emotional Detachment'. Retrieved from https://psychiatrypodcast.com/psychiatry-psychotherapy-podcast/ dealing-with-emotional-detachment.

Radwan, F. (2017). 'Body Language of the Hands'. Retrieved from https:// www.2knowmyself.com/Body_language_of_the_hands.

—— (2017). 'Body Languauge: In State of Anxiety'. Retrieved from https:// www.2knowmyself.com/body_language/body_language_anxious.

—— (2017). 'Body Language: All about Handshakes'. Retrieved from https:// www.2knowmyself.com/interpreting_body_language/body_language_ handshake.

—— (2017). 'Shaking Legs in Body Language'. Retrieved from https:// www.2knowmyself.com/shaking_legs_in_body_language.

—— (2017). 'Touching the Nose in Body Language'. Retrieved from https:// www.2knowmyself.com/body_language/body_language_negative_ evaluation.

—— (2017). 'Walking Style and Personality'. Retrieved from https:// www.2knowmyself.com/Walking_style_and_personality.

—— (2017). 'Why Do You Yawn?' Retrieved from https://www.2knowmyself. com/Body_language/body_language_of_Boredom/what_causes_ yawning.

—— (2019). 'What Does It Mean When a Woman Flips Her Hair?' Retrieved from https://www.2knowmyself.com/The_Hair_flip_gesture_in_body_ language.

—— (2019). 'Eye Contact in Body Language'. Retrieved from https://www.2knowmyself.com/Interpreting_body_language/eye_contact.

—— (2019). 'The Body Language of Self-Confidence'. Retrieved from https://www.2knowmyself.com/body_language/body_language_self_confidence.

Ratini, M. (2017). 'Salivary Gland Stones'. Retrieved from https://www.webmd.com/oral-health/guide/salivary-gland-stones-symptoms-causes-treatments.

Ravenscraft, E. (2014). 'How to Read Body Language More Effectively'. Retrieved from https://lifehacker.com/how-to-read-body-language-more-effectively-1572937449.

Rea, K., F. Aiken, and C. Borastero (1997). 'Building Therapeutic Staff: Client Relationships with Women Who Self-Harm'. Women's Health Issues 7/2: 121–125. doi: 10.1016/S1049-3867(96)00112-0.

Reiman, T. (2019). 'Distracting Body Language Behaviours'. Retrieved from http://www.bodylanguageuniversity.com/public/158.cfm.

—— (2019). 'The Human Voice Pitch'. Retrieved from http://www.bodylanguageuniversity.com/public/203.cfm.

Riegel, D. (2018). '10 Reasons You Are Talking Too Much'. Retrieved from https://www.inc.com/deborah-grayson-riegel/10-reasons-youre-talking-too-much-what-to-do-about-it.html.

Ritschel, C. (2018). 'The Subtle Body Language Signs That Somebody Doesn't Like You'. Retrieved from https://www.insider.com/how-to-tell-if-someone-doesnt-like-you-by-looking-at-their-body-language-2018-9.

Robinson, S. (2009). 'Eye for an Eye—Visual Violence'. Retrieved from https://www.psychologytoday.com/intl/blog/vitamin-eye/200907/cye-eye-visual-violence-0.

Rodewald, W. (2013). 'What Twirling Your Hair [and Other Habits] Says to Others'. Retrieved from https://stylecaster.com/beauty/body-language-cues/.

Rogers, K. (2019). 'Mouth Anatomy'. Retrieved from https://www.britannica.com/science/mouth-anatomy.

Roguski, R. (2008). 'Body Language in the Office Speaks Louder than Words'. Retrieved from http://blog.cleveland.com/business/2008/04/body_language_in_the_office_sp.html.

Ross, M. (2017). 'How to Read Body Language like an Expert'. Retrieved from https://www.fabhow.com/read-body-language-20-powerful-tips.html.

Rossow, I., K. Hawton, and M. Ystgaard (2009). 'Cannabis Use and Deliberate Self-Harm in Adolescence: A Comparative Analysis of Associations in England and Norway'. Archives of Suicide Research 13/4: 340–348. *doi: 10.1080/13811110903266475. PMID 19813111.*

Rouse, S. (2019). 'Do You Recognise Eye Blocking?' Retrieved from http://www.scottrouse.com/do-you-recognize-eye-blocking/.

Sadr, J. (2003). 'The Role of Eyebrows in Face Recognition'. *Perception*, 285–293.

Saladin, K. (2017). 'If We Close Our Eyes While Speaking to Someone, What Does this Say about Us?' Retrieved from https://www.quora.com/If-we-close-our-eyes-while-talking-to-someone-what-does-that-body-language-tell-about-us.

Saladin, K. S. (2007). *Anatomy and Physiology: The Unity of Form and Function.* New York, NY: McGraw-Hill.

Sampson, T. (2017). 'Mouth Breathing: Symptoms, Complications, and Treatments'. Retrieved from https://www.healthline.com/health/mouth-breathing.

Sandfield, F. (2003). 'Body Language Speaks Volume'. Retrieved from https://thefword.org.uk/2003/10/body_language_speaks_volumes/.

Santos, A. (2018). 'Why Do I Feel like My Temples Are Getting Squeezed, and How Do I Treat Them?' Retrieved from https://www.healthline.com/health/pressure-in-temples.

SBL (2016). 'A Guide to Body Language and Touching'. Retrieved from http://www.study-body-language.com/Body-language-touching.html.

—— (2016). 'Body Language of Legs—Sitting Positions'. Retrieved from http://www.study-body-language.com/sitting-positions.html.

—— (2016). 'Defensive Body Language'. Retrieved from http://www.study-body-language.com/Defensive-body-language.html.

—— (2016). 'Interpreting Standing Leg Movements and Positions'. Retrieved from http://www.study-body-language.com/Leg-movements.html.

—— (2016). 'Palms Position'. Retrieved from http://www.study-body-language.com/gesture.html.

—— (2016). 'Postures—Defensive Body Language'. Retrieved from http://www.study-body-language.com/Defensive-body-language.html.

—— (2019). 'Head Nod. Head Gestures—Part 2'. Retrieved from http://www.study-body-language.com/head-nod.html.

—— (2019). 'Lying and Avoiding Eye Contact—Part 1'. Retrieved from http://www.study-body-language.com/avoiding-eye-contact.html.

—— (2019). 'Mouth Expressions and Lips in Body Language'. Retrieved from http://www.study-body-language.com/body-language-lips.html.

—— (2019). 'Mouth Expressions and Lips in Body Language—Part 2'. Retrieved from http://www.study-body-language.com/body-language-lips.html.

—— (2019). 'Scrunching Your Forehead'. Retrieved from https://www.simplybodylanguage.com/scrunching-your-forehead.html.

—— (2019). 'The Eye Pupil—More Than It Sees'. Retrieved from http://www.study-body-language.com/eye-pupil.html.

—— (2019). 'The Guide to Face Expression in Body Language'. Retrieved from http://www.study-body-language.com/Face-expressions-3.html.

—— (2019). 'The Head Body Language'. Retrieved from http://www.study-body-language.com/head-body-language.html.

—— (2019). 'Using Touch in Body Language'. Retrieved from http://www.study-body-language.com/Touch-body-language.html.

Schafer, J. (2014). '9 Red Flags That You Might Be Talking to a Liar'. Retrieved from https://www.psychologytoday.com/us/blog/let-their-words-do-the-talking/201411/9-subtle-signs-someones-lying-you.

—— (2018). 'How to Tell What Someone Is Really Feeling Just by Looking at Their Lips'. Retrieved from https://www.yourtango.com/2018313187/how-read-body-language-lips.

Scharping, N. (2016). 'The Hidden Messages in a Laugh'. Retrieved from http://blogs.discovermagazine.com/d-brief/2016/04/14/your-laugh-says-a-lot-about-you/#.XNUBUKso_Mw.

Schirripa, J. (2016). '6 Ways Your Smile Reveals Your Feelings for Someone before You Do'. Retrieved from https://www.elitedaily.com/life/ways-smiles-reveal-feelings/1382561.

Segev, E. (2019). 'Understanding Hair Body Language'. Retrieved from https://mentalizer.com/understanding-hair-body-language.html.

Segre, L. (2019). 'Eye Anatomy: A Closer Look at the Parts of the Eye'. Retrieved from https://www.allaboutvision.com/resources/anatomy.htm.

Seladi-Schulman, J. (2018). 'Arm Muscles Overview'. Retrieved from https://www.healthline.com/human-body-maps/arm-muscles.

Seltzer, L. (2015). 'Trauma and the Freeze Response: Good, Bad, or Both?' Retrieved from https://www.psychologytoday.com/us/blog/evolution-the-self/201507/trauma-and-the-freeze-response-good-bad-or-both.

——(2015). 'What Does It Mean When We Stick Out Our Tongue?' Retrieved from https://www.psychologytoday.com/intl/blog/evolution-the-self/201509/what-does-it-mean-when-we-stick-our-tongues-out.

Shield, L. (2019). 'How to Be Less Clingy'. Retrieved from https://www.wikihow.com/Be-Less-Clingy.

Shmerling, R. (2018). 'Knuckle Cracking: Annoying and Harmful'. Retrieved from https://www.health.harvard.edu/blog/knuckle-cracking-annoying-and-harmful-or-just-annoying-2018051413797.

Shutterstock (2015). 'Symbolism of Colors and Color Meanings across the World'. Retrieved from https://www.shutterstock.com/blog/color-symbolism-and-meanings-around-the-world.

Skills Converged (2019). 'Body Language of Dominance'. Retrieved from https://www.skillsconverged.com/FreeTrainingMaterials/BodyLanguage/BodyLanguageofDominance.aspx.

—— (2019). 'Body Language of Lying'. Retrieved from https://www.skillsconverged.com/FreeTrainingMaterials/BodyLanguage/BodyLanguageofLying.aspx.

Smet, P et al. (1997). *Adverse Effects of Herbal Drugs, Volume 3*. Germany: Springer-Verlag Berlin Heidelberg.

Smith, B. (2019). 'Body Language'. Retrieved from https://www.streetdirectory. com/travel_guide/8526/self_improvement_and_motivation/body_ language.html.

Smith, K. (2018). 'Silence: The Secret Communication Tool'. Retrieved from https://psychcentral.com/blog/silence-the-secret-communication-tool/.

Smith, S. (2011). 'What Is Your Body Language Saying?' Retrieved from http:// edition.cnn.com/2011/LIVING/01/06/rs.body.language/index.html.

—— (2015). 'What Is Your Body Language Saying?' Retrieved from https:// www.realsimple.com/health/mind-mood/reading-body-language

Sol, M. (2019). 'Body Language: Hand Shakes'. Retrieved from https://lonerwolf. com/body-language-handshakes/.

—— (2019). 'Body Language: Hands'. Retrieved from https://lonerwolf.com/ body-language-hands/.

—— (2019). 'Body Language: Lying Signs'. Retrieved from https://lonerwolf. com/body-language-lying/.

Solanki, P. (2018). 'Decoding Men's Body Language: Facial Gestures, Postures, and More'. Retrieved from https://lovebondings.com/body-language-of-men.

Sonamics (2019). 'Body Language and Social Dynamics'. Retrieved from http:// sonamics.com/en/.

Speeli (2019). 'What Does It Mean When a Woman Flips Her Hair?' Retrieved from http://www.speeli.com/articles/view/What-does-it-mean-when-a-woman-flips-her-hair.

Sperlazza, C. (2019). 'How to Strengthen Your Vagus Nerves to Upgrade Your Whole Body'. Retrieved from https://blog.bulletproof.com/ vagus-nerve-vagal-response/.

Squeeze, H. (16 November 2013). 'Why Do You Have Eyebrows?' Retrieved from https://www.bbc.com/future/article/20131115 -why-do-you-have-eyebrows

Steber, C. (2018). '7 Things You Can Determine about Someone's Personality Based on the Way They Walk'. Retrieved from https://www.bustle.com/ p/7-things-you-can-determine-about-someones-personality-based-on-the-way-they-walk-10139056.

Stekel, W. (2013). 'Conditions of Nervous Anxiety and Their Treatment'. *Routledge, 236.* ISBN 9781136299315.

Stephen R., Brian Tracy, and Jean Hamilton (2006). 'The Interview'. In *Mission Possible: Learn How to Reach Your Potential from Some of the World's Most Successful Possibility Thinkers*, 11th edn, 8. Tennessee: Insight Publishing.

Steves, R. (2019). 'Understanding European Gestures'. Retrieved from https://www.ricksteves.com/travel-tips/sightseeing/european-gestures.

Stone, Z. (2016). '4 Body Language Gestures That Make You Look Insecure: Change Them and Become a Boss'. Retrieved from https://entrepreneurs.maqtoob.com/4-body-language-gestures-that-make-you-look-insecure-change-them-and-become-a-boss-2677ccc3add7?gi=60df1ec9ae5.

Stoute, M. (2019). 'The Seven Deadly Body Language Sins'. Retrieved from https://www.tsbmag.com/2006/05/17/the-seven-deadly-body-language-sins/.

Straker, D. (2019). 'Chest Body Language'. Retrieved from https://mentalizer.com/what-does-your-breathing-pattern-means.html.

—— (2019). 'Dominant Body Language'. Retrieved from http://changingminds.org/techniques/body/dominant_body.htm.

—— (2019). 'Foot Body Language'. Retrieved from http://changingminds.org/techniques/body/parts_body_language/feet_body_language.htm#mov.

—— (2019). 'Hips Body Language'. Retrieved from http://changingminds.org/techniques/body/parts_body_language/hip_body_language.htm.

—— (2019). 'Knee Body Language'. Retrieved from http://changingminds.org/techniques/body/parts_body_language/knee_body_language.htm.

—— (2019). 'Leg Body Language'. Retrieved from http://changingminds.org/techniques/body/parts_body_language/leg_body_language.htm.

Strong, M. (1999). *A Bright Red Scream: Self-Mutilation and the Language of Pain.* Penguin

SYN (2019). 'Non-Verbal Communication: Face and Voice'. Retrieved from https://www.skillsyouneed.com/ips/nonverbal-face-voice.html.

Syncrat (2005). 'Body Language: Footsies'. Retrieved from http://www.syncrat.com/posts/4812/footsies.

THE (2019). 'Characteristics of the Human Eye'. Retrieved from https://humaneyestructure.weebly.com/characteristics.html.

The Advertiser (2014). '10 Body Language Love Signals to Keep in Mind Next Time You're on a Date'. Retrieved from https://www.adelaidenow.com.au/lifestyle/10-body-language-love-signals-to-keep-in-mind-next-time-youre-on-a-date/news-story/da6bf2ad8bda9380d9b4ebd27c7b4fa1.

Tip Hero (2019). '11 Psychological Tricks That Basically Tell What People Are Really Thinking'. Retrieved from https://tiphero.com/11-psychological-tricks.

Toddler Sense (2019). 'Toddler Tantrums'. Retrieved from https://www.toddlersense.com/toddler_tantrums.

Tousley, S. (2019). 'Body Language Advice from an FBI Agent and Harvard Social Psychologist'. Retrieved from https://blog.hubspot.com/sales/body-language-advice.

Trauma Recovery (2019). 'Fight, Flight, Freeze Responses'. Retrieved from http://trauma-recovery.ca/impact-effects-of-trauma/fight-flight-freeze-responses/.

Trent, S. (2016). 'Throat Clearing May Indicate Deception'. Retrieved from https://www.psychologytoday.com/us/blog/let-their-words-do-the-talking/201605/throat-clearing-may-indicate-deception.

Tresidder, Jack (1997). The Hutchinson Dictionary of Symbols, 16. London: Helicon. ISBN 1-85986-059-1.

TSPT (2016). 'Body Language and Its Use in Animation'. Retrieved from https://thesilentprotagblog.wordpress.com/2016/04/10/body-language-and-its-use-in-animation/.

TTA (2019). 'Body Language 17: Playing with the Hair'. Retrieved from https://thetrustambassador.com/2019/03/02/body-language-17-playing-with-the-hair/.

TV Tropes (2019). 'Nose Tapping'. Retrieved from https://tvtropes.org/pmwiki/pmwiki.php/Main/NoseTapping.

Unfinished Success (2019). 'Body Language Communication'. Retrieved from https://www.unfinishedsuccess.com/body-language-communication/.

Van Edwards, V. (2019). 'Beware: Contempt'. Retrieved from https://gohighbrow. com/beware-contempt/.

—— (2019). 'Condescending Body Language: "I'm Better than You"'. Retrieved from https://www.scienceofpeople.com/condescending-body-language/.

—— (2019). 'Female Body Language'. Retrieved from https://www. scienceofpeople.com/female-body-language/.

Vanessa, V (2019). 'Plastic Surgery, Botox, and Facial Expressions'. Retrieved from https://www.scienceofpeople.com/plastic-surgery-botox-and-facial-expressions/.

Villnes, Z. (2018). 'Causes and Treatments for Nasolabial Folds'. Retrieved from https://www.medicalnewstoday.com/articles/320825.php.

Walker, H. (2014). 'What Causes the Brain to Have Slow Processing Speed, and How Can the Rate Be Improved?' Retrieved from https://www. scientificamerican.com/article/what-causes-the-brain-to-have-slow-processing-speed-and-how-can-the-rate-be-improved/.

Walker, T. J. (2011). 'Put Your Tongue in Your Mouth—Media Training'. Retrieved from https://www.forbes.com/sites/tjwalker/2011/05/09/keep-your-tongue-in-your-mouth-media-training/#752480a32e94.

Walton, R. E., and T. Mahmoud (2002). *Principles and Practice of Endodontics*, 3rd edn, 11–13. ISBN 0-7216-9160-9.

Wang, K. (2017). 'Handshake Politics: How World Leaders Get the "Upper Hand"'. Retrieved from https://extranewsfeed.com/handshake-politics-how-world-leaders-get-the-upper-hand-c7b42c64917f?gi=2558df041d90.

Wanshel, E. (2019). 'What Your Walking Style about Your Personality'. Retrieved from https://www.littlethings.com/walk-style-personality-quiz-speed-strides/.

Watson, K. (2018). 'Causes of an Itchy Face and How Not to Scratch It'. Retrieved from https://www.healthline.com/health/itchy-face.

Wayman, E. (2012). 'Why Do Humans Have Chins? Smithsonian'. Retrieved from https://www.smithsonianmag.com/science-nature/why-do-humans-have-chins-15140492.

Weller, C. (2016). 'A Former FBI Profiler Offers a Theory on Why So Many Politicians Use the Same Weird Hand Gesture'. Retrieved from https://www.businessinsider.com/politicians-hand-gesture-fbi-profiler-explains-2016-10?IR=T.

Wells, S. (1998). 'The Forehead'. *New Physiognomy or Signs of Character as Manifested through Temperament and External Forms and Especially in the Human Face Divine*, reprint edn, 260. Kessinger Publishing. ISBN 9780766103573.

Westside Toastmasters (2019). 'Affairs of the Heart: Signals of Attraction and Flirtation'. Retrieved from https://westsidetoastmasters.com/resources/book_of_body_language/chap15.html.

—— (2019). 'Common Gestures Seen Regularly'. Retrieved from https://westsidetoastmasters.com/resources/book_of_body_language/chap11.html.

—— (2019). 'Hand Gestures'. Retrieved from https://westsidetoastmasters.com/resources/book_of_body_language/chap6.html.

—— (2019). 'Leg Postures Reveal Our Mind's Intent'. Retrieved from https://westsidetoastmasters.com/resources/book_of_body_language/chap10.html.

—— (2019). 'The Allure of Laughter and Smiles'. Retrieved from https://westsidetoastmasters.com/resources/book_of_body_language/chap3.html.

—— (2019). 'What Arm Gestures Convey'. Retrieved from https://westsidetoastmasters.com/resources/book_of_body_language/chap4.html.

—— (2019). 'When We Are Judging or Trying to Deceive'. Retrieved from https://westsidetoastmasters.com/resources/book_of_body_language/chap7.html.

Whipple, B. (2019). 'Body Language 10: Scratching the Head'. Retrieved from https://thetrustambassador.com/2019/01/12/body-language-10-scratching-the-head/.

—— (2019). 'Body Language 11: Finger or Foot Tapping'. Retrieved from https://thetrustambassador.com/2019/01/19/body-language-11-finger-or-foot-tapping/.

—— (2019). 'Body Language 8: Chin Gestures'. Retrieved from https://thetrustambassador.com/2018/12/29/body-language-8-chin-gestures/.

Williams, G. (2019). 'Posts Tagged "Body Language Signals"'. Retrieved from https://www.themasternegotiator.com/tags/body-language-signals/.

Wilson, G. (2016). 'Body Language: Smiling vs Laughing'. Retrieved from http://theschooloflaughter.com/body-language/.

Wint, C. (2016). 'What Causes Bounding Pulse?' Retrieved from https://www.healthline.com/health/bounding-pulse.

WME (2019). 'Body Language: Importance of Your Head Position'. Retrieved from http://www.wordofmouthexperiment.com/articles/body-language/body-language-importance-your-head-position.

Wood, P. (2019). 'Body Language: 23 Must-Know Moves'. Retrieved from https://www.cbsnews.com/pictures/body-language-23-must-know-moves/2/.

Wood, R. (2018). '6 Most Obvious Body Language Signs That Women Give Out If They Are Interested in Someone'. Retrieved from https://www.mensxp.com/relationships/impress-women/46132-6-most-obvious-body-language-signs-that-women-give-out-if-they-are-interested-in-someone.html.

Writers Write (2013). 'Body Language—Eyes'. Retrieved from https://writerswrite.co.za/body-language-eyes/.

WSTM (2019). 'Clues from the Eyes'. Retrieved from https://westsidetoastmasters.com/resources/book_of_body_language/chap8.html.

YFC (2013). '3 Tricks for Improving Your Body Language in the Office'. Retrieved from https://www.businessinsider.com/3-tricks-for-improving-your-body-language-in-the-office-2013-10?IR=T.

Ying, Y. W., M. Coombs, and P. A. Lee (1999). 'Family Intergenerational Relationship of Asian American Adolescents'. *Cultural Diversity and Ethnic Minority Psychology* 5/4: 350–363.

CPSIA information can be obtained
at www.ICGtesting.com
Printed in the USA
BVHW041615270322
632569BV00022B/459